Black's Law Dictionary®

Fourth Pocket Edition

Bryan A. Garner
Editor in Chief

WEST®
A Thomson Reuters business

Mat #41148855

610 Opperman Drive
St. Paul, MN 55123
1–800–313–9378

Printed in the United States of America

ISBN 978–0–314–27544–8

Black's Law Dictionary

Fourth Pocket Edition

Bryan A. Garner, J.D., LL.D.
Editor in Chief
President, LawProse, Inc.
Distinguished Research Professor of Law,
Southern Methodist University

Jeff Newman, J.D.
Managing Editor
LawProse, Inc.

Tiger Jackson, J.D., LL.M.
Associate Editor
LawProse, Inc.

Becky R. McDaniel, J.D.
Assistant Editor
LawProse, Inc.

Preface to the Fourth Edition

Each new edition of *Black's Law Dictionary*—whether unabridged, abridged, or pocket—benefits from a continual monitoring of the legal vocabulary. At LawProse, Inc. in Dallas, Texas, my lawyer-colleagues and I are constantly researching and making incremental improvements in our legal lexicography. The entire law community owes a debt of gratitude to Thomson/West for professionalizing the updating of *Black's*, as it has done since work on the seventh unabridged edition began in 1995. A serious dictionary requires an ongoing staff of researchers, and the entire *Black's* fleet of dictionaries has now acquired a level of scholarly reliability unmatched by predecessor works.

This fourth pocket edition derives from the ninth unabridged edition—the fullest and most scholarly law dictionary to date. The entire staff at LawProse has been integrally involved in its production—not just those on the masthead, but others as well: Karolyne H.C. Garner, J.D., our general counsel; Heather Haines, J.D., our administrative assistant; and Rebekah Rutledge, our office manager. All have taken part in ensuring high standards for the work, and I am grateful to them all. Meanwhile, my gratitude is vast to my friends and colleagues at Thomson/West: Chris Parton, J.D.; Pamela Siege Chandler, J.D.; and Louis Higgins, J.D.

Much of the success of *Black's Law Dictionary* has resulted from the generosity and resourcefulness of law students who have sent me suggestions. A major reference book requires the contributions of many industrious hands and percipient eyes. So if you encounter a legal term that should be listed and defined, or if you see some way of improving an existing definition, send me your suggestions: bgarner@lawprose.org. Far from resenting corrections, my colleagues and I rejoice at them.

Presumably you've bought this book because you've decided to learn about law. My suggestion is that you approach the task as a multifaceted endeavor. Acquire the "dictionary habit": as you're reading about law, mark every word that is unfamiliar to you. Then go back and look it up. Copy the definitions into your vocabulary notebook. You'll become fully conversant with legal terminology. You'll be learning many new concepts. And don't stop with this pocket edition: get a home copy of the unabridged edition for more in-depth study. You'll be amazed at all you're learning. And with your burgeoning erudition—complemented by curricular and extracurricular reading about this fascinating discipline we call law—you'll far surpass your peers who habitually pass over words they don't know, who somehow hope for high marks despite their incomprehension.

Bryan A. Garner

Dallas, Texas
May 2011

Preface to the Third Edition

This new pocket edition of *Black's Law Dictionary* has been thoroughly updated. Every definition has been brought into line with the unabridged eighth edition of *Black's*, which itself includes 17,000 more entries than its predecessor. At LawProse, Inc., my colleagues and I closely monitor developments in legal vocabulary. And we have a small army of erudite contributors to all the editions of *Black's*: some 110 law professors and practicing lawyers have played a major role in examining and revising our definitions to ensure that they are as up-to-date and precisely worded as possible.

At LawProse, my colleague Tiger Jackson has had the laboring oar in bringing this pocket edition into line with the eighth unabridged edition. As usual, she has performed that task splendidly. My thanks to her.

And to the lawyers and law students who occasionally write in with a comment or suggestion, many thanks. We're always glad to hear from readers. To send an e-mail, see www.lawprose.org. Every reference-book author appreciates whatever help is offered.

BRYAN A. GARNER

Dallas, Texas
May 2006

Preface to the Second Edition

If dictionaries can be said to lead interesting lives, this one certainly has had one.

It began in 1994 as a book that two colleagues and I began writing from scratch, using modern lexicographic techniques. When that book was published in 1996, I began working on the unabridged *Black's Law Dictionary* (7th ed.), again with lawyers that I had trained in legal lexicography. We used the 1996 pocket edition as the starting point for that book and added thousands of new entries, which we drafted with an eye to earlier editions of *Black's*—but we drafted them essentially anew. While adding all these new terms, we inevitably improved many of the definitions from the earlier pocket edition. The seventh edition appeared in August 1999.

Then the West Group asked me to abridge the seventh edition, to replace the old paperback abridgment of the sixth edition. (For many years, *Black's* has been out in several editions—deluxe, standard, abridged, and from 1996 on, the pocket.) The new abridged edition appeared in June 2000.

The last step in the cycle, at least for now, was to produce a new pocket edition. This meant abridging the abridged edition by more than half, while keeping an eye on which terms appeared in the first pocket edition. The result, as anyone will see who bothers to compare the editions, is a textually distinct book—and, I think, much improved.

Perhaps the most important innovation is that my colleagues and I have managed to fit more than 2,000 additional entries into the book, mainly by minimizing the kinds of cross-references that can so easily fit into a bigger dictionary. So while the first pocket edition had some 7,500 main headwords, this one has more than 10,000—and the text itself is only 85 pages longer. To make this possible, we excluded most of the variants for legal terms. For those, you'll need to consult the unabridged or even the abridged seventh edition. The more useful function here, we thought, would be to include additional entries—not to list secondary variants that take up precious space.

Everyone who has worked on this project has shared a goal: to produce the most accurate, readable, and comprehensive small law dictionary ever published. Though we doubtless could have done better here and there, we think we have met our goal. We hope it meets your needs.

BRYAN A. GARNER

Dallas, Texas
February 2001

Preface to the First Edition

Every subject has its seminal reference book—the one that becomes a household word. When you think of world records, you think of *Guinness*; of encyclopedias, *Britannica*; of anatomy, *Gray's*; of music dictionaries, *Grove's*; of English-language dictionaries, *Webster* (in the U.S.) and *Oxford* (in the U.K.).

And whenever somebody thinks of law dictionaries, *Black's* seems inevitably to come to mind. Henry Campbell Black (1860–1927) first published his magnum opus in 1891, and his achievement might easily be taken for granted today. He entered a crowded field, for there were many law dictionaries then in print—several more major ones, in fact, than there are today. But who today, apart from the specialist, remembers the names of Anderson, Burrill, English, Kinney, Lawson, Rapalje, Sweet, Wharton, or even the better-known Bouvier?

What happened is that Henry Campbell Black's dictionary took the field and became incontestably supreme, partly because of his comprehensiveness, partly because of his academic standing, and partly because he had the good fortune of publishing his work with West Publishing Company.

Black's Law Dictionary has evolved over its six unabridged editions. And this pocket edition continues that evolution. Indeed, because it was compiled on modern lexicographic principles, the book you're holding is something of a radical leap forward in the evolutionary line.

Lexicographic Methods and Features

Little is known about exactly how Black and his contemporaries worked, but one thing is certain to anyone who has spent any time examining 19th-century and early-20th-century law dictionaries: a great deal of the "work" was accomplished through wholesale borrowing from other dictionaries. To cite but one example, in Bouvier (1839), Anderson (1890), Black (1891),

Kinney (1893), Shumaker & Longsdorf (1901), and several other law dictionaries of the period, the phrase *disorderly house* is defined in the following word-for-word sequence: a "house the inmates of which behave so badly as to become a nuisance to the neighborhood." Hundreds of other definitions are virtually verbatim from book to book.

Although this practice of heavy borrowing is suspect today, it may be wrong to judge these early lexicographers by modern standards. They might have copied for various reasons. First, even nonspecialist lexicographers of the time commonly borrowed from each other; that is, apart from a few notable exceptions such as Samuel Johnson (1709–1784), Noah Webster (1758–1843), and James A.H. Murray (1837–1915—the first editor of the *Oxford English Dictionary*), a high percentage of entries in early English-language dictionaries were directly traceable to even earlier dictionaries. Second, dictionary editors in the legal field were trained as common-law lawyers, under the Anglo-American system of precedent. As a result, they might have thought that accuracy precluded a reconsideration of their predecessors' words—especially if the earlier dictionary-maker cited caselaw in support of a definition. And third, notions of plagiarism were much less well defined than they are today (and, in any event, have always been looser in lexicography than elsewhere).

But the result of all this is that, as the legal language has grown, law dictionaries have generally strayed further and further afield from actual legal usage. Instead of monitoring legal language for new entries—words that emerge in a given practice area, legal slang that crops up in a certain context, words that take on meanings different from their traditional ones—compilers of law dictionaries have tended to look too much at their forerunners.

This book, however, represents a stem-to-stern (very stern) reconsideration of legal terms—an entirely fresh edition of *Black's Law Dictionary* compiled on modern lexicographic methods.

This means that my colleagues and I have done several things. We have:

- Attempted a thorough marshaling of the language of the law from original sources. Many terms make their "debut" in this edition.
- Examined the writings of specialist scholars rather than looking only at judicial decisions.
- Considered entries entirely anew rather than merely accepting what previous editions have said. We have often checked Westlaw and other sources when trying to decide which of two competing forms now predominates in legal usage.
- Imposed analytical rigor on entries by avoiding duplicative definitions and by cataloguing and numbering senses.
- Shown pronunciations that reflect how American lawyers actually say the words and phrases—not how English lawyers used to say them (and not how Latin teachers would have us say them).
- Recorded cognate forms—for example, the verb and adjective corresponding to a given noun.
- Ensured that specialized vocabularies are included—from bankruptcy to securities law, from legal realism to critical legal studies.

As a result, this book represents a balanced and up-to-date treatment of legal terms—even within the strict confines of a "pocket" dictionary.

BRYAN A. GARNER

Dallas, Texas
May 1996

Guide to the Dictionary

1. Alphabetization

All headwords, including abbreviations, are alphabetized letter by letter, not word by word. Spaces, apostrophes, hyphens, virgules, and the like are ignored. An ampersand (&) is treated as if it were the word *and*. For example:

Pan-American Convention
P & L
***Panduit* test**
per annum
P/E ratio
per capita
percentage lease
per diem
peremptory

Numerals included in a headword precede the letter "a" and are arranged in ascending numerical order:

Rule 10b–5
Rule 11
rule absolute
rulemaking
rule of 72
rule of 78

A numeral at the beginning of a headword is alphabetized as if the numeral were spelled out:

Eighth Amendment
eight-hour law
8–K
ejection

Commas break the letter-by-letter alphabetization if they are backward-looking (e.g., *attorney, power of*), but not if they are forward-looking (e.g., *right, title, and interest*).

2. Pronunciations

Boldface syllables receive primary stress:

> **oligopoly (ol-ə-gop-ə-lee),** ***n.***

If a word has more than one acceptable pronunciation, the preferred pronunciation appears first and the variant form after *or*:

> **talesman (taylz-mən** *or* **tay-leez-mən).**

A pronunciation of dubious standing is preceded by *also*:

> ***condition precedent*** **(prə-seed-ənt** *also* **pres-ə-dənt).**

For variably pronounced syllables, often only the changed syllables are included.

> ***ejusdem generis*** **(ee-jəs-dəm jen-ə-ris**
> *also* **ee-joos- or ee-yoos-).**

Brackets in pronunciations indicate an optional sound:

> **fiduciary (fi-d[y]oo-shee-er-ee),** ***adj.***

For handy reference, the pronunciation guide is located inside the front cover.

3. Dates

The parenthetical dates preceding many of the definitions show the earliest known use of the word or phrase in English. For some words, the date is merely a century (e.g., *14c*), but for most of the recently emerging vocabulary a precise year is given. The editors hope to extend this feature to most or even all the entries in future editions. Interested researchers should know that we welcome certifiable antedatings.

4. Style and Usage Tags

Two types of tags appear. First, there are usage tags:

> *Hist.* = **historical; no longer current in law**
>
> *Archaic* = **old-fashioned and declining in use**
>
> *Rare* = **very infrequent in modern usage**
>
> *Slang* = **very informal**

Second, there are many subject-matter tags that identify the field of law that a particular term or sense belongs to (e.g., *Antitrust*, *Commercial law*, *Insurance*, and *Wills & estates*). Two of these tags deserve special mention. *Roman law* indicates a term that can be traced back to the legal system of the ancient Romans. *Civil law* indicates a term that is used in modern civil-law systems, including much of the law in Louisiana.

5. Angle Brackets

Contextual illustrations of a headword are given in angle brackets:

> **avail,** *n.* **1.** Use or advantage <of little or no avail>. **2.** (*pl.*) Profits or proceeds, esp. from a sale of property <the avails of the trust fund>.

6. Bullets

Bullets are used to separate definitional information (before the bullet) from information that is not purely definitional (after the bullet), such as encyclopedic information or usage notes.

7. Cognate Forms

This dictionary lists corresponding parts of speech. For example, under the definition of *consultation*, the corresponding verb (*consult*) and adjectives (*consulting, consultative*) are listed.

If a cognate form applies to only one sense of a headword, that form is denoted as follows:

> **enjoin,** *vb.* **1.** To legally prohibit or restrain by injunction <the company was enjoined from selling its stock>. **2.** To prescribe, mandate, or strongly encourage <the graduating class was enjoined to uphold the highest professional standards>. — **enjoinment** (for sense 1), *n.* — **enjoinder** (for sense 2), *n.*

8. Subentries

Many terms in this dictionary are collected by topic. For example, the different types of contracts, such as *bilateral contract* and *gratuitous contract*, are defined under the main term *contract*. If a term has more than one sense, then the corresponding subentries are placed under the appropriate sense of that term.

9. Typefaces

The typefaces used in this dictionary are mostly self-explanatory. For instance, all headwords and cognate forms are in boldface type, and all subentries are italicized. As for headwords of foreign origin, those that are fully naturalized are in boldface Roman type, while those that are not fully naturalized are in boldface italics. Generally, small caps are used with cross-references to main entries.

10. Abbreviations

These abbreviations are used within entries:

abbr.	=	abbreviated as; abbreviation for
adj.	=	adjective
adv.	=	adverb
BrE	=	British English
ca.	=	circa
cap.	=	capitalized
cf.	=	(confer) compare with
ch.	=	chapter
conj.	=	conjunction
ed.	=	edition; editor
e.g.	=	(exempli gratia) for example
esp.	=	especially
et seq.	=	(et sequentes) and those (pages or sections) that follow
fr.	=	from; derived from
id.	=	(idem) in the same work
i.e.	=	(id est) that is
l.c.	=	lowercase
n.	=	noun
no.	=	number
¶	=	paragraph
pl.	=	plural
pp.	=	pages
p.pl.	=	past participle
prep.	=	preposition
repr.	=	reprinted
§	=	section
sing.	=	singular
specif.	=	specifically
usu.	=	usually
vb.	=	verb

Contents

Black's
Law Dictionary

Fourth Pocket Edition

A

a. **1.** (*usu. cap.* & *often ital.*) A hypothetical person <*A* deeds Blackacre to *B*>. **2.** [Latin] From; by; in; on; of; at. **3.** [Law Latin] With. **4.** [Law French] Of; at; to; for; in; with. **5.** (*cap.*) *abbr. Atlantic Reporter.*

A.2d. *abbr. Atlantic Reporter Second Series.*

AAA. *abbr.* **1.** American Arbitration Association. **2.** American Accounting Association. **3.** American Academy of Actuaries.

AALL. *abbr.* American Association of Law Libraries.

AALS. *abbr.* Association of American Law Schools.

ABA. *abbr.* **1.** American Bar Association. **2.** American Bankers Association.

abandonee (ə-ban-də-**nee**). (1848) One to whom property rights are relinquished; one to whom something is formally or legally abandoned.

abandonment, *n.* (1809) **1.** The relinquishing of a right or interest with the intention of never reclaiming it. **2.** *Family law.* The act of leaving a spouse or child willfully and without an intent to return. **3.** *Criminal law.* RENUNCIATION (3). **4.** *Contracts.* RESCISSION (2). — **abandon,** *vb.*

abatement (ə-**bayt**-mənt), *n.* (14c) **1.** The act of eliminating or nullifying. **2.** The suspension or defeat of a pending action for a reason unrelated to the merits of the claim. **3.** The act of lessening or moderating; diminution in amount or degree. **4.** *Wills & estates.* The reduction of a legacy, general or specific, as a result of the estate's being insufficient to pay all debts and legacies. — **abate,** *vb.* — **abatable,** *adj.*

abatement clause. (1890) A lease provision that releases the tenant from the rent obligation when an act of God or other specified reason precludes occupancy.

abator (ə-**bay**-tər *or* -tor). (16c) A person who eliminates a nuisance.

abduction (ab-**dək**-shən), *n.* (17c) *Criminal law.* **1.** The act of leading someone away by force or fraudulent persuasion. • Some jurisdictions have added various elements to this basic definition, such as that the abductor must have the intent to marry or defile the person, that the abductee must be a child, or that the abductor must intend to subject the abductee to concubinage or prostitution. **2.** Loosely, kidnapping. — **abduct,** *vb.* — **abductor,** *n.* — **abductee,** *n.*

aberrant behavior (a-**ber**-ənt). (1924) A single act of unplanned or thoughtless criminal behavior.

abet (ə-**bet**), *vb.* (14c) **1.** To aid, encourage, or assist (someone), esp. in the commission of a crime. **2.** To support (a crime) by active assistance. — **abetment,** *n.*

abeyance (ə-**bay**-ənts), *n.* (17c) **1.** Temporary inactivity; suspension. **2.** *Property.* A lapse in succession during which no person is vested with title. — **abeyant,** *adj.*

abide, *vb.* (bef. 12c) **1.** To tolerate or withstand. **2.** To obey; (with *by*) to act in accordance with or in conformity to. **3.** To await. **4.** To perform or execute (an order or judgment). **5.** To stay or dwell.

ability. (14c) The capacity to perform an act or service; esp., the power to carry out a legal act.

ab initio (ab i-**nish**-ee-oh), *adv.* [Latin] (16c) From the beginning.

able, *adj.* Legally competent and qualified.

ableism. Prejudice against or disregard of disabled people's needs and rights; discrimination that unreasonably favors able-bodied persons. — **ableist,** *adj.*

abnormally dangerous activity. (1957) An undertaking that necessarily carries with it a significant risk of serious harm even if reasonable care is used, and for which the actor may face strict liability for any harm caused; esp., an activity (such as dynamiting) for which the actor is held strictly liable because the activity (1) involves the risk of serious harm to persons or property, (2) cannot be performed without this risk, regardless of the precautions taken, and (3) does not ordinarily occur in the community.

abode. (13c) A home; a fixed place of residence.

abolish, *vb.* To annul, eliminate, or destroy, esp. an ongoing practice or thing.

abolition. (16c) **1.** The act of abolishing. **2.** The state of being annulled or abrogated. **3.** (*usu. cap.*) The legal termination of slavery in the United States.

abortion, *n.* (16c) **1.** An artificially induced termination of a pregnancy for the purpose of destroying an embryo or fetus. • In *Roe v. Wade*, the Supreme Court first recognized a woman's right to choose to end her pregnancy as a privacy right stemming from the Due Process Clause of the 14th Amendment. 410 U.S. 113, 93 S.Ct. 705 (1973). **2.** The spontaneous expulsion of an embryo or fetus before viability; MISCARRIAGE. — **abort,** *vb.* — **abortionist,** *n.*

above, *adj.* & *adv.* (Of an appellate court) having the power to review the case at issue; having dealt with an appeal in the case at issue. Cf. BELOW.

above-the-line, *adj.* (1973) (Of a deduction) taken after calculating gross income and before calculating adjusted gross income. Cf. BELOW-THE-LINE.

abridge, *vb.* (14c) **1.** To reduce or diminish. **2.** To condense (as a book or other writing). — **abridgment,** *n.*

abrogate (**ab**-rə-gayt), *vb.* (16c) To abolish (a law or custom) by formal or authoritative action; to annul or repeal. — **abrogation,** *n.*

abscond (ab-**skond**), *vb.* (16c) **1.** To depart secretly or suddenly, esp. to avoid arrest, prosecution, or service of process. **2.** To leave a place, usu. hurriedly, with another's money or property. — **abscondence** (ab-**skon**-dənts), *n.* — **absconder,** *n.*

absence, *n.* (14c) **1.** The state of being away from one's usual place of residence. **2.** A failure to appear, or to be available and reachable, when expected.

absentee, *n.* (17c) **1.** A person who is away from his or her usual residence; one who is absent. **2.** A person who is not present where expected. **3.** A person who either resides out of state or has departed from the state without having a representative there. — **absentee,** *adj.* — **absentee,** *adv.*

absolute, *adj.* (14c) **1.** Free from restriction, qualification, or condition <absolute ownership>. **2.** Conclusive and not liable to revision <absolute delivery>. **3.** Unrestrained in the exercise of governmental power <absolute monarchy>. — **absolute,** *n.*

absolute disparity. (1976) *Constitutional law.* The difference between the percentage of a group in the general population and the percentage of that group in the pool of prospective jurors on a venire. Cf. COMPARATIVE DISPARITY.

absolute law. (16c) A supposed law of nature thought to be unchanging in principle, although circumstances may vary the way in which it is applied.

absolve (ab- *or* əb-**zolv**), *vb.* (15c) **1.** To release from an obligation, debt, or responsibility. **2.** To free from the penalties for misconduct. — **absolver,** *n.*

absorption, *n.* (18c) **1.** The act or process of including or incorporating a thing into something else; esp., the application of rights guaranteed by the U.S. Constitution to actions by the states. **2.** *Int'l law.* The merger of one nation into another, whether voluntarily or by subjugation. **3.** *Labor law.* In a postmerger collective-bargaining agreement, a provision allowing seniority for union members in the resulting entity. **4.** *Real estate.* The rate at which property will be leased or sold on the market at a given time. **5.** *Commercial law.* A sales method by which a manufacturer pays the reseller's freight costs, which the manufacturer accounts for before quoting the reseller a price. — **absorb,** *vb.*

abstention. (16c) **1.** The act of withholding or keeping back (something or oneself); esp., the act of abstaining from voting. **2.** A federal court's relinquishment of jurisdiction when necessary to avoid needless conflict with a state's administration of its own affairs. **3.** The legal principle underlying such a relinquishment of jurisdiction. — **abstain,** *vb.*

Burford abstention. (1967) A federal court's refusal to review a state court's decision in cases involving a complex regulatory scheme and sensitive areas of state concern. *Burford v. Sun Oil Co.*, 319 U.S. 315, 63 S.Ct. 1098 (1943).

Colorado River abstention. (1976) A federal court's decision to abstain while relevant and parallel state-court proceedings are under way. *Colorado River Water Conservation Dist. v. United States*, 424 U.S. 800, 96 S.Ct. 1236 (1976).

equitable abstention. A federal court's refraining from interfering with a state administrative agency's decision on a local matter when the aggrieved party has adequate relief in the state courts.

Pullman abstention. (1963) A federal court's decision to abstain so that state courts will have an opportunity to settle an underlying state-law question whose resolution may avert the need to decide a federal constitutional question. *Railroad Comm'n v. Pullman Co.*, 312 U.S. 496, 61 S.Ct. 643 (1941).

Thibodaux abstention (**tib**-ə-doh). (1974) A federal court's decision to abstain so that state courts can decide difficult issues of public importance that, if decided by the federal court, could result in unnecessary friction between state and federal authorities. *Louisiana Power & Light Co. v. City of Thibodaux*, 360 U.S. 25, 79 S.Ct. 1070 (1959).

Younger abstention. (1972) **1.** A federal court's decision not to interfere with an ongoing state criminal proceeding by issuing an injunction or granting declaratory relief, unless the prosecution has been brought in bad faith or merely as harassment. *Younger v. Harris*, 401 U.S. 37, 91 S.Ct. 746 (1971). **2.** By extension, a federal court's decision not to interfere with a state-court civil proceeding used to enforce the criminal law, as to abate an obscene nuisance.

abstract, *n.* (15c) A concise statement of a text, esp. of a legal document; a summary.

abstraction (ab- *or* əb-**strak**-shən), *n.* (16c) **1.** The mental process of considering something without reference to a concrete instance. **2.** A theoretical idea not applied to any particular instance. **3.** The summarizing and recording of a legal instrument in public records. **4.** The act of taking with the intent to injure or defraud. — **abstract** (ab-**strakt**), *vb.*

abstract of judgment. (1812) A copy or summary of a judgment that, when filed with the appropriate public office, creates a lien on the judgment debtor's nonexempt property.

abstract of record. An abbreviated case history that is complete enough to show an appellate court that the questions presented for review have been preserved.

abstract of title. (1858) A concise statement, usu. prepared for a mortgagee or purchaser of real property, summarizing the history of a piece of land, including all conveyances, interests, liens, and encumbrances that affect title to the property.

absurdity, *n.* The state or quality of being grossly unreasonable; esp., an interpretation that would lead to an unconscionable result, esp. one that the parties or (esp. for a statute) the drafters could not have intended and certainly never considered.

abuse (ə-**byoos**), *n.* (15c) **1.** A departure from legal or reasonable use; misuse. **2.** Physical or mental maltreatment, often resulting in mental, emotional, sexual, or physical injury.

abuse of the elderly. (1971) Abuse of a senior citizen, esp. by a caregiver or relative. • Examples include deprivation of food or medication, beatings, oral assaults, and isolation.

child abuse. (1891) **1.** Intentional or neglectful physical or emotional harm inflicted on a child, including sexual molestation; esp., a parent's or caregiver's act or failure to act that results in a child's exploitation, serious physical or emotional injury, sexual abuse, or death. **2.** An act or failure to act that presents an imminent risk of serious harm to a child. • Child abuse can be either intentional or negligent.

emotional abuse. Physical or verbal abuse that causes or could cause serious emotional injury.

secondary abuse. Emotional harm suffered by children who, although they are not physically abused, witness domestic violence within their families.

sexual abuse. (1874) **1.** An illegal or wrongful sex act, esp. one performed against a minor by an adult. **2.** RAPE (2).

spousal abuse. (1978) Physical, sexual, or psychological abuse inflicted by one spouse on the other spouse; esp., wife-beating.

verbal abuse. Emotional abuse inflicted by one person on another by means of words, esp. spoken words, in a way that causes distress, fear, or similar emotions. • Verbal abuse may include name-calling, insults, threatening gestures, excessive and unfounded criticism, humiliation, and denigration. — Also sometimes termed *vulgar abuse.*

abuse (ə-**byooz**), *vb.* (15c) **1.** To damage (a thing). **2.** To depart from legal or reasonable use in dealing with (a person or thing); to misuse. **3.** To injure (a person) physically or mentally. **4.** In the context of child welfare, to hurt or injure (a child) by maltreatment.

abuse excuse. (1994) *Criminal law.* The defense that a defendant cannot tell right from wrong or control impulses because of physical or mental abuse suffered as a child. • Like the traditional excuse of insanity, the abuse excuse is asserted by a defendant in an effort to mitigate or avoid culpability for the crime charged.

abuse of discretion. (18c) **1.** An adjudicator's failure to exercise sound, reasonable, and legal decision-making. **2.** An appellate court's standard for reviewing a decision that is asserted to be grossly unsound, unreasonable, illegal, or unsupported by the evidence.

abuse of process. (1809) The improper and tortious use of a legitimately issued court process to obtain a result that is either unlawful or beyond the process's scope.

abuse-of-the-writ doctrine. (1973) *Criminal procedure.* The principle that a petition for a writ of habeas corpus may not raise claims that should have been, but were not, asserted in a previous petition.

abut (ə-**bət**), *vb.* (15c) To join at a border or boundary; to share a common boundary with. — **abutment** (ə-**bət**-mənt), *n.*

abuttals (ə-**bət**-əlz). (17c) Land boundaries; the boundary lines of a piece of land in relation to other contiguous lands.

a/c. *abbr.* Account.

academic freedom. (1863) The right (esp. of a university teacher) to speak freely about political or ideological issues without fear of loss of position or other reprisal.

acceleration, *n.* **1.** The advancing of a loan agreement's maturity date so that payment of the entire debt is due immediately. **2.** The shortening of the time for vesting in possession of an expectant interest. **3.** *Property.* The hastening of an owner's time for enjoyment of an estate because of the failure of a preceding estate. — **accelerate,** *vb.*

acceleration clause. (1905) A loan-agreement provision that requires the debtor to pay off the balance sooner than the due date if some specified event occurs, such as failure to pay an installment or to maintain insurance.

acceptance, *n.* (16c) **1.** An offeree's assent, either by express act or by implication from conduct, to the terms of an offer in a manner authorized or requested by the offeror, so that a binding contract is formed. • If an acceptance modifies the terms or adds new ones, it generally operates as a counteroffer. **2.** A buyer's assent that the goods are to be taken in performance of a contract for sale. **3.** The formal receipt of and agreement to pay a negotiable instrument. **4.** A negotiable instrument, esp. a bill of exchange, that has been accepted for payment. — **accept,** *vb.*

accommodation acceptance. (1807) The acceptance of an offer to buy goods for current or prompt shipment by shipping nonconforming goods after notifying the buyer that the shipment is intended as an accommodation. • This type of "acceptance" is not truly an acceptance under contract law, but operates instead as a counteroffer if the buyer is duly notified.

conditional acceptance. An agreement to pay a draft on the occurrence or nonoccurrence of a particular event.

express acceptance. A written or oral expression indicating that the drawee has seen the instrument and does not dispute its sufficiency.

implied acceptance. An acceptance implied by a drawee whose actions indicate an intention to comply with the request of the drawer; conduct by the drawee from which the holder is justified in concluding that the drawee intends to accept the instrument.

qualified acceptance. A conditional or partial acceptance that varies the original terms of an offer and operates as a counteroffer.

acceptance-of-the-benefits rule. (1972) The doctrine that a party may not appeal a judgment after having voluntarily and intentionally received all or some part of the relief provided by it.

accession (ak-**sesh**-ən). (16c) **1.** The act of acceding or agreeing. **2.** A coming into possession of a right or office. **3.** *Int'l law.* A method by which a nation that is not among a treaty's original signatories becomes a party to it. **4.** The acquisition of title to personal property by bestowing labor on a raw material to convert it to another thing. **5.** A property owner's right to all that is added to the property (esp. land) naturally or by labor, including land left by floods and improvements made by others. **6.** An improvement to existing personal property, such as new shafts on golf clubs.

accessory (ak-**ses**-ə-ree), *n.* (15c) **1.** Something of secondary or subordinate importance. **2.** *Criminal law.* A person who aids or contributes in the commission or concealment of a crime. • An accessory is usu. liable only if the crime is a felony. — **accessory,** *adj.* — **accessoryship,** *n.*

accessory after the fact. (17c) An accessory who was not at the scene of the crime but knows that a crime has been committed and who helps the offender try to escape arrest or punishment. 18 USCA § 3. An accessory after the fact may be prosecuted for obstructing justice. — Sometimes shortened to *accessory after.*

accessory before the fact. (17c) An accessory who assists or encourages another to commit a crime but who is not present when the offense is actually committed. • Most jurisdictions have abolished this category of accessory and instead treat such an offender as an accomplice.

accident, *n.* (14c) **1.** An unintended and unforeseen injurious occurrence; something that does not occur in the usual course of events or that could not be reasonably anticipated. **2.** *Equity practice.* An unforeseen and injurious occurrence not attributable to the victim's mistake, negligence, neglect, or misconduct; an unanticipated and untoward event that causes harm. — **accidental,** *adj.*

accidental killing. (17c) Homicide resulting from a lawful act performed in a lawful manner under a reasonable belief that no harm could occur. Cf. MALICIOUS KILLING.

accommodation, *n.* (17c) **1.** A loan or other financial favor. **2.** The act of signing an accommodation paper as surety for another. **3.** The act or an instance of making a change or provision for someone or something; an adaptation or adjustment. **4.** A convenience supplied by someone; esp., lodging and food.

public accommodation. (1859) A business that provides lodging, food, entertainment, or other services to the public; esp. (as defined by the Civil Rights Act of 1964), one that affects interstate commerce or is supported by state action.

reasonable accommodation. An adaptation, adjustment, or allowance made for a disabled person's needs or an employee's religious beliefs or practices without imposing an undue hardship on the party taking the action. • Under the Americans with Disabilities Act, a school or an employer must make reasonable accommodations for an employee's disability. Examples of reasonable accommodations that have been approved by the courts include providing additional unpaid leave, modifying the employee's work schedule, and reassigning the employee to a more appropriate, vacant position.

accommodation paper. (18c) A negotiable instrument that one party cosigns, without receiving any consideration, as surety for another party who remains primarily liable. • An accommodation paper is typically used when the cosigner is more creditworthy than the principal debtor.

accommodation party. (1812) A person who, without recompense or other benefit, signs a negotiable instrument for the purpose of being a surety for another party (called the *accommodated party*) to the instrument. • The accommodation party can sign in any capacity (i.e., as maker, drawer, acceptor, or indorser). An accommodation party is liable to all parties except the accommodated party, who impliedly agrees to pay the note or draft and to indemnify the accommodation party for all losses incurred in having to pay it.

accomplice (ə-**kom**-plis). (1854) **1.** A person who is in any way involved with another in the commission of a crime, whether as a principal in the first or second degree or as an accessory. • Although the definition includes an accessory before the fact, not all authorities treat this term as including an accessory after the fact. **2.** A person who knowingly, voluntarily, and intentionally unites with the principal offender in committing a crime and thereby becomes punishable for it.

accord, *n.* (14c) **1.** An amicable arrangement between parties, esp. between peoples or nations; compact; treaty. **2.** An offer to give or to accept a stipulated performance in the future to satisfy an obligor's existing duty, together with an acceptance of that offer. • The performance becomes what is known as a *satisfaction.* **3.** A signal used in a legal citation to introduce a case clearly supporting a proposition for which another case is being quoted directly.

accord and satisfaction. (18c) An agreement to substitute for an existing debt some alternative form of discharging that debt, coupled with the actual discharge of the debt by the substituted performance. • The new agreement is called the *accord,* and the discharge is called the *satisfaction.*

account, *n.* (14c) **1.** ACCOUNTING (3). **2.** ACCOUNTING (4). **3.** A statement by which someone seeks to describe or explain an event. **4.** A detailed statement of the debits and credits between parties to a contract or to a fiduciary relationship; a reckoning of monetary dealings. — Abbr. acct.; a/c. **5.** A course of business dealings or other relations for which records must be kept.

account in trust. An account established by an individual to hold the account's assets in trust for someone else.

account payable. (*usu. pl.*) (1936) An account reflecting a balance owed to a creditor; a debt owed by an enterprise in the normal course of business dealing. Pl. *accounts payable.*

account receivable. (*usu. pl.*) (1936) An account reflecting a balance owed by a debtor; a debt owed by a customer to an enterprise for goods or services. Pl. *accounts receivable.*

account rendered. An account produced by the creditor and presented for the debtor's examination and acceptance.

account settled. An account with a paid balance.

account stated. (17c) **1.** A balance that parties to a transaction or settlement agree on, either expressly or by implication. • The phrase also refers to the agreement itself or to the assent giving rise to the agreement. **2.** A plaintiff's claim in a suit for such a balance. **3.** *Equity practice.* A defendant's plea in response to an action for an accounting. • The defendant states that the balance due on the statement of the account has been discharged and that the defendant holds the plaintiff's release.

bank account. A deposit or credit account with a bank, such as a demand, time, savings, or passbook account. UCC § 4-104(a).

blocked account. An account at a bank or other financial institution, access to which has been restricted either by the government or by an authorized person.

custodial account. An account opened on behalf of someone else, such as one opened by a parent for a minor child, and usu. administered by a responsible third party. • Custodial accounts most often arise under the Uniform Transfers to Minors Act (1983).

deposit account. A demand, time, savings, passbook, or similar account maintained with a bank, savings-and-loan association, credit union, or like organization, other than investment property or an account evidenced by an instrument. UCC § 9-102(a)(20). — Abbr. D.A.

escrow account. A bank account, generally held in the name of the depositor and an escrow agent, that is returnable to the depositor or paid to a third person on the fulfillment of specified conditions.

joint account. (17c) A bank or brokerage account opened by two or more people, by which each party has a present right to withdraw all funds in the account and, upon the death of one party, the survivors become the owners of the account, with no right of the deceased party's heirs or devisees to share in it.

NOW account (now). An interest-bearing savings account on which the holder may write checks.

open account. (18c) **1.** An unpaid or unsettled account. **2.** An account that is left open for ongoing debit and credit entries by two parties and that has a fluctuating balance until either party finds it convenient to settle and close, at which time there is a single liability.

partial account. (18c) A preliminary accounting of an executor's or administrator's dealings with an estate.

running account. (18c) An open, unsettled account that exhibits the reciprocal demands between the parties.

accountable, *adj.* (14c) Responsible; answerable <the company was held accountable for the employee's negligence>. — **accountability,** *n.*

accountant. A person authorized under applicable law to practice public accounting; a person whose business is to keep books or accounts, to perform financial audits, to design and control accounting systems, and to give tax advice.

certified public accountant. An accountant who has satisfied the statutory and administrative requirements to be registered or licensed as a public accountant. — Abbr. CPA.

account book. A journal in which a business's transactions are recorded.

account for. (17c) **1.** To furnish a good reason or convincing explanation for; to explain the cause of. **2.** To render a reckoning of (funds held, esp. in trust). **3.** To answer for (conduct).

accounting. (18c) **1.** The act or a system of establishing or settling financial accounts; esp., the process of recording transactions in the financial records of a business and periodically extracting, sorting, and summarizing the recorded transactions to produce a set of financial records. **2.** A rendition of an account, either voluntarily or by court order. • The term frequently refers to the report of all items of property, income, and expenses prepared by a personal representative, trustee, or guardian and given to heirs, beneficiaries, or the probate court. **3.** A legal action to compel a defendant to account for and pay over money owed to the plaintiff but held by the defendant (often the plaintiff's agent); accounting for profits. **4.** More broadly, an action for the recovery of money for services performed, property sold and delivered, money loaned, or damages for the nonperformance of simple contracts. • Such an action is available when the rights of parties will be adequately protected by the payment of money. **5.** *Commercial law.* An equitable proceeding for a complete settlement of all partnership affairs, usu. in connection with partner misconduct or with a winding up. **6.** *Secured transactions.* A record that (1) is authenticated by a secured party, (2) indicates the aggregate unpaid secured obligation as of a date no more than 35 days before or after the date of the record, and (3) identifies the components of the obligations in reasonable detail. UCC § 9-102(a)(2).

accounting for profits. (1871) An action for equitable relief against a person in a fiduciary relationship to recover profits taken in a breach of the relationship.

accounting method. (1908) A system for determining income and expenses, profit and loss, asset value, appreciation and depreciation, and the like, esp. for tax purposes.

accrual accounting method (ə-**kroo**-əl). (1942) An accounting method that records entries of debits and credits when the revenue or liability arises, rather than when the income is received or an expense is paid.

capitalization accounting method. A method of determining an asset's present value by discounting its stream of expected future benefits at an appropriate rate.

cash-basis accounting method. (1954) An accounting method that considers only cash actually received as income and cash actually paid out as an expense.

completed-contract accounting method. A method of reporting profit or loss on certain long-term contracts by recognizing gross income and expenses in the tax year that the contract is completed.

cost accounting method. The practice of recording the value of assets in terms of their historical cost.

direct charge-off accounting method. A system of accounting by which a deduction for bad debts is allowed when an account has become partially or completely worthless.

equity accounting method. A method of accounting for long-term investment in common stock based on acquisition cost, investor income, net losses, and dividends.

fair-value accounting method. The valuation of assets at present actual or market value. • When this method is used to determine the value of a security or other financial instrument, it is also termed *mark-to-market accounting method.*

installment accounting method. (1954) A method by which a taxpayer can spread the recognition of gains from a sale of property over the payment period by computing the gross-profit percentage from the sale and applying it to each payment.

percentage-of-completion method. An accounting method in which revenue is recognized gradually during the completion of the subject matter of the contract.

physical-inventory accounting method. A method of counting a company's goods at the close of an accounting period.

purchase accounting method. A method of accounting for mergers whereby the total value paid or exchanged for the acquired firm's assets is recorded on the acquiring firm's books, and any difference between the fair market value of the assets acquired and the purchase price is recorded as goodwill.

accounting period. (1903) A regular span of time used for accounting purposes; esp., a period used by a taxpayer in determining income and related tax liability.

accredit (ə-**kred**-it), *vb.* **1.** To give official authorization or status to. **2.** To recognize (a school) as having sufficient academic standards to qualify graduates for higher education or for professional practice. **3.** *Int'l law.* To send (a person) with credentials as an envoy. — **accreditation** (ə-kred-i-**tay**-shən), *n.* — **accredited,** *adj.*

accretion (ə-**kree**-shən). (1830) **1.** The gradual accumulation of land by natural forces, esp. as alluvium is added to land situated on the bank of a river or on the seashore. **2.** Any increase in trust property other than increases ordinarily considered as income. **3.** A beneficiary's gain through the failure of a coheir or colegatee to take his or her share.

accrue (ə-**kroo**), *vb.* (15c) **1.** To come into existence as an enforceable claim or right; to arise <the plaintiff's cause of action for silicosis did not accrue until the plaintiff knew or had reason to know of the disease>. **2.** To accumulate periodically <the savings-account interest accrues monthly>. — **accrual,** *n.*

acct. *abbr.* Account.

accusation, *n.* (14c) **1.** A formal charge of criminal wrongdoing. • The accusation is usu. presented to a court or magistrate having jurisdiction to inquire into the alleged crime. **2.** A statement that a person has engaged in an illegal or immoral act.

accusatory body. (1877) A body (such as a grand jury) that hears evidence and determines whether a person should be charged with a crime.

accusatory part. The section of an indictment in which the offense is named.

accusatory stage. (1954) *Criminal procedure.* The point in a criminal proceeding when the suspect's right to counsel attaches. • This occurs usu. after arrest and once interrogation begins.

accuse, *vb.* (14c) To charge (a person) judicially or publicly with an offense; to make an accusation against.

accused, *n.* (16c) **1.** A person who has been blamed for wrongdoing; esp., a person who has been arrested and brought before a magistrate or who has been formally charged with a crime (as by indictment or information). **2.** A person against whom legal proceedings have been initiated.

acknowledgment. (16c) **1.** A recognition of something as being factual. **2.** An acceptance of responsibility. **3.** The act of making it known that one has received something. **4.** A formal declaration made in the presence of an authorized officer, such as a notary public, by someone who signs a document and confirms that the signature is authentic. • In most states, the officer certifies that (1) he or she personally knows the document signer or has established the signer's identity through satisfactory evidence, (2) the signer appeared before the officer on the date and in the place (usu. the county) indicated, and (3) the signer acknowledged signing the document freely. — **acknowledge,** *vb.*

ACLU. *abbr.* (1936) American Civil Liberties Union.

ACP. *abbr.* Administrative Domain-Name Challenge Panel.

ACPA. *abbr.* **1.** Anticybersquatting Consumer Protection Act. **2.** Anticounterfeiting Consumer Protection Act.

acquiescence (ak-wee-**es**-ənts). (17c) A person's tacit or passive acceptance; implied consent to an act. — **acquiesce** (ak-wee-**es**), *vb.* — **acquiescent** (ak-wee-**es**-ənt), *vb.*

acquired-rights doctrine. The principle that once a right has vested, it may not be reduced by later legislation.

acquisition, *n.* (14c) **1.** The gaining of possession or control over something. **2.** Something acquired.

acquit, *vb.* (13c) **1.** To clear (a person) of a criminal charge. **2.** To pay or discharge (a debt or claim).

acquittal, *n.* (15c) **1.** The legal certification, usu. by jury verdict, that an accused person is not guilty of the charged offense.

acquittal in fact. (17c) An acquittal by a jury verdict of not guilty.

acquittal in law. (17c) An acquittal by operation of law, as of someone who has been charged merely as an accessory after the principal has been acquitted.

implied acquittal. (1858) An acquittal in which a jury convicts the defendant of a lesser included offense without commenting on the greater offense. • Double jeopardy bars the retrial of a defendant on the higher offense after an implied acquittal.

2. *Contracts.* A release or discharge from debt or other liability; ACQUITTANCE.

acquittance, *n.* (14c) A document by which one is discharged from a debt or other obligation; a receipt or release indicating payment in full. — **acquit,** *vb.*

ACRS. *abbr.* Accelerated Cost-Recovery System.

act, *n.* (14c) **1.** Something done or performed, esp. voluntarily; a deed. **2.** The process of doing or performing; an occurrence that results from a person's will being exerted on the external world; ACTION (2).

act in pais (in **pay**). [Law French] An act performed out of court, such as a deed made between two parties on the land being transferred.

act in the law. (1829) An act that is intended to create, transfer, or extinguish a right and that is effective in law for that purpose; the exercise of a legal power.

act of the law. (17c) The creation, extinction, or transfer of a right by the operation of the law itself, without any consent on the part of the persons concerned.

administrative act. (1818) An act made in a management capacity; esp., an act made outside the actor's usual field (as when a judge supervises court personnel). • An administrative act is often subject to a greater risk of liability than an act within the actor's usual field.

bilateral act. (1895) An act that involves the consenting wills of two or more distinct parties, as with a contract, a conveyance, a mortgage, or a lease; AGREEMENT (1).

external act. (16c) An act involving bodily activity, such as speaking.

intentional act. (17c) An act resulting from the actor's will directed to that end. • An act is intentional when it is foreseen and desired by the doer, and this foresight and desire resulted in the act through the operation of the will.

internal act. (16c) An act of the mind, such as thinking.

judicial act. (16c) An act involving the exercise of judicial power.

jural act (**joor**-əl). (1860) An act taken in the context of or in furtherance of a society's legal system.

ministerial act. An act performed without the independent exercise of discretion or judgment. • If the act is mandatory, it is also termed a *ministerial duty.*

negative act. (17c) The failure to do something that is legally required; a nonoccurrence that involves the breach of a legal duty to take positive action. • This takes the form of either a forbearance or an omission.

negligent act. An act that creates an unreasonable risk of harm to another.

predicate act. An act that must be completed before legal consequences can attach to it or to another act or before further action can be taken. • In statutes, words such as "if" often precede a description of a predicate act.

tortious act. An act that subjects the actor to liability under the principles of tort law.

unilateral act. (1861) An act in which there is only one party whose will operates, as in a testamentary disposition, the exercise of a power of appointment, or the voidance of a voidable contract.

unintentional act. (1820) An act not resulting from the actor's will toward what actually takes place.

verbal act. (18c) **1.** An act performed through the medium of words, either spoken or written. **2.** *Evidence.* A statement offered to prove the words themselves because of their legal effect (e.g., the terms of a will). • For this purpose, the statement is not considered hearsay.

3. The formal product of a legislature or other deliberative body; esp., statute.

acting, *adj.* (18c) Holding an interim position; serving temporarily <an acting director>.

action. (14c) **1.** The process of doing something; conduct or behavior. **2.** A thing done; ACT (2). **3.** A civil or criminal judicial proceeding.

action at law. A civil suit stating a legal cause of action and seeking only a legal remedy.

action for money had and received. At common law, an action by which the plaintiff could recover money paid to the defendant, the money usu. being recoverable because (1) the money had been paid by mistake or under compulsion, or (2) the consideration was insufficient.

action for money paid. At common law, an action by which the plaintiff could recover money paid to a third party — not to the defendant — in circumstances in which the defendant had benefited.

action in equity. (18c) An action that seeks equitable relief, such as an injunction or specific performance, as opposed to damages.

action in personam (in pər-**soh**-nəm). (1800) **1.** An action brought against a person rather than property. • An *in personam* judgment is binding on the judgment–debtor and can be enforced against all the property of the judgment–debtor. **2.** An action in which the named defendant is a natural or legal person.

action in rem (in **rem**). (18c) An action determining the title to property and the rights of the parties, not merely among themselves, but also against all persons at any time claiming an interest in that property; a real action.

action quasi in rem (**kway**-sɪ in **rem** *or* **kway**-zɪ). (1883) An action brought against the defendant personally, with jurisdiction based on an interest in property, the objective being to deal with the particular property or to subject the property to the discharge of the claims asserted.

action to quiet title. (1837) A proceeding to establish a plaintiff's title to land by compelling the adverse claimant to establish a claim or be forever estopped from asserting it.

civil action. (16c) An action brought to enforce, redress, or protect a private or civil right; a noncriminal litigation.

collusive action. (18c) An action between two parties who have no actual controversy, being merely for the purpose of determining a legal question or receiving a precedent that might prove favorable in related litigation.

criminal action. (16c) An action instituted by the government to punish offenses against the public.

cross-action. An action brought by the defendant against the plaintiff based on the same subject matter as the plaintiff's action.

joint action. **1.** An action brought by two or more plaintiffs. **2.** An action brought against two or more defendants.

penal action. (16c) **1.** A criminal prosecution. **2.** A civil proceeding in which either the state or a common informer sues to recover a penalty from a defendant who has violated a statute. **3.**

A civil lawsuit by an aggrieved party seeking recovery of a statutory fine or a penalty, such as punitive damages.

personal action. (17c) An action brought for the recovery of debts, personal property, or damages arising from any cause.

petitory action (**pet**-ə-tor-ee). (17c) **1.** *Roman & civil law.* An action to establish and enforce title to property independently of the right to possession. **2.** *Civil law.* An action for the recognition of ownership or other real right in immovable (or sometimes movable) property.

plenary action (**plee**-nə-ree *or* **plen**-). (1837) A full hearing or trial on the merits, as opposed to a summary proceeding.

possessory action (pə-**zes**-ə-ree). (17c) An action to obtain, recover, or maintain possession of property but not title to it, such as an action to evict a nonpaying tenant.

real action. (16c) An action brought for the recovery of land or other real property; specif., an action to recover the possession of a freehold estate in real property, or seisin.

separate action. (18c) **1.** An action brought alone by each of several complainants who are all involved in the same transaction but either cannot legally join the suit or, not being required to join, choose not to join it. **2.** One of several distinct actions brought by a single plaintiff against each of two or more parties who are all liable to a plaintiff with respect to the same subject matter.

sham action. An objectively baseless lawsuit the primary purpose of which is to hinder or interfere with a competitor's business relationships. See *Professional Real Estate Investors, Inc. v. Columbia Pictures Indus., Inc.*, 508 U.S. 49, 113 S.Ct. 1920 (1993).

third-party action. (1872) An action brought as part of a lawsuit already pending but distinct from the main claim, whereby a defendant sues an entity not sued by the plaintiff when that entity may be liable to the defendant for all or part of the plaintiff's claim. • A common example is an action for indemnity or contribution.

actionable, *adj.* (16c) Furnishing the legal ground for a lawsuit or other legal action <intentional interference with contractual relations is an actionable tort>.

act of Congress. (18c) A law that is formally enacted in accordance with the legislative power granted to Congress by the U.S. Constitution.

act of God. (18c) An overwhelming, unpreventable event caused exclusively by forces of nature, such as an earthquake, flood, or tornado. • The definition has been statutorily broadened to include all natural phenomena that are exceptional, inevitable, and irresistible, the effects of which could not be prevented or avoided by the exercise of due care or foresight. 42 USCA § 9601(1).

act of hostility. An event that may be considered an adequate cause for war; *casus belli.*

act of possession. (16c) **1.** The exercise of physical control over a corporeal thing, movable or immovable, with the intent to own it. **2.** Conduct indicating an intent to claim property as one's own; esp., conduct that supports a claim of adverse possession.

actor. One who acts; a person whose conduct is in question.

bad actor. An actor who is shown or perceived to have engaged in illegal, impermissible, or unconscionable conduct. • A presumption that a person is a bad actor may be created by an adverse-inference instruction.

actual, *adj.* (14c) Existing in fact; real <actual malice>. Cf. CONSTRUCTIVE.

actually litigated. (1969) (Of a claim that might be barred by collateral estoppel) properly raised in an earlier lawsuit, submitted to the court for a determination, and determined.

actual physical control. (1880) Direct bodily power over something, esp. a vehicle. • Many jurisdictions require a showing of "actual physical control" of a vehicle by a person charged with driving while intoxicated.

actuarial method. A means of determining the amount of interest on a loan by using the loan's annual percentage rate to separately calculate the finance charge for each payment period, after crediting each payment, which is credited first to interest and then to principal.

actuary (**ak**-choo-air-ee), *n.* A statistician who determines the present effects of future contingent events; esp., one who calculates insurance and pension rates on the basis of empirically based tables. — **actuarial** (ak-choo-**air**-ee-əl), *adj.*

actus reus (**ak**-təs **ree**-əs *also* **ray**-əs). [Law Latin "guilty act"] (1902) The wrongful deed that comprises the physical components of a crime and that generally must be coupled with *mens rea* to establish criminal liability; a forbidden act.

A.D. *abbr.* Anno Domini.

ad (ad), *prep.* [Latin] At; by; for; near; on account of; to; until; upon; with relation to; concerning.

ADA. *abbr.* Americans with Disabilities Act.

ad damnum **clause** (ad **dam**-nəm). [Latin "to the damage"] (1840) A clause in a prayer for relief stating the amount of damages claimed.

addendum (ə-**den**-dəm). (17c) Something to be added, esp. to a document; a supplement.

addict (**a**-dikt), *n.* A person who habitually uses a substance, esp. a narcotic drug. — **addict** (ə-**dikt**), *vb.* — **addictive,** *adj.* — **addiction,** *n.*

addition. (17c) A structure that is attached to or connected with another building that predates the structure; an extension or annex. • Although some courts have held that an addition is merely an appurtenant structure that might not actually be in physical contact with the other building, most courts hold that there must be physical contact.

additur (**ad**-ə-tuur). [Latin "it is added to"] (1894) A trial court's order, issued usu. with the defendant's consent, that increases the jury's award of damages to avoid a new trial on grounds of inadequate damages. • The term may also refer to the increase itself, the procedure, or the court's power to make the order. Cf. REMITTITUR.

add-on clause. (1965) An installment-contract provision that converts earlier purchases into security for new purchases.

adduce (ə-**d[y]oos**), *vb.* (15c) To offer or put forward for consideration (something) as evidence or authority. — **adduction** (ə-**dək**-shən), *n.* — **adducible** (ə-**d[y]oo**-sə-bəl), *adj.*

ADEA. *abbr.* Age Discrimination in Employment Act.

ademption (ə-**demp**-shən), *n.* (16c) *Wills & estates.* The destruction or extinction of a testamentary gift by reason of a bequeathed asset's ceasing to be part of the estate at the time of the testator's death; a beneficiary's forfeiture of a legacy or bequest that is no longer operative. — **adeem** (ə-**deem**), *vb.* — **adeemed, adempted,** *adj.*

ademption by extinction. (1847) An ademption that occurs because the unique property that is the subject of a specific bequest has been sold, given away, or destroyed, or is not otherwise in existence at the time of the testator's death.

ademption by satisfaction. (1916) An ademption that occurs because the testator, while alive, has already given property to the beneficiary in lieu of the testamentary gift.

adequate, *adj.* Legally sufficient <adequate notice>.

adequate-state-grounds doctrine. (1962) A judge-made principle that prevents the U.S. Supreme Court from reviewing a state-court decision based partially on state law if a decision on a federal issue would not change the result.

ad hoc (ad **hok**), *adj.* [Latin "for this"] Formed for a particular purpose <the board created an ad hoc committee to discuss funding for the new arena>. — **ad hoc,** *adv.*

ad hominem (ad **hom**-ə-nəm), *adj.* [Latin "to the person"] (16c) Appealing to personal prejudices rather than to reason; attacking an opponent's character rather than the opponent's assertions <the brief was replete with ad hominem attacks against opposing counsel>. — **ad hominem,** *adv.*

ad infinitum (ad in-fə-**nɪ**-təm). [Latin "without limit"] To an indefinite extent <a corporation has a duration *ad infinitum* unless the articles of incorporation specify a period>.

ad interim (ad **in**-tər-im), *adv.* [Latin] *Hist.* In the meantime; temporarily.

adjacent, *adj.* Lying near or close to, but not necessarily touching.

adjective law (**aj**-ik-tiv). (1808) The body of rules governing procedure and practice; PROCEDURAL LAW.

adjourn (ə-**jərn**), *vb.* (15c) *Parliamentary law.* To end or postpone (a proceeding). — **adjournment** (ə-**jərn**-mənt), *n.*

adjourn sine die (**sɪ**-nee [or **sin**-ay] **dɪ**-ee). [Latin "without date"] To end a deliberative assembly's or court's session without setting a time to reconvene.

adjourn to a day certain. To end a deliberative assembly's or court's session while fixing a time for the next meeting.

adjudge (ə-**jəj**), *vb.* (14c) **1.** Adjudicate. **2.** To deem or pronounce to be. **3.** To award judicially.

adjudication (ə-joo-di-**kay**-shən), *n.* (17c) **1.** The legal process of resolving a dispute; the process of judicially deciding a case. **2.** JUDGMENT. — **adjudicate** (ə-**joo**-di-kayt), *vb.* — **adjudicative** (ə-**joo**-di-kə-tiv), *adj.*

adjudicator (ə-**joo**-di-kay-tər). A person whose job is to render binding decisions; one who makes judicial pronouncements.

adjunct (**aj**-əngkt), *adj.* (16c) Added as an accompanying object or circumstance; attached in a subordinate or temporary capacity <an adjunct professor>. — **adjunct,** *n.*

adjure (ə-**juur**), *vb.* (14c) To charge or entreat solemnly. — **adjuration** (aj-ə-**ray**-shən), *n.* — **adjuratory** (ə-**juur**-ə-tor-ee), *adj.* — **adjurer, adjuror** (ə-**juur**-ər), *n.*

adjuster. One appointed to ascertain, arrange, or settle a matter; esp., an independent agent or employee of an insurance company who investigates claimed losses, and negotiates and settles claims against the insurer.

ad litem (ad **lɪ**-tem *or* -təm). [Latin "for the suit"] (18c) For the purposes of the suit; pending the suit.

admeasurement (ad-**mezh**-ər-mənt), *n.* (16c) **1.** Ascertainment, assignment, or apportionment by a fixed quantity or value, or by certain limits. **2.** A writ obtained for purposes of ascertaining, assigning, or apportioning a fixed quantity or value or to establish limits; esp., a writ available against persons who usurp more than their rightful share of property. — **admeasure** (ad-**mezh**-ər), *vb.*

administration, *n.* (14c) **1.** The management or performance of the executive duties of a government, institution, or business. **2.** In public law, the practical management and direction of the executive department and its agencies. **3.** A judicial action in which a court undertakes the management and distribution of property. **4.** The management and settlement of the estate of an intestate decedent, or of a testator who has no executor, by a person legally appointed and supervised by the court. — **administer,** *vb.* — **administrative,** *adj.*

administration cum testamento annexo (kəm tes-tə-**men**-toh ə-**nek**-soh). [Latin "with the will annexed"] An administration granted when (1) a testator's will does not name any executor or when the executor named is incompetent to act, is deceased, or refuses to act, and (2) no successor executor has been named or is qualified to serve. — Abbr. c.t.a.

administration de bonis non (dee **boh**-nis **non**). [Latin "of the goods not administered"] An administration granted for the purpose of settling the remainder of an intestate estate that was not administered by the former administrator. — Abbr. d.b.n.

administration de bonis non cum testamento annexo (de **boh**-nis non kəm tes-tə-**men**-toh ə-**nek**-soh). An administration granted to settle the remainder of a testate estate not settled by a previous administrator or executor. • This type of administration arises when there is a valid will, as opposed to an *administration de bonis non,* which is granted when there is no will. — Abbr. d.b.n.c.t.a.

administration durante absentia (d[y]uu-**ran**-tee ab-**sen**-shee-ə). An administration granted during the absence of either the executor or the person who has precedence as administrator.

administration durante minore aetate (d[y]uu-**ran**-tee mi-**nor**-ee ee-**tay**-tee). An administration granted during the minority of either a child executor or the person who has precedence as administrator.

administration pendente lite (pen-**den**-tee **lɪ**-tee). An administration granted during the pendency of a suit concerning a will's validity.

ancillary administration (**an**-sə-ler-ee). (1814) An administration that is auxiliary to the administration at the place of the decedent's domicile, such as one in another state. • The purpose of this process is to collect assets, to transfer and record changed title to real property located there, and to pay any debts in that locality.

caeterorum administration (set-ə-**ror**-əm). [Latin "of the rest"] An administration granted when limited powers previously granted to an administrator are inadequate to settle the estate's residue.

domiciliary administration (dom-ə-**sil**-ee-er-ee). (1850) The handling of an estate in the state where the decedent was domiciled at death.

general administration. (18c) An administration with authority to deal with an entire estate. Cf. *special administration.*

limited administration. (18c) An administration for a temporary period or for a special purpose.

original administration. An administration that is not ancillary to a domiciliary administration.

public administration. (1893) In some jurisdictions, an administration by an officer appointed to administer for an intestate who has left no person entitled to apply for letters (or whose possible representatives refuse to serve).

special administration. (18c) An administration with authority to deal with only some of a decedent's property, as opposed to administering the whole estate. Cf. *general administration.*

temporary administration. (18c) An administration in which the court appoints a fiduciary to administer the affairs of a decedent's estate for a short time before an administrator or executor can be appointed and qualified.

administration of justice. The maintenance of right within a political community by means of the physical force of the state; the state's application of the sanction of force to the rule of right.

administrative hearing. An administrative-agency proceeding in which evidence is offered for argument or trial.

administrative law. (1896) The law governing the organization and operation of administrative agencies (including executive and independent agencies) and the relations of administrative agencies with the legislature, the executive, the judiciary, and the public. • Administrative law is divided into three parts: (1) the statutes endowing agencies with powers and establishing rules of substantive law relating to those powers; (2) the body of agency-made law, consisting of administrative rules, regulations, reports, or opinions containing findings of fact, and orders; and (3) the legal principles governing the acts of public agents when those acts conflict with private rights.

administrative-law judge. (1972) An official who presides at an administrative hearing and who has the power to administer oaths, take testimony, rule on questions of evidence, and make factual and legal determinations. 5 USCA § 556(c). — Abbr. ALJ.

administrative proceeding. (1841) A hearing, inquiry, investigation, or trial before an administrative agency, usu. adjudicatory in nature but sometimes quasi-legislative.

administrative rule. (1856) An officially promulgated agency regulation that has the force of law.

administrative tribunal. An administrative agency before which a matter may be heard or tried, as distinguished from a purely executive agency; an administrative agency exercising a judicial function.

administrator (ad-**min**-ə-stray-tər). (15c) **1.** A person who manages or heads a business, public office, or agency. **2.** A person appointed by the court to manage the assets and liabilities of an intestate decedent.

administrator ad litem (ad **lɪ**-tem *or* -təm). A special administrator appointed by the court to represent the estate's interest in an action usu. either because there is no administrator of the estate or because the current administrator has an interest in the action adverse to that of the estate.

administrator ad prosequendum (ad prahs-ə-**kwen**-dəm). An administrator appointed to prosecute or defend a certain action or actions involving the estate.

administrator cum testamento annexo (kəm tes-tə-**men**-toh ə-**nek**-soh). An administrator appointed by the court to carry out the provisions of a will when the testator has named no executor, or the executors named refuse, are incompetent to act, or have died before performing their duties.

administrator de bonis non (dee **boh**-nis **non**). An administrator appointed by the court to administer the decedent's goods that were not administered by an earlier administrator or executor. • If there is no will, the administrator bears the name *administrator de bonis non* (abbr. *administrator d.b.n.*), but if there is a will, the full name is *administrator de bonis* *non cum testamento annexo* (abbr. *administrator d.b.n.c.t.a.*).

administrator durante minore aetate (d[y]uu-**ran**-tee mi-**nor**-ee ee-**tay**-tee). An administrator who acts during the minority of a person who either is named by the testator as the estate's executor or would be appointed as the estate's administrator but for the person's youth.

ancillary administrator (**an**-sə-ler-ee). (1825) A court-appointed administrator who oversees the distribution of the part of a decedent's estate located in a jurisdiction other than where the decedent was domiciled (the place of the main administration).

domiciliary administrator. A person appointed to administer an estate in the state where the decedent was domiciled at death.

foreign administrator. An administrator appointed in another jurisdiction.

general administrator. (18c) A person appointed to administer an intestate decedent's entire estate.

public administrator. (1809) A state-appointed officer who administers intestate estates that are not administered by the decedent's relatives. • This officer's right to administer is usu. subordinate to the rights of creditors, but in a few jurisdictions the creditors' rights are subordinate.

special administrator. (18c) **1.** A person appointed to administer only a specific part of an intestate decedent's estate. **2.** A person appointed to serve as administrator of an estate solely because of an emergency or an unusual situation, such as a will contest.

administratrix (ad-min-ə-**stray**-triks *or* ad-**min**-ə-strə-triks). *Archaic.* A female administrator. Pl. **administratrixes, administratrices.**

admiralty (**ad**-mə-rəl-tee), *n.* **1.** A court that exercises jurisdiction over all maritime contracts, torts, injuries, or offenses. • The federal courts are so called when exercising their admiralty jurisdiction. **2.** The system of jurisprudence that has grown out of the practice of admiralty courts; maritime law. **3.** Narrowly, the rules governing contract, tort, and workers'-compensation claims arising out of commerce on or over navigable water. — **admiralty,** *adj.*

admissibility (ad-mis-ə-**bil**-ə-tee), *n.* (18c) The quality or state of being allowed to be entered into evidence in a hearing, trial, or other official proceeding.

conditional admissibility. (1904) The evidentiary rule that when a piece of evidence is not itself admissible, but is admissible if certain other facts make it relevant, the evidence becomes admissible on condition that counsel later introduce the connecting facts.

curative admissibility. (1904) The rule that an inadmissible piece of evidence may be admitted if offered to cure or counteract the effect of some similar piece of the opponent's evidence that itself should not have been admitted.

limited admissibility. (1910) The principle that testimony or exhibits may be admitted into evidence for a restricted purpose.

multiple admissibility. (1904) The evidentiary rule that, although a piece of evidence is inadmissible under one rule for the purpose given in offering it, it is nevertheless admissible if relevant and offered for some other purpose not forbidden by the rules of evidence.

admissible (ad-**mis**-ə-bəl), *adj.* (17c) **1.** Capable of being legally admitted; allowable; permissible. **2.** Worthy of gaining entry or being admitted.

admission (ad-**mish**-ən), *n.* (15c) **1.** Any statement or assertion made by a party to a case and offered against that party; an acknowledgment that facts are true.

admission against interest. (1828) A person's statement acknowledging a fact that is harmful to the person's position, esp. as a litigant.

admission by party-opponent. (1959) An opposing party's admission, which is not considered hearsay if it is offered against that party and is (1) the party's own statement, in either an individual or a representative capacity; (2) a statement of which the party has manifested an adoption or belief in its truth; (3) a statement by one authorized by the party to make such a statement; (4) a statement by the party's agent concerning a matter within the scope of the agency or employment and made during the existence of the relationship; or (5) a statement by a coconspirator of the party during the course of and in furtherance of the conspiracy. Fed. R. Evid. 801(d)(2).

admission by silence. (1867) The failure of a party to speak after another party's assertion of fact that, if untrue, would naturally compel a person to deny the statement.

adoptive admission. (1940) An action by a party that indicates approval of a statement made by another, and thereby acceptance that the statement is true.

extrajudicial admission. (1824) An admission made outside court proceedings.

implied admission. (18c) An admission reasonably inferable from a party's action or statement, or a party's failure to act or speak.

incidental admission. An admission made in some other connection or involved in the admission of some other fact.

incriminating admission. An admission of facts tending to establish guilt.

judicial admission. (18c) A formal waiver of proof that relieves an opposing party from having to prove the admitted fact and bars the party who made the admission from disputing it.

quasi-admission. (1813) An act or utterance, usu. extrajudicial, that creates an inconsistency with and discredits, to a greater or lesser degree, a present claim or other evidence of the person creating the inconsistency.

2. Acceptance of a lawyer by the established licensing authority, such as a state bar association, as a member of the practicing bar, usu. after the lawyer passes a bar examination and supplies adequate character references <admission to the bar>.

admonition (ad-mə-**nish**-ən), *n.* (14c) **1.** Any authoritative advice or caution from the court to the jury regarding their duty as jurors or the admissibility of evidence for consideration. **2.** A reprimand or cautionary statement addressed to counsel by a judge. — **admonish** (ad-**mon**-ish), *vb.* — **admonitory.**

adoption, *n.* (14c) **1.** *Family law.* The creation of a parent–child relationship by judicial order between two parties who usu. are unrelated; the relation of parent and child created by law between persons who are not in fact parent and child. • This relationship is brought about only after a determination that the child is an orphan or has been abandoned, or that the parents' parental rights have been terminated by court order.

adoption by estoppel. (1933) **1.** An equitable adoption of a child by one who promises or acts in a way that precludes the person and his or her estate from denying adopted status to the child. **2.** An equitable decree of adoption treating as done that which ought to have been done.

adult adoption. The adoption of one adult by another.

agency adoption. An adoption in which parental rights are terminated and legal custody is relinquished to an agency that finds and approves the adoptive parents.

black-market adoption. **1.** An illegal adoption in which an intermediary (a broker) receives payment for his or her services. **2.** Baby-selling.

closed adoption. An adoption in which the biological parent relinquishes his or her parental rights and surrenders the child to an unknown person or persons; an adoption in which there is no disclosure of the identity of the birth parents, adopting parent or parents, or child.

cooperative adoption. A process in which the birth parents and adoptive parents negotiate to reach a voluntary agreement about the degree and type of continuing contact after adoption, including direct visitation or more limited arrangements such as communication by telephone or mail, the exchange of either identifying or nonidentifying information, and other forms of contact.

de facto adoption. An adoption that falls short of the statutory requirements in a particular state.

embryo adoption. *Slang.* The receipt of a frozen embryo that is implanted into a recipient's womb.

international adoption. An adoption in which parents domiciled in one nation travel to a foreign country to adopt a child there, usu. in accordance with the laws of the child's nation.

interstate adoption. An adoption in which the prospective parents live in one state and the child lives in another state.

joint adoption. An adoption in which the prospective parents apply as a couple and are approved or rejected as a couple, as opposed to filing separate and individual applications to adopt a child.

open adoption. An adoption in which the biological mother (sometimes with the biological father) chooses the adoptive parents and in which the child often continues to have a postadoption relationship with his or her biological family.

posthumous adoption. An adoption that becomes legally final after the death of either an adoptive parent or the adopted child.

private adoption. (1865) An adoption that occurs independently between the biological mother (and sometimes the biological father) and the adoptive parents without the involvement of an agency.

second-parent adoption. An adoption by an unmarried cohabiting partner of a child's legal parent, not involving the termination of a legal parent's rights; esp., an adoption in which a lesbian, gay man, or unmarried heterosexual person adopts his or her partner's biological or adoptive child.

stepparent adoption. The adoption of a child by a stepfather or stepmother.

transracial adoption. An adoption in which at least one adoptive parent is of a race different from that of the adopted child. • Under federal law, child-placement agencies may not use race as a factor in approving adoptions. 42 USCA § 5115a.

2. *Contracts.* The process by which a person agrees to assume a contract previously made for that person's benefit, such as a newly formed corporation's acceptance of a preincorporation contract. — **adopt,** *vb.* — **adoptive,** *adj.*

adoption agency. A licensed establishment where a biological parent can voluntarily surrender a child for adoption.

adoption-registry statute. A law that provides for the release of adoption information if the biological parent, the adoptive parent, and the adoptee (after he or she reaches a certain statutorily prescribed age) all officially record their desire for its release.

adoptive-admissions rule. (1949) *Evidence.* The principle that a statement offered against an accused is not inadmissible hearsay if the accused is aware of the statement and has, by words or conduct, indicated acceptance that the statement is true.

adult (ə-**dəlt** *or* **ad**-əlt), *n.* (17c) A person who has attained the legal age of majority, generally 17 in criminal cases and 18 for other purposes. — **adult** (ə-**dəlt**), *adj.*

adultery (ə-**dəl**-tə-ree), *n.* (15c) Voluntary sexual intercourse between a married person and someone other than the person's spouse. • In many jurisdictions, adultery is a crime, but it is rarely prosecuted. — **adulterous,** *adj.* — **adulterer, adulteress,** *n.*

advance, *n.* (17c) **1.** The furnishing of money or goods before any consideration is received in return. **2.** The money or goods furnished.

advance directive. (1984) **1.** A document that takes effect upon one's incompetency and designates a surrogate decision-maker for healthcare matters. **2.** A legal document explaining one's wishes about medical treatment if one becomes incompetent or unable to communicate.

advancement, *n.* (15c) A payment or gift to an heir (esp. a child) during one's lifetime as an advance share of one's estate, with the intention of reducing, extinguishing, or diminishing the heir's claim to the estate under intestacy laws. — **advance,** *vb.*

advance sheets. (1868) A softcover pamphlet containing recently reported opinions by a court or set of courts. • Advance sheets are published during the interim between an opinion's announcement and its inclusion in a bound volume of law reports.

adventure. (17c) A commercial undertaking that has an element of risk; a venture.

adversary (**ad**-vər-ser-ee), *n.* (14c) An opponent; esp., opposing counsel. — **adversary, adversarial,** *adj.*

adversary proceeding. (1744) A hearing involving a dispute between opposing parties.

adversary system. (1936) A procedural system, such as the Anglo-American legal system, involving active and unhindered parties contesting with each other to put forth a case before an independent decision-maker. Cf. INQUISITORIAL SYSTEM.

adverse action. A decision or event that unfavorably affects a person, entity, or association.

adverse employment action. An employer's decision that substantially and negatively affects an employee's job, such as a termination, demotion, or pay cut.

adverse interest. (17c) An interest that is opposed or contrary to that of someone else.

adverse-interest rule. (1904) The principle that if a party fails to produce a witness who is within its power to produce and who should have been produced, the judge may instruct the jury to infer that the witness's evidence is unfavorable to the party's case.

adverse possession. (18c) The enjoyment of real property with a claim of right when that enjoyment is opposed to another person's claim and is continuous, exclusive, hostile, open, and notorious.

constructive adverse possession. (1823) Adverse possession in which the claim arises from the claimant's payment of taxes under color of right rather than by actual possession of the land.

advice and consent. The right of the U.S. Senate to participate in making and ratifying treaties and appointing federal officers.

advice of counsel. (17c) **1.** The guidance given by lawyers to their clients. **2.** A defense in which a party seeks to avoid liability or punishment by claiming that he or she acted reasonably and in good faith on the attorney's advice. • Such a defense usu. requires waiver of the attorney–client privilege, and the attorney cannot have knowingly participated in implementing an illegal plan.

advisement (ad-**vɪz**-mənt). (14c) Careful consideration; deliberation <the judge took the matter under advisement and promised a ruling by the next day>.

advisory committee. A committee formed to make suggestions to an executive or legislative body or to an official; esp., any one of five committees that propose to the Standing Committee on Rules of Practice and Procedure amendments to federal court rules.

advocate (**ad**-və-kit), *n.* (14c) A person who assists, defends, pleads, or prosecutes for another.

AFDC. *abbr.* Aid to Families with Dependent Children.

aff'd. *abbr.* Affirmed.

affects doctrine. (1996) *Constitutional law.* The principle allowing Congress to regulate intrastate activities that have a substantial effect on interstate commerce. • The doctrine is so called because the test is whether a given activity "affects" interstate commerce.

aff'g. *abbr.* Affirming.

affiant (ə-**fɪ**-ənt). (1807) **1.** One who makes an affidavit. **2.** COMPLAINANT (2).

affidavit (af-ə-**day**-vit). (16c) A voluntary declaration of facts written down and sworn to by the declarant before an officer authorized to administer oaths. • A great deal of evidence is submitted by affidavit, esp. in pretrial matters such as summary-judgment motions.

affidavit of inquiry. (1925) An affidavit, required in certain states before substituted service of process on an absent defendant, in which the plaintiff's attorney or a person with knowledge of the facts indicates that the defendant cannot be served within the state.

affidavit of merits. An affidavit in which a defendant asserts that he or she has a meritorious defense.

affidavit of nonprosecution. An affidavit in which a crime victim requests that the perpetrator not be prosecuted.

affidavit of notice. An affidavit stating that the declarant has given proper notice of hearing to other parties to the action.

affidavit of service. (18c) An affidavit certifying the service of a notice, summons, writ, or process.

poverty affidavit. (1887) An affidavit made by an indigent person seeking public assistance, appointment of counsel, waiver of court fees, or other free public services. 28 USCA § 1915.

search-warrant affidavit. An affidavit, usu. by a police officer or other law-enforcement agent, that sets forth facts and circumstances supporting the existence of probable cause and asks the judge to issue a search warrant.

self-proving affidavit. (1964) An affidavit attached to a will and signed by the testator and witnesses certifying that the statutory requirements of due execution of the will have been complied with. • The affidavit, which recites the facts of the will's proper execution, permits the will to be probated without the necessity of having the witnesses appear and prove due execution by their testimony.

sham affidavit. An affidavit that contradicts clear testimony given by the same witness, usu. used in an attempt to create an issue of fact in response to a motion for summary judgment.

supplemental affidavit. An affidavit made in addition to a previous one, usu. to supply additional facts.

affiliate (ə-**fil**-ee-it), *n.* (1930) A corporation that is related to another corporation by shareholdings or other means of control; a subsidiary, parent, or sibling corporation. — **affiliate** (ə-**fil**-ee-ayt), *vb.* — **affiliation** (ə-fil-ee-**ay**-shən), *n.*

affinity (ə-**fin**-ə-tee). (14c) **1.** A close agreement. **2.** The relation that one spouse has to the blood relatives of the other spouse; relationship by marriage. **3.** Any familial relation resulting from a marriage. Cf. CONSANGUINITY.

affirm, *vb.* (14c) **1.** To confirm (a judgment) on appeal. **2.** To solemnly declare rather than swear under oath.

affirmance, *n.* (16c) **1.** A ratification, reacceptance, or confirmation. **2.** The formal confirmation by an appellate court of a lower court's judgment, order, or decree.

affirmation, *n.* (15c) A solemn pledge equivalent to an oath but without reference to a supreme being or to swearing; a solemn declaration made under penalty of perjury, but without an oath. Fed. R. Evid. 603; Fed. R. Civ. P. 43(b). • While an oath is "sworn to," an affirmation is merely "affirmed," but either type of pledge may subject the person making it to the penalties for perjury. — **affirm,** *vb.* — **affirmatory,** *adj.*

affirmative, *adj.* (15c) **1.** Supporting the existence of certain facts <affirmative evidence>. **2.** Involving or requiring effort <an affirmative duty>.

affirmative action. (1961) A set of actions designed to eliminate existing and continuing discrimination, to remedy lingering effects of past discrimination, and to create systems and procedures to prevent future discrimination.

affirmative pregnant. (1807) A positive statement that ambiguously implies a negative; a statement that does not explicitly deny a charge, but instead answers an unasked question and thereby implies culpability, as when a person says "I returned your car yesterday" to the charge "You stole my car!" Cf. NEGATIVE PREGNANT.

affix (ə-**fiks**), *vb.* (16c) **1.** To attach, add to, or fasten on permanently. **2.** *Trademarks.* To attach, physically or functionally, a trademark or servicemark to the goods or services it represents. — **affixation,** *n.* (af-ik-**say**-shən).

affreightment (ə-**frayt**-mənt). The contracting of a ship to carry cargo.

AFL-CIO. *abbr.* American Federation of Labor and Congress of Industrial Organizations.

aforesaid (ə-**for**-sed), *adj.* (14c) Mentioned above; referred to previously.

aforethought (ə-**for**-thawt), *adj.* (16c) Thought of in advance; deliberate; premeditated.

a fortiori (ay for-shee-**or**-I *or* ah for-shee-**or**-ee), *adv.* [Latin] (16c) By even greater force of logic; even more so <if a 14-year-old child cannot sign a binding contract, then, *a fortiori*, a 13-year-old cannot>.

after-acquired-evidence doctrine. *Employment law.* The rule that, if an employer discharges an employee for an unlawful reason and later discovers misconduct sufficient to justify a lawful discharge, the employee cannot win reinstatement.

after-acquired property. 1. *Secured transactions.* A debtor's property that is acquired after a security transaction and becomes additional security for payment of the debt. **2.** *Bankruptcy.* Property that the bankruptcy estate acquires after commencement of the bankruptcy proceeding. **3.** *Wills & estates.* Property acquired by a person after making a will.

after-acquired-title doctrine. (1940) The principle that title to property automatically vests in a person who bought the property from a seller who acquired title only after purporting to sell the property to the buyer.

after the fact. (16c) Subsequent to an event of legal significance <accessory after the fact>.

AG. *abbr.* (1889) ATTORNEY GENERAL.

against the form of the statute. (16c) A concluding phrase in an indictment, meaning "contrary to the statutory requirements."

against the peace and dignity of the state. (18c) A concluding phrase in an indictment, used to condemn the offending conduct generally (as opposed to the specific charge of wrongdoing contained in the body of the instrument).

against the weight of the evidence. (18c) (Of a verdict or judgment) contrary to the credible evidence; not sufficiently supported by the evidence in the record.

against the will. (15c) Contrary to a person's wishes. • Indictments use this phrase to indicate that the defendant's conduct was without the victim's consent.

age, *n.* (13c) A period of time; esp., a period of individual existence or the duration of a person's life.

age of capacity. (1847) The age, usu. defined by statute as 18 years, at which a person is legally capable of agreeing to a contract, maintaining a lawsuit, or the like.

age of consent. (16c) The age, usu. defined by statute as 16 years, at which a person is legally capable of agreeing to marriage (without parental consent) or to sexual intercourse.

age of criminal responsibility. The age at which a child may be held responsible for a criminal act.

age of discretion. **1.** The age at which a person is considered responsible for certain acts and competent to exercise certain powers. **2.** Puberty.

age of majority. (16c) The age, usu. defined by statute as 18 years, at which a person attains full legal rights, esp. civil and political rights such as the right to vote.

age of reason. (1884) The age at which a person becomes able to distinguish right from wrong and is thus legally capable of committing a crime or tort.

drinking age. The age at which it is legal to purchase and consume alcoholic beverages in a given jurisdiction.

fighting age. The age at which a person becomes eligible to serve in (or liable to conscription into) a military unit.

Age Discrimination in Employment Act. A federal law prohibiting job discrimination based on a person's age, esp. unfair and discriminatory employment decisions that negatively affect someone who is 40 years old or older. 29 USCA §§ 621–634. — Abbr. ADEA.

agency. (17c) **1.** A fiduciary relationship created by express or implied contract or by law, in which one party (the *agent*) may act on behalf of another party (the *principal*) and bind that other party by words or actions.

actual agency. (1835) An agency in which the agent is in fact employed by a principal.

agency by estoppel. (1882) An agency created by operation of law and established by a principal's actions that would reasonably lead a third person to conclude that an agency exists.

agency coupled with an interest. (1844) An agency in which the agent is granted not only the power to act on behalf of a principal but also a legal interest in the estate or property involved.

agency in fact. An agency created voluntarily, as by a contract.

agency of necessity. An agency arising during an emergency that necessitates the agent's acting without authorization from the principal; the relation between a person who in exigent circumstances acts in the interest of another without being authorized to do so.

exclusive agency. (1805) The right to represent a principal — esp. either to sell the principal's products or to act as the seller's real-estate agent — within a particular market free from competition.

express agency. (18c) An actual agency arising from the principal's written or oral authorization of a person to act as the principal's agent. Cf. *implied agency.*

financing agency. A bank, finance company, or other entity that in the ordinary course of business (1) makes advances against goods or documents of title, or (2) by arrangement with either the seller or the buyer intervenes to make or collect payment due or claimed under a contract for sale, as by purchasing or paying the seller's draft, making advances against it, or taking it for collection, regardless of whether documents of title accompany the draft. UCC § 2-102(a)(20).

general agency. (18c) A principal's delegation to an agent, without restriction, to take any action connected with a particular trade, business, or employment.

implied agency. (18c) An actual agency arising from the conduct by the principal that implies an intention to create an agency relationship. Cf. *express agency.*

special agency. (1808) An agency in which the agent is authorized only to conduct a single transaction or a series of transactions not involving continuous service.

undisclosed agency. (1871) An agency relationship in which an agent deals with a third party who has no knowledge that the agent is acting on a principal's behalf. • The fact that the agency is undisclosed does not prohibit the third party from seeking redress from the principal or the agent.

2. An agent's place of business. **3.** A governmental body with the authority to implement and administer particular legislation.

federal agency. (1859) A department or other instrumentality of the executive branch of the federal government, including a government corporation and the Government Printing Office. 5 USCA § 551.

independent agency. (1902) A federal agency, commission, or board that is not under the direction of the executive, such as the Federal Trade Commission or the National Labor Relations Board.

local agency. A political subdivision of a state. • Local agencies include counties, cities, school districts, etc.

quasi-governmental agency. (1904) A government-sponsored enterprise or corporation (sometimes called a *government-controlled corporation*), such as the Federal National Mortgage Corporation.

state agency. An executive or regulatory body of a state. • State agencies include state offices, departments, divisions, bureaus, boards, and commissions.

agenda. A list of things to be done, as items to be considered at a meeting, usu. arranged in order of consideration.

agent. (15c) **1.** Something that produces an effect <an intervening agent>. **2.** One who is authorized to act for or in place of another; a representative <a professional athlete's agent>.

apparent agent. (1823) A person who reasonably appears to have authority to act for another, regardless of whether actual authority has been conferred.

bargaining agent. A labor union in its capacity of representing employees in collective bargaining.

co-agent. A person who shares with another agent the authority to act for the principal.

commercial agent. **1.** BROKER. **2.** A consular officer responsible for the commercial interests of his or her country at a foreign port.

common agent. An agent who acts on behalf of more than one principal in a transaction.

corporate agent. (1819) An agent authorized to act on behalf of a corporation; broadly, all employees and officers who have the power to bind the corporation.

del credere agent (del **kred**-ə-ray *or* **kray**-də-ray). (1822) An agent who guarantees the solvency of the third party with whom the agent makes a contract for the principal.

diplomatic agent. A national representative in one of four categories: (1) ambassadors, (2) envoys and ministers plenipotentiary, (3) ministers resident accredited to the sovereign, or (4) chargés d'affaires accredited to the minister of foreign affairs.

dual agent. An agent who represents both parties in a single transaction, esp. a buyer and a seller.

emigrant agent. One engaged in the business of hiring laborers for work outside the country or state.

escrow agent. The third-party depositary of an escrow; ESCROW (3).

fiscal agent. A bank or other financial institution that collects and disburses money and services as a depository of private and public funds on another's behalf.

foreign agent. A person who registers with the federal government as a lobbyist representing the interests of a foreign nation or corporation.

forwarding agent. A freight-forwarder who assembles less-than-carload shipments (small shipments) into carload shipments, thus taking advantage of lower freight rates.

general agent. (17c) An agent authorized to transact all the principal's business of a particular kind or in a particular place.

government agent. (1805) **1.** An employee or representative of a governmental body. **2.** A law-enforcement official, such as a police officer or an FBI agent. **3.** An informant, esp. an inmate, used by law enforcement to obtain incriminating statements from another inmate.

high-managerial agent. An agent of a corporation or other business, having authority to formulate corporate policy or supervise employees.

independent agent. (17c) An agent who exercises personal judgment and is subject to the principal only for the results of the work performed.

innocent agent. (1805) *Criminal law.* A person whose action on behalf of a principal is unlawful but does not merit prosecution because the agent had no knowledge of the principal's illegal purpose; a person who lacks the mens rea for an offense but who is tricked or coerced by the principal into committing a crime.

listing agent. (1927) The real-estate broker's representative who obtains a listing agreement with the owner.

local agent. An agent appointed to act as another's (esp. a company's) representative and to transact business within a specified district.

managing agent. (1812) A person with general power involving the exercise of judgment and discretion, as opposed to an ordinary agent who acts under the direction and control of the principal.

mercantile agent. An agent employed to sell goods or merchandise on behalf of the principal.

nonservant agent. An agent who agrees to act on the principal's behalf but is not subject to the principal's control over how the task is performed. • A principal is not liable for the physical torts of a nonservant agent.

patent agent. A specialized legal professional — not necessarily a licensed lawyer — who prepares and prosecutes patent applications before the Patent and Trademark Office • Patent agents must be licensed by the Patent and Trademark Office.

primary agent. An agent who is directly authorized by a principal. • A primary agent generally may hire a subagent to perform all or part of the agency.

private agent. An agent acting for an individual in that person's private affairs.

process agent. (1886) A person authorized to accept service of process on behalf of another.

procuring agent. A person who obtains drugs on behalf of another person and delivers the drugs to that person.

public agent. A person appointed to act for the public in matters pertaining to governmental administration or public business.

real-estate agent. An agent who represents a buyer or seller (or both, with proper disclosures) in the sale or lease of real property.

registered agent. (1809) A person authorized to accept service of process for another person, esp. a corporation, in a particular jurisdiction.

selling agent. (1839) The real-estate broker's representative who sells the property, as opposed to the agent who lists the property for sale.

settlement agent. An agent who represents the purchaser or buyer in the negotiation and closing of a real-property transaction by handling financial calculations and transfers of documents.

soliciting agent. **1.** *Insurance.* An agent with limited authority relating to the solicitation or submission of applications to an insurance company but usu. without authority to bind the insurer, as by accepting the applications on behalf of the company. **2.** An agent who solicits orders for goods or services for a principal. **3.** A managing agent of a corporation for purposes of service of process.

special agent. An agent employed to conduct a particular transaction or to perform a specified act.

specially accredited agent. An agent with whom a third person has been specially invited to deal by the principal under circumstances leading the third person to believe that he or she will be notified if the authority is altered or revoked.

statutory agent. (1844) An agent designated by law to receive litigation documents and other legal notices for a nonresident corporation. • In most states, the secretary of state is the statutory agent for such corporations.

stock-transfer agent. An organization that oversees and maintains records of transfers of shares for a corporation.

subagent. A person to whom an agent has delegated the performance of an act for the principal; a person designated by an agent to perform some duty relating to the agency.

successor agent. An agent who is appointed by a principal to act in a primary agent's stead if the primary agent is unable or unwilling to perform.

transfer agent. An organization (such as a bank or trust company) that handles transfers of shares for a publicly held corporation by issuing new certificates and overseeing the cancellation of old ones and that usu. also maintains the record of shareholders for the corporation and mails dividend checks.

undercover agent. (1930) **1.** An agent who does not disclose his or her role as an agent. **2.** A police officer who gathers evidence of criminal activity without disclosing his or her identity to the suspect.

universal agent. (18c) An agent authorized to perform all acts that the principal could personally perform.

vice-commercial agent. *Hist.* In the consular service of the United States, a consular officer who was substituted temporarily to fill the place of a commercial agent who was absent or had been relieved from duty.

3. *Patents.* A person who is not an attorney but who has fulfilled the U.S. Patent and Trademark Office requirements as a lay representative and is registered to prepare and prosecute patent applications before the PTO.

agent provocateur (**ay**-jənt prə-vok-ə-**tər** *or* **a**-zhawn praw-vaw-kə-**tuur**), *n.* (1877) **1.** An undercover agent who instigates or participates in a crime, often by infiltrating a group suspected of illegal conduct, to expose and punish criminal activity. **2.** A person who entraps another, or entices another to break the law, and then informs against the other as a lawbreaker.

aggravated, *adj.* (17c) **1.** (Of a crime) made worse or more serious by circumstances such as violence, the presence of a deadly weapon, or the intent to commit another crime <aggravated robbery>. **2.** (Of a tort) made worse or more serious by circumstances such as intention to cause harm or reckless disregard for another's safety <the defendant's negligence was aggravated by malice>. **3.** (Of an injury) harmful to a part of the body previously injured or debilitated <an aggravated bone fracture>.

aggregate (**ag**-rə-gayt), *vb.* (15c) To collect into a whole <aggregate the claims>. — **aggregate** (**ag**-rə-git), *adj.*

aggregate theory of partnership. (1913) The theory that a partnership does not have a separate legal existence (as does a corporation), but rather is only the totality of the partners who compose it.

aggregation doctrine. (1942) The rule that precludes a party from totaling all claims for purposes of meeting the minimum amount necessary to give rise to federal diversity jurisdiction under the amount-in-controversy requirement.

aggregation of claims. *Patents.* In a patent application, an excessive number of claims that do not differ significantly in scope and are essentially duplicative.

aggression. *Int'l law.* A grave breach of international law by a nation.

aggressor doctrine. (1947) The principle precluding tort recovery for a plaintiff who acts in a way that would provoke a reasonable person to use physical force for protection, unless the defendant in turn uses excessive force to repel the plaintiff.

aggrieved, *adj.* (Of a person or entity) having legal rights that are adversely affected; having been harmed by an infringement of legal rights.

aging-out, *n.* A foster child's or minor ward's reaching the age at which any legal right to care expires.

agnate, *n.* A blood relative whose connection is through the male line. —**agnatic,** *adj.*

agrarian (ə-**grair**-ee-ən), *adj.* Of or relating to land, land tenure, or a division of landed property. — **agrarian,** *n.*

agreed-boundary doctrine. (1941) The principle by which adjacent landowners resolve uncertainties over land boundaries by permanently fixing the boundaries by agreement; specif., the rule that owners of contiguous land may agree on the boundary between the parcels, as long as the actual boundary is uncertain, there is agreement between the two owners about the boundary line, there is acquiescence in the agreed line for a time exceeding the statute of limitations, and the agreed boundary is identifiable on the ground.

agreement. (15c) **1.** A mutual understanding between two or more persons about their relative rights and duties regarding past or future performances; a manifestation of mutual assent by two or more persons. **2.** The parties' actual bargain as found in their language or by implication from other circumstances, including course of dealing, usage of trade, and course of performance. UCC § 1-201(3).

agreement of sale. An agreement that obligates someone to sell and that may include a corresponding obligation for someone else to buy.

agreement to agree. **1.** An unenforceable agreement that purports to bind two parties to negotiate and enter into a contract; esp., a proposed agreement negotiated with the intent that the final agreement will be embodied in a formal written document and that neither party will be bound until the final agreement is executed. **2.** A fully enforceable agreement containing terms that are sufficiently definite as well as adequate consideration, but leaving some details to be worked out by the parties.

agreement to sell. An agreement that obligates someone to sell.

binding agreement. (18c) An enforceable contract.

business-continuation agreement. An agreement for the disposition of a business interest in the event of the owner's death, disability, retirement, or withdrawal from the business.

closing agreement. *Tax.* A written contract between a taxpayer and the Internal Revenue Service to resolve a tax dispute.

cross-purchase agreement. An agreement between a business's individual owners to purchase the interest of a withdrawing or deceased owner in order to continue operating the business.

exchange agreement. An agreement to exchange real properties, usu. like-kind properties.

formal agreement. (17c) An agreement for which the law requires not only the consent of the parties but also a manifestation of the agreement in some particular form (e.g., a signed writing), in default of which the agreement is unenforceable.

side agreement. **1.** An agreement that is ancillary to another agreement. **2.** *Int'l law.* An international accord that is specifically negotiated to supplement a broader trade treaty.

simple agreement. (18c) An agreement for which the law requires nothing for its effective operation beyond some manifestation that the parties have consented.

subordination agreement. An agreement by which one who holds an otherwise senior interest agrees to subordinate that interest to a normally lesser interest, usu. when a seller agrees to subordinate a purchase-money mortgage so that the buyer can obtain a first-mortgage loan to improve the property.

takeover agreement. An agreement under which a defaulting party's surety agrees to perform the original contract in the defaulting party's stead.

third-party business-buyout agreement. An agreement by a business's owners to sell all or part of the business to an outside person who will continue to operate it.

unconscionable agreement (ən-**kon**-shə-nə-bəl). (1817) An agreement that no promisor with any sense, and not under a delusion, would make, and that no honest and fair promisee would accept. • For commercial contexts, see UCC § 2-302.

underwriting agreement. An agreement between a corporation and an underwriter covering the terms and conditions of a new securities issue.

agribusiness. The pursuit of agriculture as an occupation or profit-making enterprise, including labor, land-use planning, and financing the cost of land, equipment, and other necessary expenses. • This term generally excludes smaller family-owned and -operated farms.

agricultural-disparagement law. A statute designed to protect food producers from and provide remedies for pecuniary harm resulting from false and malicious reports of food contamination.

Aguilar–Spinelli **test** (ah-gee-**lahr** spi-**nel**-ee *or* **ag**-wə-lahr). *Criminal procedure.* A standard for determining whether hearsay (such as an informant's tip) is sufficiently reliable to establish probable cause for an arrest or search warrant. • This two-pronged test has been replaced by a broader, totality-of-the-circumstances approach.

AICPA. *abbr.* American Institute of Certified Public Accountants.

AID. *abbr.* United States Agency for International Development.

aid and abet, *vb.* (17c) To assist or facilitate the commission of a crime, or to promote its accomplishment. • Aiding and abetting is a crime in most jurisdictions. — **aider and abettor,** *n.*

aid and comfort. (16c) Help given by someone to a national enemy in such a way that the help amounts to treason.

aider, *n.* The curing of a defect.

aider by pleading over. (1860) The cure of a pleading defect by an adversary's answering the pleading without an objection, so that the objection is waived.

aider by verdict. (1824) The cure of a pleading defect by a trial verdict, based on the presumption that the record contains adequate proof of the necessary facts even if those facts were not specifically alleged.

Aiken **exemption.** *Copyright.* An exception in the law of infringement that permits retail establishments with less than 2,000 square feet of space to play radio and television broadcasts for employees and patrons without obtaining a license. *Twentieth Century Music Corp. v. Aiken*, 422 U.S. 151, 95 S. Ct. 2040 (1975).

airbill. A document serving as a bill of lading for goods transported by air. • The term includes air consignment notes and air waybills.

air law. The part of law, esp. international law, relating to civil aviation.

air pollution. *Environmental law.* Any harmful substance or energy emitted directly or indirectly into the air, esp. if the harm is to the environment or to the public health or welfare.

air right. (1922) The right to use all or a portion of the airspace above real property.

airspace. The space that extends upward from the surface of land, esp. so far as is necessary for the owner or possessor to have reasonable use and enjoyment of the incidents of its ownership or possession.

a.k.a. *abbr.* (1955) Also known as.

alderman. A member of a city council or other local governing body.

alderwoman. A female member of a city council or other local governing body.

aleatory (**ay**-lee-ə-tor-ee), *adj.* (17c) Dependent on uncertain contingencies.

alegal, *adj.* (1991) Outside the sphere of law; not classifiable as being legal or illegal. — **alegality,** *n.*

Alford **plea.** (1971) A guilty plea that a defendant enters as part of a plea bargain, without actually admitting guilt. *North Carolina v. Alford*, 400 U.S. 25, 91 S.Ct. 160 (1970).

algorithm. *Patents.* A mathematical or logical process consisting of a series of steps designed to solve a specific type of problem.

algorithm exception. *Patents.* The general rule that an abstract mathematical function, such as an algorithm, cannot be patented.

ALI. *abbr.* American Law Institute.

alias, *n.* (17c) An assumed or additional name that a person has used or is known by.

alibi (**al**-ə-bı), *n.* [Latin "elsewhere"] (18c) **1.** A defense based on the physical impossibility of a defendant's guilt by placing the defendant in a location other than the scene of the crime at the relevant time. Fed. R. Crim. P. 12.1. **2.** The fact or state of having been elsewhere when an offense was committed.

alien (**ay**-lee-ən *or* **ayl**-yən), *n.* (14c) A person who resides within the borders of a country but is not a citizen or subject of that country; a person not owing allegiance to a particular nation.

deportable alien. An alien who has entered the United States but is subject to removal.

excludable alien. An alien ineligible for admission or entry into the United States.

illegal alien. (1901) An alien who enters a country at the wrong time or place, eludes an examination by officials, obtains entry by fraud, or enters into a sham marriage to evade immigration laws.

inadmissible alien. A deportable or excludable alien. See 8 USCA § 1182(a).

nonresident alien. (1801) A person who is neither a resident nor a citizen of the United States.

resident alien. (18c) An alien who has a legally established domicile in the United States.

alienate (**ay**-lee-ə-nayt *or* **ayl**-yə-), *vb.* (16c) To transfer or convey (property or a property right) to another. — **alienator,** *n.*

alienation (ay-lee-ə-**nay**-shən *or* ayl-yə-**nay**-shən), *n.* (14c) **1.** Withdrawal from former attachment; estrangement <alienation of affections>. **2.** Conveyance or transfer of property to another <alienation of one's estate>. — **alienative** (**ay**-lee-ə-nay-tiv *or* **ayl**-yə-), *adj.*

alienation clause. (1877) **1.** A deed provision that either permits or prohibits the further conveyance of the property. **2.** *Insurance.* A clause in an insurance policy voiding coverage if the policyholder alienates the insured property.

alienation of affections. (1867) A tort claim for willful or malicious interference with a marriage by a third party without justification or excuse. • Only a few states still allow this cause of action.

alienee (ay-lee-ə-**nee** *or* ayl-yə-**nee**), *n.* (16c) One to whom property is transferred or conveyed.

alienist. (1864) *Archaic.* A psychiatrist, esp. one who assesses a criminal defendant's sanity or capacity to stand trial.

alienor (**ay**-lee-ə-nər *or* -nor), *n.* (16c) One who transfers or conveys property to another.

alimony (**al**-ə-moh-nee). (17c) A court-ordered allowance that one spouse pays to the other spouse for maintenance and support while they are separated, while they are involved in a matrimonial lawsuit, or after they are divorced.

alimony in gross. Alimony in the form of a single and definite sum not subject to modification.

permanent alimony. Alimony payable in usu. weekly or monthly installments either indefinitely or until a time specified by court order.

rehabilitative alimony. Alimony found necessary to assist a divorced person in acquiring the education or training required to find employment outside the home or to reenter the labor force.

reimbursement alimony. Alimony designed to repay a spouse who during the marriage made financial contributions that directly enhanced the future earning capacity of the other spouse.

temporary alimony. Interim alimony ordered by the court pending an action for divorce or separation in which one party has made a claim for permanent alimony.

aliquot (**al**-ə-kwot), *adj.* (16c) Contained in a larger whole an exact number of times; fractional <5 is an aliquot part of 30>.

aliquot-part rule. (1947) The principle that a person must intend to acquire a fractional part of the ownership of property before a court can declare a resulting trust in the person's favor.

aliunde (ay-lee-**yən**-dee), *adj.* [Latin] (17c) From another source; from elsewhere <evidence aliunde>.

aliunde rule. (1943) *Evidence.* The doctrine that a verdict may not be impeached by a juror's testimony unless a foundation for the testimony is first made by competent evidence from another source.

ALJ. *abbr.* Administrative-law judge.

all and singular. (16c) Collectively and individually.

allegation, *n.* (15c) **1.** The act of declaring something to be true. **2.** Something declared or asserted as a matter of fact, esp. in a legal pleading; a party's formal statement of a factual matter as being true or provable, without its having yet been proved. — **allege,** *vb.*

disjunctive allegation. (1814) A statement in a pleading or indictment that expresses something in the alternative, usu. with the conjunction "or" <a charge that the defendant murdered or caused to be murdered is a disjunctive allegation>.

material allegation. (18c) In a pleading, an assertion that is essential to the claim, charge, or defense <a material allegation in a battery case is harmful or offensive contact with a person>.

primary allegation. (1847) The principal charge made against an adversary in a legal proceeding.

alleged (ə-**lejd**), *adj.* (15c) **1.** Asserted to be true as described <alleged offenses>. **2.** Accused but not yet tried <alleged murderer>.

***Allen* charge.** (1940) *Criminal procedure.* A supplemental jury instruction given by the court to encourage a deadlocked jury, after prolonged deliberations, to reach a verdict. *Allen v. United States*, 164 U.S. 492, 17 S.Ct. 154 (1896).

all-events test. (1954) *Tax.* A requirement that all events fixing an accrual-method taxpayer's right to receive income or incur expense must occur before the taxpayer can report an item of income or expense.

allision (ə-**lizh**-ən), *n. Maritime law.* The contact of a vessel with a stationary object such as an anchored vessel or a pier. — **allide** (ə-**lɪd**), *vb.*

allocation, *n.* (16c) A designation or apportionment for a specific purpose; esp., the crediting of a receipt or the charging of a disbursement to an account <allocation of funds>. — **allocate,** *vb.* — **allocable,** *adj.* — **allocator,** *n.*

allocution (al-ə-**kyoo**-shən), *n. Criminal procedure.* **1.** A trial judge's formal address to a convicted defendant, asking him or her to speak in mitigation of the sentence to be imposed. • This address is required under Fed. R. Crim. P. 32(c)(3)(C). **2.** An unsworn statement from a convicted defendant to the sentencing judge or jury in which the defendant can ask for mercy, explain his or her conduct, apologize for the crime, or say anything else in an effort to lessen the impending sentence. • This statement is not subject to cross-examination. — **allocutory** (ə-**lok**-yə-tor-ee), *adj.*

victim allocution. A crime victim's address to the court before sentencing, usu. urging a harsher punishment.

allodial (ə-**loh**-dee-əl), *adj.* (17c) Held in absolute ownership; pertaining to an allodium. — **allodially,** *adv.*

allodium (ə-**loh**-dee-əm), *n.* (17c) An estate held in fee simple absolute.

allograph (**al**-ə-graf). (1954) An agent's writing or signature for the principal.

allonge (a-**lawnzh**). (1859) A slip of paper sometimes attached to a negotiable instrument for the purpose of receiving further indorsements when the original paper is filled with indorsements.

all-or-nothing rule. (1954) A gloss on the rule against perpetuities holding that a class gift is invalid in its entirety if it is invalid in part. • The effect is to invalidate a class member's interest even if it vests within the period of the rule because it may be subject to partial divestment by the remote interest of another class member.

allotment, *n.* (16c) **1.** A share or portion of something, such as property previously held in common or shares in a corporation, or time assigned to speakers or sides in a deliberative assembly. **2.** In American Indian law, the selection of specific land awarded to an individual allottee from a common holding. — **allot,** *vb.*

allowance. (14c) **1.** A share or portion, esp. of money that is assigned or granted.

family allowance. (1869) A portion of a decedent's estate set aside by statute for a surviving spouse, children, or parents, regardless of any testamentary disposition or competing claims.

gratuitous allowance. A pension voluntarily granted by a public entity.

spousal allowance. (1985) A portion of a decedent's estate set aside by statute for a surviving spouse, regardless of any testamentary disposition or competing claims.

2. The sum awarded by a court to a fiduciary as payment for services. **3.** A deduction.

depletion allowance. A tax deduction for the owners of oil, gas, mineral, or timber resources corresponding to the reduced value of the property resulting from the removal of the resource.

alluvion (ə-**loo**-vee-ən). [fr. Latin *alluvio* "flood"] (16c) *Roman & civil law.* **1.** Strictly, the flow or wash of water against a shore or riverbank. **2.** An accumulation of soil, clay, or other material deposited by water; esp., in land law, an addition of land caused by the buildup of deposits from running water, the added land then belonging to the owner of the property to which it is added. — **alluvial,** *adj.* — **alluviate,** *vb.* — **alluviation,** *n.*

All Writs Act. A federal statute that gives the U.S. Supreme Court and all courts established by Congress the power to issue writs in aid of their jurisdiction and in conformity with the usages and principles of law. 28 USCA § 1651(a).

ALTA. *abbr.* American Land Title Association.

alteration. 1. *Property.* A substantial change to real estate, esp. to a structure, usu. not involving an addition to or removal of the exterior dimensions of a building's structural parts.

structural alteration. (1905) A significant change to a building or other structure, essentially creating a different building or structure.

2. An act done to an instrument, after its execution, whereby its meaning or language is changed; esp., the changing of a term in a negotiable instrument without the consent of all parties to it. • Material alterations void an instrument, but immaterial ones do not.

material alteration. (17c) **1.** A significant change in something; esp., a change in a legal instrument sufficient to alter the instrument's legal meaning or effect. **2.** An unauthorized change in an instrument or an addition to an incomplete instrument resulting in the modification of a party's obligations. UCC § 3-407.

altercation. A vehement dispute; a noisy argument.

alter ego. (1879) A corporation used by an individual in conducting personal business, the result being that a court may impose liability on the individual by piercing the corporate veil when fraud has been perpetrated on someone dealing with the corporation.

alter-ego rule. (1939) **1.** *Corporations.* The doctrine that shareholders will be treated as the owners of a corporation's property, or as the real parties in interest, whenever it is necessary to do so to prevent fraud or to do justice. **2.** *Criminal law.* The principle that one who defends another against attack stands in the position of that other person and can use only the amount of force that the other person could use under the circumstances.

altering or amending a judgment. A trial court's act of correcting a substantive mistake in a judgment, as by correcting a manifest error of law or fact. Fed. R. Civ. P. 59(e).

alternative dispute resolution. (1978) A procedure for settling a dispute by means other than litigation, such as arbitration or mediation. — Abbr. ADR.

alternative-means doctrine. (1968) *Criminal law.* The principle that when a crime may be committed in more than one way, the jury must be unanimous on the defendant's guilt but need not be unanimous on the possible different methods of committing the crime, as long as each possible method is supported by substantial evidence.

ALWD Citation Manual. A guide to American legal citation written and edited by legal-writing professionals affiliated with the Association of Legal Writing Directors. • First published in 2000 as an alternative to the *Bluebook*, it contains one citation system for all legal documents and does not distinguish between citations in law-journal footnotes and those in other writings.

a.m. *abbr.* Ante meridiem.

AMA. *abbr.* (1911) **1.** American Medical Association. **2.** Against medical advice.

amalgamation (ə-mal-gə-**may**-shən), *n.* (17c) The act of combining or uniting; consolidation. — **amalgamate,** *vb.* — **amalgamator,** *n.*

ambassador. A diplomatic officer of the highest rank, usu. designated by a government as its resident representative in a foreign state. — **ambassadorial,** *adj.* — **ambassadorship,** *n.*

ambassador extraordinary. An ambassador who is employed for a particular purpose or occasion and has limited discretionary powers.

ambassador plenipotentiary. An ambassador who has unlimited discretionary powers to act as a sovereign's or government's deputy, esp. to carry out a particular task, such as treaty negotiations.

resident ambassador. An ambassador who resides in a foreign country as the permanent representative of a sovereign or nation.

Amber Alert. A system by which the police can rapidly broadcast to the general public a report of a missing or endangered child by means of radio and television announcements.

Amber's law. A federal law that requires, among other things, life in prison without parole for two-time sex offenders whose victims are children, and reports to Congress about judges whose sentences fall below federal guidelines. • The law was named for Amber Hagerman of Texas, a nine-year-old girl who was abducted and murdered by an unknown person in 1996.

A.M. Best Company. An investment-analysis and -advisory service.

ambiguity (am-bi-**gyoo**-ə-tee), *n.* (15c) An uncertainty of meaning or intention, as in a contractual term or statutory provision. — **ambiguous** (am-**big**-yoo-əs), *adj.*

ambiguity on the factum. An ambiguity relating to the foundation of an instrument, such as a question relating to whether a testator intended for a particular clause to be part of an agreement, whether a codicil was intended to republish a former will, or whether the residuary clause was accidentally omitted.

calculated ambiguity. A purposeful use of unclear language, usu. when two negotiating parties cannot agree on clear, precise language and therefore leave a decision-maker to sort out the meaning in case of a dispute. • Strictly speaking, this is a misnomer: the more precise term is vagueness, not ambiguity.

latent ambiguity. (18c) An ambiguity that does not readily appear in the language of a document, but instead arises from a collateral matter when the document's terms are applied or executed <the contract contained a latent ambiguity: the shipping terms stated that the goods would arrive on the *Peerless*, but two ships have that name>.

patent ambiguity (**pay**-tənt). (18c) An ambiguity that clearly appears on the face of a document, arising from the language itself <the nonperformance was excused because the two different prices expressed in the contract created a patent ambiguity>.

ambit (**am**-bit). (14c) **1.** A boundary line or limit; esp., the scope of a statute or regulation, or the sphere of influence and authority of an agency, committee, department, or the like. **2.** A space surrounding a house or town.

ambulatory (**am**-byə-lə-tor-ee), *adj.* (16c) **1.** Able to walk. **2.** Capable of being altered or revised.

ameliorate (ə-**meel**-yə-rayt), *vb.* (18c) **1.** To make better. **2.** To become better — **amelioration,** *n.* — **ameliorative,** *adj.*

amenable (ə-**mee**-nə-bəl *or* -**men**-), *adj.* (16c) Legally answerable; liable to being brought to judgment. — **amenability,** *n.*

amend, *vb.* (13c) **1.** To make right; to correct or rectify. **2.** To change the wording of; specif., to formally alter (a statute, constitution, motion, etc.) by striking out, inserting, or substituting words. — **amendable,** *adj.* — **amendability,** *n.*

amendatory (ə-**men**-də-tor-ee), *adj.* Designed or serving to amend; corrective.

amendment. (17c) **1.** A formal revision or addition proposed or made to a statute, constitution, pleading, order, or other instrument; specif., a change made by addition, deletion, or correction; esp., an alteration in wording. **2.** The process of making such a revision.

a mensa et thoro (ay **men**-sə et **thor**-oh). [Latin "from board and hearth"] (17c) (Of a divorce decree) effecting a separation of the parties rather than a dissolution of the marriage.

amercement (ə-**mərs**-mənt), *n.* [fr. Law French *estre à merci* "to be at the mercy (of another)," fr. Latin *merces* "payment"] (14c) **1.** The imposition of a discretionary fine or penalty by a court, esp. on an official for misconduct. **2.** The fine or penalty so imposed. — **amerce** (ə-**mərs**), *vb.* — **amerceable** (ə- **mər**-sə-bəl), **amerciable** (ə-**mər**-see-ə-bəl), *adj.*

American Arbitration Association. A national organization that maintains a panel of arbitrators to hear labor and commercial disputes. — Abbr. AAA.

American Bar Association. A voluntary national organization of lawyers organized in 1878. • Among other things, it participates in law reform, law-school accreditation, and continuing legal education in an effort to improve legal services and the administration of justice. — Abbr. ABA.

American Bar Foundation. An outgrowth of the American Bar Association involved with sponsoring and funding projects in law-related research, education, and social studies. — Abbr. ABF.

American Civil Liberties Union. A national organization whose primary purpose is to help enforce and preserve individual rights and liberties guaranteed by federal and state constitutions. — Abbr. ACLU.

American Federation of Labor and Congress of Industrial Organizations. A voluntary affiliation of more than 100 labor unions that operate autonomously yet benefit from the affiliation's political activities and its establishment of broad policies for the national labor movement. — Abbr. AFL-CIO.

American Judicature Society. An organization made up of judges, lawyers, and lay people for the purpose of improving the administration of justice. — Abbr. AJS.

American Law Institute. An organization of lawyers, judges, and legal scholars who promote consistency and simplification of American law by publishing the Restatements of the Law, and other model codes and treatises, as well as promoting continuing legal education. — Abbr. ALI.

American rule. (1868) **1.** The general policy that all litigants, even the prevailing one, must bear their own attorney's fees. • The rule is subject to bad-faith and other statutory and contractual exceptions. **2.** The doctrine that a witness cannot be questioned on cross-examination about any fact or circumstance not connected with the matters brought out in the direct examination.

American Stock Exchange. An organized stock exchange and self-regulating organization under the Securities Exchange Act of 1934, located in New York City and engaged in national trading of corporate stocks. • It often trades in the securities of young or small companies because its listing requirements are less strict than those of the New York Stock Exchange. — Abbr. AMEX; ASE.

Americans with Disabilities Act. A federal statute that prohibits discrimination in employment, public services, and public accommodations against any person because of the person's disability ("a physical or mental impairment that substantially limits one or more of the major life activities"). 42 USCA §§ 12101–12213. — Abbr. ADA.

AMEX (**am**-eks). *abbr.* (1961) American Stock Exchange.

amicus curiae (ə-**mee**-kəs **kyoor**-ee-ɪ *or* ə-**mɪ**-kəs **kyoor**-ee-ee *also* **am**-i-kəs). [Latin "friend of the court"] (17c) A person who is not a party to a lawsuit but who petitions the court or is requested by the court to file a brief in the action because that person has a strong interest in the subject matter. — Often shortened to *amicus*. Pl. **amici curiae** (ə-**mee**-kee *or* ə-**mɪ**-sɪ *or* ə-**mɪ**-kɪ).

amnesty, *n.* (16c) A pardon extended by the government to a group or class of persons, usu. for a political offense; the act of a sovereign power officially forgiving certain classes of persons who are subject to trial but have not yet been convicted. — **amnesty,** *vb.*

Amnesty International. An international nongovernmental organization founded in the early 1960s to protect human rights throughout the world.

amortization (am-ər-tə-**zay**-shən), *n.* (1851) **1.** The act or result of gradually extinguishing a debt, such as a mortgage, usu. by contributing payments of principal each time a periodic interest payment is due.

negative amortization. An increase in a loan's principal balance caused by monthly payments insufficient to pay accruing interest.

2. The act or result of apportioning the initial cost of a usu. intangible asset, such as a patent, over the asset's useful life.

amortization schedule. A schedule of periodic payments of interest and principal owed on a debt obligation; specif., a loan schedule showing both the amount of principal and interest that is due at regular intervals over the loan term and the remaining unpaid principal balance after each scheduled payment is made.

amortize, *vb.* (1867) **1.** To extinguish (a debt) gradually, often by means of a sinking fund. **2.** To arrange to extinguish (a debt) by gradual increments.

amotion. (17c) **1.** A turning out, as the eviction of a tenant or the removal of a person from office. **2.** The common-law procedure available to shareholders to remove a corporate director for cause. **3.** The wrongful moving or carrying away of another's personal property.

amount in controversy. (1809) The damages claimed or relief demanded by the injured party in a lawsuit. 28 USCA § 1332(a).

amount realized. *Tax.* The amount received by a taxpayer for the sale or exchange of an asset, such as cash, property, services received, or debts assumed by a buyer.

AMT. *abbr.* Alternative minimum tax.

a multo fortiori (ay **məl**-toh for-shee-**or**-ɪ). [Latin] By far the stronger reason.

analog. *Patents.* A different material, usu. a chemical or DNA sequence, that produces the same result as the specified material when used in a certain way. — Also spelled *analogue.*

analytical memorandum. Research memorandum.

anarchist, *n.* (17c) One who advocates the overthrow of organized government by force or who believes in the absence of government as a political ideal. — **anarchism** (the philosophy), *n.*

anarchy, *n.* (16c) **1.** Absence of government; lawlessness. **2.** A sociopolitical theory holding that the only legitimate form of government is one under which individuals govern themselves voluntarily, free from any collective power structure enforcing compliance with social order. — **anarchic,** *adj.*

criminal anarchy. (1831) A doctrine advocating the overthrow of organized government by force or violence, by assassinating a head of government, or by some other unlawful act.

ancestry. (14c) A line of descent; lineage.

anchorage. *Maritime law.* **1.** An area where ships anchor. **2.** A duty paid by shipowners for the use of a port; a toll for anchoring.

ancient, *adj. Evidence.* (14c) Having existed for a long time without interruption, usu. at least 20 to 30 years. • Ancient items are usu. presumed to be authentic even if proof of authenticity cannot be made. Fed. R. Evid. 901(b)(8).

ancillary (**an**-sə-ler-ee), *adj.* (17c) Supplementary; subordinate. — **ancillarity** (an-sə-**la**[i]**r**-ə-tee), *n.*

and his heirs. A term of art formerly required to transfer complete title (a fee simple absolute) to real estate <A conveys Blackacre to B and his heirs>.

animal. Any living creature other than a human being.

animal ferae naturae. Wild animal.

animal mansuetae naturae. Domestic animal.

dangerous animal. An animal that has harmed or has threatened to harm a person or another animal.

domestic animal. **1.** An animal that is customarily devoted to the service of humankind at the time and in the place where it is helped. **2.** Any animal that is statutorily so designated.

domesticated animal. **1.** A feral animal that has been tamed. **2.** An animal that has customarily lived peaceably with people, such as farm animals and pets.

feral animal. A domestic animal that has returned to a wild state. • Feral animals, unlike others of their species, are usu. unsocialized to people.

vicious animal. **1.** An animal that has shown itself to be dangerous to humans. **2.** Loosely, one belonging to a breed or species that is known or reputed to be dangerous. • A vicious animal may be domestic, feral, or wild.

wild animal. **1.** An animal that, as a matter of common knowledge, is naturally untamable, unpredictable, dangerous, or mischievous. **2.** Any animal not statutorily designated as a domestic animal.

animal law, *n.* The field of law dealing with vertebrates other than humans. • The field cuts across many traditional doctrinal areas (e.g., contracts, torts, administrative law) as well as jurisprudence. Topics include wildlife-management law, laws concerning treatment of laboratory animals, and laws relating to companion animals.

animus (**an**-ə-məs). [Latin] (1816) **1.** Ill will; animosity. **2.** Intention.

annex, *n.* (16c) Something that is attached, such as a document to a report or an addition to a building.

annexation, *n.* (17c) **1.** The act of attaching; the state of being attached. **2.** *Property.* The point at which a fixture becomes a part of the realty to which it is attached. **3.** A formal act by which a nation, state, or municipality incorporates land within its dominion. **4.** The annexed land itself. — **annex,** *vb.*

annotation (an-ə-**tay**-shən), *n.* (15c) **1.** A brief summary of the facts and decision in a case, esp. one involving statutory interpretation. **2.** A note that explains or criticizes a source of law, usu. a case. • Annotations appear, for example, in the *United States Code Annotated* (USCA). **3.** A volume containing such explanatory or critical notes. — **annotate** (**an**-ə-tayt), *vb.* — **annotative**

(**an**-ə-tay-tiv), *adj.* — **annotator** (**an**-ə-tay-tər), *n.*

annuitant (ə-**n**[y]**oo**-ə-tənt), *n.* (18c) A beneficiary of an annuity.

annuity (ə-**n**[y]**oo**-ə-tee). (15c) **1.** An obligation to pay a stated sum, usu. monthly or annually, to a stated recipient. **2.** A fixed sum of money payable periodically. **3.** A right, often acquired under a life-insurance contract, to receive fixed payments periodically for a specified duration. **4.** A savings account with an insurance company or investment company, usu. established for retirement income. • Payments into the account accumulate tax-free, and the account is taxed only when the annuitant withdraws money in retirement.

annuity policy. An insurance policy providing for monthly or periodic payments to the insured to begin at a fixed date and continue through the insured's life.

annulment (ə-**nəl**-mənt), *n.* (15c) **1.** The act of nullifying or making void; voidance. **2.** A judicial or ecclesiastical declaration that a marriage is void. • An annulment establishes that the marital status never existed. — **annul** (ə-**nəl**), *vb.*

anonymous, *adj.* (17c) Not named or identified. — **anonymity** (an-ə-**nim**-ə-tee), *n.*

anonymous case. A reported case in which the word "anonymous" is substituted for at least one party's name to conceal the party's identity. See, e.g., *Anonymous v. Anonymous*, 735 N.Y.S.2d 26 (App. Div. 2001).

answer, *n.* (bef. 12c) **1.** A defendant's first pleading that addresses the merits of the case, usu. by denying the plaintiff's allegations. • An answer usu. sets forth the defendant's defenses and counterclaims.

false answer. (18c) A sham answer in a pleading.

2. A person's, esp. a witness's, response to a question posed.

evasive answer. (17c) A response that neither directly admits nor denies a question. • In discovery, this is considered a failure to answer. Fed. R. Civ. P. 37(a)(3).

unresponsive answer. (1891) *Evidence.* A response from a witness (usu. at a deposition or hearing) that is irrelevant to the question asked.

answer, *vb.* (12c) **1.** To respond to a question, a pleading, or a discovery request <the company failed to answer the interrogatories within 30 days>. **2.** To assume the liability of another <a guarantor answers for another person's debt>. **3.** To pay (a debt or other liability) <she promised to answer damages out of her own estate>.

ante (**an**-tee), *prep.* [Latin] Before. Cf. POST.

antecedent (an-tə-**see**-dənt), *adj.* (14c) Earlier; preexisting; previous. — **antecedent** (preceding thing), *n.* — **antecedence** (quality or fact of going before), *n.*

antedate (**an**-ti-dayt), *vb.* (16c) **1.** To affix with a date earlier than the true date; BACKDATE (1). **2.** To precede in time. Cf. POSTDATE. — **antedate,** *n.*

antibootleg, *adj. Copyright.* Of or pertaining to an effort to combat or discourage illegal recording, distribution, and sale of unauthorized reproductions of live and broadcast performances. — **antibootlegging,** *n.*

antibootleg statute. *Copyright.* A law, esp. a state law, that prohibits making, distributing, or selling an unauthorized recording of a live performance.

antichurning rule. *Tax.* A statutory or regulatory provision that denies certain tax advantages, esp. accelerated depreciation and amortization schedules, to taxpayers who acquire property in a transaction that does not result in a significant change in the property's ownership or use.

anticipation. **1.** The distribution or receipt of trust income before it is due. **2.** *Patents.* The prior invention or disclosure of the claimed invention by another, or the inventor's own disclosure of the claimed invention by publication, sale, or offer to sell if that disclosure predates the date of the patent-application filing by more than one year. — **anticipate,** *vb.*

anticipatory filing. The bringing of a lawsuit or regulatory action against another with the expectation that the other party is preparing an action of its own.

anticircumvention device. *Copyright.* An apparatus designed to prevent bypassing, avoiding, removing, deactivating, or impairing a technological measure that controls access to a work protected by copyright; an apparatus in a media player or receiver, such as a DVD or a TV satellite dish, designed to prevent unauthorized use or duplication of copyrighted material.

anticompetitive, *adj.* Having a tendency to reduce or eliminate competition. • This term describes the type of conduct or circumstances generally targeted by antitrust laws.

antidilution act. *Trademarks.* A statute prohibiting actions that are likely to lessen, diminish, or erode a famous mark's capacity to identify and distinguish goods and services, without regard to whether the action creates a likelihood of confusion, mistake, or deception.

antidumping law. A statute designed to protect domestic companies by preventing the sale of foreign goods at less than fair value, as defined in the statute (for example, at a price below that of the domestic market).

antihazing statute. A (usu. criminal) law that prohibits an organization or members of an organization from requiring a prospective member, as a condition of membership, to do or submit to any act that presents a substantial risk of physical or mental harm.

anti-john law. A criminal-law statute punishing prostitutes' customers.

antilapse statute. (1937) *Wills & estates.* A statute that substitutes certain heirs of some types of testamentary beneficiaries when the beneficiary has predeceased the testator and permits them to take the gift, which would otherwise fail and thus pass to the residuary beneficiary (if any) or to the intestate heirs.

antilynching law. A statute that criminalizes any unjustified act of violence by two or more people against another, regardless of race.

antinomy (an-**tin**-ə-mee), *n.* (16c) A contradiction in law or logic; esp., a conflict of authority, as between two decisions. — **antinomic** (an-ti-**nom**-ik), *adj.*

antipiracy, *adj. Copyright & Trademarks.* Of or pertaining to an effort to combat or discourage illegal reproduction, distribution, or use of copyrighted or trademarked products <an antipiracy group>.

antishelving clause. *Patents.* A provision in a patent-licensing contract, usu. one in which payment is based on royalties, requiring the licensee to put the patented article into commercial use within a specified time and to notify the patentee if the licensee decides to stop selling or manufacturing it.

antispamming law. A statute enacted to combat or criminalize the sending of unsolicited commercial e-mail. • Many states have such a law.

antistructuring statute. A federal law that forbids structuring monetary transactions with the intent to evade federal reporting requirements.

antisuit, *adj.* Of or relating to a court order forbidding the defendant in a lawsuit, pending or resolved, from filing a similar action against the same party in another jurisdiction.

antitrust law. **1.** The body of law designed to protect trade and commerce from restraints, monopolies, price-fixing, and price discrimination. • The principal federal antitrust laws are the Sherman Act (15 USCA §§ 1–7) and the Clayton Act (15 USCA §§ 12–27). **2.** (*cap.*) SHERMAN ANTITRUST ACT.

AOUSC. *abbr.* Administrative Office of the United States Courts.

APA. *abbr.* **1.** Administrative Procedure Act. **2.** Advance pricing agreement.

apartheid (ə-**pahrt**-hayt *or* ə-**pahr**-tɪt). Racial segregation; specif., a comprehensive governmental policy of racial discrimination and segregation, as it was practiced in South Africa.

APJ. *abbr.* Administrative patent judge.

a posteriori (ay pos-teer-ee-**or**-ɪ *or* ah pos-teer-ee-**or**-ee), *adv.* [Latin "from what comes after"] (16c) Inductively; from the particular to the general, or from known effects to their inferred causes <as a legal analyst, she reasoned a posteriori — from countless individual cases to generalized rules that she finally applied>. Cf. A PRIORI. — **a posteriori,** *adj.*

apparent, *adj.* (14c) **1.** Visible; manifest; obvious. **2.** Ostensible; seeming.

appeal, *n.* (13c) A proceeding undertaken to have a decision reconsidered by a higher authority; esp., the submission of a lower court's or agency's decision to a higher court for review and possible reversal <the case is on appeal>. —**appeal,** *vb.* — **appealability,** *n.*

appeal by application. An appeal for which permission must first be obtained from the reviewing court.

appeal by right. An appeal to a higher court from which permission need not be first obtained.

appeal de novo. An appeal in which the appellate court uses the trial court's record but reviews the evidence and law without deference to the trial court's rulings.

consolidated appeal. An appeal in which two or more parties, whose interests were similar enough to make a joinder practicable, proceed as a single appellant.

cross-appeal. An appeal by the appellee, usu. heard at the same time as the appellant's appeal.

delayed appeal. An appeal that takes place after the time for appealing has expired, but only when the reviewing court has granted permission because of special circumstances.

direct appeal. An appeal from a trial court's decision directly to the jurisdiction's highest court, thus bypassing review by an intermediate appellate court. • Such an appeal may be authorized, for example, when the case involves the constitutionality of a state law.

frivolous appeal. (18c) An appeal having no legal basis, usu. filed for delay to induce a judgment creditor to settle or to avoid payment of a judgment. • Federal Rule of Appellate Procedure 38 provides for the award of damages and costs if the appellate court determines that an appeal is frivolous. Fed. R. App. P. 38.

interlocutory appeal. An appeal that occurs before the trial court's final ruling on the entire case. 28 USCA § 1292(b). • Some interlocutory appeals involve legal points necessary to the determination of the case, while others involve collateral orders that are wholly separate from the merits of the action.

limited appeal. An appeal from only certain portions of a decision, usu. only the adverse or unfavorable portions.

protective appeal. A precautionary appeal filed by counsel when the client might otherwise lose an effective right to appeal.

suspensive appeal. An appeal that stays the execution of the underlying judgment.

appeals council. A commission that hears appeals of rulings by administrative-law judges in social-security matters.

appearance, *n.* (14c) *Procedure.* A coming into court as a party or interested person, or as a lawyer on behalf of a party or interested person; esp., a defendant's act of taking part in a lawsuit, whether by formally participating in it or by an answer, demurrer, or motion, or by taking postjudgment steps in the lawsuit in either the trial court or an appellate court. — **appear,** *vb.*

compulsory appearance. An appearance by one who is required to appear by having been served with process.

general appearance. A general-purpose appearance that waives a party's ability later to dispute the court's authority to enter a binding judgment against him or her.

initial appearance. A criminal defendant's first appearance in court to hear the charges read, to be advised of his or her rights, and to have bail determined. • The initial appearance is usu. required by statute to occur without undue delay. In a misdemeanor case, the initial appearance may be combined with the arraignment.

special appearance. **1.** A defendant's pleading that either claims that the court lacks personal jurisdiction over the defendant or objects to improper service of process. **2.** A defendant's showing up in court for the sole purpose of contesting the court's assertion of personal jurisdiction over the defendant.

voluntary appearance. An appearance entered by a party's own will, without the service of process.

appearance doctrine. (1972) In the law of self-defense, the rule that a defendant's use of force is justified if the defendant reasonably believed it to be justified.

appellant (ə-**pel**-ənt). (15c) A party who appeals a lower court's decision, usu. seeking reversal of that decision. Cf. APPELLEE.

appellate (ə-**pel**-it), *adj.* (18c) Of or relating to an appeal or appeals generally.

appellate division. A department of a superior court responsible for hearing appeals; an intermediate appellate court in some states, such as New York and New Jersey.

appellate rules. A body of rules governing appeals from lower courts.

appellee (ap-ə-**lee**). (16c) A party against whom an appeal is taken and whose role is to respond to that appeal, usu. seeking affirmance of the lower court's decision. Cf. APPELLANT.

appendant (ə-**pen**-dənt), *adj.* (15c) Attached or belonging to property as an additional but subsidiary right. — **appendant,** *n.*

appendix, *n.* (16c) A supplementary document attached to the end of a writing <the brief includes an appendix of exhibits>. Pl. **appendixes, appendices.**

applicant. (18c) One who requests something; a petitioner, such as a person who applies for letters of administration.

application for leave to appeal. (1882) A motion asking an appellate court to hear a party's appeal from a judgment when the party has no appeal by right or when the party's time limit for an appeal by right has expired. • The reviewing court has discretion whether to grant or reject such a motion.

application for transfer. In some jurisdictions, a request to a state's highest court to hear an appeal from an intermediate court of appeal.

applied-art doctrine. *Copyright.* The rule that a pictorial, graphic, or sculptural work that has an inherent use apart from its appearance, and is also an expressive work apart from its utility, may qualify for copyright protection. • Examples have included bookends, lamps, and sundials.

apply, *vb.* (14c) **1.** To make a formal request or motion <apply for a loan> <apply for injunctive relief>. **2.** To employ for a limited purpose <apply payments to a reduction in interest>. **3.** To put to use with a particular subject matter <apply the law to the facts>.

appointee. (18c) **1.** One who is appointed. **2.** One who receives the benefit of a power of appointment.

appointment, *n.* (15c) **1.** The designation of a person, such as a nonelected public official, for a job or duty; esp., the naming of someone to a nonelected public office.

recess appointment. An appointment, including a judicial appointment, made by the President when the Senate is not in session, subject to the Senate's later ratification.

2. An office occupied by someone who has been appointed <a high appointment in the federal government>. **3.** The act of disposing of property, in exercise of a power granted for that purpose. — **appoint,** *vb.* — **appointer** (for senses 1–3), *n.* — **appointor** (for sense 4), *n.*

Appointments Clause. (1976) The clause of the U.S. Constitution giving the President the power to nominate federal judges and various other officials. U.S. Const. art. II, § 2.

apportionment, *n.* (16c) **1.** Division into proportionate shares; esp., the division of rights and liabilities between two or more persons or entities. **2.** *Tax.* The act of allocating or attributing moneys or expenses in a given way, as when a taxpayer allocates part of profits to a particular tax year or part of the use of a personal asset to a business. **3.** Distribution of legislative seats among districts; esp., the allocation of congressional representatives among the states based on population, as required by the 14th Amendment. **4.** The division (by statute or by the testator's instruction) of an estate-tax liability among persons interested in an estate. — **apportion,** *vb.*

apportionment of liability. (1855) *Torts.* The parceling out of liability for an injury among multiple tortfeasors, and possibly the plaintiff as well. • Apportionment of liability encompasses such legal doctrines as joint and several liability, comparative responsibility, indemnity, and settlements. See Restatement (Third) of Torts: Apportionment of Liability (1999).

appraisal, *n.* (1817) **1.** The determination of what constitutes a fair price; valuation; estimation of worth. **2.** The report of such a determination. — **appraise,** *vb.* — **appraiser,** *n.*

appraisement. (17c) **1.** APPRAISAL. **2.** An ADR method used for resolving the amount or extent of liability on a contract when the issue of liability itself is not in dispute. • Unlike arbitration, appraisement is not a quasi-judicial proceeding but instead an informal determination of the amount owed on a contract.

appreciation, *n.* (18c) An increase in an asset's value, usu. because of inflation. Cf. DEPRECIATION. — **appreciate,** *vb.* — **appreciable,** *adj.*

appreciation test. (1970) *Criminal law.* A test for the insanity defense requiring proof by clear and convincing evidence that at the time of the crime, the defendant suffered from a severe mental disease or defect preventing him or her from appreciating the wrongfulness of the conduct. 18 USCA § 17.

apprehension, *n.* (14c) **1.** Seizure in the name of the law; arrest. **2.** Perception; comprehension; belief. **3.** Fear; anxiety. — **apprehend,** *vb.*

appropriation, *n.* (14c) **1.** The exercise of control over property; a taking of possession. **2.** A legislative body's act of setting aside a sum of money for a public purpose. **3.** The sum of money so voted. **4.** *Torts.* An invasion of privacy whereby one person takes the name or likeness of another for commercial gain. — **appropriate,** *vb.* — **appropriable,** *adj.* — **appropriator,** *n.*

appurtenance (ə-**pərt**-[ə-]nənts), *n.* (14c) Something that belongs or is attached to something else <the garden is an appurtenance to the land>.

appurtenant, *adj.* (14c) Annexed to a more important thing.

APR. *abbr.* Annual percentage rate.

à prendre (ah **prawn**-drə *or* -dər). [French] (17c) For taking; for seizure.

a priori (ay prI-**or**-I *or* ah pree-**or**-ee), *adv.* [Latin "from what is before"] (17c) Deductively; from the general to the particular <as an analyst, he reasoned a priori — from seemingly self-evident propositions to particular conclusions>. Cf. A POSTERIORI. — **a priori,** *adj.*

arbiter (**ahr**-bə-tər). (14c) One with the power to decide disputes, such as a judge.

arbitrage (**ahr**-bə-trahzh), *n.* The simultaneous buying and selling of identical securities in different markets, with the hope of profiting from the price difference between those markets. — **arbitrager** (**ahr**-bə-trazh-ər), **arbitrageur** (ahr-bə-trah-**zhər**), *n.*

arbitrament (ahr-**bi**-trə-mənt). (15c) **1.** The power to decide for oneself or others; the power to decide finally and absolutely. **2.** The act of deciding or settling a dispute that has been referred to arbitration. **3.** AWARD.

arbitrary, *adj.* (15c) **1.** Depending on individual discretion; specif., determined by a judge rather than by fixed rules, procedures, or law. **2.** (Of a judicial decision) founded on prejudice or preference rather than on reason or fact. • This type of decision is often termed *arbitrary and capricious.*

arbitration, *n.* (15c) A method of dispute resolution involving one or more neutral third parties who are usu. agreed to by the disputing parties and whose decision is binding. — **arbitrate,** *vb.* — **arbitral,** *adj.*

ad hoc arbitration. (1931) Arbitration of only one issue.

adjudicative-claims arbitration. (1972) Arbitration designed to resolve matters usu. handled by courts (such as a tort claim), in contrast to arbitration of labor issues, international trade, and other fields traditionally associated with arbitration.

compulsory arbitration. (1813) Arbitration required by law or forced by law on the parties.

final-offer arbitration. (1971) Arbitration in which each party must submit a "final offer" to the arbitrator, who may choose only one. • This device gives each party an incentive to make a reasonable offer or risk the arbitrator's accepting the other party's offer. The purpose of this type of arbitration is to counteract arbitrators' tendency to make compromise decisions halfway between the two parties' demands.

grievance arbitration. **1.** Arbitration that involves the violation or interpretation of an existing contract. **2.** *Labor law.* Arbitration of an employee's grievance, usu. relating to an alleged violation of the employee's rights under a collective-bargaining agreement.

judicial arbitration. Court-referred arbitration that is final unless a party objects to the award.

voluntary arbitration. (18c) Arbitration by the agreement of the parties.

arbitration act. (1807) A federal or state statute providing for the submission of disputes to arbitration.

arbitration and award. An affirmative defense asserting that the subject matter of the action has already been settled in arbitration.

arbitration board. A panel of arbitrators appointed to hear and decide a dispute according to the rules of arbitration.

arbitration bond. A performance bond executed by the parties in an arbitration.

arbitration clause. (1828) A contractual provision mandating arbitration — and thereby avoiding litigation — of disputes about the contracting parties' rights, duties, and liabilities.

arbitrator, *n.* (15c) A neutral person who resolves disputes between parties, esp. by means of formal arbitration. — **arbitratorship,** *n.*

archival copy. *Copyright.* A copy of an original piece of software, made by the consumer for backup. • An owner may make archival copies of software without infringing its copyright. 17 USCA § 117.

arguendo (ahr-gyoo-**en**-doh). [Latin "in arguing"] (1817) **1.** For the sake of argument <assuming arguendo that discovery procedures were correctly followed, the court still cannot grant the defendant's motion to dismiss>. **2.** During the course of argument <counsel mentioned arguendo that the case has been followed in three other decisions>. — Abbr. arg.

argument. (14c) **1.** A statement that attempts to persuade; esp., the remarks of counsel in analyzing and pointing out or repudiating a desired inference, for the assistance of a decision-maker. **2.** The act or process of attempting to persuade.

argumentative, *adj.* (15c) **1.** Of or relating to argument or persuasion <an argumentative tone of voice>. **2.** Expressing not only facts, but also inferences and conclusions drawn from facts <the judge sustained the prosecutor's objection to the argumentative question>.

argumentative question. A question in which the examiner interposes a viewpoint under the guise of asking a question. • This is considered an abuse of interrogation.

arise, *vb.* (bef. 12c) **1.** To originate; to stem (from) <a federal claim arising under the U.S. Constitution>. **2.** To result (from) <litigation routinely arises from such accidents>. **3.** To emerge in one's consciousness; to come to one's attention <the question of appealability then arose>.

ARM. *abbr.* Adjustable-rate mortgage.

armed, *adj.* **1.** Equipped with a weapon <an armed robber>. **2.** Involving the use of a weapon <armed robbery>.

arm-in-arm, *adj.* (2000) Of, relating to, or involving a transaction between parties whose personal interests are involved.

arm of the state. (1953) An entity created by a state and operating as an alter ego or instrumentality of the state, such as a state university or a state department of transportation. • The 11th Amendment of the U.S. Constitution generally bars suits in federal court by individuals against states. The Amendment has been interpreted as protecting arms of the state as well as the state itself. Cities and local school districts have been held not to be arms of the state.

arm's-length, *adj.* Of or relating to dealings between two parties who are not related or not on close terms and who are presumed to have roughly equal bargaining power; not involving a confidential relationship.

arraignment, *n.* (16c) The initial step in a criminal prosecution whereby the defendant is brought before the court to hear the charges and to enter a plea. — **arraign,** *vb.*

array, *n.* (14c) **1.** A panel of potential jurors; VENIRE (1). **2.** The jurors actually empaneled. **3.** A list or roster of empaneled jurors. **4.** Order; arrangement.

array, *vb.* (16c) **1.** To empanel a jury for trial. **2.** To call out the names of jurors, one by one, as they are empaneled.

arrear, *n.* (*usu. pl.*) (17c) **1.** The state of being behind in the payment of a debt or the discharge of an obligation. **2.** An unpaid or overdue debt. **3.** An unfinished duty.

arrest, *n.* (14c) **1.** A seizure or forcible restraint. **2.** The taking or keeping of a person in custody by legal authority, esp. in response to a criminal charge; specif., the apprehension of someone for the purpose of securing the administration of the law, esp. of bringing that person before a court. — **arrest,** *vb.*

citizen's arrest. (1941) An arrest of a private person by another private person on grounds that (1) a public offense was committed in the arrester's presence, or (2) the arrester has reasonable cause to believe that the arrestee has committed a felony.

false arrest. (18c) An arrest made without proper legal authority.

lawful arrest. (18c) The taking of a person into legal custody either under a valid warrant or on probable cause that the person has committed a crime. Cf. *unlawful arrest.*

malicious arrest. (18c) An arrest made without probable cause and for an improper purpose; esp., an abuse of process by which a person procures the arrest (and often the imprisonment) of another by means of judicial process, without any reasonable cause. • Malicious arrest can be grounds for an action for abuse of process, false imprisonment, or malicious prosecution.

material-witness arrest. An arrest of a witness to a crime for the purpose of inducing the witness to talk to police. • This type of arrest requires a warrant based on probable cause.

parol arrest (pə-**rohl** *or* **par**-əl). (1904) An arrest ordered by a judge or magistrate from the bench, without written complaint, and executed immediately, such as an arrest of a person who breaches the peace in open court.

pretextual arrest. (1968) An arrest of a person for a minor offense to create an opportunity to investigate the person's involvement in a more serious offense for which there is no lawful ground to make an arrest.

rearrest. A warrantless arrest of a person who has escaped from custody, violated parole or probation, or failed to appear in court as ordered.

subterfuge arrest. An arrest of a suspect for the stated purpose of obtaining evidence of one crime but with the underlying intent to search the suspect for evidence of a different crime.

unlawful arrest. The taking of a person into custody either without a valid warrant or without probable cause to believe that the person has committed a crime. Cf. *lawful arrest.*

warranted arrest. (1950) An arrest made under authority of a warrant.

warrantless arrest. (1958) A legal arrest, without a warrant, based on probable cause of a felony, or for a misdemeanor committed in a police officer's presence.

arrestee. (1844) A person who has been taken into custody by legal authority; a person who has been arrested.

arrest of judgment. (17c) The staying of a judgment after its entry; esp., a court's refusal to render or enforce a judgment because of a defect apparent from the record.

arrest record. (1930) **1.** A form completed by a police officer when a person is arrested. **2.** A cumulative list of the instances when a person has been arrested.

arrogation (ar-ə-**gay**-shən), *n.* (16c) The act of claiming or taking something without the right to do so <some commentators argue that limited military actions unilaterally ordered by the President are an arrogation of Congress's power to declare war>. — **arrogate,** *vb.*

arson, *n.* (17c) **1.** At common law, the malicious burning of someone else's dwelling house or outhouse that is either appurtenant to the dwelling house or within the curtilage. **2.** Under modern statutes, the intentional and wrongful burning of someone else's property (as to destroy a building) or one's own property (as to fraudulently collect insurance). See Model Penal Code § 220.1(1).

aggravated arson. Arson accompanied by some aggravating factor, as when the offender foresees or anticipates that one or more persons will be in or near the property being burned.

arsonable, *adj.* (1902) (Of property) of such a nature as to give rise to a charge of arson if maliciously burned <only real property, and not personal property, is arsonable>.

arsonist. (1864) One who commits arson; INCENDIARY (1).

ART. *abbr.* Assisted reproductive technology.

art. (13c) **1.** Creative expression, or the product of creative expression. **2.** An occupation or business that requires skill; a craft. **3.** *Patents.* A field of useful endeavor; the methodical application of knowledge or skill in creating something new.

prior art. *Patents.* Knowledge that is publicly known, used by others, or available on the date of invention to a person of ordinary skill in an art, including what would be obvious from that knowledge.

article, *n.* (13c) **1.** Generally, a particular item or thing. **2.** A separate and distinct part (as a clause or stipulation) of a writing, esp. in a contract, statute, or constitution. **3.** (*pl.*) An instrument containing a set of rules or stipulations. **4.** A nonfictional literary composition forming an independent part of a publication, such as a law review or journal.

Article I court. (1955) **1.** Legislative court. **2.** A type of federal legislative court that is not bound by the requirements of or protected under U.S. Const. art. III, § 2, and that performs functions similar to those of an administrative agency, such as issuing advisory opinions. U.S. Const. art. I, § 8.

Article I judge. (1958) **1.** A U.S. bankruptcy judge, magistrate judge, or administrative-law judge appointed for a term of years as authorized by Congress under Article I of the U.S. Constitution. 28 USCA §§ 151 et seq., 631 et seq. **2.** A federal judge temporarily appointed by the President without prior Senate approval.

Article III court. (1949) A federal court that, deriving its jurisdiction from U.S. Const. art. III, § 2, hears cases arising under the Constitution and the laws and treaties of the United States, cases in which the United States is a party, and cases between the states and between citizens of different states.

Article III judge. (1937) A U.S. Supreme Court, Court of Appeals, or District Court judge appointed for life under Article III of the U.S. Constitution.

articles of agreement. A writing that records matters that the parties agreed on when forming a partnership or business or transferring real property. • Unlike a contract, articles of agreement usu. contain only agreements and do not express promises of performance. They often supplement a contract.

articles of amendment. (1891) A document filed to effectuate an amendment or change to a corporation's articles of incorporation.

articles of association. (17c) **1.** Articles of incorporation. **2.** A governing document — similar to articles of incorporation — that legally creates a nonstock or nonprofit organization.

Articles of Confederation. The instrument that governed the association of the 13 original states from March 1, 1781 until the adoption of the U.S. Constitution (September 17, 1787).

articles of dissolution. (1802) A document that a dissolving corporation must file with the appropriate governmental agency, usu. the secretary of state, after the corporation has settled all its debts and distributed all its assets.

articles of impeachment. (17c) A formal document alleging the specific charges against a public official and the reasons for removing that official from office.

articles of incorporation. (18c) A governing document that sets forth the basic terms of a corporation's existence, including the number and classes of shares and the purposes and duration of the corporation.

articles of partnership. Partnership agreement.

artificial insemination. *Family law.* A process for achieving conception, whereby semen is inserted into a woman's vagina by some means other than intercourse.

ascendant (ə-**sen**-dənt), *n.* (17c) One who precedes in lineage, such as a parent or grandparent. Cf. DESCENDANT. — **ascendant,** *adj.*

collateral ascendant. (1832) Loosely, an aunt, uncle, or other relative who is not strictly an ancestor.

lineal ascendant. A blood relative in the direct line of ascent; ancestor. • Parents, grandparents, and great-grandparents are lineal ascendants.

ascent. (17c) The passing of an estate upwards to an heir in the ascending line. Cf. DESCENT.

ASE. *abbr.* American Stock Exchange.

ASFA. *abbr.* Adoption and Safe Families Act.

***Ashwander* rules.** (1953) A set of principles outlining the U.S. Supreme Court's policy of deciding constitutional questions only when necessary, and of avoiding a constitutional question if the case can be decided on the basis of another issue. • These rules were outlined in Justice Brandeis's concurring opinion in *Ashwander v. Tennessee Valley Authority*, 297 U.S. 288, 56 S.Ct. 466 (1936).

as is, *adv. & adj.* In the existing condition without modification <the customer bought the car as is>. • Under UCC § 2-316(3)(a), a seller can disclaim all implied warranties by stating that the goods are being sold "as is" or "with all faults." Generally, a sale of property "as is" means that the property is sold in its existing condition, and use of the phrase *as is* relieves the seller from liability for defects in that condition.

as of right. By virtue of a legal entitlement <the case is not one triable to a jury as of right>.

as per. (18c) In accordance with; PER (3). • This phrase has traditionally been considered a barbarism, *per* being the preferred form in commercialese <per your request>. But even *per* can be improved on <as you requested>.

aspirin wars. *Slang.* A series of false-advertising lawsuits between makers of over-the-counter pain relievers in the

1980s, all centering on the boundaries of comparative advertising.

asportation (as-pər-**tay**-shən), *n.* (18c) The act of carrying away or removing (property or a person). • Asportation is a necessary element of larceny. — **asport,** *vb.* — **asportative,** *adj.*

assailant. (16c) **1.** One who physically attacks another; one who commits an assault. **2.** One who attacks another using nonphysical means; esp., one who attacks another's position or feelings, as by criticism, argument, or abusive language.

assassination, *n.* (17c) The act of deliberately killing someone, esp. a public figure, usu. for hire or for political reasons. — **assassinate,** *vb.* — **assassin,** *n.*

assault, *n.* (14c) **1.** *Criminal & tort law.* The threat or use of force on another that causes that person to have a reasonable apprehension of imminent harmful or offensive contact; the act of putting another person in reasonable fear or apprehension of an immediate battery by means of an act amounting to an attempt or threat to commit a battery. **2.** *Criminal law.* An attempt to commit battery, requiring the specific intent to cause physical injury. **3.** Loosely, a battery. **4.** Popularly, any attack. — **assault,** *vb.* — **assaultive,** *adj.*

aggravated assault. (18c) Criminal assault accompanied by circumstances that make it more severe, such as the intent to commit another crime or the intent to cause serious bodily injury, esp. by using a deadly weapon. See Model Penal Code § 211.1(2).

assault by contact. The offense of knowingly or intentionally touching another person when the actor knows or believes that the touch will offend or provoke the other person.

assault with a deadly weapon. (1803) An aggravated assault in which the defendant, using a deadly weapon, threatens the victim with death or serious bodily injury.

assault with intent. (17c) Any of several assaults that are carried out with an additional criminal purpose in mind, such as assault with intent to murder, assault with intent to rob, assault with intent to rape, and assault with intent to inflict great bodily injury.

assault with intent to commit rape. An assault carried out with the additional criminal purpose of raping the victim.

attempted assault. (1870) An attempt to commit an assault; an attempted battery that has not progressed far enough to be an assault, as when a person intends to harm someone physically but is captured while or after trying to locate the intended victim in his or her place of employment.

civil assault. (1892) An assault considered as a tort and not as a crime. • Although the same assaultive conduct can be both a tort and a crime, this term isolates the legal elements that give rise to civil liability.

conditional assault. (1971) An assault expressing a threat on condition, such as "your money or your life."

criminal assault. (1835) An assault considered as a crime and not as a tort. • This term isolates the legal elements that give rise to criminal liability even though the act might also have been tortious.

intoxication assault. An assault that occurs when an inebriated person causes bodily injury to another person.

sexual assault. (1880) **1.** Sexual intercourse with another person who does not consent. • Several state statutes have abolished the crime of rape and replaced it with the offense of sexual assault. **2.** Offensive sexual contact with another person, exclusive of rape.

assault and battery. (16c) Loosely, a criminal battery.

assay, *n.* **1.** A proof or trial, by chemical experiments, of the purity of metals, esp. gold and silver. **2.** An examination of weights and measures.

assembly. (14c) **1.** A group of persons organized and united for some common purpose.

deliberative assembly. Parliamentary law. A body that transacts business according to parliamentary law.

unlawful assembly. (16c) A meeting of three or more persons who intend either to commit a violent crime or to carry out some act, lawful or unlawful, that will constitute a breach of the peace.

2. In many states, the lower house of a legislature.

assent, *n.* (14c) Agreement, approval, or permission; esp., verbal or nonverbal conduct reasonably interpreted as willingness. — **assent,** *vb.*

actual assent. Assent given by words or conduct intended to express willingness.

apparent assent. Assent given by language or conduct that, while not necessarily intended to express willingness, would be understood by a reasonable person to be so intended and is actually so understood.

constructive assent. (1811) Assent imputed to someone based on conduct.

express assent. (16c) Assent clearly and unmistakably communicated.

implied assent. (18c) Assent inferred from one's conduct rather than from direct expression.

mutual assent. (17c) Agreement by both parties to a contract, usu. in the form of offer and acceptance. • In modern contract law, mutual assent is determined by an objective standard — that is, by the apparent intention of the parties as manifested by their actions.

assertion, *n.* (15c) **1.** A declaration or allegation. **2.** A person's speaking, writing, acting, or failing to act with the intent of expressing a fact or opinion; the act or an instance of engaging in communicative behavior. — **assert,** *vb.* — **assertor,** *n.*

assessment, *n.* (16c) **1.** Determination of the rate or amount of something, such as a tax or damages. **2.** Imposition of something, such as a tax or fine, according to an established rate; the tax or fine so imposed. **3.** Official valuation of property for purposes of taxation. **4.** An audit or review. — **assess,** *vb.*

assessment roll. A record of taxable persons and property, prepared by a tax assessor.

assessor. (14c) **1.** An official who evaluates or makes assessments, esp. for purposes of taxation. **2.** A person who advises a judge or magistrate about scientific or technical matters during a trial. — **assessorial** (as-ə-**sor**-ee-əl), *adj.* — **assessorship,** *n.*

asset. (16c) **1.** An item that is owned and has value. **2.** (*pl.*) The entries on a balance sheet showing the items of property owned, including cash, inventory, equipment, real estate, accounts receivable, and goodwill. **3.** (*pl.*) All the property of a person (esp. a bankrupt or deceased person) available for paying debts or for distribution.

capital asset. A long-term asset used in the operation of a business or used to produce goods or services, such as equipment, land, or an industrial plant.

commercial assets. The aggregate of available property, stock in trade, cash, and other assets belonging to a merchant.

dead asset. A worthless asset; an asset that has no realizable value, such as an uncollectible account receivable.

earning asset. (*usu. pl.*) An asset (esp. of a bank) on which interest is received. • Banks consider loans to be earning assets.

frozen asset. An asset that is difficult to convert into cash because of court order or other legal process.

hidden asset. An asset carried on the books at a substantially reduced or understated value that is considerably less than market value.

illiquid asset. An asset that is not readily convertible into cash, usu. because of (1) the lack of demand, (2) the absence of an established market, or (3) the substantial cost or time required for liquidation (such as for real property, even when it is desirable).

intangible asset. Any nonphysical asset or resource that can be amortized or converted to cash, such as patents, goodwill, and computer programs, or a right to something, such as services paid for in advance.

quick asset. Cash and other current assets other than inventory.

tangible asset. An asset that has a physical existence and is capable of being assigned a value.

asset-depreciation range. (1971) *Tax.* The IRS's range of depreciation lifetimes allowed for assets placed in service between 1970 and 1980 and for assets depreciated under the Modified Accelerated Cost Recovery System. — Abbr. ADR.

asset sale and liquidation. *Mergers & acquisitions.* A merger in which a corporation's board and a majority of the stockholders approve a sale of most or all of the corporation's assets to another corporation in exchange for cash or debt.

asseverate (ə-**sev**-ə-rayt), *vb.* (1744) To state solemnly or positively; to aver. — **asseveration** (ə-sev-ə-**ray**-shən), *n.*

assign, *vb.* **1.** To convey; to transfer rights or property. **2.** To assert; to point out.

assignable, *adj.* (1809) Able to be assigned; transferable from one person to another, so that the transferee has the same rights as the transferor had.

assignee (ə-sɪ-**nee** *or* as-ə-**nee**). (14c) One to whom property rights or powers are transferred by another. • Use of the term is so widespread that it is difficult to ascribe positive meaning to it with any specificity. Courts recognize the protean nature of the term and are therefore often forced to look to the intent of the assignor and assignee in making the assignment — rather than to the formality of the use of the term *assignee* — in defining rights and responsibilities.

assignee clause. (1925) A provision of the Judiciary Act of 1789 that prevented a litigant without diversity of citizenship from assigning a claim to another who did have the required diversity. • In 1948 the assignee clause was replaced by 28 USCA § 1359, which denies federal jurisdiction when a party is improperly or collusively joined, by assignment or otherwise, merely to invoke jurisdiction.

assignment. (14c) **1.** The transfer of rights or property. **2.** The rights or property so transferred. **3.** The instrument of transfer. **4.** A task, job, or appointment. **5.** The act of assigning a task, job, or appointment. **6.** In litigation practice, a point that a litigant advances.

assignment for the benefit of creditors. (18c) Assignment of a debtor's property to another person in trust so as to consolidate and liquidate the debtor's assets for payment to creditors, any surplus being returned to the debtor. • This procedure serves as a state-law substitute for federal bankruptcy proceedings. The debtor is not discharged from unpaid debts by this procedure since creditors do not agree to any discharge.

assignment of error. (17c) A specification of the trial court's alleged errors on which the appellant relies in seeking an appellate court's reversal, vacation, or modification of an adverse judgment. Pl. **assignments of error.**

assignment-of-income doctrine. *Family law.* The common-law principle that the person who has earned income is the person taxed on it, regardless of who receives the proceeds.

assignment of rights. (18c) *Contracts.* The transfer of rights, esp. contractual rights, from one party to another.

assignor (as-ə-**nor** *or* ə-**sɪ**-nər *or* ə-sɪ-**nor**). (17c) One who transfers property rights or powers to another. — Also spelled *assigner.*

Assimilative Crimes Act. A federal statute providing that state law applies to a crime committed within a federal enclave in that state (such as a reservation or military installation) if the crime is not punishable under federal law. 18 USCA § 13.

assistance of counsel. (17c) Representation by a lawyer, esp. in a criminal case.

effective assistance of counsel. (1937) A conscientious, meaningful legal representation, whereby the defendant is advised of all rights and the lawyer performs all required tasks reasonably according to the prevailing professional standards in criminal cases. See Fed. R. Crim. P. 44; 18 USCA § 3006A.

ineffective assistance of counsel. (1957) A representation in which the defendant is deprived of a fair trial because the lawyer handles the case unreasonably, usu. either by performing incompetently or by not devoting full effort to the defendant, esp. because of a conflict of interest. • In determining whether a criminal defendant received ineffective assistance of counsel, courts generally consider several factors: (1) whether the lawyer had previously handled criminal cases; (2) whether strategic trial tactics were involved in the allegedly incompetent action; (3) whether, and to what extent, the defendant was prejudiced as a result of the lawyer's alleged ineffectiveness; and (4) whether the ineffectiveness was due to matters beyond the lawyer's control.

assisted conception. *Family law.* The fertilization of a woman's egg with a man's sperm by some means other than sexual intercourse.

assisted reproductive technology. *Family law.* Any medical means of aiding human reproduction, esp. through laboratory procedures. — Abbr. ART.

assize (ə-**sɪz**), *n.* (14c) **1.** A session of a court or council. **2.** A law enacted by such a body, usu. one setting the measure, weight, or price of a thing. **3.** The procedure provided for by such an enactment. **4.** The court that hears cases involving that procedure. **5.** A jury. **6.** A jury trial. **7.** A jury's finding. **8.** A writ.

associate, *n.* (16c) **1.** A colleague or companion. **2.** A junior member of an organization or profession; esp., a lawyer in a law firm, usu. with fewer than a certain number of years in practice, who may, upon achieving the requisite seniority, receive an offer to become a partner or shareholder.

association. (16c) **1.** The process of mentally collecting ideas, memories, or sensations. **2.** A gathering of people for a common purpose; the persons so joined. **3.** An unincorporated organization that is not a legal entity separate from the persons who compose it. • If an association has sufficient corporate attributes, such as centralized management, continuity of existence, and limited liability, it may be classified and taxed as a corporation.

benevolent association. An unincorporated, nonprofit organization that has a philanthropic or charitable purpose.

homeowners' association. **1.** An association of people who own homes in a given area and have united to improve or maintain the area's quality. **2.** An association formed by a land developer or homebuilder to manage and maintain property in which the developer or the builder owns an undivided common interest.

nonprofit association. A group organized for a purpose other than to generate income or profit, such as a scientific, religious, or educational organization.

professional association. (1837) **1.** A group of professionals organized to practice their profession together, though not necessarily in corporate or partnership form. **2.** A group of professionals organized for education, social activity, or lobbying, such as a bar association. — Abbr. P.A.

trade association. (1909) An association of business organizations having similar concerns and engaged in similar fields, formed for mutual protection, the interchange of ideas and statistics, and the establishment and maintenance of industry standards.

association-in-fact enterprise. Under RICO, a group of people or entities that have not formed a legal entity but that have a common or shared purpose and maintain an ongoing organizational structure through which the associates function as a continuing unit.

Association of American Law Schools. An organization of U.S. law schools that have each graduated at least three annual classes of students. — Abbr. AALS.

Association of Legal Writing Directors. A nonprofit corporation composed of the directors and former directors of law-school legal-writing programs, mostly in the United States.

assumed name. (17c) **1.** Alias. **2.** The name under which a business operates or by which it is commonly known.

assumpsit (ə-**səm**[**p**]-sit). [Law Latin "he undertook"] (16c) **1.** An express or implied promise, not under seal, by which one person undertakes to do some act or pay something to another. **2.** A common-law action for breach of such a promise or for breach of a contract.

general assumpsit. (18c) An action based on the defendant's breach of an implied promise to pay a debt to the plaintiff.

special assumpsit. An action based on the defendant's breach of an express contract.

assumption, *n.* (13c) **1.** A fact or statement taken as true or correct; a supposition <a logical assumption>. **2.** The act of taking (esp. someone else's debt or other obligation) for or on oneself; the agreement to so take <assumption of a debt>. — **assume,** *vb.*

implied assumption. (1852) The imposition of personal liability on a land purchaser who buys subject to a mortgage and who deducts the mortgage amount from the purchase price, so that the purchaser is treated as having assumed the debt.

assumption of the risk. (1824) *Torts.* **1.** The act or an instance of a prospective plaintiff's taking on the risk of loss, injury, or damage. **2.** The principle that one who takes on the risk of loss, injury, or damage cannot maintain an action against a party that causes the loss, injury, or damage. • Assumption of the risk was originally an affirmative defense, but in most jurisdictions it has now been wholly or largely subsumed by the doctrines of contributory or comparative negligence.

assurance, *n.* (14c) **1.** Something that gives confidence; the state of being confident or secure <self-assurance>. **2.** The act of transferring real property; the instrument by which it is transferred. **3.** A pledge or guarantee — **assure,** *vb.*

adequate assurance. **1.** *Contracts.* A circumstance or a contractual obligor's act that gives an obligee reason to be confident that the contract will be duly performed. **2.** *Bankruptcy.* Evidence that a debtor will probably be able to perform its obligations under a contract.

collateral assurance. A pledge made in addition to the principal assurance of an agreement.

further assurance. (17c) A covenant, usu. contained in a warranty deed, whereby the grantor promises to execute any document that might be needed in the future to perfect the title that the original instrument purported to transfer.

asylum. (15c) **1.** A sanctuary or shelter. **2.** Protection of usu. political refugees from arrest by a foreign jurisdiction; a nation or embassy that affords such protection. **3.** An institution for the protection and relief of the unfortunate, esp. the mentally ill.

at bar. (17c) Now before the court <the case at bar>.

at equity. According to equity; by, for, or in equity.

ATF. *abbr.* Bureau of Alcohol, Tobacco, Firearms, and Explosives.

at issue. (18c) Taking opposite sides; under dispute; in question <the federal appeals courts are at issue over a question of law>.

at-issue waiver. (1985) An exemption from the attorney–client privilege, whereby a litigant is considered to have waived the privilege by taking a position that cannot be effectively challenged without analyzing privileged information.

Atlantic Reporter. A set of regional lawbooks, part of the West Group's National Reporter System, containing every published appellate decision from Connecticut, Delaware, Maine, Maryland, New Hampshire, New Jersey, Pennsylvania, Rhode Island, and Vermont, as well as the decisions of the District of Columbia Municipal Court of Appeals, from 1885 to date. • The first series ran from 1885 to 1938; the second series is the current one. — Abbr. A.; A.2d.

at large. (14c) **1.** Free; unrestrained; not under control <the suspect is still at large>. **2.** Not limited to any particular place, person, matter, or question <at-large election>. **3.** Chosen by the voters of an entire political entity, such as a state, county, or city, rather than from separate districts within the entity <councilmember at large>. **4.** Not ordered in a topical way; at random <statutes at large>. **5.** Fully; in detail; in an extended form <there wasn't time to discuss the issue at large>.

at law. (16c) According to law; by, for, or in law.

at par, *adj.* (Of a stock or bond) issued or selling at face value.

at-risk rules, *n. pl.* (1977) Statutory limitations of a taxpayer's deductible losses to the amount the taxpayer could actually lose, to prevent the taxpayer from sheltering income.

ATS. *abbr.* At the suit of.

attach, *vb.* (14c) **1.** To annex, bind, or fasten <attach the exhibit to the pleading>. **2.** To take or seize under legal authority <attach the debtor's assets>. **3.** To become attributed; to adhere <jeopardy attaches when the jury is sworn>.

attaché (at-ə-**shay** *or* a-ta-**shay**), *n.* A person who serves as a technical adviser to an embassy.

attachment. (14c) **1.** The seizing of a person's property to secure a judgment or to be sold in satisfaction of a judgment.

attachment of wages. The attachment by a plaintiff of a defendant's earnings as an employee.

prejudgment attachment. An attachment ordered before a case is decided.

provisional attachment. A prejudgment attachment in which the debtor's property is seized so that if the creditor ultimately prevails, the creditor will be assured of recovering on the judgment through the sale of the seized property.

2. The arrest of a person who either is in contempt of court or is to be held as security for the payment of a judgment. **3.** A writ ordering legal seizure of property (esp. to satisfy a creditor's claim) or of a person. **4.** The creation of a security interest in property, occurring when the debtor agrees to the security, receives value from the secured party, and obtains rights in the collateral. UCC § 9-203. **5.** The act of affixing or connecting; something (as a document) that is affixed or connected to something else.

attachment of risk. (1900) The point when the risk of loss of purchased goods passes from the seller to the buyer. UCC § 2-509.

attainder (ə-**tayn**-dər), *n.* (15c) At common law, the act of extinguishing a person's civil rights when that person is sentenced to death or declared an outlaw for committing a felony or treason. — **attaint** (ə-**taynt**), *vb.*

attaint (ə-**taynt**), *adj.* (14c) Maligned or tarnished reputationally; under an attainder for crime.

attempt, *n.* (16c) **1.** The act or an instance of making an effort to accomplish something, esp. without success. **2.** *Criminal law.* An overt act that is done with the intent to commit a crime but that falls short of completing the crime. • Attempt is an inchoate offense distinct from the intended crime. Under the Model Penal Code, an attempt includes any act that is a substantial step toward commission of a crime, such as enticing, lying in wait for, or following the intended victim or unlawfully entering a building where a crime is expected to be committed. Model Penal Code § 5.01. — **attempt,** *vb.*

attempt to attempt. (1903) A first step made toward a criminal attempt of some sort, such as a failed effort to mail someone a note inciting that person to engage in criminal conduct. • As a general rule, courts do not recognize an attempt to commit a crime that is itself an attempt. But some jurisdictions recognize this offense, esp. when the attempted crime is defined to be an independent substantive crime.

attendant, *adj.* (15c) Accompanying; resulting <attendant circumstances>.

attenuation doctrine (ə-ten-yə-**way**-shən). (1962) *Criminal procedure.* The rule providing that evidence obtained by illegal means may nonetheless be admissible if the connection between the evidence and the illegal means is sufficiently attenuated or remote. • This is an exception to the fruit-of-the-poisonous-tree doctrine.

attest (ə-**test**), *vb.* (16c) **1.** To bear witness; testify. **2.** To affirm to be true or genuine; to authenticate by signing as a witness. — **attestation** (a-te-**stay**-shən), *n.* — **attestative** (ə-**tes**-tə-tiv), *adj.*

attestation clause. (18c) A provision at the end of an instrument (esp. a will) that is signed by the instrument's witnesses and that recites the formalities required by the jurisdiction in which the instrument might take effect (such as where the will might be probated). • The attestation strengthens the presumption that all the statutory requirements for executing the will have been satisfied.

at the courthouse door. (Of the posting of a notice of judicial sale, etc.) on the courthouse door, or in direct proximity to the door, as on a bulletin board that is located just outside the door and that is regularly used for the posting of legal notices.

attorney. (14c) **1.** Strictly, one who is designated to transact business for another; a legal agent. **2.** A person who practices law; lawyer. — Abbr. att'y. Pl. **attorneys.**

attorney ad litem (ad **lı**-tem *or* -təm). A court-appointed lawyer who represents a child during the course of a legal action, such as a divorce, termination, or child-abuse case.

attorney not of record. A lawyer who is not recognized as a party's legal representative.

attorney of record. The lawyer who appears for a party in a lawsuit and who is entitled to receive, on the party's behalf, all pleadings and other formal documents from the court and from other parties.

briefing attorney. **1.** An attorney who specializes in brief-writing, particularly appellate briefs and legal memoranda. **2.** CLERK (5).

panel attorney. (1951) A private attorney who represents an indigent defendant at the government's expense. • A panel attorney is usu. a member of an affiliated list and assigned by a court to a particular client.

research attorney. **1.** An attorney who specializes in providing legal support by researching, by writing memoranda, and by preparing drafts of documents. **2.** CLERK (5). • In some jurisdictions, a research attorney is a midlevel law clerk, above a briefing attorney but below a staff attorney.

settlement attorney. An attorney who specializes in negotiating resolutions for disputes, such as pending lawsuits, or in finalizing negotiated transactions, such as real-property sales.

staff attorney. (1934) **1.** A lawyer who works for a court, usu. in a permanent position, on matters such as reviewing motions, screening docketing statements, preparing scheduling orders, and examining habeas corpus petitions. • Staff attorneys do not rule on motions or decide cases, but they review and research factual and legal points, and recommend proposed rulings to judges, as well as drafting the orders implementing those rulings. **2.** An in-house lawyer for an organization, esp. a nonprofit organization but sometimes for a corporation. **3.** A lawyer who works for a law firm and performs the functions of an associate but who is not on a partnership track.

attorney general. (16c) The chief law officer of a state or of the United States, responsible for advising the government on legal matters and representing it in litigation. — Abbr. AG. Pl. **attorneys general.**

attorney general's opinion. (1808) **1.** An opinion furnished by the U.S. Attorney General to the President or another executive official on a request concerning a question of law. **2.** A written opinion by a state attorney general, usu. given at the request of a public official, interpreting a legal provision.

attorney's fees. (18c) The charge to a client for services performed for the client, such as an hourly fee, a flat fee, or a contingent fee.

attornment (ə-**tərn**-mənt), *n.* (16c) **1.** A tenant's agreement to hold the land as the tenant of a new landlord. **2.** A constructive delivery involving the transfer of mediate possession while a third person has immediate possession; esp., a bailee's acknowledgment that he or she will hold the goods on behalf of someone other than the bailor. — **attorn,** *vb.*

attractive-nuisance doctrine. (1903) *Torts.* The rule that a person who owns property on which there is a dangerous thing or condition that will foreseeably lure children to trespass has a duty to protect those children from the danger.

attribution, *n.* The process — outlined in the Internal Revenue Code — by which a person's or entity's stock ownership is assigned to a related family member or related entity for tax purposes. — **attribute,** *vb.* — **attributive,** *adj.*

attribution right. *Copyright.* A person's right to be credited as a work's author, to have one's name appear in connection with a work, or to forbid the use of one's name in connection with a work that the person did not create.

at will. (14c) Subject to one's discretion; as one wishes or chooses; esp. (of a legal relationship), able to be terminated or discharged by either party without cause <employment at will>.

auction, *n.* (16c) A public sale of property to the highest bidder. • Under UCC § 2-328, a sale at auction is ordinarily complete when the auctioneer so announces in a customary manner, as by pounding a hammer. — **auction,** *vb.*

auction without reserve. An auction in which the property will be sold to the highest bidder, no minimum price will limit bidding, the owner may not withdraw property after the first bid is received, the owner may not reject any bids, and the owner may not nullify the bidding by outbidding all other bidders.

auction with reserve. An auction in which the property will not be sold unless the highest bid exceeds a minimum price.

audience, *n.* A hearing before judges.

audit, *n.* (15c) A formal examination of an individual's or organization's accounting records, financial situation, or compliance with some other set of standards. — **audit,** *vb.* — **auditor,** *n.*

compliance audit. An audit conducted by a regulatory agency, an organization, or a third party to assess compliance with one or more sets of laws and regulations.

desk audit. A review of a civil-service position to determine whether its duties and responsibilities fit the prescribed job classification and pay scale.

double audit. An audit of the same subject performed separately by two independent auditors.

environmental audit. A company's voluntary self-audit to evaluate its environmental-management programs and to determine whether it is in compliance with environmental regulations.

field audit. An IRS audit conducted at the taxpayer's business premises, accountant's offices, or lawyer's offices.

independent audit. An audit conducted by an outside person or firm not connected with the person or organization being audited.

internal audit. An audit performed by an organization's personnel to ensure that internal procedures, operations, and accounting practices are in proper order.

office audit. An IRS audit of a taxpayer's return conducted in the IRS agent's office.

periodic audit. An audit conducted at regular intervals to assess a company's current condition.

post audit. An audit of funds spent on a completed capital project, the purpose being to assess the efficiency with which the funds were spent and to compare expected cash-flow estimates with actual cash flows.

tax audit. The review of a taxpayer's return by the IRS, including an examination of the taxpayer's books, vouchers, and records supporting the return.

transactional audit. An audit performed for due-diligence purposes to determine whether there are potentially significant problems with a transaction. • Transactional audits are often conducted in real-property transactions to identify any environmental problems. In that context, the audit is sometimes called a *site assessment.*

audit letter. A written request for an attorney, banker, or someone else to give financial auditors information about a person or entity being audited, including information about pending or threatened litigation. • The recipient of an audit letter usu. sends the response (called an *audit-letter response*) directly to the financial auditors.

auditor. A person or firm, usu. an accountant or an accounting firm, that formally examines an individual's or entity's financial records or status.

audit trail. (1954) The chain of evidence connecting account balances to original transactions and calculations.

***Aunt Jemima* doctrine.** *Trademarks.* The principle that a trademark is protected not only from use on a directly competing product, but also from use on a product so closely related in the marketplace that consumers would be confused into thinking that the products came from a single source. *Aunt Jemima Mills Co. v. Rigney & Co.*, 247 F. 407 (2d Cir. 1917); 15 USCA § 1114.

aural acquisition. (1968) *Criminal law.* Under the Federal Wiretapping Act, hearing or tape-recording a communication, as opposed to tracing its origin or destination. 18 USCA § 2510(4).

authentication, *n.* (18c) **1.** Broadly, the act of proving that something (as a document) is true or genuine, esp. so that it may be admitted as evidence; the condition of being so proved <authentication of the handwriting>. **2.** Specif., the assent to or adoption of a writing as one's own. — **authenticate,** *vb.*

self-authentication. (1939) Authentication without extrinsic evidence of truth or genuineness.

author. *Copyright.* The person who creates an expressive work, or the person or business that hires another to create an expressive work. • In copyright law, "author" applies to a broad range of occupations, including writers, artists, programmers, choreographers, and translators.

authority. (13c) **1.** The right or permission to act legally on another's behalf; esp., the power of one person to affect another's legal relations by acts done in accordance with the other's manifestations of assent; the power delegated by a principal to an agent <authority to sign the contract>.

actual authority. (18c) Authority that a principal intentionally confers on an agent or authority that the agent reasonably believes he or she has as a result of the agent's dealings with the principal. • Actual authority can be either express or implied.

apparent authority. (1808) Authority that a third party reasonably believes an agent has, based on the third party's dealings with the principal, even though the principal did not confer or intend to confer the authority. • Apparent authority can be created by law even when no actual authority has been conferred.

authority coupled with an interest. (17c) Authority given to an agent for valuable consideration. • This authority cannot be unilaterally terminated by the principal.

constructive authority. (1823) Authority that is inferred because of an earlier grant of authority.

express authority. (16c) Authority given to the agent by explicit agreement, either orally or in writing.

general authority. (17c) A general agent's authority, intended to apply to all matters arising in the course of the principal's business.

implied authority. (18c) Authority intentionally given by the principal to the agent as a result of the principal's conduct, such as the principal's earlier acquiescence to the agent's actions.

incidental authority. (18c) Authority needed to carry out actual or apparent authority. • For example, the actual authority to borrow money includes the incidental authority to sign commercial paper to bring about the loan.

inherent authority. (17c) Authority of an agent arising from the agency relationship.

naked authority. (18c) Authority delegated to an agent solely for the principal's benefit, without a beneficial interest in the matter for the agent. • This authority can be revoked by the principal at any time.

special authority. (18c) Authority limited to an individual transaction.

2. Governmental power or jurisdiction. **3.** A governmental agency or corporation that administers a public enterprise. **4.** A legal writing taken as definitive or decisive; esp., a judicial or administrative decision cited as a precedent.

adverse authority. (18c) Authority that is unfavorable to an advocate's position.

persuasive authority. (1842) Authority that carries some weight but is not binding on a court.

primary authority. (1826) Authority that issues directly from a law-making body; legislation and the reports of litigated cases.

secondary authority. (1826) Authority that explains the law but does not itself establish it, such as a treatise, annotation, or law-review article.

5. A source, such as a statute, case, or treatise, cited in support of a legal argument.

authorize, *vb.* (14c) **1.** To give legal authority; to empower. **2.** To formally approve; to sanction. — **authorization,** *n.*

autocracy (aw-**tok**-rə-see), *n.* (17c) Government by one person with unlimited power and authority; unlimited monarchy.

autograph, *n.* A person's own writing or signature; HOLOGRAPH.

automated transaction. (1977) A contract formed or performed, in whole or in part, by electronic means or by electronic messages in which neither party's electronic actions or messages establishing the contract are intended to be reviewed by an individual in the ordinary course. UCITA §§ 2-102(a)(7), 102:10UC; UETA § 14.

automatism (aw-**tom**-ə-tiz-əm), *n.* (1838) **1.** Action or conduct occurring without will, purpose, or reasoned intention, such as sleepwalking; behavior carried out in a state of unconsciousness or mental dissociation without full awareness. • Automatism may be asserted as a defense to negate the requisite mental state of voluntariness for commission of a crime. **2.** The state of a person who, though capable of action, is not conscious of his or her actions. — **automaton,** *n.*

automobile exception. (1970) The doctrine that when probable cause exists, a law-enforcement officer need not obtain a warrant before searching a movable vehicle (such as a car or boat) in which an individual has a lessened expectation of privacy. • This is an exception to the Fourth Amendment's warrant requirement for search and seizure; exigent circumstances are presumed to exist. Once the right to conduct a warrantless search arises, the actual search may take place at a later time.

autonomic law (aw-tə-**no m**-ik). (1832) An internal regulation that has its source in various forms of subordinate and restricted legislative authority possessed by private persons and bodies of persons. • Examples are corporate bylaws, university regulations, and the rules of the International Monetary Fund.

autonomy (aw-**tahn**-ə-mee), *n.* (17c) **1.** The right of self-government. **2.** A self-governing nation. **3.** An individual's capacity for self-determination. — **autonomous** (aw-**tahn**-ə-məs), *adj.*

autopsy (**aw**-top-see). (1678) **1.** A medical examination of a corpse to determine the cause of death, esp. in a criminal investigation. **2.** The evidence of one's own senses.

auxiliary (awg-**zil**-yə-ree), *adj.* **1.** Aiding or supporting. **2.** Subsidiary. **3.** Supplementary.

avail, *n.* (15c) **1.** Use or advantage <of little or no avail>. **2.** (*pl.*) Profits or proceeds, esp. from a sale of property <the avails of the trust fund>.

available, *adj.* Legally valid <available claims> <available defenses>.

availment, *n.* (17c) The act of making use or taking advantage of something for oneself <availment of the benefits of public office>. — **avail,** *vb.*

aver (ə-**vər**), *vb.* (15c) To assert positively, esp. in a pleading; to allege.

average, *n.* **1.** A single value that represents the midpoint of a broad sample of subjects; esp., in mathematics, the mean of a series. **2.** The ordinary or typical level; the norm. **3.** *Maritime law.* Accidental partial loss or damage to an insured ship or its cargo during a voyage. — **average,** *vb.* & *adj.*

averment (ə-**vər**-mənt), *n.* (15c) A positive declaration or affirmation of fact; esp., an assertion or allegation in a pleading.

immaterial averment. (18c) An averment that alleges something in needless detail; a statement that goes far beyond what is in issue. • This type of averment may be ordered struck from the pleading.

negative averment. (18c) An averment that is negative in form but affirmative in substance and that must be proved by the alleging party. • An example is the statement "she was not old enough to enter into the contract," which is more than just a simple denial.

a vinculo matrimonii (ay **ving**-kyə-loh ma-trə-**moh**-nee-I). [Latin] From the bond of matrimony. — Often shortened to *a vinculo.*

avoid, *vb.* (14c) To render void. • Because this legal use of *avoid* can be easily confused with the ordinary sense of the word, the verb *to void* is preferable.

avoidable, *adj.* Not inevitable; subject to prevention.

avoidance, *n.* (14c) **1.** The act of evading or escaping. **2.** The act of refraining from (something). **3.** RESCISSION (1). **4.** Voidance. **5.** ANNULMENT (1). **6.** Confession and avoidance. — **avoid,** *vb.*

avowal (ə-**vow**-əl), *n.* **1.** An open declaration. **2.** Offer of proof. — **avow,** *vb.*

avowry (ə-**vow**-ree), *n.* *Common-law pleading.* An acknowledgment — in an answer to a replevin action — that one has taken property, and a justification for that taking. — **avow,** *vb.*

avulsion (ə-**vəl**-shən), *n.* (17c) **1.** A forcible detachment or separation. **2.** A sudden removal of land caused by change in a river's course or by flood. • Land removed by avulsion remains the property of the original owner. **3.** A tearing away of a body part surgically or accidentally. — **avulse,** *vb.*

award, *n.* (14c) A final judgment or decision, esp. one by an arbitrator or by a jury assessing damages. — **award,** *vb.* (14c).

B

B2B. *abbr.* Business-to-business <a B2B transaction>.

B2C. *abbr.* Business-to-consumer <a B2C transaction>.

baby-brokering. Baby-selling.

Baby Doe. (1974) A generic pseudonym for a very young child involved in litigation. • Today a gender designation is often added: *Baby Girl Doe* or *Baby Boy Doe.* The generic term is used to shield the child's identity.

Baby FTC Act. (1988) A state statute that, like the Federal Trade Commission Act, outlaws deceptive and unfair trade practices.

Baby Moses law. Safe-haven law.

baby-selling. The exchange of money or something of value for a child. • All states have prohibitions against baby-selling. It is not considered baby-selling for prospective adoptive parents to pay money to a birth mother for pregnancy-related expenses.

baby-snatching. Child-kidnapping.

BAC. *abbr.* Blood alcohol content.

bachelor. 1. An unmarried man. **2.** The usual title of the first degree that is conferred on a university graduate. **3.** *English law.* A member of one of the orders of chivalry, such as the Order of the Bath.

bachelor of laws. LL.B.

back, *vb.* (18c) **1.** To indorse; to sign the back of a negotiable instrument. **2.** To sign so as to show acceptance or approval. **3.** To sign so as to indicate financial responsibility for (someone or something).

backdate, *vb.* (1944) **1.** To put a date earlier than the actual date on (something, as an instrument). • Under UCC § 3-113(a), backdating does not affect an instrument's negotiability. **2.** To make (something) retroactively valid.

back lands. (17c) Generally, lands lying away from — not next to — a highway or a watercourse.

backpay. The wages or salary that an employee should have received but did not because of an employer's unlawful action in setting or paying the wages or salary. — Also written *back pay.*

backspread. *Securities.* In arbitrage, a less than normal price difference in the price of a currency or commodity.

back-to-work agreement. A contract between a union and an employer covering the terms under which the employees will return to work after a strike.

bad-boy provision. *Securities.* A statutory or regulatory clause in a blue-sky law stating that certain persons, because of their past conduct, are not entitled to any type of exemption from registering their securities.

bad character. (17c) A person's propensity for or tendency toward unlawful or immoral behavior. • In limited circumstances, proof of bad character may be introduced into evidence to discredit a witness. Fed. R. Evid. 608, 609.

bad faith, *n.* (17c) Dishonesty of belief or purpose. — **bad-faith,** *adj.*

badge of fraud. (18c) A circumstance generally considered by courts as an indicator that a party to a transaction intended to hinder or defraud the other party, such as a transfer in anticipation of litigation, a transaction outside the usual course of business, or a false statement.

badge of slavery. (17c) **1.** Strictly, a legal disability suffered by a slave, such as the inability to vote or to own property. **2.**

Broadly, any act of racial discrimination — public or private — that Congress can prohibit under the 13th Amendment.

badger game. (1858) A scheme to extort money or some other benefit by arranging to catch someone in a compromising position and then threatening to make that person's behavior public.

bad-man theory. (1938) The jurisprudential doctrine or belief that a bad person's view of the law represents the best test of what the law actually is because that person will carefully calculate precisely what the rules allow and will operate up to the rules' limits. • This theory was first expounded by Oliver Wendell Holmes in his essay *The Path of the Law*, 10 Harv. L. Rev. 457 (1897).

bagman. *Slang.* (1928) A person who collects and distributes illegally obtained money; esp., an intermediary who collects a bribe for a public official.

bail, *n.* (15c) **1.** A security such as cash or a bond; esp., security required by a court for the release of a prisoner who must appear in court at a future time <bail is set at $500>.

cash bail. A sum of money (rather than a surety bond) posted to secure a prisoner's release from jail.

civil bail. A bond or deposit of money given to secure the release of a person arrested for failing to pay a court-ordered civil debt. • The bail is conditioned on the payment of the debt.

excessive bail. (17c) Bail that is unreasonably high considering both the offense with which the accused is charged and the risk that the accused will not appear for trial. • The Eighth Amendment prohibits excessive bail.

2. The process by which a person is released from custody either on the undertaking of a surety or on his or her own recognizance. **3.** Release of a prisoner on security for a future court appearance. **4.** One or more sureties for a criminal defendant.

bail, *vb.* (16c) **1.** To obtain the release of (oneself or another) by providing security for a future appearance in court. **2.** To release (a person) after receiving such security. **3.** To place (personal property) in someone else's charge or trust.

bailable, *adj.* (Of an offense or person) eligible for bail.

Bail Clause. The clause in the Eighth Amendment to the U.S. Constitution prohibiting excessive bail. • This clause was derived from similar language in England's Bill of Rights (1689).

bailee. (16c) A person who receives personal property from another, and has possession of but not title to the property.

bailer. (16c) **1.** One who provides bail as a surety for a criminal defendant's release. **2.** BAILOR (1).

bailiff. (14c) **1.** A court officer who maintains order during court proceedings. **2.** A sheriff's officer who executes writs and serves processes.

bailiwick (**bay**-lə-wik). The office, jurisdiction, or district of a bailiff; esp., a bailiff's territorial jurisdiction.

bail-jumping, *n.* (1881) The criminal offense of failing to appear in court after having been released on bail. See Model Penal Code § 242.8. — **bail-jumper,** *n.*

bailment. (16c) **1.** A delivery of personal property by one person (the *bailor*) to another (the *bailee*) who holds the property for a certain purpose, usu. under an express or implied-in-fact contract. • Unlike a sale or gift of personal property, a bailment involves a change in possession but not in title.

actual bailment. (1821) A bailment that arises from an actual or constructive delivery of property to the bailee.

bailment for hire. A bailment for which the bailee is compensated, as when one leaves a car with a parking attendant.

bailment for mutual benefit. (1868) A bailment for which the bailee is compensated and from which the bailor receives some additional benefit, as when one leaves a car with a parking attendant who will also wash the car while it is parked.

constructive bailment. (1843) A bailment that arises when the law imposes an obligation on a possessor of personal property to return the property to its rightful owner, as with an involuntary bailment.

gratuitous bailment. (1811) A bailment for which the bailee receives no compensation, as when one borrows a friend's car. • A gratuitous bailee is liable for loss of the property only if the loss is caused by the bailee's gross negligence.

involuntary bailment. (1840) A bailment that arises when a person accidentally, but without any negligence, leaves personal property in another's possession. • An involuntary bailee who refuses to return the property to the owner may be liable for conversion.

2. The personal property delivered by the bailor to the bailee. **3.** The contract or legal relation resulting from such a delivery. **4.** The act of posting bail for a criminal defendant. **5.** The documentation for the posting of bail for a criminal defendant.

bailor (bay-**lor** *or* **bay**-lər). (17c) **1.** A person who delivers personal property to another as a bailment. — Also spelled *bailer.* **2.** BAILER (1).

bailout, *n.* **1.** A rescue of an entity, usu. a corporation or an industry, from financial trouble. **2.** An attempt by a business to receive favorable tax treatment of its profits, as by withdrawing profits at capital-gain rates rather than distributing stock dividends that would be taxed at higher ordinary-income rates.

bail-point scale. A system for determining a criminal defendant's eligibility for bail, whereby the defendant either will be released on personal recognizance or will have a bail amount set according to the total number of points given, based on the defendant's background and behavior.

bail revocation. (1950) The court's cancellation of bail previously granted to a criminal defendant.

bait and switch. (1967) **1.** A sales practice whereby a merchant advertises a low-priced product to lure customers into the store only to induce them to buy a higher-priced product. • Most states prohibit the bait and switch when the original product is not actually available as advertised. **2.** The unethical practice of offering an attractive rate or premium to induce a person to apply for a loan or contract, with approval contingent on some condition, and then telling the person that the offered rate is not available but that a higher one can be substituted.

balance, *vb.* (16c) **1.** To compute the difference between the debits and credits of (an account). **2.** To equalize in number, force, or effect; to bring into proportion. **3.** To measure competing interests and offset them appropriately. — **balance,** *n.*

balance billing. A healthcare provider's practice of requiring a patient or other responsible party to pay any charges remaining after insurance and other payments and allowances have been applied to the total amount due for the provider's services.

balance of convenience. A balancing test that courts use to decide whether to issue a preliminary injunction stopping the defendant's allegedly infringing or unfair practices, weighing the benefit to the plaintiff and the public against the burden on the defendant.

balance of power. *Int'l law.* A relative equality of force between countries or groups of countries, as a result of which peace is encouraged because no country or group is in a position to predominate.

balance of sentence suspended. (1942) A sentencing disposition in which a criminal defendant is sentenced to jail but is credited with the time already served before sentencing, resulting in a suspension of the remaining sentence and release of the defendant from custody.

balance sheet. (18c) A statement of an entity's current financial position, disclosing the value of the entity's assets, liabilities, and owners' equity.

balancing test. (1951) A judicial doctrine, used esp. in constitutional law, whereby a court measures competing interests — as between individual rights and governmental powers, or between state authority and federal supremacy — and decides which interest should prevail.

ballistics. (18c) **1.** The science of the motion of projectiles, such as bullets. **2.** The study of a weapon's firing characteristics, esp. as used in criminal cases to determine a gun's firing capacity and whether a particular gun fired a given bullet.

ballot, *n.* **1.** An instrument, such as a paper or ball, used for casting a vote. **2.** The system of choosing officers by a recorded vote, such as by marking a paper.

absentee ballot. A ballot that a voter submits, sometimes by mail, before an election.

secret ballot. A vote cast in such a way that the person voting cannot be identified.

spoiled ballot. A ballot reflecting a vote that cannot be counted because it was cast in a form or manner that does not comply with the applicable rules.

3. A vote in a series of votes that is not conclusive until one candidate attains the necessary majority or supermajority <the candidate was nominated on the 21st ballot>. **4.** A list of candidates running for office <four candidates are on the ballot>. — **ballot,** *vb.*

Australian ballot. A uniform ballot printed by the government, listing all eligible candidates, and marked in secret. • Before Australian ballots became standard, candidates often printed their own ballots with only their name, and watchers at polling places could see whose ballot a voter was casting. — Loosely termed *secret ballot.*

Massachusetts ballot. A ballot in which, under each office, the candidates' names appear in alphabetical order alongside their party designations. • This is a type of Australian ballot.

office-block ballot. A ballot that lists the candidates' names under the title of the office sought without mentioning the candidates' party affiliations.

party-column ballot. A ballot that lists the candidates' names in separate columns by political party regardless of the offices sought by the candidates.

Texas ballot. A ballot that the voter marks for the candidates that he or she does not want elected. • The Texas ballot is particularly useful when the number of candidates only slightly exceeds a large number of representatives being elected.

ballot box. A locked box into which ballots are deposited.

ban, *vb.* To prohibit, esp. by legal means.

B and E. *abbr.* Breaking and entering.

bank. (15c) **1.** A financial establishment for the deposit, loan, exchange, or issue of money and for the transmission of funds; esp., a member of the Federal Reserve System. • Under securities law, a bank includes any financial institution, whether or not incorporated, doing business under federal or state law, if a substantial portion of the institution's business consists of receiving deposits or exercising fiduciary powers similar to those permitted to national banks and if the institution is supervised and examined by a state or federal banking authority; or a receiver, conservator, or other liquidating agent of any of the above institutions. 15 USCA § 78c(a)(6). **2.** The office in which such an establishment conducts transactions.

collecting bank. (1834) In the check-collection process, any bank handling an item for collection, except for the payor bank. UCC § 4-105(5).

commercial bank. (18c) A bank authorized to receive both demand and time deposits, to make loans, to engage in trust services, to issue letters of credit, to rent time-deposit boxes, and to provide similar services.

depositary bank. (1848) The first bank to which an item is transferred for collection. UCC § 4-105(2).

intermediary bank. (1896) A bank to which an item is transferred in the course of collection, even though the bank is not the depositary or payor bank. UCC § 4-105(4).

investment bank. A bank whose primary purpose is to acquire financing for businesses, esp. through the sale of securities. • An investment bank does not accept deposits and, apart from selling securities, does not deal with the public at large.

member bank. A bank that is a member of the Federal Reserve System.

mutual savings bank. A bank that has no capital stock and in which the depositors are the owners.

national bank. A bank incorporated under federal law and governed by a charter approved by the Comptroller of the Currency. • A national bank must use the term "national," "national bank," or "national association" as part of its name.

payor bank. (1911) A bank that is asked to pay the amount of a negotiable instrument and, on the bank's acceptance, is obliged to pay that amount; a bank by which an item is payable as drawn or accepted. • Because the bank is the drawee of a draft, it is also a *drawee bank.* UCC § 4-105(3).

presenting bank. (1862) A nonpayor bank that presents a negotiable instrument for payment. UCC § 4-105(6).

private bank. An unincorporated banking institution owned by an individual or a partnership and, depending on state statutes, may or may not be subject to state regulation.

savings bank. (1817) A bank that makes primarily home mortgage and some other consumer loans, receives deposits and pays interest on them, and may offer checking accounts. • Historically, savings banks did not provide any checking services.

state bank. A bank chartered by a state and supervised by the state banking department. •A state bank must have FDIC insurance on deposits but need not become a member of the Federal Reserve System to obtain the insurance. A state bank that is a member of the Federal Reserve is regulated by the state banking department and by the Federal Reserve. Nonmember state banks are regulated by both the state banking department and the FDIC.

bank, *vb.* (18c) **1.** To keep money at <he banks at the downtown branch>. **2.** To deposit (funds) in a bank <she banked the prize money yesterday>. **3.** *Slang.* To lend money to facilitate (a transaction) <who banked the deal?>. • The lender's consideration usu. consists of a fee or an interest in the property involved in the transaction.

bank examiner. A federal or state official who audits banks with respect to their financial condition, management, and policies. — Sometimes shortened to *examiner.*

bank holding company. A company that owns or controls one or more banks. • Ownership or control of 25 percent is usu. enough for this purpose. — Abbr. BHC.

banking day. (18c) **1.** The time during which a bank is open to the public for carrying on substantially all its banking functions. • Typically, if the bookkeeping and loan departments are closed by a certain hour, the remainder of that day is not part of that bank's banking day. **2.** A day on which banks are open for banking business.

banknote. A bank-issued promissory note that is payable to bearer on demand and that may circulate as money. — Also written *bank note.*

Bankr. Rep. *abbr.* Bankruptcy Reporter. — Also abbreviated B.R.

bankrupt, *n.* (16c) **1.** A person who cannot meet current financial obligations; an insolvent person. • This term was used in bankruptcy statutes until 1979, and is still commonly used by nonbankruptcy courts. But the Bankruptcy Code uses *debtor* instead of *bankrupt.* **2.** DEBTOR (2).

cessionary bankrupt. *Archaic.* A person who forfeits all property so that it may be divided among creditors. • The modern near-equivalent is Chapter 7. — **bankrupt,** *adj.* — **bankrupt,** *vb.*

bankruptcy. (18c) **1.** A statutory procedure by which a (usu. insolvent) debtor obtains financial relief and undergoes a judicially supervised reorganization or liquidation of the debtor's assets for the benefit of creditors; a case under the Bankruptcy Code (Title 11 of the United States Code).

involuntary bankruptcy. (1842) A bankruptcy case commenced by the debtor's creditors (usu. three or more), or, if the debtor is a partnership, by fewer than all the general partners. 11 USCA § 303(b).

malicious bankruptcy. An abuse of process by which a person wrongfully petitions to have another person adjudicated a bankrupt or to have a company wound up as insolvent.

voluntary bankruptcy. (18c) A bankruptcy case commenced by the debtor. 11 USCA § 301.

2. The field of law dealing with the rights of debtors who are financially unable to pay their debts and the rights of their creditors. **3.** The status of a party who has declared bankruptcy under a bankruptcy statute. **4.** Informally, the fact of being financially unable to pay one's debts and obligations as they become due; insolvency.

bankruptcy case. A proceeding commenced by filing a voluntary or involuntary petition under a bankruptcy statute.

Bankruptcy Code. Title I of the Bankruptcy Reform Act of 1978 (as amended and codified in 11 USCA), which governs bankruptcy cases filed on or after October 1, 1979. • Earlier cases were governed by the Bankruptcy Act of 1898.

Bankruptcy Court. A U.S. district court subunit comprising the bankruptcy judges within the district and exclusively concerned with administering bankruptcy proceedings.

bankruptcy crime. A crime committed in connection with a bankruptcy case, such as a trustee's embezzling from the debtor's estate. 18 USCA §§ 152–57.

bankruptcy estate. A debtor's legal and equitable interests in property at the beginning of a bankruptcy case where the property is subject to administration. See 11 USCA § 541.

bankruptcy law. **1.** Insolvency law. **2.** Traditionally, a statute that provides some relief and protection to an insolvent debtor or to the debtor's creditors.

bankruptcy plan. (1944) A detailed program of action formulated by a debtor or its creditors to govern the debtor's rehabilitation, continued operation or liquidation, and payment of debts. • The bankruptcy court must approve the plan before it is implemented.

bankruptcy proceeding. (1828) Any judicial or procedural action (such as a hearing) related to a bankruptcy.

Bank Secrecy Act. A federal statute that requires banks and other financial institutions to maintain records of customers' transactions and to report certain domestic and foreign transactions. • This act, passed by Congress in 1970, is designed to help the federal government in criminal, tax, and other regulatory investigations. 12 USCA § 1829b; 31 USCA § 5311.

bank-statement rule. (1974) *Commercial law.* The principle that if a bank customer fails to examine a bank statement and any items returned with it, and report to the bank within a reasonable time any unauthorized payments because of a material alteration or forgery, the customer may be precluded from complaining about the alteration or forgery. UCC § 4-406.

bar, *n.* (14c) **1.** In a courtroom, the railing that separates the front area, where court business is conducted, from the back area, which provides seats for observers; by extension, a similar railing in a legislative assembly. **2.** The whole body of lawyers qualified to practice in a given court or jurisdiction; the legal profession, or an organized subset of it. **3.** A particular court or system of courts. **4.** Bar examination. **5.** A barrier to or the destruction of a legal action or claim; the effect of a judgment for the defendant. **6.** A plea arresting a lawsuit or legal claim.

bar, *vb.* (16c) To prevent, esp. by legal objection.

bar association. (1872) An organization of members of the legal profession.

integrated bar association. A bar association in which membership is a statutory requirement for practicing law; a usu. statewide organization of lawyers in which membership is compulsory in order for a lawyer to have a law license.

local bar association. A voluntary bar association organized on a local level, such as an association within a county or city.

specialty bar association. A voluntary bar association for lawyers with special interests, specific backgrounds, or common practices.

state bar association. (1883) An association or group of attorneys that have been admitted to practice law in a given state; a bar association organized on a statewide level, often with compulsory membership. • State bar associations are usu. created by statute, and membership is often mandatory for those who practice law in the state. They often have authority to regulate the legal profession within the state.

voluntary bar association. A bar association that lawyers need not join to practice law.

bar examination. (1875) A written test that a person must pass before being licensed to practice law. • The exam varies from state to state. — Often shortened to *bar.*

Multistate Bar Examination. A nationally standardized part of a state bar examination given as a multiple-choice test covering broad legal subjects, including constitutional law, contracts, criminal law, evidence, property, and torts. — Abbr. MBE.

bar examiner. (1902) One appointed by the state to test applicants (usu. law-school graduates) by preparing, administering, and grading the bar examination.

bargain, *n.* (14c) An agreement between parties for the exchange of promises or performances. • A bargain is not necessarily a contract because the consideration may be insufficient or the transaction may be illegal. — **bargain,** *vb.*

bargain and sale. (16c) **1.** A negotiated transaction, usu. for goods, services, or real property. **2.** *Hist.* A written agreement for the sale of land whereby the buyer would give valuable consideration (recited in the agreement) without having to enter the land and perform livery of seisin, so that the parties equitably "raised a use" in the buyer. • The result of the transaction was to leave the legal estate in fee simple in the seller and to create an equitable estate in fee simple in the buyer until legal title was transferred to the buyer by delivery of a deed. In most jurisdictions, the bargain and sale has been replaced by the statutory deed of grant.

bargained-for exchange. *Contracts.* A benefit or detriment that the parties to a contract agree to as the price of performance. • The Restatement of Contracts (Second) defines *consideration* exclusively in terms of bargain, but it does not mention benefit or detriment.

bargaining unit. A group of employees authorized to engage in collective bargaining on behalf of all the employees of a company or an industry sector.

bargain sale. (1898) A sale of property for less than its fair market value. • For tax purposes, the difference between the sale price and the fair market value must be taken into account. And bargain sales between family members may lead to gift-tax consequences.

bargain theory of consideration. (1927) The theory that a promise or performance that is bargained for in exchange for a promise is consideration for the promise. • This theory underlies all bilateral contracts.

barratry (**bar**-ə-tree *or* **bair**-), *n.* (15c) Vexatious incitement to litigation, esp. by soliciting potential legal clients. • Barratry is a crime in most jurisdictions. — **barratrous** (**bar**-ə-trəs), *adj.*

barrister (**bar**-is-tər), *n.* (15c) In England or Northern Ireland, a lawyer who is admitted to plead at the bar and who may argue cases in superior courts. — **barristerial** (bar-ə-**steer**-ee-əl), *adj.*

barter, *n.* (15c) The exchange of one commodity for another without the use of money. — **barter,** *vb.*

base and meridian. *Property.* The east–west and north–south lines used by a surveyor to demarcate the position of the boundaries of real property. • A base line runs east to west. A meridian line runs north to south.

based on. *Copyright.* Derived from, and therefore similar to, an earlier work. • If one work is "based on" an earlier work, it infringes the copyright in the earlier work. To be based on an earlier work, a later work must embody substantially similar expression, not just substantially similar ideas.

basement court. (1995) *Slang.* A low-level court of limited jurisdiction, such as a police court, traffic court, municipal court, or small-claims court.

basis. (14c) **1.** A fundamental principle; an underlying fact or condition. **2.** *Tax.* The value assigned to a taxpayer's investment in property and used primarily for computing gain or loss from a transfer of the property. • Basis is usu. the total cost of acquiring the asset, including the purchase price plus commissions and other related expenses, less depreciation and other adjustments. When the assigned value represents the cost of acquiring the property, it is also called *cost basis*. Pl. **bases.**

adjusted basis. (1932) Basis increased by capital improvements and decreased by depreciation deductions.

adjusted cost basis. (1934) Basis resulting from the original cost of an item plus capital additions minus depreciation deductions.

carryover basis. (1952) The recipient's basis in property transferred by gift or in trust, equaling the transferor's basis.

stepped-up basis. (1951) The beneficiary's basis in property transferred by inheritance, equaling the fair market value of the property on the date of the decedent's death or on the alternate valuation date.

substituted basis. (1932) The basis of property transferred in a tax-free exchange or other specified transaction.

basis point. One-hundredth of 1%; .01%. • Basis points are used in computing investment yields (esp. of bonds) and in apportioning costs and calculating interest rates in real-estate transactions. — Abbr. bp.

bastard. (14c) **1.** A person born out of wedlock. **2.** A child born to a married woman whose husband could not be or is otherwise proved not to be the father. • Because the word is most commonly used as a slur, its use in family-law contexts is much in decline.

batable ground (**bay**-tə-bəl). (16c) Land of uncertain ownership.

Bates stamp, *n.* **1.** A self-advancing stamp machine used for affixing an identifying mark, usu. a number, to a document or to the individual pages of a document. **2.** The identifying number that is so affixed to a document or to the individual pages of a document. — Sometimes (erroneously) written *Bate stamp.* — **Bates-stamp,** *vb.*

battered-child syndrome. (1962) *Family law.* A constellation of medical and psychological conditions of a child who has suffered continuing injuries that could not be accidental and are therefore presumed to have been inflicted by someone close to the child, usu. a caregiver.

battered-woman syndrome. (1984) *Family law.* A constellation of medical and psychological conditions of a woman who has suffered physical, sexual, or emotional abuse at the hands of a spouse or partner. • This syndrome is sometimes proposed as a defense to justify or mitigate a woman's killing of a man. — Sometimes broadly termed *battered-person syndrome.*

battery, *n.* (16c) **1.** *Criminal law.* The use of force against another, resulting in harmful or offensive contact.

aggravated battery. (1811) A criminal battery accompanied by circumstances that make it more severe, such as the use of a deadly weapon or the fact that the battery resulted in serious bodily harm.

sexual battery. (1974) The forced penetration of or contact with another's sexual organs or the perpetrator's sexual organs. • In most state statutes, sexual battery is classified as both a misdemeanor and a felony.

simple battery. (1877) A criminal battery not accompanied by aggravating circumstances and not resulting in serious bodily harm.

2. *Torts.* An intentional and offensive touching of another without lawful justification. — **batter,** *vb.*

battle of the forms. (1947) The conflict between the terms of standard forms exchanged between a buyer and a seller during contract negotiations. • In its original version, UCC § 2-207 attempted to resolve battles of the forms by abandoning the common-law requirement of mirror-image acceptance and providing that a definite expression of acceptance may create a contract for the sale of goods even though it contains different or additional terms.

BEA. *abbr.* Bureau of Economic Analysis.

bear, *vb.* **1.** To support or carry <bear a heavy load>. **2.** To produce as yield <bear interest>. **3.** To give as testimony <bear witness>.

bearer. (13c) One who possesses a negotiable instrument marked "payable to bearer" or indorsed in blank.

bear hug. *Slang.* A (usu. hostile) takeover strategy in which the acquiring entity offers the target firm a price per share that is significantly higher than market value, intending to squeeze the target into accepting.

bear raid. *Slang.* High-volume stock selling by a large trader in an effort to drive down a stock price in a short time. • Bear raids are prohibited by federal law.

before the fact. (17c) In advance of an event of legal significance.

belief–action distinction. (1966) *Constitutional law.* In First Amendment law, the Supreme Court's distinction between allowing a person to follow any chosen belief and allowing the state to intervene if necessary to protect others from the practices of that belief.

belligerent, *n.* A country involved in a war or other armed international conflict. — **belligerent,** *adj.*

bellum justum (**bel**-əm **jəs**-təm). [Latin] *Int'l law.* A just war; one that the proponent considers morally and legally justifiable, such as a war against an aggressive, totalitarian regime. • The U.N. Charter outlaws the use of force except in self-defense. U.N. Charter arts. 2(4), 51 (59 Stat. 1031).

belongings. 1. Personal property; effects. **2.** All property, including realty.

below, *prep., adv.* & *adj.* (Of a lower court) having heard or having the power to hear the case at issue in the first instance. Cf. ABOVE.

below-the-line, *adj.* (1970) (Of a deduction) taken after calculating adjusted gross income and before calculating taxable income. Cf. ABOVE-THE-LINE.

bench. (13c) **1.** The raised area occupied by the judge in a courtroom. **2.** The court considered in its official capacity. **3.** Judges collectively. **4.** The judges of a particular court.

cold bench. A court, esp. an appellate court, in which the judges are largely unfamiliar with the facts and issues of a case, typically because they have not reviewed the briefs or the record.

hot bench. A court, esp. an appellate court, in which, before oral argument, the judges thoroughly familiarize themselves with the facts and issues of the case, usu. by reading the briefs and the record, and often prepare questions for counsel. • In the United States today, courts are generally expected to be hot.

lukewarm bench. A court, esp. an appellate court, in which only some of the judges, before oral argument, have familiarized themselves with the facts and issues of the case.

benchmark. 1. *Property.* A mark made on a permanent object by a surveyor to serve as a uniform reference point in making topographic surveys and tidal observations. — Formerly also written *bench mark.* **2.** A standard unit used as a basis for comparison.

bench memo. (1975) **1.** A short brief submitted by a lawyer to a trial judge, often at the judge's request. **2.** A legal memorandum prepared by an appellate judge's law clerk to help the judge in preparing for oral argument and perhaps in drafting an opinion. • A trial-court judge may similarly assign a bench memo to a law clerk, for use in preparing for hearing or trial or in drafting an opinion. **3.** A memo that summarizes the facts and issues in a case, usu. prepared for a judge by a law clerk.

bench ruling. (1971) An oral ruling issued by a judge from the bench.

beneficial, *adj.* (15c) **1.** Favorable; producing benefits. **2.** Consisting in a right that derives from something other than legal title.

beneficiary (ben-ə-**fish**-ee-er-ee *or* ben-ə-**fish**-ə-ree), *n.* (17c) **1.** A person for whose benefit property is held in trust; esp., one designated to benefit from an appointment, disposition, or assignment (as in a will, insurance policy, etc.), or to receive something as a result of a legal arrangement or instrument. **2.** A person to whom another is in a fiduciary relation, whether the relation is one of agency, guardianship, or trust. — **beneficiary,** *adj.*

contingent beneficiary. (1867) **1.** A person designated by the testator to receive a gift if the primary beneficiary is unable or unwilling to take the gift. **2.** A person designated in a life-insurance policy to receive the proceeds if the primary beneficiary is unable to do so.

creditor beneficiary. (1894) A third-party beneficiary of a contract who is owed a debt that is to be satisfied by another party's performance under the contract.

donee beneficiary. (1925) A third-party beneficiary who is intended to receive the benefit of the contract's performance as a gift from the promisee.

favored beneficiary. A beneficiary of a will who receives disproportionate amounts of the testator's property as compared with others having equal claims to the property, raising the specter of the beneficiary's undue influence over the testator.

incidental beneficiary. (1901) **1.** A third-party beneficiary who is not intended to benefit from a contract and thus does not acquire rights under the contract. **2.** A person to whom a settlor of a trust does not manifest an intention to give a beneficial interest but who may benefit from the trust's performance.

income beneficiary. (1945) A person entitled to income from property; esp., a person entitled to receive trust income.

intended beneficiary. (1845) A third-party beneficiary who is intended to benefit from a contract and thus acquires rights under the contract as well as the ability to enforce the contract once those rights have vested.

life beneficiary. (1953) One who receives payments or other benefits from a trust for life.

primary beneficiary. (1850) The person designated in a life-insurance policy to receive the proceeds when the insured dies.

third-party beneficiary. (1894) A person who, though not a party to a contract, stands to benefit from the contract's performance. • For example, if Ann and Bob agree to a contract under which Bob will render some performance to Chris, then Chris is a third-party beneficiary.

unborn beneficiary. A person who, though not yet born, is named in a general way as sharing in an estate or gift. • An example might be a grandchild not yet born when a grandparent specifies, in a will, that Blackacre is to go to "my grandchildren."

benefit, *n.* (14c) **1.** Advantage; privilege. **2.** Profit or gain; esp., the consideration that moves to the promisee.

death benefit. (*usu. pl.*) (1873) A sum or sums paid to a beneficiary from a life-insurance policy on the death of an insured.

fringe benefit. (1952) A benefit (other than direct salary or compensation) received by an employee from an employer, such as insurance, a company car, or a tuition allowance. — Often shortened (esp. in pl.) to *benefit.*

general benefit. (1925) *Eminent domain.* The whole community's benefit as a result of a taking. • It cannot be considered to reduce the compensation that is due the condemnee.

pecuniary benefit. (17c) A benefit capable of monetary valuation.

special benefit. (1857) *Eminent domain.* A benefit that accrues to the owner of the land in question and not to any others. • Any special benefits justify a reduction in the damages payable to the owner of land that is partially taken by the government during a public project.

3. Financial assistance that is received from an employer, insurance, or a public program (such as social security) in time of sickness, disability, or unemployment. — **benefit,** *vb.*

benefit of clergy. 1. At common law, the privilege of a cleric not to be tried for a felony in the King's Court. **2.** Loosely, religious approval as solemnized by church ritual <the couple had several children without benefit of clergy>. • This common use of the phrase is premised on a misunderstanding of its original meaning (sense 1).

benefit-of-the-bargain rule. (1913) **1.** The principle that a party who breaches a contract must pay the aggrieved party an amount that puts that person in the same financial position that would have resulted if the contract had been fully performed. **2.** The principle that a defrauded buyer may recover from the seller as damages the difference between the value of the property as represented and the actual value received.

BEP. *abbr.* Bureau of Engraving And Printing.

bequeath (bə-**kweeth**), *vb.* (12c) To give property (usu. personal property) by will.

bequest (bə-**kwest**), *n.* (14c) **1.** The act of giving property (usu. personal property) by will. **2.** Property (usu. personal property other than money) disposed of in a will.

charitable bequest. (18c) A bequest given to a philanthropic organization.

conditional bequest. (18c) A bequest whose effectiveness or continuation depends on the occurrence or nonoccurrence of a particular event. • An example might be a testator's gift of "the income from the farm to my daughter, Betty, until she remarries." If a condition prohibits certain legal conduct, such as using tobacco or growing a beard, it is sometimes termed a *reformation condition* or *character-improvement condition.*

demonstrative bequest. (1905) A bequest that, by its terms, must be paid out of a specific source, such as a stock fund.

executory bequest. (18c) A bequest of a future, deferred, or contingent interest in personal property.

general bequest. (18c) **1.** A bequest of a general benefit, rather than a particular asset, such as a gift of money or a gift of all the testator's stocks. **2.** A bequest payable out of the general assets of the estate.

pecuniary bequest. (18c) A testamentary gift of money; a legacy.

residuary bequest. (18c) A bequest of the remainder of the testator's estate, after the payment of the debts, legacies, and specific bequests.

specific bequest. (18c) A bequest of a specific or unique item of property, such as any real estate or a particular piece of furniture.

***Berry* rule.** (1956) The doctrine that a defendant seeking a new trial on grounds of newly discovered evidence must show that (1) the evidence is newly discovered and was unknown to the defendant at the time of trial; (2) the evidence is material rather than merely cumulative or impeaching; (3) the evidence will probably produce an acquittal; and (4) the failure to learn of the evidence was not due to the defendant's lack of diligence. *Berry v. State*, 10 Ga. 511 (1851).

bespeaks-caution doctrine. *Securities.* The principle that if soft information in a prospectus is accompanied by cautionary language that adequately warns investors that actual results or events may affect performance, then the soft information may not be materially misleading to investors. • Soft information includes forecasts, estimates, opinions, and projections about future performance.

best efforts. (17c) Diligent attempts to carry out an obligation. • As a standard, a best-efforts obligation is stronger than a good-faith obligation.

best-evidence rule. (1894) The evidentiary rule providing that, to prove the contents of a writing (or a recording or photograph), a party must produce the original writing (or a mechanical, electronic, or other familiar duplicate, such as a photocopy) unless it is unavailable, in which case secondary evidence — the testimony of the drafter or a person who read the document — may be admitted. Fed. R. Evid. 1001–1004.

bestiality (bes-chee-**al**-ə-tee). (14c) Sexual activity between a human and an animal. • Some authorities restrict the term to copulation between a human and an animal of the opposite sex.

best interests of creditors. *Bankruptcy.* A test for confirmation of a reorganization plan whereby the court inquires into whether the plan ensures that the value of property to be distributed to each creditor is at least the amount that the creditor would receive if the debtor's estate were liquidated in a Chapter 7 case.

best interests of the child. *Family law.* A standard by which a court determines what arrangements would be to a child's greatest benefit, often used in deciding child-custody and visitation matters and in deciding whether to approve an adoption or a guardianship.

best mode. *Patents.* The best way that the inventor knows to work the invention described and claimed in a patent or patent application. • Failure to disclose the best mode in an application can render a patent invalid.

bestow, *vb.* (14c) To convey as a gift. — **bestowal,** *n.*

beta testing. *Intellectual property.* The process of testing products and services, esp. software, under real-life conditions.

beth din. *Family law.* A rabbinical tribunal empowered by Jewish law to decide and enforce matters of Jewish law and custom; esp., a tribunal consisting of three rabbis who decide questions of Jewish law.

beth Torah. The judgment rendered by a panel of rabbis.

betrothal. 1. *Eccles. law.* A religious ceremony confirming an agreement to marry. **2.** *Slang.* A corporate merger agreement.

betterment. (18c) An improvement that increases the value of real property.

betterment act. (1819) A statute requiring a landowner to compensate an occupant who improves the land under a mistaken belief that the occupant is the real owner. • The compensation usu. equals the increase in the land's value generated by the improvements.

betterment tax. A tax for the improvement of highways.

beyond seas. (16c) *Hist.* (Of a person) being absent from a jurisdiction or nation. Some jurisdictions toll the statute of limitations during a defendant's absence.

BFOQ. *abbr.* Bona fide occupational qualification.

BFP. *abbr.* Bona fide purchaser.

BHC. *abbr.* Bank holding company.

BIA. *abbr.* **1.** Bureau of Indian Affairs. **2.** Board of Immigration Appeals.

bias, *n.* (16c) Inclination; prejudice; predilection. — **bias,** *vb.* — **biased,** *adj.*

bicameral, *adj.* (Of a legislature) having two legislative houses. — **bicameralism,** *n.*

bid, *n.* (18c) **1.** A buyer's offer to pay a specified price for something that may or may not be for sale. **2.** A submitted price at which one will perform work or supply goods. — **bid,** *vb.* — **bidder,** *n.*

competitive bid. A bid submitted in response to public notice of an intended sale or purchase.

firm bid. (1907) A bid that, by its terms, remains open and binding until accepted or rejected. • A firm bid commonly contains no unusual conditions that might defeat acceptance.

open bid. (1849) A bid that the bidder may alter after submission so as to meet competing bids.

sealed bid. (1849) A bid that is not disclosed until all submitted bids are opened and considered simultaneously.

bid and asked. *Securities.* A notation describing the range of prices quoted for securities in an over-the-counter stock exchange. • *Bid* denotes the highest price the buyer is willing to pay, and *asked* denotes the lowest price the seller will accept.

bidding up. (1823) The act or practice of raising the price for an auction item by making a series of progressively higher bids. • Bidding up is unlawful if the bids are made collusively by persons with an interest in raising the bids.

bid-shopping. (1964) A general contractor's effort — after being awarded a contract — to reduce its own costs by finding a subcontractor that will submit a lower bid than the one used in calculating the total contract price. • If a lower bid is obtained, the general contractor will receive a windfall profit because the savings are usu. not passed on to the property owner. The subcontractor whose bid is used in the initial proposal can seek to avoid bid-shopping by insisting that it be irrevocably named in the contract as the project's subcontractor.

biennium (bɪ-**en**-ee-əm). **1.** A two-year period. **2.** The period for which many state legislatures make appropriations.

bigamy, *n.* (13c) The act of marrying one person while legally married to another. • Bigamy is a criminal offense if it is committed knowingly. — **bigamist,** *n.* — **bigamous,** *adj.*

Big Board. The New York Stock Exchange.

bilateral, *adj.* (18c) Affecting or obligating both parties.

bill, *n.* (14c) **1.** A formal written complaint, such as a court paper requesting some specific action for reasons alleged. **2.** An equitable pleading by which a claimant brings a claim in a court of equity. • Before the merger of law and equity, the bill in equity was analogous to a declaration in law.

bill for a new trial. A bill in equity to enjoin a judgment and to obtain a new trial because of some fact that would render enforcement of the judgment inequitable.

bill in aid of execution. A bill filed by a judgment creditor to set aside a fraudulent encumbrance or conveyance.

bill in the nature of a bill of review. A postjudgment bill of review filed by someone who was neither a party to the original suit nor bound by the decree sought to be reversed.

bill in the nature of a bill of revivor. A bill filed when a litigant dies or becomes incapacitated before the litigant's interest in property could be determined. • The purpose of the bill is to resolve who holds the right to revive the original litigation in the deceased's stead.

bill in the nature of a supplemental bill. A bill bringing to court new parties and interests arising from events that occur after the suit is filed. • A *supplemental bill*, in contrast, involves parties or interests already before the court.

bill in the nature of interpleader. A bill of interpleader filed by a person claiming an interest in interpleaded property.

bill of certiorari. (18c) A bill in equity seeking removal of an action to a higher court.

bill of complaint. An original bill that begins an action in a court of equity.

bill of conformity. A bill filed by an executor or administrator who seeks the court's guidance in administering an estate. • The bill is usu. filed to adjust creditors' claims.

bill of costs. (16c) A certified, itemized statement of the amount of costs owed by one litigant to another, prepared so that the prevailing party may recover the costs from the losing party.

bill of discovery. (17c) A bill in equity seeking disclosure of facts within the opposing party's knowledge.

bill of evidence. A transcript of testimony heard at trial.

bill of exceptions. (17c) **1.** A formal written statement — signed by the trial judge and presented to the appellate court — of a party's objections or exceptions taken during trial and the grounds on which they are founded. • These bills have largely been replaced by straight appeals under the Federal Rules of Civil Procedure. **2.** In some jurisdictions, a record made to preserve error after the judge has excluded evidence.

bill of foreclosure. A bill in equity filed by a lender to have mortgaged property sold to satisfy all or part of the secured, unpaid debt.

bill of interpleader. An original bill filed by a party against two or more persons who claim from that party the same debt or duty. • The requesting party asks the court to compel the contenders to litigate and establish their rights to the debt or the duty.

bill of peace. (18c) An equitable bill filed by one who is threatened with multiple suits involving the same right, or with recurrent suits on the same right, asking the court to determine the question once and for all, and to enjoin the plaintiffs from proceeding with the threatened litigation. • One situation involves many persons having a common claim but threatening to bring separate suits; another involves one person bringing a second action on the same claim.

bill of redemption. A bill in equity filed to enforce a right to redeem real property, usu. following a mortgage foreclosure or a delinquent-tax sale.

bill of review. (17c) A bill in equity requesting that a court reverse or revise a prior decree.

bill of revivor. (17c) A bill filed for the purpose of reviving and continuing a suit in equity when the suit has been abated before final consummation. • The most common cause of such an abatement is the death of either the plaintiff or the defendant.

bill of revivor and supplement. A compound of a supplemental bill and a bill of revivor, joined for convenience. • Its distinct parts must be framed and proceeded on separately.

bill quia timet. An equitable bill used to guard against possible or prospective injuries and to preserve the means by which existing rights are protected from future or contingent violations. • It differs from an injunction, which corrects past and present — or imminent and certain — injuries. One example is a bill to perpetuate testimony.

bill to carry a decree into execution. A bill brought when a decree could not be enforced without further court order because of the parties' neglect or for some other reason.

bill to perpetuate testimony. (18c) An original bill to preserve the testimony of a material witness who may die or leave the jurisdiction before a suit is commenced, or to prevent or avoid future litigation.

bill to suspend a decree. A bill brought to set aside a decree.

bill to take testimony de bene esse (dee *or* də **bee**-nee **es**-ee *also* day **ben**-ay **es**-ay). A bill brought to take testimony pertinent to pending litigation from a witness who may be unavailable at the time of trial.

cross-bill. A bill brought by the defendant against the plaintiff in the same suit, or against other defendants in the same suit, relating to the matters alleged in the original bill.

nonoriginal bill. A bill relating to some matter already litigated by the same parties. • It is an addition to or a continuation of an original bill.

original bill. A bill relating to some matter that has never before been litigated by the same parties with the same interests.

skeleton bill of exceptions. A bill of exceptions that, in addition to the formal parts, contains only the court's directions to the clerk to copy or insert necessary documents into the record for appellate review, but does not contain the actual evidence or trial-court rulings. • For example, the statement "the clerk will insert the official transcript here" is typically a skeleton bill.

supplemental bill. A bill filed for the purpose of adding something to an original bill. • This addition usu. results from the discovery of new facts or from a new understanding of facts after the defendant has put on a defense.

supplemental bill in the nature of a bill of review.

3. A legislative proposal offered for debate before its enactment.

administration bill. A bill drafted and submitted by the executive branch.

appropriations bill. (18c) A bill that authorizes governmental expenditures. • The federal government cannot spend money unless Congress has appropriated the funds. U.S. Const. art. I, § 9, cl. 7.

budget bill. A bill designating how money will be allocated for the following fiscal year.

clean bill. A bill that has been changed so much by a legislative committee that it is better to introduce a new bill (a "clean" one) than to explain the changes made.

companion bill. A bill introduced in the other house of a bicameral legislature in a substantially identical form.

deficiency bill. An appropriations bill covering expenses omitted from the general appropriations bills, or for which insufficient appropriations were made. • An *urgent deficiency bill* covers immediate expenses usu. for one item, and a *general deficiency bill* covers a variety of items.

engrossed bill. (18c) **1.** A bill in a form ready for final passage by a legislative chamber. **2.** A bill in the form passed by one house of the legislature.

enrolled bill. (18c) A bill passed by both houses of the legislature and signed by their presiding officers.

house bill. (*often cap.*) (1871) A legislative bill being considered by a house of representatives. — Abbr. H; H.B.

must-pass bill. Legislation of vital importance, such as an appropriation without which the government will shut down. • A must-pass bill will often attract unrelated riders.

omnibus bill. (1840) **1.** A single bill containing various distinct matters, usu. drafted in this way to force the executive either to accept all the unrelated minor provisions or to veto the major provision. **2.** A bill that deals with all proposals relating to a particular subject, such as an "omnibus judgeship bill" covering all proposals for new judgeships or an "omnibus crime bill" dealing with different subjects such as new crimes and grants to states for crime control.

private bill. A bill relating to a matter of personal or local interest only.

public bill. (18c) A bill relating to public policy in the whole community.

revenue bill. (18c) A bill that levies or raises taxes. • Federal revenue bills must originate in the House of Representatives. U.S. Const. art. I, § 7, cl. 1.

senate bill. (*often cap.*) (1857) A legislative bill being considered by a senate. — Abbr. S.B.

3. An enacted statute. **4.** An itemized list of charges; an invoice. **5.** A bill of exchange; a draft. **6.** A formal document or note; an instrument. **7.** A piece of paper money. **8.** A promissory note.

billable hour. (1968) A unit of time used by an attorney, law clerk, or paralegal to account for work performed and chargeable to a client. • Billable hours are usu. divided into quarters or tenths of an hour.

billable time. (1966) An attorney's, law clerk's, or paralegal's time that is chargeable to a client.

billing cycle. The period between billings for goods sold or services rendered.

bill number. The number assigned to a proposed piece of legislation, typically designating the house in which it was introduced (S for senate or HR for house of representatives) followed by a sequential number.

bill of attainder. (17c) **1.** *Archaic.* A special legislative act that imposes a death sentence on a person without a trial. **2.** A special legislative act prescribing punishment, without a trial, for a specific person or group. • Bills of attainder are prohibited by the U.S. Constitution (art. I, § 9, cl. 3; art. I, § 10, cl. 1).

bill of entry. *Maritime law.* A written description of goods filed by an importer with customs officials to obtain permission to unload a ship's goods.

bill of indictment. (16c) An instrument presented to a grand jury and used by the jury to declare whether there is enough evidence to formally charge the accused with a crime.

bill of lading (layd-ing). (16c) A document acknowledging the receipt of goods by a carrier or by the shipper's agent and the contract for the transportation of those goods; a document that indicates the receipt of goods for shipment and that is issued by a person engaged in the business of transporting or forwarding goods. UCC § 1-201(6). • A negotiable bill of lading is a document of title. — Abbr. B/L.

bill of pains and penalties. (18c) A legislative act that, though similar to a bill of attainder, prescribes punishment less severe than capital punishment. • Bills of pains and penalties are included within the U.S. Constitution's ban on bills of attainder. U.S. Const. art I, § 9.

bill of particulars. (1831) A formal, detailed statement of the claims or charges brought by a plaintiff or a prosecutor, usu. filed in response to the defendant's request for a more specific complaint.

bill of rights. (18c) (*usu. cap.*) A section or addendum, usu. in a constitution, defining the situations in which a politically organized society will permit free, spontaneous, and individual activity, and guaranteeing that governmental powers will not be used in certain ways; esp., the first ten amendments to the U.S. Constitution.

bill of sale. (16c) An instrument for conveying title to personal property, absolutely or by way of security.

bind, *vb.* (15c) To impose one or more legal duties on (a person or institution). — **binding,** *adj.* — **bindingness,** *n.*

binder. **1.** A document in which the buyer and the seller of real property declare their common intention to bring about a transfer of ownership, usu. accompanied by the buyer's initial payment. **2.** Loosely, the buyer's initial payment in the sale of real property. **3.** An insurer's memorandum giving the insured temporary coverage while the application for an insurance policy is being processed or while the formal policy is being prepared.

binding, *adj.* (14c) **1.** (Of an agreement) having legal force. **2.** (Of an order) requiring obedience.

bind over, *vb.* (16c) **1.** To put (a person) under a bond or other legal obligation to do something, esp. to appear in court. **2.** To hold (a person) for trial; to turn (a defendant) over to a sheriff or warden for imprisonment pending further judicial action. — **binding over,** *n.* — **bindover,** *adj.*

biotechnology. *Patents.* A branch of molecular biology dealing with the use of biological processes to produce useful medical and industrial materials.

bipartite, *adj.* (16c) (Of an instrument) executed in two parts by both parties.

birth certificate. A formal document that records a person's birthdate, birthplace, and parentage.

birth control. **1.** Any means of preventing conception and pregnancy, usu. by mechanical or chemical means, but also by abstaining from intercourse. **2.** More narrowly, contraception.

birth records. (1854) Statistical data kept by a governmental entity concerning people's birthdates, birthplaces, and parentage.

biting rule. A rule of construction that once a deed or will grants a fee simple, a later provision attempting to cut down, modify, or qualify the grant will be held void.

***Bivens* action.** (1972) A lawsuit brought to redress a federal official's violation of a constitutional right. *Bivens v. Six Unknown Named Agents of the Federal Bureau of Narcotics*, 403 U.S. 388, 91 S.Ct. 1999 (1971). • A *Bivens* action allows federal officials to be sued in a manner similar to that set forth at 42 USCA § 1983 for state officials who violate a person's constitutional rights under color of state law.

B/L. *abbr.* Bill of lading.

Blackacre. (17c) A fictitious tract of land used in legal discourse (esp. law-school hypotheticals) to discuss real-property issues. • When another tract of land is needed in a hypothetical, it is often termed "Whiteacre."

blackletter law. (18c) One or more legal principles that are old, fundamental, and well settled. • The term refers to the law printed in books set in Gothic type, which is very bold and black.

blacklist, *vb.* (18c) To put the name of (a person) on a list of those who are to be boycotted or punished <the firm blacklisted the former employee>. — **blacklist,** *n.*

blackmail, *n.* (16c) A threatening demand made without justification; EXTORTION. — **blackmail,** *vb.*

Blaine amendment. A provision in a state constitution for stricter separation of church and state than is required by the Establishment Clause.

blame, *n.* **1.** An act of attributing fault; an expression of disapproval. **2.** Responsibility for something wrong. — **blame,** *vb.* — **blameworthy, blamable,** *adj.*

blanket order. 1. A judicial order that covers a broad subject or class. **2.** An order negotiated by a customer with a supplier for multiple purchases and deliveries of specified goods over a stated period, as an alternative to placing a separate order for each transaction.

blank-forms rule. *Copyright.* The principle that forms are not protectable by copyright if they are designed for recording information but do not themselves convey any information.

blasphemy (**blas**-fə-mee), *n.* (13c) Irreverence toward God, religion, a religious icon, or something else considered sacred. • Blasphemy was a crime at common law and remains so in some U.S. jurisdictions, but it is rarely if ever enforced because of its questionable constitutionality under the First Amendment. — **blaspheme** (blas-**feem** *or* **blas**-feem), *vb.* — **blasphemous** (**blas**-fə-məs), *adj.* — **blasphemer** (**blas**-fee-mər), *n.*

blending clause. (1947) A provision in a will disposing of both the testator's own property and the property over which the testator has a power of appointment, so that the two types of property are treated as a unit.

blind selling. (1946) The sale of goods without giving a buyer the opportunity to examine them.

bloc. (1903) A group of persons or political units aligned with a common interest or purpose, even if only temporarily <voting bloc>.

block, *n.* (18c) **1.** A municipal area enclosed by streets. **2.** A quantity of things bought or sold as a unit.

blockade. *Int'l law.* A belligerent's prevention of access to or egress from an enemy's ports by stationing ships to intercept vessels trying to enter or leave those ports.

***Blockburger* test.** *Criminal law.* A test, for double-jeopardy purposes, of whether a defendant can be punished separately for convictions on two charges or prosecuted later on a different charge after being convicted or acquitted on a charge involving the same incident; a comparison of two charges to see if each contains at least one element that the other does not.

blockbusting. (1954) The act or practice, usu. by a real-estate broker, of persuading one or more property owners to sell their property quickly, and often at a loss, to avoid an imminent influx of minority groups. • Blockbusting is illegal in many states.

block grant. An unrestricted grant of federal funds.

blood. (13c) A relationship between persons arising by descent from a common ancestor.

full blood. (1812) The relationship existing between persons having the same two parents; unmixed ancestry.

half blood. (17c) The relationship existing between persons having the same father or mother, but not both parents in common. — Sometimes written *half-blood.*

mixed blood. (1817) *Archaic.* The relationship between persons whose ancestors are of different races or nationalities.

blood alcohol content. (1926) The concentration of alcohol in one's bloodstream, expressed as a percentage. • Blood alcohol content is used to determine whether a person is legally intoxicated, esp. under a driving-while-intoxicated law. — Abbr. BAC.

blood-grouping test. (1930) A test used in paternity and illegitimacy cases to determine whether a particular man could be the father of a child, examples being the genetic-marker test and the human-leukocyte antigen test. • The test does not establish paternity; rather, it eliminates men who could not be the father.

blood money. 1. *Hist.* A payment given by a murderer's family to the next of kin of the murder victim. **2.** A reward given for the apprehension of a person charged with a crime, esp. capital murder.

blood test. The medical analysis of blood.

Blue Book. 1. A compilation of session laws. **2.** A volume formerly published to give parallel citation tables for a volume in the National Reporter System.

Bluebook. A citation guide that is generally considered an authoritative reference for American legal citations. • Titled *The Bluebook: A Uniform System of Citation*, the book is compiled by the editors of the *Columbia Law Review*, the *Harvard Law Review*, the *University of Pennsylvania Law Review*, and *The Yale Law Journal*.

blue chip, *n.* A corporate stock that is considered a safe investment because the corporation has a history of stability, consistent growth, and reliable earnings. — **blue-chip,** *adj.*

blue law. (1762) A statute regulating or prohibiting commercial activity on Sundays. • Once common, blue laws have declined since the 1980s when many courts held them invalid because of their origin in religion (i.e., Sunday being the Christian Sabbath). Blue laws usu. pass constitutional challenge if they are enacted to support a nonreligious purpose, such as a day of rest for workers.

blue-pencil test. (1921) A judicial standard for deciding whether to invalidate the whole contract or only the offending words. • Under this standard, only the offending words are invalidated if it would be possible to delete them simply by running a blue pencil through them, as opposed to changing, adding, or rearranging words.

blue-sky, *vb.* (1931) To approve (the sale of securities) in accordance with blue-sky laws <the company's IPO has not yet been blue-skyed>.

blue-sky, *adj.* (1906) (Of a security) having little value. • The term was first used in reference to the assets at issue in *Lowell v. People*, 131 Ill. App. 137 (1907) ("hot air and blue sky").

blue-sky law. (1912) A state statute establishing standards for offering and selling securities, the purpose being to protect citizens from investing in fraudulent schemes or unsuitable companies.

blurring, *n. Trademarks.* A form of dilution in which goodwill in a famous mark is eroded through the mark's unauthorized use by others on or in connection with dissimilar products or services. • Blurring is one type of dilution that is actionable under the Federal Trademark Dilution Act, 15 USCA § 1125(c).

board. 1. A group of persons having managerial, supervisory, or advisory powers <board of directors>. **2.** Daily meals furnished to a guest at an inn, boardinghouse, or other lodging.

board-certified, *adj.* (1938) (Of a professional) recognized by an official body as a specialist in a given field of law or medicine.

board of directors. (18c) **1.** The governing body of a corporation, elected by the shareholders to establish corporate policy, appoint executive officers, and make major business and financial decisions. **2.** The governing body of a corporation, partnership, association, or other organization, elected by the shareholders or members to establish policy, elect or appoint officers and committees, and make other governing decisions.

board of education. A state or local agency that governs and manages public schools within a state or local district.

board of health. A municipal or state agency charged with protecting the public health.

Board of Immigration Appeals. The highest administrative tribunal for interpreting and applying United States immigration law, esp. reviewing appeals from adverse decisions of immigration judges and district directors of the Department of Homeland Security.

board of legal specialization. (1969) A body, usu. an arm of a state bar association, that certifies qualified lawyers as specialists within a given field. • Typically, to qualify as a specialist, a lawyer must meet a specified level of experience, pass an examination, and provide favorable recommendations from peers.

board of pardons. (1872) A state agency, of which the governor is usu. a member, authorized to pardon persons convicted of crimes.

board of regents. A panel of persons appointed to supervise an educational institution, esp. a university.

board of review. **1.** A body that reviews administrative-agency decisions. **2.** A body that reviews property-tax assessments. **3.** In some cities, a board that reviews allegations of police misconduct.

board of trade. **1.** A federation of business executives dedicated to advancing and protecting business interests. **2.** An organization that runs a commodities exchange.

Board of Veterans' Appeals. The agency in the U.S. Department of Veterans' Appeals responsible for reviewing decisions on entitlements to veterans' benefits.

body. (15c) **1.** The main part of a written instrument, such as the central part of a statute (after the title and preamble) or the middle part of a complainant's bill in equity. **2.** A collection of laws. **3.** An artificial person created by a legal authority. **4.** An aggregate of individuals or groups. **5.** A deliberative assembly <legislative body>. **6.** An aggregate of individuals or groups <student body>. **7.** Body of a claim.

body politic. (15c) A group of people regarded in a political (rather than private) sense and organized under a common governmental authority.

boilerplate, *n.* (1893) **1.** Ready-made or all-purpose language that will fit in a variety of documents. **2.** Fixed or standardized contractual language that the proposing party often views as relatively nonnegotiable. — **boilerplate,** *adj.*

boiler-room transaction. (1988) *Slang.* A high-pressure telephone sales pitch, often of a fraudulent nature.

bolster, *vb.* To enhance (unimpeached evidence) with additional evidence. • This practice is often considered improper when lawyers seek to enhance the credibility of their own witnesses.

bona fide (**boh**-nə fɪd *or* **boh**-nə **fɪ**-dee), *adj.* [Latin "in good faith"] (17c) **1.** Made in good faith; without fraud or deceit. **2.** Sincere; genuine. — **bona fide,** *adv.*

bona fide occupational qualification. (1945) An employment qualification that, although it may discriminate against a protected class (such as sex, religion, or national origin), relates to an essential job duty and is considered reasonably necessary to the operation of the particular business. • Such a qualification is not illegal under federal employment-discrimination laws. — Abbr. BFOQ.

bona fides (**boh**-nə **fı**-deez), *n.* [Latin] Good faith.

bond, *n.* (16c) **1.** An obligation; a promise. **2.** A written promise to pay money or do some act if certain circumstances occur or a certain time elapses; a promise that is defeasible upon a condition subsequent; esp., an instrument under seal by which (1) a public officer undertakes to pay a sum of money if he or she does not faithfully discharge the responsibilities of office, or (2) a surety undertakes that if the public officer does not do so, the surety will be liable in a penal sum.

appeal bond. (18c) A bond that an appellate court may require from an appellant in a civil case to ensure payment of the costs of appeal; a bond required as a condition to bringing an appeal or staying execution of the judgment appealed from. Fed. R. App. P. 7.

bail bond. (17c) A bond given to a court by a criminal defendant's surety to guarantee that the defendant will duly appear in court in the future and, if the defendant is jailed, to obtain the defendant's release from confinement.

bid bond. A bond filed in public construction projects to ensure that the bidding contractor will enter into the contract.

discharging bond. (18c) A bond that both permits a defendant to regain possession of attached property and releases the property from the attachment lien.

executor's bond. A bond given to ensure the executor's faithful administration of the estate.

fiduciary bond. (1831) A type of surety bond required of a trustee, administrator, executor, guardian, conservator, or other fiduciary to ensure the proper performance of duties.

guaranty bond. A bond combining the features of a fidelity and a surety bond, securing both payment and performance.

indemnity bond. A bond to reimburse the holder for any actual or claimed loss caused by the issuer's or some other person's conduct.

judicial bond. (18c) A bond to indemnify an adverse party in a lawsuit against loss occasioned by delay or by deprivation of property resulting from the lawsuit.

liability bond. A bond intended to protect the assured from a loss arising from some event specified in the bond.

license bond. A bond required of a person seeking a license to engage in a specified business or to receive a certain privilege.

maintenance bond. A bond guaranteeing against construction defects for a period after the completion of the contracted-for work.

payment bond. (1877) A bond given by a surety to cover any amounts that, because of the general contractor's default, are not paid to a subcontractor or materials supplier.

peace bond. (1846) A bond required by a court from a person who has breached or threatened to breach the peace.

penal bond. (17c) A bond requiring the obligor to pay a specified sum as a penalty if the underlying obligation is not performed.

probate bond. A bond, such as that filed by an executor, required by law to be given during a probate proceeding to ensure faithful performance by the person under bond.

replevin bond (ri-**plev**-in). **1.** A bond given by a plaintiff to replevy or attach property in the defendant's possession before judgment is rendered in a replevin action. **2.** A bond given by a defendant in a replevin action to regain attached property pending the outcome of litigation.

straw bond. (1876) A bond, usu. a bail bond, that carries either a fictitious name or the name of a person who is unable to pay the sum guaranteed; a worthless or inadequate bond.

supersedeas bond (soo-pər-**see**-dee-əs). (18c) An appellant's bond to stay execution on a judgment during the pendency of the appeal. Fed. R. Civ. P. 62(d); Fed. R. App. P. 8(b). — Often shortened to *supersedeas.*

3. A long-term, interest-bearing debt instrument issued by a corporation or governmental entity, usu. to provide for a particular financial need; esp., such an instrument in which the debt is secured by a lien on the issuer's property.

annuity bond. A bond that lacks a maturity date and that perpetually pays interest.

bearer bond. (1887) A bond payable to the person holding it. • The transfer of possession transfers the bond's ownership.

callable bond. (1926) Redeemable bond.

collateral trust bond. A bond representing a debt secured by the deposit of another security with a trustee.

construction bond. A bond issued by a governmental entity for a building project.

convertible bond. (1857) A bond that can be exchanged for stock shares in the corporation that issued the bond.

corporate bond. **1.** An interest-bearing instrument containing a corporation's promise to pay a fixed sum of money at some future time. • A corporate bond may be secured or unsecured. **2.** A bond issued by a corporation, usu. having a maturity of ten years or longer.

coupon bond. A bond with attached interest coupons that the holder may present to receive interest payments.

discount bond. (1918) A bond sold at its current market value, which is less than its face value.

general-obligation bond. A municipal bond payable from general revenue rather than from a special fund. • Such a bond has no collateral to back it other than the issuer's taxing power. — Often shortened to *obligation bond.*

government bond. **1.** Savings bond. **2.** Government security.

high-yield bond. A high-risk, high-yield subordinated bond issued by a company with a credit rating below investment grade.

income bond. A corporate bond secured by the corporation's net income, after the payment of interest on senior debt.

industrial-development bond. **1.** A type of revenue bond in which interest and principal payments are backed by a corporation rather than a municipality. • This type of bond usu. finances a private business facility. **2.** A tax-exempt municipal bond that finances a usu. local industry.

investment-grade bond. A bond with a rating of BBB or better by the leading bond rating services.

junk bond. (1974) High-yield bond.

municipal bond. (1858) A bond issued by a nonfederal government or governmental unit, such as a state bond to finance local improvements. • The interest received from a municipal bond may be exempt from federal, state, and local taxes.

premium bond. (1871) A bond with a selling price above face or redemption value.

registered bond. (1865) A bond that only the holder of record may redeem, enjoy benefits from, or transfer to another.

savings bond. (1948) A nontransferable bond issued by the U.S. government.

secured bond. (1849) A bond backed by some type of security.

serial bond. (1889) A bond issued concurrently with other bonds having different maturity dates.

series bonds. (1920) A group of bonds issued under the authority of the same indenture, but offered publicly at different times and with different maturity dates and interest rates.

zero-coupon bond. (1979) A bond paying no interest. • It is sold at a discount price and later redeemed at face value, the profit being the difference.

bond, *vb.* (16c) **1.** To secure payment by providing a bond. **2.** To provide a bond for (a person).

bonded, *adj.* (1945) (Of a person or entity) acting under, or placed under, a bond.

bondholder. One who holds a government or business bond.

bond indenture. (1891) **1.** A contract between a bond issuer and a bondholder outlining a bond's face value, interest rate, maturity date, and other features. **2.** A mortgage held on specified corporate property to secure payment of the bond.

bond rating. A system of evaluating and appraising the investment value of a bond issue.

bond retirement. (1897) The cancellation of a bond that has been called or paid.

bondsman. (13c) **1.** One who guarantees a bond; a surety. **2.** *Hist.* A serf or peasant.

bond table. A schedule used in determining a bond's current value by its coupon rate, its time to maturity, and its effective yield if held to maturity.

bonitary (bahn-ə-**tair**-ee-in), *adj.* Equitable.

bonus. (18c) A premium paid in addition to what is due or expected.

book, *vb.* (13c) **1.** To record in an accounting journal (as a sale or accounting item). **2.** To record the name of (a person arrested) in a sequential list of police arrests, with details of the person's identity (usu. including a photograph and a fingerprint), particulars about the alleged offense, and the name of the arresting officer. **3.** To engage (someone) contractually as a performer or guest.

book entry. (18c) **1.** A notation made in an accounting journal. **2.** The method of reflecting ownership of publicly traded securities whereby a customer of a brokerage firm receives confirmations of transactions and monthly statements, but not stock certificates.

bookkeeping, *n.* (17c) The mechanical recording of debits and credits or the summarizing of financial information, usu. about a business enterprise.

double-entry bookkeeping. A method of bookkeeping in which every transaction recorded by a business involves one or more "debit" entries and one or more "credit" entries.

single-entry bookkeeping. A method of bookkeeping in which each transaction is recorded in a single record, such as a record of cash or credit accounts.

bookmaker. A person who determines odds and receives bets on the outcome of events, esp. sports events. — **bookmaking,** *n.*

book value. (1894) The value at which an asset is carried on a balance sheet.

boot, *n.* **1.** *Tax.* Supplemental money or property subject to tax in an otherwise tax-free exchange. **2.** *Corporations.* In a corporate reorganization, anything received other than the stock or securities of a controlled corporation. **3.** *Commercial law.* Cash or other consideration used to balance an otherwise unequal exchange.

boot camp. (1916) **1.** A camp for basic training of Navy or Marine Corps recruits. **2.** A military-like facility esp. for juvenile offenders.

bootleg, *vb. Copyright.* To make, distribute, or traffic in unauthorized sound or video recordings of live, broadcast, or recorded performances that have not been commercially released by the copyright owner. • The term strictly applies only to unauthorized copies of commercially unreleased performances. — **bootlegger,** *n.* — **bootleg; bootlegged,** *adj.*

bootstrap, *vb.* (1951) **1.** To succeed despite sparse resources. **2.** To reach an unsupported conclusion from questionable premises.

bootstrap doctrine. (1940) *Conflict of laws.* The doctrine that forecloses collateral attack on the jurisdiction of another state's court that has rendered final judgment. • The doctrine applies when a court in an earlier case has taken jurisdiction over a person, over status, or over land. It is based on the principle that under res judicata, the parties are bound by the judgment, whether the issue was the court's jurisdiction or something else. The bootstrap doctrine, however, cannot give effectiveness to a judgment by a court that had no subject-matter jurisdiction. For example, parties cannot, by appearing before a state court, "bootstrap" that court into having jurisdiction over a federal matter.

booty. 1. *Int'l law.* Movables taken from the enemy as spoils in the course of warlike operations. **2.** Property taken by force or piracy; prize or loot.

border. A boundary between one nation (or a political subdivision) and another.

border control. *Int'l law.* A country's physical manifestation of its territorial sovereignty, by which it regulates which people and goods may enter and leave.

bork (bork), *vb.* (1987) *Slang.* **1.** (Of the U.S. Senate) to reject a nominee, esp. for the U.S. Supreme Court, on grounds of the nominee's political and legal philosophy. • The term derives from the name of Robert Bork, President Ronald Reagan's unsuccessful nominee for the Supreme Court in 1987. **2.** (Of political and legal activists) to embark on a media campaign to pressure U.S. Senators into rejecting a President's nominee. **3.** Generally, to smear a political opponent.

borrow, *vb.* **1.** To take something for temporary use. **2.** To receive money with the understanding or agreement that it must be repaid, usu. with interest.

borrowed-statutes doctrine. The principle that if one state adopts a statute identical to that of another state, any settled judicial construction of that statute by the courts of the other state is binding on the courts of the state that later enacts the statute.

borrowing statute. (1934) A legislative exception to the conflict-of-laws rule holding that a forum state must apply its own statute of limitations. • A borrowing statute specifies the circumstances in which a forum state will apply another state's statute of limitations.

bottomland. (18c) Low-lying land, often located in a river's floodplain.

bound, *adj.* (15c) **1.** Constrained by a contractual or other obligation. **2.** (Of a court) constrained to follow a precedent.

bound, *n.* (*usu. pl.*) (13c) **1.** BOUNDARY. **2.** A limitation or restriction on action.

bound, *vb.* (14c) To delineate a property boundary.

boundary. (1598) A natural or artificial separation that delineates the confines of real property.

agreed boundary. A negotiated boundary by which adjacent landowners resolve uncertainties over the extent of their land.

land boundary. (18c) The limit of a landholding, usu. described by linear measurements of the borders, by points of the compass, or by stationary markers.

natural boundary. Any nonartificial thing (such as a river or ocean) that forms a boundary of a nation, a political subdivision, or a piece of property.

bounty. (13c) **1.** A premium or benefit offered or given, esp. by a government, to induce someone to take action or perform a service. **2.** A gift, esp. in a will; generosity in giving.

bounty hunter. (1930) A person who for a fee pursues someone charged with or suspected of a crime; esp., a person hired by a bail-bond company to find and arrest a criminal defendant who has breached the bond agreement by failing to appear in court as ordered.

boutique (boo-**teek**). (1984) A small specialty business; esp., a small law firm specializing in one particular aspect of law practice <a tax boutique>.

boycott, *n.* (1880) **1.** An action designed to achieve the social or economic isolation of an adversary. **2.** A concerted refusal to do business with a party to express disapproval of that party's practices. — **boycott,** *vb.*

consumer boycott. (1941) A boycott by consumers of products or services to show displeasure with the manufacturer, seller, or provider.

primary boycott. (1903) A boycott by union members who stop dealing with a former employer.

secondary boycott. (1903) A boycott of the customers or suppliers of a business so that they will withhold their patronage from that business.

bp. *abbr.* Basis point.

B.R. *abbr.* Bankruptcy Reporter. — Also abbreviated *Bankr. Rep.*

bracket creep. (1978) The process by which inflation or increased income pushes individuals into higher tax brackets.

Brady Act. A federal law establishing a national system for quickly checking the background of a prospective handgun purchaser. 18 USCA §§ 921–930.

Brady **material.** (1972) *Criminal procedure.* Information or evidence that is favorable to a criminal defendant's case and that the prosecution has a duty to disclose. • The prosecution's withholding of such information violates the defendant's due-process rights. *Brady v. Maryland*, 373 U.S. 83, 83 S.Ct. 1194 (1963).

branch. (13c) **1.** An offshoot, lateral extension, or division of an institution. **2.** A line of familial descent stemming from a common ancestor.

brand. *Trademarks.* A name or symbol used by a seller or manufacturer to identify goods or services and to distinguish them from competitors' goods or services; the term used colloquially in business and industry to refer to a corporate or product name, a business image, or a mark, regardless of whether it may legally qualify as a trademark.

Brandeis brief (**bran**-dɪs). (1930) A brief, usu. an appellate brief, that makes use of social and economic studies in addition to legal principles and citations. • The brief is named after Supreme Court Justice Louis D. Brandeis, who as an advocate filed the most famous such brief in *Muller v. Oregon*, 208 U.S. 412, 28 S.Ct. 324 (1908), in which he persuaded the Court to uphold a statute setting a maximum ten-hour workday for women.

breach, *n.* (15c) A violation or infraction of a law or obligation. — **breach,** *vb.*

breach of close. (18c) The unlawful or unauthorized entry on another person's land; a common-law trespass.

breach of contract. (17c) Violation of a contractual obligation by failing to perform one's own promise, by repudiating it, or by interfering with another party's performance.

anticipatory breach. (1889) A breach of contract caused by a party's anticipatory repudiation, i.e., unequivocally indicating that the party will not perform when performance is due. • Under these circumstances, the nonbreaching party may elect to treat the repudiation as an immediate breach and sue for damages.

continuing breach. (1817) A breach of contract that endures for a considerable time or is repeated at short intervals.

efficient breach. (1977) An intentional breach of contract and payment of damages by a party who would incur greater economic loss by performing under the contract.

immediate breach. (1820) A breach that entitles the nonbreaching party to sue for damages immediately.

material breach. (1840) A breach of contract that is significant enough to permit the aggrieved party to elect to treat the breach as total (rather than partial), thus excusing that party from further performance and affording it the right to sue for damages.

partial breach. (18c) A breach of contract that is less significant than a material breach and that gives the aggrieved party a right to damages, but does not excuse that party from performance; specif., a breach for which the injured party may substitute the remedial rights provided by law for only part of the existing contract rights.

total breach. (18c) A breach of contract for which the remedial rights provided by law are substituted for all the existing contractual rights, or can be so substituted by the injured party.

breach of covenant. (16c) The violation of an express or implied promise, usu. in a contract, either to do or not to do an act.

breach of duty. (16c) The violation of a legal or moral obligation; the failure to act as the law obligates one to act; esp., a fiduciary's violation of an obligation owed to another.

breach of promise. The violation of one's word or undertaking, esp. a promise to marry.

breach of the peace. (16c) The criminal offense of creating a public disturbance or engaging in disorderly conduct, particularly by making an unnecessary or distracting noise.

breach of trust. (17c) A trustee's violation of either the trust's terms or the trustee's general fiduciary obligations; the violation of a duty that equity imposes on a trustee, whether the violation was willful, fraudulent, negligent, or inadvertent. • A breach of trust subjects the trustee to removal and creates personal liability.

breach of warranty. (18c) A breach of an express or implied warranty relating to the title, quality, content, or condition of goods sold. UCC § 2-312.

breadth of a claim. *Patents.* The scope or extent to which a patent claim excludes others from infringing activity.

break, *vb.* (bef. 12c) **1.** To violate or disobey (a law). **2.** To nullify (a will) by court proceeding. **3.** To escape from (a place of confinement) without permission. **4.** To open (a door, gate, etc.) and step through illegally.

breakage. (1848) An allowance given by a manufacturer to a buyer for goods damaged during transit or storage.

breaking, *n. Criminal law.* (17c) In the law of burglary, the act of entering a building without permission.

breaking a case. (1950) **1.** The voicing by one appellate judge to another judge on the same panel of a tentative view on how a case should be decided. • These informal expressions assist the judges in ascertaining how close they are to agreement. **2.** The solving of a case by the police.

breaking bulk, *n.* (18c) **1.** The act of dividing a large shipment into smaller units. **2.** Larceny by a bailee, esp. a carrier, who opens containers, removes items from them, and converts the items to personal use. — **break bulk,** *vb.*

Breathalyzer. (1960) A device used to measure a person's blood alcohol content from a sample of the person's breath, esp. when the police suspect that the person was driving while intoxicated. • The term is a trademarked name. Breathalyzer test results are admissible as evidence if the test was properly administered. — **breathalyze,** *vb.*

breathing room. (1967) *Slang.* The postbankruptcy period during which a debtor may formulate a debt-repayment plan without harassment or interference by creditors.

bribe, *n.* (15c) A price, reward, gift or favor bestowed or promised with a view to pervert the judgment of or influence the action of a person in a position of trust. — **bribe,** *vb.*

bribery, *n.* (16c) The corrupt payment, receipt, or solicitation of a private favor for official action. • Bribery is a felony in most jurisdictions. See Model Penal Code § 240.1. — **bribe,** *vb.*

commercial bribery. (1927) **1.** The knowing solicitation or acceptance of a benefit in exchange for violating an oath of fidelity, such as that owed by an employee, partner, trustee, or attorney. Model Penal Code § 224.8(1). **2.** A supposedly disinterested appraiser's acceptance of a benefit that influences the appraisal of goods or services. Model Penal Code § 224.8(2). **3.** Corrupt dealing with the agents or employees of prospective buyers to secure an advantage over business competitors.

brief, *n.* (14c) A written statement setting out the legal contentions of a party in litigation, esp. on appeal; a document prepared by counsel as the basis for arguing a case, consisting of legal and factual arguments and the authorities in support of them. — **brief,** *vb.*

amicus brief. A brief, usu. at the appellate level, prepared and filed by an amicus curiae with the court's permission.

***Anders* brief.** (1969) *Criminal procedure.* A brief filed by a court-appointed defense attorney who wants to withdraw from the case on appeal based on a belief that the appeal is frivolous.

appellate brief. A brief submitted to an appeals court; specif., a brief filed by a party to an appeal pending in a court exercising appellate jurisdiction.

bench brief. An advocate's short brief, prepared for use by panelists in a moot-court competition or mock oral argument. • The brief summarizes the facts, law, and arguments for both sides on the issues.

brief on the merits. A brief that sets out the issues to be decided, the party's position, and the arguments and authorities in support.

proof brief. (1997) A preliminary appellate brief to be reviewed by the clerk of the court for compliance with applicable rules.

reply brief. (1872) A brief that responds to issues and arguments raised in the brief previously filed by one's opponent; esp., a movant's or appellant's brief filed to rebut a brief in opposition.

trial brief. (1927) Counsel's written submission, usu. just before trial, outlining the legal issues before the court and arguing one side's position.

briefmanship, *n.* The quality of the work done in producing a written legal argument.

brief-writing. (1891) The art or practice of preparing legal briefs. — **brief-writer,** *n.*

bright-line rule. (1973) A legal rule of decision that tends to resolve issues, esp. ambiguities, simply and straightforwardly, sometimes sacrificing equity for certainty.

bring an action. To sue; institute legal proceedings.

bring to book. (1865) To arrest and try (an offender) <the fugitives were brought to book and convicted>.

broker, *n.* (14c) **1.** An agent who acts as an intermediary or negotiator, esp. between prospective buyers and sellers; a person employed to make bargains and contracts between other persons in matters of trade, commerce, or navigation. **2.** *Securities.* A person engaged in the business of conducting securities transactions for the accounts of others. — **broker,** *vb.*

commercial broker. A broker who negotiates the sale of goods without having possession or control of the goods.

commission broker. A member of a stock or commodity exchange who executes buy and sell orders.

discount broker. **1.** A broker who discounts bills of exchange and promissory notes, and advances money on securities. **2.** A broker who executes buy and sell orders at commission rates lower than those of full-service brokers.

government-securities interdealer broker. A broker engaged exclusively in the business of transacting in government securities for parties who are themselves government brokers or dealers.

institutional broker. A broker who trades securities for institutional clients such as banks, mutual funds, pension funds, and insurance companies.

insurance broker. (18c) *Insurance.* A person who, for compensation, brings about or negotiates contracts of insurance as an agent for someone else, but not as an officer, salaried employee, or licensed agent of an insurance company.

money broker. A broker who negotiates the lending or raising of money for others.

mortgage broker. An individual or organization that markets mortgage loans and brings lenders and borrowers together.

note broker. A broker who negotiates the discount or sale of commercial paper.

real-estate broker. A broker who negotiates contracts of sale and other agreements (such as mortgages or leases) between buyers and sellers of real property.

registered broker. A broker registered or required to be registered under the Securities Exchange Act of 1934.

securities broker. A broker employed to buy or sell securities for a customer, as opposed to a securities dealer, who trades as a principal before selling the securities to a customer.

brokerage. (15c) **1.** The business or office of a broker. **2.** A broker's fee.

brothel. (16c) A building or business where prostitutes ply their trade; a whorehouse.

brother. (bef. 12c) A male who has one parent or both parents in common with another person.

brother-german. A full brother; the son of both of one's parents.

consanguine brother (kahn-**sang**-gwin *or* kən-**san**-gwin). *Civil law.* A brother who has the same father, but a different mother.

half brother. A brother who has the same father or the same mother, but not both.

stepbrother. The son of one's stepparent.

uterine brother (**yoo**-tər-in). *Civil law.* A brother who has the same mother, but a different father.

brother-in-law. (14c) The brother of one's spouse or the husband of one's sister. • The husband of one's spouse's sister is also sometimes considered a brother-in-law. Pl. **brothers-in-law.**

brownfield site. An abandoned, idled, or underused industrial or commercial site that is difficult to expand or redevelop because of environmental contamination.

***Bruton* error (broot-ən).** (1968) The violation of a criminal defendant's constitutional right of confrontation by admitting into evidence a nontestifying codefendant's confession that implicates both of them, where the statement is not admissible against the defendant under any exception to the hearsay rule. *Bruton v. United States,* 391 U.S. 123, 88 S.Ct. 1620 (1968).

bubble. (18c) *Slang.* A dishonest or insubstantial business project, generally founded on a fictitious or exaggerated prospectus, designed to ensnare unwary investors.

budget. (15c) **1.** A statement of an organization's estimated revenues and expenses for a specified period, usu. a year. **2.** A sum of money allocated to a particular purpose or project.

buffer zone. (1908) *Land-use planning.* An area of land separating two different zones or areas to help each blend more easily with the other, such as a strip of land between industrial and residential areas.

buggery, *n.* (14c) Sodomy or bestiality. — **bugger,** *vb.* — **bugger,** *n.*

bugging, *n.* (1955) A form of electronic surveillance by which conversations may be electronically intercepted, overheard, or recorded, usu. covertly; eavesdropping by electronic means.

building-and-loan association. (1857) A quasi-public corporation that accumulates funds through member contributions and lends money to the members buying or building homes.

building code. A law or regulation setting forth standards for the construction, maintenance, occupancy, use, or appearance of buildings and dwelling units.

building line. (1885) A boundary drawn along a curb or the edge of a municipality's sidewalks to establish how far a building must be set away from the street to maintain a uniform appearance. • This is often referred to as a *setback requirement.*

building restrictions. Regulations governing the type of structures that can be constructed on certain property.

bulk sale. (1902) A sale of a large quantity of inventory outside the ordinary course of the seller's business. • Bulk sales are regulated by Article 6 of the UCC, which is designed to prevent sellers from defrauding unsecured creditors by making these sales and then dissipating the sale proceeds.

bullpen. (1809) *Slang.* **1.** An area in a prison where inmates are kept in close confinement. **2.** A detention cell where prisoners are held until they are brought into court.

bumping. (1937) **1.** Displacement of a junior employee's position by a senior employee. **2.** An airline-industry practice of denying seats to passengers because of overbooking.

bunco. (1872) A swindling game or scheme; any trick or ploy calculated to win a person's confidence in an attempt to deceive that person.

bundle, *vb.* To sell related products or services in one transaction at an all-inclusive price.

burden, *n.* (bef. 12c) **1.** A duty or responsibility. **2.** Something that hinders or oppresses. **3.** A restriction on the use or value of land; an encumbrance. — **burden,** *vb.* — **burdensome,** *adj.*

undue burden. A substantial and unjust obstacle to the performance of a duty or enjoyment of a right.

burden of allegation. (1862) A party's duty to plead a matter in order for that matter to be heard in the lawsuit.

burden of persuasion. (1923) A party's duty to convince the fact-finder to view the facts in a way that favors that party. • In civil cases, the plaintiff's burden is usu. "by a preponderance of the evidence," while in criminal cases the prosecution's burden is "beyond a reasonable doubt." — Also loosely termed *burden of proof.*

burden of production. (1893) A party's duty to introduce enough evidence on an issue to have the issue decided by the fact-finder, rather than decided against the party in a peremptory ruling such as a summary judgment or a directed verdict.

burden of proof. (18c) **1.** A party's duty to prove a disputed assertion or charge. • The burden of proof includes both the *burden of persuasion* and the *burden of production.* **2.** Loosely, BURDEN OF PERSUASION.

middle burden of proof. A party's duty to prove a fact by clear and convincing evidence. • This standard lies between the preponderance-of-the-evidence standard and the beyond-a-reasonable-doubt standard.

burden-shifting analysis. A court's scrutiny of a complainant's evidence to determine whether it is sufficient to require the opposing party to present contrary evidence. • Burden shifting is most commonly applied in discrimination cases. If the plaintiff presents sufficient evidence of discrimination, the burden shifts to the defendant to show a legitimate, nondiscriminatory basis for its actions.

burglary, *n.* (16c) **1.** The common-law offense of breaking and entering another's dwelling at night with the intent to commit a felony. **2.** The modern statutory offense of breaking and entering any building — not just a dwelling, and not only at night — with the intent to commit a felony. • Some statutes make petit larceny an alternative to a felony for purposes of proving burglarious intent. — **burglarious** (bər-**glair**-ee-əs), *adj.* — **burglar,** *n.* (16c). — **burglarize,** *vb.*

burglary tool. (*often pl.*) (1903) An implement designed to help a person commit a burglary. • In many jurisdictions, it is illegal to possess such a tool if the possessor intends to commit a burglary.

buried-facts doctrine. *Securities.* The rule that a proxy-statement disclosure is inadequate if a reasonable shareholder could fail to understand the risks presented by facts scattered throughout the proxy.

bursting-bubble theory. (1941) *Evidence.* The principle that a presumption disappears once the presumed facts have been contradicted by credible evidence.

business. 1. A commercial enterprise carried on for profit; a particular occupation or employment habitually engaged in for livelihood or gain. **2.** Commercial enterprises. **3.** Commercial transactions. **4.** By extension, transactions or matters of a noncommercial nature.

business enterprises. The field of law dealing with various forms of business, such as corporations, limited-liability companies, and partnerships.

business-judgment rule. (1946) *Corporations.* The presumption that in making business decisions not involving direct self-interest or self-dealing, corporate directors act on an informed basis, in good faith, and in the honest belief that their actions are in the corporation's best interest. • The rule shields directors and officers from liability for unprofitable or harmful corporate transactions if the transactions were made in good faith, with due care, and within the directors' or officers' authority.

business method. *Patents.* A way or an aspect of a way in which a commercial enterprise is operated.

business plan. (1890) A written proposal explaining a new business or business idea and usu. covering financial, marketing, and operational plans.

business-purpose doctrine. (1939) *Tax.* The principle that a transaction must serve a bona fide business purpose (i.e., not just for tax avoidance) to qualify for beneficial tax treatment.

business-records exception. (1939) *Evidence.* A hearsay exception allowing business records (such as reports or memoranda) to be admitted into evidence if they were prepared in the ordinary course of business. • If there is good reason to doubt a record's reliability (e.g., the record was prepared in anticipation of litigation), the exception will not apply. Fed. R. Evid. 803(6).

business-to-business, *adj.* Of or relating to commerce between businesses, as distinguished from commerce between a business and consumers. — Abbr. B2B.

business-to-consumer, *adj.* Of or relating to commerce between a business and consumers, as distinguished from commerce between businesses. — Abbr. B2C.

business transaction. An action that affects the actor's financial or economic interests, including the making of a contract.

business visitor. *Torts.* A person who is invited or permitted to enter or remain on another's land for a purpose directly or indirectly connected with the landowner's or possessor's business dealings.

but-for test. (1925) *Tort & criminal law.* The doctrine that causation exists only when the result would not have occurred without the party's conduct.

buyer. (12c) One who makes a purchase.

buyer in ordinary course of business. (1915) A person who — in good faith and without knowledge that the sale violates a third party's ownership rights or security interest in the goods — buys from a person regularly engaged in the business of selling goods of that kind. • Pawnbrokers are excluded from the definition. UCC § 1-201(9).

buying in, *n.* (17c) The purchase of property by the original owner or an interested party at an auction or foreclosure sale. — **buy in,** *vb.*

buyout, *n.* The purchase of all or a controlling percentage of the assets or shares of a business. — **buy out,** *vb.*

leveraged buyout. (1975) The purchase of a publicly held corporation's outstanding stock by its management or outside investors, financed mainly with funds borrowed from investment bankers or brokers and usu. secured by the corporation's assets. — Abbr. LBO.

management buyout. (1976) **1.** A buyout of a corporation by its own directors and officers. **2.** A leveraged buyout of a corporation by an outside entity in which the corporation's management has a material financial interest. — Abbr. MBO.

buy–sell agreement. (1956) **1.** An arrangement between owners of a business by which the surviving owners agree to purchase the interest of a withdrawing or deceased owner. **2.** *Corporations.* A share-transfer restriction that commits the shareholder to sell, and the corporation or other shareholders to buy, the shareholder's shares at a fixed price when a specified event occurs.

by-bidding. The illegal practice of employing a person to bid at an auction for the sole purpose of stimulating bidding on the seller's property.

bylaw [fr. Danish *bye,* Old Norse *byr,* "town"] (14c) *Parliamentary law.* (*usu. pl.*) A rule or administrative provision adopted by an organization for its internal governance and its external dealings. • Although the bylaws may be an organization's most authoritative governing document, they are subordinate to a charter or articles of incorporation or association or to a constitution. The "constitution and bylaws" are sometimes a single document.

bystander. (16c) One who is present when an event takes place, but who does not become directly involved in it.

C

c. *abbr.* (1947) **1.** Circa. **2.** Copyright.

ca. *abbr.* Circa.

cabinet. (*often cap.*) (17c) The advisory council to an executive officer, esp. the President.

caducary (kə-**d[y]oo**-kə-ree), *adj.* (Of a bequest or estate) subject to, relating to, or by way of escheat, lapse, or forfeiture of property. — **caduce** (kə-**d[y]oos**), *vb.* — **caducity** (kə-**d[y]oo**-sə-tee), *n.*

c.a.f. Cost, assurance, and freight. • This term is synonymous with C.I.F.

CAFC. *abbr.* United States Court of Appeals for the Federal Circuit.

cafeteria plan. An employee fringe-benefit plan allowing a choice of basic benefits up to a certain dollar amount.

***Calandra* rule** (kə-**lan**-drə). The doctrine that a grand-jury witness may be compelled to answer questions about certain items, even though the items were obtained by the police illegally. *United States v. Calandra*, 414 U.S. 338, 94 S.Ct. 613 (1974).

calendar, *n.* (15c) **1.** (18c) A court's list of civil or criminal cases. **2.** A list of bills reported out of a legislative committee for consideration by the entire legislature.

calendar, *vb.* **1.** To place an important event on a calendar, esp. so that the event will be remembered. **2.** To place a case on a calendar.

calendar call. (1918) A court session in which the judge calls each case awaiting trial, determines its status, and assigns a trial date.

call, *n.* (13c) **1.** A request, demand, or command, esp. to come or assemble; an invitation or summons.

quorum call. A roll call to determine whether a quorum is present.

roll call. *Parliamentary law.* A calling of the roll to take attendance or a vote.

2. A demand for payment of money.

margin call. A securities broker's demand that a customer put up money or stock as collateral when the broker finances a purchase of securities. • A margin call usu. occurs when the market prices of the securities are falling.

3. A demand for the presentation of a security (esp. a bond) for redemption before the maturity date.

call, *vb.* (bef. 12c) **1.** To summon. **2.** To demand payment of money. **3.** To redeem (a bond) before maturity. — **callable,** *adj.*

call the question. *Parliamentary law.* **1.** (Of a member) to move to close debate. **2.** (Of a deliberative assembly) to adopt a motion to close debate.

call up, *vb. Parliamentary law.* To bring before a deliberative assembly business that is ready for consideration.

calumny (**kal**-əm-nee), *n.* (16c) *Archaic.* **1.** The act of maliciously misrepresenting someone's words or actions in a way that is calculated to injure that person's reputation. **2.** A false charge or imputation. — **calumnious** (kə-**ləm**-nee-əs), *adj.* — **calumniator** (kə-**ləm**-nee-ay-tər), *n.*

camera (**kam**-ə-rə). [Latin] Chamber; room.

can, *vb.* (bef. 12c) **1.** To be able to do something. **2.** To have permission (as often interpreted by courts); MAY.

cancel, *vb.* **1.** To destroy a written instrument by defacing or obliterating it. **2.** To terminate a promise, obligation, or right.

cancellation, *n.* (16c) **1.** The act of defacing or obliterating a writing (as by marking lines across it) with the intention of rendering it void. **2.** An annulment or termination of a promise or an obligation. **3.** An equitable remedy by which courts call in and annul outstanding void or rescinded instruments because they may either spawn vexatious litigation or cloud someone's title to property. **4.** *Trademarks.* The removal of a trademark from the Principal Register. — **cancel,** *vb.* — **cancelable,** *adj.*

cancellation clause. A contractual provision allowing one or both parties to annul their obligations under certain conditions.

C & F. *abbr.* Cost and freight. — Also spelled *CandF.*

candidate, *n.* An individual seeking nomination, election, or appointment to an office, membership, award, or like title or status.

canon (**kan**-ən), *n.* (bef. 12c) **1.** A rule or principle, esp. one accepted as fundamental.

canon of construction. A rule used in construing legal instruments, esp. contracts and statutes. • Although a few states have codified the canons of construction, most jurisdictions treat the canons as mere customs not having the force of law.

2. (*usu. cap.*) A maxim stating in general terms the standards of professional conduct expected of lawyers. • The Model Code of Judicial Conduct (1990) contains five canons and hundreds of specific rules. — **canonical** (kə-**non**-ə-kəl), *adj.*

canvass, *vb.* (16c) **1.** To examine in detail; scrutinize. **2.** To formally count ballots and report the returns. **3.** To solicit political support from voters or a voting district; to take stock of public opinion. — **canvass,** *n.*

cap, *n.* (1947) An upper limit, such as a statutory limit on the recovery in a tort action or on the interest a bank can charge. — **cap,** *vb.*

capacitate (kə-**pas**-ə-tayt), *vb.* (17c) To qualify; to make legally competent. — **capacitation** (kə-pas-ə-**tay**-shən), *n.*

capacity. (15c) **1.** The role in which one performs an act <in her corporate capacity>.

proprietary capacity. The capacity of a city or town when it engages in a business-like venture rather than a governmental function.

representative capacity. (17c) The position of one standing or acting for another, esp. through delegated authority <an agent acting in a representative capacity for the principal>.

2. The power to create or enter into a legal relation under the same circumstances in which a normal person would have the power to create or enter into such a relation; specif., the satisfaction of a legal qualification, such as legal age or soundness of mind, that determines one's ability to sue or be sued, to enter into a binding contract, and the like. **3.** The mental ability to understand the nature and effect of one's acts.

criminal capacity. (1853) The mental ability that a person must possess to be held accountable for a crime; the ability to understand right from wrong.

diminished capacity. (1912) An impaired mental condition — short of insanity — that is caused by intoxication, trauma, or disease and that prevents a person from having the mental state necessary to be held responsible for a crime. • In some jurisdictions, a defendant's diminished capacity can be used to determine the degree of the offense or the severity of the punishment.

testamentary capacity. (1819) The mental ability that a person must have to prepare a valid will. • This capacity is often described as the ability to recognize the natural objects of one's bounty, the nature and extent of one's estate, and the fact that one is making a plan to dispose of the estate after death. Traditionally, the phrase "of legal age and sound mind" refers to the testator's capacity.

4. The ability or power to do or experience something.

capias (**kay**-pee-əs *or* **kap**-ee-əs). [Latin "that you take"] (15c) Any of various types of writs that require an officer to take a named defendant into custody.

capital, *adj.* (16c) **1.** Of or relating to economic or financial capital <capital market>. **2.** Punishable by execution; involving the death penalty <a capital offense>.

capital, *n.* (17c) **1.** Money or assets invested, or available for investment, in a business. **2.** The total assets of a business, esp. those that help generate profits. **3.** The total amount or value of a corporation's stock; corporate equity.

capital contribution. 1. Cash, property, or services contributed by partners to a partnership. **2.** Funds made available by a shareholder, usu. without an increase in stock holdings.

capital expenditure. (1898) An outlay of funds to acquire or improve a fixed asset.

capital flight. The sending of large amounts of investment money out of a country, usu. as a result of panic caused by political turmoil or a severe recession.

capital gain. (1921) The profit realized when a capital asset is sold or exchanged.

long-term capital gain. The profit realized from selling or exchanging a capital asset held for more than a specified period, usu. one year.

short-term capital gain. The profit realized from selling or exchanging a capital asset held for less than a specified period, usu. one year. • It is treated as ordinary income under current federal tax law.

capital impairment. The financial condition of a corporation whose assets are less than the sum of its legal capital and its liabilities.

capitalism, *n.* (1849) An economic system that depends on the private ownership of the means of production and on competitive forces to determine what is produced. — **capitalist,** *adj.* & *n.*

capitalization, *n.* **1.** The act or process of capitalizing or converting something into capital. **2.** The amount or sum resulting from this act or process. **3.** The total amount of long-term financing used by a business, including stocks, bonds, retained earnings, and other funds. **4.** The total par value or stated value of the authorized or outstanding stock of a corporation.

thin capitalization. The financial condition of a firm that has a high ratio of liabilities to capital.

undercapitalization. The financial condition of a firm that does not have enough capital to carry on its business.

capitalization rate. The interest rate used in calculating the present value of future periodic payments.

capitalization ratio. The ratio between the amount of capital raised and the total capitalization of the firm.

capitalize, *vb.* **1.** To convert (earnings) into capital. **2.** To treat (a cost) as a capital expenditure rather than an ordinary and necessary expense. **3.** To determine the present value of (long-term income). **4.** To supply capital for (a business).

capital leverage. (1940) The use of borrowed funds in a business to obtain a return greater than the interest rate.

capital outlay. (1857) **1.** CAPITAL EXPENDITURE. **2.** Money expended in acquiring, equipping, and promoting a business.

capital punishment. The sentence of death for a serious crime.

capital recovery. (1942) The collection of charged-off bad debt that has been previously written off against the allowance for doubtful accounts.

capital-risk test. *Securities.* A method of determining whether a transaction constitutes an investment contract (subject to securities laws), whereby if a substantial portion of the capital used by a franchiser to start its operations is provided by a franchisee, then the transaction is treated as an investment contract.

capital structure. (1923) The mix of debt and equity by which a business finances its operations; the relative proportions of short-term debt, long-term debt, and capital stock.

capital transaction. A purchase, sale, or exchange of a capital asset.

capitated, *adj. Insurance.* Of or relating to a healthcare system that gives a medical-care provider a fixed fee per patient regardless of the treatment required.

capitation. 1. Poll tax. **2.** A method of paying a healthcare provider based on the number of members in a health-benefit plan that the provider contracts to treat. • The health plan's sponsor agrees to pay a fixed amount per person each period, regardless of what services are provided.

capitulation (kə-pich-ə-**lay**-shən), *n.* (16c) The act of surrendering or giving in. — **capitulate,** *vb.* — **capitulatory,** *adj.*

capper. 1. One who solicits business for an attorney. **2.** *Slang.* A person who acts as a lure for others (as in a gambling or confidence game).

capricious (kə-**prish**-əs), *adj.* (17c) **1.** (Of a person) characterized by or guided by unpredictable or impulsive behavior. **2.** (Of a decree) contrary to the evidence or established rules of law.

caption. (17c) **1.** The introductory part of a court paper stating the names of the parties, the name of the court, the docket or file number, and a description of the paper. Fed. R. Civ. P. 10(a). **2.** The arrest or seizure of a person by legal process.

captive, *n.* **1.** A person who is unlawfully seized and held by another. **2.** PRISONER OF WAR. **3.** An animal, esp. a wild one, that is caught and kept confined.

captive-audience doctrine. *Constitutional law.* The principle that when the listener cannot, as a practical matter, escape from intrusive speech, the speech can be restricted.

capture-and-hold rule. *Oil & gas.* For royalty-calculation purposes, the doctrine that "production" occurs when oil or gas is pumped to the surface and stored, whether at the wellhead or elsewhere on the leased property.

care, *n.* (bef. 12c) **1.** Serious attention; heed. **2.** Under the law of negligence or of obligations, the conduct demanded of a person in a given situation. • Typically, this involves a person's giving attention both to possible dangers, mistakes, and pitfalls and to ways of minimizing those risks.

great care. (15c) **1.** The degree of care that a prudent person exercises in dealing with very important personal affairs. **2.** The degree of care exercised in a given situation by someone in the business or profession of dealing with the situation.

highest degree of care. The degree of care exercised commensurate with the danger involved.

reasonable care. (17c) As a test of liability for negligence, the degree of care that a prudent and competent person engaged in the same line of business or endeavor would exercise under similar circumstances.

slight care. (17c) The degree of care a person gives to matters of minor importance; the degree of care given by a person of limited accountability.

3. *Family law.* The provision of physical or psychological comfort to another, esp. an ailing spouse, child, or parent.

caregiver. *Family law.* A person, usu. not a parent, who has and exercises custodial responsibility for a child or for an elderly or disabled person.

careless, *adj.* (bef. 12c) **1.** (Of a person) not exercising reasonable care. **2.** (Of an action or behavior) engaged in without reasonable care.

carelessness, *n.* (bef. 12c) **1.** The fact, condition, or instance of a person's either not having done what he or she ought to have done, or having done what he or she ought not to have done; heedless inattention. **2.** A person's general disposition not to do something that ought to be done.

cargo. Goods transported by a vessel, airplane, or vehicle; freight.

general cargo. Goods and materials of various types transported by carriers, often in a common load, with few or no restrictions.

hazardous cargo. Dangerous goods or materials whose carriage is usu. subject to stringent regulatory and statutory restrictions.

carjacking. The forcible theft of a vehicle from a motorist; the unlawful commandeering of an automobile. 18 USCA § 2119. — **carjack,** *vb.*

carnal knowledge. (15c) *Archaic.* Sexual intercourse, esp. with an underage female. — Sometimes shortened to *knowledge.*

carriage. Transport of freight or passengers.

carrier. 1. An individual or organization (such as a shipowner, a railroad, or an airline) that contracts to transport passengers or goods for a fee.

common carrier. (15c) A commercial enterprise that holds itself out to the public as offering to transport freight or passengers for a fee. • A common carrier is generally required by law to transport freight or passengers or freight, without refusal, if the approved fare or charge is paid.

marine carrier. A carrier operating on navigable waters subject to the jurisdiction of the United States.

private carrier. (18c) Any carrier that is not a common carrier by law. • A private carrier is not bound to accept business from the general public.

2. Insurer.

carry, *vb.* **1.** To sustain the weight or burden of; to hold or bear. **2.** To convey or transport. **3.** To possess and convey (a firearm) in a vehicle, including the locked glove compartment or trunk of a car. • The United States Supreme Court adopted this definition in interpreting the phrase *carries a firearm* as used in a statute imposing a mandatory prison term on a person who uses or carries a firearm while committing a drug-trafficking crime. *Muscarello v. U.S.*, 524 U.S. 125, 118 S.Ct. 1911 (1998).

carry away, *vb.* To take or move (stolen property, etc.). • The traditional count for larceny was that the defendant "did steal, take, and carry away" the property. A "carrying away" can be a slight movement of the property.

carryback. (1942) *Tax.* An income-tax deduction (esp. for a net operating loss) that cannot be taken entirely in a given period but may be taken in an earlier period (usu. the previous three years).

carryover. (1925) *Tax.* An income-tax deduction (esp. for a net operating loss) that cannot be taken entirely in a given period but may be taken in a later period (usu. the next five years).

carte blanche (kahrt **blah*n*sh**). [French "blank card"] **1.** A signed, blank instrument that is filled out at an agent's discretion. **2.** Full discretionary power; unlimited authority.

cartel (kahr-**tel**), *n.* (17c) **1.** A combination of producers or sellers that join together to control a product's production or price. **2.** An association of firms with common interests, seeking to prevent extreme or unfair competition, allocate markets, or share knowledge. — **cartelize** (**kahr**-tə-lɪz *or* kahr-**tel**-ɪz), *vb.*

carveout, *n.* (1966) **1.** An explicit exception to a broad rule. **2.** *Tax.* For tax purposes, the separation from property of the income derived from the property. —**carve out,** *vb.*

case. (13c) **1.** A civil or criminal proceeding, action, suit, or controversy at law or in equity.

active case. (1949) A case that is still pending.

case at bar. (16c) A case under the immediate consideration of the court.

case of first impression. (1806) A case that presents the court with an issue of law that has not previously been decided by any controlling legal authority in that jurisdiction.

case reserved. (18c) A written statement of the facts proved at trial and drawn up and stipulated to by the parties, so that certain legal issues can be decided by an appellate court.

case stated. (17c) A formal written statement of the facts in a case, submitted to the court jointly by the parties so that a decision may be rendered without trial.

inactive case. (1981) A pending case that is not proceeding toward resolution. • This may occur for several reasons, such as nonservice, want of prosecution, or (in a criminal case) the defendant's having absconded.

test case. (1894) **1.** A lawsuit brought to establish an important legal principle or right. • Such an action is frequently brought by the parties' mutual consent on agreed facts — when that is so, a test case is also sometimes termed *amicable action* or *amicable suit.* **2.** An action selected from several suits that are based on the same facts and evidence, raise the same question of law, and have a common plaintiff or a common defendant. • Sometimes, when all parties agree, the court orders a consolidation and all parties are bound by the decision in the test case.

2. A criminal investigation. **3.** An individual suspect or convict in relation to any aspect of the criminal-justice system. **4.** An argument. **5.** An instance, occurrence, or situation.

casebook. (18c) A compilation of extracts from instructive cases on a particular subject, usu. with commentary and questions about the cases, designed as a teaching aid.

casebook method. (1915) An inductive system of teaching law in which students study specific cases to learn general legal principles.

case evaluation. Assessment of a case's strengths and weaknesses, along with the cost of litigation and the amount of potential liability or recovery, typically done to decide whether to accept a case or to advise a client or potential client about how to proceed.

caseflow. (1957) **1.** The movement of cases through the judicial system, from the initial filing to the final appeal. **2.** An analysis of that movement.

case-in-chief. (1853) **1.** The evidence presented at trial by a party between the time the party calls the first witness and the time the party rests. **2.** The part of a trial in which a party presents evidence to support the claim or defense.

caselaw. (1861) The law to be found in the collection of reported cases that form all or part of the body of law within a given jurisdiction. — Also written *case law; case-law.*

caseload. (1938) The volume of cases assigned to a given court, agency, officer, judge, law firm, or lawyer.

case-management order. A court order designed to control the procedure in a case on the court's docket, esp. by limiting pretrial discovery. — Abbr. CMO.

case note. A short statement summarizing a case, esp. the relevant facts, the issues, the holding, and the court's reasoning.

case-or-controversy requirement. (1937) The constitutional requirement that, for a federal court to hear a case, the case must involve an actual dispute.

case plan. A written procedure for the care and management of a child who has been removed from his or her home and placed in foster care or in an institution.

cash, *n.* (16c) **1.** Money or its equivalent. **2.** Currency or coins, negotiable checks, and balances in bank accounts. — **cash,** *vb.*

cash equivalent. A short-term security that is liquid enough to be considered equivalent to cash.

cash-expenditure method. *Tax.* A technique used by the IRS to reconstruct a taxpayer's unreported income by comparing the amount spent on goods and services during a given period with the income reported for that period.

cash flow. (1954) **1.** The movement of cash through a business, as a measure of profitability or liquidity. **2.** The cash generated from a business or transaction. **3.** Cash receipts minus cash disbursements for a given period. — Sometimes written *cashflow.*

cashier, *n.* **1.** One who receives and records payments at a business. **2.** A bank's or trust company's executive officer, who is responsible for banking transactions.

cashier, *vb.* (16c) To dismiss from service dishonorably.

cash or deferred arrangement. A retirement-plan provision permitting an employee to have a certain amount of compensation paid in cash or contributed, on behalf of the employee, to a profit-sharing or stock-bonus plan. • A 401(k) plan is a type of cash or deferred arrangement. — Abbr. CODA.

cashout, *n.* (1971) An arrangement by a seller to receive the entire amount of equity in cash rather than retain an interest in the property. — **cash out,** *vb.*

casing. *Oil & gas.* The pipe in a wellbore hole, cemented into place to prevent pollution and to protect the hole.

casinghead gas. *Oil & gas.* Natural gas in a liquid solution with crude oil, produced at the casinghead (top) of a oil well.

castle doctrine. (1892) *Criminal law.* An exception to the retreat rule allowing the use of deadly force by a person who is protecting his or her home and its inhabitants from attack, esp. from a trespasser who intends to commit a felony or inflict serious bodily harm.

casualty. (15c) **1.** A serious or fatal accident. **2.** A person or thing injured, lost, or destroyed.

casualty gain. *Insurance.* The profit realized by an insured when the benefits paid exceed the insured property's adjusted value.

casualty pot. *Tax.* A step in evaluating tax liability in which casualty gains and losses are compared to determine whether a net loss or gain has occurred.

catch-all, *adj.* Broad; widely encompassing.

caucus (**kaw**-kəs), *n.* (18c) **1.** Representatives from a political party who assemble to nominate candidates and decide party policy. **2.** A meeting of a group, usu. within a deliberative assembly, of people aligned by party or interest to formulate a policy or strategy. — **caucus,** *vb.*

causal (**kaw**-zəl), *adj.* (16c) **1.** Of, relating to, or involving causation. **2.** Arising from a cause.

causality (kaw-**zal**-ə-tee), *n.* (17c) The principle of causal relationship; the relation between cause and effect. — **causal,** *adj.*

causa mortis (**kaw**-zə **mor**-tis), *adj.* Done or made in contemplation of one's own death.

causation (kaw-**zay**-shən). (17c) **1.** The causing or producing of an effect. **2.** CAUSALITY.

cause, *n.* (13c) **1.** Something that produces an effect or result. — **causative** (**kaw**-zə-tiv), *adj.*

but-for cause. (1924) The cause without which the event could not have occurred.

concurrent cause. (17c) One of two or more causes that simultaneously produce a result.

contributing cause. A factor that — though not the primary cause — plays a part in producing a result.

immediate cause. (16c) The last event in a chain of events, though not necessarily the proximate cause of what follows.

intervening cause. (17c) An event that comes between the initial event in a sequence and the end result, thereby altering the natural course of events that might have connected a wrongful act to an injury. • If the intervening cause is strong enough to relieve the wrongdoer of any liability, it becomes a *superseding cause.* A *dependent intervening cause* is one that is not an act and is never a superseding cause. An *independent intervening cause* is one that operates on a condition produced by an antecedent cause but in no way resulted from that cause.

proximate cause. (17c) **1.** A cause that is legally sufficient to result in liability; an act or omission that is considered in law to result in a consequence, so that liability can be imposed on the actor. **2.** A cause that directly produces an event and without which the event would not have occurred.

remote cause. (16c) A cause that does not necessarily or immediately produce an event or injury.

sole cause. (16c) The only cause that, from a legal viewpoint, produces an event or injury. • If it comes between a defendant's action and the event or injury at issue, it is treated as a *superseding cause.*

superseding cause. (1891) An intervening act or force that the law considers sufficient to override the cause for which the original tortfeasor was responsible, thereby exonerating that tortfeasor from liability.

unavoidable cause. A cause that a reasonably prudent person would not anticipate or be expected to avoid.

2. A ground for legal action.

good cause. (16c) A legally sufficient reason. • Good cause is often the burden placed on a litigant (usu. by court rule or order) to show why a request should be granted or an action excused. The term is often used in employment-termination cases.

3. A lawsuit; a case.

cause, *vb.* To bring about or effect.

cause-and-prejudice rule. (1977) *Criminal law.* The doctrine that a prisoner petitioning for a federal writ of habeas corpus on the basis of a constitutional challenge must first show that the claim rests on either a new rule of constitutional law (one that was unavailable while the case was heard in the state courts) or a fact that could not have been uncovered earlier despite due diligence, and then show by clear and convincing evidence that if the constitutional error had not occurred, the prisoner would not have been convicted. 28 USCA § 2254(e)(2).

cause célèbre (**kawz** sə-**leb** *or* **kawz** say-**leb**-rə). [French "celebrated case"] (18c) A trial or decision in which the subject matter or the characters are unusual or sensational.

cause lawyering. The practice of a lawyer who advocates for social justice by combining the activities of litigation, community organizing, public education, and lobbying to advance a cause past its current legal limitations and boundaries.

cause of action. (15c) **1.** A group of operative facts giving rise to one or more bases for suing; a factual situation that entitles one person to obtain a remedy in court from another person. **2.** A legal theory of a lawsuit.

new cause of action. A claim not arising out of or relating to the conduct, occurrence, or transaction contained in the original pleading. Fed. R. Civ. P. 15(c)).

3. Loosely, a lawsuit. — Abbr. COA.

caveat (**kav**-ee-aht *or* **kay**-vee-at *or* **kav**-ee-at). [Latin "let him or her beware"] (16c) **1.** A warning or proviso.

caveat actor (**ak**-tor). [Latin] Let the doer, or actor, beware.

caveat emptor (**emp**-tor). [Latin "let the buyer beware"] A doctrine holding that purchasers buy at their own risk. • Modern statutes and cases have greatly limited the importance of this doctrine.

caveat venditor (**ven**-di-tor). [Latin] Let the seller beware.

caveat viator (vɪ-**ay**-tor). [Latin "let the traveler beware"]. The duty of a traveler on a highway to use due care to detect and avoid defects in the way.

2. A formal notice or warning given by a party to a court or court officer requesting a suspension of proceedings. **3.** Under the Torrens system of land titles, a formal notice of an unregistered interest in land. • Once lodged with the register of deeds, this notice prevents the register from recording any dealing affecting the estate or the interest claimed. — **caveat,** *vb.*

CBA. *abbr.* Collective-bargaining agreement.

CBO. *abbr.* Congressional Budget Office.

CBT. *abbr.* Chicago Board of Trade.

CC. *abbr.* **1.** Circuit, city, civil, or county court. **2.** Chancery, civil, criminal, or Crown cases. **3.** Civil code.

CCC. *abbr.* Commodity Credit Corporation.

CCPA. *abbr.* **1.** Court of Customs and Patent Appeals. **2.** Consumer Credit Protection Act.

CCR. *abbr.* United States Commission on Civil Rights.

CD. *abbr.* Certificate of deposit.

CDC. *abbr.* Centers for Disease Control and Prevention.

CEA. *abbr.* Council of Economic Advisors.

cease-and-desist letter. A cautionary notice sent to an alleged wrongdoer, describing the offensive activity and the complainant's remedies and demanding that the activity stop.

cease-and-desist order. (1918) A court's or agency's order prohibiting a person from continuing a particular course of conduct.

cede (seed), *vb.* (18c) **1.** To surrender or relinquish. **2.** To assign or grant. — **cession (sesh**-ən), *n.* — **cessionary (sesh**-ən-er-ee), *adj.*

censor, *n.* **1.** A person who inspects publications, films, and the like for objectionable content. **2.** In the armed forces, someone who reads letters and other communications and deletes material considered a security threat. — **censorial,** *adj.* — **censorship,** *n.*

censor (**sen**-sər), *vb.* (1882) To officially inspect (esp. a book or film) and delete material considered offensive.

censure (**sen**-shər), *n.* (14c) An official reprimand or condemnation; harsh criticism <the judge's careless statements subjected her to the judicial council's censure>. — **censorious,** *adj.*

censure, *vb.* To reprimand; to criticize harshly.

census. (17c) An official count of people made for the purpose of compiling social and economic data for the political subdivision to which the people belong. Pl. **censuses.**

center-of-gravity doctrine. *Conflict of laws.* The rule that, in choice-of-law questions, the law of the jurisdiction with the most significant relationship to the transaction or event applies.

central clearing system. *Securities.* A method of facilitating securities transactions in which an agent or subsidiary of an exchange acts as a clearinghouse for member brokerage firms by clearing their checks, settling their accounts, and delivering their payments.

Central Intelligence Agency. An independent federal agency that compiles intelligence information, conducts counterintelligence activities outside the United States, and advises the President and the National Security Council on matters of foreign intelligence and national security. — Abbr. CIA.

CEO. *abbr.* Chief executive officer.

CERCLA (**sər**-klə). *abbr.* Comprehensive Environmental Response, Compensation, and Liability Act of 1980. • This statute holds responsible parties liable for the cost of cleaning up hazardous-waste sites. 42 USCA §§ 9601 et seq.

cert. *abbr.* Certiorari.

certificate, *n.* (15c) **1.** A document in which a fact is formally attested. **2.** A document certifying the bearer's status or authorization to act in a specified way. **3.** A notice by one court to another court of the action it has taken.

certificate of appealability. In an appeal from the denial of federal habeas corpus relief, a document issued by a United States circuit judge certifying that the prisoner showed that a constitutional right may have been denied. 28 USCA § 2253(c)(2).

certificate of authority. (1808) **1.** A document authenticating a notarized document that is being sent to another jurisdiction. **2.** A document issued by a state agency, usu. the secretary of state, granting an out-of-state corporation the right to do business in the state.

certificate of conference. (1979) A section of a pleading or motion filed with the court, usu. contained separately on a page near the end of the document, whereby the party filing the pleading or motion certifies to the court that the parties have attempted to resolve the matter, but that a judicial determination is needed because an agreement could not be reached. Fed. R. Civ. P. 26(c), 37.

certificate of correction. A document that corrects an error in an official document, such as a certificate of incorporation.

certificate of deposit. (1846) **1.** A banker's certificate acknowledging the receipt of money and promising to repay the depositor. **2.** A bank document showing the existence of a time deposit, usu. one that pays interest. — Abbr. CD.

certificate of incorporation. (18c) **1.** A document issued by a state authority (usu. the secretary of state) granting a corporation its legal existence and the right to function as a corporation. **2.** Articles of incorporation.

certificate of insurance. A document acknowledging that an insurance policy has been written, and setting forth in general terms what the policy covers.

certificate of occupancy. A document indicating that a building complies with zoning and building ordinances, and is ready to be occupied.

certificate of service. (1819) A section of a pleading or motion filed with the court, usu. contained separately on the last page, in which the filing party certifies to the court that a copy has been mailed to or otherwise served on all other parties. Fed. R. Civ. P. 5(d).

certificate of title. (1831) A document indicating ownership of real or personal property. UCC § 9-102(a)(10). • This document usu. identifies any liens or other encumbrances.

certification, *n.* (15c) **1.** The act of attesting. **2.** The state of having been attested. **3.** An attested statement. **4.** The writing on the face of a check by which it is certified. **5.** A procedure by which a federal appellate court asks the U.S. Supreme Court or the highest state court to review a question of law arising in a case pending before the appellate court and on which it needs guidance.

certified question. (1835) A point of law on which a federal appellate court seeks guidance from either the U.S. Supreme Court or the highest state court by the procedure of certification.

certify, *vb.* (14c) **1.** To authenticate or verify in writing. **2.** To attest as being true or as meeting certain criteria. **3.** (Of a court) to issue an order allowing a class of litigants to maintain a class action; to create (a class) for purposes of a class action. Cf. DECERTIFY. — **certified,** *adj.*

certiorari (sər-shee-ə-**rair**-ɪ *or* -**rair**-ee *or* -**rah**-ree). [Law Latin "to be more fully informed"] (15c) An extraordinary writ issued by an appellate court, at its discretion, directing a lower court to deliver the record in the case for review. • The U.S. Supreme Court uses certiorari to review most of the cases that it decides to hear. — Abbr. cert.

cert pool. A group of clerks in the U.S. Supreme Court who read petitions for certiorari and write memorandums for the justices with a synopsis of the facts and issues and often a recommendation of whether a grant of certiorari is warranted.

certworthy, *adj.* (1965) *Slang.*(Of a case or issue) deserving of review by writ of certiorari. — **certworthiness,** *n.*

cessation-of-production clause. *Oil & gas.* A lease provision that specifies what the lessee must do to maintain the lease if production stops. • The purpose of the clause is to avoid the uncertainties of the temporary-cessation-of-production doctrine.

cession (**sesh**-ən). (15c) **1.** The act of relinquishing property rights. **2.** *Int'l law.* The relinquishment or transfer of land from one nation to another, esp. after a war. as part of the price of peace. **3.** The land so relinquished or transferred.

cestui (**set**-ee *or* **ses**-twee). [French "he who"] (16c) A beneficiary. — Also spelled *cestuy.*

cestui que trust (**set**-ee [*or* **ses**-twee] kee [*or* kə] **trəst**). [Law French] (18c) *Archaic.* One who possesses equitable rights in property, usu. receiving the rents, issues, and profits from it; BENEFICIARY. Pl. **cestuis que trust** or (erroneously) **cestuis que trustent.**

cestui que use (**set**-ee [*or* **ses**-twee] kee [*or* kə] **yoos**). [Law French] (16c) *Archaic.* The person for whose use and benefit property is being held by another, who holds the legal title to the property. Pl. **cestuis que use** or (erroneously) **cestuis que usent.**

cestui que vie (**set**-ee [*or* **ses**-twee] kee [*or* kə] **vee**). [Law French] (17c) The person whose life measures the duration of a trust, gift, estate, or insurance contract.

cf. *abbr.* [Latin *confer*] (1850) Compare. • As a citation signal, *cf.* directs the reader's attention to another authority or section of the work in which contrasting, analogous, or explanatory statements may be found.

C.F. *abbr.* Cost and freight.

CFO. *abbr.* Chief financial officer.

CFP. *abbr.* Certified financial planner.

CFR. *abbr.* **1.** Code of Federal Regulations. **2.** Cost and freight.

CFTC. *abbr.* Commodity Futures Trading Commission.

ch. *abbr.* **1.** Chapter. **2.** Chancellor. **3.** Chancery. **4.** Chief.

chain-certificate method. (1966) The procedure for authenticating a foreign official record by the party seeking to admit the record as evidence at trial. See Fed. R. Civ. P. 44.

chain gang. A group of prisoners chained together to prevent their escape while working outside a prison.

chain of causation. (18c) **1.** A series of events each caused by the previous one. **2.** The causal connection between a cause and its effects.

chain of custody. (1947) **1.** The movement and location of real evidence, and the history of those persons who had it in their custody, from the time it is obtained to the time it is presented in court. **2.** The history of a chattel's possession.

chain of title. (18c) **1.** The ownership history of a piece of land, from its first owner to the present one. **2.** The ownership history of commercial paper, traceable through the indorsements. • For the holder to have good title, every prior negotiation must have been proper. If a necessary indorsement is missing or forged, the chain of title is broken and no later transferee can become a holder.

chair. *Parliamentary law.* **1.** A deliberative assembly's presiding officer. **2.** The presiding officer's seat. **3.** The officer who heads an organization. — **chair,** *vb.*

challenge, *n.* (14c) **1.** An act or instance of formally questioning the legality or legal qualifications of a person, action, or thing <a challenge to the opposing party's expert witness>.

as-applied challenge. (1974) A claim that a law or governmental policy, though constitutional on its face, is unconstitutional as applied, usu. because of a discriminatory effect; a claim that a statute is unconstitutional on the facts of a particular case or in its application to a particular party.

Batson challenge. (1987) *Procedure.* An objection that an opposing party has used a peremptory challenge to exclude a potential juror on the basis of race, ethnicity, or sex. • It is named for *Batson v. Kentucky*, 476 U.S. 79, 106 S.Ct. 1712 (1986), a criminal case in which the prosecution struck potential jurors on the basis of race. The principle of Batson was extended in later Supreme Court cases to civil litigants (*Edmonson v. Leesville Concrete Co.*, 500 U.S. 614, 111 S.Ct. 2077 (1991)) and to criminal defense attorneys (*Georgia v. McCollum*, 505 U.S. 42, 112 S.Ct. 2348 (1992)). The Court also applied it to peremptory challenges based on a juror's sex (*J.E.B. v. Alabama*, 511 U.S. 127, 114 S.Ct. 1419 (1994)). See Fed. R. Civ. P. 47(b).

constitutional challenge. (1936) A claim that a law or governmental action is unconstitutional.

facial challenge. (1973) A claim that a statute is unconstitutional on its face — that is, that it always operates unconstitutionally.

2. A party's request that a judge disqualify a potential juror or an entire jury panel.

challenge for cause. (17c) A party's challenge supported by a specified reason, such as bias or prejudice, that would disqualify that potential juror.

challenge to the array. (16c) A legal challenge to the manner in which the entire jury panel was selected, usu. for a failure to follow prescribed procedures designed to produce impartial juries drawn from a fair cross-section of the community.

challenge to the favor. A challenge for cause that arises when facts and circumstances tend to show that a juror is biased but do not warrant the juror's automatic disqualification.

peremptory challenge. (16c) One of a party's limited number of challenges that do not need to be supported by a reason unless the opposing party makes a prima facie showing that the challenge was used to discriminate on the basis of race, ethnicity, or sex.

principal challenge. A for-cause challenge that arises when facts and circumstances support a conclusive presumption of a juror's bias, resulting in automatic disqualification.

chamber, *n.* (13c) **1.** A room or compartment. **2.** A legislative or judicial body or other deliberative assembly. **3.** The hall or room where such a body conducts business. — **chamber,** *adj.*

judge's chamber. (*usu. pl.*) (17c) **1.** The private room or office of a judge. **2.** Any place where a judge transacts official business when not holding a session of the court.

lower chamber. (1885) In a bicameral legislature, the larger of the two legislative bodies, such as the House of Representatives or the House of Commons.

upper chamber. (1850) In a bicameral legislature, the smaller of the two legislative bodies, such as the Senate or the House of Lords.

chamber, *vb. Slang.* (Of a judge) to sit in one's chambers at a given location.

chamber business. (1805) Official judicial business conducted outside the courtroom.

champerty (**cham**-pər-tee), *n.* [fr. French *champs parti* "split field"] (15c) An agreement between an officious intermeddler in a lawsuit and a litigant by which the intermeddler helps pursue the litigant's claim as consideration for receiving part of any judgment proceeds; specif., an agreement to divide litigation proceeds between the owner of the litigated claim and a party unrelated to the lawsuit who supports or helps enforce the claim. — **champertous** (**cham**-pər-təs), *adj.* (17c). — **champertor** (**cham**-pər-tər), *n.* (16c).

chance, *n.* (14c) **1.** A hazard or risk. **2.** The unforeseen, uncontrollable, or unintended consequences of an act. **3.** An accident. **4.** Opportunity; hope.

chance bargain. *Contracts.* A transaction in which the parties mutually agree to accept the risk that facts and circumstances assumed by the parties at the time of contracting may not actually be what the parties believe they are.

chancellor, *n.* (14c) **1.** A judge serving on a court of chancery. **2.** A university president or CEO of an institution of higher education. **3.** In the U.S., a judge in some courts of chancery or equity. — **chancellorship,** *n.*

chance-medley. [fr. Anglo-Norman *chance medlee* "chance scuffle"] A spontaneous fight during which one participant kills another in self-defense.

chance-of-survival doctrine. (1991) The principle that a wrongful-death plaintiff need only prove that the defendant's conduct was a substantial factor in causing the death — that is, that the victim might have survived but for the defendant's conduct.

chancery (**chan**-sər-ee). (14c) **1.** A court of equity; collectively, the courts of equity. • The term is derived from the court of the Lord Chancellor, the original English court of equity. **2.** The system of jurisprudence administered in courts of equity.

change in circumstances. (1899) *Family law.* A modification in the physical, emotional, or financial condition of one or both parents, used to show the need to modify a custody or support order; esp., an involuntary occurrence that, if it had been known at the time of the divorce decree, would have resulted in the court's issuing a different decree, as when an involuntary job loss creates a need to modify the decree to provide for reduced child-support payments.

change of venue. (18c) The transfer of a case from one locale to another court in the same judicial system to cure a defect in venue, either to minimize the prejudicial impact of local sentiment or to secure a more sensible location for trial.

channel. (14c) **1.** The bed of a stream of water; the groove through which a stream flows. **2.** The line of deep water that shipping vessels follow. **3.** A water route between two islands or an island and a continent. **4.** A mode of transmitting something.

Chapter 7. 1. The chapter of the United States Bankruptcy Code allowing a trustee to collect and liquidate a debtor's nonexempt property, either voluntarily or by court order, to satisfy creditors. **2.** A bankruptcy case filed under this chapter. • An individual debtor who undergoes this type of liquidation usu. gets a fresh financial start by receiving a discharge of all debts.

Chapter 9. 1. The chapter of the United States Bankruptcy Code governing the adjustment of a municipality's debts. **2.** A bankruptcy case filed under this chapter.

Chapter 11. (1970) **1.** The chapter of the United States Bankruptcy Code allowing an insolvent business, or one that is threatened with insolvency, to reorganize its capital structure under court supervision (and subject to creditor approval) while continuing its normal operations. • Although the Code permits individual nonbusiness debtors to use Chapter 11, the vast majority of Chapter 11 cases involve business debtors. **2.** A business reorganization conducted under this chapter; REORGANIZATION (1).

Chapter 12. 1. The chapter of the United States Bankruptcy Code providing for a court-approved debt-payment relief plan for family farmers with a regular income. **2.** A bankruptcy case filed under this chapter.

Chapter 13. 1. The chapter of the United States Bankruptcy Code allowing a person's earnings to be collected by a trustee and paid to creditors by means of a court-approved debt-repayment plan if the person has a regular income. • A plan filed under Chapter 13 is sometimes called a *wage-earner's plan*, a *wage-earner plan*, or an *income-based plan*. Chapter 13 allows the debtor to propose a plan of rehabilitation to extend or reduce the balance of any obligations and to receive a discharge from unsecured debts upon completion of the payments under the plan. **2.** A bankruptcy case filed under this chapter.

Chapter 20. *Slang. Bankruptcy.* A debtor who files a Chapter 7 petition and receives a discharge, and then immediately files a Chapter 13 petition to deal with remaining nondischargeable or secured debts.

Chapter 22. *Slang. Bankruptcy.* A debtor, usu. a corporation, that files a second Chapter 11 petition shortly after a previous Chapter 11 petition has failed, because the debtor has become insolvent again or is again threatened with insolvency.

chapter surfing. *Slang.* A debtor's movement from a filing under one United

States Bankruptcy Code chapter to a filing under another.

characterization. **1.** *Conflict of laws.* The classification, qualification, and interpretation of laws that apply to the case. **2.** *Family law.* The process of classifying property accumulated by spouses as either separate or marital property (or community property).

charge, *n.* (13c) **1.** A formal accusation of an offense as a preliminary step to prosecution. **2.** An instruction or command. **3.** JURY CHARGE. **4.** An assigned duty or task; a responsibility. **5.** An encumbrance, lien, or claim. **6.** A person or thing entrusted to another's care. **7.** Price, cost, or expense. **8.** *Parliamentary law.* A deliberative assembly's mandate to a committee.

charge, *vb.* **1.** To accuse (a person) of an offense. **2.** To instruct or command. **3.** To instruct a jury on matters of law. **4.** To impose a lien or claim; to encumber. **5.** To entrust with responsibilities or duties. **6.** To demand a fee; to bill.

chargeable, *adj.* (Of an act) capable or liable of being charged as a criminal offense.

charge account. A credit arrangement by which a customer purchases goods and services and pays for them periodically or within a specified time.

charge-back, *n.* A bank's deducting of sums it had provisionally credited to a customer's account, occurring usu. when a check deposited in the account has been dishonored. UCC § 4-214.

charge conference. (1972) A meeting between a trial judge and the parties' attorneys to develop a jury charge.

charged with notice. Imputed with knowledge or awareness that is legally binding.

charge off, *vb.* To treat (an account receivable) as a loss or expense because payment is unlikely; to treat as a bad debt.

charge sheet. A police record showing the name of each person brought into custody, the nature of the accusations, and the identity of the accusers.

charging instrument. (1951) A formal document — usu. either an indictment or an information — that sets forth an accusation of a crime.

charging order. (1904) *Partnership.* A statutory procedure whereby an individual partner's creditor can satisfy its claim from the partner's interest in the partnership.

charitable, *adj.* **1.** Dedicated to a general public purpose, usu. for the benefit of needy people who cannot pay for benefits received. **2.** Involved in or otherwise relating to charity.

charitable contribution. (17c) A gratuitous transfer of property to a charitable social-welfare, religious, scientific, educational, or other qualified organization. • Such a contribution has tax value because it may result in a current income-tax deduction, may reduce federal estate taxes, and can be made free of any gift taxes.

charitable organization. (1897) *Tax.* A tax-exempt organization that (1) is organized and operated exclusively for religious, scientific, literary, educational, athletic, public-safety, or community-service purposes, (2) does not distribute earnings for the benefit of private individuals, and (3) does not participate in any way in political candidate campaigns, or engage in substantial lobbying. IRC (26 USCA) § 501(c)(3).

charitable purpose. (1877) *Tax.* The purpose for which an organization must be formed so that it qualifies as a charitable organization under the Internal Revenue Code.

charity, *n.* **1.** CHARITABLE ORGANIZATION. **2.** Aid given to the poor, the suffering, or the general community for religious, educational, economic, public-safety, or medical purposes. **3.** Goodwill.

charlatan (**shahr**-lə-tən), *n.* (17c) A person who pretends to have more knowledge or skill than he or she actually has; a quack or faker. — **charlatanism, charlatanry,** *n.*

charta (**kahr**-tə). (17c) [Law Latin] *Hist.* **1.** A charter or deed. **2.** A token by which an estate is held. **3.** A royal grant of privileges or liberties.

charter, *n.* (13c) **1.** An instrument that establishes a body politic or other organization, or that grants rights, liberties, or powers to its citizens or members. **2.** An instrument by which a municipality is incorporated, specifying its organizational structure and its highest laws. • A city charter trumps all conflicting ordinances.

home-rule charter. A local government's organizational plan or framework, analogous to a constitution, drawn by the municipality itself and adopted by popular vote of the citizenry.

3. A governmental act that creates a business or defines a corporate franchise; also, the document evidencing this act. **4.** The organic law of an organization; loosely, the highest law of any entity. **5.** A governing document granting authority or recognition from a parent organization to a subordinate or constituent organization. **6.** The leasing or hiring of an airplane, ship, or other vessel.

charter, *vb.* **1.** To establish or grant by charter <charter a bank>. **2.** To hire or rent for temporary use <charter a boat>.

charter agreement. Charterparty.

charterparty. (16c) A contract by which a ship, or a principal part of it, is leased by the owner, esp. to a merchant for the conveyance of goods on a predetermined voyage to one or more places or for a specified period of time; a special contract between the shipowner and charterer, esp. for the carriage of goods by sea.

chattel (**chat**-əl). (*usu. pl.*) (14c) Movable or transferable property; personal property.

chattel personal. (16c) A tangible good or an intangible right (such as a patent).

chattel real. (16c) A real-property interest that is less than a freehold or fee, such as a leasehold estate. • The most important chattel real is an estate for years in land, which is considered a chattel because it lacks the indefiniteness of time essential to real property.

local chattel. Personal property that is affixed to land; FIXTURE.

chattel paper. (1935) A writing that shows both a monetary obligation and a security interest in or a lease of specific goods. UCC § 9-102(1)(11). • Chattel paper is generally used in a consumer transaction when the consumer buys goods on credit. The consumer typically promises to pay for the goods by executing a promissory note, and the seller retains a security interest in the goods.

electronic chattel paper. (1998) Chattel paper evidenced by a record or records consisting of information stored in an electronic medium and retrievable in perceivable form. UCC § 9-102(a)(31).

tangible chattel paper. Chattel paper evidenced by a record or records consisting of information inscribed on a tangible medium. UCC § 9-102(a)(78).

cheating. (16c) The fraudulent obtaining of another's property by means of a false symbol or token, or by other illegal practices.

cheating by false pretenses. (1827) The intentional obtaining of both the possession and ownership of money, goods, wares, or merchandise by means of misrepresentations, with the intent to defraud.

check, *n.* (18c) A draft signed by the maker or drawer, drawn on a bank, payable on demand, and unlimited in negotiability. • Under UCC § 3-104(f), an instrument may be a check even though it is described on its face by another term, such as "money order."

bad check. (1856) A check that is not honored because the account either contains insufficient funds or does not exist.

blank check. (1819) A check signed by the drawer but left blank as to the payee or the amount, or both.

canceled check. (1839) A check bearing a notation that it has been paid by the bank on which it was drawn.

cashier's check. (1846) A check drawn by a bank on itself, payable to another person, and evidencing the payee's authorization to receive from the bank the amount of money represented by the check; a draft for which the drawer and drawee are the same bank, or different branches of the same bank.

certified check. (1841) A depositor's check drawn on a bank that guarantees the availability of funds for the check. • The guarantee may be by the drawee's signed agreement to pay the draft or by a notation on the check that it is certified.

crossed check. A check that has lines drawn across its face and writing that specifies the bank to which the check must be presented for payment. • The same effect is achieved by stamping the bank's name on the check. The check's negotiability at that bank is unaffected, but no other bank can honor it.

depository-transfer check. (1976) An unsigned, nonnegotiable check that is used by a bank to transfer funds from its branch to the collection bank.

e-check. A paper check that is supplied by a consumer to a payee (usu. a merchant) who uses the check to make an electronic funds transfer. • The payee electronically scans the check's magnetic-ink character-recognition coding to obtain the bank-routing, account, and serial numbers, then enters the amount of the check. This is usu., but not always, done at a point-of-sale terminal.

memorandum check. A check that a borrower gives to a lender for the amount of a short-term loan, with the understanding that it is not to be presented for payment but will be redeemed by the borrower when the loan falls due.

open check. A check that may be cashed by any bank.

personal check. A check drawn on a person's own account.

postdated check. A check that bears a date after the date of its issue and is payable on or after the stated date.

raised check. (1867) A check whose face amount has been increased, usu. without the knowledge of the issuer — an act that under the UCC is considered an alteration. UCC § 3-407.

registered check. A check purchased at a bank and drawn on bank funds that have been set aside to pay that check.

stale check. (1899) A check that has been outstanding for an unreasonable time — more than six months under the UCC. • Banks in jurisdictions adopting the UCC may choose not to honor such a check. UCC § 4-404.

teller's check. A draft drawn by a bank on another bank or payable at or through a bank.

traveler's check. A cashier's check that must be signed by the purchaser at the time of purchase and countersigned when cashed. UCC § 3-104(i).

check, *vb.* (14c) **1.** To control or restrain <handcuffs checked the defendant's movement>. **2.** To verify or audit <an accountant checked the invoices>. **3.** To investigate <the police checked the suspect's story>. • In this sense, *check* is typically used with *up*, *on*, or *out*. **4.** To leave for safekeeping with an attendant <the diner checked her coat at the door>.

check-kiting. (1892) The illegal practice of writing a check against a bank account with insufficient funds to cover the check, in the hope that the funds from a previously deposited check will reach the account before the bank debits the amount of the outstanding check.

check-off system. The procedure by which an employer deducts union dues directly from the employees' wages and remits those dues to the union.

checks and balances. (18c) The theory of governmental power and functions whereby each branch of government has the ability to counter the actions of any other branch, so that no single branch can control the entire government.

***Chevron* deference.** A two-part test under which a court will uphold a federal agency's construction of a federal statute if (1) the statute is ambiguous or does not address the question at issue, and (2) the agency's interpretation of the statute is reasonable. *Chevron U.S.A., Inc. v. Natural Res. Def. Council, Inc.*, 467 U.S. 837, 842–43, 104 S.Ct. 2778, 2781–82 (1984).

Chicago Board of Trade. The commodities exchange where futures contracts in a large number of agricultural products are made. — Abbr. CBT; CBOT.

Chicago Board Options Exchange. The predominant organized marketplace in the United States for trading options. — Abbr. CBOE.

chicanery (shi-**kay**-nər-ee), *n.* (17c) Trickery; deception. — **chicanerous,** *adj.*

chief, *n.* **1.** A person who is put above the rest; the leader <chief of staff>. **2.** The principal or most important part or position <commander-in-chief>. — **chief,** *adj.*

chief executive officer. (1854) A corporation's highest-ranking administrator, who manages the firm day by day and reports to the board of directors. — Abbr. CEO.

chief financial officer. The executive in charge of making a company's accounting and fiscal decisions. — Abbr. CFO.

chief information officer. The executive who supervises a company's informational infrastructure, including the system for retaining and destroying records. — Abbr. CIO.

Chief Justice of the United States. The formal title of the officer who is the Chief Justice of the Supreme Court of the United States. — Often shortened to *the Chief Justice*.

chief operating officer. A manager who supervises a company's day-to-day operations and who usu. reports to the chief executive officer. — Abbr. COO.

child. (bef. 12c) **1.** A person under the age of majority. **2.** *Hist.* At common law, a person who has not reached the age of 14. **3.** A boy or girl; a young person. **4.** A son or daughter. **5.** A baby or fetus. Pl. **children.**

abused child. A child who has been subjected to physical or mental neglect or harm.

adopted child. A child who has become the son or daughter of a parent or parents by virtue of legal or equitable adoption; adoptee.

afterborn child. (18c) A child born after execution of a will or after the time in which a class gift closes.

battered child. A child upon whom physical or sexual abuse has been inflicted, usu. by a relative, caregiver, or close family friend.

child with disabilities. Under the Individuals with Disabilities Education Act, a child who needs special-education or related services because of (1) mental retardation, (2) a hearing, language, or visual impairment, (3) a serious emotional disturbance, or (4) another health impairment or specific learning disability.

delinquent child. (1902) A child who has committed an offense that would be a crime if committed by an adult. • A delinquent child may not be subject to the jurisdiction of the juvenile court if the child is under a statutory age.

deprived child. A child who (1) lacks proper parental care or control, subsistence, education, or other care and control for his or her physical, mental, or emotional well-being, (2) has been placed for care or adoption in violation of the law, (3) has been abandoned, or (4) is without a parent, guardian, or legal custodian. Uniform Juvenile Delinquency Act, 18 USCA §§ 5031 et seq.

foster child. (12c) A child whose care and upbringing are entrusted to an adult other than the child's natural or adoptive parents, usu. by an agency.

illegitimate child. (17c) A child who was not conceived or born in lawful wedlock, nor later legitimated.

incorrigible child. (17c) A child who habitually refuses to obey his or her parents or guardians.

intended child. The child who is intended to result from a surrogacy contract.

legitimate child. (17c) **1.** At common law, a child conceived or born in lawful wedlock. **2.** Modernly, a child conceived or born in lawful wedlock, or legitimated either by the parents' later marriage or by a declaration or judgment of legitimation.

natural child. (16c) **1.** A child by birth, as distinguished from an adopted child. **2.** A child that is genetically related to the mother and father as opposed to a child conceived by donor insemination or by egg donation. **3.** *Archaic.* An illegitimate child, usu. one acknowledged by the father.

neglected child. (17c) **1.** A child whose parents or legal custodians are unfit to care for him or her because of cruelty, immorality, or incapacity. **2.** A child whose parents or legal custodians refuse to provide the necessary care and medical services for the child.

posthumous child. (17c) A child born after a parent's death. • Ordinarily, the phrase *posthumous child* suggests one born after the father's death. But in at least one case, a legally dead pregnant woman was kept on life-support machines until the child could be safely delivered; so it is possible for a mother's posthumous child to be born.

special-needs child. **1.** A child with medical problems or with a physical, mental, or emotional handicap. **2.** A child that is likely to be unadoptable because of medical problems or physical, mental, or emotional handicaps, or by reason of age or ethnic background.

stepchild. The child of one's spouse by a previous marriage. • A stepchild is generally not entitled to the same legal rights as a natural or adopted child. For example, a stepchild has no right to a share of an intestate stepparent's property.

unborn child. A child not yet born, esp. at the happening of some event.

child-abuse and -neglect reporting statute. *Family law.* A state law requiring certain persons, among them health-care providers, teachers, and child-care workers, to report suspected child abuse.

child endangerment. (1981) The placing of a child in a place or position that exposes him or her to danger to life or health.

child labor. The employment of workers under the age of majority. • This term typically focuses on abusive practices such as exploitative factory work; slavery, sale, and trafficking in children; forced or compulsory labor such as debt bondage and serfdom; and the use of children in prostitution, pornography, drug-trafficking, or anything else that might jeopardize their health, safety, or morals.

child-labor law. (1904) A state or federal statute that protects children by prescribing the necessary working conditions for children in a workplace.

Child Protective Services. A governmental agency responsible for investigating allegations of child abuse and neglect, providing family services to the parent or guardian of a child who has been abused or neglected, and administering the foster-care program. — Abbr. CPS.

child support. (1939) *Family law.* **1.** A parent's legal obligation to contribute to the economic maintenance and education of a child until the age of majority, the child's emancipation before reaching majority, or the child's completion of secondary education. • The obligation is enforceable both civilly and criminally. **2.** In a custody or divorce action, the money legally owed by one parent to the other for the expenses incurred for children of the marriage. • The right to child support is the child's right and cannot be waived, and any divorce-decree provision waiving child support is void.

decretal child support. Child support provided for in a divorce decree or modification order.

child-support-enforcement agency. *Family law.* A governmental agency that helps custodial parents collect child support.

child-support guidelines. *Family law.* Statutory provisions that govern the amount of child support that an obligor parent must pay.

child work. A minor's salutary employment, esp. within the family. • This term is sometimes used in contrast to *child labor*, the idea being that child work within the family unit can be a positive experience.

chill, *vb.* To inhibit or discourage <chill one's free-speech rights>.

chilling a sale. (1881) The act of bidders or others who combine or conspire to discourage others from attempting to buy an item so that they might buy the item themselves for a lower price.

chilling effect. (1952) **1.** *Constitutional law.* The result of a law or practice that seriously discourages the exercise of a constitutional right, such as the right to appeal or the right of free speech. **2.** Broadly, the result when any practice is discouraged.

Chinese Wall. Ethical wall.

chirograph (kɪ-rə-**graf**), *n.* **1.** *Civil law.* A handwritten instrument. **2.** A written deed, subscribed and witnessed. — **chirographic,** *adj.*

chit. (18c) **1.** A signed voucher for money received or owed, usu. for food, drink, or the like. **2.** A slip of paper with writing on it.

choate (**koh**-it *or* -ayt), *adj.* (1878) **1.** Complete in and of itself. **2.** Having ripened or become perfected. Cf. INCHOATE. — **choateness,** *n.*

choice of law. (1900) The question of which jurisdiction's law should apply in a given case.

choice-of-law clause. (1957) A contractual provision by which the parties designate the jurisdiction whose law will govern any disputes that may arise between the parties.

chop-shop, *n. Criminal law.* A garage where stolen automobiles are dismantled so that their parts can be sold separately.

chose (shohz), *n.* [French] (17c) A thing, whether tangible or intangible; a personal article; a chattel.

chose in action. (17c) **1.** A proprietary right in personam, such as a debt owed by another person, a share in a joint-stock company, or a claim for damages in tort. **2.** The right to bring an action to recover a debt, money, or thing. **3.** Personal property that one person owns but another person possesses, the owner being able to regain possession through a lawsuit.

churn, burn, and bury, *vb.* (Of a stockbroker) to make numerous risky trades in (an account) and, as a result, squander the customer's money. • The term denotes the action involved in particularly reckless churning.

churning, *n.* (1953) **1.** *Securities.* A stockbroker's excessive trading of a customer's account to earn more commissions rather than to further the customer's interests; an abuse of a customer's confidence for personal gain by frequent and numerous transactions, disproportionate to the size and nature of the customer's account. • Under securities laws, the practice is illegal — a violation of § 10(b) of the Exchange Act (15 USCA § 78j(b)). But because the fraud is the activity as a whole and there is no communication between the broker and the customer about a specific sale of securities, there is not normally a right of action for fraud based on churning. **2.** *Tax.* A transfer of property that does not result in a significant change of ownership or use of the property, usu. to make the property eligible for amortization or a more favorable method of depreciation. — **churn,** *vb.*

CIA. *abbr.* (1951) Central Intelligence Agency.

CIF. *abbr.* Cost, insurance, and freight.

CIO. *abbr.* **1.** The Congress of Industrial Organizations, which merged with the AFL in 1955. **2.** Chief information officer.

circa (**sər**-kə), *prep.* [Latin] (1861) About or around (a date, esp. an ancient one); approximately. — Abbr. ca.; c.

circuit, *n.* (15c) **1.** A judicial division in which hearings occur at several locations, as a result of which judges often travel to different locations. **2.** A judicial division of the United States — that is, one of the 13 circuits into which the U.S. courts of appeals are organized. 28 USCA § 41.

circuit mediator. An attorney-employee of a U.S. court of appeals who mediates civil cases, usu. before oral argument.

circuit-riding, *n. Hist.* The practice of a judge's traveling within a legislatively defined circuit to hear cases in one place for a time, then another, and so on.

circuity of action. (17c) A procedure allowing duplicative lawsuits, leading to unnecessarily lengthy and indirect litigation, as when a defendant fails to bring a counterclaim, but later brings a separate action to recover what could have been awarded in the original lawsuit. • Civil-procedure rules have eliminated many problems associated with circuity of action.

circumstance, *n.* (*often pl.*) (13c) An accompanying or accessory fact, event, or condition, such as a piece of evidence that indicates the probability of an event. — **circumstantial,** *adj.*

aggravating circumstance. (17c) **1.** A fact or situation that increases the degree of liability or culpability for a criminal act. **2.** A fact or situation that relates to a criminal offense or defendant and that is considered by the court in imposing punishment (esp. a death sentence).

attendant circumstance. A fact that is situationally relevant to a particular event or occurrence. • A fact-finder often reviews the attendant circumstances of a crime to learn, for example, the perpetrator's motive or intent.

exigent circumstances. (1906) **1.** A situation that demands unusual or immediate action and that may allow people to circumvent usual procedures, as when a neighbor breaks through a window of a burning house to save someone inside. **2.** A situation in which a police officer must take immediate action to effectively make an arrest, search, or seizure for which probable cause exists, and thus may do so without first obtaining a warrant. • Exigent circumstances may exist if (1) a person's life or safety is threatened, (2) a suspect's escape is imminent, or (3) evidence is about to be removed or destroyed.

extraordinary circumstances. (17c) A highly unusual set of facts that are not commonly associated with a particular thing or event.

incriminating circumstance. (1885) A fact or situation showing either that a crime was committed or that a particular person committed it.

mitigating circumstance. (17c) **1.** A fact or situation that does not justify or excuse a wrongful act or offense but that reduces the degree of culpability and thus may reduce the damages (in a civil case) or the punishment (in a criminal case). **2.** A fact or situation that does not bear on the question of a defendant's guilt but that is considered by the court in imposing punishment and esp. in lessening the severity of a sentence. **3.** *Contracts.* An unusual or unpredictable event that prevents performance, such as a labor strike.

circumvention. *Copyright.* The act of bypassing, avoiding, removing, deactivating, or impairing a technological measure or device that controls access to a work protected by U.S. copyright law.

CIT. *abbr.* Court of International Trade.

citable, *adj.* Authorized by a court to be used as legal precedent. • In general, published opinions are citable, but unpublished ones are not. — Also written *citeable.*

citation, *n.* (13c) **1.** A court-issued writ that commands a person to appear at a certain time and place to do something demanded in the writ, or to show cause for not doing so. **2.** A police-issued order to appear before a judge on a given date to defend against a stated charge, such as a traffic violation. **3.** A reference to a legal precedent or authority, such as a case, statute, or treatise, that either substantiates or contradicts a given position.

parallel citation. (1911) An additional reference to a case that has been reported in more than one reporter. • For example, whereas a *Bluebook* citation reads "*Morgan v. United States,* 304 U.S. 1 (1938)," the same reference including parallel citations reads "*Morgan v. United States,* 304 U.S. 1, 58 S.Ct. 773, 82 L.Ed. 1129 (1938)," in which the main citation is to the *U.S. Reports* and the parallel citations are to the *Supreme Court Reporter* and to the *Lawyer's Edition.*

pinpoint citation. (1961) The page on which a quotation or relevant passage appears, as opposed to the page on which a case or article begins. • For example, the number 217 is the pinpoint citation in *Baker v. Carr,* 369 U.S. 186, 217 (1962).

citation order. The appropriate ranking of the various authorities marshaled in support of a legal proposition.

citator (sI-tay-tər). A catalogued list of cases, statutes, and other legal sources showing the subsequent history and current precedential value of those sources. • Citators allow researchers to verify the authority of a precedent and to find additional sources relating to a given subject. The two most popular are Shepard's and KeyCite.

cite, *vb.* (15c) **1.** To summon before a court of law <the witness was cited for contempt>. **2.** To refer to or adduce as precedent or authority <counsel then cited the appropriate statutory provision>. **3.** To commend or honor <the soldier was cited for bravery>.

citizen, *n.* (14c) **1.** A person who, by either birth or naturalization, is a member of a political community, owing allegiance to the community and being entitled to enjoy all its civil rights and protections; a member of the civil state, entitled to all its privileges.

natural-born citizen. A person born within the jurisdiction of a national government.

naturalized citizen. A foreign-born person who attains citizenship by law.

2. For diversity-jurisdiction purposes, a corporation that was incorporated within a state or has its principal place of business there. 28 USCA § 1332(c)(1).

citizenship, *n.* **1.** The status of being a citizen. **2.** The quality of a person's conduct as a member of a community.

Citizenship Clause. (1896) The clause of the U.S. Constitution providing that all persons born or naturalized in the United States are citizens of the United States and the state they reside in. U.S. Const. amend. XIV, § 1, cl. 1.

citizen suit. An action under a statute giving citizens the right to sue violators of the law (esp. environmental law) and to seek injunctive relief and penalties.

city. 1. A municipal corporation, usu. headed by a mayor and governed by a city council; a municipality of the highest grade. **2.** The territory within a city's corporate limits. **3.** Collectively, the people who live in this territory.

city attorney. (1837) An attorney employed by a city to advise it and represent it in legal matters.

city council. A city's legislative body, usu. responsible for passing ordinances, levying taxes, appropriating funds, and generally administering city government.

city manager. A local official appointed to manage and administer the executive affairs of a municipality in accordance with the policies established by the city council or other governing body.

civic, *adj.* (1656) **1.** Of or relating to citizenship or a particular citizen <civic responsibilities>. **2.** Of or relating to a city <civic center>.

civil, *adj.* (14c) **1.** Of or relating to the state or its citizenry <civil rights>. **2.** Of or relating to private rights and remedies that are sought by action or suit, as distinct from criminal proceedings <civil litigation>. **3.** Of or relating to any of the modern legal systems derived from Roman law <Louisiana is a civil-law jurisdiction>.

civil-authority clause. *Insurance.* A clause, esp. in a fire-insurance policy, insuring against damages caused by firefighters, police, or other civil authority.

civil code. (18c) **1.** A comprehensive and systematic legislative pronouncement of the whole private, noncommercial law in a legal system of the continental civil-law tradition. **2.** (*caps.*) The code that embodies the law of France, from which a great part of the Louisiana civil code is derived. — Abbr. CC. **3.** A codification of noncriminal statutes.

civil commitment. (1945) **1.** A commitment of a person who is ill, incompetent, drug-addicted, or the like, as contrasted with a criminal sentence. **2.** A public demonstration by two people of their intent to be bound together in a marriage-like relationship. • The demonstration is usu. in the form of a ceremony, often identical to a wedding, but the relationship is usu. not legally recognized and can be dissolved without legal formalities. **3.** A residential program characterized by intense and strict supervision of sex offenders who have completed their prison sentences but are found to be likely to commit more sex crimes.

civil commotion. (16c) A public uprising by a large number of people who, acting together, cause harm to people or property. • A civil commotion usu. involves many more people than a riot.

civil defense. 1. The practice of protecting civilians from dangers caused by hostilities or disasters and helping them recover from the immediate effects of such events. **2.** The policies that underlie this practice.

civil disobedience. (1866) A deliberate but nonviolent act of lawbreaking to call attention to a particular law or set of laws believed by the actor to be of questionable legitimacy or morality.

civil disorder. (18c) A public disturbance involving three or more people who commit violent acts that cause immediate danger or injury to people or property.

civilization. (18c) The transformation of a criminal matter to a civil one by law or judgment.

civil justice. (16c) The methods by which a society redresses civil wrongs.

civil law. (14c) **1.** (*usu. cap.*) One of the two prominent legal systems in the Western world, originally administered in the Roman Empire and still influential in continental Europe, Latin America, Scotland, and Louisiana, among other parts of the world. **2.** Roman law. **3.** The body of law imposed by the state, as opposed to moral law. **4.** The law of civil or private rights, as opposed to criminal law or administrative law. — Abbr. CL.

civil liberty. (*usu. pl.*) (17c) Freedom from undue governmental interference or restraint. • This term usu. refers to freedom of speech, freedom of the press, freedom of religion, freedom of association, and other liberties associated with the Bill of Rights.

civil procedure. (18c) **1.** The body of law — usu. rules enacted by the legislature or courts — governing the methods and practices used in civil litigation. **2.** A particular method or practice used in carrying on civil litigation in a particular jurisdiction.

civil right. (*usu. pl.*) (17c) **1.** The individual rights of personal liberty guaranteed by the Bill of Rights and by the 13th, 14th, 15th, and 19th Amendments, as well as by legislation such as the Voting Rights Act. • Civil rights include esp. the right to vote, the right of due process, and the right of equal protection under the law. **2.** CIVIL LIBERTY.

civil-rights act. (1867) One of several federal statutes enacted after the Civil War (1861–1865) and, much later, during and after the civil-rights movement of the 1950s and 1960s, to implement and give further force to the basic rights guaranteed by the Constitution, and esp. prohibiting discrimination in employment and education on the basis of race, sex, religion, color, or age.

civil service, *n.* **1.** The administrative branches of a government. **2.** The group of people employed by these branches. — **civil servant,** *n.*

civil-service reform. The use of business principles and methods instead of the spoils system in the conduct of the civil service, esp. in awarding contracts and appointing officials.

civil union. *Family law.* A marriage-like relationship, often between members of the same sex, recognized by civil authorities within a jurisdiction.

C.J. *abbr.* **1.** Chief justice. **2.** Chief judge. **3.** Circuit judge. **4.** Corpus juris.

CJC. *abbr.* Code of Judicial Conduct.

CJE. *abbr.* Continuing judicial education.

C.J.S. *abbr. Corpus Juris Secundum.* — Also written CJS.

CL. *abbr.* Civil law.

***Claflin*-trust principle.** The doctrine that a trust cannot be terminated by the beneficiaries if the termination would defeat one of the settlor's material purposes in establishing the trust, even if all the beneficiaries seek its termination.

claim, *n.* (13c) **1.** The aggregate of operative facts giving rise to a right enforceable by a court. **2.** The assertion of an existing right; any right to payment or to an equitable remedy, even if contingent or provisional. **3.** A demand for money, property, or a legal remedy to which one asserts a right; esp., the part of a complaint in a civil action specifying what relief the plaintiff asks for.

stale claim. (18c) A claim that is barred by the statute of limitations or the defense of laches.

4. An interest or remedy recognized at law; the means by which a person can obtain a privilege, possession, or enjoyment of a right or thing; CAUSE OF ACTION (1).

ancillary claim. (1906) A claim that is collateral to, dependent on, or auxiliary to another claim, such as a state-law claim that is sufficiently related to a federal claim to permit federal jurisdiction over it. • The concept of ancillary federal jurisdiction is now contained in the supplemental-jurisdiction statute, 28 USCA § 1367.

colorable claim. **1.** A claim that is legitimate and that may reasonably be asserted, given the facts presented and the current law (or a reasonable and logical extension or modification of the current law). **2.** A claim in which the debtor and property holder are, as a matter of law, not adverse.

5. *Bankruptcy.* (1842) A right to payment or to an equitable remedy for breach of performance if the breach gives rise to a right to payment.

priority claim. An unsecured claim that, under bankruptcy law, must be paid before other unsecured claims.

secured claim. A claim held by a creditor who has a lien or a right of setoff against the debtor's property.

unsecured claim. **1.** A claim by a creditor who does not have a lien or a right of setoff against the debtor's property. **2.** A claim by a creditor to the extent that its lien on or right of setoff against the debtor's property is worth less than the amount of the debt.

6. *Patents.* PATENT CLAIM.

claim and delivery. (1842) A claim for the recovery of specific personal property wrongfully taken or detained, as well as for any damages caused by the taking or detention.

claimant, *n.* (15c) One who asserts a right or demand, esp. formally; esp., one who asserts a property interest in land, chattels, or tangible things.

claim check. A receipt obtained for bailed or checked property and surrendered by the holder when the bailee returns the property.

claim differentiation. *Patents.* A canon of construction presuming that each claim in a patent is different in scope and meaning from all other claims; the presumption that different terms in separate claims must have different meanings if one of the claims would otherwise be rendered superfluous.

claim dilution. *Bankruptcy.* The reduction in the likelihood that a debtor's claimants will be fully repaid, including considerations of the time value of money.

claim-jumping. 1. The extension of the borders of a mining claim to infringe on other areas or claims. **2.** The filing of a duplicate claim to take advantage of a flaw in the original claim.

claim of ownership. (1818) **1.** The possession of a piece of property with the intention of claiming it in hostility to the true owner. **2.** A party's manifest intention to take over land, regardless of title or right.

claim preclusion. Res judicata.

clandestine (klan-**des**-tin), *adj.* (16c) Secret or concealed, esp. for illegal or unauthorized purposes.

class, *n.* (17c) **1.** A group of people, things, qualities, or activities that have common characteristics or attributes.

protected class. A class of people who benefit from protection by statute, such as Title VII of the Civil Rights Act of 1964, which prohibits discrimination based on race, sex, national origin, or religion.

2. The order or rank in which people or things are arranged. **3.** A group of people, uncertain in number.

testamentary class (tes-tə-**men**-tə-ree *or* -tree). (1865) A group of beneficiaries who are uncertain in number but whose number will be ascertainable in the future, when each will take an equal or other proportionate share of the gift.

4. *Civil procedure.* A group of people who have a common legal position, so that all their claims can be efficiently adjudicated in a single proceeding.

opt-out class. A plaintiff class, certified under Federal Rule of Civil Procedure 23(b)(3), from which class members may choose to exclude themselves if they do not want to be bound by the decisions or settlements reached in the case. • Rule 23(e) permits courts to dismiss class members who request exclusion. Class members may wait until the settlement's terms are announced before choosing to opt out.

settlement class. (1971) Numerous similarly situated people for whom a claimant's representative and an adversary propose a contract specifying the payment terms for the class members' claims in exchange for the release of all claims against the adversary. • During the 1980s and 1990s, mass-tort defendants began using settlement classes as a means of foreclosing claims by some unknown number of existing and future claimants.

class action. (1909) A lawsuit in which the court authorizes a single person or a small group of people to represent the interests of a larger group. • Federal procedure has several prerequisites for maintaining a class action: (1) the class must be so large that individual suits would be impracticable, (2) there must be legal or factual questions common to the class, (3) the claims or defenses of the representative parties must be typical of those of the class, and (4) the representative parties must adequately protect the interests of the class. Fed. R. Civ. P. 23.

hybrid class action. (1937) *Hist.* A type of action in which the rights to be enforced were several and varied, but the object was to adjudicate claims that affected or might have affected the specific property in the action.

classification of patents. *Patents.* **1.** The sorting of inventions by type into broad classes and narrow subclasses, as an aid in patent searches. **2.** Any one of the several classes into which the inventions are sorted..

classified information. Data or material that, having been designated as secret or confidential, only a limited number of authorized persons may know about.

clause, *n.* (13c) A distinct section or provision of a legal document or instrument. — **clausal,** *adj.*

confidentiality clause. A clause prohibiting the parties to an agreement from disclosing to nonparties the terms of the agreement and, often, anything related to the formation of the agreement.

enabling clause. The part of a statute or constitution that gives governmental officials the power and authority to put the law into effect and to enforce it.

enacting clause. (17c) The part of a statute stating the legislative authority by which it is made and often the date when it will take effect.

nondisparagement clause. **1.** A contractual provision prohibiting the parties from publicly communicating anything negative about each other. **2.** *Family law.* A provision in a divorce decree, marital settlement agreement, parenting agreement, or similar document prohibiting either parent from criticizing the other parent in the presence of their child or children.

operative clause. A provision under an enacting or resolving clause; a provision that is not a mere recital or preamble.

partial-release clause. A provision in a mortgage or trust deed allowing a certain property or portions of a property to be removed from the effect of a lien in exchange for an agreed payment. • This clause is often found in mortgages or trust deeds for properties covered by blanket liens, such as subdivisions or condominiums.

clawback, *n.* (1953) **1.** Money taken back. **2.** The retrieval or recovery of tax allowances by additional forms of taxation. — **claw back,** *vb.*

claw-back option. The right to require repayment of funds earmarked for a specific purpose if the funds are disbursed for another purpose or in a manner inconsistent with the document governing the specified purpose.

Clayton Act. A federal statute — enacted in 1914 to amend the Sherman Act — that prohibits price discrimination, tying arrangements, and exclusive-dealing contracts, as well as mergers and interlocking directorates, if their effect might substantially lessen competition or create a monopoly in any line of commerce. 15 USCA §§ 12–27.

Cl. Ct. *abbr.* Court of Claims.

CLE. *abbr.* Continuing legal education.

clean-hands doctrine. (1914) The principle that a party cannot seek equitable relief or assert an equitable defense if that party has violated an equitable principle, such as good faith. • Such a party is described as having "unclean hands."

clean-slate rule. *Criminal procedure.* The doctrine that the double-jeopardy prohibition does not apply to the retrial of a defendant who appealed and obtained a reversal of an earlier conviction.

clear, *adj.* **1.** Free from encumbrances or claims. **2.** Free from doubt; sure. **3.** Unambiguous.

clear, *vb.* (15c) **1.** To acquit or exonerate. **2.** (Of a drawee bank) to pay (a check or draft) out of funds held on behalf of the maker. **3.** (Of a check or draft) to be paid by the drawee bank out of funds held on behalf of the maker.

clear-and-present-danger test. (1939) *Constitutional law.* The doctrine allowing the government to restrict the First Amendment freedoms of speech and press if necessary to prevent immediate and severe danger to interests that the government may lawfully protect. • This test was formulated by Justice Oliver Wendell Holmes in *Schenck v.*

United States, 249 U.S. 47, 39 S.Ct. 247 (1919).

***Clearfield Trust* doctrine.** (1957) The doctrine describing the federal courts' power to make federal common law when there is both federal lawmaking power to do so and a strong federal interest in a nationally uniform rule. *Clearfield Trust Co. v. United States*, 318 U.S. 363, 63 S.Ct. 573 (1943).

clearinghouse. (18c) **1.** A place where banks exchange checks and drafts and settle their daily balances; an association of banks or other payors regularly clearing items. See UCC § 4-104(a)(4). **2.** A stock-and-commodity exchange where the daily transactions of the brokers are cleared. **3.** Any place for the exchange of specialized information.

clearly-erroneous standard. (1950) The standard of review that an appellate court usu. applies in judging a trial court's treatment of factual issues. • Under this standard, a judgment will be upheld unless the appellate court is left with the firm conviction that an error has been committed.

clear-reflection-of-income standard. (1972) *Tax.* An income-accounting method that the IRS can force on a taxpayer if the method used does not clearly reflect income. IRC (26 USCA) § 446(b).

clemency (klem-ən-see), *n.* (15c) Mercy or leniency; esp., the power of the President or a governor to pardon a criminal or commute a criminal sentence. — **clement (klem**-ənt), *adj.*

clerk, *n.* (bef. 12c) **1.** A public official whose duties include keeping records or accounts.

city clerk. A public official who records a city's official proceedings and vital statistics.

town clerk. An officer who keeps the records, issues calls for town meetings, and performs the duties of a secretary to the town's political organization.

2. A court officer responsible for filing papers, issuing process, and keeping records of court proceedings as generally specified by rule or statute.

district clerk. The clerk of a district court within a state or federal system.

3. An employee who performs general office work. **4.** A law student or recent law-school graduate who helps a lawyer or judge with legal research, writing, and other tasks. **5.** A lawyer who assists a judge with research, writing, and case management.

elbow clerk. An individual judge's personal clerk; esp., one who works closely with the judge. • The name derives from the metaphoric expectation that the clerk is always at the judge's elbow.

pool clerk. A clerk who performs a range of duties for several judges or for the entire court.

6. SECRETARY (3).

reading clerk. A legislative officer charged with reading bills to the body.

clerk, *vb.* To work as a clerk (in sense 4 or 5).

clerkship. (1836) **1.** An internship in which a law student or recent law-school graduate assists a lawyer or judge with legal writing, research, and other tasks. **2.** *Hist.* A law student's employment as an attorney's apprentice before gaining admission to the bar. • Until shortly before World War II, a person could be admitted to the bar in many states without attending law school merely by passing the bar exam.

client, *n.* (14c) A person or entity that employs a professional for advice or help in that professional's line of work. — **cliental,** *adj.*

client control. The influence that a lawyer has over his or her client, esp. in relation to positions taken, decisions made, and general conduct with other parties and their attorneys. • Lawyers whose clients behave irrationally, as by acting vindictively or refusing even generous settlement offers, are said to have little or no client control.

client trust account. A bank account, usu. interest-bearing, in which a lawyer deposits money belonging to a client (e.g., money received from a client's debtor, from the settlement of a client's case, or from the client for later use in a business transaction).

clinical legal studies. (1972) Law-school training in which students participate in actual cases under the supervision of a practicing attorney or law professor.

close, *n.* (14c) **1.** An enclosed portion of land. **2.** The interest of a person in a particular piece of land, enclosed or not. **3.** The final price of a stock at the end of the exchange's trading day.

close, *vb.* (13c) **1.** To conclude; to bring to an end. **2.** To conclude discussion or negotiation about.

closed, *adj.* (13c) **1.** (Of a class or organization) confined to a limited number <a closed mass-tort class>. **2.** (Of a proceeding or gathering) conducted in secrecy <a closed hearing>.

close debate. *Parliamentary law.* To pass a motion that ends debate and amendment of a pending question or series of questions.

closed-shop contract. A labor agreement requiring an employer to hire and retain only union members and to discharge nonunion members.

closed source, *adj.* Of or related to software that does not include the source code and cannot be modified without either damaging the program or violating the software developer's ownership rights. • Proprietary software is usu. closed source.

close nominations. *Parliamentary law.* To end nominations from the floor by passage of a motion.

closing. The final meeting between the parties to a transaction, at which the transaction is consummated; esp., in real estate, the final transaction between the buyer and seller, whereby the conveyancing documents are concluded and the money and property transferred.

closing argument. (1828) In a trial, a lawyer's final statement to the judge or jury before deliberation begins, in which the lawyer requests the judge or jury to consider the evidence and to apply the law in his or her client's favor.

closing costs. *Real estate.* The expenses that must be paid, usu. in a lump sum at closing, apart from the purchase price and interest. • These may include taxes, title insurance, and attorney's fees.

closing of estate. (1843) *Wills & estates.* The completion of the administration of a decedent's estate, brought about by the administrator's distribution of estate assets, payment of taxes, and filing of necessary accounts with the probate court.

closing statement. (1875) **1.** CLOSING ARGUMENT. **2.** A written breakdown of the costs involved in a particular real-estate transaction, usu. prepared by a lender or an escrow agent.

cloture (**kloh**-chər), *n.* (1871) The procedure of ending debate in a legislative body and calling for an immediate vote. — Also spelled *closure.* — **cloture,** *vb.*

cloud on title. A defect or potential defect in the owner's title to a piece of land arising from some claim or encumbrance, such as a lien, an easement, or a court order.

CLS. *abbr.* Critical legal studies.

Club Fed. *Slang.* A low-security federal prison, usu. for white-collar criminals, that has a comparatively informal, relaxed atmosphere.

CMO. *abbr.* **1.** Case-management order. **2.** Collateralized mortgage obligation.

CMR. *abbr.* **1.** Court of Military Review. **2.** *Court-Martial Reports.*

co-. *prefix.* Jointly or together with <coowner>.

co. *abbr.* (*usu. cap.*) **1.** Company. **2.** County.

c/o. *abbr.* Care of.

COA. *abbr.* **1.** Contract of affreightment. **2.** Certificate of appealability. **3.** Cause of action.

coadjutor (koh-ə-**joo**-tər *or* koh-**aj**-ə-tər), *n.* (15c) A coworker or assistant — **coadjutor,** *adj.*

Coase Theorem (kohs). (1968) A proposition in economics describing the relationship between legal rules and economic efficiency. • The theorem, innovated by Ronald Coase, holds that if there are no transaction costs — such as the costs of bargaining or acquiring information — then any legal rule will produce an efficient result.

coastal-state control. *Maritime law.* The exercise of authority under international conventions for a state to stop, board, inspect, and when necessary detain vessels that are under foreign flags while they are navigating in the coastal state's territorial waters.

Coast Guard jurisdiction. The law-enforcement authority of the United States Coast Guard over the high seas and navigable waters over which the United States has jurisdiction, including the powers of stopping, searching, and seizing property, and arresting persons.

COBRA (**koh**-brə). *abbr.* CONSOLIDATED OMNIBUS BUDGET RECONCILIATION ACT OF 1985.

coconspirator. (1837) A person who engages in a criminal conspiracy with another; a fellow conspirator.

unindicted coconspirator. (1936) A person who has been identified by law enforcement as a member of a conspiracy, but who has not been named in the fellow conspirator's indictment. • Prosecutors typically name someone an unindicted coconspirator because any statement that the unindicted coconspirator has made in the course and furtherance of the conspiracy is admissible against the indicted defendants.

coconspirator's exception. (1954) An exception to the hearsay rule whereby one conspirator's acts and statements, if made during and in furtherance of the conspiracy, are admissible against a codefendant even if the statements are made in the codefendant's absence. See Fed. R. Evid. 801(d)(2)(E).

C.O.D. *abbr.* (1859) **1.** Cash on delivery; collect on delivery. **2.** Costs on delivery. **3.** Cash on demand.

code. (18c) A complete system of positive law, carefully arranged and officially promulgated; a systematic collection or revision of laws, rules, or regulations <the Uniform Commercial Code>. • Strictly, a code is a compilation not just of existing statutes, but also of much of the unwritten law on a subject, which is newly enacted as a complete system of law.

Code Adam. A procedure used by offices, stores, and other places to alert people to look for a child who has become separated from a parent or guardian and has been reported as missing somewhere within the building. • The term is a memorial to 6-year-old Adam Walsh of Florida, who in 1981 was abducted from a department store and murdered.

Code Civil. The code embodying the civil law of France, dating from 1804.

codefendant. (17c) One of two or more defendants sued in the same litigation or charged with the same crime.

code of conduct. (1919) A written set of rules governing the behavior of specified groups, such as lawyers, government employees, or corporate employees.

Code of Federal Regulations. The annual collection of executive-agency regulations published in the daily Federal Register, combined with previously issued regulations that are still in effect. — Abbr. CFR.

Code of Judicial Conduct. The body of standards governing the professional ethics and behavior of judges.

Code of Military Justice. The collection of substantive and procedural rules governing the discipline of members of the armed forces. 10 USCA §§ 801 et seq.

Code of Professional Responsibility. See Model Code of Professional Responsibility.

code state. *Hist.* A state that, at a given time, had already procedurally merged law and equity, so that equity was no longer administered as a separate system; a state in which there is only one form of civil action. • This term was current primarily in the early to mid-20th century.

codex (**koh**-deks). [Latin] *Archaic.* **1.** A code, esp. the Justinian Code. **2.** A book written on paper or parchment; esp., a volume of an ancient text.

codicil (**kod**-ə-səl *or* -sil). (15c) A supplement or addition to a will, not necessarily disposing of the entire estate but modifying, explaining, or otherwise qualifying the will in some way. • When admitted to probate, the codicil becomes a part of the will. — **codicillary** (kod-ə-**sil**-ə-ree), *adj.*

codification (kod-ə-fi-**kay**-shən), *n.* (1817) **1.** The process of compiling, arranging, and systematizing the laws of a given jurisdiction, or of a discrete branch of the law, into an ordered code. **2.** The code that results from this process. — **codify** (**kod**-ə-fɪ), *vb.* — **codifier** (**kod**-ə-fɪ-ər), *n.*

coemption (koh-**emp**-shən), *n.* (14c) The act of purchasing the entire quantity of any commodity. — **coemptional, coemptive,** *adj.*

coerce (koh-**ərs**), *vb.* To compel by force or threat.

coercion (koh-**ər**-zhən), *n.* (15c) **1.** Compulsion by physical force or threat of physical force. • An act that must be voluntary, such as signing a will, is not legally valid if done under coercion.

criminal coercion. Coercion intended to restrict another's freedom of action by: (1) threatening to commit a criminal act against that person; (2) threatening to accuse that person of having committed a criminal act; (3) threatening to expose a secret that either would subject the victim to hatred, contempt, or ridicule or would impair the victim's credit or goodwill, or (4) taking or withholding official action or causing an official to take or withhold action.

2. Conduct that constitutes the improper use of economic power to compel another to submit to the wishes of one who wields it. — **coercive,** *adj.* — **coercer,** *n.*

coexistence. *Int'l law.* The peaceful continuation of nations, peoples, or other entities or groups within an effective political-military equilibrium.

cogent (**koh**-jənt), *adj.* (17c) Compelling or convincing. — **cogency,** *n.*

cognate, *n.* (18c) One who is kin to another. — **cognate,** *adj.*

cognation (kog-**nay**-shən), *n.* (14c) Relationship by blood rather than by marriage; relationship arising through common descent from the same man and woman, whether the descent is traced through males or females. — **cognatic** (kog-**mat**-ik), *adj.*

cognitive test. (1955) *Criminal law.* A test of the defendant's ability to know certain things, specifically the nature of his or her conduct and whether the conduct was right or wrong. • This test is used in assessing whether a defendant may rely on an insanity defense.

cognizable (**kog**-ni- *or* kog-**nɪ**-zə-bəl), *adj.* (17c) **1.** Capable of being known or recognized. **2.** Capable of being identified as a group because of a common characteristic or interest that cannot be represented by others. **3.** Capable of being judicially tried or examined before a designated tribunal; within the court's jurisdiction.

cognizance (**kog**-ni-zəns), *n.* (14c) **1.** A court's right and power to try and to determine cases; jurisdiction. **2.** The taking of judicial or authoritative notice. **3.** Acknowledgment or admission of an alleged fact. **4.** *Common-law pleading.* In a replevin action, a plea by the defendant that the goods are held in bailment for another.

cognovit (kog-**noh**-vit). (18c) [Latin "he has conceded (a debt or an action)"] An acknowledgment of debt or liability in the form of a confessed judgment.

cognovit clause. (1925) A contractual provision by which a debtor agrees to jurisdiction in certain courts, waives notice requirements, and authorizes the entry of an adverse judgment in the event of a default or breach. • Cognovit clauses are outlawed or restricted in most states.

COGSA. **1.** *abbr.* Carriage of Goods by Sea Act. **2.** *Maritime law.* A country's enactment of the international convention popularly known as the Hague Rules.

cohabitation (koh-hab-ə-**tay**-shən), *n.* (15c) The fact or state of living together, esp. as partners in life, usu. with the suggestion of sexual relations. — **cohabit** (koh-**hab**-it), *vb.* — **cohabitative** (koh-**hab**-ə-tay-tiv), *adj.* — **cohabitant** (koh-**hab**-ə-tənt), *n.* — **cohabitor** (koh-**hab**-ə-tər), *n.*

illicit cohabitation. (18c) **1.** The offense committed by an unmarried man and woman who live together as husband and wife and engage in sexual intercourse. • This offense, where it still exists, is seldom prosecuted. **2.** The condition of a man and a woman who are not married to one another and live together in circumstances that make the arrangement questionable on grounds of social propriety, though not necessarily illegal.

cohort analysis (**koh**-hort). (1954) A method of measuring discrimination in the workplace by comparing, at several points in time, the pay and promotions of employees of different cognizable groups.

coif (koyf). (14c) *Hist.* **1.** A white linen headpiece formerly worn by serjeants at law (barristers of high standing) in common-law courts. **2.** The rank or order of serjeants at law.

Coinage Clause. (1863) The provision in the U.S. Constitution (art. I, § 8, cl. 5) granting to Congress the power to coin money.

coindictee. One of two or more persons who have been jointly indicted.

coinsurance clause. A provision in an insurance policy requiring a property owner to carry separate insurance up to an amount stated in the policy to qualify for full coverage.

coinsurer. An insurer who shares losses sustained under an insurance policy.

COLA. *abbr.* Cost-of-living adjustment.

cold blood. (18c) A killer's state of mind when committing a willful and premeditated homicide <a shooting in cold blood>.

collaborative law. A dispute-resolution method by which parties and their attorneys settle disputes using nonadversarial techniques to reach a binding agreement, with the understanding that if the parties cannot agree and choose to litigate instead, the attorneys involved in the negotiations will be disqualified from representing them any further.

collateral (kə-**lat**-ər-əl), *adj.* **1.** Supplementary; accompanying, but secondary and subordinate to <whether the accident victim was wearing a seat belt is a collateral issue>. **2.** Not direct in line, but on a parallel or diverging line of descent; of or relating to persons who are related by blood but are neither ancestors nor descendants <an uncle is in a collateral, not a direct, line>. — **collaterality** (kə-lat-ər-**al**-ə-tee), *n.*

collateral (kə-**lat**-ər-əl), *n.* (17c) **1.** A person collaterally related to a decedent. **2.** Property that is pledged as security against a debt; the property subject to a security interest or agricultural lien. See UCC § 9-102(a)(12).

cash collateral. Collateral consisting of cash, negotiable instruments, documents of title, securities, deposit accounts, or other cash equivalents. 11 USCA § 363(a).

cross-collateral. **1.** Security given by all parties to a contract. **2.** *Bankruptcy.* Bargained-for security that in addition to protecting a creditor's postpetition extension of credit protects the creditor's prepetition unsecured claims, which, as a result of such security, obtain priority over other creditors' prepetition unsecured claims. • Some courts allow this procedure, which is known as *cross-collateralization.*

collateral act. Any act (usu. excluding the payment of money) for which a bond or recognizance is given as security.

collateral attack. (1833) An attack on a judgment in a proceeding other than a direct appeal. • A petition for a writ of habeas corpus is one type of collateral attack.

collateral consequence. A penalty for committing a crime, in addition to the penalties included in the criminal sentence. • An example is the loss of a professional license. .

collateral-contract doctrine. (1947) The principle that in a dispute concerning a written contract, proof of a second (usu. oral) agreement will not be excluded under the parol-evidence rule if the oral agreement is independent of and not inconsistent with the written contract, and if the information in the oral agreement would not ordinarily be expected to be included in the written contract.

collateral estoppel (e-**stop**-əl). (1941) **1.** The binding effect of a judgment as to matters actually litigated and determined in one action on later controversies between the parties involving a different claim from that on which the original judgment was based. **2.** A doctrine barring a party from relitigating an issue determined against that party in an earlier action, even if the second action differs significantly from the first one.

administrative collateral estoppel. Estoppel that arises from a decision made by an agency acting in a judicial capacity.

defensive collateral estoppel. (1968) Estoppel asserted by a defendant to prevent a plaintiff from relitigating an issue previously decided against the plaintiff.

nonmutual collateral estoppel. Estoppel asserted either offensively or defensively by a nonparty to an earlier action to prevent a party to that earlier action from relitigating an issue determined against it.

offensive collateral estoppel. (1964) Estoppel asserted by a plaintiff to prevent a defendant from relitigating an issue previously decided against the defendant.

collateralize (kə-**lat**-ər-əl-ɪz), *vb.* (1941) **1.** To serve as collateral for. **2.** To make (a loan) secure with collateral. — **collateralization** (kə-lat-ər-əl-ə-**zay**-shən), *n.*

collateralized mortgage obligation. *Securities.* A bond secured by a group of mortgage obligations or pass-through securities and paid according to the payment schedule of its class (or *tranche*). — Abbr. CMO.

collateral matter. (17c) *Evidence.* Any matter on which evidence could not have been introduced for a relevant purpose. • If a witness has erred in testifying about a detail that is collateral to the relevant facts, then another party cannot call witnesses to contradict that point — cross-examination alone must suffice. Fed. R. Evid. 608(b).

collateral-negligence doctrine. (1941) The rule holding that one who engages an independent contractor is not liable for physical harm that the contractor causes if (1) the contractor's negligence consists solely of the improper manner in which the contractor's work is performed, (2) the risk of harm created is not normal to the work, and (3) the employer had no reason to contemplate the contractor's negligence when the contract was made.

collateral obligation. A liability undertaken by a person who becomes bound for another's debt.

collateral-order doctrine. (1950) A doctrine allowing appeal from an interlocutory order that conclusively determines an issue wholly separate from the merits of the action and effectively unreviewable on appeal from a final judgment.

collateral-source rule. (1951) *Torts.* The doctrine that if an injured party receives compensation for the injuries from a source independent of the tortfeasor, the payment should not be deducted from the damages that the tortfeasor must pay. • Insurance proceeds are the most common collateral source.

collation (kə-**lay**-shən), *n.* (14c) **1.** The comparison of a copy with its original to ascertain its correctness; the report of the officer who made the comparison. **2.** The taking into account of the value of advancements made by an intestate to his or her children so that the estate may be divided in accordance with the intestacy statute. — **collate** (kə-**layt**), *vb.* — **collator** (kə-**lay**-tər), *n.*

collectability. The ability of a judgment creditor to make a judgment debtor pay the amount of the judgment; the degree to which a judgment can be satisfied through collection efforts against the judgment debtor.

collection. *Banking.* The process through which an item (such as a check) passes in a payor bank.

collective bargaining. Negotiations between an employer and the representatives of organized employees to determine the conditions of employment, such as wages, hours, discipline, and fringe benefits.

collective-bargaining agreement. *Labor law.* A contract between an employer and a labor union regulating employment conditions, wages, benefits, and grievances. — Abbr. CBA.

collective punishment. (1872) A penalty inflicted on a group of persons without regard to individual responsibility for the conduct giving rise to the penalty. • Collective punishment was outlawed in 1949 by the Geneva Convention.

collision. *Maritime law.* **1.** The contact of two or more moving vessels. **2.** ALLISION.

colloquium (kə-**loh**-kwee-əm). (17c) **1.** The offer of extrinsic evidence to show that an allegedly defamatory statement referred to the plaintiff even though it did not explicitly mention the plaintiff.

2. The introductory averments in a plaintiff's pleading setting out all the special circumstances that make the challenged words defamatory. Pl. **colloquiums, colloquia.**

colloquy (**kol**-ə-kwee). (15c) Any formal discussion, such as an oral exchange between a judge, the prosecutor, the defense counsel, and a criminal defendant in which the judge ascertains the defendant's understanding of the proceedings and of the defendant's rights.

collusion (kə-**loo**-zhən), *n.* (14c) An agreement to defraud another or to do or obtain something forbidden by law. — **collude,** *vb.* — **collusive,** *adj.* — **colluder,** *n.*

colonial law. 1. Law governing a colony or colonies. **2.** The body of law in force in the 13 original U.S. colonies before the Declaration of Independence.

colon-semicolon form. *Patents.* A style of writing patent claims that uses a colon after the preamble and semicolons between every two elements.

colony, *n. Int'l law.* **1.** A dependent territorial entity subject to the sovereignty of an independent country, but considered part of that country for purposes of relations with third countries. **2.** A group of people who live in a new territory but retain ties with their parent country. **3.** The territory inhabited by such a group. — **colonize,** *vb.* — **colonial,** *adj.*

color, *n.* (13c) **1.** Appearance, guise, or semblance; esp., the appearance of a legal claim to a right, authority, or office. **2.** *Common-law pleading.* An apparent, but legally insufficient, right or ground of action, admitted in a defendant's pleading to exist for the plaintiff; esp., a plaintiff's apparent (and usu. false) right or title to property, the existence of which is pleaded by the defendant and then attacked as defective, as part of a confession and avoidance to remove the case from the jury by turning the issue from one of fact to one of law.

colorable, *adj.* (14c) **1.** (Of a claim or action) appearing to be true, valid, or right. **2.** Intended to deceive; counterfeit.

colorable imitation. *Trademarks.* Any mark, whether or not created with an intent to deceive, whose resemblance to a registered mark is likely to cause confusion or mistake.

color of authority. The appearance or presumption of authority sanctioning a public officer's actions.

color of law. (17c) The appearance or semblance, without the substance, of a legal right. • The term usu. implies a misuse of power made possible because the wrongdoer is clothed with the authority of the state. *State action* is synonymous with *color of [state] law* in the context of federal civil-rights statutes or criminal law.

color of office. The authority or power that is inherent in an office, esp. a public office. • Acts taken under the color of an office are vested with, or appear to be vested with, the authority entrusted to that office.

color of process. The appearance of validity and sufficiency surrounding a legal proceeding that is later found to be invalid.

color of title. (18c) A written instrument or other evidence that appears to establish title but does not in fact do so.

combatant (kəm-**bat**-ənt *or* **kom**-bə-tənt). (15c) *Int'l law.* A person who participates directly in hostilities. • "Legitimate" combatants are members of the armed forces or uniformed members of a militia or volunteer corps, under military command and subject to the laws of war.

enemy combatant (kəm-**bat**-ənt). A combatant captured and detained while serving in a hostile force during open warfare.

combination. 1. An alliance of individuals or corporations working together to accomplish a common (usu. economic) goal. **2.** Conspiracy.

combination in restraint of trade. *Antitrust.* An express or tacit agreement between two or more persons or entities designed to raise prices, reduce output, or create a monopoly.

comes now. *Archaic.* Traditionally, the standard commencement in pleadings <Comes now the plaintiff, Gilbert Lewis, by and through his attorneys of record, and would show unto the court the following>. • For a plural subject, the phrase is *come now* <Come now the plaintiffs, Bob and Louise Smith>. — Sometimes shortened to *comes* <Comes the State of Tennessee>.

comfort letter. 1. *Securities.* A letter from a certified public accountant certifying that no false or misleading information has been used in preparing a financial statement accompanying a securities offering. **2.** *Corporations.* A letter, esp. from a parent corporation on behalf of a subsidiary, stating its support (but short of a guarantee) for the activities and commitments of another corporation.

comity (kom-ə-tee). (16c) A practice among political entities (as nations, states, or courts of different jurisdictions), involving esp. mutual recognition of legislative, executive, and judicial acts.

Comity Clause. (1921) The clause of the U.S. Constitution giving citizens of one state the right to all privileges and immunities enjoyed by citizens of the other states. U.S. Const. art. IV, § 2, cl. 1.

comm. *abbr.* Commonwealth.

command. (14c) **1.** An order; a directive. **2.** In legal positivism, the sovereign's express desire that a person act or refrain from acting a certain way, combined with the threat of punishment for failure to comply. — **command,** *vb.*

commander-in-chief. (17c) **1.** One who holds supreme or highest command of armed forces. **2.** (*cap.*) The title of the U.S. President when acting as the constitutionally designated leader of the nation's military. U.S. Const. art. II, § 2.

Commander in Chief Clause. The clause of the U.S. Constitution appointing the President as supreme commander of the military. U.S. Const. art. II, § 2, cl. 1.

comment, *n.* (14c) **1.** NOTE (2). **2.** An explanatory statement made by the drafters of a particular statute, code section, or rule. — **commentator,** *n.*

comment on the evidence. (18c) A statement made to the jury by the judge or by counsel on the probative value of certain evidence. Fed. R. Evid. 105. • Lawyers typically make such comments in closing argument, and judges may make such comments in federal court. But most state-court judges are not permitted to do so when examining a witness, instructing the jury, and the like (in which case the comment is sometimes termed an *impermissible comment on the evidence*).

commerce. (16c) The exchange of goods and services, esp. on a large scale involving transportation between cities, states, and nations.

international commerce. Trade and other business activities between nations.

interstate commerce. (1843) Trade and other business activities between those located in different states; esp., traffic in goods and travel of people between states.

intrastate commerce. (1887) Commerce that begins and ends entirely within the borders of a single state.

Commerce Clause. (1868) U.S. Const. art. I, § 8, cl. 3, which gives Congress the exclusive power to regulate commerce among the states, with foreign nations, and with Indian tribes.

Dormant Commerce Clause. (1930) The constitutional principle that the Commerce Clause prevents state regulation of interstate commercial activity even when Congress has not acted under its Commerce Clause power to regulate that activity.

commerce power. Congress's constitutionally conferred power to regulate trade between the states.

commercial acre. *Property.* The amount of land left in a subdivided acre after deducting the amount dedicated to streets, sidewalks, utilities, etc. • The area of a commercial acre is always less than an actual acre.

commercial-activity exception. (1973) An exemption from the rule of sovereign immunity, permitting a claim against a foreign state to be adjudicated in the courts of another state if the claim arises from private acts undertaken by the foreign state, as opposed to the state's public acts.

commercial law. (18c) The substantive law dealing with the sale and distribution of goods, the financing of credit transactions on the security of the goods sold, and negotiable instruments. • Most American commercial law is governed by the Uniform Commercial Code.

commercially reasonable, *adj.* (1922) (Of a property sale) conducted in good faith and in accordance with commonly accepted commercial practice. • Under the UCC, a sale of collateral by a secured party must be done in a commercially reasonable manner, or the obligor's liability for any deficiency may be reduced or eliminated. See UCC § 9-610(b), 9-626.

commercially significant noninfringing use. *Intellectual property.* The routine use of a product in a way that does not infringe intellectual-property rights; the judicial test for determining whether the sale of a product amounts to contributory infringement.

commercial morality. Collectively, fair practices among competitors.

commercial tort claim. (1994) A claim arising in tort when the claimant is either (1) an organization, or (2) an individual whose claim arose in the course of the claimant's business or profession, and the claim does not include damages arising out of personal injury or death. UCC § 9-102(a)(13).

commercial unit. (1960) A unit of goods that by commercial usage is a single whole for purposes of sale and whose division materially impairs its character or value in the relevant market or in use. UCC § 2-105(6). • Under the UCC, "a commercial unit may be a single article (as a machine) or a set of articles (as a suite of furniture or an assortment of sizes) or a quantity (as a bale, gross, or carload) or any other unit treated in use or in the relevant market as a single whole." *Id.*

commingle, *vb.* (kə-**ming**-gəl). (17c) **1.** To put together (as funds or property) into one mass, as by mixing together a spouse's separate property with marital or community property, or mixing together the separate property of both spouses. **2.** (Of a fiduciary) to mix personal funds with those of a beneficiary or client. — Also spelled *comingle.* — **commingling** (kə-**ming**-gling), *n.*

commissary (**kom**-i-ser-ee), *n.* (14c) **1.** A person who is delegated or commissioned to perform some duty, usu. as a representative of a superior. **2.** A general store, esp. on a military base. **3.** A lunchroom. — **commissary,** *adj.*

commission, *n.* (14c) **1.** A warrant or authority, from the government or a court, that empowers the person named to execute official acts. **2.** The authority under which a person transacts business for another. **3.** A body of persons acting under lawful authority to perform certain public services.

public-service commission. A commission created by a legislature to regulate public utilities or public-service corporations.

4. The act of doing or perpetrating (as a crime). **5.** A fee paid to an agent or employee for a particular transaction, usu. as a percentage of the money received from the transaction.

commission del credere (del **kred**-ər-ay). (18c) The commission received by the seller's agent for guaranteeing a buyer's debt.

commissioner. (15c) **1.** A person who directs a commission; a member of a commission.

county commissioner. A county officer charged usu. with the management of the county's financial affairs, its police regulations, and its corporate business.

court commissioner. An officer appointed by the court esp. to hear and report facts, or to conduct judicial sales.

jury commissioner. An officer responsible for drawing and summoning the panels of potential jurors in a given county.

town commissioner. A member of the board of administrative officers charged with managing the town's business.

2. The administrative head of an organization, such as a professional sport.

commission plan. (1919) A form of municipal government whereby both legislative and executive power is vested in a small group of elected officials. • Today, commission plans are used in only a few cities.

commission to examine a witness. A judicial commission directing that a witness beyond the court's territorial jurisdiction be deposed.

commit, *vb.* **1.** To perpetrate (a crime). **2.** To send (a person) to prison or to a mental health facility, esp. by court order. **3.** *Parliamentary law.* Refer.

commitment, *n.* (14c) **1.** An agreement to do something in the future, esp. to assume a financial obligation. **2.** The act of entrusting or giving in charge. **3.** The act of confining a person in a prison, mental hospital, or other institution. **4.** The order directing an officer to take a person to a penal or mental institution.

diagnostic commitment. Pretrial or presentencing confinement of an individual, usu. to determine the individual's competency to stand trial or to determine the appropriate sentence to be rendered.

discretionary commitment. A commitment that a judge may or may not grant, depending on whether the government has proved — usu. by clear and convincing evidence — that the commitment is necessary for the well-being of the defendant or society (as when the defendant is insane and dangerous). • Most states allow discretionary commitment.

mandatory commitment. (1985) An automatically required commitment for a defendant found not guilty by reason of insanity. • This type of commitment is required under federal law, but in only a minority of states.

voluntary commitment. A commitment of a person who is ill, incompetent, drug-addicted, or the like, upon the request or with the consent of the person being committed.

committee. 1. (kə-**mit**-ee). A subordinate group to which a deliberative assembly or other organization refers business for consideration, investigation, oversight, or action <the bill was sent to legislative committee>.

committee of the whole. A special committee that comprises all the deliberative assembly's members who are present.

conference committee. A joint meeting of two legislative committees, one from each house of a bicameral legislature, usu. charged with adjusting differences in a bill passed by both houses in different versions.

credentials committee. A committee charged with preparing a roster of delegates entitled to be seated, examining contested claims to such entitlement, and preparing and issuing credentials to the delegates who appear so entitled.

executive committee. The committee of principal officers and directors who directly manage an organization's affairs between board meetings.

joint committee. A legislative committee composed of members of both houses of a legislature.

platform committee. A committee charged with developing a comprehensive statement of an organization's, usu. a political party's, public policies and principles.

program committee. The committee that plans a convention's program, usu. including both its formal business and its educational and social events.

resolutions committee. A committee charged with screening the original main motions offered for a convention's consideration.

rules committee. A committee charged with drafting rules and an agenda for the orderly conduct of a deliberative assembly's business, particularly that of a legislative body or a convention.

search committee. A committee charged with finding a suitable choice from several options, such as candidates for employment or places for a meeting.

special committee. A committee established for a particular purpose or a limited time.

standing committee. A committee that is established for ongoing business, that continues to exist from session to session, and that is usu. charged with considering business of a certain recurring kind.

subcommittee. A group within a committee to which the committee may refer business, standing in the same relation to its parent committee as the committee stands to the deliberative assembly.

2. (kəm-i-**tee**) A person who is civilly committed, usu. to a psychiatric hospital. **3.** (kəm-i-**tee**) The guardian for the person so committed.

commodity. 1. An article of trade or commerce. **2.** An economic good, esp. a raw material or an agricultural product.

common, *n.* **1.** A legal right to use another person's property, such as an easement. **2.** A tract of land set aside for the general public's use.

commonality test. The requirement that members of a group certified as a class in a class-action suit share at least one issue of law or fact whose resolution will affect all or a significant number of the putative class members.

common area. 1. *Landlord-tenant law.* The realty that all tenants may use though the landlord retains control over and responsibility for it. **2.** An area owned and used in common by the residents of a condominium, subdivision, or planned-unit development.

common-area maintenance charges. Fees paid by tenants, usu. on a pro rata basis, to compensate the landlord for the costs of operating, repairing, and maintaining common areas.

common-authority rule. The principle that a person may consent to a police officer's search of another person's property if both persons use, control, or have access to the property. • Under this rule, the consenting person must have been legally able to permit the search in his or her own right, and the defendant must have assumed the risk that a fellow occupant might permit a search.

common calling. 1. An ordinary occupation that a citizen has a right to pursue under the Privileges and Immunities Clause. **2.** A commercial enterprise that offers services to the general public, with a legal duty to serve anyone who requests the services. • For example, an innkeeper or a common carrier engages in a common calling.

common-character requirement. (1997) The rule that for a group of persons to qualify as a class in a class-action lawsuit, the appointment of the class must achieve economies of time, effort, and expense, and must promote uniformity of decision for persons similarly situated, in addition to sharing common questions of fact and law.

common design. (17c) **1.** The intention by two or more people to join in committing an unlawful act. **2.** An intention to commit more than one crime. **3.** The general design or layout of plots of land surrounding a particular tract.

common disaster. (1878) An event that causes two or more persons with related property interests (such as an insured and the beneficiary) to die at very nearly the same time, with no way of determining who died first.

common-disaster clause. (1949) A provision in a dispositive instrument, such as an insurance policy or a will, that seeks to cover the situation in which the transferor and transferee die in a common disaster.

common duty of care. (1887) A landowner's obligation to take reasonable care under the circumstances to see that a lawful visitor will be reasonably safe in using the premises for the purposes for which the visitor is permitted to be there.

common-enemy doctrine. (1905) *Property.* The rule that a landowner may repel surface waters as necessary (as during a flood), without having to consider the consequences to other landowners. • The doctrine takes its name from the idea that the floodwater is every landowner's common enemy.

common error. (1897) *Copyright.* A mistake found both in a copyrighted work and in an allegedly infringing work, the mistake being persuasive evidence of unauthorized copying.

common informer. (18c) A person who sues to recover a penalty in a penal action. • In some jurisdictions, such an action may be instituted either by the attorney general on behalf of the state or by a common informer.

common knowledge. (17c) A fact that is so widely known that a court may accept it as true without proof.

common-knowledge exception. (1929) The principle that lay testimony concerning routine or simple medical procedures is admissible to establish negligence in a medical-malpractice action. • This is a narrow exception in some jurisdictions to the rule that a medical-malpractice plaintiff must present expert testimony to establish negligence.

common law, *n.* [fr. Law French *commen ley* "common law"] (14c) **1.** The body of law derived from judicial decisions, rather than from statutes or constitutions; CASELAW <federal common law>.

federal common law. (1855) The body of decisional law derived from federal courts when adjudicating federal questions and other matters of federal concern, such as disputes between the states and foreign relations, but excluding all cases governed by state law.

general federal common law. (1890) *Hist.* In the period before *Erie v. Tompkins* (304 U.S. 64, 58 S.Ct. 817 (1938)), the judge-made law developed by federal courts in deciding disputes in diversity-of-citizenship cases. • Since *Erie*, a federal court has been bound to apply the substantive law of the state in which it sits. So even though there is a "federal common law," there is no longer a *general* federal common law applicable to all disputes heard in federal court.

2. The body of law based on the English legal system, as distinct from a civil-law system; the general Anglo-American system of legal concepts, together with the techniques of applying them, that form the basis of the law in jurisdictions where the system applies.

American common law. **1.** The body of English law that was adopted as the law of the American colonies and supplemented with local enactments and judgments. **2.** The body of judge-made law that developed during and after the United States' colonial period, esp. since independence.

3. General law common to the country as a whole, as opposed to special law that has only local application. **4.** The body of law deriving from law courts as opposed to those sitting in equity.

common-law lawyer. (19c) A lawyer who is versed in or practices under a common-law system.

common-law rule. (17c) **1.** A judge-made rule as opposed to a statutory one. **2.** A legal as opposed to an equitable rule. **3.** A general rule as opposed to one deriving from special law (such as a local custom or a rule of foreign law that, based on choice-of-law principles, is applied in place of domestic law). **4.** An old rule of English law.

common-law state. (1848) **1.** Noncode state. **2.** Any state that has not adopted a community-property regime. • The chief difference today between a community-property state and a common-law state is that in a common-law state, a spouse's interest in property held by the other spouse does not vest until (1) a divorce action has been filed, or (2) the other spouse has died.

common-nucleus-of-operative-fact test. (1966) The doctrine that a federal court will have pendent jurisdiction over state-law claims that arise from the same facts as the federal claims providing a basis for subject-matter jurisdiction.

common-source doctrine. (1938) The principle that a defendant in a trespass-to-try-title action who claims under a source common to both the defendant and the plaintiff may not demonstrate title in a third source that is paramount to the common source because doing so amounts to an attack on the source under which the defendant claims title.

commonwealth. (15c) **1.** A nation, state, or other political unit <the Commonwealth of Pennsylvania>. **2.** A political unit that has local autonomy but is voluntarily united with the United States <Puerto Rico and the Northern Mariana Islands are commonwealths>. **3.** A loose association of countries that recognize one sovereign <the British Commonwealth>. — Abbr. Commw.; comm.

commune (**kom**-yoon), *n.* (17c) A community of people who share property and responsibilities.

communication. (14c) **1.** The expression or exchange of information by speech, writing, gestures, or conduct; the process of bringing an idea to another's perception. **2.** The information so expressed or exchanged.

conditionally privileged communication. (1889) A defamatory statement made in good faith by a person with an interest in a subject to someone who also has an interest in the subject, as an employer giving a negative but accurate job review of a former employee to a potential future employer. • The privilege may be lost upon a showing of malice or bad faith.

confidential communication. (18c) A communication made within a certain protected relationship and legally protected from compelled disclosure in a legal proceeding.

ex parte communication. (1804) A communication between counsel and the court when opposing counsel is not present.

privileged communication. (1809) A communication that is protected by law from compelled disclosure in a legal proceeding, or that cannot be used against the person who made it.

communism. (19c) A political doctrine, based on Marxism, advocating the abolition of capitalism by ground-roots revolution; specif., a social and political doctrine advocating the abolition of private ownership in favor of common ownership of the means of production and the goods produced, each person contributing as able and receiving as needed.

community. (14c) **1.** A neighborhood, vicinity, or locality. **2.** A society or group of people with similar rights or interests. **3.** Joint ownership, possession, or participation.

community control. A criminal sentence whose terms include intensive and strict supervision of an offender in the community, as by restricting the offender's movements and activities and conducting electronic surveillance, and providing severe sanctions for violations of any of the sentence's terms.

community of interest. (17c) **1.** Participation in a joint venture characterized by shared liability and shared opportunity for profit. **2.** A common grievance that must be shared by all class members to maintain the class action. **3.** *Labor law.* A criterion used by the National Labor Relations Board in deciding whether a group of employees should be allowed to act as a bargaining unit. • The Board considers whether the employees have similar duties, wages, hours, benefits, skills, training, supervision, and working conditions.

community policing. (1969) A law-enforcement technique in which police officers are assigned to a particular neighborhood or area to develop relationships with the residents for the purpose of enhancing the chances of detecting and thwarting criminal activity.

community property. (1820) Assets owned in common by husband and wife as a result of its having been acquired during the marriage by means other than an inheritance or a gift to one spouse, each spouse generally holding a one-half interest in the property. • Only nine states have community-property systems: Arizona, California, Idaho, Louisiana, Nevada, New Mexico, Texas, Washington, and Wisconsin.

quasi-community property. Personal property that, having been acquired in a non-community-property state, would have been community property if acquired in a community-property state.

community-property state. (1907) A state in which spouses hold property that is acquired during marriage (other than property acquired by inheritance or individual gift) as community property.

community service. Socially valuable work performed without pay. • Community service is often required as part of a criminal sentence, esp. one that does not include incarceration.

commutation (kom-yə-**tay**-shən), *n.* (15c) **1.** An exchange or replacement. **2.** *Criminal law.* The executive's substitution in a particular case of a less severe punishment for a more severe one that has already been judicially imposed on the defendant. **3.** *Commercial & civil law.* The substitution of one form of payment for another. — **commute,** *vb.* — **commutative,** *adj.*

Commw. *abbr.* Commonwealth.

compact (kom-pakt), *n.* (14c) An agreement or covenant between two or more parties, esp. between governments or states.

family compact. An agreement to further common interests made between related people or within a group that behaves as a family.

interstate compact. (1903) A voluntary agreement between states enacted into law in the participating states upon federal congressional approval.

Compact Clause. (1925) U.S. Const. art. I, § 10, cl. 3, which forbids a state from entering into a contract with another state or a foreign country without congressional approval.

company. (13c) **1.** A corporation — or, less commonly, an association, partnership, or union — that carries on a commercial or industrial enterprise. **2.** A corporation, partnership, association, joint-stock company, trust, fund, or organized group of persons, whether incorporated or not, and (in an official capacity) any receiver, trustee in bankruptcy, or similar official, or liquidating agent, for any of the foregoing. Investment Company Act § 2(a)(8) (15 USCA § 80a-2(a)(8)). — Abbr. co.; com.

bonding company. A company that insures a party against a loss caused by a third party.

holding company. (1906) A company formed to control other companies, usu. confining its role to owning stock and supervising management.

investment company. A company formed to acquire and manage a portfolio of diverse assets by investing money collected from different sources.

joint-stock company. (18c) **1.** An unincorporated association of individuals possessing common capital, the capital being contributed by the members and divided into shares, of which each member possesses a number of shares proportionate to the member's investment. **2.** A partnership in which the capital is divided into shares that are transferable without the express consent of the partners.

limited company. (1862) A company in which the liability of each shareholder is limited to the amount individually invested. • A corporation is the most common example of a limited company.

limited-liability company. (1856) A company — statutorily authorized in certain states — that is characterized by limited liability, management by members or managers, and limitations on ownership transfer. — Abbr. L.L.C.

mutual company. A company that is owned by its customers rather than by a separate group of stockholders. • Many insurance companies are mutual companies, as are many federal savings-and-loan associations.

personal holding company. (1924) A holding company that is subject to special taxes and that usu. has a limited number of shareholders, with most of its revenue originating from passive income such as dividends, interest, rent, and royalties.

title company. (1892) A company that examines real-estate titles for any encumbrances, claims, or other flaws, and issues title insurance.

trust company. (1834) A company that acts as a trustee for people and entities and that sometimes also operates as a commercial bank.

comparable (**kom**-pər-ə-bəl), *n.* (19c) (*usu. pl.*) A piece of property used as a comparison to determine the value of a similar piece of property. — **comparable,** *adj.*

comparable worth. (1983) **1.** The analogous value that two or more employees bring to a business through their work. **2.** The idea that employees who perform identical work should receive identical pay, regardless of their sex; the doctrine that men and women who perform work of equal value should receive comparable pay.

comparative disparity. (1977) *Constitutional law.* The percentage of underrepresentation of a particular group among potential jurors on a venire, in comparison with the group's percentage of the general population. Cf. ABSOLUTE DISPARITY.

comparative-impairment test. (1974) *Conflict of laws.* A test that asks which of two or more forums would have its policies most impaired by not having its law applied in the case.

comparative law. The scholarly study of the similarities and differences between the legal systems of different jurisdictions, such as between civil-law and common-law countries.

comparative legislation. A species of comparative law seeking to define the common link for modern statutory doctrines, concerned with the development of legal study as a social science and with awakening an international legal consciousness.

comparative-negligence doctrine. (1904) *Torts.* The principle that reduces a plaintiff's recovery proportionally to the plaintiff's degree of fault in causing the damage, rather than barring recovery completely. • Most states have statutorily adopted the comparative-negligence doctrine.

comparative rectitude. (1913) *Archaic. Family law.* The degree to which one spouse is less culpable than the other in damaging the marriage, so that even though both spouses are at fault, the less culpable spouse may successfully petition for a separation or divorce.

compel, *vb.* (14c) **1.** To cause or bring about by force, threats, or overwhelming pressure. **2.** (Of a legislative mandate or judicial precedent) to convince (a court) that there is only one possible resolution of a legal dispute. — **compellable,** *adj.*

compelling need. A need so great that irreparable harm or injustice would result if it is not met. • Generally, courts decide whether a compelling need is present based on the unique facts of each case. In some jurisdictions, however, statutes define "compelling need" or provide guidelines for determining whether one exists. See, e.g., 5 USCA § 552(a)(6)(E)(v) (defining "compelling need" for an expedited response to a Freedom of Information Act request).

compelling-state-interest test. (1966) *Constitutional law.* A method for determining the constitutional validity of a law, whereby the government's interest in the law and its purpose is balanced against an individual's constitutional right that is affected by the law. • Only if the government's interest is strong enough will the law be upheld. The compelling-state-interest test is used, e.g., in equal-protection analysis when the disputed law requires strict scrutiny.

compensable (kəm-**pen**-sə-bəl), *adj.* (17c) Able or entitled to be compensated for.

compensating balance. The amount of money a borrower from a bank is required to keep on deposit as a condition for a loan or a line of credit.

compensation (kom-pən-**say**-shən), *n.* (14c) **1.** Remuneration and other benefits received in return for services rendered; esp., salary or wages. **2.** Payment of damages, or any other act that a court orders to be done by a person who has caused injury to another. • In theory, compensation makes the injured person whole. **3.** SETOFF (2). — **compensatory,** (kəm-**pen**-sə-tor-ee), **compensational** (kom-pən-**say**-shə-nəl), *adj.* — **compensate (kom**-pən-sayt), *vb.*

accrued compensation. (1919) Remuneration that has been earned but not yet paid.

deferred compensation. (1926) **1.** Payment for work performed, to be paid in the future or when some future event occurs. **2.** An employee's earnings that are taxed when received or distributed rather than when earned, such as contributions to a qualified pension or profit-sharing plan.

just compensation. (16c) Under the Fifth Amendment, a payment by the government for property it has taken under eminent domain — usu. the property's fair market value, so that the owner is theoretically no worse off after the taking.

unemployment compensation. Compensation paid at regular intervals by a state agency to an unemployed person, esp. one who has been laid off.

unreasonable compensation. (1946) *Tax.* Compensation that is not deductible as a business expense because the compensation is out of proportion to the services actually rendered or because it exceeds statutorily defined limits. IRC (26 USCA) § 162.

compensation period. The time fixed by unemployment or workers'-compensation law during which an unemployed or injured worker is entitled to receive compensation.

compensatory payment. *Family law.* A postmarital spousal payment made by the richer ex-spouse to the poorer one and treated as an entitlement rather than as a discretionary award.

competence, *n.* (17c) **1.** A basic or minimal ability to do something; qualification, esp. to testify. **2.** The capacity of an official body to do something. **3.** Authenticity. — **competent,** *adj.*

competency, *n.* (16c) **1.** The mental ability to understand problems and make decisions. **2.** A criminal defendant's ability to stand trial, measured by the capacity to understand the proceedings, to consult meaningfully with counsel, and to assist in the defense. — **competent,** *adj.*

competition. (16c) The struggle for commercial advantage; the effort or action of two or more commercial interests to obtain the same business from third parties.

fair competition. (17c) Open, equitable, and just competition between business competitors.

horizontal competition. (1930) Competition between a seller and its competitors. • The Sherman Antitrust Act prohibits unreasonable restraints on horizontal competition, such as price-fixing agreements between competitors.

perfect competition. A completely efficient market situation characterized by numerous buyers and sellers, a homogeneous product, perfect information for all parties, and complete freedom to move in and out of the market. • Antitrust scholars use the ideal as a standard for measuring market performance.

vertical competition. (1954) Competition between participants at different levels of distribution, such as manufacturer and distributor.

competitive advantage. The potential benefit from information, ideas, or devices that, if kept secret by a business, might be economically exploited to improve the business's market share or to increase its income.

compilation (kom-pə-**lay**-shən), *n.* (15c) **1.** *Copyright.* A collection of literary works arranged in an original way; esp., a work formed by collecting and assembling preexisting materials or data that are selected, coordinated, or arranged in such a way that the resulting product constitutes an original work of authorship. **2.** A collection of statutes, updated and arranged to facilitate their use. — **compile,** *vb.*

complainant (kəm-**playn**-ənt). (15c) **1.** The party who brings a legal complaint against another; esp., the plaintiff in a court of equity or, more modernly, a civil suit. **2.** A person who, under oath, signs a statement (called a "complaint") establishing reasonable grounds to believe that some named person has committed a crime.

complaint. (14c) **1.** The initial pleading that starts a civil action and states the basis for the court's jurisdiction, the basis for the plaintiff's claim, and the demand for relief. • In some states, this pleading is called a *petition.* **2.** *Criminal law.* A formal charge accusing a person of an offense. Fed. R. Crim. P. 3.

amended complaint. (1822) A complaint that modifies and replaces the original complaint by adding relevant matters that occurred before or at the time the action began. Fed. R. Civ. P. 15(d). • In some circumstances, a party must obtain the court's permission to amend its complaint.

counter-complaint. A complaint filed by a defendant against the plaintiff, alleging that the plaintiff has committed a breach and is liable to the defendant for damages.

preliminary complaint. (1833) A complaint issued by a court to obtain jurisdiction over a criminal suspect for a hearing on probable cause or on whether to bind the suspect over for trial.

supplemental complaint. (1821) An additional complaint that either corrects a defect in the original complaint or adds relevant matters that occurred after the action began. • Generally, a party must obtain the court's permission to file a supplemental complaint.

third-party complaint. (1938) A complaint filed by the defendant against a third party, alleging that the third party may be liable for some or all of the damages that the plaintiff is trying to recover from the defendant.

well-pleaded complaint. (1954) An original or initial pleading that sufficiently sets forth a claim for relief — by including the grounds for the court's jurisdiction, the basis for the relief claimed, and a demand for judgment — so that a defendant may draft an answer that is responsive to the issues presented. • In federal court, a well-pleaded complaint must raise a controlling issue of federal law, or else the court will not have federal-question jurisdiction over the lawsuit.

complementary goods. *Trademarks.* Products that are typically used together, such as pancake syrup and pancake mix, or motion-picture projectors and film. • Trademark law may prevent the use of a similar mark on complementary goods because consumers may be confused into thinking the goods come from a common source. The patent-misuse doctrine may provide a defense in an infringement suit if the plaintiff has used its patent rights to gain market control over unpatented complementary goods.

complete in itself, *adj.* (18c) (Of a legislative act) fully covering an entire subject.

complete-preemption doctrine. (1987) The rule that a federal statute's preemptive force may be so extraordinary and all-encompassing that it converts an ordinary state-common-law complaint into one stating a federal claim for purposes of the well-pleaded-complaint rule.

complicity (kəm-**plis**-ə-tee), *n.* (17c) Association or participation in a criminal act; the act or state of being an accomplice. • Under the Model Penal Code, a person can be an accomplice as a result of either that person's own conduct or the conduct of another (such as an innocent agent) for which that person is legally accountable. Model Penal Code § 2.06. — **complicitous** (kəm-**plis**-ə-təs), *adj.*

composition, *n.* (14c) **1.** An agreement between a debtor and two or more creditors for the adjustment or discharge of an obligation for some lesser amount; an agreement among the debtor and two or more creditors that the debtor will pay the creditors less than their full claims in full satisfaction of their claims. **2.** The compensation paid as part of such an agreement. — **compose,** *vb.*

composition of matter. *Patents.* One of the five types of patentable statutory subject matter, consisting of combinations of natural elements whether resulting from chemical union or from mechanical mixture, and whether the substances are gases, fluids, powders, or solids. • This classification includes chemical compounds such as drugs and fuels, physical products such as plastics and particleboard, and new life forms made by genetic engineering. Its subject matter is always the substance itself, rather than the form or shape. — Often shortened to *composition.*

compos mentis (**kom**-pəs **men**-tis), *adj.* [Latin "master of one's mind"] (17c) Of sound mind; having use of and control over one's own mental faculties. Cf. NON COMPOS MENTIS.

compound (kom- *or* kəm-**pownd**), *vb.* (14c) **1.** To put together, combine, or construct. **2.** To compute (interest) on the principal and the accrued interest. **3.** To settle (a matter, esp. a debt) by a money payment, in lieu of other liability; to adjust by agreement. **4.** To agree for consideration not to prosecute (a crime). • Compounding a felony in this way is itself a felony. **5.** Loosely, to aggravate; to make (a crime, etc.) more serious by further bad conduct.

compounder (kom- *or* kəm-**pown**-dər). (16c) **1.** One who settles a dispute; the maker of a composition. **2.** One who knows of a crime by another and agrees, for a promised or received reward, not to prosecute.

compounding a crime. (17c) The offense of either agreeing not to prosecute a crime that one knows has been committed or agreeing to hamper the prosecution.

comprehensive zoning plan. (1925) A general plan to control and direct the use and development of a large piece of property.

compromise, *n.* (15c) **1.** An agreement between two or more persons to settle matters in dispute between them. **2.** A debtor's partial payment coupled with the creditor's promise not to claim the rest of the amount due or claimed. — **compromise,** *vb.*

comp time. Time that an employee is allowed to take off from work instead of being paid for overtime already worked.

comptroller (kən-**troh**-lər). (15c) An officer of a business or a private, state, or municipal corporation who is charged with duties usu. relating to fiscal affairs, including auditing and examining accounts and reporting the financial status periodically.

compulsion, *n.* (15c) **1.** The act of compelling; the state of being compelled. **2.** An uncontrollable inclination to do something. **3.** Objective necessity; duress. — **compel,** *vb.*

compulsory (kəm-**pəl**-sə-ree), *adj.* (16c) Compelled; mandated by legal process or by statute.

compulsory-attendance law. A statute requiring minors of a specified age to attend school.

Compulsory Process Clause. (1957) The clause of the Sixth Amendment to the U.S. Constitution giving criminal defendants the subpoena power for obtaining witnesses in their favor.

comstockery (**kom**-stok-ər-ee). (*often cap.*) Censorship or attempted censorship of art or literature that is supposedly immoral or obscene.

Comstock law (kom-stok). (1878) An 1873 federal statute that prohibited mailing "obscene, lewd, or lascivious" books or pictures, as well as "any article or thing designed for the prevention of conception or procuring of abortions." • Because of the intolerance that led to this statute, the law gave rise to an English word roughly equivalent to *prudery* — namely, *comstockery.*

con. *abbr.* **1.** Confidence <con game>. **2.** Convict <ex-con>. **3.** Contra <pros and cons>. **4.** (*cap.*) Constitutional <Con. law>.

concealment, *n.* (14c) **1.** The act of refraining from disclosure; esp., an act by which one prevents or hinders the discovery of something; a cover-up. **2.** The act of removing from sight or notice; hiding. **3.** *Insurance.* The insured's intentional withholding from the insurer material facts that increase the insurer's risk and that in good faith ought to be disclosed. — **conceal,** *vb.*

active concealment. (1865) The concealment by words or acts of something that one has a duty to reveal.

fraudulent concealment. (1801) The affirmative suppression or hiding, with the intent to deceive or defraud, of a material fact or circumstance that one is legally (or, sometimes, morally) bound to reveal.

passive concealment. (1882) The act of maintaining silence when one has a duty to speak.

concealment rule. (1950) The principle that a defendant's conduct that hinders or prevents a plaintiff from discovering the existence of a claim tolls the statute of limitations until the plaintiff discovers or should have discovered the claim.

conception of invention. (1859) *Patents.* The formation in the inventor's mind of a definite and permanent idea of a complete invention that is thereafter applied in practice.

concerted action. (18c) An action that has been planned, arranged, and agreed on by parties acting together to further some scheme or cause, so that all involved are liable for the actions of one another.

concerted activity. *Labor law.* Action by employees concerning wages or working conditions. • Concerted activity is protected by the National Labor Relations Act and cannot be used as a basis for disciplining or discharging an employee.

concerted refusal to deal. *Antitrust.* An agreement between two or more persons or firms to not do business with a third party.

concession, *n.* (15c) **1.** A government grant for specific privileges. **2.** The voluntary yielding to a demand for the sake of a settlement. **3.** A rebate or abatement. — **concede,** *vb.* — **concessive,** *adj.*

concession bargaining. *Labor law.* A type of collective bargaining in which the parties negotiate the employees' giving back previously gained improvements in wages, benefits, or working conditions in exchange for some form of job security, such as protection against layoffs.

conciliation, *n.* (1803) **1.** A settlement of a dispute in an agreeable manner. **2.** A process in which a neutral person meets with the parties to a dispute and explores how the dispute might be resolved; esp., a relatively unstructured method of dispute resolution in which a third party facilitates communication between parties in an attempt to help them settle their differences. — **conciliate,** *vb.* — **conciliative, conciliatory,** *adj.* — **conciliator,** *n.*

conclude, *vb.* (16c) **1.** To ratify or formalize (a treaty, convention, or contract). **2.** To bind; estop.

conclusion, *n.* (14c) **1.** The final part of a speech or writing (such as a jury argument or a pleading). **2.** A judgment arrived at by reasoning; an inferential statement. **3.** The closing, settling, or final arranging of a treaty, contract, deal, etc.

conclusion of fact. (18c) A factual deduction drawn from observed or proven facts; an evidentiary inference.

conclusion of law. (17c) An inference on a question of law, made as a result of a factual showing, no further evidence being required; a legal inference.

conclusive, *adj.* (17c) Authoritative; decisive; convincing.

conclusory (kən-**kloo**-zə-ree *or* -sə-ree), *adj.* (1923) Expressing a factual inference without stating the underlying facts on which the inference is based.

concomitant (kən-**kom**-ə-tənt), *adj.* (17c) Accompanying; incidental <concomitant actions>. — **concomitant,** *n.*

concord (**kon**-kord *or* **kong**-), *n.* (14c) An amicable arrangement between parties, esp. between peoples or nations; a compact or treaty.

concubinage (kon-**kyoo**-bə-nij), *n.* (14c) **1.** The relationship of a man and woman who cohabit without the benefit of marriage. **2.** The state of being a concubine.

concurrence. (15c) **1.** Agreement; assent. **2.** A vote cast by a judge in favor of the judgment reached, often on grounds differing from those expressed in the opinion or opinions explaining the judgment. **3.** A separate written opinion explaining such a vote. **4.** Acceptance by one house in a bicameral legislature of an amendment passed by the other house. — **concur** (kən-**kər**), *vb.* (15c).

concurrent, *adj.* (14c) **1.** Operating at the same time; covering the same matters <concurrent prison sentences>. **2.** Having authority on the same matters <concurrent jurisdiction>.

concurrent registration. *Trademarks.* The approved recording of identical or similar marks by multiple owners if each mark was commercially used before the owners applied for registration and the risk of consumer confusion is slight. • The U.S. Patent and Trademark Office may impose restrictions on each mark's use to prevent consumer confusion.

concurrent-sentence doctrine. (1969) The principle that an appellate court affirming a conviction and sentence need not hear a challenge to a conviction on another count if the conviction on the other count carries a sentence that is equal to or less than the affirmed conviction.

condemn, *vb.* (14c) **1.** To judicially pronounce (someone) guilty. **2.** To determine and declare (property) to be assigned to public use. **3.** To adjudge (a building) as being unfit for habitation.

4. To adjudge (food or drink) as being unfit for human consumption.

condemnation (kon-dem-**nay**-shən), *n.* (14c) **1.** The act of judicially pronouncing someone guilty; conviction. **2.** The determination and declaration that certain property (esp. land) is assigned to public use, subject to reasonable compensation; the exercise of eminent domain by a governmental entity.

excess condemnation. (1921) A taking of land in excess of the boundaries of the public project as designed by the condemnor.

inverse condemnation. (1932) An action brought by a property owner for compensation from a governmental entity that has taken the owner's property without bringing formal condemnation proceedings.

quick condemnation. (1918) The immediate taking of possession of private property for public use, whereby the estimated compensation is deposited in court or paid to the condemnee until the actual amount of compensation can be established.

3. An official pronouncement that a building is unfit for habitation; the act of making such a pronouncement. **4.** The official pronouncement that a thing (such as food or drink) is unfit for use or consumption; the act of making such a pronouncement.

condemnation money. (18c) **1.** Damages that a losing party in a lawsuit is condemned to pay. **2.** Compensation paid by an expropriator of land to the landowner for taking the property.

condemnee (kon-dem-**nee**). (1890) One whose property is expropriated for public use or taken by a public-works project.

condemnor (kon-dem-**nor** *or* kən-**dem**-nər). (1890) A person or entity that expropriates property for public use. — Also spelled *condemner* (kən-**dem**-nər).

condition, *n.* (14c) **1.** A future and uncertain event on which the existence or extent of an obligation or liability depends; an uncertain act or event that triggers or negates a duty to render a promised performance. **2.** A stipulation or prerequisite in a contract, will, or other instrument, constituting the essence of the instrument.

collateral condition. A condition that requires the performance of an act having no relation to an agreement's main purpose.

compulsory condition. (1876) A condition expressly requiring that a thing be done, such as a tenant's paying rent on a certain day.

concurrent condition. (1840) A condition that must occur or be performed at the same time as another condition, the performance by each party separately operating as a condition precedent; a condition that is mutually dependent on another, arising when the parties to a contract agree to exchange performances simultaneously.

condition precedent (prə-**seed**-ənt *also* **pres**-ə-dənt). (1818) An act or event, other than a lapse of time, that must exist or occur before a duty to perform something promised arises.

condition subsequent. (1818) A condition that, if it occurs, will bring something else to an end; an event the existence of which, by agreement of the parties, discharges a duty of performance that has arisen.

constructive condition. A condition contained in an essential contractual term that, though omitted by the parties from their agreement, a court has supplied as being reasonable in the circumstances; a condition imposed by law to do justice.

express condition. (16c) **1.** A condition that is the manifested intention of the parties. **2.** A condition that is explicitly stated in an instrument; esp., a contractual condition that the parties have reduced to writing.

implied condition. (17c) A condition that is not expressly mentioned, but is imputed by law from the nature of the transaction or the conduct of the parties to have been tacitly understood between them as a part of the agreement.

implied-in-fact condition. A contractual condition that the parties have implicitly agreed to by their conduct or by the nature of the transaction.

negative condition. (17c) A condition forbidding a party from doing a certain thing, such as prohibiting a tenant from subletting leased property; a promise not to do something, usu. as part of a larger agreement.

preexisting condition. Insurance. A physical or mental condition evident during the period before the effective date of a medical-insurance policy.

3. Loosely, a term, provision, or clause in a contract. **4.** A qualification attached to the conveyance of property providing that if a particular event does or does not take place, the estate will be created, enlarged, defeated, or transferred. **5.** A state of being; an essential quality or status. — **condition,** *vb.*

dangerous condition. (1850) **1.** A property defect creating a substantial risk of injury when the property is used in a reasonably foreseeable manner. • A dangerous condition may result in waiver of sovereign immunity. **2.** A property risk that children, because of their immaturity, cannot appreciate or avoid.

conditional purpose. (16c) **1.** An intention to do something, conditions permitting. **2.** *Criminal law.* A possible defense against a crime if the conditions make committing the crime impossible (e.g., "I will steal the money if it's there," and the money is not there).

condition of employment. (1875) A qualification or circumstance required for obtaining or keeping a job.

conditions of sale. (16c) The terms under which an auction will be conducted.

condominium (kon-də-**min**-ee-əm). (1962) **1.** Ownership in common with others. **2.** A single real-estate unit in a multi-unit development in which a person has both separate ownership of a unit and a common interest, along with the development's other owners, in the common areas. Pl. (for sense 2) **condominiums.**

condonation (kon-də-**nay**-shən), *n.* (17c) A victim's express or (esp.) implied forgiveness of an offense, esp. by treating the offender as if there had been no offense. — **condone** (kən-**dohn**), *vb.* — **condonable** (kən-**dohn**-ə-bəl), *adj.*

conduct, *n.* (15c) Personal behavior, whether by action or inaction; the manner in which a person behaves. — **conduct,** *vb.*

assertive conduct. (1968) *Evidence.* Nonverbal behavior that is intended to be a statement, such as pointing one's finger to identify a suspect in a police lineup. • Assertive conduct is a statement under the hearsay rule, and thus it is not admissible unless a hearsay exception applies. Fed. R. Evid. 801(a)(2).

contumacious conduct (kon-t[y]oo-**may**-shəs). A willful disobedience of a court order.

disorderly conduct. (17c) Behavior that tends to disturb the public peace, offend public morals, or undermine public safety.

disruptive conduct. (1959) Disorderly conduct in the context of a governmental proceeding.

nonassertive conduct. (1965) *Evidence.* Nonverbal behavior that is not intended to be a statement, such as fainting while being questioned as a suspect by a police officer. • Nonassertive conduct is not a statement under the hearsay rule, and thus it is admissible. Fed. R. Evid. 801.

outrageous conduct. (18c) Conduct so extreme that it exceeds all reasonable bounds of human decency.

tortious conduct. An act or omission that subjects the actor to liability under the principles of tort law.

unprofessional conduct. (1836) Behavior that is immoral, unethical, or dishonorable, esp. when judged by the standards of the actor's profession.

unreasonably dangerous conduct. Conduct that involves undue risk under the circumstances. — Sometimes shortened to *dangerous conduct.*

wrongful conduct. (1807) An act taken in violation of a legal duty; an act that unjustly infringes on another's rights.

confederacy, *n.* (14c) **1.** A league of states or countries that have joined for mutual support or joint action; an alliance. **2.** An association of two or more persons, usu. for unlawful purposes; CONSPIRACY. **3.** The fact or condition of being allied or associated. — **confederate,** *n.*

confederation. (15c) **1.** A league or union of states or nations, each of which retains its sovereignty but also delegates some rights and powers to a central authority. **2.** An alliance; esp., in a negative sense, a conspiracy.

conference. 1. CONVENTION (3). **2.** A meeting between the two houses of a bicameral legislature.

confession, *n.* (14c) A criminal suspect's oral or written acknowledgment of guilt, often including details about the crime. — **confess,** *vb.* — **confessor,** *n.*

coerced-compliant confession. A confession by a suspect who knows that he or she is innocent but is overcome by fatigue, the questioner's tactics, or a desire for some potential benefit.

coerced confession. (1937) A confession that is obtained by threats or force.

direct confession. (17c) A statement in which an accused person acknowledges having committed the crime.

extrajudicial confession. (1813) A confession made out of court, and not as a part of a judicial examination or investigation. • Such a confession must be corroborated by some other proof of the corpus delicti, or else it is insufficient to warrant a conviction.

implied confession. A confession in which the person does not plead guilty but invokes the mercy of the court and asks for a light sentence.

indirect confession. A confession that is inferred from the defendant's conduct.

interlocking confessions. (1973) Confessions by two or more suspects whose statements are substantially the same and consistent concerning the elements of the crime.

involuntary confession. (1830) A confession induced by the police or other law-enforcement authorities who make promises to, coerce, or deceive the suspect.

judicial confession. (16c) A plea of guilty or some other direct manifestation of guilt in court or in a judicial proceeding.

naked confession. (18c) A confession unsupported by any evidence that a crime has been committed, and therefore usu. highly suspect.

oral confession. A confession that is not made in writing. • Oral confessions are admissible, though as a practical matter police interrogators prefer to take written or recorded confessions since juries typically view these as being more reliable.

plenary confession (**plee**-nə-ree *or* **plen**-ə). (1907) A complete confession; one that is believed to be conclusive against the person who made it.

threshold confession. (1962) A spontaneous confession made promptly after arrest and without interrogation by the police.

voluntary confession. A confession given freely, without any benefit or punishment promised, threatened, or expected.

confession and avoidance. (17c) A plea in which a defendant admits allegations but pleads additional facts that deprive the admitted facts of an adverse legal effect. • For example, a plea of contributory negligence (before the advent of comparative negligence) was a confession and avoidance.

confession of judgment. (18c) **1.** A person's agreeing to the entry of judgment upon the occurrence or nonoccurrence of an event, such as making a payment. **2.** A judgment taken against a debtor by the creditor, based on the debtor's written consent. **3.** The paper on which the person so agrees, before it is entered.

confidence. (14c) **1.** Assured expectation; firm trust; faith. **2.** Reliance on another's discretion; a relation of trust. **3.** A communication made in trust and not intended for public disclosure; specif., a communication protected by the attorney–client or similar privilege. — **confide,** *vb.*

confidence game. (1856) A means of obtaining money or property whereby a person intentionally misrepresents facts to gain the victim's trust so that the victim will transfer money or property to the person.

confidence man. One who defrauds a victim by first gaining the victim's confidence and then, through trickery, obtaining money or property; a swindler.

confidential, *adj.* **1.** (Of information) meant to be kept secret. **2.** (Of a relationship) characterized by trust and a willingness to confide in the other.

confidentiality, *n.* (1834) **1.** Secrecy; the state of having the dissemination of certain information restricted. **2.** The relation between lawyer and client or guardian and ward, or between spouses, with regard to the trust that is placed in the one by the other.

confidentiality agreement. *Trade secrets.* A promise not to disclose trade secrets or other proprietary information learned in the course of the parties' relationship.

confidentiality statute. A law that seals adoption records and prevents an adopted child from learning the identity of his or her biological parent and prevents the biological parent from learning the identity of the adoptive parents.

confidential source. A person who provides information to a law-enforcement agency or to a journalist on the express or implied guarantee of anonymity.

confinement, *n.* (16c) The act of imprisoning or restraining someone; the state of being imprisoned or restrained. — **confine,** *vb.*

confirmation, *n.* (14c) **1.** The act of giving formal approval. **2.** The act of verifying or corroborating; a statement that verifies or corroborates. **3.** The act of ratifying a voidable estate; a type of conveyance in which a voidable estate is made certain or a particular estate is increased. **4.** *Commercial law.* A bank's agreement to honor a letter of credit issued by another bank. — **confirm,** *vb.* — **confirmatory** (kən-**fər**-mə-tor-ee), *adj.*

confiscation (kon-fi-**skay**-shən), *n.* (16c) **1.** Seizure of property for the public treasury. **2.** Seizure of property by actual or supposed authority. — **confiscate (kon**-fə-skayt), *vb.* — **confiscatory** (kən-**fis**-kə-tor-ee), *adj.* — **confiscable**

(kən-**fis**-kə-bəl *or* **kon**-fə-skə-bəl), *adj.* — **confiscator** (**kon**-fə-skay-tər), *n.*

conflict of authority. (1822) **1.** A disagreement between two or more courts, often courts of coordinate jurisdiction, on a point of law. **2.** A disagreement between two or more treatise authors or other scholars, esp. in an area in which scholarly authority is paramount, such as public or private international law.

conflict of interest. (1843) **1.** A real or seeming incompatibility between one's private interests and one's public or fiduciary duties. **2.** A real or seeming incompatibility between the interests of two of a lawyer's clients, such that the lawyer is disqualified from representing both clients if the dual representation adversely affects either client or if the clients do not consent. See Model Rules of Prof'l Conduct 1.7(a).

thrust-upon conflict. A conflict of interest that arises during an attorney's representation of two clients but did not exist and was not reasonably foreseeable when each client's representation began, and arises through no fault of the attorney's.

conflict of laws. (1827) **1.** A difference between the laws of different states or countries in a case in which a transaction or occurrence central to the case has a connection to two or more jurisdictions. **2.** The body of jurisprudence that undertakes to reconcile such differences or to decide what law is to govern in these situations; the principles of choice of law.

conflict out, *vb.* (1981) To disqualify (a lawyer or judge) on the basis of a conflict of interest.

conforming, *adj.* (1956) Being in accordance with contractual obligations <conforming goods> <conforming conduct>. UCC § 2-102(a)(8).

conformity hearing. (1970) **1.** A court-ordered hearing to determine whether the judgment or decree prepared by the prevailing party conforms to the decision of the court. **2.** A hearing before a federal agency or department to determine whether a state-submitted plan complies with the requirements of federal law. • This type of hearing is common in cases involving social services.

Confrontation Clause. (1913) The Sixth Amendment provision generally guaranteeing a criminal defendant's right to confront an accusing witness face-to-face and to cross-examine that witness.

confusion. 1. CONFUSION OF GOODS. **2.** MERGER (9). **3.** *Trademarks.* A consumer's mistaken belief about the origin of goods or services.

forward confusion. Confusion occurring when consumers are likely to believe mistakenly that the infringing company's products are from the same source as the trademark owner's. • In forward-confusion cases, the infringing company is usu. smaller than the owner. Thus, consumers may believe the infringer to be an affiliate of the owner.

reverse confusion. Confusion occurring when consumers are likely to believe mistakenly — usu. through widespread advertising and promotion by the infringing company — that the trademark owner's products are actually those of the infringer. • Reverse confusion often injures the owner's reputation and goodwill. In an action for reverse confusion, the trademark owner is typically the smaller company.

confusion of goods. (18c) The mixture of things of the same nature but belonging to different owners so that the identification of the things is no longer possible.

congeries (kon-**jeer**-eez *or* **kon**-jə-reez). (17c) A collection or aggregation.

conglomerate (kən-**glom**-ər-it), *n.* (1967) A corporation that owns unrelated enterprises in a wide variety of industries. — **conglomerate** (kən-**glom**-ə-rayt), *vb.* — **conglomerate** (kən-**glom**-ər-it), *adj.*

congress, *n.* (16c) **1.** A formal meeting of delegates or representatives; CONVENTION (2). **2.** (*cap.*) The legislative body of the federal government, created under U.S. Const. art. I, § 1 and consisting of the Senate and the House of Representatives. — **congressional,** *adj.*

Congressional Record. The official record of the daily proceedings in the U.S. Senate and House of Representatives.

Congressional Research Service. A nonpartisan agency in the Library of Congress that researches and analyzes legislative issues for congressional committees and individual members of Congress. — Abbr. CRS.

conjectural choice, rule of. (1956) The principle that no basis for recovery is presented when all theories of causation rest only on conjecture.

conjecture (kən-**jek**-chər), *n.* (14c) A guess; supposition; surmise. — **conjecture** (kən-**jek**-chər), *vb.* — **conjectural** (kən-**jek**-chər-əl), *adj.*

conjoint (kən-**joynt**), *n.* A person connected with another in a joint interest, obligation, or undertaking, such as a cotenant or spouse. — **conjoint,** *adj.*

conjugal (**kon**-jə-gəl), *adj.* (16c) Of or relating to the married state, often with an implied emphasis on sexual relations between spouses <the prisoner was allowed a private bed for conjugal visits>.

conjugal rights. (18c) The rights and privileges arising from the marriage relationship, including the mutual rights of companionship, support, and sexual relations. • Loss of conjugal rights amounts to loss of consortium.

conjugal visit. An opportunity for physical contact granted to a prisoner and the prisoner's spouse, usu. in the form of an overnight stay at the prison.

connecting factor. (1950) *Conflict of laws.* A factual or legal circumstance that helps determine the choice of law by linking an action or individual with a state or jurisdiction. • An example of a connecting factor is a party's domicile within a state.

connecting-up doctrine. (1986) The rule allowing evidence to be conditionally admitted if the offering party promises to show relevance by adducing other evidence.

connivance (kə-**nɪ**-vənts), *n.* (16c) **1.** The act of indulging or ignoring another's wrongdoing, esp. when action should be taken to prevent it. **2.** *Family law.* As a defense to divorce, one spouse's corrupt consent, express or implied, to have the other commit adultery or some other act of sexual misconduct. • Consent is an essential element of connivance. The complaining spouse must have consented to the act complained of. — **connive** (kə-**nɪv**), *vb.*

connive (kə-**nɪv**), *vb.* **1.** To knowingly overlook another's wrongdoing. **2.** Loosely, to conspire.

consanguinity (kon-sang-**gwin**-ə-tee), *n.* (14c) The relationship of persons of the same blood or origin. — **consanguineous,** *adj.*

collateral consanguinity. (16c) The relationship between persons who have the same ancestor but do not descend or ascend from one another (for example, uncle and nephew, cousins, etc.).

lineal consanguinity. The relationship between persons who are directly descended or ascended from one another (for example, mother and daughter, great-grandfather and grandson, etc.).

conscience. (13c) **1.** The moral sense of right or wrong; esp., a moral sense applied to one's own judgment and actions. **2.** In law, the moral rule that requires justice and honest dealings between people.

conscience clause. A legislative provision that allows a person to claim an exemption from compliance, usu. on religious-freedom grounds.

conscience of the court. (17c) **1.** The court's equitable power to decide issues based on notions of fairness and justice. **2.** A standard applied by the court in deciding whether a party or a jury has acted within acceptable limits. • Thus, in some cases, a jury's award of damages is upset because it is said to "shock the conscience of the court."

conscionable (**kon**-shə-nə-bəl), *adj.* (16c) Conforming with good conscience; just and reasonable <a conscionable bargain>. — **conscionableness, conscionability,** *n.*

consensual (kən-**sen**-shoo-əl), *adj.* **1.** Having, expressing, or occurring with full consent <consensual relations>. **2.** Created or existing by mutual consent without formalities such as a written document or ceremony <consensual marriage>.

consensus. A general agreement; collective opinion.

consent, *n.* (14c) **1.** Agreement, approval, or permission as to some act or purpose, esp. given voluntarily by a competent person; legally effective assent. • Consent is an affirmative defense to assault, battery, and related torts, as well as such torts as defamation, invasion of privacy, conversion, and trespass. Consent may be a defense to a crime if the victim has the capacity to consent and if the consent negates an element of the crime or thwarts the harm that the law seeks to prevent. See Model Penal Code § 2.11. — **consensual** (kən-**sen**-shoo-əl), *adj.*

express consent. (16c) Consent that is clearly and unmistakably stated.

implied consent. (17c) **1.** Consent inferred from one's conduct rather than from one's direct expression. **2.** Consent imputed as a result of circumstances that arise, as when a surgeon removing a gall bladder discovers and removes colon cancer.

informed consent. (1938) **1.** A person's agreement to allow something to happen, made with full knowledge of the risks involved and the alternatives. • For the legal profession, informed consent is defined in Model Rule of Professional Conduct 1.0(e). **2.** A patient's knowing choice about a medical treatment or procedure, made after a physician or other healthcare provider discloses whatever information a reasonably prudent provider in the medical community would give to a patient regarding the risks involved in the proposed treatment or procedure.

parental consent. Consent given on a minor's behalf by at least one parent, or a legal guardian, or by another person properly authorized to act for the minor, for the minor to engage in or submit to a specified activity.

voluntary consent. Consent that is given freely and that has not been coerced.

2. *Parliamentary law.* Adoption.

unanimous consent. Adoption with every voter's approval, either express or implied.

consent to be sued. (1872) Agreement in advance to be sued in a particular forum.

consent to notice. (1996) A provision stating that notice required by a document may be given beforehand or to a designated person.

consequentialism. *Ethics.* An ethical theory that judges the rightness or wrongness of actions according to their consequences.

conservation. *Environmental law.* The supervision, management, and maintenance of natural resources; the protection, improvement, and use of natural resources in a way that ensures the highest social as well as economic benefits.

conservator (kən-**sər**-və-tər *or* **kon**-sər-vay-tər), *n.* (15c) A guardian, protector, or preserver. • *Conservator* is the modern equivalent of the common-law *guardian.* — **conservatorship,** *n.*

managing conservator. (1974) **1.** A person appointed by a court to manage the estate or affairs of someone who is legally incapable of doing so; guardian. **2.** In the child-custody laws of some states, the parent who has primary custody of a child, with the right to establish the child's primary domicile.

consideration, *n.* (16c) **1.** Something (such as an act, a forbearance, or a return promise) bargained for and received by a promisor from a promisee; that which motivates a person to do something, esp. to engage in a legal act. • Consideration, or a substitute such as promissory estoppel, is necessary for an agreement to be enforceable.

adequate consideration. (17c) Consideration that is fair and reasonable under the circumstances of the agreement.

fair consideration. (18c) **1.** Consideration that is roughly equal in value to the thing being exchanged; consideration given for property or for an obligation in either of the following circumstances: (1) when given in good faith as an exchange for the property or obligation, or (2) when the property or obligation is received in good faith to secure a present advance or prior debt in an amount not disproportionately small as compared with the value of the property or obligation obtained. **2.** Consideration that is honest, reasonable, and free from suspicion, but not strictly adequate or full.

future consideration. (1979) **1.** Consideration to be given in the future; esp., consideration that is due after the other party's performance. **2.** Consideration that is a series of performances, some of which will occur after the other party's performance. **3.** Consideration the specifics of which have not been agreed on between the parties.

good consideration. (18c) **1.** Consideration based on natural love or affection or on moral duty **2.** Loosely, valuable consideration; consideration that is adequate to support the bargained-for exchange between the parties.

gratuitous consideration (grə-**t**[**y**]**oo**-i-təs). (1880) Consideration that, not being founded on any detriment to the party who gives it, will not support a contract; a performance for which a party was already obligated.

grossly inadequate consideration. Consideration whose value is so much less than the fair value of the object acquired that it may not support finding that the transaction is a valid exchange.

illegal consideration. (18c) Consideration that is contrary to the law or public policy, or prejudicial to the public interest. • Such consideration does not support a contract.

immoral consideration. A consideration that so offends societal norms as to be invalid. • A contract supported by immoral consideration is usu. voidable or unenforceable.

implied consideration. (18c) Consideration that is inferred by law from the parties' actions.

inadequate consideration. (18c) Consideration that is not fair or reasonable under the circumstances of the agreement.

invented consideration. (1977) Fictional consideration created by a court to prevent the invalidation of a contract that lacks consideration.

nominal consideration. (18c) Consideration that is so insignificant as to bear no relationship to the value of what is being exchanged (e.g., $10 for a piece of real estate). • Such consideration can be valid, since courts do not ordinarily examine the adequacy of consideration (although they do often inquire into such issues as fraud and duress).

other consideration. (18c) Additional things of value to be provided under the terms of a contract, usu. unspecified in the contract, deed, or bill of sale, because they are too numerous to conveniently list, or to avoid public knowledge of the total amount of consideration.

past consideration. (18c) An act done or a promise given by a promisee before making a promise sought to be enforced. • Past consideration is not consideration for the new promise because it has not been given in exchange for this promise (although exceptions exist for new promises to pay debts barred by limitations or debts discharged in bankruptcy).

sufficient consideration. (17c) Enough consideration as a matter of law to support a contract.

valuable consideration. (17c) Consideration that is valid under the law; consideration that either confers a pecuniarily measurable benefit on one party or imposes a pecuniarily measurable detriment on the other.

2. *Parliamentary law.* The process by which a deliberative assembly disposes of a motion; deliberation.

consign (kən-**sɪn**), *vb.* (16c) **1.** To transfer to another's custody or charge. **2.** To give (goods) to a carrier for delivery to a designated recipient. **3.** To give (merchandise or the like) to another to sell, usu. with the understanding that the seller will pay the owner for the goods from the proceeds.

consignee (kon-sɪ-**nee** *or* kən-). (18c) One to whom goods are consigned.

consignment (kən-**sɪn**-mənt). (17c) **1.** The act of consigning goods for custody or sale. **2.** A quantity of goods delivered by this act, esp. in a single shipment. **3.** Under the UCC, a transaction in which a person delivers goods to a merchant for the purpose of sale, and (1) the merchant deals in goods of that kind under a name other than the name of the person making delivery, is not an auctioneer, and is not generally known by its creditor to be substantially engaged in selling others' goods, (2) with respect to each delivery, the aggregate value of the goods is $1,000 or more at the time of delivery, (3) the goods are not consumer goods immediately before delivery, and (4) the transaction does not create a security interest that secures an obligation. UCC § 9-102(a)(20).

consignor (kən-**sɪ**-nər *or* kon-sɪ-**nor**). (18c) One who dispatches goods to another on consignment.

Consolidated Omnibus Budget Reconciliation Act of 1985. A federal statute requiring employers that offer group health coverage to their employees to continue to do so for a prescribed period (usu. 18 to 36 months) after employment has terminated so that the former employee can continue to benefit from group-health rates until becoming a member of another health-insurance plan. — Abbr. COBRA.

consolidation, *n.* (15c) **1.** The act or process of uniting; the state of being united. **2.** *Legislation.* The combination into a single statutory measure of various legislative provisions that have previously been scattered in different statutes. **3.** *Civil procedure.* The court-ordered unification of two or more actions, involving the same parties and issues, into a single action resulting in a single judgment or, sometimes, in separate judgments. Fed. R. Civ. P. 42(a). **4.** *Corporations.* The unification of two or more corporations or other organizations by dissolving the existing ones and creating a single new corporation or organization. — **consolidate,** *vb.* — **consolidatory** (kən-sol-ə-**day**-tər-ee), *adj.*

consortium (kən-**sor**-shee-əm). (1836) The benefits that one person, esp. a spouse, is entitled to receive from another, including companionship, cooperation, affection, aid, financial support, and (between spouses) sexual relations.

conspicuous, *adj.* (1534) (Of a term or clause) clearly visible or obvious. • Under the UCC, a term or clause is conspicuous if it is written in a way that a reasonable person against whom it is to operate ought to notice it. UCC § 1-201(10).

conspicuous place. (18c) For purposes of posting notices, a location that is reasonably likely to be seen.

conspiracy, *n.* (14c) An agreement by two or more persons to commit an unlawful act, coupled with an intent to achieve the agreement's objective, and (in most states) action or conduct that furthers the agreement; a combination for an unlawful purpose. Model Penal Code § 5.03(7). — **conspiratorial,** *adj.* — **conspire,** *vb.*

chain conspiracy. (1959) A single conspiracy in which each person is responsible for a distinct act within the overall plan, such as an agreement to produce, import, and distribute narcotics in which each person performs only one function. • All participants are interested in the overall scheme and liable for all other participants' acts in furtherance of that scheme.

civil conspiracy. (1901) An agreement between two or more persons to commit an unlawful act that causes damage to a person or property.

seditious conspiracy. (1893) A criminal conspiracy to forcibly (1) overthrow or destroy the U.S. government, (2) oppose its authority, (3) prevent the execution of its laws, or (4) seize or possess its property. 18 USCA § 2384.

wheel conspiracy. (1959) A conspiracy in which a single member or group (the "hub") separately agrees with two or more other members or groups (the "spokes"). • The person or group at the hub is the only party liable for all the conspiracies.

conspirator, *n.* (15c) A person who takes part in a conspiracy.

constable (**kon**-stə-bəl), *n.* (13c) A peace officer responsible for minor judicial duties, such as serving writs and warrants, but with less authority and smaller jurisdiction than a sheriff. — **constabulary** (kən-**stab**-yə-ler-ee), *adj.* — **constabulary** (police station or force), *n.*

constant dollars. The value of current money expressed as a percentage of its buying power in a previous year as determined by the consumer price index. • This value is used as a measure of inflation.

constituency. 1. The body of citizens dwelling in a defined area and entitled to elect a representative. **2.** The residents of an electoral district.

constituent, *adj.* (Of a component) that helps make up or complete a unit or a whole <a constituent element of the criminal offense>.

constituent, *n.* (17c) **1.** A person who gives another the authority to act as a representative; a principal who appoints an agent. **2.** Someone who is represented by a legislator or other elected official. **3.** One part of something that makes up a whole; an element. — **constituency,** *n.*

constitution. (18c) **1.** The fundamental and organic law of a nation or state that establishes the institutions and apparatus of government, defines the scope of governmental sovereign powers, and guarantees individual civil rights and civil liberties. **2.** The written instrument embodying this fundamental law, together with any formal amendments.

flexible constitution. A constitution that has few or no special amending procedures. • The British Constitution is an example.

rigid constitution. A constitution whose terms cannot be altered by ordinary forms of legislation, only by special amending procedures. • The U.S. Constitution is an example.

unwritten constitution. **1.** The customs and values, some of which are expressed in statutes, that provide the organic and fundamental law of a state or country that does not have a single written document functioning as a constitution. **2.** The implied parts of a written constitution, encompassing the rights, freedoms, and processes considered to be essential, but not explicitly defined in the written document.

3. A nation's history of government and institutional development. • This was the standard definition before the United States produced the first written constitution. It remains current in Great Britain and other nations that have unwritten constitutions.

constitutional, *adj.* (18c) **1.** Of or relating to a constitution. **2.** Proper and valid under a constitution.

constitutional-fact doctrine. **1.** The rule that federal courts are not bound by an administrative agency's findings of fact when the facts involve whether the agency has exceeded constitutional limitations on its power, esp. regarding personal rights. **2.** The rule that a federal appellate court is not bound by a trial court's findings of fact when constitutional rights are implicated, specifically in citizenship-determination and First Amendment cases.

constitutional freedom. (1822) A basic liberty guaranteed by the Constitution or Bill of Rights, such as the freedom of speech.

constitutional guarantee. A promise contained in the United States Constitution that supports or establishes an inalienable right, such as the right to due process.

constitutionality, *n.* The quality or state of being constitutional.

constitutionalize, *vb.* (1831) **1.** To provide with a constitution. **2.** To make constitutional; to bring in line with a constitution. **3.** To make a constitutional question out of (a question of law); to subject (issue, etc.) to the burden of passing constitutional muster.

constitutional law. (18c) **1.** The body of law deriving from the U.S. Constitution and dealing primarily with governmental powers, civil rights, and civil liberties. **2.** The body of legal rules that determine the constitution of a state or country with an unwritten constitution. **3.** The field of law dealing with aspects of constitutional provisions, such as restrictions on government powers and guarantees of rights.

constitutional limitation. (18c) A constitutional provision that restricts the powers of a governmental branch, department, agency, or officer.

constitutional question. (18c) A legal issue resolvable by the interpretation of a constitution, rather than a statute.

constitutional right. (18c) A right guaranteed by a constitution; esp., one guaranteed by the U.S. Constitution or by a state constitution.

construction, *n.* (14c) **1.** The act of building by combining or arranging parts or elements; the thing so built. **2.** The act or process of interpreting or explaining the sense or intention of a writing (usu. a constitution, statute, or instrument); the ascertainment of a document's meaning in accordance with judicial standards. — **construct** (for sense 1), *vb.* — **construe** (for sense 2), *vb.*

contemporaneous construction. An interpretation given at or near the time when a writing was prepared, usu. by one or more persons involved in its preparation.

liberal construction. (17c) An interpretation that applies to a writing in light of the situation presented and that tends to effectuate the spirit and purpose of the writing.

purposive construction (**pər**-pə-siv). An interpretation that looks to the "evil" that the statute is trying to correct (i.e., the statute's purpose).

strict construction. (16c) **1.** An interpretation that considers only the literal words of a writing. **2.** A construction that considers words narrowly, usu. in their historical context. • This type of construction treats statutory and contractual words with highly restrictive readings. **3.** The philosophy underlying strict interpretation of statutes.

constructionism. A judicial approach to interpreting the text of statutes, regulations, constitutions, and the like.

liberal constructionism. Broad interpretation of a text's language, including the use of related writings to clarify the meanings of the words, and possibly also a consideration of meaning in both contemporary and current lights.

strict constructionism, *n.* (1892) The doctrinal view of judicial construction holding that judges should interpret a document or statute (esp. one involving penal sanctions) according to its literal terms, without looking to other sources to ascertain the meaning. — **strict constructionist,** *n.*

constructive, *adj.* (17c) Legally imputed; existing by virtue of legal fiction though not existing in fact. • Courts usu. give something a constructive effect for equitable reasons.

constructive-receipt doctrine. (1936) The rule that gross income under a taxpayer's control before it is actually received (such as accumulated interest income that has not been withdrawn) must be included by the taxpayer in gross income, unless the actual receipt is subject to significant constraints. IRC (26 USCA) § 451.

construe (kən-**stroo**), *vb.* (14c) To analyze and explain the meaning of (a sentence or passage).

consultation, *n.* (15c) **1.** The act of asking the advice or opinion of someone (such as a lawyer). **2.** A meeting in which parties consult or confer. **3.** *Int'l law.* The interactive methods by which states seek to prevent or resolve disputes. — **consult,** *vb.* — **consulting, consultative,** *adj.*

consultative exam. As a foundation for an expert opinion, a check-up performed by a qualified medical professional to determine whether a person has a mental or physical disability, and, if so, the extent of the disability and expectations for improvement.

consumable, *n.* (1802) A thing (such as food) that cannot be used without changing or extinguishing its substance. — **consumable,** *adj.*

consumer. (15c) A person who buys goods or services for personal, family, or household use, with no intention of resale; a natural person who uses products for personal rather than business purposes.

consumer confusion. *Trademarks.* The incorrect perception formed by a purchaser or user about a product's or service's manufacturer or origin. • The mistake usu. occurs when a product or service is marketed in a way that makes it appear to be affiliated with a well-known product, service, or provider.

consumer-contemplation test. (1979) A method of imposing product liability on a manufacturer if the evidence shows that a product's danger is greater than that which a reasonable consumer would expect.

Consumer Credit Protection Act. A federal statute that safeguards consumers in the use of credit by (1) requiring full disclosure of the terms of loan agreements, including finance charges, (2) restricting the garnishment of wages, and (3) regulating the use of credit cards. 15 USCA §§ 1601–1693. — Abbr. CCPA.

consumer-credit transaction. (1954) A transaction by which a person receives a loan to buy consumer goods or services.

consumer-goods transaction. *Secured transactions.* A transaction in which (1) an individual incurs an obligation primarily for a personal, family, or household purpose, and (2) a security interest in consumer goods secures the obligation. UCC § 9-102(a)(24).

consumer law. (1966) The area of law dealing with consumer transactions — that is, a person's obtaining credit, goods, real property, or services for personal, family, or household purposes.

consumer price index. An index that tracks the price of goods and services purchased by the average consumer and that is published monthly by the U.S. Bureau of Labor Statistics. — Abbr. CPI.

consumer product. (1949) An item of personal property that is distributed in commerce and is normally used for personal, family, or household purposes. 15 USCA § 2301(1).

Consumer Product Safety Commission. An independent federal regulatory commission that develops safety standards for consumer products and promotes research into the causes and prevention of product-related deaths, illnesses, and injuries. 15 USCA §§ 2051 et seq. — Abbr. CPSC.

consumer-protection law. (1954) A state or federal statute designed to protect consumers against unfair trade and credit practices involving consumer goods, as well as to protect consumers against faulty and dangerous goods.

consummate (**kon**-sə-mayt), *vb.* (16c) **1.** To bring to completion; esp., to make (a marriage) complete by sexual intercourse. **2.** To achieve; to fulfill. **3.** To perfect; to carry to the highest degree. — **consummate** (kən-**səm**-it *or* **kahn**-sə-mit), *adj.*

consummation of marriage. *Family law.* The first postmarital act of sexual intercourse between a husband and wife.

consumption. (14c) The act of destroying a thing by using it; the use of a thing in a way that exhausts it.

contemnor (kən-**tem**-ər *or* -nər *or* -nor). (16c) A person who is guilty of contempt before a governmental body, such as a court or legislature. — **contemn** (kən-**tem**), *vb.*

contemplation of bankruptcy. The thought of declaring bankruptcy because of the inability to continue current financial operations, often coupled with action designed to thwart the distribution of assets in a bankruptcy proceeding.

contemplation of death. (18c) The thought of dying, not necessarily from imminent danger, but as the compelling reason to transfer property to another.

contemporaneous-construction doctrine. (1956) The rule that the initial interpretation of an ambiguous statute by an administrative agency or lower court is entitled to great deference if the interpretation has been used over a long period.

contemporaneous-objection rule. (1965) The doctrine that a timely and proper objection to the admission of evidence must be made at trial for the issue of admissibility to be considered on appeal.

contemporary community standards. (1957) The gauge by which a fact-finder decides whether material is obscene, judging by its patent offensiveness and its prurience in the locale at a given time.

contempt, *n.* (14c) **1.** The act or state of despising; the condition of being despised. **2.** Conduct that defies the authority or dignity of a court or legislature. • Because such conduct interferes with the administration of justice, it is punishable, usu. by fine or imprisonment. — **contemptuous,** *adj.*

civil contempt. (1884) The failure to obey a court order that was issued for another party's benefit. • A civil-contempt proceeding is coercive or remedial in nature. The usual sanction is to confine the contemnor until he or she complies with the court order.

contempt of Congress. Deliberate interference with the duties and powers of Congress, such as a witness's refusal to answer a question from a congressional committee. • Contempt of Congress is a criminal offense. 2 USCA § 192.

criminal contempt. (1841) An act that obstructs justice or attacks the integrity of the court. • A criminal-contempt proceeding is punitive in nature.

direct contempt. (1863) A contempt (such as an assault of a testifying witness) committed in the immediate vicinity of a court; esp., a contempt committed in a judge's presence.

indirect contempt. (1896) Contempt that is committed outside of court, as when a party disobeys a court order. • Indirect contempt is punishable only after proper notice to the contemnor and a hearing.

contempt power. (1885) The power of a governmental body (such as Congress or a court) to punish someone who shows contempt for the process, orders, or proceedings of that body.

content-based restriction. (1973) *Constitutional law.* A restraint on the substance of a particular type of speech. • This type of restriction is presumptively invalid but can survive a constitutional challenge if it is based on a compelling state interest and its measures are narrowly drawn to accomplish that end.

content-valid test. A job-applicant examination that bears a close relationship to the skills required by the job. • Content-validation studies are often performed in employment-discrimination cases that contest the validity of an examination.

contest (kən-**test**), *vb.* (17c) **1.** To strive to win or hold; contend. **2.** To litigate or call into question; challenge. **3.** To deny an adverse claim or assert a defense to it in a court proceeding. — **contest (kon-**test), *n.*

contestability clause (kən-tes-tə-**bil**-ə-tee). *Insurance.* A policy provision setting forth when and under what conditions the insurer may contest a claim or void the policy based on a representation or omission made when the policy was issued.

contestant. (17c) **1.** One who contests the validity of a will, trust, or other legal instrument. **2.** *Trademarks.* One who challenges the placement of a trademark on the Principal Register. **3.** *Patents.* A party to an interference proceeding in the U.S. Patent and Trademark Office.

context, *n.* (16c) **1.** The surrounding text of a word or passage, used to determine the meaning of that word or passage <his remarks were taken out of context>. **2.** Setting or environment <in the context of foreign relations>. — **contextual,** *adj.*

context rule. *Contracts.* The principle that a court may look to extrinsic evidence to determine the intended meaning of a contract, even though the language itself is clear and unambiguous. • The court may consider (1) the subject matter and purpose of the contract, (2) the circumstances surrounding the making of the contract, (3) the subsequent conduct of the parties to the contract, (4) the reasonableness of the parties' respective interpretations, (5) statements made by the parties in preliminary negotiations, (6) usages of trade, and (7) the course of dealing between the parties. Restatement (Second) of Contracts §§ 212, 214(c) (1981).

contiguous (kən-**tig**-yoo-əs), *adj.* (17c) **1.** Touching at a point or along a boundary; ADJOINING. **2.** Near in time or sequence; successive. — **contiguity** (kon-ti-**gyoo**-ə-tee), *n.*

contingency (kən-**tin**-jən-see). (16c) **1.** An event that may or may not occur; a possibility. **2.** The condition of being dependent on chance; uncertainty. **3.** Contingent fee. — **contingent** (kən-**tin**-jənt), *adj.*

contingent fee. (17c) A fee charged for a lawyer's services only if the lawsuit is successful or is favorably settled out of court.

reverse contingent fee. A fee in which a defense lawyer's compensation depends in whole or in part on how much money the lawyer saves the client, given the client's potential liability — so that the lower the settlement or judgment, the higher the lawyer's fee.

continuance, *n.* (14c) **1.** The act of keeping up, maintaining, or prolonging. **2.** Duration; time of continuing. **3.** *Procedure.* The adjournment or postponement of a trial or other proceeding to a future date.

continuation agreement. (1942) *Partnership.* An agreement among the partners that, in the event of dissolution, the business of the partnership can be continued without the necessity of liquidation.

continuation-in-part. *Patents.* A patent application filed by the same applicant during the pendency of an earlier application, repeating a substantial part of the earlier application but adding to or subtracting from the claims. 35 USCA § 120. — Abbr. CIP.

continuing, *adj.* (14c) **1.** Uninterrupted; persisting <a continuing offense>. **2.** Not requiring renewal; enduring <continuing stockholders> <continuing jurisdiction>.

continuing judicial education. (1964) Continuing legal education for judges, usu. organized and sponsored by a governmentally subsidized body and often involving topics such as judicial writing, efficient decision-making, caseload management, and the like. — Abbr. CJE.

continuing-jurisdiction doctrine. (1966) **1.** The rule that a court retains power to enter and enforce a judgment over a party even though that party is no longer subject to a new action. **2.** *Family law.* The rule that once a court has acquired jurisdiction over a child-custody or support case, that court continues to have jurisdiction to modify orders, even if the child or a parent moves to another state.

continuing legal education. (1948) **1.** The process or system through which lawyers extend their learning beyond their law-school studies, usu. by attending seminars designed to sharpen lawyering skills or to provide updates on legal developments within particular practice areas. • In many jurisdictions, lawyers have annual or biennial requirements to devote a given number of hours (usu. 12–15) to continuing legal education. **2.** The enhanced skills or knowledge derived from this process. **3.** The business field in which educational providers supply the demand for legal seminars, books, audiotapes, and videotapes designed to further the education of lawyers. — Abbr. CLE.

continuing threat of harm. A condition or situation that presents a high risk of injury at intervals or over an extended period, whether or not an injury has actually occurred.

continuing-violation doctrine. *Employment law.* The judge-made rule that if an employer's discriminatory acts are of an ongoing nature, the statute of limitations will be extended to allow the plaintiff to recover even when a claim based on those acts would otherwise be time-barred.

continuity of business enterprise. (1980) *Tax.* A doctrine covering acquisitive reorganizations whereby the acquiring corporation must continue the target corporation's historical business or must use a significant portion of the target's business assets in a new business to qualify the acquisition as a tax-deferred transaction.

continuity of interest. (1974) **1.** *Tax.* A doctrine covering acquisitive reorganizations whereby a target corporation's shareholders must retain a share in the acquiring corporation to qualify the acquisition as a tax-deferred transaction. **2.** A judicial requirement for divisive reorganizations whereby a target corporation's shareholders must retain an interest in both the distributing and the controlled corporations to qualify the exchange as a tax-deferred transaction.

continuity-of-life doctrine. The principle that the withdrawal, incapacity, bankruptcy, or death of the owner of an entity (esp. a corporation) does not end the entity's existence.

continuous-adverse-use principle. The rule that the uninterrupted use of land — along with the other elements of adverse possession — will result in a successful claim for adverse possession.

continuous-operations clause. *Oil & gas.* A provision in an oil-and-gas lease giving the lessee the right to continue any drilling well that was begun before the lease expired and to begin drilling more wells.

continuous-representation doctrine. The principle that the limitations period for bringing a legal-malpractice action is tolled as long as the lawyer against whom the action is brought continues the representation that is related to the negligent act or omission.

continuous-treatment doctrine. (1962) The principle that the limitations period for bringing a medical-malpractice action is tolled while the patient continues treatment that is related to the negligent act or omission.

contort (**kon**-tort), *n.* **1.** (*usu. pl.*) The overlapping domain of contract law and tort law. **2.** A specific wrong that falls within that domain. **3.** *Informal.* A constitutional tort.

contra (**kon**-trə), *prep.* (15c) Against or contrary to. • As a citation signal, *contra* denotes that the cited authority supports a contrary view.

contraband (**kon**-trə-band), *n.* (16c) **1.** Illegal or prohibited trade; smuggling. **2.** Goods that are unlawful to import, export, produce, or possess. — **contraband,** *adj.*

contraband per se. Property whose possession is unlawful regardless of how it is used.

derivative contraband. Property whose possession becomes unlawful when it is used in committing an illegal act.

contract, *n.* (14c) **1.** An agreement between two or more parties creating obligations that are enforceable or otherwise recognizable at law. **2.** The writing that sets forth such an agreement. **3.** A promise or set of promises by a party to a transaction, enforceable or otherwise recognizable at law; the writing expressing that promise or set of promises. **4.** Broadly, any legal duty or set of duties not imposed by the law of tort; esp., a duty created by a decree or declaration of a court. **5.** The body of law dealing with agreements and exchange. **6.** The terms of an agreement, or any particular term. **7.** Loosely, a sale or conveyance. **8.** Loosely, an enforceable agreement between two or more parties to do or not to do a thing or set of things; a compact. — **contract,** *vb.* — **contractual,** *adj.*

accessory contract. A contract entered into primarily for the purpose of carrying out a principal contract.

adhesion contract. (1949) A standard-form contract prepared by one party, to be signed by another party in a weaker position, usu. a consumer, who adheres to the contract with little choice about the terms.

aleatory contract (**ay**-lee-ə-tor-ee). [fr. Latin *aleator* "gambler," fr. *alea* "the throwing of dice"] (1891) A contract in which at least one party's performance depends on some uncertain event that is beyond the control of the parties involved. • Most insurance contracts and life annuities are of this type.

alternative contract. (1871) A contract in which the performing party may elect to perform one of two or more specified acts to satisfy the obligation; a contract that provides more than one way for a party to complete performance, usu. permitting that party to choose the manner of performance.

best-efforts contract. A contract in which a party undertakes to use best efforts to fulfill the promises made rather than to achieve a specific result; a contract in which the adequacy of a party's performance is measured by the party's ability to fulfill the specified obligations. • Although the obligor must use best efforts, the risk of failure lies with the obligee.

bilateral contract. (1866) A contract in which each party promises a performance, so that each party is an obligor on that party's own promise and an obligee on the other's promise; a contract in which the parties obligate themselves reciprocally, so that the obligation of one party is correlative to the obligation of the other.

blanket contract. A contract covering a group of products, goods, or services for a fixed period.

build-to-print contract. A contract requiring the contractor to build a product according to exact technical specifications provided by the customer. • The design specifications are explicit and are often coupled with performance specifications, so the contractor has little discretion in how to perform. Much governmental contracting is build-to-print.

certain contract. (17c) A contract that will be performed in a stipulated manner.

collateral contract. (1809)A side agreement that relates to a contract, which, if unintegrated, can be supplemented by evidence of the side agreement; an agreement made before or at the same time as, but separately from, another contract.

construction contract. A contract setting forth the specifications for a building project's construction. • This type of contract is usu. secured by performance and payment bonds to protect both the owner and the subcontractors.

contract for deed. (1825) A conditional sales contract for the sale of real property.

contract for sale. (1808) **1.** A contract for the present transfer of property for a price. **2.** A contract to sell goods at a future time.

cost-plus contract. (1920) A contract in which payment is based on a fixed fee or a percentage added to the actual cost incurred.

destination contract. (1958) A contract in which a seller bears the risk of loss until the goods arrive at the destination. UCC § 2-509.

employment contract. (1927) A contract between an employer and employee in which the terms and conditions of employment are stated.

engineering, procurement, and construction contract. A fixed-price, schedule-intensive construction contract — typical in the construction of single-purpose projects, such as energy plants — in which the contractor agrees to a wide variety of responsibilities, including the duties to provide for the design, engineering, procurement, and construction of the facility; to prepare start-up procedures; to conduct performance tests; to create operating manuals; and to train people to operate the facility. — Abbr. EPC contract.

evergreen contract. A contract that renews itself from one term to the next in the absence of contrary notice by one of the parties.

executed contract. (18c) **1.** A contract that has been fully performed by both parties. **2.** A signed contract.

executory contract (eg-**zek**-yə-tor-ee). (18c) A contract that remains wholly unperformed or for which there remains something still to be done on both sides, often as a component of a larger transaction and sometimes memorialized by an informal letter agreement, by a memorandum, or by oral agreement.

express contract. (17c) A contract whose terms the parties have explicitly set out.

fixed-price contract. A contract in which the buyer agrees to pay the seller a definite and predetermined price regardless of increases in the seller's cost or the buyer's ability to acquire the same goods in the market at a lower price.

government contract. A contract to which a government or government agency is a party, esp. for the purchase of goods and services.

grubstake contract. A contract between two parties in which one party provides the grubstake — money and supplies — and the other party prospects for and locates minerals on public land. • Each party acquires an interest in the minerals as agreed to in the contract.

guaranteed-sale contract. A contract between a real-estate agency and a property owner in which the agency agrees to buy the property at a guaranteed price after a specified length of time if it has not been sold under the listing agreement. • The guaranteed price is usu. a substantial discount from the listed price.

illegal contract. (18c) A promise that is prohibited because the performance, formation, or object of the agreement is against the law. • Technically speaking, an illegal contract is not a contract at all because it cannot be enforced, so the phrase is a misnomer.

illusory contract. (18c) An agreement in which one party gives as consideration a promise that is so insubstantial as to impose no obligation. • The insubstantial promise renders the agreement unenforceable.

immoral contract. An agreement that so flagrantly violates societal norms as to be unenforceable.

implied contract. (17c) **1.** An implied-in-law contract. **2.** An implied-in-fact contract.

implied-in-fact contract. A contract that the parties presumably intended as their tacit understanding, as inferred from their conduct and other circumstances.

implied-in-law contract. An obligation created by law for the sake of justice; specif., an obligation imposed by law because of some special relationship between the parties or because one of them would otherwise be unjustly enriched. • An implied-in-law contract is not actually a contract, but instead is a remedy that allows the plaintiff to recover a benefit conferred on the defendant.

indemnity contract. A contract by which the promisor agrees to reimburse a promisee for some loss irrespective of a third person's liability.

installment contract. (1896) A contract requiring or authorizing the delivery of goods in separate lots, or payments in separate increments, to be separately accepted.

letter contract. In federal contract law, a written contract with sufficient provisions to permit the contractor to begin performance.

marketing contract. **1.** A business's agreement with an agency or other association for the promotion of sales of the business's goods or services. **2.** An agreement between a cooperative and its members, by which the members agree to sell through the cooperative, and the cooperative agrees to obtain an agreed price.

marriage contract. A form of mutual consent required for a matrimonial relationship to exist according to the law of the place where the consent takes place.

output contract. (1904) A contract in which a seller promises to supply and a buyer to buy all the goods or services that a seller produces during a specified period and at a set price. • The quantity term is measured by the seller's output. An output contract assures the seller of a market or outlet for the period of the contract.

parol contract (pə-**rohl** *or* **par**-əl). (18c) **1.** A contract or modification of a contract that is not in writing or is only partially in writing. **2.** At common law, a contract not under seal, although it could be in writing.

pay-or-play contract. A contract in which one party agrees to perform and the other agrees to pay for the promised performance even if performance is never demanded. • Pay-or-play contracts are usu. made in the entertainment industry.

performance contract. **1.** A contract that requires a party to act personally and does not allow substitution. • People who provide unique personal services often make performance contracts. **2.** A contract that allows the contractor to choose the means to achieve the end result. • The product's specifications may be loose and allow the contractor latitude in deciding how to perform.

precontract. (15c) A contract that precludes a party from entering into a comparable agreement with someone else.

principal contract. A contract giving rise to an accessory contract, as an agreement from which a secured obligation originates.

procurement contract. A contract in which a government receives goods or services.

requirements contract. (1932) A contract in which a buyer promises to buy and a seller to supply all the goods or services that a buyer needs during a specified period. • The quantity term is measured by the buyer's requirements. A requirements contract assures the buyer of a source for the period of the contract.

retail installment contract. A contract for the sale of goods under which the buyer makes periodic payments and the seller retains title to or a security interest in the goods.

satisfaction contract. A contract by which one party agrees to perform to the satisfaction of the other.

service contract. A contract to perform a service; esp., a written agreement to provide maintenance or repairs on a consumer product for a specified term.

severable contract. (1854) A contract that includes two or more promises each of which can be enforced separately, so that failure to perform one of the promises does not necessarily put the promisor in breach of the entire contract.

shipment contract. (1893) A contract in which a seller bears the risk of damage to the items sold only until they are brought to the place of shipment. • If a contract for the sale of goods does not address the terms of delivery, it is presumed to be a shipment contract. UCC §§ 2-319, 2-504, 2-509.

standard-form contract. (1923) A usu. preprinted contract containing set clauses, used repeatedly by a business or within a particular industry with only slight additions or modifications to meet the specific situation.

subcontract. (18c) A secondary contract made by a party to the primary contract for carrying out the primary contract, or a part of it.

substituted contract. A contract made between parties to an earlier contract so that the new one takes the place of and discharges the earlier one.

tacit contract. A contract in which conduct takes the place of written or spoken words in the offer or acceptance (or both).

take-or-pay contract. A contract requiring the buyer to either purchase and receive a minimum amount of a product ("take") or pay for this minimum without taking immediate delivery ("pay"). • These contracts are often used in the energy and oil-and-gas businesses.

third-party-beneficiary contract. A contract that directly benefits a third party and that gives the third party a right to sue any of the original contracting parties for breach.

unilateral contract. (1855) A contract in which only one party makes a promise or undertakes a performance; a contract in which no promisor receives a promise as consideration for the promise given.

valid contract. A contract that is fully operative in accordance with the parties' intent.

variable annuity contract. *Securities.* An annuity whose payments vary according to how well the fund (usu. made up of common stocks) that backs it is performing. SEC Rule 0-1(e)(1) (17 CFR § 270.0-1(e)(1)).

voidable contract. (18c) A contract that can be affirmed or rejected at the option of one of the parties; a contract that is void as to the wrongdoer but not void as to the party wronged, unless that party elects to treat it as void.

void contract. (17c) **1.** A contract that is of no legal effect, so that there is really no contract in existence at all. **2.** A contract that has been fully performed. **3.** Loosely, a voidable contract.

written contract. A contract whose terms have been reduced to writing.

contractor. (16c) **1.** A party to a contract. **2.** More specif., one who contracts to do work or provide supplies for another.

general contractor. One who contracts for the completion of an entire project, including purchasing all materials, hiring and paying subcontractors, and coordinating all the work.

Contracts Clause. (1875) The clause of the U.S. Constitution prohibiting states from passing any law that would impair private contractual obligations. • The Supreme Court has generally interpreted this clause so that states can regulate private contractual obligations if the regulation is reasonable and necessary to serve an important public purpose. U.S. Const. art. I, § 10, cl. 1.

contra proferentem (**kon**-trə prof-ə-**ren**-təm). [Latin "against the offeror"] The doctrine that, in interpreting documents, ambiguities are to be construed unfavorably to the drafter.

contrary to law. (16c) Illegal; unlawful; conflicting with established law.

contrary to the evidence. (16c) (Of an argument, finding, etc.) conflicting with the weight of the evidence presented at a contested hearing.

contravene (kon-trə-**veen**), *vb.* **1.** To violate or infringe; to defy. **2.** To come into conflict with; to be contrary to.

contributing to the delinquency of a minor. (1913) The offense of an adult's engaging in conduct involving a minor — or in the presence of a minor — likely to result in delinquent conduct. • Examples include encouraging a minor to shoplift, enabling underage drinking, and soliciting sex for money.

contribution. (14c) **1.** The right that gives one of several persons who are liable on a common debt the ability to recover proportionately from each of the others when that one person discharges the debt for the benefit of all; the right to demand that another who is jointly responsible for a third party's injury supply part of what is required to compensate the third party. **2.** One tortfeasor's right to collect from joint tortfeasors when — and to the extent that — the tortfeasor has paid more than his or her proportionate share to the injured party, the shares being determined as percentages of causal fault. **3.** The actual payment by a joint tortfeasor of a proportionate share of what is due.

contributory (kən-**trib**-yə-tor-ee), *adj.* (15c) **1.** Tending to bring about a result. **2.** (Of a pension fund) receiving contributions from both the employer and the employees.

contributory, *n.* (15c) **1.** One who contributes or who has a duty to contribute. **2.** A contributing factor.

contributory-negligence doctrine. (1911) *Torts.* The principle that completely bars a plaintiff's recovery if the damage suffered is partly the plaintiff's own fault.

control, *n.* (16c) The direct or indirect power to govern the management and policies of a person or entity, whether through ownership of voting securities, by contract, or otherwise; the power or authority to manage, direct, or oversee.

control, *vb.* (15c) **1.** To exercise power or influence over. **2.** To regulate or govern. **3.** To have a controlling interest in.

control group. (1937) The persons with authority to make decisions on a corporation's behalf.

control-group test. (1969) A method of determining whether the attorney–client privilege protects communications made by corporate employees, by providing that those communications are protected only if made by an employee who is a member of the group with authority to direct the corporation's actions as a result of that communication. • The U.S. Supreme Court rejected the control-group test in *Upjohn Co. v. United States*, 449 U.S. 383, 101 S.Ct. 677 (1981).

controlled substance. (1970) Any type of drug whose possession and use is regulated by law, including a narcotic, a stimulant, or a hallucinogen.

controlled-substance act. (1970) A federal or state statute that is designed to control the distribution, classification, sale, and use of certain drugs. • Most states have enacted these laws, which are usu. modeled on the Uniform Controlled Substances Act.

control theory. (1949) The theory that people will engage in criminal behavior unless certain personally held social controls (such as a strong investment in conventional, legitimate activities or a belief that criminal behavior is morally wrong) are in place to prevent them from doing so.

controversy. (14c) **1.** A disagreement or a dispute, esp. in public. **2.** A justiciable dispute.

public controversy. A controversy involving issues that are debated publicly and that have substantial ramifications for persons other than those engaged in it. • A participant in a public controversy may be deemed a public figure for purposes of a defamation suit arising from the controversy.

separable controversy. (1881) A claim that is separate and independent from the other claims being asserted in a suit. • This term is most often associated with the statute that permits an entire case to be removed to federal court if one of the claims, being separate and independent from the others, presents a federal question that is within the jurisdiction of the federal courts. 28 USCA § 1441(c).

3. *Constitutional law.* A case that requires a definitive determination of the law on the facts alleged for the adjudication of an actual dispute, and not merely a hypothetical, theoretical, or speculative legal issue.

controvert (**kon**-trə-vərt *or* kon-trə-**vərt**), *vb.* (16c) To dispute or contest; esp., to deny (as an allegation in a pleading) or oppose in argument.

contumacy (**kon**-t[y]uu-mə-see), *n.* (15c) Contempt of court; the refusal of a person to follow a court's order or direction. — **contumacious,** *adj.*

contumely (**kon**-t[y]uu-mə-lee *or* kən-**t[y]oo**-mə-lee), *n.* Insulting language or treatment; scornful rudeness.

convene, *vb.* (15c) **1.** To call together; to cause to assemble. **2.** *Civil law.* To bring an action.

convention. (15c) **1.** An agreement or compact, esp. one among nations; a multilateral treaty. **2.** A special deliberative assembly elected for the purpose of framing, revising, or amending a constitution. **3.** An assembly or meeting of members belonging to an organization or having a common objective. **4.** A generally accepted rule or practice; usage or custom. — **conventional,** *adj.*

conventionalism. (1837) A jurisprudential conception of legal practice and tradition holding that law is a matter of respecting and enforcing legal and social rules.

conventional law. (17c) A rule or system of rules agreed on by persons for the regulation of their conduct toward one another; law constituted by agreement as having the force of special law between the parties, by either supplementing or replacing the general law of the land.

conversion, *n.* (14c) **1.** The act of changing from one form to another; the process of being exchanged. **2.** *Tort & criminal law.* The wrongful possession or disposition of another's property as if it were one's own; an act or series of acts of willful interference, without lawful justification, with an item of property in a manner inconsistent with another's right, whereby that other person is deprived of the use and possession of the property. — **convert,** *vb.* — **conversionary,** *adj.*

constructive conversion. Conversion consisting of an action that in law amounts to the appropriation of property.

conversion by detention. Conversion by detaining property in a way that is adverse to the owner or other lawful possessor.

conversion by estoppel. A judicial determination that a conversion has taken place — though in truth one has not — because a defendant is estopped from offering a defense.

conversion by taking. Conversion by taking a chattel out of the possession of another with the intention of exercising a permanent or temporary dominion over it, despite the owner's entitlement to use it at all times.

conversion by wrongful delivery. Conversion by depriving an owner of goods by delivering them to someone else so as to change the possession.

conversion by wrongful destruction. Conversion by willfully consuming or otherwise destroying a chattel belonging to another person.

conversion by wrongful disposition. Conversion by depriving an owner of goods by giving some other person a lawful title to them.

direct conversion. The act of appropriating the property of another to one's own benefit, or to the benefit of a third person.

fraudulent conversion. Conversion that is committed by the use of fraud, either in obtaining the property or in withholding it.

involuntary conversion. The loss or destruction of property through theft, casualty, or condemnation.

technical conversion. The taking of another's personal property by one who acts in good faith and mistakenly believes that he or she is lawfully entitled to the property.

convey, *vb.* (14c) To transfer or deliver (something, such as a right or property) to another, esp. by deed or other writing; esp., to perform an act that is intended to create one or more property interests, regardless of whether the act is actually effective to create those interests.

conveyance (kən-**vay**-ənts), *n.* (15c) **1.** The voluntary transfer of a right or of property. **2.** The transfer of a property right that does not pass by delivery of a thing or merely by agreement. **3.** The transfer of an interest in real property from one living person to another, by means of an instrument such as a deed. **4.** The document (usu. a deed) by which such a transfer occurs. **5.** A means of transport; a vehicle. **6.** *Bankruptcy.* A transfer of an interest in real or personal property, including an assignment, a release, a monetary payment, or the creation of a lien or encumbrance.

conveyancer (kən-**vay**-ən-sər). (17c) A lawyer who specializes in real-estate transactions.

conveyancing (kən-**vay**-ən-sing). (17c) The act or business of drafting and preparing legal instruments, esp. those (such as deeds or leases) that transfer an interest in real property.

conveyee (kən-vay-**ee**). (18c) One to whom property is conveyed.

conveyor (kən-**vay**-ər *or* -or). (16c) One who transfers or delivers title to another.

convict (**kon**-vikt), *n.* (15c) A person who has been found guilty of a crime and is serving a sentence of confinement for that crime; a prison inmate.

conviction (kən-**vik**-shən), *n.* **1.** The act or process of judicially finding someone guilty of a crime; the state of having been proved guilty. **2.** The judgment (as by a jury verdict) that a person is guilty of a crime. **3.** A strong belief or opinion. — **convict** (kən-**vikt**), *vb.*

conviction rate. (1928) Within a given area or for a given time, the number of convictions (including plea bargains) as a percentage of the total number of prosecutions undertaken.

COO. *abbr.* Chief operating officer.

cool blood. (17c) *Criminal law.* In the law of homicide, a condition in which the defendant's emotions are not in such an excited state that they interfere with his or her faculties and reason.

***Cooley* doctrine.** (1936) *Constitutional law.* The principle that Congress has exclusive power under the Commerce Clause to regulate the national as well as the local aspects of national commercial matters, and that the states may regulate those aspects of interstate commerce so local in character as to require diverse treatment. • The Supreme Court has abandoned the *Cooley* doctrine in favor of a balancing test for Commerce Clause cases. *Cooley v. Port Bd. of Wardens*, 53 U.S. (12 How.) 299 (1851).

cooling-off period. (1913) **1.** An automatic delay between a person's taking some legal action and the consequence of that action. **2.** A period during which a buyer may cancel a purchase. **3.** An automatic delay in some states between the filing of divorce papers and the divorce hearing. **4.** *Securities.* A period (usu. at least 20 days) between the filing of a registration and the effective registration. **5.** During a dispute, a period during which no action may be taken by either side.

cooling time. (1874) *Criminal law.* Time to recover cool blood after great excitement, stress, or provocation, so that one is considered able to contemplate, comprehend, and act with reference to the consequences that are likely to follow.

cooperative, *n.* (1883) **1.** An organization or enterprise (as a store) owned by those who use its services. **2.** A dwelling (as an apartment building) owned by its residents, to whom the apartments are leased.

coowner, *n.* (1858) A person who is in concurrent ownership, possession, and enjoyment of property with one or more others; a tenant in common, a joint tenant, or a tenant by the entirety. — **coown,** *vb.* — **coownership,** *n.*

cop a plea, *vb.* (1914) *Slang.* (Of a criminal defendant) to plead guilty to a lesser charge as a means to avoid standing trial for a more serious offense.

coparcenary (koh-**pahr**-sə-ner-ee), *n.* (16c) An estate that arises when two or more persons jointly inherit from one ancestor, the title and right of possession being shared equally by all. — **coparcenary,** *adj.* — **coparcener.**(koh-**pahr**-sə-nər), *n.*

coparty. (1906) A litigant or participant in a legal transaction who has a like status with another party; a party on the same side of a lawsuit.

copayment. A fixed amount that a patient pays to a healthcare provider according to the terms of the patient's health plan.

coplaintiff. (18c) One of two or more plaintiffs in the same litigation.

coprincipal. (17c) **1.** One of two or more participants in a criminal offense who either perpetrate the crime or aid a person who does so. **2.** One of two or more persons who have appointed an agent whom they both have the right to control.

copy, *n.* (14c) **1.** An imitation or reproduction of an original. • In the law of evidence, a copy is generally admissible to prove the contents of a writing. Fed. R. Evid. 1003.

certified copy. (18c) A duplicate of an original (usu. official) document, certified as an exact reproduction usu. by the officer responsible for issuing or keeping the original.

conformed copy. (1937) An exact copy of a document bearing written explanations of things that were not or could not be copied, such as a note on the document indicating that it was signed by a person whose signature appears on the original.

examined copy. A copy (usu. of a record, public book, or register) that has been compared with the original or with an official record of an original.

true copy. A copy that, while not necessarily exact, is sufficiently close to the original that anyone can understand it.

2. *Copyright.* The physical form in which a creative work is fixed and from which the work can be reproduced or perceived, with or without the aid of a special device. 17 USCA § 101. **3.** *Copyright.* An expressive work that is substantially similar to a copyrighted work and not produced coincidentally and independently from the same source as the copyrighted work.

copyleft. *Slang.* A software license that allows users to modify or incorporate open-source code into larger programs on the condition that the software containing the source code is publicly distributed without restrictions.

copyright, *n.* (18c) **1.** The right to copy; specifically, a property right in an original work of authorship (including literary, musical, dramatic, choreographic, pictorial, graphic, sculptural, and architectural works; motion pictures and other audiovisual works; and sound recordings) fixed in any tangible medium of expression, giving the holder the exclusive right to reproduce, adapt, distribute, perform, and display the work. **2.** The body of law relating to such works. • Copyright law is governed by the Copyright Act of 1976. 17 USCA §§ 101–1332. — Abbr. c. — **copyright,** *vb.* — **copyrighted,** *adj.*

common-law copyright. A property right that arose when the work was created, rather than when it was published. • Under the Copyright Act of 1976, which took effect on January 1, 1978, common-law copyright was largely abolished for works created after the statute's effective date.

copyrightability test. A judicial test for determining whether a contributor to a joint work is an author for legal purposes, based on whether the contributor's effort is an original expression that could qualify for copyright protection on its own. • This test has been adopted by a majority of courts.

Copyright Clause. (1940) U.S. Const. art. I, § 8, cl. 8, which gives Congress the power to secure to authors the exclusive rights to their writings for a limited time.

copyright misuse. In an infringement action, an affirmative defense based on the copyright owner's use of a license to restrain trade or in any other manner that is against public policy.

copyright notice. (1889) A notice that a work is copyright-protected, usu. placed in each published copy of the work. • A copyright notice takes the form © (year of publication) (name of basic copyright owner). Since March 1, 1989, such notice is not required for a copyright to be valid (although the notice continues to provide certain procedural advantages).

copyright owner. (1886) One who holds an exclusive right or rights to copyrighted material. 17 USCA § 101.

core rights. Human rights that are generally recognized and accepted throughout the world. • These rights include freedom from extrajudicial execution, torture, and arbitrary arrest and detention. Core rights are embodied in many human rights conventions, including the Universal Declaration of Human Rights, the International Covenant on Civil and Political Rights, and the International Covenant on Economic, Social and Cultural Rights.

corespondent. (1857) **1.** A coparty who responds to a petition, such as a petition for a writ of certiorari. **2.** In some states, a coparty who responds to an appeal. **3.** *Family law.* In a divorce suit based on adultery, the person with whom the spouse is accused of having committed adultery.

cornering the market. The act or process of acquiring ownership or control of a large portion of the available supply of a commodity or security, permitting manipulation of the commodity's or security's price.

corollary (**kor**- *or* **kahr**-ə-ler-ee), *n.* (14c) A proposition that follows from a proven proposition with little or no additional proof; something that naturally follows.

coroner (**kor**- *or* **kahr**-ə-nər). (14c) A public official whose duty is to investigate the causes and circumstances of any death that occurs suddenly, suspiciously, or violently.

corpnership. [Portmanteau word probably formed fr. *corporation* + *partnership*] A limited partnership (usu. having many public investors as limited partners) whose general partner is a corporation.

corporate, *adj.* (16c) Of or relating to a corporation, esp. a business corporation.

corporate acquisition. (1911) The takeover of one corporation by another if both parties retain their legal existence after the transaction.

corporate authority. (1817) **1.** The power rightfully wielded by officers of a corporation. **2.** In some jurisdictions, a municipal officer, esp. one empowered to represent the municipality in certain statutory matters.

corporate books. (1846) Written records of a corporation's activities and business transactions.

corporate citizenship. (1889) Corporate status in the state of incorporation, though a corporation is not a constitutional citizen for the purposes of the Privileges and Immunities Clauses in Article IV § 2 and in the 14th Amendment to the U.S. Constitution.

corporate-opportunity doctrine. (1942) The rule that a corporation's directors, officers, and employees are precluded from using information gained as such to take personal advantage of any business opportunities that the corporation has an expectancy right or property interest in, or that in fairness should otherwise belong to the corporation. • In a partnership, the analogous principle is termed the *firm-opportunity doctrine.*

corporate purpose. (18c) The general scope of the business objective for which a corporation was created. • A statement of corporate purpose is commonly required in the articles of incorporation.

corporate raider. A person or business that attempts to take control of a corporation, against its wishes, by buying its stock and replacing its management.

corporate veil. (1927) The legal assumption that the acts of a corporation are not the actions of its shareholders, so that the shareholders are exempt from liability for the corporation's actions.

corporation, *n.* (15c) An entity (usu. a business) having authority under law to act as a single person distinct from the shareholders who own it and having rights to issue stock and exist indefinitely; a group or succession of persons established in accordance with legal rules into a legal or juristic person that has a legal personality distinct from the natural persons who make it up, exists indefinitely apart from them, and has the legal powers that its constitution gives it. — **incorporate,** *vb.* — **corporate,** *adj.*

acquired corporation. The corporation that no longer exists after a merger or acquisition.

admitted corporation. A corporation licensed or authorized to do business within a particular state.

aggressor corporation. A corporation that attempts to obtain control of a publicly held corporation by (1) a direct cash tender, (2) a public exchange offer to shareholders, or (3) a merger, which requires the agreement of the target's management.

business corporation. A corporation formed to engage in commercial activity for profit.

C corporation. A corporation whose income is taxed through it rather than through its shareholders. • Any corporation not electing S-corporation tax status under the Internal Revenue Code is a C corporation by default.

charitable corporation. (17c) A nonprofit corporation that is dedicated to benevolent purposes and thus entitled to special tax status under the Internal Revenue Code.

civil corporation. Any corporation other than a charitable or religious corporation.

close corporation. (1840) A corporation whose stock is not freely traded and is held by only a few shareholders (often within the same family). • The requirements and privileges of close corporations vary by jurisdiction.

collapsible corporation. (1955) A corporation formed to give a short-term venture the appearance of a long-term investment in order to portray income as capital gain, rather than profit. • The corporation is typically formed for the sole purpose of purchasing property. The corporation is usu. dissolved before the property has generated substantial income. The Internal Revenue Service treats the income earned through a collapsible corporation as ordinary income rather than as capital gain. IRC (26 USCA) § 341(a).

controlled corporation. **1.** A corporation in which the majority of the stock is held by one individual or firm. **2.** A corporation in which a substantial amount (but less than a majority) of the stock is held by one individual or firm. • Some states presume control with as little as 10%.

controlled foreign corporation. *Tax.* A foreign corporation in which more than 50% of the stock is owned by U.S. citizens who each own 10% or more of the voting stock. • These shareholders (known as *U.S. shareholders*) are required to report their pro rata share of certain passive income of the corporation. IRC (26 USCA) §§ 951–964. — Abbr. CFC.

cooperative corporation. An entity that has a corporate existence, but is primarily organized for the purpose of providing services and profits to its members and not for corporate profit. • The most common kind of cooperative corporation is formed to purchase real property, such as an apartment building, so that its shareholders may lease the apartments.

corporation by prescription. A corporation that, though lacking a charter, has acquired its corporate status through a long period of operating as a corporation. • Such an entity may engage in any enterprises that are not manifestly inconsistent with the purposes for which it is assumed to have been created.

domestic corporation. (1819) **1.** A corporation that is organized and chartered under the laws of a state. • The corporation is considered *domestic* by the chartering state. **2.** *Tax.* A corporation created or organized in the

United States or under federal or state law. IRC (26 USCA) § 7701(a)(4).

dormant corporation. **1.** An inactive corporation; a legal corporation that is presently not operating. **2.** A corporation whose authority to do business has been revoked or suspended either by operation of law (as by failure to pay franchise taxes) or by an act of the government official responsible for the corporation's authority.

dummy corporation. (1899) A corporation whose only function is to hide the principal's identity and to protect the principal from liability.

foreign corporation. (18c) A corporation that was organized and chartered under the laws of another state, government, or country <in Arizona, a California corporation is said to be a foreign corporation>.

for-profit corporation. A corporation organized for the purpose of making a profit; a business corporation.

joint-venture corporation. A corporation that has joined with one or more individuals or corporations to accomplish some specified project.

limited-liability corporation.

migratory corporation. A corporation formed under the laws of another state than that of the incorporators' residence for the purpose of carrying on a significant portion of its business in the state of the incorporators' residence or in a state other than where it was incorporated.

moneyed corporation. A corporation that uses money capital in its business, esp. one (such as a bank) that engages in the exchange or lending of money.

multinational corporation. A company with operations in two or more countries, generally allowing it to transfer funds and products according to price and demand conditions, subject to risks such as changes in exchange rates or political instability.

multistate corporation. A corporation incorporated under the laws of two or more states.

nonprofit corporation. (1908) A corporation organized for some purpose other than making a profit, and usu. afforded special tax treatment.

nonstock corporation. A corporation that does not issue shares of stock as evidence of ownership but instead is owned by its members in accordance with a charter or agreement. • Examples are mutual insurance companies, charitable organizations, and private clubs.

parent corporation. (1893) A corporation that has a controlling interest in another corporation (called a *subsidiary corporation*), usu. through ownership of more than one-half the voting stock.

private corporation. (17c) A corporation founded by and composed of private individuals principally for a nonpublic purpose, such as manufacturing, banking, and railroad corporations (including charitable and religious corporations).

professional corporation. (1958) A corporation providing services of a type requiring a professional license. • A professional corporation may be made up of architects, accountants, lawyers, physicians, veterinarians, or the like. — Abbr. P.C.

public corporation. (17c) **1.** A corporation whose shares are traded to and among the general public. **2.** A corporation that is created by the state as an agency in the administration of civil government. **3.** A government-owned corporation that engages in activities that benefit the general public, usu. while remaining financially independent. • Such a corporation is managed by a publicly appointed board.

public-service corporation. (1894) A corporation whose operations serve a need of the general public, such as public transportation, communications, gas, water, or electricity. • This type of corporation is usu. subject to extensive governmental regulation.

quasi-corporation. An entity that exercises some of the functions of a corporation but that has not been granted corporate status by statute; esp., a public corporation with limited authority and powers (such as a county or school district). — Also sometimes termed *quasi-municipal corporation.*

quasi-public corporation. A for-profit corporation providing an essential public service. • An example is an electric company or other utility.

registered corporation. (1928) A publicly held corporation, a security of which is registered under § 12 of the Securities Exchange Act of 1934. • The corporation is subject to the Act's periodic disclosure requirements and proxy regulations. 15 USCA § 78*l*.

religious corporation. A corporation created to carry out some ecclesiastical or religious purpose.

S corporation. (1961) A corporation whose income is taxed through its shareholders rather than through the corporation itself. • Only corporations with a limited number of shareholders can elect S-corporation tax status under Subchapter S of the Internal Revenue Code.

shell corporation. (1969) A corporation that has no active business and usu. exists only in name as a vehicle for another company's business operations.

sister corporation. One of two or more corporations controlled by the same, or substantially the same, owners.

small-business corporation. (1898) **1.** A corporation having no more than 75 shareholders and otherwise satisfying the requirements of the Internal Revenue Code provisions permitting a subchapter S election. IRC (26 USCA) § 1361. **2.** A corporation receiving money for stock (as a contribution to capital and paid-in surplus) totaling not more than $1,000,000, and otherwise satisfying the requirements of the Internal Revenue Code section 1244(c) thereby enabling the shareholders to claim an ordinary loss on worthless stock. IRC (26 USCA) § 1244(c).

sole corporation. A corporation having or acting through only a single member.

stock corporation. A corporation in which the capital is contributed by the shareholders and divided into shares represented by certificates.

subsidiary corporation. (1882) A corporation in which a parent corporation has a controlling share.

surviving corporation. A corporation that acquires the assets and liabilities of another corporation by a merger or takeover.

target corporation. A corporation over which control is being sought by another party.

thin corporation. A corporation with an excessive amount of debt in its capitalization.

trading corporation. A corporation whose business involves the buying and selling of goods.

tramp corporation. A corporation chartered in a state where it does not conduct business.

U.S.-owned foreign corporation. A foreign corporation in which 50% or more of the total combined voting power or total value of the stock is held directly or indirectly by U.S. citizens. IRC (26 USCA) § 904(g)(6). • If the dividend or interest income paid by a U.S. corporation is classified as a foreign source, the U.S. corporation is treated as a U.S.-owned foreign corporation. IRC (26 USCA) § 861.

corporator (**kor**-pə-ray-tər). (18c) **1.** A member of a corporation. **2.** Incorporator.

corporeal (kor-**por**-ee-əl), *adj.* (15c) Having a physical, material existence; tangible <land and fixtures are corporeal property>. Cf. INCORPOREAL. — **corporeality,** *n.*

corpus (**kor**-pəs), *n.* [Latin "body"] **1.** The property for which a trustee is responsible; the trust principal. **2.** PRINCIPAL (4). Pl. **corpora** (**kor**-pə-rə), **corpuses** (**kor**-pə-səz).

corpus delicti (**kor**-pəs də-**lik**-tɪ *or* -tee). [Latin "body of the crime"] (1818) **1.** The fact of a transgression; ACTUS REUS. **2.** Loosely, the material substance on which a crime has been committed; the physical evidence of a crime, such as the corpse of a murdered person.

corpus delicti **rule.** (1926) *Criminal law.* The doctrine that prohibits a prosecutor from proving the corpus delicti based solely on a defendant's extrajudicial statements. • The prosecution must establish the *corpus delicti* with corroborating evidence to secure a conviction.

corpus juris (**kor**-pəs **joor**-is). [Latin "body of law"] (1832) The law as the sum or collection of laws <*Corpus Juris Secundum*>. — Abbr. C.J.

correction, *n.* (14c) **1.** Generally, the act or an instance of making right what is wrong. **2.** A change in business activity or market price following and counteracting an increase or decrease in the activity or price. **3.** (*usu. pl.*) The punishment and treatment of a criminal offender through a program of imprisonment, parole, and probation. — **correct,** *vb.* — **corrective** (for senses 1 & 2), **correctional** (for sense 3), *adj.*

correctional system. A network of governmental agencies that administer a jurisdiction's prisons and parole system.

corrective advertising. Advertising that informs consumers that earlier advertisements contained a deceptive claim, and that provides consumers with corrected information. • This type of advertising may be ordered by the Federal Trade Commission.

correlative (kə-**rel**-ə-tiv), *adj.* (16c) **1.** Related or corresponding; analogous. **2.** Having or involving a reciprocal or mutually interdependent relationship.

correlative-rights doctrine. (1938) **1.** *Water law.* The principle that adjoining landowners must limit their use of a common water source to a reasonable amount. **2.** *Oil & gas.* The rule that a lessee's or landowner's right to capture oil and gas from the property is restricted by the duty to exercise that right without waste or negligence. • This is a corollary to the rule of capture.

correspondent, *n.* (17c) **1.** The writer of a letter or letters. **2.** A person employed by the media to report on events. **3.** A securities firm or financial institution that performs services for another in a place or market that the other does not have direct access to. — **correspond,** *vb.*

corroboration (kə-rob-ə-**ray**-shən), *n.* (16c) **1.** Confirmation or support by additional evidence or authority. **2.** Formal confirmation or ratification. — **corroborate,** *vb.* — **corroborative** (kə-**rob**-ə-rə-tiv), *adj.* — **corroborator** (kə-**rob**-ə-ray-tər), *n.*

corruption. (14c) **1.** Depravity, perversion, or taint; an impairment of integrity, virtue, or moral principle; esp., the impairment of a public official's duties by bribery. **2.** The act of doing something with an intent to give some advantage inconsistent with official duty and the rights of others; a fiduciary's or official's use of a station or office to procure some benefit either personally or for someone else, contrary to the rights of others. — **corrupt,** *adj.* — **corrupt,** *vb.*

corruption of blood. A defunct doctrine, now considered unconstitutional, under which a person loses the ability to inherit or pass property as a result of an attainder or of being declared civilly dead.

corruptly, *adv.* (16c) In a corrupt or depraved manner; by means of corruption or bribery. • As used in criminal-law statutes, *corruptly* usu. indicates a wrongful desire for pecuniary gain or other advantage.

corrupt-motive doctrine. (1962) *Criminal law.* The rule that conspiracy is punishable only if the agreement was entered into with an evil purpose, not merely with an intent to do the illegal act. • This doctrine has been rejected by the Model Penal Code.

corrupt-practices act. (1897) A federal or state statute that regulates campaign contributions and expenditures as well as their disclosure.

cosign, *vb.* (1967) To sign a document along with another person, usu. to assume obligations and to supply credit to the principal obligor. — **cosignature,** *n.* — **cosigner.**

cost, *n.* (13c) **1.** The amount paid or charged for something; price or expenditure.

acquisition cost. (1926) An asset's net price; the original cost of an asset.

carrying cost. **1.** *Accounting.* The variable cost of stocking one unit of inventory for one year. • Carrying cost includes the opportunity cost of the capital invested in the inventory. **2.** A current charge or noncapital expenditure made to prevent the causing or accelerating of the termination of a defeasible estate, as well as the sums spent on repairs required by the duty to avoid permissive waste.

cost of completion. (1852) *Contracts.* An element of damages based on the expense that would be incurred by the nonbreaching party to finish the promised performance.

direct cost. (1818) The amount of money for material, labor, and overhead to produce a product.

distribution cost. Any cost incurred in marketing a product or service, such as advertising, storage, and shipping.

fixed cost. (1894) A cost whose value does not fluctuate with changes in output or business activity; esp., overhead expenses such as rent, salaries, and depreciation.

indirect cost. (1884) A cost that is not specific to the production of a particular good or service but that arises from production activity in general, such as overhead allocations for general and administrative activities.

manufacturing cost. The cost incurred in the production of goods, including direct and indirect costs.

marginal cost. (1891) The additional cost incurred in producing one more unit of output.

mitigation cost. A party's expenditures to reduce an existing harm so that further damage might be halted, slowed, or diminished.

mixed cost. A cost that includes fixed and variable costs.

net book cost. The cost of property when it was first acquired or devoted to public use, minus accumulated depreciation.

net cost. The cost of an item, arrived at by subtracting any financial gain from the total cost.

opportunity cost. (1894) The cost of acquiring an asset measured by the value of an alternative investment that is forgone.

replacement cost. (1928) The cost of a substitute asset that is equivalent to an asset currently held. • The new asset has the same utility but may or may not be identical to the one replaced.

sunk cost. (1916) A cost that has already been incurred and that cannot be recovered.

transaction cost. (*usu. pl.*) A cost connected with a process transaction, such as a broker's commission, the time and effort expended to arrange a deal, or the cost involved in litigating a dispute.

unit cost. The cost of a single unit of a product or service; the total manufacturing cost divided by the number of units.

variable cost. (1953) The cost that varies in the short run in close relationship with changes in output.

2. (*pl.*) The charges or fees taxed by the court, such as filing fees, jury fees, courthouse fees, and reporter fees. **3.** (*pl.*) The expenses of litigation, prosecution, or other legal transaction, esp. those allowed in favor of one party against the other. • Some but not all states allow parties to claim attorney's fees as a litigation cost.

cost and freight. A mercantile-contract term allocating the rights and duties of the buyer and the seller of goods with respect to delivery, payment, and risk of loss, whereby the seller must (1) clear the goods for export, (2) arrange for transportation by water, and (3) pay the costs of shipping to the port of destination. — Abbr. CF; CFR; C&F; CandF.

cost approach. (1949) A method of appraising real property, based on the cost of building a new structure with the same utility, assuming that an informed buyer would pay no more for the property than it would cost to build a new structure having the same usefulness.

cost-benefit analysis. (1963) An analytical technique that weighs the costs of a proposed decision, holding, or project against the expected advantages, economic or otherwise.

cost, insurance, and freight. A mercantile-contract term allocating the rights and duties of the buyer and the seller of goods with respect to delivery, payment, and risk of loss, whereby the seller must (1) clear the goods for export, (2) arrange for transportation by water, (3) procure insurance against the buyer's risk of damage during carriage, and (4) pay the costs of shipping to the port of destination. — Abbr. CIF.

CIF destination. A contractual term denoting that the price includes in a lump sum the cost of the goods and the insurance and freight to the named destination.

cost justification. (1938) Under the Robinson-Patman Act, an affirmative defense against a charge of price discrimination dependent on the seller's showing that it incurs lower costs in serving those customers who are paying less. 15 USCA § 13(a).

cost-of-living adjustment. An automatic increase or decrease in the amount of money, usu. support or maintenance, to be paid by one party to another, the adjustment being tied to the cost-of-living-adjustment figures maintained and updated by the federal government. — Abbr. COLA.

cost-of-living clause. (1953) A provision (as in a contract or lease) that gives an automatic wage, rent, or benefit increase tied in some way to cost-of-living rises in the economy.

costs of collection. (1833) Expenses incurred in receiving payment of a note; esp., attorney's fees incurred in the effort to collect a note.

coterminous (koh-**tər**-mə-nəs), *adj.* (18c) (Of ideas or events) coextensive in time or meaning <Judge Smith's tenure was coterminous with Judge Jasper's>.

council. (12c) **1.** A deliberative assembly. **2.** An administrative or executive body.

councilor, *n.* (15c) A person who serves on a council, esp. at the local level. — **councillorship,** *n.*

counsel, *n.* (13c) **1.** Advice or assistance. **2.** One or more lawyers who represent a client.

advisory counsel. An attorney retained merely to give advice on a particular matter, as distinguished from one (such as trial counsel) actively participating in a case.

appellate counsel. (1921) A lawyer who represents a party on appeal. • The term is often used in contrast with *trial counsel.*

assigned counsel. (17c) An attorney appointed by the court to represent a person, usu. an indigent person.

corporate counsel. An in-house attorney for a corporation.

corporation counsel. A city attorney in an incorporated municipality.

Cumis counsel. An independent attorney hired by a defendant in a lawsuit in which the damages may be covered by the defendant's insurer but a conflict of interest between the defendant and the insurer makes it unreasonable for an attorney selected by the insurer to represent the defendant. *San Diego Federal Credit Union v. Cumis Ins. Society, Inc.*, 162 Cal. App. 3d 358 (1984).

general counsel. (1848) **1.** A lawyer or law firm that represents a client in all or most of the client's legal matters, but that sometimes refers extraordinary matters — such as litigation and intellectual-property cases — to other lawyers. **2.** The most senior lawyer in a corporation's legal department, usu. also a corporate officer.

independent counsel. (1920) An attorney hired to provide an unbiased opinion about a case or to conduct an impartial investigation; esp., an attorney appointed by a governmental branch or agency to investigate alleged misconduct within that branch or agency.

in-house counsel. (1974) One or more lawyers employed by a company.

junior counsel. The younger or lower-ranking of two or more attorneys employed on the same side of a case, esp. someone charged with the less important aspects of the case.

lead counsel. (1956) The more highly ranked lawyer if two or more are retained; the lawyer who manages or controls the case or cases, esp. in class actions or multidistrict litigation.

local counsel. One or more lawyers who practice in a particular jurisdiction and are retained by nonresident counsel to help prepare and try a case or to complete a transaction in accordance with that jurisdiction's law, rules, and customs.

of counsel. **1.** A lawyer employed by a party in a case; esp., one who — although not the principal attorney of record — is employed to assist in the preparation or management of the case or in its presentation on appeal. **2.** A lawyer who is affiliated with a law firm, though not as a member, partner, or associate.

special counsel. (1854) An attorney employed by the state or a political subdivision to assist in a particular case when the public interest so requires.

standby counsel. An attorney who is appointed to be prepared to represent a pro se criminal defendant if the defendant's self-representation ends.

trial counsel. (1928) A lawyer who represents a party at trial. • The term is often used in contrast with *appellate counsel.*

count, *n.* (14c) *Procedure.* **1.** The part of an indictment charging the suspect with a distinct offense. **2.** In a complaint or similar pleading, the statement of a distinct claim.

general count. A count that states the plaintiff's claim without undue particularity.

multiple counts. (1941) Several separate causes of action or charged offenses contained in a single pleading or indictment.

omnibus count (**ahm**-ni-bəs). A count that combines into one count all money claims, claims for goods sold and delivered, claims for work and labor, and claims for an account stated.

separate count. (18c) One of two or more criminal charges contained in one indictment, each charge constituting a separate indictment for which the accused may be tried.

several count. One of two or more counts in a pleading, each of which states a different cause of action.

special count. (18c) A section of a pleading in which the plaintiff's claim is stated with great particularity — usu. employed only when the pleading rules require specificity.

3. A canvassing.

count, *vb.* (17c) In pleading, to declare or state; to narrate the facts that state a claim.

counterclaim, *n.* (18c) A claim for relief asserted against an opposing party after an original claim has been made; esp., a defendant's claim in opposition to or as a setoff against the plaintiff's claim. — **counterclaim,** *vb.* — **counterclaimant,** *n.*

compulsory counterclaim. (1938) A counterclaim that must be asserted to be cognizable, usu. because it relates to the opposing party's claim and arises out of the same subject matter. • If a defendant fails to assert a compulsory counterclaim in the original action, that claim may not be brought in a later, separate action (with some exceptions). See Fed. R. Civ. P. 13(a).

permissive counterclaim. (1924) A counterclaim that need not be asserted to be cognizable, usu. because it does not arise out of the same subject matter as the opposing party's claim or involves third parties over which the court does not have jurisdiction. • Permissive counterclaims may be brought in a later, separate action. See Fed. R. Civ. P. 13(b).

counterfeit, *vb.* (14c) To unlawfully forge, copy, or imitate an item, esp. money or a negotiable instrument (such as a security or promissory note) or other officially issued item of value (such as a postage stamp or a food stamp), or to possess such an item without authorization and with the intent to deceive or defraud by presenting the item as genuine. • Counterfeiting includes producing or selling an item that displays a reproduction of a genuine trademark, usu. to deceive buyers into thinking they are purchasing genuine merchandise. See 18 USCA §§ 470 et seq. — **counterfeiting,** *n.* — **counterfeit, counterfeiter,** *n.* — **counterfeit,** *adj.*

Counterfeit Access Device and Computer Fraud and Abuse Act of 1984. A federal statute that criminalizes various computer-related activities such as accessing without permission a computer system belonging to a bank or the federal government, or using that access to improperly obtain anything of value. 18 USCA § 1030.

countermand (**kown**-tər-mand), *n.* (16c) **1.** A contradictory command that overrides or annuls a previous one. **2.** An action that has the effect of voiding something previously ordered; a revocation. — **countermand** (kown-tər-**mand** *or* **kown**-), *vb.*

counteroffer, *n.* (18c) *Contracts.* An offeree's new offer that varies the terms of the original offer and that ordinarily rejects and terminates the original offer. • A late or defective acceptance is considered a counteroffer. — **counteroffer,** *vb.* — **counterofferor,** *n.*

counterpart. (15c) **1.** In conveyancing, a corresponding part of an instrument <the other half of the indenture — the counterpart — could not be found>. **2.** One of two or more copies or duplicates of a legal instrument <this lease may be executed in any number of counterparts, each of which is considered an original>.

counterpromise, *n.* (18c) A promise made in exchange for another party's promise <a promise supported by a counterpromise is binding in its inception>. — **counterpromise,** *vb.*

countersign, *vb.* (16c) To write one's own name next to someone else's to verify the other signer's identity. — **countersignature,** *n.*

country. 1. A nation or political state; STATE (1). **2.** The territory of such a nation or state.

county. (14c) The largest territorial division for local government within a state, generally considered to be a political subdivision and a quasi-corporation.

county attorney. An attorney who represents a county in civil matters and, in some jurisdictions, prosecutes criminal offenders.

county seat. The municipality where a county's principal offices are located.

coup d'état (koo day-**tah**). [French "stroke of state"] A sudden, usu. violent, change of government through seizure of power.

coupon (**koo**-pon). An interest or dividend certificate that is attached to another instrument, such as a bond, and that may be detached and separately presented for payment of a definite sum at a specified time.

courier. A messenger, esp. one who delivers parcels, packages, and the like. • In international law, the term denotes a messenger duly authorized by a sending state to deliver a diplomatic pouch.

course of business. (17c) The normal routine in managing a trade or business.

course of dealing. (16c) An established pattern of conduct between parties in a series of transactions (e.g., multiple sales of goods over a period of years). • If a dispute arises, the parties' course of dealing can be used as evidence of how they intended to carry out the transaction.

course of employment. (17c) Events that occur or circumstances that exist as a part of one's employment; esp., the time during which an employee furthers an employer's goals through employer-mandated directives.

course of performance. (18c) A sequence of previous performance by either party after an agreement has been entered into, when a contract involves repeated occasions for performance and both parties know the nature of the performance and have an opportunity to object to it. • A course of performance accepted or acquiesced in without objection is relevant to determining the meaning of the agreement.

court, *n.* (12c) **1.** A governmental body consisting of one or more judges who sit to adjudicate disputes and administer justice. **2.** The judge or judges who sit on such a governmental body. **3.** A legislative assembly. **4.** The locale for a legal proceeding. **5.** The building where the judge or judges convene to adjudicate disputes and administer justice.

appellate court. (18c) A court with jurisdiction to review decisions of lower courts or administrative agencies.

business court. (1914) A court that handles exclusively commercial litigation. • In the late 20th century, business courts emerged as a way to unclog the general dockets and to dispose of commercial cases more efficiently and consistently.

circuit court. (17c) **1.** A court usu. having jurisdiction over several counties, districts, or states, and holding sessions in all those areas. **2.** United States Court of Appeals.

civil court. (16c) A court with jurisdiction over noncriminal cases. — Abbr. Civ. Ct.

commissioner's court. In certain states, a court having jurisdiction over county affairs and often functioning more as a managerial group than as a judicial tribunal.

commonwealth court. **1.** In some states, a court of general jurisdiction. **2.** In Pennsylvania, a court that hears suits against the state and reviews decisions of state agencies and officials.

constitutional court. (1823) A court named or described and expressly protected in a constitution; esp., Article III court.

corporation court. In some jurisdictions, a court that serves an incorporated municipality.

county court. (16c) A court with powers and jurisdiction dictated by a state constitution or statute. • The county court may govern administrative or judicial matters, depending on state law.

court above. (17c) A court to which a case is appealed.

court below. (17c) A trial court or intermediate appellate court from which a case is appealed.

court not of record. An inferior court that is not required to routinely make a record of each proceeding and usu. does not.

court of appeals. (17c) **1.** An intermediate appellate court.. **2.** In New York and Maryland, the highest appellate court within the jurisdiction.

court of claims. (*cap.*) United States Court of Federal Claims.

court of competent jurisdiction. A court that has the power and authority to do a particular act; one recognized by law as possessing the right to adjudicate a controversy.

court of equity. (16c) A court that (1) has jurisdiction in equity, (2) administers and decides controversies in accordance with the rules, principles, and precedents of equity, and (3) follows the forms and procedures of chancery. Cf. *court of law.*

court of general jurisdiction. (18c) A court having unlimited or nearly unlimited trial jurisdiction in both civil and criminal cases.

court of last resort. (17c) The court having the authority to handle the final appeal of a case, such as the U.S. Supreme Court.

court of law. (16c) **1.** Broadly, any judicial tribunal that administers the laws of a state or nation. **2.** A court that proceeds according to the course of the common law, and that is governed by its rules and principles. Cf. *court of equity.*

court of limited jurisdiction. A court with jurisdiction over only certain types of cases, or cases in which the amount in controversy is limited.

court of original jurisdiction. (18c) A court where an action is initiated and first heard.

court of record. (18c) **1.** A court that is required to keep a record of its proceedings. • The court's records are presumed accurate and cannot be collaterally impeached. **2.** A court that may fine and imprison people for contempt.

court of special session. (1813) A court that has no stated term and is not continuous, but is organized only for hearing a particular case.

criminal court. A court with jurisdiction over criminal matters.

district court. (18c) A trial court having general jurisdiction within its judicial district. — Abbr. D.C.

domestic court. (1801) A court having jurisdiction at the place of a party's residence or domicile.

drug court. A court that hears cases against nonviolent adults and juveniles, who are often first-time offenders and who are usu. charged with possession of a controlled substance or with committing a minor drug-related crime. • Drug courts focus on treatment rather than on incarceration.

examining court. (18c) A lower court (usu. presided over by a magistrate) that determines probable cause and sets bail at a preliminary hearing in a criminal case.

family court. (1923) A court having jurisdiction over matters involving divorce, child custody and support, paternity, domestic violence, and other family-law issues.

federal court. (18c) A court having federal jurisdiction, including the U.S. Supreme Court, circuit courts of appeals, district courts, bankruptcy courts, and tax courts.

foreign court. (16c) **1.** The court of a foreign nation. **2.** The court of another state.

full court. (16c) A court session that is attended by all the court's judges; an en banc court.

highest court. (16c) The court of last resort in a particular jurisdiction; a court whose decision is final and cannot be appealed because no higher court exists to consider the matter.

hot court. (1972) A court, esp. an appellate court, that is familiar with the briefs filed in the case, and therefore with the issues, before oral argument. • Typically, a hot court controls the oral argument with its questioning, as opposed to listening passively to set presentations of counsel.

inferior court. (17c) **1.** Any court that is subordinate to the chief appellate tribunal within a judicial system. **2.** A court of special, limited, or statutory jurisdiction, whose record must show the existence of jurisdiction in any given case to give its ruling presumptive validity.

intermediate court. An appellate court that is below a court of last resort.

justice court. (16c) A court, presided over by a justice of the peace, that has jurisdiction to hear minor criminal cases, matters involving small amounts of money, or certain specified claims (such as forcible-entry-and-detainer suits).

juvenile court. (1903) A court having jurisdiction over cases involving children under a specified age, usu. 18.

kangaroo court. (1849) **1.** A self-appointed tribunal or mock court in which the principles of law and justice are disregarded, perverted, or parodied. **2.** A court or tribunal characterized by unauthorized or irregular procedures, esp. so as to render a fair proceeding impossible. **3.** A sham legal proceeding.

legislative court. (1828) A court created by a statute, as opposed to one created by a constitution.

limited court. A court having special jurisdiction conferred by statute, such as a probate court.

liquidation court. Any court in which a liquidation proceeding takes place.

local court. A court whose jurisdiction is limited to a particular territory, such as a state, municipal, or county court.

magistrate's court (**maj**-i-strayts *or* -strits). (1904) **1.** A court with jurisdiction over minor criminal offenses. • Such a court also has the power to bind over for trial persons accused of more serious offenses. **2.** A court with limited jurisdiction over minor criminal and civil matters.

mayor's court. A municipal court in which the mayor presides as the judge, with jurisdiction over minor criminal (and sometimes civil) matters, traffic offenses, and the like.

military court. A court that has jurisdiction over members of the armed forces and that enforces the Code of Military Justice.

military court of inquiry. A military court that has special and limited jurisdiction and that is convened to investigate specific matters and, traditionally, to determine whether further procedures are warranted. 10 USCA § 935.

municipal court. (17c) A court having jurisdiction (usu. civil and criminal) over cases arising within the municipality in which it sits.

probate court. (18c) A court with the power to declare wills valid or invalid, to oversee the administration of estates and (in some states) to appoint guardians and approve the adoption of minors.

problem-solving court. A specialized court that matches community resources to litigants whose problems or cases may benefit from those resources.

rogue court. A court that fails to apply controlling law in making its decisions.

small-claims court. (1923) A court that informally and expeditiously adjudicates claims that seek damages below a specified monetary amount, usu. claims to collect small accounts or debts.

state court. (18c) A court of the state judicial system, as opposed to a federal court.

superior court. (18c) **1.** In some states, a trial court of general jurisdiction. **2.** In Pennsylvania, an intermediate court between the trial court and the chief appellate court.

Supreme Judicial Court. (18c) The highest appellate court in Maine and Massachusetts.

teen court. A group of teenagers who (1) hear cases involving juveniles, usu. first-time offenders, who have acknowledged their guilt or responsibility, and (2) impose sanctions within a fixed range, usu. involving counseling, community service, or restitution.

traffic court. A court with jurisdiction over prosecutions for parking violations and infractions of road law.

trial court. (18c) A court of original jurisdiction where the evidence is first received and considered.

unified family court. In some jurisdictions, a court that hears all family matters, including matters of divorce, juvenile delinquency, adoption, abuse and neglect, and criminal abuse.

World Court. International Court of Justice.

court-appointed special advocate. A trained volunteer appointed by a court to represent the interests of a child in an abuse or neglect case. — Abbr. CASA.

court calendar. (1852) A list of matters scheduled for trial or hearing; DOCKET (2).

courtesy supervision. (1970) Oversight of a parolee by a correctional agency located in a jurisdiction other than where the parolee was sentenced.

court for the trial of impeachments. (18c) A tribunal empowered to try a government officer or other person brought before it by the process of impeachment. • The U.S. Senate and the British House of Lords have this authority, as do the upper houses of most state legislatures.

courthouse steps. The figurative location of settlement negotiations that occur shortly before trial commences, regardless of the literal location of the negotiations.

court-martial, *n.* (18c) An ad hoc military court convened under military authority to try someone, particularly a member of the armed forces, accused of violating the Uniform Code of Military Justice. Pl. **courts-martial.** — **court-martial,** *vb.*

general court-martial. A proceeding that is presided over by a military judge, and no fewer than five members (who serve as jurors), and that has jurisdiction over all the members of the armed forces. • It is the highest military trial court.

special court-martial. A proceeding that is presided over by a military judge and no fewer than three members (who serve as jurors) to hear noncapital offenses and prescribe a sanction of hard labor, dismissal, or extended confinement (up to one year). • It is the intermediate level of courts-martial.

summary court-martial. A proceeding presided over by a single commissioned officer who is jurisdictionally limited in what sanctions can be imposed. • It is the lowest level of courts-martial.

Court-Martial Reports. A publication containing the opinions of the U.S. Court of Military Appeals and select decisions of the Courts of Military Review. • This publication appeared during the years 1951–1975. — Abbr. CMR.

Court of Civil Appeals. (1892) An intermediate appellate court in some states, such as Alabama and (formerly) Texas.

court of claims. (*cap.*) United States Court of Federal Claims.

Court of Common Pleas. (16c) **1.** An intermediate-level court in some states, such as Arkansas. **2.** A trial court of general jurisdiction in some states, such as Ohio, Pennsylvania, and South Carolina. — Abbr. C.P.

Court of Criminal Appeals. (1856) **1.** For each armed service, an intermediate appellate court that reviews court-martial decisions. 10 USCA §§ 859–876. **2.** In some jurisdictions, such as Texas and Oklahoma, the highest appellate court that hears criminal cases.

Court of Oyer and Terminer (**oy**-ər an[d] **tər**-mə-nər). (17c) In some states, a court of higher criminal jurisdiction.

court-packing plan. A unsuccessful proposal — made in 1937 by President Franklin D. Roosevelt — to increase the number of U.S. Supreme Court justices from nine to fifteen.

court papers. (17c) All documents that a party files with the court, including pleadings, motions, notices, and the like.

court reporter. (1894) **1.** A person who records testimony, stenographically or by electronic or other means, and when requested, prepares a transcript. **2.** Reporter of decisions.

court rules. (17c) Regulations having the force of law and governing practice and procedure in the various courts, such as the Federal Rules of Civil Procedure, the Federal Rules of Criminal Procedure, the U.S. Supreme Court Rules, and the Federal Rules of Evidence, as well as any local rules that a court promulgates.

cousin. 1. A child of one's aunt or uncle. **2.** A relative descended from one's ancestor (such as a grandparent) by two or more steps in a diverging line. **3.** Any distant relative by blood or marriage; a kinsman or kinswoman.

cousin-german. A first cousin; a child of a full sibling of one's mother or father.

cousin once removed. **1.** A child of one's cousin. **2.** A cousin of one's parent.

cousin twice removed. **1.** A grandchild of one's cousin. **2.** A cousin of one's grandparent.

second cousin. A person related to another by descending from the same great-grandfather or great-grandmother.

third cousin. A person related to another by descending from the same great-great-grandfather or great-great-grandmother.

covenant (**kəv**-ə-nənt), *n.* (14c) **1.** A formal agreement or promise, usu. in a contract or deed, to do or not do a particular act.

absolute covenant. (17c) A covenant that is not qualified or limited by any condition. Cf. *conditional covenant.*

affirmative covenant. A covenant that obligates a party to do some act; esp., an agreement that real property will be used in a certain way. Cf. *negative covenant.*

auxiliary covenant (awg-**zil**-yə-ree). A covenant that does not relate directly to the primary subject of the agreement, but to something connected to it. Cf. *principal covenant.*

collateral covenant (kə-**lat**-ə-rəl). A covenant entered into in connection with the grant of something, but that does not relate immediately to the thing granted; esp., a covenant in a deed or other sealed instrument not pertaining to the conveyed property.

concurrent covenant. (1819) A covenant that requires performance by one party at the same time as another's performance.

conditional covenant. (17c) A covenant that is qualified by a condition. Cf. *absolute covenant.*

continuing covenant. A covenant that requires the successive performance of acts, such as an agreement to pay rent in installments.

covenant not to execute. A covenant in which a party who has won a judgment agrees not to enforce it. • This covenant is most common in insurance law.

covenant not to sue. (18c) A covenant in which a party having a right of action agrees not to assert that right in litigation.

express covenant. (17c) A covenant created by the words of the parties. Cf. *implied covenant.*

implied covenant. (17c) A covenant that can be inferred from the whole agreement and the conduct of the parties. Cf. *express covenant.*

implied covenant of good faith and fair dealing. (1924) An implied covenant to cooperate with the other party to an agreement so that both parties may obtain the full benefits of the agreement; an implied covenant to refrain from any act that would injure a contracting party's right to receive the benefit of the contract.

implied negative covenant. (1890) A covenant binding a grantor not to permit use of any reserved right in a manner that might destroy the benefits that would otherwise inure to the grantee.

independent covenant. A covenant that imposes a duty that does not depend on the other party's prior performance.

inherent covenant. A covenant that relates directly to land, such as a covenant of quiet enjoyment. Cf. *collateral covenant.*

negative covenant. (18c) A covenant that requires a party to refrain from doing something; esp., in a real-estate financing transaction, the borrower's promise to the lender not to encumber or transfer the real estate as long as the loan remains unpaid. Cf. *affirmative covenant.*

noncompetition covenant. A promise, usu. in a sale-of-business, partnership, or employment contract, not to engage in the same type of business for a stated time in the same market as the buyer, partner, or employer. • Noncompetition covenants are valid to protect business goodwill in the sale of a company. In other contexts, they are generally disfavored as restraints of trade: courts generally enforce them for the duration of the business relationship, but provisions that extend beyond the termination of that relationship must be reasonable in scope, time, and territory.

positive covenant. A covenant that requires a party to do something (such as to erect a fence within a specified time).

principal covenant. A covenant that relates directly to the principal matter of an agreement. Cf. *auxiliary covenant.*

2. Treaty. **3.** A common-law action to recover damages for breach of contract under seal. **4.** A promise made in a deed or implied by law; esp., an obligation in a deed burdening or favoring a landowner. — **covenantal,** *adj.*

affirmative covenant. An agreement that real property will be used in a certain way. • An affirmative covenant is more than a restriction on the use of property. It requires the owner to undertake certain acts on the property.

covenant against encumbrances. (1807) A grantor's promise that the property has no visible or invisible encumbrances. • In a special warranty deed, the covenant is limited to encumbrances made by the grantor.

covenant appurtenant (ə-**pər**-tə-nənt). (1899) A covenant that is connected with the grantor's land; a covenant running with the land. Cf. *covenant in gross.*

covenant for further assurances. (18c) A covenant to do whatever is reasonably necessary to perfect the title conveyed if it turns out to be imperfect.

covenant for quiet enjoyment. (17c) **1.** A covenant insuring against the consequences of a defective title or any other disturbance of the title. **2.** A covenant ensuring that the tenant will not be evicted or disturbed by the grantor or a person having a lien or superior title. • This covenant is sometimes treated as being synonymous with *covenant of warranty.*

covenant for title. (18c) A covenant that binds the grantor to ensure the completeness, security, and continuance of the title transferred. • This covenant usu. includes the covenants for seisin, against encumbrances, for the right to convey, for quiet enjoyment, and of warranty.

covenant in gross. (17c) A covenant that does not run with the land. Cf. *covenant appurtenant.*

covenant of nonclaim. (1848) A covenant barring a grantor or the grantor's heirs from claiming title in the conveyed land.

covenant of seisin (**see**-zin). (18c) A covenant, usu. appearing in a warranty deed, stating that the grantor has an estate, or the right to convey an estate, of the quality and size that the grantor purports to convey. • For the covenant to be valid, the grantor must have both title and possession at the time of the grant.

covenant of warranty. (18c) A covenant by which the grantor agrees to defend the grantee against any lawful or reasonable claim of superior title by a third party and to indemnify the grantee for any loss sustained by the claim. • This covenant is sometimes treated as being synonymous with *covenant for quiet enjoyment.* The covenant is not breached if the grantor fails to defend the grantee against an invalid claim.

covenant running with the land. (18c) A covenant intimately and inherently involved with the land and therefore binding subsequent owners and successor grantees indefinitely.

restrictive covenant. (1811) A private agreement, usu. in a deed or lease, that restricts the use or occupancy of real property, esp. by specifying lot sizes, building lines, architectural styles, and the uses to which the property may be put. • Some restrictive covenants, such as race-based restrictions on transfers, are unenforceable but do not necessarily void the deed.

special covenant against encumbrances. (1860) A grantor's promise that the property is free of encumbrances created by the grantor only, not the grantor's predecessors.

covenant, *vb.* (14c) To promise or undertake in a covenant; to agree formally.

covenantee (kəv-ə-nən-**tee**). (17c) The person to whom a promise by covenant is made; one entitled to the benefit of a covenant.

covenantor (**kəv**-ə-nən-tər *or* kəv-ə-nən-**tor**). (17c) The person who makes a promise by covenant; one subject to the burden of a covenant.

coventurer (koh-**ven**-chər-ər). (1913) A person who undertakes a joint venture with one or more persons.

cover, *n.* The purchase on the open market, by the buyer in a breach-of-contract dispute, of goods to substitute for those promised but never delivered by the seller. • Under UCC § 2-712, the buyer can recover from the seller the difference between the cost of the substituted goods and the original contract price.

coverage, *n.* (1912) Inclusion of a risk under an insurance policy; the risks within the scope of an insurance policy. — **cover,** *vb.*

dependent coverage. An insurance provision for protection of an insured's dependents.

full coverage. Insurance protection that pays for the full amount of a loss with no deduction.

coverage ratio. (1975) A measurement of a firm's ability to cover its financing charges.

cover-up, *n.* Concealment of wrongdoing, esp. by a conspiracy of deception, nondisclosure, and destruction of evidence, usu. combined with a refusal to cooperate with investigators. • A cover-up often involves obstruction of justice. — **cover up,** *vb.*

CPA. *abbr.* Certified public accountant.

CPI. *abbr.* Consumer Price Index.

CPS. *abbr.* Child Protective Services.

CPSC. *abbr.* Consumer Product Safety Commission.

crack. *vb. Slang.* **1.** To open (a lock). **2.** To decode (security information); esp., to decipher or discover (a code, a password, etc. needed to break into a computer, network, server, or database). **3.** To bypass (an encryption or a security device, esp. one designed to prevent unauthorized access, as in a cable television box, or copying, as in a DVD player). **4.** To hack (a computer, network, server, or database) with the intention of causing damage or disruption.

cracking, *n.* A gerrymandering technique in which a geographically concentrated political or racial group that is large enough to constitute a district's dominant force is broken up by district lines and dispersed throughout two or more districts.

cramdown, *n.* (1954) Court confirmation of a Chapter 11 bankruptcy plan despite the opposition of certain creditors. • Under the Bankruptcy Code, a court may confirm a plan — even if it has not been accepted by all classes of creditors — if the plan (1) has been accepted by at least one impaired class, (2) does not discriminate unfairly, and (3) is fair and equitable. 11 USCA § 1129(b). — **cram down,** *vb.*

crashworthiness doctrine. (1969) *Products liability.* The principle that the manufacturer of a product will be held strictly liable for injuries occurring in a collision, even if the collision results from an independent cause, to the extent that a defect in the product causes injuries above and beyond those that would have occurred in the collision itself.

creationism. The teaching of the biblical version of the creation of the universe. • The United States Supreme Court held unconstitutional a Louisiana law that forbade the teaching of the theory of evolution unless biblical creation was also taught. The Court found the law violated the Establishment Clause of the First Amendment because it lacked a "clear secular purpose." *Edwards v. Aguillard*, 482 U.S. 578, 107 S.Ct. 2573 (1987).

creativity. *Copyright.* The degree to which a work displays imaginativeness beyond what a person of very ordinary talents might create. • Labor and expense are not elements of creativity; for that reason, they are not protected by copyright. *Feist Pubs. Inc. v. Rural Tel. Serv. Co.*, 499 U.S. 340, 111 S.Ct. 1282 (1991).

creature of statute. (1854) A doctrine, governmental agency, etc. that would not exist but for a legislative act that brought it into being.

credential. (*usu. pl.*) **1.** A document or other evidence that proves one's authority or expertise. **2.** A testimonial that a person is entitled to credit or to the right to exercise official power. **3.** The letter of credence given to an ambassador or other representative of a foreign country. — **credential,** *vb.*

credibility, *n.* (16c) The quality that makes something (as a witness or some evidence) worthy of belief. — **credible,** *adj.*

credit, *n.* (16c) **1.** Belief; trust. **2.** One's ability to borrow money; the faith in one's ability to pay debts. **3.** The time that a seller gives the buyer to make the payment that is due. **4.** The availability of funds either from a financial institution or under a letter of credit. **5.** Letter of credit. **6.** A deduction from an amount due; an accounting entry reflecting an addition to revenue or net worth. **7.** Tax credit.

credit, *vb.* (17c) **1.** To believe. **2.** To enter (as an amount) on the credit side of an account.

creditable. **1.** Worthy of being believed; credible. **2.** Capable of being ascribed or credited. **3.** Reputable; respectable.

credit balance. *Accounting.* The status of an account when the sum of the credit entries exceeds the sum of the debit entries.

credit bureau. (1874) An organization that compiles information on people's creditworthiness and publishes it in the form of reports that are used chiefly by merchants and service-providers who deal directly with customers. • The practices of credit bureaus are regulated by federal (and often state) law. Most bureaus are members of the Associated Credit Bureaus of America.

credit-card cramming. 1. A credit-card issuer's practice of charging consumers for optional goods or services that the consumers have not agreed to pay or do not understand. • For example, the credit-card crammer may offer the consumer a free service for a limited period without making it clear that if the service is not canceled when the period ends, it will be automatically renewed for a fee. **2.** A single act of charging a consumer's credit card without authorization, particularly for goods or services that the consumer did not agree to or receive.

credit-card crime. (1970) The offense of using a credit card to purchase something with knowledge that (1) the card is stolen or forged, (2) the card has been revoked or canceled, or (3) the card's use is unauthorized.

creditor. (15c) **1.** One to whom a debt is owed; one who gives credit for money or goods. **2.** A person or entity with a definite claim against another, esp. a claim that is capable of adjustment and liquidation. **3.** *Bankruptcy.* A person or entity having a claim against the debtor predating the order for relief concerning the debtor. Cf. DEBTOR.

creditor's bill. (1826) An equitable suit in which a judgment creditor seeks to reach property that cannot be reached by the process available to enforce a judgment.

creditors' committee. (1874) *Bankruptcy.* A committee comprising representatives of the creditors in a Chapter 11 proceeding, formed to negotiate the debtor's plan of reorganization. • Generally, a committee has no fewer than 3 and no more than 11 members and serves as an advisory body. 11 USCA § 1102.

credit plan. A financing arrangement under which a borrower and a lender agree to terms for a loan's repayment with interest, usu. in installments.

credit rating. An evaluation of a potential borrower's ability to repay debt, prepared by a credit bureau at the request of a lender.

credit report. 1. A credit bureau's report on a person's financial status, usu. including the approximate amounts and locations of a person's bank accounts, charge accounts, loans, and other debts, bill-paying habits, defaults, bankruptcies, foreclosures, marital status, occupation, income, and lawsuits. **2.** The report of a credit-reporting bureau, usu. including highly personal information gathered through interviews with a person's friends, neighbors, and coworkers.

credit-reporting bureau. (1904) An organization that, on request, prepares investigative reports not just on people's creditworthiness but also on personal information gathered from various sources, including interviews with neighbors, friends, and coworkers. • These reports are used chiefly by employers (for prospective employees), insurance companies (for applicants), and landlords (for prospective tenants).

credit union. A cooperative association that offers low-interest loans and other consumer banking services to persons sharing a common bond — often fellow employees and their family members. • Most credit unions are regulated by the National Credit Union Administration. State-chartered credit unions are also subject to regulation by the chartering state, and they may be regulated by state banking boards.

creditworthy, *adj.* (1924) (Of a borrower) financially sound enough that a lender will extend credit in the belief default is unlikely; fiscally healthy. — **creditworthiness,** *n.*

crier (krɪ-ər). (15c) **1.** An officer of the court who makes public pronouncements as required by the court. **2.** An auctioneer. — Also spelled *cryer.*

crime. (14c) An act that the law makes punishable; the breach of a legal duty treated as the subject-matter of a criminal proceeding.

administrative crime. (1943) An offense consisting of a violation of an administrative rule or regulation that carries with it a criminal sanction.

commercial crime. (1900) A crime that affects commerce; esp., a crime directed toward the property or revenues of a commercial establishment. • Examples include robbery of a business, embezzlement, counterfeiting, forgery, prostitution, illegal gambling, and extortion. See 26 CFR § 403.38.

common-law crime. (1827) A crime that is punishable under the common law, rather than by force of statute. Cf. *statutory crime.*

computer crime. (1971) A crime involving the use of a computer, such as sabotaging or stealing electronically stored data.

continuous crime. (1907) **1.** A crime that continues after an initial illegal act has been consummated; a crime that involves ongoing elements. • An example is illegal U.S. drug importation. The criminal act is completed not when the drugs enter the country, but when the drugs reach their final destination. **2.** A crime (such as driving a stolen vehicle) that continues over an extended period.

corporate crime. (1934) A crime committed by a corporation's representatives acting on its behalf. • Examples include price-fixing and consumer fraud. Although a corporation as an entity cannot commit a crime other than through its representatives, it can be named as a criminal defendant.

crime of omission. (18c) An offense that carries as its material component the failure to act.

crime of passion. (18c) A crime committed in the heat of an emotionally charged moment, with no opportunity to reflect on what is happening.

economic crime. A nonphysical crime committed to obtain a financial gain or a professional advantage.

hate crime. (1984) A crime motivated by the victim's race, color, ethnicity, religion, or national origin. • Certain groups have lobbied to expand the definition by statute to include a crime motivated by the victim's disability, gender, or sexual orientation.

high crime. (17c) A crime that is very serious, though not necessarily a felony. • Under the U.S. Constitution, a government officer's commission of a "high crime" is, along with treason and bribery, grounds for removal from office. U.S. Const. art. II, § 4.

honor crime. A crime motivated by a desire to punish a person who the perpetrator believes has injured a person's or group's sense of honor. • The term is most often applied to crimes committed against Muslim women by members of their own families for behavior that leads to perceived social harm, esp. loss of family honor. The term also extends to non-Muslims and covers many acts of violence, including assault, rape, infanticide, and murder. When the crime involves a death, it is also termed *honor killing.*

infamous crime (**in**-fə-məs). (16c) **1.** At common law, a crime for which part of the punishment was infamy, so that one who committed it would be declared ineligible to serve on a jury, hold public office, or testify. • Examples are perjury, treason, and fraud. **2.** A crime punishable by imprisonment in a penitentiary. • The Fifth Amendment requires a grand-jury indictment for the prosecution of infamous (or capital) crimes, which include all federal felony offenses.

instantaneous crime. (1887) A crime that is fully completed by a single act, as arson or murder, rather than a series of acts. • The statute of limitations for an instantaneous crime begins to run with its completion.

predatory crime. A crime that involves preying upon and victimizing individuals. • Examples include robbery, rape, and carjacking.

quasi-crime. (18c) *Hist.* **1.** An offense not subject to criminal prosecution (such as contempt or violation of a municipal ordinance) but for which penalties or forfeitures can be imposed. • The term includes offenses that give rise to *qui tam* actions and forfeitures for the violation of a public duty. **2.** An offense for which someone other than the actual perpetrator is held liable, the perpetrator being presumed to act on the command of the responsible party.

signature crime. (1974) A distinctive crime so similar in pattern, scheme, or modus operandi to previous crimes that it identifies a particular defendant as the perpetrator.

spontaneous crime. A criminal act that occurs suddenly and without premeditation in response to an unforeseen stimulus.

status crime. (1961) A crime of which a person is guilty by being in a certain condition or of a specific character. • An example of a status crime is vagrancy.

statutory crime. (1940) A crime punishable by statute.

street crime. (1966) A crime generally directed against a person in public, such as mugging, theft, or robbery.

victimless crime. (1964) A crime that is considered to have no direct victim, usu. because only consenting adults are involved. • Examples are possession of illicit drugs and deviant sexual intercourse between consenting adults.

violent crime. (18c) A crime that has as an element the use, attempted use, threatened use, or substantial risk of use of physical force against the person or property of another. 18 USCA § 16; USSG § 2E1.3.

crime against humanity. *Int'l law.* A brutal crime that is not an isolated incident but that involves large and systematic actions, often cloaked with official authority, and that shocks the conscience of humankind. • Among the specific crimes that fall within this category are mass murder, extermination, enslavement, deportation, and other inhumane acts perpetrated against a population, whether in wartime or not. See Statute of the International Criminal Court, art. 3 (37 ILM 999).

crime-fraud exception. (1973) The doctrine that neither the attorney–client privilege nor the attorney-work-product privilege protects attorney–client communications that are in furtherance of a current or planned crime or fraud. *Clark v. United States*, 289 U.S. 1, 53 S.Ct. 465 (1933); *In re Grand Jury Subpoena Duces Tecum*, 731 F.2d 1032 (2d Cir. 1984).

crimes against persons. (1827) A category of criminal offenses in which the perpetrator uses or threatens to use force. • Examples include murder, rape, aggravated assault, and robbery.

crimes against property. (1827) A category of criminal offenses in which the perpetrator seeks to derive an unlawful benefit from — or do damage to — another's property without the use or threat of force. • Examples include burglary, theft, and arson (even though arson may result in injury or death).

crime score. (1952) A number assigned from an established scale, indicating the relative seriousness of an offense based on the nature of the injury or the extent of property damage.

crime statistics. Figures compiled by a governmental agency to show the incidence of various types of crime within a defined geographic area during a specified time.

criminal, *adj.* (15c) **1.** Having the character of a crime; in the nature of a crime. **2.** Connected with the administration of penal justice.

criminal, *n.* (17c) **1.** One who has committed a criminal offense. **2.** One who has been convicted of a crime.

dangerous criminal. (18c) A criminal who has either committed a violent crime or used force in trying to escape from custody.

episodic criminal. (1976) **1.** A person who commits crimes sporadically. **2.** A person who commits crimes only during periods of intense stress, as in the heat of passion.

state criminal. **1.** A person who has committed a crime against the state (such as treason); a political criminal. **2.** A person who has committed a crime under state law.

criminal damage to property. (1946) **1.** Injury, destruction, or substantial impairment to the use of property (other than by fire or explosion) without the consent of a person having an interest in the property. **2.** Injury, destruction, or substantial impairment to the use of property (other than by fire or explosion) with the intent to injure or defraud an insurer or lienholder.

criminal instrument. (1901) **1.** Something made or adapted for criminal use. Model Penal Code § 5.06(1)(a). **2.** Something commonly used for criminal purposes and possessed under circumstances showing an unlawful purpose. Model Penal Code § 5.06(1)(b).

criminal-instrumentality rule. (1942) The principle that when a criminal act is committed, that act — rather than the victim's negligence that made the crime possible — will be considered to be the crime's proximate cause.

criminalistics (krim-ə-nə-**lis**-tiks), *n.* (1943) The science of crime detection, usu. involving the subjection of physical evidence to laboratory analysis, including ballistic testing, blood-fluid and tissue analysis, and other tests. — **criminalistic,** *adj.* — **criminalist** (**krim**-ə-nəl-ist), *n.*

criminality (krim-ə-**nal**-ə-tee). (17c) **1.** The state or quality of being criminal. **2.** An act or practice that constitutes a crime.

criminalization (**krim**-ə-nəl-ə-**zay**-shən), *n.* (1945) **1.** The act or an instance of making a previously lawful act criminal, usu. by passing a statute.— **criminalize (krim**-ə-nəl-ɪz), *vb.* Cf. DECRIMINALIZATION. **2.** The process by which a person develops into a criminal.

criminal justice. (16c) **1.** The methods by which a society deals with those who are accused of having committed crimes. Cf. CIVIL JUSTICE. **2.** The field of study pursued by those seeking to enter law enforcement as a profession. • Many colleges offer degrees in criminal justice, typically after two to four years of study.

criminal-justice system. (1929) The collective institutions through which an accused offender passes until the accusations have been disposed of or the assessed punishment concluded.

criminal law. (18c) The body of law defining offenses against the community at large, regulating how suspects are investigated, charged, and tried, and establishing punishments for convicted offenders.

criminal policy. (1893) The branch of criminal science concerned with protecting against crime. • It draws on information provided by criminology, and its subjects for investigation are (1) the appropriate measures of social organization for preventing harmful activities, and (2) the treatment to be accorded to those who have caused harm, i.e., whether the offenders should receive warnings, supervised probation, or medical treatment, or whether they should suffer serious deprivations of life or liberty such as imprisonment or capital punishment.

criminal procedure. (18c) The rules governing the mechanisms under which crimes are investigated, prosecuted, adjudicated, and punished. • It includes the protection of accused persons' constitutional rights.

criminal protector. (1978) An accessory after the fact to a felony; one who aids or harbors a wrongdoer after the commission of a crime.

criminal science. (1891) The study of crime with a view to discovering the causes of criminality, devising the most effective methods of reducing crime, and perfecting the means for dealing with those who have committed crimes. • The three main branches of criminal science are criminology, criminal policy, and criminal law.

criminology (krim-ə-**nol**-ə-jee), *n.* (1872) The study of crime and criminal punishment as social phenomena; the study of the causes of crime and the treatment of offenders, comprising (1) criminal biology, which examines causes that may be found in the mental and physical constitution of an offender (such as hereditary tendencies and physical defects), and (2) criminal sociology, which deals with inquiries into the effects of environment as a cause of criminality. — **criminological** (krim-ə-nə-**loj**-ə-kəl), *adj.* — **criminologist,** *n.*

crit. (1985) An adherent to the critical-legal-studies school of thought.

fem-crit. A feminist adherent of critical legal studies.

Critical Legal Studies. (1978) **1.** A school of thought advancing the idea that the legal system perpetuates the status quo in terms of economics, race, and gender by using manipulable concepts and by creating an imaginary world of social harmony regulated by law. • The Marxist wing of this school focuses on socioeconomic issues. Fem-crits emphasize gender hierarchy, whereas critical race theorists focus on racial subordination. **2.** The body of work produced by adherents to this school of thought. — Abbr. CLS.

Critical Race Theory. (1989) **1.** A reform movement within the legal profession, particularly within academia, whose adherents believe that the legal system has disempowered racial minorities. • The term first appeared in 1989. Critical race theorists observe that even if the law is couched in neutral language, it cannot be neutral because those who fashioned it had their own subjective perspectives that, once enshrined in law, have disadvantaged minorities and even perpetuated racism. **2.** The body of work produced by adherents to this theory. — Abbr. CRT.

critical stage. (1962) *Criminal procedure.* A point in a criminal prosecution when the accused's rights or defenses might be affected by the absence of legal representation. • Under the Sixth Amendment, a critical stage triggers the accused's right to appointed counsel. Examples of critical stages include preliminary hearings, jury selection, and (of course) trial.

cross-claim, *n.* (1825) A claim asserted between codefendants or coplaintiffs in a case and that relates to the subject of the original claim or counterclaim. See Fed. R. Civ. P. 13(g). — **cross-claim,** *vb.* — **cross-claimant,** *n.*

cross-collateral clause. (1965) An installment-contract provision allowing the seller, if the buyer defaults, to repossess not only the particular item sold but also every other item bought from the seller on which a balance remained due when the last purchase was made.

cross-complaint. (1854) **1.** A claim asserted by a defendant against another party to the action. **2.** A claim asserted by a defendant against a person not a party to the action for a matter relating to the subject of the action.

cross-default clause. (1979) A contractual provision under which default on one debt obligation triggers default on another obligation.

cross-examination, *n.* (18c) The questioning of a witness at a trial or hearing by the party opposed to the party who called the witness to testify. • The purpose of cross-examination is to discredit a witness before the fact-finder in any of several ways, as by bringing out contradictions and improbabilities in earlier testimony, by suggesting doubts to the witness, and by trapping the witness into admissions that weaken the testimony. The cross-examiner is typically allowed to ask leading questions but is traditionally limited to matters covered on direct examination and to credibility issues. — **cross-examine,** *vb.*

cross-offer, *n.* (1931) *Contracts.* An offer made to another in ignorance that the offeree has made the same offer to the offeror. — **cross-offer,** *vb.* — **cross-offeror,** *n.*

cross-reference, *n.* An explicit citation to a related provision within the same or a closely related document; esp., in a patent application the explicit citation in a continuing patent application to all interrelated applications, back to the original filing. • A cross-reference alone does not incorporate the disclosure of the parent application. — **cross-reference,** *vb.*

CRT. *abbr.* Critical race theory.

cruelty. (13c) The intentional and malicious infliction of mental or physical suffering on a living creature, esp. a human; abusive treatment; outrage.

cruelty to animals. A malicious or criminally negligent act that causes an animal to suffer pain or death.

extreme cruelty. (17c) As a ground for divorce, one spouse's physical violence toward the other spouse, or conduct that destroys or severely impairs the other spouse's mental health.

legal cruelty. (18c) Cruelty that will justify granting a divorce to the injured party; specif. conduct by one spouse that endangers the life, person, or health of the other spouse, or creates a reasonable apprehension of bodily or mental harm.

mental cruelty. (1898) As a ground for divorce, one spouse's course of conduct (not involving actual violence) that creates such anguish that it endangers the life, physical health, or mental health of the other spouse.

physical cruelty. (1874) As a ground for divorce, actual personal violence committed by one spouse against the other.

c.t.a. *abbr.* Administration cum testamento annexo.

Ct. Cl. *abbr.* Court of Claims.

culpable (**kəl**-pə-bəl), *adj.* (14c) **1.** Guilty; blameworthy. **2.** Involving the breach of a duty. — **culpability** (kəl-pə-**bil**-ə-tee), *n.*

culprit. (17c) **1.** A person accused or charged with the commission of a crime. **2.** A person who is guilty of a crime.

cumulative-effects doctrine. (1987) The rule that a transaction affecting interstate commerce in a trivial way may be taken together with other similar transactions to establish that the combined effect on interstate commerce is not trivial and can therefore be regulated under the Commerce Clause.

curative-admissibility doctrine. (1975) The rule that otherwise inadmissible evidence will be admitted to rebut inadmissible evidence placed before the fact-finder by the adverse party. • The doctrine applies when a motion to strike cannot cure the prejudice created by the adverse party.

curator (**kyuur**-ə-tər *or* **kyuur**-ay-tər *or* kyuu-**ray**-tor), *n.* A temporary guardian or conservator appointed by a court to care for the property or person of a minor or incapacitated person.

curatorship. (16c) The office of a curator or guardian.

cure, *vb.* (14c) To remove legal defects or correct legal errors. • For example, curing title involves removing defects from title to unmarketable land so that title becomes marketable.

currency. (17c) An item (such as a coin, government note, or banknote) that circulates as a medium of exchange.

current-cost accounting. (1938) A method of measuring assets in terms of replacement cost. • This approach accounts for inflation by recognizing price changes in a company's assets and restating the assets in terms of their current cost.

current market value. (18c) The price at which an asset can be sold within the present accounting period.

curtesy (**kər**-tə-see). (16c) At common law, a husband's right, upon his wife's death, to a life estate in the land that his wife owned during their marriage, assuming that a child was born alive to the couple. • This right has been largely abolished.

curtilage (**kər**-tə-lij). (14c) The land or yard adjoining a house, usu. within an enclosure. • Under the Fourth Amendment, the curtilage is an area usu. protected from warrantless searches.

custodial interference. *Family law.* **1.** The abduction of a child or the inducement of a minor child to leave the parent legally entitled to custody or not to return to the parent entitled to legal custody. **2.** Any hindrance to a parent's rightful access to a child.

custodial responsibility. *Family law.* Physical child custody and supervision, usu. including overnight responsibility for the child. • This term encompasses visitation and sole, joint, and shared custody. Both parents share responsibility for the child regardless of the amount of time they spend with the child.

custodian, *n.* **1.** A person or institution that has charge or custody (of a child, property, papers, or other valuables); GUARDIAN. **2.** *Bankruptcy.* A prepetition agent who has taken charge of any asset belonging to the debtor. 11 USCA § 101(11). — **custodianship,** *n.*

custody, *n.* (15c) **1.** The care and control of a thing or person for inspection, preservation, or security.

constructive custody. (1822) Custody of a person (such as a parolee or probationer) whose freedom is controlled by legal authority but who is not under direct physical control.

preventive custody. (1976) Custody intended to prevent further dangerous or criminal behavior.

protective custody. (1929) **1.** The government's confinement of a person for that person's own security or well-being, such as a witness whose safety is in jeopardy or an incompetent person who may harm him- or herself or others. **2.** *Family law.* An arrangement intended to protect a child from abuse, neglect, or danger whereby the child is placed in the safety of a foster family after being removed from a home or from the custody of the person previously responsible for the child's care. **3.** An arrangement made by law-enforcement authorities to safeguard a person in a place other than the person's home because of criminal threats to harm the person.

2. *Family law.* The care, control, and maintenance of a child awarded by a court to a responsible adult. • Custody involves legal custody (decision-making authority) and physical custody (caregiving authority), and an award of custody usu. grants both rights. In a divorce or separation proceeding between the parents, the court usu. awards custody to one of them, unless both are found to be unfit, in which case the court may award custody to a third party, typically a relative. In a case involving parental dereliction, such as abuse or neglect, the court may award custody to the state for placing the child in foster care if no responsible relative or family friend is willing and able to care for the child.

divided custody. (1905) An arrangement by which each parent has exclusive physical custody and full control of and responsibility for the child part of the time, with visitation rights in the other parent.

joint custody. (1870) An arrangement by which both parents share the responsibility for and authority over the child at all times, although one parent may exercise primary physical custody.

legal custody. **1.** CUSTODY (2). **2.** CUSTODY (3). **3.** The authority to make significant decisions on a child's behalf, including decisions about education, religious training, and healthcare.

physical custody. **1.** PHYSICAL CUSTODY (2). **2.** PHYSICAL CUSTODY (3).

sole custody. (1870) An arrangement by which one parent has full control and sole decision-making responsibility — to the exclusion of the other parent — on matters such as health, education, religion, and living arrangements.

split custody. An arrangement in which one parent has custody of one or more children, while the other parent has custody of the remaining children. • Split custody is fairly uncommon, since most jurisdictions favor keeping siblings together.

3. The detention of a person by virtue of lawful process or authority. — **custodial,** *adj.*

custody determination. *Family law.* A court order determining custody and visitation rights. • The order typically does not include any instructions on child support or other monetary obligations.

custody of the law. (17c) The condition of property or a person being under the control of legal authority (as a court or law officer).

custody proceeding. *Family law.* An action to determine who is entitled to legal or physical custody of a child. • Legal custody gives one the right to make significant decisions regarding the child, and physical custody gives one the right to physical care and control of the child.

custom, *n.* (13c) **1.** A practice that by its common adoption and long, unvarying habit has come to have the force of law. — **customary,** *adj.*

general custom. **1.** A custom that prevails throughout a country and constitutes one of the sources of the law of the land. **2.** A custom that businesses recognize and follow.

legal custom. A custom that operates as a binding rule of law, independently of any agreement on the part of those subject to it.

local custom. A custom that prevails in some defined locality only, such as a city or county, and constitutes a source of law for that place only.

2. (*pl.*) Duties imposed on imports or exports. **3.** (*pl.*) The agency or procedure for collecting such duties.

custom and usage. General rules and practices that have become the norm through unvarying habit and common use.

customary, *n.* (16c) A record of all the established legal and quasi-legal practices within a community.

customary law. (16c) Law consisting of customs that are accepted as legal requirements or obligatory rules of conduct; practices and beliefs that are so vital and intrinsic a part of a social and economic system that they are treated as if they were laws.

cyberlaw (**sɪ**-bər-law). (1994) The field of law dealing with the Internet, encompassing cases, statutes, regulations, and disputes that affect people and businesses interacting through computers. • Cyberlaw addresses issues of online speech and business that arise because of the nature of the medium, including intellectual property rights, free speech, privacy, e-commerce, and safety, as well as questions of jurisdiction.

cybersquatting. (1997) The act of reserving a domain name on the Internet, esp. a name that would be associated with a company's trademark, and then seeking to profit by selling or licensing the name to the company that has an interest in being identified with it. • The practice was banned by federal law in 1999.

cyberstalking. (1995) The act of threatening, harassing, or annoying someone through multiple e-mail messages, as through the Internet, esp. with the intent of placing the recipient in fear that an illegal act or an injury will be inflicted on the recipient or a member of the recipient's family or household.

cybertheft. (1994) The act of using an online computer service, such as one on the Internet, to steal someone else's property or to interfere with someone else's use and enjoyment of property. • Examples of cybertheft are hacking into a bank's computer records to wrongfully credit one account and debit another, and interfering with a copyright by wrongfully sending protected material over the Internet.

cy pres (see **pray** *or* sɪ). [Law French "as near as"] (1885) The equitable doctrine under which a court reforms a written instrument with a gift to charity as closely to the donor's intention as possible, so that the gift does not fail. • Courts use *cy pres* esp. in construing charitable gifts when the donor's original charitable purpose cannot be fulfilled. It is also used to distribute unclaimed portions of a class-action judgment or settlement funds to a charity that will advance the interests of the class. More recently, courts have used cy pres to distribute class-action-settlement funds not amenable to individual claims or to a meaningful pro rata distribution to a nonprofit charitable organization whose work indirectly benefits the class members and advances the public interest.

D

D. *abbr.* **1.** District. **2.** Defendant. **3.** Digest.

D.A. *abbr.* District attorney.

daily balance. (1859) The final daily accounting for a day on which interest is to be accrued or paid.

average daily balance. The average amount of money in an account (such as a bank account or credit-card account) during a given period. • This amount serves as the basis for computing interest or a finance charge for the period.

damage, *adj.* Of or relating to monetary compensation for loss or injury to a person or property.

damage, *n.* (14c) Loss or injury to person or property.

damages, *n. pl.* (16c) Money claimed by, or ordered to be paid to, a person as compensation for loss or injury. — **damage,** *adj.*

accumulative damages. Statutory damages allowed in addition to amounts available under the common law.

actual damages. (18c) An amount awarded to a complainant to compensate for a proven injury or loss; damages that repay actual losses.

additional damages. Damages usu. provided by statute in addition to direct damages. • Additional damages can include expenses resulting from the injury, consequential damages, or punitive damages.

benefit-of-the-bargain damages. (1955) Damages that a breaching party to a contract must pay to the aggrieved party, equal to the amounts that the aggrieved party would have received, including profits, if the contract had been fully performed.

compensatory damages (kəm-**pen**-sə-tor-ee). (1817) Damages sufficient in amount to indemnify the injured person for the loss suffered.

consequential damages. (17c) Losses that do not flow directly and immediately from an injurious act but that result indirectly from the act.

continuing damages. **1.** Ongoing damages arising from the same injury. **2.** Damages arising from the repetition of similar acts within a definite period.

discretionary damages. Damages (such as mental anguish or pain and suffering) that are not precisely measurable but are determined by the subjective judgment of a jury.

double damages. Damages that, by statute, are twice the amount that the fact-finder determines is owed or twice the amount of actual damages awarded.

excess damages. Damages awarded to an insured — beyond the coverage provided by an insurance policy — because the insurer did not settle the claim within policy limits.

excessive damages. A jury award that grossly exceeds the amount warranted by law based on the facts and circumstances of the case; unreasonable or outrageous damages, which are subject to reduction by remittitur.

expectation damages. (1939) Compensation awarded for the loss of what a person reasonably anticipated from a transaction that was not completed.

foreseeable damages. Damages that a breaching party knew or should have known when the contract was made would be likely to result from a breach.

future damages. (17c) Money awarded to an injured party for an injury's residual or projected effects, such as those that reduce the person's ability to function. • Examples are expected pain and suffering, loss or impairment of earning capacity, and projected medical expenses.

general damages. (18c) Damages that the law presumes follow from the type of wrong complained of; specif., compensatory damages for harm that so frequently results from the tort for which a party has sued that the harm is reasonably expected and need not be alleged or proved. • General damages do not need to be specifically claimed.

gross damages. The total damages found before adjustments and offsets.

hedonic damages (hi-**don**-ik). (1985) Damages that attempt to compensate for the loss of the pleasure of being alive. • Such damages are not allowed in most jurisdictions.

inadequate damages. Damages insufficient to fully and fairly compensate the parties; damages bearing no reasonable relation to the plaintiff's injuries, indicating prejudice, mistake, or other fact to support setting aside a jury's verdict.

incidental damages. (18c) **1.** Losses reasonably associated with or related to actual damages. **2.** A seller's commercially reasonable expenses incurred in stopping delivery or in transporting and caring for goods after a buyer's breach. UCC § 2-710. **3.** A buyer's expenses reasonably incurred in caring for goods after a seller's breach. UCC § 2-715(1).

intervening damages. Continuing damages that accrue during the pendency and prosecution of an unsuccessful appeal. • A lower court may include intervening damages in an award.

irreparable damages (i-**rep**-ə-rə-bəl). Damages that cannot be easily ascertained because there is no fixed pecuniary standard of measurement, e.g., damages for a repeated public nuisance.

liquidated damages. (18c) An amount contractually stipulated as a reasonable estimation of actual damages to be recovered by one party if the other party breaches. • If the parties to a contract have properly agreed on liquidated damages, the sum fixed is the measure of damages for a breach, whether it exceeds or falls short of the actual damages.

nominal damages. (18c) **1.** A trifling sum awarded when a legal injury is suffered but there is no substantial loss or injury to be compensated. **2.** A small amount fixed as damages for breach of contract without regard to the amount of harm.

nonpecuniary damages. Damages that cannot be measured in money.

pecuniary damages (pə-**kyoo**-nee-er-ee). (17c) Damages that can be estimated and monetarily compensated. • Although this phrase appears in many old cases, it is now widely considered a redundancy — since damages are always pecuniary.

punitive damages. (1848) Damages awarded in addition to actual damages when the defendant acted with recklessness, malice, or deceit; specif., damages assessed by way of penalizing the wrongdoer or making an example to others.

reliance damages. (1938) Damages awarded for losses incurred by the plaintiff in reliance on the contract.

rescissory damages (ri-**sis**-ə-ree *or* ri-**siz**-). Damages awarded to restore a plaintiff to the position occupied before the defendant's wrongful acts.

restitution damages. (1939) Damages awarded to a plaintiff when the defendant has been unjustly enriched at the plaintiff's expense.

speculative damages. (1804) Damages that are so uncertain to occur that they will not be awarded.

statutory damages. Damages provided by statute (such as a wrongful death and survival statute), as distinguished from damages provided under the common law.

treble damages. (18c) Damages that, by statute, are three times the amount of actual damages that the fact-finder determines is owed.

unliquidated damages. (18c) Damages that cannot be determined by a fixed formula and must be established by a judge or jury. Cf. *liquidated damages.*

damn-fool doctrine. *Insurance.* The principle that an insurer may deny (esp. liability) coverage when an insured engages in behavior that is so ill-conceived that the insurer should not be compelled to bear the loss resulting from the insured's actions.

damnify, *vb.* To cause loss or damage to; to injure <the surety was damnified by the judgment obtained against it>.

damnum (**dam**-nəm), *n.* [Latin] (1828) A loss; damage suffered. Pl. **damna.**

damnum sine injuria (**dam**-nəm **sɪ**-nee in-**joor**-ee-ə *or* **sin**-ay). [Latin "damage without wrongful act"] Loss or harm that is incurred from something other than a wrongful act and occasions no legal remedy.

danger. (13c) **1.** Peril; exposure to harm, loss, pain, or other negative result. **2.** A cause of peril; a menace.

apparent danger. (16c) **1.** Obvious danger; real danger. **2.** *Criminal law.* The perceived danger in one person's actions toward another, as a result of which it seems necessary for the threatened person to use force in self-defense.

deterrent danger. (1959) An obvious danger that an occupier of land creates to discourage trespassers, such as a barbed-wire fence or spikes on the top of a wall.

imminent danger. (16c) **1.** An immediate, real threat to one's safety that justifies the use of force in self-defense. **2.** *Criminal law.* The danger resulting from an immediate threatened injury sufficient to cause a reasonable and prudent person to defend himself or herself.

retributive danger. A concealed danger that an occupier of land creates to injure trespassers. • A retributive danger is lawful only to the extent that it could be justified if the occupier had inflicted the injury personally or directly to the trespasser. Thus, a spring gun or a land mine is an unlawful means of defending land against a trespasser.

seeming danger. Danger that a reasonable person would perceive to be real, even if it is not.

unavoidable danger. (16c) **1.** Inescapable danger. **2.** A danger that is unpreventable, esp. by a person operating a vessel.

danger-creation doctrine. (2000) The theory that if a state's affirmative conduct places a person in jeopardy, then the state may be liable for the harm inflicted on that person by a third party. • This is an exception to the general principle that the state is not liable for an injury that a third party inflicts on a member of the public.

dangerous, *adj.* (15c) **1.** (Of a condition, situation, etc.) perilous; hazardous; unsafe. **2.** (Of a person, an object, etc.) likely to cause serious bodily harm.

imminently dangerous. (1834) (Of a person, behavior, activity, or thing) reasonably certain to place life and limb in peril. • This term is relevant in several legal contexts. For example, if a mental condition renders a person imminently dangerous to self or others, he or she may be committed to a mental hospital. And the imminently dangerous behavior of pointing a gun at someone's head could subject the actor to criminal and tort liability. Further, the manufacturer of an imminently dangerous product may be held to a strict-liability standard in tort.

inherently dangerous. (1887) (Of an activity or thing) requiring special precautions at all times to avoid injury; dangerous per se.

dangerous instrumentality. (1857) An instrument, substance, or condition so inherently dangerous that it may cause serious bodily injury or death without human use or interference. • It may serve as the basis for strict liability.

dangerous-proximity test. (1973) *Criminal law.* A common-law test for the crime of attempt, focusing on whether the defendant is dangerously close to completing the offense. • Factors include the gravity of the potential crime, the apprehension of the victim, and the uncertainty of the crime's occurrence.

dangerous situation. (1898) Under the last-clear-chance doctrine, the circumstance in which a plaintiff operating a motor vehicle has reached a position (as on the path of an oncoming train) that cannot be escaped by the exercise of ordinary care.

dangerous-tendency test. (1938) A propensity of a person or animal to inflict injury. • The test is used, esp. in dog-bite cases, to determine whether an owner will be held liable for injuries caused by the owner's animal.

***Darden* hearing.** (1979) *Criminal procedure.* An ex parte proceeding to determine whether disclosure of an informant's identity is pertinent to establishing probable cause when there is otherwise insufficient evidence to establish probable cause apart from the arresting officer's testimony about an informant's communications. • The defense attorney may be excluded from the hearing but can usu. submit questions to be used by the judge in the examination. *People v. Darden*, 313 N.E.2d 49 (N.Y. 1974).

DARPA. *abbr.* Defense Advanced Research Projects Agency.

database. A compilation of information arranged in a systematic way and offering a means of finding specific elements it contains, often today by electronic means. • Unless the information itself is original, a database is not protected by U.S. copyright law. Elsewhere, it may be protected as a distinct class of "literary works," or it may be the subject of *sui generis* intellectual-property laws.

data protection. Any method of securing information, esp. information stored on a computer, from being either physically lost or seen by an unauthorized person.

date. 1. The day when an event happened or will happen. **2.** A period of time in general. **3.** An appointment at a specified time.

cutoff date. A deadline; esp., in the sale of a note or other interest-paying asset, the last date on which the seller is entitled to any interest due on the note or asset.

date of bankruptcy. (1809) *Bankruptcy.* The date when a court declares a person to be bankrupt; the date of bankruptcy adjudication.

date of injury. (1831) *Torts.* The inception date of an injury; the date of an accident causing an injury.

date of invention. *Patents.* For purposes of a patent application, the date when the creation was reduced to practice.

***date of issue.* 1.** *Commercial law.* An arbitrary date (for notes, bonds, and other documents in a series) fixed as the beginning of the term for which they run; the date that a stock or bond bears on its face, not the date on which it is actually signed, delivered, or put into circulation. **2.** *Insurance.* The date specified in the policy as the "date of issue," not the date on which the policy is executed or delivered.

date of maturity. *Commercial law.* The date when a debt falls due, such as a debt on a promissory note or bond.

date certain. A fixed or appointed day; a specified day, esp. a date fixed by an instrument such as a deed.

***Daubert* test.** (1993) *Evidence.* A method that federal district courts use to determine whether expert testimony is admissible under Federal Rule of Evidence 702, which generally requires that expert testimony consist of scientific, technical, or other specialized knowledge that will assist the fact-finder in understanding the evidence or determining a fact in issue. *Daubert v. Merrell Dow Pharms., Inc.*, 509 U.S. 579, 113 S.Ct. 2786 (1993). • Similar scrutiny must be applied to nonscientific expert testimony. *Kumho Tire Co. v. Carmichael*, 526 U.S. 137, 119 S.Ct. 1167 (1999). Variations of the *Daubert* test are applied in the trial courts of most states.

Davis–Bacon Act. A federal law originally enacted in 1931 to regulate the minimum-wage rates payable to employees of federal public-works projects. 40 USCA § 276a.

day. (bef. 12c) **1.** Any 24-hour period; the time it takes the earth to revolve once on its axis. **2.** The period between the rising and the setting of the sun. **3.** Sunlight. **4.** The period when the sun is above the horizon, along with the period in the early morning and late evening when a person's face is discernible. **5.** Any specified time period, esp. as distinguished from other periods. Cf. NIGHT.

answer day. (1859) *Civil procedure.* The last day for a defendant to file and serve a responsive pleading in a lawsuit. • Under the Federal Rules of Civil Procedure, a defendant generally must serve an answer (1) within 20 days after being served with the summons and complaint, or (2) if a defendant timely waives service at the plaintiff's request, within 60 days after the request for waiver was sent. Fed. R. Civ. P. 4(d), 12(a).

business day. A day that most institutions are open for business, usu. a day on which banks and major stock exchanges are open, excluding Saturdays, Sundays, and certain major holidays.

calendar day. A consecutive 24-hour day running from midnight to midnight.

juridical day (juu-**rid**-i-kəl). (17c) A day on which legal proceedings can be held. Cf. *nonjudicial day.*

legislative day. A day that begins when a legislative body reconvenes after a recess or adjournment, and ends when the body next recesses or adjourns until a different calendar day. • A legislative day may extend over several calendar days.

nonjudicial day. (18c) A day when courts do not sit or when legal proceedings cannot be conducted, such as a Sunday or legal holiday. Cf. *juridical day.*

peremptory day. (16c) A day assigned for trial or hearing, without further opportunity for postponement.

return day. (17c) **1.** A day on which a defendant must appear in court (as for an arraignment). **2.** A day on which a defendant must file an answer. **3.** A day on which a proof of service must be returned to court. **4.** A day on which a writ of execution must be returned to court. **5.** A day specified by law for counting votes in an election.

daybook. A merchant's original record of daily transactions.

day in court. (16c) **1.** The right and opportunity, in a judicial tribunal, to litigate a claim, seek relief, or defend one's rights. **2.** The right to be notified and given an opportunity to appear and to be heard when one's case is called.

d/b/a. *abbr.* Doing business as. • The abbreviation usu. precedes a person's or business's assumed name <Paul Smith d/b/a Paul's Dry Cleaners>.

d.b.e. *abbr.* DE BENE ESSE.

d.b.n. *abbr. Administration de bonis non.*

d.b.n.c.t.a. *abbr. Administration de bonis non cum testamento annexo.*

D.C. *abbr.* **1.** District of Columbia. **2.** District court.

DDoS. *abbr.* Distributed denial-of-service attack.

deadbeat. (1863) *Slang.* A person who does not pay debts or financial obligations (such as child-support payments, fines, and legal judgments), usu. with the suggestion that the person is also adept or experienced at evading creditors.

deadbeat dad. (1983) *Slang.* A father who has not paid or who is behind in making child-support payments.

deadbeat mom. (1987) *Slang.* **1.** A mother who has not paid or who is behind in making child-support payments. **2.** An able-bodied mother whose income is derived from welfare payments, not from gainful employment.

Deadbeat Parents Punishment Act. A 1998 federal statute that makes it a felony, punishable by up to two years in prison, for failure to pay child support if the obligor has crossed state lines in an attempt to avoid paying the support. 42 USCA § 228.

deadhand control. (1952) The convergence of various legal doctrines that allow a decedent's control of wealth to influence the conduct of a living beneficiary; esp., the use of executory interests that vest at some indefinite and remote time in the future to restrict alienability and to ensure that property remains in the hands of a particular family or organization. • Examples include the lawful use of conditional gifts, contingent future interests, and the *Claflin*-trust principle. The rule against perpetuities restricts certain types of deadhand control, which is sometimes referred to either as the power of the *mortua manus* (dead hand) or as trying to retain property *in mortua manu.*

dead letter. **1.** A law or practice that, although not formally abolished, is no longer used, observed, or enforced. **2.** A piece of mail that can be neither delivered nor returned because it lacks correct addresses for both the intended recipient and the sender.

deadlock, *n.* A state of inaction resulting from opposition, a lack of compromise or resolution, or a failure of election. — **deadlock,** *vb.*

dead man's statute. (1879) A law prohibiting the admission of a decedent's statement as evidence in certain circumstances, as when an opposing party or witness seeks to use the statement to support a claim against the decedent's estate.

deal, *n.* (15c) **1.** An act of buying and selling; the purchase and exchange of something for profit. **2.** An arrangement for mutual advantage. **3.** An indefinite quantity.

deal, *vb.* (bef. 12c) **1.** To distribute (something). **2.** To transact business with (a person or entity). **3.** To conspire with (a person or entity).

dealer, *n.* (17c) **1.** A person who purchases goods or property for sale to others; a retailer. **2.** A person or firm that buys and sells securities for its own account as a principal, and then sells to a customer.

registered dealer. A dealer registered or required to be registered under the Securities Exchange Act of 1934.

death. (bef. 12c) The ending of life; the cessation of all vital functions and signs.

accidental death. A death that results from an unusual event, one that was not voluntary, intended, expected, or foreseeable.

brain death. (1964) The bodily condition of showing no response to external stimuli, no spontaneous movements, no breathing, no reflexes, and a flat reading (usu. for a full day) on a machine that measures the brain's electrical activity.

compensable death. Workers' compensation. A death that, because it occurred in the course of employment, entitles the employee's heirs to compensation.

immediate death. (16c) **1.** Instantaneous death. **2.** A death occurring within a short time after an injury or seizure, but not instantaneously.

instantaneous death. (18c) Death occurring in an instant or within an extremely short time after an injury or seizure.

natural death. (15c) **1.** Bodily death, as opposed to civil death. **2.** Death from causes other than accident or violence; death from natural causes.

presumptive death. (1856) Death inferred from proof of the person's long, unexplained absence, usu. after seven years.

simultaneous death. (1878) The death of two or more persons in the same mishap, under circumstances that make it impossible to determine who died first.

violent death. (16c) Death accelerated by human intervention and resulting from a sharp blow, explosion, gunfire, or the like.

death case. (1907) **1.** A criminal case in which the death penalty may be or has been imposed. **2.** Wrongful-death action.

death certificate. (1888) An official document issued by a public registry verifying that a person has died, with information such as the date and time of death, the cause of death, and the signature of the attending or examining physician.

death-knell doctrine. (1972) A rule allowing an interlocutory appeal if precluding an appeal until final judgment would moot the issue on appeal and irreparably injure the appellant's rights. • Once recognized as an exception to the final-judgment rule, the doctrine was limited by the U.S. Supreme Court in *Coopers & Lybrand v. Livesay*, 437 U.S. 463, 98 S.Ct. 2454 (1978). There, the Court held that the death-knell doctrine does not permit an immediate appeal of an order denying class certification. But the doctrine still applies in some contexts. For example, the doctrine allows an immediate appeal of the denial of a temporary restraining order when the lack of an appeal would leave nothing to be considered in the trial court. *Woratzeck v. Arizona Bd. of Executive Clemency*, 117 F.3d 400 (9th Cir. 1997).

death penalty. (1848) **1.** CAPITAL PUNISHMENT. **2.** A penalty that makes a person or entity ineligible to participate in an activity that the person or entity previously participated in. • The penalty is usu. imposed because of some type of gross misconduct.

death row. (1950) The area of a prison where those who have been sentenced to death are confined.

death statute. (1910) A law that protects the interests of a decedent's family and other dependents, who may recover in damages what they would reasonably have received from the decedent if the death had not occurred.

death trap. (1835) **1.** A structure or situation involving an imminent risk of death. **2.** A situation that, although seemingly safe, is actually quite dangerous.

debarment, *n.* The act of precluding someone from having or doing something; exclusion or hindrance. — **debar,** *vb.*

debasement. (17c) **1.** The act of reducing the value, quality, or purity of something; esp., the act of lowering the value of coins by either reducing the weight of gold and silver in the coins or increasing the coins' alloy amounts. **2.** Degradation. **3.** The state of being degraded.

debate. *Parliamentary law.* Formal consideration of a motion's merits in the form of speeches for, against, or otherwise addressing the motion. — **debatable,** *adj.* — **debatability,** *n.*

controlled debate. Debate in which designated managers, usu. a partisan leader, lead each side and allot time for speeches.

extended debate. Debate that continues beyond an otherwise applicable limit.

floor debate. (1884) The legislative process of debating a proposed bill before an entire chamber rather than before a committee.

limited debate. Debate with restrictions.

de bene esse (dee **bee**-nee **es**-ee *also* day **ben**-ay **es**-ay), *adv.* [Law Latin "of well-being"] (17c) As conditionally allowed for the present; in anticipation of a future need <Willis's deposition was taken *de bene esse*>. — Abbr. *d.b.e.* — ***de bene esse,*** *adj.*

debenture (di-**ben**-chər). [fr. L. *debentur* "there are owed"] (15c) **1.** A debt secured only by the debtor's earning power, not by a lien on any specific asset. • Originally, this was the first word of a deed detailing sums acknowledged to be owed. **2.** An instrument acknowledging such a debt. **3.** A bond that is backed only by the general credit and financial reputation of the corporate issuer, not by a lien on corporate assets.

convertible debenture. (1908) A debenture that the holder may change or convert into some other security, such as stock.

convertible subordinated debenture. (1961) A debenture that is subordinate to another debt but can be converted into a different security.

sinking-fund debenture. (1893) A debenture that is secured by periodic payments into a fund established to retire long-term debt.

subordinate debenture. (1929) A debenture that is subject to the prior payment of ordinary debentures and other indebtedness.

debit. (15c) **1.** A sum charged as due or owing. **2.** In bookkeeping, an entry made on the left side of a ledger or account, noting an increase in assets or a decrease in liabilities. **3.** An account balance showing that something remains due to the holder of the account.

debit card. A card used to pay for purchases by electronic transfer from the purchaser's bank account.

debt. (13c) **1.** Liability on a claim; a specific sum of money due by agreement or otherwise. **2.** The aggregate of all existing claims against a person, entity, or state. **3.** A nonmonetary thing that one person owes another, such as goods or services. **4.** A common-law writ by which a court adjudicates claims involving fixed sums of money.

antecedent debt. **1.** *Contracts.* An old debt that may serve as consideration for a new promise if the statute of limitations has run on the old debt. **2.** *Bankruptcy.* A debtor's prepetition obligation that existed before a debtor's transfer of an interest in property.

bad debt. A debt that is uncollectible and that may be deductible for tax purposes.

bonded debt. A debt secured by a bond; a business or government debt represented by issued bonds.

community debt. A debt that is chargeable to the community of husband and wife.

consumer debt. A debt incurred by someone primarily for a personal, family, or household purpose.

contingent debt. A debt that is not presently fixed but that may become fixed in the future with the occurrence of some event.

desperate debt. **1.** Uncollectable debt. **2.** A debt taken on by one who is either insolvent or on the verge of insolvency.

distressed debt. A debt instrument issued by a company that is financially troubled and in danger of defaulting on the debt, or in bankruptcy, or likely to default or declare bankruptcy in the near future.

exigible debt. A liquidated and demandable debt; a matured claim.

fixed debt. Generally, a permanent form of debt commonly evidenced by a bond or debenture; long-term debt.

floating debt. Short-term debt that is continuously renewed to finance the ongoing operations of a business or government.

fraudulent debt. A debt created by fraudulent practices.

general debt. A governmental body's debt that is legally payable from general revenues and is backed by the full faith and credit of the governmental body.

installment debt. A debt that is to be repaid in a series of payments at regular times over a specified period.

judgment debt. A debt that is evidenced by a legal judgment or brought about by a successful lawsuit against the debtor.

liquidated debt. A debt whose amount has been determined by agreement of the parties or by operation of law.

liquid debt. A debt that is due immediately and unconditionally.

long-term debt. Generally, a debt that will not come due within the next year.

nondischargeable debt. (1908) A debt (such as one for delinquent taxes) that is not released through bankruptcy.

preferential debt. A debt that is legally payable before others, such as an employee's wages.

privileged debt. A debt that has priority over other debts if a debtor becomes insolvent; a secured debt.

public debt. A debt owed by a municipal, state, or national government.

secured debt. A debt backed by collateral.

senior debt. A debt that takes priority over other debts. • Senior debts are often secured by collateral.

short-term debt. Collectively, all debts and other liabilities that are payable within one year.

subordinate debt. A debt that is junior or inferior to other types or classes of debt. • Subordinate debt may be unsecured or have a low-priority claim against property secured by other debt instruments.

unliquidated debt. A debt that has not been reduced to a specific amount, and about which there may be a dispute.

unsecured debt. A debt not supported by collateral or other security.

debt consolidation. 1. Debt pooling. **2.** The replacement of multiple loans from one or more lenders with a single loan from one lender, usu. with a lower monthly payment and a longer repayment period.

debt instrument. (1953) A written promise to repay a debt, such as a promissory note, bill, bond, or commercial paper.

debtor. (13c) **1.** One who owes an obligation to another, esp. an obligation to pay money. **2.** *Bankruptcy.* A person who files a voluntary petition or against whom an involuntary petition is filed. **3.** *Secured transactions.* A person who either (1) has a property interest — other than a security interest or other lien — in collateral, even if the person is not an obligor, or (2) is a seller of accounts, chattel paper, payment intangibles, or promissory notes. UCC § 9-102(a)(28). — Abbr. Dr. Cf. CREDITOR.

absconding debtor. (18c) A debtor who flees from creditors to avoid having to pay a debt. • Absconding from a debt was formerly considered an act of bankruptcy.

absent debtor. A debtor who lacks the intent to defraud creditors but is beyond the geographic reach of ordinary service of process.

account debtor. A person obligated on an account, chattel paper, or general intangible. • The UCC exempts from the definition of *account debtor* a person obligated to pay a negotiable instrument, even if the instrument constitutes chattel paper. UCC § 9-102(a)(3).

new debtor. (18c) *Secured transactions.* A person who becomes bound as debtor under a security agreement previously entered into by another person. UCC §§ 9-102(a)(56), 9-203(c).

solvent debtor. A debtor who owns enough property to cover all outstanding debts and against whom a creditor can enforce a judgment.

debtor-in-possession. (1806) *Bankruptcy.* A Chapter 11 or 12 debtor that continues to operate its business as a fiduciary to the bankruptcy estate. • With certain exceptions, the debtor-in-possession has all the rights, powers, and duties of a Chapter 11 trustee. — Abbr. DIP.

debtor's examination. *Bankruptcy.* A meeting between a debtor and his or her creditors during which the creditors ask the debtor questions designed to uncover information about the location and extent of the debtor's assets and the dischargeability of debts.

debt pooling. (1957) **1.** *Bankruptcy.* An arrangement by which a person's debts are consolidated and creditors agree to accept lower monthly payments or to take less money. **2.** An arrangement under which a debtor agrees to pay (1) a sum of money periodically or otherwise to a third person who will then distribute the money among certain specified creditors in accordance with a plan, and (2) a fee to the third person for his or her services as distributor. • Debt-pooling in this manner is generally illegal if the arrangement is not made with a bank, attorney, judicial officer, retail-merchants' association, or nonprofit organization that provides debt-counseling services.

debt ratio. (1932) A corporation's total long-term and short-term liabilities divided by the firm's total assets.

debt retirement. (1928) Repayment of debt; RETIREMENT (3).

debt service. (1930) **1.** The funds needed to meet a long-term debt's annual interest expenses, principal payments, and sinking-fund contributions. **2.** Payments due on a debt, including interest and principal.

debt-to-equity ratio. (1954) A corporation's long-term debt divided by its owners' equity, calculated to assess its capitalization.

decedent (di-**see**-dənt), *n.* (16c) A dead person, esp. one who has died recently.

deceit, *n.* (14c) **1.** The act of intentionally giving a false impression. **2.** A false statement of fact made by a person knowingly or recklessly (i.e., not caring whether it is true or false) with the intent that someone else will act upon it. **3.** A tort arising from a false representation made knowingly or recklessly with the intent that another person should detrimentally rely on it. — **deceive,** *vb.*

deceptive act. (1939) As defined by the Federal Trade Commission and most state statutes, conduct that is likely to deceive a consumer acting reasonably under similar circumstances.

decertify, *vb.* (1918) **1.** To revoke the certification of. **2.** To remove the official status of (a labor union) by withdrawing the right to act as a collective-bargaining agent. **3.** (Of a court) to overrule a previous order that created a class for purposes of a class action; to officially undo (a class). Cf. CERTIFY. — **decertification,** *n.*

decision, *n.* (16c) A judicial or agency determination after consideration of the facts and the law; esp., a ruling, order, or judgment pronounced by a court when considering or disposing of a case. — **decisional,** *adj.*

appealable decision. (1870) A decree or order that is sufficiently final to receive appellate review (such as an order granting summary judgment), or an interlocutory decree or order that is immediately appealable, usu. by statute (such as an order denying immunity to a police officer in a civil-rights suit).

unreasonable decision. (1962) An administrative agency's decision that is so obviously wrong that there can be no difference of opinion among reasonable minds about its erroneous nature.

decision-making responsibility. The authority to come to a binding resolution of an issue. • For example, in child-rearing, decision-making responsibility involves the authority to make significant decisions on a child's behalf, including decisions about education, religious training, and healthcare.

declarant (di-**klair**-ənt), *n.* (17c) **1.** One who has made a statement. **2.** One who has signed a declaration, esp. one stating an intent to become a U.S. citizen. — **declarant,** *adj.*

declaration, *n.* (15c) **1.** A formal statement, proclamation, or announcement, esp. one embodied in an instrument.

declaration of alienage. A declaration by a person with dual citizenship of a wish to renounce the citizenship of one state.

declaration of default. A creditor's notice to a debtor regarding the debtor's failure to perform an obligation, such as making a payment.

declaration of dividend. (1837) A company's setting aside of a portion of its earnings or profits for distribution to its shareholders.

declaration of homestead. (1856) A statement required to be filed with a state or local authority to prove property ownership in order to claim homestead-exemption rights.

declaration of intention. (1812) An alien's formal statement resolving to become a U.S. citizen and to renounce allegiance to any other government or country.

declaration of legitimacy. (1861) A formal or legal pronouncement that a child is legitimate.

declaration of trust. (17c) **1.** The act by which the person who holds legal title to property or an estate acknowledges that the property is being held in trust for another person or for certain specified purposes. **2.** The instrument that creates a trust.

2. A document that governs legal rights to certain types of real property, such as a condominium or a residential subdivision. **3.** A listing of the merchandise that a person intends to bring into the United States. **4.** *Evidence.* An unsworn statement made by someone having knowledge of facts relating to an event in dispute.

declaration against interest. (1940) A statement by a person who is not a party to a suit and is not available to testify at trial, discussing a matter that is within the declarant's personal knowledge and is adverse to the declarant's interest. • Such a statement is admissible into evidence as an exception to the hearsay rule. Fed. R. Evid. 804(b)(3).

declaration of pain. (1891) A person's exclamation of present pain, which operates as an exception to the hearsay rule. Fed. R. Evid. 803(3).

declaration of state of mind. (1843) A person's state-of-mind statement that operates as an exception to the hearsay rule. Fed. R. Evid. 803(3).

dying declaration. (18c) A statement by a person who believes that death is imminent, relating to the cause or circumstances of the person's impending death. • The statement is admissible in evidence as an exception to the hearsay rule.

self-serving declaration. (1881) An out-of-court statement made to benefit one's own interest.

5. *Common-law pleading.* The plaintiff's first pleading in a civil action. • In most American jurisdictions, it is called a *petition* or *complaint.* **6.** A formal, written statement — resembling an affidavit but not notarized or sworn to — that attests, under penalty of perjury, to facts known by the declarant. — **declare,** *vb.* — **declaratory,** *adj.*

declaration of estimated tax. (1946) A required IRS filing by certain individuals and businesses of current estimated tax owed, accompanied by periodic payments of that amount. IRC (26 USCA) §§ 6315, 6654.

declaration of incontestability. *Trademarks.* A sworn statement submitted by the owner of a registered mark after five years of continuous use in commerce. • The statement entitles the mark to immunity from some legal challenges under the Lanham Act.

Declaration of Independence. The formal proclamation of July 4, 1776, in the name of the people of the American colonies, asserting their independence from the British Crown and announcing themselves to the world as an independent nation.

declaration of restrictions. *Property.* A statement of all the covenants, conditions, and restrictions affecting a parcel of land, usu. imposed and recorded by a developer of a subdivision. • The restrictions run with the land.

declaration of rights. An action in which a litigant requests a court's assistance not because any rights have been violated but because those rights are uncertain. • Examples include suits for a declaration of legitimacy, for declaration of nullity of marriage, and for the authoritative interpretation of a will.

Declaration of Taking Act. The federal law regulating the government's taking of private property for public use under eminent domain. 40 USCA § 3114 et seq. • Fair compensation must be paid for the property.

declaration of use. *Trademarks.* A sworn statement submitted by a registered mark's owner averring that the registered mark is currently in use in commerce.

declarator of trust (di-**klar**-ə-tər *or* di-**klair**-ə-tər *or* -tor). A common-law action against a trustee who holds property under a title *ex facie* for the trustee's own benefit.

declaratory-judgment act. (1921) A federal or state law permitting parties to bring an action to determine their legal rights and positions regarding a controversy not yet ripe for adjudication, as when an insurance company seeks a determination of coverage before deciding whether to cover a claim.

declaratory part of a law. A portion of a law clearly defining rights to be observed or wrongs to be avoided.

declaratory theory. (1895) The belief that judges' decisions never make law but instead merely constitute evidence of what the law is. • This antiquated view — held by such figures as Coke and Blackstone — is no longer accepted.

declination (dek-lə-**nay**-shən). (14c) **1.** A deviation from proper course. **2.** An act of refusal. **3.** A document filed by a fiduciary who chooses not to serve. **4.** At common law, a plea to the court's jurisdiction by reason of the judge's personal interest in the lawsuit.

deconstruction, *n.* (1969) In critical legal studies, a method of analyzing legal principles or rules by breaking down the supporting premises to show that these premises might also advance the opposite rule or result. — **deconstructionist,** *adj.* & *n.*

decorum. *Parliamentary law.* The customs of formality and courtesy observed by the members and chair in conducting business.

decoy, *n.* An undercover law-enforcement officer or agent who acts as the willing subject of an attempted or completed crime in an attempt to lure a potential criminal defendant into a situation that establishes the grounds for a prosecution.

decoy, *vb. Slang.* To entice (a person) without force; to inveigle.

decoy letter. A letter prepared and mailed to detect a criminal who has violated the postal or revenue laws.

decree, *n.* (14c) **1.** Traditionally, a judicial decision in a court of equity, admiralty, divorce, or probate — similar to a judgment of a court of law. **2.** A court's final judgment. **3.** Any court order, but esp. one in a matrimonial case.

consent decree. (1831) A court decree that all parties agree to.

custody decree. A decree awarding or modifying child custody.

decree absolute. (1826) A ripened decree nisi; a court's decree that has become unconditional because the time specified in the decree nisi has passed.

decree nisi (**nI**-sI). (18c) A court's decree that will become absolute unless the adversely affected party shows the court, within a specified time, why it should be set aside.

decree of distribution. (1841) An instrument by which heirs receive the property of a deceased person.

decree of insolvency. (18c) A probate-court decree declaring an estate's insolvency.

decree of nullity. (17c) A decree declaring a marriage to be void *ab initio.*

decree of registration. A court order that quiets title to land and directs recording of the title.

decree pro confesso (proh kən-**fes**-oh). (1821) *Equity practice.* A decree entered in favor of the plaintiff as a result of the defendant's failure to timely respond to the allegations in the plaintiff's bill; esp., a decree entered when the defendant has defaulted by not appearing in court at the prescribed time.

divorce decree. A final judgment in a suit for divorce.

decrepit (di-**krep**-it), *adj.* (15c) (Of a person) disabled; physically or mentally incompetent to such an extent that the individual would be helpless in a personal conflict with a person of ordinary health and strength.

decriminalization, *n.* (1945) The legislative act or process of legalizing an illegal act. Cf. CRIMINALIZATION (1). — **decriminalize,** *vb.*

decrowning. The act of depriving someone of a crown.

decry (di-**krɪ**), *vb.* (17c) To speak disparagingly about (someone or something).

dedication, *n.* (1809) *Property.* The donation of land or creation of an easement for public use. — **dedicate,** *vb.* — **dedicatory,** *adj.*

common-law dedication. (1858) A dedication made without a statute, consisting in the owner's appropriation of land, or an easement in it, for the benefit or use of the public, and the acceptance, by or on behalf of the land or easement.

dedication by adverse user. (1895) A dedication arising from the adverse, exclusive use by the public with the actual or imputed knowledge and acquiescence of the owner.

express dedication. (1836) A dedication explicitly manifested by the owner.

implied dedication. (1837) A dedication presumed by reasonable inference from the owner's conduct.

statutory dedication. (1852) A dedication for which the necessary steps are statutorily prescribed, all of which must be substantially followed for an effective dedication.

tacit dedication. (1926) A dedication of property for public use arising from silence or inactivity and without an express agreement.

dedition (di-**dish**-ən), *n.* [fr. Latin *deditio* "give up"] (16c) A surrender of something, such as property.

deductible, *n.* (1929) **1.** Under an insurance policy, the portion of the loss to be borne by the insured before the insurer becomes liable for payment. **2.** The insurance-policy clause specifying the amount of this portion.

deduction, *n.* (15c) **1.** The act or process of subtracting or taking away. **2.** *Tax.* An amount subtracted from gross income when calculating adjusted gross income, or from adjusted gross income when calculating taxable income. — **deductible,** *adj.*

additional standard deduction. (1956) The sum of the additional amounts that a taxpayer who turns 65 or becomes blind before the close of the taxable year is entitled to deduct.

charitable deduction. (1925) A deduction for a contribution to a charitable enterprise that has qualified for tax-exempt status in accordance with IRC (26 USCA) § 501(c)(3) and is entitled to be deducted in full by the donor from the taxable estate or from gross income.

deduction in respect of a decedent. (1949) A deduction that accrues to the point of death but is not recognizable on the decedent's final income-tax return because of the accounting method used, such as an accrued-interest expense of a cash-basis debtor.

itemized deduction. (1943) An expense (such as a medical expense, home-mortgage interest, or a charitable contribution) that can be subtracted from adjusted gross income to determine taxable income.

marital deduction. (1949) A federal tax deduction allowed for lifetime and testamentary transfers from one spouse to another. IRC (26 USCA) §§ 2056, 2523.

miscellaneous itemized deduction. (1955) Generally, an itemized deduction of job or investment expenses; a deduction other than those allowable in computing adjusted gross income, those enumerated in IRC (26 USCA) § 67(b), and personal exemptions.

standard deduction. (1944) A specified dollar amount that a taxpayer can deduct from adjusted gross income, instead of itemizing deductions, to determine taxable income.

3. The portion of a succession to which an heir is entitled before a partition. **4.** The act or process of reasoning from general propositions to a specific application or conclusion. — **deduct** (for senses 1–3), *vb.* — **deduce** (for sense 4), *vb.*

deed, *n.* (bef. 12c) **1.** Something that is done or carried out; an act or action. **2.** A written instrument by which land is conveyed. **3.** At common law, any written instrument that is signed, sealed, and delivered and that conveys some interest in property. — **deed,** *vb.*

absolute deed. (17c) A deed that conveys title without condition or encumbrance.

bargain-and-sale deed. (1972) A deed that conveys property to a buyer for valuable consideration but that lacks any guarantee from the seller about the validity of the title.

deed in lieu of foreclosure. (1934) A deed by which a borrower conveys fee-simple title to a lender in satisfaction of a mortgage debt and as a substitute for foreclosure. • This deed is often referred to simply as "deed in lieu."

deed of covenant. (17c) A deed to do something, such as a document providing for periodic payments by one party to another (usu. a charity) for tax-saving purposes.

deed of gift. (16c) A deed executed and delivered without consideration.

deed of partition. (18c) A deed that divides land held by joint tenants, tenants in common, or coparceners.

deed of reconveyance. A deed conveying title to real property from a trustee to a grantor when a loan is repaid.

deed of release. A deed that surrenders full title to a piece of property upon payment or performance of specified conditions.

deed of separation. An instrument governing a spouse's separation and maintenance.

deed of settlement. A deed to settle something, such as the distribution of property in a marriage.

deed of trust. (17c) A deed conveying title to real property to a trustee as security until the grantor repays a loan. • This type of deed resembles a mortgage.

deed poll. (16c) A deed made by and binding on only one party, or on two or more parties having similar interests. • It is so called because, traditionally, the parchment was "polled" (that is, shaved) so that it would be even at the top (unlike an indenture).

defeasible deed. (1802) A deed containing a condition subsequent causing title to the property to revert to the grantor or pass to a third party.

gift deed. (1864) A deed given for a nominal sum or for love and affection.

grant deed. (1891) A deed containing, or having implied by law, some but not all of the usual covenants of title; esp., a deed in which the grantor warrants that he or she (1) has not previously conveyed the estate being granted, (2) has not encumbered the property except as noted in the deed, and (3) will convey to the grantee any title to the property acquired after the date of the deed.

latent deed. A deed kept in a strongbox or other secret place, usu. for 20 years or more.

mortgage deed. The instrument creating a mortgage.

quitclaim deed. (18c) A deed that conveys a grantor's complete interest or claim in certain real property but that neither warrants nor professes that the title is valid.

release deed. A deed that is issued once a mortgage has been discharged, explicitly releasing and reconveying to the mortgagor the entire interest conveyed by an earlier deed of trust.

sheriff's deed. A deed that gives ownership rights in property bought at a sheriff's sale.

special warranty deed. (1808) **1.** A deed in which the grantor covenants to defend the title against only those claims and demands of the grantor and those claiming by and under the grantor. **2.** In a few jurisdictions, a quitclaim deed.

statutory deed. (1832) A warranty-deed form prescribed by state law and containing certain warranties and covenants even though they are not included in the printed form.

support deed. A deed by which a person (usu. a parent) conveys land to another (usu. a son or daughter) with the understanding that the grantee will support the grantor for life. • Support deeds often result in litigation.

tax deed. A deed showing the transfer of title to real property sold for the nonpayment of taxes.

title deed. (18c) A deed that evidences a person's legal ownership of property.

warranty deed. (1802) A deed containing one or more covenants of title; esp., a deed that expressly guarantees the grantor's good, clear title and that contains covenants concerning the quality of title, including warranties of seisin, quiet enjoyment, right to convey, freedom from encumbrances, and defense of title against all claims.

wild deed. (1914) A recorded deed that is not in the chain of title, usu. because a previous instrument connected to the chain of title has not been recorded.

deem, *vb.* (bef. 12c) **1.** To treat (something) as if (1) it were really something else, or (2) it has qualities that it does not have <although the document was not in fact signed until April 21, it explicitly states that it must be deemed to have been signed on April 14>. **2.** To consider, think, or judge <she deemed it necessary>.

deemed transferor. (1988) *Tax.* A person who holds an interest in a generation-skipping trust on behalf of a beneficiary, and whose death will trigger the imposition of a generation-skipping transfer tax. IRC (26 USCA) §§ 2601–2663.

deep pocket. (1975) **1.** (*pl.*) Substantial wealth and resources. **2.** A person or entity with substantial wealth and resources against which a claim may be made or a judgment may be taken.

deface (di-**fays**), *vb.* (14c) **1.** To mar or destroy (a written instrument, signature, or inscription) by obliteration, erasure, or superinscription. **2.** To detract from the value of (a coin) by punching, clipping, cutting, or shaving. **3.** To mar or injure (a building, monument, or other structure). — **defacement,** *n.*

de facto (di **fak**-toh *also* dee *or* day), *adj.* [Law Latin "in point of fact"] (17c) **1.** Actual; existing in fact; having effect even though not formally or legally recognized <a de facto contract> **2.** Illegitimate but in effect <a de facto government>. Cf. DE JURE.

defalcation (dee-fal-**kay**-shən), *n.* (15c) **1.** EMBEZZLEMENT. **2.** Loosely, the failure to meet an obligation; a nonfraudulent default. — **defalcate** (di-**fal**-kayt *or* dee-), *vb.* — **defalcator,** *n.*

defamacast (di-**fam**-ə-kast). (1997) Defamation by television or radio broadcast.

defamation, *n.* (14c) **1.** The act of harming the reputation of another by making a false statement to a third person. • If the alleged defamation involves a matter of public concern, the plaintiff is constitutionally required to prove both the statement's falsity and the defendant's fault. **2.** A false written or oral statement that damages another's reputation. — **defame,** *vb.*

defamation per quod. (1915) Defamation that either (1) is not apparent but is proved by extrinsic evidence showing its injurious meaning or (2) is apparent but is not a statement that is actionable per se.

defamation per se. (1928) A statement that is defamatory in and of itself and is not capable of an innocent meaning.

trade defamation. The damaging of a business by a false statement that tends to diminish the reputation of that business.

defamatory, *adj.* (16c) (Of a statement or communication) tending to harm a person's reputation, usu. by subjecting the person to public contempt, disgrace, or ridicule, or by adversely affecting the person's business.

default (di-**fawlt** *also* **dee**-fawlt), *n.* (13c) The omission or failure to perform a legal or contractual duty; esp., the failure to pay a debt when due. — **default** (di-**fawlt**), *vb.* **defaulter,** *n.*

default judgment. (16c) **1.** A judgment entered against a defendant who has failed to plead or otherwise defend against the plaintiff's claim. **2.** A judgment entered as a penalty against a party who does not comply with an order, esp. an order to comply with a discovery request.

nil-dicit default judgment (nil **dɪ**-sit). [Latin "he says nothing"] (2002) A judgment for the plaintiff entered after the defendant fails to file a timely answer, often after the defendant appeared in the case by filing a preliminary motion.

no-answer default judgment. (1979) A judgment for the plaintiff entered after the defendant fails to timely answer or otherwise appear.

post-answer default judgment. (1979) A judgment for the plaintiff entered after the defendant files an answer, but fails to appear at trial or otherwise provide a defense on the merits.

defeasance (di-**feez**-ənts), *n.* (15c) **1.** An annulment or abrogation; voidance. **2.** The fact or an instance of bringing an estate or status to an end, esp. by conditional limitation. **3.** A condition upon the fulfillment of which a deed or other instrument is defeated or made void; a contractual provision containing such a condition. — **defease,** *vb.*

defeasible, *adj.* (16c) (Of an act, right, agreement, or position) capable of being annulled or avoided. — **defeasibility,** *n.*

defeat, *vb.* **1.** To deprive (someone) of something expected, usu. by an antagonistic act. **2.** To annul or render (something) void. **3.** To vanquish; to conquer (someone or something). **4.** To frustrate (someone or something).

defect, *n.* (15c) An imperfection or shortcoming, esp. in a part that is essential to the operation or safety of a product. — **defective,** *adj.*

design defect. (1954) An imperfection occurring when the seller or distributor could have reduced or avoided a foreseeable risk of harm by adopting a reasonable alternative design, and when, as a result of not using the alternative, the product or property is not reasonably safe.

fatal defect. (18c) A serious defect capable of nullifying a contract.

hidden defect. (1896) A product imperfection that is not discoverable by reasonable inspection and for which a seller or lessor is generally liable if the flaw causes harm. • Upon discovering a hidden defect, a purchaser may revoke a prior acceptance. UCC § 2-608(1)(b).

manufacturing defect. (1925) An imperfection in a product that departs from its intended design even though all possible care was exercised in its assembly.

marketing defect. (1980) **1.** The failure to adequately warn of a potential risk of harm that is known or should have been known about a product or its foreseeable use. **2.** The failure to adequately instruct the user about how to use a product safely.

patent defect. (1827) A defect that is apparent to a normally observant person, esp. a buyer on a reasonable inspection.

product defect. (1967) An imperfection in a product that has a manufacturing defect or design defect, or is faulty because of inadequate instructions or warnings.

defective, *adj.* (14c) **1.** (Of a position, right, act, or process) lacking in legal sufficiency. **2.** (Of a product) containing an imperfection or shortcoming in a part essential to the product's safe operation.

defective condition. (1823) An unreasonably dangerous state that might well cause physical harm beyond that contemplated by the ordinary user or consumer who purchases the product.

defect of form. (17c) An imperfection in the style, manner, arrangement, or nonessential parts of a legal document, as distinguished from a substantive defect.

defect of parties. (18c) A failure to include all indispensable parties in a lawsuit.

defect of substance. (18c) An imperfection in the substantive part of a legal document, as by omitting an essential term.

defend, *vb.* (14c) **1.** To deny, contest, or oppose (an allegation or claim). **2.** To represent (someone) as an attorney.

defendant (di-**fen**-dənt). (14c) A person sued in a civil proceeding or accused in a criminal proceeding. — Abbr. D. Cf. PLAINTIFF.

John Doe defendant. An anonymous defendant labeled "John Doe" because the plaintiff does not, at the time of filing suit, know the person's name.

target defendant. In a case with multiple defendants, the one whom the plaintiff considers the primary source for any recovery of damages.

defendant in error. (18c) *Archaic.* In a case on appeal, the prevailing party in the court below.

defendant score. (1982) A number taken from an established scale, indicating the relative seriousness of the defendant's criminal history.

defendant's gain. (1882) The amount of money or the value of property that a criminal defendant has obtained by committing a crime.

defender. 1. One who defends, such as the defendant in a lawsuit, a person using self-defense, or defense counsel. **2.** PUBLIC DEFENDER.

defenestration (dee-fen-ə-**stray**-shən). (17c) The act of throwing someone or something out a window. — **defenestrate,** *vb.*

defense (di-**fen**[**t**]**s**). (16c) **1.** A defendant's stated reason why the plaintiff or prosecutor has no valid case; esp., a defendant's answer, denial, or plea <her defense was that she was 25 miles from the building at the time of the robbery>.

affirmative defense. (1837) A defendant's assertion of facts and arguments that, if true, will defeat the plaintiff's or prosecution's claim, even if all the allegations in the complaint are true. • The defendant bears the burden of proving an affirmative defense. Examples of affirmative defenses are duress (in a civil case) and insanity and self-defense (in a criminal case).

capacity defense. (1967) A defense based on the defendant's inability to be held accountable for an illegal act or the plaintiff's inability to prosecute a lawsuit (as when the plaintiff was a corporation, but has lost its corporate charter).

collateral defense (kə-**lat**-ə-rəl). *Criminal law.* A defense of justification or excuse not involving a rebuttal of the allegation and therefore collateral to the elements that the prosecutor must prove.

cultural defense. **1.** A criminal defendant's assertion that because an admitted act is not a crime in the perpetrator's culture or native land, it should not be judged by the laws of the place where it was committed. **2.** The defense that the actor's mental state at the time the alleged crime was committed was heavily influenced by cultural factors.

defense of habitation. The defense that conduct constituting a criminal offense is justified if an aggressor unjustifiably threatens the defendant's place of abode or premises and the defendant engages in conduct that is (1) harmful to the aggressor, (2) sufficient to protect that place of abode or premises, and (3) reasonable in relation to the harm threatened.

derivative defense. (1972) A defense that rebuts the criminal elements that a prosecutor must establish to justify the submission of a criminal case to a jury.

designer defense. A novel defense based on diminished capacity attributed to stress or impairment. • Examples include extraordinary reactions to snack food (the Twinkie defense), unconsciousness or sleepwalking, and postpartum psychosis.

dilatory defense (**dil**-ə-tor-ee). (1845) A defense that temporarily obstructs or delays a lawsuit but does not address the merits.

empty-suit defense. A defense in which a high-ranking officer or director in an organization claims ignorance of any wrongdoing by subordinates.

equitable defense. (18c) A defense formerly available only in a court of equity but now maintainable in a court of law. • Examples include mistake, fraud, illegality, failure of consideration, forum non conveniens, laches, estoppel, and unclean hands.

frivolous defense. (18c) A defense that has no basis in fact or law.

honesty defense. *Rare.* An assertion that the defendant acted honestly and in good faith. • This defense, almost unique to civil suits, is rarely raised.

imperfect defense. (1835) A defense that fails to meet all legal requirements and usu. results only in a reduction in grade or sentence rather than an acquittal, as when a defendant is charged with manslaughter rather than murder because the defendant, while defending another, used unreasonable force to repel the attack. Cf. *perfect defense.*

inconsistent defense. (1852) A defense so contrary to another defense that the acceptance of one requires abandonment of the other. • A person accused of murder, for example, cannot claim both self-defense and the alibi of having been in a different city when the murder took place.

issuable defense. (1847) *Common-law pleading.* A plea on the merits setting forth a legal defense.

legal defense. (17c) A complete and adequate defense in a court of law.

lesser-evils defense. (1982) The defense that, while the defendant may have caused the harm or evil that would ordinarily constitute a criminal offense, in the present case the defendant has not caused a net harm or evil because of justifying circumstances and therefore should be exculpated.

meritorious defense (mer-ə-**tor**-ee-əs). (18c) **1.** A defense that addresses the substance or essentials of a case rather than dilatory or technical objections. **2.** A defense that appears likely to succeed or has already succeeded.

ostrich defense. A criminal defendant's claim not to have known of the criminal activities of an associate.

partial defense. (1818) A defense going either to part of the action or toward mitigation of damages.

peremptory defense (pər-**emp**-tər-ee). (1860) A defense that questions the plaintiff's legal right to sue or contends that the right to sue has been extinguished.

perfect defense. (1817) A defense that meets all legal requirements and results in the defendant's acquittal. Cf. *imperfect defense.*

pretermitted defense (pree-tər-**mit**-id). (1947) A defense available to a party that must be pleaded at the right time or be waived.

sham defense. (1853) A fictitious, untrue defense, made in bad faith.

true defense. A defense admitting that a defendant committed the charged offense, but seeking to avoid punishment based on a legal excuse (such as insanity) or justification (such as self-defense).

2. A defendant's method and strategy in opposing the plaintiff or the prosecution; a doctrine giving rise to such a method or strategy. **3.** One or more defendants in a trial, as well as their counsel. **4.** *Commercial law.* A basis for avoiding liability on a negotiable instrument.

personal defense. (1950) An ordinary defense in a contract action — such as failure of consideration or nonperformance of a condition — that the maker or drawer of a negotiable instrument is precluded from raising against a person who has the rights of a holder in due course. See UCC § 3-305(b). • A personal defense can be asserted only against a transferee who is not a holder in due course.

real defense. A type of defense that is good against any possible claimant, so that the maker or drawer of a negotiable instrument can raise it even against a holder in due course. • The ten real defenses are (1) fraud in the factum, (2) forgery of a necessary signature, (3) adjudicated insanity that, under state law, renders the contract void from its inception, (4) material alteration of the instrument, (5) infancy, which renders the contract voidable under state law, (6) illegality that renders the underlying contract void, (7) duress, (8) discharge in bankruptcy, or any discharge known to the holder in due course, (9) a suretyship defense (for example, if the holder knew that one indorser was signing as a surety or accommodation party), and (10) a statute of limitations (generally three years after dishonor or acceptance on a draft and six years after demand or other due date on a note).

defense attorney. A lawyer who represents a defendant in a civil or criminal case.

defense of others. (1942) A justification defense available if one harms or threatens another when defending a third person.

defense of property. (1918) A justification defense available if one harms or threatens another when defending one's property.

defensive disclosure. *Patents.* The deliberate publication of details about an invention in order to render it prior art and preclude others from getting a patent on the same invention.

defer, *vb.* (17c) **1.** To postpone; to delay. **2.** To show deference to (another); to yield to the opinion of.

deferral state. (1977) Under the Age Discrimination in Employment Act (ADEA), a state that has its own antidiscrimination legislation and enforcement mechanism, so that the time to file a federal lawsuit under the ADEA is postponed until state remedies have been exhausted.

deferred charge. (1917) An expense not currently recognized on an income statement but carried forward on the balance sheet as an asset to be written off in the future.

deferred claim. (1900) A claim postponed to a future accounting period.

deferred credit. A credit (such as a premium on an issued bond) that is required to be spread over later accounting periods.

deferred payment. (1831) A principal-and-interest payment that is postponed; an installment payment.

deficiency, *n.* (17c) **1.** A lack, shortage, or insufficiency. **2.** A shortfall in paying taxes; the amount by which the tax properly due exceeds the sum of the amount of tax shown on a taxpayer's return. **3.** The amount still owed when the property secured by a mortgage is sold at a foreclosure sale for less than the outstanding debt; esp., the shortfall between the proceeds from a foreclosure sale and an amount consisting of the principal debt plus interest plus the foreclosure costs.

deficiency suit. (1927) An action to recover the difference between a mortgage debt and the amount realized on foreclosure.

deficit. (18c) **1.** A deficiency or disadvantage; a deficiency in the amount or quality of something. **2.** An excess of expenditures or liabilities over revenues or assets.

deficit spending. (1938) The practice of making expenditures in excess of income, usu. from borrowed funds rather than actual revenues or surplus.

defile (di-**fıl**), *vb.* (14c) **1.** To make dirty; to physically soil. **2.** To figuratively tarnish; to dishonor. **3.** To make ceremonially unclean; to desecrate. **4.** To morally corrupt (someone). — **defilement** (di-**fıl**-mənt), *n.*

defined term. In legal drafting, a word or phrase given a specific meaning for purposes of the document in which it appears; a definiendum.

definition. (14c) The meaning of a term as explicitly stated in a drafted document such as a contract, a corporate bylaw, an ordinance, or a statute; a definiens.

lexical definition. (1875) A dictionary-style definition of a word, purporting to give the full meaning of a term.

stipulative definition. (1989) A definition that, for purposes of the document in which it appears, arbitrarily clarifies a term with uncertain boundaries or that includes or excludes specified items from the ambit of the term.

deflation, *n.* A general decline in the price of goods and services. Cf. INFLATION. — **deflate,** *vb.* — **deflationary,** *adj.*

deforce, *vb.* (15c) **1.** To keep (lands) from the true owner by means of force. **2.** To oust another from possession by means of force. **3.** To detain (a creditor's money) unjustly and forcibly. — **deforciant, deforcement,** *n.*

defraud, *vb.* (14c) To cause injury or loss to (a person) by deceit. — **defraudation,** *n.*

defunct, *adj.* Dead; extinct.

degradation (deg-rə-**day**-shən). (16c) **1.** A reduction in rank, degree, or dignity; specif., censure of a clergy member by divestiture of holy orders, either by word or by a solemn divestiture of robes and other insignia. **2.** A moral or intellectual decadence or degeneration; a lessening of a person's or thing's character or quality. **3.** A wearing down of something, as by erosion.

degree. (13c) **1.** Generally, a classification or specification. **2.** An incremental measure of guilt or negligence; a level based on the seriousness of an offense. **3.** A stage in a process; a step in a series of steps toward an end. **4.** A stage in intensity. **5.** In the line of descent, a measure of removal determining the proximity of a blood or marital relationship.

equal degree. (16c) A relationship between two or more relatives who are the same number of steps away from a common ancestor.

prohibited degree. (17c) A degree of relationship so close (as between brother and sister) that marriage between the persons is forbidden by law.

6. A title conferred on a graduate of a school, college, or university, either after the completion of required studies or in honor of special achievements.

degree of care. (17c) A standard of care to be exercised in a given situation.

degree of crime. (1826) **1.** A division or classification of a single crime into several grades of guilt, according to the circumstances surrounding the crime's commission, such as aggravating factors present or the type of injury suffered. **2.** A division of crimes generally, such as felonies or misdemeanors.

degree of negligence. (18c) One of the varying levels of negligence typically designated as slight negligence, ordinary negligence, and gross negligence.

dehors (də-**hor** *or* də-**horz**). [Law French] (18c) Outside; beyond the scope of <the court cannot consider the document because it is dehors the record>.

de jure (di **juur**-ee *also* dee *or* day), *adj.* [Law Latin "as a matter of law"] (17c) Existing by right or according to law <de jure segregation during the pre-*Brown* era>. Cf. DE FACTO.

delay, *n.* (13c) **1.** The act of postponing or slowing. **2.** An instance at which something is postponed or slowed. **3.** The period during which something is postponed or slowed.

delayed funds availability. A hold that a bank places on uncollected funds that are represented by a deposited check. — Abbr. DFA.

delay rental. *Oil & gas.* A payment from the lessee to the lessor made to maintain the mineral lease from period to period during the primary term without an obligation to drill.

del credere (del **kred**-ə-ray *or* **kray**-də-ray), *adj.* [Italian] (18c) Of belief or trust.

delegate (**del**-ə-git), *n.* (15c) One who represents or acts for another person or a group.

delegatee (del-ə-gə-**tee**). (1875) An agent or representative to whom a matter is delegated.

delegation, *n.* (1612) **1.** The act of entrusting another with authority or empowering another to act as an agent or representative. **2.** A group of representatives. — **delegate** (**del**-ə-gayt) (for sense 1), *vb.* — **delegable** (**del**-ə-gə-bəl) (for sense 1), *adj.*

delegation doctrine. (1883) *Constitutional law.* The principle (based on the separation-of-powers concept) limiting Congress's ability to transfer its legislative power to another governmental branch, esp. the executive branch. • Delegation is permitted only if Congress prescribes an intelligible principle to guide an executive agency in making policy.

delegation of duties. (1893) *Contracts.* A transaction by which a party to a contract arranges to have a third party perform the party's contractual duties.

delegation of powers. (1854) A transfer of authority by one branch of government to another branch or to an administrative agency.

deleterious (del-ə-**teer**-ee-əs), *adj.* (1643) **1.** Poisonous. **2.** Unwholesome; psychologically or physically harmful.

deliberate (di-**lib**-[ə]-rit), *adj.* (15c) **1.** Intentional; premeditated; fully considered. **2.** Unimpulsive; slow in deciding.

deliberate (di-**lib**-ə-rate), *vb.* (Of a court, jury, etc.) to weigh and analyze all the evidence after closing arguments.

deliberate elicitation. (1966) *Criminal procedure.* The purposeful yet covert drawing forth of an incriminating response (usu. not during a formal interrogation) from a suspect whose Sixth Amendment right to counsel has attached but who has not waived that right. • Deliberate elicitation may occur, for example, when a police officer engages an arrested suspect in conversation on the way to the police station. Deliberate elicitation violates the Sixth Amendment. *Massiah v. United States*, 377 U.S. 201, 84 S.Ct. 1199 (1964).

deliberate speed, with all. (1817) As quickly as the maintenance of law and order and the welfare of the people will allow, esp. with respect to the desegregation of public schools. *Brown v. Board of Educ.*, 347 U.S. 483, 74 S.Ct. 686 (1954).

deliberation, *n.* (14c) The act of carefully considering issues and options before making a decision or taking some action; esp., the process by which a jury reaches a verdict, as by analyzing, discussing, and weighing the evidence. — **deliberate** (di-**lib**-ə-rayt), *vb.*

deliberative-process privilege. (1977) The principle that a decision-maker's thoughts and how they led to a decision are not subject to revelation or scrutiny.

delict (di-**likt**), *n.* [Latin *delictum* "an offense"] (16c) *Roman & civil law.* A violation of the law; esp., a wrongful act or omission giving rise to a claim for compensation; TORT. — **delictual** (di-**lik**-chə-wəl), *adj.*

deliction (di-**lik**-shən). (1966) The loss of land by gradual, natural changes, such as erosion resulting from a change in the course of a river or stream.

delimit (di-**lim**-it), *vb.* (1852) To mark (a boundary); to fix (a limit). — **delimitation,** *ni*

delinquency, *n.* (17c) **1.** A failure or omission; a violation of a law or duty. **2.** A debt that is overdue in payment.

delinquent, *adj.* (17c) **1.** (Of a person) failing to perform an obligation. **2.** (Of a person) guilty of serious antisocial or criminal conduct. **3.** (Of an obligation) past due or unperformed.

delinquent, *n.* (15c) **1.** A person who fails to perform an obligation. **2.** A person guilty of serious antisocial or criminal conduct. **3.** Juvenile delinquent.

delirium. (16c) **1.** A disordered mental state, often occurring during illness. **2.** Exaggerated excitement. **3.** A delusion; a hallucination.

delisting, *n.* The suspension of the privilege of having a security listed on an exchange. — **delist,** *vb.*

deliverance. (14c) **1.** A jury's verdict. **2.** A judicial opinion or judgment. **3.** A court's order directing that a person in custody be released; esp., such an order by an ecclesiastical court.

delivery, *n.* (15c) **1.** The formal act of transferring something, such as a deed; the giving or yielding possession or control of something to another. **2.** The thing so transferred or conveyed. — **deliver,** *vb.*

absolute delivery. (1808) A delivery that is complete upon the actual transfer of the instrument from the grantor's possession.

actual delivery. (17c) The act of giving real and immediate possession to the buyer or the buyer's agent.

conditional delivery. (18c) A delivery that passes possession subject to the happening of a specified event.

constructive delivery. (18c) An act that amounts to a transfer of title by operation of law when actual transfer is impractical or impossible. • For example, the delivery of a deposit-box key by someone who is ill and immobile may amount to a constructive delivery of the box's contents even though the box may be miles away.

second delivery. (17c) A legal delivery by the depositary of a deed placed in escrow.

symbolic delivery. (18c) The constructive delivery of the subject matter of a sale or gift by the actual delivery of an article that represents the item, that renders access to it possible, or that provides evidence of the title to it, such as the key to a warehouse or a bill of lading for goods on shipboard.

unconditional delivery. (18c) A delivery that immediately passes both possession and title and that takes effect immediately.

delivery in escrow. (1842) The physical transfer of something to an escrow agent to be held until some condition is met, at which time the agent will release it. • An example of such a delivery is a stock buyer's transfer of cash to a bank that will give the seller the cash upon receiving the stock certificates. This type of delivery creates immediate conditional rights in the promisee. The device may be used to create an option contract in which the promisee has the option.

delivery of deed. (18c) The placing of a deed in the grantee's hands or within the grantee's control. • By this act, the grantor shows an intention that the deed operates immediately as a conveyance. A deed may also be held to be delivered when the grantor manifests the intention to complete the conveyance, regardless of actual delivery.

demand, *n.* (13c) **1.** The assertion of a legal or procedural right.

contingent demand. A demand that cannot be fixed because it depends on the occurrence of a contingency.

cross-demand. (18c) A party's demand opposing an adverse party's demand.

legal demand. A lawful demand made by an authorized person.

2. A request for payment of a debt or an amount due.

demand, *vb.* (14c) **1.** To claim as one's due; to require; to seek relief. **2.** To summon; to call into court.

demand clause. (1919) A provision in a note allowing the holder to compel full payment if the maker fails to meet an installment.

demand instrument. (1924) An instrument payable on demand, at sight, or on presentation, as opposed to an instrument that is payable at a set future date.

demand letter. (1911) A letter by which one party explains its legal position in a dispute and requests that the recipient take some action (such as paying money owed), or else risk being sued. • Under some statutes (esp. consumer-protection laws), a demand letter is a prerequisite for filing a lawsuit.

demarcation line. *Int'l law.* A provisional border having the function of separating territories under different jurisdictions, usu. established when the political situation does not admit a final boundary arrangement.

démarche (day-**mahrsh**). [French "gait; walk"] An oral or written diplomatic statement, esp. one containing a demand, offer, protest, threat, or the like.

demeanor. (15c) Outward appearance or behavior, such as facial expressions, tone of voice, gestures, and the hesitation or readiness to answer questions. • In evaluating credibility, the jury may consider the witness's demeanor.

demesne (di-**mayn** *or* di-**meen**), *n.* [French] (14c) **1.** At common law, land held in one's own right, and not through a superior; esp., land attached to a manor and reserved for the court's own use. **2.** Domain; realm. — **demesnial** (di-**may**-nee-əl *or* di-**meen**-ee-əl), *adj.*

demilitarized zone. *Int'l law.* A territorial area in a country or between countries in which no military forces or military installations are stationed or maintained.

de minimis (də **min**-ə-mis), *adj.* [Latin "of the least"] (1952) **1.** Trifling; minimal. **2.** (Of a fact or thing) so insignificant that a court may overlook it in deciding an issue or case. **3.** DE MINIMIS NON CURAT LEX.

de minimis non curat lex (də **min**-ə-mis non **kyoor**-at **leks**). [Latin] The law does not concern itself with trifles.

demise (di-**mɪz**), *n.* (15c) **1.** The conveyance of an estate usu. for a term of years, a lease. **2.** The instrument by which such a conveyance is accomplished. **3.** The passing of property by descent or bequest. **4.** The death of a person or (figuratively) of a thing. — Abbr. dem. — **demise,** *vb.*

demobilization. A dismissal of troops from active service.

democracy, *n.* Government by the people, either directly or through representatives elected by the people. — **democratic,** *adj.*

demonetization. A disuse of a metal in coinage; a withdrawal of the value of a metal as money

demote, *vb.* To lower (usu. a person) in rank, position, pay, or other status.

demur (di-**mər**), *vb.* (17c) **1.** To file a demurrer. **2.** To object to the legal sufficiency of a claim alleged in a pleading without admitting or denying the truth of the facts stated. **3.** To object to the legal sufficiency of a claim alleged in a pleading while admitting the truth of the facts stated.

demurrable (di-**mər**-ə-bəl), *adj.* (1827) (Of a claim, pleading, etc.) subject to a demurrer.

demurrant (di-**mər**-ənt). One who demurs; esp., a litigant who files a demurrer.

demurrer (di-**mər**-ər). [Law French *demorer* "to wait or stay"] (16c) A pleading stating that although the facts alleged in a complaint may be true, they are insufficient for the plaintiff to state a claim for relief and for the defendant to frame an answer. • In most jurisdictions, such a pleading is now termed a *motion to dismiss*, but *demurrer* is still used in a few states, including California, Nebraska, and Pennsylvania.

speaking demurrer. (18c) A demurrer that cannot be sustained because it introduces new facts not contained in the complaint.

special demurrer. (17c) A demurrer that states grounds for an objection and specifically identifies the nature of the defect, such as that the pleading violates the rules of pleading or practice.

demurrer to evidence. (17c) A party's objection or exception that the evidence is legally insufficient to make a case. • Its effect, upon joinder in the demurrer by the opposite party, is that the jury is discharged and the demurrer is entered on record and decided by the court. A demurrer to evidence admits the truth of all the evidence and the legal deductions from that evidence.

demurrer to interrogatories. (18c) The objection or reason given by a witness for failing to answer an interrogatory.

denial, *n.* (16c) **1.** A refusal or rejection; esp., a court's refusal to grant a request presented in a motion or petition. **2.** A defendant's response controverting the facts that a plaintiff has alleged in a complaint; a repudiation.

conjunctive denial. (1860) A response that controverts all the material facts alleged in a complaint.

disjunctive denial. (1920) A response that controverts the truthfulness of two or more factual allegations of a complaint in the alternative.

general denial. (16c) A response that puts in issue all the material assertions of a complaint or petition.

qualified general denial. (1844) A general denial of all the allegations except the allegations that the pleader expressly admits.

specific denial. (1850) A separate response applicable to one or more particular allegations in a complaint.

3. A refusal or rejection <denial of an employment application>. **4.** A deprivation or withholding <denial of due process>. — **deny,** *vb.*

denial-of-service attack. A malicious strike against a computer, website, network, server, or database designed to render it inaccessible, usu. by overwhelming it with activity or by forcing it to malfunction. — Abbr. DoS attack.

distributed denial-of-service attack. A denial-of-service attack carried out by distributing a virus that causes infected computers to try to access the target computer at the same time. — Abbr. DDoS attack.

denizen (den-ə-zən).(15c) A person given certain rights in a foreign nation or living habitually in a foreign nation.

denomination. (15c) **1.** An act of naming. **2.** A collective designation, esp. of a religious sect.

denounce, *vb.* (13c) **1.** To condemn openly, esp. publicly. **2.** To declare (an act or thing) to be a crime and prescribe a punishment for it. **3.** To accuse or inform against. **4.** To give formal notice to a foreign country of the termination of (a treaty). — **denouncement,** *n.*

de novo (di **noh**-voh *or* dee), *adj.* (1536) Anew.

denumeration. (18c) An act of making a present payment.

department, *n.* (18c) **1.** A division of a greater whole; a subdivision. **2.** A country's division of territory, usu. for governmental and administrative purposes, as in the division of a state into counties. **3.** A principal branch or division of government; specif., a division of the executive branch of the U.S. government, headed by a secretary who is a member of the President's cabinet. — **departmental,** *adj.*

Department of Agriculture. The cabinet-level department of the federal government responsible for improving farm income, developing foreign markets for U.S. farm products, conducting agricultural research, and inspecting and grading food products. — Abbr. USDA.

Department of Commerce. The cabinet-level department of the federal government responsible for promoting the nation's international trade, economic growth, and technical advancement. — Abbr. DOC.

Department of Education. The cabinet-level department of the federal government responsible for advising the President on federal education policy, and administering and coordinating most federal programs of assistance to education. — Abbr. DOE.

Department of Energy. The cabinet-level department of the federal government responsible for advising the President on energy policies, plans, and programs, and for providing leadership in achieving efficient energy use, diversity in energy sources, and improved environmental quality. — Abbr. DOE.

Department of Health and Human Services. The cabinet-level department of the federal government responsible for matters of health, welfare, and income security. — Abbr. HHS.

Department of Homeland Security. The cabinet-level department of the federal government responsible for ensuring security within the U.S. borders and in its territories and possessions. — Abbr. DHS.

Department of Housing and Urban Development. The cabinet-level department of the federal government responsible for overseeing programs that are concerned with housing needs and fair-housing opportunities, and with improving and developing the nation's communities. — Abbr. HUD.

Department of Justice. The federal executive division that is responsible for federal law enforcement and related programs and services. • The U.S. Attorney General heads this department, which has separate divisions for prosecuting cases under federal antitrust laws, tax laws, environmental laws, and criminal laws. The department also has a civil division that represents the U.S. government in cases involving tort claims and commercial litigation. — Abbr. DOJ.

Department of Labor. The cabinet-level department of the federal government responsible for promoting the welfare of wage earners and for improving working conditions and opportunities for profitable employment. — Abbr. DOL.

Department of State. The cabinet-level department of the federal government responsible for advising the President in formulating and executing foreign policy.

Department of the Interior. The cabinet-level department of the federal government responsible for managing the nation's public lands and minerals, national parks, national wildlife refuges, and western water resources, and for upholding federal trust responsibilities to Indian tribes.

Department of the Treasury. The cabinet-level department of the federal government responsible for recommending tax and fiscal policies, collecting taxes, disbursing U.S. government funds, enforcing tax laws, and manufacturing coins and currency.

Department of Transportation. The federal executive division responsible for programs and policies concerning transportation. — Abbr. DOT.

Department of Veterans Affairs. The cabinet-level department of the federal government responsible for operating programs that benefit veterans of military service and their families. — Abbr. VA.

departure, *n.* (15c) **1.** A deviation or divergence from a standard rule, regulation, measurement, or course of conduct.

downward departure. (1982) In the federal sentencing guidelines, a court's imposition of a sentence more lenient than the standard guidelines propose, as when the court concludes that a criminal's history is less serious than it appears.

forbidden departure. (1996) An impermissible deviation from the federal sentencing guidelines based on race, sex, national origin, creed, religion, or socioeconomic status.

lateral departure. (1993) In the federal sentencing guidelines, a sentence allowing a defendant to avoid incarceration through community or home confinement.

upward departure. (1982) In the federal sentencing guidelines, a court's imposition of a sentence harsher than the standard guidelines propose, as when the court concludes that a criminal's history did not take into account additional offenses committed by the prisoner.

2. A variance between a pleading and a later pleading or proof. **3.** A party's desertion of the ground (either legal or factual) taken in the immediately preceding pleading and resort to another ground. — **depart,** *vb.*

dépeçage (dep-ə-**sahzh**). [French "dismemberment"] A court's application of different state laws to different issues in a legal dispute; choice of law on an issue-by-issue basis.

dependency. (16c) **1.** A land or territory geographically distinct from the country governing it, but belonging to the country and governed by its laws. **2.** A relationship between two persons or things whereby one is sustained by the other or relies on the other for support or necessities.

dependent, *n.* (16c) **1.** One who relies on another for support; one not able to exist or sustain oneself without the power or aid of someone else.

lawful dependent. (1908) **1.** One who receives an allowance or benefits from the public, such as social security. **2.** One who qualifies to receive a benefit from private funds as determined by the laws governing the distribution.

legal dependent. (1909) A person who is dependent according to the law; a person who derives principal support from another and usu. may invoke laws to enforce that support.

2. *Tax.* A person, such as a child or parent, for whom a taxpayer may be able to claim a personal exemption if the taxpayer provides more than half of the person's support during the taxable year. • Besides support, other criteria must be met as well. IRC (26 USCA) § 152. — **dependent,** *adj.*

dependent intervening cause. A cause of an accident or injury that occurs between the defendant's behavior and the injurious result, but that does not change the defendant's liability.

dependent relative revocation. (1855) A common-law doctrine that operates to undo an otherwise sufficient revocation of a will when there is evidence that the testator's revocation was conditional rather than absolute. • Typically, the doctrine applies when a testator has physically revoked the will and believes that a new will is valid, although this belief is mistaken. The doctrine undoes only the revocation; it does not always accomplish the testator's intent or validate an otherwise invalid will.

depletion, *n.* (17c) An emptying, exhausting, or wasting of an asset, esp. of a finite natural resource such as oil. — **deplete,** *vb.* — **depletive,** *adj.*

depletion reserve. *Accounting.* A charge to income reflecting the decrease in the value of a wasting asset, such as an oil reserve.

deponent (di-**poh**-nənt), *n.* (16c) **1.** One who testifies by deposition. **2.** A witness who gives written testimony for later use in court; AFFIANT. — **depone,** *vb.*

deportable, *adj.* (Of an alien) subject to removal from a country after an illegal entry.

deportation (dee-por-**tay**-shən), *n.* The act or an instance of removing a person to another country; esp., the expulsion or transfer of an alien from a country. — **deport,** *vb.*

depose (di-**pohz**), *vb.* (14c) **1.** To examine (a witness) in a deposition <the defendant's attorney will depose the plaintiff on Tuesday>. **2.** To testify; to bear witness <the affiant deposes and states that he is at least 18 years old>. **3.** To remove from office or from a position of power;

dethrone <rebels sought to depose the dictator>.

deposit, *n.* (17c) **1.** The act of giving money or other property to another who promises to preserve it or to use it and return it in kind; esp., the act of placing money in a bank for safety and convenience. **2.** The money or property so given.

demand deposit. A bank deposit that the depositor may withdraw at any time without prior notice to the bank.

direct deposit. The payment of money by transferring the payment directly into the payee's bank account, usu. by electronic transfer.

frozen deposit. A bank deposit that cannot be withdrawn, as when the financial institution is insolvent or an account is restricted.

general deposit. **1.** A bank deposit of money that is commingled with other depositors' money. **2.** A bank deposit that is to the depositor's credit, thus giving the depositor a right to the money and creating a debtor–creditor relationship between the bank and the depositor. • A bank is not required to return the actual money deposited as a general deposit, as it must with a special deposit; the bank need return only an equivalent sum.

special deposit. A bank deposit that is made for a specific purpose, that is kept separately, and that is to be returned to the depositor. • The bank serves as a bailee or trustee for a special deposit.

time deposit. A bank deposit that is to remain for a specified period or for which notice must be given to the bank before withdrawal.

3. Money placed with a person as earnest money or security for the performance of a contract. • The money will be forfeited if the depositor fails to perform.

depositary. (17c) **1.** A person or institution that one leaves money or valuables with for safekeeping <a title-insurance officer is the depositary of the funds>. • When a depositary is a company, it is often termed a *safe-deposit company.* **2.** A gratuitous bailee.

deposit in court. The placing of money or other property that represents a person's potential liability in the court's temporary custody, pending the outcome of a lawsuit.

deposition (dep-ə-**zish**-ən). (14c) **1.** A witness's out-of-court testimony that is reduced to writing (usu. by a court reporter) for later use in court or for discovery purposes. See Fed. R. Civ. P. 30; Fed. R. Crim. P. 15. **2.** The session at which such testimony is recorded.

apex deposition. (1992) The deposition of a person whose position is at the highest level of a company's hierarchy. • Courts often preclude an apex deposition unless (1) the person to be deposed has particular knowledge regarding the claim, and (2) the requesting party cannot obtain the requested — and discoverable — information through less intrusive means.

deposition de bene esse (dee **bee**-nee **es**-ee *also* day **ben**-ay **es**-ay). (18c) A deposition taken from a witness who will likely be unable to attend a scheduled trial or hearing. • If the witness is not available to attend trial, the testimony is read at trial as if the witness were present in court.

deposition on written questions. (1970) A deposition given in response to a prepared set of written questions, as opposed to a typical oral deposition. See Fed. R. Civ. P. 31.

oral deposition. (1910) A deposition given in response to oral questioning by a lawyer.

30(b)(6) deposition. (1979) Under the Federal Rules of Civil Procedure, the deposition of an organization, through the organization's designated representative. • Under Rule 30(b)(6), a party may take the deposition of an organization, such as a corporation. The notice of deposition (or subpoena) may name the organization and may specify the matters to be covered in the deposition. The organization must then designate a person to testify about those matters on its behalf. Fed. R. Civ. P. 30(b)(6). Most states authorize a similar procedure under state-court procedural rules.

3. The written record of a witness's out-of-court testimony.

depository (di-**poz**-ə-tor-ee), *n.* (17c) A place where one leaves money or valuables for safekeeping.

depository institution. 1. An organization formed under state or federal law, authorized by law to receive deposits, and supervised and examined by a government agency for the protection of depositors. **2.** A trust company or other institution authorized by law to exercise fiduciary powers similar to those of a national bank. • The term does not include an insurance company, a Morris Plan bank, an industrial loan company, or similar bank unless its deposits are insured by a federal agency.

Depository Trust Corporation. The principal central clearing agency for securities transactions on the public markets. — Abbr. DTC.

deposit ratio. The ratio of total deposits to total capital.

deposit slip. A bank's written acknowledgment of an amount received on a certain date from a depositor.

depraved, *adj.* (14c) **1.** (Of a person or crime) corrupt; perverted. **2.** (Of a crime) heinous; morally horrendous. — **depravity,** *n.*

depreciation (di-pree-shee-**ay**-shən), *n.* (1862) A decline in an asset's value because of use, wear, obsolescence, or age. Cf. APPRECIATION. — **depreciate,** *vb.* — **depreciable,** *adj.*

accelerated depreciation. Depreciation recorded using a method that writes off the cost of an asset more rapidly than the straight-line method.

accumulated depreciation. (1916) The total depreciation currently recorded on an asset.

annual depreciation. (1862) The yearly decrease in a property's value due to regular wear and tear.

economic depreciation. A reduction in the value of an asset due to a shortening of the asset's economic life.

functional depreciation. (1910) Depreciation that results from the replacement of equipment that is not yet worn out but that is obsolete in light of new technology or improved methodology allowing more efficient and satisfactory production.

depreciation method. (1915) A set formula used in estimating an asset's use, wear, or obsolescence over the asset's useful life or some portion thereof. • This method is useful in calculating the allowable annual tax deduction for depreciation.

accelerated depreciation method. (1964) A depreciation method that yields larger deductions in the earlier years of an asset's life and smaller deductions in the later years.

annuity depreciation method. A depreciation method that allows for a return of imputed interest on the undepreciated balance of an asset's value.

declining-balance depreciation method. (1947) A method of computing the annual depreciation allowance by multiplying the asset's undepreciated cost each year by a uniform rate that may not exceed double the straight-line rate or 150 percent.

double-declining depreciation method. (1996) A depreciation method that spreads over time the initial cost of a capital asset by deducting in each period twice the percentage recognized by the straight-line method and applying that double percentage to the undepreciated balance existing at the start of each period.

replacement-cost depreciation method. A depreciation method that fixes an asset's value by the price of its substitute.

sinking-fund depreciation method. A depreciation method that accounts for the time value of money by setting up a depreciation-reserve account that earns interest, resulting in a gradual yearly increase in the depreciation deduction.

straight-line depreciation method. (1930) A depreciation method that writes off the cost or other basis of the asset by deducting the expected salvage value from the initial cost of the capital asset, and dividing the difference by the asset's estimated useful life.

sum-of-the-years'-digits depreciation method. A method of calculating the annual depreciation allowance by multiplying the depreciable cost basis (cost minus salvage value) by a constantly decreasing fraction, which is represented by the remaining years of useful life at the beginning of each year divided by the total number of years of useful life at the time of acquisition.

unit depreciation method. A depreciation method — directly related to the productivity of the asset — that divides the asset's value by the estimated total number of units to be produced, and then multiplies the unit cost by the number of units sold during the year, representing the depreciation expense for the year.

units-of-output depreciation method. A method by which the cost of a depreciable asset, minus salvage value, is allocated to the accounting periods benefited based on output (as miles, hours, number of times used, and the like).

depredation. (15c) The act of plundering; pillaging.

depression. (18c) A period of economic stress that persists over an extended period, accompanied by poor business conditions and high unemployment.

deprivation. (15c) **1.** An act of taking away <deprivation of property>. **2.** A withholding of something. **3.** The state of being without something; wanting. **4.** A removal or degradation from office, esp. an ecclesiastical office.

***Deprizio* doctrine.** (1990) *Bankruptcy.* The rule that a debtor's payment to an outside creditor more than 90 days before a bankruptcy filing is voidable as a preferential transfer if the payment also benefits an inside creditor. *Levit v. Ingersoll Rand Fin. Corp.* (*In re V.N. Deprizio Constr. Co.*), 874 F.2d 1186 (7th Cir. 1989).

deputy, *n.* (15c) A person appointed or delegated to act as a substitute for another, esp. for an official. — **deputize, depute,** *vb.*

deregistration, *n.* The point at which an issuer's registration under section 12 of the Securities Exchange Act of 1934 is no longer required because of a decline in the number of holders of the issuer's securities. 15 USCA § 78*l*. — **deregister,** *vb.*

deregulation, *n.* (1963) The reduction or elimination of governmental control of business, esp. to permit free markets and competition. — **deregulate,** *vb.*

financial deregulation. The lessening of governmental oversight and intervention in the business of financial institutions.

derelict (**der**-ə-likt), *adj.* (17c) **1.** Forsaken; abandoned; cast away <derelict

property>. **2.** Lacking a sense of duty; in breach of a legal or moral obligation <the managers were derelict in their duties>. **3.** Dilapidated; run-down.

derelict, *n.* (17c) **1.** Personal property abandoned or thrown away by the owner with no intent to claim it any longer, such as a ship deserted at sea. **2.** Land uncovered by water receding from its former bed. **3.** A street person or vagrant; a hobo.

dereliction (der-ə-**lik**-shən), *n.* (16c) **1.** The forsaking of a legal or moral obligation with no intent to reassume it; abandonment. **2.** An increase of land caused by the receding of a sea, river, or stream from its usual watermark.

derelict-official act. A statute that mandates forfeiture of office if the holder willfully neglects or fraudulently fails to perform official duties.

derivative, *adj. Copyright.* Of, relating to, or constituting a work that is taken from, translated from, adapted from, or in some way further develops a previous work.

derivative, *n.* A financial instrument whose value depends on or is derived from the performance of a secondary source such as an underlying bond, currency, or commodity.

derivative action. (18c) **1.** A suit by a beneficiary of a fiduciary to enforce a right belonging to the fiduciary; esp., a suit asserted by a shareholder on the corporation's behalf against a third party (usu. a corporate officer) because of the corporation's failure to take some action against the third party. See Fed. R. Civ. P. 23.1. **2.** A lawsuit arising from an injury to another person, such as a husband's action for loss of consortium arising from an injury to his wife caused by a third person.

derivative-jurisdiction doctrine. (1964) The principle that a case is not properly removable unless it is within the subject-matter jurisdiction of the state court from which it is removed.

derogation (der-ə-**gay**-shən), *n.* (15c) **1.** The partial repeal or abrogation of a law by a later act that limits its scope or impairs its utility and force. **2.** Disparagement; depreciation in value or estimation. **3.** Detraction, prejudice, or destruction (of a grant or right). — **derogate (der-**ə-gayt), *vb.*

derogatory clause. (16c) **1.** *Contracts.* A statutory or contractual provision proclaiming that the document in which it appears, or a part of the document, cannot be repealed or amended. • Such provisions are considered ineffective. **2.** *Wills & estates.* A clause that a testator inserts secretly in a will, containing a provision that any later will not having that precise clause is invalid. • A derogatory clause seeks to protect against a later will extorted by undue influence, duress, or violence.

descendant (di-**sen**-dənt), *n.* (17c) One who follows in the bloodline of an ancestor, either lineally or collaterally. • Examples are children and grandchildren. Cf. ASCENDANT. — **descendant,** *adj.*

collateral descendant. Loosely, a blood relative who is not strictly a descendant, such as a niece or nephew.

lineal descendant. A blood relative in the direct line of descent. • Children, grandchildren, and great-grandchildren are lineal descendants.

descendibility of future interests. (1936) The legal possibility that a future interest (such as a remainder or an executory interest) can legally pass by inheritance.

descendible, *adj.* (15c) (Of property) capable of passing by descent or being inherited.

descent, *n.* (15c) **1.** The acquisition of real property by law, as by inheritance; the passing of intestate real property to heirs. **2.** The fact or process of originating from a common ancestor. Cf. ASCENT. — **descend,** *vb.*

description. (14c) **1.** A delineation or explanation of something by an account setting forth the subject's characteristics or qualities. **2.** A representation by words or drawing of something seen or heard or otherwise experienced. **3.** An enumeration or specific identification of something. **4.** LEGAL DESCRIPTION.

descriptive word. *Trademarks.* A term that portrays a general characteristic or function of a product or service. • A descriptive word may not be registered as a trademark unless it has acquired secondary meaning in the minds of consumers such that it is directly associated with one brand.

desecrate, *vb.* (17c) To divest (a thing) of its sacred character; to defile or profane (a sacred thing).

desegregation, *n.* (1951) **1.** The abrogation of policies that separate people of different races into different institutions and facilities (such as public schools). **2.** The state of having had such policies abrogated. — **desegregate,** *vb.*

desertion, *n.* (16c) The willful and unjustified abandonment of a person's duties or obligations, esp. to military service or to a spouse or family. • In family law, the five elements of spousal desertion are (1) a cessation of cohabitation, (2) the lapse of a statutory period, (3) an intention to abandon, (4) a lack of consent from the abandoned spouse, and (5) a lack of spousal misconduct that might justify the abandonment. — **desert,** *vb.*

constructive desertion. (1894) One spouse's misconduct that forces the other spouse to leave the marital abode.

criminal desertion. (18c) One spouse's willful failure without just cause to provide for the care, protection, or support of the other spouse who is in ill health or needy circumstances.

obstinate desertion. Desertion by a spouse who persistently refuses to return to the marital home, so that the other spouse has grounds for divorce.

design, *n.* (16c) **1.** A plan or scheme. **2.** Purpose or intention combined with a plan.

formed design. *Criminal law.* The deliberate and fixed intention to kill, though not necessarily a particular person.

3. The pattern or configuration of elements in something, such as a work of art. **4.** *Patents.* The drawing or the depiction of an original plan for a novel pattern, model, shape, or configuration that is chiefly decorative or ornamental. • If it meets other criteria, a design may also be protectable as a trademark. — **design,** *vb.*

design around, *vb. Patents.* To make something that performs the same function or has the same physical properties as (a patented product or process) but in a way different enough from the original that it does not infringe the patent.

designedly, *adv.* (17c) Willfully; intentionally.

design review. A process by which a building permit is withheld until the proposed building meets the architectural standards established by land-use regulations.

despoil (di-**spoil**), *vb.* (14c) To deprive (a person) of possessions illegally by violence or by clandestine means; to rob. — **despoliation** (di-spoh-lee-**ay**-shən), **despoilment,** *n.*

despot (**des**-pət), *n.* (16c) **1.** A ruler with absolute power and authority. **2.** A tyrant. — **despotic** (di-**spot**-ik), *adj.*

despotism (**des**-pə-tiz-əm). (18c) **1.** A government by a ruler with absolute, unchecked power. **2.** Total power or controlling influence.

destitute (**des**-ti-t[y]oot), *adj.* (14c) **1.** Deprived; bereft. **2.** Not possessing the necessaries of life; lacking possessions and resources; indigent.

destructibility, *n.* (18c) The capability of being destroyed by some action, turn of events, or operation of law. — **destructible,** *adj.*

destructibility of contingent remainders. (1918) *Property.* The common-law doctrine requiring a future interest to vest by the time it is to become possessory or else be totally destroyed, the interest then reverting to the grantor. • The doctrine could be avoided by the use of trustees to preserve contingent remainders. This doctrine has been abolished in all but a few American jurisdictions; the abolishing statutes are commonly termed *anti-destructibility statutes.*

desuetude (**des**-wə-t[y]ood). (15c) **1.** Lack of use; obsolescence through disuse. **2.** The doctrine holding that if a statute or treaty is left unenforced long enough, the courts will no longer regard it as having any legal effect even though it has not been repealed.

detainer. (17c) **1.** The action of detaining, withholding, or keeping something in one's custody.

unlawful detainer. (18c) The unjustifiable retention of the possession of real property by one whose original entry was lawful, as when a tenant holds over after lease termination despite the landlord's demand for possession.

2. The confinement of a person in custody. **3.** A writ authorizing a prison official to continue holding a prisoner in custody. **4.** A person who detains someone or something.

détente (day-**tahnt**). [French] **1.** The relaxation of tensions between two or more parties, esp. nations. **2.** A policy promoting such a relaxation of tensions. **3.** A period during which such tensions are relaxed.

detention, *n.* (15c) **1.** The act or fact of holding a person in custody; confinement or compulsory delay. — **detain,** *vb.*

investigative detention. (1968) The holding of a suspect without formal arrest during the investigation of the suspect's participation in a crime. • Detention of this kind is constitutional only if probable cause exists.

pretrial detention. (1962) **1.** The holding of a defendant before trial on criminal charges either because the established bail could not be posted or because release was denied. **2.** In a juvenile-delinquency case, the court's authority to hold in custody, from the initial hearing until the probable-cause hearing, any juvenile charged with an act that, if committed by an adult, would be a crime.

preventive detention. (1952) Confinement imposed usu. on a criminal defendant who has threatened to escape, poses a risk of harm, or has otherwise violated the law while awaiting trial, or on a mentally ill person who may cause harm.

secret detention. The holding of a suspect in an undisclosed place, without formal charges, a legal hearing, or access to legal counsel, and without the knowledge of anyone other than the detaining authority.

2. Custody of property; esp., an employee's custody of the employer's property without being considered as having legal possession of it.

determinable, *adj.* (15c) **1.** Liable to end upon the happening of a contingency; terminable <fee simple determinable>. **2.** Able to be determined or ascertained <the delivery date is determinable because she kept the written invoice>.

determination, *n.* (14c) A final decision by a court or administrative agency <the court's determination of the issue>.

determination letter. (1929) A letter issued by the Internal Revenue Service in response to a taxpayer's request, giving an opinion about the tax significance of a transaction, such as whether a nonprofit corporation is entitled to tax-exempt status.

deterrence, *n.* (1861) The act or process of discouraging certain behavior, particularly by fear; esp., as a goal of criminal law, the prevention of criminal behavior by fear of punishment. — **deter,** *vb.* — **deterrent,** *adj.*

general deterrence. (1949) A goal of criminal law generally, or of a specific conviction and sentence, to discourage people from committing crimes.

special deterrence. (1955) A goal of a specific conviction and sentence to dissuade the offender from committing crimes in the future.

deterrent, *n.* (1824) Something that impedes; something that prevents <a deterrent to crime>.

detinue (**det**-i-nyoo *or* -noo). (15c) A common-law action to recover personal property wrongfully taken or withheld by another.

detour, *n. Torts.* An employee's minor deviation from the employer's business for personal reasons. • Because a detour falls within the scope of employment, the employer is still vicariously liable for the employee's actions.

detraction, *n.* (14c) The removal of personal property from one state to another after transfer of title by a will or inheritance.

detriment. (15c) **1.** Any loss or harm suffered by a person or property. **2.** *Contracts.* The relinquishment of some legal right that a promisee would have otherwise been entitled to exercise.

devaluation, *n.* The reduction in the value of one currency in relation to another currency. — **devalue,** *vb.*

devastation. (17c) **1.** An executor's squandering or mismanagement of the deceased's estate. **2.** An act of destruction. **3.** WASTE (1).

development. (1885) **1.** A substantial human-created change to improved or unimproved real estate, including the construction of buildings or other structures. **2.** An activity, action, or alteration that changes undeveloped property into developed property.

deviance, *n.* (1941) The quality or state of departing from established norms, esp. in social customs. — **deviate** (**dee**-vee-ayt), *vb.* — **deviant,** *adj.* & *n.* — **deviate** (**dee**-vee-ət), *n.*

deviation doctrine. (1948) **1.** A principle allowing variation from a term of a will or trust to avoid defeating the document's purpose. **2.** A principle allowing an agent's activity to vary slightly from the scope of the principal's permission.

device. (14c) **1.** *Patents.* A mechanical invention, as differentiated in patent law from a chemical discovery. • A device may be an apparatus or an article of manufacture. **2.** A scheme to trick or deceive; a stratagem or artifice, as in the law relating to fraud.

devisable, *adj.* (16c) **1.** Capable of being bequeathed by a will. **2.** Capable of being invented. **3.** Feigned.

devise (di-**VIZ**), *n.* (15c) **1.** The act of giving property by will. **2.** The provision in a will containing such a gift. **3.** Property disposed of in a will. **4.** A will disposing of property. — **devise,** *vb.*

alternative devise. A devise that, under the terms of the will, is designed to displace another devise if one or more specified events occur.

conditional devise. (18c) A devise that depends on the occurrence of some uncertain event.

demonstrative devise. A devise, usu. of a specific amount of money or quantity of property, that is primarily payable from a designated source, but that may be payable from the estate's general assets if the designated property is insufficient.

executory devise. (17c) An interest in land, created by will, that takes effect in the future and depends on a future contingency; a limitation, by will, of a future estate or interest in land when the limitation cannot, consistently with legal rules, take effect as a remainder. • An executory devise, which is a type of conditional limitation, differs from a remainder in three ways: (1) it needs no particular estate to support it, (2) with it a fee simple or lesser estate can be limited after a fee simple, and (3) with it a remainder can be limited in a chattel interest after a particular estate for life is created in that interest.

general devise. (18c) **1.** A devise, usu. of a specific amount of money or quantity of property, that is payable from the estate's general assets. See Restatement (Third) of Property: Wills and Other Donative Transfers § 5.1 (1999). **2.** A devise that passes the testator's lands without specifically enumerating or describing them.

lapsed devise. (18c) A devise that fails because the testator outlives the named recipient.

pecuniary devise. A demonstrative devise consisting of money.

primary devise. A devise to the first person named as taker. • For example, a devise of "Blackacre to A, but if A does not survive me then to B" names A as the recipient of the primary devise and B as the recipient of the secondary or alternative devise.

residuary devise. (18c) A devise of the remainder of the testator's property left after other specific devises are taken.

specific devise. (18c) A devise that passes a particular piece of property.

devisee (dev-ə-**zee** *or* di-vɪ-**zee**). (16c) A recipient of property by will.

deviser. (16c) One who invents or contrives <the deviser of these patents>.

devisor. (16c) One who disposes of property (usu. real property) in a will.

devolution (dev-ə-**loo**-shən), *n.* (16c) The act or an instance of transferring one's rights, duties, or powers to another; the passing of such rights, duties, or powers by transfer or succession <the federal government's devolution of police power to the states>. — **devolutionary,** *adj.* — **devolutionist,** *n.*

devolve (di-**vahlv**), *vb.* (16c) **1.** To transfer (rights, duties, or powers) to another. **2.** To pass (rights, duties, or powers) by transmission or succession.

DFA. *abbr.* Delayed funds availability.

DHS. *abbr.* Department of Homeland Security.

DIA. *abbr.* Defense Intelligence Agency.

diagnosis (dɪ-əg-**noh**-sis). (17c) **1.** The determination of a medical condition (such as a disease) by physical examination or by study of its symptoms. **2.** The result of such an examination or study.

dialectic (dɪ-ə-**lek**-tik), *n.* (16c) **1.** A school of logic that teaches critical examination of the truth of an opinion, esp. by discussion or debate. **2.** An argument made by critically examining logical consequences. **3.** A logical debate. **4.** A disputant; a debater. Pl. **dialectics.**

dictum (**dik**-təm), *n.*(16c) **1.** A statement of opinion or belief considered authoritative because of the dignity of the person making it. **2.** A familiar rule; a maxim. **3.** Obiter dictum. Pl. **dicta.**

differential pricing. (1946) The setting of the price of a product or service differently for different customers.

digest, *n.* (14c) An index of legal propositions showing which cases support each proposition; a collection of summaries of reported cases, arranged by subject and subdivided by jurisdiction and court. — Abbr. D.; Dig.

Digital Millennium Copyright Act. A 1998 federal law harmonizing United States copyright protection with international law, limiting copyright liability for Internet service providers, and expanding software owners' ability to copy programs. — Abbr. DMCA.

dignitary, *adj.* Of or relating to one's interest in personal dignity, as contrasted with one's interest in freedom from physical injury and property damage.

dilatory (**dil**-ə-tor-ee), *adj.* (15c) Tending to cause delay.

diligence. (14c) **1.** A continual effort to accomplish something. **2.** Care; caution; the attention and care required from a person in a given situation. — **diligent,** *adj.*

due diligence. (18c) **1.** The diligence reasonably expected from, and ordinarily exercised by, a person who seeks to satisfy a legal requirement or to discharge an obligation. **2.** *Corporations & securities.* A prospective buyer's or broker's investigation and analysis of a target company, a piece of property, or a newly issued security.

ordinary diligence. (18c) The diligence that a person of average prudence would exercise in handling his or her own property like that at issue.

reasonable diligence. (18c) A fair degree of diligence expected from someone of ordinary prudence under circumstances like those at issue.

slight diligence. (1836) The diligence that a person of less than common prudence takes with his or her own concerns.

special diligence. The diligence expected from a person practicing in a particular field of specialty under circumstances like those at issue.

dilution. (17c) **1.** The act or an instance of diminishing a thing's strength or lessening its value. **2.** *Corporations.* The reduction in the monetary value or voting power of stock by increasing the total number of outstanding shares. **3.** *Constitutional law.* The limitation of the effectiveness of a particular group's vote by legislative reapportionment or political gerrymandering. • Such dilution violates the Equal Protection Clause. **4.** *Trademarks.* The impairment of a famous trademark's strength, effectiveness, or distinctiveness through the use of the mark on an unrelated product, usu. blurring the trademark's distinctive character or tarnishing it with an unsavory association.

dilution doctrine. *Trademarks.* The rule protecting a trademark from a deterioration in strength, as when a person seeks to use the mark for an unrelated product.

diminution (dim-ə-**n**[**y**]**oo**-shən), *n.* (14c) **1.** The act or process of decreasing, lessening, or taking away. **2.** An incompleteness or lack of certification in a court record sent from a lower court to a higher one for review. **3.** *Trademarks.* Blurring. — **diminish** (for sense 1), *vb.*

diminution-in-value method. (1980) A way of calculating damages for breach of contract based on a reduction in market value that is caused by the breach.

DIP. *abbr.* Debtor-in-Possession.

direct, *vb.* (14c) **1.** To aim (something or someone). **2.** To cause (something or someone) to move on a particular course. **3.** To guide (something or someone); to govern. **4.** To instruct (someone) with authority. **5.** To address (something or someone).

direct action. (1912) **1.** A lawsuit by an insured against his or her own insurance company rather than against the tortfeasor and the tortfeasor's insurer. **2.** A lawsuit by a person claiming against an insured but suing the insurer directly instead of pursuing compensation indirectly through the insured. **3.** A lawsuit to enforce a shareholder's rights against a corporation.

direct attack. An attack on a judgment made in the same proceeding as the one in which the judgment was entered; specif., seeking to have the judgment vacated or reversed or modified by appropriate proceedings in either the trial court or an appellate court. • Examples of direct attacks are motions for new trial and appeals.

direct examination. (1859) The first questioning of a witness in a trial or other proceeding, conducted by the party who called the witness to testify.

director (di-**rek**-tər). (15c) **1.** One who manages, guides, or orders; a chief administrator. **2.** A person appointed or elected to sit on a board that manages the affairs of a corporation or other organization by electing and exercising control over its officers.

direct order of alienation. (1852) *Real estate.* The principle that a grantee who assumes the debt on a mortgaged property is required to pay the mortgage debt if the original mortgagor defaults.

directory call. (1812) *Property.* In a land description, a general description of the areas in which landmarks or other calls are found.

directory requirement. (1865) A statutory or contractual instruction to act in a way that is advisable, but not absolutely essential — in contrast to a mandatory requirement. • A directory requirement is frequently introduced by the word *should* or, less frequently, *shall* (which is more typically a mandatory word).

direct skip. (1988) *Tax.* A generation-skipping transfer of assets, either directly or through a trust. • A direct skip may be subject to a generation-skipping transfer tax — either a gift tax or an estate tax. IRC (26 USCA) §§ 2601–2602.

disability. (16c) **1.** The inability to perform some function; esp., the inability of one person to alter a given relation with another person. **2.** An objectively measurable condition of impairment, physical or mental <his disability entitled him to workers'-compensation benefits>.

developmental disability. (1973) An impairment of general intellectual functioning or adaptive behavior.

partial disability. A worker's inability to perform all the duties that he or she could do before an accident or illness, even though the worker can still engage in some gainful activity on the job.

permanent disability. (1804) A disability that will indefinitely prevent a worker from performing some or all of the duties that he or she could do before an accident or illness.

physical disability. (1826) An incapacity caused by a physical defect or infirmity, or by bodily imperfection or mental weakness.

temporary disability. (18c) A disability that exists until an injured worker is as far restored as the nature of the injury will permit.

temporary total disability. Total disability that is not permanent.

total disability. (18c) A worker's inability to perform employment-related duties because of a physical or mental impairment.

3. Incapacity in the eyes of the law <most of a minor's disabilities are removed when he or she turns 18>.

civil disability. (18c) The condition of a person who has had a legal right or privilege revoked as a result of a criminal conviction, as when a person's driver's license is revoked after a DWI conviction.

disability compensation. Payments from public or private funds to a disabled person who cannot work, such as social-security or workers'-compensation benefits.

disablement, *n.* (15c) **1.** The act of incapacitating or immobilizing. **2.** The imposition of a legal disability.

disabling restraints. (1963) Limits on the alienation of property. • These restraints are sometimes void as being against public policy.

disaffirm (dis-ə-**fərm**), *vb.* (16c) **1.** To repudiate; to revoke consent; to disclaim the intent to be bound by an earlier transaction. **2.** To declare (a voidable contract) to be void. — **disaffirmance** (dis-ə-**fərm**-ənts), *n.*

disallow, *vb.* (14c) **1.** To refuse to allow (something). **2.** To reject (something).

disappeared person. (1944) **1.** A person who has been absent from home for a specified number of continuous years (often five or seven) and who, during that period, has not communicated with the person most likely to know his or her whereabouts. **2.** *Human-rights law.* A person who has been illegally detained or kidnapped, often by governmental authorities or soldiers, and whose current whereabouts and condition are unknown and undiscoverable.

disarmament. *Int'l law.* The negotiated or voluntary reduction of military arms, esp. nuclear weapons, to a greatly reduced level or to nil.

disaster area. (1953) A region officially declared to have suffered a catastrophic emergency, such as a flood or hurricane, and therefore eligible for government aid.

disavow (dis-ə-**vow**), *vb.* To disown; to disclaim knowledge of; to repudiate. — **disavowal,** *n.*

disbarment, *n.* (1862) The action of expelling a lawyer from the bar or from the practice of law, usu. because of some disciplinary violation. — **disbar,** *vb.*

disbursement (dis-**bərs**-mənt), *n.* The act of paying out money, commonly from a fund or in settlement of a debt or account payable. — **disburse,** *vb.*

discharge (**dis**-chahrj), *n.* (15c) **1.** Any method by which a legal duty is extinguished; esp., the payment of a debt or satisfaction of some other obligation. **2.** *Bankruptcy.* The release of a debtor from monetary obligations upon adjudication of bankruptcy; discharge in bankruptcy. **3.** The dismissal of a case. **4.** The canceling or vacating of a court order. **5.** The release of a prisoner from confinement. — **discharge** (dis-**chahrj**), *vb.*

unconditional discharge. (18c) **1.** A release from an obligation without any conditions attached. **2.** A release from confinement without any parole requirements to fulfill.

6. The relieving of a witness, juror, or jury from further responsibilities in a case. **7.** The firing of an employee.

constructive discharge. (1830) A termination of employment brought about by making the employee's working conditions so intolerable that the employee feels compelled to leave.

retaliatory discharge. (1967) A discharge that is made in retaliation for the employee's conduct (such as reporting unlawful activity by the employer to the government) and that clearly violates public policy. • Federal and state statutes may entitle an employee who is dismissed by retaliatory discharge to recover damages.

wrongful discharge. (1825) A discharge for reasons that are illegal or that violate public policy.

8. The dismissal of a member of the armed services from military service.

administrative discharge. A military-service discharge given by administrative means and not by court-martial.

bad-conduct discharge. A punitive discharge that a court-martial can give a member of the military, usu. as punishment for repeated minor offenses. — Abbr. BCD.

dishonorable discharge. The most severe punitive discharge that a court-martial can give to a member of the military.

general discharge. One of the administrative discharges given to a member of the military who does not qualify for an honorable discharge.

honorable discharge. A formal final judgment passed by the government on a soldier's entire military record, and an authoritative declaration that he or she has left the service in a status of honor. • Full veterans' benefits are given only to a person honorably discharged.

discharge in bankruptcy. (1820) **1.** The release of a debtor from personal liability for prebankruptcy debts; specif., discharge under the United States Bankruptcy Code. **2.** A bankruptcy court's decree releasing a debtor from that liability.

disciplinary proceeding. (1900) An action brought to reprimand, suspend, or expel a licensed professional or other person from a profession or other group because of unprofessional, unethical, improper, or illegal conduct.

disciplinary rule. (*often cap.*) (1890) A mandatory regulation stating the minimum level of professional conduct that a professional must sustain to avoid being subject to disciplinary action. • For lawyers, the disciplinary rules are found chiefly in the Model Code of Professional Responsibility. — Abbr. DR.

discipline, *n.* **1.** Punishment intended to correct or instruct; esp., a sanction or penalty imposed after an official finding of misconduct. **2.** The punishment or penalties (often termed "sanctions") imposed by a disciplining agency on an attorney who has breached a rule of professional ethics. **3.** Control gained by enforcing compliance or order. **4.** *Military law.* A state of mind inducing instant obedience to a lawful order, no matter how unpleasant or dangerous such compliance might be. — **discipline,** *vb.* — **disciplinary,** *adj.*

disclaimer, *n.* (15c) **1.** A renunciation of one's legal right or claim; esp., a renunciation of a patent claim, usu. to save the remainder of the application from being rejected. **2.** A repudiation of another's legal right or claim. **3.** A writing that contains such a renunciation or repudiation. **4.** RENUNCIATION (2). — **disclaim,** *vb.*

disclaimer of warranty. (1881) An oral or written statement intended to limit a seller's liability for defects in the goods sold. • In some circumstances, printed words must be specific and conspicuous to be effective.

qualified disclaimer. (1889) **1.** A disclaimer with a restriction or condition attached. • In this sense it is *qualified* because it carries the restriction or condition. **2.** A person's refusal to accept an interest in property so that he or she can avoid having to pay estate or gift taxes. • To be effective under federal tax law, the refusal must be in writing and must be executed no later than nine months from the time when the interest was created. In this sense, it is *qualified* in the sense of being within the lawful exemption. IRC (26 USCA) § 2518.

disclosure, *n.* (16c) **1.** The act or process of making known something that was previously unknown; a revelation of facts. **2.** The mandatory divulging of information to a litigation opponent according to procedural rules. — **disclose,** *vb.* — **disclosural,** *adj.*

full disclosure. A complete revelation of all material facts.

initial disclosure. *Civil procedure.* In federal practice, the requirement that parties make available to each other the following information without first receiving a discovery request: (1) the names, addresses, and telephone numbers of persons likely to have relevant, discoverable information, (2) a copy or description of all relevant documents, data compilations, and tangible items in the party's possession, custody, or control, (3) a damages computation, and (4) any relevant insurance agreements. Fed. R. Civ. P. 26(a)(1)(A)–(D).

public disclosure of private facts. (1964) The public revelation of some aspect of a person's private life without a legitimate public purpose. • The disclosure is actionable in tort if the disclosure would be highly objectionable to a reasonable person.

3. *Patents.* A document explaining how an invention works in sufficient detail for one skilled in the art to be able to understand and duplicate the invention; everything revealed about an invention in the patent application, including drawings, descriptions, specifications, references to prior art, and claims.

discontinuance (dis-kən-**tin**-yoo-ənts), *n.* (14c) **1.** The termination of a lawsuit by the plaintiff; a voluntary dismissal or nonsuit. **2.** The termination of an estate-tail by a tenant in tail who conveys a larger estate in the land than is legally allowed.

discount, *n.* (17c) **1.** A reduction from the full amount or value of something, esp. a price. **2.** An advance deduction of interest when a person lends money on a note, bill of exchange, or other commercial paper, resulting in its present value. **3.** The amount by which a security's market value is below its face value. — **discount,** *vb.*

cash discount. (1889) **1.** A seller's price reduction in exchange for an immediate cash payment. **2.** A reduction from the stated price if the bill is paid on or before a specified date.

functional discount. **1.** A supplier's price discount given to a purchaser based on the purchaser's role (such as warehousing or advertising) in the supplier's distributive system. **2.** A supplier's price discount based on the purchaser's relative distance from the supplier in the chain of distribution.

trade discount. (1889) **1.** A discount from list price offered to all customers of a given type — for example, a discount offered by a lumber dealer to building contractors. **2.** The difference between a seller's list price and the price at which the dealer actually sells goods to the trade.

volume discount. (1939) A price decrease based on a large-quantity purchase.

discoverable, *adj.* Subject to pretrial discovery <the defendant's attorney argued that the defendant's income-tax returns were not discoverable during the liability phase of the trial>.

discovery, *n.* (16c) **1.** The act or process of finding or learning something that was previously unknown. **2.** Compulsory disclosure, at a party's request, of information that relates to the litigation. • The primary discovery devices are interrogatories, depositions, requests for admissions, and requests for production. Although discovery typically comes from parties, courts also allow limited discovery from nonparties. **3.** The facts or documents disclosed. **4.** The pretrial phase of a lawsuit during which depositions, interrogatories, and other forms of discovery are conducted. — **discover,** *vb.* — **discoverable,** *adj.*

accelerated discovery. A party's production of relevant evidence to an opponent at a time earlier than would otherwise be required by rule or standing order of the court.

jurisdictional discovery. Discovery that is limited to finding facts relevant to whether the court has jurisdiction.

merits discovery. Discovery to uncover facts that support the claim or defense, or that might lead to other facts that will support the allegations of a legal proceeding.

postjudgment discovery. (1967) Discovery conducted after judgment has been rendered, usu. to determine the nature of the judgment debtor's assets or to obtain testimony for use in future proceedings.

pretrial discovery. (1939) Discovery conducted before trial to reveal facts and develop evidence. • Modern procedural rules have broadened the scope of pretrial discovery to prevent the parties from surprising each other with evidence at trial.

discovery abuse. (1975) **1.** The misuse of the discovery process, esp. by making overbroad requests for information that is unnecessary or beyond the scope of permissible disclosure or by conducting discovery for an improper purpose. **2.** The failure to respond adequately to proper discovery requests.

discovery immunity. (1975) An exemption provided by statute, caselaw, or court rules to exclude certain documents and information from being disclosed during discovery.

discovery rule. (1916) *Civil procedure.* The rule that a limitations period does not begin to run until the plaintiff discovers (or reasonably should have discovered) the injury giving rise to the claim. • The discovery rule usu. applies to injuries that are inherently difficult to detect, such as those resulting from medical malpractice.

discredit, *vb.* To destroy or impair the credibility of (a witness, a piece of evidence, or a theory); to lessen the degree of trust to be accorded to (a witness or document). — **discredit,** *n.*

discreet (di-**skreet**), *adj.* Exercising discretion; prudent; judicious; discerning.

discrete (di-**skreet**), *adj.* Individual; separate; distinct.

discretion (di-**skresh**-ən). (14c) **1.** Wise conduct and management; cautious discernment; prudence. **2.** Individual judgment; the power of free decision-making.

sole discretion. An individual's power to make decisions without anyone else's advice or consent.

3. *Criminal & tort law.* The capacity to distinguish between right and wrong, sufficient to make a person responsible for his or her own actions. **4.** A public official's power or right to act in certain circumstances according to personal judgment and conscience, often in an official or representative capacity.

administrative discretion. A public official's or agency's power to exercise judgment in the discharge of its duties.

judicial discretion. (17c) The exercise of judgment by a judge or court based on what is fair under the circumstances and guided by the rules and principles of law; a court's power to act or not act when a litigant is not entitled to demand the act as a matter of right.

prosecutorial discretion. (1966) A prosecutor's power to choose from the options available in a criminal case, such as filing charges, prosecuting, not prosecuting, plea-bargaining, and recommending a sentence to the court.

discretionary (di-**skresh**-ə-ner-ee), *adj.* (18c) (Of an act or duty) involving an exercise of judgment and choice, not an implementation of a hard-and-fast rule.

• Such an act by a court may be overturned only after a showing of abuse of discretion.

discretionary act. A deed involving an exercise of personal judgment and conscience.

discrimination, *n.* (1866) **1.** The effect of a law or established practice that confers privileges on a certain class or that denies privileges to a certain class because of race, age, sex, nationality, religion, or disability. **2.** Differential treatment; esp., a failure to treat all persons equally when no reasonable distinction can be found between those favored and those not favored.

age discrimination. Discrimination based on age. • Federal law prohibits discrimination in employment against people who are age 40 or older.

content-based discrimination. A state-imposed restriction on the content of speech, esp. when the speech concerns something of slight social value and is vastly outweighed by the public interest in morality and order. • Types of speech subject to content-based discrimination include obscenity, fighting words, and defamation. *R.A.V. v. City of St. Paul*, 505 U.S. 377, 383–84, 112 S.Ct. 2538, 2543 (1992).

invidious discrimination (in-**vid**-ee-əs). (1856) Discrimination that is offensive or objectionable, esp. because it involves prejudice or stereotyping.

racial discrimination. Discrimination based on race.

reverse discrimination. (1964) Preferential treatment of minorities, usu. through affirmative-action programs, in a way that adversely affects members of a majority group.

sex discrimination. Discrimination based on gender, esp. against women. • The Supreme Court has established an intermediate-scrutiny standard of review for gender-based classifications, which must serve an important governmental interest and be substantially related to the achievement of that objective. *Craig v. Boren*, 429 U.S. 190, 97 S.Ct. 451 (1976).

viewpoint discrimination. Content-based discrimination in which the government targets not a particular subject, but instead certain views that speakers might express on the subject; discrimination based on the content of a communication. • If restrictions on the content of speech are reasonable and not calculated to suppress a particular set of views or ideas, a governmental body may limit speech in a nonpublic forum to expressions that serve a specific purpose.

3. The effect of state laws that favor local interests over out-of-state interests. • Such a discriminatory state law may still be upheld if it is narrowly tailored to achieve an important state interest. — **discriminate,** *vb.* — **discriminatory,** *adj.*

disembodied technology. *Intellectual property.* Know-how or knowledge that is in the form of information only. • Disembodied technology includes proprietary technology and information in the public domain.

disenfranchise (dis-ən-**fran**-chɪz), *vb.* (17c) To deprive (a person) of the right to exercise a franchise or privilege, esp. to vote. — **disenfranchisement** (dis-ən-**fran**-chiz-mənt *or* -**fran**-chɪz-mənt), *n.*

disentailment (dis-ən-**tayl**-mənt), *n.* (1886) The act or process by which a tenant in tail bars the entail on an estate and converts it into a fee simple, thereby nullifying the rights of any later claimant to the fee tail. — **disentail,** *vb.*

disentitle (dis-ən-**tɪt**-əl), *vb.* (17c) To deprive (someone) of a title or claim.

disfigurement (dis-**fig**-yər-mənt). An impairment or injury to the appearance of a person or thing.

disgorgement, *n.* (15c) The act of giving up something (such as profits illegally obtained) on demand or by legal compulsion. — **disgorge,** *vb.*

dishonor, *vb.* (1814c) **1.** To refuse to accept or pay (a negotiable instrument) when presented. **2.** To deface or defile (something, such as a flag). — **dishonor,** *n.*

disincentive, *n.* (1946) A deterrent (to a particular type of conduct), often created, intentionally or unintentionally, through legislation.

disinflation. A period or process of slowing down the rate of inflation.

disinheritance, *n.* (16c) **1.** The act by which an owner of an estate deprives a would-be heir of the expectancy to inherit the estate. **2.** The state of being disinherited. — **disinherit,** *vb.*

negative disinheritance. The act by which a testator attempts to exclude a person from inheritance without disposing of the property to another.

disinter (dis-in-**tər**), *vb.* (17c) **1.** To exhume (a corpse). **2.** To remove (something) from obscurity. — **disinterment** (dis-in-**tər**-mənt), *n.*

disinterested, *adj.* (17c) Free from bias, prejudice, or partiality; not having a pecuniary interest. — **disinterest, disinterestedness,** *n.*

disinvestment, *n.* (1936) **1.** The consumption of capital. **2.** The withdrawal of investments, esp. on political grounds. — **disinvest,** *vb.*

disjoinder (dis-**joyn**-dər). (1936) The undoing of the joinder of parties or claims.

dismemberment. The cutting off of a limb or body part.

dismissal, *n.* (1885) **1.** Termination of an action or claim without further hearing, esp. before the trial of the issues involved.

dismissal agreed. A court's dismissal of a lawsuit with the acquiescence of all parties.

dismissal for want of equity. (1859) A court's dismissal of a lawsuit on substantive, rather than procedural, grounds, usu. because the plaintiff's allegations are found to be untrue or because the plaintiff's pleading does not state an adequate claim.

dismissal for want of prosecution. (1831) A court's dismissal of a lawsuit because the plaintiff has failed to pursue the case diligently toward completion. — Abbr. DWOP.

dismissal without prejudice. (1831) A dismissal that does not bar the plaintiff from refiling the lawsuit within the applicable limitations period.

dismissal with prejudice. (1898) A dismissal, usu. after an adjudication on the merits, barring the plaintiff from prosecuting any later lawsuit on the same claim. • If, after a dismissal with prejudice, the plaintiff files a later suit on the same claim, the defendant in the later suit can assert the defense of res judicata (claim preclusion).

involuntary dismissal. (1911) A court's dismissal of a lawsuit because the plaintiff failed to prosecute or failed to comply with a procedural rule or court order. Fed. R. Civ. P. 41(b).

voluntary dismissal. (1834) A plaintiff's dismissal of a lawsuit at the plaintiff's own request or by stipulation of all the parties. Fed. R. Civ. P. 41(a).

2. A release or discharge from employment.

dismissal for cause. (1877) A dismissal of a contract employee for a reason that the law or public policy has recognized as sufficient to warrant the employee's removal.

3. *Military law.* A court-martial punishment for an officer, commissioned warrant officer, cadet, or midshipman, consisting of separation from the armed services with dishonor. • A dismissal can be given only by a general court-martial and is considered the equivalent of a dishonorable discharge. — **dismiss,** *vb.*

disorder. (1877) **1.** A lack of proper arrangement. **2.** An irregularity. **3.** A public disturbance; a riot. **4.** A disturbance in mental or physical health.

disorderly house. (16c) **1.** A dwelling where people carry on activities that are a nuisance to the neighborhood. **2.** A dwelling where people conduct criminal or immoral activities. • Examples are brothels and drug houses.

disorderly person. (18c) **1.** A person guilty of disorderly conduct. **2.** A person who breaches the peace, order, decency, or safety of the public, as defined by statute.

disparagement (di-**spar**-ij-mənt), *n.* (16c) **1.** A derogatory comparison of one thing with another. **2.** The act or an instance of castigating or detracting from the reputation of, esp. unfairly or untruthfully. **3.** A false and injurious statement that discredits or detracts from the reputation of another's character, property, product, or business. • To recover in tort for disparagement, the plaintiff must prove that the statement caused a third party to take some action resulting in specific pecuniary loss to the plaintiff. — **disparage,** *vb.*

disparate impact (**dis**-pə-rit). (1973) The adverse effect of a facially neutral practice (esp. an employment practice) that nonetheless discriminates against persons because of their race, sex, national origin, age, or disability and that is not justified by business necessity. • Discriminatory intent is irrelevant in a disparate-impact claim.

disparate treatment. The practice, esp. in employment, of intentionally dealing with persons differently because of their race, sex, national origin, age, or disability. • To succeed on a disparate-treatment claim, the plaintiff must prove that the defendant acted with discriminatory intent or motive.

disparity (di-**spar**-ə-tee). (16c) Inequality; a difference in quantity or quality between two or more things.

dispensation (dis-pen-**say**-shən). An exemption from a law, duty, or penalty; permission to do something that is ordinarily forbidden.

dispense with the reading of the minutes. *Parliamentary law.* To forgo reciting the secretary's proposed minutes at the regular time.

displaced-persons camp. *Int'l. law.* In a nation in the throes of war, natural disaster, ethnic cleansing, or some similar extraordinary event, a temporary settlement where citizens who have become homeless are temporarily provided with the basic necessities of life and given assistance in resettling or emigrating.

displacement. 1. Removal from a proper place or position. **2.** A replacement; a substitution. **3.** A forced removal of a person from the person's home or country, esp. because of war. **4.** A shifting of emotional emphasis from one thing to another, esp. to avoid unpleasant or unacceptable thoughts or tendencies.

display right. (1944) *Copyright.* A copyright owner's exclusive right to show or exhibit a copy of the protected work publicly, whether directly or by technological means. • For example, this right makes it illegal to transmit a copyrighted work over the Internet without permission.

Disposing Clause. The clause of the U.S. Constitution giving Congress the power to dispose of property belonging to the federal government. U.S. Const. art. IV, § 3, cl. 2.

disposition (dis-pə-**zish**-ən), *n.* (14c) **1.** The act of transferring something to another's care or possession, esp. by deed or will; the relinquishing of property.

2. A final settlement or determination. **3.** Temperament or character; personal makeup <a surly disposition>. — **dispose,** *vb.* — **dispositive,** *adj.*

disposition without a trial. (1888) The final determination of a criminal case without a trial on the merits, as when a defendant pleads guilty or admits sufficient facts to support a guilty finding without a trial.

dispositive (dis-**poz**-ə-tiv), *adj.* (17c) **1.** Being a deciding factor; (of a fact or factor) bringing about a final determination. **2.** Of, relating to, or effecting the disposition of property by will or deed.

dispossession (dis-pə-**zesh**-ən), *n.* Deprivation of, or eviction from, rightful possession of property; the wrongful taking or withholding of possession of land from the person lawfully entitled to it; OUSTER (1). — **dispossess** (dis-pə-**zes**), *vb.*

dispossess proceeding. (1888) A summary procedure initiated by a landlord to oust a defaulting tenant and regain possession of the premises.

disprove, *vb.* To refute (an assertion); to prove (an allegation) false.

dispute, *n.* (16c) A conflict or controversy, esp. one that has given rise to a particular lawsuit. — **dispute,** *vb.*

disqualification, *n.* (18c) **1.** Something that makes one ineligible; esp., a bias or conflict of interest that prevents a judge or juror from impartially hearing a case, or that prevents a lawyer from representing a party.

vicarious disqualification. (1949) Disqualification of all the lawyers in a firm or in an office because one of the lawyers is ethically disqualified from representing the client at issue.

2. The act of making ineligible; the fact or condition of being ineligible. — **disqualify,** *vb.*

disregard, *n.* **1.** The action of ignoring or treating without proper respect or consideration. **2.** The state of being ignored or treated without proper respect or consideration. — **disregard,** *vb.*

reckless disregard. (1820) **1.** Conscious indifference to the consequences of an act. **2.** *Defamation.* Serious indifference to truth or accuracy of a publication. • "Reckless disregard for the truth" is the standard in proving the defendant's actual malice toward the plaintiff in a libel action. **3.** The intentional commission of a harmful act or failure to do a required act when the actor knows or has reason to know of facts that would lead a reasonable person to realize that the actor's conduct both creates an unreasonable risk of harm to someone and involves a high degree of probability that substantial harm will result.

disrepair. A state of being in need of restoration after deterioration or damage.

disrepute. A loss of reputation; dishonor.

disseisin (dis-**see**-zin), *n.* (14c) The act of wrongfully depriving someone of the freehold possession of property; DISPOSSESSION. — **disseise** (dis-**seez**), *vb.*

dissemble (di-**sem**-bəl), *vb.* To give a false impression about (something); to cover up (something) by deception.

dissemination (di-sem-i-**nay**-shən), *n.* **1.** The act of spreading, diffusing, or dispersing; esp., the circulation of defamatory matter. **2.** The extension of the influence or establishment of a thing, such as an idea, book, or document.

dissent (di-**sent**), *n.* (16c) **1.** A disagreement with a majority opinion, esp. among judges. **2.** A withholding of assent or approval. **3.** The act of a surviving spouse who, as statutorily authorized in many states, refuses a devise and elects instead a statutory share. — **dissent** (di-**sent**), *vb.*

dissipation, *n.* (17c) The use of an asset for an illegal or inequitable purpose, such as a spouse's use of community property for personal benefit when a divorce is imminent. — **dissipate,** *vb.*

dissolution (dis-ə-**loo**-shən), *n.* (14c) **1.** The act of bringing to an end; termination. **2.** The cancellation or abrogation of a contract, with the effect of annulling the contract's binding force and restoring the parties to their original positions. **3.** The termination of a corporation's legal existence by expiration of its charter, by legislative act, by bankruptcy, or by other means; the event immediately preceding the liquidation or winding-up process.

de facto dissolution. The termination and liquidation of a corporation's business, esp. because of an inability to pay its debts.

involuntary dissolution. The termination of a corporation administratively (for failure to file reports or pay taxes), judicially (for abuse of corporate authority, management deadlock, or failure to pay creditors), or through involuntary bankruptcy.

voluntary dissolution. A corporation's termination initiated by the board of directors and approved by the shareholders.

4. The termination of a previously existing partnership upon the occurrence of an event specified in the partnership agreement, such as a partner's withdrawal from the partnership, or as specified by law. **5.** *Patents.* The dismissal of an interference contest before a final judgment and an express award of priority. • The effect of dissolving an interference is that junior parties fail to meet their burden of proof, so the senior party retains priority. **6.** *Parliamentary law.* An adjournment sine die without any provision for reconvening the same deliberative assembly, even if another assembly of the same kind (such as a legislative body or a convention) will eventually convene. — **dissolve,** *vb.*

dissolution of marriage. Divorce.

dissuade, *vb.* To persuade (someone) not to do something <to dissuade the expert from testifying>.

distillate. *Oil & gas.* **1.** The "wet" element of natural gas that may be removed as a liquid. **2.** Any product of the process of distillation.

distinctiveness, *n. Trademarks.* The quality of a trademarked word, symbol, or device that identifies the goods of a particular merchant and distinguishes them from the goods of others. — **distinctive,** *adj.*

distinguish, *vb.* (15c) **1.** To note a significant factual, procedural, or legal difference in (an earlier case), usu. to minimize the case's precedential effect or to show that it is inapplicable. **2.** To make a distinction. — **distinction,** *n.* **distinguishable,** *adj.*

distinguishing mark. A physical indication or feature that identifies or delineates one person or thing from another.

distraction doctrine. (1999) The rule that a plaintiff may not be guilty of contributory negligence if the plaintiff's attention was diverted from a known danger by a sufficient cause.

distrain, *vb.* (13c) **1.** To force (a person, usu. a tenant), by the seizure and detention of personal property, to perform an obligation (such as paying overdue rent). **2.** To seize (goods) by distress, a legal remedy entitling the rightful owner to recover property wrongfully taken. — **distraint,** *n.*

distress, *n.* (13c) **1.** The seizure of another's property to secure the performance of a duty, such as the payment of overdue rent. **2.** The legal remedy authorizing such a seizure; the procedure by which the seizure is carried out. **3.** The property seized.

distributee (di-strib-yoo-**tee**), *n.* (1870) **1.** A beneficiary entitled to payment.

2. An heir, esp. one who obtains personal property from the estate of an intestate decedent.

distribution, *n.* (14c) **1.** The passing of personal property to an intestate decedent's heirs; specif., the process of dividing an estate after realizing its movable assets and paying out of them its debts and other claims against the estate. **2.** The act or process of apportioning or giving out. — **distribute,** *vb.*

distribution in kind. (1819) A transfer of property in its original state, such as a distribution of land instead of the proceeds of its sale.

distribution right. (1936) *Copyright.* A copyright holder's exclusive right to sell, lease, or otherwise transfer copies of the protected work to the public.

distributive clause. (1821) A will or trust provision governing the distribution of income and gifts.

distributive deviation. A trustee's authorized or unauthorized departure from the express distributional terms of a trust.

distributive finding. A jury's decision partly in favor of one party and partly in favor of another.

distributive share. (18c) **1.** The share that an heir or beneficiary receives from the legal distribution of an estate. **2.** The portion (as determined in the partnership agreement) of a partnership's income, gain, loss, or deduction that is passed through to a partner and reported on the partner's tax return. **3.** The share of assets or liabilities that a partner or partner's estate acquires after the partnership has been dissolved.

distributor. (1884) A wholesaler, jobber, or other manufacturer or supplier that sells chiefly to retailers and commercial users. — **distributorship,** *n.*

district. (17c) **1.** A territorial area into which a country, state, county, municipality, or other political subdivision is divided for judicial, political, electoral, or administrative purposes. **2.** A territorial area in which similar local businesses or entities are concentrated, such as a theater district or an arts district. — Abbr. D.

assessment district. *Tax.* A usu. municipal subdivision in which separate assessments of taxable property are made.

congressional district. (1804) A geographical unit of a state from which one member of the U.S. House of Representatives is elected.

election district. A subdivision of a state, county, or city that is established to facilitate an election or to elect governmental representatives for that subdivision.

legislative district. (1840) A geographical subdivision of a state for the purpose of electing legislative representatives.

metropolitan district. A special district, embracing parts of or entire cities and towns in a metropolitan area, created by a state to provide unified administration of one or more common services, such as water supply or public transportation.

municipal utility district. (1921) A publicly owned corporation, or a political subdivision, that provides the public with a service or services, such as water, electricity, gas, transportation, or telecommunications. — Abbr. MUD.

special district. A political subdivision that is created to bypass normal borrowing limitations, to insulate certain activities from traditional political influence, to allocate functions to entities reflecting particular expertise, and to provide a single service within a specified area <a transit authority is a special district>.

taxing district. A district — constituting the whole state, a county, a city, or other smaller unit — throughout which a particular tax or assessment is ratably apportioned and levied on the district's inhabitants.

water district. A geographical subdivision created by a state or local government entity to provide the public with a water supply.

district attorney. (18c) A public official appointed or elected to represent the state in criminal cases in a particular judicial district; PROSECUTOR (1). — Abbr. D.A.

districting. The act of drawing lines or establishing boundaries between geographic areas to create voting districts.

District of Columbia. The seat of the U.S. government, situated on the Potomac River between Maryland and Virginia. • Neither a state nor a territory, it is constitutionally subject to the exclusive jurisdiction of Congress. — Abbr. D.C.

disturbance, *n.* (13c) **1.** An act causing annoyance or disquiet, or interfering with a person's pursuit of a lawful occupation or the peace and order of a neighborhood, community, or meeting. **2.** At common law, a wrong done to an incorporeal hereditament by hindering the owner's enjoyment of it.

diverse, *adj.* **1.** Of or relating to different types. **2.** (Of a person or entity) having a different citizenship from the party or parties on the other side of the lawsuit. **3.** (Of a group of people) including people of different races, sexes, nationalities, and cultural backgrounds. — **diversity,** *n.* & *adj.*

diversification, *n.* **1.** A company's movement into a broader range of products, usu. by buying firms already serving the market or by expanding existing operations. **2.** The act of investing in a wide range of companies to reduce the risk if one sector of the market suffers losses. — **diversify,** *vb.*

diversion, *n.* (17c) **1.** A deviation or alteration from the natural course of things; esp., the unauthorized alteration of a watercourse to the detriment of a lower riparian owner, or the unauthorized use of funds. **2.** A distraction or pastime. — **divert,** *vb.*

diversion program. (1972) **1.** *Criminal law.* A program that refers certain criminal defendants before trial to community programs on job training, education, and the like, which if successfully completed may lead to the dismissal of the charges. **2.** A community-based program or set of services designed to prevent the need for court intervention in matters of child neglect, minor juvenile delinquency, truancy, or incorrigibility.

diversity of citizenship. (1876) A basis for federal-court jurisdiction that exists when (1) a case is between citizens of different states, or between a citizen of a state and an alien, and (2) the matter in controversy exceeds a specific value (now $75,000). 28 USCA § 1332. • For purposes of diversity jurisdiction, a corporation is considered a citizen of both the state of incorporation and the state of its principal place of business. An unincorporated association, such as a partnership, is considered a citizen of each state where at least one of its members is a citizen.

complete diversity. (1925) In a multiparty case, diversity between both sides to the lawsuit so that all plaintiffs have different citizenship from all defendants. • Complete diversity must exist for a federal court to have diversity jurisdiction over the matter. The rule of complete diversity was first laid down by Chief Justice Marshall in *Strawbridge v. Curtiss*, 7 U.S. (3 Cranch) 267 (1806).

manufactured diversity. (1968) Improper or collusively created diversity of citizenship for the sole or primary purpose of creating federal jurisdiction. • Manufactured diversity is prohibited by 28 USCA § 1359.

divestiture (di-**ves**-tə-chər *or* dɪ-), *n.*(17c) **1.** The loss or surrender of an asset or interest. **2.** A court order to a party to dispose of assets or property. **3.** *Antitrust.* A court order to a defendant to rid itself of property, securities, or other assets to prevent a monopoly or restraint of trade. — **divest,** *vb.*

divestment, *n.* (1844) **1.** *Property.* The cutting short of an interest in property before its normal termination. **2.** The complete or partial loss of an interest in an asset, such as land or stock. **3.** DISINVESTMENT (2). — **divest,** *vb.*

divide-and-pay-over rule. (1916) *Wills & estates.* The principle that if the only provisions in a testamentary disposition are words ordering that payment be made at some time after the testator's death, time will be of the essence and the interest is future and contingent rather than vested and immediate.

divided court. (18c) An appellate court whose opinion or decision in a particular case is not unanimous, esp. when the majority is slim, as in a 5-to-4 decision of the U.S. Supreme Court.

dividend. (17c) A portion of a company's earnings or profits distributed pro rata to its shareholders, usu. in the form of cash or additional shares.

dividend-received deduction. (1957) A deduction allowed to a corporate shareholder for dividends received from a domestic corporation. IRC (26 USCA) §§ 243–247.

dividend-reinvestment plan. (1969) A stock-purchase program that allows investors to reinvest their dividends, and perhaps convert additional voluntary payments, into shares of the entity's common stock, usu. with no sales charge, and sometimes at a discount from the stock's market price. — Abbr. DRIP; DRP.

division of powers. (18c) The allocation of power between the national government and the states. • Under the Tenth Amendment, powers not delegated to the federal government are reserved to the states or to the people. But today the Tenth Amendment provides only a limited check on Congress's power to regulate the states.

division order. *Oil & gas.* A contract for the sale of oil or gas, specifying how the payments are to be distributed.

divorce. (14c) The legal dissolution of a marriage by a court. — **divorce,** *vb.*

collaborative divorce. A divorce negotiated in a nonadversarial forum, usu. between spouses who, with or without a lawyer, are assisted as needed by a team of experts in law, mental health, and financial matters (such as taxes and real estate).

contested divorce. **1.** A divorce that one spouse opposes in court. **2.** A divorce in which the spouses litigate. • In this sense, although both spouses may want the divorce, they disagree on the terms of the divorce decree. Cf. *uncontested divorce.*

divisible divorce. (1943) A divorce whereby the marriage itself is dissolved but the issues incident to the divorce, such as alimony, child custody, and visitation, are reserved until a later proceeding.

divorce a mensa et thoro (ay **men**-sə et **thor**-oh). [Latin "(divorce) from board and hearth"] (18c) *Hist.* A partial or qualified divorce by which the parties were separated and allowed or ordered to live apart, but remained technically married. • This type of divorce, abolished in England in 1857, was the forerunner of modern judicial separation.

divorce a vinculo matrimonii (ay **ving**-kyə-loh ma-trə-**moh**-nee-ɪ). [Latin "(divorce) from the chains of marriage"] (17c) A total divorce of husband

and wife, dissolving the marriage tie and releasing the parties wholly from their matrimonial obligations. • At common law, but not always in canon law, this type of divorce bastardized any children from the marriage and was granted on grounds that existed before the marriage.

ex parte divorce (eks **pahr**-tee). (1870) A divorce proceeding in which only one spouse participates or appears in court.

fault divorce. A divorce granted to one spouse on the basis of some proven wrongful act (grounds for divorce) by the other spouse.

foreign divorce. (1831) A divorce obtained outside the state or country in which one spouse resides.

limited divorce. (1831) **1.** A divorce that ends the legal relationship of marriage by court order but does not address financial support, property distribution, or care and custody of children. **2.** Loosely, a legal separation.

mail-order divorce. (1922) *Slang.* A divorce obtained by parties who are not physically present or domiciled in the jurisdiction purporting to grant the divorce. • Such a divorce is not recognized in the United States because of the absence of the usual bases for jurisdiction.

migratory divorce. (1911) A divorce obtained in a jurisdiction other than the marital domicile; esp., a divorce obtained by a spouse who moves to, or temporarily resides in, another state or country to get the divorce.

no-fault divorce. (1969) A divorce in which the parties are not required to prove fault or grounds beyond a showing of the irretrievable breakdown of the marriage or irreconcilable differences.

uncontested divorce. A divorce that is unopposed by the spouse who did not initiate it. Cf. *contested divorce.*

divorce agreement. A contractual agreement that sets out divorcing spouses' rights and responsibilities regarding property, alimony, custody, visitation, and child support.

D.J. District judge.

DJIA. *abbr.* Dow Jones Industrial Average.

DLOP. *abbr.* Dismissal for lack of prosecution.

DNA. *abbr.* Deoxyribonucleic acid; the double-helix structure in cell nuclei that carries the genetic information of most living organisms.

DNA identification. (1987) A method of scientific identification based on a person's unique genetic makeup; specif., the comparison of a person's deoxyribonucleic acid (DNA) — a patterned chemical structure of genetic information — with the DNA in a biological specimen (such as blood, tissue, or hair) to determine whether the person is the source of the specimen. • DNA evidence is used in criminal cases for purposes such as identifying a victim's remains, linking a suspect to a crime, and exonerating an innocent suspect.

DNR order. *abbr.* Do-not-resuscitate order.

docket, *n.* (15c) **1.** A formal record in which a judge or court clerk briefly notes all the proceedings and filings in a court case.

appearance docket. (18c) A list of the parties and lawyers participating in an action, together with a brief abstract of the successive steps in the action.

judgment docket. (1826) A book that a court clerk keeps for the entry or recordation of judgments, giving official notice of existing judgment liens to interested parties.

2. A schedule of pending cases.

DWOP docket. A list of cases that the court has set for possible dismissal for want of prosecution.

preferred docket. (1993) A list of cases set for trial, arranged in order of priority. • Criminal cases are, for example, generally given precedence over civil cases on the preferred docket because of the constitutional right to a speedy trial.

3. Docket call. **4.** A written abstract that provides specific information (usu. about something attached); esp., a label.

docket, *vb.* (17c) **1.** To make a brief entry in the docket of the proceedings and filings in a court case. **2.** To abstract and enter in a book. **3.** To schedule (a case) for trial or some other event.

docket call. (1899) A court session in which attorneys (and sometimes parties) appear in court to report the status of their cases. • For example, they may announce readiness for trial or report the suit's settlement.

docket number. (1866) A number that the court clerk assigns to a case on the court's docket.

Doctor of Juridical Science. A graduate law degree, beyond the J.D. and the LL.M. — Abbr. S.J.D.; J.S.D.

Doctor of Laws. An honorary degree bestowed on one who has achieved great distinction. — Abbr. LL.D.

doctrine. (14c) **1.** A principle, esp. a legal principle, that is widely adhered to. **2.** *Archaic.* HOLDING (1).

doctrine of approximation. (1845) A doctrine that authorizes a court to vary the details of a trust's administration to preserve the trust and to carry out the donor's intentions.

doctrine of constructive service. *Employment law.* The principle that a person who contracts to work for a definite period and is wrongfully discharged after beginning work may wait until the contract period expires and then sue on the contract for the wages that the person would have earned between the time of the discharge and the expiration of the contract.

doctrine of *contra non valentem* (**kon**-trə non və-**len**-təm). (1938) The rule that a limitations or prescriptive period does not begin to run against a plaintiff who is unable to act, usu. because of the defendant's culpable act, such as concealing material information that would give rise to the plaintiff's claim.

doctrine of curative admissibility. A rule allowing a party to introduce otherwise inadmissible evidence to remove the prejudice caused by the improper admission of evidence that was offered by the opposing party. • The doctrine applies when a motion to strike cannot cure the prejudice created by the adverse party.

doctrine of election (18c). A doctrine holding that when a person has contracted with an agent without knowing of the agency and later learns the principal's identity, the person may enforce the contract against either the agent or the principal, but not both.

doctrine of entireties (en-**tɪ**-ər-teez). In customs law, the rule that when an entry consists of parts that assemble to form an article different from any of the parts, the proper classification will be of the whole article, rather than the individual components.

doctrine of equivalents. (1856) *Patents.* A judicially created theory for finding patent infringement when the accused process or product falls outside the literal scope of the patent claims.

reverse doctrine of equivalents. The doctrine preventing infringement liability when the invention is substantially described by the claims of another's patent but performs the same or a similar function in a substantially different way.

doctrine of illusory coverage. A rule requiring an insurance policy to be interpreted so that it is not merely a delusion to the insured.

doctrine of necessaries. (1870) **1.** The rule holding a parent or spouse liable to anyone who sells goods or provides medical services to that person's child or spouse if the goods or services are required for sustenance, support, or healthcare. **2.** *Archaic.* The common-law rule holding a husband or father liable to anyone who sells goods to his wife or child if the goods are required for sustenance or support.

doctrine of precedent. (18c) The rule that precedents not only have persuasive authority but also must be followed when similar circumstances arise.

doctrine of preclusion of inconsistent positions.

doctrine of revestment. A rule by which a court regains jurisdiction after the entry of final judgment when the former opposing parties have actively participated in proceedings inconsistent with the court's judgment.

doctrine of scrivener's error. (1992) A rule permitting a typographical error in a document to be reformed by parol evidence, if the evidence is precise, clear, and convincing.

doctrine of superior equities. *Insurance.* A rule by which an insurer is unable to recover from anyone whose equities are equal or superior to the insurer's; esp., a rule that a right of subrogation may be invoked against another party only if that party's guilty conduct renders the party's equity inferior to that of the insured.

document, *n.* (15c) **1.** Something tangible on which words, symbols, or marks are recorded. See Fed. R. Civ. P. 34(a). **2.** (*pl.*) The deeds, agreements, title papers, letters, receipts, and other written instruments used to prove a fact.

ancient document. (1846) *Evidence.* A document that is presumed to be authentic because its physical condition strongly suggests authenticity, it has existed for 20 or more years, and it has been maintained in proper custody (as by coming from a place where it is reasonably expected to be found). Fed. R. Evid. 901(b)(8).

foreign document. (1816) A document that originated in, or was prepared or executed in, a foreign state or country.

governing document. *Parliamentary law.* A document that defines or organizes an organization, or grants or establishes its authority and governance.

hot document. (1995) A document that directly supports a litigant's allegation.

public document. (17c) A document of public interest issued or published by a political body or otherwise connected with public business.

3. *Evidence.* Under the best-evidence rule, a physical embodiment of information or ideas, such as a letter, contract, receipt, account book, blueprint, or X-ray plate; esp., the original of such an embodiment.

document, *vb.* (18c) **1.** To support with records, instruments, or other evidentiary authorities <document the chain of custody>. **2.** To record; to create a written record of <document a file>.

document of title. (18c) A written description, identification, or declaration of goods authorizing the holder (usu. a bailee) to receive, hold, and dispose of the document and the goods it covers. • Documents of title, such as bills of lading, warehouse receipts, and delivery orders, are generally governed by Article 7 of the UCC.

negotiable document of title. A document of title that actually stands for the goods it covers, so that any transfer of the goods requires a surrender of the document. UCC § 7-104(1).

nonnegotiable document of title. A document of title that merely serves as evidence of the goods it covers. UCC § 7-104(2).

DOD. *abbr.* Department of Defense.

DOE. *abbr.* **1.** Department of Education. **2.** Department of Energy.

do equity. (Of one who seeks an equitable remedy) to treat or offer to treat the other party as fairly as is necessary, short of abandoning one's own legal rights, to bring about a fair result. • The phrase derives from the maxim, "One who seeks equity must do equity."

DOJ. *abbr.* Department of Justice.

DOL. *abbr.* Department of Labor.

dole, *n.* **1.** A share of something that is jointly owned but divisible. **2.** *Slang.* Welfare benefits received from a governmental agency.

***Dole* test.** A four-part test used to determine the constitutionality of a condition attached by Congress under its Spending Clause power to the receipt of federal money. • The spending must be in pursuit of the general welfare, and the condition must be unambiguous, related to some federal interest, and not barred by any other provision of the Constitution. *South Dakota v. Dole*, 483 U.S. 203, 107 S.Ct. 2793 (1987).

DOMA. *abbr.* Defense of Marriage Act.

domain (doh-**mayn**), *n.* (15c) **1.** The territory over which sovereignty is exercised. **2.** An estate in land. **3.** The complete and absolute ownership of land.

domain name. The words and characters that website owners designate for their registered Internet addresses.

domestic, *adj.* (15c) **1.** Of or relating to one's own country. **2.** Of or relating to one's own jurisdiction. **3.** Of or relating to the family or the household.

domestic authority. (1833) **1.** The legal power to use nondeadly force when reasonably necessary to protect a person for whom one is responsible. **2.** A defense allowing a person responsible for another (such as a parent responsible for a child) to use nondeadly force when reasonably necessary to protect the person being cared for.

domestic dispute. (1890) A disturbance, usu. at a residence and usu. within a family, involving violence and often resulting in a call to a law-enforcement agency.

domestic partnership. 1. A nonmarital relationship between two persons of the same or opposite sex who live together as a couple for a significant period of time. **2.** A relationship that an employer or governmental entity recognizes as equivalent to marriage for the purpose of extending employee-partner benefits otherwise reserved for the spouses of employees. — **domestic partner,** *n.*

domestic-partnership law. A legislative enactment, often a municipal ordinance, that grants unmarried adults living in economically or emotionally based relationships, regardless of their sexual preference, some of the rights of a civil marriage without attempting to change the traditional definition of marriage.

domicile (**dom**-ə-sɪl), *n.* (15c) **1.** The place at which a person has been physically present and that the person regards as home; a person's true, fixed, principal, and permanent home, to which that person intends to return and remain even though currently residing elsewhere. **2.** The residence of a person or corporation for legal purposes.

after-acquired domicile. (1858) A domicile established after the facts relevant to an issue arose. • An after-acquired domicile cannot be used to establish jurisdiction or choice of law.

commercial domicile. (1839) **1.** A domicile acquired by a nonresident corporation conducting enough activities to permit taxation of the corporation's property or activities located outside the bounds of the taxing state. **2.** A domicile acquired by a person or company freely residing or carrying on business in enemy territory or enemy-occupied territory.

corporate domicile. (1890) The place considered by law as the center of corporate affairs, where the corporation's functions are discharged; the legal home of a corporation, usu. its state of incorporation or the state in which it maintains its principal place of business. • For purposes of determining whether diversity jurisdiction exists in federal court, a corporation is considered a citizen of both its state of incorporation and the state of its principal place of business.

domicile of choice. (1878) **1.** A domicile established by physical presence within a state or territory, coupled with the intention to make it home. **2.** The domicile that a person chooses after reaching majority or being emancipated.

domicile of origin. (1831) The domicile of a person at birth, derived from the custodial parent or imposed by law.

domicile of succession. (1874) The domicile that determines the succession of a person's estate.

elected domicile. A contractually agreed domicile between parties for purposes of the contract.

foreign domicile. A domicile established by a citizen or subject of one sovereignty within the territory of another.

matrimonial domicile. A domicile that a husband and wife, as a married couple, have established as their home.

municipal domicile. A person's residence in a county or municipality, as distinguished from the person's state or national domicile.

national domicile. A domicile considered in terms of a particular nation rather than a locality or subdivision of a nation.

domiciliary (dom-ə-**sil**-ee-er-ee), *adj.* (18c) Of or relating to domicile.

domiciliary (dom-ə-**sil**-ee-er-ee), *n.* (1845) A person who resides in a particular place with the intention of making it a principal place of abode; one who is domiciled in a particular jurisdiction.

dominant-jurisdiction principle. (1995) The rule that the court in which a case is first filed maintains the suit, to the exclusion of all other courts that would also have jurisdiction.

dominate, *vb.* (17c) **1.** To master (someone or something); to control (someone or something). **2.** Predominate.

domination. *Patents.* The effect that an earlier patent (usu. a basic one) has on a later patent (esp. one for improvements on the patented device) because the earlier patent's claims are so broad or generic that the later patent's invention will always read on the earlier patent's claims, resulting in infringement.

dominion. (14c) **1.** Control; possession. **2.** Sovereignty. **3.** Foreign dominion.

donate, *vb.* (18c) To give (property or money) without receiving consideration for the transfer. — **donation,** *n.* — **donative (doh**-nə-tiv), *adj.*

donee (doh-**nee**). (16c) One to whom a gift is made; the recipient of a gift.

donee of power. (18c) A person who has been given a power of appointment, i.e., the power to dispose of someone else's property.

donor. (15c) **1.** One who gives something without receiving consideration for the transfer. **2.** SETTLOR (1). **3.** The person who creates or reserves a power of appointment.

do-not-resuscitate order. A document, executed by a competent person, directing that if the person's heartbeat and breathing both cease while in a hospital, nursing home, or similar facility, no attempts to restore heartbeat or breathing should be made. — Abbr. DNR order.

out-of-hospital do-not-resuscitate order. A do-not-resuscitate order, executed by a person who has been diagnosed by a physician as having a terminal condition, directing health-care professionals to withhold certain life-sustaining treatments when acting outside a hospital or similar facility. — Abbr. OOH-DNR order.

door-closing statute. (1960) A state law closing or denying access to local courts unless a plaintiff meets specified conditions; esp., a statute requiring a foreign corporation to "qualify" before doing business in the state, including registering with the secretary of state, paying a fee or tax, and appointing an agent to receive service of process.

dormant (**dor**-mənt), *adj.* (15c) Inactive; suspended; latent <a dormant judgment>. — **dormancy,** *n.*

dormant claim. (18c) A claim that is in abeyance.

DOT. *abbr.* Department of Transportation.

dotage (**doh**-tij). **1.** Senility; feebleness of a person's mind in old age. **2.** Foolish affection; excessive fondness.

double-bill, *vb.* To charge two different clients or customers the same charge; to charge two different customers for services rendered to each customer at the same time.

double-breasting. *Labor law.* The practice by a common owner of dividing its employees between two companies, one that is unionized and is party to a collective-bargaining agreement, and one that is nonunion.

double-dipping, *n.* (1975) An act of seeking or accepting essentially the same benefit twice, either from the same source or from two different sources, as in simultaneously accepting retirement and unemployment benefits. — **double-dipper,** *n.*

double-fraction problem. *Oil & gas.* A common ambiguity that arises when the owner of a fractional interest conveys or reserves a fractional interest. • For example, if the owner of an undivided half interest in minerals conveys "an undivided half interest in the minerals," it is unclear whether the intention is to convey the owner's entire half interest or half of the owner's half interest.

double jeopardy. (1847) The fact of being prosecuted or sentenced twice for substantially the same offense.

Double Jeopardy Clause. (1928) The Fifth Amendment provision stating, "nor shall any person be subject for the same offence to be twice put in jeopardy of life or limb."

double patenting. 1. Obtaining two patents covering the same invention. **2.** The issuance or obtaining of a patent for an invention that differs from an already patented invention only in some unpatentable detail.

double standard. (1900) A pair of principles that permits, esp. in a hypocritical way, greater opportunity or greater leniency for one class of people than for another, usu. based on a difference such as gender or race.

dower (**dow**-ər). (14c) At common law, a wife's right, upon her husband's death, to a life estate in one-third of the land that he owned in fee.

election dower. (1883) A widow's right to take a statutory share of her deceased husband's estate if she chooses to reject her share under a will.

Dow Jones Industrial Average. A stock-market-performance indicator that consists of the price movements in the stocks of 30 leading industrial companies in the United States. — Abbr. DJIA.

downsizing. (1975) Reducing the number of employees, usu. to decrease labor costs and to increase efficiency.

Dr. *abbr.* **1.** Debtor. **2.** Doctor.

DR. *abbr.* Disciplinary Rule.

draconian (dray- *or* drə-**koh**-nee-in), *adj.* (18c)(Of a law) harsh; severe.

draft, *n.* (17c) **1.** An unconditional written order signed by one person (the *drawer*) directing another person (the *drawee* or *payor*) to pay a certain sum of money on demand or at a definite time to a third person (the *payee*) or to bearer. • A check is the most common example of a draft.

bank draft. (1835) A draft drawn by one financial institution on another.

documentary draft. (1922) A payment demand conditioned on the presentation of a document, such as a document of title, invoice, certificate, or notice of default.

share draft. (1978) A demand that a member draws against a credit-union share account, payable to a third party. • A share draft is similar to a check that is written to draw funds out of a checking account at a bank.

sight draft. (1842) A draft that is payable on the bearer's demand or on proper presentment to the drawer.

time draft. A draft that contains a specified payment date. UCC § 3-108.

2. The compulsory enlistment of persons into military service. **3.** An initial or preliminary version.

draft, *vb.* (18c) **1.** To write or compose. **2.** To recruit or select (someone).

drafter. (1884) A person who draws or frames a legal document, such as a will, contract, or legislative bill.

drafting. (1878) The practice, technique, or skill involved in preparing legal documents — such as statutes, rules, regulations, contracts, and wills — that set forth the rights, duties, liabilities, and entitlements of persons and legal entities.

drainage district. A political subdivision authorized to levy assessments for making drainage improvements within its area.

drainage rights. The interest that a property owner has in the natural drainage and flow of water on the land.

dram-shop act. (1859) A statute allowing a plaintiff to recover damages from a commercial seller of alcoholic beverages for the plaintiff's injuries caused by a customer's intoxication.

dram-shop liability. (1995) Civil liability of a commercial seller of alcoholic beverages for personal injury caused by an intoxicated customer. • Claims based on a similar type of liability have been brought against private citizens for personal injury caused by an intoxicated social guest.

draw, *vb.* (13c) **1.** To create and sign (a draft) <draw a check to purchase goods>. **2.** To prepare or frame (a legal document) <draw up a will>. **3.** To take out (money) from a bank, treasury, or depository <she drew $6,000 from her account>. **4.** To select (a jury) <the lawyers began voir dire and had soon drawn a jury>.

drawee (draw-**ee**). (18c) The person or entity that a draft is directed to and that is requested to pay the amount stated on it. • The drawee is usu. a bank that is directed to pay a sum of money on an instrument.

drawer. (17c) One who directs a person or entity, usu. a bank, to pay a sum of money stated in an instrument — for example, a person who writes a check; the maker of a note or draft.

drawing lots. (13c) An act of selection or decision-making based on pure chance, with the result depending on the particular lot drawn.

driving under the influence. (1924) The offense of operating a motor vehicle in a physically or mentally impaired condition, esp. after consuming alcohol or drugs. • Generally, this is a lesser offense than driving while intoxicated. But in a few jurisdictions the two are synonymous. — Abbr. DUI.

drug, *n.* (14c) **1.** A substance intended for use in the diagnosis, cure, treatment, or prevention of disease. **2.** A natural or synthetic substance that alters one's perception or consciousness.

generic drug. A drug containing the active ingredients but not necessarily the same excipient substances (such as binders or capsules) as the pioneer drug marketed under a brand name.

drug abuse. The detrimental state produced by the repeated consumption of a narcotic or other potentially dangerous drug, other than as prescribed by a doctor to treat an illness or other medical condition.

drug-assistance program. 1. A governmental program to ensure access to necessary prescription medicines for needy people who are uninsured or underinsured or who otherwise lack health coverage. **2.** Rehabilitative counseling, and monitoring, usu. in a nonresidential setting, for detecting and treating users of illegal drugs.

drug-free zone. (1986) An area in which the possession or distribution of a controlled substance results in an increased penalty.

drug paraphernalia. (1920) *Criminal law.* Any type of equipment, product, or material that is primarily designed or intended for the unlawful use, manufacture, processing, or hiding of a controlled substance.

dry, *adj.* (bef. 12c) **1.** Free from moisture; desiccated <dry land>. **2.** Unfruitful; destitute of profitable interest; nominal <a dry trust>. **3.** (Of a jurisdiction) prohibiting the sale or use of alcoholic beverages <a dry county>.

dry-hole agreement. *Oil & gas.* A support agreement in which the contributing party agrees to make a cash contribution to the drilling party in exchange for geological or drilling information if the well drilled is unproductive.

DTC. *abbr.* Depository Trust Corporation.

dual-capacity doctrine. (1914) The principle that makes an employer — who is normally shielded from tort liability by workers'-compensation laws — liable in tort to an employee if the employer and employee stand in a secondary relationship that confers independent obligations on the employer.

dual citizenship. 1. A person's status as a citizen of two countries, as when the person is born in the United States to parents who are citizens of another country, or one country still recognizes a person as a citizen even though that person has acquired citizenship in another country. **2.** The status of a person who is a citizen of both the United States and the person's country of residence.

dual distributor. (1945) A firm that sells goods simultaneously to buyers on two different levels of the distribution chain; esp., a manufacturer that sells directly to both wholesalers and retailers.

dual-prosecution rule. (1981) The principle that the federal government and a state government may both prosecute a defendant for the same offense because both governments are separate and distinct entities.

dual-purpose doctrine. (1953) The principle that an employer is liable for an employee's injury that occurs during a business trip even though the trip also serves a personal purpose.

dual-sovereignty doctrine. (1957) The rule that the federal and state governments may both prosecute a person for a crime without violating the constitutional protection against double jeopardy, if the person's act violated both jurisdictions' laws.

duces tecum (**d**[y]**oo**-səs **tee**-kəm *also* **tay**-kəm). [Latin] (17c) Bring with you.

due, *adj.* (14c) **1.** Just, proper, regular, and reasonable <due care> <due notice>. **2.** Immediately enforceable <payment is due on delivery>. **3.** Owing or payable; constituting a debt <the tax refund is due from the IRS>.

due deference. The appropriate degree of respect with which a reviewing authority must consider the decision of a primary decision-maker.

due influence. (17c) The sway that one person has over another, esp. as a result of temperate persuasion, argument, or appeal to the person's affections.

duel. (15c) **1.** Trial by Combat. **2.** A single combat; specif., a prearranged combat with deadly weapons fought between two or more persons under prescribed rules, usu. in the presence of at least two witnesses, to resolve a previous quarrel or avenge a deed. • In England and the United States, death resulting from a duel is treated as murder, and seconds may be liable as accessories.

due-on-encumbrance clause. (1971) A mortgage provision giving the lender the option to accelerate the debt if the borrower further mortgages the real estate without the lender's consent.

due-on-sale clause. (1967) A mortgage provision that gives the lender the option to accelerate the debt if the borrower transfers or conveys any part of the mortgaged real estate without the lender's consent.

due posting. (1893) **1.** The stamping and placing of letters or packages in the U.S. mail. **2.** The proper entry of an item into a ledger. **3.** Proper publication; proper placement of an item (such as an announcement) in a particular place, as on a particular wall.

due process. (16c) The conduct of legal proceedings according to established rules and principles for the protection and enforcement of private rights, including notice and the right to a fair hearing before a tribunal with the power to decide the case.

economic substantive due process. (1957) The doctrine that certain social policies, such as the freedom of contract or the right to enjoy property without interference by government regulation, exist in the Due Process Clause of the 14th Amendment, particularly in the words "liberty" and "property."

procedural due process. (1934) The minimal requirements of notice and a hearing guaranteed by the Due Process Clauses of the 5th and 14th Amendments, esp. if the deprivation of a significant life, liberty, or property interest may occur.

substantive due process. (1933) The doctrine that the Due Process Clauses of the 5th and 14th Amendments require legislation to be fair and reasonable in content and to further a legitimate governmental objective.

Due Process Clause. (1890) The constitutional provision that prohibits the government from unfairly or arbitrarily depriving a person of life, liberty, or property. • There are two Due Process Clauses in the U.S. Constitution, one in the 5th Amendment applying to the federal government, and one in the 14th Amendment applying to the states (although the 5th Amendment's Due Process Clause also applies to the states under the incorporation doctrine).

due-process rights. (1930) The rights (as to life, liberty, and property) so fundamentally important as to require compliance with due-process standards of fairness and justice.

DUI. *abbr.* Driving under the influence.

duly, *adv.* In a proper manner; in accordance with legal requirements.

dummy, *adj.* (1846) Sham; make-believe; pretend.

dummy, *n.* (1866) **1.** A party who has no interest in a transaction, but participates to help achieve a legal goal. **2.** A party who purchases property and holds legal title for another.

dumping. (1857) **1.** The act of selling a large quantity of goods at less than fair value. **2.** Selling goods abroad at less than the market price at home. **3.** The disposal of waste matter into the environment.

dun (dən), *vb.* (17c) To demand payment from (a delinquent debtor). — **dun,** *n.*

***Dunaway* hearing.** (1983) *Criminal law.* A pretrial hearing to determine whether evidence was obtained in violation of Fourth Amendment protections against unreasonable search and seizure. • The name derives from *Dunaway v. New York*, 442 U.S. 200, 99 S.Ct. 2249 (1979).

duplicate (**d**[y]**oo**-pli-kit), *n.* (16c) **1.** A reproduction of an original document having the same particulars and effect as the original. See Fed. R. Evid. 101(4). **2.** A new original, made to replace an instrument that has been lost or destroyed. — **duplicate** (**d**[y]**oo**-pli-kit), *adj.*

duplicitous (d[y]oo-**plis**-i-təs), *adj.* **1.** (Of a person) deceitful; double-dealing. **2.** (Of a pleading, esp. an indictment) alleging two or more matters in one plea; characterized by double pleading.

duplicity (d[y]oo-**plis**-i-tee), *n.* (15c) **1.** Deceitfulness; double-dealing. **2.** The charging of the same offense in more than one count of an indictment. **3.** The pleading of two or more distinct grounds of complaint or defense for the same issue. • In criminal procedure, this takes the form of joining two or more offenses in the same count of an indictment.

duration. (14c) **1.** The length of time something lasts. **2.** A length of time; a continuance in time.

durational-residency requirement. (1970) The requirement that one be a state resident for a certain time, such as one year, as a precondition to the exercise of a specified right or privilege. • When applied to voting, this requirement has been held to be an unconstitutional denial of equal protection because it burdens voting rights and impairs the fundamental personal right of travel.

***Duren* test.** (1980) *Constitutional law.* A test to determine whether a jury's composition violates the fair-cross-section requirement and a criminal defendant's Sixth Amendment right to an impartial jury. • Under the test, a constitutional violation occurs if (1) a distinctive group is not fairly and reasonably represented in the jury pool in relation to its population in the community, (2) the underrepresentation is the result of a systematic exclusion of the group from the jury-selection process, and (3) the government cannot reasonably justify the discrepancy. *Duren v. Missouri*, 439 U.S. 357, 99 S.Ct. 664 (1979).

duress (d[y]uu-**res**). (13c) **1.** Strictly, the physical confinement of a person or the detention of a contracting party's property. • In the field of torts, duress is considered a species of fraud in which compulsion takes the place of deceit in causing injury. **2.** Broadly, a threat of harm made to compel a person to do something against his or her will or judgment; esp., a wrongful threat made by one person to compel a manifestation of seeming assent by another person to a transaction without real volition. • A marriage that is induced by duress is generally voidable. **3.** The use or threatened use of unlawful force — usu. that a reasonable person cannot resist — to compel someone to commit an unlawful act. • Duress is a recognized defense to a crime, contractual breach, or tort. See Model Penal Code § 2.09.

economic duress. (1929) An unlawful coercion to perform by threatening financial injury at a time when one cannot exercise free will.

moral duress. An unlawful coercion to perform by unduly influencing or taking advantage of the weak financial position of another. • Moral duress focuses on the inequities of a situation while economic duress focuses on the lack of will or capacity of the person being influenced.

duty. (13c) **1.** A legal obligation that is owed or due to another and that needs to be satisfied; an obligation for which somebody else has a corresponding right.

absolute duty. **1.** A duty to which no corresponding right attaches. **2.** A duty as to which nothing but lapse of time remains necessary to make immediate performance by the promisor obligatory.

delegable duty. (1908) A duty that may be transferred to another to perform.

duty to act. (17c) A duty to take some action to prevent harm to another, and for the failure of which one may be liable depending on the relationship of the parties and the circumstances.

duty to defend. *Insurance.* The obligation of an insurer to provide an insured with a legal defense against claims of liability, within the terms of the policy.

duty to indemnify. An obligation to compensate another for the other's loss.

duty to settle. *Insurance.* The obligation of an insurer to negotiate and settle third-party claims against an insured in good faith.

duty to speak. (16c) A requirement (not strictly a duty) to say something to correct another's false impression.

legal duty. (17c) A duty arising by contract or by operation of law; an obligation the breach of which would give a legal remedy.

nondelegable duty (non-**del**-ə-gə-bəl). (1902) **1.** *Contracts.* A duty that cannot be delegated by a contracting party to a third party. • If a contracting party purports to delegate the duty, the other party can rightfully refuse to accept performance by the third party. **2.** *Torts.* A duty that may be delegated to an independent contractor by a principal, who retains primary (as opposed to vicarious) responsibility if the duty is not properly performed. • For example, a landlord's duty to maintain common areas, though delegated to a service contractor, remains the landlord's responsibility if someone is injured by improper maintenance.

preexisting duty. (1823) A duty that one is already legally bound to perform.

2. Any action, performance, task, or observance owed by a person in an official or fiduciary capacity.

discretionary duty. A duty that allows a person to exercise judgment and choose to perform or not perform.

duty of candor (**kan**-dər). A duty to disclose material facts; esp., a duty of a director seeking shareholder approval of a transaction to disclose to the shareholders all known material facts about the transaction.

duty of good faith and fair dealing. A duty that is implied in some contractual relationships, requiring the parties to deal with each other fairly, so that neither prohibits the other from realizing the agreement's benefits.

duty of loyalty. A person's duty not to engage in self-dealing or otherwise use his or her position to further personal interests rather than those of the beneficiary.

fiduciary duty (fi-**d**[y]**oo**-shee-er-ee). A duty of utmost good faith, trust, confidence, and candor owed by a fiduciary (such as a lawyer or corporate officer) to the beneficiary (such as a lawyer's client or a shareholder); a duty to act with the highest degree of honesty and loyalty toward another person and in the best interests of the other person (such as the duty that one partner owes to another).

ministerial duty. A duty that requires neither the exercise of official discretion nor judgment.

proprietary duty. A duty owed by a governmental entity while engaged in a proprietary, rather than governmental, activity.

3. *Torts.* A legal relationship arising from a standard of care, the violation of which subjects the actor to liability. **4.** A tax imposed on a commodity or transaction, esp. on imports; impost. • A duty in this sense is imposed on things, not persons.

customs duty. A tax levied on an imported or exported commodity; esp., the federal tax levied on goods shipped into the United States.

import duty. A tax on the importation of a product.

duty to mitigate (**mit**-i-gayt). (1891) A nonbreaching party's or tort victim's duty to make reasonable efforts to limit losses resulting from the other party's breach or tort. • Not doing so precludes the party from collecting damages that might have been avoided.

dwell, *vb.* (13c) **1.** To remain; to linger. **2.** To reside in a place permanently or for some period.

dwelling-house. (15c) **1.** The house or other structure in which a person lives; a residence or abode. **2.** *Real estate.* The house and all buildings attached to or connected with the house. **3.** *Criminal law.* A building, a part of a building, a tent, a mobile home, or another enclosed space that is used or intended for use as a human habitation. • The term has referred to connected buildings in the same curtilage but now typically includes only the structures connected either directly with the house or by an enclosed passageway.

DWI. *abbr.* Driving while intoxicated.

DWOP (**dee**-wop *or* **doo**-wop). *abbr.* Dismissal for want of prosecution.

E

EAJA. *abbr.* Equal Access to Justice Act.

earmark, *n.* (16c) **1.** Originally, a mark upon the ear — a mode of marking sheep and other animals. **2.** A mark put on something (such as a coin) to distinguish it from another.

earmark, *vb.* **1.** To mark with an earmark. **2.** To set aside (esp. funds) for a specific purpose or recipient.

earnest, *n.* (13c) **1.** A nominal payment or token act that serves as a pledge or a sign of good faith, esp. as the partial purchase price of property. **2.** earnest money.

earnest money. (16c) A deposit paid (often in escrow) by a prospective buyer (esp. of real estate) to show a good-faith intention to complete the transaction, and ordinarily forfeited if the buyer defaults.

earning capacity. (1872) A person's ability or power to earn money, given the person's talent, skills, training, and experience.

earnings. (16c) Revenue gained from labor or services, from the investment of capital, or from assets.

earnings per share. *Corporations.* A measure of corporate value by which the corporation's net income is divided by the number of outstanding shares of common stock. — Abbr. EPS.

earnout agreement. (1977) An agreement for the sale of a business whereby the buyer first pays an agreed amount up front, leaving the final purchase price to be determined by the business's future profits.

earwitness. (16c) A witness who testifies about something that he or she heard but did not see.

easement (**eez**-mənt). (14c) An interest in land owned by another person, consisting in the right to use or control the land, or an area above or below it, for a specific limited purpose (such as to cross it for access to a public road). • The land benefiting from an easement is called the *dominant estate*; the land burdened by an easement is called the *servient estate.* Unlike a lease or license, an easement may last forever, but it does not give the holder the right to possess, take from, improve, or sell the land.

access easement. (1933) An easement allowing one or more persons to travel across another's land to get to a nearby location, such as a road.

affirmative easement. (1881) An easement that forces the servient-estate owner to permit certain actions by the easement holder, such as discharging water onto the servient estate. Cf. *negative easement.*

apparent easement. (1851) A visually evident easement, such as a paved trail or a sidewalk.

common easement. (18c) An easement allowing the servient landowner to share in the benefit of the easement.

continuous easement. (1863) An easement that may be enjoyed without a deliberate act by the party claiming it, such as an easement for drains, sewer pipes, lateral support of a wall, or light and air. Cf. *discontinuous easement.*

conservation easement. *Property.* A recorded, perpetual, nonpossessory interest in real property held by a government entity or by a qualified nonprofit entity that imposes restrictions or affirmative obligations on the property's owner or lessee to retain or protect natural, scenic, or open-space values of real property, ensure its availability for agricultural, forest, recreational, or open-space use, protect natural resources and habitat, maintain or enhance air or water quality, or preserve the historical, architectural, archeological, or cultural aspects of the real property.

discontinuous easement. (1867) An easement that can be enjoyed only if the party claiming it deliberately acts in some way with regard to the servient estate. • Examples are a right-of-way and the right to draw water. Cf. *continuous easement.*

easement appurtenant. (1810) An easement created to benefit another tract of land, the use of easement being incident to the ownership of that other tract. Cf. *easement in gross.*

easement by estoppel. (1907) A court-ordered easement created from a voluntary servitude after a person, mistakenly believing the servitude to be permanent, acted in reasonable reliance on the mistaken belief.

easement by necessity. (1865) An easement created by operation of law because the easement is indispensable to the reasonable use of nearby property, such as an easement connecting a parcel of land to a road.

easement in gross. (1866) An easement benefiting a particular person and not a particular piece of land. • The beneficiary need not, and usu. does not, own any land adjoining the servient estate. Cf. *easement appurtenant.*

easement of convenience. An easement that increases the facility, comfort, or convenience of enjoying the dominant estate or some right connected with it.

equitable easement. (1869) An implied easement created by equity when adjacent lands have been created out of a larger tract. • Such an easement is usu. created to allow implied privileges to continue.

exclusive easement. An easement that the holder has the sole right to use.

implied easement. (1867) An easement created by law after an owner of two parcels of land uses one parcel to benefit the other to such a degree that, upon the sale of the benefited parcel, the purchaser could reasonably expect the use to be included in the sale.

land-conservation easement. *Property.* An easement arising from an agreement between a landowner and a land trust to provide for the protection of the land in its natural state while perhaps also allowing the property to be used for agricultural or low-impact recreational activities. • The easement runs with the land.

light-and-air easement. (1940) A negative easement preventing an adjoining landowner from constructing a building that would prevent light or air from reaching the dominant estate.

mineral easement. An easement that permits the holder to enter the property to remove minerals from it.

negative easement. (1861) An easement that prohibits the servient-estate owner from doing something, such as building an obstruction. Cf. *affirmative easement.*

prescriptive easement. (1838) An easement created from an open, adverse, and continuous use over a statutory period.

quasi-easement. **1.** An easement-like right occurring when both tracts of land are owned by the same person. • A quasi-easement may become a true easement if the landowner sells one of the tracts. **2.** An obligation or license that relates to land but that is not a true easement — for example, a landowner's obligation to maintain the fence between the landowner's tract and someone else's tract.

solar easement. (1982) An easement created to protect the dominant estate's exposure to direct sunlight.

timber easement. An easement that permits the holder to cut and remove timber from another's property.

EAT. *abbr.* Earnings after taxes.

eavesdropping. (17c) The act of secretly listening to the private conversation of others without their consent.

ebb and flow. (bef. 12c) The coming and going of the tides. • This expression was formerly used to denote the limits of admiralty jurisdiction. The tidewater limitation was abandoned in *The Genesee Chief v. Fitzhugh*, 53 U.S. (12 How.) 443 (1851).

EBIT. *abbr.* Earnings before interest and taxes.

ECJ. *abbr.* European Court of Justice.

ECOA. *abbr.* Equal Credit Opportunity Act.

e-commerce. (1993) The practice of buying and selling goods and services through online consumer services on the Internet. • The *e*, a shortened form of *electronic*, has become a popular prefix for other terms associated with electronic transactions.

economic discrimination. (1919) Any form of discrimination within the field of commerce, such as boycotting a particular product or price-fixing.

economic indicator. (1903) A statistical measure (such as housing starts) used to describe the state of the economy or to predict its direction.

economic life. The duration of an asset's profitability, usu. shorter than its physical life.

economic loss. (1905) A monetary loss such as lost wages or lost profits. • The term usu. refers to a type of damages recoverable in a lawsuit. For example, in a products-liability suit, economic loss includes the cost of repair or replacement of defective property, as well as commercial loss for the property's inadequate value and consequent loss of profits or use.

economic-loss rule. (1976) *Torts.* The principle that a plaintiff cannot sue in tort to recover for purely monetary loss — as opposed to physical injury or property damage — caused by the defendant. • Many states recognize an exception to this rule when the defendant commits fraud or negligent misrepresentation, or when a special relationship exists between the parties (such as an attorney–client relationship).

economic-realities test. (1956) A method by which a court determines the true nature of a business transaction or situation by examining the totality of the commercial circumstances.

economics. The social science dealing with the production, distribution, and consumption of goods and services.

economic-substance doctrine. *Tax.* The principle that a transaction must be treated as a sham for tax purposes if (1) the transaction has no genuine business purpose, and (2) there is no reasonable possibility that it will generate a profit in the absence of tax benefits.

economy. (15c) **1.** The management or administration of the wealth and resources of a community (such as a city, state, or country). **2.** The sociopolitical organization of a community's wealth and resources. **3.** Restrained, thrifty, or sparing use of resources; efficiency.

economy of scale. (*usu. pl.*) A decline in a product's per-unit production cost resulting from increased output, usu. due to increased production facilities; savings resulting from the greater efficiency of large-scale processes.

e-contract, *n.* **1.** Point-and-click agreement. **2.** Any type of contract formed in the course of e-commerce by (1) the interaction of two or more individuals using electronic means, such as e-mail, (2) the interaction of an individual with an electronic agent, such as a computer program, or (3) the interaction of at least two electronic agents that are programmed to recognize the existence of a contract.

E.D. *abbr.* Eastern District, in reference to U.S. judicial districts.

EDI agreement. *abbr.* Electronic Data Interchange agreement; an agreement that governs the transfer or exchange of data, such as purchase orders, between parties by computer.

educational institution. 1. A school, seminary, college, university, or other educational facility, though not necessarily a chartered institution. **2.** As used in a zoning ordinance, all buildings and grounds necessary to accomplish the full scope of educational instruction, including those things essential to mental, moral, and physical development.

EEC. *abbr.* European Economic Community.

EEOC. *abbr.* Equal Employment Opportunity Commission.

effect, *n.* (14c) **1.** Something produced by an agent or cause; a result, outcome, or consequence. **2.** The result that an instrument between parties will produce on their relative rights, or that a statute will produce on existing law, as discovered from the language used, the forms employed, or other materials for construing it.

effect, *vb.* (16c) To bring about; to make happen.

effective date. (1909) The date on which a statute, contract, insurance policy, or other such instrument becomes enforceable or otherwise takes effect. • This date sometimes differs from the date on which the instrument was enacted or signed.

effects, *n. pl.* (17c) Movable property; goods.

personal effects. (1818) Items of a personal character; esp., personal property owned by a decedent at the time of death.

efficient-breach theory. (1980) *Contracts.* The view that a party should be allowed to breach a contract and pay damages, if doing so would be more economically efficient than performing under the contract.

effluent (**ef**-loo-ənt), *n.* (1859) Liquid waste that is discharged into a river, lake, or other body of water.

effluxion of time (i-**fluk**-shən). (17c) The expiration of a lease term resulting from the passage of time rather than from a specific action or event.

EFT. *abbr.* Electronic funds transfer.

e.g. *abbr.* [Latin *exempli gratia*] (17c) For example <an intentional tort, e.g., battery or false imprisonment>.

egg donation. *Family law.* A type of assisted-reproductive therapy in which eggs are removed from one woman and transplanted into the uterus of another woman who carries and delivers the child. • In egg donation, the egg is usu. fertilized in vitro.

eggshell-skull rule. (1961) *Torts.* The principle that a defendant is liable for a plaintiff's unforeseeable and uncommon reactions to the defendant's negligent or intentional act. • Under this rule, for example, if one person negligently scrapes another who turns out to be a hemophiliac, the negligent defendant is liable for the full extent of the plaintiff's injuries even though the harm to another plaintiff would have been minor.

egregious (i-**gree**-jəs), *adj.* (16c) Extremely or remarkably bad; flagrant.

egress (**ee**-gres). (16c) **1.** The act of going out or leaving. **2.** The right or ability to leave; a way of exit. Cf. INGRESS.

EIC. *abbr.* Earned-income credit.

Eighteenth Amendment. The constitutional amendment — ratified in 1919 and repealed by the 21st Amendment in 1933 — that prohibited the manufacture, sale, transportation, and possession of alcoholic beverages in the United States.

Eighth Amendment. The constitutional amendment, ratified as part of the Bill of Rights in 1791, prohibiting excessive bail, excessive fines, and cruel and unusual punishment.

EIS. *abbr.* Environmental-impact statement.

eject, *vb.* (15c) **1.** To cast or throw out. **2.** To oust or dispossess; to put or turn out of possession. **3.** To expel or thrust out forcibly (e.g., disorderly patrons). — **ejector,** *vb.*

ejection, *n.* (16c) An expulsion by action of law or by actual or threatened physical force.

ejectment. (16c) **1.** The ejection of an owner or occupier from property. **2.** A legal action by which a person wrongfully ejected from property seeks to recover possession, damages, and costs. **3.** The writ by which such an action is begun. • The essential allegations in an action for ejectment are that (1) the plaintiff has title to the land, (2) the plaintiff has been wrongfully dispossessed or ousted, and (3) the plaintiff has suffered damages.

equitable ejectment. (1820) A proceeding brought to enforce specific performance of a contract for the sale of land and for other purposes. • Though in the form of an ejectment action, this proceeding is in reality a substitute for a bill in equity.

justice ejectment. (1900) A statutory proceeding to evict a tenant who has held over after termination of the lease or breach of its conditions.

ejectment bill. (18c) *Equity practice.* A bill in equity brought to recover real property and an accounting of rents and profits, without setting out a distinct ground of equity jurisdiction (and thus demurrable).

ejector, *n.* (17c) One who ejects, puts out, or dispossesses another.

ejusdem generis (ee-**jəs**-dəm **jen**-ə-ris *also* ee-**joos**- *or* ee-**yoos**-). [Latin "of the same kind or class"] (17c) A canon of construction holding that when a general word or phrase follows a list of specifics, the general word or phrase will be interpreted to include only items of the same class as those listed.

elder law. (1986) The field of law dealing with the elderly, including such issues as estate planning, retirement benefits, social security, age discrimination, and healthcare.

election, *n.* (13c) **1.** The exercise of a choice; esp., the act of choosing from several possible rights or remedies in a way that precludes the use of other rights or remedies. **2.** The doctrine by which a person is compelled to choose between accepting a benefit under a legal instrument and retaining some property right to which the person is already entitled; an obligation imposed on a party to choose between alternative rights or claims, so that the party is entitled to enjoy only one. **3.** The process of selecting a person to occupy an office (usu. a public office), membership, award, or other title or status. — **elect,** *vb.* — **elective,** *adj.*

general election. **1.** An election that occurs at a regular interval of time. **2.** An election for all seats, as contrasted with a by-election.

municipal election. The election of municipal officers.

off-year election. An election conducted at a time other than the presidential election year.

primary election. A preliminary election in which a political party's registered voters nominate the candidate who will run in the general election. — Often shortened to *primary.*

recall election. An election in which voters have the opportunity to remove a public official from office.

runoff election. An election held after a general election, in which the two candidates who received the most votes — neither of whom received a majority — run against each other so that the winner can be determined.

special election. An election that occurs in an interim between general elections, usu. to fill a sudden vacancy in office.

election, doctrine of. A doctrine holding that when a person has contracted with an agent without knowing of the agency and later learns of the principal's identity, the person may enforce the contract against either the agent or the principal, but not both.

election board. **1.** A panel of inspectors or commissioners appointed for each election precinct to determine voter qualification, to supervise the polling, and often to ascertain and report the results. **2.** A local agency charged with conducting elections.

election contest. A challenge by an election's loser against the winner, calling for an analysis of the election returns, which may include reviewing voter qualifications or re-counting the ballots.

election fraud. (18c) Illegal conduct committed in an election, usu. in the form of fraudulent voting. • Examples include voting twice, voting under another person's name (usu. a deceased person), or voting while ineligible.

election judge. A person appointed to supervise an election at the precinct level; a local representative of an election board.

election of remedies. (18c) **1.** A claimant's act of choosing between two or more concurrent but inconsistent remedies based on a single set of facts. **2.** The affirmative defense barring a litigant from pursuing a remedy inconsistent with another remedy already pursued, when that other remedy has given the litigant an advantage over, or has damaged, the opposing party. • This doctrine has largely fallen into disrepute and is now rarely applied. **3.** The affirmative defense that a claimant cannot simultaneously recover damages based on two different liability findings if the injury is the same for both claims, thus creating a double recovery.

elective office. An office that is filled by popular election rather than by appointment.

elective share. (1931) *Wills & estates.* The percentage of a deceased spouse's estate, set by statute, that a surviving spouse (or sometimes a child) may choose to receive instead of taking under a will or in the event of being unjustifiably disinherited.

elector. (15c) **1.** A member of the electoral college chosen to elect the U.S. President and Vice President. **2.** A voter. **3.** A person who chooses between alternative rights or claims.

electoral college. (*often cap.*) (17c) The body of electors chosen from each state to formally elect the U.S. President and Vice President by casting votes based on the popular vote.

electoral process. (1851) **1.** The method by which a person is elected to public office in a democratic society. **2.** The taking and counting of votes.

electric chair. (1889) A chair that is wired so that electrodes can be fastened to a condemned person's body and a lethal charge passed through the body for the purpose of carrying out a death penalty.

electronic agent. Any electronic or automated means, such as a computer program, that can independently initiate or respond to an action or message without a human's review.

electronic transaction. (1975) A transaction formed by electronic messages in which the messages of one or both parties will not be reviewed by an individual as an expected step in forming a contract. UCC § 2A-102(a)(16).

elements of crime. (1909) The constituent parts of a crime — usu. consisting of the actus reus, mens rea, and causation — that the prosecution must prove to sustain a conviction. • The term is more broadly defined by the Model Penal Code in § 1.13(9) to refer to each component of the actus reus, causation, the mens rea, any grading factors, and the negative of any defense.

Eleventh Amendment. The constitutional amendment, ratified in 1795, prohibiting a federal court from hearing an action against a state by a person who is not a citizen of that state.

eligible, *adj.* (15c) Fit and proper to be selected or to receive a benefit; legally qualified for an office, privilege, or status. — **eligibility,** *n.*

elisor (i-**lɪ**-zər). (17c) A person appointed by a court to assemble a jury, serve a writ, or perform other duties of the sheriff or coroner if either is disqualified. — Also spelled *eslisor.*

Elkins Act. A 1903 federal law that strengthened the Interstate Commerce Act by prohibiting rebates and other forms of preferential treatment to large carriers. 49 USCA §§ 41–43 (superseded).

eloign (i-**loyn**), *vb.* (15c) **1.** To remove (a person or property) from a court's or sheriff's jurisdiction. **2.** To remove to a distance; conceal. — **eloigner,** *n.*

eloignment (i-**loyn**-mənt), *n.* (17c) The getting of a thing or person out of the way, or removing it to a distance, so as to be out of reach.

eluviation (i-loo-vee-**ay**-shən). (1899) Movement of soil caused by excessive water in the soil.

e-mail, *n.* (1982) A communication exchanged between people by computer, through either a local area network or the Internet. — **e-mail,** *vb.*

emancipate, *vb.* (17c) **1.** To set free from legal, social, or political restraint; esp., to free from slavery or bondage. **2.** To release (a child) from the control, support, and responsibility of a parent or guardian. — **emancipative, emancipatory,** *adj.* — **emancipator,** *n.*

emancipation. (17c) **1.** The act by which one who was under another's power and control is freed. **2.** A surrender and renunciation of the correlative rights and duties concerning the care, custody, and earnings of a child; the act by which a parent (historically a father) frees a child and gives the child the right to his or her own earnings.

Emancipation Proclamation. An executive proclamation, issued by President Abraham Lincoln on January 1, 1863, declaring that all persons held in slavery in designated states and districts were freed.

embargo, *n.* (16c) **1.** A government's detention of an offending nation's private ships found in the ports of the aggrieved nation. **2.** A nation's detention of all ships in its own ports, including its own, to promote safety and to preclude transportation to an offending nation. **3.** The unilateral or collective restrictions on the import or export of goods, materials, capital, or services into or from a specific country or group of countries for political or security reasons. **4.** The conscription of private property for governmental use, such as to transport troops. **5.** A temporary prohibition on disclosure. — **embargo,** *vb.*

embassy. (1534) **1.** The building in which a diplomatic body is located; esp., the residence of the ambassador. **2.** A body of diplomatic representatives headed by an ambassador; a diplomatic mission on the ambassadorial level. **3.** The mission, business, and function of an ambassador.

embezzlement, *n.* (15c) The fraudulent taking of personal property with which one has been entrusted, esp. as a fiduciary. • The criminal intent for embezzlement — unlike larceny and false pretenses — arises after taking possession (not before or during the taking). — **embezzle,** *vb.* — **embezzler,** *n.*

emblem. (15c) **1.** A flag, armorial bearing, or other symbol of a country, organization, or movement. **2.** Loosely, something that is used to symbolize something else.

embodied technology. *Intellectual property.* Know-how or knowledge that is manifest in products and equipment, including software.

embodiment. *Patents.* **1.** The tangible manifestation of an invention. **2.** The method for using this tangible form. **3.** The part of a patent application or patent that describes a concrete manifestation of the invention.

embracery (im-**brays**-ə-ree), *n.* (15c) The attempt to corrupt or wrongfully influence a judge or juror, esp. by threats or bribery.

embryo (**em**-bree-oh). A developing but unborn or unhatched animal; esp., an unborn human from conception until the development of organs (i.e., until about the eighth week of pregnancy).

emendation (ee-men-**day**-shən). (16c) Correction or revision, esp. of a text. — **emend** (i-**mend**), *vb.* (15c).

emergency doctrine. (1929) **1.** A legal principle exempting a person from the ordinary standard of reasonable care if that person acted instinctively to meet a sudden and urgent need for aid. **2.** A legal principle by which consent to medical treatment in a dire situation is inferred when neither the patient nor a responsible party can consent but a reasonable person would do so. **3.** The principle that a police officer may conduct a search without a warrant if the officer has probable cause and reasonably believes that immediate action is needed to protect life or property.

emigrant (**em**-ə-grənt), *n.* (18c) One who leaves his or her country for any reason with the intent to establish a permanent residence elsewhere. Cf. IMMIGRANT.

emigration (em-ə-**gray**-shən), *n.* (17c) The act of leaving a country with the intent not to return and to reside elsewhere. Cf. IMMIGRATION. — **emigrate,** *vb.*

emigré (**em**-ə-gray *or* em-ə-**gray**), *n.* [French] (18c) One who is forced to leave his or her country for political reasons.

eminent domain. (18c) The inherent power of a governmental entity to take privately owned property, esp. land, and convert it to public use, subject to reasonable compensation for the taking.

Eminent Domain Clause. The Fifth Amendment provision providing that private property cannot be taken for public use without just compensation.

emissary. (17c) One sent on a special mission as another's agent or representative, esp. to promote a cause or to gain information.

emit, *vb.* (16c) **1.** To give off or discharge into the air. **2.** To issue with authority. — **emission,** *n.*

emolument (i-**mol**-yə-mənt), *n.* (15c) (*usu. pl.*) Any advantage, profit, or gain received as a result of one's employment or one's holding of office.

Emoluments Clause. (1991) The clause of the United States Constitution preventing members of Congress from continuing to serve in Congress after accepting an appointment to another federal office, and also prohibiting such an appointment if the office was created or its emoluments increased while the

Senator or Representative served in Congress. U.S. Const. art. I, § 6, cl. 2.

emotional distress. (1933) A highly unpleasant mental reaction (such as anguish, grief, fright, humiliation, or fury) that results from another person's conduct; emotional pain and suffering.

empanel, *vb.* (15c) To swear in (a jury) to try an issue or case. — **empanelment, empaneling,** *n.*

emphasis added. (1945) A citation signal indicating that the writer quoting another's words has italicized or otherwise emphasized some of them.

empirical (em-**pir**-i-kəl), *adj.* (16c) Of, relating to, or based on experience, experiment, or observation <the expert's theory was not supported by empirical data>.

employ, *vb.* (15c) **1.** To make use of. **2.** To hire. **3.** To use as an agent or substitute in transacting business. **4.** To commission and entrust with the performance of certain acts or functions or with the management of one's affairs.

employee. (1822) A person who works in the service of another person (the employer) under an express or implied contract of hire, under which the employer has the right to control the details of work performance.

borrowed employee. (1932) An employee whose services are, with the employee's consent, lent to another employer who temporarily assumes control over the employee's work.

probationary employee. A recently hired employee whose ability and performance are being evaluated during a trial period of employment.

statutory employee. *Workers' compensation.* An employee who is covered, or required to be covered, by the employer's workers'-compensation insurance and who therefore has no independent tort claim against the employer for unintentional injuries suffered on the job.

employee benefit plan. (1942) A written stock-purchase, savings, option, bonus, stock-appreciation, profit-sharing, thrift, incentive, pension, or similar plan solely for employees, officers, and advisers of a company. • The term includes an employee-welfare benefit plan, an employee-pension benefit plan, or a combination of those two. See 29 USCA § 1002(3). But the term excludes any plan, fund, or program (other than an apprenticeship or training program) in which no employees are plan participants.

Employee Retirement Income Security Act. A federal statute that regulates private pension plans and employee benefit plans and that established the Pension Benefit Guaranty Corporation. 29 USCA §§ 1001 et seq. — Abbr. ERISA.

employer. (16c) A person who controls and directs a worker under an express or implied contract of hire and who pays the worker's salary or wages.

employment. (15c) **1.** The relationship between master and servant. **2.** The act of employing. **3.** The state of being employed. **4.** Work for which one has been hired and is being paid by an employer.

casual employment. Work that is occasional, irregular, or for a short time — often associated with day labor.

employment at will. Employment that is usu. undertaken without a contract and that may be terminated at any time, by either the employer or the employee, without cause.

permanent employment. Work that, under a contract, is to continue indefinitely until either party wishes to terminate it for some legitimate reason.

seasonal employment. An occupation possible only during limited parts of the year, such as a summer-camp counselor, a baseball-park vendor, or a shopping-mall Santa.

temporary employment. Work for a specific need or fixed duration, usu. agreed upon beforehand.

enablement. *Patents.* The disclosure in a patent application; specif. the description of the subject matter clear and complete enough to teach a person of ordinary skill in the art how to make and use the invention.

enact, *vb.* (15c) **1.** To make into law by authoritative act; to pass. **2.** (Of a statute) to provide. — **enactor,** *n.*

enacting words. The statutory phrasing denoting that an act is taking effect as law. • The most common enacting words are *Be it enacted that* . . . .

enactment, *n.* (18c) **1.** The action or process of making into law. **2.** A statute.

en banc (en **bangk** *or* on **bongk**). [Law French "on the bench"] *adv.* & *adj.* (1863) With all judges present and participating; in full court.

enclosure. (15c) **1.** Something enclosed in a parcel or envelope. **2.** Land surrounded by some visible obstruction; CLOSE (1). **3.** An artificial fence around one's estate.

encourage, *vb.* (15c) *Criminal law.* To instigate; to incite to action; to embolden; to help.

encroach, *vb.* (16c) **1.** To enter by gradual steps or stealth into the possessions or rights of another; to trespass or intrude. **2.** To gain or intrude unlawfully upon another's lands, property, or authority.

encroachment, *n.* (16c) **1.** An infringement of another's rights. **2.** An interference with or intrusion onto another's property.

encumbrance, *n.* (16c) A claim or liability that is attached to property or some other right and that may lessen its value, such as a lien or mortgage; any property right that is not an ownership interest. • An encumbrance cannot defeat the transfer of possession, but it remains after the property or right is transferred. — **encumber,** *vb.*

encumbrancer. (1858) One having a legal claim, such as a lien or mortgage, against property.

endangerment, *n.* (17c) The act or an instance of putting someone or something in danger; exposure to peril or harm. — **endanger,** *vb.*

endenizen (en-**den**-ə-zən), *vb.* (16c) To recognize as a legal resident; to naturalize.

endnote. (1926) A note that, instead of appearing at the bottom of the page (as a footnote does), appears at the end of the book, chapter, or paper.

endorsement, *n.* (16c) **1.** INDORSEMENT. **2.** An amendment to an insurance policy; a rider. — **endorse,** *vb.* — **endorseable,** *adj.*

endowment. (15c) A gift of money or property to an institution (such as a university) for a specific purpose, esp. one in which the principal is kept intact indefinitely and only the interest income from that principal is used. — **endow,** *vb.* (14c)

end position. (1964) One's legal and financial position on the signing of a contract, including the choices now available, such as renewal and renegotiation.

enemy. (13c) **1.** One who opposes or inflicts injury on another; an antagonist. **2.** An opposing military force. **3.** A state with which another state is at war. **4.** A person possessing the nationality of the state with which one is at war. **5.** A foreign state that is openly hostile to another whose position is being considered.

public enemy. (16c) **1.** A notorious criminal who is a menace to society; esp., one who seems more or less immune from successful prosecution. **2.** ENEMY (3). **3.** A social, health, or economic condition or problem that affects the public at large and is difficult to control.

enfeoff (en-**fef** *or* en-**feef**), *vb.* (15c) To put (a person) in legal possession of a freehold interest; to transfer a fief to.

enfeoffment (en-**fef**-mənt *or* en-**feef**-), *n.* (15c) **1.** At common law, the act or process of transferring possession and ownership of an estate in land. **2.** The property or estate so transferred. **3.** The instrument or deed by which one obtains such property or estate.

enforce, *vb.* (14c) **1.** To give force or effect to (a law, etc.); to compel obedience to. **2.** Loosely, to compel a person to pay damages for not complying with (a contract). — **enforcement,** *n.* (15c)

Enforcement of Foreign Judgments Act. A uniform law, adopted by most states, that gives the holder of a foreign judgment essentially the same rights to levy and execute on the judgment as the holder of a domestic judgment. • The Act defines a *foreign judgment* as any judgment, decree, or order (of a court in the United States or of any other court) that is entitled to full faith and credit in the state.

enforcement power. (1939) The authority by which Congress may enforce a particular constitutional amendment's provisions by appropriate legislation. • Enforcement power is granted to Congress under the 13th, 14th, 15th, 19th, 23rd, 24th, and 26th Amendments.

enfranchise, *vb.* (15c) **1.** To grant voting rights or other rights of citizenship to (a person or class). **2.** To set free, as from slavery. — **enfranchisement** (en-**fran**-chiz-mənt *or* -chɪz-mənt), *n.* (16c)

engagement, *n.* (17c) **1.** A contract or agreement involving mutual promises. **2.** An agreement to marry; the period after which a couple has agreed to marry but before they do so. — **engage,** *vb.* (15c).

engagement letter. A document identifying the scope of a professional's services to a client and outlining the respective duties and responsibilities of both.

engagement slip. (1933) A note sent by a lawyer to a court informing the court that the lawyer is professionally engaged in a second court on a given day and thus cannot appear before the first court on that day as scheduled. • The term is used in Pennsylvania.

engross, *vb.* (15c) **1.** *Hist.* To handwrite (a document, esp. a deed) in a style characterized by large letters. **2.** To prepare a copy of (a legal document, such as a deed) for execution. **3.** To prepare a copy of (a bill or mandate) before a final legislative vote. **4.** To absorb or fully occupy. — **engrossment,** *n.*

enhanced, *adj.* Made greater; increased <an enhanced sentence>.

enjoin, *vb.* (13c) **1.** To legally prohibit or restrain by injunction. **2.** To prescribe, mandate, or strongly encourage. — **enjoinment** (for sense 1), *n.* — **enjoinder** (for sense 2), *n.* — **enjoinable,** *adj.*

enjoy, *vb.* (15c) To have, possess, and use (something) with satisfaction; to occupy or have the benefit of (property).

enjoyment, *n.* (16c) **1.** Possession and use, esp. of rights or property. **2.** The exercise of a right.

adverse enjoyment. (18c) The possession or use of land under a claim of right against the property owner.

beneficial enjoyment. (18c) The possession and benefit of land or other property, but without legal title.

present enjoyment. (18c) The immediate possession and use of land or other property.

quiet enjoyment. (18c) The possession of land with the assurance that the possession will not be disturbed by a superior title.

enlarge, *vb.* (14c) **1.** To increase in size or extend in scope or duration <the court

enlarged the time allotted for closing arguments>. **2.** To free from custody or imprisonment <at common law, an action for escape lay when a prisoner was wrongly enlarged>. — **enlargement,** *n.*

enlargement of time. (18c) A usu. court-ordered extension of the time allowed to perform an action, esp. a procedural one.

enlistment, *n.* (18c) Voluntary entry into a branch of the armed services. — **enlist,** *vb.*

en masse (en **mas**). [French] (18c) In a mass; in a large group all at once; all together.

Enoch Arden law (**ee**-nək **ahrd**-ən). (1923) A statute that grants a divorce or an exemption from liability so that a person can remarry when his or her spouse has been absent without explanation for a specified number of years (usu. five or seven).

enrichment. (17c) The receipt of a benefit.

enroll, *vb.* (14c) **1.** To register or transcribe (a legal document, as a deed) into an official record on execution. **2.** To prepare (a bill passed by the legislature) for the executive's signature. — **enrollment,** *n.* — **enrolled,** *adj.*

enrolled agent. One who, though neither a certified public accountant nor an attorney, has been admitted to practice before the IRS, either by passing an examination or by working for the IRS in a technical area for at least five years.

enrolled-bill rule. (1914) The conclusive presumption that a statute, once formalized, appears precisely as the legislature intended, thereby preventing any challenge to the drafting of the bill.

entail, *n.* (14c) A fee abridged or limited to the owner's issue or class of issue rather than descending to all the heirs. — **entail,** *vb.* (14c) — **entailed,** *adj.*

enter, *vb.* (13c) **1.** To come or go into; esp., to go onto (real property) by right of entry so as to take possession <the landlord entered the defaulting tenant's premises>. **2.** To put formally before a court or on the record <the defendant entered a plea of no contest>. **3.** To become a party to <they entered into an agreement>.

enterprise, *n.* (15c) **1.** An organization or venture, esp. for business purposes. **2.** Under federal anti-racketeering law, an individual, partnership, corporation, association, union, other legal entity, or group of individuals associated in fact, although not a legal entity.

entertain, *vb.* (15c) **1.** To bear in mind or consider; esp., to give judicial consideration to. **2.** To amuse or please. **3.** To receive (a person) as a guest or provide hospitality to (a person). **4.** *Parliamentary law.* To recognize and state (a motion); to receive and take into consideration.

entertainment law. (1953) The field of law dealing with the legal and business issues in the entertainment industry (such as film, music, and theater), and involving the representation of artists and producers, the negotiation of contracts, and the protection of intellectual-property rights.

entice, *vb.* (14c) To lure or induce; esp., to wrongfully solicit (a person) to do something. — **enticement,** *n.* (14c).

entire-agreement clause. (1960) **1.** Integration clause. **2.** A provision in an insurance contract stating that the entire agreement between the insured and insurer is contained in the contract, often including the application (if attached), declarations, insuring agreement, exclusions, conditions, and endorsements.

entire-controversy doctrine. (1970) The principle that a plaintiff or defendant who does not assert all claims or defenses related to the controversy in a legal proceeding is not entitled to assert those claims or defenses in a later proceeding.

entirety (en-**tɪ**-ər-tee). (16c) **1.** The whole, as opposed to a moiety or part. **2.** Something (such as certain judgments and contracts) that the law considers incapable of being divided into parts.

entirety clause. *Oil & gas.* A mineral-lease or deed provision specifying that royalties must be apportioned if the property is subdivided after the lease is granted.

entitlement. (19c) An absolute right to a (usu. monetary) benefit, such as social security, granted immediately upon meeting a legal requirement.

entitlement program. A government program guaranteeing certain benefits, such as financial aid or government-provided services, to people or entities that meet the criteria set by law.

entity. An organization (such as a business or a governmental unit) that has a legal identity apart from its members or owners.

corporate entity. A corporation's status as an organization existing independently of its shareholders. • As a separate entity, a corporation can, in its own name, sue and be sued, lend and borrow money, and buy, sell, lease, and mortgage property.

public entity. A governmental entity, such as a state government or one of its political subdivisions.

entity assumption. (1972) The presumption that a business is a unit separate from its owners and from other firms.

entity theory of partnership. (1916) The theory that a partnership is an entity with a legal existence apart from the partners who make it up.

entrapment, *n.* (1899) **1.** A law-enforcement officer's or government agent's inducement of a person to commit a crime, by means of fraud or undue persuasion, in an attempt to later bring a criminal prosecution against that person. **2.** The affirmative defense of having been so induced. • To establish entrapment (in most states), the defendant must show that he or she would not have committed the crime but for the fraud or undue persuasion. — **entrap,** *vb.*

entrepreneur (on-trə-prə-**nər** *or* -**noor**), *n.* (19c) One who initiates and assumes the financial risks of a new enterprise and who usu. undertakes its management.

entrust, *vb.* (16c) To give (a person) the responsibility for something, usu. after establishing a confidential relationship. — **entrustment,** *n.*

entry, *n.* (13c) **1.** The act, right, or privilege of entering real property.

lawful entry. (17c) **1.** The entry onto real property by a person not in possession, under a claim or color of right, and without force or fraud. **2.** The entry of premises under a search warrant.

open entry. (18c) A conspicuous entry onto real property to take possession; an entry that is neither clandestine nor carried out by secret artifice or stratagem and that (by law in some states) is accomplished in the presence of two witnesses.

unlawful entry. (17c) **1.** The crime of entering another's real property, by fraud or other illegal means, without the owner's consent. **2.** An alien's crossing of a border into a country without proper documents.

2. An item written in a record; a notation. **3.** The placement of something before the court or on the record. **4.** *Copyright.* The deposit of a title of work with the Register of Copyrights to secure its protection. **5.** *Immigration.* Any entrance of an alien into the United States, whether voluntary or involuntary. **6.** *Criminal law.* The unlawful coming into a building to commit a crime.

entry of judgment. (17c) The ministerial recording of a court's final decision, usu. by noting it in a judgment book or civil docket.

enumerate (i-**n**[y]**oo**-mə-rayt), *vb.* To count off or designate one by one; to list. — **enumeration,** *n.*

enunciate (i-**nən**-see-ayt), *vb.* (17c) **1.** To state publicly; to announce or proclaim. **2.** To articulate or pronounce. — **enunciation,** *n.*

en ventre sa mere (on **von**-trə sa **mair**). [Law French "in utero"] (18c)(Of a fetus) in the mother's womb <child *en ventre sa mere*>. • This phrase refers to an unborn child, usu. in the context of a discussion of that child's rights.

en vie (on **vee**). [Law French "in life"] Alive.

environmental crime. (1972) *Environmental law.* A statutory offense involving harm to the environment, such as a violation of the criminal provisions in the Clean Air Act Amendments of 1970, the Federal Water Pollution Control Act of 1972 (commonly called the Clean Water Act), or the Endangered Species Act of 1973.

environmental effect. (1967) *Environmental law.* A natural or artificial disturbance of the physical, chemical, or biological components that make up the environment.

environmental-impact statement. (1971) *Environmental law.* **1.** A document that the National Environmental Policy Act (42 USCA § 4332(2)(c)) requires a federal agency to produce for a major project or legislative proposal so that better decisions can be made about the positive and negative environmental effects of an undertaking. **2.** In some states, a public document used by a government agency to analyze the significant environmental effects of a proposed project, to identify alternatives, and to disclose possible ways to reduce or avoid possible environmental damage. — Abbr. EIS.

environmental law. (1971) The field of law dealing with the maintenance and protection of the environment, including preventive measures such as the requirements of environmental-impact statements, as well as measures to assign liability and provide cleanup for incidents that harm the environment.

Environmental Protection Agency. An independent federal agency in the executive branch responsible for setting pollution-control standards in the areas of air, water, solid waste, pesticides, radiation, and toxic materials; enforcing laws enacted to protect the environment; and coordinating the antipollution efforts of state and local governments. — Abbr. EPA.

envoy (**en**-voy). (17c) **1.** A high-ranking diplomat sent to a foreign country to execute a special mission or to serve as a permanent diplomatic representative. **2.** A messenger or representative.

eo instante (**ee**-oh in-**stan**-tee). [Latin] At that very instant.

E.O.M. *abbr.* End of month. • This appears as a payment term in some sales contracts.

eo nomine (**ee**-oh **nahm**-ə-nee). [Latin] (17c) By or in that name.

EPA. *abbr.* Environmental Protection Agency.

e pluribus unum (ee **ploor**-ə-bəs [y]**oo**-nəm). [Latin] One out of many. • This is the motto on the official seal of the United States and on several U.S. coins.

equal-access rule. (1989) *Criminal law.* The doctrine that contraband found on a defendant's premises will not support a conviction if other persons have the same access to the premises as the defendant. • To invoke this defense successfully, the defendant must show that other persons did in fact have equal access to the premises; speculative evidence that trespassers might have come onto the premises will not bar a conviction.

Equal Access to Justice Act. A 1980 federal statute that allows a prevailing party in certain actions against the government to recover attorney's fees and expert-witness fees. — Abbr. EAJA.

Equal Credit Opportunity Act. A federal statute that prohibits creditors from discriminating against credit applicants on the basis of race, color, religion, national origin, age, sex, or marital status with respect to any aspect of a credit transaction. 15 USCA §§ 1691(a)–(f). — Abbr. ECOA.

Equal Employment Opportunity Commission. An independent federal commission that investigates claims of employment discrimination based on race, color, religion, sex, national origin, or age and enforces antidiscrimination statutes through lawsuits. • It was created by Title VII of the Civil Rights Act of 1964. The EEOC encourages mediation and other nonlitigious means of resolving employment disputes. A claimant must file a charge of discrimination with the EEOC before pursuing a claim under Title VII of the Civil Rights Act and certain other employment-related statutes. — Abbr. EEOC.

equal-footing doctrine. (1949) The principle that a state admitted to the Union after 1789 enters with the same rights, sovereignty, and jurisdiction within its borders as did the original 13 states.

equality before the law. (18c) The status or condition of being treated fairly according to regularly established norms of justice; esp., in British constitutional law, the notion that all persons are subject to the ordinary law of the land administered by the ordinary law courts, that officials and others are not exempt from the general duty of obedience to the law, that discretionary governmental powers must not be abused, and that the task of superintending the operation of law rests with an impartial, independent judiciary.

equalization, *n.* (18c) **1.** The raising or lowering of assessed values to achieve conformity with values in surrounding areas. **2.** *Tax.* The adjustment of an assessment or tax to create a rate uniform with another.

equalization board. (1875) A local governmental agency responsible for adjusting the tax rates in different districts to ensure an equitable distribution of the tax burden.

equally divided. (16c) **1.** (Of property) apportioned per capita — not per stirpes — among heirs on the testator's death. **2.** (Of a court, legislature, or other group) having the same number of votes on each side of an issue or dispute.

Equal Pay Act. A federal law mandating that all who perform substantially the same work must be paid equally. 29 USCA § 206.

equal protection. (1866) The 14th Amendment guarantee that the government must treat a person or class of persons the same as it treats other persons or classes in like circumstances. • In today's constitutional jurisprudence, equal protection means that legislation that discriminates must have a rational basis for doing so. And if the legislation affects a fundamental right (such as the right to vote) or involves a suspect classification (such as race), it is unconstitutional unless it can withstand strict scrutiny.

Equal Protection Clause. (1899) The 14th Amendment provision requiring the states to give similarly situated persons or classes similar treatment under the law.

Equal Time Act. A federal law requiring that a broadcasting-facility licensee who permits a legally qualified candidate for public office to use the facility for broadcasting must afford an equal opportunity to all other candidates for the office. 47 USCA § 315.

equipment, *n.* (17c) The articles or implements used for a specific purpose or activity (esp. a business operation). • Under the UCC, *equipment* includes goods if (1) the goods are used in or bought for a business enterprise (including farming or a profession) or by a debtor that is a nonprofit organization or a governmental subdivision or agency, and (2) the goods are not inventory, farm products, or consumer goods. UCC § 9-102(a)(33).

equitable (**ek**-wi-tə-bəl), *adj.* (16c) **1.** Just; consistent with principles of justice and right. **2.** Existing in equity; available or sustainable by an action in equity, or under the rules and principles of equity.

equitable-adjustment theory. (1979) The doctrine that in settling a federal contract dispute, the contracting officer should make a fair adjustment within a reasonable time before the contractor has to settle with its subcontractors, suppliers, and other creditors.

equitable distribution. (1893) *Family law.* The division of marital property by a court in a divorce proceeding, under statutory guidelines that provide for a fair, but not necessarily equal, allocation of the property between the spouses. • With equitable distribution, when a marriage ends in divorce, property acquired during the marriage is divided equitably between the spouses regardless of who holds title to the property.

equitable recoupment. (1878) A principle that diminishes a party's right to recover a debt to the extent that the party holds money or property of the debtor to which the party has no right.

equitable right to setoff. (1895) The right to cancel cross-demands, usu. used by a bank to take from a customer's deposit accounts the amount equal to the customer's debts that have matured and that are owed to that bank.

equitable tolling. (1967) **1.** The doctrine that the statute of limitations will not bar a claim if the plaintiff, despite diligent efforts, did not discover the injury until after the limitations period had expired. **2.** The doctrine that if a plaintiff files a suit first in one court and then refiles in another, the statute of limitations does not run while the litigation is pending in the first court if various requirements are met.

equity, *n.* (14c) **1.** Fairness; impartiality; evenhanded dealing. **2.** The body of principles constituting what is fair and right; natural law. **3.** The recourse to principles of justice to correct or supplement the law as applied to particular circumstances. **4.** The system of law or body of principles originating in the English Court of Chancery and superseding the common and statute law (together called "law" in the narrower sense) when the two conflict. **5.** A right, interest, or remedy recognizable by a court of equity.

contravening equity (kon-trə-**veen**-ing). (1888) A right or interest that is inconsistent with or contrary to a right sought to be enforced.

countervailing equity (kown-tər-**vayl**-ing). (1824) A contrary and balancing equity, equally deserving of consideration.

latent equity (**lay**-tənt). (18c) An equitable claim or right known only by the parties for and against whom it exists, or that has been concealed from one who is interested in the subject matter.

perfect equity. (1821) An equitable title or right that, to be a legal title, lacks only the formal conveyance or other investiture that would make it cognizable at law; esp., the equity of a real-estate purchaser who has paid the full amount due but has not yet received a deed.

6. The right to decide matters in equity; equity jurisdiction. **7.** The amount by which the value of or an interest in property exceeds secured claims or liens; the difference between the value of the property and all encumbrances upon it. **8.** An ownership interest in property, esp. in a business. **9.** A share in a publicly traded company.

equity of exoneration (eg-zon-ə-**ray**-shən). The right of a person who is secondarily liable on a debt to make the primarily liable party discharge the debt or reimburse any payment that the secondarily liable person has made.

equity of partners. The right of each partner to have the firm's property applied to the firm's debts.

equity of redemption. *Real estate.* The right of a mortgagor in default to recover property before a foreclosure sale by paying the principal, interest, and other costs that are due.

equity of subrogation. (1850) The right of a person who is secondarily liable on a debt, and who pays the debt, to personally enforce any right that the original creditor could have pursued against the debtor, including the right to foreclose on any security held by the creditor and any right that the creditor may have to contribution from others who are liable for the debt.

equity-of-the-statute rule. (1959) In statutory construction, the principle that a statute should be interpreted according to the legislators' purpose and intent, even if this interpretation goes beyond the literal meaning of the text.

equity participation. (1947) The inclusion of a lender in the equity ownership of a project as a condition of the lender's granting a loan.

equity ratio. 1. The percentage relationship between a purchaser's equity value (esp. the amount of a down payment) and the property value. **2.** The measure of a shareholder's equity divided by total equity.

equity to a settlement. (1838) A wife's equitable right, arising when her husband sues in equity for the reduction of her equitable estate to his own possession, to have all or part of that estate settled upon herself and her children.

equivocal (i-**kwiv**-ə-kəl), *adj.* (17c) **1.** Of doubtful character; questionable. **2.** Having more than one meaning or sense; ambiguous.

erase, *vb.* (14c) **1.** To rub or scrape out (something written); to obliterate. **2.** To obliterate (recorded material). **3.** To seal (criminal records) from disclosure. — **erasure,** *n.*

ergo (**ər**-goh *or* **air**-goh), *adv.* [Latin] Therefore; thus.

***Erie* doctrine** (**eer**-ee). (1943) The principle that a federal court exercising diversity jurisdiction over a case that does not involve a federal question must apply the substantive law of the state where the court sits. *Erie R.R. v. Tompkins*, 304 U.S. 64, 58 S.Ct. 817 (1938).

ERISA (ee- *or* ə-**ris**-ə). *abbr.* Employee Retirement Income Security Act.

erosion. (1841) The wearing away of something by action of the elements; esp., the gradual eating away of soil by the operation of currents or tides.

err (ər), *vb.* (14c) To make an error; to be incorrect or mistaken.

errant (**er**-ənt), *adj.* (14c) **1.** Fallible; incorrect; straying from what is proper <an errant judicial holding>. **2.** Traveling <a knight errant>.

errata sheet. (1932) An attachment to a deposition transcript containing the deponent's corrections upon reading the transcript and the reasons for those corrections.

erratum (i-**ray**-təm *or* i-**rah**-təm), *n.* [Latin "error"] (16c) An error that needs correction. Pl. **errata** (i-**ray**-tə *or* i-**rah**-tə).

error, *n.* (13c) **1.** An assertion or belief that does not conform to objective reality; a belief that what is false is true or that what is true is false; MISTAKE.

error in corpore (**kor**-pə-ree). (18c) A mistake involving the identity of a particular object, as when a party buys a horse believing it to be the one that the party had already examined and ridden, when in fact it is a different horse.

error in negotio (ni-**goh**-shee-oh). (1944) A mistake about the type of contract that the parties actually wanted to enter.

error in qualitate (kwah-lə-**tay**-tee). A mistake affecting the quality of the contractual object.

error in quantitate (kwahn-tə-**tay**-tee). A mistake affecting the amount of the contractual object.

2. A mistake of law or of fact in a tribunal's judgment, opinion, or order.

assigned error. An alleged error that occurred in a lower court and is pointed out in an appellate brief as grounds for reversal.

Caldwell error. The constitutionally impermissible error of resting a death sentence on a determination made by a sentencer who has been led to believe that the responsibility for determining the appropriateness of the defendant's death sentence lies elsewhere. *Caldwell v. Mississippi*, 472 U.S. 320, 105 S.Ct. 2633 (1985).

clear error. (18c) A trial judge's decision or action that appears to a reviewing court to have been unquestionably erroneous.

clerical error. (18c) An error resulting from a minor mistake or inadvertence, esp. in writing or copying something on the record, and not from judicial reasoning or determination.

cross-error. (1838) An error brought by the party responding to a writ of error.

cumulative error. The prejudicial effect of two or more trial errors that may have been harmless individually.

harmless error. (1851) An error that does not affect a party's substantive rights or the case's outcome. • A harmless error is not grounds for reversal.

invited error. (1893) An error that a party cannot complain of on appeal because the party, through conduct, encouraged or prompted the trial court to make the erroneous ruling.

manifest constitutional error. (1985) An error by the trial court that has an identifiably negative impact on the trial to such a degree that the constitutional rights of a party are compromised.

manifest error. (18c) An error that is plain and indisputable, and that amounts to a complete disregard of the controlling law or the credible evidence in the record.

plain error. (1801) An error that is so obvious and prejudicial that an appellate court should address it despite the parties' failure to raise a proper objection at trial.

reversible error. (1855) An error that affects a party's substantive rights or the case's outcome, and thus is grounds for reversal if the party properly objected at trial.

substantial error. An error that affects a party's substantive rights or the outcome of the case. • A substantial error may require reversal on appeal.

3. An appeal <a proceeding in error>.

escalator clause. (1930) **1.** A contractual provision that makes pricing flexible by increasing or decreasing the contract price according to changing market conditions, such as higher or lower taxes or operating costs. **2.** A provision in a divorce decree or divorce agreement providing for the automatic increase of alimony payments upon the occurrence of any of various triggering events, such as cost-of-living increases or an increase in the obligor's salary. • Escalation clauses for child support are often unenforceable. **3.** *Oil & gas.* A provision in a long-term gas contract allowing the base price of the gas to be adjusted as the market changes.

escape, *n.* (14c) **1.** The act or an instance of breaking free from confinement, restraint, or an obligation. **2.** An unlawful departure from legal custody without the use of force. **3.** At common law, a criminal offense committed by a peace officer who allows a prisoner to depart unlawfully from legal custody. — **escape,** *vb.*

escape clause. (1945) A contractual provision that allows a party to avoid performance under specified conditions; specif., an insurance-policy provision — usu. contained in the "other insurance" section of the policy — requiring the insurer to provide coverage only if no other coverage is available.

escheat (es-**cheet**), *n.* (14c) **1.** Reversion of property (esp. real property) to the state upon the death of an owner who has neither a will nor any legal heirs. **2.** Property that has so reverted. — **escheat,** *vb.* — **escheatable,** *adj.*

escrow (**es**-kroh), *n.* (16c) **1.** A legal document or property delivered by a promisor to a third party to be held by the third party for a given amount of time or until the occurrence of a condition, at which time the third party is to hand over the document or property to the promisee <the agent received the escrow two weeks before the closing date>. **2.** An account held in trust or as security <the earnest money is in escrow>. **3.** The holder of such a document, property, or deposit <the attorney performed the function of escrow>. **4.** The general arrangement under which a legal document or property is delivered to a third person until the occurrence of a condition <creating an escrow>. — **escrow,** *vb.*

escrow agreement. (1882) The instructions given to the third-party depositary of an escrow.

espionage (**es**-pee-ə-nahzh). (18c) The practice of using spies to collect information about what another government or company is doing or plans to do.

industrial espionage. (1962) *Intellectual property.* One company's spying on another to steal trade secrets or other proprietary information.

Espionage Act. A federal law that criminalizes and punishes espionage, spying, and related crimes. 18 USCA §§ 793 et seq.

espousals (ə-**spow**-zəlz), *n.* (14c) Mutual promises between a man and a woman to marry one another.

esquire (**es**-kwɪr *or* e-**skwɪr**). (15c) (*usu. cap. as an honorific*) A title of courtesy commonly appended after the name of a lawyer. — Abbr. Esq.

establish, *vb.* (14c) **1.** To settle, make, or fix firmly; to enact permanently. **2.** To make or form; to bring about or into existence. **3.** To prove; to convince.

establishment, *n.* (15c) **1.** The act of establishing; the state or condition of being established. **2.** An institution or place of business. **3.** A group of people who are in power or who control or exercise great influence over something.

Establishment Clause. (1959) The First Amendment provision that prohibits the federal and state governments from establishing an official religion, or from favoring or disfavoring one view of religion over another. U.S. Const. amend. I.

estate. (15c) **1.** The amount, degree, nature, and quality of a person's interest in land or other property; esp., a real-estate interest that may become possessory, the ownership being measured in terms of duration.

concurrent estate. (18c) Ownership or possession of property by two or more persons at the same time. • In modern practice, there are three types of concurrent estates: tenancy in common, joint tenancy, and tenancy by the entirety.

contingent estate. (17c) An estate that vests only if a specified event does or does not happen.

defeasible estate. (17c) An estate that may come to an end before its maximum duration has run because of the operation of a special limitation, a condition subsequent, or an executory limitation. • If an estate is defeasible by operation of a special limitation, it is called a *determinable estate.*

derivative estate. (18c) A particular interest that has been carved out of another, larger estate.

determinable estate. (17c) An estate that is defeasible by operation of a special limitation.

equitable estate. (17c) An estate recognized in equity, such as a trust beneficiary's interest.

equitable life estate. An interest in real or personal property that lasts for the life of the holder of the estate and that is equitable as opposed to legal in its creation. • An example is a life estate held by a trust beneficiary.

estate on condition. (18c) An estate that vests, is modified, or is defeated upon the occurrence or nonoccurrence of some specified event. • While an estate on limitation can revert without any action by the grantor or the grantor's heirs, an estate on condition requires the entry of the grantor or the grantor's heirs to end the estate whenever the condition occurs.

estate on condition expressed. (18c) A contingent estate in which the condition upon which the estate will fail is stated explicitly in the granting instrument.

estate on condition implied. (18c) A contingent estate having some condition that is so inseparable from the estate's essence that it need not be expressed in words.

estate on limitation. (18c) An estate that automatically reverts back to the grantor according to a provision, usu. regarding the passage of a determined time period, designated by words such as "during," "while," and "as long as."

joint estate. (15c) Any of the following five types of estates: (1) a joint tenancy, (2) a tenancy in common, (3) an estate in coparcenary (a common-law estate in which coheirs hold as tenants in common), (4) a tenancy by the entirety, or (5) an estate in partnership.

life estate. (18c) An estate held only for the duration of a specified person's life, usu. the possessor's.

life estate pur autre vie (pər **oh**-trə **vee**). (1888) A life estate for which the measuring life — the life whose duration determines the duration of the estate — is someone's other than the possessor's.

next eventual estate. (1836) An estate taking effect upon an event that terminates the accumulation of undisposed rents and profits; an estate taking effect when the existing estate terminates.

possessory estate. (18c) An estate giving the holder the right to possess the property, with or without an ownership interest in the property.

vested estate. (18c) An estate with a present right of enjoyment or a present fixed right of future enjoyment.

2. All that a person or entity owns, including both real and personal property.

3. The property that one leaves after death; the collective assets and liabilities of a dead person.

decedent's estate. (18c) The real and personal property that a person possesses at the time of death and that passes to the heirs or testamentary beneficiaries.

residuary estate. (18c) The part of a decedent's estate remaining after payment of all debts, expenses, statutory claims, taxes, and testamentary gifts (special, general, and demonstrative) have been made.

taxable estate. (18c) A decedent's gross estate reduced by allowable deductions (such as administration costs and ESOP deductions). IRC (26 USCA) § 2051. • The taxable estate is the amount that is subject to the federal unified transfer tax at death.

4. A tract of land, esp. one affected by an easement.

dominant estate. (18c) An estate that benefits from an easement. Cf. *servient estate.*

servient estate (**sər**-vee-ənt). (18c) An estate burdened by an easement. Cf. *dominant estate.*

estate freeze. (1986) An estate-planning maneuver whereby an owner of a closely held business exchanges common stock for dividend-paying preferred stock and gives the common stock to his or her children, thus seeking to guarantee an income in retirement and to avoid estate tax on future appreciation in the business's value.

estate in lands. (16c) **1.** Property that one has in lands, tenements, or hereditaments. **2.** The conditions or circumstances under which a tenant stands in relation to the leased property.

estate planning. (1938) **1.** The preparation for the distribution and management of a person's estate at death through the use of wills, trusts, insurance policies, and other arrangements, esp. to reduce administration costs and transfer-tax liability. **2.** A branch of law that involves the arrangement of a person's estate, taking into account the laws of wills, taxes, insurance, property, and trusts.

estop (e-**stop**), *vb.* (15c) To bar or prevent by estoppel.

estoppel (e-**stop**-əl), *n.* (16c) **1.** A bar that prevents one from asserting a claim or right that contradicts what one has said or done before or what has been legally established as true. **2.** A bar that prevents the relitigation of issues. **3.** An affirmative defense alleging good-faith reliance on a misleading representation and an injury or detrimental change in position resulting from that reliance.

equitable estoppel. (18c) A defensive doctrine preventing one party from taking unfair advantage of another when, through false language or conduct, the person to be estopped has induced another person to act in a certain way, with the result that the other person has been injured in some way.

estoppel by contract. A bar that prevents a person from denying a term, fact, or performance arising from a contract that the person has entered into.

estoppel by deed. Estoppel that prevents a party to a deed from denying anything recited in that deed if the party has induced another to accept or act under the deed; esp., estoppel that prevents a grantor of a warranty deed, who does not have title at the time of the conveyance but who later acquires title, from denying that he or she had title at the time of the transfer.

estoppel by election. The intentional exercise of a choice between inconsistent alternatives that bars the person making the choice from the benefits of the one not selected.

estoppel by laches. (1894) An equitable doctrine by which some courts deny relief to a claimant who has unreasonably delayed or been negligent in asserting a claim.

estoppel by misrepresentation. An estoppel that arises when one makes a false statement that induces another person to believe something and that results in that person's reasonable and detrimental reliance on the belief.

estoppel by negligence. An estoppel arising when a negligent person induces someone to believe certain facts, and then the other person reasonably and detrimentally relies on that belief.

estoppel by representation. An estoppel that arises when one makes a statement or admission that induces another person to believe something and that results in that person's reasonable and detrimental reliance on the belief; esp., equitable estoppel.

estoppel by silence. (1872) Estoppel that arises when a party is under a duty to speak but fails to do so.

judicial estoppel. (1886) Estoppel that prevents a party from contradicting previous declarations made during the same or an earlier proceeding if the change in position would adversely affect the proceeding or constitute a fraud on the court.

legal estoppel. Estoppel recognized in law (as distinguished from equitable estoppel or estoppel in pais), such as an estoppel resulting from a recital or other statement in a deed or official record, and precluding any denial or assertion concerning a fact.

promissory estoppel. (1924) The principle that a promise made without consideration may nonetheless be enforced to prevent injustice if the promisor should have reasonably expected the promisee to rely on the promise and if the promisee did actually rely on the promise to his or her detriment.

quasi-estoppel. (1823) An equitable doctrine preventing one from repudiating an act or assertion if it would harm another who reasonably relied on the act or assertion.

technical estoppel. **1.** An estoppel arising from a matter of record or from a deed made by the party who is claimed to be estopped. • Estoppels by deed or by record are called "technical" because the rules of estoppel apply with certainty in appropriate cases. **2.** Collateral estoppel.

estoppel certificate. (1897) A signed statement by a party (such as a tenant or a mortgagee) certifying for another's benefit that certain facts are correct, such as that a lease exists, that there are no defaults, and that rent is paid to a certain date. • A party's delivery of this statement estops that party from later claiming a different state of facts.

estrange, *vb.* **1.** To separate, to keep away (a person or thing), or to keep away from (a person or thing). **2.** To destroy or divert affection, trust, and loyalty. — **estrangement,** *n.*

estreat (e-**street**), *n.* (15c) A copy or duplicate of some original writing or record, esp. of a fine or amercement imposed by a court, extracted from the record, and certified to one who is authorized and required to collect it.

estreat, *vb.* (16c) To take out a forfeited recognizance from the recordings of a court and return it to the court to be prosecuted.

estrepe (e-**streep**), *vb.* (17c) **1.** To strip; to despoil; to commit waste upon an estate, as by cutting down trees or removing buildings. **2.** To injure the value of a reversionary interest by stripping or spoiling the estate.

estrepement (e-**streep**-mənt), *n.* (16c) A species of aggravated waste, by stripping or devastating land to the injury of the reversioner, esp. pending a suit for possession.

et al. (et **al** *or* **ahl**). *abbr.* **1.** [Latin *et alii* or *et alia*] And other persons <the office of Thomas Webb et al.>. **2.** [Latin *et alibi*] And elsewhere.

et cetera (et **set**-ər-ə). [Latin "and others"] (12c) And other things. • The term usu. indicates additional, unspecified items in a series. — Abbr. etc.

ethical, *adj.* (16c) **1.** Of or relating to moral obligations that one person owes another; esp., in law, of or relating to legal ethics. **2.** In conformity with moral norms or standards of professional conduct.

ethical consideration. (*often cap.*) A structural component of the ethical canons set forth in the legal profession's Model Code of Professional Responsibility, containing a goal or ethical principle intended to guide a lawyer's professional conduct. • Ethical considerations are often used in the interpretation and application of the Model Rules of Professional Conduct. — Abbr. EC.

ethical wall. (1988) A screening mechanism maintained by an organization, esp. a law firm, to protect client confidences from improper disclosure to lawyers or staff who are not involved in a particular representation.

ethnic cleansing. (1991) The officially sanctioned forcible and systematic diminution or elimination of targeted ethnic minorities from a geographic area, usu. by confiscating real and personal property, ordering or condoning mass murders and mass rapes, and expelling the survivors.

et seq. (et **sek**). *abbr.* [Latin *et sequens* "and the following one," *et sequentes* (masc.) "and the following ones," or *et sequentia* (neuter) "and the following ones"] (18c) And those (pages or sections) that follow <11 USCA §§ 101 et seq.>.

et uxor (et **ək**-sor). [Latin] *Archaic.* And wife. • This phrase was formerly common in case names and legal documents (esp. abstracts of title) involving a husband and wife jointly. It usu. appears in its abbreviated form, *et ux.* <conveyed the land to Donald Baird *et ux.*>.

EU. *abbr.* European Union.

eureka moment. *Slang.* The instant when an inventor realizes the answer to a question or the significance of a discovery.

euro (**yuur**-oh). (1981) The official currency of most countries in the European Union.

Eurodollar. (1960) United States currency held in a bank outside the U.S., usu. in Europe, and used to settle international transactions.

European Court of Human Rights. The judicial body of the Council of Europe.

European law. (1844) **1.** The law of the European Union. **2.** More broadly, the law of the European Union, together with the conventions of the Council of Europe, including the European Convention on Human Rights. **3.** More broadly still, all the law current in Europe, including the law of European organizations, the North Atlantic Treaty Organization, and all the bilateral and multilateral conventions in effect, as well as European customary law.

European Union. An association of European nations whose purpose is to achieve full economic unity (and eventual political union) by agreeing to eliminate barriers to the free movement of capital, goods, and labor among the member-nations. — Abbr. EU.

euthanasia (yoo-thə-**nay**-zhə), *n.* (1869) The act or practice of causing or hastening the death of a person who suffers from an incurable or terminal disease or condition, esp. a painful one, for reasons of mercy. — **euthanasic** (yoo-thə-**nay**-zik), *adj.*

active euthanasia. Euthanasia performed by a facilitator (such as a healthcare practitioner) who not only provides the means of death but also carries out the final death-causing act.

passive euthanasia. The act of allowing a terminally ill person to die by either withholding or withdrawing life-sustaining support such as a respirator or feeding tube.

voluntary euthanasia. Euthanasia performed with the terminally ill person's consent.

euthanize (**yoo**-thə-nɪz), *vb.* (1873) To put to death by euthanasia. • This term is used chiefly in reference to animals.

evasive, *adj.* (17c) Tending or seeking to evade; elusive; shifting. • If a pleading requiring a response is evasive, the responding party may move for a more definite statement. Fed. R. Civ. P. 12(e).

even date. The same date. • This jargonistic phrase is sometimes used in one instrument to refer to another instrument with the same date, esp. when both relate to the same transaction (as a deed and a mortgage).

evict, *vb.* (15c) **1.** To expel (a person, esp. a tenant), from real property, usu. by legal process. **2.** *Archaic.* To recover (property or title) from a person by legal process. — **evictor,** *n.*

eviction. (16c) The act or process of legally dispossessing a person of land or rental property.

actual eviction. (18c) A physical expulsion of a person from land or rental property.

constructive eviction. (1826) **1.** A landlord's act of making premises unfit for occupancy, often with the result that the tenant is compelled to leave. **2.** The inability of a land purchaser to obtain possession because of paramount outstanding title.

retaliatory eviction. (1966) An eviction, nearly always illegal, commenced in response to a tenant's complaints or involvement in activities with which the landlord does not agree.

summary eviction. (1907) An eviction accomplished through a simplified legal procedure, without the formalities of a full trial.

total eviction. (1832) An eviction that wholly deprives the tenant of any right in the premises.

evidence, *n.* (14c) **1.** Something (including testimony, documents and tangible objects) that tends to prove or disprove the existence of an alleged fact. **2.** The collective mass of things, esp. testimony and exhibits, presented before a tribunal in a given dispute. **3.** The body of law regulating the admissibility of what is offered as proof into the record of a legal proceeding. — **evidence,** *vb.*

admissible evidence. (18c) Evidence that is relevant and is of such a character (e.g., not unfairly prejudicial, based on hearsay, or privileged) that the court should receive it.

best evidence. (17c) Evidence of the highest quality available, as measured by the nature of the case rather than the thing being offered as evidence.

character evidence. (1949) Evidence regarding someone's general personality traits or propensities, of a praiseworthy or blameworthy nature; evidence of a person's moral standing in a community. Fed. R. Evid. 404, 405, 608.

circumstantial evidence. (18c) **1.** Evidence based on inference and not on personal knowledge or observation. **2.** All evidence that is not given by eyewitness testimony.

clear and convincing evidence. (17c) Evidence indicating that the thing to be proved is highly probable or reasonably certain. • This is a greater burden than preponderance of the evidence, the standard applied in most civil trials, but less than evidence beyond a reasonable doubt, the norm for criminal trials.

conclusive evidence. (17c) **1.** Evidence so strong as to overbear any other evidence to the contrary. **2.** Evidence that so preponderates as to oblige a fact-finder to come to a certain conclusion.

concomitant evidence. (17c) Evidence that, at the time of the act, the alleged doer of the act was present and actually did it.

conflicting evidence. (1803) Evidence that comes from different sources and is often irreconcilable.

corroborating evidence. (17c) Evidence that differs from but strengthens or confirms what other evidence shows (esp. that which needs support).

credible evidence. (17c) Evidence that is worthy of belief; trustworthy evidence.

critical evidence. (18c) Evidence strong enough that its presence could tilt a juror's mind. • Under the Due Process Clause, an indigent criminal defendant is usu. entitled to an expert opinion of the merits of critical evidence.

cumulative evidence. (18c) Additional evidence that supports a fact established by the existing evidence (esp. that which does not need further support).

demeanor evidence. (1909) The behavior and appearance of a witness on the witness stand, to be considered by the fact-finder on the issue of credibility.

demonstrative evidence (di-**mon**-strə-tiv). (17c) Physical evidence that one can see and inspect (i.e. an explanatory aid, such as a chart, map, and some computer simulations) and that, while of probative value and usu. offered to clarify testimony, does not play a direct part in the incident in question.

derivative evidence. (1961) Evidence that is discovered as a result of illegally obtained evidence and is therefore inadmissible because of the primary taint.

direct evidence. (16c) Evidence that is based on personal knowledge or observation and that, if true, proves a fact without inference or presumption.

documentary evidence. (18c) Evidence supplied by a writing or other document, which must be authenticated before the evidence is admissible.

evidence-in-chief. (18c) Evidence used by a party in making its case-in-chief.

exclusive evidence. (18c) The only facts that have, or are allowed by law to have, any probative force at all on a particular matter in issue.

exculpatory evidence (ek-**skəl**-pə-tor-ee). (18c) Evidence tending to establish a criminal defendant's innocence. Fed. R. Crim. P. 16. • The prosecution has a duty to disclose exculpatory evidence in its possession or control when the evidence may be material to the outcome of the case.

expert evidence. (16c) Evidence about a scientific, technical, professional, or other specialized issue given by a person qualified to testify because of familiarity with the subject or special training in the field. Fed. R. Evid. 702–705.

extrajudicial evidence. (18c) Evidence that does not come directly under judicial cognizance but nevertheless constitutes an intermediate link between judicial evidence and the fact requiring proof. • It includes all facts that are known to the tribunal only by way of inference from some form of judicial evidence.

extrinsic evidence. (17c) **1.** Evidence relating to a contract but not appearing on the face of the contract because it comes from other sources, such as statements between the parties or the circumstances surrounding the agreement. • Extrinsic evidence is usu. not admissible to contradict or add to the terms of an unambiguous document. **2.** Evidence that is not legitimately before the court. **3.** Evidence that is calculated to impeach a witness's credibility, adduced by means other than cross-examination of the witness. • The means may include evidence in documents and recordings and the testimony of other witnesses. See Fed. R. Evid. 608(b) & note.

fabricated evidence. (18c) False or deceitful evidence that is unlawfully created, usu. after the relevant event, in an attempt to achieve or avoid liability or conviction.

forensic evidence. (18c) Evidence used in court; esp., evidence arrived at by scientific or technical means, such as ballistic or medical evidence.

foundational evidence. (1946) Evidence that determines the admissibility of other evidence.

habit evidence. (1921) Evidence of one's regular response to a repeated specific situation. Fed. R. Evid. 406.

illegally obtained evidence. (1924) Evidence obtained by violating a statute or a person's constitutional or other right, esp. the Fourth Amendment guarantee against unreasonable searches, the Fifth Amendment right to remain silent, or the Sixth Amendment right to counsel.

immaterial evidence. (18c) **1.** Evidence lacking in probative value. **2.** Evidence offered to prove a matter that is not in issue.

impeachment evidence. (1861) Evidence used to undermine a witness's credibility. Fed. R. Evid. 607–610.

incompetent evidence. (18c) Evidence that is for any reason inadmissible.

incriminating evidence. (1878) Evidence tending to establish guilt or from which a fact-trier can infer guilt.

inculpatory evidence (in-**kəl**-pə-tor-ee). (1849) Evidence showing or tending to show one's involvement in a crime or wrong.

indispensable evidence. (18c) Evidence without which a particular fact cannot be proved.

insufficient evidence. (17c) Evidence that is inadequate to prove or support a finding of something.

intrinsic evidence. (17c) **1.** Evidence brought out by the examination of the witness testifying. **2.** Evidence existing within a writing.

irrelevant evidence. Evidence not tending to prove or disprove a matter in issue. Fed. R. Evid. 401–403.

judicial evidence. (17c) Evidence produced in court, consisting of all facts brought to the attention of or admitted into evidence before the tribunal.

legal evidence. (17c) **1.** Admissible evidence. **2.** All admissible evidence, both oral and documentary, of such a character that it reasonably and substantially proves the point rather than merely raising suspicion or conjecture.

material evidence. (17c) Evidence having some logical connection with the facts of consequence or the issues.

mathematical evidence. (18c) **1.** Loosely, evidence that establishes its conclusions with absolute certainty. **2.** Evidence pertaining to mathematical or statistical matters, or probabilities.

medical evidence. (18c) Evidence furnished by a doctor, nurse, or other qualified medical person testifying in a professional capacity as an expert, or by a standard treatise on medicine or surgery.

moral evidence. (17c) Loosely, evidence that depends on a belief, rather than complete and absolute proof. • Generally, moral evidence is testimonial.

multiple evidence. (1926) Evidence with probative or other value on more than one issue but usu. admitted into evidence for one specific purpose. • Impeachment evidence, for example, may not be probative on a particular issue but may nonetheless affect the jury's perceptions of several issues.

negative evidence. (17c) Evidence suggesting that an alleged fact does not exist, such as a witness's testifying that he or she did not see an event occur. • Negative evidence is generally regarded as weaker than positive evidence because a positive assertion that a witness saw an event is a stronger statement than an assertion that a witness did not see it. But a negative assertion will sometimes be considered positive evidence, depending on the witness's opportunity to see the event. For instance, testimony that the witness watched the entire game and saw no riot in the stands is stronger than testimony stating only that the witness did not see a riot.

newly discovered evidence. (18c) Evidence existing at the time of a motion or trial but then unknown to a party, who, upon later discovering it, may assert it as grounds for reconsideration or a new trial. See Fed. R. Civ. P. 60(b).

opinion evidence. (1955) A witness's belief, thought, inference, or conclusion concerning a fact or facts. Fed. R. Evid. 701–705.

original evidence. (18c) A witness's statement that he or she perceived a fact in issue by one of the five senses, or that the witness was in a particular physical or mental state.

parol evidence (pə-**rohl** *or* **par**-əl). (18c) Evidence of oral statements.

partial evidence. (17c) Evidence that establishes one of a series of facts.

preappointed evidence. (1850) Evidence prescribed in advance (as by statute) for the proof of certain facts.

preliminary evidence. (18c) Evidence that is necessary to begin a hearing or trial and that may be received conditionally in anticipation of other evidence linking it to issues in the case. Fed. R. Evid. 104.

presumptive evidence. (17c) **1.** Evidence deemed sufficient to establish another fact unless discredited by other evidence. **2.** *Archaic.* Circumstantial evidence as distinct from testimonial evidence.

prima facie evidence (**prɪ**-mə **fay**-shə). (18c) Evidence that will establish a fact or sustain a judgment unless contradictory evidence is produced.

privileged evidence. (1897) Evidence that is exempt from production to an opposing party or tribunal (with certain, limited exceptions) because it is covered by one or more statutory or common-law protections, such as the attorney–client privilege.

probative evidence (**proh**-bə-tiv). (1877) Evidence that tends to prove or disprove a point in issue.

proffered evidence (**prof**-ərd). (1904) **1.** Evidence that is offered to the court to obtain a ruling on its admissibility. **2.** Evidence whose admissibility depends on the existence or nonexistence of a preliminary fact.

prospectant evidence (prə-**spek**-tənt). (1924) Evidence that, before someone does an act, suggests that the person might or might not do the act. • This evidence typically falls into any of five categories: (1) moral character or disposition, (2) physical and mental capacity, (3) habit or custom, (4) emotion or motive, and (5) plan, design, or intention.

real evidence. (17c) Physical evidence (such as clothing or a knife wound) that itself plays a direct part in the incident in question.

rebuttal evidence. (1859) Evidence offered to disprove or contradict the evidence presented by an opposing party. • Rebuttal evidence is introduced in the rebutting party's answering case; it is not adduced, e.g., through cross-examination during the case-in-chief of the party to be rebutted.

relevant evidence. (18c) Evidence tending to prove or disprove a matter in issue. • Relevant evidence is both probative and material and is admissible unless excluded by a specific statute or rule. Fed. R. Evid. 401–403.

reputation evidence. (1888) Evidence of what one is thought by others to be. • Reputation evidence may be introduced as proof of character when character is in issue or is used circumstantially. Fed. R. Evid. 405(a).

retrospectant evidence (re-trə-**spek**-tənt). (1929) Evidence that, although it occurs after an act has been done, suggests that the alleged doer of the act actually did it.

satisfactory evidence. (17c) Evidence that is sufficient to satisfy an unprejudiced mind seeking the truth.

scientific evidence. (17c) Fact or opinion evidence that purports to draw on specialized knowledge of a science or to rely on scientific principles for its evidentiary value.

secondary evidence. (17c) Evidence that is inferior to the primary or best evidence and that becomes admissible when the primary or best evidence is lost or inaccessible. • Examples include a copy of a lost instrument or testimony regarding a lost instrument's contents.

secret evidence. (1983) Classified information that may be used against a defendant in an immigration proceeding but withheld from the defendant, the defendant's lawyer, and the public on national-security grounds. • The use of secret evidence was made easier under the Anti-Terrorism and Effective Death Penalty Act of 1996.

signature evidence. Highly distinctive evidence of a person's prior bad acts. • While ordinarily inadmissible, signature evidence will be admitted if it shows, for example, that two crimes were committed through the same planning, design, scheme, or modus operandi, and in such a way that the prior act and the current act are uniquely identifiable as those of the defendant. See Fed. R. Evid. 404(b).

slight evidence. (18c) A small quantity of evidence; esp., the small amount of evidence sufficient to remove a presumption from a case or for a rational fact-finder to conclude that something essential has not been established beyond a reasonable doubt.

state's evidence. (1886) Testimony provided by one criminal defendant — under a promise of immunity or reduced sentence — against another criminal defendant.

substantial evidence. (17c) **1.** Evidence that a reasonable mind could accept as adequate to support a conclusion; evidence beyond a scintilla. **2.** The product of adequately controlled investigations, including clinical studies, carried out by qualified experts that establish the effectiveness of a drug under FSA regulations. 21 USCA § 355(e).

substantive evidence (**səb**-stən-tiv). Evidence offered to help establish a fact in issue, as opposed to evidence directed to impeach or to support a witness's credibility.

tainted evidence. (1876) Evidence that is inadmissible because it was directly or indirectly obtained by illegal means.

tangible evidence. Physical evidence that is either real or demonstrative.

testimonial evidence. (1831) A person's testimony offered to prove the truth of the matter asserted; esp., evidence elicited from a witness.

traditionary evidence. (18c) Evidence derived from a deceased person's former statements or reputation. • Traditionary evidence is admissible to prove ancestry, ancient boundaries, or similar facts, usu. when no living witnesses are available to testify.

unwritten evidence. (18c) Evidence given orally, in court or by deposition.

evidence code. A relatively comprehensive set of statutory provisions or rules governing the admissibility of evidence at hearings and trials.

evidence of title. (17c) The means by which the ownership of land is satisfactorily demonstrated within a given jurisdiction.

evidencing feature. *Evidence.* A group of circumstances that, when taken as a whole, form a composite feature that can be reliably associated with a single object. • This term appears more frequently in criminal cases than in civil. In criminal cases, it usu. refers to evidence that establishes a perpetrator's identity, but in civil cases it often refers to evidence that an event did or did not occur.

evidentiary (ev-i-**den**-shə-ree), *adj.* (1810) **1.** Having the quality of evidence; constituting evidence; evidencing. **2.** Pertaining to the rules of evidence or the evidence in a particular case.

evince, *vb.* (17c) To show, indicate, or reveal.

ex. (18c) **1.** Former. **2.** Without. **3.** From. **4.** (*usu. cap.*) *abbr.* Exhibit. **5.** *abbr.* Example.

exaction, *n.* (15c) **1.** The act of demanding more money than is due; extortion. **2.** A fee, reward, or other compensation arbitrarily or wrongfully demanded. — **exact,** *vb.*

examination. (14c) **1.** The questioning of a witness under oath. **2.** *Bankruptcy.* The questioning of a debtor, esp. at the first meeting of creditors, concerning such matters as the bankrupt's debts and assets. **3.** An inquiry made at the U.S. Patent and Trademark Office, upon application for a patent, into the alleged invention's novelty and utility, and whether it interferes with any other pending application or in-force patent. **4.** *Banking.* The government's fact-finding mechanism for determining the soundness of a bank's finances and management. **5.** *Insurance.* A periodic investigation by a state insurance commission into the affairs and soundness of an insurance company licensed in that state. **6.** Preliminary hearing. **7.** A test, such as a bar examination.

examination system. *Patents.* A patent system in which an invention is subjected to official scrutiny to determine whether it qualifies for patent protection.

examiner. (16c) **1.** One authorized to conduct an examination; esp., a person appointed by the court, esp. a court of equity, to administer an oath and take testimony. **2.** A patent officer responsible for determining the patentability of an invention submitted to the patent office. **3.** Medical examiner. **4.** Bank examiner.

examining board. (1851) An appointed group of public officials responsible for conducting the tests required by those applying for occupational and professional licenses.

ex ante (eks **an**-tee), *adj.* & *adv.* [Latin "from before"] (1937) Based on assumption and prediction, on how things appeared beforehand, rather than in hindsight; subjective; prospective <from an *ex ante* perspective>.

ex cathedra (eks kə-**thee**-drə *or* **kath**-ə-drə), *adv.* & *adj.* [Latin "from the chair"] (17c) By virtue of one's high office or position; with authority <ex cathedra pronouncements>.

exception, *n.* (14c) **1.** A formal objection to a court's ruling by a party who wants to preserve an overruled objection or rejected proffer for appeal. • To make an exception or objection, attorneys sometimes say, "I except" or "I object." *Exception* properly refers only to an objection made after an initial objection or proffer is made and overruled. In most courts, an exception is no longer required to preserve the initial objection.

dilatory exception (**dil**-ə-tor-ee). (1822) *Louisiana law.* An exception intended to delay but not dismiss an action.

general exception. (16c) **1.** An objection pointing out a substantive defect in an opponent's pleading, such as the insufficiency of the claim or the court's lack of subject-matter jurisdiction; an objection to a pleading for want of substance. **2.** An objection in which the excepting party does not specify the grounds of the objection.

peremptory exception. (16c) *Louisiana law.* A defensive pleading asserting that no legal remedy exists for the plaintiff's alleged injury, that res judicata or prescription bars the claim, or that an indispensable party has not been included in the litigation.

2. Something that is excluded from a rule's operation.

statutory exception. (18c) A provision in a statute exempting certain persons or conduct from the statute's operation.

3. The retention of an existing right or interest, by and for the grantor, in real property being granted to another. — **except,** *vb.*

exceptionable (ek-**sep**-shən-ə-bəl), *adj.* (17c) Liable to objection; objectionable.

Excessive Fines Clause. (1986) The clause of the Eighth Amendment to the U.S. Constitution prohibiting the imposition of excessive fines.

excess of jurisdiction. (17c) **1.** A court's acting beyond the limits of its power, usu. in one of three ways: (1) when the court has no power to deal with the kind of matter at issue, (2) when the court has no power to deal with the particular person concerned, or (3) when the judgment or order issued is of a kind that the court has no power to issue. **2.** A court's departure from recognized and established requirements of law, despite apparent adherence to procedural form, the effect of which is a deprivation of one's constitutional right.

excess of privilege. (1889) **1.** An excessive publication of a privileged statement — that is, beyond the limits of the privilege. **2.** The improper and malicious use of the privilege to publish a statement.

exchange, *n.* (14c) *Commercial law.* **1.** The act of transferring interests, each in consideration for the other. **2.** Money or negotiable instruments presented as payment; currency. **3.** The interchange or conversion of money. **4.** The payment of a debt using a bill of exchange or credit rather than money. **5.** An organization that brings together buyers and sellers of securities, commodities, and the like to promote uniformity in the customs and usages of merchants, to facilitate the speedy adjustment of business disputes, to gather and disseminate valuable commercial and economic information, and to secure to its members the benefits of cooperation in the furtherance of their legitimate pursuits. **6.** The building or hall where members of an exchange meet every business day to buy and sell for themselves, or as brokers for their customers, for present and future delivery. — **exchange,** *vb.*

excise, *n.* (15c) A tax imposed on the manufacture, sale, or use of goods (such as a cigarette tax), or on an occupation or activity (such as a license tax or an attorney occupation fee).

excited utterance. (1800) A statement about a startling event made under the stress and excitement of the event. • An excited utterance may be admissible as a hearsay exception. Fed. R. Evid. 803(2).

excludable, *adj.* (1916) **1.** (Of evidence) subject to exclusion <excludable hearsay>. **2.** (Of an alien) ineligible for admission or entry into a country.

exclusion, *n.* **1.** *Tax.* An item of income excluded from gross income.

annual exclusion. (1940) The amount allowed as nontaxable gift income during the calendar year. IRC (26 USCA) § 2503.

2. *Evidence.* A trial judge's determination that an item offered as evidence may not be presented to the trier of fact (esp. the jury). **3.** *Insurance.* An insurance-policy provision that excepts certain events or conditions from coverage. — **exclude,** *vb.* — **exclusionary,** *adj.*

exclusionary rule. (1855) **1.** *Evidence.* Any rule that excludes or suppresses evidence <despite many exceptions, hearsay has long been inadmissible under an exclusionary rule>. **2.** *Criminal procedure.* A rule that excludes or suppresses evidence obtained in violation of an accused person's constitutional rights <in accordance with the exclusionary rule, the court did not admit the drugs into evidence because they had been obtained during a warrantless search of the defendant's home>.

exclusive control. (1890) Under the doctrine of res ipsa loquitur, a defendant's sole management of and responsibility for the instrumentality causing harm. • Exclusive control is a prerequisite to the doctrine's applicability.

exclusive-dealing arrangement. (1943) An agreement requiring a buyer to purchase all needed goods or services from one seller.

ex contractu (eks kən-**trak**-t[y]oo). [Latin "from a contract"] Arising from a contract <action *ex contractu*>.

exculpate (**ek**-skəl-payt *or* ek-**skəl**-payt), *vb.* (17c) To free from blame or accusation. — **exculpation** (ek-skəl-**pay**-shən), *n.* — **exculpatory** (ek-**skəl**-pə-tor-ee), *adj.*

exculpatory clause. (1891) A contractual provision relieving a party from liability resulting from a negligent or wrongful act.

exculpatory-no doctrine. (1977) *Criminal law.* The principle that a person cannot be charged with making a false statement for falsely denying guilt in response to an investigator's question. • This doctrine is based on the Fifth Amendment right against self-incrimination. But the U.S. Supreme Court has overruled this doctrine in federal law. *Brogan v. United States*, 522 U.S. 398, 118 S.Ct. 805 (1998).

excusable, *adj.* (14c) (Of an illegal act or omission) not punishable under the specific circumstances.

excuse (ek-**skyoos**), *n.* (14c) **1.** A reason that justifies an act or omission or that relieves a person of a duty. **2.** *Criminal law.* A defense that arises because the defendant is not blameworthy for having acted in a way that would otherwise be criminal. • The following defenses are the traditional excuses: duress, entrapment, infancy, insanity, and involuntary intoxication. — **excuse** (ek-**skyooz**), *vb.* — **excusatory** (ek-**skyooz**-ə-tor-ee), *adj.*

excuss (ek-**skəs**), *vb.* (18c) To seize and detain by law.

ex delicto (eks də-**lik**-toh), *adj. & adv.* [Latin "from a wrong"] Arising from a crime or tort <action *ex delicto*>.

execute, *vb.* (14c) **1.** To perform or complete (a contract or duty). **2.** To change (as a legal interest) from one form to another. **3.** To make (a legal document) valid by signing; to bring (a legal document) into its final, legally enforceable form. **4.** To put to death, esp. by legal sentence. **5.** To enforce and collect on (a money judgment).

executed, *adj.* (16c) **1.** (Of a document) that has been signed <an executed will>. **2.** That has been done, given, or performed <executed consideration>.

execution, *n.* (14c) **1.** The act of carrying out or putting into effect (as a court order or a securities transaction). **2.** Validation of a written instrument, such as a contract or will, by fulfilling the necessary legal requirements. **3.** Judicial enforcement of a money judgment, usu. by seizing and selling the judgment debtor's property. **4.** A court order directing a sheriff or other officer to enforce a judgment, usu. by seizing and selling the judgment debtor's property. **5.** *Criminal law.* The carrying out of a death sentence. — **execute,** *vb.*

execution clause. The part of a deed containing the date, seal (if required), and signatures of the grantor, grantor's spouse, and witnesses.

executioner. (16c) A person who puts another person to death to carry out a death sentence; a person who carries out capital punishment on the state's behalf.

executive, *n.* (18c) **1.** The branch of government responsible for effecting and enforcing laws; the person or persons who constitute this branch.

chief executive. (1876) The head of the executive branch of a government, such as the President of the United States.

2. A corporate officer at the upper levels of management. — **executive,** *adj.*

executive administration. Collectively, high public officials who administer the chief departments of the government.

executive agency. An executive-branch department whose activities are subject to statute and whose contracts are subject to judicial review. • One example is the National Aeronautics and Space Agency.

executive agreement. (1942) An international agreement entered into by the President, without approval by the Senate, and usu. involving routine diplomatic or military matters.

executive branch. (18c) The branch of government charged with administering and carrying out the law; EXECUTIVE (1).

executive director. A salaried employee who serves as an organization's chief administrative and operating officer and heads its professional staff.

executive employee. An employee whose duties include some form of managerial authority and active participation in the control, supervision, and management of the business.

executive order. (1862) An order issued by or on behalf of the President, usu. intended to direct or instruct the actions of executive agencies or government officials, or to set policies for the executive branch to follow. — Abbr. ex. ord.

executive power. (17c) *Constitutional law.* The power to see that the laws are duly executed and enforced. • Under federal law, this power is vested in the President; in the states, it is vested in the governors. The President's enumerated powers are found in the U.S. Constitution, art. II, § 2; governors' executive powers are provided for in state constitutions. The other two great powers of government are the legislative power and the judicial power.

executor, *n.* (13c) **1.** (**ek**-sə-kyoo-tər) One who performs or carries out some act. **2.** (eg-**zek**-yə-tər) A person named by a testator to carry out the provisions in the testator's will. — Abbr. *exor.*

acting executor. (18c) One who assumes the role of executor — usu. temporarily — but is not the legally appointed executor or the executor-in-fact.

executor de son tort (də sawn [*or* son] **tor**[**t**]). [Law French "executor of his own wrong"] (17c) A person who, without legal authority, takes on the responsibility to act as an executor or administrator of a decedent's property, usu. to the detriment of the estate's beneficiaries or creditors.

executor lucratus (loo-**kray**-təs). An executor who has assets of the testator, the latter having become liable by wrongfully interfering with another's property.

general executor. (18c) An executor who has the power to administer a decedent's entire estate until its final settlement.

independent executor. (1877) An executor who, unlike an ordinary executor, can administer the estate with very little supervision by the probate court.

joint executor. (17c) One of two or more persons named in a will as executor of an estate.

limited executor. (18c) An executor whose appointment is restricted in some way, such as time, place, or subject matter.

literary executor. *Copyright.* A limited-purpose executor appointed to manage copyrighted materials in an estate.

special executor. (18c) An executor whose power is limited to a portion of the decedent's estate.

substituted executor. (18c) An executor appointed to act in the place of an executor who cannot or will not perform the required duties.

executory (eg-**zek**-yə-tor-ee), *adj.* (16c) **1.** Taking full effect at a future time <executory judgment>. **2.** To be performed at a future time; yet to be completed <executory contract>.

executory interest. (1833) A future interest, held by a third person, that either cuts off another's interest or begins after the natural termination of a preceding estate.

shifting executory interest. An executory interest that operates in defeasance of an interest created simultaneously in a third person.

springing executory interest. An executory interest that operates in defeasance of an interest left in the transferor.

executory unilateral accord. (1940) An offer to enter a contract; OFFER (2).

exemplar (eg-**zem**-plər *or* -plahr), *n.* (15c) **1.** An ideal or typical example; a standard specimen <handwriting exemplars>. **2.** Nontestimonial identification evidence, such as fingerprints, voiceprints, and DNA samples.

exemplary, *adj.* (16c) **1.** Serving as an ideal example; commendable <exemplary behavior>. **2.** Serving as a warning or deterrent; admonitory <exemplary damages>.

exemplary damages. Punitive damages.

exemplification, *n.* (16c) An official transcript of a public record, authenticated as a true copy for use as evidence. — **exemplify,** *vb.*

exempli gratia (eg-**zem**-plı **gray**-shee-ə *or* ek-**sem**-plee **grah**-tee-ə). [Latin] (17c) For example; for instance. — Abbr. e.g. or (rarely) ex. gr.

exempt, *adj.* (14c) Free or released from a duty or liability to which others are held <persons exempt from military service> <property exempt from

sequestration>. — **exempt,** *vb.* — **exemptive,** *adj.*

exemption. (14c) **1.** Freedom from a duty, liability, or other requirement; an exception. **2.** A privilege given to a judgment debtor by law, allowing the debtor to retain certain property without liability. **3.** *Tax.* An amount allowed as a deduction from adjusted gross income, used to determine taxable income.

dependency exemption. (1920) A tax exemption granted to an individual taxpayer for each dependent whose gross income is less than the exemption amount and for each child who is younger than 19 or, if a student, younger than 24.

personal exemption. (1920) An amount allowed as a deduction from an individual taxpayer's adjusted gross income.

exemption clause. (1840) A contractual provision providing that a party will not be liable for damages for which that party would otherwise have ordinarily been liable.

exemption law. (1839) A law describing what property of a debtor cannot be attached by a judgment creditor or trustee in bankruptcy to satisfy a debt.

exempt organization. An organization that is either partially or completely exempt from federal income taxation.

exempt property. (1839) **1.** A debtor's holdings and possessions that, by law, a creditor cannot attach to satisfy a debt. • All the property that creditors may lawfully reach is known as *nonexempt property.* Many states provide a homestead exemption that excludes a person's house and household items, up to a certain amount, from the liens of most creditors. The purpose of the exemption is to prevent debtors from becoming destitute. **2.** Personal property that a surviving spouse is automatically entitled to receive from the decedent's estate.

exercise, *vb.* (14c) **1.** To make use of; to put into action <exercise the right to vote>. **2.** To implement the terms of; to execute <exercise the option to buy the commodities>. — **exercise,** *n.*

exercise of judgment. (17c) The use of sound discretion — that is, discretion exercised with regard to what is right and equitable rather than arbitrarily or willfully.

ex facie (eks **fay**-shee-ee *or* -shee *or* -shə). [Latin] (1861) *Archaic.* On the face of it; evidently; apparently.

ex facto (eks **fak**-toh). [Latin "from a fact"] From or in consequence of a fact or action; actually; de facto.

ex gratia (eks **gray**-shee-ə *or* **grah**-tee-ə). [Latin "by favor"] (18c) As a favor; not legally necessary.

ex gratia payment. (1916) A payment not legally required; esp., an insurance payment not required to be made under an insurance policy.

exhaustion of remedies. (1876) The doctrine that, if an administrative remedy is provided by statute, a claimant must seek relief first from the administrative body before judicial relief is available.

exhaustion of state remedies. (1944) The doctrine that an available state remedy must be exhausted in certain types of cases before a party can gain access to a federal court.

exhibit, *n.* (17c) **1.** A document, record, or other tangible object formally introduced as evidence in court. **2.** A document attached to and made part of a pleading, motion, contract, or other instrument.

exhibitionism, *n.* (1893) The indecent display of one's body. — **exhibitionist,** *adj.* & *n.*

exhibit list. (1929) **1.** A pretrial filing that identifies by number and description the exhibits a party intends to offer into evidence at trial. **2.** A document prepared during a trial by the clerk or a courtroom deputy to identify by number and description the exhibits that the parties have entered into evidence.

exhumation (eks-hyoo-**may**-shən *or* eg-zyoo-), *n.* (18c) The removal from the earth of something buried, esp. a human corpse; disinterment.

exigency (**ek**-sə-jən-see), *n.* (16c) A state of urgency; a situation requiring immediate action.

exigent, *adj.* (17c) Requiring immediate action or aid; urgent <exigent circumstances>.

exile, *n.* (14c) **1.** Expulsion from a country, esp. from the country of one's origin or longtime residence; banishment. **2.** A person who has been banished. **3.** A prolonged voluntary absence from one's home country. — **exile,** *vb.*

exit, *n.* (16c) **1.** A way out; egress. **2.** In a docket entry, an issuance of something (as a writ or process). • For example, *exit attachment* denotes that a writ of attachment has been issued in the case. — **exit,** *vb.*

ex officio (eks ə-**fish**-ee-oh), *adv.* & *adj.* [Latin] (16c) By virtue or because of an office; by virtue of the authority implied by office.

ex officio justice. (1855) A judge who serves on a commission or board only because the law requires the presence of a judge rather than because the judge was selected for the position.

ex officio service (eks ə-**fish**-ee-oh). (1845) A service that the law imposes on an official by virtue of the office held, such as that of a local justice of the peace to perform marriage ceremonies.

exonerate (eg-**zon**-ə-rayt), *vb.* (16c) **1.** To free from responsibility. **2.** To free from encumbrances. — **exonerative** (eg-**zon**-ər-ay-tiv *or* -ə-tiv), *adj.* — **exoneration** (eg-zon-ə-**ray**-shən). (16c)

ex. ord. (*often cap.*) *abbr.* Executive order.

exordium (eg-**zor**-dee-əm). [Latin] (16c) An introduction in a discourse or writing, esp. in a will. • In a will, the exordium usu. contains statements of the testator's name and capacity to make the will.

ex parte (eks **pahr**-tee), *adv.* [Latin "from the part"] (18c) On or from one party only, usu. without notice to or argument from the adverse party <the judge conducted the hearing ex parte>.

ex parte, *adj.* (17c) Done or made at the instance and for the benefit of one party only, and without notice to, or argument by, any person adversely interested; of or relating to court action taken by one party without notice to the other, usu. for temporary or emergency relief <an ex parte hearing> <an ex parte injunction>. • Despite the traditional one-sidedness of ex parte matters, some courts now require notice to the opposition before what they call an "ex parte hearing." — **ex parte,** *adv.*

expatriate (ek-**spay**-tree-it), *n.* (18c) An expatriated person; esp., a person who lives permanently in a foreign country.

expatriate (ek-**spay**-tree-ayt), *vb.* (1812) **1.** To withdraw (oneself) from residence in or allegiance to one's native country; to leave one's home country to live elsewhere. **2.** To banish or exile (a person). — **expatriation,** *n.*

expectancy, *n.* (1811) **1.** *Property.* An estate with a reversion, a remainder, or an executory interest. **2.** *Wills & estates.* The possibility that an heir apparent, an heir presumptive, or a presumptive next of kin will acquire property by devolution on intestacy, or the possibility that a presumptive beneficiary will acquire property by will. **3.** *Insurance.* The probable number of years in one's life.

expectant, *adj.* (14c) Having a relation to, or being dependent on, a contingency; contingent.

expectation, *n.* (16c) **1.** The act of looking forward; anticipation. **2.** A basis on which something is expected to happen; esp., the prospect of receiving wealth, honors, or the like.

expectation of privacy. (1965) A belief in the existence of the right to be free of governmental intrusion in regard to a particular place or thing.

expediment (ek-**sped**-ə-mənt), *n.* (1848) The whole of one's goods and chattels.

expel, *vb.* (15c) To drive out or away; to eject, esp. with force.

expenditure. (18c) **1.** The act or process of paying out; disbursement. **2.** A sum paid out.

expense, *n.* (14c) An expenditure of money, time, labor, or resources to accomplish a result; esp., a business expenditure chargeable against revenue for a specific period. — **expense,** *vb.*

accrued expense. (1880) An expense incurred but not yet paid.

business expense. (1858) An expense incurred to operate and promote a business; esp., an expenditure made to further the business in the taxable year in which the expense is incurred.

capital expense. (1913) An expense made by a business to provide a long-term benefit; a capital expenditure.

deferred expense. (1925) A cost incurred by a business when the business expects to benefit from that cost over a period beyond the current year.

educational expense. (1882) A deductible expense incurred either to maintain or improve an existing job skill or to meet a legally imposed job requirement.

entertainment expense. An expense incurred while providing entertainment relating directly to or associated with a business purpose.

extraordinary expense. (16c) An unusual or infrequent expense, such as a write-off of goodwill or a large judgment. • As used in a constitutional provision authorizing a state to incur extraordinary expenses, the term denotes an expense for the general welfare compelled by an unforeseen condition such as a natural disaster or war.

funeral expense. (*usu. pl.*) (18c) An expense necessarily and reasonably incurred in procuring the burial, cremation, or other disposition of a corpse, including the funeral or other ceremonial rite, a casket and vault, a monument or tombstone, a burial plot and its care, and a visitation (or wake).

general administrative expense. (*usu. pl.*) (1907) An expense incurred in running a business, as distinguished from an expense incurred in manufacturing or selling; overhead.

medical expense. (1853) **1.** An expense for medical treatment or healthcare, such as drug costs and health-insurance premiums. **2.** (*usu. pl.*) In civil litigation, any one of many possible medical costs that the plaintiff has sustained or reasonably expects to incur because of the defendant's allegedly wrongful act, including charges for visits to physicians' offices, medical procedures, hospital bills, medicine, and recuperative therapy needed in the past and in the future.

moving expense. (1903) An expense incurred in changing one's residence.

operating expense. (1861) An expense incurred in running a business and producing output.

ordinary and necessary expense. (1826) An expense that is normal or usual and helpful or appropriate for the operation of a particular trade or business and that is paid or incurred during the taxable year.

organizational expense. (1941) An expense incurred while setting up a corporation or other entity.

out-of-pocket expense. (1905) An expense paid from one's own funds.

prepaid expense. (1919) An expense (such as rent, interest, or insurance) that is paid before the due date or before a service is rendered.

travel expense. (1905) An expense (such as for meals, lodging, and transportation) incurred while away from home in the pursuit of a trade or business.

expenses of administration. (18c) Expenses incurred by a decedent's representatives in administering the estate.

expenses of receivership. (18c) Expenses incurred by a receiver in conducting the business, including rent and fees incurred by the receiver's counsel and by any master, appraiser, and auditor.

expense stop. (1990) A lease provision establishing the maximum expenses to be paid by the landlord, beyond which the tenant must bear all remaining expenses.

expert, *n.* (16c) A person who, through education or experience, has developed skill or knowledge in a particular subject, so that he or she may form an opinion that will assist the fact-finder. Fed. R. Evid. 702. — **expertise** (ek-spər-**teez**), *n.*

consulting expert. (1897) An expert who, though retained by a party, is not expected to be called as a witness at trial. • A consulting expert's opinions are generally exempt from the scope of discovery. Fed. R. Civ. P. 26(b)(4)(B).

impartial expert. (1870) An expert who is appointed by the court to present an unbiased opinion. Fed. R. Evid. 706.

testifying expert. (1952) An expert who is identified by a party as a potential witness at trial. • As a part of initial disclosures in federal court, a party must provide to all other parties a wide range of information about a testifying expert's qualifications and opinion, including all information that the witness considered in forming the opinion. Fed. R. Civ. P. 26(a)(2)(b).

expiration, *n.* A coming to an end; esp., a formal termination on a closing date. — **expire,** *vb.*

expiration date. (1803) The date on which an offer, option, or the like ceases to exist.

exploitation, *n.* (19c) The act of taking advantage of something; esp., the act of taking unjust advantage of another for one's own benefit. — **exploit,** *vb.* — **exploitative,** *adj.*

export, *n.* (17c) **1.** A product or service created in one country and transported to another.

domestic export. A product originally grown or manufactured in the United States, as distinguished from a product originally imported into the United States and then exported.

2. The process of transporting products or services to another country.

export, *vb.* (15c) **1.** To send or carry abroad. **2.** To send, take, or carry (a good or commodity) out of the country; to transport (merchandise) from one country to another in the course of trade. **3.** To carry out or convey (goods) by sea.

exportation. (17c) The act of sending or carrying goods and merchandise from one country to another.

export declaration. (1920) A document — required by federal law — containing details of an export shipment.

ex post, *adj.* [Latin "from after"] (1937) Based on knowledge and fact; viewed after the fact, in hindsight; objective; retrospective.

ex post facto (eks pohst **fak**-toh), *adj.* (18c) Done or made after the fact; having retroactive force or effect.

ex post facto, *adv.* [Latin "from a thing done afterward"] (17c) After the fact; retroactively.

Ex Post Facto Clause. (1848) One of two clauses in the U.S. Constitution forbidding the enactment of ex post facto laws. U.S. Const. art. I, § 9, cl. 3; art. I, § 10, cl. 1.

ex post facto law. (18c) A law that impermissibly applies retroactively, esp. in a way that negatively affects a person's rights, as by criminalizing an action that was legal when it was committed. • Ex post facto criminal laws are prohibited by the U.S. Constitution. But retrospective civil laws may be allowed.

exposure. (17c) The amount of liability or other risk to which a person is subject.

express, *adj.* (14c) Clearly and unmistakably communicated; directly stated. — **expressly,** *adv.*

express abrogation. (1857) The repeal of a law or provision by a later one that refers directly to it; abrogation by express provision or enactment.

expressed, *adj.* (16c) Declared in direct terms; stated in words; not left to inference or implication.

expressio unius est exclusio alterius (ek-**spres[h]**-ee-oh yoo-**nɪ**-əs est ek-**skloo**-zhee-oh al-tə-**rɪ**-əs). [Law Latin] A canon of construction holding that to express or include one thing implies the exclusion of the other, or of the alternative. • For example, the rule that "each citizen is entitled to vote" implies that noncitizens are not entitled to vote.

express republication. (18c) A testator's repeating of the acts essential to a will's valid execution, with the avowed intent of republishing the will.

expropriation, *n.* (15c) **1.** A governmental taking or modification of an individual's property rights, esp. by eminent domain. **2.** A voluntary surrender of rights or claims; the act of renouncing or divesting oneself of something previously claimed as one's own. — **expropriate,** *vb.* — **expropriator,** *n.*

expulsion, *n.* (15c) An ejectment or banishment, either through depriving a person of a benefit or by forcibly evicting a person. — **expulsive,** *adj.*

expunge (ek-**spənj**), *vb.* (17c) **1.** To erase or destroy. **2.** *Parliamentary law.* To declare (a vote or other action) null and outside the record, so that it is noted in the original record as expunged, and redacted from all future copies. — **expungement** (ek-**spənj**-mənt), **expunction** (ek-**spəngk**-shən), *n.*

expungement of record. (1966) The removal of a conviction (esp. for a first offense) from a person's criminal record.

expurgation (ek-spər-**gay**-shən), *n.* (15c) The act or practice of purging or cleansing, as by publishing a book without its obscene passages. — **expurgate** (**eks**-pər-gayt), *vb.* — **expurgator** (**eks**-pər-gay-tər), *n.*

ex rel. *abbr.* [Latin *ex relatione* "by or on the relation of"] (1838) On the relation or information of. • A suit *ex rel.* is typically brought by the government upon the application of a private party (called a *relator*) who is interested in the matter.

extension, *n.* (17c) **1.** The continuation of the same contract for a specified period. **2.** *Patents.* A continuation of the life of a patent for an additional statutorily allowed period. **3.** *Tax.* A period of additional time to file an income-tax return beyond its due date. **4.** A period of additional time to take an action, make a decision, accept an offer, or complete a task. — **extend,** *vb.*

extension agreement. (1869) An agreement providing additional time for the basic agreement to be performed.

extenuate (ek-**sten**-yoo-ayt), *vb.* (16c) To make less severe; to mitigate. — **extenuation** (ek-sten-yoo-**ay**-shən), *n.*

externality. (*usu. pl.*) (1957) A consequence or side effect of one's economic activity, causing another to benefit without paying or to suffer without compensation.

negative externality. (1970) An externality that is detrimental to another, such as water pollution created by a nearby factory.

positive externality. (1970) An externality that benefits another, such as the advantage received by a neighborhood when a homeowner attractively landscapes the property.

extinct, *adj.* (15c) **1.** No longer in existence or use. **2.** (Of a debt) lacking a claimant.

extinguishment, *n.* (16c) The cessation or cancellation of some right or interest. • For example, the extinguishment of a legacy occurs when the item bequeathed no longer exists or no longer belongs to the testator's estate. — **extinguish,** *vb.*

extinguishment of lien. (1800) A lien's discharge by operation of law.

extirpation (ek-stər-**pay**-shən), *n.* (16c) **1.** The act of completely removing or destroying something. **2.** Damage to land intentionally done by a person who has lost the right to the land.

extortion, *n.* (14c) **1.** The offense committed by a public official who illegally obtains property under the color of office; esp., an official's collection of an unlawful fee. **2.** The act or practice of obtaining something or compelling some action by illegal means, as by force or coercion. — **extort,** *vb.* (15c). — **extortionate,** *adj.*

extra (**ek**-strə), *prep.* [Latin] (1852) Beyond; except; without; out of; additional.

extradite (**ek**-strə-dɪt), *vb.* (1864) **1.** To surrender or deliver (a fugitive) to another jurisdiction. **2.** To obtain the surrender of (a fugitive) from another jurisdiction.

extradition (ek-strə-**dish**-ən). (18c) The official surrender of an alleged criminal by one state or nation to another having jurisdiction over the crime charged; the return of a fugitive from justice, regardless of consent, by the authorities where the fugitive is found.

international extradition. Extradition in response to a demand made by the executive of one nation on the executive of another nation.

interstate extradition. Extradition in response to a demand made by the governor of one state on the governor of another state.

Extradition Clause. (1878) The clause of the U.S. Constitution providing that any accused person who flees to another state must, on request of the executive authority of the state where the crime was committed, be returned to that state. U.S. Const. art. IV, § 2, cl. 2.

extradition treaty. (1847) A treaty governing the preconditions for, and exceptions to, the surrender of a fugitive from justice by the country where the fugitive is found to another country claiming criminal jurisdiction over the fugitive.

extrahazardous, *adj.* (1831) Especially or unusually dangerous. • This term is often applied to exceptionally dangerous railroad crossings.

extrajudicial, *adj.* (17c) Outside court; outside the functioning of the court system.

extrajudicial statement. (1838) Any utterance made outside of court.

extralegal, *adj.* (17c) Beyond the province of law.

extraneous question. (1808) A question that is beyond or beside the point to be decided.

extraordinary repair. (1828) As used in a lease, a repair that is made necessary by some unusual or unforeseen occurrence that does not destroy the building but merely renders it less suited to its intended use; a repair that is beyond the usual, customary, or regular kind.

extrapolate (ek-**strap**-ə-layt), *vb.* (19c) **1.** To estimate an unknown value or quantity on the basis of the known range, esp. by statistical methods. **2.** To deduce an unknown legal principle from a known case. **3.** To speculate about possible results, based on known facts. — **extrapolative** (-lay-tiv *or* -lə-tiv), **extrapolatory** (-lə-tor-ee), *adj.* — **extrapolator** (-lay-tər), *n.* — **extrapolation** (ek-strap-ə-**lay**-shən), *n.* (19c).

extraterritorial, *adj.* (19c) Beyond the geographic limits of a particular jurisdiction. — **extraterritoriality,** *n.* (19c).

extrinsic, *adj.* (17c) From outside sources; of or relating to outside matters.

eye of the law. (16c) The law as a personified thinker; legal contemplation <dead people are no longer persons in the eye of the law>.

eyewitness. (16c) One who personally observes an event.

eyewitness identification. (1939) A naming or description by which one who has seen an event testifies from memory about the person or persons involved.

F

F. *abbr.* The first series of the *Federal Reporter,* which includes federal decisions (trial and appellate) from 1880 to 1924.

F.2d. *abbr.* The second series of the *Federal Reporter,* which includes federal appellate decisions from 1924 to 1993.

F.3d. *abbr.* The third series of the *Federal Reporter,* which includes federal appellate decisions from 1993.

FAA. *abbr.* **1.** Federal Aviation Administration. **2.** Federal Arbitration Act. **3.** Free of All Average.

fabricate, *vb.* (15c) To invent, forge, or devise falsely. • To fabricate a story is to create a plausible version of events that is advantageous to the person relating those events. The term is softer than *lie.*

face, *n.* (13c) **1.** The surface of anything, esp. the front, upper, or outer part <the face of a clock>. **2.** By extension, the apparent or explicit part of a writing or record <the fraud must appear on the face of the record>. **3.** The inscribed side of a document, instrument, or judgment <although the contract appeared valid on its face, the buyer did not have the legal capacity to enter into it>.

face amount. 1. Par value. **2.** *Insurance.* The amount payable under an insurance policy.

face value. 1. Face amount. **2.** Par value.

facial, *adj.* (19c) Apparent; of or relating to the face of things; prima facie.

facial attack. (1966) A challenge to the sufficiency of a complaint, such as a motion to dismiss in federal practice.

facially sufficient, *adj.* (1972) (Of a document) appearing valid on its face.

facilitate, *vb.* (17c) *Criminal law.* To make the commission of a crime easier. — **facilitator,** *n.* — **facilitation,** *n.*

facsimile (fak-**sim**-ə-lee). (17c) **1.** An exact copy. **2.** FAX.

fact. (15c) **1.** Something that actually exists; an aspect of reality. • Facts include not just tangible things, actual occurrences, and relationships, but also states of mind such as intentions and opinions. **2.** An actual or alleged event or circumstance, as distinguished from its legal effect, consequence, or interpretation. **3.** An evil deed; a crime.

adjudicative fact (ə-**joo**-di-kay-tiv *or* -kə-tiv). (1959) A controlling or operative fact, rather than a background fact; a fact that concerns the parties to a judicial or administrative proceeding and that helps the court or agency determine how the law applies to those parties.

dispositive fact (dis-**poz**-ə-tiv). (1946) **1.** A fact that confers rights or causes the loss of rights. • A dispositive fact may be either an investitive or a divestitive fact. **2.** A fact that is decisive of a legal matter; evidence that definitively resolves a legal issue or controversy.

divestitive fact (di-**ves**-tə-tiv *or* dɪ-). (1973) A fact that causes the loss of rights; an act or event modifying or extinguishing a legal relation.

evaluative fact. (1986) A fact used to assess an action as being reasonable or negligent.

evidentiary fact (ev-i-**den**-shə-ree) (1855) **1.** A fact that is necessary for or leads to the determination of an ultimate fact. **2.** A fact that furnishes evidence of the existence of some other fact.

exonerative fact (eg-**zon**-ər-ə-tiv *or* -ay-tiv). (1980) A divestitive fact that extinguishes a duty.

fact in evidence. (18c) A fact that a tribunal considers in reaching a conclusion;

a fact that has been admitted into evidence in a trial or hearing.

fact in issue. (*usu. pl.*) (17c) A fact to be determined by a fact-finder.

impositive fact. An investitive fact that imposes duties.

inferential fact. (1858) A fact established by conclusions drawn from other evidence rather than from direct testimony or evidence; a fact derived logically from other facts.

investitive fact (in-**ves**-tə-tiv). (1939) A fact that confers rights.

judicially noticed fact. A fact that is not established by admissible evidence but may be accepted by the court because the fact is generally known within the trial court's territorial jurisdiction, or because its validity can be determined from sources whose accuracy cannot be reasonably questioned. See Fed. R. Evid. 201(b).

jurisdictional fact. (*usu. pl.*) (1837) A fact that must exist for a court to properly exercise its jurisdiction over a case, party, or thing.

legal fact. (18c) A fact that triggers a particular legal consequence.

legislative fact. (1828) A fact that explains a particular law's rationality and that helps a court or agency determine the law's content and application.

material fact. (1848) A fact that is significant or essential to the issue or matter at hand.

operative fact. (1857) A fact that affects an existing legal relation, esp. a legal claim.

physical fact. (1857) A fact having a physical existence, such as a fingerprint left at a crime scene.

predicate fact (**pred**-ə-kit). (1899) **1.** A fact from which a presumption or inference arises. **2.** A fact necessary to the operation of an evidentiary rule. • For example, there must actually be a conspiracy for the co-conspirator exception to the hearsay rule to apply.

presumed fact. A fact whose existence can be justifiably inferred from facts established by evidence.

primary fact. (18c) A fact that can be established by direct testimony and from which inferences are made leading to ultimate facts.

private fact. (16c) A fact that has not been made public.

probative fact (**proh**-bə-tiv). (1858) A fact in evidence used to prove an ultimate fact, such as skid marks used to show speed as a predicate to a finding of negligence.

public fact. (1955) For the purpose of an invasion-of-privacy claim, a fact that is in a public record or in the public domain.

simulated fact. (1943) A fabricated fact intended to mislead; a lie.

ultimate fact. (18c) A fact essential to the claim or the defense.

undisputed fact. (18c) An uncontested or admitted fact.

fact-finder. (1926) One or more persons — such as jurors in a trial or administrative-law judges in a hearing — who hear testimony and review evidence to rule on a factual issue.

fact-finding. (1909) **1.** The process of taking evidence to determine the truth about a disputed point of fact. **2.** A method of alternative dispute resolution in which an impartial third party determines and studies the facts and positions of disputing parties that have reached an impasse, with a view toward clarifying the issues and helping the parties work through their dispute.

faction. (16c) A number of citizens, whether a majority or a minority, who are united and motivated by a common impulse or interest that is adverse to the rights of others or to the permanent or aggregate interests of the community. • This definition is adapted from *The Federalist*, No. 10.

factor, *n.* (15c) **1.** An agent or cause that contributes to a particular result. **2.** An agent who is employed to sell property for the principal and who possesses or controls the property; a person who receives and sells goods for a commission. • A factor differs from a broker because the factor possesses or controls the property. **3.** One who buys accounts receivable at a discount. **4.** A garnishee. **5.** A person in charge of managing property, esp. real property.

factoring, *n.* The buying of accounts receivable at a discount.

factorize (**fak**-tə-rɪz), *vb.* (19c) Garnish. — **factorization,** *n.*

factorizing process. (1837) A procedure or legal process by which a third party, rather than the creditor, attaches a debtor's property; GARNISHMENT.

factum (**fak**-təm), *n.* [Latin] (18c) **1.** A fact, such as a person's physical presence in a new domicile. **2.** An act or deed, such as the due execution of a will. **3.** A statement of facts. **4.** Brief. Pl. **facta.**

fail, *vb.* (13c) **1.** To be deficient or unsuccessful; to fall short. **2.** To become insolvent or bankrupt. **3.** To lapse.

failure. (17c) **1.** Deficiency; lack; want. **2.** An omission of an expected action, occurrence, or performance.

failure of consideration. (1803) A seriously deficient contractual performance that causes a contract's basis or inducement to cease to exist or to become worthless. • Scholars disapprove of this term as misleading, since *failure of performance* is more accurate. Unlike *consideration*, the phrase *failure of consideration* relates not to the formation of a contract but to its performance.

partial failure of consideration. (1808) A party's incomplete performance of a contract with multiple, severable performances, so that if some of the performances are not accomplished, the appropriate part of the agreement can be apportioned to whatever has been completed.

total failure of consideration. (1809) A situation in which the contract is indivisible so that a complete lack of consideration voids the contract.

failure of issue. (17c) *Archaic.* The fact of a person's dying when the person has no surviving children or other descendants who are eligible to inherit the person's estate.

indefinite failure of issue. (18c) A failure of issue whenever it happens, without any certain period within which it must happen.

failure-of-proof defense. (1982) The defense that a party's proof does not establish a fact essential to a claim or defense.

failure to protect. *Family law.* The refusal or inability of a parent or guardian to prevent abuse of a child under his or her care.

failure to thrive. (1967) *Family law.* **1.** A medical and psychological condition in which a child's height, weight, and motor development fall significantly below average growth rates. • Failure to thrive is sometimes asserted as a ground for alleging abuse or neglect by a parent or caregiver. **2.** A condition, occurring during the first three years of a child's life, in which the child suffers marked retardation or ceases to grow.

faint pleader. (17c) A false, fraudulent, or collusive manner of pleading.

fair, *adj.* (bef. 12c) **1.** Impartial; just; equitable; disinterested. **2.** Free of bias or prejudice.

fair-and-equitable requirement. (17c) *Bankruptcy.* A Bankruptcy Code standard requiring a forced, nonconsensual Chapter 11 plan (a "cramdown" plan) to provide adequately for each class of interests that has not accepted the plan. 11 USCA § 1129(b).

fair comment. (18c) A statement based on the writer's or speaker's honest opinion about a matter of public concern. • Fair comment is a defense to libel or slander.

Fair Credit Billing Act. A federal law that facilitates the correction of billing errors by credit-card companies and makes those companies more responsible for the quality of goods purchased by cardholders. 15 USCA §§ 1666–1666j.

fair-credit-reporting act. (1971) A federal or state law that regulates disclosure and use of consumer-credit information and ensures the right of consumers to have access to and to correct their credit reports. — Abbr. FCRA.

fair-cross-section requirement. (1975) *Constitutional law.* The principle that a person's right to an impartial jury, guaranteed by the Sixth Amendment, includes a requirement that the pool of potential jurors fairly represent the composition of the jurisdiction's population. • The pool of potential jurors need not precisely match the composition of the jurisdiction. But the representation of each group must be fair — no group should be systematically excluded or underrepresented. A minimal disparity in a particular group's representation, such as an absolute disparity of 10%, will not ordinarily violate this principle unless some aggravating factor exists.

fair dealing, *n.* (17c) **1.** The conduct of business with full disclosure, usu. by a corporate officer with the corporation. **2.** A fiduciary's transacting of business so that, although the fiduciary might derive a personal benefit, all interested persons are fully apprised of that potential and of all other material information about the transaction. **3.** *Canadian law.* FAIR USE.

Fair Debt Collection Practices Act. A federal statute that regulates debt-collection practices, and defines the rights of consumers who are contacted by debt collectors. 15 USCA §§ 1692–1692p. — Abbr. FDCPA.

Fair Labor Standards Act. A federal law, enacted in 1938, that regulates minimum wages, overtime pay, and the employment of minors. 29 USCA §§ 201–219. — Abbr. FLSA.

fairness doctrine. (1965) *Hist.* A federal law, based on an FCC rule, requiring the broadcast media to furnish a reasonable opportunity for the discussion of conflicting views on issues of public importance. • The FCC abandoned the fairness doctrine in 1987.

fair on its face. (18c) (Of a document) having the appearance of being regular or legal and not capable of being shown to be defective without extraneous evidence.

fair play. Equity, candor, and fidelity in dealings with another.

fair play and substantial justice. (1945) The fairness requirement that a court must meet in its assertion of personal jurisdiction over a nonresident defendant to comport with due process. *International Shoe Co. v. Washington,* 326 U.S. 310, 66 S.Ct. 154 (1945).

fair-report privilege. (1980) A defense to liability for publishing defamatory matter from a report of an official or judicial proceeding, when the report is a full, fair, and accurate account of the proceeding.

fair-trade agreement. (1937) A commercial agreement that a seller will sell all of a producer's goods at or above a specified minimum price. • Fair-trade agreements were valid until 1975, when the Consumer Goods Pricing Act made them illegal. 15 USCA §§ 1, 45.

fair trial. (17c) A trial by an impartial and disinterested tribunal in accordance with regular procedures; esp., a criminal trial in which the defendant's constitutional and legal rights are respected.

fair use. (1869) *Copyright.* A reasonable and limited use of a copyrighted work without the author's permission, such as quoting from a book in a book review or using parts of it in a parody. 17 USCA § 107.

fair-value law. A statute allowing a credit against a deficiency for the amount that the fair market value of land exceeds the price at foreclosure.

fair warning. (1931) *Criminal law.* The requirement that a criminal statute define an offense with enough precision so that a reasonable person can know what conduct is prohibited and so that a reasonably skilled lawyer can predict what conduct falls within the statute's scope.

Faithfully Executed Clause. (1967) The clause of the U.S. Constitution providing that the President must take care that the laws are carried out faithfully. U.S. Const. art. II, § 3.

faith-healing exemption. *Family law.* In a child-abuse or child-neglect statute, a provision that a parent who provides a child with faith healing (in place of standard medical treatment) will not, for that reason alone, be charged with abuse or neglect.

fake, *n.* (19c) Something that is not what it purports to be.

fake, *vb.* (19c) To make or construct falsely.

fallacy. Any unsound, and usu. deceptive, argument or inference. • The presence of a fallacy in a legal argument is a defect — often fatal and usu. deceptive — in the legal reasoning.

formal fallacy. A fallacy involving flaws in the form of the argument, such as a violation of the formal rules of syllogistic reasoning.

material fallacy. A fallacy involving flaws in the factual content of a logical argument.

false, *adj.* (12c) **1.** Untrue. **2.** Deceitful; lying. **3.** Not genuine; inauthentic.

false advertising, *n.* (1911) **1.** The tortious and sometimes criminal act of distributing an advertisement that is untrue, deceptive, or misleading; esp., under the Lanham Trademark Act, an advertising statement that tends to mislead consumers about the characteristics, quality, or geographic origin of one's own or someone else's goods, services, or commercial activity. **2.** At common law, a statement in a defendant's advertising about its own goods or services intended to deceive or confuse customers into buying those goods or services instead of the plaintiff's, and causing actual damage to the plaintiff, esp. the loss of sales.

False Claims Act. A federal statute establishing civil and criminal penalties against persons who bill the government falsely, deliver less to the government than represented, or use a fake record to decrease an obligation to the government. 18 USCA §§ 286–287; 31 USCA §§ 3729–3733. • The Act may be enforced either by the attorney general or by a private person in a qui tam action.

false designation of origin. *Trademarks.* A mark, design, or similar element that creates a misleading or erroneous impression of a good or product's source.

false imprisonment. (14c) A restraint of a person in a bounded area without justification or consent. • False imprisonment is a common-law misdemeanor and a tort. It applies to private as well as governmental detention.

false judgment. *Hist.* A writ filed to obtain review of a judgment of a court not of record.

false light. (1962) *Torts.* In an invasion-of-privacy action, a plaintiff's allegation that the defendant attributed to the plaintiff views that he or she does not hold and placed the plaintiff before the public in a highly offensive and untrue manner.

false-memory syndrome. The supposed recovery of memories of traumatic or stressful episodes that did not actually occur, often in session with a mental-health therapist.

false pretenses. (18c) The crime of knowingly obtaining title to another's personal property by misrepresenting a fact with the intent to defraud.

false report. (1827) *Criminal law.* The criminal offense of informing law enforcement about a crime that did not occur.

false return. (16c) **1.** A process server's or other court official's recorded misrepresentation that process was served, that some other action was taken, or that something is true. **2.** A tax return on which taxable income is incorrectly reported or the tax is incorrectly computed.

falsify, *vb.* (15c) To make something false; to counterfeit or forge. — **falsification,** *n.*

falsifying a record. (18c) The crime of making false entries or otherwise tampering with a public record with the intent to deceive or injure, or to conceal wrongdoing. 18 USCA §§ 1506, 2071, 2073; Model Penal Code § 224.4.

***falsus in uno* doctrine** (**fal**-səs [*or* **fawl**-səs] in **yoo**-noh). [fr. Latin *falsus in uno, falsus in omnibus* "false in one thing, false in all"] The principle that if the jury believes that a witness's testimony on a material issue is intentionally deceitful, the jury may disregard all of that witness's testimony.

family, *n.* (14c) **1.** A group of persons connected by blood, by affinity, or by law, esp. within two or three generations. **2.** A group consisting of parents and their children. **3.** A group of persons who live together and have a shared commitment to a domestic relationship. — **familial,** *adj.*

blended family. (1985) The combined families of persons with children from earlier marriages or relationships.

extended family. (1942) **1.** The immediate family together with the collateral relatives who make up a clan. **2.** The immediate family together with collateral relatives and close family friends.

immediate family. (18c) **1.** A person's parents, spouse, children, and siblings. **2.** A person's parents, spouse, children, and siblings, as well as those of the person's spouse. • Stepchildren and adopted children are usu. immediate family members. For some purposes, such as taxes, a person's immediate family may also include the spouses of children and siblings.

family arrangement. (1817) An informal agreement among family members, usu. to distribute property in a manner other than what the law provides for.

family-expense statute. (1901) **1.** A state law that permits a charge against the property of a spouse for family debts such as rent, food, clothing, and tuition. **2.** A section of the federal tax code providing that a person may not deduct expenses incurred for family, living, or personal purposes. IRC (26 USCA) § 262.

family law. (1919) **1.** The body of law dealing with marriage, divorce, adoption, child custody and support, child abuse and neglect, paternity, juvenile delinquency, and other domestic-relations issues. **2.** (More broadly) the bodies of law dealing with wills and estates, property, constitutional rights, contracts, employment, and finance as they relate to families.

family leave. (1981) An unpaid leave of absence from work taken to have or care for a baby or to care for a sick family member.

family of marks. *Trademarks.* A group of trademarks that share a recognizable characteristic so that they are recognized by consumers as identifying a single source.

family-partnership rules. (1946) Laws or regulations designed to prevent the shifting of income among partners, esp. family members, who may not be dealing at arm's length.

family-purpose rule. (1927) *Torts.* The principle that a vehicle's owner is liable for injuries or damage caused by a family member's negligent driving. • Many states have abolished this rule.

family support. A combined award of child support and alimony that does not apportion the amount of each.

Fannie Mae (**fan**-ee **may**). Federal National Mortgage Association.

FAPE. *abbr.* Free appropriate public education. • This is a right of children with disabilities to have access to free education, guaranteed by the Rehabilitation Act of 1973 and the Individuals with Disabilities Education Act. See 34 C.F.R. § 100.33; 34 C.F.R. § 300.13.

FAR. (*often pl.*) *abbr.* Federal aviation regulation.

farming operation. (1859) *Bankruptcy.* A business engaged in farming, tillage of soil, dairy farming, ranching, raising of crops, poultry, or livestock, and production of poultry or livestock products in an unmanufactured state. 11 USCA § 101(21).

farm out, *vb.* (17c) To turn over something (such as an oil-and-gas lease) for performance by another.

FAS. *abbr.* **1.** Free alongside ship. **2.** Fetal alcohol syndrome.

FASB (**faz**-bee). *abbr.* Financial Accounting Standards Board.

fascism. A totalitarian political ideology under which all economic and social aspects of life come under rigid government control or direction, and the state's interests supersede individual interests.

fast-tracking, *n.* (1996) A court's method of accelerating the disposition of cases in an effort to clear its docket. • For example, a judge might order that all discovery must be finished within 90 days and that trial is set for 30 days later. — **fast-track,** *vb.*

fatal, *adj.* (14c) **1.** Of or relating to death; producing death <the decision had fatal consequences> <fatal blow>. **2.** Providing grounds for legal invalidity <a fatal defect in the contract>.

father. (bef. 12c) A male parent.

acknowledged father. The admitted biological father of a child born to unmarried parents.

biological father. (1951) The man whose sperm impregnated the child's biological mother.

legal father. (16c) The man recognized by law as the male parent of a child. • A man is the legal father of a child if he was married to the child's natural mother when the child was born, if he has recognized or acknowledged the child, or if he has been declared the child's natural father in a paternity action. If a man consents to the artificial insemination of his wife, he is the legal father of the child that is born as a result of the artificial insemination even though he may not be the genetic father of the child.

presumed father. (1937) The man presumed to be the father of a child for any of several reasons: (1) because he was married to the child's natural mother when the child was conceived or born (even though the marriage may have been invalid), (2) because the man married the mother after the child's birth and agreed either to have his name on the birth certificate or to support the child, or (3) because the man welcomed the child into his home and held out the child as his own.

putative father (**pyoo**-tə-tiv). (16c) The alleged biological father of a child born out of wedlock.

stepfather. (bef. 12c) The husband of one's mother by a later marriage.

***Fatico* hearing** (**fat**-ə-koh). (1979) *Criminal procedure.* A sentencing hearing at which the prosecution and the defense may present evidence about what the defendant's sentence should be. *United States v. Fatico*, 603 F.2d 1053 (2d Cir. 1979).

fault. (13c) An error or defect of judgment or of conduct; any deviation from prudence or duty resulting from inattention, incapacity, perversity, bad faith, or mismanagement.

fault-first method. (1996) A means by which to apply a settlement credit to a jury verdict, by first reducing the amount of the verdict by the percentage of the plaintiff's comparative fault, then subtracting from the remainder the amount of any settlements the plaintiff has received on the claim.

fault of omission. (17c) Negligence resulting from a negative act.

***Fauntleroy* doctrine.** The principle that a state must give full faith and credit to another state's judgment, if the other state had proper jurisdiction, even though the judgment is based on a claim that is illegal in the state in which enforcement is sought. *Fauntleroy v. Lum*, 210 U.S. 230, 28 S.Ct. 641 (1908).

faux (foh), *adj.* [Law French] *Hist.* False or counterfeit.

favorite of the law. (18c) A person or status entitled to generous and preferential treatment in legal doctrine.

favoritism. (18c) Preference or selection, usu. invidious, based on factors other than merit.

fax, *n.* (1948) **1.** A method of transmitting over telephone lines an exact copy of a printing. **2.** A machine used for such transmission. **3.** The communication sent or received by such a machine. — **fax,** *vb.*

FBI. *abbr.* Federal Bureau of Investigation.

F. Cas. *abbr. Federal Cases*, a series of reported decisions (1789–1880) predating the *Federal Reporter.*

FCC. *abbr.* Federal Communications Commission.

FDA. *abbr.* Food and Drug Administration.

f/d/b/a. *abbr.* Formerly doing business as.

FDIC. *abbr.* Federal Deposit Insurance Corporation.

feasance (**fee**-zənts), *n.* (16c) The doing or execution of an act, condition, or obligation. — **feasor,** *n.*

feasibility standard. (1978) *Bankruptcy.* The requirement that, to obtain bankruptcy-court approval, a Chapter 11 reorganization plan must be workable and have a reasonable likelihood of success.

feasor (**fee**-zər), *n.* (1808) An actor; a person who commits an act.

featherbedding. (1921) A union practice designed to increase employment and guarantee job security by requiring employers to hire or retain more employees than are needed. • Featherbedding is restricted by federal law but is an unfair labor practice only if, for example, a union exacts pay from an employer for services not performed or not to be performed.

FEC. *abbr.* Federal Election Commission.

Fed. *abbr.* **1.** Federal. **2.** Federal Reserve System.

Fed. Appx. *abbr. Federal Appendix.*

Fed. Cir. *abbr.* United States Court of Appeals for the Federal Circuit.

federal, *adj.* (18c) Of or relating to a system of associated governments with a vertical division of governments into national and regional components having different responsibilities; esp., of or relating to the national government of the United States. — Abbr. Fed.

Federal Acquisition Regulation. (*usu. pl.*) A federal regulation that governs contracting methods, requirements, and procedures with the federal government. 48 CFR ch. 1.

Federal Appendix. A set of reports containing all the full-text "unpublished" opinions that West receives from the federal circuit courts of appeals. • These are the opinions not designated for publication in the *Federal Reporter.* Coverage began January 1, 2001. — Abbr. Fed. Appx.

Federal Arbitration Act. A federal statute providing for the enforcement of private agreements to arbitrate disputes related to interstate commercial and maritime matters. 9 USCA §§ 1–16. — Abbr. FAA.

Federal Aviation Act. A federal law establishing the Federal Aviation Administration (FAA) to be responsible for regulation of aircraft and air travel, including aircraft safety, certification of aircraft personnel, and airport development. 49 USCA §§ 44720 et seq.

Federal Bureau of Investigation. A division of the U.S. Department of Justice charged with investigating all violations of federal laws except those specifically assigned to another federal agency. — Abbr. FBI.

Federal Bureau of Prisons. The U.S. government unit responsible for the custody and care of federal offenders, whether incarcerated in federal correctional and detention centers or in state-run or privately operated facilities.

Federal Circuit. Court of Appeals for the Federal Circuit.

Federal Claims, U.S. Court of. United States Court of Federal Claims.

federal-comity doctrine. (1976) The principle requiring federal district courts to refrain from interfering in each other's affairs.

Federal Communications Commission. An independent federal commission that regulates interstate and foreign communications by radio, television, wire, satellite, and cable. — Abbr. FCC.

federal crime. (1860) A criminal offense under a federal statute. • Most federal crimes are codified in Title 18 of the U.S. Code.

Federal Deposit Insurance Corporation. A federal corporation that protects bank and thrift deposits by insuring accounts up to $100,000, examining banks that are not members of the Federal Reserve System, and liquidating failed institutions. — Abbr. FDIC.

Federal Election Commission. A ten-member independent federal commission that certifies payments to qualifying presidential campaigns in primary and general elections and to national-nominating conventions, audits campaign expenditures, and enforces laws requiring public disclosure of financial activities of presidential campaigns and political parties. 2 USCA § 437c. — Abbr. FEC.

Federal Emergency Management Agency. A unit in the Department of Homeland Security responsible for coordinating all emergency-preparedness activities of the federal government through its ten regional offices. — Abbr. FEMA.

Federal Energy Regulatory Commission. An independent five-member commission in the U.S. Department of Energy responsible for licensing hydroelectric-power projects and for setting interstate rates on (1) transporting and selling natural gas for resale, (2) transporting and selling electricity at wholesale, and (3) transporting oil by pipeline. — Abbr. FERC.

Federal Home Loan Bank. One of 12 federally chartered banks created in 1932 to extend secured loans (advances) to savings institutions that are members of the system and to community financial institutions that finance small businesses, small farms, and small agribusinesses. — Abbr. FHLB.

Federal Home Loan Mortgage Corporation. A corporation that purchases both conventional and federally insured first mortgages from members of the Federal Reserve System and other approved banks. — Abbr. FHLMC.

Federal Housing Administration. The HUD division that encourages mortgage lending by insuring mortgage loans on homes meeting the agency's standards. — Abbr. FHA.

Federal Housing Finance Board. A five-member independent federal board that supervises the 12 Federal Home Loan Banks. • Formerly known as the Federal Home Loan Bank Board, it was established by the Federal Home Loan Bank Act of 1932. That Act was amended by the Financial Institutions Reform, Recovery, and Enforcement Act of 1989. 12 USCA §§ 1421 et seq.

Federal Insurance Contributions Act. The federal act imposing the social-security tax on employers and employees. IRC (26 USCA) §§ 3101–3127. — Abbr. FICA.

federalism. (1787) The legal relationship and distribution of power between the national and regional governments within a federal system of government.

cooperative federalism. (1947) Distribution of power between the federal government and the states in which each recognizes the powers of the other while jointly engaging in certain governmental functions.

Federalist Society. A national association of lawyers, law students, and others committed to conservative and libertarian viewpoints on political and social matters. • The group is based in Washington, D.C.

Federal Judicial Code. The portion (Title 28) of the U.S. Code dealing with the organization, jurisdiction, venue, and procedures of the federal court system, as well as court officers, personnel, and the Department of Justice.

Federal Kidnapping Act. A federal law punishing kidnapping for ransom or reward when the victim is transported interstate or internationally.

Federal Labor Relations Authority. An agency that protects the right of federal employees to organize, engage in collective bargaining, and select their own union representatives. — Abbr. FLRA.

Federal Land Bank. (1914) One of a system of 12 regional banks created in 1916 to provide mortgage loans to farmers. • The system is now merged with federal intermediate credit banks to create the Federal Farm Credit System.

federal law. (18c) The body of law consisting of the U.S. Constitution, federal statutes and regulations, U.S. treaties, and federal common law.

Federal Maritime Commission. An independent federal agency that regulates the waterborne foreign and domestic commerce of the United States by (1) ensuring that U.S. international trade is open to all countries on fair and equitable terms, (2) guarding against unauthorized monopolies in U.S. waterborne commerce, and (3) ensuring that financial responsibility is maintained to clean up oil spills and indemnify injured passengers. — Abbr. FMC.

Federal Mediation and Conciliation Service. An independent federal agency that tries to prevent the interruption of interstate commerce that could result from a labor–management dispute by helping the parties reach a settlement without resorting to a job action or strike. • The Service can intervene on its own authority or at the request of a party to the dispute. It also helps employers and unions select qualified arbitrators. The Service was established by the Labor Management Relations Act of 1947. 29 USCA § 172. — Abbr. FMCS.

Federal Mine Safety and Health Review Commission. An independent five-member commission that (1) monitors compliance with occupational safety and health standards in the nation's surface and underground coal, metal, and nonmetal mines, and (2) adjudicates disputes that arise under the Federal Mine Safety and Health Amendments Act of 1977. —Abbr. FMSHRC.

Federal National Mortgage Association. A privately owned and managed corporation chartered by the U.S. government that provides a secondary mortgage market for the purchase and sale of mortgages guaranteed by the Veterans Administration and those insured under the Federal Housing Administration. — Abbr. FNMA.

Federal Parent Locator Service. A federal program created to help enforce child-support obligations. 42 USCA § 653. — Abbr. FPLS.

federal prison camp. A federal minimum-security detention facility. • Federal prison camps, which often do not have walls or fences, usu. house nonviolent inmates who are serving sentences shorter than a year plus one day and who are not considered escape risks.

Federal Protective Service. A law-enforcement agency in the U.S. Department of Homeland Security responsible for protecting ambassadors, diplomatic staffs, and embassy property. • It was transferred from the General Services Administration in 2003.

federal question. In litigation, a legal issue involving the interpretation and application of the U.S. Constitution, an act of Congress, or a treaty. • Jurisdiction over federal questions rests with the federal courts. 28 USCA § 1331.

Federal Railroad Administration. A unit in the U.S. Department of Transportation responsible for promulgating and enforcing rail-safety regulations; administering rail-related financial-aid programs; conducting research on rail safety; and rehabilitating rail passenger service for the Northeast corridor. — Abbr. FRA.

Federal Register. A daily publication containing presidential proclamations and executive orders, federal-agency regulations of general applicability and legal effect, proposed agency rules, and documents required by law to be published. — Abbr. Fed. Reg.

Federal Reporter. See F.

Federal Reporter Second Series. See F.2D.

Federal Reporter Third Series. See F.3D.

Federal Reserve Board of Governors. The board that supervises the Federal Reserve System and sets national monetary and credit policy. • The board consists of seven members nominated by the President and confirmed by the Senate for 14-year terms. — Abbr. FRB.

federal reserve note. (1913) The paper currency in circulation in the United States. • Non-interest-bearing promissory notes are payable to their bearer on demand. The Federal Reserve Banks issue the notes in denominations of $1, $2, $5, $10, $20, $50, and $100.

Federal Reserve System. The central bank that sets credit and monetary policy by fixing the reserves to be maintained by depository institutions, determining the discount rate charged by Federal Reserve Banks, and regulating the amount of credit that may be extended on any security. — Abbr. FRS; Fed.

Federal Rules Decisions. See F.R.D.

Federal Rules Enabling Act. A 1934 statute granting the U.S. Supreme Court the authority to adopt rules of civil procedure for federal courts. • For the rulemaking power of federal courts today, see 28 USCA §§ 2071, 2072. See also Fed. R. Civ. P. 83; Fed. R. Crim. P. 57.

Federal Rules of Appellate Procedure. The rules governing appeals to the U.S. courts of appeals from lower courts, some federal-agency proceedings, and applications for writs. — Abbr. Fed. R. App. P.; FRAP.

Federal Rules of Bankruptcy Procedure. The rules governing proceedings instituted under the Bankruptcy Code. — Abbr. Fed. R. Bankr. P.

Federal Rules of Civil Procedure. The rules governing civil actions in the U.S. district courts. — Abbr. Fed. R. Civ. P.; FRCP.

Federal Rules of Criminal Procedure. The rules governing criminal proceedings in the U.S. district courts. — Abbr. Fed. R. Crim. P.

Federal Rules of Evidence. The rules governing the admissibility of evidence at trials in federal courts. — Abbr. Fed. R. Evid.; FRE.

Federal Savings and Loan Insurance Corporation. A federal agency created in 1934 to insure deposits in savings-and-loan associations and savings banks. • When this agency became insolvent in 1989, its assets and liabilities were transferred to an insurance fund managed by the FDIC. — Abbr. FSLIC.

Federal Supplement. See F.SUPP.

Federal Supplement 2d. See F.SUPP.2D.

Federal Tort Claims Act. A statute that limits federal sovereign immunity and allows recovery in federal court for tort damages caused by federal employees, but only if the law of the state where the injury occurred would hold a private person liable for the injury. 28 USCA §§ 2671–2680 — Abbr. FTCA.

Federal Trade Commission. An independent five-member federal commission that administers various laws against business monopolies, restraint of trade, and deceptive trade practices. — Abbr. FTC.

federal transfer. The federal district court's right to move a civil action filed there to any other district or division where the plaintiff could have brought the action originally. 28 USCA § 1404(a).

Federal Transit Administration. A unit in the U.S. Department of Transportation responsible for increasing public-transit ridership through demonstration projects and financial assistance. — Abbr. FTA.

federation. (18c) A league or union of states, groups, or peoples united under a strong central authority but retaining limited regional sovereignty, esp. over local affairs.

Fed. R. App. P. *abbr.* Federal Rules of Appellate Procedure.

Fed. R. Bankr. P. *abbr.* Federal Rules of Bankruptcy procedure.

Fed. R. Civ. P. *abbr.* Federal Rules of Civil procedure.

Fed. R. Crim. P. *abbr.* Federal Rules of Criminal Procedure.

Fed. Reg. *abbr.* Federal Register.

Fed. R. Evid. *abbr.* Federal Rules of Evidence.

fee. (14c) **1.** A charge for labor or services, esp. professional services.

docket fee. (1836) A fee charged by a court for filing a claim.

expert-witness fee. A fee paid for the professional services of an expert witness.

fixed fee. (18c) **1.** A flat charge for a service; a charge that does not vary with the amount of time or effort required to complete the service. **2.** In a construction contract, a predetermined amount that is added to costs for calculating payments due under the contract.

franchise fee. (1894) **1.** A fee paid by a franchisee to a franchisor for franchise rights. • Franchise fees are regulated by state laws. **2.** A fee paid to the government for a government grant of a franchise, such as the one required for operating a radio or television station.

jury fee. (1806) A fee, usu. a minimal one, that a party to a civil suit must pay the court clerk to be entitled to a jury trial.

loan-origination fee. A fee charged by a lender to cover the administrative costs of making a loan.

origination fee. (1921) A fee charged by a lender for preparing and processing a loan.

probate fee. Compensation paid with a probate court's approval to an attorney who performs probate-related services to the estate.

success fee. A bonus paid to a representative who performs exceptionally well in gaining favorable results; esp., a bonus that a client pays to an attorney if the attorney obtains something of value to the client. • For instance, a client might agree to pay a success fee for success in litigation, for favorable negotiations in a transaction, or for the successful conclusion of a corporate merger, acquisition, or loan.

witness fee. **1.** A statutory fee that must be tendered with a subpoena for the subpoena to be binding. **2.** A fee paid by a party to a witness as reimbursement for reasonable expenses (such as travel, meals, lodging, and loss of time) incurred as a result of the witness's having to attend and testify at a deposition or trial. • Any other payment to a nonexpert witness is considered unethical.

2. A heritable interest in land; esp., a fee simple absolute.

base fee. (16c) A fee that has some qualification connected to it and that terminates whenever the qualification terminates. • An example of the words creating a base fee are "to A and his heirs, tenants of the manor of Tinsleydale," which would terminate when A or his heirs are no longer tenants of the manor of Tinsleydale. Among the base fees at common law are the fee simple subject to a condition subsequent and the conditional fee.

feemail (**fee**-mayl). (1994) *Slang.* **1.** An attorney's fee extorted by intimidation, threats, or pressure. **2.** The act or process of extorting such a fee.

fee simple. (15c) An interest in land that, being the broadest property interest allowed by law, endures until the current holder dies without heirs; esp., a fee simple absolute.

fee simple absolute. (18c) An estate of indefinite or potentially infinite duration (e.g., "to Albert and his heirs").

fee simple conditional. (17c) An estate restricted to some specified heirs, exclusive of others (e.g., "to Albert and his female heirs").

fee simple defeasible (di-**fee**-zə-bəl). (18c) An estate that ends either because there are no more heirs of the person to whom it is granted or because a special limitation, condition subsequent, or executory limitation takes effect before the line of heirs runs out.

fee simple determinable. (18c) An estate that will automatically end and revert to the grantor if some specified event occurs (e.g., "to Albert and his heirs while the property is used for charitable purposes"); an estate in fee simple subject to a special limitation. • The future interest retained by the grantor is called a *possibility of reverter.*

fee simple subject to a condition subsequent. (1874) An estate subject to the grantor's power to end the estate if some specified event happens (e.g., "to Albert and his heirs, upon condition that no alcohol is sold on the premises"). • The future interest retained by the grantor is called a *power of termination* (or a *right of entry*).

fee simple subject to an executory limitation. (1856) A fee simple defeasible that is subject to divestment in favor of someone other than the grantor if a specified event happens (e.g., "to Albert and his heirs, but if the property is ever used as a parking lot, then to Bob").

fee tail. (15c) An estate that is heritable only by specified descendants of the original grantee, and that endures until its current holder dies without issue (e.g., "to Albert and the heirs of his body").

***Feist* doctrine.** (1991) *Copyright.* The rule that "sweat of the brow" will not support U.S. copyright protection in an unoriginal collection of facts. *Feist Pubs. v. Rural Tel. Serv. Co.*, 499 U.S. 340, 111 S. Ct. 1282 (1991).

fellow-officer rule. (1971) *Criminal procedure.* The principle that an investigative stop or an arrest is valid even if the law-enforcement officer lacks personal knowledge to establish reasonable suspicion or probable cause as long as the officer is acting on the knowledge of another officer and the collective knowledge of the law-enforcement office.

fellow-servant rule. (1905) A common-law doctrine holding that an employer is not liable for an employee's injuries caused by a negligent coworker. • This doctrine has generally been abrogated by workers'-compensation statutes.

felon, *n.* (13c) A person who has been convicted of a felony.

felonious (fə-**loh**-nee-əs), *adj.* (16c) **1.** Of, relating to, or involving a felony. **2.** Constituting or having the character of a felony. **3.** Proceeding from an evil heart or purpose; malicious; villainous. **4.** Wrongful; (of an act) done without excuse or color of right.

felonious restraint. (1971) **1.** The offense of knowingly and unlawfully restraining a person under circumstances that expose the person to serious bodily harm. Model Penal Code § 212.2(a). **2.** The offense of holding a person in involuntary servitude. Model Penal Code § 212.2(b).

felony, *n.* (14c) A serious crime usu. punishable by imprisonment for more than one year or by death.

atrocious felony. (1814) *Archaic.* A serious, usu. cruel felony involving personal violence. • The common practice today is to refer to the specific type of crime alleged (e.g., first-degree murder or aggravated sexual assault).

serious felony. (1874) A major felony, such as burglary of a residence or an assault that causes great bodily injury. • In many jurisdictions, a defendant's prior serious-felony convictions can be used to enhance another criminal charge.

felony injury to a child. The act of causing or allowing a child to suffer in circumstances likely to produce great bodily harm or death, or inflicting unjustifiable pain or mental suffering in those circumstances.

felony-murder rule. (1943) The doctrine holding that any death resulting from the commission or attempted commission of a felony is murder.

FEMA. *abbr.* Federal Emergency Management Agency.

female genital mutilation. (1979) **1.** Female circumcision. **2.** The act of cutting, or cutting off, one or more female sexual organs. • Female genital mutilation is practiced primarily among certain tribes in Africa, but it also occurs among some immigrant populations in the United States and in other Western nations. — Abbr. FGM.

fence, *n.* (14c) **1.** A person who receives stolen goods, usu. with the intent to sell them in a legitimate market. **2.** A place where stolen goods are sold. — **fence,** *vb.*

FERC (fərk). *abbr.* Federal Energy Regulatory Commission.

FERPA. *abbr.* Family Educational Rights and Privacy Act.

fertile-octogenarian rule. (1856) The legal fiction, assumed under the rule against perpetuities, that a woman can become pregnant as long as she is alive. • The case that gave rise to this fiction was *Jee v. Audley*, 1 Cox 324, 29 Eng. Rep. 1186 (ch. 1787).

feticide (**fee**-tə-sɪd). (1842) **1.** The act or an instance of killing a fetus, usu. by assaulting and battering the mother; esp., the act of unlawfully causing the death of a fetus. **2.** An intentionally induced miscarriage. — **feticidal,** *adj.*

fetter, *n.* (*usu. pl.*) (bef. 12c) A chain or shackle for the feet. — **fetter,** *vb.*

fetus. (14c) A developing but unborn mammal, esp. in the latter stages of development. — Also spelled *foetus.*

ff. *abbr.* And the pages following.

FHA. *abbr.* **1.** Farmers Home Administration. **2.** Federal Housing Administration.

FHLB. *abbr.* Federal Home Loan Bank.

FHLMC. *abbr.* Federal Home Loan Mortgage Corporation.

fiat (**fee**-aht *or* **fee**-at *or* **fɪ**-at *or* **fɪ**-ət), *n.* [Latin "let it be done"] (17c) **1.** An order or decree, esp. an arbitrary one. **2.** A court decree, esp. one relating to a routine matter such as scheduling.

FICA (**fɪ**-kə). *abbr.* Federal Insurance Contributions Act.

fiducial, *adj.* (16c) Of, relating to, or characterized by confidence in and reliance on another person or thing.

fiduciary (fi-**d**[**y**]**oo**-shee-er-ee), *n.* (17c) **1.** A person who is required to act for the benefit of another person on all matters within the scope of their relationship; one who owes to another the duties of good faith, trust, confidence, and candor <the corporate officer is a fiduciary to the corporation>. **2.** One who must exercise a high standard of care in managing another's money or property <the beneficiary sued the fiduciary for investing in speculative securities>. — **fiduciary,** *adj.*

fieri facias (**fɪ**-ə-rɪ **fay**-shee-əs). [Latin "that you cause to be done"] (15c) A writ of execution that directs a marshal or sheriff to seize and sell a defendant's property to satisfy a money judgment. — Abbr. *fi. fa.*; *Fi. Fa.*

FIFO (**fɪ**-foh). *abbr.* First-in, first-out.

Fifteenth Amendment. The constitutional amendment, ratified in 1870, guaranteeing all citizens the right to vote regardless of race, color, or prior condition of servitude.

Fifth Amendment. The constitutional amendment, ratified with the Bill of Rights in 1791, providing that a person cannot be (1) required to answer for a capital or otherwise infamous offense unless a grand jury issues an indictment or presentment, (2) subjected to double jeopardy, (3) compelled to engage in self-incrimination on a criminal matter, (4) deprived of life, liberty, or property without due process of law, or (5) deprived of private property for public use without just compensation.

50-percent rule. (1975) The principle that liability for negligence is apportioned in accordance with the percentage of fault that the fact-finder assigns to each party, that the plaintiff's recovery will be reduced by the percentage of negligence assigned to the plaintiff, and that the plaintiff's recovery is barred if the plaintiff's percentage of fault is 50% or more.

fighting words. (1917) **1.** Inflammatory speech that might not be protected by the First Amendment's free-speech guarantee because it might incite a violent response. **2.** Inflammatory speech that is pleadable in mitigation — but not in defense — of a suit for assault.

file, *n.* (17c) **1.** A court's complete and official record of a case. **2.** A lawyer's complete record of a case. **3.** A portion or section of a lawyer's case record. **4.** A case.

file, *vb.* (16c) **1.** To deliver a legal document to the court clerk or record custodian for placement into the official record. **2.** To commence a lawsuit. **3.** To record or deposit something in an organized retention system or container for preservation and future reference. **4.** *Parliamentary law.* To acknowledge and deposit (a report, communication, or other document) for information and reference only without necessarily taking any substantive action.

file wrapper. *Patents & Trademarks.* The complete record of proceedings in the Patent and Trademark Office from the initial application to the issued patent or trademark.

filibuster (fil-ə-bəs-tər), *n.* (18c) A dilatory tactic, esp. prolonged and often irrelevant speechmaking, employed in an attempt to obstruct legislative action. — **filibuster,** *vb.*

filing, *n.* (18c) A particular document (such as a pleading) in the file of a court clerk or record custodian <the lawyer argued that the plaintiff's most recent filing was not germane to the issue before the court>.

filing fee. (1864) A sum of money required to be paid to the court clerk before a proceeding can start.

filing status. *Tax.* One of the four categories under which a person files an income tax return. • Under federal law, the four categories are: (1) single; (2) head of household; (3) married filing a joint return; and (4) married filing separate returns.

finality doctrine. (1942) The rule that a court will not judicially review an administrative agency's action until it is final.

final-judgment rule. (1931) The principle that a party may appeal only from a district court's final decision that ends the litigation on the merits. • Under this rule, a party must raise all claims of error in a single appeal. 28 USCA § 1291.

finance, *n.* (18c) **1.** That aspect of business concerned with the management of money, credit, banking, and investments. **2.** The science or study of the management of money, credit, banking, and investments.

finance, *vb.* (19c) To raise or provide funds.

finance charge. An additional payment, usu. in the form of interest, paid by a retail buyer for the privilege of purchasing goods or services in installments. • This phrase is increasingly used as a euphemism for *interest.*

finance company. (20c) A nonbank company that deals in loans either by making them or by purchasing notes from another company that makes the loans directly to borrowers.

Financial Accounting Standards Board. The independent body of accountants responsible for establishing, interpreting, and improving standards for financial accounting and reporting. — Abbr. FASB.

financial institution. (1821) A business, organization, or other entity that manages money, credit, or capital, such as a bank, credit union, savings-and-loan association, securities broker or dealer, pawnbroker, or investment company.

financial intermediary. (1873) A financial entity — usu. a commercial bank — that advances the transfer of funds between borrowers and lenders, buyers and sellers, and investors and savers.

financial planner. A person whose business is advising clients about personal finances and investments. • Upon completing a certification program, such a person is called a *certified financial planner.* — Abbr. CFP.

financial-responsibility act. (1930) A state statute conditioning license and registration of motor vehicles on proof of insurance or other financial accountability.

financial-responsibility clause. (1946) *Insurance.* A provision in an automobile insurance policy stating that the insured has at least the minimum amount of liability insurance coverage required by a state's financial-responsibility law.

financial restatement. A report correcting material errors in a financial statement, esp. to adjust profits and losses after an accounting procedure has been disallowed.

financial statement. A balance sheet, income statement, or annual report that summarizes an individual's or organization's financial condition on a specified date or for a specified period by reporting assets and liabilities.

financing, *n.* (19c) **1.** The act or process of raising or providing funds. **2.** Funds that are raised or provided. — **finance,** *vb.*

financing statement. (1954) A document filed in the public records to notify third parties, usu. prospective buyers and lenders, of a secured party's security interest in goods or real property. See UCC § 9-102(a)(39).

finder. (13c) **1.** An intermediary who brings together parties for a business opportunity, such as two companies for a merger, a borrower and a financial institution, an issuer and an underwriter of securities, or a seller and a buyer of real estate. • A finder differs from a broker-dealer because the finder merely brings two parties together to make their own contract, while a broker-dealer usu. participates in the negotiations. **2.** A person who discovers an object, often a lost or mislaid chattel.

finder's fee. (1937) **1.** The amount charged by one who brings together parties for a business opportunity. **2.** The amount charged by a person who locates a lost or missing item and returns it to its owner.

finder's-fee contract. (1959) An agreement between a finder and one of the parties to a business opportunity.

finding of fact. (18c) A determination by a judge, jury, or administrative agency of a fact supported by the evidence in the record, usu. presented at the trial or hearing.

fine, *n.* (13c) **1.** An amicable final agreement or compromise of a fictitious or actual suit to determine the true possessor of land. **2.** A fee paid by a tenant to the landlord at the commencement of the tenancy to reduce the rent payments. **3.** A pecuniary criminal punishment or civil penalty payable to the public treasury. — **fine,** *vb.*

excessive fine. (16c) **1.** *Criminal law.* A fine that is unreasonably high and disproportionate to the offense committed. • The Eighth Amendment proscribes excessive fines. **2.** A fine or penalty that seriously impairs one's earning capacity, esp. from a business.

fine print. (1951) The part of an agreement or document — usu. in small, light print that is not easily noticeable — referring to disclaimers, restrictions, or limitations.

fingerprint, *n.* (1859) **1.** The distinctive pattern of lines on a human fingertip. **2.** The impression of a fingertip made on any surface. **3.** An ink impression of the pattern of lines on a fingertip, usu. taken during the booking procedure after an arrest. — **fingerprint,** *vb.* — **fingerprinting,** *n.*

FIO. *abbr.* Free in and out. • This bill-of-lading term means that the shipper supervises and pays for loading and unloading of cargo.

FIOS. *abbr.* Free in and out stowed. • This bill-of-lading term means that the shipper supervises and pays for loading, unloading, and stowing.

firefighter's rule. A doctrine holding that a firefighter, police officer, or other emergency professional may not hold a person, usu. a property owner, liable for unintentional injuries suffered by the professional in responding to the situation created or caused by the person.

firm, *n.* (18c) **1.** The title under which one or more persons conduct business jointly. **2.** The association by which persons are united for business purposes. • Traditionally, this term has referred to a partnership, as opposed to a company. But today it frequently refers to a company.

First Amendment. The constitutional amendment, ratified with the Bill of Rights in 1791, guaranteeing the freedoms of speech, religion, press, assembly, and petition.

first chair, *n.* (1952) *Slang.* The lead attorney in court for a given case <despite having worked at the firm for six years, the associate had yet to be first chair in a jury trial>. — **first-chair,** *vb.*

first-degree sexual conduct. (1979) Sexual battery that involves an aggravating factor, as when the perpetrator commits the offense against a minor or when the perpetrator commits the offense in the course of committing another crime, such as a burglary.

first-in, first-out. An accounting method that assumes that goods are sold in the order in which they were purchased — that is, the oldest items are sold first. — Abbr. FIFO.

first-sale doctrine. (1963) **1.** *Copyright.* The rule that the purchaser of a physical copy of a copyrighted work, such as a book or CD, may give or sell that copy to someone else without infringing the copyright owner's exclusive distribution rights. **2.** *Patents.* The principle that the buyer of a patented article has the right to use, repair, and resell the article without interference from the patentee.

first-to-file rule. (1969) *Civil procedure.* **1.** The principle that, when two suits are brought by the same parties, regarding the same issues, in two courts of proper jurisdiction, the court that first acquires jurisdiction usu. retains the suit, to the exclusion of the other court. • The court with the second-filed suit ordinarily stays proceedings or abstains. But an exception exists if the first-filed suit is brought merely in anticipation of the true plaintiff's suit and amounts to an improper attempt at forum-shopping. **2.** The doctrine allowing a party to a previously filed lawsuit to enjoin another from pursuing a later-filed action.

first-to-file system. *Patents.* The practice of granting priority to the first person to file a patent application. • Most of the world uses a first-to-file patent system; the only major exception is the United States, which grants priority to the first inventor.

first-to-invent system. *Patents.* The practice of awarding a patent to the first person to create an invention, rather than the first to file a patent application. • Because the first inventor is not necessarily the first person to file for a patent, an interference hearing is held to decide who is entitled to the patent. This system is used only in the United States.

FISA. *abbr.* Foreign Intelligence Surveillance Act.

FISC. *abbr.* United States Foreign Intelligence Surveillance Court.

fisc (fisk), *n.* [Latin *fiscus*] The public treasury. — Also spelled *fisk.*

fiscal (**fis**-kəl), *adj.* (16c) **1.** Of or relating to financial matters. **2.** Of or relating to public finances or taxation.

fishing expedition. An attempt, through broad discovery requests or random questions, to elicit information from another party in the hope that something relevant might be found; esp., such an attempt that exceeds the scope of discovery allowed by procedural rules.

fix bail, *vb.* (18c) To set the amount and terms of bail <after hearing the officer's testimony, the judge fixed bail for the defendant at $100,000>.

fixture. (18c) Personal property that is attached to land or a building and that is regarded as an irremovable part of the real property, such as a fireplace built into a home. See UCC § 9-102(a)(41).

tenant's fixture. (1832) Removable personal property that a tenant affixes to the leased property but that the tenant can detach and take away.

trade fixture. (1839) Removable personal property that a tenant attaches to leased land for business purposes, such as a display counter. • Despite its name, a trade fixture is not usu. treated as a fixture — that is, as irremovable.

fixture filing. (1972) The act or an instance of recording, in public real-estate records, a security interest in personal property that is intended to become a fixture. See UCC § 9-102(a)(40). • The creditor files a financing statement in the real-property records of the county where a mortgage on the real estate would be filed. A fixture-filing financing statement must contain a description of the real estate.

FKA. *abbr.* Formerly known as. — Also rendered *F/K/A*; *fka*; *f/k/a.*

flag desecration. The act of mutilating, defacing, burning, or flagrantly misusing a flag. • Flag desecration is constitutionally protected as a form of free speech. *United States v. Eichman,* 496 U.S. 310, 110 S.Ct. 2404 (1990).

flag state. *Maritime law.* The state under whose flag a ship is registered. • A ship may fly the flag of one state only.

flip, *vb. Slang.* **1.** To buy and then immediately resell securities or real estate in an attempt to turn a profit. **2.** To refinance consumer loans. **3.** To turn state's evidence.

float, *n.* (1915) **1.** The sum of money represented by outstanding or uncollected checks. **2.** The delay between a transaction and the withdrawal of funds to cover the transaction. **3.** The amount of a corporation's shares that are available for trading on the securities market.

float, *vb.* (1833) **1.** (Of a currency) to attain a value in the international exchange market solely on the basis of supply and demand <the IMF allowed the peso to float>. **2.** To issue (a security) for sale on the market <PDQ Corp. floated a new series of preferred shares>. **3.** To arrange or negotiate (a loan) <the bank floated a car loan to Alice despite her poor credit history>.

floodgate. (*usu. pl.*) (13c) A restraint that prevents a release of a usu. undesirable result <the new law opened the floodgates of litigation>.

floodplain. (19c) Land that is subject to floodwaters because of its level topography and proximity to a river or arroyo; esp., level land that, extending from a riverbank, is inundated when the flow of water exceeds the channel's capacity.

floor. (18c) **1.** *Parliamentary law.* The part of the hall where the members of a deliberative body meet to debate issues and conduct business; esp., a legislature's central meeting place where the members sit and conduct business, as distinguished from the galleries, corridors, or lobbies. **2.** The trading area where stocks and commodities are bought and sold on an exchange. **3.** The lowest limit.

flotsam (**flot**-səm). (17c) Goods and debris, esp. those from a shipwreck, that float on the surface of a body of water.

FLRA. *abbr.* Federal Labor Relations Authority.

FLSA. *abbr.* Fair Labor Standards Act.

flyspeck, *n. Insurance.* A potential trivial defect in title to real property, as a result of which a title-insurance company is likely to exclude any risk from that defect before issuing a policy. — **flyspeck,** *vb.*

FmHA. *abbr.* Farmers Home Administration.

FMSHRC. *abbr.* Federal Mine Safety and Health Review Commission.

FNMA. *abbr.* Federal National Mortgage Association.

FOB. *abbr.* Free on board.

FOIA (**foy**-ə). *abbr.* Freedom of Information Act.

foiable (**foy**-ə-bəl), *adj.* (1981) *Slang.* (Of documents) subject to disclosure under the Freedom of Information Act (FOIA).

follow, *vb.* (bef. 12c) To conform to or comply with; to accept as authority.

Food and Drug Administration. A division of the U.S. Public Health Service in the Department of Health and Human Services responsible for ensuring that food is safe, pure, and wholesome; that human and animal drugs, biological products, and medical devices are safe and effective; and that certain other products, such as electronic products that emit radiation, are safe. — Abbr. FDA.

Food, Drug, and Cosmetic Act. A 1938 federal law prohibiting the transportation in interstate commerce of adulterated or misbranded food, drugs, or cosmetics. — Abbr. FDCA.

fool's test. The test formerly used by federal courts and by the Federal Trade Commission to determine whether an advertisement is deceptive, by asking whether even a fool might believe it. • The name comes from Isaiah: "wayfaring men, though fools, shall not err therein."

footprint. (16c) **1.** *Evidence.* The impression made on a surface of soil, snow, etc., by a human foot or a shoe, boot, or any other foot covering. **2.** *Real estate.* The shape of a building's base.

for account of. (1826) A form of indorsement on a note or draft introducing the name of the person entitled to receive the proceeds.

Foraker Act (**for**-ə-kər). The original (1900) federal law providing Puerto Rico with a civil government, but keeping it outside the U.S. customs area. See 48 USCA §§ 731–752.

forbearance, *n.* (16c) **1.** The act of refraining from enforcing a right, obligation, or debt. • Strictly speaking, *forbearance* denotes an intentional negative act, while *omission* or *neglect* is an unintentional negative act. **2.** The act of tolerating or abstaining. — **forbear,** *vb.*

for cause. For a legal reason or ground. • The phrase expresses a common standard governing the removal of a civil servant or an employee under contract. — **for-cause,** *adj.*

force, *n.* (14c) Power, violence, or pressure directed against a person or thing.

actual force. (16c) Force consisting in a physical act, esp. a violent act directed against a robbery victim.

constructive force. (1802) Threats and intimidation to gain control or prevent resistance; esp., threatening words or gestures directed against a robbery victim.

deadly force. (16c) Violent action known to create a substantial risk of causing death or serious bodily harm. • Generally, a person may use deadly force in self-defense or in defense of another only if retaliating against another's deadly force.

excessive force. (16c) Unreasonable or unnecessary force under the circumstances.

intervening force. Force that actively produces harm to another after the actor's negligent act or omission has been committed.

irresistible force. (16c) Force that cannot be foreseen or controlled, esp. that which prevents the performance of a contractual obligation; FORCE MAJEURE.

nondeadly force. (1961) **1.** Force that is neither intended nor likely to cause death or serious bodily harm; force intended to cause only minor bodily harm. **2.** A threat of deadly force, such as displaying a knife.

reasonable force. (17c) Force that is not excessive and that is appropriate for protecting oneself or one's property. • The use of reasonable force will not render a person criminally or tortiously liable.

unlawful force. (16c) Force that is directed against a person without that person's consent, and that is a criminal offense or an actionable tort. Model Penal Code § 3.11.

force and effect, *n.* (16c) Legal efficacy. • The term is now generally regarded as a redundant legalism.

force majeure (fors ma-**zhər**). [Law French "a superior force"] (1883) An event or effect that can be neither anticipated nor controlled. • The term includes both acts of nature (e.g., floods and hurricanes) and acts of people (e.g., riots, strikes, and wars).

force-majeure clause. (1916) A contractual provision allocating the risk of loss if performance becomes impossible or impracticable, esp. as a result of an event or effect that the parties could not have anticipated or controlled.

forcible detainer. The wrongful retention of possession of property by one originally in lawful possession, often with threats or actual use of violence.

forcible entry. (17c) **1.** The act or an instance of violently and unlawfully taking possession of lands and tenements against the will of those in lawful possession. **2.** The act of entering land in another's possession by the use of force against another or by breaking into the premises.

forcible entry and detainer. (17c) **1.** The act of violently taking and keeping possession of lands and tenements without legal authority. **2.** A quick and simple legal proceeding for regaining possession of real property from someone who has wrongfully taken, or refused to surrender, possession.

foreclosure (for-**kloh**-zhər). (18c) A legal proceeding to terminate a mortgagor's interest in property, instituted by the lender (the mortgagee) either to gain title or to force a sale in order to satisfy the unpaid debt secured by the property. — **foreclose,** *vb.* (15c).

equitable foreclosure. (1876) A foreclosure method in which the court orders the property sold, and the proceeds are applied first to pay the costs of the lawsuit and sale and then to the mortgage debt.

judicial foreclosure. (1839) A costly and time-consuming foreclosure method by which the mortgaged property is sold through a court proceeding requiring many standard legal steps such as the filing of a complaint, service of process, notice, and a hearing.

mortgage foreclosure. (1842) A foreclosure of the mortgaged property upon the mortgagor's default.

nonjudicial foreclosure. (1916) A foreclosure method that does not require court involvement.

power-of-sale foreclosure. (1946) A foreclosure process by which, according to the mortgage instrument and a state statute, the mortgaged property is sold at a nonjudicial public sale by a public official, the mortgagee, or a trustee, without the stringent notice requirements, procedural burdens, or delays of a judicial foreclosure.

strict foreclosure. (1823) A rare procedure that gives the mortgagee title to the mortgaged property — without first conducting a sale — after a defaulting mortgagor fails to pay the mortgage debt within a court-specified period.

tax foreclosure. (1869) A public authority's seizure and sale of property for nonpayment of taxes.

foreclosure decree. (1847) **1.** Generally, a decree ordering a judicial foreclosure sale. **2.** A decree ordering the strict foreclosure of a mortgage.

foreign, *adj.* (13c) **1.** Of or relating to another country <foreign affairs>. **2.** Of or relating to another jurisdiction <the Arizona court gave full faith and credit to the foreign judgment from Mississippi>. — **foreigner,** *n.*

foreign-earned-income exclusion. (1964) The Internal Revenue Code provision that excludes from taxation a limited amount of income earned by nonresident taxpayers outside the United States. • The taxpayer must elect between this exclusion and the foreign tax credit. IRC (26 USCA) § 911(a), (b).

Foreign Emoluments Clause. The clause of the U.S. Constitution prohibiting titles of nobility and the acceptance of a gift, title, or other benefit from a foreign power. U.S. Const. art. I, § 9, cl. 8. — Sometimes shortened to *Emoluments Clause.*

foreign exchange. (17c) **1.** The process of making international monetary transactions; esp., the conversion of one currency to that of a different country. **2.** Foreign currency or negotiable instruments payable in foreign currency, such as traveler's checks.

Foreign Intelligence Surveillance Act. A 1978 federal statute that established new procedures and courts to authorize electronic surveillance of foreign intelligence operations in the United States. • The Act established the Foreign Intelligence Surveillance Court and the Foreign Intelligence Court of Review. It allows the Attorney General to obtain warrants that authorize electronic surveillance of suspected foreign-intelligence operatives without public disclosure and without a showing of probable cause that criminal activity is involved. — Abbr. FISA.

foreign law. 1. Generally, the law of another country. **2.** *Conflict of laws.* The law of another state or of a foreign country.

foreign object. (17c) An item that appears where it does not belong; esp., an item introduced into a living body, such as a sponge that is left in a patient's body during surgery.

foreign service. (19c) United States Foreign Service.

foreign substance. (17c) A substance found in a body, organism, or thing where it is not supposed to be found <the plaintiff sued because she thought she saw — and later confirmed that she had found — a foreign substance (namely, a piece of glass) in her hamburger>.

foreman. (15c) A person who directs the work of employees; an overseer, crew chief, or superintendent. — **foremanship,** *n.*

forensic (fə-**ren**-sik *also* -zik), *adj.* [fr. Latin *forensis* "public," fr. Latin *forum* "court"] (17c) **1.** Used in or suitable to courts of law or public debate <forensic psychiatry>. **2.** Rhetorical; argumentative <Tietjen's considerable forensic skills>. **3.** *Hist.* Exterior; foreign.

forensic engineering. (1976) The use of engineering principles or analysis in a lawsuit, usu. through an expert witness's testimony.

forensic linguistics. (1973) The science or technique that evaluates the linguistic characteristics of written or oral communications, usu. to determine identity or authorship.

forensic medicine. (1845) The branch of medicine that establishes or interprets evidence using scientific or technical facts, such as ballistics.

forensic pathology. (1959) The specific branch of medicine that establishes or interprets evidence dealing with diseases and disorders of the body, esp. those that cause death.

forensics (fə-**ren**-siks *also* -ziks). (1963) **1.** The art of argumentative discourse. **2.** The branch of law enforcement dealing with legal evidence relating to firearms and ballistics.

foreseeability, *n.* (1928) The quality of being reasonably anticipatable. • Foreseeability, along with actual causation, is an element of proximate cause in tort law. — **foreseeable,** *adj.*

forfeiture (**for**-fi-chər), *n.* (14c) **1.** The divestiture of property without compensation. **2.** The loss of a right, privilege, or property because of a crime, breach of obligation, or neglect of duty. • Title is instantaneously transferred to another, such as the government, a corporation, or a private person. **3.** Something (esp. money or property) lost or confiscated by this process; a penalty. — **forfeit,** *vb.* — **forfeitable,** *adj.*

civil forfeiture. (1867) An in rem proceeding brought by the government against property that either facilitated a crime or was acquired as a result of criminal activity.

criminal forfeiture. (1866) A governmental proceeding brought against a person to seize property as punishment for the person's criminal behavior.

4. A destruction or deprivation of some estate or right because of the failure to perform some contractual obligation or condition.

forfeiture clause. (1804) A contractual provision stating that, under certain circumstances, one party must forfeit something to the other. • Forfeiture clauses are often held to be void, although they are similar to conditions and other qualifications of estates in land.

forgery, *n.* (16c) **1.** The act of fraudulently making a false document or altering a real one to be used as if genuine. • Though forgery was a misdemeanor at common law, modern statutes typically make it a felony. **2.** A false or altered document made to look genuine by someone with the intent to deceive. **3.** Under the Model Penal Code, the act of fraudulently altering, authenticating, issuing, or transferring a writing without appropriate authorization. • Under the explicit terms of the Code, *writing* can include items such as coins and credit cards. Model Penal Code § 224.1(1). — **forge,** *vb.* — **forger,** *n.*

form, *n.* (13c) **1.** The outer shape or structure of something, as distinguished from its substance or matter <courts are generally less concerned about defects in form than defects in substance>. **2.** Established behavior or procedure, usu. according to custom or rule <the prosecutor followed the established form in her closing argument>. **3.** A model; a sample; an example <attorneys often draft pleadings by using a form instead of starting from scratch>. **4.** The customary method of drafting legal documents, usu. with fixed words, phrases, and sentences <Jones prepared the contract merely by following the state bar's form>. **5.** A legal document with blank spaces to be filled in by the drafter <the divorce lawyer used printed forms that a secretary could fill in>.

formality. (16c) **1.** A small point of practice that, though seemingly unimportant, must usu. be observed to achieve a particular legal result. **2.** *Copyright.* (*usu. pl.*) A procedural requirement formerly required before receiving U.S. copyright protection. • Formalities included (1) a copyright notice appearing on the work, (2) actual publication, (3) registration with the Copyright Office, and (4) deposit of the work with the Library of Congress. The formality requirements eroded during the 20th century. Today, none are required, although registration remains a prerequisite for an infringement suit by U.S. authors in the United States.

formal law. (17c) Procedural law.

formbook. A book that contains sample legal documents, esp. transaction-related documents such as contracts, deeds, leases, wills, trusts, and securities disclosure documents.

former adjudication. (18c) A judgment in a prior action that resulted in a final determination of the rights of the parties or essential fact questions and serves to bar relitigation of the issues relevant to that determination. • Collateral estoppel and res judicata are the two types of former adjudication.

former jeopardy. (1870) The fact of having previously been prosecuted for the same offense. • A defendant enters a plea of former jeopardy to inform the court that a second prosecution is improper.

fornication, *n.* (14c) Voluntary sexual intercourse between two unmarried persons. — **fornicate,** *vb.* — **fornicator,** *n.*

forswearing (for-**swair**-ing), *n.* (14c) The act of repudiating or renouncing under oath. — **forswear,** *vb.*

forthwith, *adv.* (14c) **1.** Immediately; without delay. **2.** Directly; promptly; within a reasonable time under the circumstances.

fortuitous event. (1856) **1.** A happening that, because it occurs only by chance or accident, the parties could not reasonably have foreseen. **2.** An event that, so far as contracting parties are aware, depends on chance. **3.** *Louisiana law.* An event that could not have been reasonably foreseen at the time a contract was made. La. Civ. Code art. 1875.

forum, *n.* (15c) **1.** A public place, esp. one devoted to assembly or debate. **2.** A court or other judicial body; a place of jurisdiction. Pl. **forums, fora.**

forum conveniens (**for**-əm kən-**vee**-nee-enz). [Latin "a suitable forum"] The court in which an action is most appropriately brought, considering the best interests and convenience of the parties and witnesses.

forum non conveniens (**for**-əm non kən-**vee**-nee-enz). [Latin "an unsuitable court"] *Civil procedure.* The doctrine that an appropriate forum — even though competent under the law — may divest itself of jurisdiction if, for the convenience of the litigants and the witnesses, it appears that the action should proceed in another forum in which the action might also have been properly brought in the first place.

forum-selection clause. (1970) A contractual provision in which the parties establish the place (such as the country, state, or type of court) for specified litigation between them.

forum-shopping. (1954) The practice of choosing the most favorable jurisdiction or court in which a claim might be heard. • A plaintiff might engage in forum-shopping, for example, by filing suit in a jurisdiction with a reputation for high jury awards or by filing several similar suits and keeping the one with the preferred judge.

foster, *adj.* (bef. 12c) **1.** (Of a relationship) involving parental care given by someone not related by blood or legal adoption <foster home>. **2.** (Of a person) giving or receiving parental care to or from someone not related by blood or legal adoption <foster parent> <foster child>. — **foster,** *vb.* (12c).

fosterage, *n.* (17c) **1.** The act of caring for another's child. **2.** The entrusting of a child to another. **3.** The condition of being in the care of another. **4.** The act of encouraging or promoting.

foster care. (1876) **1.** A federally funded child-welfare program providing substitute care for abused and neglected children who have been removed by court order from their parents' or guardians' care or for children voluntarily placed by their parents in the temporary care of the state because of a family crisis. 42 USCA §§ 670–679a. **2.** The area of social services concerned with meeting the needs of children who participate in these types of programs.

foster-care placement. (1968) The (usu. temporary) act of placing a child in a home with a person or persons who provide parental care for the child.

foster home. (19c) A household in which foster care is provided to a child who has been removed from his or her birth or adoptive parents, usu. for abuse or neglect. • A foster home is usu. an individual home, but it can also be a group home.

foundation. (14c) **1.** The basis on which something is supported; esp., evidence or testimony that establishes the admissibility of other evidence <laying the foundation>. **2.** A fund established for charitable, educational, religious, research, or other benevolent purposes; an endowment.

founded on, *adj.* (16c) Having as a basis <the suit was founded on the defendant's breach of contract>.

four corners. (1874) The face of a written instrument.

four-corners rule. (1948) **1.** The principle that a document's meaning is to be gathered from the entire document and not from its isolated parts. **2.** The principle that no extraneous evidence should be used to interpret an unambiguous document.

Fourteenth Amendment. The constitutional amendment, ratified in 1868, whose primary provisions effectively apply the Bill of Rights to the states by prohibiting states from denying due process and equal protection and from abridging the privileges and immunities of U.S. citizenship. • The amendment also gave Congress the power to enforce these provisions, leading to legislation such as the civil-rights acts.

Fourth Amendment. The constitutional amendment, ratified with the Bill of Rights in 1791, prohibiting unreasonable searches and seizures and the issuance of warrants without probable cause.

fourth estate. (1821) The journalistic profession; the news media.

four unities. (1852) The four qualities needed to create a joint tenancy at common law — interest, possession, time, and title.

FPLS. *abbr.* Federal Parent Locator Service.

fractional, *adj.* (1815) (Of a tract of land) covering an area less than the acreage reflected on a survey; pertaining to any irregular division of land containing either more or less than the conventional amount of acreage.

frame, *vb.* (14c) **1.** To plan, shape, or construct; esp., to draft or otherwise draw up (a document). **2.** To incriminate (an innocent person) with false evidence, esp. fabricated. — **framable, frameable,** *adj.*

franchise (**fran**-chɪz), *n.* (14c) **1.** The right to vote. **2.** The government-conferred right to engage in a specific business or to exercise corporate powers. **3.** The sole right granted by the owner of a trademark or tradename to engage in business or to sell a good or service in a certain area. **4.** The business or territory controlled by the person or entity that has been granted such a right.

commercial franchise. A franchise using local capital and management by contracting with third parties to operate a facility identified as offering a particular brand of goods or services.

sports franchise. **1.** A franchise granted by a professional sports league to field a team in that league. **2.** The team itself.

franchise, *vb.* (14c) To grant (to another) the sole right of engaging in a certain business or in a business using a particular trademark in a certain area.

franchise agreement. (1905) The contract between a franchisor and franchisee establishing the terms and conditions of the franchise relationship. • State and federal laws regulate franchise agreements.

***Franks* hearing.** (1979) A hearing to determine whether a police officer's affidavit used to obtain a search warrant that yields incriminating evidence was based on false statements by the police officer. *Franks v. Delaware*, 438 U.S. 154, 98 S.Ct. 2674 (1978).

FRAP (frap). *abbr.* Federal Rules of Appellate Procedure.

fratricide (**fra**-trə-sɪd *or* **fray**-). (15c) **1.** The killing of one's brother or sister. **2.** One who has killed one's brother or sister. — **fratricidal,** *adj.*

fraud, *n.* (14c) **1.** A knowing misrepresentation of the truth or concealment of a material fact to induce another to act to his or her detriment. • Fraud is usu. a tort, but in some cases (esp. when the conduct is willful) it may be a crime. **2.** A misrepresentation made recklessly without belief in its truth to induce another person to act. **3.** A tort arising from a knowing misrepresentation, concealment of material fact, or reckless misrepresentation made to induce another to act to his or her detriment. **4.** Unconscionable dealing; esp., in contract law, the unfair use of the power arising out of the parties' relative positions and resulting in an unconscionable bargain. — **fraudulent,** *adj.*

actual fraud. (17c) A concealment or false representation through a statement or conduct that injures another who relies on it in acting.

affiliate click fraud. Click fraud committed by a third party who agrees to host the ad in exchange for payment based on the number of clicks.

affinity fraud. A fraud in which the perpetrator tailors the fraud to target members of a particular group united by common traits or interests that produce inherent trust. • The perpetrator often is or pretends to be a member of the group. Investment scams such as Ponzi or pyramid schemes are common forms of affinity fraud. When a religious group is targeted, it is usu. called *religious-affinity fraud.*

bank fraud. The criminal offense of knowingly executing, or attempting to execute, a scheme or artifice to defraud a financial institution, or to obtain property owned by or under the control of a financial institution, by means of false or fraudulent pretenses, representations, or promises. 18 USCA § 1344.

bankruptcy fraud. (1815) A fraudulent act connected to a bankruptcy case; esp., any of several proscribed acts performed knowingly and fraudulently in a bankruptcy case, such as concealing assets or destroying, withholding, or falsifying documents in an effort to defeat bankruptcy-code provisions. See 18 USCA § 152.

civil fraud. (18c) **1.** FRAUD (3). **2.** *Tax.* An intentional — but not willful — evasion of taxes. • The distinction between an intentional (i.e., *civil*) and willful (i.e., *criminal*) fraud is not always clear, but *civil fraud* carries only a monetary, noncriminal penalty.

click fraud. A scheme in which a person or robot repeatedly clicks on a merchant's pay-per-click advertisement on a website for purposes other than viewing the website or making a purchase.

constructive fraud. (18c) Unintentional deception or misrepresentation that causes injury to another.

criminal fraud. (18c) Fraud that has been made illegal by statute and that subjects the offender to criminal penalties such as fines and imprisonment. • An example is the willful evasion of taxes accomplished by filing a fraudulent tax return.

extrinsic fraud. (1851) **1.** Deception that is collateral to the issues being considered in the case; intentional misrepresentation or deceptive behavior outside the transaction itself (whether a contract or a lawsuit), depriving one party of informed consent or full participation. • For example, a person might engage in extrinsic fraud by convincing a litigant not to hire counsel or answer by dishonestly saying the matter will not be pursued. **2.** Deception that prevents a person from knowing about or asserting certain rights.

fraud in law. (17c) Fraud that is presumed under the circumstances, as when a debtor transfers assets and thereby impairs creditors' efforts to collect sums due.

fraud in the factum. (1848) Fraud occurring when a legal instrument as actually executed differs from the one intended for execution by the person who executes it, or when the instrument may have had no legal existence. • Compared to fraud in the inducement, fraud in the factum occurs only rarely, as when a blind person signs a mortgage when misleadingly told that the paper is just a letter.

fraud in the inducement. (1831) Fraud occurring when a misrepresentation leads another to enter into a transaction with a false impression of the risks, duties, or obligations involved; an intentional misrepresentation of a material risk or duty reasonably relied on, thereby injuring the other party without vitiating the contract itself, esp. about a fact relating to value.

fraud on the community. *Family law.* In a community-property state, the deliberate hiding or fraudulent transfer of community assets before a divorce or death for the purpose of preventing the other spouse from claiming a half-interest ownership in the property.

fraud on the court. (1810) In a judicial proceeding, a lawyer's or party's misconduct so serious that it undermines or is intended to undermine the integrity of the proceeding. • Examples are bribery of a juror and introduction of fabricated evidence.

fraud on the market. **1.** Fraud occurring when an issuer of securities gives out misinformation that affects the market price of stock, the result being that people who buy or sell are effectively misled even though they did not rely on the statement itself or anything derived from it other than the market price. **2.** The securities-law claim based on such fraud.

insurance fraud. Fraud committed against an insurer, as when an insured lies on a policy application or fabricates a claim.

intrinsic fraud. (1832) Deception that pertains to an issue involved in an original action. • Examples include the use of fabricated evidence, a false return of service, perjured testimony, and false receipts or other commercial documents.

mail fraud. (1918) An act of fraud using the U.S. Postal Service, as in making false representations through the mail to obtain an economic advantage. 18 USCA §§ 1341–1347.

promissory fraud. (1934) A promise to perform made when the promisor had no intention of performing the promise.

wire fraud. (1955) An act of fraud using electronic communications, as by making false representations on the telephone to obtain money. • The federal Wire Fraud Act provides that any artifice to defraud by means of wire or other electronic communications (such as radio or television) in foreign or interstate commerce is a crime. 18 USCA § 1343.

fraudulent conveyance. (17c) **1.** A transfer of property for little or no consideration, made for the purpose of hindering or delaying a creditor by putting the property beyond the creditor's reach; a transaction by which the owner of real or personal property seeks to place the property beyond the reach of creditors. **2.** *Bankruptcy.* A prebankruptcy transfer or obligation made or incurred by a debtor for little or no consideration or with the actual intent to hinder, delay, or defraud a creditor. • A bankruptcy trustee may recover such a conveyance from the transferee if the requirements of 11 USCA § 548 are met.

FRB. *abbr.* Federal Reserve Board of Governors.

FRCA. *abbr.* Fair-Credit-Reporting Act.

FRCP. *abbr.* Federal Rules of Civil Procedure.

F.R.D. *abbr.* Federal Rules Decisions; a series of reported federal court decisions (beginning in 1938) that construe or apply the Federal Rules of Civil and Criminal Procedure. • Also included are rule changes, ceremonial proceedings of federal courts, and articles on federal-court practice and procedure. — Often written *FRD.*

FRE. *abbr.* Federal Rules of Evidence.

Freddie Mac. Federal Home Loan Mortgage Corporation.

free, *adj.* (bef. 12c) **1.** Having legal and political rights; enjoying political and civil liberty. **2.** Not subject to the constraint or domination of another; enjoying personal freedom; emancipated. **3.** Characterized by choice, rather than by compulsion or constraint. **4.** Unburdened. **5.** Not confined by force or restraint. **6.** Unrestricted and unregulated. **7.** Costing nothing; gratuitous. — **freely,** *adv.* — **freely,** *adv.*

free alongside ship. A mercantile-contract term allocating the rights and duties of the buyer and the seller of goods with respect to delivery, payment, and risk of loss, whereby the seller must clear the goods for export, and deliver the goods to the wharf beside the buyer's chosen vessel. UCC § 2-319. — Abbr. FAS.

freedom of association. (1889) The right to join with others in a common undertaking that would be lawful if pursued individually. • This right is protected by the First Amendment to the U.S. Constitution. The government may not prohibit outsiders from joining an association, but the insiders do not necessarily have a right to exclude others.

freedom of choice. (1817) **1.** The liberty embodied in the exercise of one's rights. **2.** The parents' opportunity to select a school for their child in a unitary, integrated school system that is devoid of de jure segregation. **3.** The liberty to exercise one's right of privacy, esp. the right to have an abortion.

freedom of contract. (1879) The doctrine that people have the right to bind themselves legally; a judicial concept that contracts are based on mutual agreement and free choice, and thus should not be hampered by external control such as governmental interference.

freedom of expression. (1877) The freedom of speech, press, assembly, or religion as guaranteed by the First Amendment; the prohibition of governmental interference with those freedoms.

Freedom of Information Act. The federal statute that establishes guidelines for public disclosure of documents and materials created and held by federal agencies. 5 USCA § 552. — Abbr. FOIA.

freedom of religion. (16c) The right to adhere to any form of religion or none, to practice or abstain from practicing religious beliefs, and to be free from governmental interference with or promotion of religion, as guaranteed by the First Amendment and Article VI, § 3 of the U.S. Constitution.

freedom of speech. (17c) The right to express one's thoughts and opinions without governmental restriction, as guaranteed by the First Amendment.

freedom of the press. (17c) The right to print and publish materials without governmental intervention, as guaranteed by the First Amendment.

freedom of the seas. *Int'l law.* The principle that the seas beyond territorial waters are not subject to any country's control. • Ships on the high seas are subject only to the jurisdiction of the country whose flag they fly, except in cases of piracy, hijacking, hot pursuit from territorial waters, slave trading, and certain rights of approach by warships.

free enterprise. (1890) A private and consensual system of production and distribution, usu. conducted for a profit in a competitive environment that is relatively free of governmental interference.

Free Exercise Clause. (1950) The constitutional provision (U.S. Const. amend. I) prohibiting the government from interfering in people's religious practices or forms of worship.

freehold, *n.* (15c) **1.** An estate in land held in fee simple, in fee tail, or for term of life; any real-property interest that is or may become possessory. **2.** The tenure by which such an estate is held.

movable freehold. (18c) The land a seashore owner acquires or loses as water recedes or approaches.

freeman. (bef. 12c) **1.** A person who possesses and enjoys all the civil and political rights belonging to the people under a free government. **2.** A person who is not a slave.

free on board. (ca. 1924) A mercantile-contract term allocating the rights and duties of the buyer and the seller of goods with respect to delivery, payment, and risk of loss, whereby the seller must clear the goods for export, and the buyer must arrange for transportation. — Abbr. FOB.

FOB destination. A mercantile term denoting that the seller is required to pay the freight charges as far as the buyer's named destination.

FOB shipping. A mercantile term denoting that the seller is required to bear the risk of placing the goods on a carrier.

free rider. One who obtains an economic benefit at another's expense without contributing to it. — Also written *free-rider.*

free trade, *n.* (17c) The open and unrestricted import and export of goods without barriers, such as quotas or tariffs, other than those charged only as a revenue source, as opposed to those designed to protect domestic businesses.

free-trade zone. A duty-free area within a country to promote commerce, esp. transshipment and processing, without entering into the country's market.

freeze, *n.* (1942) **1.** A period when the government restricts or immobilizes certain commercial activity.

credit freeze. (1922) A period when the government restricts bank-lending.

wage-and-price freeze. (1943) A period when the government forbids the increase of wages and prices.

2. A recapitalization of a closed corporation so that the value of its existing capital is concentrated primarily in preferred stock rather than in common stock. — **freeze,** *vb.*

fresh complaint. (1853) A reasonably prompt lodging of a grievance; esp., a victim's prompt report of a sexual assault to someone trustworthy.

fresh pursuit. (17c) **1.** The right of a police officer to make a warrantless search of a fleeing suspect or to cross jurisdictional lines to arrest a fleeing suspect. **2.** The right of a person to use reasonable force to retake property that has just been taken.

fresh start. (1857) *Bankruptcy.* The favorable financial status obtained by a debtor who receives a release from personal liability on prepetition debts or who reorganizes debt obligations through the confirmation and completion of a bankruptcy plan.

friendly fire. (1976) **1.** A fire burning where it is intended to burn, yet capable of causing unintended damage. **2.** Military or police gunfire that injures one's own side.

friendly suit. (18c) A lawsuit in which all the parties have agreed beforehand to allow a court to resolve the issues. • Friendly suits are often filed by settling parties who wish to have a judgment entered.

friend of the court. (1816) **1.** AMICUS CURIAE. **2.** In some jurisdictions, an official who investigates and advises the court in domestic-relations cases involving minors. • The friend of the court may also help enforce court orders in those cases.

frisk, *n.* (18c) A pat-down search to discover a concealed weapon.

frivolous, *adj.* (15c) Lacking a legal basis or legal merit; not serious; not reasonably purposeful <a frivolous claim>.

frolic (**frol**-ik), *n. Torts.* An employee's significant deviation from the employer's business for personal reasons. • A frolic is outside the scope of employment, and thus the employer is not vicariously liable for the employee's actions.

front, *n.* (14c) **1.** The side or part of a building or lot that is open to view, that is the principal entrance, or that faces out to the open (as to a lake or ocean); the foremost part of something <the property's front was its most valuable attribute>. **2.** A person or group that serves to conceal the true identity or activity of the person or group in control <the political party was a front for the terrorist group>. **3.** A political association similar to a party <popular front>.

frontage (**frən**-tij). (17c) **1.** The part of land abutting a street or highway or lying between a building's front and a street or highway. **2.** The linear distance of a frontage.

frontager (**frən**-tij-ər), *n.* (17c) A person owning or occupying land that abuts a highway, river, seashore, or the like.

front-foot rule. (1872) The principle that an improvement cost is to be apportioned among several properties in proportion to their frontage, without regard to the benefits conferred on each property.

fruit-and-the-tree doctrine. (1979) *Tax.* The rule that an individual who earns income cannot assign that income to another person to avoid taxation.

fruit-of-the-poisonous-tree doctrine. (1948) *Criminal procedure.* The rule that evidence derived from an illegal search, arrest, or interrogation is inadmissible because the evidence (the "fruit") was tainted by the illegality (the "poisonous tree"). • Under this doctrine, for example, a murder weapon is inadmissible if the map showing its location and used to find it was seized during an illegal search.

frustration, *n.* (16c) **1.** The prevention or hindering of the attainment of a goal, such as contractual performance.

commercial frustration. (1918) An excuse for a party's nonperformance because of some unforeseeable and uncontrollable circumstance.

self-induced frustration. (1926) A breach of contract caused by one party's action that prevents the performance. • The phrase is something of a misnomer, since *self-induced frustration* is not really a type of frustration at all but is instead a breach of contract.

temporary frustration. (1950) An occurrence that prevents performance and legally suspends the duty to perform for the duration of the event. • If the burden or circumstance is substantially different after the event, then the duty may be discharged.

2. *Contracts.* The doctrine that if a party's principal purpose is substantially frustrated by unanticipated changed circumstances, that party's duties are discharged and the contract is considered terminated. — **frustrate,** *vb.*

FSLIC. *abbr.* Federal Savings and Loan Insurance Corporation.

F.Supp. *abbr. Federal Supplement,* a series of reported decisions of the federal district courts (from 1932 to 1998), the U.S. Court of Claims (1932 to 1960), and the U.S. Customs Court (from 1949 to 1998, but renamed the Court of International Trade in 1980). • It is the first of the *Federal Supplement* series.

F.Supp.2d. *abbr.* The second series of the *Federal Supplement,* which includes decisions of federal district courts and the Court of International Trade from 1997 to the present. • Some of the F.Supp. volumes contain cases from 1998 and some of the F.Supp.2d volumes contain cases decided in 1997.

FTC. *abbr.* Federal Trade Commission.

FTCA. *abbr.* Federal Tort Claims Act.

FTDA. *abbr.* Federal Trademark Dilution Act.

fugitive. (14c) **1.** A person who flees or escapes; a refugee. **2.** A criminal suspect or a witness in a criminal case who flees, evades, or escapes arrest, prosecution, imprisonment, service of process, or the giving of testimony, esp. by fleeing the jurisdiction or by hiding. See 18 USCA § 1073.

Fugitive Felon Act. A federal statute that makes it a felony to flee across state lines to avoid state-felony prosecution or confinement, or to avoid giving testimony in a state-felony case. 18 USCA § 1073.

fugue (fyoog). (16c) An abnormal state of consciousness in which one appears to function normally but on recovery has no memory of what one did while in that condition.

Full Faith and Credit Clause. (1896) U.S. Const. art. IV, § 1, which requires states to give effect to the acts, public records, and judicial decisions of other states.

Full Faith and Credit for Child-Support Orders Act. A 1994 federal statute designed to facilitate interstate child-support collection. 28 USCA § 1738B.

fully administered. (17c) A plea by an executor or administrator that he or she has completely and legally disposed of all the assets of the estate and that the estate has no remaining assets from which a new claim could be satisfied.

function, *n.* (16c) **1.** Activity that is appropriate to a particular business or profession. **2.** Office; duty; the occupation of an office.

fund, *n.* (17c) **1.** A sum of money or other liquid assets established for a specific purpose.

blended fund. A fund created by income from more than one source, usu. from the sale of a testator's real and personal property.

contingent fund. (18c) **1.** A fund created by a municipality for expenses that will necessarily arise during the year but that cannot be appropriately classified under any of the specific purposes for which taxes are collected. **2.** A fund segregated by a business to pay unknown costs that may arise in the future.

fund in court. (18c) **1.** Contested money deposited with the court. **2.** Money deposited to pay a contingent liability.

general fund. (17c) **1.** A government's primary operating fund; a state's assets furnishing the means for the support of government and for defraying the legislature's discretionary appropriations. • A general fund is distinguished from assets of a special character, such as trust, escrow, and special-purpose funds. **2.** A nonprofit entity's assets that are not earmarked for a specific purpose.

general revenue fund. (1855) The fund out of which a municipality pays its ordinary and incidental expenses.

guaranty fund. A private deposit-insurance fund, raised primarily by assessments on banks, and used to pay the depositors of an insolvent bank.

paid-in fund. A reserve cash fund established by a mutual insurance company to pay unforeseen losses. • The fund is in lieu of a capital stock account.

public fund. (*usu. pl.*) **1.** The revenue or money of a governmental body. **2.** The securities of a state or national government.

revolving fund. (1928) A fund whose moneys are continually expended and then replenished, such as a petty-cash fund.

sinking fund. (18c) A fund consisting of regular deposits that are accumulated with interest to pay off a long-term corporate or public debt. — Abbr. SF.

unsatisfied-judgment fund. (1953) A fund established by a state to compensate persons for losses stemming from an automobile accident caused by an uninsured or underinsured motorist.

2. (*usu. pl.*) Money or other assets, such as stocks, bonds, or working capital, available to pay debts, expenses, and the like. **3.** A pool of investments owned in common and managed for a fee; mutual fund.

fund, *vb.* (18c) **1.** To furnish money to (an individual, entity, or venture), esp. to finance a particular project. **2.** To use resources in a manner that produces interest. **3.** To convert (a debt, esp. an open account) into a long-term debt that bears interest at a fixed rate.

fundamental-fairness doctrine. (1969) The rule that applies the principles of due process to a judicial proceeding. • The term is commonly considered synonymous with *due process.*

fundamental law. (17c) The organic law that establishes the governing principles of a nation or state; esp., constitutional law.

fundamental-miscarriage-of-justice exception. The doctrine allowing a federal court in a habeas corpus proceeding to address a claim of constitutional error that, although ordinarily unreviewable, is subject to review because of a state-court procedural default that rendered the proceedings basically unfair.

fundamental right. (17c) **1.** A right derived from natural or fundamental law. **2.** *Constitutional law.* A significant component of liberty, encroachments of which are rigorously tested by courts to ascertain the soundness of purported governmental justifications. • A fundamental right triggers strict scrutiny to determine whether the law violates the Due Process Clause or the Equal Protection Clause of the 14th Amendment. As enunciated by the Supreme Court, fundamental rights include voting, interstate travel, and various aspects of privacy (such as marriage and contraception rights).

fungible (**fən**-jə-bəl), *adj.* (18c) Commercially interchangeable with other property of the same kind <corn and wheat are fungible goods, whereas land is not>. — **fungible,** *n.*

furlough (**fər**-loh). (17c) **1.** A leave of absence from military or other employment duty. **2.** A brief release from prison. — **furlough,** *vb.*

future-advance clause. (1911) A contractual term in a security agreement covering additional loaned amounts on present collateral or collateral to be acquired in the future, regardless of whether the secured party is obliged to make the advances; esp., a provision in an open-end mortgage or deed of trust allowing the borrower to borrow additional sums in the future, secured under the same instrument and by the same security. • This type of clause makes a new security agreement unnecessary when the secured creditor makes a future loan to the debtor.

futures, *n.* **1.** Standardized assets (such as commodities, stocks, or foreign currencies) bought or sold for future acceptance or delivery. **2.** Futures contract. **3.** Future claimants, esp. those who would become members of a class of persons injured by a defendant and thus included in a class action.

G

GAAP (gap). *abbr.* Generally accepted accounting principles.

GAAS (gas). *abbr.* Generally accepted auditing standards.

gage (gayj), *n.* (14c) A pledge, pawn, or other thing deposited as security for performance.

gag order. (1952) **1.** A judge's order directing parties, attorneys, witnesses, or journalists to refrain from publicly discussing the facts of a case. • When directed to the press, such an order is generally unconstitutional under the First Amendment. **2.** A judge's order that an unruly defendant be bound and gagged during trial to prevent further interruptions.

gain, *n.* (14c) **1.** An increase in amount, degree, or value.

pecuniary gain. (18c) **1.** A gain of money or of something having monetary value. **2.** *Criminal law.* Any monetary or economic gain that serves as an impetus for the commission of an offense. • In most states, an offense and its punishment are aggravated if the offense was committed for pecuniary gain. Murder, for example, is often aggravated to capital murder if the murderer is paid to commit the crime.

2. Excess of receipts over expenditures or of sale price over cost. **3.** *Tax.* The excess of the amount realized from a sale or other disposition of property over the property's adjusted value. IRC (26 USCA) § 1001.

extraordinary gain. (16c) A gain that is both unusual and infrequent, such as the gain realized from selling a large segment of a business.

ordinary gain. (1945) A gain from the sale or exchange of a noncapital asset.

recognized gain. (1951) The portion of a gain that is subject to income taxation. IRC (26 USCA) § 1001(c).

***Gallagher* agreement.** (1977) A contract that gives one codefendant the right to settle with the plaintiff for a fixed sum at any time during trial and that guarantees payment of the sum regardless of the trial's outcome. *City of Tucson v. Gallagher*, 493 P.2d 1197 (Ariz. 1972).

gambling, *n.* (18c) The act of risking something of value, esp. money, for a chance to win a prize. • Gambling is regulated by state and federal law. 18 USCA §§ 1081 et seq.

gambling device. Any thing, such as cards, dice, or an electronic or mechanical contrivance, that allows a person to play a game of chance in which money may be won or lost. • Gambling devices are regulated by law, and the use or possession of a gambling device can be illegal.

game, *n.* (13c) **1.** Wild animals and birds considered as objects of pursuit, for food or sport; esp., animals for which one must have a license to hunt. **2.** A contest, for amusement or for a prize, whose outcome depends on the skill, strength, or luck of the players.

game of chance. A game whose outcome is determined by luck rather than skill.

game of skill. A game in which the outcome is determined by a player's superior knowledge or ability, not chance.

percentage game. A game of chance from which the house collects an amount calculated as a percentage of the wagers made or the sums won. • Percentage games are illegal in many states.

game law. (18c) A federal or state law that regulates the hunting of game, esp. one that forbids the capturing or killing of specified game either entirely or seasonally, describes the means for killing or capturing game in season, or restricts the number and type of game animals that may be killed or captured in season. 16 USCA §§ 661–667; 18 USCA §§ 41–47.

gamete intrafallopian transfer. (ca. 1984) A procedure in which mature eggs are implanted in a woman's fallopian tubes and fertilized with semen. — Abbr. GIFT.

ganancial (gə-**nan**-shəl), *adj.* (1843) Of, relating to, or consisting of community property <a spouse's ganancial rights>.

gang. (15c) A group of persons who go about together or act in concert, esp. for antisocial or criminal purposes. • Many gangs have common identifying signs and symbols, such as hand signals and distinctive colors.

gangster. A member of a criminal gang or an organized-crime syndicate.

GAO. *abbr.* General Accountability Office.

gap-filler. (15c) A rule that supplies a contractual term that the parties failed to include in the contract. • For example, if the contract does not contain a sales price, UCC § 2-305(1) establishes the price as being a reasonable one at the time of delivery.

gap period. (1978) *Bankruptcy.* The duration of time between the filing of an involuntary bankruptcy petition and the entry of the order for relief.

gap report. (1984) In the making of federal court rules, a report that explains any changes made by an advisory committee in the language of a proposed amendment to a procedural rule after its publication for comment.

gap theory. *Insurance.* The principle that a tortfeasor will be considered underinsured if his or her liability-insurance coverage — although legally adequate — is less than the injured party's underinsured-motorist coverage. • This principle allows an injured party to invoke underinsured-motorist coverage.

***Garcia* hearing** (gahr-**see**-ə). (1981) *Criminal procedure.* A hearing held to ensure that a defendant who is one of two or more defendants represented by the same attorney understands (1) the risk of a conflict of interest inherent in this type of representation, and (2) that he or she is entitled to the services of an attorney who does not represent anyone else in the defendant's case. *United States v. Garcia*, 517 F.2d 272 (5th Cir. 1975).

garnish, *vb.* [Old French *garnir* "to warn" "to prepare"] (16c) To subject (property) to garnishment; to attach (property held by a third party) in order to satisfy a debt. — **garnishable,** *adj.*

garnishee (gahr-ni-**shee**), *n.* (17c) A person or institution (such as a bank) that is indebted to or is bailee for another whose property has been subjected to garnishment.

garnisher. (16c) A creditor who initiates a garnishment action to reach the debtor's property that is thought to be held or owed by a third party (the *garnishee*).

garnishment, *n.* (16c) **1.** A judicial proceeding in which a creditor (or potential creditor) asks the court to order a third party who is indebted to or is bailee for the debtor to turn over to the creditor any of the debtor's property (such as wages or bank accounts) held by that third party. • A plaintiff initiates a garnishment action as a means of either prejudgment seizure or postjudgment collection.

wrongful garnishment. (1896) **1.** An improper or tortious garnishment. **2.** A cause of action against a garnisher for improperly or tortiously filing a garnishment proceeding.

2. The judicial order by which such a turnover is effected.

gas chamber. (ca. 1945) A small, sealed room in which a capital punishment is carried out by strapping the prisoner into a chair and releasing poisonous fumes.

GATT (gat). *abbr.* General Agreement on Tariffs and Trade.

g.b.h. *abbr.* Grievous bodily harm.

GBMI. *abbr.* Guilty but mentally ill.

General Accounting Office. General Accountability Office.

General Accountability Office. An office in the legislative branch of the federal government responsible for auditing the receipt and disbursement of U.S. government funds and conducting investigations for members of Congress and congressional committees. — Abbr. GAO.

General Agreement on Tariffs and Trade. A multiparty international agreement — signed originally in 1948 — that promotes international trade by lowering import duties and providing equal access to markets. • More than 150 nations are parties to the agreement. — Abbr. GATT.

general assembly. 1. The name of the legislative body in many states. **2.** (*cap.*) The deliberative body of the United Nations.

General Counsel's Memorandum. *Tax.* **1.** A written discussion, issued by the office of the Chief Counsel of the IRS, on the merits of a legal issue involving tax law. **2.** A written explanation, issued by the office of the Chief Counsel of the IRS, explaining the IRS's positions in revenue rulings and technical advice memorandums.

General Court. The name of the legislatures of Massachusetts and New Hampshire. • "General Court" was a common colonial-era term for a body that exercised judicial and legislative functions.

generalia specialibus non derogant (jen-ə-**ray**-lee-ə spesh-ee-**ay**-lə-bəs non **der**-ə-gənt). [Latin "general things do not derogate from specific things"] The doctrine holding that general words in a later statute do not repeal an earlier statutory provision dealing with a special subject.

General Land Office. A former U.S. Interior Department division that exercised executive power relating to the public lands, including their survey, patenting, and sale or other disposition.

generally accepted accounting principles. (1930) The conventions, rules, and procedures that define approved accounting practices at a particular time. — Abbr. GAAP.

generally accepted auditing standards. The guidelines issued by the American Institute of Certified Public Accountants establishing an auditor's professional qualities and the criteria for the auditor's examination and required reports. — Abbr. GAAS.

general maritime law. The body of U.S. legal precedents and doctrines developed through caselaw in maritime and admiralty litigation. • General maritime law is a branch of federal common law. It is distinguished from statutory law.

general principle of law. 1. A principle widely recognized by peoples whose legal order has attained a certain level of sophistication. **2.** *Int'l law.* A principle that gives rise to international legal obligations. **3.** A principle recognized in all kinds of legal relations, regardless of the legal system to which it belongs (state law, federal law, international law, etc.).

General Services Administration. The independent federal agency that constructs and operates buildings; manages government property and records; procures and distributes supplies; and provides management services in communications, traffic, and automatic data processing. — Abbr. GSA.

general-verdict rule. (1930) The principle that when a jury returns a general verdict on multiple causes of action (or theories of recovery), it is presumed on appeal that the jury found in the prevailing party's favor on each cause of action.

General Welfare Clause. (1898) U.S. Const. art. I, § 8, cl. 1, which empowers Congress to levy taxes and pay debts in order to provide for the country's general welfare. • The Supreme Court has broadly interpreted this clause to allow Congress to create, for example, the social-security system.

general words. (18c) Semantically broad expression; esp., language used in deeds to convey not only the specific property described in the conveyance but also all easements, privileges, and appurtenances that may belong to the property.

generation. (14c) **1.** A single degree or stage in the succession of persons in natural descent. **2.** The average time span between the birth of parents and the birth of their children.

generation-skipping transfer. (1979) *Wills & trusts.* A conveyance of assets to a "skip person," that is, a person more than one generation removed from the transferor. • For example, a conveyance either directly or in trust from a grandparent to a grandchild is a generation-skipping transfer subject to a generation-skipping transfer tax. IRC (26 USCA) §§ 2601–2663.

generic, *adj.* (1846) *Trademarks.* **1.** Common or descriptive, and thus not eligible for trademark protection; nonproprietary <a generic name>. **2.** Not having a trademark or brand name <generic drugs>. — **genericness,** *n.* (20c).

generic-drug law. (1977) A statute that allows pharmacists to substitute a generic drug for a brand-name drug under specified conditions. • Most states have enacted generic-drug laws to ensure that less-expensive generic drugs are available to consumers.

genericide (jə-**ner**-ə-sɪd). *Trademarks.* The loss or cancellation of a trademark that no longer distinguishes the owner's product from others' products. • Genericide occurs when a trademark becomes such a household name that the consuming public begins to think of the mark not as a brand name but as a synonym for the product itself. Examples of trademarks that have been "killed" by genericide include *aspirin* and *escalator.*

generic name. (1872) *Trademarks.* A term that describes something generally without designating the thing's source or creator, such as the word *car* or *sink.* • A generic name cannot be protected as a trademark for the thing it denotes; e.g., *Apple* can be a trademark for computers but not for apples.

genetic engineering. (ca. 1951) A method of creating new life forms and organic matter by gene-splicing and other techniques. • The Supreme Court has ruled that those creations are patentable. *Diamond v. Chakrabarty,* 447 U.S. 303, 100 S.Ct. 2204 (1980).

genetic-marker test. A medical method of testing tissue samples used in paternity and illegitimacy cases to determine whether a particular man could be the father of a child. • This test represents a medical advance over blood-grouping tests. It analyzes DNA and is much more precise in assessing the probability of paternity. — Abbr. GMT.

Geneva Conventions of 1949 (jə-**nee**-və). Four international agreements dealing with the protection of wounded members of the armed forces, the treatment of prisoners of war, and the protection of civilians during international armed conflicts.

genocide (**jen**-ə-sɪd). (ca. 1944) *Int'l law.* An international crime involving acts causing serious physical and mental harm with the intent to destroy, partially or entirely, a national, ethnic, racial, or religious group. • The widely ratified Genocide Convention of 1948 defines the crime.

gentlemen's agreement. (1886) An unwritten agreement that, while not legally enforceable, is secured by the good faith and honor of the parties.

gentrification, *n.* (1973) The restoration and upgrading of a deteriorated or aging urban neighborhood by middle-class or affluent persons, resulting in increased property values and often in displacement of lower-income residents. — **gentrify,** *vb.*

genuine, *adj.* (17c) **1.** (Of a thing) authentic or real; having the quality of what a given thing purports to be or to have <the plaintiff failed to question whether the exhibits were genuine>. **2.** (Of an instrument) free of forgery or counterfeiting <the bank teller could not determine whether the signature on the check was genuine>. UCC § 1-201(18).

genuine issue of material fact. (1938) *Civil procedure.* In the law of summary judgments, a triable, substantial, or real question of fact supported by substantial evidence. • An issue of this kind precludes entry of summary judgment.

geodetic-survey system (jee-ə-**det**-ik). (1990) A federally created land-description method consisting of nationwide marks (or *benches*) made at longitude and latitude points. • The geodetic-survey system integrates most of the real property in the United States into one unified form of measurement.

german (**jər**-mən), *adj.* (14c) Having the same parents or grandparents; closely related.

germane (jər-**mayn**), *adj.* (14c) Relevant; pertinent. • Under parliamentary law, debate and amendments are in order only if they are germane to the motion under consideration.

gerrymandering (**jer**-ee-man-dər-ing *or* **ger**-ee-), *n.* (1812) **1.** The practice of dividing a geographical area into electoral districts, often of highly irregular shape, to give one political party an unfair advantage by diluting the opposition's voting strength. **2.** The practice of dividing any geographical or jurisdictional area into political units (such as school districts) to give some group a special advantage. — **gerrymander,** *vb.*

ghosting. The assumption of the identity of a deceased person to conceal one's true identity.

GIFT. *abbr.* Gamete intrafallopian transfer.

gift, *n.* (12c) **1.** The voluntary transfer of property to another without compensation. **2.** A thing so transferred. — **gift,** *vb.*

anatomical gift. (1971) A testamentary donation of a bodily organ or organs, esp. for transplant or for medical research.

charitable gift. An inter vivos or testamentary donation to a nonprofit organization for the relief of poverty, the advancement of education, the advancement of religion, the promotion of health, governmental, or municipal purposes, and other purposes the accomplishment of which is beneficial to the community.

class gift. (1949) A gift to a group of persons, uncertain in number at the time of the gift but to be ascertained at a future time, who are all to take in definite proportions, the share of each being dependent on the ultimate number in the group.

completed gift. (1952) A gift that is no longer in the donor's possession and control. • Only a completed gift is taxable under the gift tax.

gift causa mortis (**kaw**-zə **mor**-tis). (18c) A gift made in contemplation of the donor's imminent death. • The three essentials are that (1) the gift must be made with a view to the donor's present illness or peril, (2) the donor must actually die from that illness or peril, without ever recovering, and (3) there must be a delivery. Even though *causa mortis* is the more usual word order in modern law, the correct Latin phrasing is *mortis causa* — hence *gift mortis causa.*

gift in trust. (18c) A gift of legal title to property to someone who will act as trustee for the benefit of a beneficiary.

gift over. (18c) A property gift (esp. by will) that takes effect after the expiration of a preceding estate in the property (such as a life estate or fee simple determinable) <to Sarah for life, with gift over to Don in fee>.

inter vivos gift (**in**-tər **vɪ**-vohs *or* **vee**-vohs). (1848) A gift of personal property made during the donor's lifetime and delivered to the donee with the intention of irrevocably surrendering control over the property.

onerous gift (**ohn**-ə-rəs *or* **on**-ə-rəs). A gift made subject to certain conditions imposed on the recipient.

prenuptial gift (pree-**nəp**-shəl). (1921) A gift of property from one spouse to another before marriage. • In community-property states, prenuptial gifts are often made to preserve the property's classification as separate property.

split gift. (1957) *Tax.* A gift that is made by one spouse to a third person and that, for gift-tax purposes, both spouses treat as being made one-half by each spouse; a gift in which the spouses combine their annual gift-tax exclusions.

substitute gift. (1934) A testamentary gift to one person in place of another who is unable to take under the will for some reason.

taxable gift. (1922) A gift that, after adjusting for the annual exclusion and applicable deductions, is subject to the federal unified transfer tax. IRC (26 USCA) § 2503.

testamentary gift (tes-tə-**men**-tə-ree *or* -tree). (18c) A gift made in a will.

vested gift. (1820) An absolute gift, being neither conditional nor contingent, though its use or enjoyment might not occur until sometime in the future.

gift enterprise. (1858) **1.** A scheme for the distribution of items by chance among those who have purchased shares in the scheme. **2.** A merchant's scheme to increase sales without lowering prices by giving buyers tickets that carry a chance to win a prize.

gifting club. A type of pyramid scheme or Ponzi scheme in which recruits make "gifts" of money to other club members with the expectation that future recruits will make "gifts" to the present recruits.

gilt-edged, *adj.* (Of a security) having the highest rating for safety of investment; exceptionally safe as an investment.

Ginnie Mae (**jin**-ee **may**). Government National Mortgage Association.

gist (jist). (18c) **1.** The ground or essence (of a legal action) <the gist of the crime>. **2.** The main point <she skimmed the brief to get the gist of it>. • This noun derives from the Law French verb *giser* "to lie."

give, *vb.* (13c) **1.** To voluntarily transfer (property) to another without compensation. **2.** To confer by a formal act. **3.** To present for another to consider. **4.** (Of a jury) to impose or award by verdict.

give, devise, and bequeath, *vb.* (17c) To transfer property by will <I give, devise, and bequeath all the rest, residue, and remainder of my estate to my beloved daughter Sarah>. • This wording has long been criticized as redundant. In modern usage, *give* ordinarily suffices.

glass ceiling. (1984) An actual or supposed upper limit of professional advancement, esp. for women, as a result of discriminatory practices.

Glass–Steagall Act. A federal statute that protects bank depositors by restricting the securities-related business of commercial banks, specif. by prohibiting banks from owning brokerage firms or engaging in the brokerage business. 12 USCA § 378.

gloss, *n.* (16c) **1.** A note inserted between the lines or in the margin of a text to explain a difficult or obscure word in the text <this edition of Shakespeare's works is bolstered by its many glosses on Elizabethan English>. **2.** A collection of explanations; a glossary <the hornbook's copious gloss>. **3.** (*usu. pl.*) A pronouncement about meaning; an interpretation <the statutory language needs no gloss>.

GMI. *abbr.* Guilty but mentally ill.

GNMA. *abbr.* Government National Mortgage Association.

GNP. *abbr.* Gross national product.

go forward, *vb.* (1964) To commence or carry on with the presentation of a case in court <after the lunch recess, the judge instructed the plaintiff to go forward with its case>.

go hence without day. (18c) (Of a defendant to a lawsuit) to be finished with legal proceedings without any further settings on the court's calendar. • Thus, a defendant who "goes hence without day" succeeds in getting a case finally resolved, usu. by dismissal. The phrase derives from the Law French phrase *aller sans jour*, and over time defendants came to use it to request that the case against them be dismissed without the necessity of a day in court.

going-and-coming rule. (1927) **1.** The principle that torts committed by an employee while commuting to or from work are generally outside the scope of employment. **2.** The principle that denies workers'-compensation benefits to an employee injured while commuting to or from work.

going concern. (1881) A commercial enterprise actively engaging in business with the expectation of indefinite continuance.

going price, *n.* (18c) The prevailing or current market value of something.

going private. The process of changing a public corporation into a close corporation by terminating the corporation's status with the SEC as a publicly held corporation and by having its outstanding publicly held shares acquired by a single shareholder or a small group.

going public. The process of a company's selling stock to the investing public for the first time (after filing a registration statement under applicable securities laws), thereby becoming a public corporation.

golden handshake. *Corporations.* A generous compensation package offered to an employee, usu. as an inducement to retire or upon dismissal.

golden parachute. (1981) *Corporations.* An employment-contract provision that grants an upper-level executive lucrative severance benefits — including long-term salary guarantees or bonuses — if control of the company changes hands (as by a merger).

golden rule. The principle that, in construing written instruments, a court should adhere to the grammatical and ordinary sense of the words unless that adherence would lead to some manifest absurdity; esp., in statutory construction, the principle that if a statute's literal meaning would lead to an absurd or unjust result, or even to an inconsistency within the statute itself, the statute should be interpreted in a way that avoids such a result or inconsistency.

golden-rule argument. A jury argument in which a lawyer asks the jurors to reach a verdict by imagining themselves or someone they care about in the place of the injured plaintiff or crime victim. • Because golden-rule arguments ask the jurors to become advocates for the plaintiff or victim and to ignore their obligation to exercise calm and reasonable judgment, these arguments are widely condemned and are considered improper in most states.

gold standard. (19c) A monetary system in which currency is convertible into its legal equivalent in gold or gold coin. • The United States adopted the gold standard in 1900 and abandoned it in 1934.

good, *adj.* (bef. 12c) **1.** Sound or reliable <a good investment>. **2.** Valid, effectual, and enforceable; sufficient under the law <good title>.

good and workmanlike. (18c) (Of a product or service) characterized by quality craftsmanship; constructed or performed in a skillful way or method.

good behavior. (16c) **1.** A standard by which judges are considered fit to continue their tenure, consisting in the avoicance of criminal behavior. **2.** Orderly conduct, which in the context of penal law allows a prisoner to reduce the time spent in prison.

good faith, *n.* (18c) A state of mind consisting in (1) honesty in belief or purpose, (2) faithfulness to one's duty or obligation, (3) observance of reasonable commercial standards of fair dealing in a given trade or business, or (4) absence of intent to defraud or to seek unconscionable advantage. — **good-faith,** *adj.*

good-faith exception. (1980) *Criminal procedure.* An exception to the exclusionary rule whereby evidence obtained under a warrant later found to be invalid (esp. because it is not supported by probable cause) is nonetheless admissible if the police reasonably relied on the notion that the warrant was valid. • The Supreme Court adopted the good-faith exception in *United States v. Leon*, 468 U.S. 897, 104 S.Ct. 3405 (1984).

good moral character, *n.* (18c) **1.** A pattern of behavior that is consistent with the community's current ethical standards and that shows an absence of deceit or morally reprehensible conduct. **2.** A pattern of behavior conforming to a profession's ethical standards and showing an absence of moral turpitude.

goods. (bef. 12c) **1.** Tangible or movable personal property other than money; esp., articles of trade or items of merchandise <goods and services>. • The sale of goods is governed by Article 2 of the UCC. **2.** Things that have value, whether tangible or not <the importance of social goods varies from society to society>.

bulky goods. Goods that are obviously difficult to move because of their nature, their number, or their location.

capital goods. Goods (such as equipment and machinery) used for the production of other goods or services.

consumer goods. Goods bought or used primarily for personal, family, or household purposes, and not for resale or for producing other goods. UCC § 9-102(23).

distressed goods. Goods sold at unusually low prices or at a loss.

durable goods. Consumer goods that are designed to be used repeatedly over a long period, such as automobiles or refrigerators.

fungible goods (**fən**-jə-bəl). Goods that are interchangeable with one another; goods that, by nature or trade usage, are the equivalent of any other like unit, such as coffee or grain. UCC § 1-201(b)(18).

household goods. Goods that are used in connection with a home.

nonconforming goods. Goods that fail to meet contractual specifications, allowing the buyer to reject the tender of the goods or to revoke their acceptance. UCC §§ 2-601, 2-608.

soft goods. Consumer goods (such as clothing) that are not durable goods.

Good Samaritan doctrine (sə-**mar**-i-tən). (1952) *Torts.* The principle that a person who is injured while attempting to aid another in imminent danger, and who then sues the one whose negligence created the danger, will not be charged with contributory negligence unless the rescue attempt is an unreasonable one or the rescuer acts unreasonably in performing the attempted rescue.

good-samaritan law. (1965) A statute that exempts from liability a person (such as an off-duty physician) who voluntarily renders aid to another in imminent danger but negligently causes injury while rendering the aid.

goods and chattels (**chat**-əlz), *n.* (16c) Loosely, personal property of any kind; occasionally, tangible personal property only.

good-soldier defense. An excuse theory based on the assertion that a defendant was following orders, esp. of a military or corporate superior. • The term is a derisive label rather than a valid defense. Following an order does not relieve a defendant of responsibility for wrongful acts unless there are circumstances that would amount to coercion.

good-time law. A statute allowing a prisoner's sentence to be reduced by a stated number of days for each month or year of good behavior while incarcerated.

goodwill. (bef. 12c) A business's reputation, patronage, and other intangible assets that are considered when appraising the business, esp. for purchase; the ability to earn income in excess of the income that would be expected from the business viewed as a mere collection of assets.

govern, *vb.* (14c) (Of a precedent) to control a point in issue <the *Smith* case will govern the outcome of the appeal>.

governing body. 1. GOVERNMENT (2). **2.** A group of (esp. corporate) officers or persons having ultimate control.

government. (14c) **1.** The structure of principles and rules determining how a state or organization is regulated. **2.** The sovereign power in a nation or state. **3.** An organization through which a body of people exercises political authority; the machinery by which sovereign power is expressed. • In this sense, the term refers collectively to the political organs of a country regardless of their function or level, and regardless of the subject matter they deal with.

de facto government (di **fak**-toh). **1.** A government that has taken over the regular government and exercises sovereignty over a nation. **2.** An independent government established and exercised by a group of a country's inhabitants who have separated themselves from the parent state.

de jure government. A functioning government that is legally established.

federal government. **1.** A national government that exercises some degree of control over smaller political units that have surrendered some degree of power in exchange for the right to participate in national political matters. **2.** The U.S. government.

local government. The government of a particular locality, such as a city, county, or parish; a governing body at a lower level than the state government. • The term includes a school district, fire district, transportation authority, and any other special-purpose district or authority.

provisional government. A government temporarily established to govern until a permanent one is organized to replace it.

republican government. A government in the republican form; specif., a government by representatives chosen by the people.

state government. The government of a state of the United States.

4. The executive branch of the U.S. government. **5.** The prosecutors in a given criminal case. **6.** An academic course devoted to the study of government; political science.

government-agency defense. *Torts.* An affirmative defense that immunizes a contractor from liability upon proof that the contractor acted on the government's behalf as an agent or as a government officer. • This defense is extremely limited because of the difficulty of establishing the government–agent relationship.

governmental function. (1817) *Torts.* A government agency's conduct that is expressly or impliedly mandated or authorized by constitution, statute, or other law and that is carried out for the benefit of the general public. • Generally, a governmental entity is immune from tort liability for governmental acts.

governmental-function theory. (1936) *Constitutional law.* A principle by which private conduct is characterized as state action, esp. for due-process and equal-protection purposes, when a private party is exercising a public function. • Under this theory, for example, a political party (which is a private entity) cannot exclude voters from primary elections on the basis of race.

governmental instrumentality. (1854) A constitutionally or legislatively created agency that is immune from certain kinds of liability, as for taxes or punitive damages.

government-contractor defense. An affirmative defense that immunizes a government contractor from civil liability under state law when the contractor complies with government specifications. • Immunization is extended when two conditions are satisfied: (1) the supplier warned the government about any dangers presented by the goods about which the supplier had knowledge but the government did not, and (2) the government itself is immune from liability under the *Feres* doctrine. Essentially, this federal common-law defense, which has been applied in cases of negligence, strict liability, and breach of warranty, extends sovereign immunity over the contractor.

Government National Mortgage Association. A federally owned corporation in the U.S. Department of Housing and Urban Development responsible for guaranteeing mortgage-backed securities composed of FHA-insured or VA-guaranteed mortgage loans. — Abbr. GNMA.

government of laws. The doctrine that government must operate according to established, consistent legal principles and not according to the interests of those who happen to be in power at a given time; esp., the doctrine that judicial decisions must be based on the law, regardless of the character of the litigants or the personal predilections of the judge.

Government Printing Office. An office in the legislative branch of the federal government responsible for printing and distributing congressional publications and publications of other agencies of the United States government. — Abbr. GPO.

governor. (14c) The chief executive official of a U.S. state.

GPO. *abbr.* Government Printing Office.

grab law. (1884) The various means of debt collection involving remedies outside the scope of federal bankruptcy law, such as attachment and garnishment; aggressive collection practices.

grace period. (1945) A period of extra time allowed for taking some required action (such as making payment) without incurring the usual penalty for being late.

grade, *n. Criminal law.* An incremental step in the scale of punishments for offenses, based on a particular offense's seriousness.

grading. The fixing of a criminal offense at a level of seriousness, such as first degree, second degree, or third degree (in reference to a felony), or Class A, Class B, or Class C (in reference to a misdemeanor).

graft, *n.* (14c) **1.** The act of using a position of trust to gain money or property dishonestly; esp., a public official's fraudulent acquisition of public funds. **2.** Money or property gained illegally or unfairly.

grand, *adj.* (17c) Of or relating to a crime involving the theft of money or property valued more than a statutorily established amount, and therefore considered more serious than those involving a lesser amount <grand theft>.

grandfather, *vb.* (1953) To cover (a person) with the benefits of a grandfather clause <the statute sets the drinking age at 21 but grandfathers those who are 18 or older on the statute's effective date>.

grandfather clause. (1900) **1.** *Hist.* A clause in the constitutions of some Southern states exempting from suffrage restrictions the descendants of men who could vote before the Civil War. • The U.S. Supreme Court held that a clause of this kind in the Oklahoma Constitution violated the 15th Amendment. *Guinn v. United States,* 238 U.S. 347, 35 S.Ct. 926 (1915). **2.** A provision that creates an exemption from the law's effect for something that existed before the law's effective date; specif., a statutory or regulatory clause that exempts a class of persons or transactions because of circumstances existing before the new rule or regulation takes effect. **3.** In a government contract, a provision that immunizes the contractor against any changes in federal law that would otherwise adversely affect the contract. **4.** In a construction contract, a general and inclusive provision that makes a party responsible for dealing with risks, whether expected or unexpected.

grand jury. (15c) A body of (usu. 16 to 23) people who are chosen to sit permanently for at least a month — and sometimes a year — and who, in ex parte proceedings, decide whether to issue indictments. See Fed. R. Crim. P. 6. • If the grand jury decides that evidence is strong enough to hold a suspect for trial, it returns a bill of indictment (a *true bill*) charging the suspect with a specific crime.

investigative grand jury. (1960) A grand jury whose primary function is to examine possible crimes and develop evidence not currently available to the prosecution.

runaway grand jury. (1959) A grand jury that acts essentially in opposition to the prosecution, as by calling its own witnesses, perversely failing to return an indictment that the prosecution has requested, or returning an indictment that the prosecution did not request.

screening grand jury. (1990) A grand jury whose primary function is to decide whether to issue an indictment.

special grand jury. (1854) A grand jury specially summoned, usu. when the regular grand jury either has already been discharged or has not been drawn; a grand jury with limited authority.

Grand Jury Clause. (1949) The clause of the Fifth Amendment to the U.S. Constitution requiring an indictment by a grand jury before a person can be tried for serious offenses.

grandparent rights. A grandfather's or grandmother's rights in seeking visitation with a grandchild. • By statute in most states, in certain circumstances a grandparent may seek court-ordered visitation with a grandchild. But the United States Supreme Court has held that the primary, constitutionally protected right of decision-making regarding association with a child lies with the child's parents.

Granger Cases (**grayn**-jər). Six U.S. Supreme Court decisions holding that the police power of the states enabled them, through legislation, to regulate fees charged by common carriers, warehouses, and grain elevators.

grant, *n.* (13c) **1.** An agreement that creates a right or interest in favor of a person or that effects a transfer of a right or interest from one person to another. • Examples include leases, easements, charges, patents, franchises, powers, and licenses. **2.** The formal transfer of real property. **3.** The document by which a transfer is effected; esp., DEED. **4.** The property or property right so transferred.

grant, *vb.* (13c) **1.** To give or confer (something), with or without compensation. **2.** To formally transfer (real property) by deed or other writing. **3.** To permit or agree to. **4.** To approve, warrant, or order (a request, motion, etc.).

grantback, *n.* (1956) A license-agreement provision requiring the licensee to assign or license back to the licensor any improvements that the licensee might make to a patent or other proprietary right.

grantee. (15c) One to whom property is conveyed.

grant-in-aid. (19c) A sum of money given by a governmental agency to a person or institution for a specific purpose; esp., federal funding for a state public program.

granting clause. (18c) The words that transfer an interest in a deed or other instrument, esp. an oil-and-gas lease.

grantor. (17c) One who conveys property to another.

gratuitous (grə-**t[y]oo**-ə-təs), *adj.* (17c) **1.** Done or performed without obligation to do so; given without consideration in circumstances that do not otherwise impose a duty <gratuitous promise>. **2.** Done unnecessarily <gratuitous obscenities>. — **gratuity,** *n.*

gravamen (grə-**vay**-mən). (17c) The substantial point or essence of a claim, grievance, or complaint.

gravity. (16c) Seriousness of harm, an offense, etc., as judged from an objective, legal standpoint.

graymail. (1978) A criminal defendant's threat to reveal classified information during the trial in the hope of forcing the government to drop the criminal charge.

greenback, *n.* (ca. 1862) *Slang.* A legal-tender note of the United States; any note issued by a federal reserve bank. • The term was coined in 1862 when the backs of American paper currency were first printed in green ink.

green card. (1969) A registration card evidencing a resident alien's status as a permanent U.S. resident.

greenfield site. (ca. 1962) **1.** Land that has never been developed. • Such land is presumably uncontaminated. **2.** Property acquired as an investment, esp. for establishing a new business.

greenmail. (1983) **1.** The act or practice of buying enough stock in a company to threaten a hostile takeover and then selling the stock back to the corporation at an inflated price. **2.** The money paid for stock in the corporation's buyback. **3.** A shareholder's act of filing or threatening to file a derivative action and then seeking a disproportionate settlement.

Gresham's law. (19c) The principle that a debased currency will drive out valuable currency. • This economic principle is popularly attributed to Sir Thomas Gresham (1519–1579), even though earlier writers such as Oresme and Copernicus discussed it.

grievance, *n.* (14c) **1.** An injury, injustice, or wrong that gives ground for a complaint <a petition for a redress of grievances>. **2.** The complaint itself

<the client filed a grievance with the state-bar committee>. **3.** *Labor law.* A complaint that is filed by an employee or the employee's union representative and that usu. concerns working conditions, esp. an alleged violation of a collective-bargaining agreement.

grievance procedure. *Labor law.* A process, consisting of several steps, for the resolution of an employee's complaint.

grievant, *n.* (1958) *Labor law.* An employee who files a grievance and submits it to the grievance procedure outlined in a collective-bargaining agreement.

grieve, *vb.* To contest under a grievance procedure. — **grievable,** *adj.*

grift, *vb.* (1915) *Slang.* To obtain money or other property illicitly by adroit use of a scam, confidence game, or other fraudulent means. — **grifter,** *n.*

gross national product. (1947) The market value of all goods and services produced in a country within a year, used to measure a country's economic development and wealth. — Abbr. GNP.

gross receipts. *Tax.* The total amount of money or other consideration received by a business taxpayer for goods sold or services performed in a taxable year, before deductions. IRC (26 USCA) § 448; 26 C.F.R. § 1.448-1T (f)(2)(iv).

gross-rent multiplier. The ratio between the market value of rent-producing property and its annual gross rental income. • The gross-rent multiplier is used as a method to estimate a property's market value. — Abbr. GRM.

gross up, *vb.* (1987) *Slang. Tax.* To add back to a decedent's gross estate the gift taxes paid by the decedent or the decedent's estate on gifts made by the decedent or the decedent's spouse during the three-year period preceding the decedent's death. IRC (26 USCA) § 2035.

ground, *n.* (*usu. pl.*) (13c) The reason or point that something (as a legal claim or argument) relies on for validity <grounds for divorce> <several grounds for appeal>.

ground, *vb.* (14c) **1.** To provide a basis for (something, such as a legal claim or argument) <the decision was grounded on public policy>. **2.** To base (something, such as a legal principle or judicial decision) on <the court grounded the decision on common law> <strict liability is grounded on public policy>.

groundless, *adj.* (17c) (Of a legal claim or argument) lacking a basis or a rationale <groundless cause of action>.

group litigation. (1936) A set of lawsuits on behalf of or against numerous persons recognized as one litigating entity, such as a civil-rights group.

growth. The gain, increase, or expansion in value of securities or of a business.

growth industry. (1954) An industry or business sector whose revenues and earnings are rising at a faster rate than average.

growth management. (1974) *Land-use planning.* The regulation of a community's rate of growth through zoning ordinances, impact fees, and other measures.

GSA. *abbr.* General Services Administration.

guarantee (gar-ən-**tee**), *n.* (17c) **1.** The assurance that a contract or legal act will be duly carried out. **2.** Something given or existing as security, such as to fulfill a future engagement or a condition subsequent. **3.** One to whom a guaranty is made.— **guarantee,** *vb.* (18c).

guarantee clause. (1887) **1.** A provision in a contract, deed, or mortgage by which one person promises to pay the obligation of another. **2.** (*cap.*) U.S. Const. art. IV, § 4, under which the federal government ensures for the states both a republican form of government and protection from invasion or internal insurrection.

guarantee of title. *Property.* A warranty that the title to a piece of real property is vested in a particular person, given by a title company or abstract company, and based on a title searcher's opinion of the status of the property's title. The guarantee is usu. backed by insurance to cover damages resulting from the title searcher's oversight or negligence in finding recorded legal instruments.

guarantor. (19c) One who makes a guaranty or gives security for a debt. • While a surety's liability begins with that of the principal, a guarantor's liability does not begin until the principal debtor is in default.

guarantor of collectibility. (1881) One who guarantees a debtor's solvency and is under a duty to pay only if the creditor is unable to collect from the principal debtor after exhausting all legal remedies, including demand, suit, judgment, and any supplementary proceedings.

guarantor of payment. (1814) One who guarantees payment of a negotiable instrument when it is due without the holder first seeking payment from another party. • A guarantor of payment is liable only if "payment guaranteed" or equivalent words are added to the guarantor's indorsement.

guaranty (**gar**-ən-tee), *n.* (16c) A promise to answer for the payment of some debt, or the performance of some duty, in case of the failure of another who is liable in the first instance. • The term is most common in finance and banking contexts. While a warranty relates to things (not persons), is not collateral, and need not be in writing, a guaranty is an undertaking that a person will pay or do some act, is collateral to the duty of the primary obligor, and must be in writing.

absolute guaranty. (18c) **1.** An unqualified promise that the principal will pay or perform. **2.** A guarantor's contractual promise to perform some act for the creditor — such as paying money or delivering property — if the principal debtor defaults.

conditional guaranty. (1813) A guaranty that requires the performance of some condition by the creditor before the guarantor will become liable.

contingent guaranty. (1843) A guaranty in which the guarantor will not be liable unless a specified event occurs.

continuing guaranty. (1817) A guaranty that governs a course of dealing for an indefinite time or by a succession of credits.

cross-stream guaranty. A guaranty made by a company for the obligation of another company when both are owned by the same parent company or individual.

downstream guaranty. **1.** A parent corporation's guaranty of a subsidiary's obligations. **2.** A guaranty made for a company by a guarantor who is also a partner, member, or stockholder of the company.

general guaranty. (17c) **1.** A guaranty addressed to no specific person, so that anyone who acts on it can enforce it. **2.** A guaranty for the principal's default on obligations that the principal undertakes with anyone.

good-guy guaranty. A limited guaranty by a third-person that leased property or collateral will be kept in good condition and returned to the lessor or lender if a default occurs. • Good-guy guaranties are most commonly associated with real-property leases.

guaranty of collection. (1843) A guaranty that is conditioned on the creditor's having first exhausted legal remedies against the principal debtor before suing the guarantor.

guaranty of payment. (1811) A guaranty that is not conditioned on the creditor's exhausting legal remedies against the principal debtor before suing the guarantor.

irrevocable guaranty (i-**rev**-ə-kə-bəl). (1898) A guaranty that cannot be terminated unless the other parties consent.

limited guaranty. (1831) An agreement to answer for a debt arising from a single transaction.

revocable guaranty. (1936) A guaranty that the guarantor may terminate without any other party's consent.

special guaranty. (18c) **1.** A guaranty addressed to a particular person or group of persons, who are the only ones who can enforce it. **2.** A guaranty that names a definite person as obligee and that can be accepted only by the person named.

specific guaranty. (18c) A guaranty of a single debt or obligation.

upstream guaranty. A guaranty made by a corporate subsidiary for the parent corporation's obligations.

guardian, *n.* (15c) One who has the legal authority and duty to care for another's person or property, esp. because of the other's infancy, incapacity, or disability. • A guardian may be appointed either for all purposes or for a specific purpose.

foreign guardian. A guardian appointed by a court in a state other than the one in which the ward is domiciled. • A foreign guardian cares for the ward's property that is located in the state of appointment.

general guardian. A guardian who has general care and control of the ward's person and estate.

guardian ad litem (ad **lɪ**-tem *or* -təm). (18c) A guardian, usu. a lawyer, appointed by the court to appear in a lawsuit on behalf of an incompetent or minor party. — Abbr. GAL.

guardian by election. A guardian chosen by a ward who would otherwise be without one.

guardian in socage. New York law. A guardian for a child who has acquired lands by descent. • A guardian is usu. a relative who could not possibly inherit from the child. This type of guardianship applies to both the person and the property of the child and, historically, lasted only until the child was 14, when the child was allowed to select a guardian; now it lasts until the child reaches age 18 or is emancipated.

guardian of the estate. A guardian responsible for taking care of the property of someone who is incapable of caring for his or her own property because of infancy, incapacity, or disability.

guardian of the person. A guardian responsible for taking care of someone who is incapable of caring for himself or herself because of infancy, incapacity, or disability.

partial guardian. A guardian whose rights, duties, and powers are strictly limited to those specified in a court order.

quasi-guardian. A guardian who assumes that role without any authority. • Such a person may be made to account as guardian.

special guardian. (17c) A guardian who has special or limited powers over the ward's person or estate.

standby guardian. A parent-designated guardian appointed to assume responsibility for a child at a future date if the child's parent becomes incapable of caring for the child but who does not divest the parent of custodial rights.

statutory guardian. A guardian appointed by a court having special statutory jurisdiction.

successor guardian. An alternate guardian named in a parent's will against the possibility that the first nominee cannot or will not serve as guardian.

testamentary guardian. A guardian nominated by a parent's will for the person and property of a child until the child reaches the age of majority.

guardianship. (15c) **1.** The fiduciary relationship between a guardian and a ward or other incapacitated person, whereby the guardian assumes the power to make decisions about the ward's person or property. **2.** The duties and responsibilities of a guardian.

ancillary guardianship. A subservient and subsidiary guardianship in a state other than that in which guardianship is originally granted.

guardianship of the estate. A guardianship in which the guardian can make decisions only about matters regarding the ward's assets and property.

guardianship of the person. A guardianship in which the guardian is authorized to make all significant decisions affecting the ward's well-being, including the ward's physical custody, education, health, activities, personal relationships, and general welfare.

plenary guardianship. A guardianship in which the guardian can make decisions about both the ward's estate and the ward's person.

standby guardianship. A guardianship in which a parent designates a guardian to assume responsibility for a child at a future date, if the child's parent becomes incapable of caring for the child, but without divesting the parent of custodial rights.

guest. (13c) **1.** A person who is entertained or to whom hospitality is extended. **2.** A person who pays for services at an establishment, esp. a hotel or restaurant. **3.** A nonpaying passenger in a motor vehicle.

social guest. *Torts.* A guest who is invited to enter or remain on another person's property primarily for private entertainment as opposed to entertainment open to the general public.

guest statute. (1914) A law that bars a nonpaying passenger in a noncommercial vehicle from suing the host-driver for damages resulting from the driver's ordinary negligence. • Though once common, guest statutes remain in force in only a few states.

guilt, *n.* (bef. 12c) The fact or state of having committed a wrong, esp. a crime <the state's burden was to prove guilt beyond a reasonable doubt>. Cf. INNOCENCE.

guilt phase. (1960) The part of a criminal trial during which the fact-finder determines whether the defendant committed a crime.

guilty, *adj.* (bef. 12c) **1.** Having committed a crime; responsible for a crime <guilty of armed robbery>. **2.** Responsible for a civil wrong, such as a tort or breach of contract <guilty of fraudulent misrepresentation>. — **guiltily,** *adv.*

guilty, *n.* **1.** A plea of a criminal defendant who does not contest the charges. **2.** A jury verdict convicting the defendant of the crime charged.

guilty but mentally ill. (1977) A form of verdict in a criminal case whereby the jury rejects the defendant's insanity defense but still recommends psychiatric treatment because the defendant is mentally ill. — Abbr. GBMI; GMI.

gun-control law. (1968) A statute or ordinance that regulates the sale, possession, or use of firearms. • Gun-control laws vary widely among the states, and many cities have gun-control ordinances. Federal law restricts and regulates the illegal sale, possession, and use of firearms. 18 USCA §§ 921–930.

H

H. *abbr.* **1.** House of Representatives. **2.** House report.

habeas corpus (**hay**-bee-əs **kor**-pəs). [Law Latin "that you have the body"] (18c) A writ employed to bring a person before a court, most frequently to ensure that the person's imprisonment or detention is not illegal (*habeas corpus ad subjiciendum*). • In addition to being used to test the legality of an arrest or commitment, the writ may be used to obtain judicial review of (1) the regularity of the extradition process, (2) the right to or amount of bail, or (3) the jurisdiction of a court that has imposed a criminal sentence. — Abbr. H.C. — Sometimes shortened to *habeas*.

habendum clause (hə-**ben**-dəm). (1829) **1.** The part of an instrument, such as a deed or will, that defines the extent of the interest being granted and any conditions affecting the grant. • The introductory words to the clause are ordinarily *to have and to hold*. **2.** *Oil & gas.* The provision in an oil-and-gas lease defining how long the interest granted to the lessee will extend. • Modern oil-and-gas leases typically provide for a primary term — a fixed number of years during which the lessee has no obligation to develop the premises — and a secondary term (for "so long thereafter as oil and gas produced") once development takes place. Most jurisdictions require production of paying quantities to keep the lease in effect.

habitability. (1890) The condition of a building in which inhabitants can live free of serious defects that might harm health and safety.

habitation. (14c) **1.** The act of inhabiting; occupancy. **2.** A dwelling place; a domicile. **3.** *Civil law.* A nontransferable and nonheritable right to dwell in the house of another. La. Civ. Code art. 630.

habitual, *adj.* (17c) **1.** Customary; usual <habitual late sleeper>. **2.** Recidivist <habitual offender>.

hack, *vb.* To surreptitiously break into the computer, network, servers, or database of another person or organization. — **hacker,** *n.*

had. Commenced or begun, as used in a statute providing that no legal proceeding may be *had* (usu. followed by the words *or maintained*) <no action for foreclosure may be had or maintained until the debtor has been given at least 30 days' notice>.

***Hadley v. Baxendale* rule.** (1930) *Contracts.* The principle that consequential damages will be awarded for breach of contract only if it was foreseeable at the time of contracting that this type of damage would result from the breach. *Hadley v. Baxendale*, 9 Exch. 341 (1854). • *Hadley v. Baxendale* is best known for its impact on a nonbreaching party's ability to recover consequential damages, but the case also confirmed the principle that the nonbreaching party may recover damages that arise naturally from the breach.

Hague Academy of International Law (hayg). A center for advanced studies in international law, both public and private, aimed at facilitating the comprehensive and impartial examination of problems of international legal relations.

Hague Convention. The short name for any one of the many numerous international conventions that address different legal issues and attempt to standardize procedures between nations.

Hague Convention on the Civil Aspects of International Child Abduction. An international convention (concluded in 1980) that seeks to counteract cross-border child-snatching by noncustodial parents.

Hague Tribunal. *Int'l law.* A permanent court of arbitration established by the Hague Peace Conference of 1899 to facilitate immediate recourse to arbitration to settle international differences.

haircut. 1. *Securities.* The discount required by the National Association of Securities Dealers on the value of stock that a brokerage firm holds in its own account at the time of filing a monthly report about the firm's net capital condition. **2.** The difference between the amount of a loan and the market value of the collateral securing the loan.

hale, *v.* To compel (a person) to go, esp. to court <hale a party into court>.

halfway house. (1970) A transitional housing facility designed to rehabilitate people who have recently left a prison or medical-care facility, or who otherwise need help in adjusting to a normal life.

hallmark. (18c) **1.** An official stamp affixed by goldsmiths and silversmiths on articles made of gold or silver to show genuineness. **2.** A mark of genuineness.

hammer, *n. Slang.* A forced sale; a sale at public auction <her jewelry was brought to the hammer>.

hand down, *vb.* (17c) To announce or file (a judgment) in a case.

Hand formula. (1972) A balancing test for determining whether conduct has created an unreasonable risk of harm, first formulated by Judge Learned Hand in *United States v. Carroll Towing Co.*, 159 F.2d 169 (2d Cir. 1947). • Under this test, an actor is negligent if the burden of taking adequate precautions against the harm is outweighed by the probable gravity of the harm multiplied by the probability that the harm will occur.

hands-off agreement. (1986) A noncompete contractual provision between an employer and a former employee prohibiting the employee from using information learned during his or her employment to divert or to steal customers from the former employer.

hand up, *vb.* (1930) (Of a grand jury) to deliver (an indictment) to a criminal court.

hang, *vb.* (1848) (Of a jury) to be unable to reach a verdict <the jury was hung after 12 hours of continuous deliberation>.

hanging, *n.* The killing of someone by suspending the person above the ground by a rope around the person's neck. • Death is caused by asphyxiation (by being hoisted from the ground) or by a sudden breaking of the cervical vertebrae (by being dropped from a height).

happiness, right to pursue. (1829) The constitutional right to pursue any lawful business or activity — in any manner not inconsistent with the equal rights of others — that might yield the highest enjoyment, increase one's prosperity, or allow the development of one's faculties.

happy-slapping. *Slang.* An assault on a randomly chosen victim by a person or group while another person films the assault with the intention of later broadcasting or selling copies of the recording.

harassment (hə-**ras**-mənt *or* **har**-əs-mənt). (18c) Words, conduct, or action (usu. repeated or persistent) that, being directed at a specific person, annoys, alarms, or causes substantial emotional distress in that person and serves no legitimate purpose. • Harassment is actionable in some circumstances, as when a creditor uses threatening or abusive tactics to collect a debt. — **harass** (hə-**ras** *or* **har**-əs), *vb.*

harboring, *n.* (14c) The act of affording lodging, shelter, or refuge to a person, esp. a criminal or illegal alien.

harboring an illegal alien. The act of providing concealment from detection by law-enforcement authorities or shelter, employment, or transportation to help a noncitizen remain in the United States unlawfully, while knowing about or recklessly disregarding the noncitizen's illegal immigration status. • The crime of harboring an illegal alien does not require that the offender be involved in the smuggling of illegal aliens into the country. 8 USCA § 1324.

hard case. (1836) A lawsuit involving equities that tempt a judge to stretch or even disregard a principle of law at issue. • Hence the expression, "Hard cases make bad law."

hard labor. (18c) Work imposed on prisoners as additional punishment, usu. for misconduct while in prison.

hard-look doctrine. (1979) *Administrative law.* The principle that a court should carefully review an administrative-agency decision to ensure that the decision did not result from expediency, pressure, or whim.

hard sell. A sales practice characterized by slogans, aggressiveness, intimidation, and urgent decision-making.

hardship. (13c) **1.** Privation; suffering or adversity. **2.** The asperity with which a proposed construction of law would bear on a particular case, sometimes forming a basis (also known as an argument *ab inconvenienti*) against the construction. **3.** *Family law.* A condition that makes it onerous or impossible for a child-support obligor to make the required child-support payment. **4.** *Zoning.* A ground for a variance under some zoning statutes if the zoning ordinance as applied to a particular property is unduly oppressive, arbitrary, or confiscatory; esp., a ground for granting a variance, based on the impossibility or prohibitive expense of conforming the property or its use to the zoning regulation.

harm, *n.* (bef. 12c) Injury, loss, damage; material or tangible detriment.

accidental harm. **1.** Harm not caused by a purposeful act. **2.** Harm not caused by a tortious act.

bodily harm. (16c) Physical pain, illness, or impairment of the body.

physical harm. (18c) Any physical injury or impairment of land, chattels, or the human body.

social harm. (1933) An adverse effect on any social interest that is protected by the criminal law.

harmful behavior. Conduct that could injure another person, esp. a child.

cumulatively harmful behavior. *Family law.* Seriously harmful parental (or caregiver) behavior that, if continued for a significant period, will over time cause serious harm to a child.

immediately harmful behavior. *Family law.* Seriously harmful parental (or caregiver) behavior that could have caused serious injury to a child but that, because of the intervention of an outside force or a fortuitous event, did not result in any injury.

seriously harmful behavior. *Family law.* Parental (or caregiver) behavior that could cause serious injury to a child in the person's care. • Some examples of seriously harmful behavior are physical battering, physical neglect, sexual abuse, and abandonment.

harmony. (14c) Agreement or accord; conformity <the decision in *Jones* is in harmony with earlier Supreme Court precedent>. — **harmonize,** *vb.*

Hatch Act. A federal statute, enacted in 1939, that restricts political-campaign activities by federal employees and limits contributions by individuals to political campaigns. 5 USCA §§ 1501–1508.

have the floor. *Parliamentary law.* To be entitled to speak after being recognized by the chair.

hazard, *n.* (14c) **1.** Danger or peril; esp., a contributing factor to a peril.

extraordinary hazard. *Workers' compensation.* An unusual occupational danger that is increased by the acts of employees other than the injured worker.

imminent hazard. An immediate danger; esp., in environmental law, a situation in which the continued use of a pesticide will probably result in unreasonable adverse effects on the environment or will involve an unreasonable danger to the survival of an endangered species. 7 USCA § 136(1).

occupational hazard. (1917) A danger or risk that is peculiar to a particular calling or occupation. • Occupational hazards include both accidental injuries and occupational diseases.

2. *Insurance.* The risk or probability of loss or injury, esp. a loss or injury covered by an insurance policy.

moral hazard. A hazard that has its inception in mental attitudes, such as dishonesty, carelessness, and insanity.

physical hazard. A hazard that has its inception in the material world, such as location, structure, occupancy, exposure, and the like.

hazardous substance. (1882) A toxic pollutant; an imminently dangerous chemical or mixture.

hazard pay. (1956) Special compensation for work done under unpleasant or unsafe conditions.

hazing, *n.* (1850) The practice of physically or emotionally abusing newcomers to an organization as a means of initiation. • In the early 19th century, *hazing* referred to beating. Hazing was a well-established custom in fraternities at Ivy League universities by the mid-19th century. (One college magazine referred to "the absurd and barbarous custom of hazing, which has long prevailed in the college." 1 Harvard Mag. 413 (1860)). The first death from hazing was reported at Yale in 1892 (*N.Y. Daily News*, June 28, 1892). In the late 20th century, many colleges and universities banned hazing and many states passed antihazing statutes establishing criminal penalties.

H.C. *abbr.* **1.** House of Commons. 2. Habeas corpus.

HDC. *abbr.* Holder in due course.

he. (bef. 12c) A pronoun of the masculine gender, traditionally used and construed in statutes to include both sexes, as well as corporations. • It may also be read as *they.* Because of the trend toward nonsexist language, fastidious drafters avoid using the generic pronouns *he*, *him*, and *his* unless the reference is only to a male person.

headlease. (1909) A primary lease under which a sublease has been granted.

headlessor. (1933) A lessor on a lease of property that has been subleased.

head money. (16c) A tax on people who fit within a designated class; a poll tax.

headnote. (1855) A case summary that appears before the printed judicial opinion in a law report, addresses a point of law, and usu. includes the relevant facts bearing on that point of law.

head of family. A person who supports one or more people related by birth, adoption, or marriage and with whom those persons maintain their permanent domicile. • The phrase *head of family* appears most commonly in homestead law. For a person to have the status of head of family, there must, of necessity, be at least two people in the family.

head of household. (1847) **1.** The primary income-provider within a family. **2.** For income-tax purposes, an unmarried or separated person (other than a surviving spouse) who provides a home for dependents for more than one-half of the taxable year.

headright. (1930) In American Indian law, a tribemember's right to a pro rata portion of income from a tribal trust fund set up under the Allotment Act of 1906.

health. (bef. 12c) **1.** The state of being sound or whole in body, mind, or soul. **2.** Freedom from pain or sickness.

public health. (17c) **1.** The health of the community at large. **2.** The healthful or sanitary condition of the general body of people or the community en masse; esp., the methods of maintaining the health of the community, as by preventive medicine and organized care for the sick. • Many cities have a "public health department" or other agency responsible for maintaining the public health; federal laws dealing with health are administered by the Department of Health and Human Services.

healthcare-insurance receivable. An interest in or claim under an insurance policy, being a right to payment of a monetary obligation for healthcare goods or services provided. UCC § 9-104(c).

health law. (18c) A statute, ordinance, or code that prescribes sanitary standards and regulations for the purpose of promoting and preserving the community's health.

health-maintenance organization. (1973) A group of participating healthcare providers that furnish medical services to enrolled members of a group health-insurance plan. — Abbr. HMO.

health officer. A government official charged with executing and enforcing health laws.

hearing. (13c) **1.** A judicial session, usu. open to the public, held for the purpose of deciding issues of fact or of law, sometimes with witnesses testifying <the court held a hearing on the admissibility of DNA evidence in the murder case>. **2.** *Administrative law.* Any setting in which an affected person presents arguments to a decision-maker <a hearing on zoning variations>. **3.** In legislative practice, any proceeding in which legislators or their designees receive testimony about legislation that might be enacted <the shooting victim spoke at the Senate's hearing on gun control>. **4.** *Equity practice.* A trial.

adjudication hearing. (1947) **1.** *Administrative law.* An agency proceeding in which a person's rights and duties are decided after notice and an opportunity to be heard. **2.** In child-abuse and neglect proceedings, the trial stage at which the court hears the state's allegations and evidence and decides whether the state has the right to intervene on behalf of the child. **3.** In a juvenile-delinquency case, a hearing at which the court hears evidence of the charges and makes a finding of whether the charges are true or not true.

contested hearing. A hearing in which at least one of the parties has objections regarding one or more matters before the court.

custody hearing. (1935) *Family law.* A judicial examination of the facts relating to child custody, typically in a divorce or separation proceeding. • Child-neglect and dependency matters are also often dealt with in custody hearings.

detention hearing. (1959) **1.** *Criminal law.* A hearing to determine whether an accused should be released pending trial. **2.** *Family law.* A hearing held by a juvenile court to determine whether a juvenile accused of delinquent conduct should be detained, continued in confinement, or released pending an adjudicatory hearing.

disposition hearing. (1960) *Family law.* **1.** In child-abuse and neglect proceedings, after an adjudication hearing at which the state proves its allegations, a hearing at which the court hears evidence and enters orders for the child's care, custody, and control. • Typically, the judge determines a plan for services aimed at reunifying or rehabilitating the family. **2.** In a juvenile-delinquency case, after an adjudication hearing at which the state proves its case against the juvenile or after a juvenile's pleading true to the charges against him, a hearing at which the court determines what sanctions, if any, will be imposed on the juvenile.

evidentiary hearing. (1952) A hearing at which evidence is presented, as opposed to a hearing at which only legal argument is presented.

exclusionary hearing. (1963) A pretrial hearing conducted to review and determine the admissibility of alleged illegally obtained evidence.

fair hearing. (1831) A judicial or administrative hearing conducted in accordance with due process.

full hearing. (17c) A hearing at which the parties are allowed notice of each other's claims and are given ample opportunity to present their positions with evidence and argument.

hearing de novo (dee *or* di **noh**-voh). (18c) **1.** A reviewing court's decision of a matter anew, giving no deference to a lower court's findings. **2.** A new hearing of a matter, conducted as if the original hearing had not taken place.

independent-source hearing. *Criminal procedure.* A hearing to determine whether evidence was obtained illegally, and if so, whether the evidence is admissible.

neglect hearing. (1952) *Family law.* A judicial hearing involving alleged child abuse or some other situation in which a child has not been properly cared for by a parent or person legally responsible for the child's care.

omnibus hearing. (1969) *Criminal procedure.* A hearing designed to bring judicial oversight to a criminal case at an early stage to make certain that the case is being handled expeditiously and properly.

permanency hearing. (1832) *Family law.* Under the Adoption and Safe Families Act, a judicial proceeding to determine the future, permanent status of a child in foster care.

public hearing. (18c) A hearing that, within reasonable limits, is open to anyone who wishes to observe.

review hearing. *Family law.* After a finding of child abuse or neglect, a hearing to assess the progress in the case plan.

revocation hearing. (1928) *Criminal procedure.* A hearing held to determine whether a parolee should be returned to prison for violating the terms of parole.

shelter hearing. *Family law.* A hearing shortly after the state's removal of a child for suspected abuse or neglect.

suppression hearing. (1955) *Criminal procedure.* A pretrial hearing in which a criminal defendant seeks to prevent the introduction of evidence alleged to have been seized illegally.

termination-of-parental-rights hearing. *Family law.* A trial or court proceeding, usu. initiated by a state agency, that seeks to sever the legal ties between a parent and child, usu. so that the child can be adopted.

transfer hearing. (1968) *Criminal procedure.* In a juvenile-court case, a hearing to determine whether the case should be transferred to adult criminal court so that the juvenile may be tried as an adult.

uncontested hearing. A hearing in which either (1) the parties are in agreement as to all matters before the court, or (2) one of the parties has failed to appear despite notice.

unfair hearing. (1915) A hearing that is not conducted in accordance with due process, as when the defendant is denied the opportunity to prepare or consult with counsel.

hearsay. (16c) **1.** Traditionally, testimony that is given by a witness who relates not what he or she knows personally, but what others have said, and that is therefore dependent on the credibility of someone other than the witness. • Such testimony is generally inadmissible under the rules of evidence. **2.** In federal law, a statement (either a verbal assertion or nonverbal assertive conduct), other than one made by the declarant while testifying at the trial or hearing, offered in evidence to prove the truth of the matter asserted. Fed. R. Evid. 801(c).

double hearsay. (1921) A hearsay statement that contains further hearsay statements within it, none of which is admissible unless exceptions to the rule against hearsay can be applied to each level <the double hearsay was the report's statement that Amy had heard Joe admit running the red light>. Fed. R. Evid. 805.

hearsay exception. Any of several deviations from the hearsay rule, allowing the admission of otherwise inadmissible statements because the circumstances surrounding the statements provide a basis for considering the statements reliable.

tender-years hearsay exception. A hearsay exception for an out-of-court statement by a child ten years of age or younger, usu. describing an act of physical or sexual abuse, when the child is unavailable to testify and the court determines that the time, content, and circumstances of the statement make it reliable.

hearsay rule. (1896) The rule that no assertion offered as testimony can be received unless it is or has been open to test by cross-examination or an opportunity for cross-examination, except as provided otherwise by the rules of evidence, by court rules, or by statute. • The chief reasons for the rule are that out-of-court statements amounting to hearsay are not made under oath and are not subject to cross-examination. Fed. R. Evid. 802. Rule 803 provides 23 explicit exceptions to the hearsay rule, regardless of whether the out-of-court declarant is available to testify, and Rule 804 provides five more exceptions for situations in which the declarant is unavailable to testify.

heartbalm statute. A state law that abolishes the rights of action for monetary damages as solace for the emotional trauma occasioned by a loss of love and relationship. • The abolished rights of action include alienation of affections, breach of promise to marry, criminal conversation, and seduction of a person over the legal age of consent. Many states today have enacted heartbalm statutes primarily because of the highly speculative nature of the injury and the potential for abusive prosecution, as well as the difficulties of determining the cause of a loss.

heat of passion. (bef. 12c) Rage, terror, or furious hatred suddenly aroused by some immediate provocation, usu. another person's words or actions. • At common law, the heat of passion could serve as a mitigating circumstance that would reduce a murder charge to manslaughter.

hedge, *vb.* (17c) To use two compensating or offsetting transactions to ensure a position of breaking even; esp., to make advance arrangements to safeguard oneself from loss on an investment, speculation, or bet, as when a buyer of commodities insures against unfavorable price changes by buying in advance at a fixed rate for later delivery. — **hedging,** *n.*

hedge fund. (1967) A specialized investment group — usu. organized as a limited partnership or offshore investment company — that offers the possibility of high returns through risky techniques such as selling short or buying derivatives. • Most hedge funds are not registered with the SEC and are therefore restricted in marketing their services to the public.

heedlessness, *n.* (16c) The quality of being thoughtless and inconsiderate; esp., conduct involving the disregard of others' rights or safety. • Heedlessness is often construed to involve the same degree of fault as recklessness. — **heedless,** *adj.*

hegemony (hi-**jem**-ə-nee), *n.* (16c) **1.** Influence, authority, or supremacy over others <the hegemony of capitalism>. **2.** The striving for leadership or predominant authority of one state of a confederacy or union over the others; political domination <the former Soviet Union's hegemony over Eastern Europe>. — **hegemonic** (hej-ə-**mon**-ik), *adj.*

heinous (**hay**-nəs), *adj.* (14c) (Of a crime or its perpetrator) shockingly atrocious or odious. — **heinousness,** *n.*

heir (air). (13c) **1.** A person who, under the laws of intestacy, is entitled to receive an intestate decedent's property. **2.** Loosely (in common-law jurisdictions), a person who inherits real or personal property, whether by will or by intestate succession. **3.** Popularly, a person who has inherited or is in line to inherit great wealth. **4.** *Civil law.* A person who succeeds to the rights and occupies the place of, or is entitled to succeed to the estate of, a decedent, whether by an act of the decedent or by operation of law. • The term *heir* under the civil law has a more expansive meaning than under the common law.

afterborn heir. (18c) One born after the death of an intestate from whom the heir is entitled to inherit.

beneficiary heir (ben-ə-**fish**-ee-er-ee). *Civil law.* An heir who accepts an inheritance but whose liability for estate debts is limited to the value of the inheritance.

coheir (koh-**air**). One of two or more persons to whom an inheritance descends.

collateral heir. (17c) One who is neither a direct descendant nor an ancestor of the decedent, but whose kinship is through a collateral line, such as a brother, sister, uncle, aunt, nephew, niece, or cousin. Cf. *lineal heir.*

expectant heir. (17c) An heir who has a reversionary or future interest in property, or a chance of succeeding to it.

forced heir. *Civil law.* (1813) A person whom the testator or donor cannot disinherit because the law reserves part of the estate for that person. • In Louisiana, only descendants are forced heirs.

heir apparent. (14c) An heir who is certain to inherit unless he or she dies first or is excluded by a valid will.

heir by adoption. A person who has been adopted by (and thus has become an heir to) the deceased. • By statute in most jurisdictions, an adopted child has the same right of succession to intestate property as a biological child unless the deceased clearly expresses a contrary intention. Jurisdictions differ on whether an adopted child may also inherit from his or her biological parents or family. The clear majority view, however, is that upon adoption, a complete severance of rights and obligations occurs and the child forfeits inheritance from all biological relatives.

heir by devise. (1842) One to whom lands are given by will.

heir conventional. *Civil law.* One who takes a succession because of a contract or settlement entitling him or her to it.

heir of the blood. (16c) An heir who succeeds to an estate because of consanguinity with the decedent, in either the ascending or descending line.

heir presumptive. (17c) An heir who will inherit if the potential intestate dies immediately, but who may be excluded if another, more closely related heir is born.

heirs and assigns. (16c) A term of art formerly required to create a fee simple <A conveys Blackacre to B and his heirs and assigns>.

irregular heir. *Hist. Louisiana law.* A person or entity who has a statutory right to take property from an estate in default of the testamentary or legal heirs.

joint heir. (16c) **1.** A coheir. **2.** A person who is or will be an heir to both of two designated persons at the death of the survivor of them, the word *joint* being here applied to the ancestors rather than the heirs.

known heir. (16c) An heir who is present to claim an inheritance, the extent of which depends on there being no closer relative.

laughing heir. (1943) *Slang.* An heir distant enough to feel no grief when a relative dies and leaves an inheritance (generally viewed as a windfall) to the heir.

lineal heir. (16c) A person who is either an ancestor or a descendant of the decedent, such as a parent or a child. Cf. *collateral heir.*

natural heir. (16c) An heir by consanguinity as distinguished from an heir by adoption or a statutory heir (such as a person's spouse).

pretermitted heir (pree-tər-**mit**-id). (1841) A child or spouse who has been omitted from a will, as when a testator makes a will naming his or her two children and then, sometime later, has two more children who are not mentioned in the will.

prospective heir. (1855) An heir who may inherit but may be excluded; an heir apparent or an heir presumptive.

testamentary heir (tes-tə-**men**-tə-ree *or* -tree). *Civil law.* A person who is appointed as an heir in the decedent's will.

unconditional heir. *Civil law.* A person who chooses — expressly or tacitly — to inherit without any reservation or without making an inventory.

heirloom. (15c) An item of personal property that by local custom, contrary to the usual legal rule, descends to the heir along with the inheritance, instead of passing to the executor or administrator of the last owner.

heirship. (13c) **1.** The quality or condition of being an heir. **2.** The relation between an ancestor and an heir.

hell-or-high-water clause. (1980) A clause in a personal-property lease requiring the lessee to continue to make full rent payments to the lessor even if the thing leased is unsuitable, defective, or destroyed.

hell-or-high-water rule. (1960) **1.** The principle that a personal-property lessee must pay the full rent due, regardless of any claim against the lessor, unless the lessee proves unequal bargaining power or unconscionability. **2.** *Insurance.* The principle that an insured's automobile-liability policy will cover the insured while using a vehicle owned by another if the insured uses the vehicle in a manner within the scope of the permission granted.

henceforth, *adv.* (14c) From now on <the newly enacted rule will apply henceforth>.

hereafter, *adv.* (bef. 12c) **1.** From now on; henceforth <because of the highway construction, she will hereafter take the

bus to work>. **2.** At some future time <the court will hereafter issue a ruling on the gun's admissibility>. **3.** Hereinafter <the exhibits hereafter referred to as Exhibit A and Exhibit B>.

hereby, *adv.* (13c) By this document; by these very words <I hereby declare my intention to run for public office>.

hereditament (her-ə-**dit**-ə-mənt *or* hə-**red**-i-tə-mənt). (15c) **1.** Any property that can be inherited; anything that passes by intestacy. **2.** Real property; land.

hereditary, *adj.* (15c) Of or relating to inheritance; that descends from an ancestor to an heir.

herein, *adv.* (bef. 12c) In this thing (such as a document, section, or paragraph) <the due-process arguments stated herein should convince the court to reverse the judgment>. • This term is inherently ambiguous.

hereinafter, *adv.* (16c) Later in this document <the buyer agrees to purchase the property described hereinafter>.

hereof, *adv.* (bef. 12c) Of this thing (such as a provision or document) <the conditions hereof are stated in section 3>.

hereto, *adv.* (12c) To this document <the exhibits are attached hereto>.

heretofore, *adv.* (13c) Up to now; before this time <a question that has not heretofore been decided>.

hereunder, *adv.* (15c) **1.** Later in this document <review the provisions hereunder before signing the consent form>. **2.** In accordance with this document <notice hereunder must be provided within 30 days after the loss>.

herewith, *adv.* (bef. 12c) With or in this document <enclosed herewith are three copies>.

heritable (**her**-i-tə-bəl), *adj.* (14c) **1.** (Of property) capable of being inherited. **2.** (Of a person) capable of inheriting.

hermeneutics (hər-mə-**n[y]oo**-tiks), *n.* (18c) The art of interpreting texts, esp. as a technique used in critical legal studies. — **hermeneutical, hermeneutic,** *adj.*

heterologous, *adj. Patents.* Of, relating to, or constituting the DNA of a foreign organism.

heuristic (hyuu-**ris**-tik), *adj.* (1821) Of or relating to a method of learning or problem-solving by using trial-and-error and other experimental techniques <heuristic discovery methods>.

HEW. *abbr.* The Department of Health, Education, and Welfare, a former agency of the U.S. government created in 1953. • When the Department of Education was created in 1979, the name of HEW was changed to the Department of Health and Human Services (HHS).

HGN test. *abbr.* Horizontal-gaze nystagmus test.

HHS. *abbr.* Department of Health And Human Services.

HIDC. *abbr.* Holder in due course.

high–low agreement. (1980) A settlement in which a defendant agrees to pay the plaintiff a minimum recovery in return for the plaintiff's agreement to accept a maximum amount regardless of the outcome of the trial.

highway. (bef. 12c) **1.** Broadly, any main route on land, on water, or in the air. **2.** A free and public roadway or street that every person may use. **3.** The main public road connecting towns or cities. **4.** The entire width between boundaries of every publicly maintained way when part is open to public use for purposes of vehicular traffic.

highwayman. (17c) A highway robber; a person who robs on a public road.

hijack, *vb.* (1923) **1.** To commandeer (a vehicle or airplane), esp. at gunpoint. **2.** To steal or rob from (a vehicle or airplane in transit). **3.** *Hist.* To rob by trickery or violence; esp., to rob (a smuggler or bootlegger) and take illegal goods.

HIPAA (**hip**-ə). *abbr.* Health Insurance Portability and Accountability Act.

hire, *vb.* (bef. 12c) **1.** To engage the labor or services of another for wages or other payment. **2.** To procure the temporary use of property, usu. at a set price. **3.** To grant the temporary use of services <hire themselves out>.

hired gun. (1971) *Slang.* **1.** An expert witness who testifies favorably for the party paying his or her fee, often because of that financial relationship rather than because of the facts. **2.** A lawyer who stops at nothing to accomplish the client's goals, regardless of moral consequences.

hireling, *n.* A person who is hired or serves for wages, esp. one who works only for the sake of payments.

His Honor; Her Honor. (1827) **1.** A third-person title customarily given to a judge. **2.** A third-person title customarily given to the mayor of a city. **3.** A third-person title given by the Massachusetts Constitution to the lieutenant governor of the commonwealth.

historic-preservation law. An ordinance prohibiting the demolition or exterior alteration of certain historic buildings or of all buildings in a historic district.

historic site. A building, structure, area, or property that is significant in the history, architecture, archaeology, or culture of a country, state, or city, and has been so designated by statute. • A historic site usu. cannot be altered without the permission of the appropriate authorities.

hit, *n.* (bef. 12c) **1.** A physical strike. **2.** *Criminal law.* A murder committed for money or on orders from a gang leader. **3.** *Criminal law.* An instance of the taking of a drug. **4.** *Intellectual property.* A single instance of a computer's connection to a Web page. **5.** *Intellectual property.* A Web page identified by an Internet search engine as containing words matching a user's query. **6.** A creative work that is a popular or a commercial success.

hit-and-run statute. A law requiring a motorist involved in an accident to remain at the scene and to give certain information to the police and others involved.

hitherto, *adv.* (13c) Until now; heretofore.

HLA test. Human-leukocyte antigen test.

HMO. *abbr.* Health-maintenance organization.

hoard, *vb.* (bef. 12c) To acquire and hold (goods) beyond one's reasonable needs, usu. because of an actual or anticipated shortage or price increase.

hodgepodge. (15c) **1.** Hotchpot. **2.** An unorganized mixture.

hodgepodge act. (1883) A statute that deals with incongruous subjects.

hold, *vb.* (bef. 12c) **1.** To possess by a lawful title <Sarah holds the account as her separate property>. **2.** (Of a court) to adjudge or decide as a matter of law (as opposed to fact) <this court thus holds the statute to be unconstitutional>. **3.** To direct and bring about officially; to conduct according to law <we must hold an election every two years>. **4.** To keep in custody or under an obligation <I will ask the judge to hold you accountable>. **5.** To take or have an estate from another; to have an estate on condition of paying rent or performing service <James holds Hungerstream Manor under lease>. **6.** To conduct or preside at; to convoke, open, and direct the operations of <Judge Brown holds court four days a week>. **7.** To possess or occupy; to be in possession and administration of <Jones holds the office of treasurer>.

holdback, *n.* An amount withheld from the full payment of a contract pending the other party's completion of some obligation, esp. to ensure that a contractor finishes the work agreed on beforehand. — **hold back,** *vb.*

holder. (14c) **1.** A person who has legal possession of a negotiable instrument and is entitled to receive payment on it. **2.** A person with legal possession of a document of title or an investment security. **3.** A person who possesses or uses property.

holder for value. (18c) A person who has given value in exchange for a negotiable instrument. • Under the UCC, examples of "giving value" include acquiring a security interest in the instrument and accepting the instrument in payment of an antecedent claim. UCC § 3-303(a).

holder in due course. (1882) A person who in good faith has given value for a negotiable instrument that is complete and regular on its face, is not overdue, and, to the possessor's knowledge, has not been dishonored. • Under UCC § 3-305, a holder in due course takes the instrument free of all claims and personal defenses, but subject to real defenses. — Abbr. HDC; HIDC.

holder in good faith. (18c) One who takes property or an instrument without knowledge of any defect in its title.

hold harmless, *vb.* (18c) To absolve (another party) from any responsibility for damage or other liability arising from the transaction; indemnify.

hold-harmless agreement. (1939) A contract in which one party agrees to indemnify the other.

holding, *n.* (15c) **1.** A court's determination of a matter of law pivotal to its decision; a principle drawn from such a decision. Cf. OBITER DICTUM. **2.** A ruling on evidence or other questions presented at trial. **3.** (*usu. pl.*) Legally owned property, esp. land or securities.

holding charge. (1949) A criminal charge of some minor offense filed to keep the accused in custody while prosecutors take time to build a bigger case and prepare more serious charges.

holding over. A tenant's action in continuing to occupy the leased premises after the lease term has expired.

holding period. (1935) *Tax.* The time during which a capital asset must be held to determine whether gain or loss from its sale or exchange is long-term or short-term.

hold order. (1945) A notation in a prisoner's file stating that another jurisdiction has charges pending against the prisoner and instructing prison officials to alert authorities in that other jurisdiction instead of releasing the prisoner.

hold out, *vb.* (16c) **1.** To represent (oneself or another) as having a certain legal status, as by claiming to be an agent or partner with authority to enter into transactions <even though he was only a promoter, Schwartz held himself out as the principal>. **2.** To refuse to yield or submit; to stand firm <Womack held out for a higher salary and better benefits>.

holograph (**hol**-ə-graf), *n.* (17c) A document (such as a will or deed) that is handwritten by its author. — **holographic,** *adj.*

home. (bef. 12c) A dwelling place.

home office. A corporation's principal office or headquarters.

Home Owners Warranty. A warranty and insurance program that, among other coverage, insures a new home for ten years against major structural defects. • The program was developed by the Home Owners Warranty Corporation, a subsidiary of the National Association of Home Builders. Builders often provide this type of coverage, and many states provide similar warranty protection by statute. — Abbr. HOW.

home rule. (1860) A state legislative provision or action allocating a measure of autonomy to a local government, conditional on its acceptance of certain terms.

homestead. (bef. 12c) **1.** The house, outbuildings, and adjoining land owned and occupied by a person or family as a residence.

business homestead. (1882) The premises on which a family's business is located. • In some states, business homesteads are exempt from execution or judicial sale for most kinds of debt.

constitutional homestead. (1851) A homestead, along with its exemption from forced sale, conferred on the head of a household by a state constitution.

probate homestead. (1881) A homestead created by a probate court from a decedent's estate for the benefit of the decedent's surviving spouse and minor children.

2. A surviving spouse's right of occupying the family home for life. • In some states, the right is extended to other dependents of a decedent.

homestead law. (1847) A statute exempting a homestead from execution or judicial sale for debt, unless all owners, usu. a husband and wife, have jointly mortgaged the property or otherwise subjected it to creditors' claims.

home-study report. *Family law.* A summary of an investigation into a child's home, family environment, and background, usu. prepared by a social worker when a child has been removed from his or her home because of abuse or neglect, but also prepared after a similar investigation of the home of potential adoptive parents.

homicide (**hom**-ə-sɪd), *n.* (14c) **1.** The killing of one person by another. **2.** A person who kills another. — **homicidal,** *adj.*

criminal homicide. (1850) **1.** Homicide prohibited and punishable by law, such as murder or manslaughter. **2.** The act of purposely, knowingly, recklessly, or negligently causing the death of another human being. Model Penal Code § 210.1.

excusable homicide. (18c) Homicide resulting from a person's lawful act, committed without intention to harm another.

felonious homicide. (18c) Homicide committed unlawfully, without legal justification or excuse. • This is the category into which murder and manslaughter fall.

homicide by abuse. (1989) Homicide in which the perpetrator, under circumstances showing an extreme indifference to human life, causes the death of the perpetrator's dependent — usu. a child or mentally retarded person.

homicide per infortunium (pər in-for-**t[y]oo**-nee-əm). [Latin "homicide by misfortune"] (1856) The unintentional killing of another while engaged in a lawful act; accidental killing.

innocent homicide. (1884) Homicide that does not involve criminal guilt.

justifiable homicide. (18c) **1.** The killing of another in self-defense when faced with the danger of death or serious bodily injury. **2.** A killing mandated or permitted by the law, such as execution for a capital crime or killing to prevent a crime or a criminal's escape.

negligent homicide. (1859) Homicide resulting from the careless performance of a legal or illegal act in which the danger of death is apparent; the killing of a human being by criminal negligence.

nonfelonious homicide. A killing that is legally either excusable or justifiable.

reckless homicide. (1866) The unlawful killing of another person with conscious indifference toward that person's life.

vehicular homicide. (1952) The killing of a person as a result of the unlawful or negligent operation of a motor vehicle.

victim-precipitated homicide. A killing provoked by the victim who consciously intended to die at the hands of another person. • This term applies loosely to any assisted suicide. Unlike most types of homicide, the victim bears some of the responsibility for causing his or her own death.

willful homicide. (1860) The act of intentionally causing a person's death, with or without legal justification.

Hon. *abbr.* Honorable.

honor, *vb.* (13c) **1.** To accept or pay (a negotiable instrument) when presented. **2.** To recognize, salute, or praise.

Honorable. (15c) A title of respect given to judges, members of the U.S. Congress, ambassadors, and the like. — Abbr. Hon.

honorarium (on-ə-**rair**-ee-əm), *n.* (17c) **1.** A payment of money or anything else of value made to a person for services rendered for which fees cannot legally be or are not traditionally paid. **2.** A voluntary reward for that for which no remuneration could be collected by law; a voluntary donation in consideration of services that admit of no compensation in money. Pl. **honoraria; honorariums.**

honorary, *adj.* (16c) (Of a title or status) conferred in recognition of merit or service, but without the attendant rights, powers, or duties; nominal <honorary member>.

horizontal equality. In per capita distribution of an estate, parity of distribution among members of the same generation.

horizontal-gaze nystagmus test (nis-**tag**-məs). (1985) *Criminal law.* A field-sobriety test for intoxication, in which the suspect is told to focus on an object (such as a pencil) and to track its movement, usu. from side to side, by moving only the eyes. • Intoxication is indicated if the eyes jerk or twitch while tracking the object. — Abbr. HGN test.

hornbook. (16c) **1.** A book explaining the basics of a given subject. **2.** A textbook containing the rudimentary principles of an area of law.

hornbook law. Blackletter law.

hornbook method. (1895) A method of legal instruction characterized by a straightforward presentation of legal doctrine, occasionally interspersed with questions. • The hornbook method predominates in civil-law countries, and in certain fields of law, such as procedure and evidence.

horseshedding, *n.* (1931) The instructing of a witness favorable to one's case (esp. a client) about the proper method of responding to questions while giving testimony. — **horseshed,** *vb.*

hospiticide (hah-**spit**-ə-sɪd), *n.* (17c) **1.** The murder of a host by a guest. **2.** A host who murders a guest.

hostage. (13c) **1.** An innocent person held captive by another who threatens to kill or harm that person if one or more demands are not met. • Hostage-taking is a federal crime. 18 USCA § 1203. **2.** *Int'l law.* A person who is given or taken into an enemy's custody, in time of war, with his or her freedom or life to stand as security for the performance of some agreement made to the enemy by the belligerent power giving the hostage.

hostile, *adj.* (16c) **1.** Adverse. **2.** Showing ill will or a desire to harm. **3.** Antagonistic; unfriendly.

hostility. (15c) **1.** A state of enmity between individuals or nations. **2.** An act or series of acts displaying antagonism. **3.** (*usu. pl.*) Acts of war.

hot cargo. (1938) *Labor law.* Goods produced or handled by an employer with whom a union has a dispute.

hot-cargo agreement. (1957) *Labor law.* A voluntary agreement between a union and a neutral employer by which the latter agrees to exert pressure on another employer with whom the union has a dispute, as by ceasing or refraining from handling, using, selling, transporting, or otherwise dealing in any of the products of an employer that the union has labeled as unfair. • Most agreements of this type were prohibited by the Landrum–Griffin Act of 1959.

hotchpot (**hoch**-pot), *n.* (16c) **1.** The blending of items of property to secure equality of division, esp. as practiced either in cases of divorce or in cases in which advancements of an intestate's property must be made up to the estate by a contribution or by an accounting. **2.** In a community-property state, the property that falls within the community estate.

hot news. *Intellectual property.* Extremely time-sensitive or transient information that is usu. reliable for very brief periods, such as stock quotations.

hot-potato rule. The principle that a lawyer may not unreasonably withdraw from representing a client. • The term comes from the rule's classic formulation: "a firm may not drop a client like a 'hot potato,' especially if it is in order to keep happy a far more lucrative client." *Picker Int'l, Inc. v. Varian Assocs., Inc.*, 670 F. Supp. 1363, 1365 (N.D. Ohio 1987). An exception may be allowed for a conflict of interest arising from circumstances beyond the control of the lawyer or the law firm.

house. (bef. 12c) **1.** A home, dwelling, or residence. **2.** A branch of a legislature or a quorum of such a branch; esp., the lower chamber of a bicameral legislature. **3.** House of Representatives.

house arrest. (1936) The confinement of a person who has been accused or convicted of a crime to his or her home, usu. by attaching an electronically monitored bracelet to the person.

housebreaking. (17c) The crime of breaking into a dwelling or other secured building, with the intent to commit a felony inside; burglary. — **housebreaker,** *n.*

houseburning. The common-law misdemeanor of intentionally burning one's own house that is within city limits or that is close enough to other houses that they might be in danger of catching fire (even though no actual damage to them may result).

household, *n.* (14c) **1.** A family living together. **2.** A group of people who dwell under the same roof. **3.** The contents of a house.

house of delegates. (18c) **1.** (*often cap.*) The convention of many learned or professional associations, including the American Bar Association <the ABA House of Delegates>. **2.** (*cap.*) The lower chamber of the state legislature in Maryland, Virginia, and West Virginia.

House of Representatives. (18c) **1.** The lower chamber of the U.S. Congress, composed of 435 members — apportioned among the states on the basis of population — who are elected to two-year terms. **2.** The lower house of a state legislature. — Abbr. H.R.; H.

HOW. *abbr.* Homeowner's warranty.

howsoever, *adv.* (14c) In whatever way; however.

H.R. *abbr.* House of Representatives.

HUD. *abbr.* Department of Housing and Urban Development.

hue and cry. (15c) *Hist.* **1.** The public uproar that, at common law, a citizen was expected to initiate after discovering a crime. **2.** The pursuit of a felon accompanying such an uproar. **3.** A written proclamation for the capture of a felon.

human-leukocyte antigen test. A medical process of analyzing the blood sample of a man in a paternity or legitimacy case by comparing certain indicators with the child's blood. — Abbr. HLA test.

human rights. (18c) The freedoms, immunities, and benefits that, according to modern values (esp. at an international level), all human beings should be able to claim as a matter of right in the society in which they live.

husband. (13c) A married man; a man who has a lawful spouse living.

common-law husband. The husband in a common-law marriage; a man who contracts an informal marriage with a woman and then holds himself out to the community as being married to her.

husbandry. (14c) **1.** Agriculture or farming; cultivation of the soil for food. **2.** Generally, care of a household; careful management of resources.

hush money. (18c) *Slang.* A bribe to suppress the dissemination of certain information; a payment to secure silence.

Hyde Amendment. A federal law that prohibits the use of Medicaid funds for abortions except when necessary to save the mother's life, and that prohibits federally funded family-planning programs from providing abortion counseling. • The bill was sponsored by Representative Henry Hyde of Illinois.

***Hydraflow* test.** (1996) A principle for deciding when an inadvertent disclosure of a privileged document is a waiver of the attorney–client privilege, whereby the court considers the reasonableness of the precautions taken to prevent the inadvertent disclosure, the number of disclosures involved, the extent of the disclosure, the promptness of any efforts to remedy the disclosure, and whether justice would be best served by permitting the disclosing party to retrieve the document. *Hydraflow, Inc. v. Enidine, Inc.*, 145 F.R.D. 626 (W.D.N.Y. 1993).

hypothecate (hɪ-**poth**-ə-kayt), *vb.* (17c) To pledge (property) as security or collateral for a debt, without delivery of title or possession.

hypothesis (hɪ-**poth**-ə-səs). (16c) **1.** A supposition based on evidence but not proven; a proposed explanation, supported by evidence, that serves as a starting point for investigation. **2.** A theory or supposition proposed for the sake of debate.

hypothetical, *n.* (17c) A proposition or statement that is presumed true for the sake of logical analysis or debate. • Hypotheticals are often used as teaching tools to illustrate the application of legal principles or to explore the potential consequences of words and actions.

hypothetical-person defense. (1979) An entrapment defense in which the defendant asserts that an undercover law-enforcement officer (or person acting at the law-enforcement officer's direction) encouraged the defendant to engage in the criminal conduct either by making false representations designed to convince the defendant that the conduct was not prohibited, or by using persuasive methods that created a substantial risk that the charged offense would be committed by a person who was not otherwise inclined to commit it. • This defense has been adopted by a minority of states and by the Model Penal Code. See Model Penal Code § 2.13.

hypothetical question. (1826) A trial device that solicits an expert witness's opinion based on assumptions treated as facts established by evidence.

I

IABA. *abbr.* Inter-American Bar Association.

ibid. (**ib**-id). *abbr.* [Latin *ibidem*] (17c) In the same place. • This abbreviation, used in citations (mostly outside law), denotes that the reference is to a work cited immediately before, and that the cited matter appears on the same page of the same book (unless a different page is specified).

ICC. *abbr.* **1.** Interstate Commerce Commission. **2.** International criminal court.

ICJ. *abbr.* International Court of Justice.

id. (id). *abbr.* [Latin *idem*] (17c) The same. • *Id.* is used in a legal citation to refer to the authority cited immediately before <*id.* at 55>.

IDEA. *abbr.* Individuals with Disabilities Education Act.

idea–expression dichotomy. *Copyright.* The fundamental rule that copyright law protects only specific expressions of an idea, not the idea itself.

idem sonans (ɪ-dem **soh**-nanz), *adj.* [Latin] (1856) (Of words or names) sounding the same, regardless of spelling <the names Gene and Jean are *idem sonans*>.

idem sonans (ɪ-dem **soh**-nanz), *n.* [Latin] (1848) A legal doctrine preventing a variant spelling of a name in a document from voiding the document if the misspelling is pronounced the same way as the true spelling.

identification of goods. (1887) A process that enables a buyer to obtain an identifiable (and therefore insurable) interest in goods before taking possession from the seller. • The goods are identified in any manner agreed to by the parties. UCC § 2-501.

identify, *vb.* (18c) **1.** To prove the identity of (a person or thing) <the witness identified the weapon>. **2.** To look upon as being associated (with) <the plaintiff was identified with the environmental movement>. **3.** To specify (certain goods) as the object of a contract <identify the appliances to the contract>.

identity. (16c) **1.** The identical nature of two or more things; esp., in patent law, the sameness in two devices of the function performed, the way it is performed, and the result achieved. • Under the doctrine of equivalents, infringement may be found even if the accused device is not identical to the claimed invention. **2.** *Evidence.* The authenticity of a person or thing.

identity of interests. (18c) *Civil procedure.* A relationship between two parties who are so close that suing one serves as notice to the other, so that the other may be joined in the suit. Fed. R. Civ. P. 15(c)(1)(c).

identity of parties. (1803) *Civil procedure.* A relationship between two parties who are so close that a judgment against one prevents later action against the other because of res judicata.

identity theft. The unlawful taking and use of another person's identifying information for fraudulent purposes.

i.e. *abbr.* [Latin *id est*] (17c) That is <the federal government's highest judicial body, i.e., the Supreme Court>.

IFP. *abbr.* In forma pauperis.

ignominy (**ig**-nə-min-ee). Public disgrace or dishonor. — **ignominious,** *adj.*

ignoramus (ig-nə-**ray**-məs). [Law Latin] *Hist.* We do not know. • This notation, when written on a bill of indictment, indicated the grand jury's rejection of the bill.

ignorantia facti excusat (ig-nə-**ran**-shee-ə **fak**-tɪ ek-**skyoo**-sat *or* -zat).

[Latin] Ignorance of fact is an excuse; whatever is done under a mistaken impression of a material fact is excused or provides grounds for relief.

ignorantia juris (ig-nə-**ran**-shee-ə **joor**-is). [Latin] Ignorance of law.

ignorantia juris non excusat (ig-nə-**ran**-shee-ə **joor**-is non ek-**skyoo**-sat *or* -zat). [Latin] Lack of knowledge about a legal requirement or prohibition is never an excuse to a criminal charge. • In English, the idea is commonly rendered *ignorance of the law is no excuse.*

ignoratio elenchi (ig-nə-**ray**-shee-oh e-**leng**-kɪ *or* ig-nə-**rah**-tee-oh i-**leng**-kee). [Law Latin "ignorance of the conclusion to be proved"] (16c) An advocate's misunderstanding of an opponent's position, manifested by an argument that fails to address the opponent's point; the overlooking of an opponent's counterargument. • This fallacy of logic often involves an advocate's trying to prove something that is immaterial to the point to be decided.

ignore, *vb.* (1801) **1.** To refuse to notice, recognize, or consider. **2.** (Of a grand jury) to reject (an indictment) as groundless; to no-bill (a charge).

ignoring, *n. Family law.* A parent's or caregiver's pattern of depriving a child of essential intellectual or emotional stimulation or of otherwise stifling a child's emotional growth and intellectual development, essentially by being unavailable.

IIED. *abbr.* Intentional infliction of emotional distress.

ill, *adj.* (Of a pleading) defective, bad, or null.

illation (i-**lay**-shən). (16c) **1.** The act or process of inferring. **2.** An inference; that which is inferred.

illegal, *adj.* Forbidden by law; unlawful <illegal dumping> <an illegal drug>.

illegal entry. (18c) **1.** *Criminal law.* The unlawful act of going into a building with the intent to commit a crime. **2.** *Immigration.* The unauthorized entrance of an alien into the United States by arriving at the wrong time or place, by evading inspection, or by fraud.

illegality, *n.* (17c) **1.** An act that is not authorized by law. **2.** The state of not being legally authorized. **3.** The state or condition of being unlawful. • The affirmative defense of illegality must be expressly set forth in the response to the opponent's pleading. Fed. R. Civ. P. 8(c).

illegal per se. Unlawful in and of itself.

illegitimacy. (17c) **1.** Unlawfulness. **2.** The status of a person who is born outside a lawful marriage and who is not later legitimated by the parents.

illegitimate, *adj.* (16c) **1.** (Of a child) born out of lawful wedlock and never having been legitimated. **2.** Against the law; unlawful. **3.** Improper. **4.** Incorrectly inferred. **5.** *Ecclesiastical law.* (Of a child) born within a marriage that is regarded as an invalid sacrament from its inception.

illicit (i[l]-**lis**-ət), *adj.* (16c) Illegal or improper <illicit relations>.

illusory (i-**loo**-sə-ree), *adj.* (17c) Deceptive; based on a false impression.

illusory-transfer doctrine. The rule that the law disregards an inter vivos gift over which the donor retains so much control that there is no good-faith intent to relinquish the transferred property. • The illusory-transfer doctrine is usu. applied to inter vivos trusts in which the settlor retains an excessive control or an interest — for instance, one in which the settlor retains the income for life, the power to revoke, and substantial managerial powers. The leading case on this doctrine is *Newman v. Dore,* 9 N.E.2d 966 (N.Y. 1937).

IMF. *abbr.* International Monetary Fund.

immaterial, *adj.* (1893) (Of evidence) tending to prove some fact that is not properly at issue; lacking any logical connection with the consequential facts. — **immateriality,** *n.*

immediate, *adj.* (15c) **1.** Occurring without delay; instant <an immediate acceptance>. **2.** Not separated by other persons or things <her immediate neighbor>. **3.** Having a direct impact; without an intervening agency <the immediate cause of the accident>. — **immediacy, immediateness,** *n.*

immediate control. (1962) *Criminal procedure.* **1.** The area within an arrestee's reach. • A police officer may conduct a warrantless search of this area to ensure the officer's safety and to prevent the arrestee from destroying evidence. **2.** Vehicular control that is close enough to allow the driver to instantly govern the vehicle's movements. • A driver's failure to maintain immediate control over the vehicle could be evidence of negligence.

immediately-apparent requirement. (1978) *Criminal procedure.* The principle that a police officer must have probable cause to believe that an item is contraband before seizing it. • This plain-view exception to the warrant requirement was first announced in *Coolidge v. New Hampshire*, 403 U.S. 443, 91 S.Ct. 2022 (1971).

immemorial (im-ə-**mor**-ee-əl), *adj.* (17c) Beyond memory or record; very old.

immigrant. (18c) A person who enters a country to settle there permanently; a person who immigrates.

alien immigrant. An immigrant who has not yet been naturalized.

immigration, *n.* (17c) The act of entering a country with the intention of settling there permanently. — **immigrate,** *vb.* — **immigrant,** *n.*

Immigration and Nationality Act. A comprehensive federal law regulating immigration, naturalization, and the exclusion of aliens. 8 USCA §§ 1101–1537.

Immigration and Naturalization Service. A former U.S. Department of Justice agency that administered the Immigration and Nationality Act and operated the U.S. Border Patrol. — Abbr. INS.

immoral subject matter. 1. *Patents.* Inventions that do not have a socially beneficial use. • In the past, patents were denied for some categories of inventions, such as gambling devices and fraudulent products, esp. medicines. The doctrine is rarely used today. **2.** *Trademarks.* Scandalous subject matter.

immovable, *n.* (*usu. pl.*) (16c) Property that cannot be moved; an object so firmly attached to land that it is regarded as part of the land. — **immovable,** *adj.*

immunity. (14c) **1.** Any exemption from a duty, liability, or service of process; esp., such an exemption granted to a public official or governmental unit. — **immune,** *adj.*

absolute immunity. (17c) A complete exemption from civil liability, usu. afforded to officials while performing particularly important functions, such as a representative enacting legislation and a judge presiding over a lawsuit.

congressional immunity. (1969) Either of two special immunities given to members of Congress: (1) the exemption from arrest while attending a session of the body to which the member belongs, excluding an arrest for treason, breach of the peace, or a felony, or (2) the exemption from arrest or questioning for any speech or debate entered into during a legislative session. U.S. Const. art. I, § 6, cl. 1.

constitutional immunity. (1852) Immunity created by a constitution.

diplomatic immunity. (1911) The general exemption of diplomatic ministers from the operation of local law, the exception being that a minister who is plotting against the security of the host nation may be arrested and sent out of the country.

discretionary immunity. (1965) A qualified immunity for a public official's acts, granted when the act in question required the exercise of judgment in carrying out official duties (such as planning and policy-making). 28 USCA § 2680(a).

executive immunity. (1941) **1.** The absolute immunity of the U.S. President or a state governor from civil damages for actions that are within the scope of official responsibilities. **2.** The qualified immunity from civil claims against lesser executive officials, who are liable only if their conduct violates clearly established constitutional or statutory rights.

foreign immunity. The immunity of a foreign sovereign, its agents, and its instrumentalities from litigation in U.S. courts.

intergovernmental immunity. (1935) The immunity between the federal and state governments based on their independent sovereignty.

judicial immunity. (1850) The immunity of a judge from civil liability arising from the performance of judicial duties.

legislative immunity. (1890) The immunity of a legislator from civil liability arising from the performance of legislative duties.

prosecutorial immunity. The absolute immunity of a prosecutor from civil liability for decisions made and actions taken in a criminal prosecution.

qualified immunity. (1877) Immunity from civil liability for a public official who is performing a discretionary function, as long as the conduct does not violate clearly established constitutional or statutory rights.

sovereign immunity. (1857) **1.** A government's immunity from being sued in its own courts without its consent. • Congress has waived most of the federal government's sovereign immunity. **2.** A state's immunity from being sued in federal court by the state's own citizens.

2. *Torts.* A doctrine providing a complete defense to a tort action. • Unlike a privilege, immunity does not negate the tort, and it must be raised affirmatively or it will be waived.

charitable immunity. (1935) The immunity of a charitable organization from tort liability. • This immunity has been eliminated or restricted in most states.

corporate immunity. A corporate officer's immunity from personal liability for a tortious act committed while acting in good faith and within the course of corporate duties.

husband–wife immunity. (1951) The immunity of one spouse from a tort action by the other spouse for personal injury.

parental immunity. (1930) **1.** The principle that children cannot sue their parents, and that parents cannot sue their children, for tort claims. **2.** The principle that parents are not liable for damages caused by the ordinary negligence of their minor child.

3. *Criminal law.* Freedom from prosecution granted by the government in exchange for the person's testimony. • By granting immunity, the government can compel testimony — despite the Fifth Amendment right against self-incrimination — because that testimony can no longer incriminate the witness.

pocket immunity. (1983) Immunity that results from the prosecutor's decision not to prosecute, instead of from a formal grant of immunity.

testimonial immunity. (1938) Immunity from the use of the compelled testimony against the witness. • Any information derived from that testimony, however, is generally admissible against the witness.

transactional immunity. (1966) Immunity from prosecution for any event or transaction described in the compelled testimony. • This is the broadest form of immunity.

use immunity. (1970) Immunity from the use of the compelled testimony (or any information derived from that testimony) in a future prosecution against the witness. • After granting use immunity, the government can still prosecute if it shows that its evidence comes from a legitimate independent source.

immunize, *vb.* (1892) To grant immunity to.

impact rule. (1865) *Torts.* The common-law requirement that physical contact must have occurred to allow damages for negligent infliction of emotional distress. • This rule has been abandoned in most jurisdictions.

impair, *vb.* (17c) To diminish the value of (property or a property right). • This term is commonly used in reference to diminishing the value of a contractual obligation to the point that the contract becomes invalid or a party loses the benefit of the contract.

impairing the morals of a minor. (1931) The offense of an adult's engaging in sex-related acts, short of intercourse, with a minor. • Examples of this conduct are fondling, taking obscene photographs, and showing pornographic materials.

impairment, *n.* (14c) The fact or state of being damaged, weakened, or diminished <impairment of collateral>. — **impair,** *vb.*

impartial, *adj.* (16c) Unbiased; disinterested.

impartible (im-**pahr**-tə-bəl), *adj.* (14c) Indivisible <an impartible estate>.

impeachment. (16c) **1.** The act (by a legislature) of calling for the removal from office of a public official, accomplished by presenting a written charge of the official's alleged misconduct; esp., the initiation of a proceeding in the U.S. House of Representatives against a federal official, such as the President or a judge. • Congress's authority to remove a federal official stems from Article II, Section 4 of the Constitution, which authorizes the removal of an official for "Treason, Bribery, or other high Crimes and Misdemeanors." The grounds upon which an official can be removed do not, however, have to be criminal in nature. They usu. involve some type of abuse of power or breach of the public trust. Articles of impeachment — which can be approved by a simple majority in the House — serve as the charging instrument for the later trial in the Senate. If the President is impeached, the Chief Justice of the Supreme Court presides over the Senate trial. The defendant can be removed from office by the vote of a two-thirds majority of the senators who are present. In the United Kingdom, impeachment is by the House of Commons and trial by the House of Lords. But no case has arisen there since 1801, and many British scholars consider impeachment obsolete. **2.** The act of discrediting a witness, as by catching the witness in a lie or by demonstrating that the witness has been convicted of a criminal offense. **3.** The act of challenging the accuracy or authenticity of evidence. — **impeach,** *vb.* (14c). — **impeachable,** *adj.*

impeachment of verdict. (1821) A party's attack on a verdict, alleging impropriety by a member of the jury.

impediment (im-**ped**-ə-mənt). (14c) A hindrance or obstruction; esp., some fact (such as legal minority) that bars a marriage if known beforehand and, if discovered after the ceremony, renders the marriage void or voidable.

imperative theory of law. (1909) The theory that law consists of the general commands issued by a country or other political community to its subjects and enforced by courts with the sanction of physical force. • Imperative theorists believe that if there are rules predating or independent of the country, those rules may closely resemble law or even substitute for it, but they are not law.

impersonation. (18c) The act of impersonating someone.

false impersonation. (1878) The crime of falsely representing oneself as another person, usu. a law-enforcement officer, for the purpose of deceiving someone. See 18 USCA §§ 912–917.

impertinent matter. (18c) *Procedure.* In pleading, matter that is not relevant to the action or defense. • A federal court may strike any impertinent matter from a pleading. Fed. R. Civ. P. 12(f).

impinge, *vb.* (17c) To encroach or infringe (*on* or *upon*) <impinge on the defendant's rights>.

implead, *vb.* (14c) To bring (someone) into a lawsuit; esp., to bring (a new party) into the action.

impleader, *n.* (1918) A procedure by which a third party is brought into a lawsuit, esp. by a defendant who seeks to shift liability to someone not sued by the plaintiff. Fed. R. Civ. P. 14.

implicate, *vb.* (15c) **1.** To show (a person) to be involved in (a crime, misfeasance, etc.). **2.** To be involved or affected.

implication. (15c) **1.** The act of showing involvement in something, esp. a crime or misfeasance. **2.** An inference drawn from something said or observed.

necessary implication. (18c) An implication so strong in its probability that anything to the contrary would be unreasonable.

implied, *adj.* (16c) Not directly expressed; recognized by law as existing inferentially.

implied in law, *n.* (1806) Imposed by operation of law and not because of any inferences that can be drawn from the facts of the case.

implied-license doctrine. 1. The principle that a person's specific conduct may be tantamount to a grant of permission to do something. **2.** The principle that in some specified circumstances a statute can be construed as supplying a necessary authority by operation of law.

imply, *vb.* (14c) **1.** To express or involve indirectly; to suggest. **2.** (Of a court) to impute or impose on equitable or legal grounds. **3.** To read into (a document). — **implication,** *n.*

import, *n.* (16c) **1.** A product brought into a country from a foreign country where it originated <imports declined in the third quarter>. **2.** The process of bringing foreign goods into a country <the import of products affects the domestic economy in significant ways>. **3.** The meaning; esp., the implied meaning <the court must decide the import of that obscure provision>. **4.** Importance; significance <time will tell the relative import of Judge Posner's decisions in American law>.

imported litigation. (1927) One or more lawsuits brought in a state that has no interest in the dispute.

importer. (15c) A person or entity that brings goods into a country from a foreign country and pays customs duties.

Import–Export Clause. (1945) U.S. Const. art. I, § 10, cl. 2, which prohibits states from taxing imports or exports. • The Supreme Court has liberally interpreted this clause, allowing states to tax imports as long as the tax does not discriminate in favor of domestic goods.

importune (im-por-**t[y]oon**), *vb.* (16c) To solicit forcefully; to request persistently, and sometimes irksomely.

impose, *vb.* (17c) To levy or exact (a tax or duty).

imposition. (14c) An impost or tax.

impossibility. (14c) **1.** The fact or condition of not being able to occur, exist, or be done. **2.** A fact or circumstance that cannot occur, exist, or be done. **3.** *Contracts.* A fact or circumstance that excuses performance because (1) the subject or means of performance has deteriorated, has been destroyed, or is no longer available, (2) the method of delivery or payment has failed, (3) a law now prevents performance, or (4) death or illness prevents performance. • Increased or unexpected difficulty and expense do not usu. qualify as an impossibility and thus do not excuse performance. **4.** The doctrine by which such a fact or circumstance excuses contractual performance. **5.** *Criminal law.* A fact or circumstance preventing the commission of a crime.

factual impossibility. (1932) Impossibility due to the fact that the illegal act cannot physically be accomplished, such as trying to pick an empty pocket. • Factual impossibility is not a defense to the crime of attempt.

legal impossibility. (1831) **1.** Impossibility due to the fact that what the defendant intended to do is not illegal even though the defendant might have believed that he or she was committing a crime. • This type of legal impossibility is a defense to the crimes of attempt, conspiracy, and solicitation. **2.** Impossibility due to the fact that an element required for an attempt has not been satisfied. • This is a defense to the crime of attempt.

objective impossibility. Impossibility due to the nature of the performance and not to the inability of the individual promisor.

subjective impossibility. Impossibility due wholly to the inability of the individual promisor and not to the nature of the performance.

supervening impossibility. Impossibility arising after the formation of a contract but before the time when the promisor's performance is due, and arising because of facts that the promisor had no reason to anticipate and did not contribute to the occurrence of.

impossibility-of-performance doctrine. (1960) The principle that a party may be released from a contract on the ground that uncontrollable circumstances have rendered performance impossible.

impound, *vb.* (15c) **1.** To place (something, such as a car or other personal property) in the custody of the police or the court, often with the understanding that it will be returned intact at the end of the proceeding. **2.** To take and retain possession of (something, such as a forged document to be produced as evidence) in preparation for a criminal prosecution.

impoundment. (17c) **1.** The action of impounding; the state of being impounded. **2.** *Constitutional law.* The President's refusal to spend funds appropriated by Congress. • Although not authorized by the Constitution and seldom used, impoundment effectively gives the executive branch a line-item veto over legislative spending.

impracticability (im-prak-ti-kə-**bil**-ə-tee). (17c) *Contracts.* **1.** A fact or circumstance that excuses a party from performing an act, esp. a contractual duty, because (though possible) it would cause extreme and unreasonable difficulty. • For performance to be truly impracticable, the duty must become much more difficult or much more expensive to perform, and this difficulty or expense must have been unanticipated. **2.** The doctrine by which such a fact or circumstance excuses performance.

commercial impracticability. (1913) The occurrence of a contingency whose nonoccurrence was an assumption in the contract, as a result of which one party cannot perform.

imprescriptible (im-prə-**skrip**-tə-bəl), *adj.* (16c) Not subject to prescription; not capable of being acquired by prescription.

impressment (im-**pres**-mənt), *n.* (18c) **1.** The act of forcibly taking (something) for public service. **2.** A court's imposition of a constructive trust on equitable grounds. **3.** *Archaic.* The method by which armed forces were formerly expanded, when so-called press-gangs seized men off the streets and forced them to join the army or navy. — **impress,** *vb.*

imprimatur (im-pri-**may**-tər *or* -**mah**-tər). [Latin "let it be printed"] (17c) **1.** A license required to publish a book. • Once required in England, the imprimatur is now encountered only rarely in countries that censor the press. **2.** A general grant of approval; commendatory license or sanction.

imprison, *vb.* (14c) To confine (a person) in prison.— **imprisonment,** *n.* (14c).

improper, *adj.* (15c) **1.** Incorrect; unsuitable or irregular. **2.** Fraudulent or otherwise wrongful.

improve, *vb.* (16c) **1.** To increase the value or enhance the appearance of something. **2.** To develop (land), whether or not the development results in an increase or a decrease in value. — **improver,** *n.*

improved value. (1834) *Real estate.* In the appraisal of property, the value of the land plus the value of any improvements.

improvement. (16c) An addition to real property, whether permanent or not; esp., one that increases its value or utility or that enhances its appearance.

general improvement. (17c) An improvement whose primary purpose or effect is to benefit the public generally, though it may incidentally benefit property owners in its vicinity.

local improvement. (1831) A real-property improvement, such as a sewer or sidewalk, financed by special assessment, and specially benefiting adjacent property.

necessary improvement. (17c) An improvement made to prevent the deterioration of property.

public improvement. An improvement made to property owned by the state or any other political entity, such as a municipality.

valuable improvement. (18c) An improvement that adds permanent value to the freehold.

voluntary improvement. An improvement whose only purpose is ornamental.

improvidence (im-**prahv**-ə-dənts). (15c) A lack of foresight and care in the management of property, esp. as grounds for removing an estate administrator.

improvident (im-**prahv**-ə-dənt), *adj.* (16c) **1.** Lacking foresight and care in the management of property. **2.** Of or relating to a judgment arrived at by using misleading information or a mistaken assumption.

impugn (im-**pyoon**), *vb.* (14c) To challenge or call into question (a person's character, the truth of a statement, etc.). — **impugnment,** *n.*

impulse, *n.* (17c) A sudden urge or inclination that prompts an unplanned action.

uncontrollable impulse. (1844) An impulse so overwhelming that it cannot be resisted.

impunity (im-**pyoo**-nə-tee). (16c) Exemption from punishment; immunity from the detrimental effects of one's actions.

impute (im-**pyoot**), *vb.* (14c) To ascribe or attribute; to regard (usu. something undesirable) as being done, caused, or possessed by. — **imputation,** *n.* — **imputable,** *adj.*

in, *prep.* Under or based on the law of <to bring an action in contract>.

in absentia (in ab-**sen**-shee-ə *or* ab-**sen**-shə). [Latin] (1886) In the absence of (someone); in (someone's) absence <tried in absentia>.

in action. (18c) (Of property) attainable or recoverable through litigation.

inadequate remedy at law. (1817) A remedy (such as money damages) that does not sufficiently correct the wrong, as a result of which an injunction may be available to the disadvantaged party.

inadmissible, *adj.* (18c) **1.** (Of a thing) not allowable or worthy of being admitted. **2.** (Of evidence) excludable by some rule of evidence. **3.** (Of an alien) ineligible for admission into a country or (if the alien has already entered illegally) subject to removal.

inadvertence, *n.* (15c) An accidental oversight; a result of carelessness.

inadvertent discovery. (1971) *Criminal procedure.* A law-enforcement officer's unexpected finding of incriminating evidence in plain view. • Even though this type of evidence is obtained without a warrant, it can be used against the accused under the plain-view exception to the warrant requirement.

inalienable, *adj.* (17c) Not transferable or assignable.

inarbitrable, *adj.* (18c) **1.** (Of a dispute) not capable of being arbitrated; not subject to arbitration. **2.** Not subject to being decided.

in arrears (in ə-**reerz**), *adj.* & *adv.* (17c) **1.** Behind in the discharging of a debt or other obligation <the tenants were in arrears with the rent>. **2.** At the end of a term or period instead of the beginning <the interests, fees, and costs are payable in arrears>.

inauguration (i-naw-gyə-**ray**-shən), *n.* (16c) **1.** A formal ceremony inducting someone into office. **2.** A formal ceremony introducing something into public use. **3.** The formal commencement of a period of time or course of action. — **inaugurate** (i-**naw**-gyə-rayt), *vb.* — **inauguratory** (i-**naw**-gyə-rə-tor-ee), *adj.* — **inaugurator** (i-**naw**-gyə-ray-tər), *n.*

in being. (17c) Existing in life <life in being plus 21 years>. • In property law, this term includes children conceived but not yet born.

in blank. (1836) (Of an indorsement) not restricted to a particular indorsee.

Inc. *abbr.* Incorporated.

in camera (in **kam**-ə-rə), *adv.* & *adj.* [Law Latin "in a chamber"] (1872) **1.** In the judge's private chambers. **2.** In the courtroom with all spectators excluded. **3.** (Of a judicial action) taken when court is not in session.

in camera inspection. (1953) A trial judge's private consideration of evidence.

incapacitated person. (1834) A person who is impaired by an intoxicant, by mental illness or deficiency, or by physical illness or disability to the extent that personal decision-making is impossible.

incapacitation, *n.* (18c) **1.** The action of disabling or depriving of legal capacity. **2.** The state of being disabled or lacking legal capacity. — **incapacitate,** *vb.*

incapacity. (17c) **1.** Lack of physical or mental capabilities. **2.** Lack of ability to have certain legal consequences attach to one's actions.

testimonial incapacity. (1867) The lack of capacity to testify.

in capita. Individually.

incarceration, *n.* (16c) The act or process of confining someone; imprisonment. — **incarcerate,** *vb.* — **incarcerator,** *n.*

shock incarceration. (1985) Incarceration in a military-type setting, usu. for three to six months, during which the offender is subjected to strict discipline, physical exercise, and hard labor.

incendiary (in-**sen**-dee-er-ee), *n.* (15c) **1.** One who deliberately and unlawfully sets fire to property. **2.** An instrument (such as a bomb) or chemical agent designed to start a fire. — **incendiary,** *adj.*

incentive pay plan. (1948) A compensation plan in which increased productivity is rewarded with higher pay.

incest, *n.* (13c) **1.** Sexual relations between family members or close relatives, including children related by adoption. **2.** Intermarriage between persons related in any degree of consanguinity or affinity within which marriage is prohibited. — **incestuous,** *adj.*

in chief. (17c) **1.** Principal, as opposed to collateral or incidental. **2.** Denoting the part of a trial in which the main body of evidence is presented.

inchoate (in-**koh**-it), *adj.* (16c) Partially completed or imperfectly formed; just begun. — **inchoateness,** *n.*

incident, *adj.* (15c) Dependent upon, subordinate to, arising out of, or otherwise connected with (something else, usu. of greater importance) <the utility easement is incident to the ownership of the tract>.

incident, *n.* (15c) **1.** A discrete occurrence or happening <an incident of copyright infringement> **2.** A dependent, subordinate, or consequential part (of something else) <child support is a typical incident of divorce>.

incidental, *adj.* (17c) Subordinate to something of greater importance; having a minor role.

incident of ownership. (*usu. pl.*) (1821) Any right of control that may be exercised over a transferred life-insurance policy so that the policy's proceeds will be included in a decedent's gross estate for estate-tax purposes.

incident to employment. *Workers' compensation.* A risk that is related to or connected with a worker's job duties.

incite, *vb.* (15c) To provoke or stir up (someone to commit a criminal act, or the criminal act itself).

incitement, *n.* (15c) **1.** The act or an instance of provoking, urging on, or stirring up. **2.** *Criminal law.* The act of persuading another person to commit a crime. — **inciteful,** *adj.*

inciter. (15c) A person who incites another to commit a crime; an aider or abettor.

incivism (**in**-si-viz-əm). (18c) Unfriendliness toward one's own country or its government; lack of good citizenship.

inclusionary-approach rule. (1981) The principle that evidence of a prior crime, wrong, or act is admissible for any purpose other than to show a defendant's criminal propensity as long as it is relevant to some disputed issue and its probative value outweighs its prejudicial effect.

incognito (in-kog-**nee**-toh *or* in-**kog**-ni-toh), *adj.* or *adv.* [Latin "unknown"] (17c) Without making one's name or identity known.

income. (16c) The money or other form of payment that one receives, usu. periodically, from employment, business, investments, royalties, gifts, and the like.

accrued income. (1869) Money earned but not yet received.

accumulated income. Income that is retained in an account; esp., income that a trust has generated, but that has not yet been reinvested or distributed by the trustee.

accumulated taxable income. The income of a corporation as adjusted for certain items (such as excess charitable contributions), less the dividends-paid deduction and the accumulated-earnings credit.

active income. (1972) **1.** Wages; salary. **2.** Income from a trade or business.

adjusted gross income. (1940) Gross income minus allowable deductions specified in the tax code. — Abbr. AGI.

adjusted ordinary gross income. A corporation's gross income less capital gains and certain expenses. — Abbr. AOGI.

aggregate income. (1926) The combined income of a husband and wife who file a joint tax return.

current income. Income that is due within the present accounting period.

deferred income. (1918) Money received at a time later than when it was earned, such as a check received in January for commissions earned in November.

disposable income. (1960) Income that may be spent or invested after payment of taxes and other primary obligations.

distributable net income. (1918) The amount of distributions from estates and trusts that the beneficiaries will have to include in income.

dividend income. (1930) The income resulting from a dividend distribution and subject to tax.

earned income. (1894) Money derived from one's own labor or active participation; earnings from services. Cf. *unearned income* (2).

exempt income. (1947) Income that is not subject to income tax.

fixed income. Money received at a constant rate, such as a payment from a pension or annuity.

gross income. (1843) Total income from all sources before deductions, exemptions, or other tax reductions.

imputed income. (1948) The benefit one receives from the use of one's own property, the performance of one's services, or the consumption of self-produced goods and services.

income in respect of a decedent. (1945) Income earned by a person, but not collected before death. • This income is included in the decedent's gross estate for estate-tax purposes. For income-tax purposes, it is taxed to the estate or, if the estate does not collect the income, it is taxed to the eventual recipient.

net income. (18c) Total income from all sources minus deductions, exemptions, and other tax reductions. • Income tax is computed on net income.

net operating income. Income derived from operating a business, after subtracting operating costs.

nonoperating income. Business income derived from investments rather than operations.

ordinary income. (1860) **1.** For business-tax purposes, earnings from the normal operations or activities of a business. **2.** For individual income-tax purposes, income that is derived from sources such as wages, commissions, and interest (as opposed to income from capital gains).

other income. Income not derived from an entity's principal business, such as earnings from dividends and interest.

passive income. (1958) Income derived from a business, rental, or other income-producing activity that the earner does not directly participate in or has no immediate control over.

passive investment income. Investment income that does not involve or require active participation, such as gross receipts from royalties, rental income, dividends, interest, annuities, and gains from the sale or exchange of securities.

personal income. (1851) The total income received by an individual from all sources.

portfolio income. (1978) Income not derived in the ordinary course of a trade or business, such as interest earned on savings, dividends, royalties, capital gains, or other investment sources.

prepaid income. (1935) Income received but not yet earned.

previously taxed income. An S corporation's undistributed taxable income taxed to the shareholders as of the last day of the corporation's tax year. — Abbr. PTI.

real income. Income adjusted to allow for inflation or deflation so that it reflects true purchasing power.

regular income. Income that is received at fixed or specified intervals.

split income. (1949) An equal division between spouses of earnings reported on a joint tax return, allowing for equal tax treatment in community-property and common-law states.

taxable income. (1856) Gross income minus all allowable deductions and exemptions. • Taxable income is multiplied by the applicable tax rate to compute one's tax liability.

unearned income. (1921) **1.** Earnings from investments rather than labor. **2.** Income received but not yet earned; money paid in advance.

unrelated-business income. (1952) *Tax.* Gross income earned by a nonprofit corporation from activities unrelated to its nonprofit functions. • A nonprofit corporation's income is tax-exempt only to the extent that it is produced by activities directly related to its nonprofit purpose.

income approach. (1951) A method of appraising real property based on capitalization of the income that the property is expected to generate.

income averaging. *Tax.* A method of computing tax by averaging a person's current income with that of preceding years.

income-basis method. A method of computing the rate of return on a security using the interest and price paid rather than the face value.

income-shifting. (1957) The practice of transferring income to a taxpayer in a lower tax bracket, such as a child, to reduce tax liability. • Often this is accomplished by forming a Clifford trust.

income statement. (1863) A statement of all the revenues, expenses, gains, and losses that a business incurred during a given period.

income-withholding order. (1986) A court order providing for the withholding of a person's income by an employer, usu. to enforce a child-support order.

in common. (16c) Shared equally with others, undivided into separately owned parts.

incommunicado (in-kə-myoo-ni-**kah**-doh), *adj.* [Spanish] (1844) **1.** Without any means of communication. **2.** (Of a prisoner) having the right to communicate with only a few designated people.

incommutable (in-kə-**myoot**-ə-bəl), *adj.* (18c) (Of an offense) not capable of being commuted.

incompatibility, *n.* (1875) Conflict in personality and disposition, usu. leading to the breakup of a marriage. • Every state now recognizes some form of incompatibility as a no-fault ground for divorce.

Incompatibility Clause. The clause of the U.S. Constitution prohibiting a person from simultaneously holding offices in both the executive and legislative branches of the federal government. U.S. Const. art. I, § 6, par. 2, cl. 2.

incompetence, *n.* (17c) **1.** The state or fact of being unable or unqualified to do something. **2.** Incompetency.

incompetency, *n.* (17c) Lack of legal ability in some respect, esp. to stand trial or to testify. — **incompetent,** *adj.*

incompetent, *adj.* (16c) **1.** (Of a witness) unqualified to testify. **2.** (Of evidence) inadmissible.

inconclusive, *adj.* (18c) (Of evidence) not leading to a conclusion or definite result.

inconsistent, *adj.* (17c) Lacking agreement among parts; not compatible with another fact or claim.

incorporate, *vb.* (14c) **1.** To form a legal corporation <she incorporated the family business>. **2.** To combine with something else <incorporate the exhibits into the agreement>. **3.** To make the terms of another (esp. earlier) document part of a document by specific reference <the codicil incorporated the terms of the will>; esp., to apply the provisions of the Bill of Rights to the states by interpreting the 14th Amendment's Due Process Clause as encompassing those provisions.

incorporation, *n.* (15c) **1.** The formation of a legal corporation. **2.** *Constitutional law.* The process of applying the provisions of the Bill of Rights to the states by interpreting the 14th Amendment's Due Process Clause as encompassing those provisions.

selective incorporation. Incorporation of certain provisions of the Bill of Rights. • Justice Benjamin Cardozo, who served from 1932 to 1938, first advocated this approach.

total incorporation. Incorporation of all of the Bill of Rights. • Justice Hugo Black, who served on the U.S. Supreme Court from 1937 to 1971, first advocated this approach.

3. Incorporation by reference. — **incorporate,** *vb.*

incorporation by reference. (1886) A method of making a secondary document part of a primary document by including in the primary document a statement that the secondary document should be treated as if it were contained within the primary one.

incorporator. (1883) A person who takes part in the formation of a corporation, usu. by executing the articles of incorporation.

incorporeal (in-kor-**por**-ee-əl), *adj.* (15c) Having a conceptual existence but no physical existence; intangible. — **incorporeality,** *n.*

incorrigibility (in-kor-ə-jə-**bil**-ə-tee *or* in-kahr-), *n.* (14c) Serious or persistent misbehavior by a child, making reformation by parental control impossible or unlikely. — **incorrigible,** *adj.*

increment (in[g]-krə-mənt), *n.* (15c) A unit of increase in quantity or value. — **incremental,** *adj.*

unearned increment. An increase in the value of real property due to population growth.

incriminate (in-**krim**-ə-nayt), *vb.* (18c) **1.** To charge (someone) with a crime. **2.** To identify (oneself or another) as being involved in the commission of a crime or other wrongdoing. — **incriminatory,** *adj.* — **incrimination,** *n.* (18c).

incriminating, *adj.* (18c) Demonstrating or indicating involvement in criminal activity <incriminating evidence>.

inculpate (in-**kəl**-payt *or* **in**-kəl-payt), *vb.* (18c) **1.** To accuse. **2.** To implicate (oneself or another) in a crime or other wrongdoing; incriminate. — **inculpation,** *n.* — **inculpatory** (in-**kəl**-pə-tor-ee), *adj.*

incumbent (in-**kəm**-bənt), *n.* (15c) One who holds an official post, esp. a political one. — **incumbency,** *n.* — **incumbent,** *adj.*

incur, *vb.* (15c) To suffer or bring on oneself (a liability or expense). — **incurrence,** *n.* — **incurrable,** *adj.*

in custodia legis (in kə-**stoh**-dee-ə **lee**-jis). [Latin] In the custody of the law <the debtor's automobile was *in custodia legis* after being seized by the sheriff>. • The phrase is traditionally used in reference to property taken into the court's charge during pending litigation over it.

indebtedness (in-**det**-id-nis). (17c) **1.** The condition or state of owing money. **2.** Something owed; a debt.

indecency, *n.* (16c) The state or condition of being outrageously offensive, esp. in a vulgar or sexual way. • Unlike obscene material, indecent speech is protected under the First Amendment. — **indecent,** *adj.*

indecent advertising. 1. Signs, broadcasts, or other forms of communication that use grossly objectionable words, symbols, pictures, or the like to sell or promote goods, services, events, etc. **2.** *Archaic.* In some jurisdictions, the statutory offense of advertising the sale of abortifacients and (formerly) contraceptives.

indecent exposure. (1828) An offensive display of one's body in public, esp. of the genitals.

indecent liberties. (18c) Improper behavior, usu. toward another person, esp. of a sexual nature.

indefeasible (in-də-**feez**-ə-bəl), *adj.* (16c) (Of a claim or right) not vulnerable to being defeated, revoked, or lost <an indefeasible estate>.

in delicto (in də-**lik**-toh). [Latin] In fault.

indemnification (in-dem-nə-fi-**kay**-shən), *n.* (18c) **1.** The action of compensating for loss or damage sustained. **2.** The compensation so made. — **indemnificatory,** *adj.*

indemnify (in-**dem**-nə-fɪ), *vb.* (17c) **1.** To reimburse (another) for a loss suffered because of a third party's or one's own act or default; hold harmless. **2.** To promise to reimburse (another) for such a loss. **3.** To give (another) security against such a loss. — **indemnifiable,** *adj.*

indemnitee (in-dem-nə-**tee**). (1884) One who receives indemnity from another.

indemnitor (in-**dem**-nə-tər *or* -tor). (1827) One who indemnifies another.

indemnity (in-**dem**-nə-tee), *n.* (15c) **1.** A duty to make good any loss, damage, or liability incurred by another. **2.** The right of an injured party to claim reimbursement for its loss, damage, or liability from a person who has such a duty. **3.** Reimbursement or compensation for loss, damage, or liability in tort; esp., the right of a party who is secondarily liable to recover from the party who is primarily liable for reimbursement of expenditures paid to a third party for injuries resulting from a violation of a common-law duty. — **indemnitory,** *adj.*

contractual indemnity. Indemnity that is expressly provided for in an agreement.

double indemnity. (1859) The payment of twice the basic benefit in the event of a specified loss, esp. as in an insurance contract requiring the insurer to pay twice the policy's face amount in the case of accidental death.

equitable indemnity. A doctrine allowing a defendant in a tort action to allocate blame to a codefendant or cross-defendant, and thereby to proportionally reduce legal responsibility, even in the absence of contractual indemnity.

implied indemnity. Indemnity arising from equitable considerations and based on the parties' relationship, as when a guarantor pays a debt to a creditor that the principal debtor should have paid.

indemnity against liability. (1838) A right to indemnity that arises on the indemnitor's default, regardless of whether the indemnitee has suffered a loss.

indemnity clause. (1860) A contractual provision in which one party agrees to answer for any specified or unspecified liability or harm that the other party might incur.

indemnity principle. *Insurance.* The doctrine that an insurance policy should not confer a benefit greater in value than the loss suffered by the insured.

indenture (in-**den**-chər), *n.* (14c) **1.** A formal written instrument made by two or more parties with different interests, traditionally having the edges serrated, or indented, in a zigzag fashion to reduce the possibility of forgery and to distinguish it from a deed poll. **2.** A deed or elaborate contract signed by two or more parties.

corporate indenture. A document containing the terms and conditions governing the issuance of debt securities, such as bonds or debentures.

debenture indenture. (1938) An indenture containing obligations not secured by a mortgage or other collateral. • It is a long-term financing vehicle that places the debenture holder in substantially the same position as a bondholder secured by a first mortgage.

trust indenture. A document containing the terms and conditions governing a trustee's conduct and the trust beneficiaries' rights.

3. *Hist.* A contract by which an apprentice or other person, such as a servant, is bound to a master, usu. for a term of years or other limited period. — **indentured,** *adj.*

independence, *n.* (17c) The state or quality of being independent; esp., a country's freedom to manage all its affairs, whether external or internal, without control by other countries.

independent, *adj.* (17c) **1.** Not subject to the control or influence of another. **2.** Not associated with another (often larger) entity. **3.** Not dependent or contingent on something else.

independent advice. (1871) Counsel that is impartial and not given to further the interests of the person giving it.

independent contractor. (1841) One who is entrusted to undertake a specific project but who is left free to do the assigned work and to choose the method for accomplishing it. • It does not matter whether the work is done for pay or gratuitously. Unlike an employee, an independent contractor who commits a wrong while carrying out the work usu. does not create liability for the one who did the hiring.

independent creation. *Copyright.* A defense asserting that a later work is not a derivative of an allegedly infringed work, but is a product of coincidentally parallel labor.

independent-living program. *Family law.* A training course designed to enable foster children who are near the age of majority to leave the foster-care system and manage their own affairs as adults. • Independent living programs provide education, training, and financial and employment counseling.

independent-significance doctrine. (1968) *Wills & estates.* The principle that effect will be given to a testator's disposition that is not done solely to avoid the requirements of a will.

independent-source rule. (1968) *Criminal procedure.* The rule providing — as an exception to the fruit-of-the-poisonous-tree doctrine — that evidence obtained by illegal means may nonetheless be admissible if that evidence is also obtained by legal means unrelated to the original illegal conduct.

indeterminate, *adj.* (14c) Not definite; not distinct or precise.

indeterminate conditional release. A release from prison granted once the prisoner fulfills certain conditions. • The release can be revoked if the prisoner breaches other conditions.

indeterminate sentencing. (1941) The practice of not imposing a definite term of confinement, but instead prescribing a range for the minimum and maximum term, leaving the precise term to be fixed in some other way, usu. based on the prisoner's conduct and apparent rehabilitation while incarcerated.

index, *n.* (14c) **1.** An alphabetized listing of the topics or other items included in a single book or document, or in a series of volumes, usu. found at the end of the book, document, or series <index of authorities>.

grantee–grantor index. (1961) An index, usu. kept in the county clerk's or recorder's office, alphabetically listing by grantee the volume and page number of the grantee's recorded property transactions.

grantor–grantee index. (1944) An index, usu. kept in the county clerk's or recorder's office, alphabetically listing by grantor the volume and page number of the grantor's recorded property transactions.

tract index. (1858) An index, usu. kept in the county clerk's or recorder's office, listing, by location of each parcel of land, the volume and page number of the recorded property transactions affecting the parcel.

2. A number, usu. expressed in the form of a percentage or ratio, that indicates or measures a series of observations, esp. those involving a market or the economy <cost-of-living index> <stock index>.

indexing. 1. The practice or method of adjusting wages, pension benefits, insurance, or other types of payments to compensate for inflation. **2.** The practice of investing funds to track or mirror an index of securities.

index of authorities. (1881) An alphabetical list of authorities cited in a book or brief, usu. with subcategories for cases, statutes, and treatises.

indicator. (17c) *Securities.* An average or index that shows enough of a correlation to market trends or economic conditions that it can help analyze market performance.

indicia (in-**dish**-ee-ə), *n. pl.* (17c) (*pl.*) Signs; indications <the purchase receipts are indicia of ownership>.

indicia of title. A document that evidences ownership of personal or real property.

indict (in-**dɪt**), *vb.* (17c) To charge (a person) with a crime by formal legal process, esp. by grand-jury presentation. — **indictee** (in-dɪ-**tee**), *n.* (16c). — **indictor** (in-**dɪt**-ər *or* in-**dɪ**-tor), *n.* (17c).

indictment (in-**dɪt**-mənt), *n.* (14c) **1.** The formal written accusation of a crime, made by a grand jury and presented to a court for prosecution against the accused person. See Fed. R. Crim. P. 7. **2.** The act or process of preparing or bringing forward such a formal written accusation.

barebones indictment. (1963) An indictment that cites only the language of the statute allegedly violated; an indictment that does not provide a factual statement.

duplicitous indictment (d[y]oo-**plis**-ə-təs). (1914) **1.** An indictment containing two or more offenses in the same count. **2.** An indictment charging the same offense in more than one count.

joint indictment. (17c) An indictment that charges two or more people with an offense.

indifference. (15c) A lack of interest in or concern about something; apathy.

deliberate indifference. **1.** *Criminal law.* (1951) The careful preservation of one's ignorance despite awareness of circumstances that would put a reasonable person on notice of a fact essential to a crime. **2.** *Criminal law.* Awareness of and disregard for the risk of harm to another person's life, body, or property. **3.** *Torts.* Conscious disregard of the harm that one's actions could do to the interests or rights of another.

indigency, *n.* (17c) The state or condition of a person who lacks the means of subsistence; extreme hardship or neediness; poverty. • For purposes of the Sixth Amendment right to appointed counsel, *indigency* refers to a defendant's inability to afford an attorney. — **indigent,** *adj.* & *n.*

indigent (**in**-di-jənt), *n.* (15c) **1.** A poor person. **2.** A person who is found to be financially unable to pay filing fees and court costs and so is allowed to proceed *in forma pauperis.* • The Supreme Court has recognized an indigent petitioner's right to have certain fees and costs waived in divorce and termination-of-parental-rights cases. *Boddie v. Connecticut,* 401 U.S. 371, 91 S.Ct. 780 (1971); *M.L.B. v. S.L.J.,* 519 U.S. 102, 117 S.Ct. 555 (1996). — **indigent,** *adj.*

indignity (in-**dig**-ni-tee), *n.* (16c) *Family law.* A ground for divorce consisting in one spouse's pattern of behavior calculated to humiliate the other.

indispensable-element test. *Criminal law.* A common-law test for the crime of attempt, based on whether the defendant acquires control over any thing that is essential to the crime. • Under this test, for example, a person commits a crime by buying the explosives with which to detonate a bomb.

individual, *adj.* (15c) **1.** Existing as an indivisible entity. **2.** Of or relating to a single person or thing, as opposed to a group.

individualized education program. *Family law.* A specially designed plan of educational instruction for a child with disabilities. — Abbr. IEP.

individual retirement account. (1974) A savings or brokerage account to which a person may contribute up to a specified amount of earned income each year. • The contributions, along with any interest earned in the account, are not taxed until the money is withdrawn after a participant reaches 59½ (or before then, if a 10% penalty is paid). — Abbr. IRA.

education individual retirement account. An individual retirement account from which withdrawals may be made tax-free if the withdrawn funds are used for education costs.

Roth IRA. (1991) An IRA in which contributions are nondeductible when they are made.

Individuals with Disabilities Education Act. A federal statute that governs the public education of children with physical or mental handicaps and attempts to ensure that these children receive a free public education that meets their unique needs. 20 USCA §§ 1400–1485. — Abbr. IDEA.

indivisible, *adj.* (14c) Not separable into parts; held by two or more people in undivided shares <an indivisible debt>.

indorse, *vb.* (16c) To sign (a negotiable instrument), usu. on the back, either to accept responsibility for paying an obligation memorialized by the instrument or to make the instrument payable to someone other than the payee.

indorsee (in-dor-**see**). (18c) A person to whom a negotiable instrument is transferred by indorsement.

indorsement, *n.* (16c) **1.** The placing of a signature, sometimes with an additional notation, on the back of a negotiable instrument to transfer or guarantee the instrument or to acknowledge payment. **2.** The signature or notation itself. — **indorse,** *vb.*

accommodation indorsement. (1888) An indorsement to an instrument by a third party who acts as surety for another party who remains primarily liable.

blank indorsement. An indorsement that names no specific payee, thus making the instrument payable to the bearer and negotiable by delivery only. UCC § 3-205(b).

conditional indorsement. (1894) An indorsement that restricts the instrument in some way, as by limiting how the instrument can be paid or transferred; an indorsement giving possession of the instrument to the indorsee, but retaining title until the occurrence of some condition named in the indorsement. • Wordings that indicate this type of indorsement are "Pay to Brad Jones when he becomes 18 years of age" and "Pay to Brigitte Turner, or order, unless before payment I give you notice to the contrary."

irregular indorsement. (1842) An indorsement by a person who signs outside the chain of title and who therefore is neither a holder nor a transferor of the instrument. • An irregular indorser is generally treated as an accommodation party.

qualified indorsement. (1806) An indorsement that passes title to the instrument but limits the indorser's liability to later holders if the instrument is later dishonored. • Typically, a qualified indorsement is made by writing "without recourse" or "sans recourse" over the signature. UCC § 3-415(b).

restrictive indorsement. (18c) An indorsement that includes a condition (e.g., "pay Josefina Cardoza only if she has worked 8 full hours on April 13") or any other language restricting further negotiation (e.g., "for deposit only").

special indorsement. (18c) An indorsement that specifies the person to receive payment or to whom the goods named by the document must be delivered. UCC § 3-205(a).

trust indorsement. (1945) An indorsement stating that the payee becomes a trustee for a third person (e.g., "pay Erin Ray in trust for Kaitlin Ray"); a restrictive indorsement that limits the instrument to the use of the indorser or another person.

unauthorized indorsement. (1840) An indorsement made without authority, such as a forged indorsement.

unqualified indorsement. (1839) An indorsement that does not limit the indorser's liability on the paper.

unrestrictive indorsement. (1844) An indorsement that includes no condition or language restricting negotiation.

indorser. (18c) A person who transfers a negotiable instrument by indorsement; specif., one who signs a negotiable instrument other than as maker, drawer, or acceptor.

accommodation indorser. (1820) An indorser who acts as surety for another person.

inducement, *n.* (15c) **1.** The act or process of enticing or persuading another person to take a certain course of action. **2.** *Contracts.* The benefit or advantage that causes a promisor to enter into a contract. **3.** *Criminal law.* An enticement or urging of another person to commit a crime. **4.** The preliminary statement in a pleading; esp., in an action for defamation, the plaintiff's allegation that extrinsic facts gave a defamatory meaning to a statement that is not defamatory on its face, or, in a criminal indictment, a statement of preliminary facts necessary to show the criminal character of the alleged offense. — **induce,** *vb.*

induction. (14c) **1.** The act or process of initiating <the induction of three new members into the legal fraternity>. **2.** The act or process of reasoning from specific instances to general propositions <after looking at several examples, the group reasoned by induction that it is a very poor practice to begin a new paragraph by abruptly bringing up a new case>. — **induct,** *vb.* (14c).

industrial relations. All dealings and relationships between an employer and its employees, including collective bargaining about issues such as safety and benefits.

Ineligibility Clause. The clause of the U.S. Constitution that prohibits a member of Congress from accepting an appointment to an executive office that was created, or the compensation for which was increased, during the member's service in Congress. U.S. Const. art. I, § 6.

inequitable (in-**ek**-wi-tə-bəl), *adj.* (17c) Not fair; opposed to principles of equity.

in equity. (15c) In a chancery court rather than a court of law; before a court exercising equitable jurisdiction.

inequity (in-**ek**-wi-tee), *n.* (16c) **1.** Unfairness; a lack of equity. **2.** An instance of injustice.

in esse (in **es**-ee *also* **es**-ay). [Latin "in being"] (16c) In actual existence; IN BEING <the court was concerned only with the rights of the children *in esse*>.

in evidence. Having been admitted into evidence.

inevitable-disclosure doctrine. *Trade secrets.* The legal theory that a key employee, once hired by a competitor, cannot avoid misappropriating the former employer's trade secrets. • To justify an injunction, the plaintiff must prove that the former employee has confidential information and will not be able to avoid using that knowledge to unfairly compete against the plaintiff. Most courts have rejected this controversial doctrine on grounds that it effectively turns a nondisclosure agreement into a disfavored noncompetition agreement.

inevitable-discovery rule. (1873) *Criminal procedure.* The rule providing — as an exception to the fruit-of-the-poisonous-tree doctrine — that evidence obtained by illegal means may nonetheless be admissible if the prosecution can show that the evidence would eventually have been legally obtained anyway.

in extremis (in ek-**stree**-mis). [Latin "in extremity"] (16c) **1.** In extreme circumstances. **2.** Near the point of death; on one's deathbed. • Unlike *in articulo mortis,* the phrase *in extremis* does not always mean at the point of death.

in fact. (18c) Actual or real; resulting from the acts of parties rather than by operation of law.

infamous (**in**-fə-məs), *adj.* (14c) **1.** (Of a person) having a bad reputation. **2.** (Of a person) deprived of some or all rights of citizenship after conviction for a serious crime. **3.** (Of conduct) that is punishable by imprisonment.

infamy (**in**-fə-mee), *n.* (18c) **1.** Disgraceful repute. **2.** The loss of reputation or position resulting from a person's being convicted of an infamous crime.

infancy. (14c) **1.** MINORITY (1). **2.** Early childhood. **3.** The beginning stages of anything.

infant, *n.* (14c) **1.** A newborn baby. **2.** Minor.

infanticide (in-**fant**-ə-sɪd). (17c) **1.** The act of killing a newborn child, esp. by the parents or with their consent. • In archaic usage, the word referred also to the killing of an unborn child. **2.** The practice of killing newborn children. **3.** One who kills a newborn child. — **infanticidal,** *adj.*

infect, *vb.* (14c) **1.** To contaminate <the virus infected the entire network>. **2.** To taint with crime <one part of the city has long been infected with illegal drug-dealing>. **3.** To make (a ship or cargo) liable in the seizure of contraband, which is only a part of its cargo <claiming that the single package of marijuana had infected the ship, the Coast Guard seized the entire vessel>. — **infection,** *n.* — **infectious,** *adj.*

infer, *vb.* (16c) To conclude from facts or from factual reasoning; to draw as a conclusion or inference.

inference (**in**-fər-ənts), *n.* (16c) **1.** A conclusion reached by considering other facts and deducing a logical consequence from them.

adverse inference. A detrimental conclusion drawn by the fact-finder from a party's failure to produce evidence that is within the party's control. • Some courts allow the inference only if the party's failure is attributable to bad faith.

2. The process by which such a conclusion is reached; the process of thought by which one moves from evidence to proof. — **infer,** *vb.* — **inferential,** *adj.* — **inferrer,** *n.*

inference-on-inference rule. (1940) The principle that a presumption based on another presumption cannot serve as a basis for determining an ultimate fact.

inference-stacking. The practice or an instance of piling one or more inferences on each other to arrive at a legal conclusion.

infidelity. (15c) Unfaithfulness to an obligation; esp., marital unfaithfulness.

in fine (in **fɪ**-nee *or* **fɪn**), *adv.* [Latin] **1.** In short; in summary. **2.** At the end (of a book, chapter, section, etc.).

infirmative, *adj. Rare.* (Of evidence) tending to weaken or invalidate a criminal accusation <an infirmative fact>.

infirmative hypothesis. *Criminal law.* An approach to a criminal case in which the defendant's innocence is assumed, and incriminating evidence is explained in a manner consistent with that assumption.

infirmity (in-**fər**-mə-tee), *n.* (14c) Physical weakness caused by age or disease; esp., in insurance law, an applicant's ill health that is poor enough to deter an insurance company from insuring the applicant. — **infirm,** *adj.*

in flagrante delicto (in flə-**gran**-tee də-**lik**-toh). [Latin "while the crime is ablaze"] (18c) In the very act of committing a crime or other wrong; red-handed.

inflammatory (in-**flam**-ə-tor-ee), *adj.* (18c) Tending to cause strong feelings of anger, indignation, or other type of upset; tending to stir the passions. • Evidence can be excluded if its inflammatory nature outweighs its probative value.

inflation, *n.* (14c) A general increase in prices coinciding with a fall in the real value of money. Cf. DEFLATION. — **inflationary,** *adj.*

cost-push inflation. Inflation caused by a rise in production costs.

demand-pull inflation. Inflation caused by an excess of demand over supply.

inflation rate. The pace of change in the prices of goods and services in a particular period. • The primary indexes for measuring the rate are the Consumer Price Index and the Producer Price Index.

infliction of emotional distress. 1. Intentional infliction of emotional distress. **2.** Negligent infliction of emotional distress.

informal, *adj.* (16c) Not done or performed in accordance with normal forms or procedures.

informant. (17c) One who informs against another; esp., one who confidentially supplies information to the police about a crime, sometimes in exchange for a reward or special treatment.

in forma pauperis (in **for**-mə **paw**-pə-ris), *adv.* [Latin "in the manner of a pauper"] (16c) In the manner of an indigent who is permitted to disregard filing fees and court costs. — Abbr. IFP.

information. (15c) A formal criminal charge made by a prosecutor without a grand-jury indictment.

Information Analysis and Infrastructure Protection Directorate. The division of the U.S. Department of Homeland Security responsible for analyzing intelligence information gathered from the Central Intelligence Agency, the Defense Intelligence Agency, the Federal Bureau of Investigation, the National Security Administration, and other sources, and for issuing warnings about threats of terrorist attack. — Abbr. IAIP.

information and belief, on. (1827) (Of an allegation or assertion) based on secondhand information that the declarant believes to be true.

informer. (14c) **1.** Informant. **2.** A private citizen who brings a penal action to recover a penalty.

infra (**in**-frə), *adv.* & *adj.* [Latin "below"] (18c) Later in this text. • *Infra* is used as a citational signal to refer to a later-cited authority.

infraction, *n.* (17c) A violation, usu. of a rule or local ordinance and usu. not punishable by incarceration. — **infract,** *vb.*

civil infraction. An act or omission that, though not a crime, is prohibited by law and is punishable. • In some states, many traffic violations are classified as civil infractions.

infrastructure. The underlying framework of a system; esp., public services and facilities (such as highways, schools, bridges, sewers, and water systems) needed to support commerce as well as economic and residential development.

infringement, *n.* (1861) *Intellectual property.* An act that interferes with one of the exclusive rights of a patent, copyright, or trademark owner. — **infringe,** *vb.*

contributory infringement. The act of participating in, or contributing to, the infringing acts of another person.

domain-name infringement. Infringement of another's trademark or servicemark by the use of a confusingly similar Internet domain name.

infringement by sale. *Patents.* The unauthorized sale, resale, or offer of a possessory interest in a patented invention.

innocent infringement. The act of violating an intellectual-property right without knowledge or awareness that the act constitutes infringement.

literal infringement. *Patents.* Infringement in which every element and every limitation of a patent claim is present, exactly, in the accused product or process.

vicarious infringement. A person's liability for an infringing act of someone else, even though the person has not directly committed an act of infringement.

willful infringement. An intentional and deliberate infringement of another person's intellectual property.

in full. Constituting the whole or complete amount <payment in full>.

in futuro (in fyə-**tyoor**-oh), *adv.* [Latin] In the future.

ingress (**in**-gres). (15c) **1.** The act of entering. **2.** The right or ability to enter; access.

ingress, egress, and regress. (17c) The right of a lessee to enter, leave, and reenter the land in question.

in gross. **1.** Undivided; still in one large mass. **2.** (Of a servitude) personal as distinguished from appurtenant to land.

inhabit, *vb.* (14c) To dwell in; to occupy permanently or habitually as a residence.

inhere (in-**heer**), *vb.* (15c) To exist as a permanent, inseparable, or essential attribute or quality of a thing; to be intrinsic to something.

inherently dangerous activity. An activity that can be carried out only by the exercise of special skill and care and that involves a grave risk of serious harm if done unskillfully or carelessly.

inherent-powers doctrine. The principle that allows courts to deal with diverse matters over which they are thought to have intrinsic authority, such as (1) procedural rulemaking, (2) internal budgeting of the courts, (3) regulating the practice of law; and (4) general judicial housekeeping. • The power is based on interpretations of art. I, § 8, cl. 18 of the Constitution.

inherit, *vb.* (14c) **1.** To receive (property) from an ancestor under the laws of intestate succession upon the ancestor's death. **2.** To receive (property) as a bequest or devise.

inheritable, *adj.* Heritable.

inheritance. (14c) **1.** Property received from an ancestor under the laws of intestacy. **2.** Property that a person receives by bequest or devise.

inheritor (in-**hair**-i-tər), *n.* (15c) A person who inherits; HEIR.

initiative (i-**nish**-ə-tiv *or* i-**nish**-ee-ə-tiv). (1889) An electoral process by which a percentage of voters can propose legislation and compel a vote on it by the legislature or by the full electorate.

injunction (in-**jəngk**-shən), *n.* (16c) A court order commanding or preventing an action. • To get an injunction, the complainant must show that there is no plain, adequate, and complete remedy at law and that an irreparable injury will result unless the relief is granted.

antisuit injunction. An injunction prohibiting a litigant from instituting other, related litigation, usu. between the same parties on the same issues.

ex parte injunction. (1854) A preliminary injunction issued after the court has heard from only the moving party.

mandatory injunction. (1843) An injunction that orders an affirmative act or mandates a specified course of conduct. Cf. *prohibitory injunction.*

permanent injunction. (1846) An injunction granted after a final hearing on the merits. • Despite its name, a permanent injunction does not necessarily last forever.

preliminary injunction. (1828) A temporary injunction issued before or during trial to prevent an irreparable injury from occurring before the court has a chance to decide the case. • A preliminary injunction will be issued only after the defendant receives notice and an opportunity to be heard.

preventive injunction. (1882) An injunction designed to prevent a loss or injury in the future.

prohibitory injunction. (1843) An injunction that forbids or restrains an act. • This is the most common type of injunction.

quia-timet injunction (**kwɪ**-ə **tɪ**-mət *or* **kwee**-ə **tim**-et). [Latin "because he fears"] (1913) An injunction granted to prevent an action that has been threatened but has not yet violated the plaintiff's rights.

reparative injunction (ri-**par**-ə-tiv). (1955) An injunction requiring the defendant to restore the plaintiff to the position that the plaintiff occupied before the defendant committed a wrong.

injunctive, *adj.* (15c) That has the quality of directing or ordering; of or relating to an injunction.

in jure (in **joor**-ee). [Latin "in law"] According to the law.

injuria absque damno (in-**joor**-ee-ə **abs**-kwee **dam**-noh). [Latin "injury without damage"] A legal wrong that will not sustain a lawsuit because no harm resulted from it.

injury, *n.* (14c) **1.** The violation of another's legal right, for which the law provides a remedy; a wrong or injustice. **2.** Any harm or damage. — **injure,** *vb.* — **injurious,** *adj.*

accidental injury. (1800) An injury resulting from external, violent, and unanticipated causes; esp., a bodily injury caused by some external force or agency operating contrary to a person's intentions, unexpectedly, and not according to the usual order of events.

advertising injury. Harm resulting from (1) oral or written speech that slanders or libels a person, or disparages a person's goods, products, or services; (2) oral or written speech that violates a person's right of privacy; (3) misappropriation of advertising ideas or style of doing business; or (4) infringement of copyright, esp. in a name or slogan.

bodily injury. (16c) Physical damage to a person's body.

civil injury. (17c) Physical harm or property damage caused by breach of a contract or by a criminal offense redressable through a civil action.

compensable injury (kəm-**pen**-sə-bəl). *Workers' compensation.* An injury caused by an accident arising from the employment and in the course of the employee's work, and for which the employee is statutorily entitled to receive compensation.

continual injury. An injury that recurs at repeated intervals.

continuing injury. (1824) An injury that is still in the process of being committed. • An example is the constant smoke or noise of a factory.

direct injury. (17c) **1.** An injury resulting directly from violation of a legal right. **2.** An injury resulting directly from a particular cause, without any intervening causes.

injury in fact. (1809) An actual or imminent invasion of a legally protected interest, in contrast to an invasion that is conjectural or hypothetical.

irreparable injury (i-**rep**-ər-ə-bəl). (17c) An injury that cannot be adequately measured or compensated by money and is therefore often considered remediable by injunction.

legal injury. (18c) Violation of a legal right.

malicious injury. (16c) **1.** An injury resulting from a willful act committed with knowledge that it is likely to injure another or with reckless disregard of the consequences. **2.** Malicious mischief.

pecuniary injury. An injury that can be adequately measured or compensated by money.

permanent injury. (17c) **1.** A completed wrong whose consequences cannot be remedied for an indefinite period. **2.** *Property.* A lasting injury to land that causes it to revert to the grantor or vests immediate right of possession in a remainderman.

personal injury. (16c) *Torts.* **1.** In a negligence action, any harm caused to a person, such as a broken bone, a cut, or a bruise; bodily injury. **2.** Any invasion of a personal right, including mental suffering and false imprisonment. **3.** For purposes of workers' compensation, any harm (including a worsened preexisting condition) that arises in the scope of employment. — Abbr. PI.

public injury. A loss or an injury stemming from a breach of a duty or violation of a right that affects the community as a whole.

reparable injury (**rep**-ər-ə-bəl). (1832) An injury that can be adequately compensated by money.

scheduled injury. A partially disabling injury for which a predetermined amount of compensation is allowed under a workers'-compensation statute.

serious bodily injury. (1843) Serious physical impairment of the human body; esp., bodily injury that creates a substantial risk of death or that causes serious, permanent disfigurement or protracted loss or impairment of the function of any body part or organ. Model Penal Code § 210.0(3).

temporary injury. An injury that may be abated or discontinued at any time by either the injured party or the wrongdoer.

in kind, *adv.* (17c) **1.** In goods or services rather than money <payment in cash or in kind>. **2.** In a similar way; with an equivalent of what has been offered or received <returned the favor in kind>. — **in-kind,** *adj.* <in-kind repayment>.

in law. (15c) Existing in law or by force of law; in the contemplation of the law.

in-law, *n.* (1894) A relative by marriage.

in lieu of. (13c) Instead of or in place of; in exchange or return for <the creditor took a note in lieu of cash>.

in limine (in **lim**-ə-nee), *adv.* [Latin "at the outset"] (18c) Preliminarily; presented to only the judge, before or during trial.

in-limine, *adj.* (Of a motion or order) raised preliminarily, esp. because of an issue about the admissibility of evidence believed by the movant to be prejudicial.

in loco parentis (in **loh**-koh pə-**ren**-tis), *adv.* & *adj.* [Latin "in the place of a parent"] (1818) Of, relating to, or acting as a temporary guardian or caretaker of a child, taking on all or some of the responsibilities of a parent.

inmate. (16c) **1.** A person confined in a prison, hospital, or similar institution. **2.** *Archaic.* A person living inside a place; one who lives with others in a dwelling.

in mercy, *adv.* (17c) At a judge's discretion concerning punishment. • A judgment formerly noted (using the Law Latin phrase *in misericordia*) which litigant lost by stating that the unsuccessful party was in the court's mercy. A plaintiff held in mercy for a false claim, for example, was said to be *in misericordia pro falso clamore suo.*

in mortua manu (in **mor**-choo-ə **man**-yoo), *adj.* & *adv.* [Law Latin "in a dead hand"] *Hist.* (Of property) perpetually controlled according to a decedent's directions.

innocence, *n.* (14c) The absence of guilt; esp., freedom from guilt for a particular offense.

actual innocence. (1839) *Criminal law.* The absence of facts that are prerequisites for the sentence given to a defendant.

legal innocence. (1813) *Criminal law.* The absence of one or more procedural or legal bases to support the sentence given to a defendant. • In the context of a petition for writ of habeas corpus or other attack on the sentence, legal innocence is often contrasted with actual innocence. Actual innocence, which focuses on the facts underlying the sentence, can sometimes be used to obtain relief from the death penalty based on trial-court errors that were not objected to at trial, even if the petitioner cannot meet the elements of the cause-and-prejudice rule. But legal innocence, which focuses on the applicable law and procedure, is not as readily available. Inadvertence or a poor trial strategy resulting in the defendant's failure to assert an established legal principle will not ordinarily be sufficient to satisfy the cause-and-prejudice rule or to establish the right to an exception from that rule.

innocent, *adj.* (14c) Free from guilt; free from legal fault.

innocent-construction rule. The doctrine that an allegedly libelous statement will be given an innocuous interpretation if the statement is either ambiguous or harmless.

innominate obligations. (1949) Obligations having no specific classification or name because they are not strictly contractual, delictual, or quasi-contractual. • An example is the obligation of a trustee to a beneficiary.

innuendo (in-yoo-**en**-doh). [Latin "by hinting"] (17c) **1.** An oblique remark or indirect suggestion, usu. of a derogatory nature. **2.** An explanatory word or passage inserted parenthetically into a legal document. • In criminal law, an innuendo is a statement in an indictment showing the application or meaning of matter previously expressed, the meaning of which would not otherwise be clear. In the law of defamation, an innuendo is the plaintiff's explanation of a statement's defamatory meaning when that meaning is not apparent from the statement's face. For example, the innuendo of the statement "David burned down his house" can be shown by pleading that the statement was understood to mean that David was defrauding his insurance company (the fact that he had insured his house is pleaded and proved by *inducement*).

inoperative, *adj.* (17c) Having no force or effect; not operative.

in pais (in **pay** *or* **pays**). [Law French "in the country"] Outside court or legal proceedings.

in pari delicto (in **par**-ı də-**lik**-toh), *adv.* [Latin "in equal fault"] Equally at fault.

***in pari delicto* doctrine,** *n.* [Latin] (1917) The principle that a plaintiff who has participated in wrongdoing may not recover damages resulting from the wrongdoing.

in pari materia (in **par**-ı mə-**teer**-ee-ə). [Latin "in the same matter"] **1.** *adj.* On the same subject; relating to the same matter. • It is a canon of construction that statutes that are *in pari materia* may be construed together, so that inconsistencies in one statute may be resolved by looking at another statute on the same subject. **2.** *adv.* Loosely, in conjunction with <the Maryland constitutional provision is construed *in pari materia* with the Fourth Amendment>.

in perpetuity (in pər-pə-**t[y]oo**-ə-tee). (14c) Forever.

in personam (in pər-**soh**-nəm), *adj.* [Latin "against a person"] (18c) **1.** Involving or determining the personal rights and obligations of the parties. **2.** (Of a legal action) brought against a person rather than property. — **in personam,** *adv.*

in posse (in **pos**-ee). [Latin] Not currently existing, but ready to come into existence under certain conditions in the future; potential.

in praesenti (in pri-**zen**-tı *or* pree-). [Latin] At present; right now.

inquest. (13c) **1.** An inquiry by a coroner or medical examiner, sometimes with the aid of a jury, into the manner of death of a person who has died under suspicious circumstances, or who has died in prison. **2.** An inquiry into a certain matter by a jury empaneled for that purpose. **3.** The finding of such a specially empaneled jury. **4.** A proceeding, usu. ex parte, to determine, after the defendant has defaulted, the amount of the plaintiff's damages.

grand inquest. An impeachment proceeding.

inquisition. (14c) **1.** The record of the finding of the jury sworn by the coroner to inquire into a person's death. **2.** A judicial inquiry, esp. in a derogatory sense. **3.** A persistent, grueling examination conducted without regard for the examinee's dignity or civil rights.

inquisitorial system. (1846) A system of proof-taking used in civil law, whereby the judge conducts the trial, determines what questions to ask, and defines the scope and the extent of the inquiry.

in re (in **ree** *or* **ray**). [Latin "in the matter of"] (1877) (Of a judicial proceeding) not formally including adverse parties, but rather involving something (such as an estate). • The term is often used in case citations, esp. in uncontested proceedings <*In re Butler's Estate*>.

in rem (in **rem**), *adj.* [Latin "against a thing"] (18c) Involving or determining the status of a thing, and therefore the rights of persons generally with respect to that thing. — **in rem,** *adv.*

quasi in rem (**kway**-SI in **rem** *or* **kway**-ZI). [Latin "as if against a thing"] (1804) Involving or determining the rights of a person having an interest in property located within the court's jurisdiction.

insane, *adj.* (16c) Mentally deranged; suffering from one or more delusions or false beliefs that (1) have no foundation in reason or reality, (2) are not credible to any reasonable person of sound mind, and (3) cannot be overcome in a sufferer's mind by any amount of evidence or argument.

insane delusion. (1838) An irrational, persistent belief in an imaginary state of facts resulting in a lack of capacity to undertake acts of legal consequence, such as making a will.

insanity, *n.* (16c) Any mental disorder severe enough that it prevents a person from having legal capacity and excuses the person from criminal or civil responsibility. • Insanity is a legal, not a medical, standard.

emotional insanity. (1872) Insanity produced by a violent excitement of the emotions or passions, although reasoning faculties may remain unimpaired; a passion that for a period creates complete derangement of intellect. • Emotional insanity is sometimes described as an irresistible impulse to do an act.

temporary insanity. (18c) Insanity that exists only at the time of a criminal act.

insanity defense. *Criminal law.* (1912) An affirmative defense alleging that a mental disorder caused the accused to commit the crime. See 18 USCA § 17; Fed. R. Crim. P. 12.2. • Unlike other defenses, a successful insanity defense may not result in an acquittal but instead in a special verdict ("not guilty by reason of insanity") that usu. leads to the defendant's commitment to a mental institution.

insecurity clause. (1872) A loan-agreement provision that allows the creditor to demand immediate and full payment of the loan balance if the creditor has reason to believe that the debtor is about to default, as when the debtor suddenly loses a significant source of income.

inside information. Information about a company's financial or market situation obtained not from public disclosure, but from a source within the company or a source that owes the company a duty to keep the information confidential.

insider. (1848) **1.** *Securities.* A person who has knowledge of facts not available to the general public. **2.** One who takes part in the control of a corporation, such as an officer or director, or one who owns 10% or more of the corporation's stock. **3.** *Bankruptcy.* An entity or person who is so closely related to a debtor that any deal between them will not be considered an arm's-length transaction and will be subject to close scrutiny.

insider trading. The use of material, nonpublic information in trading the shares of a company by a corporate insider or other person who owes a fiduciary duty to the company. • This is the classic definition. The Supreme Court has also approved a broader definition, known as the "misappropriation theory": the deceitful acquisition and misuse of information that properly belongs to persons to whom one owes a duty. Thus, under the misappropriation theory, it is insider trading for a lawyer to trade in the stock of XYZ Corp. after learning that a client of the lawyer's firm is planning a takeover of XYZ. But under the classic definition, that is not insider trading because the lawyer owed no duty to XYZ itself.

insolvency, *n.* (17c) **1.** The condition of being unable to pay debts as they fall due or in the usual course of business. **2.** The inability to pay debts as they mature.

balance-sheet insolvency. Insolvency created when the debtor's liabilities exceed its assets.

equity insolvency. Insolvency created when the debtor cannot meet its obligations as they fall due.

inspection. (14c) A careful examination of something, such as goods (to determine their fitness for purchase) or items produced in response to a discovery request (to determine their relevance to a lawsuit).

inspection right. (1898) The legal entitlement in certain circumstances to examine articles or documents, such as a consumer's right to inspect goods before paying for them.

installment, *n.* (18c) A periodic partial payment of a debt.

installment sale. (1893) A conditional sale in which the buyer makes a down payment followed by periodic payments and the seller retains title or a security interest until all payments have been received.

instance, *n.* (14c) **1.** An example or occurrence <there were 55 instances of reported auto theft in this small community last year>. **2.** The act of instituting legal proceedings <court of first instance>. **3.** Urgent solicitation or insistence <she applied for the job at the instance of her friend>.

instant, *adj.* This; the present (case, judgment, order, etc.); now being discussed.

instanter (in-**stan**-tər), *adv.* (17c) Instantly; at once.

institutionalize, *vb.* (1865) **1.** To place (a person) in an institution. **2.** To give (a rule or practice) official sanction.

institutional lender. A business, esp. a bank, that routinely makes loans to the general public.

institutional litigant. (1858) An organized group that brings lawsuits not merely to win but also to bring about a change in the law or to defend an existing law.

instrument. (15c) **1.** A written legal document that defines rights, duties, entitlements, or liabilities, such as a contract, will, promissory note, or share certificate. **2.** *Commercial law.* An unconditional promise or order to pay a fixed amount of money, with or without interest or other fixed charges described in the promise or order. • Under the UCC, a promise or order must meet several other specifically listed requirements to qualify as an instrument. UCC § 3-104(a). **3.** A means by which something is achieved, performed, or furthered.

inchoate instrument. (1834) An unrecorded instrument that must, by law, be recorded to serve as effective notice to third parties.

incomplete instrument. (1822) A paper that, although intended to be a negotiable instrument, lacks an essential element. • An incomplete instrument may be enforced if it is subsequently completed. UCC § 3-115.

indispensable instrument. The formal written evidence of an interest in intangibles, so necessary to represent the intangible that the enjoyment, transfer, or enforcement of the intangible depends on possession of the instrument.

perfect instrument. (18c) An instrument (such as a deed or mortgage) that is executed and filed with a public registry.

sealed instrument. At common law and under some statutes, an instrument to which the bound party has affixed a personal seal, usu. recognized as providing indisputable evidence of the validity of the underlying obligations. • Many states have abolished the common-law distinction between sealed and unsealed instruments. The UCC provides that the laws applicable to sealed instruments do not apply to negotiable instruments or contracts for the sale of goods. UCC § 2-203.

instrumentality, *n.* **1.** A thing used to achieve an end or purpose. **2.** A means or agency through which a function of another entity is accomplished, such as a branch of a governing body.

insubordination. (18c) **1.** A willful disregard of an employer's instructions, esp. behavior that gives the employer cause to terminate a worker's employment. **2.** An act of disobedience to proper authority; esp., a refusal to obey an order that a superior officer is authorized to give.

insular, *adj.* (17c) **1.** Of, relating to, from, or constituting an island <insular origin>. **2.** Isolated from, uninterested in, or ignorant of things outside a limited scope <insular viewpoint>.

insurance. (17c) **1.** A contract by which one party (the *insurer*) undertakes to indemnify another party (the *insured*) against risk of loss, damage, or liability arising from the occurrence of some specified contingency, and usu. to defend the insured or to pay for a defense regardless of whether the insured is ultimately found liable. **2.** The amount for which someone or something is covered by such an agreement. — **insure,** *vb.*

accident insurance. Insurance that indemnifies against bodily injury caused by an accident.

automobile insurance. An agreement to indemnify against one or more kinds of loss associated with the use of an automobile, including damage to a vehicle and liability for personal injury.

aviation insurance. Insurance that protects the insured against a loss connected with the use of an aircraft. • This type of insurance can be written to cover a variety of risks, including bodily injury, property damage, and hangarkeepers' liability.

broad-form insurance. (1959) Comprehensive insurance. • This type of insurance usu. takes the form of an endorsement to a liability or property policy, broadening the coverage that is typically available.

burial insurance. Insurance that pays for the holder's burial and funeral expenses.

casualty insurance. An agreement to indemnify against loss resulting from a broad group of causes such as legal liability, theft, accident, property damage, and workers' compensation. • The meaning of casualty insurance has become blurred because of the rapid increase in different types of insurance coverage.

collision insurance. (1921) Automobile insurance that covers damage to the insured's vehicle resulting from a rollover or collision with any object, but does not cover a personal injury or damage to other property.

commercial insurance. **1.** An indemnity agreement in the form of a deed or bond to protect against a loss caused by a party's breach of contract. **2.** A form of coverage that allows an insurer to adjust the premium rates at will, and doesn't require the insured to accept the premium or renew the coverage from period to period.

comprehensive insurance. (1924) Insurance that combines coverage against many kinds of losses that may also be insured separately. • This is commonly used, for example, in an automobile-insurance policy.

compulsory insurance. (1887) Statutorily required insurance; esp., motor-vehicle liability insurance that a state requires as a condition to register the vehicle.

convertible insurance. (1926) Insurance that can be changed to another form without further evidence of insurability, usu. referring to a term-life-insurance policy that can be changed to permanent insurance without a medical examination.

crop insurance. Insurance that protects against loss to growing crops from natural perils such as hail and fire.

deposit insurance. (1933) A federally sponsored indemnification program to protect depositors against the loss of their money, up to a specified maximum, if the bank or savings-and-loan association fails or defaults.

directors and officers' liability insurance. An agreement to indemnify corporate directors and officers against judgments, settlements, and fines arising from negligence suits, shareholder actions, and other business-related suits. — Often shortened to *D&O liability insurance*; *D&O insurance.*

disability insurance. Coverage purchased to protect a person from a loss of income during a period of incapacity for work.

double insurance. (18c) Insurance coverage by more than one insurer for the same interest and for the same insured. • Except with life insurance, the insured is entitled to only a single indemnity from a loss, and to recover this, the insured may either (1) sue each insurer for its share of the loss, or (2) sue one or more of the insurers for the entire amount, leaving any paying insurers to recover from the others their respective shares of the loss.

employers'-liability insurance. **1.** An agreement to indemnify an employer against an employee's claim not covered under the workers'-compensation system. **2.** An agreement to indemnify against liability imposed on an employer for an employee's negligence that injures a third party.

excess insurance. (1916) An agreement to indemnify against any loss that exceeds the amount of coverage under another policy. Cf. *primary insurance.*

extended-term insurance. (1925) Insurance that remains in effect after a default in paying premiums, as long as the policy has cash value to pay premiums. • Many life-insurance policies provide this feature to protect against forfeiture of the policy if the insured falls behind in premium payments.

family-income insurance. An agreement to pay benefits for a stated period following the death of the insured. • At the end of the payment period, the face value is paid to the designated beneficiary.

fidelity insurance. An agreement to indemnify an employer against a loss arising from the lack of integrity or honesty of an employee or of a person holding a position of trust, such as a loss from embezzlement.

fire insurance. An agreement to indemnify against property damage caused by fire, wind, rain, or other similar disaster.

fleet insurance. Insurance that covers a number of vehicles owned by the same entity.

flood insurance. Insurance that indemnifies against a loss caused by a flood. • This type of insurance is often sold privately but subsidized by the federal government.

fraternal insurance. Life or health insurance issued by a fraternal benefit society to its members.

general-disability insurance. Disability insurance that provides benefits to a person who cannot perform any job that the person is qualified for.

government insurance. Life insurance underwritten by the federal government to military personnel, veterans, and government employees.

group insurance. A form of insurance offered to a member of a group, such as the employees of a business, as long as that person remains a member of the group. • Group insurance is typically health or life (usu. term life) insurance issued under a master policy between the insurer and the employer, who usu. pays all or part of the premium for the insured person. Other groups, such as unions and associations, often offer group insurance to their members.

health insurance. Insurance covering medical expenses resulting from sickness or injury.

homeowner's insurance. Insurance that covers both damage to the insured's residence and liability claims made against the insured (esp. those arising from the insured's negligence).

liability insurance. An agreement to cover a loss resulting from the insured's liability to a third party, such as a loss incurred by a driver who injures a pedestrian. • The insured's claim under the policy arises once the insured's liability to a third party has been asserted.

Lloyd's insurance. (1897) Insurance provided by insurers as individuals, rather than as a corporation. • The insurers' liability is several but not joint. Most states either prohibit or strictly regulate this type of insurance.

malpractice insurance (mal-**prak**-tis). (1943) An agreement to indemnify a professional person, such as a doctor or lawyer, against negligence claims.

mortgage insurance. **1.** An agreement to pay off a mortgage if the insured dies or becomes disabled. **2.** An agreement to provide money to the lender if the mortgagor defaults on the mortgage payments.

mutual insurance. A system of insurance (esp. life insurance) whereby the policyholders become members of the insurance company, each paying premiums into a common fund from which each can draw in the event of a loss.

no-fault auto insurance. An agreement to indemnify for a loss due to personal injury or property damage arising from the use of an automobile, regardless of who caused the accident.

paid-up insurance. (1871) Insurance that remains in effect even though no more premiums are due.

primary insurance. Insurance that attaches immediately on the happening of a loss; insurance that is not contingent on the exhaustion of an underlying policy.

renewable term insurance. Insurance that the insured may continue at the end of a term, but generally at a higher premium. • The insured usu. has the right to renew for additional terms without a medical examination.

replacement insurance. (1938) Insurance under which the value of the loss is measured by the current cost of replacing the insured property.

self-insurance. A plan under which a business maintains its own special fund to cover any loss. • Unlike other forms of insurance, there is no contract with an insurance company.

terrorism insurance. Insurance that indemnifies against losses sustained because of an act of terrorism. • Terrorism insurance has been available since the 1970s; it was (and is) required for U.S. airports of almost all sizes. In the mid-1980s, terrorism insurance was offered to individuals, originally as a form of travel insurance that provided compensation for terrorism-related cancellations or changes in itinerary when traveling to or in certain countries.

title insurance. (1889) An agreement to indemnify against loss arising from a defect in title to real property, usu. issued to the buyer of the property by the title company that conducted the title search.

unemployment insurance. (1897) A type of social insurance that pays money to workers who are unemployed for reasons unrelated to job performance. • Individual states administer unemployment insurance, which is funded by payroll taxes.

insurance adjuster. (1934) A person who determines the value of a loss to the insured and settles the claim against the insurer.

insurance agent. (1866) A person authorized by an insurance company to sell its insurance policies.

insurance certificate. (1865) **1.** A document issued by an insurer as evidence of insurance or membership in an insurance or pension plan. **2.** A document issued by an insurer to a shipper as evidence that a shipment of goods is covered by a marine insurance policy.

insurance commissioner. (1889) A public official who supervises the insurance business conducted in a state.

insurance company. (18c) A corporation or association that issues insurance policies.

insurance policy. (1869) **1.** A contract of insurance. **2.** A document detailing such a contract.

accident policy. A type of business or personal policy that insures against loss resulting directly from accidental bodily injuries sustained during the policy term.

basic-form policy. (1997) A policy that offers limited coverage against loss. • A basic-form policy generally covers damages from fire, windstorm, explosion, riot, aircraft, vehicles, theft, or vandalism.

blanket policy. (1894) An agreement to indemnify all property, regardless of location.

block policy. An all-risk policy that covers groups of property (such as property held in bailment or a business's merchandise) against most perils.

broad-form policy. (1950) A policy that offers broad protection with few limitations. • This policy offers greater coverage than a basic-form policy, but less than an open-perils policy.

claims-made policy. (1974) An agreement to indemnify against all claims made during a specified period, regardless of when the incidents that gave rise to the claims occurred.

closed policy. An insurance policy whose terms cannot be changed.

commercial general-liability policy. A comprehensive policy that covers most commercial risks, liabilities, and causes of loss. • This type of policy covers both business losses and situations in which a business is liable to a third party for personal injury or property damage. First introduced in 1986, this policy has largely replaced comprehensive general-liability policies.

completed-operations policy. A policy usu. purchased by a building contractor to cover accidents arising out of a job or an operation that the contractor has completed.

comprehensive general-liability policy. (1943) A broad-coverage commercial insurance policy covering a variety of general risks, esp. bodily injury and property damage to a third party for which the business entity is liable. • This policy was first offered in 1940. It has largely been replaced by the commercial-general liability policy.

concurrent policy. (1937) One of two or more insurance policies that cover the same risk.

homeowner's policy. A multiperil policy providing coverage for a variety of risks, including loss by fire, water, burglary, and the homeowner's negligent conduct.

incontestable policy. (1897) A policy containing a provision that prohibits the insurer from contesting or canceling the policy on the basis of statements made in the application.

joint life policy. (1927) A life-insurance policy that matures and becomes due upon the death of any of those jointly insured.

lapsed policy. (1873) **1.** An insurance policy on which there has been a default in premium payments. **2.** An insurance policy that, because of statutory provisions, remains in force after a default in premium payments.

life policy. A life-insurance policy that requires lifetime annual fixed premiums and that becomes payable only on the death of the insured.

limited policy. (1884) An insurance policy that specifically excludes certain classes or types of loss.

manuscript policy. (1962) An insurance policy containing nonstandard provisions that have been negotiated between the insurer and the insured.

master policy. (1926) An insurance policy that covers multiple insureds under a group-insurance plan.

multiperil policy. (1951) An insurance policy that covers several types of losses, such as a homeowner's policy that covers losses from fire, theft, and personal injury.

occurrence policy. An agreement to indemnify for any loss from an event that occurs within the policy period, regardless of when the claim is made.

open-perils policy. (1997) A property insurance policy covering all risks against loss except those specifically excluded from coverage.

standard policy. (1893) **1.** An insurance policy providing insurance that is recommended or required by state law, usu. regulated by a state agency. **2.** An insurance policy that contains standard terms used for similar insurance policies nationwide, usu. drafted by an insurance industrial association such as Insurance Services Office.

term policy. A life-insurance policy that gives protection for a specified period, but that does not have a cash value or reserve value.

insurance pool. (1935) A group of several insurers that, to spread the risk, combine and share premiums and losses.

insurance rating. (1905) The process by which an insurer arrives at a policy premium for a particular risk.

insured, *n.* (17c) A person who is covered or protected by an insurance policy.

additional insured. (1929) A person who is covered by an insurance policy but who is not the primary insured.

class-one insured. (1982) In a motor-vehicle policy, the named insured and any relative residing with the named insured.

class-two insured. (1985) In a motor-vehicle policy, a person lawfully occupying a vehicle at the time of an accident.

named insured. (1899) A person designated in an insurance policy as the one covered by the policy.

primary insured. The individual or entity whose name appears first in the declarations of an insurance policy.

insurer. (17c) One who agrees, by contract, to assume the risk of another's loss and to compensate for that loss.

excess insurer. An insurer who is liable for settling any part of a claim not covered by an insured's primary insurer.

primary insurer. An insurer who is contractually committed to settling a claim up to the applicable policy limit before any other insurer becomes liable for any part of the same claim.

quasi-insurer. (1830) A service provider who is held to strict liability in the provision of services, such as an innkeeper or a common carrier.

insurgent, *n.* (18c) A person who, for political purposes, engages in armed hostility against an established government. — **insurgent,** *adj.* — **insurgency,** *n.*

insuring clause. A provision in an insurance policy or bond reciting the risk assumed by the insurer or establishing the scope of the coverage.

insurrection. (15c) A violent revolt against an oppressive authority, usu. a government.

intake, *n.* (1943) **1.** The official screening of a juvenile charged with an offense in order to determine where to place the juvenile pending formal adjudication or informal disposition. **2.** The body of officers who conduct this screening.

intake day. (1985) The day on which new cases are assigned to the courts.

intangible, *adj.* (17c) Not capable of being touched; impalpable; incorporeal.

intangible, *n.* (1914) Something that lacks a physical form; an abstraction, such as responsibility; esp., an asset that is not corporeal, such as intellectual property.

general intangible. (1935) Any personal property other than goods, accounts, chattel paper, documents, instruments, investment property, rights to proceeds of written letters of credit, and money. • Some examples are goodwill, things in action, and literary rights. UCC § 9-102(a)(42).

payment intangible. (1996) A general intangible under which the account debtor's principal obligation is a monetary obligation. UCC § 9-102(a)(61).

integrated contract. (1930) One or more writings constituting a final expression of one or more terms of an agreement.

completely integrated contract. (1950) An integrated agreement adopted by the parties as a full and exclusive statement of the terms of the agreement.

partially integrated contract. (1958) An agreement in which some, but not all, of the terms are integrated; any agreement other than a completely integrated agreement.

integration. (17c) **1.** The process of making whole or combining into one. **2.** *Contracts.* The full expression of the parties' agreement, so that all earlier agreements are superseded, the effect being that neither party may later contradict or add to the contractual terms.

complete integration. (1930) The fact or state of fully expressing the intent of the parties.

partial integration. (1910) The fact or state of not fully expressing the parties' intent. • Parol (extrinsic) evidence is admissible to clear up ambiguities with respect to the terms that are not integrated.

3. *Wills & estates.* The combining of more than one writing into a single document to form the testator's last will and testament. **4.** The incorporation of different races into existing institutions (such as public schools) for the purpose of reversing the historical effects of racial discrimination.

integration clause. (1941) A contractual provision stating that the contract represents the parties' complete and final agreement and supersedes all informal understandings and oral agreements relating to the subject matter of the contract.

integration rule. (1899) The rule that if the parties to a contract have embodied their agreement in a final document, any other action or statement is without effect and is immaterial in determining the terms of the contract.

intellectual property. (1808) **1.** A category of intangible rights protecting commercially valuable products of the human intellect. • The category comprises primarily trademark, copyright, and patent rights, but also includes trade-secret rights, publicity rights, moral rights, and rights against unfair competition. **2.** A commercially valuable product of the human intellect, in a concrete or abstract form, such as a copyrightable work, a protectable trademark, a patentable invention, or a trade secret. — Abbr. IP.

intend, *vb.* (14c) **1.** To have in mind a fixed purpose to reach a desired objective; to have as one's purpose <Daniel intended to become a lawyer>. **2.** To contemplate that the usual consequences of one's act will probably or necessarily follow from the act, whether or not those consequences are desired for their own sake <although he activated the theater's fire alarm only on a dare, the jury found that Wilbur intended to cause a panic>. **3.** To signify or mean <the parties intended for the writing to supersede their earlier handshake deal>.

intended to be recorded. (18c) (Of a deed or other instrument) not yet filed with a public registry, but forming a link in a chain of title.

intended-use doctrine. (1967) *Products liability.* The rule imposing a duty on a manufacturer to develop a product so that it is reasonably safe for its intended or foreseeable users. • In determining the scope of responsibility, the court considers the defendant's marketing scheme and the foreseeability of the harm.

intendment (in-**tend**-mənt). (14c) **1.** The sense in which the law understands something. **2.** A decision-maker's inference about the true meaning or intention of a legal instrument. **3.** A person's expectations when interacting with others within the legal sphere.

intent. (13c) **1.** The state of mind accompanying an act, esp. a forbidden act. • While motive is the inducement to do some act, intent is the mental resolution or determination to do it. When the intent to do an act that violates the law exists, motive becomes immaterial.

constructive intent. (1864) A legal principle that actual intent will be presumed when an act leading to the result could have been reasonably expected to cause that result.

criminal intent. (17c) **1.** MENS REA. **2.** An intent to commit an actus reus without any justification, excuse, or other defense.

donative intent. The intent to surrender dominion and control over the gift that is being made.

general intent. (17c) The intent to perform an act even though the actor does not desire the consequences that result. • This is the state of mind required for the commission of certain common-law crimes not requiring a specific intent or not imposing strict liability. General intent usu. takes the form of recklessness (involving actual awareness of a risk and the culpable taking of that risk) or negligence (involving blameworthy inadvertence).

immediate intent. (18c) The intent relating to a wrongful act; the part of the total intent coincident with the wrongful act itself.

implied intent. (18c) A person's state of mind that can be inferred from speech or conduct, or from language used in an instrument to which the person is a party.

intent to kill. (16c) An intent to cause the death of another; esp., a state of mind that, if found to exist during an assault, can serve as the basis for an aggravated-assault charge.

larcenous intent. (1832) A state of mind existing when a person (1) knowingly takes away the goods of another without any claim or pretense of a right to do so, and (2) intends to permanently deprive the owner of them or to convert the goods to personal use.

manifest intent. (17c) Intent that is apparent or obvious based on the available circumstantial evidence, even if direct evidence of intent is not available.

predatory intent. *Antitrust.* A business's intent to injure a competitor by unfair means, esp. by sacrificing revenues to drive a competitor out of business.

specific intent. (18c) The intent to accomplish the precise criminal act that one is later charged with.

testamentary intent. (1830) A testator's intent that a particular instrument function as his or her last will and testament.

transferred intent. (1932) Intent that the law may shift from an originally intended wrongful act to a wrongful act actually committed. • For example, if a person intends to kill one person but kills another inadvertently, the intent may be transferred to the actual act.

ulterior intent. (1848) The intent that passes beyond a wrongful act and relates to the objective for the sake of which the act is done; MOTIVE. • For example, a thief's immediate intent may be to steal another's money, but the ulterior intent may be to buy food with that money.

2. A lawmaker's state of mind and purpose in drafting or voting for a measure.

original intent. (17c) The mental state of the drafters or enactors of the U.S. Constitution, a statute, or another document.

intention, *n.* (14c) The willingness to bring about something planned or foreseen; the state of being set to do something. — **intentional,** *adj.*

intentional, *adj.* (17c) Done with the aim of carrying out the act.

intentional infliction of emotional distress. (1958) The tort of intentionally or recklessly causing another person severe emotional distress through one's extreme or outrageous acts.

intent to publish. *Defamation.* The intent to communicate (defamatory words, etc.) to a third person or with knowledge that the communication will probably reach third persons.

inter alia (**in**-tər **ay**-lee-ə *or* **ah**-lee-ə), *adv.* [Latin] (17c) Among other things.

inter alios (**in**-tər **ay**-lee-əs *or* **ah**-lee-əs), *adv.* [Latin] (17c) Among other persons.

Inter-American Bar Association. An organization of lawyers from North America, Central America, and South America whose purpose is to promote education, cooperation, and professional exchanges among lawyers from different American countries. — Abbr. IABA.

intercept, *vb.* (15c) **1.** To divert (money) from a payee to satisfy a financial obligation of the payee. **2.** To covertly receive or listen to (a communication). • The term usu. refers to covert reception by a law-enforcement agency.

intercourse. (15c) **1.** Dealings or communications, esp. between businesses, governmental entities, or the like. **2.** Physical sexual contact, esp. involving the penetration of the vagina by the penis.

interdict (in-tər-**dikt**), *vb.* (15c) **1.** To forbid or restrain. **2.** To intercept and seize (contraband, etc.). — **interdiction,** *n.*

interest, *n.* (15c) **1.** The object of any human desire; esp., advantage or profit of a financial nature <conflict of interest>. **2.** A legal share in something; all or part of a legal or equitable claim to or right in property <right, title, and interest>. • Collectively, the word includes any aggregation of rights, privileges, powers, and immunities; distributively, it refers to any one right, privilege, power, or immunity.

absolute interest. (18c) An interest that is not subject to any condition.

beneficial interest. (18c) A right or expectancy in something (such as a trust or an estate), as opposed to legal title to that thing. • For example, a person with a beneficial interest in a trust receives income from the trust but does not hold legal title to the trust property.

contingent interest. (18c) An interest that the holder may enjoy only upon the occurrence of a condition precedent.

controlling interest. Sufficient ownership of stock in a company to control policy and management; esp., a greater-than-50% ownership interest in an enterprise.

direct interest. (17c) A certain, absolute interest.

entire interest. (17c) A whole interest or right, without diminution.

equitable interest. (17c) An interest held by virtue of an equitable title or claimed on equitable grounds, such as the interest held by a trust beneficiary.

expectation interest. (1836) The interest of a nonbreaching party in being put in the position that would have resulted if the contract had been performed.

financial interest. An interest involving money or its equivalent; esp., an interest in the nature of an investment.

future interest. (17c) A property interest in which the privilege of possession or of other enjoyment is future and not present.

inalienable interest. (1848) An interest that cannot be sold or traded.

inchoate interest. (1800) A property interest that has not yet vested.

insurable interest. (18c) A legal interest in another person's life or health or in the protection of property from injury, loss, destruction, or pecuniary damage. • To take out an insurance policy, the purchaser or the potential insured's beneficiary must have an insurable interest. If a policy does not have an insurable interest as its basis, it will usu. be considered a form of wagering and thus be held unenforceable.

joint interest. An interest that is acquired at the same time and by the same title as another person's.

junior interest. An interest that is subordinate to a senior interest.

legal interest. (17c) **1.** An interest that has its origin in the principles, standards, and rules developed by courts of law as opposed to courts of chancery. **2.** An interest recognized by law, such as legal title.

legally protected interest. A property interest that the law will protect against impairment or destruction, whether in law or in equity.

liberty interest. (1960) An interest protected by the due-process clauses of state and federal constitutions.

present interest. (17c) **1.** A property interest in which the privilege of possession or enjoyment is present and not merely future; an interest entitling the holder to immediate possession. **2.** A trust interest in which the beneficiary has the immediate beneficial enjoyment of the trust's proceeds. **3.** A trust interest in which the trustee has the immediate right to control and manage the property in trust.

proprietary interest. (17c) A property right; specif., the interest held by a property owner together with all appurtenant rights, such as a stockholder's right to vote the shares.

reliance interest. (1936) The interest of a nonbreaching party in being put in the position that would have resulted if the contract had not been made, including out-of-pocket costs.

restitution interest. A nonbreaching party's interest in preventing the breaching party from retaining a benefit received under the contract and thus being unjustly enriched.

reversionary interest. A future interest left in the transferor or successor in interest.

senior interest. An interest that takes precedence over others; esp., a debt security or preferred share that has a higher claim on a corporation's assets and earnings than that of a junior obligation or common share.

terminable interest. (1883) An interest that may be terminated upon the lapse of time or upon the occurrence of some condition.

undivided interest. (18c) An interest held under the same title by two or more persons, whether their rights are equal or unequal in value or quantity.

vested interest. (18c) An interest for which the right to its enjoyment, either present or future, is not subject to the happening of a condition precedent.

3. The compensation fixed by agreement or allowed by law for the use or detention of money, or for the loss of money by one who is entitled to its use; esp., the amount owed to a lender in return for the use of borrowed money.

accrued interest. (18c) Interest that is earned but not yet paid, such as interest that accrues on real estate and that will be paid when the property is sold if, in the meantime, the rental income does not cover the mortgage payments.

add-on interest. (1952) Interest that is computed on the original face amount of a loan and that remains the same even as the principal declines. • A $10,000 loan with add-on interest at 8% payable over three years would require equal annual interest payments of $800 for three years, regardless of the unpaid principal amount.

compound interest. (17c) Interest paid on both the principal and the previously accumulated interest. Cf. *simple interest.*

conventional interest. (1878) Interest at a rate agreed to by the parties themselves, as distinguished from that prescribed by law.

gross interest. (1884) A borrower's interest payment that includes administrative, service, and insurance charges.

imputed interest. (1968) Interest income that the IRS attributes to a lender regardless of whether the lender actually receives interest from the borrower.

interest as damages. (1841) Interest allowed by law in the absence of a promise to pay it, as compensation for a delay in paying a fixed sum or a delay in assessing and paying damages.

prejudgment interest. Statutorily prescribed interest accrued either from the date of the loss or from the date when the complaint was filed up to the date the final judgment is entered.

prepaid interest. (1887) Interest paid before it is earned.

qualified residence interest. (1993) *Tax.* Interest paid on debt that is secured by one's home and that was incurred to purchase, build, improve, or refinance the home.

simple interest. (17c) Interest paid on the principal only and not on accumulated interest.

unearned interest. (1880) Interest received by a financial institution before it is earned.

interest-analysis technique. (1964) *Conflict of laws.* A method of resolving choice-of-law questions by reviewing a state's laws and the state's interests in enforcing those laws to determine whether that state's laws or those of another state should apply.

interest-coverage ratio. The ratio between a company's pretax earnings and the annual interest payable on bonds and loans.

interest rate. (1886) The percentage that a borrower of money must pay to the lender in return for the use of the money, usu. expressed as a percentage of the principal payable for a one-year period.

annual percentage rate. (1941) The actual cost of borrowing money, expressed in the form of an annualized interest rate. — Abbr. APR.

contract rate. (1856) The interest rate printed on the face of a bond certificate.

discount rate. (1913) **1.** The interest rate at which a member bank may borrow money from the Federal Reserve. • This rate controls the supply of money available to banks for lending. **2.** The percentage of a commercial paper's face value paid by an issuer who sells the instrument to a financial institution. **3.** The interest rate used in calculating present value.

effective rate. (1912) The actual annual interest rate, which incorporates compounding when calculating interest, rather than the stated rate or coupon rate.

floating rate. (1921) A varying interest rate that is tied to a financial index such as the prime rate.

illegal rate. (1867) An interest rate higher than the rate allowed by law.

legal rate. (1857) **1.** The interest rate imposed as a matter of law when none is provided by contract. **2.** The maximum interest rate, set by statute, that may be charged on a loan.

lock rate. (2000) A mortgage-application interest rate that is established and guaranteed for a specified period.

nominal rate. (1872) The interest rate stated in a loan agreement or on a bond, with no adjustment made for inflation.

prime rate. (1952) The interest rate that a commercial bank holds out as its lowest rate for a short-term loan to its most creditworthy borrowers, usu. large corporations. • This rate, which can vary slightly from bank to bank, often dictates other interest rates for various personal and commercial loans.

real rate. (1895) An interest rate that has been adjusted for inflation over time.

variable rate. (1970) An interest rate that varies at preset intervals in relation to the current market rate (usu. the prime rate).

interference, *n.* (18c) **1.** The act of meddling in another's affairs. **2.** An obstruction or hindrance. **3.** *Patents.* An administrative proceeding in the U.S. Patent and Trademark Office to determine who is entitled to the patent when two or more applicants claim the same invention, or when an application interferes with an existing patent. **4.** *Trademarks.* An administrative proceeding in the U.S. Patent and Trademark Office to determine whether a mark one party wants to register will cause confusion among consumers with another party's mark. — **interfere,** *vb.*

intergovernmental-immunity doctrine. (1939) *Constitutional law.* The principle that both the federal government and the states are independent sovereigns, and that neither sovereign may intrude on the other in certain political spheres.

interim, *adj.* (16c) Done, made, or occurring for an intervening time; temporary or provisional <an interim director>.

interim-occupancy agreement. (1962) A contract governing an arrangement (called a *leaseback*) whereby the seller rents back property from the buyer.

interlineation (in-tər-lin-ee-**ay**-shən), *n.* (15c) **1.** The act of writing something between the lines of an earlier writing. **2.** Something written between the lines of an earlier writing. — **interline,** *vb.*

interlocutory (in-tər-**lok**-yə-tor-ee), *adj.* (15c) (Of an order, judgment, appeal, etc.) interim or temporary; not constituting a final resolution of the whole controversy.

Interlocutory Appeals Act. A federal statute, enacted in 1958, that grants discretion to a U.S. court of appeals to review an interlocutory order in a civil case if the trial judge states in writing that the order involves a controlling question of law on which there is substantial ground for difference of opinion, and that an immediate appeal from the order may materially advance the termination of the litigation. 28 USCA § 1292(b).

interloper, *n.* (16c) **1.** One who interferes without justification. **2.** One who trades illegally. — **interlope,** *vb.*

intermediary (in-tər-**mee**-dee-er-ee), *n.* (18c) A mediator or go-between; a third-party negotiator. — **intermediate** (in-tər-**mee**-dee-ayt), *vb.*

intermediate scrutiny. (1974) *Constitutional law.* A standard lying between the extremes of rational-basis review and strict scrutiny. • Under the standard, if a statute contains a quasi-suspect classification (such as gender or legitimacy), the classification must be substantially related to the achievement of an important governmental objective.

intermediation. (17c) **1.** Any process involving an intermediary. **2.** The placing of funds with a financial intermediary that reinvests the funds, such as a bank that lends the funds to others or a mutual fund that invests the funds in stocks, bonds, or other instruments.

intern, *n.* (1889) An advanced student or recent graduate who is apprenticing to gain practical experience before entering a specific profession. — **internship,** *n.*

intern, *vb.* (1866) **1.** To segregate and confine a person or group, esp. those suspected of hostile sympathies in time of war. **2.** To work in an internship.

internal-affairs doctrine. *Conflict of laws.* The rule that in disputes involving a corporation and its relationships with its shareholders, directors, officers, or agents, the law to be applied is the law of the state of incorporation.

Internal Revenue Code. Title 26 of the U.S. Code, containing all current federal tax laws. — Abbr. IRC.

Internal Revenue Service. A unit in the U.S. Department of the Treasury responsible for enforcing and administering the internal-revenue laws and other tax laws except those relating to alcohol, tobacco, firearms, and explosives. — Abbr. IRS.

internal-security act. (1950) A statute illegalizing and controlling subversive activities of organizations whose purpose is believed to be to overthrow or disrupt the government. • In the United States, many provisions in such statutes have been declared unconstitutional. One such law was repealed in 1993. See 50 USCA § 781.

international agreement. (1871) A treaty or other contract between different countries, such as GATT or NAFTA.

International Court of Justice. The 15-member permanent tribunal that is the principal judicial organ of the United Nations. • The Court sits in the Hague, Netherlands. It has jurisdiction to decide disputes submitted to it by nations, and to render advisory opinions requested by the United Nations and its specialized agencies. The U.N. Security Council has the express power to enforce the Court's judgments. — Abbr. ICJ.

international crime. *Int'l law.* A grave breach of international law, such as genocide or a crime against humanity, made a punishable offense by treaties or applicable rules of customary international law. • An international crime occurs when three conditions are satisfied: (1) the criminal norm must derive either from a treaty concluded under international law or from customary international law, and must have direct binding force on individuals without intermediate provisions of municipal law, (2) the provision must be made for the prosecution of acts penalized by international law in accordance with the principle of universal jurisdiction, so that the international character of the crime might show in the mode of prosecution itself (e.g., before the International Criminal Court), and (3) a treaty establishing liability for the act must bind the great majority of countries.

International Criminal Court. A court established by a treaty known as the Statute of the International Criminal Court (effective 2002), with jurisdiction over genocides, crimes against humanity, war crimes, and aggression. It sits in The Hague, Netherlands. — Abbr. ICC.

International Criminal Police Organization. An international law-enforcement group founded in 1923 and headquartered in Lyons, France. • The organization gathers and shares information on transnational criminals for more than 180 member nations.

international economic law. (1939) International law relating to investment, economic relations, economic development, economic institutions, and regional economic integration.

international law. (18c) The legal system governing the relationships between nations; more modernly, the law of international relations, embracing not only nations but also such participants as international organizations and individuals (such as those who invoke their human rights or commit war crimes).

International Law Commission. A body created in 1947 by the United Nations for the purpose of encouraging the progressive development and codification of international law.

international legal community. (1928) **1.** The collective body of countries whose mutual legal relations are based on sovereign equality. **2.** More broadly, all organized entities having the capacity to take part in international legal relations. **3.** An integrated organization on which a group of countries, by international treaty, confer part of their powers for amalgamated enterprise. •

In this sense, the European Union is a prime example.

International Monetary Fund. A U.N. specialized agency established to stabilize international exchange rates and promote balanced trade. — Abbr. IMF.

international organization. (1907) *Int'l law.* **1.** An intergovernmental association of countries, established by and operated according to multilateral treaty, whose purpose is to pursue the common aims of those countries. • Examples include the World Health Organization, the International Civil Aviation Organization, and the Organization of Petroleum Exporting Countries. **2.** Loosely, an intergovernmental or nongovernmental international association.

international relations. (1880) **1.** World politics. **2.** Global political interaction, primarily among sovereign nations. **3.** The academic discipline devoted to studying world politics, embracing international law, international economics, and the history and art of diplomacy.

internecine (in-tər-**nee**-sin *or* in-tər-**nee**-sɪn *or* in-tər-**nes**-een), *adj.* (17c) **1.** Deadly; characterized by mass slaughter. **2.** Mutually deadly; destructive of both parties. **3.** Loosely, of or relating to conflict within a group.

internment (in-**tərn**-mənt), *n.* The government-ordered detention of people suspected of disloyalty to the government, such as the confinement of Japanese Americans during World War II. — **intern,** *vb.*

inter partes (in-tər **pahr**-teez), *adv.* [Latin "between parties"] (1816) Between two or more parties; with two or more parties in a transaction. — ***inter partes,*** *adj.*

interplea. (17c) A pleading by which a stakeholder places the disputed property into the court's registry; the plea made by an interpleader.

interplead, *vb.* (16c) **1.** (Of a claimant) to assert one's own claim regarding property or an issue already before the court. **2.** (Of a stakeholder) to institute an interpleader action, usu. by depositing disputed property into the court's registry to abide the court's decision about who is entitled to the property.

interpleader, *n.* (16c) **1.** A suit to determine a right to property held by a usu. disinterested third party (called a *stakeholder*) who is in doubt about ownership and who therefore deposits the property with the court to permit interested parties to litigate ownership. • Typically, a stakeholder initiates an interpleader both to determine who should receive the property and to avoid multiple liability. Fed. R. Civ. P. 22. **2.** Loosely, a party who interpleads.

interpolation (in-tər-pə-**lay**-shən), *n.* (17c) The act of inserting words into a document to change or clarify the meaning. — **interpolate,** *vb.* — **interpolative,** *adj.* — **interpolator,** *n.*

interposition, *n.* (14c) The act of submitting something (such as a pleading or motion) as a defense to an opponent's claim. — **interpose,** *vb.*

interpretation, *n.* (14c) **1.** The process of determining what something, esp. the law or a legal document, means; the ascertainment of meaning to be given to words or other manifestations of intention.

authentic interpretation. (1967) An interpretation arrived at by asking the drafter or drafting body what the intended meaning was.

comparative interpretation. (1933) A method of statutory construction by which parts of the statute are compared to each other, and the statute as a whole is compared to other documents from the same source on a similar subject.

customary interpretation. (1902) Interpretation based on earlier rulings on the same subject.

extensive interpretation. (17c) A liberal interpretation that applies a statutory provision to a case not falling within its literal words.

grammatical interpretation. (1830) Interpretation that is based exclusively on the words themselves.

liberal interpretation. (18c) Interpretation according to what the reader believes the author reasonably intended, even if, through inadvertence, the author failed to think of it.

logical interpretation. (1870) Interpretation that departs from the literal words on the ground that there may be other, more satisfactory evidence of the author's true intention.

restrictive interpretation. (17c) An interpretation that is bound by a principle or principles existing outside the interpreted text. Cf. *unrestrictive interpretation.*

strict interpretation. (16c) Interpretation according to what the reader believes the author must have been thinking at the time of the writing, and no more. • Typically, this type of reading gives a text a narrow meaning.

unrestrictive interpretation. (1968) Interpretation in good faith, without reference to any specific principle.

2. The understanding one has about the meaning of something. **3.** A translation, esp. oral, from one language to another. **4.** Characterization. — **interpret,** *vb.* — **interpretative, interpretive,** *adj.*

interpretation clause. (1827) A legislative or contractual provision giving the meaning of frequently used words or explaining how the document as a whole is to be construed.

interpretivism. (1978) A doctrine of constitutional interpretation holding that judges must follow norms or values expressly stated or implied in the language of the Constitution.

interrogation, *n.* (15c) The formal or systematic questioning of a person; esp., intensive questioning by the police, usu. of a person arrested for or suspected of committing a crime. • The Supreme Court has held that, for purposes of the Fifth Amendment right against self-incrimination, interrogation includes not only express questioning but also words or actions that the police should know are reasonably likely to elicit an incriminating response. *Rhode Island v. Innis*, 446 U.S. 291, 100 S.Ct. 1082 (1980). — **interrogate,** *vb.* — **interrogative,** *adj.*

custodial interrogation. (1966) Police questioning of a detained person about the crime that he or she is suspected of having committed. • Miranda warnings must be given before a custodial interrogation.

investigatory interrogation. (1962) Routine, nonaccusatory questioning by the police of a person who is not in custody.

noncustodial interrogation. (1966) Police questioning of a suspect who has not been detained and can leave at will. • Miranda warnings are usu. not given before a noncustodial interrogation.

interrogator (in-**ter**-ə-gay-tər). (18c) One who poses questions to another.

interrogatory (in-tə-**rog**-ə-tor-ee), *n.* (16c) A written question (usu. in a set of questions) submitted to an opposing party in a lawsuit as part of discovery. See Fed. R. Civ. P. 33.

cross-interrogatory. (17c) An interrogatory from a party who has received a set of interrogatories.

special interrogatory. (18c) A written jury question whose answer is required to supplement a general verdict. • This term is not properly used in federal practice, which authorizes interrogatories and special verdicts, but not special interrogatories. Fed. R. Civ. P. 49.

in terrorem (in te-**ror**-əm), *adv.* & *adj.* [Latin "in order to frighten"] (17c) By way of threat; as a warning.

***in terrorem* clause.** No-contest clause.

inter se (**in**-tər **see** *or* **say**). [Latin "between or among themselves"] (1845) (Of a right or duty) owed between the parties rather than to others.

interspousal, *adj.* (1906) Between husband and wife.

interstate, *adj.* (1844) Between two or more states or residents of different states.

interstate agreement. (1876) An agreement between states.

Interstate Agreement on Detainers Act. A law, originally enacted in 1956, that allows the federal government, certain states, and the District of Columbia to temporarily obtain custody of a prisoner for trial even though the prisoner is already incarcerated elsewhere.

Interstate Commerce Commission. The now-defunct federal agency established by the Interstate Commerce Act in 1887 to regulate surface transportation between states by certifying carriers and pipelines and by monitoring quality and pricing. • In December 1995, when Congress eliminated this agency, the Surface Transportation Board (STB) — a three-member board that is a division of the Department of Transportation — assumed most of the agency's duties. — Abbr. ICC.

interstate income-withholding order. (1994) A court order entered to enforce a support order of a court of another state by withholding income of the defaulting person.

interstate law. (1866) **1.** International law. **2.** The rules and principles used to determine controversies between residents of different states.

intervenor. (17c) One who voluntarily enters a pending lawsuit because of a personal stake in it.

intervention, *n.* (1860) **1.** The entry into a lawsuit by a third party who, despite not being named a party to the action, has a personal stake in the outcome. **2.** The legal procedure by which such a third party is allowed to become a party to the litigation. **3.** *Int'l law.* One nation's interference by force, or threat of force, in another nation's internal affairs or in questions arising between other nations. — **intervene,** *vb.* — **interventionary,** *adj.*

humanitarian intervention. An intervention by the international community to curb abuses of human rights within a country, even if the intervention infringes the country's sovereignty.

inter vivos (**in**-tər **vɪ**-vohs *or* **vee**-vohs), *adj.* [Latin "between the living"] (1837) Of or relating to property conveyed not by will or in contemplation of an imminent death, but during the conveyor's lifetime. — ***inter vivos,*** *adv.*

intestacy (in-**tes**-tə-see). (18c) The state or condition of a person's having died without a valid will.

intestate (in-**tes**-tayt), *adj.* (14c) **1.** Of or relating to a person who has died without a valid will. **2.** Of or relating to the property owned by a person who died without a valid will. **3.** Of or relating to intestacy.

intestate, *n.* (17c) One who has died without a valid will.

partial intestate. One who has died with a valid will that does not dispose of all of his or her net probate estate.

intestate law. (18c) The relevant statute governing succession to estates of those who die without a valid will.

in the course of employment. (1911) *Workers' compensation.* (Of an accident) having happened to an on-the-job employee within the scope of employment.

intimidation, *n.* (17c) Unlawful coercion; extortion. — **intimidate,** *vb.* — **intimidatory,** *adj.* — **intimidator,** *n.*

in toto (in **toh**-toh), *adv.* [Latin "in whole"] (18c) Completely; as a whole <the company rejected the offer *in toto*>.

intoxicant, *n.* (1863) A substance (esp. liquor) that deprives a person of the ordinary use of the senses or of reason.

intoxication, *n.* (15c) A diminished ability to act with full mental and physical capabilities because of alcohol or drug consumption; drunkenness. See Model Penal Code § 2.08. — **intoxicate,** *vb.*

involuntary intoxication. (1870) The ingestion of alcohol or drugs against one's will or without one's knowledge. • Involuntary intoxication is an affirmative defense to a criminal or negligence charge.

pathological intoxication. (1947) An extremely exaggerated response to an intoxicant. • This may be treated as involuntary intoxication if it is unforeseeable.

public intoxication. (1885) The condition of a person who is under the influence of drugs or alcohol in a place open to the general public.

voluntary intoxication. (18c) A willing ingestion of alcohol or drugs to the point of impairment done with the knowledge that one's physical and mental capabilities would be impaired. • Voluntary intoxication is not a defense to a general-intent crime, but may be admitted to refute the existence of a particular state of mind for a specific-intent crime.

intra vires (**in**-trə **vɪ**-reez), *adj.* [Latin "within the powers (of)"] (1877) Of or referring to an action taken within a corporation's or person's scope of authority. — **intra vires,** *adv.*

introduce into evidence. (18c) To have (a fact or object) admitted into the trial record, allowing it to be considered by the jury or the court in reaching a decision.

introductory clause. The first paragraph of a contract, which typically begins with words such as "This Agreement is made on [date] between [parties' names]."

intromission (in-trə-**mish**-ən). (16c) **1.** The transactions of an employee or agent with funds provided by an employer or principal; loosely, dealing in the funds of another. **2.** *Scots law.* The act of handling or dealing with the affairs or property of another; the possession of another's property, with or without legal authority.

intrusion, *n.* (15c) **1.** A person's entering without permission. **2.** In an action for invasion of privacy, a highly offensive invasion of another person's seclusion or private life.— **intrude,** *vb.* — **intrusive,** *adj.*

inure (in-**yoor**), *vb.* (15c) **1.** To take effect; to come into use <the settlement proceeds must inure to the benefit of the widow and children>. **2.** To make accustomed to something unpleasant; to habituate <abused children become inured to violence>. — **inurement,** *n.*

in utero (in **yoo**-tə-roh). [Latin "in the uterus"] In the womb; during gestation or before birth <child *in utero*>.

invalid (in-**val**-id), *adj.* (17c) **1.** Not legally binding. **2.** Without basis in fact.

invalid (**in**-və-lid), *n.* (18c) A person who, because of serious illness or other disability, lacks the physical or mental capability of managing his or her day-to-day life.

invasion. (17c) A hostile or forcible encroachment on the rights of another.

invasion of privacy. (1862) An unjustified exploitation of one's personality or intrusion into one's personal activities, actionable under tort law and sometimes under constitutional law.

inveigle (in-**vay**-gəl), *vb.* (16c) To lure or entice through deceit or insincerity. — **inveiglement,** *n.*

invention, *n.* (14c) *Patents.* **1.** A patentable device or process created through independent effort and characterized by an extraordinary degree of skill or ingenuity; a newly discovered art or operation. • *Invention* embraces the concept of nonobviousness. **2.** The act or process of creating such a device or process. **3.** Generally, anything that is created or devised. — **invent,** *vb.*

invest, *vb.* (17c) **1.** To supply with authority or power <the U.S. Constitution invests the President with the power to conduct foreign affairs>. **2.** To apply (money) for profit <Jillson invested her entire savings in the mutual fund>. **3.** To make an outlay of money for profit <Baird invested in stocks>.

investigate, *vb.* (16c) **1.** To inquire into (a matter) systematically; to make (a suspect) the subject of a criminal inquiry. **2.** To make an official inquiry.

investment. (16c) **1.** An expenditure to acquire property or assets to produce revenue; a capital outlay.

fixed-dollar investment. An investment whose value is the same when sold as it was when purchased.

fixed-income investment. An investment (including preferred stock) that pays a fixed dividend throughout its life and is not redeemable unless the corporation makes a special call.

net investment. **1.** The net cash required to start a new project. **2.** The gross investment in capital goods less capital consumption, including depreciation.

2. The asset acquired or the sum invested.

investment adviser. A person who, for pay, advises others, either directly or through publications or writings, about the value of securities or the advisability of investing in, purchasing, or selling securities, or who is in the business of issuing reports on securities.

investment banker. A person or institution that underwrites, sells, or assists in raising capital for businesses, esp. for new issues of stocks or bonds; a trader at an investment bank.

investor. (17c) **1.** A buyer of a security or other property who seeks to profit from it without exhausting the principal. **2.** Broadly, a person who spends money with an expectation of earning a profit.

accredited investor. An investor treated under the Securities Act of 1933 as being knowledgeable and sophisticated about financial matters, esp. because of the investor's large net worth.

institutional investor. One who trades large volumes of securities, usu. by investing other people's money into large managed funds.

sophisticated investor. *Securities.* An investor who has sufficient knowledge and experience of financial matters to be capable of evaluating a security's qualities.

inviolable (in-**vɪ**-ə-lə-bəl), *adj.* (15c) Safe from violation; incapable of being violated. — **inviolability,** *n.*

inviolate (in-**vɪ**-ə-lit), *adj.* (15c) Free from violation; not broken, infringed, or impaired.

invitation, *n. Torts.* In the law of negligence, the enticement of others to enter, remain on, or use property or its structures; conduct that justifies others in believing that the possessor wants them to enter. — **invite,** *vb.*

invitation to negotiate. (1902) *Contracts.* A solicitation for one or more offers, usu. as a preliminary step to forming a contract. —**invite,** *vb.*

invitee (in-vɪ-**tee**). (1837) A person who has an express or implied invitation to enter or use another's premises, such as a business visitor or a member of the public to whom the premises are held open. • The occupier has a duty to inspect the premises and to warn the invitee of dangerous conditions.

public invitee. (1937) An invitee who is invited to enter and remain on property for a purpose for which the property is held open to the public.

in vitro fertilization. A procedure by which an egg is fertilized outside a woman's body and then inserted into the womb for gestation. — Abbr. IVF.

in vivo fertilization. The process in which an egg is fertilized inside a woman's body.

invoice, *n.* (16c) An itemized list of goods or services furnished by a seller to a buyer, usu. specifying the price and terms of sale; a bill of costs. — **invoice,** *vb.*

involuntary, *adj.* (15c) Not resulting from a free and unrestrained choice; not subject to control by the will. — **involuntariness,** *n.*

in witness whereof. (16c) The traditional beginning of the concluding clause (termed the *testimonium clause*) of a will or contract, esp. a deed.

IOU (ɪ-oh-**yoo**). [abbr. "I owe you"] (17c) **1.** A memorandum acknowledging a debt. **2.** The debt itself.

IP. *abbr.* Intellectual property.

IPO. *abbr.* Initial public offering.

ipse dixit (**ip**-see **dik**-sit). [Latin "he himself said it"] (15c) Something asserted but not proved <his testimony that she was a liar was nothing more than an *ipse dixit*>.

ipsissima verba (ip-**sis**-ə-mə **vər**-bə). [Latin "the very (same) words"] (1807) The exact words used by somebody being quoted <on its face, the *ipsissima verba* of the statute supports the plaintiff's position on the ownership issue>.

ipso facto (**ip**-soh **fak**-toh). [Latin "by the fact itself"] (16c) By the very nature of the situation <if 25% of all contractual litigation is caused by faulty drafting, then, *ipso facto*, the profession needs to improve its drafting skills>.

IRA (ɪ-ahr-**ay** *or* **ɪ**-rə). *abbr.* Individual Retirement Account.

IRAC (**ɪ**-rak). A mnemonic acronym used mostly by law students and their writing instructors, esp. as a method of answering essay questions on law exams. • The acronym is commonly said to stand for either (1) issue, rule, application, conclusion, or (2) issue, rule, analysis, conclusion.

IRC. *abbr.* Internal Revenue Code.

irreconcilable differences. (1975) Persistent and unresolvable disagreements between spouses, leading to the breakdown of the marriage. • These differences may be cited — without specifics — as grounds for no-fault divorce. At least 33 states have provided that irreconcilable differences are a basis for divorce.

irrecusable, *adj.* (18c) (Of an obligation) that cannot be avoided, although made without one's consent, such as the obligation to not strike another without some lawful excuse. Cf. RECUSABLE (1).

irrefragable (i-**ref**-rə-gə-bəl), *adj.* (16c) Unanswerable; not to be controverted; impossible to refute.

irregular, *adj.* (14c) Not in accordance with law, method, or usage; not regular.

irrelevance, *n.* (1847) The quality or state of being inapplicable to a matter under consideration.

irrelevant (i-**rel**-ə-vənt), *adj.* (16c) **1.** (Of evidence) having no probative value; not tending to prove or disprove a matter in issue. **2.** (Of a pleaded allegation) having no substantial relation to the action, and will not affect the court's decision. — **irrelevance,** *n.*

irreparable-injury rule (i-**rep**-ə-rə-bəl). (1969) The principle that equitable relief (such as an injunction) is available only when no adequate legal remedy (such as monetary damages) exists.

irresistible-impulse test. (1892) *Criminal law.* A test for insanity, holding that a person is not criminally responsible for an act if mental disease prevented that person from controlling potentially criminal conduct.

irretrievable breakdown of the marriage. (1973) *Family law.* A ground for divorce that is based on incompatibility between marriage partners and in many states is the sole ground for no-fault divorce.

irrevocable (i-**rev**-ə-kə-bəl), *adj.* (14c) Unalterable; committed beyond recall. — **irrevocability,** *n.*

IRS. *abbr.* Internal Revenue Service.

issue, *n.* (16c) **1.** A point in dispute between two or more parties. • In an appeal, an issue may take the form of a separate and discrete question of law or fact, or a combination of both.

collateral issue. (18c) A question or issue not directly connected with the matter in dispute.

deep issue. (1944) The fundamental issue to be decided by a court in ruling on a point of law. • A deep issue is usu. briefly phrased in separate sentences, with facts interwoven (in chronological order) to show precisely what problem is to be addressed. Cf. *surface issue.*

general issue. (16c) **1.** A plea (often a general denial) by which a party denies the truth of every material allegation in an opposing party's pleading. **2.** The issue arising from such a plea.

immaterial issue. (18c) An issue not necessary to decide the point of law. Cf. *material issue.*

issue of fact. (17c) A point supported by one party's evidence and controverted by another's.

issue of law. (18c) A point on which the evidence is undisputed, the outcome depending on the court's interpretation of the law.

legal issue. (17c) A legal question, usu. at the foundation of a case and requiring a court's decision.

material issue. An issue that must be decided in order to resolve a controversy. • The existence of a material issue of disputed fact precludes summary judgment. Cf. *immaterial issue.*

special issue. (17c) At common law, an issue arising from a specific allegation in a pleading. • Special issues are no longer used in most jurisdictions.

surface issue. A superficially stated issue phrased in a single sentence, without many facts, and usu. beginning with the word *whether.* Cf. *deep issue.*

ultimate issue. (17c) A not-yet-decided point that is sufficient either in itself or in connection with other points to resolve the entire case.

2. A class or series of securities that are simultaneously offered for sale.

new issue. A stock or bond sold by a corporation for the first time, often to raise working capital.

original issue. The first issue of securities of a particular type or series.

3. *Wills & estates.* Lineal descendants; offspring. **4.** *Commercial law.* The first delivery of a negotiable instrument by its maker or holder.

issue, *vb.* (14c) **1.** To accrue <rents issuing from land> **2.** To be put forth officially <without probable cause, the search warrant will not issue> **3.** To send out or distribute officially <issue process> <issue stock>. — **issuance,** *n.*

IVF. *abbr.* In vitro fertilization.

J

J. *abbr.* **1.** Judge. **2.** Justice. **3.** Judgment. **4.** Jus. **5.** Journal.

JA. *abbr.* **1.** Judge Advocate. **2.** Joint account.

***Jackson–Denno* hearing.** (1965) A court proceeding, held outside the jury's presence to determine whether the defendant's confession was voluntary and therefore admissible as evidence. *Jackson v. Denno*, 378 U.S. 368, 84 S.Ct. 1774 (1964).

***Jackson* standard.** (1980) *Criminal law.* The principle that the standard of review on appeal — when a criminal defendant claims that there is insufficient evidence to support the conviction — is to determine whether, after considering the evidence in the light most favorable to the prosecution, any rational trier of fact could have found the essential elements of the crime beyond a reasonable doubt. *Jackson v. Virginia*, 443 U.S. 307, 99 S.Ct. 2781 (1979).

Jacob Wetterling Crimes Against Children and Sexually Violent Offender Registration Act. A 1989 federal statute requiring each state to create a sex-offender registry of sexually violent offenders, particularly those who have been convicted of sex crimes against minors, and to disclose information about registered sex offenders for public-safety purposes. • The Act mandates a minimum registration period of 10 years, beginning on the offender's date of release from custody or supervision. It was amended in 1996 by Megan's Law, which added the disclosure requirement.

JAG. *abbr.* Judge Advocate General.

JAG Manual. Manual of the Judge Advocate General.

jail, *n.* (13c) A local government's detention center where persons awaiting trial or those convicted of misdemeanors are confined. — **jail,** *vb.*

jail credit. (1950) Time spent by a criminal defendant in confinement while awaiting trial. • This time is usu. deducted from the defendant's final sentence (if convicted).

jailhouse lawyer. A prison inmate who seeks release through legal procedures or who gives legal advice to other inmates.

***James* hearing.** (1981) A court proceeding held to determine whether the out-of-court statements of a coconspirator should be admitted into evidence, by analyzing whether there was a conspiracy, whether the declarant and the defendant were part of the conspiracy, and whether the statement was made in furtherance of the conspiracy. *United States v. James*, 590 F.2d 575 (5th Cir. 1979); Fed. R. Evid. 801(d)(2)(E).

Jane Doe. A fictitious name for a female party to a legal proceeding, used because the party's true identity is unknown or because her real name is being withheld.

Janus-faced (**jay**-nəs fayst), *adj.* (17c) Having two contrasting or contradictory aspects; two-faced.

J.D. *abbr.* Juris doctor.

***Jencks* material.** (1961) *Criminal procedure.* A prosecution witness's written or recorded pretrial statement that a criminal defendant, upon filing a motion after the witness has testified, is entitled to have in preparing to cross-examine the witness. • The defense may use a statement of this kind for impeachment purposes. *Jencks v. United States*, 353 U.S. 657, 77 S.Ct. 1007 (1957); Jencks Act, 18 USCA § 3500.

reverse Jencks material. *Criminal procedure.* A defense witness's written or recorded pretrial statement that a prosecutor is entitled to have in preparing to cross-examine the witness.

jeopardy. (14c) The risk of conviction and punishment that a criminal defendant faces at trial. • Jeopardy attaches in a jury trial when the jury is empaneled, and in a bench trial when the first witness is sworn.

***Jewell* instruction** (**joo**-wəl). (1977) *Criminal procedure.* A court's instruction to the jury that the defendant can be found to have the requisite criminal mental state despite being deliberately ignorant of some of the facts surrounding the crime.

Jim Crow law. (1891) *Hist.* A law enacted or purposely interpreted to discriminate against blacks, such as a law requiring separate restrooms for blacks and whites. • Jim Crow laws are unconstitutional under the 14th Amendment.

JJ. *abbr.* **1.** Judges. **2.** Justices.

JNOV. *abbr.* Judgment *non obstante veredicto.*

job action. *Labor law.* A concerted, temporary action by employees (such as a sickout or work slowdown), intended to pressure management to concede to the employees' demands without resorting to a strike.

John Doe. A fictitious name used in a legal proceeding to designate a person whose identity is unknown, to protect a person's known identity, or to indicate that a true defendant does not exist.

joinder, *n.* (17c) The uniting of parties or claims in a single lawsuit. — **join,** *vb.*

collusive joinder. (1883) Joinder of a defendant, usu. a nonresident, in order to have a case removed to federal court.

compulsory joinder. (1901) The necessary joinder of a party if either of the following is true: (1) in that party's absence, those already involved in the lawsuit cannot receive complete relief; or (2) the absent party claims an interest in the subject of an action, so that party's absence might either impair the protection of that interest or leave some other party subject to multiple or inconsistent obligations. Fed. R. Civ. P. 19(a).

fraudulent joinder. (1836) The bad-faith joinder of a party, usu. a resident of the state, to prevent removal of a case to federal court.

joinder of issue. **1.** The submission of an issue jointly for decision. **2.** The acceptance or adoption of a disputed point as the basis of argument in a controversy. **3.** The taking up of the opposite side of a case, or of the contrary view on a question.

joinder of offenses. The charging of an accused with two or more crimes as multiple counts in a single indictment or information. • Unless later severed, joined offenses are tried together at a single trial. Fed. R. Crim. P. 8(a).

joinder of remedies. The joinder of alternative claims, such as breach of contract and quantum meruit, or of one claim with another prospective claim, such as a creditor's claim against a debtor to recover on a loan and the creditor's claim against a third party to set aside the transfer of the loan's collateral.

permissive joinder. (1903) The optional joinder of parties if (1) their claims or the claims asserted against them are asserted jointly, severally, or in respect of the same transaction or occurrence, and (2) any legal or factual question common to all of them will arise. Fed. R. Civ. P. 20.

joint, *adj.* (14c) **1.** (Of a thing) common to or shared by two or more persons or entities <joint bank account>. **2.** (Of a person or entity) combined, united, or sharing with another <joint heirs>.

joint administration. *Bankruptcy.* The management of two or more bankruptcy estates, usu. involving related debtors, under one docket for purposes of handling various administrative matters, including notices to creditors, to conclude the cases more efficiently. Fed. R. Bankr. P. 1015.

joint and several, *adj.* (17c) (Of liability, responsibility, etc.) apportionable at an adversary's discretion either among two or more parties or to only one or a few select members of the group; together and in separation.

joint enterprise. (17c) **1.** *Criminal law.* An undertaking by two or more persons who set out to commit an offense they have conspired to. **2.** *Torts.* An undertaking by two or more persons with an equal right to direct and benefit from the endeavor, as a result of which one participant's negligence may be imputed to the others. **3.** Joint venture. **4.** A joint venture for noncommercial purposes.

joint inventor. *Patents.* A person who collaborates with another or others in developing an invention. • All joint inventors must be identified on a patent application.

joint participation. (1971) *Civil-rights law.* A pursuit undertaken by a private person in concert with a governmental entity or state official, resulting in the private person's performing public functions and thereby being subject to claims under the civil-rights laws.

jointure (**joyn**-chər). (15c) **1.** *Archaic.* A woman's freehold life estate in land, made in consideration of marriage in lieu of dower and to be enjoyed by her only after her husband's death. **2.** A settlement under which a wife receives such an estate. **3.** An estate in lands given jointly to a husband and wife before they marry.

joint venture. (18c) A business undertaking by two or more persons engaged in a single defined project. • The necessary elements are: (1) an express or implied agreement; (2) a common purpose that the group intends to carry out; (3) shared profits and losses; and (4) each member's equal voice in controlling the project.

joker. (1904) **1.** An ambiguous clause inserted in a legislative bill to render it inoperative or uncertain in some respect without arousing opposition at the time of passage. **2.** A rider or amendment that is extraneous to the subject of the bill.

Jones Act. *Maritime law.* A federal statute that allows a seaman injured during the course of employment to recover damages for the injuries in a negligence action against the employer. • If a seaman dies from such injuries, the seaman's personal representative may maintain an action against the employer. 46 USCA app. § 688.

journal. (15c) **1.** A book or record kept, usu. daily, as of the proceedings of a legislature or the events of a ship's voyage. **2.** *Accounting.* In double-entry bookkeeping, a book in which original entries are recorded before being transferred to a ledger. **3.** A periodical or magazine, esp. one published for a scholarly or professional group. — Abbr. J.

joyriding, *n.* (1909) The illegal driving of someone else's automobile without permission, but with no intent to deprive the owner of it permanently. See Model Penal Code § 223.9. — **joyride,** *vb.* — **joyrider,** *n.*

J.P. *abbr.* Justice of the peace.

J.S.D. [Law Latin *juris scientiae doctor*] *abbr.* Doctor of Juridical Science.

J.U.D. [Law Latin *juris utriusque doctor* "doctor of both laws"] *abbr.* A doctor of both civil and canon law.

judge, *n.* (14c) A public official appointed or elected to hear and decide legal matters in court. — Abbr. J. (and, in plural, JJ.).

administrative patent judge. *Patents.* A U.S. Patent and Trademark Office adjudicator charged with conducting interference and appeal proceedings. — Abbr. APJ.

associate judge. (18c) An appellate judge who is neither a chief judge nor a presiding judge.

bankruptcy judge. (1873) A judicial officer appointed by a U.S. Court of Appeals to preside over cases filed under the Bankruptcy Code and proceedings related to bankruptcy cases that are referred by the U.S. district court. • A bankruptcy judge is appointed for a term of 14 years. 28 USCA §§ 151 et seq.

chief judge. (15c) The judge who presides over the sessions and deliberations of a court, while also overseeing the administration of the court. — Abbr. C.J.

circuit judge. (18c) **1.** A judge who sits on a circuit court; esp., a federal judge who sits on a U.S. court of appeals. **2.** *Hist.* A special judge added to a court for the purpose of holding trials, but without being a regular member of the court. — Abbr. C.J.

county judge. (18c) A local judge having criminal or civil jurisdiction, or sometimes both, within a county.

de facto judge (di **fak**-toh). (1829) A judge operating under color of law but whose authority is procedurally defective, such as a judge appointed under an unconstitutional statute.

district judge. (18c) A judge in a federal or state judicial district. — Abbr. D.J.

family-court judge. A judge who sits on a court that has jurisdiction exclusively over matters involving domestic relations, such as divorce and child-custody matters.

hanging judge. (18c) *Slang.* A judge who is harsh (sometimes corruptly so) with defendants, esp. those accused of capital crimes.

inferior judge. A judge who sits on a lower court.

juvenile-court judge. A judge who sits on a court that has jurisdiction exclusively over matters involving juveniles, such as suits involving child abuse and neglect, matters involving status offenses, and, sometimes, suits to terminate parental rights.

lay judge. (16c) A judge who is not a lawyer.

military judge. A commissioned officer of the armed forces who is on active duty and is a member of a bar of a federal court or of the highest court of a state.

municipal judge. (18c) A local judge having criminal or civil jurisdiction, or sometimes both, within a city.

presiding judge. (18c) **1.** A judge in charge of a particular court or judicial district; esp., the senior active judge on a three-member panel that hears and decides cases. **2.** A chief judge. — Abbr. P.J.

probate judge. (18c) A judge having jurisdiction over probate, inheritance, guardianships, and the like.

senior judge. (18c) **1.** The judge who has served for the longest time on a given court. **2.** A federal or state judge who qualifies for senior status and chooses this status over retirement.

special judge. (17c) A judge appointed or selected to sit, usu. in a specific case, in the absence or disqualification of the regular judge or otherwise as provided by statute.

trial judge. (17c) The judge before whom a case is tried. • This term is used most commonly on appeal from the judge's rulings.

visiting judge. (1888) A judge appointed by the presiding judge of an administrative region to sit temporarily on a given court, usu. in the regular judge's absence.

judge advocate. (17c) *Military law.* **1.** An officer of a court-martial who acts as a prosecutor. **2.** A legal adviser on a military commander's staff. **3.** Any officer in the Judge Advocate General's Corps or in a department of a U.S. military branch. — Abbr. JA.

Judge Advocate General. *Military law.* The senior legal officer and chief legal adviser of the Army, Navy, or Air Force. — Abbr. JAG.

judge-made law. (1817) **1.** The law established by judicial precedent rather than by statute. **2.** The law that results when judges construe statutes contrary to legislative intent.

judgeship. (17c) **1.** The office or authority of a judge. **2.** The period of a judge's incumbency.

judge-shopping. (1962) The practice of filing several lawsuits asserting the same claims — in a court or a district with multiple judges — with the hope of having one of the lawsuits assigned to a favorable judge and of nonsuiting or voluntarily dismissing the others.

judgment. (13c) A court's final determination of the rights and obligations of the parties in a case. • The term *judgment* includes an equitable decree and any order from which an appeal lies. Fed. R. Civ. P. 54. — Abbr. J.

accumulative judgment. (1921) A second or additional judgment against a person who has already been convicted, the execution of which is postponed until the completion of any prior sentence.

agreed judgment. (1945) A settlement that becomes a court judgment when the judge sanctions it. • In effect, an agreed judgment is merely a contract acknowledged in open court and ordered to be recorded, but it binds the parties as fully as other judgments.

declaratory judgment. (1886) A binding adjudication that establishes the rights and other legal relations of the parties without providing for or ordering enforcement. • Declaratory judgments are often sought, for example, by insurance companies in determining whether a policy covers a given insured or peril.

deferred judgment. (1896) A judgment placing a convicted defendant on probation, the successful completion of which will prevent entry of the underlying judgment of conviction.

deficiency judgment. (1865) A judgment against a debtor for the unpaid balance of the debt if a foreclosure sale or a sale of repossessed personal property fails to yield the full amount of the debt due.

domestic judgment. A judgment rendered by the courts of the state or country where the judgment or its effect is at issue.

dormant judgment. (18c) A judgment that has not been executed or enforced within the statutory time limit. • As a result, any judgment lien may have been lost and execution cannot be issued unless the judgment creditor first revives the judgment.

erroneous judgment. (17c) A judgment issued by a court with jurisdiction to issue it, but containing an improper application of law. • This type of judgment is not void, but can be corrected by a trial court while the court retains plenary jurisdiction, or in a direct appeal.

excess judgment. *Insurance.* A judgment that exceeds all of the defendant's insurance coverage.

executory judgment (eg-**zek**-yə-tor-ee). (18c) A judgment that has not been carried out, such as a yet-to-be fulfilled order for the defendant to pay the plaintiff.

final judgment. (18c) A court's last action that settles the rights of the parties and disposes of all issues in controversy, except for the award of costs (and, sometimes, attorney's fees) and enforcement of the judgment.

foreign judgment. A decree, judgment, or order of a court in a state, country, or judicial system different from that where the judgment or its effect is at issue.

interlocutory judgment (in-tər-**lok**-[y]ə-tor-ee). (17c) An intermediate judgment that determines a preliminary or subordinate point or plea but does not finally decide the case. • A judgment or order given on a provisional or accessory claim or contention is generally interlocutory.

irregular judgment. A judgment that may be set aside because of some irregularity in the way it was rendered, such as a clerk's failure to send a defendant notice that a default judgment has been rendered.

judgment as a matter of law. (1873) A judgment rendered during a jury trial — either before or after the jury's verdict — against a party on a given issue when there is no legally sufficient basis for a jury to find for that party on that issue. • In federal practice, the term *judgment as a matter of law* has replaced both the directed verdict and the judgment notwithstanding the verdict. Fed. R. Civ. P. 50.

judgment in rem (in **rem**). (18c) A judgment that determines the status or condition of property and that operates directly on the property itself.

judgment nil capiat per billa (nil **kap**-ee-ət pər **bil**-ə). (1816) Judgment that the plaintiff take nothing by the bill; a take-nothing judgment in a case instituted by a bill.

judgment nil capiat per breve (nil **kap**-ee-ət pər **breev** *or* **bree**-vee). (1916) Judgment that the plaintiff take nothing by the writ; a take-nothing judgment in a case instituted by a writ.

judgment nisi (**nɪ**-sɪ). (18c) A provisional judgment that, while not final or absolute, may become final on a party's motion.

judgment notwithstanding the verdict. (18c) A judgment entered for one party even though a jury verdict has been rendered for the opposing party. — Abbr. JNOV; judgment N.O.V.

judgment nunc pro tunc. A judgment entered on a day after the time when it should have been entered, as of the earlier date.

judgment of acquittal. (17c) A judgment, rendered on the defendant's motion or court's own motion, that acquits the defendant of the offense charged when the evidence is insufficient. Fed. R. Crim. P. 29.

judgment of conviction. (1806) **1.** The written record of a criminal judgment, consisting of the plea, the verdict or findings, the adjudication, and the sentence. Fed. R. Crim. P. 32(d)(1). **2.** A sentence in a criminal case.

judgment of discontinuance. A judgment dismissing a plaintiff's action based on interruption in the proceedings occasioned by the plaintiff's failure to continue the suit at the appointed time or times.

judgment of dismissal. (1809) A final determination of a case (against the plaintiff in a civil action or the government in a criminal action) without a trial on its merits.

judgment of nolle prosequi (**nahl**-ee **prahs**-ə-kwɪ). (1869) A judgment entered against a plaintiff who, after appearance but before judgment on the merits, has decided to abandon prosecution of the lawsuit.

judgment on the merits. (18c) A judgment based on the evidence rather than on technical or procedural grounds.

judgment on the pleadings. (18c) A judgment based solely on the allegations and information contained in the pleadings, and not on any outside matters. Fed. R. Civ. P. 12(c).

judgment on the verdict. (17c) A judgment for the party receiving a favorable jury verdict.

judgment quasi in rem (**kway**-sɪ [*or* -zɪ] in **rem**). (1905) A judgment based on the court's jurisdiction over the defendant's interest in property rather than on its jurisdiction over the defendant or the property.

judgment quod recuperet (kwod ri-**kyoo**-pər-it). Judgment that the plaintiff recover.

money judgment. (1869) A judgment for damages subject to immediate execution, as distinguished from equitable or injunctive relief.

nunc pro tunc judgment (**nəngk** proh **təngk**). (1828) A procedural device by which the record of a judgment is amended to accord with what the judge actually said and did, so that the record will be accurate.

personal judgment. (1829) **1.** A judgment that imposes personal liability on a defendant and that may therefore be satisfied out of any of the defendant's property within judicial reach. **2.** A judgment resulting from an action in which a court has personal jurisdiction over the parties. **3.** A judgment against a person as distinguished from a judgment against a thing, right, or status.

take-nothing judgment. (1938) A judgment for the defendant providing that the plaintiff recover nothing in damages or other relief.

valid judgment. **1.** A judgment that will be recognized by common-law states as long as it is in force in the state where the judgment was rendered. **2.** A judicial act rendered by a court having jurisdiction over the parties and over the subject matter in a proceeding in which the parties have had a reasonable opportunity to be heard.

voidable judgment. (17c) A judgment that, although seemingly valid, is defective in some material way; esp., a judgment that, although rendered by a court having jurisdiction, is irregular or erroneous.

void judgment. (18c) A judgment that has no legal force or effect, the invalidity of which may be asserted by any party whose rights are affected at any time and any place, whether directly or collaterally. • From its inception, a void judgment continues to be absolutely null. It is incapable of being confirmed, ratified, or enforced in any manner or to any degree. One source of a void judgment is the lack of subject-matter jurisdiction.

judgment creditor. (18c) A person having a legal right to enforce execution of a judgment for a specific sum of money.

judgment debtor. (18c) A person against whom a money judgment has been entered but not yet satisfied.

judgment-proof, *adj.* (18c) (Of an actual or potential judgment debtor) unable to satisfy a judgment for money damages because the person has no property, does not own enough property within the court's jurisdiction to satisfy the judgment, or claims the benefit of statutorily exempt property.

judicator (**joo**-di-kay-tər), *n.* (18c) A person authorized to act or serve as a judge.

judicatory (**joo**-di-kə-tor-ee), *adj.* (17c) **1.** Of or relating to judgment. **2.** Allowing a judgment to be made; giving a decisive indication.

judicatory (**joo**-di-kə-tor-ee), *n.* (16c) **1.** A court; any tribunal with judicial authority <a church judicatory>. **2.** The administration of justice <working toward a more efficient judicatory>.

judicature (**joo**-di-kə-chər). (16c) **1.** The action of judging or of administering justice through duly constituted courts. **2.** JUDICIARY (3). **3.** A judge's office, function, or authority.

judicial (joo-**dish**-əl), *adj.* (14c) **1.** Of, relating to, or by the court or a judge <judicial duty> <judicial demeanor>. **2.** In court <the witness's judicial confession>. **3.** Legal <the Attorney General took no judicial action>. **4.** Of or relating to a judgment <an award of judicial interest at the legal rate>.

judicial activism, *n.* (1949) A philosophy of judicial decision-making whereby judges allow their personal views about public policy, among other factors, to guide their decisions, usu. with the suggestion that adherents of this philosophy tend to find constitutional violations and are willing to ignore precedent. — **judicial activist,** *n.*

judicial activity report. A regular report, usu. monthly or quarterly, on caseload and caseflow within a given court or court system.

judicial administration. The process of doing justice through a system of courts.

Judicial Article. (1881) Article III of the U.S. Constitution, which creates the Supreme Court, vests in Congress the right to create inferior courts, provides for life tenure for federal judges, and specifies the powers and jurisdiction of the federal courts.

judicial branch. (18c) The branch of government consisting of the courts, whose function is to ensure justice by interpreting, applying, and generally administering the laws; judiciary.

judicial bypass. (1977) A procedure permitting a person to obtain a court's approval for an act that would ordinarily require the approval of someone else, such as a law that requires a minor to notify a parent before obtaining an abortion but allows an appropriately qualified minor to obtain a court order permitting the abortion without parental notice.

judicial-bypass provision. *Family law.* **1.** A statutory provision that allows a court to assume a parental role when the parent or guardian cannot or will not act on behalf of a minor or an incompetent. **2.** A statutory provision that allows a minor to circumvent the necessity of obtaining parental consent by obtaining judicial consent.

judicial cognizance. Judicial notice.

Judicial Conference of the United States. The policy-making body of the federal judiciary, responsible for surveying the business of the federal courts, making recommendations to Congress on matters affecting the judiciary, and supervising the work of the Administrative Office of the United States Courts.

judicial council. (1925) A regularly assembled group of judges whose mission is to increase the efficiency and effectiveness of the courts on which they sit; esp., a semiannual assembly of a federal circuit's judges called by the circuit's chief judge. 28 USCA § 332.

judicial document. A court-filed paper that is subject to the right of public access because it is or has been both relevant to the judicial function and useful in the judicial process. See *Lugosch v. Pyramid Co. of Onandaga*, 435 F.3d 110, 119 (2d Cir. 2006).

judicial economy. (1942) Efficiency in the operation of the courts and the judicial system; esp., the efficient management of litigation so as to minimize duplication of effort and to avoid wasting the judiciary's time and resources. • A court can enter a variety of orders to promote judicial economy. For instance, a court may consolidate two cases for trial to save the court and the parties from having two trials, or it may order a separate trial on certain issues if doing so would provide the opportunity to avoid a later trial that would be more complex and time-consuming.

judicial-economy exception. (1981) An exemption from the final-judgment rule, by which a party may seek immediate appellate review of a nonfinal order if doing so might establish a final or nearly final disposition of the entire suit.

judicialize, *vb.* **1.** To pattern (procedures, etc.) after a court of law. **2.** To bring (something not traditionally within the judicial system) into the judicial system. — **judicialization,** *n.*

judicial notice. (17c) A court's acceptance, for purposes of convenience and without requiring a party's proof, of a well-known and indisputable fact; the court's power to accept such a fact. Fed R. Evid. 201.

Judicial Panel on Multidistrict Litigation. A panel of federal judges responsible for transferring civil actions having common questions of fact from one district court to another to consolidate pretrial proceedings. • The panel was created in 1968. The Chief Justice appoints its members. 28 USCA § 1407. — Abbr. JPML.

judicial power. (16c) **1.** The authority vested in courts and judges to hear and decide cases and to make binding judgments on them; the power to construe and apply the law when controversies arise over what has been done or not done under it. **2.** A power conferred on a public officer involving the exercise of judgment and discretion in deciding questions of right in specific cases affecting personal and proprietary interests.

judicial question. (18c) A question that is proper for determination by the courts, as opposed to a moot question or one properly decided by the executive or legislative branch. Cf. POLITICAL QUESTION.

judicial restraint. (18c) **1.** A restraint imposed by a court, as by a restraining order, injunction, or judgment. **2.** The principle that, when a court can resolve a case based on a particular issue, it should do so, without reaching unnecessary issues. **3.** A philosophy of judicial decision-making whereby judges avoid indulging their personal beliefs about the public good and instead try merely to interpret the law as legislated and according to precedent. Cf. JUDICIAL ACTIVISM.

judicial review. (1851) **1.** A court's power to review the actions of other branches or levels of government; esp., the courts' power to invalidate legislative and executive actions as being unconstitutional. **2.** The constitutional doctrine providing for this power. **3.** A court's review of a lower court's or an administrative body's factual or legal findings.

de novo judicial review. (1955) A court's nondeferential review of an administrative decision, usu. through a review of the administrative record plus any additional evidence the parties present.

plenary review. Appellate review by all the members of a court rather than a panel.

judiciary (joo-**dish**-ee-er-ee *or* joo-**dish**-ə-ree), *n.* (18c) **1.** The branch of government responsible for interpreting the laws and administering justice. **2.** A system of courts. **3.** A body of judges. — **judiciary,** *adj.*

judicious (joo-**dish**-əs), *adj.* (16c) Well-considered; discreet; wisely circumspect. — **judiciousness,** *n.*

jump bail, *vb.* (1889) (Of an accused) to fail to appear in court at the appointed time after promising to appear and posting a bail bond.

jump citation. Pinpoint citation.

junior, *adj.* (13c) Lower in rank or standing; subordinate.

jural (**joor**-əl), *adj.* (17c) **1.** Of or relating to law or jurisprudence; legal. **2.** Of or relating to rights and obligations.

jural agent. (2004) An official — someone who has the appropriate authoritative status in society to enforce or affect the society's legal system — who engages in a jural act. • Common examples include judges, legislators, and police officers acting in their official capacities.

jurat (**joor**-at). (18c) [fr. Latin *jurare* "to swear"] A certification added to an affidavit or deposition stating when and before what authority the affidavit or deposition was made. • A jurat typically says "Subscribed and sworn to before me this _____ day of [month], [year]," and the officer (usu. a notary public) thereby certifies three things: (1) that the person signing the document did so in the officer's presence, (2) that the signer appeared before the officer on the date indicated, and (3) that the officer administered an oath or affirmation to the signer, who swore to or affirmed the contents of the document.

witness jurat. A subscribing witness's certificate acknowledging the act of witnessing. • Even though this certificate is technically an acknowledgment and not a true jurat, the phrase *witness jurat* is commonly used.

juratorial (joor-ə-**toh**-ri-əl) *adj.* Of or pertaining to a jury.

juratory (**joor**-ə-tor-ee), *adj.* Of, relating to, or containing an oath.

jure (**joor**-ee), *adv.* [Latin] **1.** By right; in right. **2.** By law.

juridical (juu-**rid**-i-kəl), *adj.* (16c) **1.** Of or relating to judicial proceedings or to the administration of justice. **2.** Of or relating to law; legal. Cf. NONJURIDICAL.

juridical link. (1947) A legal relationship between members of a group, such as those in a potential class action, sufficient to make a single suit more efficient or effective than multiple suits.

jurimetrics (joor-ə-**me**-triks), *n.* (1949) The use of scientific or empirical methods, including measurement, in the study or analysis of legal matters. — **jurimetrician** (joor-ə-me-**trish**-ən), **jurimetricist** (joor-ə-**me**-trə-sist), *n.*

juris (**joor**-is), *adj.* [Latin] **1.** Of law. **2.** Of right.

juriscenter (**joor**-ə-sen-tər *or* joor-ə-**sen**-tər), *n. Conflict of laws.* The jurisdiction that is most appropriately considered a couple's domestic center of gravity for matrimonial purposes.

jurisdiction, *n.* (14c) **1.** A government's general power to exercise authority over all persons and things within its territory; esp., a state's power to create interests that will be recognized under common-law principles as valid in other states. **2.** A court's power to decide a case or issue a decree. **3.** A geographic area within which political or judicial authority may be exercised. **4.** A political or judicial subdivision within such an area. — **jurisdictional,** *adj.*

agency jurisdiction. The regulatory or adjudicative power of a government administrative agency over a subject matter or matters.

ancillary jurisdiction. (1835) A court's jurisdiction to adjudicate claims and proceedings related to a claim that is properly before the court. • For example, if a plaintiff brings a lawsuit in federal court based on a federal question (such as a claim under Title VII), the defendant may assert a counterclaim over which the court would not otherwise have jurisdiction (such as a state-law claim of stealing company property). The concept of ancillary jurisdiction has now been codified, along with the concept of pendent jurisdiction, in the supplemental-jurisdiction statute. 28 USCA § 1367.

anomalous jurisdiction. (1864) **1.** Jurisdiction that is not granted to a court by statute, but that is inherent in the court's authority to govern lawyers and other officers of the court, such as the power to issue a preindictment order suppressing illegally seized property. **2.** An appellate court's provisional jurisdiction to review the denial of a motion to intervene in a lower-court case, so that if the court finds that the denial was correct, then its jurisdiction disappears — and it must dismiss the appeal for want of jurisdiction — because an order denying a motion to intervene is not a final, appealable order.

appellate jurisdiction. (18c) The power of a court to review and revise a lower court's decision. • For example, U.S. Const. art. III, § 2 vests appellate jurisdiction in the Supreme Court, while 28 USCA §§ 1291–1295 grant appellate jurisdiction to lower federal courts of appeals. Cf. *original jurisdiction.*

arising-in jurisdiction. A bankruptcy court's jurisdiction over issues relating to the administration of the bankruptcy estate, and matters that occur only in a bankruptcy case. 28 USCA §§ 157, 1334.

assistant jurisdiction. The incidental aid provided by an equity court to a court of law when justice requires both legal and equitable processes and remedies.

concurrent jurisdiction. (17c) **1.** Jurisdiction that might be exercised simultaneously by more than one court over the same subject matter and within the same territory, a litigant having the right to choose the court in which to file the action. **2.** Jurisdiction shared by two or more states, esp. over the physical boundaries (such as rivers or other bodies of water) between them. Cf. *exclusive jurisdiction.*

consent jurisdiction. (1855) Jurisdiction that parties have agreed to, either by accord, by contract, or by general appearance. • Parties may not, by agreement, confer subject-matter jurisdiction on a federal court that would not otherwise have it.

continuing jurisdiction. (1855) A court's power to retain jurisdiction over a matter after entering a judgment, allowing the court to modify its previous rulings or orders.

criminal jurisdiction. (16c) A court's power to hear criminal cases.

default jurisdiction. *Family law.* In a child-custody matter, jurisdiction conferred when it is in the best interests of the child and either (1) there is no other basis for jurisdiction under the Uniform Child Custody Jurisdiction Act or the Parental Kidnapping Prevention Act, or (2) when another state has declined jurisdiction in favor of default jurisdiction.

delinquency jurisdiction. The power of the court to hear matters regarding juvenile acts that, if committed by an adult, would be criminal.

diversity jurisdiction. (1927) A federal court's exercise of authority over a case involving parties who are citizens of different states and an amount in controversy greater than a statutory minimum. 28 USCA § 1332.

emergency jurisdiction. *Family law.* A court's ability to take jurisdiction of a child who is physically present in the state when that child has been abandoned or when necessary to protect the child from abuse. • Section 3(a)(3) of the Uniform Child Custody Jurisdiction Act allows for emergency jurisdiction. It is usu. temporary, lasting only as long as is necessary to protect the child.

equity jurisdiction. (18c) In a common-law judicial system, the power to hear certain civil actions according to the procedure of the court of chancery, and to resolve them according to equitable rules.

exclusive jurisdiction. (18c) A court's power to adjudicate an action or class of actions to the exclusion of all other courts. Cf. *concurrent jurisdiction.*

extraterritorial jurisdiction. (1818) A court's ability to exercise power beyond its territorial limits.

federal jurisdiction. (1800) **1.** The exercise of federal-court authority. **2.** The area of study dealing with the jurisdiction of federal courts.

federal-juvenile-delinquency jurisdiction. A federal court's power to hear a case in which a person under the age of 18 violates federal law. • In such a case, the federal court derives its jurisdictional power from 18 USCA §§ 5031 et seq. The Act severely limits the scope of federal-juvenile-delinquency jurisdiction because Congress recognizes that juvenile delinquency is essentially a state issue. The acts that typically invoke federal jurisdiction are (1) acts committed on federal lands (military bases, national parks, Indian reservations), and (2) acts that violate federal drug laws or other federal criminal statutes.

federal-question jurisdiction. (1941) The exercise of federal-court power over claims arising under the U.S. Constitution, an act of Congress, or a treaty. 28 USCA § 1331.

foreign jurisdiction. (16c) **1.** The powers of a court of a sister state or foreign country. **2.** Extraterritorial process, such as long-arm service of process.

general jurisdiction. (16c) **1.** A court's authority to hear a wide range of cases, civil or criminal, that arise within its geographic area. **2.** A court's authority to hear all claims against a defendant, at the place of the defendant's domicile or the place of service, without any showing that a connection exists between the claims and the forum state.

general personal jurisdiction. Jurisdiction arising when a person's continuous and systematic contacts with a forum state enable the forum state's courts to adjudicate a claim against the person, even when the claim is not related to the person's contacts with the forum state.

home-state jurisdiction. *Family law.* In interstate child-custody disputes governed by the Uniform Child Custody Jurisdiction and Enforcement Act, jurisdiction based on the child's having been a resident of the state for at least six consecutive months immediately before the commencement of the suit.

in rem jurisdiction (in **rem**). (1930) A court's power to adjudicate the rights to a given piece of property, including the power to seize and hold it.

international jurisdiction. A court's power to hear and determine matters between different countries or persons of different countries.

legislative jurisdiction. A legislature's general sphere of authority to enact laws and conduct all business related to that authority, such as holding hearings.

limited jurisdiction. (16c) Jurisdiction that is confined to a particular type of case or that may be exercised only under statutory limits and prescriptions.

long-arm jurisdiction. Jurisdiction over a nonresident defendant who has had some contact with the jurisdiction in which the petition is filed.

original jurisdiction. (17c) A court's power to hear and decide a matter before any other court can review the matter.

pendent jurisdiction (**pen**-dənt). (1942) A court's jurisdiction to hear and determine a claim over which it would not otherwise have jurisdiction, because the claim arises from the same transaction or occurrence as another claim that is properly before the court. • For example, if a plaintiff brings suit in federal court claiming that the defendant, in one transaction, violated both a federal and a state law, the federal court has jurisdiction over the federal claim (under federal-question jurisdiction) and also has jurisdiction over the state claim that is pendent to the federal claim. Pendent jurisdiction has now been codified as supplemental jurisdiction. 28 USCA § 1367.

pendent-party jurisdiction. (1973) A court's jurisdiction to adjudicate a claim against a party who is not otherwise subject to the court's jurisdiction, because the claim by or against that party arises from the same transaction or occurrence as another claim that is properly before the court. • Pendent-party jurisdiction has been a hotly debated subject, and was severely limited by the U.S. Supreme Court in *Finley v. United States*, 490 U.S. 545, 109 S.Ct. 2003 (1990). The concept is now codified in the supplemental-jurisdiction statute, and it applies to federal-question cases but not to diversity-jurisdiction cases. 28 USCA § 1367. Neither pendent-party jurisdiction nor supplemental jurisdiction may be used to circumvent the complete-diversity requirement in cases founded on diversity jurisdiction.

personal jurisdiction. A court's power to bring a person into its adjudicative process; jurisdiction over a defendant's personal rights, rather than merely over property interests.

plenary jurisdiction (**plee**-nə-ree *or* **plen**-ə-ree). A court's full and absolute power over the subject matter and the parties in a case.

primary jurisdiction. The power of an agency to decide an issue in the first instance when a court, having concurrent jurisdiction with the agency, determines that it would be more pragmatic for the agency to handle the case initially.

probate jurisdiction. Jurisdiction over matters relating to wills, settlement of decedents' estates, and (in some states) guardianship and the adoption of minors.

quasi-in-rem jurisdiction (**kway**-sɪ in **rem** *or* **kway**-zɪ). (1918) Jurisdiction over a person but based on that person's interest in property located within the court's territory.

significant-connection jurisdiction. *Family law.* In a child-custody matter, jurisdiction based on (1) the best interests of the child, (2) at least one parent's (or litigant's) significant connection to the state, and (3) the presence in the state of substantial evidence about the child's present or future care, protection, training, and personal relationships.

spatial jurisdiction. Jurisdiction based on the physical territory that an entity's authority covers.

specific jurisdiction. (1828) Jurisdiction that stems from the defendant's having certain minimum contacts with the forum state so that the court may hear a case whose issues arise from those minimum contacts. Cf. *general jurisdiction.*

specific personal jurisdiction. Jurisdiction based on a person's minimum contacts with the forum state when the claim arises out of or is related to those contacts.

state jurisdiction. **1.** The exercise of state-court authority. **2.** A court's power to hear all matters, both civil and criminal, arising within its territorial boundaries.

status-offense jurisdiction. The power of the court to hear matters regarding noncriminal conduct committed by a juvenile.

subject-matter jurisdiction. (1936) Jurisdiction over the nature of the case and the type of relief sought; the extent to which a court can rule on the conduct of persons or the status of things. Cf. *personal jurisdiction.*

summary jurisdiction. (18c) **1.** A court's jurisdiction in a summary proceeding. **2.** The court's authority to issue a judgment or order (such as a finding of contempt) without the necessity of a trial or other process.

supplemental jurisdiction. (1836) Jurisdiction over a claim that is part of the same case or controversy as another claim over which the court has original jurisdiction. • Since 1990, federal district courts have had supplemental jurisdiction which includes jurisdiction over both ancillary and pendent claims. 28 USCA § 1367.

temporal jurisdiction. Jurisdiction based on the court's having authority to adjudicate a matter when the underlying event occurred.

territorial jurisdiction. **1.** Jurisdiction over cases arising in or involving persons residing within a defined territory. **2.** Territory over which a government, one of its courts, or one of its subdivisions has jurisdiction.

transient jurisdiction (**tran**-shənt). Personal jurisdiction over a defendant who is served with process while in the forum state only temporarily (such as during travel).

voluntary jurisdiction. **1.** Jurisdiction exercised over unopposed matters. **2.** *Eccles. law.* Jurisdiction that does not require a judicial proceeding, as with granting a license or installing a nominee to a benefice.

jurisdictional limits. (1800) The geographic boundaries or the constitutional or statutory limits within which a court's authority may be exercised.

jurisdiction clause. (1861) **1.** At law, a statement in a pleading that sets forth the court's jurisdiction to act in the case. **2.** *Equity practice.* The part of the bill intended to show that the court has jurisdiction, usu. by an averment that adequate relief is unavailable outside equitable channels.

Juris Doctor (**joor**-is **dok**-tər). (1895) Doctor of law — the law degree most commonly conferred by an American law school. — Abbr. J.D.

jurisprude (**joor**-is-prood), *n.* (1937) **1.** A person who makes a pretentious display of legal knowledge or who is overzealous about the importance of legal doctrine. **2.** Jurisprudent.

jurisprudence (joor-is-**prood**-ənts), *n.* (17c) **1.** Originally (in the 18th century), the study of the first principles of the law of nature, the civil law, and the law of nations. **2.** More modernly, the study of the general or fundamental elements of a particular legal system, as opposed to its practical and concrete details. **3.** The study of legal systems in general. **4.** Judicial precedents considered collectively. **5.** In German literature, the whole of legal knowledge. **6.** A system, body, or division of law. **7.** Caselaw.

analytical jurisprudence. (1876) A method of legal study that concentrates on the logical structure of law, the meanings and uses of its concepts, and the formal terms and the modes of its operation.

equity jurisprudence. (1826) **1.** The legal science treating the rules, principles, and maxims that govern the decisions of a court of equity. **2.** The cases and controversies that are considered proper subjects of equity. **3.** The nature and form of the remedies that equity grants.

ethical jurisprudence. (1826) The branch of legal philosophy concerned with the law from the viewpoint of its ethical significance and adequacy.

• This area of study brings together moral and legal philosophy.

expository jurisprudence. (18c) The scholarly exposition of the contents of an actual legal system as it now exists or once existed.

feminist jurisprudence. (1978) A branch of jurisprudence that examines the relationship between women and law, including the history of legal and social biases against women, the elimination of those biases in modern law, and the enhancement of women's legal rights and recognition in society.

general jurisprudence. (18c) **1.** The scholarly study of the fundamental elements of a given legal system. **2.** The scholarly study of the law, legal theory, and legal systems generally.

historical jurisprudence. (1823) The branch of legal philosophy concerned with the history of the first principles and conceptions of a legal system, dealing with (1) the general principles governing the origin and development of law, and (2) the origin and development of the legal system's first principles.

particular jurisprudence. (18c) The scholarly study of the legal system within a particular jurisdiction, the focus being on the fundamental assumptions of that system only.

positivist jurisprudence. (1931) A theory that denies validity to any law that is not derived from or sanctioned by a sovereign or some other determinate source.

sociological jurisprudence. (1907) A philosophical approach to law stressing the actual social effects of legal institutions, doctrines, and practices. • This influential approach was started by Roscoe Pound in 1906 and became a precursor to legal realism.

jurisprudent, *n.* (17c) A person learned in the law; a specialist in jurisprudence.— **jurisprudential** (joor-is-proo-**den**-shəl), *adj.*

jurist. (15c) **1.** A person who has thorough knowledge of the law; esp., a judge or an eminent legal scholar. **2.** Jurisprudent. — **juristic,** *adj.* (1831).

juror (**joor**-ər *also* **joor**-or). (14c) A person serving on a jury panel.

grand juror. A person serving on a grand jury.

petit juror (**pet**-ee). A trial juror, as opposed to a grand juror.

presiding juror. The juror who chairs the jury during deliberations and speaks for the jury in court by announcing the verdict.

stealth juror. A juror, esp. one in a high-profile case, who deliberately fails to disclose a relevant bias in order to qualify as a juror and bases a decision on that bias rather than on the facts and law.

jury, *n.* (15c) A group of persons selected according to law and given the power to decide questions of fact and return a verdict in the case submitted to them.

advisory jury. (1892) A jury empaneled to hear a case when the parties have no right to a jury trial. See Fed. R. Civ. P. 39(c). • The judge may accept or reject the advisory jury's verdict.

blue-ribbon jury. (1940) A jury consisting of jurors who are selected for their special qualities, such as advanced education or special training, sometimes used in a complex civil case (usu. by stipulation of the parties) and sometimes also for a grand jury (esp. one investigating governmental corruption). • A blue-ribbon jury is not allowed in criminal trials because it would violate the defendant's right to trial by a jury of peers. An even more elite group of jurors, involving specialists in a technical field, is called a *blue-blue-ribbon jury.*

coroner's jury. (17c) A jury summoned by a coroner to investigate the cause of death.

death-qualified jury. *Criminal law.* A jury that is fit to decide a case involving the death penalty because the jurors have no absolute ideological bias against capital punishment.

hung jury. (1854) A jury that cannot reach a verdict by the required voting margin.

impartial jury. (17c) A jury that has no opinion about the case at the start of the trial and that bases its verdict on competent legal evidence.

inquest jury. (1873) A jury summoned from a particular district to appear before a sheriff, coroner, or other ministerial officer and inquire about the facts concerning a death.

mixed jury. (1878) A jury composed of both men and women or persons of different races.

petit jury (**pet**-ee). (15c) A jury (usu. consisting of 6 or 12 persons) summoned and empaneled in the trial of a specific case. Cf. GRAND JURY.

rogue jury. A jury that ignores the law and evidence in reaching a capricious verdict. • Unlike jury nullification, a rogue jury's verdict is not based on a desire to achieve a just, fair, or moral outcome.

shadow jury. (1974) A group of mock jurors paid to observe a trial and report their reactions to a jury consultant hired by one of the litigants. • The shadow jurors, who are matched as closely as possible to the real jurors, provide counsel with information about the jury's likely reactions to the trial.

special jury. (17c) A jury chosen from a panel that is drawn specifically for that case. • Such a jury is usu. empaneled at a party's request in an unusually important or complicated case.

struck jury. (18c) A jury selected by allowing the parties to alternate in striking from a list any person whom a given party does not wish to have on the jury, until the number is reduced to the appropriate number (traditionally 12).

jury box. The enclosed part of a courtroom where the jury sits. — Also spelled *jury-box.*

jury charge. (1883) **1.** Jury instruction. **2.** A set of jury instructions.

jury duty. (1829) **1.** The obligation to serve on a jury. **2.** Actual service on a jury.

jury-fixing. (1887) The act or an instance of illegally procuring the cooperation of one or more jurors who actually influence the outcome of the trial. — **jury-fixer,** *n.*

jury instruction. (*usu. pl.*) (1943) A direction or guideline that a judge gives a jury concerning the law of the case.

additional instruction. (1821) A jury charge, beyond the original instructions, that is usu. given in response to the jury's question about the evidence or some point of law.

affirmative converse instruction. (1966) An instruction presenting a hypothetical that, if true, commands a verdict in favor of the defendant. • An affirmative converse instruction usu. begins with language such as "your verdict must be for the defendant if you believe ...."

affirmative instruction. (1835) An instruction that removes an issue from the jury's consideration, such as an instruction that whatever the evidence, the defendant cannot be convicted under the indictment count to which the charge is directed.

argumentative instruction. (1888) An instruction that assumes facts not in evidence, that singles out or unduly emphasizes a particular issue, theory, or defense, or that otherwise invades the jury's province regarding the weight, probative value, or sufficiency of the evidence.

cautionary instruction. (1881) **1.** A judge's instruction to the jurors to disregard certain evidence or consider it for specific purposes only. **2.** A judge's instruction for the jury not to be influenced by outside factors and not to talk to anyone about the case while the trial is in progress.

curative instruction. (1890) A judge's instruction that is intended to correct an erroneous instruction.

disparaging instruction. A jury charge that discredits or defames a party to a lawsuit.

formula instruction. (1927) A jury charge derived from a standardized statement of the law on which the jury must base its verdict.

general instruction. Any jury instruction that does not present a question or issue to be answered.

mandatory instruction. (1895) An instruction requiring a jury to find for one party and against the other if the jury determines that, based on a preponderance of the evidence, a given set of facts exists.

model jury instruction. (1964) A form jury charge usu. approved by a state bar association or similar group regarding matters arising in a typical case.

ostrich instruction. (1966) *Criminal procedure. Slang.* An instruction stating that a defendant who deliberately avoided acquiring actual knowledge can be found to have acted knowingly.

peremptory instruction. (1829) A court's explicit direction that a jury must obey, such as an instruction to return a verdict for a particular party.

single-juror instruction. (1980) An instruction stating that if any juror is not reasonably satisfied with the plaintiff's evidence, then the jury cannot render a verdict for the plaintiff.

special instruction. (1807) An instruction on some particular point or question involved in the case, usu. in response to counsel's request for such an instruction.

standard instruction. (1914) A jury instruction that has been regularly used in a given jurisdiction.

willful-blindness instruction. An instruction that an otherwise culpable defendant may be held accountable for a crime if the defendant deliberately avoided finding out about the crime.

jury nullification. (1982) A jury's knowing and deliberate rejection of the evidence or refusal to apply the law either because the jury wants to send a message about some social issue that is larger than the case itself or because the result dictated by law is contrary to the jury's sense of justice, morality, or fairness.

jury-packing. (1887) The act or an instance of contriving to have a jury composed of persons who are predisposed toward one side or the other.

jury pardon. (1974) A rule that permits a jury to convict a defendant of a lesser offense than the offense charged if sufficient evidence exists to convict the defendant of either offense.

jury process. (18c) **1.** The procedure by which jurors are summoned and their attendance is enforced. **2.** The papers served on or mailed to potential jurors to compel their attendance.

jury question. (18c) **1.** An issue of fact that a jury decides. **2.** A special question that a court may ask a jury that will deliver a special verdict.

jury wheel. (1873) A physical device or electronic system used for storing and randomly selecting names of potential jurors.

jus (jəs *also* joos *or* yoos), *n.* [Latin "law, right"] **1.** Law in the abstract. **2.** A system of law. **3.** A legal right, power, or principle. — Abbr. J. — Also spelled *ius.* Pl. ***jura*** (**joor**-ə *also* **yoor**-ə).

jus necessitatis (jəs nə-ses-i-**tay**-tis), *n.* [Latin] A person's right to do what is required for which no threat of legal punishment is a dissuasion. • This idea implicates the proverb that necessity knows no law (*necessitas non habet legem*), so that an act that would be objectively understood as necessary is not wrongful even if done with full and deliberate intention.

jus sanguinis (jəs **sang**-gwə-nis), *n.* [Latin "right of blood"] The rule that a child's citizenship is determined by the parents' citizenship. • Most nations follow this rule. Cf. JUS SOLI.

jus soli (jəs **soh**-lɪ), *n.* [Latin "right of the soil"] The rule that a child's citizenship is determined by place of birth. • This is the U.S. rule, as affirmed by the 14th Amendment to the Constitution. Cf. JUS SANGUINIS.

just, *adj.* (14c) Legally right; lawful; equitable.

just deserts (di-**zərts**). (16c) What one really deserves; esp., the punishment that a person deserves for having committed a crime.

jus tertii (jəs **tər**-shee-ɪ), *n.* [Latin] **1.** The right of a third party. **2.** The doctrine that, particularly in constitutional law, courts do not decide what they do not need to decide.

justice. (17c) **1.** The fair and proper administration of laws.

commutative justice (kə-**myoo**-tə-tiv *or* **kom**-yə-tay-tiv). (1856) Justice concerned with the relations between persons and esp. with fairness in the exchange of goods and the fulfillment of contractual obligations.

distributive justice. (16c) Justice owed by a community to its members, including the fair allocation of common advantages and sharing of common burdens.

personal justice. (16c) Justice between parties to a dispute, regardless of any larger principles that might be involved.

popular justice. (17c) Demotic justice, which is usu. considered less than fully fair and proper even though it satisfies prevailing public opinion in a particular case.

positive justice. (17c) Justice as it is conceived, recognized, and incompletely expressed by the civil law or some other form of human law.

social justice. (1902) **1.** Justice that conforms to a moral principle, such as that all people are equal. **2.** One or more equitable resolutions sought on behalf of individuals and communities who are disenfranchised, underrepresented, or otherwise excluded from meaningful participation in legal, economic, cultural, and social structures, with the ultimate goal of removing barriers to participation and effecting social change.

substantial justice. (17c) Justice fairly administered according to rules of substantive law, regardless of any procedural errors not affecting the litigant's substantive rights; a fair trial on the merits.

2. A judge, esp. of an appellate court or a court of last resort. — Abbr. J. (and, in plural, JJ.

associate justice. (18c) An appellate-court justice other than the chief justice.

chief justice. (15c) The presiding justice of an appellate court, usu. the highest appellate court in a jurisdiction and esp. the U.S. Supreme Court. — Abbr. C.J.

circuit justice. (18c) **1.** A justice who sits on a circuit court. **2.** A U.S. Supreme Court justice who has jurisdiction over one or more of the federal circuits, with power to issue injunctions, grant bail, or stay execution in those circuits.

justice of the peace. (15c) A local judicial officer having jurisdiction over minor criminal offenses and minor civil disputes, and authority to perform routine civil functions (such as administering oaths and performing marriage ceremonies). — Abbr. J.P.

justiciability (jə-stish-ee-ə-**bil**-ə-tee *or* jə-stish-ə-**bil**-ə-tee), *n.* (15c) The quality or state of being appropriate or suitable for adjudication by a court. — **justiciable** (jə-**stish**-ee-ə-bəl *or* jəs-**tish**-ə-bəl), *adj.*

justification, *n.* (14c) **1.** A lawful or sufficient reason for one's acts or omissions; any fact that prevents an act from being wrongful. **2.** A showing, in court, of a sufficient reason why a defendant acted in a way that, in the absence of the reason, would constitute the offense with which the defendant is charged. Model Penal Code § 3.02. **3.** A surety's proof of having enough money or credit to provide security for the party for whom it is required. — **justify,** *vb.* — **justificatory** (jəs-**ti**-fi-kə-tor-ee), *adj.*

defensive-force justification. A justification defense available when an aggressor has threatened harm to the particular interest that is the subject of the defense — usu. to the actor (self-defense), to other persons (defense of others), or to property (defense of property).

imperfect justification. (1853) A reason or cause that is insufficient to completely justify a defendant's behavior but that can be used to mitigate criminal punishment.

judicial-authority justification. A justification defense available when an actor has engaged in conduct constituting an offense in order to comply with a court order.

public-authority justification. A justification defense available when an actor has been specifically authorized to engage in the conduct constituting an offense in order to protect or further a public interest.

justification defense. *Criminal & tort law.* A defense that arises when the defendant has acted in a way that the law does not seek to prevent. • Traditionally, the following defenses were justifications: consent, self-defense, defense of others, defense of property, necessity (choice of evils), the use of force to make an arrest, and the use of force by public authority. — Sometimes shortened to *justification.*

juvenile (**joo**-və-nəl *or* -nɪl), *n.* (18c) A person who has not reached the age (usu. 18) at which one should be treated as an adult by the criminal-justice system; MINOR. — **juvenile,** *adj.* — **juvenility** (joo-və-**nil**-ə-tee), *n.*

juvenile delinquency. (1816) Antisocial behavior by a minor; esp., behavior that would be criminally punishable if the actor were an adult, but instead is usu. punished by special laws pertaining only to minors.

juvenile-justice system. The collective institutions through which a youthful offender passes until any charges have been disposed of or the assessed punishment has been concluded. • The system comprises juvenile courts (judges and lawyers), law enforcement (police), and corrections (probation officers and social workers).

K

K. *abbr.* Contract.

k/a. *abbr.* Known as.

keeper. (15c) One who has the care, custody, or management of something and who usu. is legally responsible for it.

Keogh plan (**kee**-oh). (1952) A tax-deferred retirement program developed for the self-employed. • This plan is also known as an *H.R. 10 plan*, after the House of Representatives bill that established the plan.

***Ker–Frisbie* rule.** (1974) The principle that the government's power to try a criminal defendant is not impaired by the defendant's having been brought back illegally to the United States from a foreign country. *Ker v. Illinois*, 119 U.S. 436, 7 S.Ct. 225 (1886); *Frisbie v. Collins*, 342 U.S. 519, 72 S.Ct. 509 (1952).

KeyCite, *vb.* (1997) To determine the subsequent history of (a case, statute, etc.) by using the online citator of the same name to establish that the point being researched is still good law. — **KeyCiting,** *n.*

key money. (1948) **1.** Payment (as rent or security) required from a new tenant in exchange for a key to the leased property. **2.** Payment made (usu. secretly) by a prospective tenant to a landlord or current tenant to increase the chance of obtaining a lease in an area where there is a housing shortage. • Key money in the first sense is a legal transaction; key money in the second sense is usu. an illegal bribe that violates housing laws.

key-number system. (1909) A legal-research indexing system developed by West Publishing Company (now the West Group) to catalogue American caselaw with headnotes. • In this system, a number designates a point of law, allowing a researcher to find all reported cases addressing a particular point by referring to its number.

key person. An important officer or employee; a person primarily responsible for a business's success.

kickback, *n.* (1920) A return of a portion of a monetary sum received, esp. as a result of coercion or a secret agreement.

kickout clause. (1983) A contractual provision allowing a party to end or modify the contract if a specified event occurs.

kidnapping. (17c) **1.** At common law, the crime of forcibly abducting a person from his or her own country and sending the person to another. • This offense amounted to false imprisonment aggravated by moving the victim to another country. **2.** The crime of seizing and taking away a person by force or fraud. — **kidnap,** *vb.* (17c).

aggravated kidnapping. (1943) Kidnapping accompanied by some aggravating factor (such as a demand for ransom or injury of the victim).

child-kidnapping. (1978) The kidnapping of a minor, often without the element of force or fraud (as when someone walks off with another's baby).

kidnapping by cesarean. The kidnapping of a newborn baby by a person who causes the unlawful and forcible delivery of the baby by cesarean section without the mother's consent.

kidnapping for ransom. (1909) The offense of unlawfully seizing a person and then confining the person, usu. in a secret place, while attempting to extort ransom.

parental kidnapping. (1984) The kidnapping of a child by one parent in violation of the other parent's custody or visitation rights.

simple kidnapping. (1943) Kidnapping not accompanied by an aggravating factor.

kill, *vb.* (14c) To end life; to cause physical death. • The word is also used figuratively in putting an end to something <opponents were able to kill the proposed amendment>.

kin, *n.* (bef. 12c) **1.** One's relatives; family. **2.** A relative by blood, marriage, or adoption, though usu. by blood only; a kinsman or kinswoman.

kindred. 1. Kin. **2.** Kinship.

kinship. Relationship by blood, marriage, or adoption.

kiting. 1. Check-kiting. **2.** *Slang. Commercial law.* Raising money on credit, often by using accommodation paper.

***Klaxon* doctrine** (**klak**-sən). (1966) *Conflict of laws.* The principle that a federal court exercising diversity jurisdiction must apply the choice-of-law rules of the state where the court sits. • In *Klaxon Co. v. Stentor Elec. Mfg. Co.*, the Supreme Court extended the rule of *Erie v. Tompkins* to choice-of-law issues. 313 U.S. 487, 61 S.Ct. 1020 (1941).

kleptomania (klep-tə-**may**-nee-ə), *n.* (1830) A compulsive urge to steal, esp. without economic motive. — **kleptomaniac,** *n.* & *adj.*

knock-and-announce rule. (1969) *Criminal procedure.* The requirement that the police knock at the door and announce their identity, authority, and purpose before entering a residence to execute an arrest or search warrant.

knock-for-knock agreement. (1949) An arrangement between insurers whereby each will pay the claim of its insured without claiming against the other party's insurance.

knock off, *vb.* (1879) **1.** To make an unauthorized copy of (another's product), usu. for sale at a substantially lower price than the original. **2.** *Slang.* To murder. **3.** *Slang.* To rob or burglarize.

knockoff, *n.* (1966) *Intellectual property.* An unauthorized counterfeit and usu. inferior copy of another's product, esp. one protected by patent, trademark, trade dress, or copyright, usu. passed off at a substantially lower price than the original.

know all men by these presents. (16c) Take note. • This archaic form of address — a loan translation of the Latin *noverint universi per praesentes* — was traditionally used to begin certain legal documents such as bonds and powers of attorney, but in modern drafting style the phrase is generally considered deadwood.

know-how. (1838) The information, practical knowledge, techniques, and skill required to achieve some practical end, esp. in industry or technology.

knowing, *adj.* (14c) **1.** Having or showing awareness or understanding; well-informed. **2.** Deliberate; conscious. — **knowingly,** *adv.*

knowledge. (14c) **1.** An awareness or understanding of a fact or circumstance; a state of mind in which a person has no substantial doubt about the existence of a fact.

actual knowledge. (16c) **1.** Direct and clear knowledge, as distinguished from constructive knowledge <the employer, having witnessed the accident, had actual knowledge of the worker's injury>. **2.** Knowledge of information that would lead a reasonable person to inquire further <under the discovery rule, the limitations period begins to run once the plaintiff has actual knowledge of the injury>.

constructive knowledge. (18c) Knowledge that one using reasonable care or diligence should have, and therefore that is attributed by law to a given person <the court held that the partners had constructive knowledge of the

partnership agreement even though none of them had read it>.

imputed knowledge. (18c) Knowledge attributed to a given person, esp. because of the person's legal responsibility for another's conduct <the principal's imputed knowledge of its agent's dealings>.

personal knowledge. (17c) Knowledge gained through firsthand observation or experience, as distinguished from a belief based on what someone else has said. • Rule 602 of the Federal Rules of Evidence requires lay witnesses to have personal knowledge of the matters they testify about. An affidavit must also be based on personal knowledge, unless the affiant makes it clear that a statement relies on "information and belief."

reckless knowledge. (1911) A person's awareness that a prohibited circumstance may exist, regardless of which the person accepts the risk and goes on to act.

scientific knowledge. (17c) *Evidence.* Knowledge that is grounded on scientific methods that have been supported by adequate validation. • Four primary factors are used to determine whether evidence amounts to scientific knowledge: (1) whether it has been tested; (2) whether it has been subjected to peer review and publication; (3) the known or potential rate of error; and (4) the degree of acceptance within the scientific community.

superior knowledge. (17c) Knowledge greater than that of another person, esp. so as to adversely affect that person <in its fraud claim, the subcontractor alleged that the general contractor had superior knowledge of the equipment shortage>.

2. *Archaic.* Carnal knowledge.

known-loss doctrine. *Insurance.* A principle denying insurance coverage when the insured knows before the policy takes effect that a specific loss has already happened or is substantially certain to happen.

L

L. *abbr.* **1.** Law (5). **2.** Locus. **3.** Latin.

label, *n.* (17c) **1.** *Trademarks.* An informative display of written or graphic matter, such as a logo, title, or similar marking, affixed to goods or services to identify their source. **2.** Any writing (such as a codicil) attached to a larger writing. **3.** A narrow slip of paper or parchment attached to a deed or writ in order to hold a seal.

labeling. Under the Federal Food, Drug, and Cosmetic Act, any label or other written, printed, or graphic matter that is on a product or its container, or that accompanies the product. • To come within the Act, the labeling does not need to accompany the product. It may be sent before or after delivery of the product, as long as delivery of the product and the written material are part of the same distribution program.

labor, *n.* **1.** Work of any type, including mental exertion. • The term usu. refers to work for wages as opposed to profits. **2.** Workers considered as an economic unit or a political element.

labor agreement. Collective-bargaining agreement.

labor dispute. (1907) A controversy between an employer and its employees concerning the terms or conditions of employment, or concerning the association or representation of those who negotiate or seek to negotiate the terms or conditions of employment.

laborer. (14c) **1.** A person who makes a living by physical labor. **2.** Worker.

labor law. The field of law governing the relationship between employers and employees, esp. law governing the dealings of employers and the unions that represent employees.

labor–management relations. (1947) The broad spectrum of activities concerning the relationship between employers and employees, both union and nonunion.

Labor–Management Relations Act. A federal statute, enacted in 1947, that regulates certain union activities, permits suits against unions for proscribed acts, prohibits certain strikes and boycotts, and provides steps for settling strikes involving national emergencies. 29 USCA §§ 141 et seq.

labor-relations act. (1935) A statute regulating relations between employers and employees. • Although the Labor–Management Relations Act is the chief federal labor-relations act, various states have enacted these statutes as well.

Lacey Act. A federal law, originally enacted in 1900, that permits states to enforce their own game laws prohibiting the importation of animals from other states or countries. 16 USCA §§ 661 et seq.

laches (lach-iz). [Law French "remissness; slackness"] (14c) **1.** Unreasonable delay in pursuing a right or claim — almost always an equitable one — in a way that prejudices the party against whom relief is sought. **2.** The equitable doctrine by which a court denies relief to a claimant who has unreasonably delayed in asserting the claim, when that delay has prejudiced the party against whom relief is sought.

laissez-faire (les-ay-**fair**), *n.* [French "let (people) do (as they choose)"] (1825) **1.** Governmental abstention from interfering in economic or commercial affairs. **2.** The doctrine favoring such abstention. — **laissez-faire,** *adj.*

laity (**lay**-ə-tee). (15c) Collectively, persons who are not members of the clergy.

lame duck. (1910) An elected official serving out a term after a successor has been elected.

land, *n.* (bef. 12c) **1.** An immovable and indestructible three-dimensional area consisting of a portion of the earth's surface, the space above and below the surface, and everything growing on or permanently affixed to it. **2.** An estate or interest in real property.

accommodation land. (1843) Land that is bought by a builder or speculator who erects houses or improvements on it and then leases it at an increased rent.

acquired land. Land acquired by the government from private hands or from another governmental entity; esp., property acquired by the federal government from private or state ownership. • This term is frequently contrasted with *public domain.*

arable land (**ar**-ə-bəl). (16c) Land fit for cultivation.

enclosed land. (17c) Land that is actually enclosed and surrounded with fences.

fast land. (*often pl.*) (16c) Land that is above the high-water mark and that, when flooded by a government project, is subjected to a governmental taking.

federal land. (*usu. pl.*) Land owned by the United States government. • Federal lands are classified as public lands (also termed "lands in the public domain") or acquired federal lands, depending on how the land was obtained.

improved land. (17c) Land that has been developed; esp., land occupied by buildings and structures. • The improvements may or may not enhance the value of the land.

mineral land. (18c) Land that contains deposits of valuable minerals in quantities justifying the costs of extraction and using the land for mining, rather than agricultural or other purposes.

public land. (17c) Lands or land interests held by the government, without regard to how the government acquired ownership; unappropriated land belonging to the federal or state government.

riparian land. **1.** Land that includes part of the bed of a watercourse or lake. **2.** Land that borders on a public watercourse or public lake whose bed is owned by the public.

school land. (18c) Public real estate set apart for sale or exploitation by a state to establish and fund public schools.

seated land. (1822) Land that is occupied, cultivated, improved, reclaimed, farmed, or used as a place of residence, with or without cultivation.

settled land. Any land — or any interest in it — that is the subject of any document that limited it to, or put it into trust for, a person by way of succession.

swamp and overflowed land. (1853) Land that, because of its boggy, marshy, fenlike character, is unfit for cultivation, requiring drainage or reclamation to render it available for beneficial use. • Such lands were granted out of the U.S. public domain to the littoral states by acts of Congress in 1850 and thereafter. 43 USCA §§ 981 et seq.

unimproved land. **1.** Raw land that has never been developed, and usu. that lacks utilities. **2.** Land that was formerly developed but has now been cleared of all buildings and structures.

land bank. (1921) **1.** A bank created under the Federal Farm Loan Act to make loans at low interest rates secured by farmland. **2.** A program in which land is retired from agricultural production for conservation or tree-cultivation purposes.

land department. A federal or state bureau that determines factual matters regarding the control and transfer of public land.

landed, *adj.* (15c) **1.** (Of a person) having an estate in land. **2.** (Of an estate, etc.) consisting of land.

land flip. (1988) *Real estate.* A transaction in which a piece of property is purchased for one price and immediately sold, usu. to a fictitious entity, for a much higher price, to dupe a lender or later purchaser into thinking that the property is more valuable than it actually is.

land grant. (1862) A donation of public land to an individual, a corporation, or a subordinate government.

private land grant. (1861) A land grant to a natural person.

landholder. (17c) One who possesses or owns land.

landing. (15c) **1.** A place on a river or other navigable water for loading and unloading goods, or receiving and delivering passengers and watercraft. **2.** The termination point on a river or other navigable water for these purposes. **3.** The act or process of coming back to land after a voyage or flight.

landlocked, *adj.* (17c) **1.** Surrounded by land, with no way to get in or out except by crossing the land of another. **2.** (Of a country) surrounded by other nations, with no access to major navigable waterways.

landlord. (bef. 12c) One who leases real property to another.

absentee landlord. A landlord who does not live on the leased premises; usu., one who lives far away.

landlord–tenant relationship. (1921) The legal relationship between the lessor and lessee of real estate. • The relationship is contractual, created by a lease (or agreement for lease) for a term of years, from year to year, for life, or at will, and exists when one person occupies the premises of another with the lessor's permission or consent, subordinated to the lessor's title or rights. There must be a landlord's reversion, a tenant's estate, transfer of possession and control of the premises, and (generally) an express or implied contract.

landman. (1923) *Oil & gas.* A person responsible for acquiring oil and gas leases, negotiating arrangements for development of leases, and managing leased properties. • In this field, both men and women are commonly known as *landmen.*

landmark. (bef. 12c) **1.** A feature of land (such as a natural object, or a monument or marker) that demarcates the boundary of the land. **2.** A historically significant building or site.

landmark decision. (1913) A judicial decision that significantly changes existing law. • Examples are *Brown v. Board of Educ.*, 347 U.S. 483, 74 S.Ct. 686 (1954) (holding that segregation in public schools violates the Equal Protection Clause), and *Palsgraf v. Long Island R.R.*, 162 N.E. 99 (N.Y. 1928) (establishing that a defendant's duty in a negligence action is limited to plaintiffs within the apparent zone of danger — that is, plaintiffs to whom damage could be reasonably foreseen).

land office. (17c) A government office in which sales of public land are recorded.

land-poor, *adj.* (1873) (Of a person) owning a substantial amount of unprofitable or encumbered land, but lacking the money to improve or maintain the land or to pay the charges due on it.

Landrum–Griffin Act. A federal law, originally enacted in 1959 as the Labor–Management Reporting and Disclosure Act, designed to (1) curb corruption in union leadership and undemocratic conduct in internal union affairs, (2) outlaw certain types of secondary boycotts, and (3) prevent so-called hot-cargo provisions in collective-bargaining agreements.

lands, *n. pl.* (14c) **1.** At common law, property less extensive than either tenements or hereditaments. **2.** By statute in some states, land including tenements and hereditaments.

lands, tenements, and hereditaments. (16c) Real property. • The term was traditionally used in wills, deeds, and other instruments.

land trust certificate. An instrument granting the holder a share of the benefits of property ownership, while the trustee retains legal title.

land-use planning. (1939) The deliberate, systematic development of real estate through methods such as zoning, environmental-impact studies, and the like.

language. (14c) **1.** Any organized means of conveying or communicating ideas, esp. by human speech, written characters, or sign language. **2.** The letter or grammatical import of a document or instrument, as distinguished from its spirit.

Lanham Act (lan-əm). A federal trademark statute, enacted in 1946, that provides for a national system of trademark registration and protects the owner of a federally registered mark against the use of similar marks if any confusion might result or if the strength of a strong mark would be diluted. • The Lanham Act's scope is independent of and concurrent with state common law. 15 USCA §§ 1051 et seq.

lapidation (lap-ə-**day**-shən), *n.* An execution by stoning a person to death. — **lapidate (lap**-ə-dayt), *vb.*

lapping. (1939) An embezzlement technique by which an employee takes funds from one customer's accounts receivable and covers it by using a second customer's payment to pay the first account, then a third customer's payment to pay the second account, and so on.

lapse, *n.* (16c) **1.** The termination of a right or privilege because of a failure to exercise it within some time limit or because a contingency has occurred or not occurred. **2.** *Wills & estates.* The failure of a testamentary gift, esp. when the beneficiary dies before the testator.

lapse, *vb.* (18c) **1.** (Of an estate or right) to pass away or revert to someone else because conditions have not been fulfilled or because a person entitled to possession has failed in some duty. **2.** (Of a devise, grant, etc.) to become void.

larcenable (lahr-sə-nə-bəl), *adj.* (1920) Subject to larceny.

larcenist, *n.* (1803) One who commits larceny.

larcenous (lahr-sə-nəs), *adj.* (18c) **1.** Of, relating to, or characterized by larceny. **2.** (Of a person) contemplating or tainted with larceny; thievish.

larceny (lahr-sə-nee), *n.* (15c) The unlawful taking and carrying away of someone else's personal property with the intent to deprive the possessor of it permanently.

aggravated larceny. (1831) Larceny accompanied by some aggravating factor (as when the theft is from a person).

constructive larceny. (1827) Larceny in which the perpetrator's felonious intent to appropriate the goods is construed from the defendant's conduct at the time of asportation, although a felonious intent was not present before that time.

grand larceny. (1828) Larceny of property worth more than a statutory cutoff amount, usu. $100.

larceny by trick. (1898) Larceny in which the taker misleads the rightful possessor, by misrepresentation of fact, into giving up possession of (but not title to) the goods.

larceny from the person. (18c) Larceny in which the goods are taken directly from the person, but without violence or intimidation, the victim usu. being unaware of the taking.

mixed larceny. (18c) **1.** Larceny accompanied by aggravation or violence to the person. **2.** Larceny involving a taking from a house.

petit larceny. (16c) Larceny of property worth less than an amount fixed by statute, usu. $100. — Also spelled *petty larceny.*

simple larceny. (18c) Larceny unaccompanied by aggravating factors; larceny of personal goods unattended by an act of violence.

larger parcel. (1895) *Eminent domain.* A portion of land that is not a complete parcel, but is the greater part of a bigger tract, entitling the owner to damages both for the parcel taken and for its severance from the larger tract. • To grant both kinds of damages, a court generally requires the owner to show unity of ownership, unity of use, and contiguity of the land. But some states and the federal courts do not require contiguity when there is strong evidence of unity of use.

Larrison **rule** (**lar**-ə-sən). (1952) *Criminal law.* The doctrine that a defendant may be entitled to a new trial on the basis of newly discovered evidence of false testimony by a government witness if the jury might have reached a different conclusion without the evidence and it unfairly surprised the defendant at trial. *Larrison v. United States,* 24 F.2d 82 (7th Cir. 1928).

lascivious (lə-**siv**-ee-əs), *adj.* (15c) (Of conduct) tending to excite lust; lewd; indecent; obscene.

last-clear-chance doctrine. (1904) *Torts.* The rule that a plaintiff who was contributorily negligent may nonetheless recover from the defendant if the defendant had the last opportunity to prevent the harm but failed to use reasonable care to do so (in other words, if the defendant's negligence is later in time than the plaintiff's).

last-employer rule. The doctrine that liability for an occupational injury or illness falls to the employer who exposed the worker to the injurious substance just before the first onset of the disease or injury.

last illness. (1904) The sickness ending in the person's death.

last-in, first-out. (1934) An accounting method that assumes that the most recent purchases are sold or used first, matching current costs against current revenues. — Abbr. LIFO.

last-injurious-exposure rule. Last-employer rule.

last-in-time-marriage presumption. *Family law.* A presumption that the most recently contracted marriage is valid.

last-link doctrine. (1985) The rule that an attorney need not divulge nonprivileged information if doing so would reveal information protected by the attorney–client privilege, particularly if the information would provide essential evidence to support indicting or convicting the client of a crime.

last-opportunity doctrine. Last-clear-chance doctrine.

last-straw doctrine. *Employment law.* The rule that the termination of employment may be justified by a series of incidents of poor performance, not one of which alone would justify termination, followed by a final incident showing a blatant disregard for the employer's interests.

last-treatment rule. The doctrine that, for an ongoing physician–patient relationship, the statute of limitations on a medical-malpractice claim begins to run when the treatment stops or the relationship ends.

late, *adj.* (bef. 12c) **1.** Tardy; coming after an appointed or expected time. **2.** (Of a person) only recently having died.

latent (**lay**-tənt), *adj.* (15c) Concealed; dormant <a latent defect>.

laundry list. (1958) *Slang.* An enumeration of items, as in a statute or court opinion <Texas's consumer-protection law contains a laundry list of deceptive trade practices>.

law. (bef. 12c) **1.** The regime that orders human activities and relations through systematic application of the force of politically organized society, or through social pressure, backed by force, in such a society; the legal system <respect and obey the law>. **2.** The aggregate of legislation, judicial precedents, and accepted legal principles; the body of authoritative grounds of judicial and administrative action; esp., the body of rules, standards, and principles that the courts of a particular jurisdiction apply in deciding controversies brought before them <the law of the land>. **3.** The set of rules or principles dealing with a specific area of a legal system <copyright law>. **4.** The judicial and administrative process; legal action and proceedings <when settlement negotiations failed, they submitted their dispute to the law>. **5.** A statute <Congress passed a law>. — Abbr. L. **6.** Common law <law but not equity>. **7.** The legal profession <she spent her entire career in law>.

enacted law. Law that has its source in legislation; written law.

general law. **1.** Law that is neither local nor confined in application to particular persons. • Even if there is only one person or entity to which a given law applies when enacted, it is general law if it purports to apply to all persons or places of a specified class throughout the jurisdiction. **2.** A statute that relates to a subject of a broad nature.

internal law. Law that regulates the domestic affairs of a country.

special law. A law that pertains to and affects a particular case, person, place, or thing, as opposed to the general public.

tacit law. A law that derives its authority from the people's consent, without a positive enactment.

unenacted law. Law that does not have its source in legislation.

unwritten law. A rule, custom, or practice that has not been enacted in the form of a statute or ordinance. • The term traditionally includes caselaw.

written law. Statutory law, together with constitutions and treaties, as opposed to judge-made law.

law and economics. (*often cap.*) (1979) **1.** A discipline advocating the economic analysis of the law, whereby legal rules are subjected to a cost-benefit analysis to determine whether a change from one legal rule to another will increase or decrease allocative efficiency and social wealth. • Originally developed as an approach to antitrust policy, law and economics is today used by its proponents to explain and interpret a variety of legal subjects. **2.** The field or movement in which scholars devote themselves to this discipline. **3.** The body of work produced by these scholars.

law and literature. (*often cap.*) (1997) **1.** Traditionally, the study of how lawyers and legal institutions are depicted in literature; esp., the examination of law-related fiction as sociological evidence of how a given culture, at a given time, views law. **2.** More modernly, the application of literary theory to legal texts, focusing esp. on lawyers' rhetoric, logic, and style, as well as legal syntax and semantics. **3.** The field or movement in which scholars devote themselves to this study or application. **4.** The body of work produced by these scholars.

law arbitrary. A law not found in the nature of things, but imposed by the legislature's mere will; a bill not immutable.

lawbook. (16c) A book, usu. a technical one, about the law; esp., a primary legal text such as a statute book or book that reports caselaw.

lawbreaker, *n.* (15c) A person who violates or has violated the law.

law clerk. 1. CLERK (4). **2.** Paralegal.

law commission. (*often cap.*) An official or quasi-official body of people formed to propose legal reforms intended to improve the administration of justice.

law court. 1. COURT (1). **2.** COURT (2).

law-craft, *n.* (16c) The practice of law.

law enforcement. (1895) **1.** The detection and punishment of violations of the law. • This term is not limited to the enforcement of criminal laws. For example, the Freedom of Information Act contains an exemption from disclosure for information compiled for law-enforcement purposes and furnished in confidence. That exemption is valid for the enforcement of a variety of noncriminal laws (such as national-security laws) as well as criminal laws. See 5 USCA § 552(b)(7). **2.** CRIMINAL JUSTICE (2). **3.** Police officers and other members of the executive branch of government charged with carrying out and enforcing the criminal law.

Law Enforcement Assistance Administration. A former federal agency (part of the Department of Justice) that was responsible for administering law-enforcement grants under the Omnibus Crime Control and Safe Streets Act of 1968. • It has been replaced by a variety of federal agencies, including the National Institute of Corrections and National Institute of Justice.

Law Enforcement Information Network. A computerized communications system that some states use to document driver's-license records, automobile registrations, wanted-persons' files, and the like. — Abbr. LEIN.

law-enforcement officer. A person whose duty is to enforce the laws and preserve the peace.

law firm. (1852) An association of lawyers who practice law together, usu. sharing clients and profits, in a business organized traditionally as a partnership but often today as either a professional corporation or a limited-liability company.

captive law firm. A law firm staffed by employees of an insurance company. • These lawyers typically defend insureds in lawsuits covered under the insurer's liability policies. The insurer's use of a captive firm to defend an insured raises ethical questions about whether the lawyers will act in the insured's best interests. — Often shortened to *captive firm*.

Law French. (17c) The corrupted form of the Norman French language that arose in England in the centuries after William the Conqueror invaded England in 1066 and that was used for several centuries as the primary language of the English legal system; the Anglo-French used in medieval England in judicial proceedings, pleadings, and lawbooks.

lawful, *adj.* (13c) Not contrary to law; permitted by law.

lawful admission. (1899) *Immigration.* Legal entry into the country, including under a valid immigrant visa. • Lawful admission is one of the requirements for an immigrant to receive a naturalization order and certificate. 8 USCA §§ 1101(a)(20), 1427(a)(1), 1429.

lawful age. (16c) **1.** Age of capacity. **2.** Age of majority.

lawful authorities. (16c) Those persons (such as the police) with the right to exercise public power, to require obedience to their lawful commands, and to command or act in the public name.

lawful fence. (17c) A strong, substantial, and well-suited barrier that is sufficient to prevent animals from escaping property and to protect the property from trespassers.

lawful goods. (16c) Property that one may legally hold, sell, or export; property that is not contraband.

lawgiver. (14c) **1.** A legislator, esp. one who promulgates an entire code of laws. **2.** A judge with the power to interpret law. — **lawgiving,** *adj.* & *n.*

law journal. 1. A legal periodical or magazine, esp. one published by a bar association. — Abbr. L.J. **2.** LAW REVIEW (1).

Law Latin. (16c) A corrupted form of Latin formerly used in law and legal documents, including judicial writs, royal charters, and private deeds. • It primarily consists of a mixture of Latin, French, and English words used in English sentence structures.

law list. (18c) **1.** A published compilation of the names and addresses of practicing lawyers and other information of interest to the profession, such as legal organizations, court calendars, rosters of specialists, court reporters, and the like. **2.** A legal directory that provides biographical information about lawyers, such as Martindale-Hubbell. • Many states and large cities have law lists or directories.

law of persons. (17c) The law relating to persons; the law that pertains to the different statuses of persons.

law of property. The category of law dealing with proprietary rights in rem, such as personal servitudes, predial servitudes, and rights of real security.

law of the case. (18c) **1.** The doctrine holding that a decision rendered in a former appeal of a case is binding in a later appeal. **2.** An earlier decision giving rise to the application of this doctrine.

law of the circuit. (1861) **1.** The law as announced and followed by a U.S. Circuit Court of Appeals. **2.** The rule that one panel of judges on a U.S. Circuit Court of Appeals should not overrule a decision of another panel of judges on the same court. **3.** The rule that an opinion of one U.S. Circuit Court of Appeals is not binding on another circuit but may be considered persuasive.

law of the land. (15c) **1.** The law in effect in a country and applicable to its members, whether the law is statutory, administrative, or case-made. **2.** Due process of law.

law of the place. (1947) Under the Federal Tort Claims Act, the state law applicable to the place where the injury occurred. • Under the Act, the federal government waives its sovereign immunity for specified injuries, including certain wrongful acts or omissions of a government employee causing injury that the United States, if it were a private person, would be liable for under the law of the state where the incident occurred. 28 USCA § 1346(b).

law of the sea. The body of international law governing how nations use and control the sea and its resources.

law of the trial. A legal theory or court ruling that is not objected to and is used or relied on in a trial <neither party objected to the court's jury instruction, so it became the law of the trial>.

law of things. The law pertaining to things; the law that is determined by changes in the nature of things.

law practice. (17c) An attorney's professional business, including the relationships that the attorney has with clients and the goodwill associated with those relationships.

law reform. (1846) The process of, or a movement dedicated to, streamlining, modernizing, or otherwise improving a body of law generally or the code governing a particular branch of the law;

specif., the investigation and discussion of the law on a topic (e.g., bankruptcy), usu. by a commission or expert committee, with the goal of formulating proposals for change to improve the operation of the law.

law review. (1845) **1.** A journal containing scholarly articles, essays, and other commentary on legal topics by professors, judges, law students, and practitioners. • Law reviews are usu. published at law schools and edited by law students. **2.** The law-student staff and editorial board of such a journal.

law school. (17c) An institution for formal legal education and training. • Graduates who complete the standard program, usu. three years in length, receive a Juris Doctor (or, formerly, a Bachelor of Laws).

accredited law school. (1905) A law school approved by the state and the Association of American Law Schools, or by the state and the American Bar Association. • In all states except California, only graduates of an accredited law school may take the bar examination.

Law School Admissions Test. A standardized examination purporting to measure the likelihood of success in law school. • Most American law schools use the results of this examination in admissions decisions. — Abbr. LSAT.

laws of war. *Int'l law.* The rules and principles agreed on by most nations for regulating matters inherent in or incident to the conduct of a public war, such as the relations of neutrals and belligerents, blockades, captures, prizes, truces and armistices, capitulations, prisoners, and declarations of war and peace.

law-talk, *n.* **1.** Legalese. **2.** Discussion that is heavily laced with lawyers' concerns and legal references.

law writer. (1852) A person who writes on legal subjects, usu. from a technical, nonpopular point of view.

lawyer, *n.* (14c) One who is licensed to practice law. — **lawyerly, lawyerlike,** *adj.* — **lawyerdom,** *n.*

certified military lawyer. A person qualified to act as counsel in a general court-martial.

criminal lawyer. (18c) A lawyer whose primary work is to represent criminal defendants. • This term is rarely if ever applied to prosecutors despite their integral involvement in the criminal-justice system.

headnote lawyer. Slang. A lawyer who relies on the headnotes of judicial opinions rather than taking the time to read the opinions themselves.

public-interest lawyer. An attorney whose practice is devoted to advocacy on behalf of a public institution or nongovernmental organization, or to advising and representing indigent clients and others who have limited access to legal aid. • Public-interest lawyers often practice in fields such as civil rights and immigration law.

transactional lawyer. (1990) A lawyer who works primarily on transactions such as licensing agreements, mergers, acquisitions, joint ventures, and the like.

lawyer, *vb.* (18c) **1.** To practice as a lawyer. **2.** To supply with lawyers. — **lawyering,** *n.*

lawyer-referral service. A program, usu. offered by a bar association, that helps nonindigent clients clarify their legal problems and provides either contact information for lawyers who practice in the appropriate field or information about government agencies or consumer organizations that may be able to provide services.

lawyer-witness rule. (1982) The principle that an attorney who will likely be called as a fact witness at trial may not participate as an advocate in the case, unless the testimony will be about an uncontested matter or the amount of attorney's fees in the case, or if disqualifying the attorney would create a substantial hardship for the client. • The rule permits an attorney actively participating in the case to be a witness on merely formal matters but discourages testimony on other matters on behalf of a client. *Model Rules of Professional Conduct* Rule 3.7 (1983).

lay, *adj.* (14c) **1.** Not ecclesiastical; not of the clergy. **2.** Not expert, esp. with reference to law or medicine; nonprofessional.

lay, *vb.* (14c) To allege or assert.

lay damages, *vb.* To allege damages, esp. in the complaint.

laying a foundation. *Evidence.* Introducing evidence of certain facts needed to render later evidence relevant, material, or competent. • For example, propounding a hypothetical question to an expert is necessary before the expert may render an opinion.

laying of the venue. (18c) A statement in a complaint naming the district or county in which the plaintiff proposes that any trial of the matter should occur.

layman. (15c) **1.** A person who is not a member of the clergy. **2.** A person who is not a member of a profession or an expert on a particular subject.

layoff. (1868) The termination of employment at the employer's instigation; esp., the termination — either temporary or permanent — of many employees in a short time. — **lay off,** *vb.*

mass layoff. *Labor law.* Under the Worker Adjustment and Retraining Notification Act, a reduction in force that results in the loss of work at a single site, of 30 days or more, for at least 500 full-time employees, or 50 or more full-time employees if they make up at least 33%of the employees at that site. 29 USCA § 2101(a)(3).

LBO. *abbr.* Leveraged buyout.

LC. *abbr.* **1.** Letter of credit. **2.** Letter of credence. — Also written L/C.

L-Claim proceeding. (1997) A hearing under the Racketeer Influenced and Corrupt Organizations Act, intended to ensure that property ordered to be forfeited belongs solely to the defendant. • A petition for an L-Claim proceeding is filed by a third party who claims an interest in the property. The purpose is not to divide the assets among competing claimants, and general creditors of the defendant are not be allowed to maintain an L-Claim petition. The name refers to its legal basis in subsection *l* of RICO's penalty provision. 18 USCA § 1963(*l*)(2).

LEAA. *abbr.* Law Enforcement Assistance Administration.

leaching (**leech**-ing). (18c) The process by which moving fluid separates the soluble components of a material. • Under CERCLA, leaching is considered a release of contaminants. The term is sometimes used to describe the migration of contaminating materials, by rain or groundwater, from a fixed source, such as a landfill. 42 USCA § 9601(22).

leading case. (17c) **1.** A judicial decision that first definitively settled an important legal rule or principle and that has since been often and consistently followed. • An example is *Miranda v. Arizona*, 384 U.S. 436, 86 S.Ct. 1602 (1966) (creating the exclusionary rule for evidence improperly obtained from a suspect being interrogated while in police custody). **2.** An important, often the most important, judicial precedent on a particular legal issue. **3.** Loosely, a reported case that is cited as the dispositive authority on an issue being litigated.

leading question. (1824) A question that suggests the answer to the person being interrogated; esp., a question that may be answered by a mere "yes" or "no." • Leading questions are generally allowed only in cross-examination.

leads doctrine. *Tax.* In a tax-evasion case, the rule that the government must investigate all the taxpayer's leads that are reasonably accessible and that, if true, would establish the taxpayer's innocence, or the government risks having the trial judge presume that any leads not investigated are true and exonerating.

league. (15c) **1.** A covenant made by nations, groups, or individuals for promoting common interests or ensuring mutual protection. **2.** An alliance or association of nations, groups, or individuals formed by such a covenant. **3.** A unit of distance, usu. measuring about three miles (chiefly, nautical).

leakage. (15c) **1.** The waste of a liquid caused by its leaking from a storage container. **2.** An allowance against duties granted by customs to an importer of liquids for losses sustained by this waste. **3.** *Intellectual property.* Loss in value of a piece of intellectual property because of unauthorized copying.

leapfrog development. (1976) An improvement of land that requires the extension of public facilities from their current stopping point, through undeveloped land that may be scheduled for future development, to the site of the improvement.

learned (**lər**-nid), *adj.* (14c) **1.** Having a great deal of learning; erudite. • A lawyer might refer to an adversary as a "learned colleague" or "learned opponent" — a comment that, depending on the situation and tone of voice, may be either a genuine compliment or a sarcastic slight. **2.** Well-versed in the law and its history.

learned-treatise rule. (1946) *Evidence.* An exception to the hearsay rule, by which a published text may be established as authoritative, either by expert testimony or by judicial notice. • Under the Federal Rules of Evidence, a statement in a published treatise, periodical, or pamphlet on sciences or arts (such as history or medicine) can be established as authoritative — and thereby admitted into evidence for the purpose of examining or cross-examining an expert witness — by expert testimony or by the court's taking judicial notice of the authoritative nature or reliability of the text. If the statement is admitted into evidence, it may be read into the trial record, but it may not be received as an exhibit. Fed. R. Evid. 803(18).

lease, *n.* (14c) **1.** A contract by which a rightful possessor of real property conveys the right to use and occupy the property in exchange for consideration, usu. rent. • The lease term can be for life, for a fixed period, or for a period terminable at will. **2.** Such a conveyance plus all covenants attached to it. **3.** The written instrument memorializing such a conveyance and its covenants. **4.** The piece of real property so conveyed. **5.** A contract by which the rightful possessor of personal property conveys the right to use that property in exchange for consideration.

assignable lease. (1915) A lease that the lessee can transfer to a successor.

building lease. A long-term lease of land that includes a covenant to erect or alter a building or other improvement.

commercial lease. (1909) A lease for business purposes.

community lease. (1919) A lease in which a number of lessors owning interests in separate tracts execute a lease in favor of a single lessee.

concurrent lease. (1946) A lease that begins before a previous lease ends, entitling the new lessee to be paid all rents that accrue on the previous lease after the new lease begins, and to remedies against the holding tenant.

consumer lease. (1972) **1.** A lease of goods by a person who is in the business of selling or leasing a product primarily for the lessee's personal or household use. UCC § 2A-103(1)(e). **2.** A residential — rather than commercial — lease.

durable lease. (1816) A lease that reserves a rent payable annually, usu. with a right of reentry for nonpayment.

finance lease. (1966) A fixed-term lease used by a business to finance capital equipment. • The lessor's service is usu. limited to financing the asset, and the lessee pays maintenance costs and taxes and has the option of purchasing the asset at lease-end for a nominal price. Finance leases strongly resemble security agreements and are written almost exclusively by financial institutions as a way to help a commercial customer obtain an expensive capital item that the customer might not otherwise be able to afford. UCC § 2A-103(1)(g).

full-service lease. (1967) A lease in which the lessor agrees to pay all maintenance expenses, insurance premiums, and property taxes.

graduated lease. (1930) A lease in which rent varies depending on future contingencies, such as operating expenses or gross income.

gross lease. (1939) A lease in which the lessee pays a flat amount for rent, out of which the lessor pays all the expenses (such as fuel, water, and electricity).

ground lease. (1840) A long-term (usu. 99-year) lease of land only. • Such a lease typically involves commercial property, and any improvements built by the lessee usu. revert to the lessor.

index lease. A lease that provides for increases in rent according to the increases in the consumer price index.

leveraged lease. (1972) A lease that is collateral for the loan through which the lessor acquired the leased asset, and that provides the lender's only recourse for nonpayment of the debt; a lease in which a creditor provides nonrecourse financing to the lessor (who has substantial leverage in the property) and in which the lessor's net investment in the lease, apart from nonrecourse financing, declines during the early years and increases in later years.

master lease. (1935) A contract that establishes a leasehold's basic terms and conditions applicable to all related contracts for rental properties.

mineral lease. A lease in which the lessee has the right to explore for and extract oil, gas, or other minerals. • The rent usu. is based on the amount or value of the minerals extracted.

mining lease. A lease of a mine or mining claim, in which the lessee has the right to work the mine or claim, usu. with conditions on the amount and type of work to be done. • The lessor is compensated with either fixed rent or royalties based on the amount of ore mined.

month-to-month lease. (1914) A tenancy with no written contract. • Rent is paid monthly, and usu. one month's notice by the landlord or tenant is required to terminate the tenancy.

net lease. A lease in which the lessee pays rent plus property expenses (such as taxes and insurance).

net-net-net lease. A lease in which the lessee pays all the expenses, including mortgage interest and amortization, leaving the lessor with an amount free of all claims.

oil-and-gas lease. (1892) A lease granting the right to extract oil and gas from a specified piece of land. • Although called a "lease," this interest is typically considered a determinable fee in the minerals rather than a grant of possession for a term of years.

operating lease. A lease of property (esp. equipment) for a term that is shorter than the property's useful life. • Under an operating lease, the lessor is typically responsible for paying taxes and other expenses on the property.

perpetual lease. **1.** An ongoing lease not limited in duration. **2.** A grant of lands in fee with a reservation of a rent in fee; a fee farm.

proprietary lease. A lease between a cooperative apartment association and a tenant.

reversionary lease. A lease that will take effect when a prior lease terminates.

sandwich lease. (1976) A lease in which the lessee subleases the property to a third party, esp. for more rent than under the original lease.

short lease. (17c) A lease of brief duration, often less than six months.

timber lease. (1853) A real-property lease that contemplates that the lessee will cut timber on the leased premises.

lease, *vb.* (16c) **1.** To grant the possession and use of (land, buildings, rooms, movable property, etc.) to another in return for rent or other consideration. **2.** To take a lease of; to hold by a lease.

leaseback, *n.* (1947) The sale of property on the understanding, or with the express option, that the seller may lease the property from the buyer immediately upon the sale.

leasehold, *n.* (18c) A tenant's possessory estate in land or premises, the four types being the tenancy for years, the periodic tenancy, the tenancy at will, and the tenancy at sufferance.

leasehold improvements. (1845) Beneficial changes to leased property (such as a parking lot or driveway) made by or for the benefit of the lessee. • The phrase is used in a condemnation proceeding to determine the share of compensation to be allocated to the lessee.

leasehold interest. (18c) **1.** Leasehold; esp., for purposes of eminent domain, the lessee's interest in the lease itself, measured by the difference between the total remaining rent and the rent the lessee would pay for similar space for the same period. **2.** A lessor's or lessee's interest under a lease contract. UCC § 2A-103.

leasehold value. The value of a leasehold interest. • This term usu. applies to a long-term lease when the rent paid under the lease is lower than current market rates. Some states permit the lessee to claim the leasehold interest from the landlord in a condemnation proceeding, unless the lease prohibits such a claim. Other states prohibit these claims by statute.

lease-purchase agreement. (1939) A rent-to-own purchase plan under which the buyer takes possession of the goods with the first payment and takes ownership with the final payment; a lease of property (esp. equipment) by which ownership of the property is transferred to the lessee at the end of the lease term. • Such a lease is usu. treated as an installment sale. Under a capital lease, the lessee is responsible for paying taxes and other expenses on the property.

least-intrusive-means doctrine. (1978) A doctrine requiring the government to exhaust all other investigatory means before seeking sensitive testimony, as by compelling an attorney to testify before a grand jury on matters that may be protected by the attorney–client privilege.

least-intrusive-remedy doctrine. (1989) The rule that a legal remedy should provide the damaged party with appropriate relief, without unduly penalizing the opposing party or the jurisdiction's legal system, as by striking only the unconstitutional portion of a challenged statute while leaving the rest intact.

least-restrictive environment. Under the Individuals with Disabilities Education

Act, the school setting that, to the greatest extent appropriate, educates a disabled child together with children who are not disabled. 20 USCA § 1412(5).

least-restrictive-means test. (1972) The rule that a law or governmental regulation should be crafted in a way that will protect individual civil liberties as much as possible and should be only as restrictive as necessary to accomplish a legitimate governmental purpose.

leave, *n.* (bef. 12c) **1.** Departure; the act of going away. **2.** Extended absence for which one has authorization; esp., a voluntary vacation from military duties with the chance to visit home; furlough. **3.** Permission.

leave, *vb.* (bef. 12c) **1.** To give by will; to bequeath or devise. • This usage has historically been considered loose by the courts, and it is not always given testamentary effect. **2.** To be survived by. **3.** To depart; voluntarily go away; quit (a place). **4.** To depart willfully with the intent not to return. **5.** To deliver (a summons, money, an article, etc.) by dropping off at a certain place.

leave no issue, *vb.* (16c) To die without any surviving child or other descendant. • The spouse of a deceased child is usu. not issue.

leave of absence. (18c) A worker's temporary absence from employment or duty with the intention to return. • Salary level and seniority typically are unaffected by a leave of absence.

leave of court. (18c) Judicial permission to follow a nonroutine procedure.

ledger (**lej**-ər). (16c) A book or series of books used for recording financial transactions in the form of debits and credits.

legacy (**leg**-ə-see), *n.* (15c) A gift by will, esp. of personal property and often of money.

absolute legacy. A legacy given without condition and intended to vest immediately.

accumulated legacy. A legacy that has not yet been paid to a legatee.

additional legacy. A second legacy given to a legatee in the same will (or in a codicil to the same will) that gave another legacy. • An additional legacy is supplementary to another and is not considered merely a repeated expression of the same gift.

alternate legacy. (1983) A legacy by which the testator allows the legatee to choose one of two or more items.

conditional legacy. (17c) A legacy that will take effect or be defeated subject to the occurrence or nonoccurrence of an event.

contingent legacy. (18c) A legacy that depends on an uncertain event and thus has not vested. • An example is a legacy given to one's granddaughter "if she attains the age of 21.

demonstrative legacy (di-**mon**-strə-tiv). (18c) A legacy paid from a particular source if that source has enough money.

general legacy. (18c) A gift of personal property that the testator intends to come from the estate's general assets, payable in money or items indistinguishable from each other, such as shares of publicly traded stock.

lapsed legacy. (18c) A legacy to a legatee who dies either before the testator dies or before the legacy is payable. • It falls into the residual estate unless the jurisdiction has an antilapse statute.

modal legacy (**moh**-dəl). A legacy accompanied by directions about the manner in which it will be applied to the legatee's benefit.

pecuniary legacy (pi-**kyoo**-nee-er-ee). (18c) A legacy of a sum of money.

residuary legacy (ri-**zij**-oo-er-ee). (18c) A legacy of the estate remaining after the satisfaction of all claims and all specific, general, and demonstrative legacies.

specific legacy. (18c) A legacy of a specific or unique item of property, such as any real estate or a particular piece of furniture.

substitutional legacy. (1894) A legacy that replaces a different legacy already given to a legatee.

trust legacy. A legacy of personal property to trustees to be held in trust, with the income usu. paid to a specified beneficiary.

vested legacy. (18c) A legacy given in such a way that the legatee has a fixed, indefeasible right to its payment. • A legacy is said to be vested when the testator's words making the bequest convey a transmissible interest, whether present or future, to the legatee. Thus, a legacy to be paid when the legatee reaches the age of 21 is a vested legacy because it is given unconditionally and absolutely. Although the legacy is vested, the legatee's enjoyment of it is deferred.

void legacy. (18c) A legacy that never had any legal existence. • The subject matter of such a legacy is treated as a part of the estate and passes under the residuary clause of a will or (in the absence of a residuary clause) under the rules for intestate succession.

legal, *adj.* (15c) **1.** Of or relating to law; falling within the province of law. **2.** Established, required, or permitted by law; lawful. **3.** Of or relating to law as opposed to equity.

legal act. (15c) **1.** Any act not condemned as illegal. • For example, a surgeon's incision is a legal act, while stabbing is an illegal one. **2.** An action or undertaking that creates a legally recognized obligation; an act that binds a person in some way.

legal-acumen doctrine (**lee**-gəl ə-**kyoo**-mən). (1905) The principle that if a defect in, or the invalidity of, a claim to land cannot be discovered without legal expertise, then equity may be invoked to remove the cloud created by the defect or invalidity.

legal-advice exception. 1. The rule that an attorney may withhold as privileged the client's identity and information regarding fees, if there is a strong probability that disclosing the information would implicate the client in the criminal activity for which the attorney was consulted. **2.** An exemption contained in open-meetings legislation, permitting a governmental body to meet in closed session to consult with its attorney about certain matters.

legal age. (18c) **1.** Age of capacity. **2.** Age of majority.

legal aid. (1890) Free or inexpensive legal services provided to those who cannot afford to pay full price.

legal assistant. (1939) **1.** Paralegal. **2.** A legal secretary.

legal-certainty test. (1964) *Civil procedure.* A test designed to determine whether the amount in controversy satisfies the minimum needed to establish the court's jurisdiction. • The amount claimed in the complaint will control unless there is a "legal certainty" that the claim is actually less than the minimum amount.

legal citology (sɪ-**tol**-ə-jee). (1996) The study of citations (esp. in footnotes) and their effect on legal scholarship. — **legal citologist** (sɪ-**tol**-ə-jist), *n.*

legal conclusion. (17c) A statement that expresses a legal duty or result but omits the facts creating or supporting the duty or result.

legal correlative. A legal status that has a corresponding or reciprocal status, such as a right that corresponds to a duty. • Wesley Newcomb Hohfeld of Yale Law School first introduced the bases for the concept of legal correlatives in two articles published in the *Yale Law Journal* in 1913 and 1917.

legal custody. 1. CUSTODY (2). **2.** CUSTODY (3). **3.** Decision-making responsibility.

legal death. 1. Brain death. **2.** Civil death.

legal description. (18c) A formal description of real property, including a description of any part subject to an easement or reservation, complete enough that a particular piece of land can be located and identified.

legal-elements test. (1980) *Criminal law.* A method of determining whether one crime is a lesser included offense in relation to another crime, by examining the components of the greater crime to analyze whether a person who commits the greater crime necessarily commits the lesser one too.

legal entity. (18c) A body, other than a natural person, that can function legally, sue or be sued, and make decisions through agents. • A typical example is a corporation.

legalese (lee-gə-**leez**). (1914) The jargon characteristically used by lawyers, esp. in legal documents.

legal ethics. (1828) **1.** Standards of professional conduct applicable to members of the legal profession. • Ethical rules consist primarily of the ABA Model Rules of Professional Conduct and the earlier ABA Model Code of Professional Responsibility, together with related regulatory judgments and opinions. The Model Rules of Professional Conduct have been enacted into law, often in a modified form, in most states. **2.** The study of such standards. **3.** A lawyer's practical observance of or conformity to established standards of professional conduct.

legal etiquette. The professional courtesy that lawyers have traditionally observed in their professional conduct, shown through civility and a strong sense of honor.

legal fiction. (17c) An assumption that something is true even though it may be untrue, made esp. in judicial reasoning to alter how a legal rule operates; specif., a device by which a legal rule or institution is diverted from its original purpose to accomplish indirectly some other object.

legal formalism, *n.* (1895) The theory that law is a set of rules and principles independent of other political and social institutions. — **legal formalist,** *n.*

legal holiday. (1867) A day designated by law as exempt from court proceedings, issuance of process, and the like.

legal-injury rule. (1956) The doctrine that the statute of limitations on a claim does not begin to run until the claimant has sustained some legally actionable damage.

legalism, *n.* (1928) **1.** Formalism carried almost to the point of meaninglessness; an inclination to exalt the importance of law or formulated rules in any area of action. **2.** A mode of expression characteristic of lawyers; a jargonistic phrase characteristic of lawyers, such as "pursuant to."

legalist, *n.* (1829) A person who views things from a legal or formalistic standpoint; esp., one who believes in strict adherence to the letter of the law rather than its spirit.

legalistic, *adj.* (17c) Characterized by legalism; exalting the importance of law or formulated rules in any area of action.

legality. (15c) **1.** Strict adherence to law, prescription, or doctrine; the quality of being legal. **2.** The principle that a person may not be prosecuted under a criminal law that has not been previously published.

legalize, *vb.* (18c) **1.** To make lawful; to authorize or justify by legal sanction. **2.**

To imbue with the spirit of the law; to make legalistic. — **legalization,** *n.*

legal list. A group of investments in which institutions and fiduciaries (such as banks and insurance companies) may legally invest according to state statutes.

legally, *adv.* (16c) In a lawful way; in a manner that accords with the law.

legally determined, *adj.* (17c) (Of a claim, issue, etc.) decided by legal process.

legally incapacitated person. (1919) A person, other than a minor, who is temporarily or permanently impaired by mental illness, mental deficiency, physical illness or disability, or alcohol or drug use to the extent that the person lacks sufficient understanding to make or communicate responsible personal decisions or to enter into contracts.

legal memory. (1882) The period during which a legal right or custom can be determined or established. • Traditionally, common-law legal memory began in the year 1189, but in 1540 it became a steadily moving period of 60 years.

legal mind. (18c) The intellect, legal capacities, and attitudes of a well-trained lawyer — often used as a personified being.

legal moralism. (1963) The theory that a government or legal system may prohibit conduct that is considered immoral.

legal order. (16c) **1.** Traditionally, a set of regulations governing a society and those responsible for enforcing them. **2.** Modernly, such regulations and officials plus the processes involved in creating, interpreting, and applying the regulations.

legal paternalism. (1913) The theory that a government or legal system is justified in controlling the individual and private affairs of citizens. • This theory is often associated with legal positivists.

legal positivism, *n.* (1939) The theory that legal rules are valid only because they are enacted by an existing political authority or accepted as binding in a given society, not because they are grounded in morality or in natural law. — **legal positivist,** *n.*

legal practitioner. A lawyer.

legal proceeding. (17c) Any proceeding authorized by law and instituted in a court or tribunal to acquire a right or to enforce a remedy.

legal realism, *n.* (1930) The theory that law is based, not on formal rules or principles, but instead on judicial decisions that should derive from social interests and public policy. — **legal realist,** *n.*

legal research. (18c) **1.** The finding and assembling of authorities that bear on a question of law. **2.** The field of study concerned with the effective marshaling of authorities that bear on a question of law.

legal science. (18c) The field of study that, as one of the social sciences, deals with the institutions and principles that particular societies have developed (1) for defining the claims and liabilities of persons against one another in various circumstances, and (2) for peaceably resolving disputes and controversies in accordance with principles accepted as fair and right in the particular community at a given time.

legal secretary. (1897) An employee in a law office whose responsibilities include typing legal documents and correspondence, keeping records and files, and performing other duties supportive of the employer's law practice.

Legal Services Corporation. A nonprofit federal corporation that provides financial aid in civil cases to those who cannot afford legal assistance through grants to legal-aid and other organizations and by contracting with individuals, firms, corporations, and organizations to provide legal services.

legal tender. (18c) The money (bills and coins) approved in a country for the payment of debts, the purchase of goods, and other exchanges for value.

legal theory. (1804) **1.** General jurisprudence. **2.** The principle under which a litigant proceeds, or on which a litigant bases its claims or defenses in a case.

Legal Writing Institute. A nonprofit corporation founded in 1984 to promote the exchange of information and ideas about the teaching of legal writing. — Abbr. LWI.

legatee (leg-ə-**tee**). (17c) **1.** One who is named in a will to take personal property; one who has received a legacy or bequest. **2.** Loosely, one to whom a devise of real property is given.

general legatee. A person whose bequest is of a specified quantity to be paid out of the estate's personal assets.

residuary legatee (ri-**zij**-oo-er-ee). (18c) A person designated to receive the residue of a decedent's estate.

specific legatee. (18c) The recipient, under a will, of designated property that is transferred by the owner's death.

universal legatee. A residuary legatee that receives the entire residuary estate.

legislate, *vb.* (180) **1.** To make or enact laws. **2.** To bring (something) into or out of existence by making laws; to attempt to control (something) by legislation. — **legislative,** *adj.*

legislation. (17c) **1.** The process of making or enacting a positive law in written form, according to some type of formal procedure, by a branch of government constituted to perform this process. **2.** The law so enacted. **3.** The whole body of enacted laws.

ancillary legislation. (1860) Legislation that is auxiliary to principal legislation.

general legislation. (18c) Legislation that applies to the community at large.

judicial legislation. (18c) The making of new legal rules by judges.

local and special legislation. (1853) Legislation that affects only a specific geographic area or a particular class of persons.

pork-barrel legislation. (1961) Legislation that favors a particular local district by allocating funds or resources to projects (such as constructing a highway or a post office) of economic value to the district and of political advantage to the district's legislator.

subordinate legislation. (18c) **1.** Legislation that derives from any authority other than the sovereign power in a state and that therefore depends for its continued existence and validity on some superior or supreme authority. **2.** Regulation.

supreme legislation. (17c) Legislation that derives directly from the supreme or sovereign power in a state and is therefore incapable of being repealed, annulled, or controlled by any other legislative authority.

4. A proposed law being considered by a legislature. **5.** The field of study concentrating on statutes.

legislative branch. (18c) The branch of government responsible for enacting laws; legislature.

legislative council. A state agency that studies legislative problems and plans legislative strategy between regular legislative sessions.

legislative counsel. (1839) A person or group charged with helping legislators fulfill their legislative duties, such as by performing research, drafting bills, and the like.

legislative districting. (1962) The process of dividing a state into territorial districts to be represented in the state or federal legislature.

legislative-equivalency doctrine. (2003) The rule that a law should be amended or repealed only by the same procedures that were used to enact it.

legislative function. 1. The duty to determine legislative policy. **2.** The duty to form and determine future rights and duties.

legislative history. (1844) The background and events leading to the enactment of a statute, including hearings, committee reports, and floor debates. • Legislative history is sometimes recorded so that it can later be used to aid in interpreting the statute.

legislative intent. (1812) The design or plan that the legislature had at the time of enacting a statute.

dormant legislative intent. The intent that the legislature would have had if a given ambiguity, inconsistency, or omission had been called to the legislators' minds. — Sometimes shortened to *dormant intent.*

legislative investigation. A formal inquiry conducted by a legislative body incident to its legislative authority. • A legislature has many of the same powers as a court to support a legislative inquiry, including the power to subpoena and cross-examine a witness and to hold a witness in contempt.

legislative power. (17c) *Constitutional law.* The power to make laws and to alter them; a legislative body's exclusive authority to make, amend, and repeal laws. • Under federal law, this power is vested in Congress, consisting of the House of Representatives and the Senate. A legislative body may delegate a portion of its lawmaking authority to agencies within the executive branch for purposes of rulemaking and regulation. But a legislative body may not delegate its authority to the judicial branch, and the judicial branch may not encroach on legislative duties.

legislative rule. An administrative rule created by an agency's exercise of delegated quasi-legislative authority. • A legislative rule has the force of law.

legislator, *n.* (17c) One who makes laws within a given jurisdiction; a member of a legislative body. — **legislatorial** (lej-is-lə-**tor**-ee-əl), *adj.*

legislature. (17c) The branch of government responsible for making statutory laws. • The federal government and most states have bicameral legislatures, usu. consisting of a house of representatives and a senate.

legisprudence (lee-jis-**proo**-dənts). (1950) The systematic analysis of statutes within the framework of jurisprudential philosophies about the role and nature of law.

legist (**lee**-jist). (15c) **1.** One learned or skilled in the law; a lawyer. **2.** Jurist.

legitimacy. (17c) **1.** Lawfulness. **2.** The status of a person who is born within a lawful marriage or who acquires that status by later action of the parents; legal kinship between a child and its parent or parents.

legitimate (lə-**jit**-ə-mət), *adj.* (15c) **1.** Complying with the law; lawful. **2.** Genuine; valid. **3.** Born of legally married parents.

legitimation, *n.* (16c) **1.** The act of making something lawful; authorization. **2.** The act or process of authoritatively declaring a person legitimate, esp. a child whose parentage has been unclear. — **legitimate** (lə-**jit**-ə-mayt), *vb.*

lemon law. (18c) **1.** A statute designed to protect a consumer who buys a substandard automobile, usu. by requiring the manufacturer or dealer either to replace the vehicle or to refund the full purchase price. **2.** By extension, a statute designed to protect a consumer who buys any product of inferior quality.

***Lemon* test.** (1971) A legal standard for judging the state's violation of the Establishment Clause of the First Amendment. • The *Lemon* test has most often been used in school-related cases. It employs a three-pronged test to determine the state's action: (1) Does the state's action have a religious purpose? (2) Does the state's action have the primary effect of either promoting or inhibiting religion? (3) Does the state's action create an "excessive entanglement" between church and state? *Lemon v. Kurtzman*, 403 U.S. 602, 91 S.Ct. 2105 (1971). In recent years, the Court has not overturned *Lemon* but has declined to apply it when deciding Establishment Clause cases.

lend, *vb.* (bef. 12c) **1.** To allow the temporary use of (something), sometimes in exchange for compensation, on condition that the thing or its equivalent be returned. **2.** To provide (money) temporarily on condition of repayment, usu. with interest. — **lender,** *n.*

lend-lease. (1941) A mutually beneficial exchange made between friendly parties; esp., an arrangement made in 1941, under the Lend-Lease Act, whereby U.S. destroyers were lent to Great Britain in exchange for Britain's leasing of land to the United States for military bases.

lenient, *adj.* Tolerant; mild; merciful.

lenient test. (1996) The principle that the attorney–client privilege applicable to a document or other communication will be waived only by a knowing or intentional disclosure, and will not usu. be waived by an inadvertent disclosure.

lenity (**len**-ə-tee). (16c) The quality or condition of being lenient; mercy or clemency.

lese majesty (leez **maj**-əs-tee). [Law French "injured majesty"] (16c) **1.** A crime against the state, esp. against the ruler. **2.** An attack on a custom or traditional belief.

lessee (le-**see**). (15c) One who has a possessory interest in real or personal property under a lease; tenant.

less-lethal, *n. Jargon.* A weapon that inflicts pain or discomfort short of death, as by firing bean bags or rubber bullets, or by discharging electromagnetic, acoustic, or other energy so that the target may be incapacitated but usu. not seriously injured.

lessor (**les**-or *or* le-**sor**). (14c) One who conveys real or personal property by lease; esp., landlord.

lessor's interest. (1821) The present value of the future income under a lease, plus the present value of the property after the lease expires.

let, *n.* (12c) An impediment or obstruction <free to act without let or hindrance>.

let, *vb.* (bef. 12c) **1.** To allow or permit. **2.** To offer (property) for lease; to rent out. **3.** To award (a contract), esp. after bids have been submitted.

lethal, *adj.* (16c) Deadly; fatal.

lethal injection. (1898) An injection of a deadly substance into a prisoner in order to carry out a sentence of capital punishment.

letter. (13c) **1.** A written communication that is usu. enclosed in an envelope, sealed, stamped, and delivered (esp., an official written communication) <an opinion letter>. **2.** (*usu. pl.*) A written instrument containing or affirming a grant of some power or right <letters testamentary>. **3.** Strict or literal meaning <the letter of the law>.

letter of credit. (17c) *Commercial law.* An instrument under which the issuer (usu. a bank), at a customer's request, agrees to honor a draft or other demand for payment made by a third party (the *beneficiary*), as long as the draft or demand complies with specified conditions, and regardless of whether any underlying agreement between the customer and the beneficiary is satisfied. • Letters of credit are governed by Article 5 of the UCC. — Abbr. LC; L/C. — Often shortened to *credit*.

letter of intent. (1942) A written statement detailing the preliminary understanding of parties who plan to enter into a contract or some other agreement; a noncommittal writing preliminary to a contract. — Abbr. LOI.

letter of request. 1. A document issued by one court to a foreign court, requesting that the foreign court (1) take evidence from a specific person within the foreign jurisdiction or serve process on an individual or corporation within the foreign jurisdiction and (2) return the testimony or proof of service for use in a pending case. See Fed. R. Civ. P. 28. **2.** An instrument by which an inferior court withdraws or waives jurisdiction so that a matter can be heard in the court immediately above. Pl. **letters of request.**

letter of the law. (17c) The strictly literal meaning of the law, rather than the intention or policy behind it.

letter ruling. (1950) *Tax.* A written statement issued by the IRS to an inquiring taxpayer, explaining the tax implications of a particular transaction.

letters. (16c) *Wills & estates.* A court order giving official authority to a fiduciary to conduct appointed tasks. • Examples are letters of administration, letters of conservatorship, letters of guardianship, and letters testamentary. Unif. Probate Code § 1-201(23).

letters of administration. (16c) A formal document issued by a probate court to appoint the administrator of an estate.

letters of administration c.t.a. (1894) Letters of administration appointing an administrator *cum testamento annexo* (with the will annexed) either because the will does not name an executor or because the named executor does not qualify.

letters of administration d.b.n. (1877) Letters of administration appointing an administrator *de bonis non* (concerning goods not yet administered) because the named executor failed to complete the estate's probate.

letters of guardianship. (18c) A court order appointing a guardian to care for the well-being, property, and affairs of a minor or an incapacitated adult. • It defines the scope of the guardian's rights and duties, including the extent of control over the ward's education and medical issues.

letters patent. (15c) A governmental grant of the exclusive right to use an invention or design.

letters testamentary. (17c) A probate-court order approving the appointment of an executor under a will and authorizing the executor to administer the estate.

level of abstraction. *Copyright.* The degree to which a work describes an idea or process in a general rather than concrete way. • Judge Learned Hand posited that from any work one can restate the idea in more and more abstract ways, omitting more and more details, until one is left with an uncopyrightable idea rather than a protectable work of originality. See *Nichols v. Universal Pictures Corp.*, 45 F.2d 119 (1930).

leverage, *n.* (1830) **1.** Positional advantage; effectiveness. **2.** The use of credit or borrowed funds (such as buying on margin) to improve one's speculative ability and to increase an investment's rate of return. **3.** The advantage obtained from using credit or borrowed funds rather than equity capital. **4.** The ratio between a corporation's debt and its equity capital. **5.** The effect of this ratio on common-stock prices.

leverage, *vb.* (1957) **1.** To provide (a borrower or investor) with credit or funds to improve speculative ability and to seek a high rate of return. **2.** To supplement (available capital) with credit or outside funds. **3.** To fund (a company) with debt as well as shareholder equity. **4.** *Antitrust.* To use power in one market to gain an unfair advantage in another market. **5.** *Insurance.* To manipulate two coverages, as by an insurer's withholding settlement of one claim to influence a claim arising under another source of coverage.

leverage contract. (1975) An agreement for the purchase or sale of a contract for the future delivery of a specified commodity, usu. silver, gold, or another precious metal, in a standard unit and quantity, for a particular price, with no right to a particular lot of the commodity. • A leverage contract operates much like a futures contract, except that there is no designated contract market for leverage contracts. The market sets the uniform terms of a futures contract. But in a leverage contract, the individual merchant sets the terms, does not guarantee a repurchase market, and does not guarantee to continue serving or acting as the broker for the purchaser. Leverage contracts are generally forbidden for agricultural commodities. 7 USCA § 23(a).

levy (**lev**-ee), *n.* (13c) **1.** The imposition of a fine or tax; the fine or tax so imposed. **2.** The enlistment of soldiers into the military; the soldiers so enlisted. **3.** The legally sanctioned seizure and sale of property; the money obtained from such a sale. — **levy,** *vb.* (14c). — **leviable** (**lev**-ee-ə-bəl), *adj.*

wrongful levy. (18c) A levy on a third party's property that is not subject to a writ of execution.

lewd, *adj.* (14c) Obscene or indecent; tending to moral impurity or wantonness <lewd behavior>.

lewdness. (16c) Gross, wanton, and public indecency that is outlawed by many state statutes; a sexual act that the actor knows will likely be observed by someone who will be affronted or alarmed by it. See Model Penal Code § 251.1.

lex (leks), *n.* [Latin "law"] **1.** Law, esp. statutory law. **2.** Positive law, as opposed to natural law. • Strictly speaking, *lex* is a statute, whereas *jus* is law in general (as well as a right). **3.** A system or body of laws, written or unwritten, that are peculiar to a jurisdiction or to a field of human activity. **4.** A collection of uncodified laws within a jurisdiction.

lex domicilii (**leks** dom-ə-**sil**-ee-ɪ). [Latin] (18c) **1.** The law of the country where a person is domiciled. **2.** The determination of a person's rights by establishing where, in law, that person is domiciled. See Restatement (Second) of Conflict of Laws §§ 11 et seq. (1971).

lex fori (**leks for**-ɪ). [Latin] (1803) The law of the forum; the law of the jurisdiction where the case is pending.

LEXIS (**lek**-sis). A proprietary online computer service that provides access to databases of legal information, including federal and state caselaw, statutes, and secondary materials.

lex loci (**leks loh**-sɪ). [Latin] (18c) **1.** The law of the place; local law. **2.** *Lex loci contractus.*

lex loci contractus (**leks loh**-sɪ kən-**trak**-təs). [Latin] The law of the place where a contract is executed or to be performed.

lex loci delicti (**leks loh**-sɪ də-**lik**-tɪ). [Latin] The law of the place where the tort or other wrong was committed. — Often shortened to *lex delicti.*

liability, *n.* (18c) **1.** The quality or state of being legally obligated or accountable; legal responsibility to another or to society, enforceable by civil remedy or criminal punishment. **2.** (*often pl.*) A financial or pecuniary obligation; debt.

accomplice liability. (1958) Criminal responsibility of one who acts with another before, during, or (in some jurisdictions) after a crime. See 18 USCA § 2.

accrued liability. (1877) A debt or obligation that is properly chargeable in a given accounting period but that is not yet paid.

alternative liability. (1929) Liability arising from the tortious acts of two or more parties — when the plaintiff proves that one of the defendants has caused harm but cannot prove which one caused it — resulting in a shifting of the burden of proof to each defendant. Restatement (Second) of Torts § 433B(3) (1965).

civil liability. (1817) **1.** Liability imposed under the civil, as opposed to the criminal, law. **2.** The state of being legally obligated for civil damages.

contingent liability. (18c) A liability that will occur only if a specific event happens; a liability that depends on the occurrence of a future and uncertain event. • In financial statements, contingent liabilities are usu. stated in footnotes.

derivative liability. (1886) Liability for a wrong that a person other than the one wronged has a right to redress. • Examples include liability to a widow in a wrongful-death action and liability to a corporation in a shareholder's derivative suit.

enterprise liability. (1941) **1.** Liability imposed on each member of an industry responsible for manufacturing a harmful or defective product, allotted by each manufacturer's market share of the industry. **2.** Criminal liability imposed on a business (such as a corporation or partnership) for certain offenses, such as public-welfare offenses or offenses for which the legislature specifically intended to impose criminal sanctions. See Model Penal Code § 2.07.

joint and several liability. (1819) Liability that may be apportioned either among two or more parties or to only one or a few select members of the group, at the adversary's discretion.

joint liability. (18c) Liability shared by two or more parties.

limited liability. (1833) Liability restricted by law or contract; esp., the liability of a company's owners for nothing more than the capital they have invested in the business.

market-share liability. (1980) Liability that is imposed, usu. severally, on each member of an industry, based on each member's share of the market or respective percentage of the product that is placed on the market.

official liability. Liability of an officer or receiver for a breach of contract or a tort committed during the officer's or receiver's tenure, but not involving any personal liability.

personal liability. (18c) Liability for which one is personally accountable and for which a wronged party can seek satisfaction out of the wrongdoer's personal assets.

primary liability. (1834) Liability for which one is directly responsible, as opposed to secondary liability.

remedial liability. Liability arising from a proceeding whose object contains no penal element. • The two types of proceedings giving rise to this liability are specific enforcement and restitution.

secondary liability. (1830) Liability that does not arise unless the primarily liable party fails to honor its obligation.

several liability. (1819) Liability that is separate and distinct from another's liability, so that the plaintiff may bring a separate action against one defendant without joining the other liable parties.

shareholder's liability. **1.** The statutory, added, or double liability of a shareholder for a corporation's debts, despite full payment for the stock. **2.** The liability of a shareholder for any unpaid stock listed as fully owned on the stock certificate, usu. occurring either when the shareholder agrees to pay full par value for the stock and obtains the certificate before the stock is paid for, or when partially paid-for stock is intentionally issued by a corporation as fully paid, the consideration for it being entirely fictitious.

strict liability. (1844) Liability that does not depend on actual negligence or intent to harm, but that is based on the breach of an absolute duty to make something safe.

tortious liability. Liability that arises from the breach of a duty that (1) is fixed primarily by the law, (2) is owed to persons generally, and (3) when breached, is redressable by an action for unliquidated damages.

vicarious liability (vɪ-**kair**-ee-əs). (1890) Liability that a supervisory party (such as an employer) bears for the actionable conduct of a subordinate or associate (such as an employee) based on the relationship between the two parties.

liability limit. *Insurance.* The maximum amount of coverage that an insurance company will provide on a single claim under an insurance policy.

liable (**lɪ**-ə-bəl *also* **lɪ**-bəl), *adj.* (15c) **1.** Responsible or answerable in law; legally obligated. **2.** (Of a person) subject to or likely to incur (a fine, penalty, etc.).

libel (**lɪ**-bəl), *n.* (14c) A defamatory statement expressed in a fixed medium, esp. writing but also a picture, sign, or electronic broadcast. — **libel,** *vb.* (16c). — **libelous,** *adj.*

criminal libel. At common law, a malicious libel that is designed to expose a person to hatred, contempt, or ridicule and that may subject the author to criminal sanctions. • Because of constitutional protections of free speech, libel is no longer criminally prosecuted.

false-implication libel. Libel that creates a false implication or impression even though each statement in the article, taken separately, is true.

group libel. (1940) Libel that defames a class of persons, esp. because of their race, sex, national origin, religious belief, or the like. • Civil liability for group libel is rare because the plaintiff must prove that the statement applied particularly to him or her.

libel per quod (pər **kwod**). (1927) **1.** Libel that is actionable only on allegation and proof of special damages. **2.** Libel in which the defamatory meaning is not apparent from the statement on its face but rather must be proved from extrinsic circumstances.

libel per se (pər **say**). (1843) **1.** Libel that is actionable in itself, requiring no proof of special damages. **2.** Libel that is defamatory on its face, such as the statement "Frank is a thief."

trade libel. Trade defamation that is written or recorded.

liberal, *adj.* (14c) **1.** (Of a condition, state, opinion, etc.) not restricted; expansive; tolerant. **2.** (Of a person or entity) opposed to conservatism; advocating expansive freedoms and individual expression. **3.** (Of an act, etc.) generous. **4.** (Of an interpretation, construction, etc.) not strict or literal; loose.

liberty. (14c) **1.** Freedom from arbitrary or undue external restraint, esp. by a government. **2.** A right, privilege, or immunity enjoyed by prescription or by grant; the absence of a legal duty imposed on a person.

natural liberty. (16c) The power to act as one wishes, without any restraint or control, unless by nature.

personal liberty. (16c) One's freedom to do as one pleases, limited only by the government's right to regulate the public health, safety, and welfare.

political liberty. (17c) A person's freedom to participate in the operation of government, esp. in elections and in the making and administration of laws.

religious liberty. (17c) Freedom — as guaranteed by the First Amendment — to express, without external control other than one's own conscience, any or no system of religious opinion and to engage in or refrain from any form of religious observance or public or private religious worship, as long as it is consistent with the peace and order of society.

Liberty Clause. (1971) The Due Process Clause in the 14th Amendment to the U.S. Constitution.

Library of Congress. A library on the U.S. Capitol grounds responsible for conducting research for members of Congress and congressional committees.

license, *n.* (15c) **1.** A permission, usu. revocable, to commit some act that would otherwise be unlawful; esp., an agreement (not amounting to a lease or profit à prendre) that it is lawful for the licensee to enter the licensor's land to do some act that would otherwise be illegal, such as hunting game. **2.** The certificate or document evidencing such permission. — **license,** *vb.*

bare license. (17c) A license in which no property interest passes to the licensee, who is merely not a trespasser. • It is revocable at will.

blanket license. *Copyright.* A license granted by a performing-rights society, such as ASCAP or BMI, to use all works in the society's portfolio in exchange for a fixed percentage of the user's revenues.

cross-license. *Patents.* An agreement between two or more patentees to exchange licenses for their mutual benefit and use of the licensed products.

exclusive license. (18c) A license that gives the licensee the sole right to perform the licensed act, often in a defined territory, and that prohibits the licensor from performing the licensed act and from granting the right to anyone else; esp., such a license of a copyright, patent, or trademark right.

license coupled with an interest. (1836) An irrevocable license in real estate that confers the right (not the mere permission) to perform an act or acts upon the property; esp., a license incidental to the ownership of an interest in a chattel located on the land with respect to which the license exists.

open-source license. A license that allows open-source software users to copy, distribute, or modify the source code, and publicly distribute derived works based upon the source code. • Open-source licenses usu. do not require royalty or other fees on distribution.

shrink-wrap license. (1984) A license printed on the outside of a software package to advise the buyer that by opening the package, the buyer becomes legally bound to abide by the terms of the license. • Shrink-wrap licenses usu. seek to (1) prohibit users from making unauthorized copies of the software, (2) prohibit modifications to the software, (3) limit use of the software to one computer, (4) limit the manufacturer's liability, and (5) disclaim warranties.

licensee. (1864) **1.** One to whom a license is granted. **2.** One who has permission to enter or use another's premises, but only for one's own purposes and not for the occupier's benefit.

bare licensee. (1864) A licensee whose presence on the premises the occupier tolerates but does not necessarily approve, such as one who takes a shortcut across another's land.

licensee by invitation. (1894) One who is expressly or impliedly permitted to enter another's premises to transact business with the owner or occupant or to perform an act benefiting the owner or occupant.

licensee by permission. (1894) One who has the owner's permission or passive consent to enter the owner's premises for one's own convenience, curiosity, or entertainment.

license fee. 1. A monetary charge imposed by a governmental authority for the privilege of pursuing a particular occupation, business, or activity. **2.** A charge of this type accompanied by a requirement that the licensee take some action, or be subjected to regulations or restrictions.

licensing. (15c) **1.** The sale of a license authorizing another to use something (such as computer software) protected by copyright, patent, or trademark. **2.** A governmental body's process of issuing a license.

licentiate (lɪ-**sen**-shee-ət), *n.* (16c) One who has obtained a license or authoritative permission to exercise some function, esp. to practice a profession.

licentious (lɪ-**sen**-shəs), *adj.* (16c) Lacking or ignoring moral or legal restraint, esp. in sexual activity; lewd; lascivious. — **licentiousness,** *n.*

licit (**lis**-it), *adj.* (15c) Not forbidden by law; permitted; legal. — **licitly,** *adv.*

licitation (lis-ə-**tay**-shən). (17c) The offering for sale or bidding for purchase at an auction; esp., in civil law, a judicial sale of property held in common. See La. Civ. Code art. 811.

lie, *vb.* (bef. 12c) **1.** To tell an untruth; to speak or write falsely <she lied on the witness stand>. **2.** To have foundation in the law; to be legally supportable, sustainable, or proper <in such a situation, an action lies in tort>. **3.** To exist; to reside <final appeal lies with the Supreme Court>.

lien (leen *or* **lee**-ən), *n.* (16c) A legal right or interest that a creditor has in another's property, lasting usu. until a debt or duty that it secures is satisfied. — **lien,** *vb.* — **lienable, liened,** *adj.*

lienholder. (1830) A person having or owning a lien.

lien of a covenant. (1916) The beginning portion of a covenant, stating the names of the parties and the character of the covenant.

lien-stripping. *Bankruptcy.* The practice of splitting a mortgagee's secured claim into secured and unsecured components and reducing the claim to the market value of the debtor's residence, thereby allowing the debtor to modify the terms of the mortgage and reduce the amount of the debt. • The U.S. Supreme Court has prohibited lien-stripping in all Chapter 7 cases (*Nobelman v. American Savs. Bank*, 508 U.S. 324, 113 S.Ct. 2106 (1993)) and in Chapter 13 cases involving a debtor's principal residence (*Dewsnup v. Timm*, 502 U.S. 410, 112 S.Ct. 773 (1992)), and the Bankruptcy Reform Act of 1994 modified the Bankruptcy Code to prohibit lien-stripping in Chapter 11 cases involving an individual's principal residence.

lien theory. (1882) The idea that a mortgage resembles a lien, so that the mortgagee acquires only a lien on the property and the mortgagor retains both legal and equitable title unless a valid foreclosure occurs.

lieutenant governor. (16c) A deputy or subordinate governor, sometimes charged with such duties as presiding over the state legislature, but esp. important as the governor's successor if the governor dies, resigns, or becomes disabled.

life-care contract. (1950) An agreement in which one party is assured of care and maintenance for life in exchange for transferring property to the other party.

life expectancy. 1. The period that a person of a given age and sex is expected to live, according to actuarial tables. **2.** The period that a given person is expected to live, taking into account individualized characteristics such as heredity, past and present diseases, and other relevant medical data.

life in being. (1836) Under the rule against perpetuities, anyone alive when a future interest is created, whether or not the person has an interest in the estate.

life insurance. (1809) An agreement between an insurance company and the policyholder to pay a specified amount to a designated beneficiary on the insured's death.

corporate-owned life insurance. A life-insurance policy bought by a company on an employee's life, naming the company as beneficiary. — Abbr. COLI.

credit life insurance. Life insurance on a borrower, usu. in a consumer installment loan, in which the amount due is paid if the borrower dies.

endowment life insurance. Life insurance that is payable either to the insured at the end of the policy period or to the insured's beneficiary if the insured dies before the period ends.

joint life insurance. (1920) Life insurance on two or more persons, payable to the survivor or survivors when one of the policyholders dies.

key-employee life insurance. Life insurance taken out by a company on an essential or valuable employee, with the company as beneficiary.

national-service life insurance. Life insurance available to a person in active U.S. military service on or after October 8, 1940, and issuable at favorable rates.

ordinary life insurance. **1.** Life insurance having an investment-sensitive cash value, such as whole life insurance or universal life insurance. • Ordinary insurance is one of three main categories of life insurance. **2.** Whole-life insurance.

single-premium life insurance. Life insurance that is paid for in one installment rather than a series of premiums over time.

term life insurance. Life insurance that covers the insured for only a specified period. • It pays a fixed benefit to a named beneficiary upon the insured's death but is not redeemable for a cash value during the insured's life.

universal life insurance. Term life insurance in which the premiums are paid from the insured's earnings from a money-market fund.

variable life insurance. Life insurance in which the premiums are invested in securities and whose death benefits thus depend on the securities' performance, though there is a minimum guaranteed death benefit.

whole life insurance. Life insurance that covers an insured for life, during which the insured pays fixed premiums, accumulates savings from an invested portion of the premiums, and receives a guaranteed benefit upon death, to be paid to a named beneficiary. • Such a policy may provide that at a stated time, premiums will end or benefits will increase.

life interest. (18c) An interest in real or personal property measured by the duration of the holder's or another named person's life.

life of a writ. The effective period during which a writ may be levied. • That period usu. ends on the day that the law or the writ itself provides that it must be returned to court.

life-sustaining procedure. (1976) A medical procedure that uses mechanical or artificial means to sustain, restore, or substitute for a vital function and that serves only or mainly to postpone death.

life table. An actuarial table that gives the probable proportions of people who will live to different ages.

life tenant. (16c) A person who, until death, is beneficially entitled to property; the holder of a life estate.

equitable life tenant. (1880) A life tenant not automatically entitled to possession but who makes an election allowed by law to a person of that status — such as a spouse — and to whom a court will normally grant possession if security or an undertaking is given.

legal life tenant. (1886) A life tenant who is automatically entitled to possession by virtue of a legal estate.

LIFO (**lɪ**-foh). *abbr.* Last-in, first-out.

light most favorable. (1861) The standard of scrutinizing or interpreting a verdict by accepting as true all evidence and inferences that support it and disregarding all contrary evidence and inferences.

like, *adj.* (12c) **1.** Equal in quantity, quality, or degree; corresponding exactly <like copies>. **2.** Similar or substantially similar <like character>.

like-kind exchange. (1963) An exchange of trade, business, or investment property (except inventory or securities) for property of the same kind, class, or character. IRC (26 USCA) § 1031.

like-kind property. (1946) *Tax.* Property that is of such a similar kind, class, or character to other property that a gain from an exchange of the property is not recognized for federal income-tax purposes.

likelihood-of-confusion test. *Trademarks.* A test for trademark infringement, based on the probability that a substantial number of ordinarily prudent buyers will be misled or confused about the source of a product.

likelihood-of-success-on-the-merits test. *Civil procedure.* The rule that a litigant who seeks a preliminary injunction, or seeks to forestall the effects of a judgment during appeal, must show a reasonable probability of success in the litigation or appeal.

limine out (**lim**-ə-nee), *vb.* (1997) (Of a court) to exclude (evidence) by granting a motion in limine.

limit, *n.* (14c) **1.** A restriction or restraint. **2.** A boundary or defining line. **3.** The extent of power, right, or authority. — **limit,** *vb.* — **limited,** *adj.*

limitation. (14c) **1.** The act of limiting; the state of being limited. **2.** A restriction. **3.** A statutory period after which a lawsuit or prosecution cannot be brought in court. **4.** *Property.* The restriction of the extent of an estate; the creation by deed or devise of a lesser estate out of a fee simple.

collateral limitation. *Hist.* A limitation that makes the duration of an estate dependent on another event (other than the life of the grantee), such as an estate to A until B turns 21.

conditional limitation. (18c) **1.** Executory limitation. **2.** A lease provision that automatically terminates the lease if a specified event occurs, such as if the lessee defaults.

executory limitation. (18c) A restriction that causes an estate to automatically end and revest in a third party upon the happening of a specified event.

limitation over. (17c) An additional estate created or contemplated in a conveyance, to be enjoyed after the first estate expires or is exhausted. • An example of language giving rise to a limitation over is "to A for life, remainder to B.

special limitation. (17c) A restriction that causes an estate to end automatically and revert to the grantor upon the happening of a specified event.

supplanting limitation. A limitation involving a secondary gift that is expressed in a clause following the original gift and that is typically introduced by the words "but if," "and if," or "in case."

limitation-of-damages clause. (1933) A contractual provision by which the parties agree on a maximum amount of damages recoverable for a future breach of the agreement.

limitation-of-liability act. (1897) A federal or state law that limits the type of damages that may be recovered, the liability of particular persons or groups, or the time during which an action may be brought.

limitation-of-remedies clause. (1974) A contractual provision that restricts the remedies available to the parties if a party defaults. • Under the UCC, such a clause is valid unless it fails of its essential purpose or it unconscionably limits consequential damages.

line, *n.* (14c) **1.** A demarcation, border, or limit. **2.** A person's occupation or business. **3.** In manufacturing, a series of closely related products. **4.** The ancestry of a person; lineage.

collateral line. (16c) A line of descent connecting persons who are not directly related to each other as ascendants or descendants, but who are descendants of a common ancestor.

direct line. (17c) A line of descent traced through only those persons who are related to each other directly as ascendants or descendants.

maternal line. (17c) A person's ancestry or relationship with another traced through the mother.

paternal line. (17c) A person's ancestry or relationship with another traced through the father.

lineage (lin-ee-əj). (14c) Ancestry and progeny; family, ascending or descending.

lineal (lin-ee-əl), *adj.* (15c) Derived from or relating to common ancestors, esp. in a direct line; hereditary.

lineal, *n.* (18c) A lineal descendant; a direct blood relative.

line of credit. (1917) The maximum amount of borrowing power extended to a borrower by a given lender, to be drawn upon by the borrower as needed.

lineup. (1915) A police identification procedure in which a criminal suspect and other physically similar persons are shown to the victim or a witness to determine whether the suspect can be identified as the perpetrator of the crime.

linguistic profiling. Profiling based on vocal characteristics that suggest a speaker's race, sex, or national, ethnic, or regional origin.

link-in-chain principle. (1962) *Criminal procedure.* The principle that a criminal defendant's Fifth Amendment right against self-incrimination protects the defendant not only from answering directly incriminating questions but also from giving answers that might connect the defendant to criminal activity in the chain of evidence.

liquid, *adj.* (1879) **1.** (Of an asset) capable of being readily converted into cash. **2.** (Of a person or entity) possessing assets that can be readily converted into cash.

liquidate, *vb.* (16c) **1.** To settle (an obligation) by payment or other adjustment; to extinguish (a debt). **2.** To ascertain the precise amount of (debt, damages, etc.) by litigation or agreement. **3.** To determine the liabilities and distribute the assets of (an entity), esp. in bankruptcy or dissolution. **4.** To convert (a nonliquid asset) into cash. **5.** To wind up the affairs of (a corporation, business, etc.). **6.** *Slang.* To get rid of (a person), esp. by killing.

liquidated, *adj.* (18c) **1.** (Of an amount or debt) settled or determined, esp. by agreement. **2.** (Of an asset or assets) converted into cash.

liquidated amount. A figure readily computed, based on an agreement's terms.

liquidated-damages clause. (1873) A contractual provision that determines in advance the measure of damages if a party breaches the agreement. • Traditionally, courts have upheld such a clause unless the agreed-on sum is deemed a penalty for one of the following reasons: (1) the sum grossly exceeds the probable damages on breach, (2) the same sum is made payable for any variety of different breaches (some major, some minor), or (3) a mere delay in payment has been listed among the events of default.

liquidation, *n.* (16c) **1.** The act of determining by agreement or by litigation the exact amount of something (as a debt or damages) that before was uncertain. **2.** The act of settling a debt by payment or other satisfaction. **3.** The act or process of converting assets into cash, esp. to settle debts. **4.** *Bankruptcy.* The process — under Chapter 7 of the Bankruptcy Code — of collecting a debtor's nonexempt property, converting that property to cash, and distributing the cash to the various creditors.

liquidator. (1858) A person appointed to wind up a business's affairs, esp. by selling off its assets.

liquidity. 1. The quality or state of being readily convertible to cash. **2.** *Securities.* The characteristic of having enough units in the market that large transactions can occur without substantial price variations.

liquidity ratio. The ratio between a person's or entity's assets that are held in cash or liquid form and the amount of the person's or entity's current liabilities, indicating the ability to pay current debts as they come due.

lis (lis). [Latin] (17c) A piece of litigation; a controversy or dispute.

lis pendens (lis **pen**-dənz). [Latin] (17c) **1.** A pending lawsuit. **2.** The jurisdiction, power, or control acquired by a court over property while a legal action is pending. **3.** A notice, recorded in the chain of title to real property, required or permitted in some jurisdictions to warn all persons that certain property is the subject matter of litigation, and that any interests acquired during the pendency of the suit are subject to its outcome.

list, *n.* (13c) **1.** A roll or register, as of names. **2.** A docket of cases ready for hearing or trial.

list, *vb.* (bef. 12c) **1.** To set down or enter (information) in a list. **2.** To register (a security) on an exchange so that it may be publicly traded. **3.** To place (property) for sale under an agreement with a real-estate agent or broker.

listing. (1891) **1.** *Real estate.* An agreement between a property owner and an agent, whereby the agent agrees to try to secure a buyer or tenant for a specific property at a certain price and terms in return for a fee or commission.

exclusive-agency listing. A listing providing that one agent has the right to be the only person, other than the owner, to sell the property during a specified period.

multiple listing. A listing providing that the agent will allow other agents to try to sell the property. • Under this agreement, the original agent gives the selling agent a percentage of the commission or some other stipulated amount.

net listing. A listing providing that the agent agrees to sell the owner's property for a set minimum price, any amount over the minimum being retained by the agent as commission.

open listing. A listing that allows selling rights to be given to more than one agent at a time, obligates the owner to pay a commission when a specified broker makes a sale, and reserves the owner's right to personally sell the property without paying a commission.

2. *Securities.* The contract between a firm and a stock exchange by which the trading of the firm's securities on the exchange is handled. **3.** *Tax.* The creation of a schedule or inventory of a person's taxable property; the list of a person's taxable property.

list of creditors. (1818) A schedule giving the names and addresses of creditors, along with amounts owed them. • This list is required in a bankruptcy proceeding.

literal, *adj.* (16c) According to expressed language. • Literal performance of a condition requires exact compliance with its terms.

literary property. 1. The physical property in which an intellectual production is embodied, such as a book, screenplay, or lecture. **2.** An owner's exclusive right to possess, use, and dispose of such a production.

litigable (lit-ə-gə-bəl), *adj.* (18c) Able to be contested or disputed in court. — **litigability,** *n.*

litigant. (17c) A party to a lawsuit.

vexatious litigant. A litigant who repeatedly files frivolous lawsuits.

litigation, *n.* (17c) **1.** The process of carrying on a lawsuit. **2.** A lawsuit itself. — **litigate,** *vb.* — **litigatory, litigational,** *adj.*

complex litigation. Litigation involving several parties who are separately represented, and usu. involving multifarious factual and legal issues.

litigation-hold letter. A writing that orders the segregation and retention of certain documents and data that are or may be relevant to a threatened or pending litigation or an official investigation.

litigator. (16c) **1.** A trial lawyer. **2.** A lawyer who prepares cases for trial, as by conducting discovery and pretrial motions, trying cases, and handling appeals.

litigious (li-**tij**-əs), *adj.* (14c) Prone to legal disputes; contentious. — **litigiousness, litigiosity** (li-tij-ee-**os**-ə-tee), *n.*

littoral (lit-ər-əl), *adj.* (17c) Of or relating to the coast or shore of an ocean, sea, or lake. — **littoral,** *n.*

livery (liv-ə-ree *or* **liv**-ree). (15c) **1.** The delivery of the possession of real property. **2.** *Hist.* An heir's writ, upon reaching the age of majority, to obtain seisin of his lands from the king. **3.** The boarding and care of horses for a fee. **4.** A business that rents vehicles.

living separate and apart. (18c) (Of spouses) living away from each other, along with at least one spouse's intent to dissolve the marriage.

living will. (1972) An instrument, signed with the formalities statutorily required for a will, by which a person directs that his or her life not be artificially prolonged by extraordinary measures when there is no reasonable expectation of recovery from extreme physical or mental disability. • Most states have living-will legislation.

L.J. *abbr.* Law journal.

LL.B. *abbr.* Bachelor of Laws. • This was formerly the law degree ordinarily conferred by American law schools. It is still the normal degree in British law schools.

L.L.C. *abbr.* Limited-liability company.

LL.D. *abbr.* Doctor of Laws.

LL.M. *abbr.* Master of Laws.

Lloyd's of London. *Insurance.* **1.** A London insurance mart where individual underwriters gather to quote rates and write insurance on a wide variety of risks. **2.** A voluntary association of merchants, shipowners, underwriters, and brokers formed not to write policies but instead to issue a notice of an endeavor to members who may individually underwrite a policy by assuming shares of the total risk of insuring a client.

Lloyd's underwriters. An unincorporated association of underwriters who, under a common name, engage in the insurance business through an attorney-in-fact having authority to obligate the underwriters severally, within specified limits, on insurance contracts that the attorney makes or issues in the common name.

L.L.P. *abbr.* Limited-liability partnership.

load, *n.* An amount added to a security's price or to an insurance premium in order to cover the sales commission and expenses.

loan, *n.* (12c) **1.** An act of lending; a grant of something for temporary use. **2.** A thing lent for the borrower's temporary use; esp., a sum of money lent at interest.

accommodation loan. (1834) A loan for which the lender receives no consideration in return.

add-on loan. (1972) A loan in which the interest is calculated at the stated rate for the loan agreement's full term for the full principal amount, and then the interest is added to the principal before installment payments are calculated, resulting in an interest amount higher than if it were calculated on the monthly unpaid balance.

amortized loan. (1930) A loan calling for periodic payments that are applied first to interest and then to principal, as provided by the terms of the note.

balloon loan. An installment loan in which one or more of the later repayments are much larger than earlier payments; esp., a loan featuring a string of payments that are too small to amortize the entire loan within the loan period, coupled with a large final lump-sum payment of the outstanding balance.

bridge loan. A short-term loan that is used to cover costs until more permanent financing is arranged or to cover a portion of costs that are expected to be covered by an imminent sale.

building loan. A type of bridge loan used primarily for erecting a building. • The loan is typically advanced in parts as work progresses and is used to pay the contractor, subcontractors, and material suppliers.

call loan. (1869) A loan for which the lender can demand payment at any time, usu. with 24 hours' notice, because there is no fixed maturity date.

commercial loan. (1875) A loan that a financial institution gives to a business, generally for 30 to 90 days.

consolidation loan. (1875) A loan whose proceeds are used to pay off other individual loans, thereby creating a more manageable debt.

consumer loan. (1957) A loan that is given to an individual for family, household, personal, or agricultural purposes and that is generally governed by truth-in-lending statutes and regulations.

day loan. A short-term loan to a broker to finance daily transactions.

home-equity loan. (1984) A line of bank credit given to a homeowner, using as collateral the homeowner's equity in the home.

installment loan. (1916) A loan that is to be repaid in usu. equal portions over a specified period.

interest-free loan. (1946) Money loaned to a borrower at no charge or, under the Internal Revenue Code, with a charge that is lower than the market rate. IRC (26 USCA) § 7872.

interest-only loan. A loan for which the borrower pays only the interest on the principal balance of the loan for a stated period, usu. a few years. • At the end of the stated period, the principal balance is unchanged. An interest-only loan features low initial payments in return for significantly larger payments later or a balloon payment at the end of the term.

liar's loan. A loan that involves no background check and can be obtained by claiming that one meets the lender's income and other requirements.

mortgage loan. (1846) A loan secured by a mortgage or deed of trust on real property.

NINJA loan. abbr. No-income, no-job, no-assets loan.

no-doc loan. **1.** A loan for which a borrower provides only minimal proof of ability to repay. • The name is short for "no documentation." **2.** Liar's loan.

nonperforming loan. (1984) An outstanding loan that is not being repaid.

nonrecourse loan. (1941) A secured loan that allows the lender to attach only the collateral, not the borrower's personal assets, if the loan is not repaid.

participation loan. (1928) A loan issued by two or more lenders.

recourse loan. A loan that allows the lender, if the borrower defaults, not only to attach the collateral but also to seek judgment against the borrower's (or guarantor's) personal assets.

revolver loan. (1985) A single loan that a debtor takes out in lieu of several lines of credit or other loans from various creditors, and that is subject to review and approval at certain intervals.

revolving loan. (1927) A loan that is renewed at maturity.

secured loan. (1862) A loan that is secured by property or securities.

short-term loan. (1902) A loan with a due date of less than one year, usu. evidenced by a note.

signature loan. An unsecured loan based solely on the borrower's promise or signature.

subprime loan. A loan, esp. a mortgage or home-equity loan, made to one whose financial condition and creditworthiness are poor, creating a high risk of default. • A subprime loan usu. has an adjustable interest rate that is low at inception, to help a financially weak borrower qualify, then rises over the life of the loan.

term loan. A loan with a specified due date, usu. of more than one year. • Such a loan typically cannot be repaid before maturity without incurring a penalty.

veteran's loan. A federally guaranteed loan extended to armed-forces veterans for the purchase of a home.

loan-amortization schedule. (1958) A schedule that divides each loan payment into an interest component and a principal component.

loan commitment. (1940) A lender's binding promise to a borrower to lend a specified amount of money at a certain interest rate, usu. within a specified period and for a specified purpose (such as buying real estate).

loan for consumption. (1840) An agreement by which a lender delivers goods to a borrower who consumes them and who is obligated to return goods of the same quantity, type, and quality.

loan for exchange. (1915) A contract by which a lender delivers personal property to a borrower who agrees to return similar property, usu. without compensation for its use.

loan for use. (1837) An agreement by which a lender delivers an asset to a borrower who must use it according to its normal function or according to the agreement, and who must return it when finished using it. • No interest is charged.

loan participation. (1934) The coming together of multiple lenders to issue a large loan (called a *participation loan*) to one borrower, thereby reducing each lender's individual risk.

loan-receipt agreement. (1943) *Torts.* A settlement agreement by which the defendant lends money to the plaintiff interest-free, the plaintiff not being obligated to repay the loan unless he or she recovers money from other tortfeasors responsible for the same injury.

loansharking, *n.* (1914) The practice of lending money at excessive and esp. usurious rates, and often using threats or extortion to enforce repayment. — **loan-shark,** *vb.* — **loan shark,** *n.*

loan-to-value ratio. The ratio, usu. expressed as a percentage, between the amount of a mortgage loan and the value of the property pledged as security for the mortgage.

loan value. *Insurance.* **1.** The maximum amount that may be lent safely on property or life insurance without jeopardizing the lender's need for protection from the borrower's default. **2.** The amount of money an insured can borrow against the cash value of his or her life-insurance policy.

lobby, *vb.* (1837) **1.** To talk with or curry favor with a legislator, usu. repeatedly or frequently, in an attempt to influence the legislator's vote. **2.** To support or oppose (a measure) by working to influence a legislator's vote. **3.** To try to influence (a decision-maker). — **lobbying,** *n.* — **lobbyist,** *n.*

lobbying act. (1948) A federal or state law governing the conduct of lobbyists, usu. by requiring them to register and file activity reports. • An example is the Federal Regulation of Lobbying Act, 12 USCA § 261.

local concern. (1833) An activity conducted by a municipality in its proprietary capacity.

locality of a lawsuit. (1939) The place where a court may exercise judicial authority.

locality rule. 1. The doctrine that, in a professional-malpractice suit, the standard of care applicable to the professional's conduct is the reasonable care exercised by similar professionals in the same vicinity and professional community. **2.** The doctrine that, in determining the appropriate amount of attorney's fees to be awarded in a suit, the proper basis is the rate charged by similar attorneys for similar work in the vicinity.

local law. 1. A statute that relates to or operates in a particular locality rather than the entire state. **2.** A statute that applies to particular persons or things rather than an entire class of persons or things. **3.** The law of a particular jurisdiction, as opposed to the law of a foreign state. **4.** *Conflict of laws.* The body of standards, principles, and rules — excluding conflict-of-laws rules — that the state courts apply to controversies before them. Restatement (Second) of Conflict of Laws § 4(1) (1971).

local option. An option that allows a municipality or other governmental unit to determine a particular course of action without the specific approval of state officials.

local rule. (1819) **1.** A rule based on the physical conditions of a state and the character, customs, and beliefs of its people. **2.** A rule by which an individual court supplements the procedural rules applying generally to all courts within the jurisdiction.

location. (16c) **1.** The specific place or position of a person or thing. **2.** The act or process of locating. **3.** *Real estate.* The designation of the boundaries of a particular piece of land, either on the record or on the land itself.

locative calls (**lok**-ə-tiv). (1807) *Property.* In land descriptions, specific descriptions that fix the boundaries of the land.

Lochnerize (**lok**-nər-ɪz), *vb.* (1976) To examine and strike down economic legislation under the guise of enforcing the Due Process Clause, esp. in the manner of the U.S. Supreme Court during the early 20th century. • The term takes its name from the decision in *Lochner v. New York*, 198 U.S. 45, 25 S.Ct. 539 (1905), in which the Court invalidated New York's maximum-hours law for bakers. — **Lochnerization,** *n.*

lockbox. (1872) **1.** A secure box, such as a post-office box, strongbox, or safe-deposit box. **2.** A facility offered by a financial institution for quickly collecting and consolidating checks and other funds from a party's customers.

lockdown. (1977) The temporary confinement of prisoners in their cells during a state of heightened alert caused by an escape, riot, or other emergency.

lockout. (1854) **1.** An employer's withholding of work and closing of a business because of a labor dispute. **2.** Loosely, an employee's refusal to work because the employer unreasonably refuses to abide by an expired employment contract while a new one is being negotiated.

locus (**loh**-kəs). [Latin "place"] (18c) The place or position where something is done or exists. — Abbr. L.

locus delicti (**loh**-kəs də-**lik**-tɪ). [Latin "place of the wrong"] The place where an offense was committed; the place where the last event necessary to make the actor liable occurred.

locus in quo (**loh**-kəs in **kwoh**). [Latin "place in which"] (18c) The place where something is alleged to have occurred.

locus standi (**loh**-kəs **stan**-dɪ *or* -dee). [Latin "place of standing"] (1835) The right to bring an action or to be heard in a given forum; standing.

lodestar. (14c) **1.** A guiding star; an inspiration or model. **2.** A reasonable amount of attorney's fees in a given case, usu. calculated by multiplying a reasonable number of hours worked by the prevailing hourly rate in the community for similar work, and often considering such additional factors as the degree of skill and difficulty involved in the case, the degree of its urgency, its novelty, and the like.

logical-cause doctrine. (1980) The principle that, if the plaintiff proves that an injury occurred and proves a logical cause of it, a party desiring to defeat the claim cannot succeed merely by showing that there is another imaginable cause, but must also show that the alternative cause is more probable than the cause shown by the plaintiff.

logical positivism. (1931) A philosophical system or movement requiring that meaningful statements be in principle verifiable.

logical-relationship standard. (1976) *Civil procedure.* A test applied to determine whether a defendant's counterclaim is compulsory, by examining whether both claims are based on the same operative facts or whether those facts activate additional rights, otherwise dormant, for the defendant. • One of the most important factors considered is whether hearing the claims together would promote judicial economy and efficiency. Fed. R. Civ. P. 13(a).

logrolling, *n.* (1812) **1.** The exchanging of political favors; esp., the trading of votes among legislators to gain support of measures that are beneficial to each legislator's constituency. **2.** The legislative practice of including several propositions in one measure or proposed constitutional amendment so that the legislature or voters will pass all of them, even though these propositions might not have passed if they had been submitted separately. — **logroll,** *vb.*

loitering, *n.* (14c) The criminal offense of remaining in a certain place (such as a public street) for no apparent reason. • Loitering statutes are generally held to be unconstitutionally vague. — **loiter,** *vb.*

lollipop syndrome. (1986) *Family law.* A situation in which one or both parents, often in a custody battle, manipulate the child with gifts, fun, good times, and minimal discipline in an attempt to win over the child.

long, *adj.* **1.** Holding a security or commodity in anticipation of a rise in price. **2.** Of or relating to a purchase of securities or commodities in anticipation of rising prices.

long-arm, *adj.* Of, relating to, or arising from a long-arm statute.

long-arm statute. (1951) A statute providing for jurisdiction over a nonresident defendant who has had contacts with the territory where the statute is in effect. • Most state long-arm statutes extend this jurisdiction to its constitutional limits.

lookout, *n.* (17c) A careful, vigilant watching.

look-through principle. (1993) *Tax.* A doctrine for allocating transfer-gains taxes on real estate by looking beyond the entity possessing legal title to identify the beneficial owners of the property.

loophole. (17c) An ambiguity, omission, or exception (as in a law or other legal document) that provides a way to avoid a rule without violating its literal requirements; esp., a tax-code provision that allows a taxpayer to legally avoid or reduce income taxes.

looseleaf service. (1927) A type of lawbook having pages that are periodically replaced with updated pages, designed to cope with constant change and increasing bulk.

loss. (bef. 12c) **1.** An undesirable outcome of a risk; the disappearance or diminution of value, usu. in an unexpected or relatively unpredictable way. • When the loss is a decrease in value, the usual method of calculating the loss is to ascertain the amount by which a thing's original cost exceeds its later selling price. **2.** *Tax.* The excess of a property's adjusted value over the amount realized from its sale or other disposition. IRC (26 USCA) § 1001. **3.** *Insurance.* The amount of financial detriment caused by an insured person's death or an insured property's damage, for which the insurer becomes liable. **4.** The failure to maintain possession of a thing.

actual loss. (18c) A loss resulting from the real and substantial destruction of insured property.

capital loss. (1921) The loss realized upon selling or exchanging a capital asset.

casualty loss. (1934) For tax purposes, the total or partial destruction of an asset resulting from an unexpected or unusual event, such as an automobile accident or a tornado.

consequential loss. (1829) A loss arising from the results of damage rather than from the damage itself. • A consequential loss is proximate when the natural and probable effect of the wrongful conduct, under the circumstances, is to set in operation the intervening cause from which the loss directly results. When the loss is not the natural and probable effect of the wrongful conduct, the loss is remote.

constructive total loss. (1805) Such serious damage to the insured property that the cost of repairs would exceed the value of the thing repaired.

direct loss. (18c) A loss that results immediately and proximately from an event.

extraordinary loss. (17c) A loss that is both unusual and infrequent, such as a loss resulting from a natural disaster.

net operating loss. (1921) The excess of operating expenses over revenues, the amount of which can be deducted from gross income if other deductions do not exceed gross income.

ordinary loss. (1850) *Tax.* A loss incurred from the sale or exchange of an item that is used in a trade or business. • The loss is deductible from ordinary income, and thus is more beneficial to the taxpayer than a capital loss.

out-of-pocket loss. (1921) The difference between the value of what the buyer paid and the market value of what was received in return.

paper loss. (1924) A loss that is realized only by selling something (such as a security) that has decreased in market value.

total loss. (1924) The complete destruction of insured property so that nothing of value remains and the subject matter no longer exists in its original form. • Generally, a loss is total if, after the damage occurs, no substantial remnant remains standing that a reasonably prudent uninsured owner, desiring to rebuild, would use as a basis to restore the property to its original condition.

loss leader. (1922) A good or commodity sold at a very low price, usu. below cost, to attract customers to buy other items.

loss-of-bargain rule. (1903) The doctrine that damages for a breach of a contract should put the injured party in the position it would have been in if both parties had performed their contractual duties.

loss-of-chance doctrine. (1987) A rule in some states providing a claim against a doctor who has engaged in medical malpractice that, although it does not result in a particular injury, decreases or eliminates the chance of surviving or recovering from the preexisting condition for which the doctor was consulted.

loss of consortium (kən-**sor**-shee-əm). (1878) **1.** A loss of the benefits that one spouse is entitled to receive from the other, including companionship, cooperation, aid, affection, and sexual relations. **2.** A similar loss of benefits that one is entitled to receive from a parent or child.

loss-payable clause. *Insurance.* An insurance-policy provision that authorizes the payment of proceeds to someone other than the named insured, esp. to someone who has a security interest in the insured property.

lost, *adj.* (16c) **1.** (Of property) beyond the possession and custody of its owner and not locatable by diligent search. **2.** (Of a person) missing. **3.** *Parliamentary law.* (Of a motion) rejected; not adopted.

lost-chance doctrine. (1985) **1.** Loss-of-chance doctrine. **2.** A rule permitting a claim, in limited circumstances, against someone who fails to come to the aid of a person who is in imminent danger of being injured or killed.

lost earning capacity. (1908) A person's diminished earning power resulting from an injury.

lost profits. *Contracts.* A measure of damages that allows a seller to collect the profits that would have been made on the sale if the buyer had not breached. UCC § 2-708(2).

lost-volume seller. (1974) A seller of goods who, after a buyer has breached a sales contract, resells the goods to a different buyer who would have bought identical goods from the seller's inventory even if the original buyer had not breached. • Such a seller is entitled to lost profits, rather than contract price less market price, as damages from the original buyer's breach. UCC § 2-708(2).

lot. (bef. 12c) **1.** A tract of land, esp. one having specific boundaries or being used for a given purpose.

minimum lot. A lot that has the least amount of square footage allowed by a local zoning law.

nonconforming lot. A previously lawful lot that now violates an amended or newly adopted zoning ordinance.

2. An article that is the subject of a separate sale, lease, or delivery, whether or not it is sufficient to perform the contract. UCC §§ 2-105(5); 2A-103(1)(s). **3.** A specified number of shares or a specific quantity of a commodity designated for trading.

odd lot. A number of shares of stock or the value of a bond that is less than a round lot.

round lot. The established unit of trading for stocks and bonds. • A round lot of stock is usu. 100 shares, and a round lot of bonds is usu. $1,000 or $5,000 par value.

lot line. (1829) A land boundary that separates one tract from another.

lottery. (16c) A method of raising revenues, esp. state-government revenues, by selling tickets and giving prizes (usu. cash prizes) to those who hold tickets with winning numbers that are drawn at random.

lower-of-cost-or-market method. (1958) A means of pricing or costing inventory by which inventory value is set at either acquisition cost or market cost, whichever is lower.

lowest responsible bidder. (1844) A bidder who has the lowest price conforming to the contract specifications and who is financially able and competent to complete the work, as shown by the bidder's prior performance.

loyalty, *n.* (15c) Faithfulness or allegiance to a person, cause, duty, or government. — **loyal,** *adj.*

loyalty oath. Oath of allegiance.

L.P. *abbr.* Limited partnership.

L.R. *abbr.* Law Reports.

LSAT. *abbr.* Law-School Admissions Test.

Ltd. *abbr.* Limited — used in company names to indicate limited liability.

lucid interval. (17c) **1.** A brief period during which an insane person regains sanity sufficient to have the legal capacity to contract and act on his or her own behalf. **2.** A period during which a person has enough mental capacity to understand the concept of marriage and the duties and obligations it imposes. **3.** A period during which an otherwise incompetent person regains sufficient testamentary capacity to execute a valid will.

lucrative (**loo**-krə-tiv), *adj.* (15c) Profitable; remunerative.

lumping. *Criminal procedure.* The imposition of a general sentence on a criminal defendant.

lunatic, *n. Archaic.* An insane person.

LWI. *abbr.* Legal Writing Institute.

lying in wait. *Criminal law.* The series of acts involved in watching, waiting for, and hiding from someone, with the intent of killing or inflicting serious bodily injury on that person.

lynch, *vb.* (1836) (Of a mob) to kill (somebody) without legal authority, usu. by hanging.

lynch law. (1811) The administration of summary punishment, esp. death, for an alleged crime, without legal authority.

M

M. *abbr.* Mortgage.

mace-proof, *vb.* To exempt from an arrest; to secure against an arrest.

machination (mak-ə-**nay**-shən). (15c) **1.** An act of planning a scheme, esp. for an evil purpose. **2.** The scheme so planned.

machine. (16c) *Patents.* A device or apparatus consisting of fixed and moving parts that work together to perform some function. • Machines are one of the statutory categories of inventions that can be patented.

MACRS. *abbr.* Modified Accelerated Cost Recovery System.

magisterial (maj-ə-**steer**-ee-əl), *adj.* (17c) Of or relating to the character, office, powers, or duties of a magistrate.

magistracy (**maj**-ə-strə-see). (16c) **1.** The office, district, or power of a magistrate. **2.** A body of magistrates.

magistral, *adj.* (16c) **1.** Of or relating to a master or masters. **2.** Formulated by a physician. **3.** Magisterial.

magistrate (**maj**-ə-strayt), *n.* (14c) **1.** The highest-ranking official in a government, such as the king in a monarchy, the president in a republic, or the governor in a state. **2.** A local official who possesses whatever power is specified in the appointment or statutory grant of authority. **3.** A judicial officer with strictly limited jurisdiction and authority, often on the local level and often restricted to criminal cases. **4.** Judicial officer. — **magisterial** (maj-ə-**stir**-ee-əl), *adj.*

committing magistrate. (18c) A judicial officer who conducts preliminary criminal hearings and may order that a defendant be released for lack of evidence, sent to jail to await trial, or released on bail.

district-court magistrate. (1932) In some states, a quasi-judicial officer given the power to set bail, accept bond, accept guilty pleas, impose sentences for traffic violations and similar offenses, and conduct informal hearings on civil infractions.

federal magistrate. United States Magistrate Judge.

investigating magistrate. (1908) A quasi-judicial officer responsible for examining and sometimes ruling on certain aspects of a criminal proceeding before it comes before a judge.

police magistrate. (18c) A judicial officer who has jurisdiction to try minor criminal offenses, breaches of police regulations, and similar violations.

Magistrate Judge, U.S. United States Magistrate Judge.

Magnuson–Moss Warranty Act (**mag**-nə-sən–**maws** *or* –**mos**). A federal statute requiring that a written warranty of a consumer product fully and conspicuously disclose, in plain language, the terms and conditions of the warranty, including whether the warranty is full or limited, according to standards given in the statute. 15 USCA §§ 2301–2312.

mailbox rule. (1975) **1.** *Contracts.* The principle that an acceptance becomes effective — and binds the offeror — once it has been properly mailed. • The mailbox rule does not apply, however, if the offer specifies that an acceptance is not effective until received. **2.** The principle that when a pleading or other document is filed or served by mail, filing or service is deemed to have occurred on the date of mailing.

mail cover. (1959) A process by which the U.S. Postal Service provides a government agency with information on the face of an envelope or package (such as a postmark) for the agency's use in locating a fugitive, identifying a coconspirator, or obtaining other evidence necessary to solve a crime.

maim, *n.* (14c) *Archaic.* The type of strength-diminishing injury required to support a charge of mayhem; esp., serious injury to a body part that is necessary for fighting. — **maim,** *vb.*

main pot. *Tax.* A step in evaluating tax liability in which qualified transactions are compared to determine whether a net gain or loss has occurred. IRC (26 USCA) § 1231.

mainstreaming. (1973) The practice of educating a disabled student in classes with students who are not disabled, in a regular-education setting, as opposed to a special-education class.

maintainor. (15c) *Criminal law.* A person who meddles in someone else's litigation by providing money or other assistance; a person who is guilty of maintenance.

maintenance, *n.* (14c) **1.** The continuation of something, such as a lawsuit. **2.** The continuing possession of something, such as property. **3.** The assertion of a position or opinion; the act of upholding a position in argument. **4.** The care and work put into property to keep it operating and productive; general repair and upkeep. **5.** Financial support given by one person to another, usu. paid as a result of a legal separation or divorce; esp. alimony. • Maintenance may end after a specified time or upon the death, cohabitation, or remarriage of the receiving party.

maintenance in gross. (1914) A fixed amount of money to be paid upon divorce by one former spouse to the other, in a lump sum or in installments.

separate maintenance. (17c) Money paid by one married person to another for support if they are no longer living together as spouses.

6. Improper assistance in prosecuting or defending a lawsuit given to a litigant by someone who has no bona fide interest in the case; meddling in someone else's litigation.

maintenance fee. 1. A periodic payment required to maintain a privilege, such as a license. **2.** A charge for keeping an improvement in working condition or a residential property in habitable condition. **3.** A fee charged for reinvesting earnings and dividends in mutual funds.

major disaster. A catastrophe, such as a hurricane, tornado, storm, flood, earthquake, drought, or fire, so severe that it warrants disaster assistance from the federal government. 40 CFR § 109.

majority. (16c) **1.** The status of one who has attained the age (usu. 18) at which one is entitled to full civic rights and considered legally capable of handling one's own affairs. **2.** A number that is more than half of a total; a group of more than 50 percent <the candidate received 50.4 percent of the votes.

absolute majority. A majority of all those who are entitled to vote in a particular election, regardless of how many voters actually cast ballots.

simple majority. A numerical majority of those actually voting.

supermajority. A fixed proportion greater than half (often two-thirds or a percentage greater than 50%), required for a measure to pass.

veto-proof majority. A legislative majority large enough that it can override an executive veto.

majority rule. (1848) **1.** The principle that a majority of a group has the power to make decisions that bind the group. **2.** The constitutional principle that each voter is entitled to a share of the franchise equal to that of each other voter. **3.** *Corporations.* The common-law principle that a director or officer owes no fiduciary duty to a shareholder with respect to a stock transaction.

major life activity. (1979) A basic activity that an average person in the general population can perform with little or no difficulty, such as seeing, hearing, sleeping, eating, walking, traveling, or working. • A person who is substantially limited in a major life activity is protected from discrimination under a variety of disability laws, most significantly the Americans with Disabilities Act and the Rehabilitation Act.

make, *vb.* (bef. 12c) **1.** To cause (something) to exist <to make a record>. **2.** To enact (something) <to make law>. **3.** To acquire (something) <to make money on execution>. **4.** To legally perform, as by executing, signing, or delivering (a document) <to make a contract>.

maker. (14c) **1.** One who frames, promulgates, or ordains (as in *lawmaker*). **2.** A person who signs a promissory note.

accommodation maker. (1829) One who signs a note as a surety.

prime maker. (1972) The person who is primarily liable on a note or other negotiable instrument.

make-whole doctrine. *Insurance.* The principle that, unless the insurance policy provides otherwise, an insurer will not receive any of the proceeds from the settlement of a claim, except to the extent that the settlement funds exceed the amount necessary to fully compensate the insured for the loss suffered.

maladministration. Poor management or regulation by a public officer; specif., an official's abuse of power.

mala fides (**mal**-ə **fɪ**-deez), *n.* Bad faith.

malapportionment, *n.* (1959) The improper or unconstitutional apportionment of a legislative district. — **malapportion,** *vb.*

malfeasance (mal-**fee**-zənts), *n.* (17c) A wrongful or unlawful act; esp. wrongdoing or misconduct by a public official; misfeasance in public office. — **malfeasant** (mal-**fee**-zənt), *adj.* — **malfeasor** (mal-**fee**-zər), *n.*

malfunction theory. (1979) *Products-liability law.* A principle permitting a products-liability plaintiff to prove that a product was defective by proving that the product malfunctioned, instead of requiring the plaintiff to prove a specific defect.

malice, *n.* (14c) **1.** The intent, without justification or excuse, to commit a wrongful act. **2.** Reckless disregard of the law or of a person's legal rights. **3.** Ill will; wickedness of heart. — **malicious,** *adj.* (13c).

actual malice. (18c) **1.** The deliberate intent to commit an injury, as evidenced by external circumstances. **2.** *Defamation.* Knowledge (by the person who utters or publishes a defamatory statement) that a statement is false, or reckless disregard about whether the statement is true.

express malice. (17c) **1.** *Criminal law.* The intent to kill or seriously injure arising from a deliberate, rational mind. **2.** Actual malice. **3.** *Defamation.* The bad-faith publication of defamatory material.

general malice. (17c) Malice that is necessary for any criminal conduct; malice that is not directed at a specific person.

implied malice. (17c) Malice inferred from a person's conduct.

particular malice. (16c) Malice that is directed at a particular person.

transferred malice. (1961) Malice directed to one person or object but instead harming another in the way intended for the first.

universal malice. (17c) The state of mind of a person who determines to take a life on slight provocation, without knowing or caring who may be the victim.

malice aforethought. (17c) The requisite mental state for common-law murder, encompassing any one of the following: (1) the intent to kill, (2) the intent to inflict grievous bodily harm, (3) extremely reckless indifference to the value of human life (the so-called "abandoned and malignant heart"), or (4) the intent to commit a dangerous felony (which leads to culpability under the felony-murder rule).

malice exception. (1977) A limitation on a public official's qualified immunity, by which the official can face civil liability for willfully exercising discretion in a way that violates a known or well-established right.

malicious, *adj.* **1.** Substantially certain to cause injury. **2.** Without just cause or excuse

malicious act. (17c) An intentional, wrongful act done willfully or intentionally against another without legal justification or excuse.

malicious killing. (17c) An intentional killing without legal justification or excuse.

malicious mischief. (18c) The common-law misdemeanor of intentionally destroying or damaging another's property. See Model Penal Code § 220.3.

malicious prosecution. (17c) **1.** The institution of a criminal or civil proceeding for an improper purpose and without probable cause. **2.** The tort claim resulting from the institution of such a proceeding.

malinger, *vb.* (1820) To feign illness or disability, esp. in an attempt to avoid an obligation or to continue receiving disability benefits.

malpractice (mal-**prak**-tis). (17c) An instance of negligence or incompetence on the part of a professional. • To succeed in a malpractice claim, a plaintiff must also prove proximate cause and damages.

legal malpractice. A lawyer's failure to render professional services with the skill, prudence, and diligence that an ordinary and reasonable lawyer would use under similar circumstances.

medical malpractice. A doctor's failure to exercise the degree of care and skill that a physician or surgeon of the same medical specialty would use under similar circumstances.

maltreatment. (18c) Bad treatment (esp. improper treatment by a surgeon) resulting from ignorance, neglect, or willfulness.

malum in se (**mal**-əm in **say** *or* **see**), *n.* [Latin "evil in itself"] (17c) A crime or an act that is inherently immoral, such as murder, arson, or rape. Pl. ***mala in se.*** — ***malum in se,*** *adj.*

malum prohibitum (**mal**-əm proh-**hib**-i-təm), *n.* [Latin "prohibited evil"] (18c) An act that is a crime merely because it is prohibited by statute, although the act itself is not necessarily immoral. Pl. ***mala prohibita.*** — ***malum prohibitum,*** *adj.*

malversation (mal-vər-**say**-shən), *n.* [French "ill behavior"] Official corruption; misbehavior by an official in the exercise of the duties of the office. — **malverse,** *vb.*

malware. (1990) *Slang.* Malicious technology.

managed care. (1982) A system of comprehensive healthcare provided by a health-maintenance organization, a preferred-provider organization, or a similar group.

management. (16c) The people in an organization who are vested with a certain amount of discretion and independent judgment in managing its affairs.

middle management. People who exercise some discretion and independent judgment in carrying out top management's directives.

top management. The highest level of a company's management, at which major policy decisions and long-term business plans are made.

manager. (16c) **1.** A person who administers or supervises the affairs of a business, office, or other organization.

general manager. A manager who has overall control of a business, office, or other organization, including authority over other managers. • A general manager is usu. equivalent to a president or chief executive officer of a corporation.

2. A legislator appointed to a conference committee charged with adjusting differences in a bill passed by both houses in different versions. **3.** *Parliamentary law.* A member who displays the evidence against another member who is charged with misconduct and faces possible disciplinary action.

M & A. *abbr.* Mergers and acquisitions.

mandamus (man-**day**-məs), *n.* [Latin "we command"] (16c) A writ issued by a court to compel performance of a particular act by a lower court or a governmental officer or body, usu. to correct a prior action or failure to act. Pl. **mandamuses.** — **mandamus,** *vb.*

mandate, *n.* (16c) **1.** An order from an appellate court directing a lower court to take a specified action. **2.** A judicial command directed to an officer of the court to enforce a court order. **3.** In politics, the electorate's overwhelming show of approval for a given political candidate or platform. — **mandate,** *vb.* — **mandatory,** *adj.* (15c).

mandate rule. (1958) The doctrine that, after an appellate court has remanded a case to a lower court, the lower court must follow the decision that the appellate court has made in the case, unless new evidence or an intervening change in the law dictates a different result.

mandatory waiver. The mandatory transfer, without judicial discretion, of a case from juvenile court to criminal court once the prosecutor has charged a juvenile with one of certain statutorily enumerated serious crimes.

manifestation of intention. (1826) *Wills & estates.* The external expression of the testator's intention, as distinguished from an undisclosed intention.

manifest-disregard doctrine. (1983) The principle that an arbitration award will be vacated if the arbitrator knows the applicable law and deliberately chooses to disregard it, but will not be vacated for a mere error or misunderstanding of the law.

manifest-error-or-clearly-wrong rule. (1981) In some jurisdictions, the doctrine that an appellate court cannot set aside a trial court's finding of fact unless a review of the entire record reveals that the finding has no reasonable basis.

manifest injustice. A direct, obvious, and observable error in a trial court, such as a defendant's guilty plea that is involuntary or is based on a plea agreement that the prosecution has rescinded.

manifest weight of the evidence. A deferential standard of review under which a verdict will be reversed or disregarded only if another outcome is obviously correct and the verdict is clearly unsupported by the evidence.

Mann Act. A federal law, enacted originally in 1910, making it illegal to transport an individual in interstate or foreign commerce for prostitution or other criminal sexual activity. 18 USCA § 2421–2424.

Mansfield rule. (1968) The doctrine that a juror's testimony or affidavit about juror misconduct may not be used to challenge the verdict.

manslaughter, *n.* (15c) The unlawful killing of a human being without malice aforethought. — **manslaughter,** *vb.*

involuntary manslaughter. (18c) Homicide in which there is no intention to kill or do grievous bodily harm, but that is committed with criminal negligence or during the commission of a crime not included within the felony-murder rule.

misdemeanor manslaughter. (1947) Unintentional homicide that occurs during the commission of a misdemeanor (such as a traffic violation).

voluntary manslaughter. (18c) An act of murder reduced to manslaughter because of extenuating circumstances such as adequate provocation (arousing the "heat of passion") or diminished capacity.

manufacturer. (17c) A person or entity engaged in producing or assembling new products. • A federal law has broadened the definition to include those who act for (or are controlled by) any such person or entity in the distribution of new products, as well as those who import new products for resale. 42 USCA § 4902(6).

***Mapp* hearing.** (1971) *Criminal procedure.* A hearing held to determine whether evidence implicating the accused was obtained as the result of an illegal search and seizure, and should therefore be suppressed. *Mapp v. Ohio*, 367 U.S. 643, 81 S.Ct. 1684 (1961).

margin, *n.* (14c) **1.** A boundary or edge. **2.** A measure or degree of difference. **3.** PROFIT MARGIN. **4.** The difference between a loan's face value and the market value of the collateral that secures the loan. **5.** Cash or collateral required to be paid to a securities broker by an investor to protect the broker against losses from securities bought on credit. **6.** The amount of an investor's equity in securities bought on credit through the broker. — **margin,** *vb.* — **marginal, margined,** *adj.*

marginal note. A brief notation, in the nature of a subheading, placed in the margin of a printed statute to give a brief indication of the matters dealt with in the section or subsection beside which it appears.

marital, *adj.* (17c) Of or relating to the marriage relationship.

marital agreement. (1866) An agreement between spouses or two people engaged to be married concerning the division and ownership of marital property during marriage or upon dissolution by death or divorce; esp. a premarital contract or separation agreement primarily concerned with dividing marital property in the event of divorce.

marital-privacy doctrine. A principle that limits governmental intrusion into private family matters, such as those involving sexual relations between married persons. • First recognized in *Griswold v. Connecticut*, 381 U.S. 479, 85 S.Ct. 1678 (1965), the doctrine formerly deterred state intervention into incidents involving domestic violence. Today, with the trend toward individual privacy rights, the doctrine does not discourage governmental protection from domestic violence.

marital rights. (18c) Rights and incidents (such as property or cohabitation rights) arising from the marriage contract.

mariticide. (1992) **1.** The murder of one's husband. **2.** A woman who murders her husband. — **mariticidal,** *adj.*

maritime law. The body of law governing marine commerce and navigation, the carriage at sea of persons and property, and marine affairs in general; the rules governing contract, tort, and workers'-compensation claims or relating to commerce on or over water.

mark, *n.* (bef. 12c) **1.** A symbol, impression, or feature on something, usu. to identify it or distinguish it from something else. **2.** Trademark. **3.** Servicemark.

marked money. (1883) Money that bears a telltale mark so that the money can be traced, usu. to a perpetrator of a crime, as when marked money is given to a kidnapper as ransom.

market, *n.* (bef. 12c) **1.** A place of commercial activity in which goods or services are bought and sold <the farmers' market>. **2.** A geographic area or demographic segment considered as a place of demand for particular goods or services; esp. prospective purchasers of goods, wherever they are <the foreign market for microchips>. **3.** The opportunity for buying and selling goods or services; the extent of economic demand <a strong job market for accountants>. **4.** A securities or commodities exchange <the stock market closed early because of the blizzard>. **5.** The business of such an exchange; the enterprise of buying and selling securities or commodities <the stock market is approaching an all-time high>. **6.** The price at which the buyer and seller of a security or commodity agree <the market for wheat is $8 per bushel>.

bear market. A securities market characterized by falling prices over a prolonged period.

black market. An illegal market for goods that are controlled or prohibited by the government, such as the underground market for prescription drugs.

bull market. A securities market characterized by rising prices over a prolonged period.

buyer's market. A market in which supply significantly exceeds demand, resulting in lower prices.

common market. An economic association formed by several nations to reduce or eliminate trade barriers among them, and to establish uniform trade barriers against nonmembers.

derivative market. A market for the exchange of derivative instruments.

discount market. The portion of the money market in which banks and other financial institutions trade commercial paper.

financial market. A market for the exchange of capital and debt instruments.

foreign-exchange market. A market where various currencies are traded internationally.

futures market. A commodity exchange in which futures contracts are traded; a market for a trade (e.g., commodities futures contracts and stock options) that is negotiated at the current price but calls for delivery at a future time.

gray market. A market in which the seller uses legal but sometimes unethical methods to avoid a manufacturer's distribution chain and thereby sell goods (esp. imported goods) at prices lower than those envisioned by the manufacturer.

money market. The financial market for dealing in short-term negotiable instruments such as commercial paper, certificates of deposit, banker's acceptances, and U.S. Treasury securities.

open market. A market in which any buyer or seller may trade and in which prices and product availability are determined by free competition.

public market. A market open to both buyers and sellers.

secondary market. The market for goods or services that have previously been available for buying and selling; esp. the securities market in which previously issued securities are traded among investors.

seller's market. A market in which demand exceeds (or approaches) supply, resulting in raised prices.

soft market. A market (esp. a stock market) characterized by falling or drifting prices and low volume.

spot market. A market (esp. in commodities) in which payment or delivery is immediate.

marketability. (1877) Salability; the probability of selling property, goods, securities, or services at specified times, prices, and terms. — **marketable,** *adj.* (16c).

marketable-title act. (1957) A state statute providing that a person can establish good title to land by searching the public records only back to a specified time (such as 40 years).

market approach. (1958) A method of appraising real property, by surveying the market and comparing the property to similar pieces of property that have been recently sold, and making appropriate adjustments for differences between the properties, including location, size of the property, and the dates of sale.

marketing, *n.* (16c) **1.** The act or process of promoting and selling, leasing, or licensing products or services. **2.** The part of a business concerned with meeting customers' needs. **3.** The area of study concerned with the promotion and selling of products or services.

market-participant doctrine. (1983) The principle that, under the Commerce Clause, a state does not discriminate against interstate commerce by acting as a buyer or seller in the market, by operating a proprietary enterprise, or by subsidizing private business. • Under the Dormant Commerce Clause principle, the Commerce Clause — art. I, § 8, cl. 3 of the U.S. Constitution — disallows most state regulation of, or discrimination against, interstate commerce. But if the state is participating in the market instead of regulating it, the Dormant Commerce Clause analysis does not apply, and the state activity will generally stand.

marketplace of ideas. (1949) A forum in which expressions of opinion can freely compete for acceptance without governmental restraint. • Although Justice Oliver Wendell Holmes was the first jurist to discuss the concept as a metaphor for explaining freedom of speech, the phrase *marketplace of ideas* dates in American caselaw only from 1954.

market power. (1915) The ability to reduce output and raise prices above the competitive level — specif., above marginal cost — for a sustained period, and to make a profit by doing so.

market share. (1954) The percentage of the market for a product that a firm supplies, usu. calculated by dividing the firm's output by the total market output.

marksman. 1. A person who signs documents with some kind of character or symbol instead of writing his or her name. **2.** A highly skilled shooter.

***Marks* rule.** The doctrine that, when the U.S. Supreme Court issues a fractured, plurality opinion, the opinion of the justices concurring in the judgment on the narrowest grounds — that is, the legal standard with which a majority of the Court would agree — is considered the Court's holding. *Marks v. United States,* 430 U.S. 188, 97 S.Ct. 990 (1977).

mark up, *vb.* (1868) **1.** To increase (the price of goods, etc.) **2.** To revise or amend (a legislative bill, a rule, etc.). **3.** To place (a case) on the trial calendar.

markup, *n.* (1916) **1.** An amount added to an item's cost to determine its selling price. **2.** A session of a congressional committee during which a bill is revised and put into final form before it is reported to the appropriate house.

marriage, *n.* (13c) **1.** The legal union of a couple as spouses. • The essentials of a valid marriage are (1) parties legally capable of contracting to marry, (2) mutual consent or agreement, and (3) an actual contracting in the form prescribed by law. Marriage has important consequences in many areas of the law, such as torts, criminal law, evidence, debtor–creditor relations, property, and contracts.

common-law marriage. (17c) A marriage that takes legal effect, without license or ceremony, when two people capable of marrying live together as husband and wife, intend to be married, and hold themselves out to others as a married couple.

covenant marriage. (1990) A special type of marriage in which the parties agree to more stringent requirements for marriage and divorce than are otherwise imposed by state law for ordinary marriages. • Most laws require premarital counseling. A divorce will be granted only after the couple has undergone marital counseling and has been separated for a specified period (usu. at least 18 months).

green-card marriage. *Slang.* A sham marriage in which a U.S. citizen marries a foreign citizen for the sole purpose of allowing the foreign citizen to become a permanent U.S. resident. • The Marriage Fraud Amendments were enacted to regulate marriages entered into for the purpose of circumventing U.S. immigration laws. 8 USCA §§ 1154 (h), 1255(e).

marriage of convenience. (18c) **1.** A marriage entered into for social or financial advantages rather than out of mutual love. **2.** Loosely, an ill-considered marriage that, at the time, is convenient for the parties involved.

plural marriage. (1862) A marriage in which one spouse is already married to someone else; a bigamous or polygamous union; polygamy.

same-sex marriage. The ceremonial union of two people of the same sex; a marriage or marriage-like relationship between two women or two men.

sham marriage. (18c) A purported marriage in which all the formal requirements are met or seemingly met, but in which the parties go through the ceremony with no intent of living together as husband and wife.

voidable marriage. (1845) A marriage that is initially invalid but that remains in effect unless terminated by court order.

void marriage. (17c) A marriage that is invalid from its inception, that cannot be made valid, and that can be terminated by either party without obtaining a divorce or annulment.

2. Marriage ceremony. — **marital,** *adj.*

ceremonial marriage. (1876) A wedding that follows all the statutory requirements and that has been solemnized before a religious or civil official.

civil marriage. (17c) A wedding ceremony conducted by an official, such as a judge, or by some other authorized person — as distinguished from one solemnized by a member of the clergy.

proxy marriage. (1924) A wedding in which someone stands in for an absent bride or groom, as when one party is stationed overseas in the military.

marriage article. (1831) A premarital stipulation between spouses who intend to incorporate the stipulation in a postnuptial agreement.

marriage bonus. *Tax.* The difference between the reduced income-tax liability owed by a married couple filing a joint income-tax return and the greater amount they would have owed had they been single and filed individually.

marriage ceremony. (17c) The religious or civil proceeding that solemnizes a marriage.

marriage certificate. (1821) A document that is executed by the religious or civil official presiding at a marriage ceremony and filed with a public authority (usu. the county clerk) as evidence of the marriage.

marriage license. (17c) A document, issued by a public authority, that grants a couple permission to marry.

marriage mill. A place that facilitates hasty, often secret, marriages by requiring few or no legal formalities. • Marriage-mill unions may be voidable but are rarely void in the absence of absolute impediments to marriage.

marriage penalty. *Tax.* The difference between the greater income-tax liability owed by a married couple filing a joint income-tax return and the lesser amount they would owe had they been single and filed individually.

married women's property acts. (*sometimes cap.*) Statutes enacted to remove a married woman's legal disabilities; esp. statutes that abolished the common-law prohibitions against a married woman's contracting, suing and being sued, or acquiring, holding, and conveying property in her own right, free from any restrictions by her husband.

***Marsden* motion.** A criminal defendant's request that a court dismiss or replace a court-appointed attorney on grounds that the attorney is not completely or adequately representing the defendant. *People v. Marsden*, 465 P.2d 44 (Cal. 1970).

marshal, *n.* (13c) **1.** A law-enforcement officer with duties similar to those of a sheriff. **2.** A judicial officer who provides court security, executes process, and performs other tasks for the court. — **marshalship,** *n.*

United States Marshal. A federal official who carries out the orders of a federal court.

marshal, *vb.* (15c) To arrange or rank in order.

marshaling the evidence. (1892) **1.** Arranging all of a party's evidence in the order that it will be presented at trial. **2.** The practice of formulating a jury charge so that it arranges the evidence to give more credence to a particular interpretation.

martial law (mahr-shəl). (1933) **1.** The law by which during wartime the army, instead of civil authority, governs the country because of a perceived need for military security or public safety. • The military assumes control purportedly until civil authority can be restored. **2.** A body of firm, strictly enforced rules that are imposed because of a perception by the country's rulers that civil government has failed, or might fail, to function. • Martial law is usu. imposed when the rulers foresee an invasion, insurrection, economic collapse, or other breakdown of the rulers' desired social order. **3.** The law by which the army in wartime governs foreign territory that it occupies. **4.** Loosely, military law.

Martindale-Hubbell Law Directory. A set of books, traditionally published annually, containing a roster and ratings of lawyers and law firms in most cities of the United States, corporate legal departments, government lawyers, foreign lawyers, and lawyer-support providers, as well as a digest of the laws of the states, the District of Columbia, and territories of the United States, and a digest of the laws of many foreign jurisdictions, including Canada and its provinces.

***Martinez* report.** A report that a court may require a pro se party to file in order to clarify a vague or incomprehensible complaint. *Martinez v. Aaron*, 570 F.2d 317 (10th Cir. 1978).

Mary Carter agreement. (1972) A contract (usu. a secret one) by which one or more, but not all, codefendants settle with the plaintiff and obtain a release, along with a provision granting them a portion of any recovery from the nonparticipating codefendants. • In a Mary Carter agreement, the participating codefendants agree to remain parties to the lawsuit and, if no recovery is awarded against the nonparticipating codefendants, to pay the plaintiff a settled amount. Such an agreement is void as against public policy in some states but is valid in others if disclosed to the jury. *Booth v. Mary Carter Paint Co.*, 202 So. 2d 8 (Fla. Dist. Ct. App. 1967).

***Massiah* rule.** (1966) The principle that an attempt to elicit incriminating statements (usu. not during a formal interrogation) from a suspect whose right to counsel has attached but who has not waived that right violates the Sixth Amendment. *Massiah v. United States*, 377 U.S. 201, 84 S.Ct. 1199 (1964).

master, *n.* (bef. 12c) **1.** One who has personal authority over another's services; specif., a principal who employs another to perform one or more services and who controls or has the right to control the physical conduct of the other in the performance of the services; employer. **2.** A parajudicial officer (such as a referee, an auditor, an examiner, or an assessor) specially appointed to help a court with its proceedings. • A master may take testimony, hear and rule on discovery disputes, enter temporary orders, and handle other pretrial matters, as well as computing interest, valuing annuities, investigating encumbrances on land titles, and the like — usu. with a written report to the court. Fed. R. Civ. P. 53.

special master. (1833) A master appointed to assist the court with a particular matter or case.

standing master. (1848) A master appointed to assist the court on an ongoing basis.

master and servant. (16c) The relation between two persons, one of whom (the master) has authority over the other (the servant), with the power to direct the time, manner, and place of the services. • This relationship is similar to that of principal and agent, but that terminology applies to employments in which the employee has some discretion, while the servant is almost completely under the control of the master. Also, an agent usu. acts for the principal in business relations with third parties, while a servant does not.

master limited partnership. Publicly traded partnership.

Master of Laws. A law degree conferred on those completing graduate-level legal study, beyond the J.D. or LL.B. — Abbr. LL.M.

master plan. (1914) *Land-use planning.* A municipal plan for housing, industry, and recreation facilities, including their projected environmental impact.

master's report. A master's formal report to a court, usu. containing a recommended decision in a case as well as findings of fact and conclusions of law.

matching principle. (1979) *Tax.* A method for handling expense deductions, by which the depreciation in a given year is matched by the associated tax benefit.

material, *adj.* (14c) **1.** Of or relating to matter; physical. **2.** Having some logical connection with the consequential facts. **3.** Of such a nature that knowledge of the item would affect a person's decision-making; significant; essential. — **materiality,** *n.*

materialman. A person who supplies materials used in constructing or repairing a structure or vehicle.

maternal, *adj.* (15c) Of, relating to, or coming from one's mother.

maternal-preference presumption. *Family law.* The belief that custody of a child, regardless of age, should generally be awarded to the mother in a divorce unless she is found to be unfit. • Most jurisdictions no longer adhere to the maternal-preference presumption.

maternity (mə-**tər**-ni-tee). (17c) **1.** The state or condition of being a mother, esp. a biological one; motherhood. **2.** The section of a hospital devoted to the care of mothers and infants during and after childbirth. **3.** Attribution right.

***Mathews v. Eldridge* test.** (1980) *Constitutional law.* The principle for determining whether an administrative procedure provides due-process protection, by analyzing (1) the nature of the private interest that will be affected by the governmental action, (2) the risk of an erroneous deprivation through the procedure used, (3) the probable value of additional or substitute procedural safeguards, (4) the governmental function involved, and (5) the administrative burden and expense that would be created by requiring additional or substitute procedural safeguards. *Mathews v. Eldridge*, 424 U.S. 319, 96 S.Ct. 893 (1976).

matricide (**ma**-trə-sɪd), *n.* (16c) **1.** The act of killing one's own mother. **2.** One who kills his or her mother. — **matricidal,** *adj.*

matrimonial res. (1893) **1.** The marriage estate. **2.** The state of marriage; the legal relationship between married persons, as opposed to the property and support obligations arising from the marriage.

matrimony, *n.* (14c) The ceremony or state of being married. — **matrimonial,** *adj.*

matter, *n.* (13c) **1.** A subject under consideration, esp. involving a dispute or litigation; case. **2.** Something that is to be tried or proved; an allegation forming the basis of a claim or defense.

matter of fact. (16c) A matter involving a judicial inquiry into the truth of alleged facts.

matter of form. A matter concerned only with formalities or noncritical characteristics <the objection that the motion was incorrectly titled related to a matter of form>.

matter of law. A matter involving a judicial inquiry into the applicable law.

matter of record. A matter that has been entered on a judicial or other public record and therefore can be proved by producing that record.

matter of substance. A matter concerning the merits or critical elements, rather than mere formalities.

new matter. A litigant's claim or defense that goes beyond the issues raised in the original litigation, either by raising a new issue with new facts to be proved or by raising a defense that does not implicate an element of the original claims.

special matter. Common-law pleading. Out-of-the-ordinary evidence that a defendant is allowed to enter, after notice to the plaintiff, under a plea of the general issue.

matter of course. (17c) Something done as a part of a routine process or procedure.

mature, *vb.* (1861) (Of a debt or obligation) to become due. — **maturity,** *n.* — **mature,** *adj.*

mature-minor doctrine. *Family law.* A rule holding that an adolescent, though not having reached the age of majority, may make decisions about his or her health and welfare if the adolescent demonstrates an ability to articulate reasoned preferences on those matters. • The mature-minor doctrine was recognized as constitutionally protected in medical decisions (abortion rights). Not all states recognize the common-law mature-minor doctrine.

maxim (**mak**-sim). (16c) A traditional legal principle that has been frozen into a concise expression. • Examples are "possession is nine-tenths of the law" and *caveat emptor* ("let the buyer beware").

maximum medical improvement. (1955) The point at which an injured person's condition stabilizes, and no further recovery or improvement is expected, even with additional medical intervention.

may, *vb.* (bef. 12c) **1.** To be permitted to. **2.** To be a possibility. **3.** Loosely, is required to; shall; must. • In dozens of cases, courts have held *may* to be synonymous with *shall* or *must*, usu. in an effort to effectuate legislative intent.

mayhem (**may**-hem), *n.* (15c) **1.** The crime of maliciously injuring a person's body, esp. to impair or destroy the victim's capacity for self-defense. • Modern statutes usu. treat this as a form of aggravated battery. **2.** Violent destruction. **3.** Rowdy confusion or disruption. — **maim** (for sense 1), *vb.*

May it please the court. (17c) An introductory phrase that lawyers use when first addressing a court, esp. when presenting oral argument to an appellate court.

mayor, *n.* (14c) An official who is elected or appointed as the chief executive of a city, town, or other municipality. — **mayoral** (**may**-ər-əl), *adj.* — **mayoralty** (**may**-ər-əl-tee), *n.* (14c).

MBE. *abbr.* Multistate Bar Examination.

McDonnell Douglas **test.** *Employment law.* The principle for applying a shifting burden of proof in employment-discrimination cases, essentially requiring the plaintiff to come forward with evidence of discrimination and the defendant to come forward with evidence showing that the employment action complained of was taken for nondiscriminatory reasons. • Under this test, the plaintiff must first establish a prima facie case of discrimination, as by showing that the plaintiff is a member of a protected group and suffered an adverse employment action. If the plaintiff satisfies that burden, then the defendant must articulate a legitimate, nondiscriminatory reason for the employment action complained of. If the defendant satisfies that burden, then the plaintiff must prove that the defendant's stated reason is just a pretext for discrimination and that discrimination was the real reason for the employment action. *McDonnell Douglas Corp. v. Green*, 411 U.S. 792, 93 S.Ct. 1817 (1973).

McNaghten **rules** (mik-**nawt**-ən). (1917) *Criminal law.* The doctrine that a person is not criminally responsible for an act when a mental disability prevented the person from knowing either (1) the nature and quality of the act or (2) whether the act was right or wrong. • The federal courts and most states have adopted this test in some form. *McNaghten's Case*, 8 Eng. Rep. 718 (H.L. 1843). — Also spelled *McNaughten rules*; *M'Naghten rules*; *M'Naughten rules.*

M.D. *abbr.* (15c) **1.** Middle District, usu. in reference to U.S. judicial districts. **2.** Doctor of medicine.

meander line (mee-**an**-dər). (1865) A survey line (not a boundary line) on a portion of land, usu. following the course of a river or stream.

meaning. (14c) The sense of anything, but esp. of words; that which is conveyed (or intended to be conveyed) by a written or oral statement or other communicative act.

objective meaning. The meaning that would be attributed to an unambiguous document (or portion of a document) by a disinterested reasonable person who is familiar with the surrounding circumstances. • A party to a contract is often held to its objective meaning, which it is considered to have had reason to know, even if the party subjectively understood or intended something else.

plain meaning. The meaning attributed to a document (usu. by a court) by giving the words their ordinary sense, without referring to extrinsic indications of the author's intent.

subjective meaning. The meaning that a party to a legal document attributes to it when the document is written, executed, or otherwise adopted.

means, *n.* (14c) **1.** Available resources, esp. for the payment of debt; income. **2.** Something that helps to attain an end; an instrument; a cause.

measure of damages. (18c) The basis for calculating damages to be awarded to someone who has suffered an injury.

measuring life. (1922) Under the rule against perpetuities, the last beneficiary to die who was alive at the testator's death and who usu. holds a preceding interest.

mediate powers (**mee**-dee-it). (1820) Subordinate powers incidental to primary powers, esp. as given by a principal to an agent; powers necessary to accomplish the principal task.

mediation (mee-dee-**ay**-shən), *n.* (14c) A method of nonbinding dispute resolution involving a neutral third party who tries to help the disputing parties reach a mutually agreeable solution. — **mediate** (**mee**-dee-ayt), *vb.* — **mediatory** (**mee**-dee-ə-tor-ee), *adj.* — **mediator** (**mee**-dee-ay-tər), *n.* (14c).

Medicaid. (1966) A cooperative federal–state program that pays for medical expenses for qualifying individuals who cannot afford private medical services. • The program is authorized under the Social Security Act.

medical directive. Advance directive.

medical-emergency exception. (1975) *Criminal law.* The principle that a police officer does not need a warrant to enter a person's home if the entrance is made to render aid to someone whom the officer reasonably believes to be in need of immediate assistance.

medical examiner. (1820) A public official who investigates deaths, conducts autopsies, and helps the state prosecute homicide cases. • Medical examiners have replaced coroners in many states.

Medicare. (1953) A federal program — established under the Social Security Act — that provides health insurance for the elderly and the disabled.

medicolegal (med-i-koh-**lee**-gəl), *adj.* (1835) Involving the application of medical science to law.

medigap insurance. (1975) *Slang.* A private insurance policy for Medicare patients to cover the costs not covered by Medicare.

medium of exchange. (18c) Anything generally accepted as payment in a transaction and recognized as a standard of value.

med. mal. Medical malpractice.

meeting of the minds. (1830) *Contracts.* Actual assent by both parties to the formation of a contract, meaning that they agree on the same terms, conditions, and subject matter. • This was required under the traditional subjective theory of assent, but modern contract doctrine requires only objective manifestations of assent.

Megan's law (**meg**-ənz *or* **may**-gənz). (1994) A statute that requires sex offenders who are released from prison to register with a local board and that provides the means to disseminate information about the registrants to the community in which they dwell.

memorandum. (15c) **1.** An informal written note or record outlining the terms of a transaction or contract <the memorandum indicated the developer's intent to buy the property at its appraised value>. • To satisfy the statute of frauds, a memorandum can be written in any form, but it must (1) identify the parties to the contract, (2) indicate the contract's subject matter, (3) contain the contract's essential terms, and (4) contain the signature of the party against whom enforcement is sought. **2.** An informal written communication used esp. in offices <the firm sent a memorandum reminding all lawyers to turn in their timesheets>. — Often shortened to *memo*. **3.** A party's written statement of its legal arguments presented to the court, usu. in the form of a brief <memorandum of law>. Pl. **memoranda, memorandums.**

persuasive memorandum. A memorandum written to sway the reader to accept the writer's position on a stated problem.

research memorandum. A memorandum whose purpose is analyze a legal issue and inform the reader about possible approaches and outcomes. • This type of memorandum is usu. an in-house document.

memorandum in error. A document alleging a factual error, usu. accompanied by an affidavit of proof.

memorial, *n.* (17c) **1.** An abstract of a legal record, esp. a deed; memorandum. **2.** A written statement of facts presented to a legislature or executive as a petition.

menacing, *n.* (14c) An attempt to commit common-law assault.

mendacity (men-**das**-ə-tee), *n.* (16c) **1.** The quality of being untruthful. **2.** A lie; falsehood. — **mendacious** (men-**day**-shəs), *adj.*

mens (menz), *n.* [Latin] Mind; intention; will.

mens rea (**menz ree**-ə). [Law Latin "guilty mind"] (1861) The state of mind that the prosecution, to secure a conviction, must prove that a defendant had when committing a crime; criminal intent or recklessness. • *Mens rea* is the second of two essential elements of every crime at common law, the other being the *actus reus*. Pl. ***mentes reae*** (**men**-teez **ree**-ee).

mental abuse. Emotional abuse.

mental illness. (1847) **1.** A disorder in thought or mood so substantial that it impairs judgment, behavior, perceptions of reality, or the ability to cope with the ordinary demands of life. **2.** Mental disease that is severe enough to necessitate care and treatment for the afflicted person's own welfare or the welfare of others in the community.

mental reservation. (17c) One party's silent understanding or exception to the meaning of a contractual provision.

mentition (men-**tish**-ən), *n.* [fr. Latin *mentitio* "lying"] (17c) The act of lying.

mercantile paper. Commercial paper.

mercenary (**mər**-sə-ner-ee). (14c) *Int'l law.* A professional soldier hired by someone other than his or her own government to fight in a foreign country.

merchandise (**mər**-chən-dɪz *also* -dɪs). (13c) **1.** In general, a movable object involved in trade or traffic; that which is passed from one person to another by purchase and sale. **2.** In particular, that which is dealt in by merchants; an article of trading or the class of objects in which trade is carried on by physical transfer; collectively, mercantile goods, wares or commodities, or any subjects of regular trade, animate as well as inanimate. **3.** Purchase and sale; trade; traffic, dealing, or advantage from dealing.

merchant. (13c) One whose business is buying and selling goods for profit; esp. a person or entity that holds itself out as having expertise peculiar to the goods in which it deals and is therefore held by the law to a higher standard of expertise than that of a nonmerchant. • Because the term relates solely to goods, a supplier of services is not considered a merchant.

merchantable (**mər**-chənt-ə-bəl), *adj.* (15c) Fit for sale in the usual course of trade at the usual selling prices; marketable. — **merchantability,** *n.*

merchant exception. (1973) *Contracts.* In a sale of goods, an exemption from the statute of frauds whereby a contract between merchants is enforceable if, within a reasonable time after they reach an oral agreement, a written confirmation of the terms is sent, to which the recipient does not object within ten days of receiving it. UCC § 2-201.

merchant's defense. (1972) The principle that a store owner will not be held liable for reasonably detaining a suspected shoplifter, to facilitate an investigation by a law-enforcement officer, if probable cause exists to suspect the detained person of wrongfully removing merchandise from the store.

mercy. (13c) Compassionate treatment, as of criminal offenders or of those in distress; esp. imprisonment, rather than death, imposed as punishment for capital murder.

mercy rule. (1981) *Evidence.* The principle that a defendant is entitled to offer character evidence as a defense to a criminal charge. Fed. R. Evid. 404(a)(1).

mere right. An abstract right in property, without possession or even the right of possession.

meretricious (mer-ə-**trish**-əs), *adj.* (17c) **1.** Involving prostitution <a meretricious encounter>. **2.** (Of a romantic relationship) involving either unlawful sexual connection or lack of capacity on the part of one party <a meretricious marriage>. **3.** Superficially attractive but fake nonetheless; alluring by false show <meretricious advertising claims>.

merger. (18c) **1.** The act or an instance of combining or uniting. **2.** *Contracts.* The substitution of a superior form of contract for an inferior form, as when a written contract supersedes all oral agreements and prior understandings. **3.** *Contracts.* The replacement of a contractual duty or of a duty to compensate with a new duty between the same parties, based on different operative facts, for the same performance or for a performance differing only in liquidating a duty that was previously unliquidated. **4.** *Property.* The absorption of a lesser estate into a greater estate when both become the same person's property. **5.** *Criminal law.* The absorption of a lesser included offense into a more serious offense when a person is charged with both crimes, so that the person is not subject to double jeopardy. **6.** *Civil procedure.* The effect of a judgment for the plaintiff, which absorbs any claim that was the subject of the lawsuit into the judgment, so that the plaintiff's rights are confined to enforcing the judgment. **7.** The joining of the procedural aspects of law and equity. **8.** The absorption of one organization (esp. a corporation) that ceases to exist into another that retains its own name and identity and acquires the assets and liabilities of the former. **9.** The merger of rights and duties in the same person, resulting in the extinction of obligations; esp. the blending of the rights of a creditor and debtor, resulting in the extinguishment of the creditor's right to collect the debt. • As originally developed in Roman law, a merger resulted from the marriage of a debtor and creditor, or when a debtor became the creditor's heir. **10.** The absorption of a contract into a court order, so that an agreement between the parties (often a marital agreement incident to a divorce or separation) loses its separate identity as an enforceable contract when it is incorporated into a court order.

meritorious (mer-ə-**tor**-ee-əs), *adj.* (15c) **1.** (Of an act, etc.) meriting esteem or reward. **2.** (Of a case, etc.) meriting a legal victory; having legal worth.

merits. (18c) The elements or grounds of a claim or defense; the substantive considerations to be taken into account in deciding a case, as opposed to extraneous or technical points, esp. of procedure <trial on the merits>.

merit system. (1879) The practice of hiring and promoting employees, esp. government employees, based on their competence rather than political favoritism.

Merit Systems Protection Board. The independent federal agency that oversees personnel practices of the federal government and hears and decides appeals from adverse personnel actions taken against federal employees. • Its functions were transferred from the former Civil Service Commission under Reorganization Plan No. 2 of 1978. — Abbr. MSPB.

mesne (meen), *adj.* (16c) Occupying a middle position; intermediate or intervening, esp. in time of occurrence or performance.

messuage (**mes**-wij). (14c) A dwelling house together with the curtilage, including any outbuildings.

metalaw (**met**-ə-law). (1956) A hypothetical set of legal principles based on the rules of existing legal systems and designed to provide a framework of agreement for these different systems.

mete out, *vb.* (bef. 15c) To dispense or measure out (justice, punishment, etc.).

metes and bounds (meets). (15c) The territorial limits of real property as measured by distances and angles from designated landmarks and in relation to adjoining properties.

MFN. *abbr.* Most-favored nation.

mild exigency. (1984) A circumstance that justifies a law-enforcement officer's departure from the knock-and-announce rule, such as the likelihood that the building's occupants will try to escape, resist arrest, or destroy evidence.

military law. The branch of public law governing military discipline and other rules regarding service in the armed forces.

Military Rules of Evidence. The rules of evidence applicable to military law and courts-martial. — Abbr. MRE.

militate (**mil**-ə-tayt), *vb.* (16c) To exert a strong influence.

militia (mə-**lish**-ə), *n.* (16c) A body of citizens armed and trained, esp. by a state, for military service apart from the regular armed forces. • The Constitution recognizes a state's right to form a "well-regulated militia" but also grants Congress the power to activate, organize, and govern a federal militia. U.S. Const. amend. II; U.S. Const. art. I, § 8, cl. 15–16.

reserve militia. All persons who are not exempt from military service and not actively serving in the armed forces or national guard.

Militia Clause. (1918) One of two clauses of the U.S. Constitution giving Congress the power to call forth, arm, and maintain a military force to enforce compliance with its laws, suppress insurrections, and repel invasions. U.S. Const. art. I, § 8, cls. 15 and 16.

***Mimms* order.** (1993) A police officer's command for a motorist to get out of the vehicle. • A *Mimms* order need not be independently justified if the initial stop was lawful. *Pennsylvania v. Mimms*, 434 U.S. 106, 98 S.Ct. 330 (1977).

mineral, *n.* (15c) **1.** Any natural inorganic matter that has a definite chemical composition and specific physical properties that give it value. **2.** A subsurface material that is explored for, mined, and exploited for its useful properties and commercial value. **3.** Any natural material that is defined as a mineral by statute or caselaw.

mineral entry. (1882) The right of entry on public land to mine valuable mineral deposits.

mineral interest. *Oil & gas.* The right to search for, develop, and remove minerals from land or to receive a royalty based on the production of minerals. • Mineral interests are granted by an oil-and-gas lease.

minimal participant. (1987) *Criminal law.* Under the federal sentencing guidelines, a defendant who is among the least culpable of a group of criminal actors, as when the defendant does not understand the scope or structure of the criminal enterprise or the actions of the other members of the group. • The offense level for a crime of a minimal participant can be decreased by four levels. U.S. Sentencing Guidelines Manual § 3B1.2(a).

mini-*Miranda* requirement. *Debtor–creditor law.* A debt collector's obligation when communicating with a debtor to inform the debtor that (1) the communication is from a debt collector seeking to collect a debt and (2) any information received will be used for that purpose. • This disclosure is required by the Fair Debt Collection Practices Act.

minimization requirement. (1972) *Criminal law.* The mandate that police officers acting under an eavesdropping warrant must use the wiretap in a way that will intercept the fewest possible conversations that are not subject to the warrant.

minimum contacts. (1945) A nonresident defendant's forum-state connections, such as business activity or actions foreseeably leading to business activity, that are substantial enough to bring the defendant within the forum-state court's personal jurisdiction without offending traditional notions of fair play and substantial justice. *International Shoe Co. v. Washington*, 326 U.S. 310, 66 S.Ct. 154 (1945).

ministerial, *adj.* (16c) Of or relating to an act that involves obedience to instructions or laws instead of discretion, judgment, or skill <the court clerk's ministerial duties include recording judgments on the docket>.

ministerial-function test. (1990) The principle that the First Amendment bars judicial resolution of a Title VII employment-discrimination claim based on a religious preference, if the employee's responsibilities are religious in nature, as in spreading faith, supervising a religious order, and the like. 42 USCA § 2000e-1(a).

minitrial. (1990) A private, voluntary, and informal form of dispute resolution in which each party's attorney presents an abbreviated version of its case to a neutral third party and to the opponent's representatives, who have settlement authority.

minor, *n.* (16c) A person who has not reached full legal age; a child or juvenile.

emancipated minor. (1817) A minor who is self-supporting and independent of parental control, usu. as a result of a court order.

minority. (15c) **1.** The state or condition of being under legal age. **2.** A group having fewer than a controlling number of votes. **3.** A group that is different in some respect (such as race or religious belief) from the majority and that is sometimes treated differently as a result; a member of such a group.

minor participant. (1960) *Criminal law.* Under the federal sentencing guidelines, a defendant who is less culpable for a crime than the other members of the group committing the crime, but who has more culpability than a minimal participant.

mint, *n.* (15c) **1.** A government-authorized place for coining money. **2.** A large supply, esp. of money.

mintage. (16c) **1.** The mint's charge for coining money. **2.** The product of minting; money.

minute book. (16c) **1.** A book in which a court clerk enters minutes of court proceedings. **2.** A record of the subjects discussed and actions taken at a corporate directors' or shareholders' meeting.

***Miranda* hearing** (mə-**ran**-də). (1966) A pretrial proceeding held to determine whether the *Miranda* rule has been followed and thus whether the prosecutor may introduce into evidence the defendant's statements to the police made after arrest.

***Miranda* rule.** (1966) The doctrine that a criminal suspect in police custody must be informed of certain constitutional rights before being interrogated. • The suspect must be advised of the right to remain silent, the right to have an attorney present during questioning, and the right to have an attorney appointed if the suspect cannot afford one. If the suspect is not advised of these rights or does not validly waive them, any evidence obtained during the interrogation cannot be used against the suspect at trial (except for impeachment purposes). *Miranda v. Arizona*, 384 U.S. 436, 86 S.Ct. 1602 (1966).

Mirandize (mə-**ran**-dɪz), *vb.* (1971) *Slang.* To read or recite (to an arrestee) rights under the *Miranda* rule.

mirror-image rule. (1972) *Contracts.* The doctrine that the acceptance of a contractual offer must be positive, unconditional, unequivocal, and unambiguous, and must not change, add to, or qualify the terms of the offer; the common-law principle that for a contract to be formed, the terms of an acceptance must correspond exactly with those of the offer. • In modern commercial contexts, the mirror-image rule has been replaced by a UCC provision that allows parties to enforce their agreement despite minor discrepancies between the offer and the acceptance.

misadventure. (13c) **1.** A mishap or misfortune. **2.** Homicide committed accidentally by a person doing a lawful act and having no intent to injure; accidental killing.

misallege, *vb.* To erroneously assert (a fact, a claim, etc.).

misapplication, *n.* (17c) The improper or illegal use of funds or property lawfully held. — **misapply,** *vb.*

misappropriation, *n.* (18c) **1.** The application of another's property or money dishonestly to one's own use. **2.** *Intellectual property.* The common-law tort of using the noncopyrightable information or ideas that an organization collects and disseminates for a profit to compete unfairly against that organization, or copying a work whose creator has not yet claimed or been granted exclusive rights in the work. *Int'l News Serv. v. Associated Press*, 248 U.S. 215, 29 S.Ct. 68 (1918). — **misappropriate,** *vb.*

misbranding, *n.* The act or an instance of labeling one's product falsely or in a misleading way. • Misbranding is prohibited by federal and state law. — **misbrand,** *vb.*

miscarriage. (16c) Spontaneous and involuntary premature expulsion of a nonviable fetus.

miscarriage of justice. (1862) A grossly unfair outcome in a judicial proceeding, as when a defendant is convicted despite a lack of evidence on an essential element of the crime.

miscegenation (mi-sej-ə-**nay**-shən). (1863) A marriage between persons of different races, formerly considered illegal in some jurisdictions. • In 1967, the U.S. Supreme Court held that laws banning interracial marriages are unconstitutional. *Loving v. Virginia*, 388 U.S. 1, 87 S.Ct. 1817 (1967).

mischarge. (1939) An erroneous jury instruction that may be grounds for reversing a verdict.

mischief (**mis**-chəf). (14c) **1.** A condition in which a person suffers a wrong or is under some hardship, esp. one that a statute seeks to remove or for which equity provides a remedy <this legislation

seeks to eliminate the mischief of racially restrictive deed covenants>. **2.** Injury or damage caused by a specific person or thing <the vandals were convicted of criminal mischief>. **3.** The act causing such injury or damage <their mischief damaged the abbey>.

mischief rule. (1974) In statutory construction, the doctrine that a statute should be interpreted by first identifying the problem (or "mischief") that the statute was designed to remedy and then adopting a construction that will suppress the problem and advance the remedy.

misconduct (mis-**kon**-dəkt). (17c) **1.** A dereliction of duty; unlawful or improper behavior.

affirmative misconduct. (1897) **1.** An affirmative act of misrepresentation or concealment of a material fact; intentional wrongful behavior. • Some courts hold that there must be an ongoing pattern of misrepresentation or false promises, as opposed to an isolated act of providing misinformation. **2.** With respect to a claim of estoppel against the federal government, a misrepresentation or concealment of a material fact by a government employee — beyond a merely innocent or negligent misrepresentation.

juror misconduct. (1954) A juror's violation of the court's charge or the law, committed either during trial or in deliberations after trial, such as (1) communicating about the case with outsiders, witnesses, attorneys, bailiffs, or judges, (2) bringing into the jury room information relating to the case but not in evidence, and (3) conducting experiments regarding theories of the case outside the court's presence.

official misconduct. (1830) A public officer's corrupt violation of assigned duties by malfeasance, misfeasance, or nonfeasance.

wanton misconduct. (1844) An act, or a failure to act when there is a duty to do so, in reckless disregard of another's rights, coupled with the knowledge that injury will probably result.

willful and wanton misconduct. (1866) Conduct committed with an intentional or reckless disregard for the safety of others, as by failing to exercise ordinary care to prevent a known danger or to discover a danger.

willful misconduct. (1804) Misconduct committed voluntarily and intentionally.

willful misconduct of an employee. (1884) The deliberate disregard by an employee of the employer's interests, including its work rules and standards of conduct, justifying a denial of unemployment compensation if the employee is terminated for the misconduct.

2. An attorney's dishonesty or attempt to persuade a court or jury by using deceptive or reprehensible methods.

miscontinuance. (16c) A continuance erroneously ordered by a court.

miscreant (**mis**-kree-ənt). (14c) **1.** A wrongdoer. **2.** An apostate; an unbeliever.

misdate. (16c) To erroneously date (a document, etc.).

misdelivery. (1867) Delivery not according to contractual specifications; esp. delivery to the wrong person or delivery of goods in a damaged condition. • This concept applies to contracts of carriage and contracts of sale, lease, etc., requiring delivery in some form.

misdemeanant (mis-də-**mee**-nənt), *n.* (1819) A person who has been convicted of a misdemeanor.

misdemeanor (mis-di-**mee**-nər). (16c) A crime that is less serious than a felony and is usu. punishable by fine, penalty, forfeiture, or confinement (usu. for a brief term) in a place other than prison (such as a county jail).

gross misdemeanor. (18c) A serious misdemeanor, though not a felony.

serious misdemeanor. (1893) One of a class of misdemeanors having more severe penalties than most other misdemeanors.

misdemeanor-manslaughter rule. (1967) The doctrine that a death occurring during the commission of a misdemeanor (or sometimes a nondangerous felony) is involuntary manslaughter. • Many states and the Model Penal Code have abolished this rule.

misdescription. (1848) **1.** A contractual error or falsity that deceives, injures, or materially misleads one of the contracting parties. **2.** A bailee's inaccurate identification, in a document of title, of goods received from the bailor. **3.** An inaccurate legal description of land in a deed.

misfeasance (mis-**fee**-zənts), *n.* (16c) **1.** A lawful act performed in a wrongful manner. **2.** More broadly, a transgression or trespass; malfeasance. — **misfeasant,** *adj.* — **misfeasor,** *n.*

misfeasance in public office. (1880) The tort of excessive, malicious, or negligent exercise of statutory powers by a public officer.

misjoinder (mis-**joyn**-dər). (18c) **1.** The improper union of parties in a civil case. **2.** The improper union of offenses in a criminal case.

mislay, *vb.* (15c) To deposit (property, etc.) in a place not afterwards recollected; to lose (property, etc.) by forgetting where it was placed.

misleading, *adj.* (16c) (Of an instruction, direction, etc.) delusive; calculated to be misunderstood.

misnomer (mis-**noh**-mər). (15c) A mistake in naming a person, place, or thing, esp. in a legal instrument. • In federal pleading — as well as in most states — misnomer of a party can be corrected by an amendment, which will relate back to the date of the original pleading. Fed. R. Civ. P. 15(c)(3).

misperformance. (17c) A faulty attempt to discharge an obligation (esp. a contractual one).

mispleading. (16c) Pleading incorrectly. • A party who realizes that its pleading is incorrect can usu. amend the pleading, as a matter of right, within a certain period, and can thereafter amend with the court's permission.

misprision (mis-**prizh**-ən). (15c) **1.** Concealment or nondisclosure of a serious crime by one who did not participate in the crime.

clerical misprision. (18c) A court clerk's mistake or fraud that is apparent from the record.

misprision of felony. (16c) Concealment or nondisclosure of someone else's felony. See 18 USCA § 4.

misprision of treason. (16c) Concealment or nondisclosure of someone else's treason.

negative misprision. (18c) The wrongful concealment of something that should be revealed <misprision of treason>.

positive misprision. (18c) The active commission of a wrongful act <seditious conduct against the government is positive misprision>.

2. Seditious conduct against the government. **3.** An official's failure to perform the duties of public office. **4.** Misunderstanding; mistake.

misprisor (mis-**prɪ**-zər). One who commits misprision of felony.

misreading. An act of fraud in which a person incorrectly reads the contents of an instrument to an illiterate or blind person with the intent to deceitfully obtain that person's signature.

misrecital. (16c) An incorrect statement of a factual matter in a contract, deed, pleading, or other instrument.

misrepresentation, *n.* (17c) **1.** The act of making a false or misleading assertion about something, usu. with the intent to deceive. • The word denotes not just written or spoken words but also any other conduct that amounts to a false assertion. **2.** The assertion so made; an assertion that does not accord with the facts. — **misrepresent,** *vb.*

fraudulent misrepresentation. (18c) A false statement that is known to be false or is made recklessly — without knowing or caring whether it is true or false — and that is intended to induce a party to detrimentally rely on it.

innocent misrepresentation. (1809) A false statement that the speaker or writer does not know is false; a misrepresentation that, though false, was not made fraudulently.

material misrepresentation. (18c) **1.** *Contracts.* A false statement that is likely to induce a reasonable person to assent or that the maker knows is likely to induce the recipient to assent. **2.** *Torts.* A false statement to which a reasonable person would attach importance in deciding how to act in the transaction in question or to which the maker knows or has reason to know that the recipient attaches some importance. See Restatement (Second) of Torts § 538 (1979).

negligent misrepresentation. (1888) A careless or inadvertent false statement in circumstances where care should have been taken.

missing-evidence rule. (1981) The doctrine that, when a party fails at trial to present evidence that the party controls and that would have been proper to present, the jury is entitled to infer that the evidence would have been unfavorable to that party.

missing person. 1. Someone whose whereabouts are unknown and, after a reasonable time, seem to be unascertainable. **2.** Someone whose continuous and unexplained absence entitles the heirs to petition a court to declare the person dead and to divide up the person's property.

missing-witness rule. (1961) The doctrine that, when a party fails at trial to present a witness who is available only to that party and whose testimony would have been admissible, the jury is entitled to infer that the witness's testimony would have been unfavorable to that party.

mistake, *n.* (17c) **1.** An error, misconception, or misunderstanding; an erroneous belief. **2.** *Contracts.* The situation in which either (1) the parties to a contract did not mean the same thing, or (2) at least one party had a belief that did not correspond to the facts or law. • As a result, the contract may be voidable.

basic mistake. A mistake of fact or of law constituting the basis on which a transaction rests.

essential mistake. (1818) *Contracts.* A mistake serious enough that no real consent could have existed, so that there was no real agreement.

mistake of fact. (1808) **1.** A mistake about a fact that is material to a transaction; any mistake other than a mistake of law. **2.** The defense asserting that a criminal defendant acted from an innocent misunderstanding of fact rather than from a criminal purpose.

mistake of law. (18c) **1.** A mistake about the legal effect of a known fact or situation. **2.** The defense asserting that a defendant did not understand the criminal consequences of certain conduct. • This defense is generally not as effective as a mistake of fact.

mutual mistake. (18c) **1.** A mistake in which each party misunderstands the other's intent. **2.** A mistake that is shared and relied on by both parties to a contract. • A court will often revise or nullify a contract based on a mutual mistake about a material term.

unessential mistake. (1928) *Contracts.* A mistake that does not relate to the nature of the contents of an agreement, but only to some external circumstance, so that the mistake has no effect on the validity of the agreement.

unilateral mistake. (1885) A mistake by only one party to a contract. • A unilateral mistake is generally not as likely to be a ground for voiding the contract as is a mutual mistake.

mistrial. (17c) **1.** A trial that the judge brings to an end, without a determination on the merits, because of a procedural error or serious misconduct occurring during the proceedings. **2.** A trial that ends inconclusively because the jury cannot agree on a verdict.

misunderstanding. (13c) **1.** A flawed interpretation of meaning or significance. **2.** A situation in which the words or acts of two people suggest assent, but one or both of them in fact intend something different from what the words or acts express. **3.** A quarrel; an instance of usu. mild wrangling.

misuse, *n.* (14c) **1.** *Products liability.* A defense alleging that the plaintiff used the product in an improper, unintended, or unforeseeable manner. **2.** *Patents.* The use of a patent either to improperly extend the granted monopoly to nonpatented goods or to violate antitrust laws.

misuser. (17c) An abuse of a right or office, as a result of which the person having the right might lose it.

mitigate (**mit**-ə-gayt), *vb.* (15c) To make less severe or intense. — **mitigation,** *n.* — **mitigatory** (**mit**-ə-gə-tor-ee), *adj.*

mitigation-of-damages doctrine. (1978) The principle requiring a plaintiff, after an injury or breach of contract, to make reasonable efforts to alleviate the effects of the injury or breach.

mitigation of punishment. (18c) *Criminal law.* A reduction in punishment due to mitigating circumstances that reduce the criminal's level of culpability, such as the existence of no prior convictions.

mitigator. A factor tending to show that a criminal defendant, though guilty, is less culpable than the act alone would indicate.

mixed law. A law concerning both persons and property.

mixed-motive doctrine. *Employment law.* The principle that, when the evidence in an employment-discrimination case shows that the complained-of employment action was based in part on a nondiscriminatory reason and in part on a discriminatory reason, the plaintiff must show that discrimination was a motivating factor for the employment action and, if the plaintiff makes that showing, then the defendant must show that it would have taken the same action without regard to the discriminatory reason.

mixed question. (18c) **1.** Mixed question of law and fact. **2.** An issue involving conflicts of foreign and domestic law.

mixed question of law and fact. (1805) An issue that is neither a pure question of fact nor a pure question of law. • Mixed questions of law and fact are typically resolved by juries. — Often shortened to *mixed question.*

MJOA. *abbr.* Motion for judgment of acquittal.

MLA. *abbr.* Motion for leave to appeal.

M.O. *abbr.* Modus operandi.

mock trial. (18c) **1.** A fictitious trial organized to allow law students, or sometimes lawyers, to practice the techniques of trial advocacy. **2.** A fictitious trial, arranged by a litigant's attorney, to assess trial strategy, to estimate the case's value or risk, and to evaluate the case's strengths and weaknesses.

mode. (17c) A manner of doing something.

model act. (1931) A statute drafted by the National Conference of Commissioners on Uniform State Laws and proposed as guideline legislation for the states to borrow from or adapt to suit their individual needs.

Model Code of Professional Responsibility. A set of guidelines for lawyers, organized in the form of canons, disciplinary rules, and ethical considerations. • Published by the ABA in 1969, this code has been replaced in most states by the Model Rules of Professional Conduct as the ethical standards by which lawyers are regulated and disciplined, although the Model Code continues to be used to interpret and apply the Model Rules.

Model Penal Code. A proposed criminal code drafted by the American Law Institute and used as the basis for criminal-law revision by many states. — Abbr. MPC.

Model Rules of Professional Conduct. A set of ethical guidelines for lawyers, organized in the form of 52 rules — some mandatory, some discretionary — together with explanatory comments. • Published by the ABA in 1983, these rules have generally replaced the Model Code of Professional Responsibility and have been adopted as law, sometimes with modifications, by most states. The Model Code of Professional Responsibility is sometimes used to interpret and apply the Model Rules.

moderator. (16c) One who presides at a meeting or assembly.

modification. (17c) **1.** A change to something; an alteration. **2.** A qualification or limitation of something.

modification order. *Family law.* A postdivorce order that changes the terms of child support, custody, visitation, or alimony.

modus (**moh**-dəs), *n.* [Latin "mode"] *Criminal procedure.* The part of a charging instrument describing the manner in which an offense was committed.

modus operandi (**moh**-dəs op-ə-**ran**-dɪ *or* -dee). [Latin "a manner of operating"] (17c) A method of operating or a manner of procedure; esp. a pattern of criminal behavior so distinctive that investigators attribute it to the work of the same person. — Abbr. M.O. Pl. **modi operandi.**

moiety (**moy**-ə-tee). (15c) **1.** A half of something (such as an estate). **2.** A portion less than half; a small segment. **3.** In federal customs law, a payment made to an informant who assists in the seizure of contraband, the payment being no more than 25% of the contraband's net value (up to a maximum of $250,000). 19 USCA § 1619.

moiety act. (1875) *Criminal law.* A law providing that a portion (such as half) of an imposed fine will inure to the benefit of the informant.

mole. (1922) A person who uses a long affiliation with an organization to gain access to and betray confidential information.

molestation. (15c) **1.** The persecution or harassment of someone. **2.** The act of making unwanted and indecent advances to or on someone, esp. for sexual gratification. — **molest,** *vb.* — **molester,** *n.*

child molestation. (1951) Any indecent or sexual activity on, involving, or surrounding a child, usu. under the age of 14. See Fed. R. Evid. 414(d).

money. (14c) **1.** The medium of exchange authorized or adopted by a government as part of its currency; esp. domestic currency. UCC § 1-201(24). **2.** Assets that can be easily converted to cash. **3.** Capital that is invested or traded as a commodity. **4.** (*pl.*) Funds; sums of money.

money demand. (1821) A claim for a fixed, liquidated sum, as opposed to a damage claim that must be assessed by a jury.

money-laundering, *n.* (1974) The act of transferring illegally obtained money through legitimate people or accounts so that its original source cannot be traced.

money-market account. An interest-bearing account at a bank or other financial institution.

money order. (1802) A negotiable draft issued by an authorized entity (such as a bank, telegraph company, post office, etc.) to a purchaser, in lieu of a check to be used to pay a debt or otherwise transmit funds upon the credit of the issuer.

money service business, *n.* A nonbank entity that provides mechanisms for people to make payments or to obtain currency or cash in exchange for payment instruments.

money supply. The total amount of money in circulation in the economy.

monopolization, *n.* (18c) The act or process of obtaining a monopoly. • In federal antitrust law, monopolization is an offense with two elements: (1) the possession of monopoly power — that is, the power to fix prices and exclude competitors — within the relevant market, and (2) the willful acquisition or maintenance of that power, as distinguished from growth or development as a consequence of a superior product, business acumen, or historical accident. *United States v. Grinnell Corp.*, 384 U.S. 563, 86 S.Ct. 1698 (1966). — **monopolize,** *vb.* — **monopolist** (mə-**nop**-ə-list), *n.*

monopoly, *n.* (16c) **1.** Control or advantage obtained by one supplier or producer over the commercial market within a given region. **2.** The market condition existing when only one economic entity produces a particular product or provides a particular service. • The term is now commonly applied also to situations that approach but do not strictly meet this definition.

monopsony (mə-**nop**-sə-nee), *n.* (1933) A market situation in which one buyer controls the market. — **monopsonistic,** *adj.*

monument, *n.* (15c) **1.** A written document or record, esp. a legal one. **2.** Any natural or artificial object that is fixed permanently in land and referred to in a legal description of the land. — **monumental,** *adj.*

Moody's Investor's Service. An investment-analysis and advisory service.

moot, *adj.* (16c) **1.** *Archaic.* Open to argument; debatable. **2.** Having no practical significance; hypothetical or academic. — **mootness,** *n.*

moot, *vb.* (bef. 12c) **1.** *Archaic.* To raise or bring forward (a point or question) for discussion. **2.** To render (a question) moot or of no practical significance.

moot court. (18c) **1.** A fictitious court held usu. in law schools to argue moot or hypothetical cases, esp. at the appellate level. **2.** A practice session for an appellate argument in which a lawyer presents the argument to other lawyers, who first act as judges by asking questions and who later provide criticism on the argument.

mootness doctrine. (1963) The principle that American courts will not decide moot cases — that is, cases in which there is no longer any actual controversy.

moral certainty. (17c) Absolute certainty.

morality. (14c) **1.** Conformity with recognized rules of correct conduct. **2.** The character of being virtuous, esp. in sexual matters. **3.** A system of duties; ethics.

private morality. (18c) A person's ideals, character, and private conduct, which are not valid governmental concerns if the individual is to be considered sovereign over body and mind and if the need to protect the individual's physical or moral well-being is insufficient to justify governmental intrusion.

public morality. (18c) **1.** The ideals or general moral beliefs of a society. **2.** The ideals or actions of an individual to the extent that they affect others.

moral law. (15c) A collection of principles defining right and wrong conduct; a standard to which an action must conform to be right or virtuous.

moral turpitude. (17c) Conduct that is contrary to justice, honesty, or morality.

moral-wrong doctrine. (1962) The doctrine that if a wrongdoer acts on a mistaken understanding of the facts, the law will not exempt the wrongdoer from culpability when, if the facts had been as the actor believed them to be, his or her conduct would nevertheless be immoral.

moratorium (mor-ə-**tor**-ee-əm). (1875) **1.** An authorized postponement, usu. a lengthy one, in the deadline for paying a debt or performing an obligation. **2.** The period of this delay. **3.** The suspension of a specific activity. Pl. **moratoriums, moratoria.**

moratory (**mor**-ə-tor-ee), *adj.* (1891) Of or relating to a delay; esp. of or relating to a moratorium.

Morgan presumption. (1948) A presumption that shifts the burden of proof by requiring the person against whom it operates to produce sufficient evidence to outweigh the evidence that supports the presumed fact, as in requiring a criminal defendant who was arrested while in possession of an illegal substance — and is thereby presumed to have knowingly possessed it — to produce sufficient evidence to entitle the jury to find that the defendant's evidence outweighs the evidence of knowing possession. See Edmund M. Morgan, *Instructing the Jury Upon Presumptions and Burdens of Proof*, 47 Harv. L. Rev. 59, 82–83 (1933).

mortgage (**mor**-gij), *n.* (15c) **1.** A conveyance of title to property that is given as security for the payment of a debt or the performance of a duty and that will become void upon payment or performance according to the stipulated terms. **2.** A lien against property that is granted to secure an obligation (such as a debt) and that is extinguished upon payment or performance according to stipulated terms. **3.** An instrument (such as a deed or contract) specifying the terms of such a transaction. **4.** Loosely, the loan on which such a transaction is based. **5.** The mortgagee's rights conferred by such a transaction. **6.** Loosely, any real-property security transaction, including a deed of trust. — Abbr. M. — **mortgage,** *vb.*

adjustable-rate mortgage. A mortgage in which the lender can periodically adjust the mortgage's interest rate in accordance with fluctuations in some external market index.

balloon-payment mortgage. A mortgage requiring periodic payments for a specified time and a lump-sum payment of the outstanding balance at maturity.

consolidated mortgage. A mortgage created by combining two or more mortgages.

conventional mortgage. A mortgage, not backed by government insurance, by which the borrower transfers a lien or title to the lending bank or other financial institution. • These mortgages, which feature a fixed periodic payment of principal and interest throughout the mortgage term, are typically used for home financing.

exploding adjustable-rate mortgage. An adjustable-rate mortgage for which the lender resets the interest rate so high that the borrower can no longer make payments.

FHA mortgage. A mortgage that is insured fully or partially by the Federal Housing Administration.

fixed-rate mortgage. A mortgage with an interest rate that remains the same over the life of the mortgage regardless of market conditions. — Abbr. FRM.

flexible-rate mortgage. **1.** Adjustable-rate mortgage. **2.** Renegotiable-rate mortgage.

interest-only mortgage. A balloon-payment mortgage on which the borrower must at first make only interest payments, but must make a lump-sum payment of the full principal at maturity.

second mortgage. A mortgage that is junior to a first mortgage on the same property, but that is senior to any later mortgage.

VA mortgage. A veteran's mortgage that is guaranteed by the Veterans Administration.

mortgage commitment. (1939) A lender's written agreement with a borrower stating the terms on which it will lend money for the purchase of specified real property, usu. with a time limitation.

mortgage-contingency clause. (1965) A real-estate-sale provision that conditions the buyer's performance on obtaining a mortgage loan.

mortgage discount. (1928) The difference between the mortgage principal and the amount the mortgage actually sells for; the up-front charge by a lender at a real-estate closing for the costs of financing.

mortgagee (mor-gə-**jee**). (16c) One to whom property is mortgaged; the mortgage creditor, or lender.

mortgagee in possession. (18c) A mortgagee who takes control of mortgaged land by agreement with the mortgagor, usu. upon default of the loan secured by the mortgage.

mortmain (**mort**-mayn). [French "dead-hand"] (15c) The condition of lands or tenements held in perpetuity by an ecclesiastical or other corporation.

mortmain statute. (1839) A law that limits gifts and other dispositions of land to corporations (esp. charitable ones) and that prohibits corporations from holding land in perpetuity.

most favored nation. A treaty status granted to a nation, usu. in international trade, allowing it to enjoy the privileges that the other party accords to other nations under similar circumstances. • The primary effect of most-favored-nation status is lower trade tariffs. — Abbr. MFN.

most-favored-tenant clause. (1962) A commercial-lease provision ensuring that the tenant will be given the benefit of any negotiating concessions given to other tenants.

most-significant-contacts test. Most-significant-relationships test.

most-significant-relationship test. (1968) *Conflict of laws.* The doctrine that, to determine the state law to apply to a dispute, the court should determine which state has the most substantial connection to the occurrence and the parties.

mother. (bef. 12c) A woman who has given birth to, provided the egg for, or legally adopted a child. • The term is sometimes interpreted as including a pregnant woman who has not yet given birth.

biological mother. (1965) The woman who provides the egg that develops into an embryo. • With today's genetic-engineering techniques, the biological mother may not be the birth mother, but she is usu. the legal mother.

birth mother. (1958) The woman who carries an embryo during the gestational period and who delivers the child.

stepmother. (bef. 12c) The wife of one's father by a later marriage.

surrogate mother. (1914) **1.** A woman who carries out the gestational function and gives birth to a child for another; esp. a woman who agrees to provide her uterus to carry an embryo throughout pregnancy, typically on behalf of an infertile couple, and who relinquishes any parental rights she may have upon the birth of the child. **2.** A person who performs the role of a mother.

Mother Hubbard clause. (1939) **1.** A clause stating that a mortgage secures all the debts that the mortgagor may at any time owe to the mortgagee. **2.** *Oil & gas.* A provision in an oil-and-gas lease protecting the lessee against errors in the description of the property by providing that the lease covers all the land owned by the lessor in the area. **3.** A court's written declaration that any relief not expressly granted in a specific ruling or judgment is denied.

motion. (18c) **1.** A written or oral application requesting a court to make a specified ruling or order.

calendar motion. (1930) A motion relating to the time of a court appearance.

cross-motion. A competing request for relief or orders similar to that requested by another party against the cross-moving party, such as a motion for summary judgment or for sanctions.

dilatory motion (**dil**-ə-tor-ee). (18c) **1.** A motion made solely for the purpose of delay or obstruction. **2.** A motion that delays the proceedings.

ex parte motion (eks **pahr**-tee). (1831) A motion made to the court without notice to the adverse party; a motion that a court considers and rules on without hearing from all sides.

omnibus motion. (1889) A motion that makes several requests or asks for multiple forms of relief.

posttrial motion. (1889) A motion made after judgment is entered, such as a motion for new trial.

show-cause motion. A motion filed with the court requesting that a litigant be required to appear and explain why that litigant has failed to comply with a legal requirement.

speaking motion. (1935) A motion that addresses matters not raised in the pleadings.

special motion. (16c) A motion specifically requiring the court's discretion upon hearing, as distinguished from one granted as a matter of course.

2. *Parliamentary law.* A proposal made in a meeting, in a form suitable for its consideration and action, that the meeting (or the organization for which the meeting is acting) take a certain action or view.

motion for directed verdict. (1904) A party's request that the court enter judgment in its favor before submitting the case to the jury because there is no legally sufficient evidentiary foundation on which a reasonable jury could find for the other party. • Under the Federal Rules of Civil Procedure, the equivalent court paper is known as a motion for judgment as a matter of law. — Abbr. MDV.

motion for judgment as a matter of law. (1956) A party's request that the court enter a judgment in its favor before the case is submitted to the jury, or after a contrary jury verdict, because there is no legally sufficient evidentiary basis on which a jury could find for the other party. • Under the Federal Rules of Civil Procedure, a party may move for judgment as a matter of law anytime before the case has been submitted to the jury. This kind of motion was formerly known as a *motion for directed verdict* (and still is in many jurisdictions). If the motion is denied and the case is submitted to the jury, resulting in an unfavorable verdict, the motion may be renewed within ten days after entry of the judgment. This aspect of the motion replaces the court paper formerly known as a *motion for judgment notwithstanding the verdict.* Fed. R. Civ. P. 50.

motion for judgment notwithstanding the verdict. (1822) A party's request that the court enter a judgment in its favor despite the jury's contrary verdict because there is no legally sufficient evidentiary basis for a jury to find for the other party. • Under the Federal Rules of Civil Procedure, this procedure has been replaced by the provision for a motion for judgment as a matter of law, which must be presented before the case has been submitted to the jury but can be reasserted if it is denied and the jury returns an unfavorable verdict. Fed. R. Civ. P. 50.

motion for judgment of acquittal. (1923) A criminal defendant's request, at the close of the government's case or the close of all evidence, to be acquitted because there is no legally sufficient evidentiary basis on which a reasonable jury could return a guilty verdict. • If the motion is granted, the government has no right of appeal. Fed. R. Crim. P. 29(a). — Abbr. MJOA.

motion for judgment on the pleadings. (1923) A party's request that the court rule in its favor based on the pleadings on file, without accepting evidence, as when the outcome of the case rests on the court's interpretation of the law. Fed. R. Civ. P. 12(c).

motion for leave to appeal. (1874) A request that an appellate court review an interlocutory order that meets the standards of the collateral-order doctrine. — Abbr. MLA.

motion for more definite statement. (1904) A party's request that the court require an opponent to amend a vague or ambiguous pleading to which the party cannot reasonably be required to respond. Fed. R. Civ. P. 12(e).

motion for new trial. (18c) A party's postjudgment request that the court vacate the judgment and order a new trial for such reasons as factually insufficient evidence, newly discovered evidence, and jury misconduct. • In many jurisdictions, this motion is required before a party can raise such a matter on appeal.

motion for protective order. (1948) A party's request that the court protect it from potentially abusive action by the other party, usu. relating to discovery, as when one party seeks discovery of the other party's trade secrets. • A court will sometimes craft a protective order to protect one party's trade secrets by ordering that any secret information exchanged in discovery be used only for purposes of the pending suit and not be publicized.

motion for relief from the judgment. (1867) A party's request that the court correct a clerical mistake in the judgment — that is, a mistake that results in the judgment's incorrectly reflecting the court's intentions — or relieve the party from the judgment because of such matters as (1) inadvertence, surprise, or excusable neglect, (2) newly discovered evidence that could not have been discovered through diligence in time for a motion for new trial, (3) the judgment's being the result of fraud, misrepresentation, or misconduct by the other party, or (4) the judgment's being void or having been satisfied or released. Fed. R. Civ. P. 60.

motion for repleader. (18c) *Common-law pleading.* An unsuccessful party's posttrial motion asking that the pleadings begin anew because the issue was joined on an immaterial point.

motion for summary judgment. (1842) A request that the court enter judgment without a trial because there is no genuine issue of material fact to be decided by a fact-finder — that is, because the evidence is legally insufficient to support a verdict in the nonmovant's favor. • In federal court and in most state courts, the movant-defendant must point out in its motion the absence of evidence on an essential element of the plaintiff's claim, after which the burden shifts to the nonmovant-plaintiff to produce evidence raising a genuine fact issue. But if a party moves for summary judgment on its own claim or defense, then it must establish each element of the claim or defense as a matter of law. Fed. R. Civ. P. 56. — Abbr. MSJ.

motion in arrest of judgment. (17c) **1.** A defendant's motion claiming that a substantial error appearing on the face of the record vitiates the whole proceeding and the judgment. **2.** A postjudgment motion in a criminal case claiming that the indictment is insufficient to sustain a judgment or that the verdict is somehow insufficient.

motion in limine (in **lim**-ə-nee). (18c) A pretrial request that certain inadmissible evidence not be referred to or offered at trial. • Typically, a party makes this motion when it believes that mere mention of the evidence during trial would be highly prejudicial and could not be remedied by an instruction to disregard. If, after the motion is granted, the opposing party mentions or attempts to offer the evidence in the jury's presence, a mistrial may be ordered. A ruling on a motion in limine does not always preserve evidentiary error for appellate purposes. To raise such an error on appeal, a party may be required to formally object when the evidence is actually admitted or excluded during trial.

motion to alter or amend the judgment. (1950) A party's request that the court correct a substantive error in the judgment, such as a manifest error of law or fact. • Under the Federal Rules of Civil Procedure, a motion to alter or amend the judgment must be filed within ten days after the judgment is entered. It should not ordinarily be used to correct clerical errors in a judgment. Those types of errors — that is, errors that result in the judgment not reflecting the court's intention — may be brought in a motion for relief from the judgment, which does not have the ten-day deadline. A motion to alter or amend the judgment is usu. directed to substantive issues regarding the judgment, such as an intervening change in the law or newly discovered evidence that was not available at trial. Fed. R. Civ. P. 59(e).

motion to compel discovery. (1960) A party's request that the court force the party's opponent to respond to the party's discovery request (as to answer interrogatories or produce documents). Fed. R. Civ. P. 37(a).

motion to dismiss. (18c) A request that the court dismiss the case because of settlement, voluntary withdrawal, or a procedural defect. • Under the Federal Rules of Civil Procedure, a plaintiff may voluntarily dismiss the case (under Rule 41(a)) or the defendant may ask the court to dismiss the case, usu. based on one of the defenses listed in Rule 12(b). These defenses include lack of personal or subject-matter jurisdiction, improper venue, insufficiency of process, the plaintiff's failure to state a claim on which relief can be granted, and the failure to join an indispensable party. A defendant will frequently file a motion to dismiss for failure to state a claim, which is governed by Rule 12(b)(6), claiming that even if all the plaintiff's allegations are true, they would not be legally sufficient to state a claim on which relief might be granted. — Abbr. MTD.

motion to lift the stay. (1969) *Bankruptcy.* A party's request that the bankruptcy court alter the automatic bankruptcy stay to allow the movant to act against the debtor or the debtor's property, as when a creditor seeks permission to foreclose on a lien because its security interest is not adequately protected.

motion to quash (kwahsh). (18c) A party's request that the court nullify process or an act instituted by the other party, as in seeking to nullify a subpoena.

motion to remand. (1816) In a case that has been removed from state court to federal court, a party's request that the federal court return the case to state court, usu. because the federal court lacks jurisdiction or because the procedures for removal were not properly followed. 28 USCA § 1447(c).

motion to strike. (1806) **1.** *Civil procedure.* A party's request that the court delete insufficient defenses or immaterial, redundant, impertinent, or scandalous statements from an opponent's pleading. Fed. R. Civ. P. 12(f). **2.** *Evidence.* A request that inadmissible evidence be deleted from the record and that the jury be instructed to disregard it.

motion to suppress. (18c) A request that the court prohibit the introduction of illegally obtained evidence at a criminal trial.

motion to transfer venue. (1934) A request that the court transfer the case to another district or county, usu. because the original venue is improper under the applicable venue rules or because of local prejudice.

motion to withdraw. 1. An attorney's request for a court's permission to cease representing a client in a lawsuit. **2.** A defendant's formal request for a court's permission to change the defendant's plea or strike an admission.

motive. (14c) Something, esp. willful desire, that leads one to act.

bad motive. (18c) A person's knowledge that an act is wrongful while the person commits the act.

malicious motive. (18c) A motive for bringing a prosecution, other than to do justice.

movable, *n.* (*usu. pl.*) (15c) Property that can be moved or displaced, such as personal goods.

intangible movable. A physical thing that can be moved but that cannot be touched in the usual sense. • Examples are light and electricity.

movant (**moov**-ənt). (1875) One who makes a motion to the court or a deliberative body.

move, *vb.* (15c) **1.** To make an application (to a court) for a ruling, order, or some other judicial action. **2.** To make a motion.

MPC. *abbr.* Model Penal Code.

MRE. *abbr.* Military Rules of Evidence.

MSHA. *abbr.* Mine Safety and Health Administration.

MSJ. *abbr.* Motion for Summary Judgment.

MSPB. *abbr.* Merit Systems Protection Board.

MTD. *abbr.* Motion to Dismiss.

MUD. *abbr.* Municipal Utility District.

mug book. (1947) A collection of mug shots of criminal suspects maintained by law-enforcement agencies (such as the FBI and police departments) to be used in identifying criminal offenders.

mulct (məlkt), *n.* (16c) A fine or penalty.

mulct, *vb.* (17c) **1.** To punish by a fine. **2.** To deprive or divest of, esp. fraudulently.

mule. *Slang.* A person hired to smuggle contraband, esp. a controlled substance, and deliver it to the distributor at a destination point.

multidisciplinary practice. A fee-sharing association of lawyers and nonlawyers in a firm that delivers both legal and nonlegal services. • Rule 5.4 of the Model Rules of Professional Conduct effectively bars multidisciplinary practice. Under this rule, a lawyer cannot (1) share legal fees with nonlawyers, (2) form a partnership involving the practice of law with nonlawyers, (3) form a law firm in which a nonlawyer has an interest, or (4) allow a nonlawyer to direct the lawyer's professional judgment. — Abbr. MDP.

multidistrict litigation. (1966) *Civil procedure.* Federal-court litigation in which civil actions pending in different districts and involving common fact questions are transferred to a single district for coordinated pretrial proceedings, after which the actions are returned to their original districts for trial. 28 USCA § 1407. — Abbr. MDL.

multifarious (məl-tə-**fair**-ee-əs), *adj.* (16c) **1.** (Of a single pleading) improperly joining distinct matters or causes of action, and thereby confounding them. **2.** Improperly joining parties in a lawsuit. **3.** Diverse; many and various. — **multifariousness,** *n.*

multilateral, *adj.* (1827) Involving more than two parties.

multipartite, *adj.* (17c) (Of a document, etc.) divided into many parts.

multiplicity (məl-tə-**plis**-i-tee), *n. Criminal procedure.* The improper charging of the same offense in more than one count of a single indictment or information. • Multiplicity violates the Fifth Amendment protection against double jeopardy. — **multiplicitous** (məl-tə-**plis**-i-təs), *adj.*

multiplicity of actions. (17c) The existence of two or more lawsuits litigating the same issue against the same defendant.

municipal corporation. A city, town, or other local political entity formed by charter from the state and having the autonomous authority to administer the state's local affairs; esp., a public corporation created for political purposes and endowed with political powers to be exercised for the public good in the administration of local civil government.

municipal function. The duties and responsibilities that a municipality owes its members.

municipality. (18c) **1.** Municipal corporation. **2.** The governing body of a municipal corporation.

muniment (**myoo**-nə-mənt). (15c) A document (such as a deed or charter) evidencing the rights or privileges of a person, family, or corporation.

muniment of title. (1806) Documentary evidence of title, such as a deed or a judgment regarding the ownership of property.

murder, *n.* (bef. 12c) The killing of a human being with malice aforethought. Model Penal Code § 210.2. — **murder,** *vb.* — **murderous,** *adj.*

depraved-heart murder. (1975) A murder resulting from an act so reckless and careless of the safety of others that it demonstrates the perpetrator's complete lack of regard for human life.

felony murder. (1926) Murder that occurs during the commission of a dangerous felony (often limited to rape, kidnapping, robbery, burglary, and arson).

first-degree murder. (1895) Murder that is willful, deliberate, or premeditated, or that is committed during the course of another dangerous felony.

mass murder. (1917) A murderous act or series of acts by which a criminal kills many victims at or near the same time, usu. as part of one act or plan.

murder by torture. (1901) A murder preceded by the intentional infliction of pain and suffering on the victim.

second-degree murder. (1909) Murder that is not aggravated by any of the circumstances of first-degree murder.

serial murder. (1977) A murder in which a criminal kills one of many victims over time, often as part of a pattern in which the criminal targets victims who have some similar characteristics.

third-degree murder. (1933) A wrong that did not constitute murder at common law. • Only a few states have added to their murder statutes a third degree of murder. The other states classify all murders in two degrees. Manslaughter is not a degree of the crime of murder, but instead is a distinct offense.

unintentional murder. **1.** A killing for which malice is implied because the person acted with intent to cause serious physical injury or knew that the conduct was substantially certain to cause death or serious physical injury. • In some jurisdictions, this term is applied generally to several grades of killings without express intent. **2.** Depraved-heart murder. **3.** Felony murder. **4.** Voluntary manslaughter.

willful murder. (16c) The unlawful and intentional killing of another without excuse or mitigating circumstances.

mutation, *n.* A significant and basic alteration; esp. in property law, the alteration of a thing's status, such as from separate property to community property. — **mutate,** *vb.* — **mutational,** *adj.*

mutatis mutandis (myoo-**tay**-tis myoo-**tan**-dis). [Latin] (16c) All necessary changes having been made; with the necessary changes <what was said regarding the first contract applies *mutatis mutandis* to all later ones>.

mute, *n.* (17c) **1.** A person who cannot speak. **2.** A person (esp. a prisoner) who stands silent when required to answer or plead.

mutilation, *n.* (16c) **1.** The act or an instance of rendering a document legally ineffective by subtracting or altering — but not completely destroying — an essential part through cutting, tearing, burning, or erasing. **2.** *Criminal law.* The act of cutting off or permanently damaging a body part, esp. an essential one. — **mutilate,** *vb.* — **mutilator,** *n.*

mutiny (**myoo**-tə-nee), *n.* (16c) **1.** An insubordination or insurrection of armed forces, esp. sailors, against the authority of their commanders; a forcible revolt by members of the military against constituted authority, usu. their commanding officers. **2.** Loosely, any uprising against authority. — **mutinous,** *adj.*

mutual, *adj.* (16c) **1.** Generally, directed by each toward the other or others; reciprocal. **2.** (Of a condition, credit covenant, promise, etc.) reciprocally given, received, or exchanged. **3.** (Of a right, etc.) belonging to two parties; common. — **mutuality,** *n.*

mutual-agreement program. (1978) A prisoner-rehabilitation plan in which the prisoner agrees to take part in certain self-improvement activities to receive a definite parole date.

mutual association. A mutually owned, cooperative savings and loan association, with the deposits being shares of the association. • A mutual association is not allowed to issue stock and is usu. regulated by the Office of Thrift Supervision, an agency of the U.S. Treasury Department.

mutual combat. (17c) A consensual fight on equal terms — arising from a moment of passion but not in self-defense — between two persons armed with deadly weapons. • A murder charge may be reduced to voluntary manslaughter if death occurred by mutual combat.

mutual demands. (17c) Countering demands between two parties at the same time <a claim and counterclaim in a lawsuit are mutual demands>.

mutual fund. (1934) **1.** An investment company that invests its shareholders' money in a usu. diversified selection of securities. — Often shortened to *fund*. **2.** Loosely, a share in such a company.

bond fund. A mutual fund that invests primarily in specialized corporate bonds or municipal bonds.

common-stock fund. A mutual fund that invests only in common stock.

dual fund. A closed-end mutual fund that invests in two classes of stock — stock that pays dividends and stock that increases in investment value without dividends. • A dual fund combines characteristics of an income fund and a growth fund.

growth fund. A mutual fund that typically invests in well-established companies whose earnings are expected to increase. • Growth funds usu. pay small dividends but offer the potential for large share-price increases.

income fund. A mutual fund that typically invests in securities that consistently produce a steady income, such as bonds or dividend-paying stocks.

index fund. A mutual fund that invests in the stock of companies constituting a specific market index, such as Standard & Poor's 500 stocks, and thereby tracks the stock average.

load fund. A mutual fund that charges a commission, usu. ranging from 4 to 9%, either when shares are purchased (a *front-end load*) or when they are redeemed (a *back-end load*).

money-market fund. A mutual fund that invests in low-risk government securities and short-term notes.

no-load fund. A mutual fund that does not charge any sales commission (although it may charge fees to cover operating costs).

performance fund. A mutual fund characterized by an aggressive purchase of stocks expected to show near-term growth.

regional fund. A mutual fund that concentrates its investments in a specific geographic area or a particular economic area.

utility fund. A mutual fund that invests only in public-utility securities.

mutuality. (16c) The state of sharing or exchanging something; a reciprocation; an interchange <mutuality of obligation>.

mutuality doctrine. (1926) The collateral-estoppel requirement that, to bar a party from relitigating an issue determined against that party in an earlier action, both parties must have been in privity with one another in the earlier proceeding.

mutuality of debts. *Bankruptcy.* For purposes of setoff, the condition in which debts are owed between parties acting in the same capacity, even though the debts are not of the same character and did not arise out of the same transaction.

mutuality of estoppel. (1852) The collateral-estoppel principle that a judgment is not conclusively in favor of someone unless the opposite decision would also be conclusively against that person.

mutuality of obligation. (1838) The agreement of both parties to a contract to be bound in some way.

mutuality of remedy. (1819) The availability of a remedy, esp. equitable relief, to both parties to a transaction, sometimes required before either party can be granted specific performance.

N

n.a. *abbr.* (1947) **1.** (*cap.*) National Association. **2.** Not applicable. **3.** Not available. **4.** Not allowed.

NAFTA (**naf**-tə). *abbr.* North American Free Trade Agreement.

naked, *adj.* (14c) (Of a legal act or instrument) lacking confirmation or validation <naked ownership of property>.

naked contract. *Nudum pactum.*

naked licensee. Bare licensee.

naked ownership. Imperfect ownership.

naked promise. Gratuitous promise.

naked trust. Passive trust.

named-perils policy. Multiperil insurance policy.

named plaintiff. Class representative.

Napoleonic Code. **1.** (*usu. pl.*) The codification of French law commissioned by Napoleon in the 19th century, including the *Code civil* (1804), the *Code de procédure civil* (1806), the *Code de commerce* (1807), the *Code pénal* (1810), and the *Code d'instruction crimenelle* (1811). **2.** Loosely, CIVIL CODE (2).

narcoanalysis (nahr-koh-ə-**nal**-ə-sis). (1936) The process of injecting a "truth-serum" drug into a patient to induce semiconsciousness, and then interrogating the patient.

narcotic, *n.* (14c) **1.** An addictive drug, esp. an opiate, that dulls the senses and induces sleep. **2.** (*usu. pl.*) A drug that is controlled or prohibited by law. — **narcotic,** *adj.*

narrowly tailored, *adj.* (1972) (Of a content-neutral restriction on the time, place, or manner of speech in a designated public forum) being only as broad as is reasonably necessary to promote a substantial governmental interest that would be achieved less effectively without the restriction; no broader than absolutely necessary.

NASA. *abbr.* National Aeronautics And Space Administration.

NASD. *abbr.* National Association of Securities Dealers.

NASDAQ (**naz**-dak). *abbr.* National Association of Securities Dealers Automated Quotations.

nation, *n.* (14c) **1.** A large group of people having a common origin, language, and tradition and usu. constituting a political entity. • When a nation is coincident with a state, the term *nation-state* is often used. **2.** A community of people inhabiting a defined territory and organized under an independent government; a sovereign political state. — **national,** *adj.* (16c).

national, *n.* **1.** A member of a nation. **2.** A person owing permanent allegiance to and under the protection of a state. 8 USCA § 1101(a)(21).

National Aeronautics and Space Administration. The independent federal agency that conducts research into space flight and that builds and flies space vehicles. • NASA was created by the National Aeronautics and Space Act of 1958. — Abbr. NASA.

National Archives and Records Administration. An independent federal agency that sets procedures for preserving governmental records that are important for legal and historical reasons; helps federal agencies manage their records; provides record-storage access; and manages the Presidential Libraries system. • The agency, run by the Archivist of the United States, retains only a small percentage of the federal records produced each year. It publishes the *United States Statutes at Large*, the *Federal Register*, the *Code of Federal*

Regulations, the weekly *Compilation of Presidential Documents*, the annual *Public Papers of the President*, and the *United States Government Manual*. — Abbr. NARA.

National Association of Securities Dealers Automated Quotations. A computerized system for recording transactions and displaying price quotations for a group of actively traded securities on the over-the-counter market. — Abbr. NASDAQ.

National Association of Women Lawyers. An organization, formed in 1899, devoted to the interests of female lawyers and their families. — Abbr. NAWL.

National Bar Association. An organization of primarily African-American lawyers, founded in 1925 to promote education, professionalism, and the protection of civil rights. — Abbr. NBA.

National Capital Region. The District of Columbia and six nearby counties: Montgomery and Prince George's in Maryland, and Fairfax, Loudoun, Prince William, and Arlington in Virginia. — Abbr. NCR.

National Conference of Commissioners on Uniform State Laws. An organization that drafts and proposes statutes for adoption by individual states, with the goal of making the laws on various subjects uniform among the states.

national debt. (18c) The total financial obligation of the federal government, including such instruments as Treasury bills, notes, and bonds, as well as foreign debt.

national defense. 1. All measures taken by a nation to protect itself against its enemies. **2.** A nation's military establishment.

National Guard. The U.S. militia, which is maintained as a reserve for the U.S. Army and Air Force. • Its members are volunteers, recruited and trained on a statewide basis and equipped by the federal government. A state may request the National Guard's assistance in quelling disturbances, and the federal government may order the National Guard into active service in times of war or other national emergency.

National Institute of Corrections. A federal organization (established within the Bureau of Prisons) whose responsibilities include helping federal, state, and local authorities improve correctional programs, conducting research on correctional issues such as crime prevention, and conducting workshops for law-enforcement personnel, social workers, judges, and others involved in treating and rehabilitating offenders. 18 USCA §§ 4351–4353.

nationality. (17c) The relationship between a citizen of a nation and the nation itself, customarily involving allegiance by the citizen and protection by the state; membership in a nation. • This term is often used synonymously with *citizenship*.

Nationality Act. Immigration and Nationality Act.

nationalization, *n.* (1847) **1.** The act of bringing an industry under governmental control or ownership. **2.** The act of giving a person the status of a citizen.

nationalize, *vb.* (1809) **1.** To bring (an industry) under governmental control or ownership. **2.** To give (a person) the status of a citizen; naturalize.

National Labor Relations Act. A federal statute regulating the relations between employers and employees and establishing the National Labor Relations Board. 29 USCA §§ 151–169. • The statute is also known as the Wagner Act of 1935. It was amended by the Taft–Hartley Act of 1947 and the Landrum–Griffin Act of 1959. — Abbr. NLRA.

National Labor Relations Board. An independent five-member federal board created to prevent and remedy unfair labor practices and to safeguard employees' rights to organize into labor unions. 29 USCA § 153. — Abbr. NLRB.

National Lawyers Guild. An association of lawyers, law students, and legal workers dedicated to promoting a left-wing political and social agenda. • Founded in 1937, it now comprises some 4,000 members.

National Mediation Board. An independent federal board that mediates labor–management disputes in the airline and railroad industries and provides administrative and financial support in adjusting grievances in the railroad industry. 45 USCA §§ 154–163. — Abbr. NMB.

National Oceanic and Atmospheric Administration. A unit in the U.S. Department of Commerce responsible for monitoring the environment in order to make accurate and timely weather forecasts and to protect life, property, and the environment. — Abbr. NOAA.

national origin. (1880) The country in which a person was born, or from which the person's ancestors came. • This term is used in several antidiscrimination statutes, including Title VII of the Civil Rights Act of 1964, which prohibits discrimination because of an individual's "race, color, religion, sex, or national origin." 42 USCA § 2000e-2.

national park. (1868) A scenic, natural, historic, and recreational area owned by the United States and set aside for permanent protection.

National Reporter System. A series of lawbooks, published by the West Group, containing every published appellate decision of the federal and state courts in the United States. • For federal courts, the system includes the *Supreme Court Reporter, Federal Reporter, Federal Claims Reporter, Federal Supplement, Federal Rules Decisions, Bankruptcy Reporter, Military Justice Reporter,* and *Veterans Appeals Reporter.* For state courts, the system includes the *Atlantic Reporter, California Reporter, New York Supplement, North Eastern Reporter, North Western Reporter, Pacific Reporter, South Eastern Reporter, Southern Reporter,* and *South Western Reporter.*

National Science Foundation. An independent federal foundation that promotes progress in science and engineering through grants, contracts, and other agreements awarded to universities, colleges, academic consortia, and nonprofit and small-business institutions. — Abbr. NSF.

National Security Agency. A unit in the U.S. Department of Defense responsible for protecting U.S. information systems as well as producing foreign intelligence information. • The agency uses code makers and code breakers. — Abbr. NSA.

National Security Council. An agency in the Executive Office of the President responsible for advising the President on national-security matters. • It was created by the National Security Act of 1947. 50 USCA § 402. — Abbr. NSC.

national-security letter. A document that is issued by an FBI official, or by a senior official of another federal agency, and that functions as a subpoena requiring the recipient, usu. a business, to turn over specific business documents. • The Department of Justice provides guidelines for the issuance of a national-security letter, which is not typically reviewed by a court or magistrate. Federal law prohibits the letter's recipient from disclosing the existence of the letter, except to an attorney. — Abbr. NSL.

National Transportation Safety Board. An independent five-member federal board that investigates air, rail, water, highway, pipeline, and hazardous-waste accidents; conducts studies; and makes recommendations to government agencies, the transportation industry, and others on safety measures and practices. 49 USCA §§ 1101–1155. — Abbr. NTSB.

native-born, *adj.* **1.** Born within the territorial jurisdiction of a country. **2.** Born of parents who convey rights of citizenship to their offspring, regardless of the place of birth.

natural affection. (16c) The love naturally existing between close relatives, such as parent and child. • Natural affection is not consideration for a contract.

Natural Born Citizen Clause. (1988) The clause of the U.S. Constitution barring persons not born in the United States from the presidency. U.S. Const. art. II, § 1, cl. 5.

natural consequence. (16c) Something that predictably occurs as the result of an act <plaintiff's injuries were the natural consequence of the car wreck>.

natural-death act. (1977) A statute that allows a person to prepare a living will instructing a physician to withhold life-sustaining procedures if the person should become terminally ill.

naturalization. (16c) The granting of citizenship to a foreign-born person under statutory authority.

Naturalization Clause. (1849) The constitutional provision stating that every person born or naturalized in the United States is a citizen of the United States and of the state of residence. U.S. Const. amend. XIV, § 1.

naturalize, *vb.* (16c) To grant the rights, privileges, and duties of citizenship to (one previously a noncitizen); to make (a noncitizen) a citizen under statutory authority. — **naturalization,** *n.*

natural law. (15c) **1.** A physical law of nature. **2.** A philosophical system of legal and moral principles purportedly deriving from a universalized conception of human nature or divine justice rather than from legislative or judicial action; moral law embodied in principles of right and wrong.

natural object. A person likely to receive a portion of another person's estate based on the nature and circumstances of their relationship.

naval law. A system of regulations governing naval forces.

navy. (14c) **1.** A fleet of ships. **2.** The military sea force of a country, including its collective ships and its corps of officers and enlisted personnel; esp. (*usu. cap.*), the division of the U.S. armed services responsible primarily for seagoing forces. • The U.S. Constitution gives Congress the power to establish a navy and make laws governing the naval forces. U.S. Const. art. I, § 8, cl. 13–14.

Navy Department. A division of the Department of Defense that oversees the operation and efficiency of the Navy, including the Marine Corps component (and the U.S. Coast Guard when operating as a naval service). • Established in 1798, the Department is headed by the Secretary of the Navy, who is appointed by the President and reports to the Secretary of Defense.

N.B. *abbr.* [Latin *nota bene*] (17c) Note well; take notice — used in documents to call attention to something important.

N.D. *abbr.* Northern District, in reference to a U.S. judicial district.

N.E. *abbr. North Eastern Reporter.*

necessaries. (14c) **1.** Things that are indispensable to living <an infant's necessaries include food, shelter, and clothing>. **2.** Things that are essential to maintaining the lifestyle to which one is accustomed <a multimillionaire's necessaries may include a chauffeured limousine and a private chef>. • The term includes whatever is reasonably needed for subsistence, health, comfort, and education, considering the person's age, station in life, and medical condition, but it excludes (1) anything purely ornamental, (2) anything solely for pleasure, (3) what the person is already supplied with, (4) anything that concerns someone's estate or business as opposed to personal needs, and (5) borrowed money.

necessary and proper, *adj.* (16c) Being appropriate and well adapted to fulfilling an objective.

Necessary and Proper Clause. (1926) The clause of the U.S. Constitution permitting Congress to make laws "necessary and proper" for the execution of its enumerated powers. U.S. Const. art. I, § 8, cl. 18. • The Supreme Court has broadly interpreted this clause to grant Congress the implied power to enact any law reasonably designed to achieve an express constitutional power. *McCulloch v. Maryland*, 17 U.S. (4 Wheat.) 316 (1819).

necessary inference. (17c) A conclusion that is unavoidable if the premise on which it is based is taken to be true.

necessary repair. (16c) An improvement to property that is both needed to prevent deterioration and proper under the circumstances.

necessities. (14c) **1.** Indispensable things of any kind. **2.** NECESSARIES (1).

necessitous, *adj.* (17c) Living in a state of extreme want; hard up.

necessity. 1. *Criminal law.* A justification defense for a person who acts in an emergency that he or she did not create and who commits a harm that is less severe than the harm that would have occurred but for the person's actions. **2.** *Torts.* A privilege that may relieve a person from liability for trespass or conversion if that person, having no alternative, harms another's property in an effort to protect life or health.

manifest necessity. (17c) A sudden and overwhelming emergency, beyond the court's and parties' control, that makes conducting a trial or reaching a fair result impossible and that therefore authorizes the granting of a mistrial.

moral necessity. (17c) A necessity arising from a duty incumbent on a person to act in a particular way.

physical necessity. (17c) A necessity involving an actual, tangible force that compels a person to act in a particular way.

private necessity. (16c) *Torts.* A necessity that involves only the defendant's personal interest and thus provides only a limited privilege.

public necessity. (16c) *Torts.* A necessity that involves the public interest and thus completely excuses the defendant's liability.

née (nay), *adj.* [French] (17c) (Of a woman) born. • This term is sometimes used after a married woman's name to indicate her maiden name <Mrs. Robert Jones, née Thatcher>. — Also spelled *nee.*

negate, *vb.* (17c) **1.** To deny. **2.** To nullify; to render ineffective.

negative-pledge clause. (1935) **1.** A provision requiring a borrower, who borrows funds without giving security, to refrain from giving future lenders any security without the consent of the first lender. **2.** A provision, usu. in a bond indenture, stating that the issuing entity will not pledge its assets if it will result in less security to the bondholders under the indenture agreement.

negative pregnant. (17c) A denial implying its affirmative opposite by seeming to deny only a qualification of the allegation and not the allegation itself. • An example is the statement, "I didn't steal the money last Tuesday," the implication being that the theft might have happened on another day.

neglect, *n.* (16c) **1.** The omission of proper attention to a person or thing, whether inadvertent, negligent, or willful; the act or condition of disregarding. **2.** The failure to give proper attention, supervision, or necessities, esp. to a child, to such an extent that harm results or is likely to result. — **neglect,** *vb.* — **neglectful,** *adj.*

child neglect. (1930) The failure of a person responsible for a minor to care for the minor's emotional or physical needs. • Child neglect is a form of child abuse.

culpable neglect. (18c) Censurable or blameworthy neglect; neglect that is less than gross carelessness but more than the failure to use ordinary care.

developmental neglect. Failure to provide necessary emotional nurturing and physical or cognitive stimulation, as a result of which a child could suffer from serious developmental delays.

educational neglect. Failure to ensure that a child attends school in accordance with state law.

excusable neglect. (1855) A failure — which the law will excuse — to take some proper step at the proper time (esp. in neglecting to answer a lawsuit) not because of the party's own carelessness, inattention, or willful disregard of the court's process, but because of some unexpected or unavoidable hindrance or accident or because of reliance on the care and vigilance of the party's counsel or on a promise made by the adverse party.

inexcusable neglect. (18c) Unjustifiable neglect; neglect that implies more than unintentional inadvertence.

medical neglect. Failure to provide medical, dental, or psychiatric care that is necessary to prevent or to treat serious physical or emotional injury or illness.

physical neglect. Failure to provide necessaries, the lack of which has caused or could cause serious injury or illness.

willful neglect. (18c) Intentional or reckless failure to carry out a legal duty, esp. in caring for a child.

negligence, *n.* (14c) **1.** The failure to exercise the standard of care that a reasonably prudent person would have exercised in a similar situation; any conduct that falls below the legal standard established to protect others against unreasonable risk of harm, except for conduct that is intentionally, wantonly, or willfully disregardful of others' rights. **2.** A tort grounded in this failure, usu. expressed in terms of the following elements: duty, breach of duty, causation, and damages.

active negligence. (1875) Negligence resulting from an affirmative or positive act, such as driving through a barrier.

advertent negligence. (1909) Negligence in which the actor is aware of the unreasonable risk that he or she is creating; recklessness.

casual negligence. A plaintiff's failure to (1) pay reasonable attention to his or her surroundings, so as to discover the danger created by the defendant's negligence, (2) exercise reasonable competence, care, diligence, and skill to avoid the danger once it is perceived, or (3) prepare as a reasonable person would to avoid future dangers.

collateral negligence. An independent contractor's negligence, for which the employer is generally not liable.

comparative negligence. (1862) A plaintiff's own negligence that proportionally reduces the damages recoverable from a defendant.

concurrent negligence. (1831) The negligence of two or more parties acting independently but causing the same damage.

contributory negligence. (1822) **1.** A plaintiff's own negligence that played a part in causing the plaintiff's injury and that is significant enough (in a few jurisdictions) to bar the plaintiff from recovering damages. • In most jurisdictions, this defense has been superseded by comparative negligence. **2.** *Rare.* The negligence of a third party — neither the plaintiff nor the defendant — whose act or omission played a part in causing the plaintiff's injury.

criminal negligence. (1838) Gross negligence so extreme that it is punishable as a crime. • For example, involuntary manslaughter or other negligent homicide can be based on criminal negligence, as when an extremely careless automobile driver kills someone.

culpable negligence. (17c) **1.** Negligent conduct that, while not intentional, involves a disregard of the consequences likely to result from one's actions. **2.** Criminal negligence.

gross negligence. (16c) **1.** A lack of slight diligence or care. **2.** A conscious, voluntary act or omission in reckless disregard of a legal duty and of the consequences to another party, who may typically recover exemplary damages. **3.** Criminal negligence.

imputed negligence. (18c) Negligence of one person charged to another; negligence resulting from a party's special relationship with another party who is originally negligent — so that, for example, a parent might be held responsible for some acts of a child.

inadvertent negligence. (18c) Negligence in which the actor is not aware of the unreasonable risk that he or she is creating, but should have foreseen and avoided it.

joint negligence. (18c) The negligence of two or more persons acting together to cause an accident.

negligence in law. Failure to observe a duty imposed by law.

negligence per se. (1841) Negligence established as a matter of law, so that breach of the duty is not a jury question. • Negligence per se usu. arises from a statutory violation.

ordinary negligence. (16c) **1.** Lack of ordinary diligence; the failure to use ordinary care. • The term is most commonly used to differentiate between *negligence* and *gross negligence.* **2.** NEGLIGENCE (1).

passive negligence. (18c) Negligence resulting from a person's failure or omission in acting, such as failing to remove hazardous conditions from public property.

simple negligence. **1.** *Inadvertent negligence.* **2.** NEGLIGENCE (1).

slight negligence. (18c) The failure to exercise the great care of an extraordinarily prudent person, resulting in liability in special circumstances (esp. those involving bailments or carriers) in which lack of ordinary care would not result in liability; lack of great diligence.

subsequent negligence. (1827) The negligence of the defendant when, after the defendant's initial negligence and the plaintiff's contributory negligence, the defendant discovers — or should have discovered — that the plaintiff was in a position of danger and fails to exercise due care in preventing the plaintiff's injuries.

negligence rule. (1914) *Commercial law.* The principle that if a party's negligence contributes to an unauthorized signing or a material alteration in a negotiable instrument, that party is estopped from raising this issue against later parties who transfer or pay the instrument in good faith. • Examples of negligence include leaving blanks or spaces on the amount line of the instrument, erroneously mailing the instrument to a person with the same name as the payee, and failing to follow internal procedures designed to prevent forgeries.

negligent, *adj.* (14c) Characterized by a person's failure to exercise the degree of care that someone of ordinary prudence would have exercised in the same circumstance. — **negligently,** *adv.*

negligent entrustment. (1944) The act of leaving a dangerous article (such as a gun or car) with a person who the lender knows, or should know, is likely to use it in an unreasonably risky manner.

negligent hiring. *Torts.* An employer's lack of care in selecting an employee who the employer knew or should have known was unfit for the position, thereby creating an unreasonable risk that another person would be harmed.

negligent infliction of emotional distress. (1970) The tort of causing another severe emotional distress through one's negligent conduct. • Most courts will allow a plaintiff to recover damages for emotional distress if the defendant's conduct results in physical contact with the plaintiff or, when no contact occurs, if the plaintiff is in the zone of danger.

negotiable, *adj.* (18c) **1.** (Of a written instrument) capable of being transferred by delivery or indorsement when the transferee takes the instrument for value, in good faith, and without notice of conflicting title claims or defenses. **2.** (Of a deal, agreement, etc.) capable of being accomplished. **3.** (Of a price or deal) subject to further bargaining and possible change.

negotiable instrument. (18c) A written instrument that (1) is signed by the maker or drawer, (2) includes an unconditional promise or order to pay a specified sum of money, (3) is payable on demand or at a definite time, and (4) is payable to order or to bearer. UCC § 3-104(a). • Among the various types of negotiable instruments are bills of exchange, promissory notes, bank checks, certificates of deposit, and other negotiable securities.

negotiable words. (1819) The terms and phrases that make a document a negotiable instrument.

negotiation, *n.* (16c) **1.** A consensual bargaining process in which the parties attempt to reach agreement on a disputed or potentially disputed matter. • Negotiation usu. involves complete autonomy for the parties involved, without the intervention of third parties. **2.** (*usu. pl.*) Dealings conducted between two or more parties for the purpose of reaching an understanding. **3.** The transfer of an instrument by delivery or indorsement whereby the transferee takes it for value, in good faith, and without notice of conflicting title claims or defenses. — **negotiate,** *vb.* — **negotiable,** *adj.* — **negotiability,** *n.*

neighbor principle. (1963) The doctrine that one must take reasonable care to avoid acts or omissions that one can reasonably foresee will be likely to injure one's neighbor. • According to this principle, *neighbor* includes all persons who are so closely and directly affected by the act that the actor should reasonably think of them when engaging in the act or omission in question.

neither party. A docket entry reflecting the parties' agreement not to continue to appear to prosecute and defend a lawsuit. • This entry is equivalent to a dismissal.

nepotism (**nep**-ə-tiz-əm), *n.* (17c) Bestowal of official favors on one's relatives, esp. in hiring. — **nepotistic** (nep-ə-**tis**-tik), *adj.*

nerve-center test. A method courts sometimes use to determine the location of a company's principal place of business by examining where the company's central decision-making authority lies. • Factors include the locations where the corporate officers, directors, and (sometimes) shareholders reside, and where they direct and control the corporation's activities.

net, *n.* (15c) **1.** An amount of money remaining after a sale, minus any deductions for expenses, commissions, and taxes. **2.** The gain or loss from a sale of stock. **3.** Net weight.

net assets. Net worth.

neutral, *adj.* (15c) **1.** Indifferent. **2.** (Of a judge, mediator, arbitrator, or actor) refraining from taking sides in a dispute. **3.** Impartial; unbiased. • The term frequently applies to statutes that regulate or restrict speech.

content-neutral. (Of a regulation or discrimination) applicable to all speech, regardless of viewpoint and subject matter.

neutral, *n.* (15c) **1.** A person or country taking no side in a dispute; esp., a country that is at peace and is committed to aid neither of two or more belligerents. **2.** A nonpartisan arbitrator typically selected by two other arbitrators — one of whom has been selected by each side in the dispute.

neutralization. (1817) **1.** The act of making something ineffective. **2.** *Evidence.* The cancellation of unexpected harmful testimony from a witness by showing, usu. by cross-examination, that the witness has made conflicting statements. • For example, a prosecutor may attempt to neutralize testimony of a state witness who offers unexpected adverse testimony.

neutral principles. (1959) *Constitutional law.* Rules grounded in law, as opposed to rules based on personal interests or beliefs.

new-debtor syndrome. Conduct showing a debtor's bad faith in filing for bankruptcy, as a result of which the court may dismiss the bankruptcy petition. • An example is the debtor's formation of a corporation, immediately before the bankruptcy filing, solely to take advantage of the bankruptcy laws.

new-rule principle. (1989) *Criminal procedure.* A doctrine barring federal courts from granting habeas corpus relief to a state prisoner because of a rule, not dictated by existing precedent, announced after the prisoner's conviction and sentence became final.

new ruling. (1931) *Criminal procedure.* A Supreme Court ruling not dictated by precedent existing when the defendant's conviction became final and thus not applicable retroactively to habeas cases. • For example, when the Court in *Ford v. Wainwright*, 477 U.S. 399, 106 S.Ct. 2595 (1986), ruled that the Eighth Amendment prohibits execution of insane prisoners, this new ruling was nonretroactive because it departed so widely from prior doctrine. *Teague v. Lane*, 489 U.S. 288, 109 S.Ct. 1060 (1989).

newspaper. (17c) A publication for general circulation, usu. in sheet form, appearing at regular intervals, usu. daily or weekly, and containing matters of general public interest, such as current events.

newspaper of general circulation. (1838) A newspaper that contains news and information of interest to the general public, rather than to a particular segment, and that is available to the public within a certain geographic area. • Legal notices (such as a class-action notice) are often required by law to be published in a newspaper of general circulation.

official newspaper. A newspaper designated to contain all the public notices, resolves, acts, and advertisements of a state or municipal legislative body.

New York Stock Exchange. An association of member firms that handle the purchase and sale of securities both for themselves and for customers. • This exchange, the dominant one in the United States, trades in only large companies having at least one million outstanding shares. — Abbr. NYSE.

New York Supplement. A set of regional lawbooks, part of the West Group's National Reporter System, containing every published appellate decision from intermediate and lower courts of record in New York, from 1888 to date. • The first series ran from 1888 to 1937; the second series is the current one. — Abbr. N.Y.S.; N.Y.S.2d.

next friend. (16c) A person who appears in a lawsuit to act for the benefit of an incompetent or minor plaintiff, but who is not a party to the lawsuit and is not appointed as a guardian.

next-in, first-out. A method of inventory valuation (but not a generally accepted accounting principle) whereby the cost of goods is based on their replacement cost rather than their actual cost. — Abbr. NIFO.

next of kin. (18c) **1.** The person or persons most closely related to a decedent by blood or affinity. **2.** An intestate's heirs — that is, the person or persons entitled to inherit personal property from a decedent who has not left a will.

nexus, *n.* (17c) A connection or link, often a causal one. Pl. **nexuses; nexus**.

nexus test. (1975) The standard by which a private person's act is considered state action — and may give rise to liability for violating someone's constitutional rights — if the conduct is so closely related to the government's conduct that the choice to undertake it may fairly be said to be that of the state. • While similar to the symbiotic-relationship test, the nexus test focuses on the particular act complained of, instead of on the overall relationship of the parties. Still, some courts use the terms and analyses interchangeably.

NGO. *abbr.* Nongovernmental organization.

NIFO (**nɪ**-foh). *abbr.* Next-in, first-out.

night. (bef. 12c) **1.** The time from sunset to sunrise. **2.** Darkness; the time when a person's face is not discernible. • This definition was used in the common-law definition of certain offenses, such as burglary. **3.** Thirty minutes after sunset and thirty minutes before sunrise, or a similar definition as set forth by statute, as in a statute requiring specific authorization for night searches. **4.** Evening.

nihil dicit (**nɪ**-hil **dɪ**-sit), *n.* [Latin "he says nothing"] **1.** The failure of a defendant to answer a lawsuit. **2.** *Nil dicit* default judgment.

nihil est (**nɪ**-hil est). [Latin "there is nothing"] A form of return by a sheriff or constable who was unable to serve a writ because nothing was found to levy on.

nil (nil). [Latin] (16c) Nothing. • This word is a contracted form of *nihil*.

nimmer. (14c) A petty thief; pilferer; pickpocket.

Nineteenth Amendment. The constitutional amendment, ratified in 1920, providing that a citizen's right to vote cannot be denied or abridged by the United States, or by any state within it, on the basis of sex.

ninety-day letter. (1933) Statutory notice of a tax deficiency sent by the IRS to a taxpayer. • During the 90 days after receiving the notice, the taxpayer must pay the taxes (and, if desired, seek a refund) or challenge the deficiency in tax court. IRC (26 USCA) §§ 6212, 6213.

Ninth Amendment. The constitutional amendment, ratified with the Bill of Rights in 1791, providing that rights listed in the Constitution must not be construed in a way that denies or disparages unlisted rights, which are retained by the people.

nisi (**nɪ**-sɪ), *adj.* [Latin "unless"] (18c) (Of a court's ex parte ruling or grant of relief) having validity unless the adversely affected party appears and shows cause why it should be withdrawn <a decree *nisi*>.

nisi prius (**nɪ**-sɪ **prɪ**-əs). [Latin "unless before then"] (16c) A civil trial court in which, unlike in an appellate court, issues are tried before a jury. • The term is obsolete in the United States except in New York and Oklahoma.

NLRB. *abbr.* National Labor Relations Board.

NMB. *abbr.* National Mediation Board.

NOAA. *abbr.* National Oceanic and Atmospheric Administration.

no-action letter. (1959) A letter from the staff of a governmental agency stating that if the facts are as represented in a person's request for an agency ruling, the staff will advise the agency not to take action against the person. • Typically, a no-action letter is requested from the SEC on such matters as shareholder proposals, resales of stock, and marketing techniques.

no actus reus (noh **ak**-təs **ree**-əs). A plea in which a criminal defendant either denies involvement with a crime or asserts that the harm suffered is too remote from the criminal act to be imputable to the defendant.

no bill, *n.* (18c) A grand jury's notation that insufficient evidence exists for an indictment on a criminal charge <the grand jury returned a no bill instead of the indictment the prosecutors expected>. — **no-bill,** *vb.*

no-bonus clause. *Landlord–tenant law.* A lease provision that takes effect upon governmental condemnation, limiting the lessee's damages to the value of any improvements to the property and preventing the lessee from recovering the difference between the lease's fixed rent and the property's market rental value.

no-claim, *n.* The lack of a claim. • Legal philosophers devised this term to denote the opposite of a claim.

no contest. (1931) A criminal defendant's plea that, while not admitting guilt, the defendant will not dispute the charge. • This plea is often preferable to a guilty plea, which can be used against the defendant in a later civil lawsuit.

no-contest clause. (1929) A provision designed to threaten one into action or inaction; esp., a testamentary provision that threatens to dispossess any beneficiary who challenges the terms of the will.

no-duty, *n.* Liberty not to do an act.

no-duty doctrine. (1966) *Torts.* **1.** The rule that a defendant who owes no duty to the plaintiff is not liable for the plaintiff's injury. **2.** The rule that the owner or possessor of property has no duty to warn or protect an invitee from known or obvious hazards.

***Noerr–Pennington* doctrine.** (1967) The principle that the First Amendment shields from liability (esp. under antitrust laws) companies that join together to lobby the government. • The doctrine derives from a line of Supreme Court cases beginning with *Eastern R.R. Presidents Conference v. Noerr Motor Freight, Inc.*, 365 U.S. 127, 81 S.Ct. 523 (1961), and *United Mine Workers v. Pennington*, 381 U.S. 657, 85 S.Ct. 1585 (1965).

no evidence. (15c) **1.** The lack of a legally sufficient evidentiary basis for a reasonable fact-finder to rule in favor of the party who bears the burden of proof <there is no evidence in the record about his whereabouts at midnight>. • Under the Federal Rules of Civil Procedure, a party can move for judgment as a matter of law to claim that the other party — who bears the burden of proof — has been fully heard and has not offered sufficient evidence to prove one or more essential elements of the suit or defense. Fed. R. Civ. P. 50. Though such a contention is usu. referred to as a no-evidence motion, the issue is not whether there was actually no evidence, but rather whether the evidence was sufficient for the fact-finder to be able to reasonably rule in favor of the other party. **2.** Evidence that has no value in an attempt to prove a matter in issue <that testimony is no evidence of an alibi>.

no-eyewitness rule. (1956) *Torts.* The largely defunct principle that if no direct evidence shows what a dead person did to avoid an accident, the jury may infer that the person acted with ordinary care for his or her own safety. • In a jurisdiction where the rule persists, a plaintiff in a survival or wrongful-death action can assert the rule to counter a defense of contributory negligence.

no-fault, *adj.* (1967) Of or relating to a claim that is adjudicated without any determination that a party is blameworthy <no-fault divorce>.

no funds. An indorsement marked on a check when there are insufficient funds in the account to cover the check.

NOL. Net operating loss.

nolens volens (**noh**-lenz **voh**-lenz), *adv.* & *adj.* [Latin] (16c) Willing or unwilling <*nolens volens*, the school district must comply with the court's injunction>.

nolition (noh-**lish**-ən). (17c) The absence of volition; unwillingness.

nolle prosequi (**nahl**-ee **prahs**-ə-kwɪ), *n.* [Latin "not to wish to prosecute"] (17c) **1.** A legal notice that a lawsuit or prosecution has been abandoned. **2.** A docket entry showing that the plaintiff or the prosecution has abandoned the action.

nolle prosequi (**nahl**-ee **prahs**-ə-kwɪ), *vb.* (1875) To abandon (a suit or prosecution); to have (a case) dismissed by a *nolle prosequi* <the state *nolle prosequied* the charges against Johnson>.

nolo contendere (**noh**-loh kən-**ten**-də-ree). [Latin "I do not wish to contend"] (1829) No contest.

NOM clause. *abbr.* No-oral-modification clause.

nominal (nahm-ə-nəl), *adj.* (17c) **1.** Existing in name only <he was the nominal leader but had no real authority>. **2.** (Of a price or amount) trifling, esp. as compared to what would be expected <the lamp sold for a nominal price of ten cents>. **3.** Of or relating to a name or term <a nominal definition>. — **nominally,** *adv.*

nomination.(15c) **1.** The act of proposing a person for election or appointment. **2.** The act of naming or designating a person for an office, membership, award, or like title or status. — **nominate,** *vb.* (16c).

nominee (nom-i-**nee**), *n.* (17c) **1.** A person who is proposed for an office, membership, award, or like title or status. • An individual seeking nomination, election, or appointment is a *candidate.* A candidate for election becomes a *nominee* after being formally nominated. **2.** A person designated to act in place of another, usu. in a very limited way. **3.** A party who holds bare legal title for the benefit of others or who receives and distributes funds for the benefit of others.

nomographer (nə-**mog**-rə-fər). (17c) **1.** A person who drafts laws. **2.** A person skilled in nomography.

nomography (nə-**mog**-rə-fee). (1832) **1.** The art of drafting laws. **2.** A treatise on the drafting of laws.

non (non). [Latin] (14c) Not; no. • This term negates, sometimes as a separate word and sometimes as a prefix.

nonability. (17c) **1.** The lack of legal capacity, esp. to sue on one's own behalf. **2.** A plea or exception raising a lack of legal capacity.

nonacceptance. (17c) **1.** The refusal or rejection of something, such as a contract offer; rejection. **2.** A buyer's rejection of goods because they fail to conform to contractual specifications. See UCC § 2-601(a). **3.** A drawee's failure or refusal to receive and pay a negotiable instrument.

nonaccess. *Family law.* (17c) Absence of opportunity for sexual intercourse. •

Nonaccess is often used as a defense by the alleged father in paternity cases.

nonacquiescence (non-ak-wee-**es**-ənts). *Administrative law.* An agency's policy of declining to be bound by lower-court precedent that is contrary to the agency's interpretation of its organic statute, but only until the Supreme Court has ruled on the issue.

nonadmission. (16c) **1.** The failure to acknowledge something. **2.** The refusal to allow something, such as evidence in a legal proceeding.

nonage (**non**-ij). Minority.

nonbailable, *adj.* (1811) **1.** (Of a person) not entitled to bail <the defendant was nonbailable because of a charge of first-degree murder>. **2.** (Of an offense) not admitting of bail <murder is a nonbailable offense>.

nonbillable time. (1947) An attorney's or paralegal's time that is not chargeable to a client.

noncapital, *adj.* (1865) (Of a crime) not involving or deserving of the death penalty <noncapital murder>.

noncitable, *adj.* Not authorized by a court to be used as legal precedent. • In general, unpublished opinions are noncitable, although court rules vary.

noncitizen. (1850) A person who is not a citizen of a particular place.

nonclaim. (15c) A person's failure to pursue a right within the legal time limit, resulting in that person's being barred from asserting the right.

noncombatant, *n.* (1811) **1.** An armed-service member who serves in a nonfighting capacity. **2.** A civilian in wartime.

non compos mentis (non **kom**-pəs **men**-tis), *adj.* [Latin "not master of one's mind"] (17c) **1.** Insane. **2.** Incompetent.

nonconformity. (17c) The failure to comply with something, as in a contract specification.

nonconsensual, *adj.* (1920) Not occurring by mutual consent <nonconsensual sexual relations>.

nonconstitutional, *adj.* (1879) Of or relating to some legal basis or principle other than those of the U.S. Constitution or a state constitution <the appellate court refused — on nonconstitutional procedural grounds — to hear the defendant's argument about cruel and unusual punishment>.

nonconsumable, *n.* (1902) A thing (such as land, a vehicle, or a share of stock) that can be enjoyed without any change to its substance other than a natural diminution over time; nonfungible. — **nonconsumable,** *adj.*

noncontractual, *adj.* (1883) Not relating to or arising from a contract <a noncontractual obligation>.

noncontributory, *adj.* (1907) **1.** Not involved in something. **2.** (Of an employee benefit plan) funded solely by the employer.

noncustodial, *adj.* **1.** (1960) (Of an interrogation, etc.) not taking place while a person is in custody. **2.** Of or relating to someone, esp. a parent, who does not have sole or primary custody.

nondelegable (non-**del**-ə-gə-bəl), *adj.* (1902) (Of a power, function, etc.) not capable of being entrusted to another's care.

nondelivery. (18c) A failure to transfer or convey something, such as goods.

nondirection. (18c) The failure of a judge to properly instruct a jury on a necessary point of law.

nondisclosure. (1908) **1.** The failure or refusal to reveal something that either might be or is required to be revealed. **2.** Nondisclosure agreement.

nondisclosure agreement. *Trade secrets.* A contract or contractual provision containing a person's promise not to disclose any information shared by or discovered from a trade-secret holder, including all information about trade secrets, procedures, or other internal or proprietary matters. • Employees and some nonemployees, such as beta-testers and contractors, are frequently required to sign nondisclosure agreements. — Abbr. NDA.

nondiverse, *adj.* (1947) **1.** Of or relating to similar types <the attorney's practice is nondiverse: she handles only criminal matters>. **2.** (Of a person or entity) having the same citizenship as the party or parties on the other side of a lawsuit <the parties are nondiverse because both plaintiff and defendant are California citizens>.

nonfeasance (non-**feez**-ənts), *n.* (16c) The failure to act when a duty to act existed. — **nonfeasant,** *adj.* — **nonfeasor,** *n.*

nonforfeitable, *adj.* (1871) Not subject to forfeiture.

nonfungible (non-**fən**-jə-bəl), *adj.* Not commercially interchangeable with other property of the same kind <a piece of land is regarded as nonfungible>. — **nonfungible,** *n.*

nongovernmental organization. *Int'l law.* Any scientific, professional, business, or public-interest organization that is neither affiliated with nor under the direction of a government; an international organization that is not the creation of an agreement among countries, but rather is composed of private individuals or organizations. — Abbr. NGO.

noninterpretivism, *n.* (1978) In constitutional interpretation, the doctrine holding that judges are not confined to the Constitution's text or preratification history but may instead look to evolving social norms and values as the basis for constitutional judgments. — **noninterpretivist,** *n.*

nonintervention. (1831) *Int'l law.* The principle that a country should not interfere in the internal affairs of another country. • The U.N. Charter binds it from intervening "in matters which are essentially within the domestic jurisdiction of any state . . . ." U.N. Charter art. 2(7).

nonjoinder. (1823) The failure to bring a person who is a necessary party into a lawsuit. Fed. R. Civ. P. 12(b)(7), 19.

nonjuridical (non-juu-**rid**-i-kəl), *adj.* (1853) **1.** Not of or relating to judicial proceedings or to the administration of justice <the dispute was nonjuridical>. **2.** Not of or relating to the law; not legal <a natural person is a nonjuridical entity>.

nonjusticiable (non-jəs-**tish**-ee-ə-bəl *or* non-jəs-**tish**-ə-bəl), *adj.* (1915) Not proper for judicial determination <the controversy was nonjusticiable because none of the parties had suffered any harm>.

nonlawyer. A person who is not a lawyer.

nonleviable (non-**lev**-ee-ə-bəl), *adj.* (1860) (Of property or assets) exempt from execution, seizure, forfeiture, or sale, as in bankruptcy.

nonmonetary item. (1965) An asset or liability whose price fluctuates over time (such as land, equipment, inventory, and warranty obligations).

nonmovant (non-**moov**-ənt). (1955) A litigating party other than the one that has filed the motion currently under consideration <the court, in ruling on the plaintiff's motion for summary judgment, properly resolved all doubts in the nonmovant's favor>.

nonnegotiable, *adj.* (1859) **1.** (Of an agreement or term) not subject to change <the kidnapper's demands were nonnegotiable>. **2.** (Of an instrument or note) incapable of transferring by indorsement or delivery.

non obstante veredicto (non ahb-**stan**-tee [*or* əb-**stan**-tee] ver-ə-**dik**-toh). [Latin] (15c) Notwithstanding the verdict. — Abbr. n.o.v.; NOV.

nonobviousness. *Patents.* **1.** An invention's quality of being sufficiently different from the prior art that, at the time the invention was made, it would not have been obvious to a person having ordinary skill in the art relevant to the invention. **2.** The requirement that this quality must be demonstrated for an invention to be patentable. The test of obviousness involves examining the scope and content of the prior art, the differences between the prior art and the patent claims, and the level of ordinary skill in the art. 35 USCA § 103.

nonoccupant visitor. (1996) *Criminal procedure.* A person who owns, co-owns, is employed by, or is a patron of a business enterprise where a search is being conducted in accordance with a search warrant.

nonoccupational, *adj.* (1918) **1.** Not relating to one's job. **2.** Of or relating to a general-disability policy providing benefits to an individual whose disability prevents that individual from working at any occupation.

nonoccupier. (1958) One who does not occupy a particular piece of land; esp., an entrant on land who is either an invitee or a licensee.

nonparticipating, *adj.* (1859) Of or relating to not taking part in something; specif., not sharing or having the right to share in profits or surpluses. — Often shortened to *nonpar.*

nonpayment. (15c) Failure to deliver money or other valuables, esp. when due, in discharge of an obligation.

nonperformance. (16c) Failure to discharge an obligation (esp. a contractual one).

nonprivity (non-**priv**-ə-tee). (1902) The fact or state of not being in privity of contract with another; lack of privity.

horizontal nonprivity. (1982) The lack of privity occurring when the plaintiff is not a buyer within the distributive chain, but one who consumes, uses, or is otherwise affected by the goods. • For example, a houseguest who becomes ill after eating meat that her host bought from the local deli is in horizontal nonprivity with the deli.

vertical nonprivity. (1982) The lack of privity occurring when the plaintiff is a buyer within the distributive chain who did not buy directly from the defendant. • For example, someone who buys a drill from a local hardware store and later sues the drill's manufacturer is in vertical nonprivity with the manufacturer.

nonprobate, *adj.* (1919) **1.** Of or relating to some method of transmitting property at death other than by a gift by will <nonprobate distribution>. **2.** Of or relating to the property so disposed <nonprobate assets>.

non prosequitur (non prə-**sek**-wə-tər *or* proh-). [Latin "he does not prosecute"] (18c) The judgment rendered against a plaintiff who has not pursued the case. — Often shortened to *non pros.*

nonpublic forum. (1978) *Constitutional law.* Public property that is not designated or traditionally considered an arena for public communication, such as a jail or a military base. • The government's means of regulating a nonpublic forum need only be reasonable and viewpoint-neutral to be constitutional.

non-purchase-money, *adj.* (1941) Not pertaining to or being an obligation secured by property obtained by a loan <non-purchase-money mortgage>.

nonrecognition provision. (1932) *Tax.* A statutory rule that allows all or part of a realized gain or loss not to be recognized for tax purposes. • Generally, this type of provision only postpones the recognition of the gain or loss.

nonrecourse, *adj.* (1926) Of or relating to an obligation that can be satisfied only out of the collateral securing the obligation and not out of the debtor's other assets.

nonrenewal. (1819) A failure to renew something, such as a lease or an insurance policy.

non sequitur (non **sek**-wə-tər). [Latin "it does not follow"] (16c) **1.** An inference or conclusion that does not logically follow from the premises. **2.** A remark or response that does not logically follow from what was previously said.

nonservice. (18c) The failure to serve a summons, warrant, or other process in a civil or criminal case.

nonskip person. (1988) *Tax.* A person who is not a skip person for purposes of the generation-skipping transfer tax. IRC (26 USCA) § 2613(b).

nonsolicitation agreement. A promise, usu. in a contract for the sale of a business, a partnership agreement, or an employment contract, to refrain, for a specified time, from either (1) enticing employees to leave the company, or (2) trying to lure customers away.

nonstaple. *Patents.* An unpatented thing or material that is a component of a patented product or is used in a patented process, but that has little or no other practical use. • Patentees have a limited right to control the market for nonstaples through tying agreements. But if the thing supplied is a staple, the tying agreement is restraint of trade. 35 USCA § 271(d).

nonstatutory, *adj.* **1.** Enforceable by some legal precept other than enacted law, such as precedent or trade custom. **2.** *Patents.* Unpatentable for not meeting some statutory requirement, e.g., novelty, utility, nonobviousness, or enabling description. **3.** *Patents.* Of or relating to an equitable defense to an infringement claim, esp. estoppel, inequitable conduct, or laches.

nonsuit, *n.* (15c) **1.** A plaintiff's voluntary dismissal of a case or of a defendant, without a decision on the merits. • Under the Federal Rules of Civil Procedure, a voluntary dismissal is equivalent to a nonsuit. Fed. R. Civ. P. 41(a). **2.** A court's dismissal of a case or of a defendant because the plaintiff has failed to make out a legal case or to bring forward sufficient evidence. — **nonsuit,** *vb.*

nonsupport. (1909) *Family law.* The failure to support a person for whom one is legally obliged to provide, such as a child, spouse, or other dependent. • Nonsupport is a crime in most states.

nonunion, *adj.* (1863) **1.** (Of a person or thing) not belonging to or affiliated with a labor union <a nonunion worker> <a nonunion contract>. **2.** (Of a position or belief) not favoring labor unions <she will not alter her nonunion stance>. **3.** (Of a product) not made by labor-union members <the equipment was of nonunion manufacture>.

nonuse. (16c) **1.** The failure to exercise a right <nonuse of the easement>. **2.** The condition of not being put into service <the equipment was in nonuse>.

nonuser. The failure to exercise a right (such as a franchise or easement), as a result of which the person having the right might lose it <the government may not revoke a citizen's voting right because of nonuser>.

no-oral-modification clause. (1969) A contractual provision stating that the parties cannot make any oral modifications or alterations to the agreement. — Abbr. NOM clause.

no-pass, no-play rule. (1984) A state law requiring public-school students who participate in extracurricular activities (such as sports or band) to maintain a minimum grade-point average or else lose the privilege to participate.

no recourse. **1.** The lack of means by which to obtain reimbursement from, or a judgment against, a person or entity <the bank had no recourse against the individual executive for collection of the corporation's debts>. **2.** A notation indicating that such means are lacking <the bill was indorsed "no recourse">.

no-retreat rule. (1973) *Criminal law.* The doctrine that the victim of a murderous assault may use deadly force in self-defense if there is no reasonable alternative to avoid the assailant's threatened harm. • A majority of American jurisdictions have adopted this rule.

no-right, *n.*(1913) The absence of right against another in some particular respect. • A no-right is the correlative of a privilege.

norm. (1821) **1.** A model or standard accepted (voluntarily or involuntarily) by society or other large group, against which society judges someone or something. • An example of a norm is the standard for right or wrong behavior. **2.** An actual or set standard determined by the typical or most frequent behavior of a group.

normal law. (1904) The law as it applies to persons who are free from legal disabilities.

normal mind. (1887) A mental capacity that is similar to that of the majority of people who can handle life's ordinary responsibilities.

normative, *adj.* (1852) Establishing or conforming to a norm or standard <Rawls's theory describes normative principles of justice>.

North American Free Trade Agreement. A 1994 agreement between the United States, Canada, and Mexico, designed to phase out all tariffs and eliminate many nontariff barriers (such as quotas) inhibiting the free trade of goods between the participating nations. — Abbr. NAFTA.

North Eastern Reporter. A set of regional lawbooks, part of the West Group's National Reporter System, containing every published appellate decision from Illinois, Indiana, Massachusetts, New York, and Ohio, from 1885 to date. • The first series ran from 1885 to 1936; the second series is the current one. — Abbr. N.E.; N.E.2d.

North Western Reporter. A set of regional lawbooks, part of the West Group's National Reporter System, containing every published appellate decision from Iowa, Michigan, Minnesota, Nebraska, North Dakota, South Dakota, and Wisconsin, from 1879 to date. • The first series ran from 1879 to 1941; the second series is the current one. — Abbr. N.W.; N.W.2d.

noscitur a sociis (**nos**-ə-tər ay [*or* ah] **soh**-shee-is). [Latin "it is known by its associates"] (18c) A canon of construction holding that the meaning of an unclear word or phrase should be determined by the words immediately surrounding it.

notarial, *adj.* (15c) Of or relating to the official acts of a notary public <a notarial seal>.

notarial act. (18c) An official function of a notary public, such as placing a seal on an affidavit.

notarize, *vb.* (Of a notary public) to attest to the authenticity of (a signature, mark, etc.).

notary public (**noh**-tə-ree), *n.* (16c) A person authorized by a state to administer oaths, certify documents, attest to the authenticity of signatures, and perform official acts in commercial matters, such as protesting negotiable instruments. — Abbr. n.p. Pl. **notaries public.** — **notarize,** *vb.* — **notarial,** *adj.*

notary seal. (18c) **1.** The imprint or embossment made by a notary public's seal. **2.** A device, usu. a stamp or embosser, that makes an imprint on a notarized document.

embossed seal. (1959) **1.** A notary seal that is impressed onto a document, raising the impression above the surface. • An embossed seal clearly identifies the original document because the seal is only faintly reproducible. For this reason, this type of seal is required in some states and on some documents notarized for federal purposes. **2.** The embossment made by this seal.

rubber-stamp seal. (1948) **1.** In most states, a notary public's official seal, which is ink-stamped onto documents and is therefore photographically reproducible. • It typically includes the notary's name, the state seal, the words "Notary Public," the name of the county where the notary's bond is filed, and the expiration date of the notary's commission. **2.** The imprint made by this seal.

note, *n.* (17c) **1.** A written promise by one party (the *maker*) to pay money to another party (the *payee*) or to bearer. • A note is a two-party negotiable instrument, unlike a draft (which is a three-party instrument).

accommodation note. A note that an accommodating party has signed and thereby assumed secondary liability for; accommodation paper.

balloon note. A note requiring small periodic payments but a very large final payment. • The periodic payments usu. cover only interest, while the final payment (the balloon payment) represents the entire principal.

promissory note. (18c) An unconditional written promise, signed by the maker, to pay absolutely and in any event a certain sum of money either to, or to the order of, the bearer or a designated person.

2. A scholarly legal essay shorter than an article and restricted in scope, explaining or criticizing a particular set of cases or a general area of the law, and usu. written by a law student for publication in a law review. **3.** A minute or memorandum intended for later reference; MEMORANDUM (1).

note, *vb.* (13c) **1.** To observe carefully or with particularity. **2.** To put down in writing.

not found. Words placed on a bill of indictment, meaning that the grand jury has insufficient evidence to support a true bill.

not guilty. (15c) **1.** A defendant's plea denying the crime charged. **2.** A jury verdict acquitting the defendant because the prosecution failed to prove the defendant's guilt beyond a reasonable doubt.

not guilty by reason of insanity. (1844) **1.** A not-guilty verdict, based on mental illness, that usu. does not release the defendant but instead results in commitment to a mental institution. **2.** A criminal defendant's plea of not guilty that is based on the insanity defense. — Abbr. NGRI.

3. *Common-law pleading.* A defendant's plea denying both an act of trespass alleged in a plaintiff's declaration and the plaintiff's right to possess the property at issue. **4.** A general denial in an ejectment action.

notice, *n.* (16c) **1.** Legal notification required by law or agreement, or imparted by operation of law as a result of some fact (such as the recording of an instrument); definite legal cognizance, actual or constructive, of an existing right or title <under the lease, the tenant must give the landlord written notice 30 days before vacating the premises>. • A person has notice of a fact or condition if that person (1) has actual knowledge of it; (2) has received information about it; (3) has reason to know about it; (4) knows about a related fact; or (5) is considered as having been able to ascertain it by checking an official filing or recording. **2.** The condition of being so notified, whether or not actual awareness exists <all prospective buyers were on notice of the judgment lien>. **3.** A written or printed announcement <the notice of sale was posted on the courthouse bulletin board>.

actual notice. (18c) **1.** Notice given directly to, or received personally by, a party. **2.** *Property.* Notice given by open possession and occupancy of real property.

commercial-law notice. Under the UCC, notice of a fact arising either as a result of actual knowledge or notification of the fact, or as a result of circumstances under which a person would have reason to know of the fact. UCC § 1-201(25).

constructive notice. (18c) Notice arising by presumption of law from the existence of facts and circumstances that a party had a duty to take notice of, such as a registered deed or a pending lawsuit; notice presumed by law to have been acquired by a person and thus imputed to that person.

direct notice. (17c) Actual notice of a fact that is brought directly to a party's attention.

due notice. (17c) Sufficient and proper notice that is intended to and likely to reach a particular person or the public; notice that is legally adequate given the particular circumstance.

express notice. (18c) Actual knowledge or notice given to a party directly, not arising from any inference, duty, or inquiry.

fair notice. (17c) **1.** Sufficient notice apprising a litigant of the opposing party's claim. **2.** The requirement that a pleading adequately apprise the opposing party of a claim. • A pleading must be drafted so that an opposing attorney of reasonable competence would be able to ascertain the nature and basic issues of the controversy and the evidence probably relevant to those issues. **3.** Fair warning.

immediate notice. **1.** Notice given as soon as possible. **2.** More commonly, and esp. on notice of an insurance claim, notice that is reasonable under the circumstances.

implied notice. (18c) Notice that is inferred from facts that a person had a means of knowing and that is thus imputed to that person; actual notice of facts or circumstances that, if properly followed up, would have led to a knowledge of the particular fact in question.

imputed notice. (1831) Information attributed to a person whose agent, having received actual notice of the information, has a duty to disclose it to that person. • For example, notice of a hearing may be imputed to a witness because it was actually disclosed to that witness's attorney of record.

inquiry notice. (1945) Notice attributed to a person when the information would lead an ordinarily prudent person to investigate the matter further; esp., the time at which the victim of an alleged securities fraud became aware of facts that would have prompted a reasonable person to investigate.

personal notice. (17c) Oral or written notice, according to the circumstances, given directly to the affected person.

public notice. (16c) Notice given to the public or persons affected, usu. by publishing in a newspaper of general circulation. • This notice is usu. required, for example, in matters of public concern.

reasonable notice. Notice that is fairly to be expected or required under the particular circumstances.

record notice. (1855) Constructive notice of the contents of an instrument, such as a deed or mortgage, that has been properly recorded.

short notice. Notice that is inadequate or not timely under the circumstances.

notice, *vb.* (15c) **1.** To give legal notice to or of <the plaintiff's lawyer noticed depositions of all the experts that the defendant listed>. **2.** To realize or give attention to <the lawyer noticed that the witness was leaving>.

notice-and-comment period. *Administrative law.* The statutory time frame during which an administrative agency publishes a proposed regulation and receives public comment on the regulation. • The regulation cannot take effect until after this period expires.

notice filing. The perfection of a security interest under Article 9 of the UCC by filing only a financing statement, as opposed to a copy or abstract of the security agreement. • The financing statement must contain (1) the debtor's signature, (2) the secured party's name and address, (3) the debtor's name and mailing address, and (4) a description of the types of, or items of, collateral.

notice-of-alibi rule. (1969) The principle that, upon written demand from the government, a criminal defendant who intends to call an alibi witness at trial must give notice of who that witness is and where the defendant claims to have been at the time of the alleged offense. • The government is, in turn, obligated to give notice to the defendant of any witness it intends to call to rebut the alibi testimony. See Fed. R. Crim. P. 12.1.

notice of appeal. (18c) A document filed with a court and served on the other parties, stating an intention to appeal a trial court's judgment or order. • In most jurisdictions, filing a notice of appeal is the act by which the appeal is perfected. For instance, the Federal Rules of Appellate Procedure provide that an appeal is taken by filing a notice of appeal with the clerk of the district court from which the appeal is taken, and that the clerk is to send copies of the notice to all the other parties' attorneys, as well as the court of appeals. Fed. R. App. P. 3(a), (d).

notice of appearance. (1844) **1.** *Procedure.* A party's written notice filed with the court or oral announcement on the record informing the court and the other parties that the party wants to participate in the case. **2.** *Bankruptcy.* A written notice filed with the court or oral announcement in open court by a person who wants to receive all pleadings in a particular case. • This notice is usu. filed by an attorney for a creditor who wants to be added to the official service list. **3.** A pleading filed by an attorney to notify the court and the other parties that he or she represents one or more parties in the lawsuit. — Abbr. NOA.

notice of completion. *Construction law.* A written and recorded announcement that a building project is finished, thereby limiting the time for filing mechanic's liens against the property. • The time for filing a lien begins to run when the notice of completion is filed.

notice of dishonor. (1804) Notice to the indorser of an instrument that acceptance or payment has been refused. • This notice — along with presentment and actual dishonor — is a condition of an indorser's secondary liability. UCC § 3-503(a).

notice of motion. (18c) Written certification that a party to a lawsuit has filed a motion or that a motion will be heard or considered by the court at a particular time. • Under the Federal Rules of Civil Procedure, the requirement that a motion be made in writing is fulfilled if the motion is stated in a written notice of the hearing on the motion. Also, the courts in most jurisdictions require all motions to include a certificate, usu. referred to as a certificate of service, indicating that the other parties to the suit have been given notice of the motion's filing. Notice of any hearing or other submission of the motion must usu. be provided to all parties by the party requesting the hearing or submission. Fed. R. Civ. P. 5(d), 7(b)(1); Fed. R. Civ. P. Form 19.

notice of nonresponsibility. *Construction law.* A written disclaimer that, if posted conspicuously and recorded, relieves a property owner from liability for work or materials used on the property without the owner's authorization. • It protects an owner against mechanic's liens that could arise when repairs or improvements are made by a tenant or other person in possession.

notice of orders or judgments. (1854) Written notice of the entry of an order or judgment, provided by the court clerk or one of the parties. • Notice of a judgment is usu. provided by the clerk of the court in which the judgment was entered. If the court does not provide notice, a party is usu. required to provide it. Under the Federal Rules of Civil Procedure and the Federal Rules of Criminal Procedure, the clerk is required to provide immediate notice of any order or judgment to any party to the case who is not in default. Fed. R. Civ. P. 77(d); Fed. R. Crim. P. 49(c).

notice of protest. **1.** A statement, given usu. by a notary public to a drawer or indorser of a negotiable instrument, that the instrument was neither paid nor accepted; information provided to the drawer or indorser that protest was made for nonacceptance or nonpayment of a note or bill. **2.** A shipowner's or crew's declaration under oath that damages to their vessel or cargo were the result of perils of the sea and that the shipowner is not liable for the damages.

notice of removal. (1892) The pleading by which the defendant removes a case from state court to federal court. • A notice of removal is filed in the federal district court in the district and division in which the suit is pending. The notice must contain a short and plain statement of the grounds for removal and must include a copy of all process, pleadings, and orders that have been served on the removing party while the case has been pending. The removing party must also notify the state court and other parties to the suit that the notice of removal has been filed. A notice of removal must be filed, if at all, within 30 days after the defendant is served with process in the suit. 28 USCA § 1446; *Murphy Bros., Inc. v. Michetti Pipe Stringing, Inc.*, 526 U.S. 344, 119 S.Ct. 1322 (1999).

notice of trial. (17c) A document issued by a court informing the parties of the date on which the lawsuit is set for trial. • While the court typically provides the notice to all parties, it may instead instruct one party to send the notice to all the others.

notice-prejudice rule. A doctrine barring an insurer from using late notice as a reason to deny an insured's claim unless the insurer can show that it was prejudiced by the untimely notice.

notice statute. (1864) A recording act providing that the person with the most recent valid claim, and who purchased without notice of an earlier, unrecorded claim, has priority. • About half the states have notice statutes.

notice to appear. (17c) A summons or writ by which a person is cited to appear in court. • This is an informal phrase sometimes used to refer to the summons or other initial process by which a person is notified of a lawsuit. The Federal Rules of Civil Procedure require the summons to state that the defendant must appear and defend within a given time and that failure to do so will result in a default judgment. Fed. R. Civ. P. 4(a).

notice to plead. (18c) A warning to a defendant, stating that failure to file a responsive pleading within a prescribed time will result in a default judgment. •

The Federal Rules of Civil Procedure require the summons to notify the defendant that failure to appear and defend within a prescribed time will result in a default judgment. Fed. R. Civ. P. 4(a).

notice to quit. (18c) **1.** A landlord's written notice demanding that a tenant surrender and vacate the leased property, thereby terminating the tenancy. **2.** A landlord's notice to a tenant to pay any back rent within a specified period (often seven days) or else vacate the leased premises.

notify, *vb.* (14c) To inform (a person or group) in writing or by any method that is understood.

notoriety. (16c) **1.** The state of being generally, and often unfavorably, known and spoken of. **2.** A person in such a state.

notorious, *adj.* (15c) **1.** Generally known and spoken of, usu. unfavorably. **2.** (Of the possession of property) so conspicuous as to impute notice to the true owner.

not sufficient funds. (1845) The notation of dishonor (of a check) indicating that the drawer's account does not contain enough money to cover payment. — Abbr. NSF.

novation (noh-**vay**-shən), *n.* (16c) The act of substituting for an old obligation a new one that either replaces an existing obligation with a new obligation or replaces an original party with a new party. • A novation may substitute (1) a new obligation between the same parties, (2) a new debtor, or (3) a new creditor. — **novate** (noh-**vayt** *or* **noh**-vayt), *vb.* — **novatory** (**noh**-və-tor-ee), *adj.*

novelty. (14c) **1.** *Trade secrets.* The newness of information that is generally unused or unknown and that gives its owner a competitive advantage in a business field. • In the law of trade secrets, novelty does not require independent conception or even originality. A rediscovered technique with marketable applications can qualify as a novelty and be protected as a trade secret. **2.** *Patents.* Newness of an invention both in form and in function or performance; the strict statutory requirement that this originality be demonstrated before an invention is patentable. • Proving novelty is one purpose of the rigorous and expensive examination process. If the invention has been previously patented, described in a publication, known or used by others, or sold, it is not novel. 35 USCA § 102.

noxious (**nok**-shəs), *adj.* (15c) **1.** Harmful to health; injurious. **2.** Unwholesome; corruptive. **3.** *Archaic.* Guilty.

n.p. *abbr.* **1.** *Nisi prius.* **2.** Notary public.

NPV. *abbr.* Net present value.

n.r. *abbr.* **1.** New reports. **2.** Not reported. **3.** Nonresident.

NRC. *abbr.* Nuclear Regulatory Commission.

n.s. *abbr.* **1.** New series. • This citation form indicates that a periodical has been renumbered in a new series. **2.** New style.

NSA. *abbr.* National Security Agency.

NSC. *abbr.* National Security Council.

NSF. *abbr.* **1.** National Science Foundation. **2.** Not sufficient funds.

NSL. *abbr.* National-security letter.

NTSB. *abbr.* National Transportation Safety Board.

nude, *adj.* (15c) **1.** Naked; unclothed. **2.** Lacking in consideration or in some essential particular. **3.** Mere; lacking in description or specification.

nudum pactum (**n**[y]**oo**-dəm **pak**-təm). [Latin "bare agreement"] (17c) An agreement that is unenforceable as a contract because it is not "clothed" with consideration.

nugatory (**n**[y]**oo**-gə-tor-ee), *adj.* (17c) Of no force or effect; useless; invalid.

nuisance. (14c) **1.** A condition, activity, or situation (such as a loud noise or foul odor) that interferes with the use or enjoyment of property; esp., a nontransitory condition or persistent activity that either injures the physical condition of adjacent land or interferes with its use or with the enjoyment of easements on the land or of public highways. • Liability might or might not arise from the condition or situation. **2.** Loosely, an act or failure to act resulting in an interference with the use or enjoyment of property. • In this sense, the term denotes the action causing the interference, rather than the resulting condition <the Slocums' playing electric guitars in their yard constituted a nuisance to their neighbors>. **3.** The class of torts arising from such conditions, acts, or failures to act when they occur unreasonably.

abatable nuisance. (1871) **1.** A nuisance so easily removable that the aggrieved party may lawfully cure the problem without notice to the liable party, such as overhanging tree branches. **2.** A nuisance that reasonable persons would regard as being removable by reasonable means.

absolute nuisance. (18c) **1.** Interference with a property right that a court considers fixed or invariable, such as a riparian owner's right to use a stream in its natural condition. **2.** Nuisance per se. **3.** Interference in a place where it does not reasonably belong, even if the interfering party is careful.

anticipatory nuisance. A condition that, although not yet at the level of a nuisance, is very likely to become one, so that a party may obtain an injunction prohibiting the condition.

attractive nuisance. (1901) A dangerous condition that may attract children onto land, thereby causing a risk to their safety.

continuing nuisance. (1837) A nuisance that is either uninterrupted or frequently recurring. • It need not be constant or unceasing, but it must occur often enough that it is almost continuous.

mixed nuisance. (1894) A condition that is both a private nuisance and a public nuisance, so that it is dangerous to the community at large but also causes particular harm to private individuals.

nuisance in fact. (1855) A nuisance existing because of the circumstances of the use or the particular location.

nuisance per se (pər **say**). (18c) Interference so severe that it would constitute a nuisance under any circumstances; a nuisance regardless of location or circumstances of use, such as a leaky nuclear-waste storage facility.

permanent nuisance. (18c) A nuisance that cannot readily be abated at reasonable expense.

private nuisance. (18c) A condition that interferes with a person's enjoyment of property; esp., a structure or other condition erected or put on nearby land, creating or continuing an invasion of the actor's land and amounting to a trespass to it. • The condition constitutes a tort for which the adversely affected person may recover damages or obtain an injunction.

public nuisance. (17c) An unreasonable interference with a right common to the general public, such as a condition dangerous to health, offensive to community moral standards, or unlawfully obstructing the public in the free use of public property. • Such a nuisance may lead to a civil injunction or criminal prosecution.

qualified nuisance. (1944) A condition that, though lawful in itself, is so negligently permitted to exist that it creates an unreasonable risk of harm and, in due course, actually results in injury to another. • It involves neither an intentional act nor a hazardous activity.

recurrent nuisance. A nuisance that occurs from time to time with distinct intervals between occurrences, rather than being continuous or only briefly interrupted.

temporary nuisance. (1879) A nuisance that can be corrected by a reasonable expenditure of money or labor.

null, *adj.* (16c) Having no legal effect; without binding force; VOID <the contract was declared null and void>. • The phrase *null and void* is a common redundancy.

nulla bona (**nəl**-ə **boh**-nə). [Latin "no goods"] (18c) A form of return by a sheriff or constable upon an execution when the judgment debtor has no seizable property within the jurisdiction.

nulla poena sine lege (**nəl**-ə **pee**-nə **sɪ**-nee **lee**-jee *or* **sin**-ay **lay**-gay). [Latin] No punishment without a law authorizing it.

nullification (nəl-i-fi-**kay**-shən), *n.* (18c) **1.** The act of making something void; specif., the action of a state in abrogating a federal law, on the basis of state sovereignty. **2.** The state or condition of being void. — **nullify,** *vb.*

nullification doctrine. The theory — espoused by southern states before the Civil War — advocating a state's right to declare a federal law unconstitutional and therefore void.

nullity (**nəl**-ə-tee). (16c) **1.** Something that is legally void <the forged commercial transfer is a nullity>. **2.** The fact of being legally void <she filed a petition for nullity of marriage>.

numbers game. A type of lottery in which a person bets that on a given day a certain series of numbers will appear from some arbitrarily chosen source, such as stock-market indexes or the U.S. Treasury balance. • The game creates a fund from which the winner's share is drawn and is subject to regulation as a lottery.

numerosity (n[y]oo-mər-**ahs**-ə-tee). (1958) The requirement in U.S. district courts that, for a case to be certified as a class action, the party applying for certification must show, among other things, that the class of potential plaintiffs is so large that the joinder of all of them into the suit is impracticable.

nunc pro tunc (**nəngk** proh **təngk** *or* **nuungk** proh **tuungk**). [Latin "now for then"] Having retroactive legal effect through a court's inherent power <the court entered a *nunc pro tunc* order to correct a clerical error in the record>.

nuncupative (**nəng**-kyə-pay-tiv *or* nəng-**kyoo**-pə-tiv), *adj.* [fr. Latin *nuncupare* "to name"] (15c) Stated by spoken word; declared orally.

nuptial (**nəp**-shəl), *adj.* (15c) Of or relating to marriage.

Nuremberg defense (**n[y]ər**-əm-bərg). The defense asserted by a member of the military that the soldier was following orders given by superiors. • The term derives from the Nuremberg war-crimes trials after World War II.

nurturing-parent doctrine. *Family law.* The principle that, although a court deciding on child support generally disregards a parent's motive in failing to maximize earning capacity, the court will not impute income to a custodial parent who remains at home or works less than full-time in order to provide a better environment for a child. • The doctrine is fact-specific; courts apply it case by case.

N.W. *abbr. North Western Reporter.*

NYS. *abbr. New York Supplement.*

NYSE. *abbr.* New York Stock Exchange.

O

oath. (bef. 12c) **1.** A solemn declaration, accompanied by a swearing to God or a revered person or thing, that one's statement is true or that one will be bound to a promise. **2.** A statement or promise made by such a declaration. **3.** A form of words used for such a declaration. **4.** A formal declaration made solemn without a swearing to God or a revered person or thing; affirmation.

assertory oath (ə-**sər**-tə-ree). (18c) An oath by which one attests to some factual matter, rather than making a promise about one's future conduct.

corporal oath (**kor**-pər-əl). (16c) An oath made solemn by touching a sacred object, esp. the Bible.

extrajudicial oath. (17c) An oath that, although formally sworn, is taken outside a legal proceeding or outside the authority of law.

judicial oath. (17c) An oath taken in the course of a judicial proceeding, esp. in open court.

nonjudicial oath. An oath taken out of court, esp. before an officer ex parte.

oath of allegiance. An oath by which one promises to maintain fidelity to a particular sovereign or government. • This oath is most often administered to a high public officer, to a soldier or sailor, or to an alien applying for naturalization.

oath of office. (16c) An oath taken by a person about to enter into the duties of public office, by which the person promises to perform the duties of that office in good faith.

pauper's oath. (1844) An affidavit or verification of poverty by a person requesting public funds or services.

promissory oath. (15c) An oath that binds the party to observe a specified course of conduct in the future.

purgatory oath. An oath taken to clear oneself of a charge or suspicion.

Oath or Affirmation Clause. (1974) The clause of the U.S. Constitution requiring members of Congress and the state legislatures, and all members of the executive or judicial branches — state or local — to pledge by oath or affirmation to support the Constitution. U.S. Const. art. VI, cl. 3.

obiter (**oh**-bit-ər), *adv.* [Latin "by the way"] (16c) Incidentally; in passing <the judge said, obiter, that a nominal sentence would be inappropriate>.

obiter dictum (**ob**-i-tər **dik**-təm). [Latin "something said in passing"] (18c) A judicial comment made while delivering a judicial opinion, but one that is unnecessary to the decision in the case and therefore not precedential (although it may be considered persuasive). Cf. HOLDING (1). Pl. **obiter dicta.**

object (**ob**-jekt), *n.* (15c) **1.** A person or thing to which thought, feeling, or action is directed. **2.** Something sought to be attained or accomplished; an end, goal, or purpose.

object (əb-**jekt**), *vb.* (15c) **1.** To state in opposition; to put forward as an objection. **2.** To state or put forward an objection, esp. to something in a judicial proceeding. — **objector,** *n.*

objection, *n.* (1837) A formal statement opposing something that has occurred, or is about to occur, in court and seeking the judge's immediate ruling on the point. • The party objecting must usu. state the basis for the objection to preserve the right to appeal an adverse ruling.

continuing objection. (1940) A single objection to all the questions in a given line of questioning. • A judge may allow a lawyer to make a continuing objection when the judge has overruled an objection applicable to many questions, and the lawyer wants to preserve the objection for the appellate record.

general objection. (18c) An objection made without specifying any grounds in support of the objection. • A general objection preserves only the issue of relevancy.

speaking objection. (1958) An objection that contains more information (often in the form of argument) than needed by the judge to sustain or overrule it. • Many judges prohibit lawyers from using speaking objections, and sometimes even from stating the grounds for objections, because of the potential for influencing the jury.

specific objection. (1894) An objection that is accompanied by a statement of one or more grounds in support of the objection.

objectionable, *adj.* (18c) Open to opposition, esp. adverse reason or contrary argument.

objection in point of law. (17c) A defensive pleading by which the defendant admits the facts alleged by the plaintiff but objects that they do not make out a legal claim.

objective, *adj.* (17c) **1.** Of, relating to, or based on externally verifiable phenomena, as opposed to an individual's perceptions, feelings, or intentions. **2.** Without bias or prejudice; disinterested.

objective ethics. Moral absolutism.

objective theory of contract. (1904) The doctrine that a contract is not an agreement in the sense of a subjective meeting of the minds but is instead a series of external acts giving the objective semblance of agreement.

object of a right. (1880) The thing in respect of which a right exists; the subject matter of a right.

obligation, *n.* (18c) **1.** A legal or moral duty to do or not do something. **2.** A formal, binding agreement or acknowledgment of a liability to pay a certain amount or to do a certain thing for a particular person or set of persons; esp., a duty arising by contract. — **obligate,** *vb.* (16c)

absolute obligation. (17c) An obligation requiring strict fulfillment according to the terms of the engagement, without any alternatives to the obligor.

accessory obligation. (17c) An obligation that is incidental to another obligation. • For example, a mortgage to secure payment of a bond is an accessory obligation. The primary obligation is to pay the bond itself.

alternative obligation. (18c) An obligation that can be satisfied in at least two different ways, at the choice of the obligor.

conditional obligation. (17c) An obligation that depends on an uncertain event.

contractual obligation. An obligation arising from a contract or agreement.

conventional obligation. (18c) An obligation that results from agreement of the parties; a contractual obligation.

current obligation. (18c) An obligation that is presently enforceable, but not past due.

determinate obligation. An obligation that has a specific thing as its object.

heritable obligation. (18c) An obligation that may be enforced by a successor of the creditor or against a successor of the debtor.

indeterminate obligation. An obligation by which the obligor is bound to deliver one of a certain species of items. • For example, an obligation to deliver a pre-1509 edition of

Vocabularium Iuris can be discharged by delivering any edition published before that date.

joint obligation. (18c) **1.** An obligation that binds two or more debtors to a single performance for one creditor. **2.** An obligation that binds one debtor to a single performance for two or more creditors.

moral obligation. (18c) A duty that is based only on one's conscience and that is not legally enforceable; an obligation with a purely moral basis, as opposed to a legal one.

obediential obligation (ə-bee-dee-**en**-shəl). (18c) An obligation imposed on a person because of a situation or relationship, such as an obligation of parents to care for their children.

perfect obligation. A legally enforceable obligation; one that is recognized and sanctioned by positive law.

personal obligation. **1.** An obligation performable only by the obligor, not by the obligor's heirs or representatives. **2.** An obligation in which the obligor is bound to perform without encumbering his or her property for its performance.

primary obligation. (17c) **1.** An obligation that arises from the essential purpose of the transaction between the parties. **2.** A fundamental contractual term imposing a requirement on a contracting party from which other obligations may arise.

secondary obligation. (17c) A duty, promise, or undertaking that is incident to a primary obligation; esp., a duty to make reparation upon a breach of contract.

simple obligation. (17c) An obligation that does not depend on an outside event; an unconditional obligation.

single obligation. (17c) An obligation with no penalty attached for nonperformance, as when one party simply promises to pay 20 dollars to another.

statutory obligation. (18c) An obligation — whether to pay money, perform certain acts, or discharge duties — that is created by or arises out of a statute, rather than based on an independent contractual or legal relationship.

obligatory (ə-**blig**-ə-tor-ee), *adj.* (14c) **1.** Legally or morally binding. **2.** Required; mandatory. **3.** Creating or recording an obligation.

oblige (ə-**blıj**), *vb.* (14c) **1.** To bind by legal or moral duty; obligate. **2.** To bind by doing a favor or service.

obligee (ob-lə-**jee**). (16c) **1.** One to whom an obligation is owed; a promisee, creditor, or donor beneficiary. **2.** *Archaic.* One who is obliged to do something; OBLIGOR (1).

obligor (ob-lə-**gor** *or* **ob**-lə-gor). (16c) **1.** One who has undertaken an obligation; a promisor or debtor. UCC § 9-102(a)(59). **2.** *Archaic.* One who obliges another to do something; OBLIGEE (1).

oblique (oh-**bleek** *or* ə-**bleek**), *adj.* (15c) **1.** Not direct in descent; collateral <an oblique heir>. **2.** Indirect; circumstantial <oblique evidence>.

obloquy (**ob**-lə-kwee). (15c) **1.** Abusive or defamatory language; CALUMNY. **2.** The state or condition of being ill spoken of; disgrace or bad repute.

obnoxious, *adj.* (16c) **1.** Offensive; objectionable <obnoxious behavior>. **2.** Contrary; opposed <a practice obnoxious to the principle of equal protection under the law>. **3.** *Archaic.* Exposed to harm; liable to something undesirable <actions obnoxious to criticism>.

obscene, *adj.* (16c) Extremely offensive under contemporary community standards of morality and decency; grossly repugnant to the generally accepted notions of what is appropriate. • Under the Supreme Court's three-part test, material is legally obscene — and therefore not protected under the First Amendment — if, taken as a whole, the material (1) appeals to the prurient interest in sex, as determined by the average person applying contemporary community standards; (2) portrays sexual conduct, as specifically defined by the applicable state law, in a patently offensive way; and (3) lacks serious literary, artistic, political, or scientific value. *Miller v. California*, 413 U.S. 15, 93 S.Ct. 2607 (1973).

obscenity, *n.* (16c) **1.** The characteristic or state of being morally abhorrent or socially taboo, esp. as a result of referring to or depicting sexual or excretory functions. **2.** Something (such as an expression or act) that has this characteristic.

commercialized obscenity. (1956) Obscenity produced and marketed for sale to the public.

observe, *vb.* (14c) To adhere to or abide by (a law, rule, or custom).

obsolescence (ob-sə-**les**-ənts). (1832) **1.** The process or state of falling into disuse or becoming obsolete. **2.** A diminution in the value or usefulness of property, esp. as a result of technological advances. • For tax purposes, obsolescence is usu. distinguished from physical deterioration. — **obsolescent,** *adj.* (18c). — **obsolete,** *adj.* (17c).

economic obsolescence. Obsolescence that results from external economic factors, such as decreased demand or changed governmental regulations.

functional obsolescence. Obsolescence that results either from inherent deficiencies in the property, such as inadequate equipment or design, or from technological improvements available after the use began.

planned obsolescence. A system or policy of deliberately producing consumer goods that will wear out or become outdated after limited use, thus inducing consumers to buy new items more frequently.

obstruction of justice. (1854) Interference with the orderly administration of law and justice, as by giving false information to or withholding evidence from a police officer or prosecutor, or by harming or intimidating a witness or juror. • Obstruction of justice is a crime in most jurisdictions.

obstruction of process. Interference of any kind with the lawful service or execution of a writ, warrant, or other process. • Most jurisdictions make this offense a crime.

obtest (ob- *or* əb-**test**), *vb.* (16c) **1.** To call to or invoke as a witness. **2.** To ask for earnestly; beseech; implore. **3.** To protest.

obviate (**ob**-vee-ayt), *vb.* (16c) **1.** To dispose of or do away with (a thing); to anticipate and prevent from arising. **2.** To make unnecessary. — **obviation,** *n.* — **obviator,** *n.*

obvious error. A standard of review that applies to unobjected-to actions and omissions at trial that are so seriously prejudicial as to result in manifest injustice.

obviousness, *n.* (1921) *Patents.* The quality or state of being easily apparent to a person with ordinary skill in a given art, considering the scope and content of the prior art, so that the person could reasonably believe that, at the time it was conceived, the invention was to be expected. See 35 USCA 5103. — **obvious,** *adj.*

OCC. *abbr.* Office of the Comptroller of the Currency.

occupancy. (16c) **1.** The act, state, or condition of holding, possessing, or residing in or on something; actual possession, residence, or tenancy, esp. of a dwelling or land. **2.** The act of taking possession of something that has no owner (such as abandoned property) so as to acquire legal ownership. **3.** The period or term during which one owns, rents, or otherwise occupies property. **4.** The state or condition of being occupied. **5.** The use to which property is put.

occupant. (16c) **1.** One who has possessory rights in, or control over, certain property or premises. **2.** One who acquires title by occupancy.

general occupant. (18c) A person who occupies land in the interim arising after the death of a *pur autre vie* tenant but before the death of the person who serves as the measuring life for the estate. • The *pur autre vie* tenant does not state who may occupy the land after the death of the first tenant; the land can be occupied by the first possessor of the land.

special occupant. (18c) A person specifically designated in a conveyance as being entitled to a life estate if the conveyee dies before the end of the life estate; specif., a *pur autre vie* tenant's heir who occupies land in the interim between the death of the tenant and the death of the person who serves as the measuring life for the estate. • A special occupancy can arise when the grant to the *pur autre vie* tenant provides that possession is for the life of the tenant, then to the tenant's heirs.

occupation. (14c) **1.** An activity or pursuit in which a person is engaged; esp., a person's usual or principal work or business.

dangerous occupation. An occupation that involves an appreciable risk of death or serious bodily injury.

2. The possession, control, or use of real property; occupancy. **3.** The seizure and control of a territory by military force; the condition of territory that has been placed under the authority of a hostile army. **4.** The period during which territory seized by military force is held.

occupational disease. (1901) A disease that is contracted as a result of exposure to debilitating conditions or substances in the course of employment.

Occupational Safety and Health Administration. A unit in the U.S. Department of Labor responsible for setting and enforcing workplace safety and health standards and for helping employers comply. • It was created under the Occupational Safety and Health Act of 1970. — Abbr. OSHA (**oh**-shə).

occupying claimant. (1801) A person who claims the right under a statute to recover for the cost of improvements done to land that is later found not to belong to the person.

occurrence rule. *Civil procedure.* The rule that a limitations period begins to run when the alleged wrongful act or omission occurs, rather than when the plaintiff discovers the injury. • This rule applies, for example, to most breach-of-contract claims.

o/d. *abbr.* **1.** OVERDRAFT (1). **2.** OVERDRAFT (2).

OD. *abbr.* **1.** Overdose. **2.** OVERDRAFT (1). **3.** OVERDRAFT (2).

odd-lot doctrine. *Workers' compensation.* The doctrine that permits a finding of total disability for an injured claimant who, though able to work sporadically, cannot obtain regular employment and steady income and is thus considered an "odd lot" in the labor market.

odium (**oh**-dee-əm). (17c) **1.** The state or fact of being hated. **2.** A state of disgrace, usu. resulting from detestable conduct. **3.** Hatred or strong aversion accompanied by loathing or contempt. — **odious,** *adj.*

OEQ. *abbr.* Office of Environmental Quality.

of course. (16c) **1.** Following the ordinary procedure <the writ was issued as a matter of course>. **2.** Naturally; obviously; clearly <we'll appeal that ruling, of course>.

offender. (15c) A person who has committed a crime.

adult offender. (1831) **1.** A person who has committed a crime after reaching the age of majority. **2.** A person who, having committed a crime while a minor, has been convicted after reaching the age of majority. **3.** A juvenile who has committed a crime and is tried as an adult rather than as a juvenile.

career offender. (1965) Under the federal-sentencing guidelines, an adult who, after being convicted of two violent felonies or controlled-substance felonies, commits another such felony. U.S. Sentencing Guidelines Manual § 4B1.1.

first offender. (1884) A person who authorities believe has committed a crime but who has never before been convicted of a crime. • First offenders are often treated leniently at sentencing or in plea negotiations.

habitual offender. **1.** A person who commits the same or a similar offense a certain number of times in a certain period, as set by statute, and is therefore eligible for an enhanced sentence. **2.** Recidivist.

repeat offender. (1956) A person who has been convicted of a crime more than once; recidivist.

situational offender. (1945) A first-time offender who is unlikely to commit future crimes.

status offender. (1967) A youth who engages in conduct that — though not criminal by adult standards — is considered inappropriate enough to bring a charge against the youth in juvenile court; a juvenile who commits a status offense.

youthful offender. (1885) **1.** A person in late adolescence or early adulthood who has been convicted of a crime. • A youthful offender is often eligible for special programs not available to older offenders, including community supervision, the successful completion of which may lead to erasing the conviction from the offender's record. **2.** Juvenile delinquent.

offense (ə-**fents**). (14c) A violation of the law; a crime, often a minor one.

acquisitive offense. (1981) An offense characterized by the unlawful appropriation of another's property. • This is a generic term that refers to a variety of crimes (such as larceny) rather than a particular one.

allied offense. (1896) A crime with elements so similar to those of another that the commission of the one is automatically the commission of the other.

bailable offense. (18c) A criminal charge for which a defendant may be released from custody after providing proper security.

capital offense. (16c) A crime for which the death penalty may be imposed.

cognate offense. (1866) A lesser offense that is related to the greater offense because it shares several of the elements of the greater offense and is of the same class or category. • For example, shoplifting is a cognate offense of larceny because both crimes require the element of taking property with the intent to deprive the rightful owner of that property.

compound offense. An offense composed of one or more separate offenses. • For example, robbery is a compound offense composed of larceny and assault.

continuing offense. (18c) A crime (such as a conspiracy) that is committed over a period of time, so that the last act of the crime controls when the statute of limitations begins to run.

cumulative offense. (1833) An offense committed by repeating the same act at different times.

divisible offense. (1847) A crime that includes one or more crimes of lesser grade. • For example, murder is a divisible offense comprising assault, battery, and assault with intent to kill.

extraneous offense. (1881) An offense beyond or unrelated to the offense for which a defendant is on trial.

graded offense. (1891) A crime that is divided into various degrees of severity with corresponding levels of punishment, such as murder (first-degree and second-degree) or assault (simple and aggravated).

inchoate offense. (1809) A step toward the commission of another crime, the step in itself being serious enough to merit punishment. • The three inchoate offenses are attempt, conspiracy, and solicitation. The term is sometimes criticized.

index offense. (1980) One of eight classes of crimes reported annually by the FBI in the Uniform Crime Report. • The eight classes are murder (and nonnegligent homicide), rape, robbery, aggravated assault, burglary, larceny-theft, arson, and auto theft.

indictable offense. (18c) A crime that can be prosecuted only by indictment. • In federal court, such an offense is one punishable by death or by imprisonment for more than one year or at hard labor. Fed. R. Crim. P. 7(a).

joint offense. (18c) An offense (such as conspiracy) committed by the participation of two or more persons.

lesser included offense. (1908) A crime that is composed of some, but not all, of the elements of a more serious crime and that is necessarily committed in carrying out the greater crime <battery is a lesser included offense of murder>. • For double-jeopardy purposes, a lesser included offense is considered the "same offense" as the greater offense, so that acquittal or conviction of either offense precludes a separate trial for the other.

liquor offense. Any crime involving the inappropriate use or sale of intoxicating liquor.

major offense. An offense the commission of which involves one or more lesser included offenses, as murder may include assault and battery.

multiple offense. (1908) An offense that violates more than one law but that may require different proof so that an acquittal or conviction under one statute does not exempt the defendant from prosecution under another.

negligent offense. A violation of law arising from a defective discharge of duty or from criminal negligence.

object offense. The crime that is the object of the defendant's attempt, solicitation, conspiracy, or complicity. • For example, murder is the object offense in a charge of attempted murder.

offense against property. (1837) A crime against another's personal property. • The common-law offenses against property were larceny, embezzlement, cheating, cheating by false pretenses, robbery, receiving stolen goods, malicious mischief, forgery, and uttering forged instruments. Although the term *crimes against property*, a common term in modern usage, includes crimes against real property, the term *offense against property* is traditionally restricted to personal property.

offense against public justice and authority. A crime that impairs the administration of justice. • The common-law offenses of this type were obstruction of justice, barratry, maintenance, champerty, embracery, escape, prison breach, rescue, misprision of felony, compounding a crime, subornation of perjury, bribery, and misconduct in office.

offense against the habitation. (1849) A crime against another's house — traditionally either arson or burglary.

offense against the person. (1854) A crime against the body of another human being. • The common-law offenses against the person were murder, manslaughter, mayhem, rape, assault, battery, robbery, false imprisonment, abortion, seduction, kidnapping, and abduction.

offense against the public health, safety, comfort, and morals. A crime traditionally viewed as endangering the whole of society. • The common-law offenses of this type were nuisance, bigamy, adultery, fornication, lewdness, illicit cohabitation, incest, miscegenation, sodomy, bestiality, buggery, abortion, and seduction.

offense against the public peace. (18c) A crime that tends to disturb the peace. • The common-law offenses of this type were riot, unlawful assembly, dueling, rout, affray, forcible entry and detainer, and libel on a private person.

petty offense. (17c) A minor or insignificant crime. 18 USCA § 19.

predicate offense. **1.** An earlier offense that can be used to enhance a sentence levied for a later conviction. • Predicate offenses are defined by statute and are not uniform from state to state. **2.** Lesser included offense.

public offense. (16c) An act or omission forbidden by law.

public-welfare offense. (1933) A minor offense that does not involve moral delinquency and is prohibited only to secure the effective regulation of conduct in the interest of the community. • An example is driving a car with one brake-light missing.

same offense. **1.** For double-jeopardy purposes, the same criminal act, omission, or transaction for which the person has already stood trial. **2.** For sentencing and enhancement-of-punishment purposes, an offense that is quite similar to a previous one.

separate offense. (18c) **1.** An offense arising out of the same event as another offense but containing some differences in elements of proof. • A person may be tried, convicted, and sentenced for each separate offense. **2.** An offense arising out of a different event entirely from another offense under consideration.

serious offense. (18c) An offense not classified as a petty offense and usu. carrying at least a six-month sentence.

sexual offense. (1885) An offense involving unlawful sexual conduct, such as prostitution, indecent exposure, incest, pederasty, and bestiality.

status offense. (1960) **1.** Status crime. **2.** A minor's violation of the juvenile code by doing some act that would not be considered illegal if an adult did it, but that indicates that the minor is beyond parental control. • Examples include running away from home, truancy, and incorrigibility.

strict-liability offense. An offense for which the action alone is enough to warrant a conviction, with no need to prove a mental state. • For example, illegal parking is a strict-liability offense.

substantive offense (s**ə**b-stən-tiv). (18c) A crime that is complete in itself and is not dependent on another crime for one of its elements.

summary offense. (1928) An offense (such as a petty misdemeanor) that can be prosecuted without an indictment.

unrelated offense. (1896) A crime that is independent from the charged offense.

violent offense. (1965) A crime characterized by extreme physical force, such as murder, forcible rape, and assault and battery with a dangerous weapon.

offensive (ə-**fen**-siv), *adj.* (16c) **1.** Of or for attack <an offensive weapon>. **2.** Unpleasant or disagreeable to the senses; obnoxious <an offensive odor>. **3.** Causing displeasure, anger, or resentment; esp., repugnant to the prevailing sense of what is decent or moral <patently offensive language and photographs>.

offensive-use waiver. (1993) An exemption from the attorney–client privilege, whereby a litigant is considered to have waived the privilege by seeking affirmative relief, if the claim relies on privileged information that would be outcome-determinative and that the opposing party has no other way to obtain.

offer, *n.* (15c) **1.** The act or an instance of presenting something for acceptance <the prosecutor's offer of immunity>. **2.** A promise to do or refrain from doing some specified thing in the future, conditioned on an act, forbearance, or return promise being given in exchange for the promise or its performance; a display of willingness to enter into a contract on specified terms, made in a way that would lead a reasonable person to understand that an acceptance, having been sought, will result in a binding contract <she accepted the $750 offer on the Victorian armoire>.

irrevocable offer (i-**rev**-ə-kə-bəl). (1885) An offer that includes a promise to keep it open for a specified period, during which the offer cannot be withdrawn without the offeror's becoming subject to liability for breach of contract. • Traditionally, this type of promise must be supported by consideration to be enforceable, but under UCC § 2-205, a merchant's signed, written offer giving assurances that it will be held open — but lacking consideration — is nonetheless irrevocable for the stated period (or, if not stated, for a reasonable time not exceeding three months).

offer to all the world. (1861) An offer, by way of advertisement, of a reward for the rendering of specified services, addressed to the public at large. • As soon as someone renders the services, a contract is made.

standing offer. (1842) An offer that is in effect a whole series of offers, each of which is capable of being converted into a contract by a distinct acceptance.

3. A price at which one is ready to buy or sell; BID <she lowered her offer to $200>. **4.** ATTEMPT (2) <an offer to commit battery>. — **offer,** *vb.* — **offeror,** *n.*

offeree (ah-fər-**ee**). (1882) One to whom an offer is made.

offering, *n.* (15c) **1.** The act of making an offer; something offered for sale. **2.** The sale of an issue of securities.

offer of compromise. (18c) An offer by one party to settle a dispute amicably (usu. by paying money) to avoid or end a lawsuit or other legal action.

offer of judgment. (1971) A settlement offer by one party to allow a specified judgment to be taken against the party. • In federal procedure (and in many states), if the adverse party rejects the offer, and if a judgment finally obtained by that party is not more favorable than the offer, then that party must pay the costs incurred after the offer was made. Fed. R. Civ. P. 68.

offer of performance. (18c) *Contracts.* One party's reasonable assurance to the other, through words or conduct, of a present ability to fulfill contractual obligations.

offer of proof. (17c) *Procedure.* A presentation of evidence for the record (but outside the jury's presence) usu. made after the judge has sustained an objection to the admissibility of that evidence, so that the evidence can be preserved on the record for an appeal of the judge's ruling. • An offer of proof, which may also be used to persuade the court to admit the evidence, consists of three parts: (1) the evidence itself, (2) an explanation of the purpose for which it is offered (its relevance), and (3) an argument supporting admissibility. Such an offer may include tangible evidence or testimony (through questions and answers, a lawyer's narrative description, or an affidavit). Fed. R. Evid. 103(a)(2).

offeror (ah-fər-**or**). (1882) One who makes an offer.

office. (13c) **1.** A position of duty, trust, or authority, esp. one conferred by a governmental authority for a public purpose. **2.** (*often cap.*) A division of the U.S. government ranking immediately below a department. **3.** A place where business is conducted or services are performed.

ministerial office. An office that does not include authority to exercise judgment, only to carry out orders given by a superior office, or to perform duties or acts required by rules, statutes, or regulations.

office of honor. An uncompensated public position of considerable dignity and importance to which public trusts or interests are confided.

Office of Management and Budget. An office in the Executive Office of the President responsible for helping the President prepare the annual federal budget and supervising its administration. • It was originally established by Reorganization Plan No.1 of 1939 as the Bureau of the Budget. — Abbr. OMB.

Office of Personnel Management. The independent federal agency that administers the personnel system of the government by helping agencies recruit and evaluate employees; manage retirement and health-benefit systems; coordinate temporary assignments; conduct investigations; and develop leadership in the federal executive service. • The agency was established by Reorganization Plan No. 2 of 1978 and given various functions of the former U.S. Civil Service Commission by Executive Order 12107 of 1978. — Abbr. OPM.

Office of Special Counsel. An independent federal agency that investigates activities prohibited by the civil-service laws, rules, and regulations and, if the investigation warrants it, litigates the matter before the Merit Systems Protection Board. • The agency was established by Reorganization Plan No. 2 of 1978. — Abbr. OSC.

Office of the Comptroller of the Currency. An office in the U.S. Department of the Treasury responsible for regulating approximately 2,600 national banks by examining them; approving or denying applications for bank charters, branches, or mergers; closing banks that fail to follow rules and regulations; and regulating banking practices. — Abbr. OCC.

Office of the United States Trade Representative. An office in the Executive Office of the President responsible for setting and administering overall trade policy. • It was established under Reorganization Plan No. 3 of 1979. 19 USCA § 2171.

office practice. (1872) A law practice that primarily involves handling matters outside of court, such as negotiating and drafting contracts, preparing wills and trusts, setting up corporations and partnerships, and advising on tax or employment issues; a transactional-law practice.

office practitioner. (1933) A lawyer who does not litigate; an attorney whose work is accomplished primarily in the office, without court appearances.

officer. (14c) **1.** A person who holds an office of trust, authority, or command. • In public affairs, the term refers esp. to a person holding public office under a national, state, or local government, and authorized by that government to exercise some specific function. In corporate law, the term refers esp. to a person elected or appointed by the board of directors to manage the daily operations of a corporation, such as a CEO, president, secretary, or treasurer.

administrative officer. **1.** An officer of the executive department of government, usu. of inferior rank. **2.** A ministerial or executive officer, as distinguished from a judicial officer.

corporate officer. An officer of a corporation, such as a CEO, president, secretary, or treasurer.

fiscal officer. **1.** The person (such as a state or county treasurer) charged with the collection and distribution of public money. **2.** The person (such as a chief financial officer) whose duties are to oversee the financial matters of a corporation or business.

hearing officer. **1.** Administrative-law judge. **2.** Judicial officer.

judicial officer. (17c) **1.** A judge or magistrate. **2.** Any officer of the court, such as a bailiff or court reporter. **3.** A person, usu. an attorney, who serves in an appointive capacity at the pleasure of an appointing judge, and whose actions and decisions are reviewed by that judge.

juvenile officer. (1911) A juvenile-court employee, sometimes a social worker or probation officer, who works with the judge to direct and develop the court's child-welfare work.

ministerial officer. An officer who primarily executes mandates issued by the officer's superiors.

probation officer. A government officer who supervises the conduct of a probationer.

2. *Military law.* One who holds a commission in the armed services, or a military post higher than that of the lowest ranks; a person who has a command in the armed forces.

commissioned officer. An officer in the armed forces who holds grade and office under a presidential commission.

general officer. A military officer whose command extends to a body of forces composed of several regiments. • Examples are generals, lieutenant-generals, major-generals, and brigadiers.

noncommissioned officer. An enlisted person in the Army, Air Force, or Marine Corps in certain pay grades above the lowest pay grade. • Examples are sergeants and corporals.

warrant officer. A person who holds a commission or warrant in a warrant-officer grade. • A warrant officer's rank is below a second lieutenant or ensign but above cadets, midshipmen, and enlisted personnel.

officer of the court. (16c) A person who is charged with upholding the law and administering the judicial system. • Typically, *officer of the court* refers to a judge, clerk, bailiff, sheriff, or the like, but the term also applies to a lawyer, who is obliged to obey court rules and who owes a duty of candor to the court.

official (ə-**fish**-əl), *adj.* (16c) **1.** Of or relating to an office or position of trust or authority <official duties>. **2.** Authorized or approved by a proper authority <a company's official policy>.

official, *n.* (14c) **1.** One who holds or is invested with a public office; a person elected or appointed to carry out some portion of a government's sovereign powers.. **2.** One authorized to act for a corporation or organization, esp. in a subordinate capacity. **3.** (*usu. cap.*) Official principal.

officiousness (ə-**fish**-əs-nəs), *n.* (16c) Interference in the affairs of others without justification under the circumstances. — **officious,** *adj.*

off point. (1951) Not discussing the precise issue at hand; irrelevant.

offset, *n.* (18c) Something (such as an amount or claim) that balances or compensates for something else; setoff. — **offset,** *vb.* (17c).

of record. (16c) **1.** Recorded in the appropriate records <counsel of record>. **2.** (Of a court) that has proceedings taken down stenographically or otherwise documented <court of record>.

of the essence. (18c) (Of a contractual requirement) so important that if the requirement is not met, the promisor will be held to have breached the contract and a rescission by the promisee will be justified <time is of the essence>.

Old-Age and Survivors' Insurance. (1935) A system of insurance, subsidized by the federal government, that provides retirement benefits for persons who reach retirement age and payments to survivors upon the death of the insured. • This was the original name for the retirement and death benefits established by the Social Security Act of 1935. As the scope of these benefits expanded, the name changed to Old Age, Survivors, and Disability Insurance (OASDI), and then to Old Age, Survivors, Disability, and Health Insurance (OASDHI). Today, the system is most often referred to as *Social Security.* — Abbr. OASI.

OMB. *abbr.* Office of Management and Budget.

ombudsman (**om**-bədz-mən). (1872) **1.** An official appointed to receive, investigate, and report on private citizens' complaints about the government. **2.** A similar appointee in a nongovernmental organization (such as a company or university).

omission, *n.* (14c) **1.** A failure to do something; esp., a neglect of duty <the complaint alleged that the driver had committed various negligent acts and omissions>. **2.** The act of leaving something out <the contractor's omission of the sales price rendered the contract void>. **3.** The state of having been left out or of not having been done <his omission from the roster caused no harm>. **4.** Something that is left out, left undone, or otherwise neglected <the many omissions from the list were unintentional>. — **omit,** *vb.* — **omissive, omissible,** *adj.*

omnibus (**om**-ni-bəs), *adj.* (1842) Relating to or dealing with numerous objects or items at once; including many things or having various purposes.

omnibus clause. (1880) **1.** A provision in an automobile-insurance policy that extends coverage to all drivers operating the insured vehicle with the owner's permission. **2.** Residuary clause.

OMVI. *abbr.* Operating a motor vehicle while intoxicated.

OMVUI. *abbr.* Operating a motor vehicle while under the influence.

on all fours. (Of a law case) squarely on point (with a precedent) on both facts and law; nearly identical in all material ways <our client's case is on all fours with the Supreme Court's most recent opinion>.

on demand. (17c) When presented or upon request for payment <this note is payable on demand>.

one-action rule. In debtor-creditor law, the principle that when a debt is secured by real property, the creditor must foreclose on the collateral before proceeding against the debtor's unsecured assets.

one-day, one-trial method. (1976) A system of summoning and using jurors whereby a person answers a jury summons and participates in the venire for one day only, unless the person is actually empaneled for a trial, in which event the juror's service lasts for the entire length of the trial.

180-day rule. *Criminal procedure.* **1.** A rule that, in some jurisdictions, allows a person charged with a felony to be released on personal recognizance if the person has been in jail for 180 days without being brought to trial, and if the delay has not resulted from the defendant's own actions. **2.** A rule requiring all pending charges against a prison inmate to be brought to trial in 180 days or to be dismissed with prejudice.

one-party consent rule. The principle that one party to a telephone or other conversation may secretly record the conversation. • This principle applies in most but not all states.

one-person, one-vote rule. (1965) *Constitutional law.* The principle that the Equal Protection Clause requires legislative voting districts to have about the same population. *Reynolds v. Sims*, 377 U.S. 533, 84 S.Ct. 1362 (1964).

onerous (**oh**-nər-əs *or* **on**-ər-əs), *adj.* (14c) **1.** Excessively burdensome or troublesome; causing hardship <onerous discovery requests>. **2.** Having or involving obligations that outweigh the advantages <onerous property>. **3.** *Civil law.* Done or given in return for something of equivalent value; supported by consideration <an onerous contract>. — **onerousness,** *n.*

one-satisfaction rule. (1965) The principle that a plaintiff is only entitled to only one recovery for a particular harm, and that the plaintiff must elect a single remedy if the jury has awarded more than one. • This rule is, for example, one of the foundations of a defendant's right to have a jury verdict reduced by the amount of any settlements the plaintiff has received from other entities for the same injury.

one-subject rule. The principle that a statute should embrace only one topic, which should be stated in its title.

one-year rule. *Patents.* The statutory requirement that a patent application must be filed within one year after any publication, public use, sale, or offer for sale of the invention. • If an inventor waits longer than a year, the patent is blocked by this "statutory bar." 35 USCA §§ 102(b).

onomastic (on-ə-**mas**-tik), *adj.* (16c) **1.** Of or relating to names or nomenclature. **2.** (Of a signature on an instrument) in a handwriting different from that of the body of the document; esp., designating an autograph signature alone, as distinguished from the main text in a different hand or in typewriting. — **onomastics** (for sense 1), *n.*

on or about. (17c) Approximately; at or around the time specified. • This language is used in pleading to prevent a variance between the pleading and the proof, usu. when there is any uncertainty about the exact date of a pivotal event. When used in nonpleading contexts, the phrase is mere jargon.

on pain of. (14c) Or else suffer punishment for noncompliance. • This phrase usu. follows a command or condition <ordered to cease operations on pain of a $2,000 fine>.

on point. (1927) Discussing the precise issue now at hand; apposite <this opinion is not on point as authority in our case>.

onset date. The beginning of a period of disability for purposes of disability payments by the Social Security Administration.

on the brief. (Of a lawyer) having participated in preparing a given brief. • The names of all the lawyers on the brief are typically listed on the front cover.

on the merits. (18c) (Of a judgment) delivered after the court has heard and evaluated the evidence and the parties' substantive arguments.

on the pleadings. (18c) (Of a judgment) rendered for reasons that are apparent from the faces of the complaint and answer, without hearing or evaluating the evidence or the substantive arguments.

onus (**oh**-nəs). (17c) **1.** A burden; a load. **2.** A disagreeable responsibility; an obligation. **3.** *Onus probandi.*

onus probandi (**oh**-nəs prə-**ban**-dɪ). [Latin] (18c) Burden of proof. — Often shortened to *onus.*

open, *adj.* (bef. 12c) **1.** Manifest; apparent; notorious. **2.** Visible; exposed to public view; not clandestine. **3.** Not closed, settled, fixed, or terminated.

open and notorious. (16c) **1.** NOTORIOUS (2). **2.** (Of adultery) known and recognized by the public and flouting the accepted standards of morality in the community.

open court. (15c) **1.** A court that is in session, presided over by a judge, attended by the parties and their attorneys, and engaged in judicial business. • *Open court* usu. refers to a proceeding in which formal entries are made on the record. The term is distinguished from a court that is hearing evidence in camera or from a judge that is exercising merely magisterial powers. **2.** A court session that the public is free to attend. • Most state constitutions have open-court provisions guaranteeing the public's right to attend trials.

open-door law. Sunshine law.

open-end, *adj.* (1931) **1.** Allowing for future changes or additions <open-end credit plan>. **2.** Continually issuing or redeeming shares on demand at the current net asset value <open-end investment company>.

open-fields doctrine. (1963) *Criminal procedure.* The rule permitting a warrantless search of the area outside a property owner's curtilage. • Unless there is some other legal basis for the search, it must exclude the home and any adjoining land (such as a yard) that is within an enclosure or otherwise protected from public scrutiny.

opening statement. (1848) At the outset of a trial, an advocate's statement giving the fact-finder a preview of the case and of the evidence to be presented. • Although the opening statement is not supposed to be argumentative, lawyers — purposefully or not — often include some form of argument. The term is thus sometimes referred to as *opening argument.*

open-records act. A statute providing for public access to view and copy government records maintained by public agencies.

open season. (1846) A specific time of year when it is legal to hunt or catch game or fish.

open source, *adj.* (1998) Of or related to software that includes human-readable source code and can be freely revised.

open-source software. (1998) Software that is usu. not sold for profit, includes both human-readable source code and machine-readable object code, and allows users to freely copy, modify, or distribute the software. • Even though open-source software is made widely available for free, it may be protected by federal trademark law. See *Planetary Motion Inc. v. Techplosion Inc.*, 261 F.3d 1188 (11th Cir. 2001).

open space. (17c) Undeveloped (or mostly undeveloped) urban or suburban land that is set aside and permanently restricted to agricultural, recreational, or conservational uses. • The land may be publicly or privately owned. Access may be restricted or unrestricted. Open spaces are not necessarily in a natural state: the term includes land used for public parks, gardens, farms, and pastures. But it does not include structures such as parking lots, swimming pools, or tennis courts.

operability. *Patents.* The ability of an invention to work as described. • A patent examiner may challenge the operability of an invention and require some proof, such as a demonstration of a working model.

operation of law. (17c) The means by which a right or a liability is created for a party regardless of the party's actual intent <because the court didn't rule on the motion for rehearing within 30 days, it was overruled by operation of law>.

operative, *adj.* (15c) **1.** Being in or having force or effect; esp., designating the part of a legal instrument that gives effect to the transaction involved <the operative provision of the contract>. **2.** Having principal relevance; essential to the meaning of the whole <*may* is the operative word of the statute>.

operative construction. 1. The interpretation of a writing or agreement, esp. a contract, statute, or regulation, that is being relied on by the parties, a court, or an administrative agency. **2.** The doctrine that the interpretation of a statute or regulation made by an administrative agency charged with enforcing it is entitled to judicial deference unless it is arbitrary and capricious.

operative words. In a transactional document, the words that actually effect the transaction.

opinion. (14c) **1.** A court's written statement explaining its decision in a given case, usu. including the statement of facts, points of law, rationale, and dicta. — Abbr. op.

advisory opinion. (1837) **1.** A nonbinding statement by a court of its interpretation of the law on a matter submitted for that purpose. • Federal courts are constitutionally prohibited from issuing advisory opinions by the case-or-controversy requirement, but other courts, such as the International Court of Justice, render them routinely. **2.** A written statement, issued only by an administrator of an employee benefit plan, that interprets ERISA and applies it to a specific factual situation. • Only the parties named in the request for the opinion can rely on it, and its reliability depends on the accuracy and completeness of all material facts.

depublished opinion. An intermediate appellate court's opinion that has been struck from the official reports, esp. by the highest court.

dissenting opinion. (1817) An opinion by one or more judges who disagree with the decision reached by the majority.

extrajudicial opinion. **1.** An opinion that is beyond the court's authority to render. • Such opinions are void. **2.** A judge's personal or scholarly opinion expressed in a medium other than a judicial opinion.

majority opinion. (1882) An opinion joined in by more than half the judges considering a given case.

memorandum opinion. (1912) A unanimous appellate opinion that succinctly states the decision of the court; an opinion that briefly reports the court's conclusion, usu. without elaboration because the decision follows a well-established legal principle or does not relate to any point of law.

per curiam opinion (pər **kyoor**-ee-əm). (1860) An opinion handed down by an appellate court without identifying the individual judge who wrote the opinion.

plurality opinion. (1908) An opinion lacking enough judges' votes to constitute a majority, but receiving more votes than any other opinion.

seriatim opinions (seer-ee-**ay**-tim). (1832) A series of opinions written individually by each judge on the bench, as opposed to a single opinion speaking for the court as a whole.

slip opinion. **1.** A court opinion that is published individually after being rendered and then collectively in advance sheets before being released for publication in a reporter. • Unlike an unpublished opinion, a slip opinion can usu. be cited as authority. **2.** *Archaic.* A preliminary draft of a court opinion not yet ready for publication.

unpublished opinion. (1849) An opinion that the court has specifically designated as not for publication. • Court rules usu. prohibit citing an unpublished opinion as authority. Such an opinion is considered binding only on the parties to the particular case in which it is issued.

2. A formal expression of judgment or advice based on an expert's special knowledge; esp., a document, usu. prepared at a client's request, containing a lawyer's understanding of the law that applies to a particular case.

adverse opinion. An outside auditor's opinion that a company's financial statements do not conform with generally accepted accounting principles or do not accurately reflect the company's financial position.

audit opinion. A certified public accountant's opinion regarding the audited financial statements of an entity.

coverage opinion. A lawyer's opinion on whether a particular event is covered by a given insurance policy.

infringement opinion. *Patents.* A patent attorney's opinion about the probable outcome of an infringement hearing or trial on whether a particular product or process infringes one or more claims of another's patent.

legal opinion. (18c) A written document in which an attorney provides his or her understanding of the law as applied to assumed facts. • The attorney may be a private attorney or attorney representing the state or other governmental entity. Private attorneys frequently render legal opinions on the ownership of real estate or minerals, insurance coverage, and corporate transactions. A party may be entitled to rely on a legal opinion, depending on factors such as the identity of the parties to whom the opinion was addressed, the nature of the opinion, and the law governing the opinion.

patentability opinion. *Patents.* A patent attorney's or patent agent's opinion on the patent office's probable holding about the allowability of a patent application's claims. • The opinion is almost a mini-examination report because it is based on consideration of the invention's subject matter, prior art, etc.

title opinion. (1927) A lawyer's or title company's opinion on the state of title for a given piece of real property, usu. describing whether the title is clear and marketable or whether it is encumbered.

3. A person's thought, belief, or inference, esp. a witness's view about a facts in dispute, as opposed to personal knowledge of the facts themselves.

expert opinion. An opinion offered by a witness whose knowledge, skill, experience, training, and education qualify the witness to help a fact-finder understand the evidence or decide a factual dispute.

fixed opinion. (1807) A bias or prejudice that disqualifies a potential juror.

opinion rule. (1896) *Evidence.* The principle that a witness should testify to facts, not opinions, and that a nonexpert witness's opinions are often excludable from evidence. • Traditionally, this principle is regarded as one of the important exclusionary rules in evidence law. It is based on the idea that a witness who has observed data should provide the most factual evidence possible, leaving the jury to draw inferences and conclusions from the evidence. Under this system, the witness's opinion is unnecessary. Today, opinions are admissible if rationally based on a witness's perceptions and helpful to the fact-finder.

OPM. *abbr.* Office of Personnel Management.

opponent. (16c) **1.** An adverse party in a contested matter. **2.** A party that is challenging the admissibility of evidence. • In this sense, the word is an antonym of *proponent*. **3.** *Parliamentary law.* A member who speaks against a pending motion.

opportunity. The fact that the alleged doer of an act was present at the time and place of the act.

opportunity to be heard. (17c) The chance to appear in a court or other tribunal and present evidence and argument before being deprived of a right by governmental authority. • The opportunity to be heard is a fundamental requirement of procedural due process. It ordinarily includes the right to receive fair notice of the hearing, to secure the assistance of counsel, and to cross-examine adverse witnesses.

opposition. 1. *Patents.* An action or procedure by which a third party can request a patent application's refusal or an issued patent's annulment. **2.** *Trademarks.* A procedure by which a third party can contest a trademark after it has been approved but before it has been placed on the Principal Register.

oppression. (14c) **1.** The act or an instance of unjustly exercising authority or power. **2.** An offense consisting in the abuse of discretionary authority by a public officer who has an improper motive, as a result of which a person is injured. • This offense does not include extortion, which is typically a more serious crime. **3.** *Contracts.* Coercion to enter into an illegal contract. • Oppression is grounds for the recovery of money paid or property transferred under an illegal contract. **4.** *Corporations.* Unfair treatment of minority shareholders (esp. in a close corporation) by the directors or those in control of the corporation. — **oppress,** *vb.* — **oppressive,** *adj.*

opt in, *vb.* (1966) To choose to participate in (something).

option, *n.* (17c) **1.** The right or power to choose; something that may be chosen <the lawyer was running out of options for settlement>. **2.** An offer that is included in a formal or informal contract; esp., a contractual obligation to keep an offer open for a specified period, so that the offeror cannot revoke the offer during that period <the option is valid because it is supported by consideration>. **3.** The right conveyed by such a contract <Pitts declined to exercise his option to buy the house>. **4.** The right (but not the obligation) to buy or sell a given quantity of securities, commodities, or other assets at a fixed price within a specified time <trading stock options is a speculative business>.

call option. An option to buy something (esp. securities) at a fixed price even if the market rises; the right to require another to sell.

futures option. An option to buy or sell a futures contract.

lease option. In a contract for rental property, a clause that gives the renter the right to buy the property at a fixed price, usu. at or after a fixed time.

nonforfeiture option. A policyholder's option, upon the lapse of premium payments, to continue an insurance policy for a shorter period than the original term, to surrender the policy for its cash value, to continue the policy for a reduced amount, or to take some other action rather than forfeit the policy.

option to purchase real property. A contract by which an owner of realty enters an agreement with another allowing the latter to buy the property at a specified price within a specified time, or within a reasonable time in the future, but without imposing an obligation to purchase upon the person to whom it is given.

put option. An option to sell something (esp. securities) at a fixed price even if the market declines; the right to require another to buy. — Often shortened to *put*.

settlement option. *Insurance.* A life-insurance-policy clause providing choices in the method of paying benefits to a beneficiary, as by lump-sum payment or periodic installments.

option, *vb.* (1888) To grant or take an option on (something) <Ward optioned his first screenplay to the studio for $50,000>.

option agreement. *Corporations.* A share-transfer restriction that commits the shareholder to sell, but not the corporation or other shareholders to buy, the shareholder's shares at a fixed price when a specified event occurs.

opt out, *vb.* (1922) To choose not to participate in (something) <with so many plaintiffs opting out of the class, the defendant braced itself for multiplicitous lawsuits>.

oral, *adj.* (17c) Spoken or uttered; not expressed in writing.

oral argument. (1823) An advocate's spoken presentation before a court (esp. an appellate court) supporting or opposing the legal relief at issue.

order, *n.* (16c) **1.** A command, direction, or instruction. **2.** A written direction or command delivered by a court or judge. • The word generally embraces final decrees as well as interlocutory directions or commands.

administrative order. **1.** An order issued by a government agency after an adjudicatory hearing. **2.** An agency regulation that interprets or applies a statutory provision.

antiharassment order. A type of restraining order available to victims of harassment or stalking, usu. forbidding a person to contact, surveil, or approach the victim.

dismissal order. A court order ending a lawsuit without a decision on the merits.

ex parte order (eks **pahr**-tee). (18c) An order made by the court upon the application of one party to an action without notice to the other.

filiation order. *Family law.* A court's determination of paternity, usu. including a direction to pay child support.

final order. (16c) An order that is dispositive of the entire case.

interim order. A temporary court decree that remains in effect for a specified time or until a specified event occurs.

interlocutory order (in-tər-**lok**-yə-tor-ee). (17c) An order that relates to some intermediate matter in the case; any order other than a final order.

show-cause order. (1925) An order directing a party to appear in court and explain why the party took (or failed to take) some action or why the court should or should not grant some relief.

temporary order. A court order issued during the pendency of a suit, before the final order or judgment has been entered.

ordered, adjudged, and decreed. (17c) The traditional words used to introduce a court decision <It is therefore ordered, adjudged, and decreed that Martin must return the overpayment to Hurley>.

Order of the Coif (koyf). An honorary legal organization whose members are selected on the basis of their law-school grades.

ordinance (**or**-də-nənts). (14c) An authoritative law or decree; esp., a municipal regulation. • Municipal governments can pass ordinances on matters that the state government allows to be regulated at the local level. A municipal ordinance carries the state's authority and has the same effect within the municipality's limits as a state statute.

ordinary, *adj.* (15c) **1.** Occurring in the regular course of events; normal; usual. **2.** (Of a judge) having jurisdiction by right of office rather than by delegation. **3.** (Of jurisdiction) original or immediate, as opposed to delegated.

ordinary-meaning rule. 1. The rule that when a word is not defined in a statute or other legal instrument, the court normally construes it in accordance with its ordinary or natural meaning. **2.** Plain-meaning rule.

ordinary skill in the art. *Patents.* The level of technical knowledge, experience, and expertise possessed by a typical engineer, scientist, designer, etc. in a technology that is relevant to an invention.

ore tenus (**or**-ee **tee**-nəs *or* **ten**-əs), *adv.* & *adj.* [Latin "by word of mouth"] (17c) **1.** Orally; by word of mouth; *viva voce* <pleading carried on ore tenus>. **2.** Made or presented orally <ore tenus evidence>.

ore tenus rule. (1964) The presumption that a trial court's findings of fact are correct and should not be disturbed unless clearly wrong or unjust.

organic law. (1831) **1.** The body of laws (as in a constitution) that define and establish a government; fundamental law. **2.** *Civil law.* Decisional law; caselaw.

organized crime. (1867) **1.** Widespread criminal activities that are coordinated and controlled through a central syndicate. **2.** Persons involved in these criminal activities; a syndicate of criminals who rely on their unlawful activities for income.

organized labor. 1. Workers who are affiliated by membership in a union. **2.** A union, or unions collectively, considered as a political force.

originalism. (1980) *Constitutional law.* The theory that the U.S. Constitution should be interpreted according to the intent of those who drafted and adopted it.

originality. (18c) *Copyright.* **1.** The quality or state of being the product of independent creation and having a minimum degree of creativity. • Originality is a requirement for copyright protection. But this is a lesser standard than that of novelty in patent law: to be original, a work does not have to be novel or unique. **2.** The degree to which a product claimed for copyright is the result of an author's independent efforts.

origination clause. (*often cap.*) (1984) **1.** The constitutional provision that all bills for increasing taxes and raising revenue must originate in the House of Representatives, not the Senate (U.S. Const. art. I, § 7, cl. 1). • The Senate may, however, amend revenue bills. **2.** A provision in a state constitution requiring that revenue bills originate in the lower house of the state legislature.

orphan, *n.* (15c) **1.** A child whose parents are dead. **2.** A child with one dead parent and one living parent. **3.** A child who has been deprived of parental care and has not been legally adopted; a child without a parent or guardian.

OSHA (**oh**-shə). *abbr.* **1.** Occupational Safety and Health Act of 1970. **2.** Occupational Safety and Health Administration.

OTC. *abbr.* Over-the-counter.

other-insurance clause. An insurance-policy provision that attempts to limit coverage if the insured has other coverage for the same loss. • The three major other-insurance clauses are the pro rata clause, the excess clause, and the escape clause.

other-property rule. The principle that tort recovery is unavailable if the only damage caused by a product defect is to the product itself. See *East River S.S. Corp. v. Transamerica Delaval, Inc.*, 476 U.S. 858, 106 S. Ct. 2295 (1986).

OUI. *abbr.* Operating under the influence.

our federalism. (*often cap.*) (1971) The doctrine holding that a federal court must refrain from hearing a constitutional challenge to state action if federal adjudication would be considered an improper intrusion into the state's right to enforce its own laws in its own courts.

oust, *vb.* (15c) To put out of possession; to deprive of a right or inheritance.

ouster. (16c) **1.** The wrongful dispossession or exclusion of someone (esp. a cotenant) from property (esp. real property); dispossession. **2.** The removal of a public or corporate officer from office.

outbuilding. (17c) A detached building (such as a shed or garage) within the grounds of a main building.

outcome-determinative test. (1959) *Civil procedure.* A test used to determine whether an issue is substantive for purposes of the *Erie* doctrine by examining the issue's potential effect on the outcome of the litigation.

outlaw, *n.* (bef. 12c) **1.** A person who has been deprived of the benefit and protection of the law; a person under a sentence of outlawry. **2.** A lawless person or habitual criminal; esp., a fugitive from the law. **3.** *Int'l law.* A person, organization, or nation under a ban or restriction because it is considered to be in violation of international law or custom.

outlaw, *vb.* (18c) **1.** To deprive (someone) of the benefit and protection of the law; to declare an outlaw <outlaw the fugitive>. **2.** To make illegal <outlaw fireworks within city limits>. **3.** To remove from legal jurisdiction or enforcement; to deprive of legal force <outlaw a claim under the statute>.

out-of-court, *adj.* (1950) Not done or made as part of a judicial proceeding <an out-of-court settlement>.

out of order. (18c) **1.** (Of a motion) not in order <the motion is out of order because it conflicts with the bylaws>. • A motion may be "out of order" because it is inherently inappropriate for the deliberative assembly's consideration at any time (e.g., because it proposes an unlawful action). A motion that is not appropriate simply because it is brought before the meeting at the wrong time but that may be appropriate for consideration at another time is more precisely referred to as "not in order." **2.** (Of a person) guilty of a breach of decorum or other misconduct during a meeting <the member is out of order>.

out-of-pocket rule. (1940) The principle that a defrauded buyer may recover from the seller as damages the difference between the amount paid for the property and the actual value received.

outsourcing agreement. An agreement between a business and a service provider in which the service provider promises to provide necessary services, esp. data processing and information management, using its own staff and equipment, and usu. at its own facilities.

outstanding, *adj.* (18c) **1.** Unpaid; uncollected <outstanding debts>. **2.** Publicly issued and sold <outstanding shares>.

over, *adj.* (bef. 12c) (Of a property interest) intended to take effect after the failure or termination of a prior estate; preceded by some other possessory interest <a limitation over> <a gift over>.

overage, *n.* (1909) **1.** An excess or surplus, esp. of goods or merchandise. **2.** A percentage of retail sales paid to a store's landlord in addition to fixed rent.

overbreadth doctrine. (1970) *Constitutional law.* The doctrine holding that if a statute is so broadly written that it deters free expression, then it can be struck down on its face because of its chilling effect — even if it also prohibits acts that may legitimately be forbidden. • The Supreme Court has used this doctrine to invalidate a number of laws, including those that would disallow peaceful picketing or require loyalty oaths.

overdraft. (1843) **1.** A withdrawal of money from a bank in excess of the balance on deposit. **2.** The amount of money so withdrawn. — Abbr. (in senses 1 & 2) OD; o/d. **3.** A line of credit extended by a bank to a customer (esp. an established or institutional customer) who might overdraw on an account.

overdraw, *vb.* (18c) To draw on (an account) in excess of the balance on deposit; to make an overdraft.

overhead, *n.* (1907) Business expenses (such as rent, utilities, or support-staff salaries) that cannot be allocated to a particular product or service; fixed or ordinary operating costs.

overinclusive, *adj.* (1949) (Of legislation) extending beyond the class of persons intended to be protected or regulated; burdening more persons than necessary to cure the problem <an overinclusive classification>.

overinsurance. 1. Insurance (esp. from the purchase of multiple policies) that exceeds the value of the thing insured. **2.** Excessive or needlessly duplicative insurance.

overreaching, *n.* (16c) **1.** The act or an instance of taking unfair commercial advantage of another, esp. by fraudulent means. **2.** The act or an instance of defeating one's own purpose by going too far. — **overreach,** *vb.*

override (oh-vər-**rīd**), *vb.* (14c) To prevail over; to nullify or set aside.

override (**oh**-vər-rīd), *n.* (1931) **1.** A commission paid to a manager on a sale made by a subordinate. **2.** A commission paid to a real-estate broker who listed a property when, within a reasonable amount of time after the expiration of the listing, the owner sells that property directly to a buyer with whom the broker had negotiated during the term of the listing. **3.** ROYALTY (2).

overrule, *vb.* (16c) **1.** To rule against; to reject <the judge overruled all of the defendant's objections>. **2.** (Of a court) to overturn or set aside (a precedent) by expressly deciding that it should no longer be controlling law <in *Brown v. Board of Education*, the Supreme Court overruled *Plessy v. Ferguson*>.

oversubscription. A situation in which there are more subscribers to a new issue of securities than there are securities available for purchase.

overt, *adj.* (14c) Open and observable; not concealed or secret <the conspirators' overt acts>.

overt act. (17c) *Criminal law.* **1.** An act that indicates an intent to kill or seriously harm another person and thus gives that person a justification to use self-defense. **2.** An outward act, however innocent in itself, done in furtherance of a conspiracy, treason, or criminal attempt. • An overt act is usu. a required element of these crimes.

over-the-counter, *adj.* **1.** Not listed or traded on an organized securities exchange; traded between brokers and dealers who negotiate directly <over-the-counter stocks>. **2.** (Of drugs) sold legally without a doctor's prescription <over-the-counter cough medicine>. — Abbr. OTC.

overtime. 1. The hours worked by an employee in excess of a standard day or week. • Under the Fair Labor Standards Act, employers must pay extra wages (usu. 1½ times the regular hourly rate) to certain employees (usu. nonsalaried ones) for each hour worked in excess of 40 hours per week. **2.** The extra wages paid for excess hours worked.

overtry, *vb.* (1911) (Of a trial lawyer) to try a lawsuit by expending excessive time, effort, and other resources to explore minutiae, esp. to present more evidence than the fact-trier can assimilate, the result often being that the adversary gains arguing points by disputing the minutiae.

overturn, *vb.* (1842) To overrule or reverse <the court overturned a long-established precedent>.

OWI. *abbr.* Operating while intoxicated.

owing, *adj.* (15c) That is yet to be paid; owed; due <a balance of $5,000 is still owing>.

own, *vb.* (bef. 12c) To rightfully have or possess as property; to have legal title to.

owner. (bef. 12c) One who has the right to possess, use, and convey something; a person in whom one or more interests are vested. • An owner may have complete property in the thing or may have parted with some interests in it (as by granting an easement or making a lease).

adjoining owner. (18c) A person who owns land abutting another's; abutter.

beneficial owner. (18c) **1.** One recognized in equity as the owner of something because use and title belong to that person, even though legal title may belong to someone else; esp., one for whom property is held in trust. **2.** A corporate shareholder who has the power to buy or sell the shares, but who is not registered on the corporation's books as the owner.

general owner. (18c) One who has the primary or residuary title to property; one who has the ultimate ownership of property.

legal owner. (17c) One recognized by law as the owner of something; esp., one who holds legal title to property for the benefit of another.

limited owner. (1836) A tenant for life; the owner of a life estate.

record owner. (1863) **1.** A property owner in whose name the title appears in the public records. **2.** Stockholder of record.

sole and unconditional owner. (1871) *Insurance.* The owner who has full equitable title to, and exclusive interest in, the insured property.

special owner. (18c) One (such as a bailee) with a qualified interest in property.

owners' association. (1968) **1.** The basic governing entity for a condominium or planned unit developments. • It is usu. an unincorporated association or a nonprofit corporation. **2.** Homeowners' association.

owners' equity. (1935) The aggregate of the owners' financial interests in the assets of a business entity; the capital contributed by the owners plus any retained earnings. • Owners' equity is calculated as the difference in value between a business entity's assets and its liabilities.

ownership. (16c) The bundle of rights allowing one to use, manage, and enjoy property, including the right to convey it to others. • Ownership implies the right to possess a thing, regardless of any actual or constructive control. Ownership rights are general, permanent, and heritable.

beneficial ownership. (18c) **1.** A beneficiary's interest in trust property. **2.** A corporate shareholder's power to buy or sell the shares, though the shareholder is not registered on the corporation's books as the owner.

contingent ownership. (1886) Ownership in which title is imperfect but is capable of becoming perfect on the fulfillment of some condition; conditional ownership.

corporeal ownership. (1894) The actual ownership of land or chattels.

incorporeal ownership. (1931) The ownership of rights in land or chattels.

joint ownership. (18c) Undivided ownership shared by two or more persons. • Typically, an owner's interest, at death, passes to the surviving owner or owners by virtue of the right of survivorship.

ownership in common. (1838) Ownership shared by two or more persons whose interests are divisible. • Typically their interests, at death, pass to the dead owner's heirs or successors.

qualified ownership. (18c) Ownership that is shared, restricted to a particular use, or limited in the extent of its enjoyment.

trust ownership. (1893) A trustee's interest in trust property.

vested ownership. (1867) Ownership in which title is perfect.

oyer (**oy**-ər *or* **oh**-yər). [fr. Old French *oïr* "to hear"] (15c) *Hist.* **1.** A criminal trial held under a commission of oyer and terminer. **2.** The reading in open court of a document (esp. a deed) that is demanded by one party and read by the other. **3.** *Common-law pleading.* A prayer to the court by a party opposing a profert, asking to have the instrument on which the opponent relies read aloud.

oyer and terminer (**oy**-ər an[d] **tər**-mə-nər). [Law French *oyer et terminer* "to hear and determine"] (15c) **1.** Commission of Oyer and Terminer. **2.** Court of Oyer And Terminer.

oyez (**oh**-yes *or* **oh**-yez *or* **oh**-yay). [Law French] (15c) Hear ye. • The utterance *oyez, oyez, oyez* is usu. used in court by the public crier to call the courtroom to order when a session begins or when a proclamation is about to be made.

P

P. *abbr. Pacific Reporter.*

P.A. *abbr.* Professional association.

PAC (pak). *abbr.* Political-action committee.

PACER. *abbr.* Public Access to Court Electronic Records.

Pacific Reporter. A set of regional lawbooks, part of the West Group's National Reporter System, containing every officially published appellate decision from Alaska, Arizona, California, Colorado, Hawaii, Idaho, Kansas, Montana, Nevada, New Mexico, Oklahoma, Oregon, Utah, Washington, and Wyoming, from 1883 to date. • The first series ran from 1883 to 1931; the second series ran until 2000; the third series is the current one. — Abbr. P.; P.2d; P.3d.

pack, *vb.* (16c) To choose or arrange (a tribunal, jurors, etc.) to accomplish a desired result <pack a jury>.

packing, *n.* A gerrymandering technique in which a dominant political or racial group minimizes minority representation by concentrating the minority into as few districts as possible.

pact. (15c) An agreement between two or more parties; esp., an agreement (such as a treaty) between two or more nations or governmental entities.

pad, *vb.* (1831) *Slang.* (Of a lawyer, paralegal, etc.) to overstate the number of (billable hours worked). — **padding,** *n.*

pain and suffering. (1825) Physical discomfort or emotional distress compensable as an element of noneconomic damages in torts.

palimony (**pal**-ə-moh-nee). [Portmanteau word from *pal* + *alimony*] (1977) A court's award of post-relationship support or compensation for services, money, and goods contributed during a long-term nonmarital relationship, esp. where a common-law marriage cannot be established. The term originated in the press coverage of *Marvin v. Marvin*, 557 P.2d 106 (Cal. 1976).

***Palsgraf* rule** (**pawlz**-graf). (1932) *Torts.* The principle that negligent conduct resulting in injury will lead to liability only if the actor could have reasonably foreseen that the conduct would cause the injury. • In *Palsgraf v. Long Island R.R.*, 162 N.E. 99 (N.Y. 1928), two railroad attendants negligently dislodged a package of fireworks from a man they were helping board a train. The package exploded on impact and knocked over some scales that fell on Mrs. Palsgraf. The New York Court of Appeals, in a 4–3 majority opinion written by Chief Justice Benjamin Cardozo, held that the attendants could not have foreseen the possibility of injury to Palsgraf and therefore did not breach any duty to her. In the dissenting opinion, Justice William S. Andrews asserted that the duty to exercise care is owed to all, and thus a negligent act will subject the actor to liability to all persons proximately harmed by it, whether or not the harm is foreseeable. Both opinions have been widely cited to support the two views expressed in them.

pander, *n.* (15c) One who engages in pandering.

pandering (**pan**-dər-ing), *n.* (17c) **1.** The act or offense of recruiting a prostitute, finding a place of business for a prostitute, or soliciting customers for a prostitute. **2.** The act or offense of selling or distributing textual or visual material (such as magazines or videotapes) openly advertised to appeal to the recipient's sexual interest. — **pander,** *vb.*

P & L. *abbr.* Profit and loss.

panel. (14c) **1.** A list of persons summoned as potential jurors; venire. **2.** A group of persons selected to serve on a jury; jury. **3.** A set of judges selected from a complete court to decide a specific case; esp., a group of three judges designated to sit for an appellate court.

panelation (pan-əl-**ay**-shən). (2003) The act of empaneling a jury.

panel-shopping. (1974) The practice of choosing the most favorable group of judges to hear an appeal.

panhandling. The act or practice of approaching or stopping strangers and begging for money or food. — **panhandler,** *n.* — **panhandle,** *vb.*

paper. (14c) **1.** Any written or printed document or instrument. **2.** A negotiable document or instrument evidencing a debt; esp., commercial documents or negotiable instruments considered as a group. **3.** (*pl.*) Court papers.

bankable paper. Notes, checks, bank bills, drafts, and other instruments received as cash by banks.

bearer paper. An instrument payable to the person who holds it rather than to the order of a specific person. • Bearer paper is negotiated simply by delivering the instrument to a transferee.

commercial paper. **1.** An instrument, other than cash, for the payment of money. • Commercial paper — typically existing in the form of a draft (such as a check) or a note (such as a certificate of deposit) — is governed by Article 3 of the UCC. But even though the UCC uses the term *commercial paper* when referring to negotiable instruments of a particular kind (drafts, checks, certificates of deposit, and notes as defined by Article 3), the term long predates the UCC as a business and legal term in common use. Before the UCC, it was generally viewed as synonymous with *negotiable paper* or *bills and notes.* It was sometimes applied even to nonnegotiable instruments. **2.** Such instruments collectively. **3.** Loosely, a short-term unsecured promissory note, usu. issued and sold by one company to meet another company's immediate cash needs.

paper standard. A monetary system based entirely on paper; a system of currency that is not convertible into gold or other precious metal.

parajudge. United States Magistrate Judge.

paralegal, *n.* (1967) A person who has some education in law and assists a lawyer in duties related to the practice of law but who is not a licensed attorney. — **paralegal,** *adj.*

paralegalize, *vb. Slang.* To proofread, cite-check, and otherwise double-check the details in (a legal document).

parcel, *n.* (15c) **1.** A small package or bundle. **2.** A tract of land; esp., a continuous tract or plot of land in one possession, no part of which is separated from the rest by intervening land in another's possession.

parcel, *vb.* (15c) To divide and distribute (goods, land, etc.).

pardon, *n.* (14c) The act or an instance of officially nullifying punishment or other legal consequences of a crime. • A pardon is usu. granted by the chief executive of a government. — **pardon,** *vb.*

parens patriae (**par**-enz **pay**-tree-ee *or* **pa**-tree-ɪ). [Latin "parent of his or her country"] (18c) **1.** *Roman law.* The emperor as the embodiment of the state. **2.** The state regarded as a sovereign; the state in its capacity as provider of protection to those unable to care for themselves <the attorney general acted as *parens patriae* in the administrative hearing>. **3.** A doctrine by which a government has standing to prosecute a lawsuit on behalf of a citizen, esp. on behalf of someone who is under a legal disability to prosecute the suit <*parens* *patriae* allowed the state to institute proceedings>. • The state ordinarily has no standing to sue on behalf of its citizens, unless a separate, sovereign interest will be served by the suit.

parent. (15c) The lawful father or mother of someone. • In ordinary usage, the term denotes more than responsibility for conception and birth. The term commonly includes (1) either the natural father or the natural mother of a child, (2) either the adoptive father or the adoptive mother of a child, (3) a child's putative blood parent who has expressly acknowledged paternity, and (4) an individual or agency whose status as guardian has been established by judicial decree.

adoptive parent. (18c) A parent by virtue of legal adoption.

biological parent. The woman who provides the egg or the man who provides the sperm to form the zygote that grows into an embryo.

birth parent. Either the biological father or the mother who gives birth to a child.

custodial parent. The parent awarded physical custody of a child in a divorce.

de facto parent. An adult who (1) is not the child's legal parent, (2) has, with consent of the child's legal parent, resided with the child for a significant period, and (3) has routinely performed a share of the caretaking functions at least as great as that of the parent who has been the child's primary caregiver without any expectation of compensation for this care.

foster parent. (17c) An adult who, though without blood ties or legal ties, cares for and rears a child, esp. an orphaned or neglected child who might otherwise be deprived of nurture, usu. under the auspices and direction of an agency and for some compensation or benefit.

noncustodial parent. In the child-custody laws of some states, a parent without the primary custody rights of a child; esp., the parent not awarded physical custody of a child in a divorce. • The noncustodial parent is typically awarded visitation with the child.

surrogate parent. (1972) **1.** A person who carries out the role of a parent by court appointment or the voluntary assumption of parental responsibilities. **2.** Surrogate mother.

parental-autonomy doctrine. The principle that a parent has a fundamental right to raise his or her child and to make all decisions regarding that child free from governmental intervention, unless (1) the child's health and welfare are jeopardized by the parent's decisions, or (2) public health, welfare, safety, and order are threatened by the parent's decisions. • The Supreme Court first recognized the doctrine of parental autonomy over the family in *Meyer v. Nebraska*, 262 U.S. 390, 43 S.Ct. 625 (1923).

parental-consent statute. A statute that requires a minor to obtain his or her parent's consent before receiving elective medical treatment, such as an abortion. • Without parental consent, a physician or other medical professional commits a battery upon a child when giving nonemergency medical treatment. To pass constitutional muster, a parental-consent statute must include a judicial-bypass provision. *Planned Parenthood of Southeastern Pa. v. Casey*, 505 U.S. 833, 112 S. Ct. 2791 (1992).

parental-discipline privilege. A parent's right to use reasonable force or to impose reasonable punishment on a child in a way that is necessary to control, train, and educate. • Several factors are used to determine the reasonableness of the action, including whether the actor is the parent; the child's age, sex, and physical and mental state; the severity and foreseeable consequences of the punishment; and the nature of the misconduct.

parent-alienation syndrome. A situation in which one parent has manipulated a child to fear or hate the other parent; a condition resulting from a parent's actions that are designed to poison a child's relationship with the other parent.

Parental Kidnapping Prevention Act. A federal law, enacted in 1980, providing a penalty for child-kidnapping by a noncustodial parent and requiring states to recognize and enforce a child-custody order rendered by a court of another state. 28 USCA § 1738A; 42 USCA §§ 654, 655, 663. — Abbr. PKPA.

parental-liability statute. (1963) A law obliging parents to pay damages for torts (esp. intentional ones) committed by their minor children. • All states have these laws, but most limit the parents' monetary liability to about $3,000 per tort.

parental-notification statute. A law that requires a physician to notify a minor's parent of her intention to have an abortion.

parental-preference doctrine. (1974) The principle that custody of a minor child should ordinarily be granted to a fit parent rather than another person. • The preference can be rebutted by proof that the child's best interests are to the contrary.

parental-privilege doctrine. The parent's right to discipline his or her child reasonably, to use reasonable child-rearing practices free of governmental interference, and to exercise decision-making authority over the child.

parental-responsibility statute. (1956) **1.** A law imposing criminal sanctions (such as fines) on parents whose minor children commit crimes as a result of the parents' failure to exercise sufficient control over them. **2.** Parental-liability statute.

parental rights. (18c) A parent's rights to make all decisions concerning his or her child, including the right to determine the child's care and custody, the right to educate and discipline the child, and the right to control the child's earnings and property.

parentela (par-ən-**tee**-lə), *n. pl.* [Law Latin] (15c) Persons who can trace descent from a common ancestor.

parentelic method (par-ən-**tee**-lik *or* -**tel**-ik). (1935) A scheme of computation used to determine the paternal or maternal collaterals entitled to inherit when a childless intestate decedent is not survived by parents or their issue. • Under this method, the estate passes to grandparents and their issue; if there are none, to great-grandparents and their issue; and so on down each line until an heir is found.

parenticide (pə-**ren**-tə-sɪd). (17c) **1.** The act of murdering one's parent. **2.** A person who murders his or her parent. — **parenticidal,** *adj.*

parenting plan. A plan that allocates custodial responsibility and decision-making authority for what serves the child's best interests and that provides a mechanism for resolving any later disputes between parents.

parimutuel betting (par-i-**myoo**-choo-əl). A system of gambling in which bets placed on a race are pooled and then paid (less a management fee and taxes) to those holding winning tickets.

parliament. (12c) The supreme legislative body of some nations; esp. (*cap.*), in the United Kingdom, the national legislature consisting of the monarch, the House of Lords, and the House of Commons.

parliamentarian. (17c) *Parliamentary law.* A consultant trained in parliamentary law who advises the chair and others on matters of parliamentary law and procedure. • The parliamentarian, who is often a professional, only advises and never "rules" on procedural issues.

parliamentary law. The body of rules and precedents governing the proceedings of legislative bodies and other deliberative assemblies.

parliamentary procedure. 1. Parliamentary law. **2.** Parliamentary law as applied in a particular organization, including the parliamentary authority and other rules that the organization adopts.

parody. (16c) *Intellectual property.* A transformative use of a well-known work for purposes of satirizing, ridiculing, critiquing, or commenting on the original work, as opposed to merely alluding to the original to draw attention to the later work. • In constitutional law, a parody is protected as free speech. In copyright law, a work must meet the definition of a parody and be a fair use of the copyrighted material, or else it may constitute infringement.

parol (pə-**rohl** *or* **par**-əl), *adj.* (16c) **1.** Oral; unwritten <parol evidence>. **2.** Not under seal <parol contract>.

parol (pə-**rohl** *or* **par**-əl), *n.* (15c) An oral statement or declaration.

parole (pə-**rohl**), *n.* (17c) The conditional release of a prisoner from imprisonment before the full sentence has been served. — **parole,** *vb.* — **parolee** (pə-roh-**lee**), *n.* (1903).

parole board. (1898) A governmental body that decides whether prisoners may be released from prison before completing their sentences.

parole revocation. (1930) The administrative or judicial act of returning a parolee to prison because of the parolee's failure to abide by the conditions of parole (as by committing a new offense).

parol-evidence rule. (1893) *Contracts.* The common-law principle that a writing intended by the parties to be a final embodiment of their agreement cannot be modified by evidence of earlier or contemporaneous agreements that might add to, vary, or contradict the writing.

***Parratt–Hudson* doctrine.** (1986) The principle that a state actor's random, unauthorized deprivation of someone's property does not amount to a due-process violation if the state provides an adequate postdeprivation remedy. *Parratt v. Taylor,* 451 U.S. 527, 101 S.Ct. 1908 (1984); *Hudson v. Palmer,* 468 U.S. 517, 104 S.Ct. 3194 (1984).

parricide (**par**-ə-sɪd), *n.* (16c) **1.** The act of killing a close relative, esp. a parent. **2.** One who kills such a relative. — **parricidal,** *adj.*

particeps (**pahr**-tə-seps), *n.* [Latin] **1.** A participant. **2.** A part owner.

particeps criminis (**pahr**-tə-seps **krim**-ə-nis), *n.* [Latin "partner in crime"] (17c) **1.** An accomplice or accessory. Pl. ***participes criminis*** (pahr-**tis**-ə-peez). **2.** The doctrine that one participant in an unlawful activity cannot recover in a civil action against another participant in the activity. • This is a civil doctrine only, having nothing to do with criminal responsibility.

particulars of sale. (18c) A document that describes the various features of a thing (such as a house) that is for sale.

partition, *n.* (15c) **1.** Something that separates one part of a space from another. **2.** The act of dividing; esp., the division of real property held jointly or in common by two or more persons into individually owned interests. — **partition,** *vb.* — **partible,** *adj.*

partner. (13c) **1.** One who shares or takes part with another, esp. in a venture with shared benefits and shared risks; an associate or colleague. **2.** One of two or more persons who jointly own and carry on a business for profit. **3.** One of two persons who are married or who live together; a spouse or companion.

general partner. (1804) A partner who ordinarily takes part in the daily operations of the business, shares in the profits and losses, and is personally responsible for the partnership's debts and other liabilities.

junior partner. (18c) A partner whose participation is limited with respect to both profits and management.

limited partner. (1822) A partner who receives profits from the business but does not take part in managing the business and is not liable for any amount greater than his or her original investment.

liquidating partner. (1825) The partner appointed to settle the accounts, collect the assets, adjust the claims, and pay the debts of a dissolving or insolvent firm.

name partner. (1945) A partner whose name appears in the name of the partnership.

nominal partner. (18c) A person who is held out as a partner in a firm or business but who has no actual interest in the partnership.

quasi-partner. (1809) A person who joins others in an enterprise that appears to be, but is not, a partnership. • A joint venturer, for example, is a quasi-partner.

secret partner. (18c) A partner whose connection with the firm is concealed from the public.

senior partner. (18c) A high-ranking partner, as in a law firm.

silent partner. (18c) A partner who shares in the profits but who has no active voice in management of the firm and whose existence is often not publicly disclosed.

surviving partner. (17c) The partner who, upon the partnership's dissolution because of another partner's death, serves as a trustee to administer the firm's remaining affairs.

partnership. (16c) A voluntary association of two or more persons who jointly own and carry on a business for profit. • Under the Uniform Partnership Act, a partnership is presumed to exist if the persons agree to share proportionally the business's profits or losses.

collapsible partnership. (1962) *Tax.* A partnership formed by partners who intend to dissolve it before they realize any income. IRC (26 USCA) § 751.

family partnership. (1902) A business partnership in which the partners are related. IRC (26 USCA) § 704(e).

general partnership. (18c) A partnership in which all partners participate fully in running the business and share equally in profits and losses (though the partners' monetary contributions may vary).

limited-liability partnership. (1910) A partnership in which a partner is not liable for a negligent act committed by another partner or by an employee not under the partner's supervision. — Abbr. L.L.P.

limited partnership. (18c) A partnership composed of one or more persons who control the business and are personally liable for the partnership's debts (called *general partners*), and one or more persons who contribute capital and share profits but who cannot manage the business and are liable only for the amount of their contribution (called *limited partners*). — Abbr. L.P.

partnership at will. (1849) A partnership that any partner may dissolve at any time without thereby incurring liability.

partnership by estoppel. (1872) A partnership implied by law when one or more persons represent themselves as partners to a third party who relies on that representation. • A person who is deemed a partner by estoppel becomes liable for any credit extended to the partnership by the third party.

partnership for a term. A partnership that exists for a specified duration or until a specified event occurs.

publicly traded partnership. A partnership whose interests are traded either over-the-counter or on a securities exchange. • These partnerships may be treated as corporations for income-tax purposes. IRC (26 USCA) § 7704(a). — Abbr. PTP.

partnership agreement. (1802) A contract defining the partners' rights and duties toward one another — not the partners' relationship with third parties.

partnership association. (1812) A business organization that combines the features of a limited partnership and a close corporation. • Partnership associations are statutorily authorized in only a few states.

partner's lien. (1870) A partner's right to have the partnership property applied in payment of the partnership's debts and to have whatever is due the firm from fellow partners deducted from what would otherwise be payable to them for their shares.

part-performance doctrine. (1935) The equitable principle by which a failure to comply with the statute of frauds is overcome by a party's execution, in reliance on an opposing party's oral promise, of a substantial portion of an oral contract's requirements.

party. (13c) **1.** One who takes part in a transaction <a party to the contract>.

party of the first part. (18c) *Archaic.* The party named first in a contract; esp., the owner or seller.

party of the second part. (18c) *Archaic.* The party named second in a contract; esp., the buyer.

2. One by or against whom a lawsuit is brought <a party to the lawsuit>.

adverse party. (15c) A party whose interests are opposed to the interests of another party to the action.

aggrieved party. (17c) A party entitled to a remedy; esp., a party whose personal, pecuniary, or property rights have been adversely affected by another person's actions or by a court's decree or judgment.

fictitious party. A person who is named in a writ, complaint, or record as a party in a suit, but who does not actually exist, or a person who is named as a plaintiff but is unaware of the suit and did not consent to be named.

indispensable party. (1821) A party who, having interests that would inevitably be affected by a court's judgment, must be included in the case. • If such a party is not included, the case must be dismissed. Fed. R. Civ. P. 19(b).

innocent party. (16c) A party who did not consciously or intentionally participate in an event or transaction.

interested party. (17c) A party who has a recognizable stake (and therefore standing) in a matter.

necessary party. (18c) A party who, being closely connected to a lawsuit, should be included in the case if feasible, but whose absence will not require dismissal of the proceedings.

nominal party. (18c) A party to an action who has no control over it and no financial interest in its outcome; esp., a party who has some immaterial interest in the subject matter of a lawsuit and who will not be affected by any judgment, but who is nonetheless joined in the lawsuit to avoid procedural defects. • An example is the disinterested stakeholder in a garnishment action.

party opponent. (18c) An adversary in a legal proceeding.

party to be charged. (1923) A defendant in an action to enforce a contract falling within the statute of frauds.

prevailing party. (17c) A party in whose favor a judgment is rendered, regardless of the amount of damages awarded.

proper party. (1823) A party who may be joined in a case for reasons of judicial economy but whose presence is not essential to the proceeding.

real party in interest. (1804) A person entitled under the substantive law to enforce the right sued upon and who generally, but not necessarily, benefits from the action's final outcome.

3. POLITICAL PARTY.

par value. The value of an instrument or security as shown on its face; esp., the arbitrary dollar amount assigned to a stock share by the corporate charter, or the principal of a bond at maturity.

pass, *vb.* (14c) **1.** To pronounce or render an opinion, ruling, sentence, or judgment <the court refused to pass on the constitutional issue, deciding the case instead on procedural grounds>. **2.** To transfer or be transferred <the woman's will passes title to the house to her nephew, much to her husband's surprise>. **3.** To enact (a legislative bill or resolution); to adopt <Congress has debated whether to pass a balanced-budget amendment to the Constitution>. **4.** To approve or certify (something) as meeting specified requirements <the mechanic informed her that the car had passed inspection>. **5.** To publish, transfer, or circulate (a thing, often a forgery) <he was found guilty of passing counterfeit bills>. **6.** To forgo or proceed beyond <the case was passed on the court's trial docket because the judge was presiding over a criminal trial>. **7.** Abstain.

passim (**pas**-im), *adv.* [Latin] (17c) Here and there; throughout (the cited work). • In modern legal writing, the citation signal *see generally* is preferred to *passim* as a general reference, although *passim* can be useful in a brief's index of authorities to show that a given authority is cited throughout the brief.

passing off, *n.* (1900) *Intellectual property.* The act or an instance of falsely representing one's own product as that of another in an attempt to deceive potential buyers. — **pass off,** *vb.*

reverse passing off. The act or an instance of falsely representing another's product as one's own in an attempt to deceive potential buyers.

passive, *adj.* Not involving active participation; esp., of or relating to a business enterprise in which an investor does not have immediate control over the activity that produces income.

passive activity. (1962) *Tax.* A business activity in which the taxpayer does not materially participate and therefore does not have immediate control over the income.

pass-through, *adj.* (1951) (Of a seller's or lessor's costs) chargeable to the buyer or lessee.

past recollection recorded. *Evidence.* A document concerning events that a witness once knew about but can no longer remember. • The document itself is evidence and, despite being hearsay, may be admitted and read into the record if it was prepared or adopted by the witness when the events were fresh in the witness's memory. Fed. R. Evid. 803(5).

***Pate* hearing.** A proceeding in which the trial court seeks to determine whether a criminal defendant is competent to stand trial. *Pate v. Robinson*, 383 U.S. 375, 86 S.Ct. 836 (1966); 18 USCA § 4241.

patent (**pay**-tənt), *adj.* (14c) Obvious; apparent <a patent ambiguity>.

patent (**pat**-ənt), *n.* (14c) **1.** The governmental grant of a right, privilege, or authority. **2.** The official document so granting. **3.** The right to exclude others from making, using, marketing, selling, offering for sale, or importing an invention for a specified period (20 years from the date of filing), granted by the federal government to the inventor if the device or process is novel, useful, and nonobvious. 35 USCA §§ 101–103.

blocking patent. One of two patents, neither of which can be effectively practiced without infringing the other.

business-method patent. A U.S. patent that describes and claims a series of process steps that, as a whole, constitutes a method of doing business.

combination patent. A patent granted for an invention that unites existing components in a novel and nonobvious way.

Community patent. An international patent issued by the European Patent Office.

cyberpatent. **1.** Business-method patent. **2.** Internet patent.

design patent. A patent granted for a new, original, and ornamental design for an article of manufacture; a patent that protects a product's appearance or nonfunctional aspects. 36 USCA § 171.

fencing patent. A patent procured for some aspect of an invention that the inventor does not intend to produce but that the inventor wants to prevent competitors from using in making improvements.

improvement patent. A patent having claims directed to an improvement on a preexisting invention.

Internet patent. A type of utility patent granted on an invention that combines business methods and software programs for Internet applications.

method patent. A patent having method or process claims that define a series of actions leading to a tangible physical result.

paper patent. A patent granted for a discovery or invention that has never been used commercially.

pioneer patent. A patent covering a function or a major technological advance never before performed, a wholly novel device, or subject matter of such novelty and importance as to mark a distinct step in the progress of the art, as distinguished from a mere improvement or perfection of what had gone before.

plant patent. A patent granted for the invention or discovery of a new and distinct variety of asexually reproducing plant. 36 USCA § 161.

process patent. A patent for a method of treating specified materials to produce a certain result; a patent outlining a means of producing a physical result independently of the producing mechanism.

submarine patent. *Slang.* A patent that is delayed in prosecution by the applicant in order to let an infringing user continue to develop its business, with the intention of taking in later-invented technology once the patent finally "surfaces" from the U.S. Patent and Trademark Office.

utility patent. A patent granted for one of the following types of inventions: a process, a machine, a manufacture, or a composition of matter (such as a new chemical). • Utility patents are the most commonly issued patents. 35 USCA § 101.

patentable subject matter. Things that by law can be patented; any machine, process, manufacture, or material composition, or an improvement to such things, that (1) is discovered or invented, (2) is new and useful, and (3) meets the statutory conditions and requirements to qualify for a patent. • Patents may be issued for "any new and useful process, machine, manufacture, or composition of matter, or any new and useful improvement thereof." 35 USCA § 101. Patents may not be issued for laws of nature, naturally occurring materials, physical phenomena, or abstract ideas and formulas. But if a naturally occurring material is processed in a way that gives it a new use, that process may be patentable.

Patent Act. The current federal statute governing patent registrations and rights, enacted in 1952. 35 USCA §§ 1 et seq. • The Act reversed several Supreme Court doctrines of patentability by eliminating the synergism and "flash of genius" requirements for combination patents (§ 103), making "means-plus-function" claims valid once again (§ 112), and narrowing the patent-misuse doctrine of contributory infringement (§ 271).

Patent and Copyright Clause. (1929) The constitutional provision granting Congress the authority to promote the advancement of science and the arts by establishing a national system for patents and copyrights. U.S. Const. art. I, § 8, cl. 8.

Patent and Trademark Office. The Department of Commerce agency that examines patent and trademark applications, issues patents, registers trademarks, and furnishes patent and trademark information and services to the public. — Abbr. PTO.

patent attorney. A lawyer who drafts and prosecutes patent applications, and who represents inventors in infringement suits and interference hearings. • In addition to a law license, a patent attorney must have a scientific or technical background, pass the patent bar examination, and be licensed by the U.S. Patent and Trademark Office.

patent claim. A formal statement describing the novel features of an invention and defining the scope of the patent's protection <claim #3 of the patent describes an electrical means for driving a metal pin>.

patentee (pat-ən-**tee**). One who either has been granted a patent or has succeeded in title to a patent. • Although it might seem helpful to distinguish a patentee as a person to whom a patent is issued and a patent-holder as the owner of a patent, including the original grantee's assigns, the Patent Act explicitly includes all title-holders under the term "patentee." 35 USCA § 100(d).

patent medicine. A packaged drug that is protected by trademark and is available without prescription.

patent-misuse doctrine. An equitable rule that patentees should not be allowed to use their patent to effectively broaden the scope of their monopoly in restraint of trade or otherwise against the public interest.

patent pending. (1917) The designation given to an invention while the Patent and Trademark Office is processing the patent application. • No protection against infringement exists, however, unless an actual patent is granted.

paternal, *adj.* (15c) Of, relating to, or coming from one's father <paternal property>.

paternalism, *n.* (1873) A government's policy or practice of taking responsibility for the individual affairs of its citizens, esp. by supplying their needs or regulating their conduct in a heavy-handed manner. — **paternalistic,** *adj.*

paternity (pə-**tər**-ni-tee). (15c) The state or condition of being a father, esp. a biological one; fatherhood.

paternity suit. (1945) A court proceeding to determine whether a person is the father of a child (esp. one born out of wedlock), usu. initiated by the mother in an effort to obtain child support.

paternity test. (1926) A test, usu. involving DNA identification or tissue-typing, for determining whether a given man is the biological father of a particular child.

pathology (pə-**thol**-ə-jee), *n.* (17c) The branch of medical study that examines the origins, symptoms, and nature of diseases. — **pathological** (path-ə-**loj**-i-kəl), *adj.* — **pathologist** (pə-**thol**-ə-jist), *n.*

patient-litigant exception. (1951) An exemption from the doctor–patient privilege, whereby the privilege is lost when the patient sues the doctor for malpractice.

patient's bill of rights. (1973) A general statement of patient rights voluntarily adopted by a healthcare provider or mandated by statute, covering such matters as access to care, patient dignity and confidentiality, personal safety, consent to treatment, and explanation of charges.

patricide (**pa**-trə-sɪd), *n.* (16c) **1.** The act of killing one's own father. **2.** One who kills his or her father. — **patricidal,** *adj.*

patrimony (**pa**-trə-moh-nee). (14c) An estate inherited from one's father or other ancestor; legacy or heritage.

Patriot Act. USA Patriot Act.

patron. (15c) **1.** A regular customer or client of a business. **2.** A licensee invited or permitted to enter leased land for the purpose for which it is leased. **3.** A person who protects or supports some person or thing.

patronage (**pay**-trə-nij). (16c) **1.** The giving of support, sponsorship, or protection. **2.** All the customers of a business; clientele. **3.** The power to appoint persons to governmental positions or to confer other political favors.

patronizing a prostitute. (1956) The offense of requesting or securing the performance of a sex act for a fee; prostitution.

pattern, *n.* (1883) A mode of behavior or series of acts that are recognizably consistent <a pattern of racial discrimination>.

pattern of racketeering activity. (1972) Two or more related criminal acts that amount to, or pose a threat of, continued criminal activity.

pattern-or-practice case. A lawsuit, often a class action, in which the plaintiff attempts to show that the defendant has systematically engaged in discriminatory activities, esp. by means of policies and procedures. • Typically, such a case involves employment discrimination, housing discrimination, or school segregation. A plaintiff must usu. show that a defendant's behavior forms a pattern of actions or is embedded in routine practices but inferences of executive or official complicity may be drawn from a consistent failure to respond to complaints or implement corrective measures.

pauper. (16c) A very poor person, esp. one who receives aid from charity or public funds; indigent.

pawn, *n.* (15c) **1.** An item of personal property deposited as security for a debt; a pledge or guarantee. • In modern usage, the term is usu. restricted to the pledge of jewels and other personal chattels to pawnbrokers as security for a small loan. **2.** The act of depositing personal property in this manner. **3.** The condition of being held on deposit as a pledge. **4.** Pignus. — **pawn,** *vb.*

pawnbroker, *n.* One who lends money, usu. at a high interest rate, in exchange for personal property that is deposited as security by the borrower. — **pawnbroking,** *n.*

payable, *adj.* (14c) (Of a sum of money or a negotiable instrument) that is to be paid. • An amount may be payable without being due.

payable after sight. (18c) Payable after acceptance or protest of nonacceptance.

payable on demand. (17c) Payable when presented or upon request for payment; payable at any time.

payable to bearer. (18c) Payable to anyone holding the instrument.

payable to order. (17c) Payable only to a specified payee.

payee. (18c) One to whom money is paid or payable; esp., a party named in commercial paper as the recipient of the payment.

payment. (14c) **1.** Performance of an obligation by the delivery of money or some other valuable thing accepted in partial or full discharge of the obligation. **2.** The money or other valuable thing so delivered in satisfaction of an obligation.

advance payment. (16c) A payment made in anticipation of a contingent or fixed future liability or obligation.

balloon payment. (1935) A final loan payment that is usu. much larger than the preceding regular payments and that discharges the principal balance of the loan.

conditional payment. (17c) Payment of an obligation only on condition that something be done. • Generally, the payor reserves the right to demand the payment back if the condition is not met.

constructive payment. (1827) A payment made by the payor but not yet credited by the payee. • For example, a rent check mailed on the first of the month is a constructive payment even though the landlord does not deposit the check until ten days later.

direct payment. (18c) **1.** A payment made directly to the payee, without using an intermediary, such as a child-support payment made directly to the obligee parent rather than through the court. **2.** A payment that is absolute and unconditional on the amount, the due date, and the payee.

down payment. (1926) The portion of a purchase price paid in cash (or its equivalent) at the time the sale agreement is executed.

installment payment. One of a series of periodic payments made under an installment plan.

involuntary payment. (18c) A payment obtained by fraud or duress.

lump-sum payment. (1914) A payment of a large amount all at once, as opposed to a series of smaller payments over time.

payment in due course. (1816) A payment to the holder of a negotiable instrument at or after its maturity date, made by the payor in good faith and without notice of any defect in the holder's title.

payment into court. (1829) A party's money or property deposited with a court for distribution after a proceeding according to the parties' settlement or the court's order.

payola (pay-**oh**-lə). (1937) An indirect and secret payment for a favor, esp. one relating to business; a bribe.

payor. (16c) One who pays; esp., a person responsible for paying a negotiable instrument.

payroll. 1. A list of employees to be paid and the amount due to each of them. **2.** The total compensation payable to a company's employees for one pay period.

PBS. *abbr.* **1.** Public Buildings Service. **2.** Public Broadcasting Service.

P.C. *abbr.* **1.** Professional corporation. **2.** Political correctness.

P.D. *abbr.* **1.** Public defender. **2.** Police department.

peace officer. A civil officer (such as a sheriff or police officer) appointed to maintain public tranquility and order; esp., a person designated by public authority to keep the peace and arrest persons guilty or suspected of crime.

peacetime. A period in which a country has declared neither a war nor a national emergency, even if the country is involved in a conflict or quasi-conflict.

peculation (pek-yə-**lay**-shən), *n.* (17c) Embezzlement, esp. by a public official. — **peculate** (**pek**-yə-layt), *vb.* — **peculative** (**pek**-yə-lə-tiv), *adj.* — **peculator** (**pek**-yə-lay-tər), *n.*

peculiar-risk doctrine. (1958) The principle that an employer will be liable for injury caused by an independent contractor if the employer failed to take reasonable precautions against a risk that is peculiar to the contractor's work and that the employer should have recognized.

pecuniary (pi-**kyoo**-nee-er-ee), *adj.* (16c) Of or relating to money; monetary.

pederasty (**ped**-ər-as-tee), *n.* (17c) Anal intercourse between a man and a boy. • Pederasty is illegal in all states. — **pederast** (**ped**-ə-rast), *n.*

pedophilia. (1906) **1.** A sexual disorder consisting in the desire for sexual gratification by molesting children, esp. prepubescent children. **2.** An adult's act of child molestation. • Pedophilia can but does not necessarily involve intercourse. The American Psychiatric Association applies both senses to perpetrators who are at least 16 years old and at least five years older than their victims. — **pedophile,** *n.*

Peeping Tom. (18c) A person who spies on another (as through a window), usu. for sexual pleasure; voyeur.

peer, *n.* **1.** A person who is of equal status, rank, or character with another. **2.** A member of the British nobility. — **peerage** (**peer**-ij), *n.*

peer-reviewed journal. (1980) A publication whose practice is to forward submitted articles to disinterested experts who screen them for scholarly or scientific reliability so that articles actually published have already withstood expert scrutiny and comment.

peer-review organization. (1978) A governmental agency that monitors health-regulation compliance by private hospitals requesting public funds (such as Medicare payments). — Abbr. PRO.

penal (**pee**-nəl), *adj.* (15c) Of, relating to, or being a penalty or punishment, esp. for a crime.

penal code. (18c) A compilation of criminal laws, usu. defining and categorizing the offenses and setting forth their respective punishments.

penalty. (15c) **1.** Punishment imposed on a wrongdoer, usu. in the form of imprisonment or fine; esp., a sum of money exacted as punishment for either a wrong to the state or a civil wrong (as distinguished from compensation for the injured party's loss). • Though usu. for crimes, penalties are also sometimes imposed for civil wrongs.

civil penalty. (17c) A fine assessed for a violation of a statute or regulation.

statutory penalty. (18c) A penalty imposed for a statutory violation; esp., a penalty imposing automatic liability on a wrongdoer for violation of a statute's terms without reference to any actual damages suffered.

2. An extra charge against a party who violates a contractual provision.

prepayment penalty. (1948) A charge assessed against a borrower who elects to pay off a loan before it is due.

3. Excessive stipulated damages that a contract purports to impose on a party that breaches. • If the damages are excessive enough to be considered a penalty, a court will usu. not enforce that particular provision of the contract. Some contracts specify that a given sum of damages is intended "as liquidated damages and not as a penalty" — but even that language is not foolproof. **4.** Penalty clause.

penalty clause. (1843) A contractual provision that assesses against a defaulting party an excessive monetary charge unrelated to actual harm. • Penalty clauses are generally unenforceable.

penalty phase. (1959) The part of a criminal trial in which the fact-finder determines the punishment for a defendant who has been found guilty.

penalty point. A punishment levied for a traffic offense and accumulated on the driver's record. • If a driver receives a statutorily set number of points, the driver's license may be restricted, suspended, or terminated.

pend, *vb.* (18c) (Of a lawsuit) to be awaiting decision or settlement.

pendency (**pen**-dən-see), *n.* (17c) The state or condition of being pending or continuing undecided.

pendent (**pen**-dənt), *adj.* (18c) **1.** Not yet decided; pending <a pendent action>. **2.** Of or relating to pendent jurisdiction or pendent-party jurisdiction <pendent parties>. **3.** Contingent; dependent <pendent upon a different claim>.

pendente lite (pen-**den**-tee **lɪ**-tee), *adv.* [Latin "while the action is pending"] During the proceeding or litigation; in a manner contingent on the outcome of litigation.

pending, *adj.* (17c) Remaining undecided; awaiting decision <a pending case>.

pending, *prep.* (17c) **1.** Throughout the continuance of; during <in escrow pending arbitration>. **2.** While awaiting; until <the injunction was in force pending trial>.

penetration, *n.* **1.** *Criminal law.* The entry of the penis or some other part of the body or a foreign object into the vagina or other bodily orifice. • This is the typical meaning today in statutes defining sexual offenses. **2.** The depth reached by a bullet or other projectile in something against which the projectile is fired. **3.** The act of piercing or passing something into or through a body or object. — **penetrate,** *vb.*

penitentiary (pen-ə-**ten**-shə-ree), *n.* (1807) A correctional facility or other place of long-term confinement for convicted criminals; prison. — **penitentiary,** *adj.*

***Pennoyer* rule** (pə-**noy**-ər). (1968) The principle that a court may not issue a personal judgment against a defendant over whom it has no personal jurisdiction. *Pennoyer v. Neff,* 95 U.S. 714 (1877).

***Pennsylvania* rule.** *Torts.* The principle that a tortfeasor who violates a statute in the process of causing an injury has the burden of showing that the violation did not cause the injury. *The Pennsylvania,* 86 U.S. (19 Wall.) 125, 136 (1874).

penology (pee-**nol**-ə-jee), *n.* (1838) The study of penal institutions, crime prevention, and the punishment and rehabilitation of criminals, including the art of fitting the right treatment to an offender. — **penological** (pee-nə-**loj**-i-kəl), *adj.* — **penologist** (pee-**nol**-ə-jist), *n.*

pen register. (1953) A mechanical device that logs dialed telephone numbers by monitoring electrical impulses.

pension. (16c) A fixed sum paid regularly to a person (or to the person's beneficiaries), esp. by an employer as a retirement benefit.

vested pension. A pension in which an employee (or employee's estate) has rights to benefits purchased with the employer's contributions to the plan, even if the employee is no longer employed by this employer at the time of retirement. • The vesting of qualified pension plans is governed by ERISA.

Pension Benefit Guaranty Corporation. A self-financing federal corporation that guarantees payment of pension benefits in covered benefit pension plans. — Abbr. PBGC.

pension plan. **1.** Under ERISA, any plan, fund, or program established or maintained by an employer or an employee organization that provides retirement income to employees or results in a deferral of income by employees extending to the termination of employment or beyond. 29 USCA § 1002(2)(A). **2.** Under the Internal Revenue Code, an employer's plan established and maintained primarily to provide systematically for the payment of definitely determinable benefits to employees over a period of years, usu. for life, after retirement.

penumbra (pi-**nəm**-brə), *n.* (18c) A surrounding area or periphery of uncertain extent. • In constitutional law, the Supreme Court has ruled that the specific guarantees in the Bill of Rights have penumbras containing implied rights, esp. the right of privacy. Pl. **penumbras, penumbrae** (pi-**nəm**-bree). — **penumbral** (pi-**nəm**-brəl), *adj.*

peonage (**pee**-ə-nij), *n.* (1844) Illegal and involuntary servitude in satisfaction of a debt. — **peon,** *n.*

people. (*usu. cap.*) (1801) The citizens of a state as represented by the prosecution in a criminal case <*People v. Snyder*>.

people's court. (1912) A court in which individuals can resolve small disputes.

people-smuggling. The crime of helping a person enter a country illegally in return for a fee.

peppercorn. A small or insignificant thing or amount; nominal consideration.

per (pər), *prep.* [Latin] (14c) **1.** Through; by <the dissent, per Justice Thomas>. **2.** For each; for every <55 miles per hour>. **3.** In accordance with the terms of; according to <per the contract>.

per annum (pər **an**-əm), *adv.* [Latin] (16c) By, for, or in each year; annually.

P/E ratio. *abbr.* Price–earnings ratio.

per capita (pər **kap**-i-tə), *adj.* [Latin "by the head"] (17c) **1.** Divided equally among all individuals, usu. in the same class <the court will distribute the property to the descendants on a per capita basis>.

per capita with representation. (1935) Divided equally among all members of a class of takers, including those who have predeceased the testator, so that no family stocks are cut off by the prior death of a taker. • For example, if T (the testator) has three children — A, B, and C — and C has two children but predeceases T, C's children will still take C's share when T's estate is distributed.

2. Allocated to each person; possessed by each individual <the average annual per capita income has increased over the last two years>. — **per capita,** *adv.*

per contra (pər **kon**-trə). [Latin] (16c) On the other hand; to the contrary; by contrast.

per curiam (pər **kyoor**-ee-əm), *adv.* & *adj.* [Latin] (15c) By the court as a whole.

per curiam, *n.* Per curiam opinion.

per diem (pər **dɪ**-əm *or* **dee**-əm), *adv.* [Latin] (15c) By the day; for each day.

per diem, *adj.* (18c) Based on or calculated by the day <per diem interest>.

per diem, *n.* (1812) **1.** A monetary daily allowance, usu. to cover expenses. **2.** A daily fee.

perdurable (pər-**d[y]uur**-ə-bəl), *adj.* (15c) (Of an estate in land) lasting or enduring; durable; permanent.

peremptory (pər-**emp**-tə-ree), *adj.* (15c) **1.** Final; absolute; conclusive; incontrovertible <the king's peremptory order>. **2.** Not requiring any shown cause; arbitrary <peremptory challenges>.

perfect (pər-**fekt**), *vb.* (14c) To take all legal steps needed to complete, secure, or record (a claim, right, or interest); to provide necessary public notice in final conformity with the law <perfect a security interest> <perfect the title>.

perfect attestation clause. (1875) A testamentary provision asserting that all actions required to make a valid testamentary disposition have been performed.

perfection. Validation of a security interest as against other creditors, usu. by filing a statement with some public office or by taking possession of the collateral.

automatic perfection. The self-operative perfection of a purchase-money security interest without filing or without possession of the collateral. • The security interest is perfected simply by the attachment of the security interest, without any additional steps.

temporary perfection. The continuous perfection of a security interest for a limited period. UCC § 9-304(4).

perfect-tender rule. (1970) *Commercial law.* The principle that a buyer may reject a seller's goods if the quality, quantity, or delivery of the goods fails to conform precisely to the contract. • Although the perfect-tender rule was adopted by the UCC (§ 2-601), other Code provisions — such as the seller's right to cure after rejection — have softened the rule's impact.

performance, *n.* (16c) **1.** The successful completion of a contractual duty, usu. resulting in the performer's release from any past or future liability; EXECUTION (2).

defective performance. (1832) A performance that, whether partial or full, does not wholly comply with the contract.

future performance. (17c) Performance in the future of an obligation that will become due under a contract.

part performance. (18c) **1.** The accomplishment of some but not all of one's contractual obligations. **2.** A party's execution, in reliance on an opposing party's oral promise, of enough of an oral contract's requirements that a court may hold the statute of frauds not to apply. **3.** Part-performance doctrine.

substantial performance. (18c) Performance of the primary, necessary terms of an agreement.

vicarious performance. Performance carried by an employee, agent, or other nominee.

2. The equitable doctrine by which acts consistent with an intention to fulfill an obligation are construed to be in fulfillment of that obligation, even if the party was silent on the point. **3.** A company's earnings. **4.** The ability of a corporation to maintain or increase earnings.

peril. (13c) **1.** Exposure to the risk of injury, damage, or loss <the perils of litigation>.

inescapable peril. (1933) A danger that one cannot avoid without another's help.

2. *Insurance.* The cause of a risk of loss to person or property; esp., the cause of a risk such as fire, accident, theft, forgery, earthquake, flood, or illness <insured against all perils>.

periphrasis (pə-**rif**-rə-sis), *n.* (16c) A roundabout way of writing or speaking; circumlocution. — **periphrastic** (per-ə-**fras**-tik), *adj.*

perjury (**pər**-jər-ee), *n.* (14c) The act or an instance of a person's deliberately making material false or misleading statements while under oath. — **perjure** (**pər**-jər), *vb.* — **perjured** (**pər**-jərd), **perjurious** (pər-**juur**-ee-əs), *adj.* — **perjuror** (**pər**-jər-ər), *n.*

perjury-trap doctrine. (1989) The principle that a perjury indictment against a person must be dismissed if the prosecution secures it by calling that person as a grand-jury witness in an effort to obtain evidence for a perjury charge, esp. when the person's testimony does not relate to issues material to the grand-jury's ongoing investigation.

***Perlman* doctrine.** The principle that a discovery order directed at a disinterested third party is immediately appealable on the theory that the third party will not risk contempt by refusing to comply. • The doctrine originated in *Perlman v. United States*, 247 U.S. 7, 13, 38 S.Ct. 417, 420 (1918). The Court reasoned that the third party's ability to protect his or her rights would be thwarted if the party could not appeal immediately.

permission. (15c) **1.** The act of permitting. **2.** A license or liberty to do something; authorization.

express permission. Permission that is clearly and unmistakably granted by actions or words, oral or written.

implied permission. **1.** Permission that is inferred from words or actions. **2.** Implied consent.

3. Conduct that justifies others in believing that the possessor of property is willing to have them enter if they want to do so.

permit (**pər**-mit), *n.* (17c) A certificate evidencing permission; a license <a gun permit>.

permit (pər-**mit**), *vb.* (15c) **1.** To consent to formally <permit the inspection to be carried out>. **2.** To give opportunity for <lax security permitted the escape>. **3.** To allow or admit of <if the law so permits>.

perp (pərp), *n. Slang.* Perpetrator <the police brought in the perp for questioning>.

perpetrate, *vb.* (16c) To commit or carry out (an act, esp. a crime) <find whoever perpetrated this heinous deed>. — **perpetration,** *n.* — **perpetrator,** *n.* (16c).

perpetuation of testimony. The means or procedure for preserving for future use witness testimony that might otherwise be unavailable at trial.

perquisite (**pər**-kwi-zit). (16c) A privilege or benefit given in addition to one's salary or regular wages.

per quod (pər **kwod**), *adv.* & *adj.* [Latin "whereby"] (17c) Requiring reference to additional facts; (of libel or slander) actionable only on allegation and proof of special damages.

per se (pər **say**), *adv.* & *adj.* [Latin] (16c) **1.** Of, in, or by itself; standing alone, without reference to additional facts. **2.** As a matter of law.

persecution, *n.* Violent, cruel, and oppressive treatment directed toward a person or group of persons because of their race, religion, sexual orientation, politics, or other beliefs. — **persecute,** *vb.*

person. (13c) **1.** A human being.

disabled person. (1872) A person who has a mental or physical impairment.

displaced person. A person who remains within an internationally recognized state border after being forced to flee a home or place of habitual residence because of armed conflict, internal strife, the government's systematic violations of human rights, or a natural or man-made disaster.

interested person. (1844) A person having a property right in or claim against a thing, such as a trust or decedent's estate. • The meaning may expand to include an entity, such as a business that is a creditor of a decedent. — Abbr. IP.

person in loco parentis (in **loh**-koh pə-**ren**-tis). (1827) A person who acts in place of a parent, either temporarily (as a schoolteacher does) or indefinitely (as a stepparent does); a person who has assumed the obligations of a parent without formally adopting the child.

person of incidence. (1880) The person against whom a right is enforceable; a person who owes a legal duty. • The meaning may expand to include an entity, such as an insurance company.

person of inherence (in-**heer**-ənts). (1909) The person in whom a legal right is vested; the owner of a right. • The meaning may expand to include an entity.

person of interest. A person who is the subject of a police investigation but who has not been identified by investigators as being suspected of committing the crime itself.

2. The living body of a human being <contraband found on the smuggler's person>. **3.** An entity (such as a corporation) that is recognized by law as having most of the rights and duties of a human being. • In this sense, the term includes partnerships and other associations, whether incorporated or unincorporated.

artificial person. (17c) An entity, such as a corporation, created by law and given certain legal rights and duties of a human being; a being, real or imaginary, who for the purpose of legal reasoning is treated more or less as a human being.

personable, *adj.* (16c) Having the status of a legal person (and thus the right to plead in court, enter into contracts, etc.) <a personable entity>.

personal, *adj.* (14c) **1.** Of or affecting a person <personal injury>. **2.** Of or constituting personal property <personal belongings>.

personality. (1870) The legal status of one regarded by the law as a person; the legal conception by which the law regards a human being or an artificial entity as a person.

personal law. (18c) The law that governs a person's family matters, usu. regardless of where the person goes. • In common-law systems, personal law refers to the law of the person's domicile. In civil-law systems, it refers to the law of the individual's nationality (and so is sometimes called *lex patriae*).

Personal Responsibility and Work Opportunity Reconciliation Act. A 1996 federal law that overhauled the welfare system, as well as requiring states to provide a means for collecting child support by (1) imposing liens on a child-support obligor's assets, and (2) facilitating income-withholding. • The Act did away with Aid to Families with Dependent Children in favor of Temporary Assistance to Needy Families. It also limited the length of time that persons could receive welfare and tied states' receipt of federal child-support funds to their implementing enhanced paternity-establishment services. — Abbr. PRWORA.

personal service. (16c) **1.** Actual delivery of the notice or process to the person to whom it is directed. **2.** An act done personally by an individual. • In this sense, a personal service is an economic service involving either the intellectual or manual personal effort of an individual, as opposed to the salable product of the person's skill.

personalty (**pərs**-ən-əl-tee). (16c) Personal property as distinguished from real property.

quasi-personalty. Things that are considered movable by the law, though fixed to real property either actually (as with a fixture) or fictitiously (as with a lease for years).

persona non grata (pər-**sohn**-ə non **grah**-də), *n.* [Latin] An unwanted person; esp., a diplomat who is not acceptable to a host country. Pl. **personae non gratae.**

person-endangering state of mind. (1990) An intent to kill, inflict great bodily injury, act in wanton disregard of an unreasonable risk to others, or perpetrate a dangerous felony.

person with ordinary skill in the art. *Patents.* A fictional construct of the patent laws, denoting someone who has reasonably developed abilities in the field of the invention at issue.

per stirpes (pər **stər**-peez), *adv.* & *adj.* [Latin "by roots or stocks"] (17c) Proportionately divided between beneficiaries according to their deceased ancestor's share.

persuasion. (14c) The act of influencing or attempting to influence others by reasoned argument; the act of persuading. — **persuade,** *vb.*

pertinent, *adj.* (15c) Pertaining to the issue at hand; relevant <pertinent testimony>.

petit (**pet**-ee *or* **pet**-it), *adj.* [Law French "minor, small"] (15c) Petty.

petition, *n.* (15c) **1.** A formal written request presented to a court or other official body.

certiorari petition. A petition seeking discretionary review from an appellate court.

involuntary petition. (1868) A petition filed in a bankruptcy court by a creditor seeking to declare a debtor bankrupt.

juvenile petition. (1945) A juvenile-court petition alleging delinquent conduct by the accused.

petition for probate. A written application by which a party requests that a court admit a will to probate.

voluntary petition. (1842) A petition filed with a bankruptcy court by a debtor seeking protection from creditors.

2. In some states, the first pleading in a lawsuit; COMPLAINT (1). — **petition,** *vb.*

petitioner. (15c) A party who presents a petition to a court or other official body, esp. when seeking relief on appeal.

petition in bankruptcy. A formal written request, presented to a bankruptcy court, seeking protection for an insolvent debtor.

pettifogger (**pet**-i-fog-ər), *n.* (16c) **1.** A lawyer lacking in education, ability, sound judgment, or common sense. **2.** A lawyer who clouds an issue with insignificant details. — **pettifoggery** (pet-i-**fog**-ər-ee), *n.*

petty, *adj.* (16c) Relatively insignificant or minor <a petty crime>.

Philadelphia lawyer. (1788) A shrewd and learned lawyer. • This term can have positive or negative connotations today, but when it first appeared (in colonial times), it carried only a positive sense deriving from Philadelphia's position as America's center of learning and culture.

phishing, *n. Slang.* The sending of a fraudulent electronic communication that appears to be a genuine message from a legitimate entity or business for the purpose of inducing the recipient to disclose sensitive personal information.

phonorecord (**foh**-noh-rek-ərd). (1968) A physical object (such as a phonographic record, cassette tape, or compact disc) from which fixed sounds can be perceived, reproduced, or otherwise communicated directly or with a machine's aid. • The term is fairly common in copyright contexts since it is defined in the U.S. Copyright Act of 1976 (17 USCA § 101).

p.h.v. *abbr.* Pro hac vice.

physical custody. (1884) **1.** Custody of a person (such as an arrestee) whose freedom is directly controlled and limited. **2.** *Family law.* The right to have the child live with the person awarded custody by the court. **3.** Possession of a child during visitation.

physical-facts rule. (1923) *Evidence.* The principle that oral testimony may be disregarded when it is inconsistent or irreconcilable with the physical evidence in the case.

physical-proximity test. (1955) *Criminal law.* A common-law test for the crime of attempt, focusing on how much more the defendant would have needed to do to complete the offense.

P.I. *abbr.* **1.** Personal injury. **2.** Private investigator.

picketing. (1832) The demonstration by one or more persons outside a business or organization to protest the entity's activities or policies and to pressure the entity to meet the protesters' demands; esp., an employees' demonstration aimed at publicizing a labor dispute and influencing the public to withhold business from the employer.

pickpocket. (16c) A thief who steals money or property from the person of another, usu. by stealth but sometimes by physical diversion such as bumping into or pushing the victim.

piercing the corporate veil. (1928) The judicial act of imposing personal liability on otherwise immune corporate officers, directors, or shareholders for the corporation's wrongful acts.

pignorate (**pig**-nə-rayt), *vb.* (17c) **1.** To give over as a pledge; to pawn. **2.** To take in pawn. — **pignorative,** *adj.*

pignus (**pig**-nəs), *n.* [Latin "pledge"] A bailment in which goods are delivered to secure the payment of a debt or performance of an engagement, accompanied by a power of sale in case of default. • This type of bailment is for the benefit of both parties. Pl. ***pignora*** or ***pignera.***

pilferage (**pil**-fər-ij), *n.* (18c) **1.** The act or an instance of stealing. **2.** The item or items stolen. — **pilfer** (**pil**-fər), *vb.*

pillage (**pil**-ij), *n.* **1.** The forcible seizure of another's property, esp. in war; esp., the wartime plundering of a city or territory. **2.** The property so seized or plundered; BOOTY. — **pillage,** *vb.*

pilot. **1.** A person in control of an airplane. **2.** *Maritime law.* A person in control of a vessel.

pilotage (**pɪ**-lə-tij). **1.** The navigating of vessels; the business of navigating vessels. **2.** Compensation that a pilot receives for navigating a vessel, esp. into and out of harbor or through a channel or passage.

pimp, *n.* (17c) A person who solicits customers for a prostitute, usu. in return for a share of the prostitute's earnings. — **pimp,** *vb.* — **pimping,** *n.*

pinkerton. *Slang.* A private detective or security guard, usu. one who is armed. • The name comes from the Pinkerton Detective Agency, the first private detective agency in the United States, established in 1852.

***Pinkerton* rule.** (1979) *Criminal law.* The doctrine imposing liability on a conspirator for all offenses committed in furtherance of the conspiracy, even if those offenses are actually performed by coconspirators. *Pinkerton v. United States*, 328 U.S. 640, 66 S.Ct. 1180 (1946).

pink slip. *Slang.* A notice of employment termination given to an employee by an employer.

piracy, *n.* (16c) **1.** Robbery, kidnapping, or other criminal violence committed at sea. **2.** A similar crime committed aboard a plane or other vehicle. **3.** Hijacking.

air piracy. (1948) The crime of using force or threat to seize control of an aircraft; the hijacking of an aircraft, esp. one in flight.

4. The unauthorized and illegal reproduction or distribution of materials protected by copyright, patent, or trademark law. — **pirate,** *vb.* — **piratical** (pɪ-**rat**-ə-kəl), *adj.* — **pirate,** *n.*

video piracy. The illegal copying and sale or rental of copyrighted motion pictures.

pirate recording. *Copyright.* An unauthorized copy of the sounds on a copyright-protected recording, including digital duplication made available over the Internet.

PITI. *abbr.* Principal, interest, taxes, and insurance — the components of a monthly mortgage payment.

PKPA. *abbr.* Parental Kidnapping Prevention Act.

P.L. *abbr.* Public law.

place of abode. (16c) A person's residence or domicile.

place of business. (16c) A location at which one carries on a business.

principal place of business. (1825) The place of a corporation's chief executive offices, which is typically viewed as the "nerve center.

place of contracting. (18c) The country or state in which a contract is entered into. • The place of contracting is not necessarily the place where the document is signed; another location may be designated in the contract.

place of delivery. (17c) The place where goods sold are to be sent by the seller. • If no place is specified in the contract, the seller's place of business is usu. the place of delivery. UCC § 2-308.

place of employment. (17c) The location at which work done in connection with a business is carried out; the place where some process or operation related to the business is conducted.

place of performance. The place where a promise is to be performed, either by specific provision or by interpretation of the language of the promise.

place of wrong. The place, esp. the state, where the last event necessary to make an actor liable for an alleged tort takes place.

plagiarism. (17c) The deliberate and knowing presentation of another person's original ideas or creative expressions as one's own. — **plagiarize** (**play**-jə-rɪz), *vb.* — **plagiarist** (**play**-jə-rist), *n.*

plain-feel doctrine. (1984) *Criminal procedure.* The principle that a police officer, while conducting a legal pat-down search, may seize any contraband that the officer can immediately and clearly identify, by touch but not by manipulation, as being illegal or incriminating.

plain-language law. (1978) Legislation requiring nontechnical, readily comprehensible language in consumer contracts such as residential leases or insurance policies.

plain-language movement. (1978) **1.** The loosely organized campaign to encourage legal writers and business writers to write clearly and concisely — without legalese — while preserving accuracy and precision. **2.** The body of persons involved in this campaign.

plain-meaning rule. (1937) **1.** The rule that if a writing, or a provision in a writing, appears to be unambiguous on its face, its meaning must be determined from the writing itself without resort to any extrinsic evidence. • Though often applied, this rule is often condemned as simplistic because the meaning of words varies with the verbal context and the surrounding circumstances, not to mention the linguistic ability of the users and readers (including judges). **2.** Ordinary-meaning rule.

plaintiff. (14c) The party who brings a civil suit in a court of law. — Abbr. pltf. Cf. DEFENDANT.

involuntary plaintiff. A plaintiff who is joined in a lawsuit by court order when the party's joinder is imperative for the litigation and the party is subject to the court's jurisdiction but refuses to join the suit voluntarily.

plaintiff in error. (17c) *Archaic.* **1.** Appellant. **2.** Petitioner.

plain-view doctrine. (1963) *Criminal procedure.* The rule permitting a police officer's warrantless seizure and use as evidence of an item seen in plain view from a lawful position or during a legal search when the officer has probable cause to believe that the item is evidence of a crime.

planned-unit development. A land area zoned for a single-community subdivision with flexible restrictions on residential, commercial, and public uses. — Abbr. PUD.

planning board. A local government body responsible for approving or rejecting proposed building projects.

Plant Patent Act. *Patents.* The 1930 federal law that extended patent protection for developing "any distinct and new" varieties of asexually reproducing plants. 35 USCA §§ 161–164. — Abbr. PPA.

plat. (15c) **1.** A small piece of land; PLOT (1). **2.** A map describing a piece of land and its features, such as boundaries, lots, roads, and easements.

platform. A statement of principles and policies adopted by a political party as the basis of the party's appeal for public support.

plat map. (1941) A document that gives the legal descriptions of pieces of land by lot, street, and block number.

plea, *n.* (13c) **1.** An accused person's formal response of "guilty," "not guilty," or "no contest" to a criminal charge.

blind plea. (1972) A guilty plea made without the promise of a concession from either the judge or the prosecutor.

guilty plea. (1942) An accused person's formal admission in court of having committed the charged offense. • A guilty plea must be made voluntarily and only after the accused has been informed of and understands his or her rights. It ordinarily has the same effect as a guilty verdict and conviction after a trial on the merits. A guilty plea is usu. part of a plea bargain.

negotiated plea. (1956) The plea agreed to by a criminal defendant and the prosecutor in a plea bargain.

nolo plea. A plea by which the defendant does not contest or admit guilt. See Fed. R. Crim. P. 11(b); nolo contendere.

not-guilty plea. (1912) An accused person's formal denial in court of having committed the charged offense. • The prosecution must then prove all elements of the charged offense beyond a reasonable doubt if the defendant is to be convicted.

2. At common law, the defendant's responsive pleading in a civil action. **3.** A factual allegation offered in a case; a pleading.

anomalous plea. (1851) An equitable plea in which a party states new facts and negates some of the opponent's stated facts. • Partly confession and avoidance and partly traverse, the plea is appropriate when the plaintiff, in the bill, has anticipated the plea, and the defendant then traverses the anticipatory matters.

common plea. (17c) A common-law plea in a civil action as opposed to a criminal prosecution.

dilatory plea (**dil**-ə-tor-ee). (16c) A plea that does not challenge the merits of a case but that seeks to delay or defeat the action on procedural grounds.

double plea. (16c) A plea consisting in two or more distinct grounds of complaint or defense for the same issue.

issuable plea. (17c) A plea on the merits presenting a cognizable complaint to the court.

jurisdictional plea. (1900) A plea asserting that the court lacks jurisdiction either over the defendant or over the subject matter of the case.

negative plea. (16c) A plea that traverses some material fact or facts stated in the bill.

nonissuable plea. (1841) A plea on which a court ruling will not decide the case on the merits, such as a plea in abatement.

peremptory plea. (18c) A plea that responds to the merits of the plaintiff's claim.

plea in abatement. (17c) A plea that objects to the place, time, or method of asserting the plaintiff's claim but does not dispute the claim's merits. • A defendant who successfully asserts a plea in abatement leaves the claim open for continuation in the current action or reassertion in a later action if the defect is cured.

plea in discharge. (18c) A plea that the defendant has previously satisfied and discharged the plaintiff's claim.

plea in equity. (17c) A special defense relying on one or more reasons why the suit should be dismissed, delayed, or barred. • The various kinds are (1) pleas to the jurisdiction, (2) pleas to the person, (3) pleas to the form of the bill, and (4) pleas in bar of the bill. Pleas in equity generally fall into two classes: *pure pleas* and *anomalous pleas.*

plea in estoppel. (1831) *Common-law pleading.* A plea that neither confesses nor avoids but rather pleads a previous inconsistent act, allegation, or denial on the part of the adverse party to preclude that party from maintaining an action or defense.

plea in suspension. (1875) A plea that shows some ground for not proceeding in the suit at the present time and prays that the proceedings be stayed until that ground is removed, such as a party's being a minor or the plaintiff's being an alien enemy.

plea of privilege. (17c) A plea that raises an objection to the venue of an action.

plea of release. (18c) A plea that admits the claim but sets forth a written discharge executed by a party authorized to release the claim.

plea puis darrein continuance (**pwis dar**-ayn kən-**tin**-yoo-ənts). [Law French "plea since the last continuance"] (18c) A plea that alleges new defensive matter that has arisen during a continuance of the case and that did not exist at the time of the defendant's last pleading.

plea to the declaration. (1820) A plea in abatement that objects to the declaration and applies immediately to it.

plea to the person of the defendant. (1872) A plea in abatement alleging that the defendant has a legal disability to be sued.

plea to the person of the plaintiff. (1821) A plea in abatement alleging that the plaintiff has a legal disability to sue.

plea to the writ. (17c) A plea in abatement that objects to the writ (summons) and applies (1) to the form of the writ for a matter either apparent on the writ's face or outside the writ, or (2) to the way in which the writ was executed or acted on.

pure plea. (18c) An equitable plea that affirmatively alleges new matters that are outside the bill. • If proved, the effect is to end the controversy by dismissing, delaying, or barring the suit. A pure plea must track the allegations of the bill, not evade it or mistake its purpose. Originally, this was the only plea known in equity.

rolled-up plea. (1929) *Defamation.* A defendant's plea claiming that the statements complained of are factual and that, to the extent that they consist of comment, they are fair comment on a matter of public interest.

special plea. (16c) A plea alleging one or more new facts rather than merely disputing the legal grounds of the action or charge. • All pleas other than general issues are special pleas.

plea bargain, *n.* (1963) A negotiated agreement between a prosecutor and a criminal defendant whereby the defendant pleads guilty to a lesser offense or to one of multiple charges in exchange for some concession by the prosecutor, usu. a more lenient sentence or a dismissal of the other charges. — **plea-bargain,** *vb.* — **plea-bargaining,** *n.*

charge bargain. (1890) A plea bargain in which a prosecutor agrees to drop some of the counts or reduce the charge to a less serious offense in exchange for a plea of either guilty or no contest from the defendant.

sentence bargain. (1973) A plea bargain in which a prosecutor agrees to recommend a lighter sentence in exchange for a plea of either guilty or no contest from the defendant.

plead, *vb.* (13c) **1.** To make a specific plea, esp. in response to a criminal charge. **2.** To assert or allege in a pleading. **3.** To file or deliver a pleading.

pleader. (13c) **1.** A party who asserts a particular pleading. **2.** A person who pleads in court on behalf of another.

pleading, *n.* (16c) **1.** A formal document in which a party to a legal proceeding (esp. a civil lawsuit) sets forth or responds to allegations, claims, denials, or defenses.

accusatory pleading. (1908) An indictment, information, or complaint by which the government begins a criminal prosecution.

amended pleading. (1809) A pleading that replaces an earlier pleading and that contains matters omitted from or not known at the time of the earlier pleading.

anomalous pleading. (1845) A pleading that is partly affirmative and partly negative in its allegations.

argumentative pleading. A pleading that states allegations rather than facts, and thus forces the court to infer or hunt for supporting facts.

articulated pleading. (1953) A pleading that states each allegation in a separately numbered paragraph.

defective pleading. (17c) A pleading that fails to meet minimum standards of sufficiency or accuracy in form or substance.

hypothetical pleading. A pleading asserting that if a certain fact is true, then a certain result must follow. • Hypothetical pleadings are generally improper.

pleading to the merits. A responsive pleading that addresses the plaintiff's cause of action, in whole or in part.

responsive pleading. (1833) A pleading that replies to an opponent's earlier pleading.

sham pleading. (1825) An obviously frivolous or absurd pleading that is made only for purposes of vexation or delay.

shotgun pleading. (1964) A pleading that encompasses a wide range of contentions, usu. supported by vague factual allegations.

supplemental pleading. (1841) A pleading that either corrects a defect in an earlier pleading or addresses facts arising since the earlier pleading was filed. • Unlike an amended pleading, a supplemental pleading merely adds to the earlier pleading and does not replace it.

2. A system of defining and narrowing the issues in a lawsuit whereby the parties file formal documents alleging their respective positions.

alternative pleading. (1868) A form of pleading whereby the pleader alleges two or more independent claims or defenses that are not necessarily consistent with each other, such as alleging both intentional infliction of emotional distress and negligent infliction of emotional distress based on the same conduct. Fed. R. Civ. P. 8(e)(2).

artful pleading. (1950) A plaintiff's disguised phrasing of a federal claim as solely a state-law claim in order to prevent a defendant from removing the case from state court to federal court.

code pleading. (1860) A procedural system requiring that the pleader allege merely the facts of the case giving rise to the claim or defense, not the legal conclusions necessary to sustain the claim or establish the defense.

equity pleading. (18c) The system of pleading used in courts of equity. • In most jurisdictions, rules unique to equity practice have been largely supplanted by one set of rules of court, esp. where law courts and equity courts have merged.

issue pleading. (1916) The common-law method of pleading, the main purpose of which was to frame an issue.

notice pleading. (1918) A procedural system requiring that the pleader give only a short and plain statement of the claim showing that the pleader is entitled to relief, and not a complete detailing of all the facts. Fed. R. Civ. P. 8(a).

3. The legal rules regulating the statement of the plaintiff's claims and the defendant's defenses.

plead over, *vb.* (17c) To fail to notice a defective allegation in an opponent's pleading before responding to the pleading.

plead the Fifth. Take the Fifth.

plea in bar. (17c) A plea that seeks to defeat the plaintiff's or prosecutor's action completely and permanently.

general plea in bar. (18c) A criminal defendant's plea of not guilty by which the defendant denies every fact and circumstance necessary to be convicted of the crime charged.

special plea in bar. (17c) A plea that, rather than addressing the merits and denying the facts alleged, sets up some extrinsic fact showing why a criminal defendant cannot be tried for the offense charged.

plea of tender. (18c) At common law, a pleading asserting that the defendant has consistently been willing to pay the debt demanded, has offered it to the plaintiff, and has brought the money into court ready to pay the plaintiff.

plebiscite (**pleb**-ə-sɪt *or* **pleb**-ə-sit), *n.* (1860) **1.** A binding or nonbinding referendum on a proposed law, constitutional amendment, or significant public issue. **2.** *Int'l law.* A direct vote of a country's electorate to decide a question of public importance, such as union with another country or a proposed change to the constitution. — **plebiscitary** (plə-**bi**-sə-ter-ee), *adj.*

pledge, *n.* (14c) **1.** A formal promise or undertaking. **2.** The act of providing something as security for a debt or obligation. **3.** A bailment or other deposit of personal property to a creditor as security for a debt or obligation; PAWN (2). **4.** The item of personal property so deposited; PAWN (1). **5.** The thing so provided. **6.** A security interest in personal property represented by an indispensable instrument, the interest being created by a bailment or other deposit of personal property for the purpose of securing the payment of a debt or the performance of some other duty. — **pledge,** *vb.* — **pledgeable,** *adj.*

plenary (**plee**-nə-ree *or* **plen**-ə-ree), *adj.* (15c) **1.** Full; complete; entire <plenary authority>. **2.** (Of an assembly) intended to have the attendance of all members or participants <plenary session>.

plenipotentiary (plen-ə-pə-**ten**-shee-er-ee). A person who has full power to do a thing; a person fully commissioned to act for another.

plot, *n.* (bef. 12c) **1.** A measured piece of land; LOT (1). **2.** A plan forming the basis of a conspiracy.

plot plan. (1925) A plan that shows a proposed or present use of a plot of land, esp. of a residential area.

plottage. (1916) The increase in value achieved by combining small, undeveloped tracts of land into larger tracts.

plow back, *vb.* To reinvest earnings and profits into a business instead of paying them out as dividends or withdrawals.

plurality. (1803) The greatest number (esp. of votes), regardless of whether it is a simple or an absolute majority.

plural marriage. Polygamy.

pluries (**pluur**-ee-eez), *n.* [Latin "many times"] (15c) A third or subsequent writ issued when the previous writs have been ineffective; a writ issued after an alias writ.

PM. *abbr.* **1.** Postmaster. **2.** Prime minister.

P.O. *abbr.* **1.** Post office. **2.** Purchase order.

pocket part. (1931) A supplemental pamphlet inserted usu. into the back inside cover of a lawbook, esp. a treatise or code, to update the material in the main text until the publisher issues a new edition of the entire work. • Legal publishers frequently leave a little extra room inside their hardcover books so that pocket parts may later be added.

P.O.D. *abbr.* Pay on delivery.

poena (**pee**-nə). [Latin] (1859) Punishment; penalty.

point, *n.* (13c) **1.** A pertinent and distinct legal proposition, issue, or argument <point of error>. **2.** *Parliamentary law.* Any of several kinds of requests made in a deliberative body.

point of clarification. A question about procedure or substance.

point of information. An inquiry asking a question about a motion's merits or effect.

point of order. A request suggesting that the meeting or a member is not following the applicable rules and asking the chair enforce the rules.

point of privilege. A motion that raises a question of privilege.

procedural point. A request that raises a personal privilege relating to a member's ability to participate effectively in the meeting, such as the member's ability to see or hear the proceedings.

3. One percent of the face value of a loan (esp. a mortgage loan), paid up front to the lender as a service charge or placement fee <the borrower hoped for only a two-point fee on the mortgage>. **4.** A unit used for quoting stock, bond, or commodity prices <the stock closed up a few points today>. **5.** A payment to secure a loan, stated as a percentage of the loan's face amount.

point-and-click agreement. (2000) An electronic version of a shrink-wrap license in which a computer user agrees to the terms of an electronically displayed agreement by pointing the cursor to a particular location on the screen and then clicking.

point of error. (18c) An alleged mistake by a lower court asserted as a ground for appeal.

point of fact. A discrete factual proposition at issue in a case.

point of law. (16c) A discrete legal proposition at issue in a case.

reserved point of law. (1821) An important or difficult point of law that arises during trial but that the judge sets aside for future argument or decision so that testimony can continue.

point source. *Environmental law.* The discernible and identifiable source from which pollutants are discharged.

point system. (1955) *Criminal law.* A system that assigns incremental units to traffic violations, the accumulation of a certain number within a year resulting in the automatic suspension of a person's driving privileges.

poison pill. A corporation's defense against an unwanted takeover bid whereby shareholders are granted the right to acquire equity or debt securities at a favorable price to increase the bidder's acquisition costs.

***Polaroid* test.** *Trademarks.* A judicial test for trademark infringement, analyzing eight factors: (1) strength of the mark, (2) similarity between the marks, (3) proximity of the products' markets, (4) effects on market expansion (ability to "bridge the gap"), (5) actual confusion, (6) the defendant's good or bad faith, (7) quality of the products, and (8) sophistication of the buyer. *Polaroid Corp. v. Polarad Electronics Corp.*, 287 F.2d 492, 495 (2d Cir. 1961).

police, *n.* **1.** The governmental department charged with the preservation of public order, the promotion of public safety, and the prevention and detection of crime. **2.** The officers or members of this department. — **police,** *vb.*

police officer. A peace officer responsible for preserving public order, promoting public safety, and preventing and detecting crime.

police power. (1821) **1.** The inherent and plenary power of a sovereign to make all laws necessary and proper to preserve the public security, order, health, morality, and justice. • It is a fundamental power essential to government, and it cannot be surrendered by the legislature or irrevocably transferred away from government. **2.** A state's Tenth Amendment right, subject to due-process and other limitations, to establish and enforce laws protecting the public's health, safety, and general welfare, or to delegate this right to local governments. **3.** Loosely, the power of the government to intervene in the use of privately owned property, as by subjecting it to eminent domain.

policy. (14c) **1.** The general principles by which a government is guided in its management of public affairs. **2.** A document containing a contract of insurance; insurance policy. **3.** A type of lottery in which bettors select numbers to bet on and place the bet with a "policy writer.

policyholder. One who owns an insurance policy, regardless of whether that person is the insured party.

policy of the law. PUBLIC POLICY (1).

political-action committee. (1839) An organization formed by a special-interest group to raise and contribute money to the campaigns of political candidates who the group believes will promote its interests. — Abbr. PAC.

political correctness, *n.* (1979) **1.** The inclination to avoid language and practices that might offend anyone's political sensibilities, esp. in racial or sexual matters. **2.** An instance in which a person conforms to this inclination. — Abbr. P.C. — **politically correct,** *adj.*

political law. Political science.

political offense. (18c) A crime directed against the security or government of a nation, such as treason, sedition, or espionage.

political party. An organization of voters formed to influence the government's conduct and policies by nominating and electing candidates to public office.

political question. (1808) A question that a court will not consider because it involves the exercise of discretionary power by the executive or legislative branch of government.

political science. (17c) The branch of learning concerned with the study of the principles and conduct of government.

political subdivision. (1827) A division of a state that exists primarily to discharge some function of local government.

politics. 1. The science of the organization and administration of the state. **2.** The activity or profession of engaging in political affairs.

polity (**pol**-ə-tee). (16c) **1.** The total governmental organization as based on its goals and policies. **2.** A politically organized body or community.

polity approach. (1975) A method of resolving church-property disputes by which a court examines the structure of the church to determine whether the church is independent or hierarchical, and then resolves the dispute in accordance with the decision of the proper church-governing body.

poll, *n.* (18c) **1.** A sampling of opinions on a given topic, conducted randomly or obtained from a specified group. **2.** The act or process of voting at an election. **3.** The result of the counting of votes. **4.** (*usu. pl.*) The place where votes are cast.

poll, *vb.* (17c) **1.** To ask how each member of (a group) individually voted. **2.** To question (people) so as to elicit votes, opinions, or preferences. **3.** To receive (a given number of votes) in an election.

pollicitation. *Contracts.* (15c) The offer of a promise.

pollute, *vb.* To corrupt or defile; esp., to contaminate the soil, air, or water with noxious substances. — **pollution,** *n.* — **polluter,** *n.*

polyandry (**pol**-ee-an-dree). (17c) The condition or practice of having more than one husband at the same time.

polygamy (pə-**lig**-ə-mee), *n.* (16c) **1.** The state or practice of having more than one spouse simultaneously. **2.** *Hist.* The fact or practice of having more than one spouse during one's lifetime, though never simultaneously. • Until the third century, polygamy included remarriage after a spouse's death because a valid marriage bond was considered indissoluble. — **polygamous,** *adj.* — **polygamist,** *n.*

polygraph, *n.* (1923) A device used to evaluate truthfulness by measuring and recording involuntary physiological changes in the human body during interrogation. — **polygraphic,** *adj.* — **polygraphy,** *n.*

polygyny (pə-**lij**-ə-nee). (18c) The condition or practice of having more than one wife at the same time.

Ponzi scheme (**pon**-zee). (1920) A fraudulent investment scheme in which money contributed by later investors generates artificially high dividends or returns for the original investors, whose example attracts even larger investments. • Money from the new investors is used directly to repay or pay interest to earlier investors, usu. without any operation or revenue-producing activity other than the continual raising of new funds.

pool, *n.* (1868) **1.** An association of individuals or entities who share resources and funds to promote their joint undertaking; esp., an association of persons engaged in buying or selling commodities. **2.** A gambling scheme in which numerous persons contribute stakes for betting on a particular event (such as a sporting event).

pooling, *n. Oil & gas.* The bringing together of small tracts of land or fractional mineral interests over a producing reservoir for the purpose of drilling an oil or gas well.

compulsory pooling. Pooling done by order of a regulatory agency.

voluntary pooling. Pooling arranged by agreement of the owners of mineral interests.

pooling agreement. A contractual arrangement by which corporate shareholders agree that their shares will be voted as a unit.

porcupine provision. A clause in a corporation's charter or bylaws designed to prevent a takeover without the consent of the board of directors.

pornography, *n.* (1842) Material (such as writings, photographs, or movies) depicting sexual activity or erotic behavior in a way that is designed to arouse sexual excitement. • Pornography is protected speech under the First Amendment unless it is determined to be legally obscene. — **pornographic,** *adj.*

child pornography. (1967) Material depicting a person under the age of 18 engaged in sexual activity. • Child pornography is not protected by the First Amendment — even if it falls short of the legal standard for obscenity — and those directly involved in its distribution can be criminally punished.

virtual child pornography. Material that includes a computer-generated image that appears to be a minor engaged in sexual activity but that in reality does not involve a person under the age of 18.

port. 1. A harbor where ships load and unload cargo. **2.** Any place where persons and cargo are allowed to enter a country and where customs officials are stationed.

foreign port. **1.** One exclusively within the jurisdiction of another country or state. **2.** A port other than a home port.

free port. A port located outside a country's customs frontier, so that goods may be delivered usu. free of import duties or taxes, without being subjected to customs-control procedures; free-trade zone.

home port. The port that is either where a vessel is registered or where its owner resides.

port of call. A port at which a ship stops during a voyage.

port of delivery. The port that is the terminus of any particular voyage and where the ship unloads its cargo.

port of departure. The port from which a vessel departs on the start of a voyage.

port of destination. The port at which a voyage is to end. • This term generally includes any stopping places at which the ship receives or unloads cargo.

port of discharge. The place where a substantial part of the cargo is discharged.

portable business. (1983) A portfolio of legal business that an attorney can take from one firm or geographic location to another, with little loss in client relationships.

port authority. (1870) A state or federal agency that regulates traffic through a port or that establishes and maintains airports, bridges, tollways, and public transportation.

portfolio. (1848) **1.** The various securities or other investments held by an investor at any given time. • An investor will often hold several different types of investments in a portfolio for the purpose of diversifying risk. **2.** The role within the government of a high official <minister without portfolio>.

port-state control. *Maritime law.* The exercise of authority under international conventions for a state to stop, board, inspect, and when necessary detain vessels sailing under foreign flags while they are navigating in the port state's territorial waters or are in one of its ports.

posit, *vb.* **1.** To presume true or to offer as true. **2.** To present as an explanation.

positive law. (14c) A system of law promulgated and implemented within a particular political community by political superiors, as distinct from moral law or law existing in an ideal community or in some nonpolitical community. • Positive law typically consists of enacted law — the codes, statutes, and regulations that are applied and enforced in the courts.

positivism. (1846) The doctrine that all true knowledge is derived from observable phenomena, rather than speculation or reasoning. — **positivistic,** *adj.*

posse (**pos**-ee). [Latin] (16c) **1.** A possibility. **2.** Power; ability. **3.** Posse comitatus.

posse comitatus (**pos**-ee kom-ə-**tay**-təs), *n.* [Latin "power of the county"] (16c) A group of citizens who are called together to help the sheriff keep the peace or conduct rescue operations.

Posse Comitatus Act. A federal law that, with a few exceptions, prohibits the Army or Air Force from directly participating in civilian law-enforcement operations, as by making arrests, conducting searches, or seizing evidence. 18 USCA § 1385. — Abbr. PCA.

possess, *vb.* (14c) To have in one's actual control; to have possession of.

possession. (14c) **1.** The fact of having or holding property in one's power; the exercise of dominion over property. **2.** The right under which one may exercise control over something to the exclusion of all others; the continuing exercise of a claim to the exclusive use of a material object. **3.** (*usu. pl.*) Something that a person owns or controls; PROPERTY (2). **4.** A territorial dominion of a state or nation.

actual possession. (16c) Physical occupancy or control over property.

bona fide possession. (1815) Possession of property by a person who in good faith does not know that the property's ownership is disputed.

constructive possession. (18c) Control or dominion over a property without actual possession or custody of it.

criminal possession. (1811) The unlawful possession of certain prohibited articles, such as illegal drugs or drug paraphernalia, firearms, or stolen property.

derivative possession. (1851) Lawful possession by one (such as a tenant) who does not hold title.

exclusive possession. (18c) The exercise of exclusive dominion over property, including the use and benefit of the property.

hostile possession. (1812) Possession asserted against the claims of all others, esp. the record owner.

immediate possession. (17c) Possession that is acquired or retained directly or personally.

immemorial possession. Possession that began so long ago that no one still living witnessed its beginning.

incorporeal possession. (1964) Possession of something other than a material object, such as an easement over a neighbor's land, or the access of light to the windows of a house.

mediate possession (**mee**-dee-it). Possession of a thing through someone else, such as an agent. • In every instance of mediate possession, there is a direct possessor (such as an agent) as well as a mediate possessor (the principal).

naked possession. (16c) The mere possession of something, esp. real estate, without any apparent right or colorable title to it.

notorious possession. (18c) Possession or control that is evident to others; possession of property that, because it is generally known by people in the area where the property is located, gives rise to a presumption that the actual owner has notice of it.

peaceable possession. (16c) Possession (as of real property) not disturbed by another's hostile or legal attempts to recover possession; esp., wrongful possession that the rightful possessor has appeared to tolerate.

pedal possession. (1839) Actual possession, as by living on the land or by improving it. • This term usu. appears in adverse-possession contexts.

possession in fact. (17c) Actual possession that may or may not be recognized by law. • For example, an employee's possession of an employer's property is for some purposes not legally considered possession, the term *detention* or *custody* being used instead.

possession in law. (16c) **1.** Possession that is recognized by the law either because it is a specific type of possession in fact or because the law for some special reason attributes the advantages and results of possession to someone who does not in fact possess. **2.** Constructive possession.

possession of a right. (17c) The continuing exercise and enjoyment of a right. • This type of possession is often unrelated to an ownership interest in property. For example, a criminal defendant possesses the right to demand a trial by jury.

scrambling possession. (1823) **1.** A wrongful possession that the rightful possessor has not appeared to tolerate. **2.** Possession that is uncertain because it is in dispute. • With scrambling possession, the dispute is over who actually has possession — not over whether a party's possession is lawful.

possessor. (15c) One who has possession of real or personal property; esp., a person who is in occupancy of land with the intent to control it or has been but no longer is in that position, but no one else has gained occupancy or has a right to gain it. — **possessorial** (pos-ə-**sor**-ee-əl), *adj.*

legal possessor. (17c) One with the legal right to possess property, such as a buyer under a conditional sales contract, as contrasted with the legal owner who holds legal title.

possessor bona fide (**boh**-nə fɪ-dee). A possessor who believes that no other person has a better right to the possession.

possessor mala fide (**mal**-ə fɪ-dee). A possessor who knows that someone else has a better right to the possession.

possessory claim. (1833) Title to public land held by a claimant who has filed a declaratory statement but has not paid for the land.

possessory interest. (18c) **1.** The present right to control property, including the right to exclude others, by a person who is not necessarily the owner. **2.** A present or future right to the exclusive use and possession of property.

possibility. (14c) **1.** An event that may or may not happen. **2.** A contingent interest in real or personal property.

naked possibility. (18c) A mere chance or expectation that a person will acquire future property. • A conveyance of a naked possibility is usu. void for lack of subject matter, as in a deed conveying all rights to a future estate not yet in existence.

possibility coupled with an interest. (18c) An expectation recognized in law as an estate or interest, as occurs in an executory devise or in a shifting or springing use. • This type of possibility may be sold or assigned.

remote possibility. (17c) A limitation dependent on two or more facts or events that are contingent and uncertain; a double possibility.

possibility of reverter. (18c) A reversionary interest that is subject to a condition precedent; specif., a future interest retained by a grantor after conveying a fee simple determinable, so that the grantee's estate terminates automatically and reverts to the grantor if the terminating event ever occurs. • In this type of interest, the grantor transfers an estate whose maximum potential duration equals that of the grantor's own estate and attaches a special limitation that operates in the grantor's favor.

POSSLQ (**pahs**-əl-kyoo). *abbr.* A person of opposite sex sharing living quarters. • Although this term (which is used by the Census Bureau) is intended to include only a person's roommate of the opposite sex to whom the person is not married, the phrase literally includes those who are married. This overbreadth has occasionally been criticized.

post. [Latin] (14c) After.

post, *vb.* (17c) **1.** To publicize or announce by affixing a notice in a public place <foreclosure notice was posted at the county courthouse>. **2.** To transfer (accounting entries) from an original record to a ledger <post debits and credits>. **3.** To place in the mail <post a letter>. **4.** To make a payment or deposit; to put up <post bail>.

postconviction-relief proceeding. (1964) A state or federal procedure for a prisoner to request a court to vacate or correct a conviction or sentence.

postdate, *vb.* (17c) To put a date on (an instrument, such as a check) that is later than the actual date.

posterity, *n.* (14c) **1.** Future generations collectively. **2.** All the descendants of a person to the furthest generation.

post hoc (pohst hok). [Latin fr. *post hoc, ergo propter hoc* "after this, therefore because of this"] (1844) **1.** *adv.* After this; subsequently. **2.** *adj.* Of or relating to the fallacy of assuming causality from temporal sequence; confusing sequence with consequence.

posthumous (**pos**-chə-məs), *adj.* Occurring or existing after death; esp., (of a child) born after the father's death.

posting. (17c) **1.** *Accounting.* The act of transferring an original entry to a ledger. **2.** The act of mailing a letter. **3.** A method of substituted service of process by displaying the process in a prominent place (such as the courthouse door) when other forms of service have failed. **4.** A publication method, as by displaying municipal ordinances in designated localities. **5.** The act of providing legal notice, as by affixing notices of judicial sales at or on the courthouse door. **6.** The procedure for processing a check, including one or more of the following steps: (1) verifying any signature, (2) ascertaining that sufficient funds are available, (3) affixing a "paid" or other stamp, (4) entering a charge or entry to a customer's account, and (5) correcting or reversing an entry or erroneous action concerning the check.

postmortem, *adj.* (1824) Done or occurring after death <a postmortem examination>.

postmortem, *n.* AUTOPSY (1).

postnuptial (pohst-**nəp**-shəl), *adj.* (1807) Made or occurring during marriage <a postnuptial contract>.

postnuptial agreement (pohst-**nəp**-shəl). (1834) An agreement entered into during marriage to define each spouse's property rights in the event of death or divorce. • The term commonly refers to an agreement between spouses during the marriage at a time when separation or divorce is not imminent. When dissolution is intended as the result, it is more properly called a *property settlement* or *marital agreement.*

postpone, *vb.* (15c) **1.** To put off to a later time. **2.** To place lower in precedence or importance; esp., to subordinate (a lien) to a later one. — **postponement,** *n.*

post-terminal sitting. A court session held after the normal term.

potentially responsible party. *Environmental law.* A person or entity that may be required to clean up a polluted site because the person or entity (1) owns or operates on the site, (2) arranged for the disposal of a hazardous substance on the site, (3) transported a hazardous substance to the site, or (4) contributed in any other way to contaminate the site. — Abbr. PRP.

pound, *n.* (12c) **1.** A place where impounded property is held until redeemed. **2.** A place for the detention of stray animals. **3.** A measure of weight equal to 16 avoirdupois ounces or 7,000 grains. **4.** The basic monetary unit of the United Kingdom, equal to 100 pence.

poundage fee. (18c) A percentage commission awarded to a sheriff for moneys recovered under judicial process, such as execution or attachment.

pour out, *vb.* (1978) *Slang.* To deny (a claimant) damages or relief in a lawsuit <the plaintiff was poured out of court by the jury's verdict of no liability>.

poverty. 1. The condition of being indigent; the scarcity of the means of subsistence <war on poverty>. **2.** Dearth of something desirable <a poverty of ideas>.

power. (13c) **1.** The ability to act or not act; esp., a person's capacity for acting in such a manner as to control someone else's responses. **2.** Dominance, control, or influence over another; control over one's subordinates. **3.** The legal right or authorization to act or not act; a person's or organization's ability to alter, by an act of will, the rights, duties, liabilities, or other legal relations either of that person or of another.

agent's power. The ability of an agent or apparent agent to act on behalf of the principal in matters connected with the agency or apparent agency.

concurrent power. (1812) A political power independently exercisable by both federal and state governments in the same field of legislation.

congressional power. The authority vested in the U.S. Senate and House of Representatives to enact laws and take other constitutionally permitted actions. U.S. Const. art. I.

delegated power. Power normally exercised by an authority that has temporarily conferred the power on a lower authority.

derivative power. Power that arises only from a grant of authority. • Power may be derived, for example, by an agent from a principal, or by a head of state from constitutional or statutory provisions.

discretionary power. A power that a person may choose to exercise or not, based on the person's judgment.

enumerated power. (1805) A political power specifically delegated to a governmental branch by a constitution.

implied power. (1807) A political power that is not enumerated but that nonetheless exists because it is needed to carry out an express power.

incident power. (17c) A power that, although not expressly granted, must exist because it is necessary to the accomplishment of an express purpose.

inherent power. (17c) A power that necessarily derives from an office, position, or status.

investigatory power (in-**ves**-tə-gə-tor-ee). (*usu. pl.*) The authority conferred on a governmental agency to inspect and compel disclosure of facts germane to an investigation.

naked power. (18c) The power to exercise rights over something (such as a trust) without having a corresponding interest in that thing.

plenary power (**plee**-nə-ree *or* **plen**-ə-ree). (16c) Power that is broadly construed; esp., a court's power to dispose of any matter properly before it.

power coupled with an interest. (18c) A power to do some act, conveyed along with an interest in the subject matter of the power. • A power coupled with an interest is not held for the benefit of the principal, and it is irrevocable due to the agent's interest in the subject property. For this reason, some authorities assert that it is not a true agency power.

power of revocation (rev-ə-**kay**-shən). (17c) A power that a person reserves in an instrument (such as a trust) to revoke the legal relationship that the person has created.

public power. A power vested in a person as an agent or instrument of the functions of the state.

quasi-judicial power. (152) An administrative agency's power to adjudicate the rights of those who appear before it.

quasi-legislative power. (1864) An administrative agency's power to engage in rulemaking. 5 USCA § 553.

reserved power. (1831) A political power that is not enumerated or prohibited by a constitution, but instead is reserved by the constitution for a specified political authority, such as a state government.

restraining power. A power to restrict the acts of others.

resulting power. A political power derived from the aggregate powers expressly or impliedly granted by a constitution.

special power. (18c) **1.** An agent's limited authority to perform only specific acts or to perform under specific restrictions. **2.** Limited power of appointment.

spending power. (1923) The power granted to a governmental body to spend public funds; esp., the congressional power to spend money for the payment of debt and provision of the common defense and general welfare of the United States. U.S. Const. art. I, § 8, cl. 1.

taxing power. (18c) The power granted to a governmental body to levy a tax; esp., the congressional power to levy and collect taxes as a means of effectuating Congress's delegated powers. U.S. Const. art. I, § 8, cl. 1.

4. A document granting legal authorization. **5.** An authority to affect an estate in land by (1) creating some estate independently of any estate that the holder of the authority possesses, (2) imposing a charge on the estate, or (3) revoking an existing estate.

appendant power (ə-**pen**-dənt). (17c) **1.** A power that gives the donee a right to appoint estates that attach to the donee's own interest. **2.** A power held by a donee who owns the property interest in the assets subject to the power, and whose interest can be divested by the exercise of the power. • The appendant power is generally viewed as adding nothing to the ownership and thus is not now generally recognized as a true power.

beneficial power. (18c) A power that is executed for the benefit of the power's donee, as distinguished from a *trust power*, which is executed for the benefit of someone other than the power's donee (i.e., a trust beneficiary).

power in gross. (18c) A power held by a donee who has an interest in the assets subject to the power but whose interest cannot be affected by the exercise of the power. • An example is a life tenant with a power over the remainder.

6. Physical strength. **7.** Moral or intellectual force. **8.** A person of influence <a power in the community>. **9.** One of the great nations of the world <one of the world's two great powers>. **10.** The military or unit of it, such as a troop of soldiers.

power of alienation. (16c) The capacity to sell, transfer, assign, or otherwise dispose of property.

power of appointment. (18c) A power created or reserved by a person having property subject to disposition, enabling the donee of the power to designate transferees of the property or shares in which it will be received; esp., a power conferred on a donee by will or deed to select and determine one or more recipients of the donor's estate or income.

general power of appointment. (18c) A power of appointment by which the donee can appoint — that is, dispose of the donor's property — in favor of anyone at all, including oneself or one's own estate; esp., a power that authorizes the alienation of a fee to any alienee.

limited power of appointment. (1830) A power of appointment that either does not allow the entire estate to be conveyed or restricts to whom the estate may be conveyed; esp., a power by which the donee can appoint to only the person or class specified in the instrument creating the power, but cannot appoint to oneself or one's own estate.

testamentary power of appointment (tes-tə-**men**-tə-ree *or* -tree). (1858) A power of appointment created by a will.

power of attorney. (18c) **1.** An instrument granting someone authority to act as agent or attorney-in-fact for the grantor. • An ordinary power of attorney is revocable and automatically terminates upon the death or incapacity of the principal. **2.** The authority so granted; specif., the legal ability to produce a change in legal relations by doing whatever acts are authorized. Pl. **powers of attorney.**

durable power of attorney. (1980) A power of attorney that remains in effect during the grantor's incompetency.

general power of attorney. (18c) A power of attorney that authorizes an agent to transact business for the principal.

irrevocable power of attorney (i-**rev**-ə-kə-bəl). (18c) A power of attorney that the principal cannot revoke.

special power of attorney. (18c) A power of attorney that limits the agent's authority to only a specified matter.

springing power of attorney. A power of attorney that becomes effective only when needed, at some future date or upon some future occurrence, usu. upon the principal's incapacity.

power-of-sale clause. (1883) A provision in a mortgage or deed of trust permitting the mortgagee or trustee to sell the property without court authority if the payments are not made.

power of termination. (1919) A future interest retained by a grantor after conveying a fee simple subject to a condition subsequent, so that the grantee's estate terminates (upon breach of the condition) only if the grantor exercises the right to retake it.

PPO. *abbr.* **1.** Preferred-provider organization. **2.** Permanent protective order.

practicable, *adj.* (16c) (Of a thing) reasonably capable of being accomplished; feasible.

practice, *n.* (15c) **1.** The procedural methods and rules used in a court of law <local practice requires that an extra copy of each motion be filed with

the clerk>. **2.** Practice of law <where is your practice?>.

practice act. (1881) A statute governing practice and procedure in courts. • Practice acts are usu. supplemented with court rules such as the Federal Rules of Civil Procedure.

practice book. (1873) A volume devoted to the procedures in a particular court or category of courts, usu. including court rules, court forms, and practice directions.

practice of law. (17c) The professional work of a duly licensed lawyer, encompassing a broad range of services such as conducting cases in court, preparing papers necessary to bring about various transactions from conveying land to effecting corporate mergers, preparing legal opinions on various points of law, drafting wills and other estate-planning documents, and advising clients on legal questions. • The term also includes activities that comparatively few lawyers engage in but that require legal expertise, such as drafting legislation and court rules.

unauthorized practice of law. (1928) The practice of law by a person, typically a nonlawyer, who has not been licensed or admitted to practice law in a given jurisdiction. — Abbr. UPL.

practitioner. (16c) A person engaged in the practice of a profession, esp. law or medicine.

praecipe (**pree**-sə-pee *or* **pres**-ə-pee), *n.* [Latin "command"] (15c) **1.** At common law, a writ ordering a defendant to do some act or to explain why inaction is appropriate. **2.** A written motion or request seeking some court action, esp. a trial setting or an entry of judgment. — **praecipe,** *vb.*

praxis (**prak**-sis). [Greek "doing; action"] (1933) In critical legal studies, practical action; the practice of living the ethical life in conjunction and in cooperation with others.

prayer for relief. (18c) A request addressed to the court and appearing at the end of a pleading; esp., a request for specific relief or damages.

general prayer. (18c) A prayer for additional unspecified relief, traditionally using language such as, "Plaintiff additionally prays for such other and further relief to which she may show herself to be justly entitled." • The general prayer typically follows a special prayer.

special prayer. (18c) A prayer for the particular relief to which a plaintiff claims to be entitled.

prayer of process. (18c) A conclusion in a bill in equity requesting the issuance of a subpoena if the defendant fails to answer the bill.

preamble (**pree**-am-bəl), *n.* (14c) An introductory statement in a constitution, statute, or other document explaining the document's basis and objective; esp., a statutory recital of the inconveniences for which the statute is designed to provide a remedy. — **preambulary** (pree-**am**-byə-ler-ee), **preambular** (pree-**am**-byə-lər), *adj.*

precarious, *adj.* (17c) Dependent on the will or pleasure of another; uncertain.

precatory (**prek**-ə-tor-ee), *adj.* (17c) (Of words) requesting, recommending, or expressing a desire for action, but usu. in a nonbinding way. • An example of precatory language is "it is my wish and desire to . . . ."

precedence (**pres**-ə-dənts *or* prə-**seed**-ənts), *n.* (16c) **1.** The order or priority in place or time observed by or for persons of different statuses (such as political dignitaries) on the basis of rank during ceremonial events. **2.** Generally, the act or state of going before something else according to some system of priorities. **3.** The order in which persons may claim the right to administer an intestate's estate.

precedent (prə-**seed**-ənt *also* **pres**-ə-dənt), *adj.* (14c) Preceding in time or order <condition precedent>.

precedent (**pres**-ə-dənt), *n.* (16c) **1.** The making of law by a court in recognizing and applying new rules while administering justice. **2.** A decided case that furnishes a basis for determining later cases involving similar facts or issues. — **precedential,** *adj.*

binding precedent. (17c) A precedent that a court must follow. • For example, a lower court is bound by an applicable holding of a higher court in the same jurisdiction.

declaratory precedent. (1900) A precedent that is merely the application of an already existing legal rule.

original precedent. (17c) A precedent that creates and applies a new legal rule.

persuasive precedent. (1905) A precedent that is not binding on a court, but that is entitled to respect and careful consideration.

precedent sub silentio (səb sə-**len**-shee-oh). (1825) A legal question that was neither argued nor explicitly discussed in a judicial decision but that seems to have been silently ruled on and might therefore be treated as a precedent.

superprecedent. **1.** A precedent that defines the law and its requirements so effectively that it prevents divergent holdings in later legal decisions on similar facts or induces disputants to settle their claims without litigation. **2.** A precedent that has become so established in the law by a long line of reaffirmations that it is very difficult to overturn it; specif., a precedent that has been reaffirmed many times and whose rationale has been extended to cover cases in which the facts are dissimilar, even wholly unrelated, to those of the precedent. • For example, *Roe v. Wade* has been called a superprecedent because it has survived more than three dozen attempts to overturn it and has been relied on in decisions protecting gay rights and the right to die.

3. Doctrine of precedent. **4.** A form of pleading or property-conveyancing instrument. • Precedents are often compiled in book form and used by lawyers as guides for preparing similar documents.

precept (**pree**-sept). (14c) **1.** A standard or rule of conduct; a command or principle <several legal precepts govern here>. **2.** A writ or warrant issued by an authorized person demanding another's action, such as a judge's order to an officer to bring a party before the court <the sheriff executed the precept immediately>.

precinct. A geographical unit of government, such as an election district, a police district, or a judicial district.

précis (pray-**see** *or* **pray**-see), *n.* [French] (18c) A concise summary of a text's essential points; an abstract. Pl. **précis** (pray-**seez** *or* **pray**-seez).

predecease, *vb.* To die before (another) <she predeceased her husband>.

predial (**pree**-dee-əl), *adj.* (15c) Of, consisting of, relating to, or attached to land <predial servitude>.

predicate act. (1977) **1.** Predicate offense. **2.** Lesser included offense. **3.** Under RICO, one of two or more related acts of racketeering necessary to establish a pattern.

prediction theory. 1. Bad-man theory. **2.** Predictive theory of law.

predictive theory of law. (1956) The view that the law is nothing more than a set of predictions about what the courts will decide in given circumstances. • This theory is embodied in Holmes's famous pronouncement, "The prophecies of what the courts will do in fact, and nothing more pretentious, are what I mean by the law." Oliver Wendell

Holmes, *The Path of the Law*, 10 Harv. L. Rev. 457, 460–61 (1897).

predisposition. (17c) A person's inclination to engage in a particular activity; esp., an inclination that vitiates a criminal defendant's claim of entrapment.

predominant-purpose test. An assessment of whether Article 2 of the UCC applies to an exchange, conducted by considering whether the exchange's chief aspect, viewed in light of all the circumstances, is the sale of goods. • If goods account for most of the exchange's value, it is probably a sale; if services account for most of the value, it probably is not.

preemption (pree-**emp**-shən), *n.* (18c) **1.** The right to buy before others. **2.** The purchase of something under this right. **3.** An earlier seizure or appropriation. **4.** The occupation of public land so as to establish a preemptive title. **5.** *Constitutional law.* The principle (derived from the Supremacy Clause) that a federal law can supersede or supplant any inconsistent state law or regulation. — **preempt,** *vb.* — **preemptive,** *adj.*

preemption claimant. (1824) One who has settled on land subject to preemption, intending in good faith to acquire title to it.

preemption right. (18c) The privilege to take priority over others in claiming land subject to preemption. • The privilege arises from the holder's actual settlement of the land.

preexisting-duty rule. (1990) *Contracts.* The rule that if a party does or promises to do what the party is already legally obligated to do — or refrains or promises to refrain from doing what the party is already legally obligated to refrain from doing — the party has not incurred detriment.

prefer, *vb.* (14c) **1.** To put forward or present for consideration; esp. (of a grand jury), to bring (a charge or indictment) against a criminal suspect. **2.** To give priority to, such as to one creditor over another.

preference. 1. The act of favoring one person or thing over another; the person or thing so favored. **2.** Priority of payment given to one or more creditors by a debtor; a creditor's right to receive such priority. **3.** *Bankruptcy.* Preferential transfer.

insider preference. A transfer of property by a bankruptcy debtor to an insider more than 90 days before but within one year after the filing of the bankruptcy petition.

liquidation preference. A preferred shareholder's right, once the corporation is liquidated, to receive a specified distribution before common shareholders receive anything.

preferential rule. (1959) *Evidence.* A rule that prefers one kind of evidence to another. • It may work provisionally, as when a tribunal refuses to consider one kind of evidence until another kind (presumably better) is shown to be unavailable, or it may work absolutely, as when the tribunal refuses to consider anything but the better kind of evidence.

preferential transfer. *Bankruptcy.* A prebankruptcy transfer made by an insolvent debtor to or for the benefit of a creditor, thereby allowing the creditor to receive more than its proportionate share of the debtor's assets; specif., an insolvent debtor's transfer of a property interest for the benefit of a creditor who is owed on an earlier debt, when the transfer occurs no more than 90 days before the date when the bankruptcy petition is filed or (if the creditor is an insider) within one year of the filing, so that the creditor receives more than it would otherwise receive through the distribution of the bankruptcy estate. • Under the circumstances described in 11 USCA § 547, the bankruptcy trustee may recover — for the estate's benefit — a preferential transfer from the transferee.

preferred-provider organization. (1984) A group of healthcare providers (such as doctors, hospitals, and pharmacies) that agree to provide medical services at a discounted cost to covered persons in a given geographic area. — Abbr. PPO.

prehearing conference. (1946) An optional conference for the discussion of procedural and substantive matters on appeal, usu. held in complex civil, criminal, tax, and agency cases.

prejudice, *n.* (14c) **1.** Damage or detriment to one's legal rights or claims.

legal prejudice. (18c) A condition that, if shown by a party, will usu. defeat the opposing party's action; esp., a condition that, if shown by the defendant, will defeat a plaintiff's motion to dismiss a case without prejudice.

undue prejudice. (17c) The harm resulting from a fact-trier's being exposed to evidence that is persuasive but inadmissible (such as evidence of prior criminal conduct) or that so arouses the emotions that calm and logical reasoning is abandoned.

2. A preconceived judgment formed with little or no factual basis; a strong bias. — **prejudice,** *vb.* — **prejudicial,** *adj.*

prejudicial publicity. (1935) Extensive media attention devoted to an upcoming civil or criminal trial.

preliminary hearing. A criminal hearing (usu. conducted by a magistrate) to determine whether there is sufficient evidence to prosecute an accused person.

preliminary inquiry. *Military law.* The initial investigation of a reported or suspected violation of the Uniform Code of Military Justice.

preliminary statement. (1834) The introductory part of a brief or memorandum in support of a motion, in which the advocate summarizes the essence of what follows.

premarital, *adj.* Of, relating to, or occurring before marriage.

prematurity. 1. The circumstance existing when the facts underlying a plaintiff's complaint do not yet create a live claim. **2.** The affirmative defense based on this circumstance.

premeditated, *adj.* (16c) Done with willful deliberation and planning; consciously considered beforehand <a premeditated killing>.

premeditation, *n.* (15c) Conscious consideration and planning that precedes some act (such as committing a crime). — **premeditate,** *vb.*

premise (**prem**-is), *n.* (14c) A previous statement or contention from which a conclusion is deduced. — **premise** (**prem**-is *or* pri-**mɪz**), *vb.*

premises (**prem**-ə-siz). (15c) **1.** Matters (usu. preliminary facts or statements) previously referred to in the same instrument <wherefore, premises considered, the plaintiff prays for the following relief>. **2.** The part of a deed that describes the land being conveyed, as well as naming the parties and identifying relevant facts or explaining the reasons for the deed. **3.** A house or building, along with its grounds <smoking is not allowed on these premises>.

premises liability. (1950) A landowner's or landholder's tort liability for conditions or activities on the premises.

premium, *n.* **1.** The periodic payment required to keep an insurance policy in effect. **2.** A sum of money paid in addition to a regular price, salary, or other amount; a bonus. **3.** The amount by which a security's market value exceeds its face value. **4.** The amount paid to buy a securities option.

premium rate. *Insurance.* The price per unit of life insurance. • Life insurers use three factors — the interest factor, the mortality factor, and the risk factor — to calculate premium rates.

prenatal injury. Harm to a fetus or an embryo.

prenuptial (pree-**nəp**-shəl), *adj.* (1857) Made or occurring before marriage; premarital.

prenuptial agreement. (1882) An agreement made before marriage usu. to resolve issues of support and property division if the marriage ends in divorce or by the death of a spouse.

prepaid legal services. (1963) An arrangement — usu. serving as an employee benefit — that enables a person to make advance payments for future legal services.

preparation. *Criminal law.* The act or process of devising the means necessary to commit a crime.

prepayment clause. (1935) A loan-document provision that permits a borrower to satisfy a debt before its due date.

prepetition (pree-pə-**tish**-ən), *adj.* (1938) Occurring before the filing of a petition (esp. in bankruptcy) <prepetition debts>.

preponderance (pri-**pon**-dər-ənts), *n.* (17c) Superiority in weight, importance, or influence. — **preponderate** (pri-**pon**-dər-ayt), *vb.* — **preponderant** (pri-**pon**-dər-ənt), *adj.*

preponderance of the evidence. (18c) The greater weight of the evidence, not necessarily established by the greater number of witnesses testifying to a fact but by evidence that has the most convincing force; superior evidentiary weight that, though not sufficient to free the mind wholly from all reasonable doubt, is still sufficient to incline a fair and impartial mind to one side of the issue rather than the other. • This is the burden of proof in most civil trials, in which the jury is instructed to find for the party that, on the whole, has the stronger evidence, however slight the edge may be.

prerogative (pri-**rog**-ə-tiv), *n.* (15c) An exclusive right, power, privilege, or immunity, usu. acquired by virtue of office. — **prerogative,** *adj.*

prescribable (pri-**skrıb**-ə-bəl), *adj.* (1890) (Of a right) that can be acquired or extinguished by prescription.

prescribe, *vb.* **1.** To dictate, ordain, or direct; to establish authoritatively (as a rule or guideline). **2.** To claim ownership through prescription. **3.** To invalidate or otherwise make unenforceable through prescription. **4.** To become invalid or otherwise unenforceable through prescription.

prescription, *n.* (15c) **1.** The act of establishing authoritative rules. **2.** A rule so established. **3.** The effect of the lapse of time in creating and destroying rights. **4.** The extinction of a title or right by failure to claim or exercise it over a long period. **5.** The acquisition of title to a thing (esp. an intangible thing such as the use of real property) by open and continuous possession over a statutory period.

prescriptive right. (17c) A right obtained by prescription <after a nuisance has been continuously in existence for 20 years, a prescriptive right to continue it is acquired as an easement appurtenant to the land on which it exists>.

presence, *n.* **1.** The state or fact of being in a particular place and time. **2.** Close physical proximity coupled with awareness.

constructive presence. **1.** *Criminal law.* Legal imputation of having been at a crime scene, based on having been close enough to the scene to have aided and abetted the crime's commission. **2.** *Wills & estates.* Legal imputation of a witness's having been in the room when a will was signed, based on the fact that the testator and the witness were able to see each other at the time of the signing. • This principle was commonly employed until the 20th century, when the presence-of-the-testator rule became dominant.

presence-of-defendant rule. The principle that a felony defendant is entitled to be present at every major stage of the criminal proceeding. Fed. R. Crim. P. 43.

presence of the court. (18c) The company or proximity of the judge or other courtroom official. • For purposes of contempt, an action is in the presence of the court if it is committed within the view of the judge or other person in court and is intended to disrupt the court's business.

presence-of-the-testator rule. The principle that a testator must be aware (through sight or other sense) that the witnesses are signing the will. • Many jurisdictions interpret this requirement liberally, and the Uniform Probate Code has dispensed with it.

present, *adj.* (14c) **1.** Now existing; at hand <a present right to the property>. **2.** Being considered; now under discussion <the present appeal does not deal with that issue>. **3.** In attendance; not elsewhere <all present voted for him>.

presentation. (15c) The delivery of a document to an issuer or named person for the purpose of initiating action under a letter of credit; PRESENTMENT (3).

presentence hearing. (1940) A proceeding at which a judge or jury receives and examines all relevant information regarding a convicted criminal and the related offense before passing sentence.

presentence-investigation report. (1943) A probation officer's detailed account of a convicted defendant's educational, criminal, family, and social background, conducted at the court's request as an aid in passing sentence. See Fed. R. Crim. P. 32(c). — Abbr. PSI; PIR.

presenter. *Commercial law.* Any person presenting a document (such as a draft) to an issuer for honor. UCC § 5-102.

presentment (pri-**zent**-mənt). (15c) **1.** The act of presenting or laying before a court or other tribunal a formal statement about a matter to be dealt with legally. **2.** *Criminal procedure.* A formal written accusation returned by a grand jury on its own initiative, without a prosecutor's previous indictment request. • Presentments are obsolete in the federal courts. **3.** The formal production of a negotiable instrument for acceptance or payment.

presentment for acceptance. (18c) Production of an instrument to the drawee, acceptor, or maker for acceptance. • This type of presentment may be made anytime before maturity, except that with bills payable at sight, after demand, or after sight, presentment must be made within a reasonable time.

presentment for payment. (18c) Production of an instrument to the drawee, acceptor, or maker for payment. • This type of presentment must be made on the date when the instrument is due.

present recollection refreshed. (1908) *Evidence.* A witness's memory that has been enhanced by showing the witness a document that describes the relevant events. • The document itself is merely a memory stimulus and is not admitted in evidence. Fed. R. Evid. 612.

presents, *n. pl.* (14c) *Archaic.* The instrument under consideration. • This is usu. part of the phrase *these presents,* which is part of the longer phrase *know all men by these presents* (itself a loan translation from the Latin *noverint universi per praesentes*).

present sense impression. (1942) *Evidence.* One's perception of an event or condition, formed during or immediately after the fact. • A statement containing a present sense impression is admissible even if it is hearsay. Fed. R. Evid. 803(1).

preside, *vb.* (15c) **1.** To occupy the place of authority, esp. as a judge during a hearing or trial <preside over the proceedings>. **2.** To exercise management or control <preside over the estate>.

president, *n.* **1.** The chief political executive of a government; the head of state. **2.** The chief executive officer of a corporation or other organization. **3.** CHAIR. — **presidential,** *adj.*

President of the United States. The highest executive officer of the federal government of the United States.

press, *n.* The news media; print and broadcast news organizations collectively.

Press Clause. The First Amendment provision that "Congress shall make no law . . . abridging the freedom . . . of the press." U.S. Const. amend I.

presume, *vb.* To assume beforehand; to suppose to be true in the absence of proof.

presumption. (15c) A legal inference or assumption that a fact exists, based on the known or proven existence of some other fact or group of facts. • Most presumptions are rules of evidence calling for a certain result in a given case unless the adversely affected party overcomes it with other evidence. A presumption shifts the burden of production or persuasion to the opposing party, who can then attempt to overcome the presumption.

conclusive presumption. (18c) A presumption that cannot be overcome by any additional evidence or argument.

conflicting presumption. (1830) One of two or more presumptions that would lead to opposite results.

heeding presumption. (1990) A rebuttable presumption that an injured product user would have followed a warning label had the product manufacturer provided one.

mixed presumption. (1838) A presumption containing elements of both law and fact.

natural presumption. (16c) A deduction of one fact from another, based on common experience.

permissive presumption. (1827) A presumption that a trier of fact is free to accept or reject from a given set of facts.

presumption of fact. A type of rebuttable presumption that may be, but as a matter of law need not be, drawn from another established fact or group of facts.

presumption of intent. (18c) A permissive presumption that a criminal defendant who intended to commit an act did so.

presumption of law. (16c) A legal assumption that a court is required to make if certain facts are established and no contradictory evidence is produced.

procedural presumption. A presumption that may be rebutted by credible evidence.

rebuttable presumption. (1852) An inference drawn from certain facts that establish a prima facie case, which may be overcome by the introduction of contrary evidence.

statutory presumption. (1819) A rebuttable or conclusive presumption that is created by statute.

presumption of death. (18c) A presumption that arises on the unexpected disappearance and continued absence of a person for an extended period, commonly seven years.

presumption of innocence. (18c) *Criminal law.* The fundamental principle that a person may not be convicted of a crime unless the government proves guilt beyond a reasonable doubt, without any burden placed on the accused to prove innocence.

presumption of maternity. *Family law.* The presumption that the woman who has given birth to a child is both the genetic mother and the legal mother of the child.

presumption of natural and probable consequences. (1980) *Criminal law.* The presumption that *mens rea* may be derived from proof of the defendant's conduct.

presumption of paternity. (1829) *Family law.* The presumption that the father of a child is the man who (1) is married to the child's mother when the child was conceived or born (even though the marriage may have been invalid), (2) married the mother after the child's birth and agreed either to have his name on the birth certificate or to support the child, or (3) welcomed the child into his home and later held out the child as his own.

presumption of survivorship. (1844) The presumption that one of two or more victims of a common disaster survived the others, based on the supposed survivor's youth, good health, or other reason rendering survivorship likely.

presumption of validity. *Patents.* The doctrine that the holder of a patent is entitled to a statutory presumption that the patent is valid and that the burden is on a challenger to prove invalidity.

presumptive (pri-**zəmp**-tiv), *adj.* (15c) **1.** Giving reasonable grounds for belief or presumption. **2.** Based on a presumption. — **presumptively,** *adv.*

pretermission (pree-tər-**mish**-ən). (18c) **1.** The condition of one who is pretermitted, as an heir of a testator. **2.** The act of omitting an heir from a will.

pretermit (pree-tər-**mit**), *vb.* (15c) **1.** To ignore or disregard purposely <the court pretermitted the constitutional question by deciding the case on procedural grounds>. **2.** To neglect, overlook, or omit accidentally <the third child was pretermitted in the will>. • Although in ordinary usage sense 1 prevails, in legal contexts (esp. involving heirs) sense 2 is usual.

pretermitted-heir statute. (1955) A state law that, under certain circumstances, grants an omitted heir the right to inherit a share of the testator's estate, usu. by treating the heir as though the testator had died intestate.

pretext (**pree**-tekst), *n.* (16c) A false or weak reason or motive advanced to hide the actual or strong reason or motive. — **pretextual** (pree-**teks**-choo-əl), *adj.*

pretrial conference. (1938) An informal meeting at which opposing attorneys confer, usu. with the judge, to work toward the disposition of the case by discussing matters of evidence and narrowing the issues that will be tried. See Fed. R. Civ. P. 16; Fed. R. Crim. P. 17.1.

pretrial hearing. Pretrial conference.

pretrial intervention. 1. DIVERSION PROGRAM (1). **2.** Deferred judgment.

pretrial order. (1939) A court order setting out the claims and defenses to be tried, the stipulations of the parties, and the case's procedural rules, as agreed to by the parties or mandated by the court at a pretrial conference. See Fed. R. Civ. P. 16(e).

prevail, *vb.* (17c) **1.** To obtain the relief sought in an action; to win a lawsuit. **2.** To be commonly accepted or predominant.

prevarication (pri-var-ə-**kay**-shən), *n.* (16c) The act or an instance of lying or avoiding the truth; equivocation. — **prevaricate** (pri-**var**-ə-kayt), *vb.* — **prevaricator** (pri-**var**-ə-kay-tər), *n.*

prevent, *vb.* To hinder or impede.

prevention doctrine. (1979) *Contracts.* The principle that each contracting party has an implied duty to not do anything that prevents the other party from performing its obligation.

preventive law. A practice of law that seeks to minimize a client's risk of litigation or secure more certainty with regard to the client's legal rights and duties. • Emphasizing planning, counseling, and the nonadversarial resolution of disputes, preventive law focuses on the lawyer's role as adviser and negotiator.

price. The amount of money or other consideration asked for or given in exchange for something else; the cost at which something is bought or sold.

market price. The prevailing price at which something is sold in a specific market.

suggested retail price. The sales price recommended to a retailer by a manufacturer of the product.

wholesale price. The price that a retailer pays for goods purchased (usu. in bulk) from a wholesaler for resale to consumers at a higher price.

price discrimination. (1915) The practice of offering identical or similar goods to different buyers at different prices when the costs of producing the goods are the same.

price-fixing. (1889) The artificial setting or maintenance of prices at a certain level, contrary to the workings of the free market. • Price-fixing is usu. illegal per se under antitrust law.

horizontal price-fixing. (1935) Price-fixing among competitors on the same level, such as retailers throughout an industry.

vertical price-fixing. (1936) Price-fixing among parties in the same chain of distribution, such as manufacturers and retailers attempting to control an item's resale price.

price index. An index of average prices as a percentage of the average prevailing at some other time (such as a base year).

price leadership. (1942) A market condition in which an industry leader establishes a price that others in the field adopt as their own. • Price leadership alone does not violate antitrust laws without other evidence of an intent to create a monopoly.

price support. (1927) The artificial maintenance of prices (as of a particular commodity) at a certain level, esp. by governmental action (as by subsidy).

price war. (1895) A period of sustained or repeated price-cutting in an industry (esp. among retailers), designed to undersell competitors or force them out of business.

prima facie (**prɪ**-mə **fay**-shə *or* **fay**-shee), *adv.* [Latin] (15c) At first sight; on first appearance but subject to further evidence or information <the agreement is prima facie valid>.

prima facie, *adj.* (18c) Sufficient to establish a fact or raise a presumption unless disproved or rebutted <a prima facie showing>.

prima facie case. (1805) **1.** The establishment of a legally required rebuttable presumption. **2.** A party's production of enough evidence to allow the fact-trier to infer the fact at issue and rule in the party's favor.

prima facie presumption. Rebuttable presumption.

primary caregiver. *Family law.* **1.** The parent who has had the greatest responsibility for the daily care and rearing of a child. **2.** The person (including a nonparent) who has had the greatest responsibility for the daily care and rearing of a child.

primary-caregiver doctrine. *Family law.* The presumption that, in a custody dispute, the parent who is a child's main caregiver will be the child's custodian, assuming that he or she is a fit parent.

primary committee. *Bankruptcy.* A group of creditors organized to help the debtor draw up a reorganization plan.

prime, *vb.* To take priority over <Watson's preferred mortgage primed Moriarty's lien>.

primogeniture (prɪ-mə-**jen**-ə-chər). (15c) **1.** The state of being the firstborn child among siblings. **2.** The common-law right of the firstborn son to inherit his ancestor's estate, usu. to the exclusion of younger siblings.

principal, *adj.* Chief; primary; most important.

principal, *n.* (14c) **1.** One who authorizes another to act on his or her behalf as an agent.

apparent principal. A person who, by outward manifestations, has made it reasonably appear to a third person that another is authorized to act as the person's agent.

disclosed principal. (1858) A principal whose identity is revealed by the agent to a third party. • A disclosed principal is always liable on a contract entered into by the agent with the principal's authority, but the agent is usu. not liable.

partially disclosed principal. (1934) A principal whose existence — but not actual identity — is revealed by the agent to a third party.

undisclosed principal. (1835) A principal whose identity is kept secret by the agent; a principal for whom the other party has no notice that the agent is acting. • An undisclosed principal and the agent are both liable on a contract entered into by the agent with the principal's authority.

2. One who commits or participates in a crime.

principal in the first degree. (18c) The perpetrator of a crime.

principal in the second degree. (18c) One who helped the perpetrator at the time of the crime.

3. One who has primary responsibility on an obligation, as opposed to a surety or indorser. **4.** The corpus of an estate or trust. **5.** The amount of a debt, investment, or other fund, not including interest, earnings, or profits.

Principal Register. *Trademarks.* The list of distinctive marks approved for federal trademark registration.

Printers Ink Statute. A model statute drafted in 1911 and adopted in a number of states making it a misdemeanor to print an advertisement that contains a false or deceptive statement.

prior, *adj.* (17c) **1.** Preceding in time or order <under this court's prior order>. **2.** Taking precedence <a prior lien>.

prior, *n.* (1919) *Criminal law. Slang.* A previous conviction <because the defendant had two priors, the judge automatically enhanced his sentence>.

prior-appropriation doctrine. (1959) The rule that, among the persons whose properties border on a waterway, the earliest users of the water have the right to take all they can use before anyone else has a right to it.

priority. (15c) **1.** The status of being earlier in time or higher in degree or rank; precedence. **2.** *Commercial law.* An established right to such precedence; esp., a creditor's right to have a claim paid before other creditors of the same debtor receive payment. **3.** The doctrine that, as between two courts, jurisdiction should be accorded the court in which proceedings are first begun. **4.** *Patents & Trademarks.* The status of being first to invent something (and therefore be potentially eligible for patent protection) or to use a mark in trade (and therefore be potentially eligible for trademark registration).

prior restraint. (1833) A governmental restriction on speech or publication before its actual expression. • Prior restraints violate the First Amendment unless the speech is obscene, is defamatory, or creates a clear and present danger to society.

prior-use doctrine. (1856) The principle that, without legislative authorization, a government agency may not appropriate property already devoted to a public use.

prison. (bef. 12c) A state or federal facility of confinement for convicted criminals, esp. felons.

private prison. (1865) A prison that is managed by a private company, not by a governmental agency.

prison breach. (17c) A prisoner's forcible breaking and departure from a place of lawful confinement; the offense of escaping from confinement in a prison or jail.

prison camp. (1864) A usu. minimum-security camp for the detention of trustworthy prisoners who are often employed on government projects.

prisoner. 1. A person who is serving time in prison. **2.** A person who has been apprehended by a law-enforcement officer and is in custody, regardless of whether the person has yet been put in prison.

prisoner of conscience. *Human-rights law.* A person who is imprisoned because of his or her beliefs, race, sex, ethnic origin, language, or religion. • The range of "beliefs" that fall within this definition is not settled but may include political ideologies and objections to military service, esp. in wartime.

prisoner of war. A person, usu. a soldier, who is captured by or surrenders to the enemy in wartime. — Abbr. POW.

privacy. The condition or state of being free from public attention to intrusion into or interference with one's acts or decisions.

privacy law. (1936) **1.** A federal or state statute that protects a person's right to be left alone or that restricts public access to personal information such as tax returns and medical records. **2.** The area of legal studies dealing with a person's right to be left alone and with restricting public access to personal information such as tax returns and medical records.

private, *adj.* (14c) **1.** Relating or belonging to an individual, as opposed to the public or the government. **2.** (Of a company) not having shares that are freely available on an open market. **3.** Confidential; secret.

private-attorney-general doctrine. The equitable principle that allows the recovery of attorney's fees to a party who brings a lawsuit that benefits a significant number of people, requires private enforcement, and is important to society as a whole.

private judging. (1979) A type of alternative dispute resolution whereby the parties hire a private individual to hear and decide a case.

private law. (18c) The body of law dealing with private persons and their property and relationships.

private sector. (1930) The part of the economy or an industry that is free from direct governmental control.

privation (prɪ-**vay**-shən). (15c) **1.** The act of taking away or withdrawing. **2.** The condition of being deprived.

privatization (prɪ-və-tə-**zay**-shən), *n.* (1942) The act or process of converting a business or industry from governmental ownership or control to private enterprise. — **privatize,** *vb.*

privilege. (bef. 12c) **1.** A special legal right, exemption, or immunity granted to a person or class of persons; an exception to a duty.

absolute privilege. (18c) A privilege that immunizes an actor from suit, no matter how wrongful the action might be, and even though it is done with an improper motive.

deliberative-process privilege. (1977) A privilege permitting the government to withhold documents relating to policy formulation to encourage open and independent discussion among those who develop government policy.

judicial privilege. (1845) *Defamation.* **1.** The privilege protecting any statement made in the course of and with reference to a judicial proceeding by any judge, juror, party, witness, or advocate. **2.** Litigation privilege.

legislative privilege. (1941) *Defamation.* The privilege protecting (1) any statement made in a legislature by one of its members, and (2) any paper published as part of legislative business.

litigation privilege. A privilege protecting the attorneys and parties in a lawsuit against tort claims based on certain acts done and statements made when related to the litigation. • The privilege is most often applied to defamation claims but may be extended to encompass other torts, such as invasion of privacy and disclosure of trade secrets. The facts of each case determine whether the privilege applies and whether it is qualified or absolute.

official privilege. (1927) The privilege immunizing from a defamation lawsuit any statement made by one state officer to another in the course of official duty.

privilege from arrest. (1840) An exemption from arrest, as that enjoyed by members of Congress during legislative sessions. U.S. Const. art. I, § 6, cl. 1.

qualified privilege. (1865) A privilege that immunizes an actor from suit only when the privilege is properly exercised in the performance of a legal or moral duty.

special privilege. (17c) A privilege granted to a person or class of persons to the exclusion of others and in derogation of the common right.

testimonial privilege. (1907) A right not to testify based on a claim of privilege; a privilege that overrides a witness's duty to disclose matters within the witness's knowledge, whether at trial or by deposition.

viatorial privilege (vɪ-ə-**tor**-ee-əl). (1904) A privilege that overrides a person's duty to attend court in person and to testify.

2. An affirmative defense by which a defendant acknowledges at least part of the conduct complained of but asserts that the defendant's conduct was authorized or sanctioned by law; esp., in tort law, a circumstance justifying or excusing an intentional tort. **3.** An evidentiary rule that gives a witness the option to not disclose the fact asked for, even though it might be relevant; the right to prevent disclosure of certain information in court, esp. when the information was originally communicated in a professional or confidential relationship. • Assertion of an evidentiary privilege can be overcome by proof that an otherwise privileged communication was made in the presence of a third party to whom the privilege would not apply.

accountant–client privilege. (1956) The protection afforded to a client from an accountant's unauthorized disclosure of materials submitted to or prepared by the accountant. • The privilege is not widely recognized.

attorney–client privilege. (1934) The client's right to refuse to disclose and to prevent any other person from disclosing confidential communications between the client and the attorney. • The privilege is widely recognized.

doctor–patient privilege. (1954) The right to exclude from discovery and evidence in a legal proceeding any confidential communication that a patient makes to a physician for the purpose of diagnosis or treatment, unless the patient consents to the disclosure.

executive privilege. (1909) A privilege, based on the constitutional doctrine of separation of powers, that exempts the executive branch of the federal government from usual disclosure requirements when the matter to be disclosed involves national security or foreign policy.

informant's privilege. (1962) The qualified privilege that a government can invoke to prevent disclosure of the identity and communications of its informants. • In exercising its power to formulate evidentiary rules for federal criminal cases, the U.S. Supreme Court has consistently declined to hold that the government must disclose the identity of informants in a preliminary hearing or in a criminal trial. *McCray v. Illinois*, 386 U.S. 300, 312, 87 S.Ct. 1056, 1063 (1967). A party can, however, usu. overcome the privilege by demonstrating that the need for the information outweighs the public interest in maintaining the privilege.

joint-defense privilege. (1975) The rule that a defendant can assert the attorney–client privilege to protect a confidential communication made to a codefendant's lawyer if the communication was related to the defense of both defendants.

journalist's privilege. (1970) **1.** A reporter's protection, under constitutional or statutory law, from being compelled to testify about confidential information or sources. **2.** A publisher's protection against defamation lawsuits when the publication makes fair comment on the actions of public officials in matters of public concern.

marital privilege. (1902) **1.** The privilege allowing a spouse not to testify, and to prevent another person from testifying, about confidential communications between the spouses during the marriage. **2.** The privilege allowing a spouse not to testify in a criminal case as an adverse witness against the other spouse, regardless of the subject matter of the testimony. **3.** The privilege immunizing from a defamation lawsuit any statement made between husband and wife.

peer-review privilege. (1979) A privilege that protects from disclosure the proceedings and reports of a medical facility's peer-review committee, which reviews and oversees the patient care and medical services provided by the staff.

political-vote privilege. A privilege to protect from compulsory disclosure a vote cast in an election by secret ballot.

priest–penitent privilege. (1958) The privilege barring a clergy member from testifying about a confessor's communications.

privacy privilege. A defendant's right not to disclose private information unless the plaintiff can show that (1) the information is directly relevant to the case, and (2) the plaintiff's need for the information outweighs the defendant's need for nondisclosure. • This privilege is recognized in California but in few other jurisdictions.

privilege against self-incrimination. *Criminal law.* **1.** RIGHT AGAINST SELF-INCRIMINATION. **2.** A criminal defendant's right not to be asked any questions by the judge or prosecution unless the defendant chooses to testify.

psychotherapist–patient privilege. (1968) A privilege that a person can invoke to prevent the disclosure of a confidential communication made in the course of diagnosis or treatment of a mental or emotional condition by or at the direction of a psychotherapist. • The privilege can be overcome under certain conditions, as when the examination is ordered by a court.

self-critical-analysis privilege. (1982) A privilege protecting individuals and entities from divulging the results of candid assessments of their compliance with laws and regulations, to the extent that the assessments are internal, the results were intended from the outset to be confidential, and the information is of a type that would be curtailed if it were forced to be disclosed. • This privilege is founded on the public policy that it is beneficial to permit individuals and entities to confidentially evaluate their compliance with the law, so that they will monitor and improve their compliance with it.

state-secrets privilege. (1959) A privilege that the government may invoke against the discovery of a material that, if divulged, could compromise national security.

tax-return privilege. A privilege to refuse to divulge the contents of a tax return or certain related documents. • The privilege is founded on the public policy of encouraging honest tax returns.

privileged, *adj.* **1.** Not subject to the usual rules or liabilities; esp., not subject to disclosure during the course of a lawsuit <a privileged document>. **2.** Enjoying or subject to a privilege.

Privileges and Immunities Clause. (1911) The constitutional provision (U.S. Const. art. IV, § 2, cl. 1) prohibiting a state from favoring its own citizens by discriminating against other states' citizens who come within its borders.

Privileges or Immunities Clause. (1918) The constitutional provision (U.S. Const. amend. XIV, § 1) prohibiting state laws that abridge the privileges or immunities of U.S. citizens. • The clause was effectively nullified by the Supreme Court in the *Slaughter-House Cases*, 83 U.S. (16 Wall.) 36 (1873).

privity (**priv**-ə-tee). (16c) **1.** The connection or relationship between two parties, each having a legally recognized interest in the same subject matter (such as a transaction, proceeding, or piece of property); mutuality of interest <privity of contract>.

horizontal privity. (1968) *Commercial law.* The legal relationship between a party and a nonparty who is related to the party (such as a buyer and a member of the buyer's family).

privity of blood. (16c) **1.** Privity between an heir and an ancestor. **2.** Privity between coparceners.

privity of contract. (17c) The relationship between the parties to a contract, allowing them to sue each other but preventing a third party from doing so.

privity of estate. (17c) A mutual or successive relationship to the same right in property, as between grantor and grantee or landlord and tenant.

privity of possession. (1818) Privity between parties in successive possession of real property. • The existence of this type of privity is often at issue in adverse-possession claims.

vertical privity. (1968) **1.** *Commercial law.* The legal relationship between parties in a product's chain of distribution (such as a manufacturer and a seller). **2.** Privity between one who signs a contract containing a restrictive covenant and one who acquires the property burdened by it.

2. Joint knowledge or awareness of something private or secret, esp. as implying concurrence or consent <privity to a crime>.

privy (**priv**-ee), *n. pl.* (15c) A person having a legal interest of privity in any action, matter, or property; a person who is in privity with another. Pl. **privies.**

prize. 1. Something of value awarded in recognition of a person's achievement. **2.** A vessel or cargo captured at sea or seized in port by the forces of a nation at war, and therefore liable to being condemned or appropriated as enemy property.

prize law. The system of laws applicable to the capture of prize at sea, dealing with such matters as the rights of captors and the distribution of the proceeds.

prize money. 1. A dividend from the proceeds of a captured vessel, paid to the captors. **2.** Money offered as an award.

PRO. *abbr.* Peer-review organization.

pro (proh). [Latin] (15c) For.

probable cause. (16c) **1.** *Criminal law.* A reasonable ground to suspect that a person has committed or is committing a crime or that a place contains specific items connected with a crime. • Under the Fourth Amendment, probable cause — which amounts to more than a bare suspicion but less than evidence that would justify a conviction — must be shown before an arrest warrant or search warrant may be issued. **2.** *Torts.* A reasonable belief in the existence of facts on which a claim is based and in the legal validity of the claim itself. **3.** A reasonable basis to support issuance of an administrative warrant based on either (1) specific evidence of an existing violation of administrative rules, or (2) evidence showing that a particular business meets the legislative or administrative standards permitting an inspection of the business premises.

probable-cause hearing. 1. Preliminary hearing. **2.** Shelter hearing.

probable consequence. (16c) An effect or result that is more likely than not to follow its supposed cause.

probable-desistance test. (1974) *Criminal law.* A common-law test for the crime of attempt, focusing on whether the defendant has exhibited dangerous behavior indicating a likelihood of committing the crime.

probate (**proh**-bayt), *n.* (15c) **1.** The judicial procedure by which a testamentary document is established to be a valid will; the proving of a will to the satisfaction of the court.

informal probate. (1974) Probate designed to operate with minimal input and supervision of the probate court. • Most modern probate codes encourage this type of administration, with an independent personal representative.

small-estate probate. (2004) An informal procedure for administering small estates, less structured than the normal process and usu. not requiring the assistance of an attorney.

2. Loosely, a personal representative's actions in handling a decedent's estate. **3.** Loosely, all the subjects over which probate courts have jurisdiction.

probate, *vb.* (18c) **1.** To admit (a will) to proof. **2.** To administer (a decedent's estate). **3.** To grant probation to (a criminal); to reduce (a sentence) by means of probation.

probate estate. (1930) A decedent's property subject to administration by a personal representative.

net probate estate. The probate estate after the following deductions: (1) family allowances, (2) exempt property, (3) homestead allowances, (4) claims against the estate, and (5) taxes for which the estate is liable.

probate law. The body of statutes, rules, cases, etc. governing all subjects over which a probate court has jurisdiction.

probation. (16c) **1.** A court-imposed criminal sentence that, subject to stated conditions, releases a convicted person into the community instead of sending the criminal to jail or prison. — **probationary,** *adj.*

bench probation. (1966) Probation in which the offender agrees to certain conditions or restrictions and reports only to the sentencing judge rather than a probation officer.

shock probation. (1972) Probation that is granted after a brief stay in jail or prison.

2. The act of judicially proving a will. — **probate,** *adj.*

probationer. A convicted criminal who is on probation.

probation termination. (1970) The ending of a person's status as a probationer by (1) the routine expiration of the probationary period, (2) early termination by court order, or (3) probation revocation.

probative (proh-bə-tiv), *adj.* (17c) Tending to prove or disprove. — **probativeness, probativity,** *n.*

pro bono (proh **boh**-noh), *adv.* & *adj.* [Latin *pro bono publico* "for the public good"] (1966) Being or involving uncompensated legal services performed esp. for the public good.

procedural law. (1896) The rules that prescribe the steps for having a right or duty judicially enforced, as opposed to the law that defines the specific rights or duties themselves.

procedure. (16c) **1.** A specific method or course of action. **2.** The judicial rule or manner for carrying on a civil lawsuit or criminal prosecution.

proceeding. (16c) **1.** The regular and orderly progression of a lawsuit, including all acts and events between the time of commencement and the entry of judgment. **2.** Any procedural means for seeking redress from a tribunal or agency. **3.** An act or step that is part of a larger action. **4.** The business conducted by a court or other official body; a hearing. **5.** *Bankruptcy.* A particular dispute or matter arising within a pending case — as opposed to the case as a whole.

collateral proceeding. (18c) A proceeding brought to address an issue incidental to the principal proceeding.

competency proceeding. (1925) A proceeding to assess a person's mental capacity. • A competency hearing may be held either in a criminal context to determine a defendant's competency to stand trial or as a civil proceeding to assess whether a person should be committed to a mental-health facility or should have a guardian appointed to manage the person's affairs.

contempt proceeding. (1859) A judicial or quasi-judicial hearing conducted to determine whether a person has committed contempt.

criminal proceeding. (16c) A proceeding instituted to determine a person's guilt or innocence or to set a convicted person's punishment; a criminal hearing or trial.

ex parte proceeding (eks **pahr**-tee). (18c) A proceeding in which not all parties are present or given the opportunity to be heard.

in camera proceeding (in **kam**-ə-rə). (1958) A proceeding held in a judge's chambers or other private place.

informal proceeding. (18c) A trial conducted in a more relaxed manner than a typical court trial, such as an administrative hearing or a trial in small-claims court.

judicial proceeding. (16c) Any court proceeding; any proceeding initiated to procure an order or decree, whether in law or in equity.

posttrial proceeding. Action on a case that occurs after the trial is completed.

proceeding in rem. A proceeding brought to affect all persons' interests in a thing that is subject to the power of a state.

proceeding quasi in rem. A proceeding brought to affect particular persons' interests in a thing.

quasi-criminal proceeding. Procedure. A civil proceeding that is conducted in conformity with the rules of a criminal proceeding because a penalty analogous to a criminal penalty may apply, as in some juvenile proceedings. • For example, juvenile delinquency is classified as a civil offense. But like a defendant in a criminal trial, an accused juvenile faces a potential loss of liberty. So criminal procedure rules apply.

special proceeding. (18c) **1.** A proceeding that can be commenced independently of a pending action and from which a final order may be appealed immediately. **2.** A proceeding involving statutory or civil remedies or rules rather than the rules or remedies ordinarily available under rules of procedure; a proceeding providing extraordinary relief.

summary proceeding. (17c) A nonjury proceeding that settles a controversy or disposes of a case in a relatively prompt and simple manner.

supplementary proceeding. (17c) **1.** A proceeding held in connection with the enforcement of a judgment, for the purpose of identifying and locating the debtor's assets available to satisfy the judgment. **2.** A proceeding that in some way supplements another.

proceeds (**proh**-seedz), *n.* (13c) **1.** The value of land, goods, or investments when converted into money; the amount of money received from a sale. **2.** Something received upon selling, exchanging, collecting, or otherwise disposing of collateral. UCC § 9-102(a)(67).

net proceeds. (18c) The amount received in a transaction minus the costs of the transaction (such as expenses and commissions).

process, *n.* (14c) **1.** The proceedings in any action or prosecution. **2.** A summons or writ, esp. to appear or respond in court.

process server. (17c) A person authorized by law or by a court to formally deliver process to a defendant or respondent.

procurement (proh-**kyoor**-mənt), *n.* (14c) **1.** The act of getting or obtaining something or of bringing something about. **2.** The act of persuading or inviting another, esp. a woman or child, to have illicit sexual intercourse. — **procure,** *vb.*

procurer. (15c) One who induces or prevails upon another to do something, esp. to engage in an illicit sexual act.

produce (prə-**doos**), *vb.* (15c) **1.** To bring into existence; to create. **2.** To provide (a document, witness, etc.) in response to subpoena or discovery request. **3.** To yield (as revenue). **4.** To bring (oil, etc.) to the surface of the earth.

producer price index. An index of wholesale price changes, issued monthly by the U.S. Bureau of Labor Statistics.

product. (1825) Something that is distributed commercially for use or consumption and that is usu. (1) tangible personal property, (2) the result of fabrication or processing, and (3) an item that has passed through a chain of commercial distribution before ultimate use or consumption.

defective product. (1903) A product that is unreasonably dangerous for normal use, as when it is not fit for its intended purpose, inadequate instructions are provided for its use, or it is inherently dangerous in its design or manufacture.

production of suit. (1830) *Common-law pleading.* The plaintiff's burden to produce evidence to confirm the allegations made in the declaration.

products liability, *n.* (1925) **1.** A manufacturer's or seller's tort liability for any damages or injuries suffered by a buyer, user, or bystander as a result of a defective product. **2.** The legal theory by which liability is imposed on the manufacturer or seller of a defective product. **3.** The field of law dealing with this theory. — **products-liability,** *adj.*

strict products liability. (1964) Products liability arising when the buyer proves that the goods were unreasonably dangerous and that (1) the seller was in the business of selling goods, (2) the goods were defective when they were in the seller's hands, (3) the defect caused the plaintiff's injury, and (4) the product was expected to and did reach the consumer without substantial change in condition.

profane, *adj.* (Of speech or conduct) irreverent to something held sacred.

profanity. Obscene, vulgar, or insulting language; blasphemy. • Profanity is distinguished from mere vulgarity and obscenity by the additional element of irreverence toward or mistreatment of something sacred.

profert (**proh**-fərt). (18c) *Common-law pleading.* A declaration on the record stating that a party produces in court the deed or other instrument relied on in the pleading.

profess, *vb.* (16c) To declare openly and freely; to confess.

profession. (15c) **1.** A vocation requiring advanced education and training; esp., one of the three traditional learned professions — law, medicine, and the ministry. **2.** Collectively, the members of such a vocation.

professional, *n.* (1846) A person who belongs to a learned profession or whose occupation requires a high level of training and proficiency.

proffer (**prof**-ər), *vb.* (14c) To offer or tender (something, esp. evidence) for immediate acceptance. — **proffer,** *n.*

profiling. 1. Racial profiling. **2.** Linguistic profiling.

profit, *n.* (13c) **1.** The excess of revenues over expenditures in a business transaction; GAIN (2). **2.** A servitude that gives the right to pasture cattle, dig for minerals, or otherwise take away some part of the soil; PROFIT À PRENDRE. • A profit may be either appurtenant or in gross.

profit à prendre (a **prawn**-drə *or* ah **prahn**-dər). [Law French "profit to take"] (*usu. pl.*) (17c) A right or privilege to go on another's land and take away something of value from its soil or from the products of its soil (as by mining, logging, or hunting). Pl. **profits à prendre.**

profiteering, *n.* (1814) The taking advantage of unusual or exceptional circumstances to make excessive profits, as in the selling of scarce goods at inflated prices during war. — **profiteer,** *vb.*

profit margin. 1. The difference between the cost of something and the price for which it is sold. **2.** The ratio, expressed as a percentage, between this difference and the selling price.

profit-sharing plan. An employee benefit plan that allows an employee to share in the company's profits.

qualified profit-sharing plan. A plan in which an employer's contributions are not taxed to the employee until distribution.

pro forma (proh **for**-mə), *adj.* [Latin "for form"] (16c) **1.** Made or done as a formality. **2.** (Of an invoice or financial statement) provided in advance to describe items, predict results, or secure approval.

progeny (**proj**-ə-nee), *n. pl.* (14c) **1.** Children or descendants; offspring <only one of their progeny attended law school>. **2.** In a figurative sense, a line of precedents that follow a leading case <*Erie* and its progeny>.

prognosis (prog-**noh**-sis). (17c) **1.** The process of forecasting the probable outcome of a present medical condition (such as a disease). **2.** The forecast of such an outcome.

pro hac vice (proh hahk **vee**-chay *or* hak **vɪ**-see *also* hahk **vees**). [Latin] (17c) For this occasion or particular purpose. • The phrase usu. refers to a lawyer who has not been admitted to practice in a particular jurisdiction but who is admitted there temporarily for the purpose of conducting a particular case.

prohibition. (15c) **1.** A law or order that forbids a certain action. **2.** An extraordinary writ issued by an appellate court to prevent a lower court from exceeding its jurisdiction or to prevent a nonjudicial officer or entity from exercising a power. **3.** (*cap.*) The period from 1920 to 1933, when the manufacture, transport, and sale of alcoholic beverages in the United States was forbidden by the 18th Amendment to the Constitution. • The 18th Amendment was repealed by the 21st Amendment.

prolicide (**proh**-lə-sɪd). (1826) **1.** The killing of offspring; esp., the crime of killing a child shortly before or after birth. **2.** One who kills a child shortly before or after birth. — **prolicidal,** *adj.*

prolixity (proh-**lik**-sə-tee). (14c) The unnecessary and superfluous stating of facts and legal arguments in pleading or evidence.

promise, *n.* (15c) **1.** The manifestation of an intention to act or refrain from acting in a specified manner, conveyed in such a way that another is justified in understanding that a commitment has been made; a person's assurance that the person will or will not do something. • A binding promise — one that the law will enforce — is the essence of a contract. **2.** The words in a promissory note expressing the maker's intention to pay a debt. • A mere written acknowledgment that a debt is due is insufficient to constitute a promise. — **promise,** *vb.*

aleatory promise (**ay**-lee-ə-tor-ee). A promise conditional on the happening of a fortuitous event, or on an event that the parties believe is fortuitous.

alternative promise. (17c) A contractual promise to do one of two or more things, any one of which qualifies as consideration.

collateral promise. A promise to guarantee the debt of another, made primarily without benefit to the party making the promise.

conditional promise. (16c) A promise that is conditioned on the occurrence of an event other than the lapse of time. • A conditional promise is not illusory as long as the condition is not entirely within the promisor's control.

corresponding promise. A mutual promise calling for the performance of an act substantially similar to the act called for by the other mutual promise, both acts being in pursuit of a common purpose.

dependent promise. (1829) A promise to be performed by a party only when another obligation has first been performed by another party.

gratuitous promise. (17c) A promise made in exchange for nothing; a promise not supported by consideration.

illusory promise. (1841) A promise that appears on its face to be so insubstantial as to impose no obligation on the promisor; an expression cloaked in promissory terms but actually containing no commitment by the promisor. • An illusory promise typically, by its terms, makes performance optional with the promisor. For example, if a guarantor promises to make good on the principal debtor's obligation "as long as I think it's in my commercial interest," the promisor is not really bound.

implied promise. (18c) A promise created by law to render a person liable on a contract so as to avoid fraud or unjust enrichment.

mutual promises. (16c) Promises given simultaneously by two parties, each promise serving as consideration for the other.

new promise. A previously unenforceable promise that a promisor revives and agrees to fulfill, as when a debtor agrees to pay a creditor an amount discharged in the debtor's bankruptcy.

unconditional promise. (1802) A promise that either is unqualified or requires nothing but the lapse of time to make the promise presently enforceable. • A party who makes an unconditional promise must perform that promise even though the other party has not performed according to the bargain.

promisee (prom-is-**ee**). (18c) One to whom a promise is made.

promisor (prom-is-**or**). (17c) One who makes a promise; esp., one who undertakes a contractual obligation.

promissory, *adj.* (15c) Containing or consisting of a promise <the agreement's promissory terms>.

promoter. (14c) **1.** A person who encourages or incites. **2.** A founder or organizer of a corporation or business venture; one who takes the entrepreneurial initiative in founding or organizing a business or enterprise.

promulgate (prə-**məl**-gayt *or* **prom**-əl-gayt), *vb.* (16c) **1.** To declare or announce publicly; to proclaim. **2.** To put (a law or decree) into force or effect. **3.** (Of an administrative agency) to carry out the formal process of rulemaking by publishing the proposed regulation, inviting public comments, and approving or rejecting the proposal. — **promulgation** (prom-əl-**gay**-shən *or* proh-məl-), *n.*

pronounce, *vb.* (14c) To announce formally <pronounce judgment>.

proof, *n.* (13c) **1.** The establishment or refutation of an alleged fact by evidence; the persuasive effect of evidence in the mind of a fact-finder. **2.** Evidence that determines the judgment of a court. **3.** An attested document that constitutes legal evidence.

affirmative proof. (18c) Evidence establishing the fact in dispute by a preponderance of the evidence.

conditional proof. (1931) A fact that amounts to proof as long as there is no other fact amounting to disproof.

double proof. (1955) **1.** *Bankruptcy.* Proof of claims by two or more creditors against the same debt. • This violates the general rule that there can be only one claim with respect to a single debt. **2.** *Evidence.* Corroborating government evidence (usu. by two witnesses) required to sustain certain convictions.

negative proof. (16c) Proof that establishes a fact by showing that its opposite is not or cannot be true.

positive proof. (17c) Direct or affirmative proof.

proof beyond a reasonable doubt. (1834) Proof that precludes every reasonable hypothesis except that which it tends to support.

proof of acknowledgment. (18c) An authorized officer's certification — based on a third party's testimony — that the signature of a person (who usu. does not appear before the notary) is genuine and was freely made.

proof of service. (18c) **1.** A document filed (as by a sheriff) in court as evidence that process has been successfully served on a party. **2.** Certificate of service.

pro per., *adv.* & *adj. Pro persona.*

pro per., *n.* **1.** Pro se. **2.** *Propria persona.*

proper law. *Conflict of laws.* The substantive law that, under the principles of conflict of laws, governs a transaction.

proper lookout, *n.* (1842) The duty of a vehicle operator to exercise caution to avoid collisions with pedestrians or other vehicles.

proper means. *Trade secrets.* Any method of discovering trade secrets that does not violate property-protection statutes or standards of commercial ethics.

pro persona (proh pər-**soh**-nə), *adv.* & *adj.* [Latin] For one's own person; on one's own behalf <a *pro persona* brief>.

property. (14c) **1.** The right to possess, use, and enjoy a determinate thing (either a tract of land or a chattel); the right of ownership. **2.** Any external thing over which the rights of possession, use, and enjoyment are exercised.

abandoned property. (1841) Property that the owner voluntarily surrenders, relinquishes, or disclaims.

common property. (17c) **1.** Real property that is held by two or more persons with no right of survivorship. **2.** Common area.

distressed property. (1927) Property that must be sold because of mortgage foreclosure or because it is part of an insolvent estate.

incorporeal property. (18c) **1.** An in rem proprietary right that is not classified as corporeal property. • Incorporeal property is traditionally broken down into two classes: (1) *jura in re aliena* (encumbrances), whether over material or immaterial things, examples being leases, mortgages, and servitudes; and (2) *jura in re propria* (full ownership over immaterial things), examples being patents, copyrights, and trademarks. **2.** A legal right in property having no physical existence. • Patent rights, for example, are incorporeal property.

intangible property. (1843) Property that lacks a physical existence. • Examples include stock options and business goodwill.

lost property. (1810) Property that the owner no longer possesses because of accident, negligence, or carelessness, and that cannot be located by an ordinary, diligent search.

marital property. (1855) Property that is acquired during marriage and that is subject to distribution or division at the time of marital dissolution. • Generally, it is property acquired after the date of the marriage and before a spouse files for separation or divorce.

mislaid property. (1915) Property that has been voluntarily relinquished by the owner with an intent to recover it later — but that cannot now be found.

mixed property. (18c) Property with characteristics of both real property and personal property — such as heirlooms and fixtures.

personal property. (18c) **1.** Any movable or intangible thing that is subject to ownership and not classified as real property. **2.** *Tax.* Property not used in a taxpayer's trade or business or held for income production or collection.

private property. (17c) Property — protected from public appropriation — over which the owner has exclusive and absolute rights.

public property. (17c) State- or community-owned property not restricted to any one individual's use or possession.

qualified property. A temporary or special interest in a thing (such as a right to possess it), subject to being totally extinguished by the occurrence of a specified contingency over which the qualified owner has no control.

qualified-terminable-interest property. (1982) Property that passes by a QTIP trust from a deceased spouse to the surviving spouse and that (if the executor so elects) qualifies for the marital deduction provided that the surviving spouse is entitled to receive all income in payments made at least annually for life and that no one has the power to appoint the property to anyone other than the surviving spouse. — Abbr. QTIP.

real property. (18c) Land and anything growing on, attached to, or erected on it, excluding anything that may be severed without injury to the land. • Real property can be either corporeal (soil and buildings) or incorporeal (easements).

tangible personal property. (1843) Corporeal personal property of any kind; personal property that can be seen, weighed, measured, felt, or touched, or is in any other way perceptible to the senses, such as furniture, cooking utensils, and books.

tangible property. (1802) Property that has physical form and characteristics.

terminable property. Property (such as a leasehold) whose duration is not perpetual or indefinite but is limited in time or is liable to termination upon the occurrence of some specified event.

property of the debtor. *Bankruptcy.* Property that is owned or (in some instances) possessed by the debtor, including property that is exempted from the bankruptcy estate. 11 USCA § 541(b).

property of the estate. *Bankruptcy.* The debtor's tangible and intangible property interests (including both legal and equitable interests) that fall under the bankruptcy court's jurisdiction because they were owned or held by the debtor when the bankruptcy petition was filed. 11 USCA § 541.

property settlement. 1. A judgment in a divorce case determining the distribution of the marital property between the divorcing parties. • A property settlement includes a division of the marital debts as well as assets. **2.** A contract that divides up the assets of divorcing spouses and is incorporated into a divorce decree. **3.** Marital agreement.

prophylactic (proh-fə-**lak**-tik), *adj.* (16c) Formulated to prevent something <a prophylactic rule>. — **prophylaxis** (proh-fə-**lak**-sis), **prophylactic,** *n.*

propinquity (prə-**ping**-kwə-tee). (15c) The state of being near; specif., kindred or parentage <degrees of propinquity>.

proponent, *n.* (16c) **1.** A person who puts forward a legal instrument for consideration or acceptance; esp., one who offers a will for probate. **2.** A person who puts forward a proposal; one who argues in favor of something. **3.** *Parliamentary law.* A member who speaks in favor of a pending motion. — **propone** (prə-**pohn**), *vb.*

proportionality review. (1976) *Criminal law.* An appellate court's analysis of whether a death sentence is arbitrary, capricious, or excessive by comparing the case in which it was imposed with similar cases in which the death penalty was approved or disapproved.

proportional representation. 1. An electoral system that allocates legislative seats to each political group in proportion to its popular voting strength. **2.** Proportional voting. • The term refers to two related but distinguishable concepts: proportional *outcome* (having members of a group elected in proportion to their numbers in the electorate) and proportional *involvement* (more precisely termed *proportional voting* and denoting the electoral system also known as *single transferable voting*).

proposal. Something offered for consideration or acceptance.

propound (prə-**pownd**), *vb.* (16c) **1.** To offer for consideration or discussion. **2.** To make a proposal. **3.** To put forward (a will) as authentic.

propria persona (**proh**-pree-ə pər-**soh**-nə), *adj.* & *adv.* [Latin] In his own person; pro se. — Sometimes shortened to *pro per.* — Abbr. *p.p.*

proprietary (prə-**prɪ**-ə-ter-ee), *adj.* (15c) **1.** Of or relating to a proprietor <the licensee's proprietary rights>. **2.** Of, relating to, or holding as property <the software designer sought to protect its proprietary data>.

proprietary function. (1902) *Torts.* A municipality's conduct that is performed for the profit or benefit of the municipality, rather than for the benefit of the general public.

proprietary power. Power coupled with an interest.

proprietary software. Software that cannot be used, redistributed, or modified without permission.

proprietor, *n.* (16c) An owner, esp. one who runs a business. — **proprietorship,** *n.*

pro rata (proh **ray**-tə *or* **rah**-tə *or* **ra**-tə), *adv.* (16c) Proportionately; according to an exact rate, measure, or interest <the liability will be assessed pro rata between the defendants>. — **pro rata,** *adj.*

prorate (**proh**-rayt *or* proh-**rayt**), *vb.* (1858) To divide, assess, or distribute proportionately <prorate taxes between the buyer and the seller>. — **proration,** *n.*

prorogation (proh-rə-**gay**-shən). (14c) The act of putting off to another day; esp., the discontinuance of a legislative session until its next term. — **prorogative,** *adj.*

prorogue (proh-**rohg** *or* prə-), *vb.* (15c) **1.** To postpone or defer. **2.** To suspend or discontinue a legislative session.

proscribe, *vb.* (15c) To outlaw or prohibit; to forbid.

proscription, *n.* (14c) **1.** The act of prohibiting; the state of being prohibited. **2.** A prohibition or restriction. — **proscriptive,** *adj.*

pro se (proh **say** *or* **see**), *adv.* & *adj.* [Latin] (1817) For oneself; on one's own behalf; without a lawyer <the defendant proceeded pro se> <a pro se defendant>.

pro se, *n.* (1857) One who represents oneself in a court proceeding without the assistance of a lawyer <the third case on the court's docket involving a pro se>.

prosecute, *vb.* (15c) **1.** To commence and carry out a legal action <because the plaintiff failed to prosecute its contractual claims, the court dismissed the suit>. **2.** To institute and pursue a criminal action against (a person) <the notorious felon has been prosecuted in seven states>. **3.** To engage in; carry on <the company prosecuted its business for 12 years before going bankrupt>. — **prosecutory,** *adj.*

prosecution. (16c) **1.** The commencement and carrying out of any action or scheme <the prosecution of a long, bloody war>. **2.** A criminal proceeding in which an accused person is tried <the conspiracy trial involved the prosecution of seven defendants>.

sham prosecution. (1903) A prosecution that seeks to circumvent a defendant's double-jeopardy protection by appearing to be prosecuted by another sovereignty, when it is in fact controlled by the sovereignty that already prosecuted the defendant for the same crime.

vindictive prosecution. (1834) A prosecution in which a person is singled out under a law or regulation because the person has exercised a constitutionally protected right.

3. The government attorneys who initiate and maintain a criminal action against an accused defendant <the prosecution rests>. **4.** *Patents.* The process of applying for a patent through the U.S. Patent and Trademark Office and negotiating with the patent examiner.

prosecutor, *n.* (16c) **1.** A legal officer who represents the state or federal government in criminal proceedings.

public prosecutor. **1.** PROSECUTOR (1). **2.** District attorney.

special prosecutor. (1859) A lawyer appointed to investigate and, if justified, seek indictments in a particular case.

2. A private person who institutes and carries on a legal action, esp. a criminal action. — **prosecutorial,** *adj.*

prosecutorial misconduct. (1963) *Criminal law.* A prosecutor's improper or illegal act (or failure to act), esp. involving an attempt to avoid required disclosure or to persuade the jury to wrongly convict a defendant or assess an unjustified punishment.

prosecutorial vindictiveness. *Criminal law.* The act or an instance of intentionally charging a more serious crime or seeking a more severe penalty in retaliation for a defendant's lawful exercise of a constitutional right.

prospective, *adj.* (18c) **1.** Effective or operative in the future <prospective application of the new statute>. **2.** Anticipated or expected; likely to come about <prospective clients>.

prospectus (prə-**spek**-təs). A printed document that describes the main features of an enterprise (esp. a corporation's business) and that is distributed to prospective buyers or investors; esp., a written description of a securities offering. • Under SEC regulations, a publicly traded corporation must provide a prospectus before offering to sell stock in the corporation. Pl. **prospectuses.**

newspaper prospectus. A summary prospectus that the SEC allows to be disseminated through advertisements in newspapers, magazines, or other periodicals sent through the mails as second-class matter (though not distributed by the advertiser), when the securities involved are issued by a foreign national government with which the United States maintains diplomatic relations.

preliminary prospectus. A prospectus for a stock issue that has been filed but not yet approved by the SEC.

prostitute, *n.* (16c) A person who engages in sexual acts in exchange for money or anything else of value.

child prostitute. A child who is offered or used for sex acts in exchange for money. • Some people object to this phrase because the term "prostitute" suggests a degree of voluntariness or choice on the child's part, which is often not true. An alternative without those connotations is *prostituted child.*

prostitution, *n.* (16c) **1.** The act or practice of engaging in sexual activity for money or its equivalent; commercialized sex. **2.** The act of debasing. — **prostitute,** *vb.* — **prostitute,** *n.*

pro tanto (proh **tan**-toh), *adv.* & *adj.* [Latin] (17c) To that extent; for so much; as far as it goes <the debt is pro tanto discharged> <a pro tanto payment>.

protectionism. (1844) The protection of domestic businesses and industries against foreign competition by imposing high tariffs and restricting imports. — **protectionist,** *adj.*

protection money. (18c) **1.** A bribe paid to an officer as an inducement not to interfere with the criminal activities of the briber. **2.** Money extorted from a business owner by one who promises to "protect" the business premises, with the implied threat that if the owner does not pay, the person requesting the payment will harm the owner or damage the premises.

protective order. (1884) **1.** A court order prohibiting or restricting a party from engaging in conduct (esp. a legal procedure such as discovery) that unduly annoys or burdens the opposing party or a third-party witness. **2.** RESTRAINING ORDER (1).

blanket protective order. A protective order that covers a broad subject or class.

emergency protective order. A temporary protective order granted on an expedited basis, usu. after an ex parte hearing (without notice to the other side), most commonly to provide injunctive relief from an abuser in a domestic-violence case; esp., a short-term restraining order that is issued at the request of a law-enforcement officer in response to a domestic-violence complaint from a victim who is in immediate danger. — Abbr. EPO.

permanent protective order. A protective order of indefinite duration granted after a hearing with notice to both sides; esp., a court order that prohibits an abuser from contacting or approaching the protected person for a long period, usu. years. Despite the name, permanent orders often have expiration dates set by state law. An order may also require the abuser to perform certain acts such as attending counseling or providing financial support for the protected person. — Abbr. PPO.

protective sweep. (1973) A police officer's quick and limited search — conducted after the officer has lawfully entered the premises — based on a reasonable belief that such a search is necessary to protect the officer or others from harm.

protégé. A person protected by or under the care or training of another person or an entity, esp. one who is established or influential.

pro tempore (proh **tem**-pə-ree), *adv.* & *adj.* [Latin] (15c) For the time being; appointed to occupy a position temporarily <a judge pro tempore>. — Abbr. pro tem.

protest, *n.* (15c) **1.** A formal statement or action expressing dissent or disapproval. **2.** A notary public's written statement that, upon presentment, a negotiable instrument was neither paid nor accepted. **3.** A formal statement, usu. in writing, disputing a debt's legality or validity but agreeing to make payment while reserving the right to recover the amount at a later time. • The disputed debt is described as *under protest.* **4.** *Tax.* A taxpayer's statement to the collecting officer that payment is being made unwillingly because the taxpayer believes the tax to be invalid. — **protest,** *vb.*

protestation (prot-ə-**stay**-shən). (14c) *Common-law pleading.* A declaration by which a party makes an oblique allegation or denial of some fact, claiming that it does or does not exist or is or is not legally sufficient, while not directly affirming or denying the fact.

provable, *adj.* (15c) Capable of being proved.

prove, *vb.* (13c) To establish or make certain; to establish the truth of (a fact or hypothesis) by satisfactory evidence.

prove up, *vb.* (1832) To present or complete the proof of (something) <deciding not to put a doctor on the stand, the plaintiff attempted to prove up his damages with medical records only>.

prove-up, *n.* The establishment of a prima facie claim. • A prove-up is necessary when a factual assertion is unopposed because even without opposition, the claim must be supported by evidence.

provided, *conj.* (15c) **1.** On the condition or understanding (that) <we will sign the contract provided that you agree to the following conditions>. **2.** Except (that) <all permittees must be at least 18 years of age, provided that those with a bona fide hardship must be at least 15 years of age>. **3.** And <a railway car must be operated by a full crew if it extends for more than 15 continuous miles, provided that a full crew must consist of at least six railway workers>.

provision. (15c) **1.** A clause in a statute, contract, or other legal instrument. **2.** A stipulation made beforehand.

provisional, *adj.* (16c) **1.** Temporary <a provisional injunction>. **2.** Conditional <a provisional government>.

provisional exit. *Criminal procedure.* A prisoner's temporary release from prison for a court appearance, hospital treatment, work detail, or other purpose requiring a release with the expectation of return.

proviso (prə-vɪ-zoh). (15c) **1.** A limitation, condition, or stipulation upon whose compliance a legal or formal document's validity or application may depend. **2.** In drafting, a provision that begins with the words *provided that* and supplies a condition, exception, or addition.

provocation, *n.* (15c) **1.** The act of inciting another to do something, esp. to commit a crime. **2.** Something (such as words or actions) that affects a person's reason and self-control, esp. causing the person to commit a crime impulsively. — **provoke,** *vb.* — **provocative,** *adj.*

adequate provocation. (1842) Something that would cause a reasonable person to act without self-control and lose any premeditated state of mind.

proximate (**prok**-sə-mit), *adj.* (17c) **1.** Immediately before or after. **2.** Very near or close in time or space. — **proximateness,** *n.*

proximate consequence. (1840) A result following an unbroken sequence from some (esp. negligent) event.

proximity. (15c) The quality or state of being near in time, place, order, or relation.

proxy, *n.* (15c) **1.** One who is authorized to act as a substitute for another; esp., in corporate law, a person who is authorized to vote another's stock shares. **2.** The grant of authority by which a person is so authorized. **3.** The document granting this authority.

PRP. *abbr.* Potentially responsible party.

prudent, *adj.* (14c) Circumspect or judicious in one's dealings; cautious. — **prudence,** *n.*

prudent-investor rule. (1960) *Trusts.* The principle that a fiduciary must invest in only those securities or portfolios of securities that a reasonable person would buy.

prudent-operator standard. Reasonably-prudent-operator standard.

prudent person. Reasonable person.

prudent-person rule. Prudent-investor rule.

prurient (**pruur**-ee-ənt), *adj.* (17c) Characterized by or arousing inordinate or unusual sexual desire <films appealing to prurient interests>. — **prurience,** *n.*

p.s. *abbr.* (*usu. cap.*) **1.** Public statute; PUBLIC LAW (2). **2.** Postscript.

pseudonym (**sood**-ə-nim), *n.* A fictitious name or identity. — **pseudonymous** (soo-**don**-ə-məs), *adj.* — **pseudonymity** (sood-ə-**nim**-ə-tee), *n.*

psychiatric (sɪ-kee-**at**-rik), *adj.* Of or relating to the study or treatment of mental, emotional, and behavioral disorders by medical doctors trained in the field of psychiatry.

psychiatric examination. *Criminal law.* An analysis performed by a psychiatrist to determine a defendant's mental state.

psychopath (sɪ-kə-path), *n.* (1885) **1.** A person with a mental disorder characterized by an extremely antisocial personality that often leads to aggressive, perverted, or criminal behavior. **2.** Loosely, a person who is mentally ill or unstable. — **psychopathy** (sɪ-**kop**-ə-thee), *n.* — **psychopathic** (sɪ-kə-**path**-ik), *adj.*

PTO. *abbr.* Patent and Trademark Office.

Pub. L. *abbr.* Public law.

public, *adj.* (14c) **1.** Relating or belonging to an entire community, state, or nation. **2.** Open or available for all to use, share, or enjoy. **3.** (Of a company) having shares that are available on an open market.

public, *n.* (16c) **1.** The people of a nation or community as a whole <a crime against the public>. **2.** A place open or visible to the public <in public>.

publication, *n.* (14c) **1.** Generally, the act of declaring or announcing to the public. **2.** *Copyright.* The offering or distribution of copies of a work to the public. • At common law, publication marked the dividing line between state and federal protection, but the Copyright Act of 1976 superseded most of common-law copyright and thereby diminished the significance of publication. Under the Act, an original work is considered published only when it is first made publicly available without restriction. **3.** *Defamation.* The communication of defamatory words to someone other than the person defamed. **4.** *Wills & estates.* The formal declaration made by a testator when signing the will that it is the testator's will.

public-convenience-and-necessity standard. (1964) A common criterion used by a governmental body to assess whether a particular request or project should be granted or approved.

public defender. (1827) A lawyer or staff of lawyers, usu. publicly appointed and paid, whose duty is to represent indigent criminal defendants. — Abbr. P.D.

public domain. (17c) **1.** Government-owned land. **2.** *Hist.* Government lands that are open to entry and settlement. • Today virtually all federal lands are off-limits to traditional entry and settlement. **3.** *Intellectual property.* The universe of inventions and creative works that are not protected by intellectual-property rights and are therefore available for anyone to use without charge.

public-duty doctrine. (1976) *Torts.* The rule that a governmental entity (such as a state or municipality) cannot be held liable for an individual plaintiff's injury resulting from a governmental officer's or employee's breach of a duty owed to the general public rather than to the individual plaintiff.

public figure. (1871) A person who has achieved fame or notoriety or who has voluntarily become involved in a public controversy. • A public figure (or public official) suing for defamation must prove that the defendant acted with actual malice. *New York Times Co. v. Sullivan*, 376 U.S. 254, 84 S.Ct. 710 (1964).

all-purpose public figure. A person who achieves such pervasive fame or notoriety that he or she becomes a public figure for all purposes and in all contexts. • For example, a person who occupies a position with great persuasive power and influence may become an all-purpose public figure whether or not the person actively seeks attention. *Gertz v. Robert Welch, Inc.*, 418 U.S. 323, 345, 94 S.Ct. 2997, 3009 (1974).

limited-purpose public figure. (1979) A person who, having become involved in a particular public issue, has achieved fame or notoriety only in relation to that particular issue.

public forum. (1935) *Constitutional law.* A public place where people traditionally gather to express ideas and exchange views. • To be constitutional, the government's regulation of a public forum must be narrowly tailored to serve a significant government interest and must usu. be limited to time-place-or-manner restrictions.

designated public forum. (1985) Public property that has not traditionally been open for public assembly and debate but that the government has opened for use by the public as a place for expressive activity, such as a public-university facility or a publicly owned theater. • Unlike a traditional public forum, the government does not have to retain the open character of a designated public forum. Also, the subject matter of the expression permitted in a designated public forum may be limited to accord with the character of the forum; reasonable, content-neutral time, place, and manner restrictions are generally permissible. But any prohibition based on the content of the expression must be narrowly drawn to effectuate a compelling state interest, as with a traditional public forum.

traditional public forum. (1973) Public property that has by long tradition — as opposed to governmental designation — been used by the public for assembly and expression, such as a public street, public sidewalk, or public park. • To be constitutional, the government's content-neutral restrictions of the time, place, or manner of expression must be narrowly tailored to serve a significant government interest, and leave open ample alternative channels of communication. Any government regulation of expression that is based on the content of the expression must meet the much higher test of being necessary to serve a compelling state interest.

public-function test. (1966) In a suit under 42 USCA § 1983, the doctrine that a private person's actions constitute state action if the private person performs functions that are traditionally reserved to the state.

public interest. (16c) **1.** The general welfare of the public that warrants recognition and protection. **2.** Something in which the public as a whole has a stake; esp., an interest that justifies governmental regulation.

public-interest exception. (1957) The principle that an appellate court may consider and decide a moot case — although such decisions are generally prohibited — if (1) the case involves a question of considerable public importance, (2) the question is likely to arise in the future, and (3) the question has evaded appellate review.

public-interest law. Legal practice that advances social justice or other causes for the public good, such as environmental protection. • Although public-interest law primarily encompasses private not-for-profit work, the term is sometimes used to include the work of government agencies such as public-defender offices.

public law. (16c) **1.** The body of law dealing with the relations between private individuals and the government, and with the structure and operation of the government itself; constitutional law, criminal law, and administrative law taken together. **2.** A statute affecting the general public. • Federal public laws are first published in *Statutes at Large* and are eventually collected by subject in the U.S. Code. — Abbr. Pub. L.; P.L. **3.** Constitutional law.

public office. A position whose occupant has legal authority to exercise a government's sovereign powers for a fixed period.

public policy. (16c) **1.** Broadly, principles and standards regarded by the legislature or by the courts as being of fundamental concern to the state and the whole of society. • Courts sometimes use the term to justify their decisions, as when declaring a contract void because it is "contrary to public policy." **2.** More narrowly, the principle that a person should not be allowed to do anything that would tend to injure the public at large.

public purpose. (18c) An action by or at the direction of a government for the benefit of the community as a whole.

public safety. (16c) The welfare and protection of the general public, usu. expressed as a governmental responsibility <Department of Public Safety>.

public-safety exception. (1984) *Evidence.* An exception to the *Miranda* rule, allowing into evidence an otherwise suppressible statement by a defendant concerning information that the police needed at the time it was made in order to protect the public. • If, for example, a victim tells the police that an assailant had a gun, and upon the suspect's arrest the police find a holster but no gun, they would be entitled immediately to ask where the gun is. Under the public-safety exception, the suspect's statement of the gun's location would be admissible.

public sector. (1934) The part of the economy or an industry that is controlled by the government.

public service. (16c) **1.** A service provided or facilitated by the government for the general public's convenience and benefit. **2.** Government employment; work performed for or on behalf of the government. **3.** Broadly, any work that serves the public good, including government work and public-interest law.

public writing. The written acts or records of a government (or its constituent units) that are not constitutionally or statutorily protected from disclosure. • Laws and judicial records, for example, are public writings. A private writing that becomes part of a public record may be a public writing in some circumstances.

publish, *vb.* (14c) **1.** To distribute copies (of a work) to the public. **2.** To communicate (defamatory words) to someone other than the person defamed. **3.** To declare (a will) to be the true expression of one's testamentary intent. **4.** To make (evidence) available to a jury during trial.

PUC. *abbr.* Public Utilities Commission.

PUD. *abbr.* **1.** Planned-unit development. **2.** Municipal utility district.

puffing. (18c) **1.** The expression of an exaggerated opinion — as opposed to a factual misrepresentation — with the intent to sell a good or service. • Puffing involves expressing opinions, not asserting something as a fact. Although there is some leeway in puffing goods, a seller may not misrepresent them or say that they have attributes that they do not possess. **2.** Secret bidding at an auction by or on behalf of a seller; BY-BIDDING.

puisne (**pyoo**-nee), *adj.* [Law French] (16c) Junior in rank; subordinate.

punishable, *adj.* (15c) **1.** (Of a person) subject to a punishment <there is no dispute that Jackson remains punishable for these offenses>. **2.** (Of a crime or tort) giving rise to a specified punishment <a felony punishable by imprisonment for up to 20 years>. — **punishability,** *n.*

punishment, *n.* (15c) **1.** A sanction — such as a fine, penalty, confinement, or loss of property, right, or privilege — assessed against a person who has violated the law.

corporal punishment. (16c) Physical punishment; punishment that is inflicted upon the body (including imprisonment).

cruel and unusual punishment. (17c) Punishment that is torturous, degrading, inhuman, grossly disproportionate to the crime in question, or otherwise shocking to the moral sense of the community.

cumulative punishment. (1842) Punishment that increases in severity when a person is convicted of the same offense more than once.

deterrent punishment. (1896) **1.** *Criminal law.* Punishment intended to deter the offender and others from committing crimes and to make an example of the offender so that like-minded people are warned of the consequences of crime. **2.** *Torts.* Punishment intended to deter a tortfeasor from repeating a behavior or failing to remove a hazard that led to an injury.

excessive punishment. (17c) Punishment that is not justified by the gravity of the offense or the defendant's criminal record.

infamous punishment. (16c) Punishment by imprisonment, usu. in a penitentiary.

preventive punishment. (1893) Punishment intended to prevent a repetition of wrongdoing by disabling the offender.

reformative punishment. (1919) Punishment intended to change the character of the offender.

retributive punishment. (1887) Punishment intended to satisfy the community's retaliatory sense of indignation that is provoked by injustice.

2. *Family law.* A negative disciplinary action administered to a minor child by a parent.

punitive, *adj.* (16c) Involving or inflicting punishment.

punitive statute. Penal statute.

pur (pər *or* poor). [Law French] By; for.

pur autre vie (pər **oh**-trə [*or* **oh**-tər] **vee**). [Law French "for another's life"] For or during a period measured by another's life <a life estate *pur autre vie*>.

purchase, *n.* (15c) **1.** The act or an instance of buying. **2.** The acquisition of real property by one's own or another's act (as by will or gift) rather than by descent or inheritance. — **purchase,** *vb.*

purchase agreement. (1909) A sales contract.

purchase money. (17c) The initial payment made on property secured by a mortgage.

purchase order. (1916) A document authorizing a seller to deliver goods with payment to be made later. — Abbr. P.O.

purchaser. (14c) **1.** One who obtains property for money or other valuable consideration; a buyer.

bona fide purchaser. (18c) One who buys something for value without notice of another's claim to the property and without actual or constructive notice of any defects in or infirmities, claims, or equities against the seller's title; one who has in good faith paid valuable consideration for property without notice of prior adverse claims. — Abbr. BFP.

2. One who acquires real property by means other than descent, gift, or inheritance.

pure-comparative-negligence doctrine. (1976) The principle that liability for negligence is apportioned in accordance with the percentage of fault that the fact-finder assigns to each party and that a plaintiff's percentage of fault reduces the amount of recoverable damages but does not bar recovery.

purge, *vb.* (13c) To exonerate (oneself or another) of guilt <the judge purged the defendant of contempt>.

purport (**pər**-port), *n.* (15c) The idea or meaning that is conveyed or expressed, esp. by a formal document.

purport (pər-**port**), *vb.* (17c) To profess or claim, esp. falsely; to seem to be <the

document purports to be a will, but it is neither signed nor dated>.

purported, *adj.* (1885) Reputed; rumored.

purpose. (13c) An objective, goal, or end; specif., the business activity that a corporation is chartered to engage in.

purpose clause. An introductory clause to a statute explaining its background and stating the reasons for its enactment.

purpresture (pər-**pres**-chər). (14c) An encroachment upon public rights and easements by appropriation to private use of that which belongs to the public.

purse-snatching. The stealing of a handbag or other similar item by seizing or grabbing it from a victim's physical possession and then fleeing, often without harm or threat of harm to the victim. • Purse-snatching is usu. a type of larceny. But if the perpetrator uses great force to take the bag or injures or threatens to injure the victim, it may instead be classified as a robbery.

pursuant to. (16c) **1.** In compliance with; in accordance with; under <she filed the motion pursuant to the court's order>. **2.** As authorized by; under <pursuant to Rule 56, the plaintiff moves for summary judgment>. **3.** In carrying out <pursuant to his responsibilities, he ensured that all lights had been turned out>.

pursuit. (14c) **1.** An occupation or pastime. **2.** The act of chasing to overtake or apprehend.

pursuit of happiness. (18c) The principle — announced in the Declaration of Independence — that a person should be allowed to pursue the person's desires (esp. in regard to an occupation) without unjustified interference by the government.

purview (**pər**-vyoo). (15c) **1.** Scope; area of application. **2.** The body of a statute following the preamble.

pusher. A person who sells illicit drugs.

put, *n.* Put option.

putative (**pyoo**-tə-tiv), *adj.* (15c) Reputed; believed; supposed.

putative-father registry. *Family law.* An official roster in which an unwed father may claim possible paternity of a child for purposes of receiving notice of a prospective adoption of the child.

put in, *vb.* (15c) To place in due form before a court; to place among the records of a court.

put out. EVICT (1).

put the question. (Of the chair) to formally state a question in its final form for the purpose of taking a vote.

putting in fear. (17c) The threatening of another person with violence to compel the person to hand over property.

pyramiding. A speculative method used to finance a large purchase of stock or a controlling interest by pledging an investment's unrealized profit.

pyramiding inferences, rule against. (1959) *Evidence.* A rule prohibiting a fact-finder from piling one inference on another to arrive at a conclusion. • Today this rule is followed in only a few jurisdictions.

pyramid scheme. (1949) A property-distribution scheme in which a participant pays for the chance to receive compensation for introducing new persons to the scheme, as well as for when those new persons themselves introduce participants.

Q

Q. *abbr.* (16c) QUESTION (1). • This abbreviation is almost always used in deposition and trial transcripts to denote each question asked by the examining lawyer.

Q-and-A. *abbr.* (1837) Question-and-answer.

qcf. *abbr.* *Quare clausum fregit.*

QD. *abbr.* [Latin *quasi dicat*] (16c) As if he should say.

QDRO (**kwah**-droh). *abbr.* Qualified domestic-relations order.

QED. *abbr.* [Latin *quod erat demonstrandum*] (17c) Which was to be demonstrated or proved.

Q.T. *abbr.* Qui tam action.

QTIP (**kyoo**-tip). *abbr.* Qualified-terminable-interest property.

qua (kway *or* kwah). [Latin] (17c) In the capacity of; as <the fiduciary, qua fiduciary, is not liable for fraud, but he may be liable as an individual>.

quaere (**kweer**-ee), *vb.* [Latin] (17c) Inquire; query; examine. • This term was often used in the syllabus of a reported case to show that a point was doubtful or open to question.

qualification. (16c) **1.** The possession of qualities or properties (such as fitness or capacity) inherently or legally necessary to make one eligible for a position or office, or to perform a public duty or function <voter qualification requires one to meet residency, age, and registration requirements>. **2.** A modification or limitation of terms or language; esp., a restriction of terms that would otherwise be interpreted broadly <the contract contained a qualification requiring the lessor's permission before exercising the right to sublet>. **3.** CHARACTERIZATION (1). — **qualify,** *vb.*

qualified, *adj.* (16c) **1.** Possessing the necessary qualifications; capable or competent <a qualified medical examiner>. **2.** Limited; restricted <qualified immunity>. — **qualify,** *vb.* — **qualifiedly** (**kwah**-lə-fɪd-lee *or* -fɪ-əd-lee), *adv.*

qualified domestic-relations order. (1984) A state-court order or judgment that relates to alimony, child support, or some other state domestic-relations matter and that (1) recognizes or provides for an alternate payee's right to receive all or part of any benefits due a participant under a pension, profit-sharing, or other retirement benefit plan, (2) otherwise satisfies § 414 of the Internal Revenue Code, and (3) is exempt from the ERISA rule prohibiting the assignment of plan benefits. — Abbr. QDRO.

qualified fee. **1.** Fee simple determinable. **2.** Base fee.

qualified medical child-support order. A family-court order that enables a nonemployee custodial parent — without the employee parent's consent — to enroll the child, make claims, and receive payments as needed under the employee parent's group health plan, all at the employee parent's expense. — Abbr. QMCSO.

qualified opinion. An audit-report statement containing exceptions or qualifications to certain items in the accompanying financial statement.

qualified plan. **1.** Qualified pension plan. **2.** Qualified profit-sharing plan.

qualifying event. Any one of several specified occasions that, but for the continuation-of-coverage provisions under the Consolidated Omnibus Budget Reconciliation Act of 1985 (COBRA), would result in a loss of benefits to a covered employee under a qualified benefit plan. • These occasions include employment termination, a reduction in work hours, the employee's separation or divorce, the employee's death, and the employer's bankruptcy. IRC (26 USCA) § 4980B(f)(3).

quality. 1. The particular character or properties of a person, thing, or act, often essential for a particular result. **2.** The character or degree of excellence of a person or substance, esp. in comparison with others.

quality of estate. (18c) **1.** The period when the right of enjoying an estate is conferred upon the owner, whether at present or in the future. **2.** The manner in which the owner's right of enjoyment of an estate is to be exercised, whether solely, jointly, in common, or in coparcenary.

quantitative rule. (1919) An evidentiary rule requiring that a given type of evidence is insufficient unless accompanied by additional evidence before the case is closed.

quantum (**kwon**-təm). [Latin "an amount"] The required, desired, or allowed amount; portion or share <a quantum of evidence>. Pl. **quanta** (**kwon**-tə).

quantum meruit (**kwon**-təm **mer**-oo-it). [Latin "as much as he has deserved"] (17c) **1.** The reasonable value of services; damages awarded in an amount considered reasonable to compensate a person who has rendered services in a quasi-contractual relationship. **2.** A claim or right of action for the reasonable value of services rendered. **3.** At common law, a count in an assumpsit action to recover payment for services rendered to another person.

quantum valebant (**kwon**-təm və-**lee**-bant *or* -bənt). [Latin "as much as they were worth"] (18c) **1.** The reasonable value of goods and materials. **2.** At common law, a count in an assumpsit action to recover payment for goods sold and delivered to another. • *Quantum valebant* — although less common than *quantum meruit* — is still used today as an equitable remedy to provide restitution for another's unjust enrichment.

quarantine. (17c) **1.** The isolation of a person or animal afflicted with a communicable disease or the prevention of such a person or animal from coming into a particular area, the purpose being to prevent the spread of disease. • Federal, state, and local authorities are required to cooperate in the enforcement of quarantine laws. 42 USCA § 243(a). **2.** A place where a quarantine is in force. — **quarantine,** *vb.*

quare (**kwair**-ee). [Latin] Why; for what reason; on what account. • This was used in various common-law writs, esp. writs in trespass.

quare clausum fregit (**kwair**-ee **klaw**-zəm **free**-jit). [Latin] Why he broke the close. — Abbr. *qu. cl. fr.*; *q.c.f.*

quarter, *n.* In the law of war, the act of showing mercy to a defeated enemy by sparing lives and accepting a surrender <to give no quarter>. — **quarter,** *vb.* — **quartering,** *n. Hist.*

quash (kwahsh), *vb.* (13c) **1.** To annul or make void; to terminate <quash an indictment> <quash proceedings>. **2.** To suppress or subdue; to crush <quash a rebellion>. — **quashal** (**kwahsh**-əl), *n.*

quasi (**kway**-sɪ *or* **kway**-zɪ *also* **kwah**-zee). [Latin "as if"] (15c) Seemingly but not actually; in some sense or degree; resembling; nearly.

quasi-judicial, *adj.* (1820) Of, relating to, or involving an executive or administrative official's adjudicative acts. • Quasi-judicial acts, which are valid if there is no abuse of discretion, often determine the fundamental rights of citizens. They are subject to review by courts.

quasi-judicial act. (1840) **1.** A judicial act performed by an official who is not a judge. **2.** An act performed by a judge who is not acting entirely in a judicial capacity.

quasi-legislative, *adj.* (1934) (Of an act, function, etc.) not purely legislative in nature <the administrative agency's rulemaking, being partly adjudicative, is not entirely legislative — that is, it is quasi-legislative>.

qu. cl. fr. *abbr.* Quare clausum fregit.

question. (14c) **1.** A query directed to a witness. — Abbr. Q.

categorical question. (18c) **1.** Leading question. **2.** (*often pl.*) One of a series of questions, on a particular subject, arranged in systematic or consecutive order.

cross-question. (17c) A question asked of a witness during cross-examination. — Abbr. XQ.

direct question. (17c) A question asked of a witness during direct examination.

2. An issue in controversy; a matter to be determined. **3.** *Parliamentary law.* A motion that the chair has stated for a meeting's consideration in a form that the meeting can adopt or reject; a pending motion. • A question is technically only a "motion" until the chair states it for the meeting's consideration. But for most purposes, the parliamentary terms "motion" and "question" are interchangeable.

question-and-answer. (17c) **1.** The portion of a deposition or trial transcript in which evidence is developed through a series of questions asked by the lawyer and answered by the witness. — Abbr. Q-and-A. **2.** The method for developing evidence during a deposition or at trial, requiring the witness to answer the examining lawyer's questions, without offering unsolicited information. **3.** The method of instruction used in many law-school classes, in which the professor asks questions of one or more students and then follows up each answer with another question.

question of fact. (17c) **1.** An issue that has not been predetermined and authoritatively answered by the law. • An example is whether a particular criminal defendant is guilty of an offense or whether a contractor has delayed unreasonably in constructing a building. **2.** An issue that does not involve what the law is on a given point. **3.** A disputed issue to be resolved by the jury in a jury trial or by the judge in a bench trial. **4.** An issue capable of being answered by way of demonstration, as opposed to a question of unverifiable opinion.

question of law. (17c) **1.** An issue to be decided by the judge, concerning the application or interpretation of the law <a jury cannot decide questions of law, which are reserved for the court>. **2.** A question that the law itself has authoritatively answered, so that the court may not answer it as a matter of discretion <the enforceability of an arbitration clause is a question of law>. **3.** An issue about what the law is on a particular point; an issue in which parties argue about, and the court must decide, what the true rule of law is <both parties appealed on the question of law>. **4.** An issue that, although it may turn on a factual point, is reserved for the court and excluded from the jury; an issue that is exclusively within the province of the judge and not the jury <whether a contractual ambiguity exists is a question of law>.

quia (**kwɪ**-ə *or* **kwee**-ə). [Latin] *Hist.* Because; whereas. • This term was used to point out the consideration in a conveyance.

quia timet (**kwɪ**-ə **tɪ**-mət *or* **kwee**-ə **tim**-et). [Latin "because he fears"] (17c) A legal doctrine that allows a person to seek equitable relief from future probable harm to a specific right or interest.

quick-asset ratio. The ratio between an entity's current or liquid assets (such as cash and accounts receivable) and its current liabilities.

quickening. The first motion felt in the womb by the mother of the fetus, usu. occurring near the middle of the pregnancy.

quid pro quo (**kwid** proh **kwoh**), *n.* [Latin "something for something"] (16c) An action or thing that is exchanged for another action or thing of more or less equal value; a substitute <the discount was given as a quid pro quo for the extra business>.

quiet, *vb.* **1.** To pacify or silence (a person, etc.). **2.** To make (a right, position, title, etc.) secure or unassailable by removing disturbing causes or disputes.

quit, *adj.* (13c) (Of a debt, obligation, or person) acquitted; free; discharged.

quit, *vb.* (15c) **1.** To cease (an act, etc.); to stop <he didn't quit stalking the victim until the police intervened>. **2.** To leave or surrender possession of (property) <the tenant received a notice to quit but had no intention of quitting the premises>.

qui tam action (**kwɪ** tam *or* **kee**-tam). [Latin *qui tam pro domino rege quam pro se ipso in hac parte sequitur* "who as well for the king as for himself sues in this matter"] (18c) An action brought under a statute that allows a private person to sue for a penalty, part of which the government or some specified public institution will receive. — Often shortened to *qui tam* (Q.T.).

quitclaim, *n.* (14c) **1.** A formal release of one's claim or right. **2.** Quitclaim deed.

quitclaim, *vb.* (14c) **1.** To relinquish or release (a claim or right). **2.** To convey all of one's interest in (property), to whatever extent one has an interest; to execute a quitclaim deed.

quittance. (13c) **1.** A release or discharge from a debt or obligation. **2.** The document serving as evidence of such a release.

quoad (**kwoh**-ad). [Latin] As regards; with regard to <with a pledge, the debtor continues to possess *quoad* the world at large>.

quoad hoc (**kwoh**-ad **hok**). [Latin] (17c) As to this; with respect to this; so far as this is concerned. • A prohibition *quoad hoc* is a prohibition of certain things among others, such as matters brought in an ecclesiastical court that should have been brought in a temporal court.

quondam (**kwon**-dəm), *adj.* Having been formerly; former <the quondam ruler>.

quorum, *n.* (17c) *Parliamentary law.* The minimum number of members (usu. a majority of all the members) who must be present for a deliberative assembly to legally transact business. Pl. **quorums.**

quota. (17c) **1.** A proportional share assigned to a person or group; an allotment <the university's admission standards included a quota for in-state residents>. **2.** A quantitative restriction; a minimum or maximum number <Faldo met his sales quota for the month>.

export quota. A restriction on the products that can be sold to foreign countries. • In the United States, export quotas can be established by the federal government for various purposes, including national defense, price support, and economic stability.

import quota. A restriction on the volume of a certain product that can be brought into the country from a foreign country. • In the United States, the President may establish a quota on an item that poses a threat of serious injury to a domestic industry.

quotation. (17c) **1.** A statement or passage that is exactly reproduced, attributed, and cited. **2.** The amount stated as a stock's or commodity's current price.

market quotation. The most current price at which a security or commodity trades.

3. A contractor's estimate for a given job.

quo warranto (kwoh wə-**ran**-toh *also* kwoh **wahr**-ən-toh). [Law Latin "by what authority"] (15c) **1.** A common-law writ used to inquire into the authority by which a public office is held or a franchise is claimed. **2.** An action by which the state seeks to revoke a corporation's charter. • The Federal Rules of Civil Procedure are applicable to proceedings for quo warranto "to the extent that the practice in such proceedings is not set forth in statutes of the United States and has therefore conformed to the practice in civil actions." Fed. R. Civ. P. 81(a)(2).

q.v. *abbr.* [Latin *quod vide*] (17c) Which see — used in non-*Bluebook* citations for cross-referencing. Pl. **qq.v.**

R

R. *abbr. Trademarks.* When contained in a circle (and often superscripted), the symbol indicating that a trademark or servicemark is registered in the U.S. Patent and Trademark Office.

race-notice statute. (1968) A recording law providing that the person who records first, without notice of prior unrecorded claims, has priority.

race statute. (1944) A recording act providing that the person who records first, regardless of notice, has priority.

race to the courthouse.(1961) **1.** *Bankruptcy.* The competition among creditors to make claims on assets, usu. motivated by the advantages to be gained by those who act first in preference to other creditors. **2.** *Civil procedure.* The competition between disputing parties, both of whom know that litigation is inevitable, to prepare and file a lawsuit in a favorable or convenient forum before the other side files in one that is less favorable or less convenient.

racial profiling. The law-enforcement practice of using race, national origin, or ethnicity as a salient basis for suspicion of criminal activity.

racket, *n.* (1819) **1.** An organized criminal activity; esp., the extortion of money by threat or violence. **2.** A dishonest or fraudulent scheme, business, or activity.

racketeer, *n.* (1924) A person who engages in racketeering. — **racketeer,** *vb.*

Racketeer Influenced and Corrupt Organizations Act. A law designed to attack organized criminal activity and preserve marketplace integrity by investigating, controlling, and prosecuting persons who participate or conspire to participate in racketeering. 18 USCA §§ 1961–1968. • Enacted in 1970, the federal RICO statute applies only to activity involving interstate or foreign commerce. Since then, many states have adopted laws (sometimes called "little RICO" acts) based on the federal statute. The federal and most state RICO acts provide for enforcement not only by criminal prosecution but also by civil lawsuit, in which the plaintiff can sue for treble damages. — Abbr. RICO.

racketeering, *n.* (1897) **1.** A system of organized crime traditionally involving the extortion of money from businesses by intimidation, violence, or other illegal methods. **2.** A pattern of illegal activity (such as bribery, extortion, fraud, and murder) carried out as part of an enterprise (such as a crime syndicate) that is owned or controlled by those engaged in the illegal activity. See 18 USCA §§ 1951–1960.

rack rent, *n.* Rent equal to or nearly equal to the full annual value of the property; excessively or unreasonably high rent. — **rack-rent,** *vb.* — **rack-renter,** *n.*

raffle, *n.* A form of lottery in which each participant buys one or more chances to win a prize.

raid, *n.* **1.** A sudden attack or invasion by law-enforcement officers, usu. to make an arrest or to search for evidence of a crime. **2.** An attempt by a business or union to lure employees or members from a competitor. **3.** An attempt by a group of speculators to cause a sudden fall in stock prices by concerted selling.

railroad, *vb.* **1.** To transport by train. **2.** To send (a measure) hastily through a legislature so that there is little time for consideration and debate. **3.** To convict (a person) hastily, esp. by the use of false charges or insufficient evidence.

rainmaker, *n.* A lawyer who generates a large amount of business for a law firm, usu. through wide contacts within the business community. — **rainmaking,** *n.*

raise, *vb.* (12c) **1.** To increase in amount or value <the industry raised prices>. **2.** To gather or collect <the charity raised funds>. **3.** To bring up for discussion or consideration; to introduce or put forward <the party raised the issue in its pleading>. **4.** To create or establish <the person's silence raised an inference of consent>. **5.** To increase the stated amount of (a negotiable instrument) by fraudulent alteration <the indorser raised the check>.

raising an instrument. The act of fraudulently altering a negotiable instrument, esp. a check, to increase the amount stated as payable.

rake-off, *n.* (1887) A percentage or share taken, esp. from an illegal transaction; an illegal bribe, payoff, or skimming of profits. — **rake off,** *vb.*

rally, *n.* A sharp rise in price or trading (as of stocks) after a declining market.

Rambo lawyer. *Slang.* A lawyer, esp. a litigator, who uses aggressive, unethical, or illegal tactics in representing a client and who lacks courtesy and professionalism in dealing with other lawyers.

ram raid. *Slang.* The smashing of a shop window or other commercial premises with a vehicle in order to break in and steal cash or goods. • The term is most common in Britain, Ireland, and Australia.

R and D. *abbr.* Research and development.

rank and file. 1. The enlisted soldiers of an armed force, as distinguished from the officers. **2.** The general membership of a union.

ransom, *n.* (13c) **1.** Money or other consideration demanded or paid for the release of a captured person or property. **2.** The release of a captured person or property in exchange for payment of a demanded price.

ransom, *vb.* (14c) **1.** To obtain the release of (a captive) by paying a demanded price. **2.** To release (a captive) upon receiving such a payment. **3.** To hold and demand payment for the release of (a captive).

rap, *n.* (1903) *Slang.* **1.** Legal responsibility for a criminal act <he took the rap for his accomplices>. **2.** A criminal charge <a murder rap>. **3.** A criminal conviction; esp., a prison sentence <a 20-year rap for counterfeiting>.

rape, *n.* (15c) **1.** At common law, unlawful sexual intercourse committed by a man with a woman not his wife through force and against her will. • The common-law crime of rape required at least a slight penetration of the penis into the vagina. Also at common law, a husband could not be convicted of raping his wife. — Formerly termed *rapture*; *ravishment.* **2.** Unlawful sexual activity (esp. intercourse) with a person (usu. a female) without consent and usu. by force or threat of injury. — **rape,** *vb.* — **rapist,** *n.*

acquaintance rape. (1980) Rape committed by someone known to the victim, esp. by the victim's social companion.

command rape. Coerced or forced sexual contact between a superior member and subordinate member of the armed forces.

date rape. (1975) Rape committed by a person who is escorting the victim on a social occasion. • Loosely, *date rape* also sometimes refers to what is more accurately called *acquaintance rape* or *relationship rape.*

marital rape. (1936) A husband's sexual intercourse with his wife by force or without her consent.

rape by means of fraud. An instance of sexual intercourse that has been induced by fraud.

relationship rape. (1999) Rape committed by someone with whom the victim has had a significant association, often (though not always) of a romantic nature. • This term encompasses all types of relationships, including family, friends, dates, cohabitants, and spouses, in which the victim has had more than brief or perfunctory interaction with the other person. Thus it does not extend to those with whom the victim has had only brief encounters or a nodding acquaintance.

spousal rape. Marital rape.

statutory rape. (1873) Unlawful sexual intercourse with a person under the age of consent (as defined by statute), regardless of whether it is against that person's will. • Generally, only an adult may be convicted of this crime.

3. *Archaic.* The act of seizing and carrying off a person (esp. a woman) by force; abduction. **4.** The act of plundering or despoiling a place.

rapprochement (ra-prosh-**mah*n***). [French] The establishment or restoration of cordial relations between two or more nations.

rap sheet. (1960) *Slang.* A person's criminal record.

rat. *Slang.* STOOL PIGEON (1).

ratable (**ray**-tə-bəl), *adj.* (16c) **1.** Proportionate <ratable distribution>. **2.** Capable of being estimated, appraised, or apportioned <because hundreds of angry fans ran onto the field at the same time, blame for the goalpost's destruction is not ratable>. **3.** Taxable <the government assessed the widow's ratable estate>.

ratchet theory. (1977) *Constitutional law.* The principle that Congress, in exercising its enforcement power under the 14th Amendment, can increase but not dilute the scope of 14th Amendment guarantees as previously defined by the Supreme Court. • The theory was stated by Justice Brennan in *Katzenbach v. Morgan*, 384 U.S. 641, 86 S.Ct. 1717 (1966), but was repudiated by the Supreme Court in *City of Boerne v. Flores*, 521 U.S. 507, 117 S.Ct.2157 (1997).

rate, *n.* (15c) **1.** Proportional or relative value; the proportion by which quantity or value is adjusted <rate of inflation>. **2.** An amount paid or charged for a good or service <the rate for a business-class fare is $550>. **3.** INTEREST RATE <the rate on the loan increases by 2% after five years>. — **rate,** *vb.*

rate base. The investment amount or property value on which a company, esp. a public utility, is allowed to earn a particular rate of return.

rate of return. The annual income from an investment, expressed as a percentage of the investment.

fair rate of return. The amount of profit that a public utility is permitted to earn, as determined by a public utility commission.

ratification, *n.* (15c) **1.** Adoption or enactment, esp. where the act is the last in a series of necessary steps or consents. **2.** Confirmation and acceptance of a previous act, thereby making the act valid from the moment it was done. **3.** *Contracts.* A person's binding adoption of an act already completed but either not done in a way that originally produced a legal obligation or done by a third party having at the time no authority to act as the person's agent. — **ratify,** *vb.* — **ratifiable,** *adj.*

ratiocination (rash-ee-os-ə-**nay**-shən), *n.* (16c) The process or an act of reasoning. — **ratiocinative** (rash-ee-**os**-ə-nay-tiv), *adj.* — **ratiocinate** (rash-ee-**os**-ə-nayt), *vb.*

ratio decidendi (**ray**-shee-oh des-ə-**den**-dɪ), *n.* [Latin "the reason for deciding"] (18c) **1.** The principle or rule of law on which a court's decision is founded <many poorly written judicial opinions do not contain a clearly ascertainable *ratio decidendi*>. **2.** The rule of law on which a later court thinks that a previous court founded its decision; a general rule without which a case must have been decided otherwise <this opinion recognizes the Supreme Court's *ratio decidendi* in the school desegregation cases>. — Often shortened to *ratio*. Pl. ***rationes decidendi*** (**ray**-shee-oh-neez des-ə-**den**-dɪ).

rational-basis test. (1947) *Constitutional law.* The criterion for judicial analysis of a statute that does not implicate a fundamental right or a suspect or quasi-suspect classification under the Due Process or Equal Protection Clause, whereby the court will uphold a law if it bears a reasonable relationship to the attainment of a legitimate governmental objective.

rational-choice theory. (1979) The theory that behavioral choices, including the choice to engage in criminal activity, are based on purposeful decisions that the potential benefits outweigh the risks.

rDNA. *abbr.* Recombinant DNA technology.

re (ree *or* ray), *prep.* (18c) Regarding; in the matter of. • In the title of a case, it usu. signifies a legal proceeding regarding the disposition of real or personal property or a change in legal status. In American caselaw, the abbreviation commonly used is *in re* <In re Estate of Kirk>. In business correspondence, the term signals the subject matter <re: Board Meeting>.

REA. *abbr.* Rural Electrification Administration.

readjustment, *n.* (18c) Voluntary reorganization of a financially troubled corporation by the shareholders themselves, without a trustee's or a receiver's intervention. — **readjust,** *vb.*

read law. **1.** To prepare for a legal career by working in a lawyer's office as a clerk while studying legal texts on one's own time. • Most American lawyers in the 18th and 19th centuries obtained their legal educations solely by reading law. Today, few American states allow applicants to take the bar exam without attending law school. **2.** To study law at a law school.

ready, willing, and able. (1829) (Of a prospective buyer) legally and financially capable of consummating a purchase.

reaffirmation, *n.* (1857) **1.** Approval of something previously decided or agreed to; renewal <the Supreme Court's reaffirmation of this principle is long overdue>. **2.** *Bankruptcy.* An agreement between the debtor and a creditor by which the debtor promises to repay a prepetition debt that would otherwise be discharged at the conclusion of the bankruptcy <the debtor negotiated a reaffirmation so that he could keep the collateral>. — **reaffirm,** *vb.*

reaffirmation hearing. *Bankruptcy.* A hearing at which the debtor and a creditor present a reaffirmation of a dischargeable debt for the court's approval. • The reaffirmation hearing is usu. held simultaneously with the discharge hearing.

real, *adj.* (15c) **1.** Of or relating to things (such as lands and buildings) that are fixed or immovable <real property> <a real action>. **2.** Actual; genuine; true <real authority>. **3.** (Of money, income, etc.) measured in terms of purchasing power rather than nominal value; adjusted for inflation <real wages>.

real-estate investment trust. A company that invests in and manages a portfolio of real estate, with the majority of the trust's income distributed to its shareholders. — Abbr. REIT.

real-estate-mortgage investment conduit. An entity that holds a fixed pool of mortgages or mortgage-backed securities (such as collateralized mortgage obligations), issues interests in itself to investors, and receives favorable tax treatment by passing its income through to those investors. • Real-estate-mortgage investment conduits were created by the Tax Reform Act of 1986. — Abbr. REMIC.

real-estate mortgage trust. A real-estate investment trust that buys and sells the mortgages on real property rather than the real property itself. — Abbr. REMT.

real-estate syndicate. A group of investors who pool their money to buy and sell real property. • Most real-estate syndicates operate as limited partnerships or real-estate investment trusts.

realignment (ree-ə-**lIn**-mənt), *n.* The process by which a court, usu. in determining diversity jurisdiction, identifies and rearranges the parties as plaintiffs and defendants according to their ultimate interests. — **realign,** *vb.*

realization, *n.* (18c) **1.** Conversion of noncash assets into cash assets. **2.** *Tax.* An event or transaction, such as the sale or exchange of property, that substantially changes a taxpayer's economic position so that income tax may be imposed or a tax allowance granted. — **realize,** *vb.*

real law. The law of real property; real-estate law.

real party in interest. PARTY (2).

real-party-in-interest rule. The principle that the person entitled by law to enforce a substantive right should be the one under whose name the action is prosecuted. Fed. R. Civ. P. 17(a).

real things. (18c) Property that is fixed and immovable, such as lands and buildings; real property.

realtor (**reel**-tər). **1.** (*cap.*) *Servicemark.* A real-estate agent who is a member of the National Association of Realtors. **2.** Loosely, any real-estate agent or broker.

realty. Land and anything growing on, attached to, or erected on it, that cannot be removed without injury to the land.

reapportionment, *n.* (1874) Realignment of a legislative district's boundaries to reflect changes in population and ensure proportionate representation by elected officials. See U.S. Const. art. I, § 2, cl. 3. — **reapportion,** *vb.*

reargument, *n.* (18c) The presentation of additional arguments, which often suggest that a controlling legal principle has been overlooked, to a court (usu. an appellate court) that has already heard initial arguments. — **reargue,** *vb.*

reasonable, *adj.* (14c) **1.** Fair, proper, or moderate under the circumstances <reasonable pay>. **2.** According to reason <your argument is reasonable but not convincing>. **3.** (Of a person) having the faculty of reason <a reasonable person would have looked both ways before crossing the street>. — **reasonableness,** *n.*

reasonable accommodation. ACCOMMODATION.

reasonable cause. PROBABLE CAUSE (1).

reasonable-consumer test. The prevailing test for determining whether advertisement is deceptive, determined by asking whether the reasonable consumer would believe that the claim is true.

reasonable doubt. (18c) The doubt that prevents one from being firmly convinced of a defendant's guilt, or the belief that there is a real possibility that a defendant is not guilty. • "Beyond a reasonable doubt" is the standard used by a jury to determine whether a criminal defendant is guilty. See Model Penal Code § 1.12. In deciding whether guilt has been proved beyond a reasonable doubt, the jury must begin with the presumption that the defendant is innocent.

reasonable-expectations doctrine. The principle that an ambiguous or inconspicuous term in a contract should be interpreted to favor the weaker party's objectively reasonable expectations from the contract, even though the explicit language of the terms may not support those expectations. • This principle is most often applied when interpreting insurance policies, consumer contracts, and other types of adhesion contracts.

reasonable-inference rule. (1945) An evidentiary principle providing that a jury, in deciding a case, may properly consider any reasonable inference drawn from the evidence presented at trial.

reasonable medical probability. (1949) In proving the cause of an injury, a standard requiring a showing that the injury was more likely than not caused by a particular stimulus, based on the general consensus of recognized medical thought.

reasonable person. A hypothetical person used as a legal standard, esp. to determine whether someone acted with negligence; specif., a person who exercises the degree of attention, knowledge, intelligence, and judgment that society requires of its members for the protection of their own and of others' interests. • The reasonable person acts sensibly, does things without serious delay, and takes proper but not excessive precautions.

reasonable time. (1951) **1.** *Contracts.* The time needed to do what a contract requires to be done, based on subjective circumstances. • If the contracting parties do not fix a time for performance, the law will usu. presume a reasonable time. **2.** *Commercial law.* The time during which the UCC permits a party to accept an offer, inspect goods, substitute conforming goods for rejected goods, and the like.

reasonable-use theory. (1933) *Property.* The principle that owners of riparian land may make reasonable use of their water if this use does not affect the water available to lower riparian owners.

reasonably-prudent-operator standard. *Oil & gas.* The test generally applied to determine a lessee's compliance with implied lease covenants by considering what a reasonable, competent operator in the oil-and-gas industry would do under the circumstances, acting in good faith and with economic motivation, and taking into account the lessor's interests as well as that of the operator.

reason to know. Information from which a person of ordinary intelligence — or of the superior intelligence that the person may have — would infer that the fact in question exists or that there is a substantial enough chance of its existence that, if the person exercises reasonable care, the person can assume the fact exists.

rebut, *vb.* (14c) To refute, oppose, or counteract (something) by evidence, argument, or contrary proof <rebut the opponent's expert testimony>.

rebuttal, *n.* (1830) **1.** In-court contradiction of an adverse party's evidence. **2.** The time given to a party to present contradictory evidence or arguments. **3.** The arguments contained in a reply brief.

rebutter. (16c) **1.** *Common-law pleading.* The defendant's answer to a plaintiff's surrejoinder; the pleading that followed the rejoinder and surrejoinder, and that might in turn be answered by the surrebutter. **2.** One who rebuts.

rebutting evidence. Rebuttal evidence.

recall, *n.* (1902) **1.** Removal of a public official from office by popular vote. **2.** A manufacturer's request to consumers for the return of defective products for repair or replacement. **3.** Revocation of a judgment for factual or legal reasons. — **recall,** *vb.*

recall of mandate. The extraordinary action by an appellate court of withdrawing the order it issued to the trial court upon deciding an appeal, usu. after the deadline has passed for the losing party to seek a rehearing.

recant (ri-**kant**), *vb.* (16c) **1.** To withdraw or renounce (prior statements or testimony) formally or publicly. **2.** To withdraw or renounce prior statements or testimony formally or publicly. — **recantation,** *n.*

recapitalization, *n.* An adjustment or recasting of a corporation's capital structure — that is, its stocks, bonds, or other securities — through amendment of the articles of incorporation or merger with a parent or subsidiary. — **recapitalize,** *vb.*

recaption. (17c) **1.** At common law, lawful seizure of another's property for a second time to secure the performance of a duty; a second distress. **2.** Peaceful retaking, without legal process, of one's own property that has been wrongfully taken.

recapture, *n.* **1.** The act or an instance of retaking or reacquiring; recovery. **2.** The lawful taking by the government of earnings or profits exceeding a specified amount; esp., the government's recovery of a tax benefit (such as a deduction or credit) by taxing income or property that no longer qualifies for the benefit. — **recapture,** *vb.*

receipt, *n.* (14c) **1.** The act of receiving something <my receipt of the document was delayed by two days>. **2.** A written acknowledgment that something has been received <keep the receipt for the gift>. **3.** (*usu. pl.*) Something received; INCOME <post the daily receipts in the ledger>.

receipt, *vb.* (18c) **1.** To acknowledge in writing the receipt of (something, esp. money) <the bill must be receipted>. **2.** To give a receipt for (something, esp. money) <the bookkeeper receipted the payments>.

receiptor (ri-**see**-tər). (1814) A person who receives from a sheriff another's property seized in garnishment and agrees to return the property upon demand or execution.

receivable, *adj.* **1.** Capable of being admitted or accepted <receivable evidence>. **2.** Awaiting receipt of payment <accounts receivable>. **3.** Subject to a call for payment <a note receivable>.

receivable, *n.* (14c) An amount owed, esp. by a business's customer.

receiver. (18c) A disinterested person appointed by a court, or by a corporation or other person, for the protection or collection of property that is the subject of diverse claims (for example, because it belongs to a bankrupt or is otherwise being litigated).

receivership. (15c) **1.** The state or condition of being in the control of a receiver. **2.** The position or function of being a receiver appointed by a court or under a statute. **3.** A proceeding in which a court appoints a receiver.

receiving stolen property. (1847) The criminal offense of acquiring or controlling property known to have been stolen by another person.

reception. (1931) The adoption in whole or in part of the law of one jurisdiction by another jurisdiction. • In the legal idiom, it is most common to speak of the reception of Roman law.

recess (**ree**-ses), *n.* (17c) **1.** A brief break in judicial proceedings. **2.** *Parliamentary law.* A motion that suspends but does not end a meeting, and that usu. provides for resumption of the meeting. **3.** *Parliamentary law.* The interval between such a motion's adoption and the meeting's reconvening. — **recess** (ri-**ses**), *vb.*

recession. (1929) A period characterized by a sharp slowdown in economic activity, declining employment, and a decrease in investment and consumer spending.

recharacterization. A court's determination that an insider's loan to an entity in liquidation (such as a corporation or partnership) should be treated as a capital contribution, not as a loan, thereby entitling the insider to only part of the liquidation proceeds payable after all the business's debts have been discharged.

recidivism (ri-**sid**-ə-viz-əm), *n.* (1886) A tendency to relapse into a habit of criminal activity or behavior. — **recidivous, recidivist,** *adj.*

recidivist (ri-**sid**-ə-vist), *n.* (1880) One who has been convicted of multiple criminal offenses, usu. similar in nature; a repeat offender.

reciprocal (ri-**sip**-rə-kəl), *adj.* (16c) **1.** Directed by each toward the other or others; MUTUAL <reciprocal trusts>. **2.** BILATERAL <a reciprocal contract>. **3.** Corresponding; equivalent <reciprocal discovery>.

reciprocal dealing. A business arrangement in which a buyer having greater economic power than a seller agrees to buy something from the seller only if the seller buys something in return.

reciprocity (res-ə-**pros**-i-tee). (18c) **1.** Mutual or bilateral action. **2.** The mutual concession of advantages or privileges for purposes of commercial or diplomatic relations.

recital. (16c) **1.** An account or description of some fact or thing <the recital of the events leading up to the accident>. **2.** A preliminary statement in a contract or deed explaining the reasons for entering into it or the background of the transaction, or showing the existence of particular facts <the recitals in the settlement agreement should describe the underlying dispute>. — **recite,** *vb.*

reckless, *adj.* (bef. 12c) Characterized by the creation of a substantial and unjustifiable risk of harm to others and by a conscious (and sometimes deliberate) disregard for or indifference to that risk; heedless; rash. • Reckless conduct is much more than mere negligence: it is a gross deviation from what a reasonable person would do. — **recklessly,** *adv.*

reckless disregard. DISREGARD.

reckless driving. (1902) The criminal offense of operating a motor vehicle in a manner that shows conscious indifference to the safety of others.

reckless endangerment. (1968) The criminal offense of putting another person at substantial risk of death or serious injury. • This is a statutory, not a common-law, offense.

reckless indifference. Deliberate indifference.

reckless negligence. Gross negligence.

recklessness, *n.* (bef. 12c) **1.** Conduct whereby the actor does not desire harmful consequence but nonetheless foresees the possibility and consciously takes the risk. • Recklessness involves a greater degree of fault than negligence but a lesser degree of fault than intentional wrongdoing. **2.** The state of mind in which a person does not care about the consequences of his or her actions.

reclamation (rek-lə-**may**-shən), *n.* (1848) **1.** The act or an instance of improving the value of economically useless land by physically changing the land, such as irrigating a desert. **2.** *Commercial law.* A seller's limited right to retrieve goods delivered to a buyer when the buyer is insolvent. UCC § 2-702(2). **3.** The act or an instance of obtaining valuable materials from waste materials. — **reclaim,** *vb.*

recognition, *n.* (16c) **1.** Confirmation that an act done by another person was authorized. **2.** The formal admission that a person, entity, or thing has a particular status; esp. a nation's act in formally acknowledging the existence of another nation or national government. **3.** *Parliamentary law.* The chair's acknowledgment that a member is entitled to the floor <the chair recognizes the delegate from Minnesota>. **4.** *Tax.* The act or an instance of accounting for a taxpayer's realized gain or loss for the purpose of income-tax reporting. **5.** An employer's acknowledgment that a union has the right to act as a bargaining agent for employees. **6.** *Int'l law.* Official action by a country acknowledging, expressly or by implication, *de jure* or *de facto*, the existence of a government or a country, or a situation such as a change of territorial sovereignty. — **recognize,** *vb.*

recognizance (ri-**kog**-nə-zənts). (14c) A bond or obligation, made in court, by which a person promises to perform some act or observe some condition, such as to appear when called, to pay a debt, or to keep the peace; specif., an in-court acknowledgment of an obligation in a penal sum, conditioned on the performance or nonperformance of a particular act. • Most commonly, a recognizance takes the form of a bail bond that guarantees an unjailed criminal defendant's return for a court date <the defendant was released on his own recognizance>.

personal recognizance. (18c) The release of a defendant in a criminal case in which the court takes the defendant's word that he or she will appear for a scheduled matter or when told to appear. • This type of release dispenses with the necessity of the person's posting money or having a surety sign a bond with the court.

recollection, *n.* (17c) **1.** The action of recalling something to the mind, esp. through conscious effort. **2.** Something recalled to the mind. — **recollect,** *vb.*

recommit. *Parliamentary law.* To refer (a motion) back to a committee that has considered it.

recompense (**rek**-əm-pents), *n.* (15c) Repayment, compensation, or retribution for something, esp. an injury or loss. — **recompense,** *vb.*

reconciliation (rek-ən-sil-ee-**ay**-shən), *n.* (14c) **1.** Restoration of harmony between persons or things that had been in conflict <a reconciliation between the plaintiff and the defendant is unlikely even if the lawsuit settles before trial>. **2.** *Family law.* Voluntary resumption, after a separation, of full marital relations between spouses <the court dismissed the divorce petition after the parties' reconciliation>. **3.** *Accounting.* An adjustment of accounts so that they agree, esp. by allowing for outstanding items <reconciliation of the checking account and the bank statement>. — **reconcile** (**rek**-ən-sɪl), *vb.*

reconciliation agreement. *Family law.* A contract between spouses who have had marital difficulties but who now wish to save the marital relationship, usu. by specifying certain economic actions that might ameliorate pressures on the marriage. • Many states have statutes prohibiting enforcement of contracts for domestic services, so if the agreement governs anything other than economic behavior, it may be unenforceable.

reconsider, *vb.* To discuss or take up (a matter) again <legislators voted to reconsider the bill>. — **reconsideration,** *n.*

reconstruction. 1. The act or process of rebuilding, re-creating, or reorganizing something. **2.** (*cap.*) The process by which the Southern states that had seceded during the Civil War were readmitted into the Union during the years following the war (i.e., from 1865 to 1877) <the 13th, 14th, and 15th Amendments to the U.S. Constitution are a lasting legacy of Reconstruction>.

reconversion. The notional or imaginary process by which an earlier constructive conversion (a change of personal into real property or vice versa) is annulled and the converted property restored to its original character.

reconveyance, *n.* (16c) The restoration or return of something (esp. an estate or title) to a former owner or holder. — **reconvey,** *vb.*

record, *n.* (13c) **1.** A documentary account of past events, usu. designed to memorialize those events. **2.** Information that is inscribed on a tangible medium or that, having been stored in an electronic or other medium, is retrievable in perceivable form. UCC § 2A-102(a)(34). **3.** The official report of the proceedings in a case, including the filed papers, a verbatim transcript of the trial or hearing (if any), and tangible exhibits.

defective record. (18c) **1.** A trial record that fails to conform to requirements of appellate rules. **2.** A flawed real-estate title resulting from a defect on the property's record in the registry of deeds.

public record. (16c) A record that a governmental unit is required by law to keep, such as land deeds kept at a county courthouse. • Public records are generally open to view by the public.

reporter's record. In some jurisdictions, a trial transcript.

silent record. Criminal procedure. A record that fails to disclose that a defendant voluntarily and knowingly entered a plea, waived a right to counsel, or took any other action affecting his or her rights.

record, *vb.* To deposit (an original or authentic official copy of a document) with an authority.

recorder. (15c) **1.** A municipal judge with the criminal jurisdiction of a magistrate or a police judge and sometimes also with limited civil jurisdiction. **2.** A municipal or county officer who keeps public records such as deeds, liens, and judgments.

court recorder. (18c) A court official who records court activities using electronic recording equipment, usu. for the purpose of preparing a verbatim transcript.

recorder of deeds. Register of deeds.

recording act. (1802) A law that establishes the requirements for recording a deed or other property interest and the standards for determining priorities between persons claiming interests in the same property (usu. real property). • Recording acts — the three main types of which are the *notice statute*, the *race statute*, and the *race-notice statute* — are designed to protect bona fide purchasers from earlier unrecorded interests.

recording agent. Insurance agent.

recording officer. SECRETARY (3).

recording statute. Recording act.

record of decision. *Environmental law.* A public document, generated under CERCLA, describing a federal agency's decision regarding an environmental problem, identifying the remedies considered and which one is best, stating whether practical means to minimize or prevent environmental harms caused by the chosen remedy have been adopted, and summarizing a plan for monitoring and enforcing any measures required to mitigate environmental harm. — Abbr. ROD.

record on appeal. The record of a trial-court proceeding as presented to the appellate court for review.

recoupment (ri-**koop**-mənt), *n.* (17c) **1.** The recovery or regaining of something, esp. expenses. **2.** The withholding, for equitable reasons, of all or part of something that is due. **3.** Reduction of a plaintiff's damages because of a demand by the defendant arising out of the same transaction. **4.** The right of a defendant to have the plaintiff's claim reduced or eliminated because of the plaintiff's breach of contract or duty in the same transaction. **5.** An affirmative defense alleging such a breach. — **recoup,** *vb.*

recourse (**ree**-kors *or* ri-**kors**). (14c) **1.** The act of seeking help or advice. **2.** Enforcement of, or a method for enforcing, a right. **3.** The right of a holder of a negotiable instrument to demand payment from the drawer or indorser if the instrument is dishonored. **4.** The right to repayment of a loan from the borrower's personal assets, not just from the collateral that secured the loan.

recover, *vb.* (14c) **1.** To get back or regain in full or in equivalence <the landlord recovered higher operating costs by raising rent>. **2.** To obtain by a judgment or other legal process <the plaintiff recovered punitive damages in the lawsuit>. **3.** To obtain (a judgment) in one's favor <the plaintiff recovered a judgment against the defendant>. **4.** To obtain damages or other relief; to succeed in a lawsuit or other legal proceeding <the defendant argued that the plaintiff should not be allowed to recover for his own negligence>.

recoverable, *adj.* (14c) Capable of being recovered, esp. as a matter of law <court costs and attorney's fees are recoverable under the statute>. — **recoverability,** *n.*

recovered-memory syndrome. Repressed-memory syndrome.

recovery. (15c) **1.** The regaining or restoration of something lost or taken away. **2.** The obtainment of a right to something (esp. damages) by a judgment or decree. **3.** An amount awarded in or collected from a judgment or decree.

double recovery. (1813) **1.** A judgment that erroneously awards damages twice for the same loss, based on two different theories of recovery. **2.** Recovery by a party of more than the maximum recoverable loss that the party has sustained.

recrimination (ri-krim-i-**nay**-shən), *n.* **1.** *Family law. Archaic.* In a divorce suit, a countercharge that the complainant has been guilty of an offense constituting a ground for divorce. • Recriminations are now virtually obsolete because of the prevalence of no-fault divorce. **2.** *Criminal law.* An accused person's counteraccusation against the accuser. • The accusation may be for the same or a different offense. — **recriminatory,** *adj.*

recross-examination. (1869) A second cross-examination, after redirect examination. — Often shortened to *recross.*

rectification (rek-tə-fi-**kay**-shən), *n.* (18c) **1.** A court's equitable correction of a contractual term that is misstated; the judicial alteration of a written contract to make it conform to the true intention of the parties when, in its original form, it did not reflect this intention. • As an equitable remedy, the court alters the terms as written so as to express the true intention of the parties. The court might do this when the rent is wrongly recorded in a lease or when the area of land is incorrectly cited in a deed. **2.** A court's slight modification of words of a statute as a means of carrying out what the court is convinced must have been the legislative intent. • For example, courts engage in rectification when they read *and* as *or* or *shall* as *may,* as they frequently must do because of unfastidious drafting. — **rectify,** *vb.*

recusable (ri-**kyoo**-zə-bəl), *adj.* (1863) **1.** (Of an obligation) arising from a party's voluntary act and that can be avoided. **2.** (Of a judge) capable of being disqualified from sitting on a case. **3.** (Of a fact) providing a basis for disqualifying a judge from sitting on a case.

recusal (ri-**kyoo**-zəl), *n.* (1949) Removal of oneself as judge or policy-maker in a particular matter, esp. because of a conflict of interest.

recusant (**rek**-yə-zənt *or* ri-**kyoo**-zənt), *adj.* (16c) Refusing to submit to an authority or comply with a command <a recusant witness>.

recuse (ri-**kyooz**), *vb.* (16c) **1.** To remove (oneself) as a judge in a particular case because of prejudice or conflict of interest <the judge recused himself from the trial>. **2.** To challenge or object to (a judge) as being disqualified from hearing a case because of prejudice or a conflict of interest <the defendant filed a motion to recuse the trial judge>.

redaction (ri-**dak**-shən), *n.* (18c) **1.** The careful editing of a document, esp. to remove confidential references or offensive material. **2.** A revised or edited document. — **redactional,** *adj.* — **redact,** *vb.*

reddendum (ri-**den**-dəm). [Latin "that must be given back or yielded"] (17c) A clause in a deed by which the grantor reserves some new thing (esp. rent) out of what had been previously granted.

redelivery. (15c) An act or instance of giving back or returning something; restitution.

redemise, *n.* (18c) An act or instance of conveying or transferring back (an estate) already demised. — **redemise,** *vb.*

redemption, *n.* (16c) **1.** The act or an instance of reclaiming or regaining possession by paying a specific price. **2.** *Bankruptcy.* A debtor's right to repurchase property from a buyer who obtained the property at a forced sale initiated by a creditor. **3.** *Securities.* The reacquisition of a security by the issuer. • Redemption usu. refers to the repurchase of a bond before maturity, but it may also refer to the repurchase of stock and mutual-fund shares. **4.** *Property.* The payment of a defaulted mortgage debt by a borrower who does not want to lose the property. — **redeemable, redemptive, redemptional** *adj.* — **redeem,** *vb.*

statutory redemption. (1851) The statutory right of a defaulting mortgagor to recover property, within a specified period, after a foreclosure or tax sale, by paying the outstanding debt or charges.

tax redemption. (1867) A taxpayer's recovery of property taken for nonpayment of taxes, accomplished by paying the delinquent taxes and any interest, costs, and penalties.

red herring. (1884) An irrelevant legal or factual issue, usu. intended to distract or mislead.

redirect examination. (1865) A second direct examination, after cross-examination, the scope ordinarily being limited to matters covered during cross-examination. — Often shortened to *redirect.*

redisseisin (ree-dis-**see**-zin), *n.* (16c) **1.** A disseisin by one who has already dispossessed the same person of the same estate. **2.** A writ to recover an estate that has been dispossessed by redisseisin. — **redisseise** (ree-dis-**seez**), *vb.*

redistribution. The act or process of distributing something again or anew <redistribution of wealth>.

redistrict, *vb.* To organize into new districts, esp. legislative ones; reapportion.

redistricting. Reapportionment.

redlining, *n.* (1973) **1.** Credit discrimination (usu. unlawful discrimination) by an institution that refuses to provide loans or insurance on properties in areas that are considered to be poor financial risks or to the people who live in those areas. **2.** The process, usu. automated, of creating, for an existing document, an interim version that shows, through strike-outs and other typographical features, all deletions and insertions made in the most recent revision. — **redline,** *vb.*

redraft, *n.* (17c) A second negotiable instrument offered by the drawer after the first instrument has been dishonored. — **redraft,** *vb.*

redress (ri-**dres** *or* **ree**-dres), *n.* (14c) **1.** Relief; remedy <money damages, as opposed to equitable relief, is the only redress available>. **2.** A means of seeking relief or remedy <if the statute of limitations has run, the plaintiff is without redress>. — **redressable,** *adj.* — **redress** (ri-**dres**), *vb.*

penal redress. A form of penal liability requiring full compensation of the injured person as an instrument for punishing the offender; compensation paid to the injured person for the full value of the loss (an amount that may far exceed the wrongdoer's benefit).

restitutionary redress. Money paid to one who has been injured, the amount being the pecuniary value of the benefit to the wrongdoer.

red tape. A bureaucratic procedure required to be followed before official action can be taken; esp. rigid adherence to time-consuming rules and regulations; excessive bureaucracy. • The phrase originally referred to the red ribbons that lawyers and government officials once used to tie their papers together.

reductio ad absurdum (ri-**dək**-shee-oh *or* ri-**dək**-tee-oh ad ab-**sər**-dəm). [Latin "reduction to the absurd"] (18c) In logic, disproof of an argument by showing that it leads to a ridiculous conclusion.

reduction in force. Layoff.

reduction to practice. *Patents.* The embodiment of the concept of an invention, either by physical construction and operation or by filing a patent application with a disclosure adequate to teach a person reasonably skilled in the art how to make and work the invention without undue experimentation.

reenactment rule. (1941) In statutory construction, the principle that when reenacting a law, the legislature implicitly adopts well-settled judicial or administrative interpretations of the law.

reentry, *n.* (15c) **1.** The act or an instance of retaking possession of land by someone who formerly held the land and who reserved the right to retake it when the new holder let it go. **2.** A landlord's resumption of possession of leased premises upon the tenant's default under the lease. — **reenter,** *vb.*

reexamination, *n.* (17c) **1.** Redirect examination. **2.** *Patents.* A proceeding by the U.S. Patent and Trademark Office to determine whether prior art renders one or more claims of an already-issued patent invalid; specif., an administrative procedure by which a party can seek review of a patent on the basis of prior art by the PTO. — **reexamine,** *vb.*

reexecution. (18c) The equitable remedy by which a lost or destroyed deed or other instrument is replaced. • Equity compels the party or parties to execute a new deed or instrument if a claimant properly proves a right under one that has been lost or destroyed.

referee. (17c) A type of master appointed by a court to assist with certain proceedings. • In some jurisdictions, referees take testimony before reporting to the court.

reference, *n.* (16c) **1.** The act of sending or directing to another for information, service, consideration, or decision; specif., the act of sending a case to a master or referee for information or decision.

general reference. (18c) A court's reference of a case to a referee, usu. with all parties' consent, to decide all issues of fact and law. • The referee's decision stands as the judgment of the court.

special reference. (1831) A court's reference of a case to a referee for decisions on specific questions of fact. • The special referee makes findings and reports them to the trial judge, who treats them as advisory only and not as binding decisions.

2. An order sending a case to a master or referee for information or decision. **3.** Mention or citation of one document or source in another document or source. **4.** *Patents.* Information — such as that contained in a publication, another patent, or another patent application — that a patent examiner considers to be anticipatory prior art or proof of unpredictability in the art that forms a basis for one or more of an applicant's claims to be rejected. — **refer,** *vb.*

referendum. (1847) **1.** The process of referring a state legislative act, a state constitutional amendment, or an important public issue to the people for final approval by popular vote. **2.** A vote taken by this method. Pl. **referendums, referenda.**

referral. (1927) The act or an instance of sending or directing to another for information, service, consideration, or decision <referral of the client to an employment-law specialist> <referral of the question to the board of directors>.

refinancing, *n.* An exchange of an old debt for a new debt, as by negotiating a different interest rate or term or by repaying the existing loan with money acquired from a new loan. — **refinance,** *vb.*

reformation (ref-ər-**may**-shən), *n.* (1829) An equitable remedy by which a court will modify a written agreement to reflect the actual intent of the parties, usu. to correct fraud or mutual mistake in the writing, such as an incomplete property description in a deed. • In cases of mutual mistake, the actual intended agreement must usu. be established by clear and convincing evidence. In cases of fraud, there must be clear evidence of what the agreement would have been but for the fraud. — **reform,** *vb.*

reformatory, *n.* (1834) A penal institution in which young offenders, esp. minors, are disciplined and trained or educated.

refugee. A person who flees or is expelled from a country, esp. because of persecution, and seeks haven in another country.

refund, *n.* **1.** The return of money to a person who overpaid, such as a taxpayer who overestimated tax liability or whose employer withheld too much tax from earnings. **2.** The money returned to a person who overpaid. **3.** The act of refinancing, esp. by replacing outstanding securities with a new issue of securities. — **refund,** *vb.*

refusal. (15c) **1.** The denial or rejection of something offered or demanded. **2.** An opportunity to accept or reject something before it is offered to others; the right or privilege of having this opportunity.

refute, *vb.* (16c) **1.** To prove (a statement) to be false. **2.** To prove (a person) to be wrong.

Reg. *abbr.* **1.** Regulation. **2.** Register.

reg, *n.* (*usu. pl.*) (1904) *Slang.* REGULATION (3) <review not only the tax code but also the accompanying regs>.

regard, *n.* (14c) Attention, care, or consideration <without regard for the consequences>.

regime (rə-**zheem** *or* ray-**zheem**). (18c) **1.** A system of rules, regulations, or government <the community-property regime>. **2.** A particular administration or government, esp. an authoritarian one. — Also spelled *régime.*

register, *n.* (16c) **1.** A governmental officer who keeps official records <each county employs a register of deeds and wills>.

probate register. (1887) One who serves as the clerk of a probate court and, in some jurisdictions, as a quasi-judicial officer in probating estates.

register of deeds. (18c) A public official who records deeds, mortgages, and other instruments affecting real property.

register of wills. (18c) A public official who records probated wills, issues letters testamentary and letters of administration, and serves generally as clerk of the probate court. • The register of wills exists only in some states.

2. Probate judge. **3.** A book in which all docket entries are kept for the various cases pending in a court. — Abbr. Reg.

register, *vb.* (14c) **1.** To enter in a public registry <register a new car>. **2.** To enroll formally <five voters registered yesterday>. **3.** To make a record of <counsel registered three objections>. **4.** (Of a lawyer, party, or witness) to check in with the clerk of court before a judicial proceeding <please register at the clerk's office before entering the courtroom>. **5.** To file (a new security issue) with the Securities and Exchange Commission or a similar state agency <the company hopes to register its securities before the end of the year>.

Register of Copyrights. The federal official who is in charge of the U.S. Copyright Office, which issues regulations and processes applications for copyright registration.

Register of the Treasury. An officer of the U.S. Treasury whose duty is to keep accounts of receipts and expenditures of public money, to record public debts, to preserve adjusted accounts with vouchers and certificates, to record warrants drawn on the Treasury, to sign and issue government securities, and to supervise the registry of vessels under federal law. 31 USCA § 161.

registrant. (1890) One who registers; esp., one who registers something for the purpose of securing a right or privilege granted by law upon official registration.

registrar. (17c) A person who keeps official records; esp., a school official who maintains academic and enrollment records.

registration, *n.* **1.** The act of recording or enrolling <the county clerk handles registration of voters>.

criminal registration. The requirement in some communities that any felon who spends any time in the community must register his or her name with the police. • Since the late 1980s, many states have adopted strict registration laws for convicted sex offenders.

2. *Securities.* The complete process of preparing to sell a newly issued security to the public. — **register,** *vb.*

registration system. *Patents.* A patent system in which an invention is given patent protection when it is registered, without being subjected to official examination. • The United States operated under a registration system from 1790 until 1793.

regress, *n.* (14c) **1.** The act or an instance of going or coming back; return or reentry <free entry, egress, and regress>. **2.** The right or liberty of going back; reentry. — **regress** (ri-**gres**), *vb.*

regulation, *n.* (17c) **1.** The act or process of controlling by rule or restriction <the federal regulation of the airline industry>.

self-regulation. The process by which an identifiable group of people, such as licensed lawyers, govern or direct their own activities by rules; specif., an organization's or industry's control, oversight, or direction of itself according to rules and standards that it establishes. • Self-regulation is often subject to the oversight of various governmental agencies.

2. Bylaw <the CEO referred to the corporate regulation>. **3.** A rule or order, having legal force, usu. issued by an administrative agency <Treasury regulations explain and interpret the Internal Revenue Code>. — Abbr. (usu.

cap.) reg. — **regulatory, regulable,** *adj.* — **regulate,** *vb.*

proposed regulation. A draft administrative regulation that is circulated among interested parties for comment. — Abbr. prop. reg.

regulatory search. Administrative search.

rehabilitation, *n.* (1940) **1.** *Criminal law.* The process of seeking to improve a criminal's character and outlook so that he or she can function in society without committing other crimes <rehabilitation is a traditional theory of criminal punishment, along with deterrence and retribution>. **2.** *Evidence.* The restoration of a witness's credibility after the witness has been impeached <the inconsistencies were explained away during the prosecution's rehabilitation of the witness>. **3.** *Bankruptcy.* The process of reorganizing a debtor's financial affairs — under Chapter 11, 12, or 13 of the Bankruptcy Code — so that the debtor may continue to exist as a financial entity, with creditors satisfying their claims from the debtor's future earnings <the corporation's rehabilitation was successful>. — **rehabilitative,** *adj.* — **rehabilitate,** *vb.*

rehearing. (17c) A court's second or subsequent hearing of a case, a motion, or an appeal, usu. to consider an alleged error or omission in the court's judgment or opinion. — Abbr. reh'g.

reh'g. *abbr.* Rehearing.

rei (**ree**-ɪ). *pl. Reus.*

reification (ree-ə-fi-**kay**-shən), *n.* (1846) **1.** Mental conversion of an abstract concept into a material thing. **2.** *Civil procedure.* Identification of the disputed thing in a nonpersonal action and attribution of an in-state situs to it for jurisdictional purposes. **3.** *Commercial law.* Embodiment of a right to payment in a writing (such as a negotiable instrument) so that a transfer of the writing also transfers the right. — **reify** (**ree**-ə-fɪ *or* **ray**-), *vb.*

reimbursement, *n.* **1.** Repayment. **2.** Indemnification. — **reimburse,** *vb.*

reinstate, *vb.* To place again in a former state or position; to restore. — **reinstatement,** *n.*

reinvestment. 1. The addition of interest earned on a monetary investment to the principal sum. **2.** A second, additional, or repeated investment; esp., the application of dividends or other distributions toward the purchase of additional shares (as of a stock or a mutual fund).

reissue. 1. An abstractor's certificate attesting to the correctness of an abstract. • A reissue is an important precaution when the abstract comprises an original abstract brought down to a certain date and then several later continuations or extensions. **2.** Reissue patent.

REIT (reet). *abbr.* REAL-ESTATE INVESTMENT TRUST.

rejection. (16c) **1.** A refusal to accept a contractual offer. **2.** A refusal to accept tendered goods as contractual performance. • Under the UCC, a buyer's rejection of nonconforming goods must be made within a reasonable time after tender or delivery, and notice of the rejection must be given to the seller. **3.** *Parliamentary law.* Failure of adoption or ratification. **4.** *Patents.* A patent examiner's finding in an office action that a claim in an application is unpatentable. — **reject,** *vb.*

rejoinder, *n.* (15c) *Common-law pleading.* The defendant's answer to the plaintiff's reply (or replication). — **rejoin,** *vb.*

relation back, *n.* (18c) **1.** The doctrine that an act done at a later time is, under certain circumstances, treated as though it occurred at an earlier time. • In federal civil procedure, an amended pleading may relate back, for purposes of the statute of limitations, to the time when the original pleading was filed. Fed. R. Civ. P. 15(c). **2.** A judicial application of that doctrine. — **relate back,** *vb.*

relationship. The nature of the association between two or more people; esp., a legally recognized association that makes a difference in the participants' legal rights and duties of care.

attorney–client relationship. The formal legal representation of a person by a lawyer. • An attorney–client relationship may be found, for disciplinary purposes, without any formal agreement.

confidential relationship. **1.** Fiduciary relationship. **2.** *Trade secrets.* A relationship in which one person has a duty to the other not to disclose proprietary information. • A confidential relationship can be expressly established, as by the terms of an employment contract. It can also be implied when one person knows or should know that the information is confidential, and the other person reasonably believes that the first person has consented to keep the information confidential. A confidential relationship might be implied, for instance, between two people negotiating the sale of a business.

doctor–patient relationship. The association between a medical provider and one who is being diagnosed or treated. • The relationship imposes a duty on the doctor to ensure that the patient gives informed consent for treatment.

employer–employee relationship. The association between a person employed to perform services in the affairs of another, who in turn has the right to control the person's physical conduct in the course of that service. • At common law, the relationship was termed "master-servant."

fiducial relationship. Trust relationship.

fiduciary relationship. (1846) A relationship in which one person is under a duty to act for the benefit of another on matters within the scope of the relationship. • Fiduciary relationships — such as trustee–beneficiary, guardian–ward, principal–agent, and attorney–client — require an unusually high degree of care. Fiduciary relationships usu. arise in one of four situations: (1) when one person places trust in the faithful integrity of another, who as a result gains superiority or influence over the first, (2) when one person assumes control and responsibility over another, (3) when one person has a duty to act for or give advice to another on matters falling within the scope of the relationship, or (4) when there is a specific relationship that has traditionally been recognized as involving fiduciary duties, as with a lawyer and a client or a stockbroker and a customer.

master–servant relationship. Employer-employee relationship.

parent–child relationship. The association between an adult and a minor in the adult's care, esp. an offspring or an adoptee. • The relationship imposes a high duty of care on the adult, including the duties to support, to rescue, to supervise and control, and to educate.

professional relationship. An association that involves one person's reliance on the other person's specialized training. • Examples include one's relationship with a lawyer, doctor, insurer, banker, and the like.

special relationship. A nonfiduciary relationship having an element of trust, arising esp. when one person trusts another to exercise a reasonable degree of care and the other knows or ought to know about the reliance.

trust relationship. An association based on one person's reliance on the other person's specialized training.

relative, *n.* (14c) A person connected with another by blood or affinity; a person who is kin with another.

blood relative. (1863) One who shares an ancestor with another.

collateral relative. (18c) A relative who is not in the direct line of descent, such as a cousin.

relative by affinity. (1821) A person who is related solely as the result of a marriage and not by blood or adoption. • A person is a relative by affinity (1) to any blood or adopted relative of his or her spouse, and (2) to any spouse of his or her blood and adopted relatives. Based on the theory that marriage makes two people one, the relatives of each spouse become the other spouse's relatives by affinity.

relative of the half blood. A collateral relative who shares one common ancestor. • A half brother, for example, is a relative of the half blood.

relative-convenience doctrine. The principle that an injunction or other equitable relief may be denied if granting it would cause one party great inconvenience but denying it would cause the other party little or no inconvenience.

relative-responsibility statute. A law requiring adult children to support or provide basic necessities for their indigent elderly parents.

relator. (17c) **1.** The real party in interest in whose name a state or an attorney general brings a lawsuit. **2.** The applicant for a writ, esp. a writ of mandamus, prohibition, or quo warranto. **3.** A person who furnishes information on which a civil or criminal case is based; an informer.

release, *n.* (14c) **1.** Liberation from an obligation, duty, or demand; the act of giving up a right or claim to the person against whom it could have been enforced <the employee asked for a release from the noncompete agreement>. **2.** The relinquishment or concession of a right, title, or claim <Benson's effective release of the claim against Thompson's estate precluded his filing a lawsuit>. **3.** A written discharge, acquittance, or receipt; specif., a writing — either under seal or supported by sufficient consideration — stating that one or more of the worker's contractual or compensatory rights are discharged <Jones signed the release before accepting the cash from Hawkins>. **4.** A written authorization or permission for publication <the newspaper obtained a release from the witness before printing his picture on the front page>. **5.** The act of conveying an estate or right to another, or of legally disposing of it <the release of the easement on February 14>. **6.** A deed or document effecting a conveyance <the legal description in the release was defective>. **7.** The action of freeing or the fact of being freed from restraint or confinement <he became a model citizen after his release from prison>. **8.** A document giving formal discharge from custody <after the sheriff signed the release, the prisoner was free to go>. — **release,** *vb.*

conditional release. (18c) **1.** A discharge from an obligation based on some condition, the failure of which defeats the release. **2.** An early discharge of a prison inmate, who is then subject to the rules and regulations of parole.

marginal release. Property. An entry made in the margin of a property record by the recorder of deeds to show that a claim against the property has been satisfied.

mutual release. A simultaneous exchange of releases of legal claims held by two or more parties against each other.

partial release. (1837) A release of a portion of a creditor's claims against property; esp., a mortgagee's release of specified parcels covered by a blanket mortgage.

Pierringer release. A release that allows a defendant in a negligence suit to settle with the plaintiff for a share of the damages and insulates the settling defendant against contribution claims by nonsettling defendants. • This type of release was first described in *Pierringer v. Hoger,* 124 N.W.2d 106, 110–11 (Wis. 1963). It is used in some jurisdictions that do not have contribution statutes.

study release. (1970) A program that allows a prisoner to be released for a few hours at a time to attend classes at a nearby college or technical institution.

unconditional release. (1871) The final discharge of a prison inmate from custody.

9. *Environmental law.* The injection of contaminants or pollutants into the environment as a side effect of operations such as manufacturing, mining, or farming.

release of mortgage. A written document that discharges a mortgage upon full payment by the borrower and that is publicly recorded to show that the borrower has full equity in the property.

release on recognizance. (1913) The pretrial release of an arrested person who promises, usu. in writing but without supplying a surety or posting bond, to appear for trial at a later date. — Abbr. ROR.

release to uses. (1830) Conveyance of property, by deed of release, by one party to another for the benefit of the grantor or a third party.

releasor. (17c) One who releases property or a claim to another.

relegation, *n.* (16c) **1.** Banishment or exile, esp. a temporary one. **2.** Assignment or delegation. — **relegate,** *vb.*

relevant, *adj.* (16c) Logically connected and tending to prove or disprove a matter in issue; having appreciable probative value — that is, rationally tending to persuade people of the probability or possibility of some alleged fact. — **relevance, relevancy,** *n.*

reliance, *n.* (17c) Dependence or trust by a person, esp. when combined with action based on that dependence or trust. — **rely,** *vb.*

detrimental reliance. (1941) Reliance by one party on the acts or representations of another, causing a worsening of the first party's position. • Detrimental reliance may serve as a substitute for consideration and thus make a promise enforceable as a contract.

reliction (ri-**lik**-shən). (17c) **1.** A process by which a river or stream shifts its location, causing the recession of water from its bank. **2.** The alteration of a boundary line because of the gradual removal of land by a river or stream.

relief. (14c) **1.** A payment made by an heir of a feudal tenant to the feudal lord for the privilege of succeeding to the ancestor's tenancy. **2.** Aid or assistance given to those in need, esp., financial aid provided by the state. **3.** The redress or benefit, esp. equitable in nature (such as an injunction or specific performance), that a party asks of a court.

affirmative relief. (1842) The relief sought by a defendant by raising a counterclaim or cross-claim that could have been maintained independently of the plaintiff's action.

alternative relief. (1851) Judicial relief that is mutually exclusive with another form of judicial relief. • In pleading, a party may request alternative relief, as by asking for both specific performance and damages that would be averted by specific performance. Fed. R. Civ. P. 8(a).

coercive relief. (1886) Judicial relief, either legal or equitable, in the form of a personal command to the defendant that is enforceable by physical restraint.

declaratory relief. A unilateral request to a court to determine the legal status or ownership of a thing.

extraordinary relief. Judicial relief that exceeds what is typically or customarily granted but is warranted by the unique or extreme circumstances of a situation. • The types of extraordinary relief most frequently sought are injunctions and extraordinary writs, esp. mandamus.

interim relief. (1886) Relief that is granted on a preliminary basis before an order finally disposing of a request for relief.

therapeutic relief. (1889) The relief, esp. in a settlement, that requires the defendant to take remedial measures as opposed to paying damages. • An example is a defendant-corporation (in an employment-discrimination suit) that agrees to undergo sensitivity training.

religion. A system of faith and worship usu. involving belief in a supreme being and usu. containing a moral or ethical code; esp., such a system recognized and practiced by a particular church, sect, or denomination. • In construing the protections under the Establishment Clause and the Free Exercise Clause, courts have interpreted the term *religion* quite broadly to include a wide variety of theistic and nontheistic beliefs.

state religion. A religion promoted, taught, or enforced by a government's acts to the exclusion of other religions.

Religion Clause. In the Bill of Rights, the provision stating that "Congress shall make no law respecting an establishment of religion or prohibiting the free exercise thereof." U.S. Const. amend. I. • Some writers use the plural form, "Religion Clauses," to mean both the Establishment Clause and the Free Exercise Clause, thus emphasizing the asserted common purpose of the two provisions.

religious-exemption statute. Faith-healing exemption.

Religious Test Clause. The clause of the U.S. Constitution that prohibits the use of a religious test as a qualification to serve in any office or public trust. U.S. Const. art. VI, par. 3, cl. 2.

relinquishment, *n.* (15c) The abandonment of a right or thing. — **relinquish,** *vb.*

relitigate, *vb.* (1826) To litigate (a case or matter) again or anew. — **relitigation,** *n.*

remainder. (15c) *Property.* **1.** A future interest arising in a third person — that is, someone other than the estate's creator, its initial holder, or the heirs of either — who is intended to take after the natural termination of the preceding estate. • For example, if a grant is "to A for life, and then to B," B's future interest is a remainder. If there is only one preceding estate and the remainder vests on that estate's expiration, the remainder is also termed an *executed estate.*

accelerated remainder. (1901) A remainder that has passed to the remainderman, as when the gift to the preceding beneficiary fails.

alternative remainder. (1830) A remainder in which the disposition of property is to take effect only if another disposition does not take effect.

charitable remainder. (1932) A remainder, usu. from a life estate, that is given to a charity; for example, "to Jane for life, and then to the American Red Cross.

contingent remainder. (18c) A remainder that is either given to an unascertained person or made subject to a condition precedent. • An example is "to A for life, and then, if B has married before A dies, to B."

cross-remainder. (18c) A future interest that results when particular estates are given to two or more persons in different parcels of land, or in the same land in undivided shares, and the remainders of all the estates are made to vest in the survivor or survivors. • Two examples of devises giving rise to cross-remainders are (1) "to A and B for life, with the remainder to the survivor and her heirs," and (2) "Blackacre to A and Whiteacre to B, with the remainder of A's estate to B on A's failure of issue, and the remainder of B's estate to A on B's failure of issue." • If no tenants or issue survive, the remainder vests in a third party (sometimes known as the *ulterior remainderman*). Each tenant in common has a reciprocal, or *cross*, remainder in the share of the others. This type of remainder could not be created by deed unless expressly stated. It could, however, be implied in a will.

defeasible remainder. (18c) A vested remainder that will be destroyed if a condition subsequent occurs. • An example is "to A for life, and then to B, but if B ever sells liquor on the land, then to C."

indefeasible remainder. (1898) A vested remainder that is not subject to a condition subsequent; specif., a remainder in which the remainderman is certain to acquire a present interest sometime in the future and will be entitled to retain the interest permanently.

remainder subject to open. (1838) A vested remainder that is given to a class of persons whose numbers may change over time and that is to be shared equally by each member of the class. • An example is "to A for life, and then equally to all of B's children." The class must have at least one member, but more can be added over time.

vested remainder. (18c) A remainder that is given to an ascertained person and that is not subject to a condition precedent. • An example is "to A for life, and then to B."

2. The property in a decedent's estate that is not otherwise specifically devised or bequeathed in a will.

remainder interest. (1815) The property that passes to a beneficiary after the expiration of an intervening income interest. • For example, if a grantor places real estate in trust with income to A for life and remainder to B upon A's death, then B has a remainder interest.

remainderman. (18c) A person who holds or is entitled to receive a remainder.

ulterior remainderman. A third party whose future interest in a property vests only if all the preceding reciprocal interests expire.

remand (ri-**mand** *also* **ree**-mand), *n.* (18c) **1.** The act or an instance of sending something (such as a case, claim, or person) back for further action. **2.** An order remanding a case, claim, or person.

remand (ri-**mand**), *vb.* (15c) **1.** To send (a case or claim) back to the court or tribunal from which it came for some further action <the appellate court reversed the trial court's opinion and remanded the case for new trial>. **2.** To recommit (an accused person) to custody after a preliminary examination <the magistrate, after denying bail, remanded the defendant to custody>.

remanet (**rem**-ə-net). (16c) **1.** A case or proceeding whose hearing has been postponed. **2.** A remainder or remnant.

remediable, *adj.* (15c) Capable of being remedied, esp. by law. — **remediability,** *n.*

remedial, *adj.* (17c) **1.** Affording or providing a remedy; providing the means of obtaining redress <a remedial action>. **2.** Intended to correct, remove, or lessen a wrong, fault, or defect. **3.** Of or relating to a means of enforcing an existing substantive right.

remedial action. *Environmental law.* An action intended to bring about or restore long-term environmental quality; esp., under CERCLA, a measure intended to permanently alleviate pollution when a hazardous substance has been released or might be released into the environment, so as to prevent or minimize any further release of hazardous substances and thereby minimize the risk to public health or to the environment. 42 USCA § 9601(24); 40 CFR § 300.6.

remedial law. (17c) **1.** A law providing a means to enforce rights or redress injuries. **2.** A law that corrects or modifies an existing law; esp., a law providing a new or different remedy when the existing remedy, if any, is inadequate.

remediation. *Environmental law.* The restoration of polluted land, water, or air to its former state, or as nearly so as is practical.

remedies, *n.* The field of law dealing with the means of enforcing rights and redressing wrongs.

remedy, *n.* (13c) **1.** The means of enforcing a right or preventing or redressing a wrong; legal or equitable relief. **2.** Remedial action. — **remedy,** *vb.*

adequate remedy at law. (18c) A legal remedy (such as an award of damages) that provides sufficient relief to the petitioning party, thus preventing the party from obtaining equitable relief.

administrative remedy. (1880) A nonjudicial remedy provided by an administrative agency. • Ordinarily, if an administrative remedy is available, it must be exhausted before a court will hear the case.

concurrent remedy. (18c) One of two or more legal or equitable actions available to redress a wrong.

cumulative remedy. (18c) A remedy available to a party in addition to another remedy that still remains in force.

equitable remedy. (18c) A remedy, usu. a nonmonetary one such as an injunction or specific performance, obtained when available legal remedies, usu. monetary damages, cannot adequately redress the injury. • Historically, an equitable remedy was available only from a court of equity.

extrajudicial remedy. A remedy not obtained from a court, such as repossession.

extraordinary remedy. (16c) A remedy — such as a writ of mandamus or habeas corpus — not available to a party unless necessary to preserve a right that cannot be protected by a standard legal or equitable remedy.

judicial remedy. (18c) A remedy granted by a court.

legal remedy. (17c) A remedy historically available in a court of law, as distinguished from a remedy historically available only in equity.

provisional remedy. (18c) A temporary remedy awarded before judgment and pending the action's disposition, such as a temporary restraining order, a preliminary injunction, a prejudgment receivership, or an attachment.

remedy over. (18c) A remedy that arises from a right of indemnification or subrogation. • For example, if a city is liable for injuries caused by a defect in a street, the city has a "remedy over" against the person whose act or negligence caused the defect.

self-help remedy. Extrajudicial remedy.

specific remedy. (18c) A remedy whereby the injured party is awarded the very performance that was contractually promised or whereby the injury threatened or caused by a tort is prevented or repaired.

speedy remedy. (18c) A remedy that, under the circumstances, can be pursued expeditiously before the aggrieved party has incurred substantial detriment.

substitutional remedy. (1987) A remedy intended to give the promisee something as a replacement for the promised performance or to give the plaintiff something in lieu of preventing or repairing an injury.

remise (ri-**mɪz**), *vb.* (15c) To give up, surrender, or release (a right, interest, etc.) <the quitclaim deed provides that the grantor remises any rights in the property>.

remission. (13c) **1.** A cancellation or extinguishment of all or part of a financial obligation; a release of a debt or claim. **2.** A pardon granted for an offense. **3.** Relief from a forfeiture or penalty. **4.** A diminution or abatement of the symptoms of a disease.

remit, *vb.* (14c) **1.** To pardon or forgive <the wife could not remit her husband's infidelity>. **2.** To abate or slacken; to mitigate <the receipt of money damages remitted the embarrassment of being fired>. **3.** To refer (a matter for decision) to some authority, esp. to send back (a case) to a lower court <the appellate court remitted the case to the trial court for further factual determinations>. **4.** To send or put back to a previous condition or position <a landlord's breach of a lease does not justify the tenant's refusal to pay rent; instead, the tenant is remitted to the right to recover damages>. **5.** To transmit (as money) <upon receiving the demand letter, she promptly remitted the amount due>. — **remissible** (for senses 1–4), *adj.* — **remittable** (for sense 5), *adj.*

remittance. (18c) **1.** A sum of money sent to another as payment for goods or services. **2.** An instrument (such as a check) used for sending money. **3.** The action or process of sending money to another person or place.

remittee. (18c) One to whom payment is sent.

remitter. (16c) **1.** The principle by which a person having two titles to an estate, and entering on it by the later or more defective title, is deemed to hold the estate by the earlier or more valid title. **2.** The act of sending back a case to a lower court. **3.** One who sends payment to someone else.

remittitur (ri-**mit**-i-tər). (18c) **1.** An order awarding a new trial, or a damages amount lower than that awarded by the jury, and requiring the plaintiff to choose between those alternatives <the defendant sought a remittitur of the $100 million judgment>. **2.** The process by which a court requires either that the case be retried, or that the damages awarded by the jury be reduced.

remittitur of record. (1848) The action of sending the transcript of a case back from an appellate court to a trial court; the notice for doing so.

remonetization, *n.* The restoration of a precious metal (such as gold or silver) to its former use as legal tender. — **remonetize,** *vb.*

remonstrance (ri-**mon**-strənts), *n.* (16c) **1.** A presentation of reasons for opposition or grievance. **2.** A formal document stating reasons for opposition or grievance. **3.** A formal protest against governmental policy, actions, or officials. — **remonstrate** (ri-**mon**-strayt), *vb.*

remote, *adj.* (15c) **1.** Far removed or separated in time, space, or relation. **2.** Slight. **3.** *Property.* Beyond the 21 years after some life in being by which a devise must vest.

remote cause. CAUSE (1).

remoteness of consequence. *Torts.* The lack of proximate causation with respect to an alleged act by a defendant. • Even if the plaintiff proves every other element for tortious liability, the defendant will not be liable if the harm suffered by the plaintiff is too far removed from the defendant's conduct.

removal, *n.* (16c) **1.** The transfer or moving of a person or thing from one location, position, or residence to another. **2.** The transfer of an action from state to federal court. 28 USCA § 1441. — **remove,** *vb.*

civil-rights removal. (1964) Removal of a case from state to federal court because a person: (1) has been denied or cannot enforce a civil right in the state court, (2) is being sued for performing an act under color of authority derived from a law providing for equal rights, or (3) is being sued for refusing to perform an act that would be inconsistent with equal rights.

removal action. *Environmental law.* An action, esp. under CERCLA, intended to bring about the short-term abatement and cleanup of pollution (as by removing and disposing of toxic materials).

remuneration (ri-myoo-nə-**ray**-shən), *n.* (15c) **1.** Payment; compensation. **2.** The act of paying or compensating. — **remunerative,** *adj.* — **remunerate,** *vb.*

rencounter (ren-**kown**-tər). (16c) A hostile meeting or contest; a battle or combat. — Also spelled *rencontre* (ren-**kon**-tər).

render, *vb.* **1.** To transmit or deliver <render payment>. **2.** (Of a judge) to deliver formally <render a judgment>. **3.** (Of a jury) to agree on and report formally <render a verdict>. **4.** To pay as due <render an account>.

rendition, *n.* (17c) **1.** The action of making, delivering, or giving out, such as a legal decision. **2.** The return of a fugitive from one state to the state where the fugitive is accused or was convicted of a crime.

extraordinary rendition. The transfer, without formal charges, trial, or court approval, of a person suspected of being a terrorist or supporter of a terrorist group to a foreign nation for imprisonment and interrogation on behalf of the transferring nation. • When an innocent person is subjected to extraordinary rendition, it is also termed *erroneous extradition.* When a transfer is made to a nation notorious for human-rights violations, it may be colloquially termed *torture by proxy* or *torture flight.*

rendition of judgment. (18c) The judge's oral or written ruling containing the judgment entered.

renege (ri-**nig** *or* ri-**neg**), *vb.* (16c) To fail to keep a promise or commitment; to back out of a deal.

renegotiation, *n.* (1934) **1.** The act or process of negotiating again or on different terms; a second or further negotiation. **2.** The reexamination and adjustment of a government contract to eliminate or recover excess profits by the contractor. — **renegotiate,** *vb.*

renewal, *n.* (17c) **1.** The act of restoring or reestablishing. **2.** *Parliamentary law.* The introduction or consideration of a question already disposed of. **3.** The recreation of a legal relationship or the replacement of an old contract with a new contract, as opposed to the mere extension of a previous relationship or contract. — **renew,** *vb.*

renounce, *vb.* (14c) **1.** To give up or abandon formally (a right or interest); to disclaim <renounce an inheritance>. **2.** To refuse to follow or obey; to decline to recognize or observe <renounce one's allegiance>.

rent, *n.* (13c) Consideration paid, usu. periodically, for the use or occupancy of property (esp. real property).

rentage. (17c) Rent or rental.

rental, *n.* (14c) **1.** The amount received as rent. **2.** The income received from rent. **3.** A record of payments received from rent. — **rental,** *adj.*

rent control. (1931) A restriction imposed, usu. by municipal legislation, on the maximum rent that a landlord may charge for rental property, and often on a landlord's power of eviction.

rents, issues, and profits. (17c) The total income or profit arising from the ownership or possession of property.

rent strike. (1964) A refusal by a group of tenants to pay rent until grievances with the landlord are heard or settled.

renunciation (ri-nən-see-**ay**-shən), *n.* (14c) **1.** The express or tacit abandonment of a right without transferring it to another. **2.** *Wills & estates.* The act of waiving a right under a will. • At one time, one *renounced* an inheritance by intestacy and *disclaimed* a gift by will. Today *disclaim* is common in both situations. **3.** *Criminal law.* Complete and voluntary abandonment of criminal purpose — sometimes coupled with an attempt to thwart the activity's success — before a crime is committed. • Renunciation can be an affirmative defense to attempt, conspiracy, and the like. Model Penal Code § 5.01(4). **4.** Anticipatory repudiation. — **renunciative, renunciatory,** *adj.* — **renounce,** *vb.*

reorganization, *n.* **1.** *Bankruptcy.* A financial restructuring of a corporation, esp. in the repayment of debts, under a plan created by a trustee and approved by a court.

haircut reorganization. A restructuring that reduces the principal amount of indebtedness owed to creditors. • The more common usage is simply *haircut* <we took a haircut on that deal>.

2. *Tax.* A restructuring of a corporation, as by a merger or recapitalization, in order to improve its tax treatment under the Internal Revenue Code. • The Code classifies the various types of reorganizations with different letters. IRC (26 USCA) § 368(a)(1).

reorganization plan. *Bankruptcy.* A plan of restructuring submitted by a corporation for approval by the court in a Chapter 11 case.

rep. *abbr.* **1.** Report. **2.** Reporter. **3.** Representative. **4.** Republic.

reparation (rep-ə-**ray**-shən). (14c) **1.** The act of making amends for a wrong. **2.** (*usu. pl.*) Compensation for an injury or wrong, esp. for wartime damages or breach of an international obligation.

repeal, *n.* (16c) RESCIND (2); esp., abrogation of an existing law by legislative act. — **repeal,** *vb.*

express repeal. (17c) Repeal by specific declaration in a new statute or main motion.

implied repeal. (18c) Repeal by irreconcilable conflict between an old law or main motion and a more recent law or motion.

repealing clause. (17c) A statutory provision that repeals an earlier statute.

replead, *vb.* (16c) **1.** To plead again or anew; to file a new pleading, esp. to correct a defect in an earlier pleading. **2.** To make a repleader.

repleader (ree-**plee**-dər). (17c) *Common-law pleading.* A court order or judgment — issued on the motion of a party who suffered an adverse judgment — requiring the parties to file new pleadings because of some defect in the original pleadings.

repleviable (ri-**plev**-ee-ə-bəl), *adj.* (16c) Capable of being replevied; recoverable by replevin <repleviable property>. — Also spelled *replevisable* (ri-**plev**-ə-sə-bəl).

replevin (ri-**plev**-in), *n.* (17c) **1.** An action for the repossession of personal property wrongfully taken or detained by the defendant, whereby the plaintiff gives security for and holds the property until the court decides who owns it.. **2.** A writ obtained from a court authorizing the retaking of personal property wrongfully taken or detained.

personal replevin. (1844) At common law, an action to replevy a person out of prison or out of another's custody. • Personal replevin has been largely superseded by the writ of habeas corpus as a means of investigating the legality of an imprisonment.

replevin in cepit (in **see**-pit). (18c) An action for the repossession of property that is both wrongfully taken and wrongfully detained.

replevin in detinet (in **det**-i-net). (18c) An action for the repossession of property that is rightfully taken but wrongfully detained.

replevy, *vb.* (16c) **1.** To recover possession of (goods) by a writ of replevin. **2.** To recover (goods) by replevin. **3.** *Archaic.* To bail (a prisoner).

repliant (ri-**plı**-ənt). (16c) A party who makes a replication (i.e., a common-law reply).

replication (rep-lə-**kay**-shən). (15c) A plaintiff's or complainant's reply to a defendant's plea or answer; REPLY (2).

reply, *n.* (18c) **1.** *Civil procedure.* In federal practice, the plaintiff's response to the defendant's counterclaim (or, by court order, to the defendant's or a third party's answer). Fed. R. Civ. P. 7(a). **2.** *Common-law pleading.* The plaintiff's response to the defendant's plea or answer. • The reply is the plaintiff's second pleading, and it is followed by the defendant's rejoinder. — **reply,** *vb.*

repo (**ree**-poh). **1.** Repossession. **2.** Repurchase agreement.

report, *n.* (14c) **1.** A formal oral or written presentation of facts or a recommendation for action <according to the treasurer's report, there is $300 in the bank>.

committee report. *Parliamentary law.* A report from a committee to a deliberative assembly on business referred to the committee or on a matter otherwise under its charge.

informational report. *Parliamentary law.* A report without a recommendation for action.

majority report. *Parliamentary law.* A committee report, as distinguished from a minority report.

minority report. *Parliamentary law.* A report by a member or members who dissent from a committee report, setting forth their views, and sometimes proposing an alternative recommendation. • Some organizations require that a minority must reach a certain size (or obtain permission) before it can file a report. A typical minimum is one-fourth of the committee's members, which guarantees that not more than one minority report will result.

officer's report. *Parliamentary law.* A report from an officer to an organization or deliberative assembly on business relating to the officer's duties or on a matter otherwise under the officer's charge.

report with recommendation. *Parliamentary law.* A report accompanied by a recommendation for action.

2. A written account of a court proceeding and judicial decision <the law clerk sent the court's report to counsel for both sides>. **3.** (*usu. pl.*) A published volume of judicial decisions by a particular court or group of courts <U.S. Reports>.

official report. (*usu. pl.*) The governmentally approved set of reported cases within a given jurisdiction.

4. (*usu. pl.*) A collection of administrative decisions by one or more administrative agencies. — Abbr. rep. — **report,** *vb.*

reporter. (14c) **1.** A person responsible for making and publishing a report; esp., a lawyer-consultant who prepares drafts of official or semi-official writings such as court rules or Restatements. **2.** Reporter of decisions. **3.** REPORT (3). — Abbr. rep.; rptr.

reporter of decisions. (1839) The person responsible for publishing a court's opinions. • The position began historically — in the years before systematic reporting of decisions was introduced — when lawyers attended the sessions of particular courts, were accredited to them by the judges, and reported the decisions of that court. Today, the reporter of decisions holds an administrative post as a court employee. The reporter often has duties that include verifying citations, correcting spelling and punctuation, and suggesting minor editorial improvements before judicial opinions are released or published.

reporter's record. 1. Record. **2.** Transcript.

reporter's syllabus. Headnote.

repose (ri-**pohz**), *n.* (16c) **1.** Cessation of activity; temporary rest. **2.** A statutory period after which an action cannot be brought in court, even if it expires before the plaintiff suffers any injury.

repository (ri-**poz**-ə-tor-ee). (15c) A place where something is deposited or stored; a warehouse or storehouse.

repossession, *n.* (15c) The act or an instance of retaking property; esp., a seller's retaking of goods sold on credit when the buyer has failed to pay for them. — **repossess,** *vb.*

representation, *n.* (16c) **1.** A presentation of fact — either by words or by conduct — made to induce someone to act, esp. to enter into a contract; esp., the manifestation to another that a fact, including a state of mind, exists <the buyer relied on the seller's representation that the roof did not leak>.

affirmative representation. (1842) A representation asserting the existence of certain facts pertaining to a given subject matter.

material representation. (18c) A representation to which a reasonable person would attach importance in deciding his or her course of action in a transaction.

promissory representation. (1842) A representation about what one will do in the future; esp., a representation made by an insured about what will happen during the time of coverage, stated as a matter of expectation and amounting to an enforceable promise.

2. The act or an instance of standing for or acting on behalf of another, esp. by a lawyer on behalf of a client <Clarence Darrow's representation of John Scopes>.

concurrent representation. The simultaneous representation of more than one person in the same matter.

3. The fact of a litigant's having such a close alignment of interests with another person that the other is considered as having been present in the litigation <the named plaintiff provided adequate representation for the absent class members>.

adequate representation. (1939) A close alignment of interests between actual parties and potential parties in a lawsuit, so that the interests of potential parties are sufficiently protected by the actual parties. • The concept of adequate representation is often used in procedural contexts. For example, if a case is to be certified as a class action, there must be adequate representation by the named plaintiffs of all the potential class members. Fed. R. Civ. P. 23(a)(4). And if a nonparty is to intervene in a lawsuit, there must not already be adequate representation of the nonparty by an existing party. Fed. R. Civ. P. 24(a)(2).

virtual representation. (1934) A party's maintenance of an action on behalf of others with a similar interest, as a class representative does in a class action.

4. The assumption by an heir of the rights of his or her predecessor <each

child takes a share by representation>. — **represent,** *vb.*

representative, *n.* (17c) **1.** One who stands for or acts on behalf of another <the owner was the football team's representative at the labor negotiations>.

accredited representative. (1846) A person with designated authority to act on behalf of another person, group, or organization, usu. by being granted that authority by law or by the rules of the group or organization.

class representative. (1942) A person who sues on behalf of a group of plaintiffs in a class action.

lawful representative. (17c) **1.** A legal heir. **2.** An executor, administrator, or other legal representative.

legal–personal representative. (18c) **1.** When used by a testator referring to personal property, an executor or administrator. **2.** When used by a testator referring to real property, one to whom the real estate passes immediately upon the testator's death. **3.** When used concerning the death of a mariner at sea, the public administrator, executor, or appointed administrator in the seaman's state of residence.

personal representative. (18c) A person who manages the legal affairs of another because of incapacity or death, such as the executor of an estate. • Technically, an executor is a personal representative named in a will, while an administrator is a personal representative not named in a will.

registered representative. (1945) A person approved by the SEC and stock exchanges to sell securities to the public.

2. A member of a legislature, esp. of the lower house <one senator and one representative attended the rally>. — Abbr. rep.

representative action. (1911) **1.** Class action. **2.** DERIVATIVE ACTION (1).

representative capacity. CAPACITY (1).

repressed-memory syndrome. A memory disorder characterized by an intermittent and extensive inability to recall important personal information, usu. following or concerning a traumatic or highly stressful occurrence, when the memory lapses cannot be dismissed as normal forgetfulness. • The theoretical basis for this syndrome was proposed by Sigmund Freud in 1895. The American Psychiatric Association has recognized the syndrome officially by the medical term *dissociative amnesia.* — Abbr. RMS.

reprieve (ri-**preev**), *n.* (16c) Temporary postponement of the carrying out of a criminal sentence, esp. a death sentence. — **reprieve,** *vb.*

reprimand, *n.* (17c) In professional responsibility, a form of disciplinary action — imposed after trial or formal charges — that declares the lawyer's conduct improper but does not limit his or her right to practice law; a mild form of lawyer discipline that does not restrict the lawyer's ability to practice law. — **reprimand,** *vb.*

private reprimand. An unpublished communication between a disciplinary agency and a wrongdoing attorney, admonishing the attorney about the improper conduct.

public reprimand. A published notice, appearing usu. in a legal newspaper or bar journal, admonishing the attorney about improper conduct and describing the impropriety for the benefit of other members of the legal profession.

reprisal (ri-**prɪ**-zəl). **1.** (*often pl.*) *Int'l law.* The use of force, short of war, against another country to redress an injury caused by that country. **2.** (*often pl.*) *Int'l law.* An act of forceful retaliation for injury or attack by another country;

formerly, in war, the killing of prisoners in response to an enemy's war crimes (now unlawful). **3.** Any act or instance of retaliation, as by an employer against a complaining employee.

reproductive rights. A person's constitutionally protected rights relating to the control of his or her procreative activities; specif., the cluster of civil liberties relating to pregnancy, abortion, and sterilization, esp. the personal bodily rights of a woman in her decision whether to become pregnant or bear a child. • The phrase includes the idea of being able to make reproductive decisions free from discrimination, coercion, or violence. Human-rights scholars increasingly consider many reproductive rights to be protected by international human-rights law.

republic, *n.* A system of government in which the people hold sovereign power and elect representatives who exercise that power. — Abbr. rep. — **republican,** *adj.*

republication, *n.* (18c) **1.** The act or an instance of publishing again or anew. **2.** *Wills & estates.* Reestablishment of the validity of a previously revoked will by repeating the formalities of execution or by using a codicil. **3.** *Defamation.* The act or an instance of repeating or spreading more widely a defamatory statement. — **republish,** *vb.*

repudiate, *vb.* (16c) To reject or renounce (a duty or obligation); esp., to indicate an intention not to perform (a contract).

repudiation (ri-pyoo-dee-**ay**-shən), *n.* (16c) A contracting party's words or actions that indicate an intention not to perform the contract in the future; a threatened breach of contract. — **repudiatory** (ri-**pyoo**-dee-ə-tor-ee), **repudiable** (ri-**pyoo**-dee-ə-bəl), *adj.*

anticipatory repudiation. (1913) Repudiation of a contractual duty before the time for performance, giving the injured party an immediate right to damages for total breach, as well as discharging the injured party's remaining duties of performance.

total repudiation. (1859) An unconditional refusal by a party to perform the acts required by a contract.

repugnancy (ri-**pəg**-nən-see). (1865) An inconsistency or contradiction between two or more parts of a legal instrument (such as a contract or statute).

repugnant (ri-**pəg**-nənt), *adj.* (14c) Inconsistent or irreconcilable with; contrary or contradictory to <the court's interpretation was repugnant to the express wording of the statute>.

reputation, *n.* (14c) The esteem in which a person is held by others. • Evidence of reputation may be introduced as proof of character whenever character evidence is admissible. Fed. R. Evid. 405. — **reputational,** *adj.*

request for admission. (1939) *Civil procedure.* In pretrial discovery, a party's written factual statement served on another party who must admit, deny, or object to the substance of the statement. • Ordinarily, many requests for admission appear in one document. The admitted statements, along with any statements not denied or objected to, will be treated by the court as established and therefore do not have to be proved at trial. Fed. R. Civ. P. 36. — Abbr. RFA.

request for instructions. (1942) *Procedure.* During trial, a party's written request that the court instruct the jury on the law as set forth in the request. See Fed. R. Civ. P. 51. — Abbr. RFI.

request for production. (1944) *Procedure.* In pretrial discovery, a party's written request that another party provide specified documents or other tangible things for inspection and copying. Fed. R. Civ. P. 34. — Abbr. RFP.

request for proposal. An invitation to prospective suppliers or contractors to submit proposals or bids to provide goods or services. • Unlike most invitations for bids, an RFP requires bidders to give more information than the proposed price. For instance, bidders may have to provide evidence of good financial condition, acceptable technical capability, stock availability, and customer satisfaction. — Abbr. RFP.

required-records doctrine. (1945) The principle that the privilege against self-incrimination does not apply when one is being compelled to produce business records that are kept in accordance with government regulations and that involve public aspects.

required-request law. A law mandating that hospital personnel discuss with a deceased patient's relatives the possibility of an anatomical gift.

res (rays *or* reez *or* rez), *n.* [Latin "thing"] (17c) **1.** An object, interest, or status, as opposed to a person <jurisdiction of the res — the real property in Colorado>. **2.** The subject matter of a trust; CORPUS (1) <the stock certificate is the res of the trust>. Pl. **res.**

resale, *n.* (17c) **1.** The act of selling goods or property — previously sold to a buyer who breached the sales contract — to someone else. UCC § 2-706. **2.** A retailer's selling of goods, previously purchased from a manufacturer or wholesaler, usu. to consumers or to someone else further down the chain of distribution. — **resell,** *vb.*

rescind (ri-**sind**), *vb.* (17c) **1.** To abrogate or cancel (a contract) unilaterally or by agreement. **2.** To make void; to repeal or annul <rescind the legislation>. **3.** *Parliamentary law.* To void, repeal, or nullify a main motion adopted earlier. — **rescindable,** *adj.*

rescission (ri-**sizh**-ən), *n.* (17c) **1.** A party's unilateral unmaking of a contract for a legally sufficient reason, such as the other party's material breach, or a judgment rescinding the contract. **2.** An agreement by contracting parties to discharge all remaining duties of performance and terminate the contract. — **rescissory** (ri-**sis**-ə-ree *or* ri-**siz**-), *adj.*

equitable rescission. (1889) Rescission that is decreed by a court of equity.

legal rescission. (1849) **1.** Rescission that is effected by the agreement of the parties. **2.** Rescission that is decreed by a court of law, as opposed to a court of equity.

rescript (**ree**-skript), *n.* (17c) **1.** A judge's written order to a court clerk explaining how to dispose of a case. **2.** An appellate court's written decision, usu. unsigned, that is sent down to the trial court. **3.** A duplicate or counterpart; a rewriting.

rescue, *n.* (14c) **1.** The act or an instance of saving or freeing someone from danger or captivity. **2.** The forcible and unlawful freeing of a person from arrest or imprisonment. **3.** The forcible retaking by the owner of goods that have been lawfully distrained. — **rescue,** *vb.*

rescue doctrine. (1926) *Torts.* The principle that a tortfeasor who negligently endangered a person is liable for injuries to someone who reasonably attempted to rescue the person in danger.

resentencing, *n.* (1878) The act or an instance of imposing a new or revised criminal sentence. — **resentence,** *vb.*

reservation. (15c) **1.** The creation of a new right or interest (such as an easement), by and for the grantor, in real property being granted to another.

implied reservation. (1867) An implied easement that reserves in a landowner an easement across a portion of sold land, such as a right-of-way over land lying between the seller's home and the only exit. • An implied reservation arises only if the seller could have expressly reserved an easement, but for some reason failed to do so.

2. The establishment of a limiting condition or qualification; esp., a nation's formal declaration, upon signing or ratifying a treaty, that its willingness to become a party to the treaty is conditioned on the modification or amendment of one or more provisions of the treaty as applied in its relations with other parties to the treaty. **3.** A tract of public land that is not open to settlers but is set aside for a special purpose; esp., a tract of land set aside for use by indigenous peoples.

reserve, *n.* Something retained or stored for future use; esp., a fund of money set aside by a bank or an insurance company to cover future liabilities.

Reserved Power Clause. Tenth Amendment.

resettlement, *n.* (17c) **1.** The settlement of one or more persons in a new or former place. **2.** The reopening of an order or decree for the purpose of correcting a mistake or adding something omitted. — **resettle,** *vb.*

res gestae (rays **jes**-tee *also* **jes**-tı), *n. pl.* [Latin "things done"] (17c) The events at issue, or other events contemporaneous with them. • In evidence law, words and statements about the res gestae are usu. admissible under a hearsay exception (such as present sense impression or excited utterance). Where the Federal Rules of Evidence or state rules fashioned after them are in effect, the use of *res gestae* is now out of place. See Fed. R. Evid. 803(1), (2).

residence. (14c) **1.** The act or fact of living in a given place for some time <a year's residence in New Jersey>. **2.** The place where one actually lives, as distinguished from a domicile <she made her residence in Oregon>. • *Residence* usu. just means bodily presence as an inhabitant in a given place; *domicile* usu. requires bodily presence plus an intention to make the place one's home. A person thus may have more than one residence at a time but only one domicile. Sometimes, though, the two terms are used synonymously. **3.** A house or other fixed abode; a dwelling <a three-story residence>. **4.** The place where a corporation or other enterprise does business or is registered to do business <Pantheon Inc.'s principal residence is in Delaware>.

residency. (14c) **1.** A place of residence, esp. an official one <the diplomat's residency>. **2.** RESIDENCE (1) <one year's residency to be eligible for in-state tuition>.

resident, *adj.* **1.** Affiliated with or working for a particular person or company <resident agent>. **2.** Dwelling in a place other than one's home on a long-term basis <the hospital's resident patient>.

resident, *n.* (15c) **1.** A person who lives in a particular place. **2.** A person who has a home in a particular place. • In sense 2, a resident is not necessarily either a citizen or a domiciliary.

residential care. *Family law.* Foster-care placement involving residence in a group home or institution. • This type of foster care is most commonly used for adolescents who have been adjudged to be delinquents or status offenders.

residential cluster. *Land-use planning.* An area of land developed as a unit with group housing and open common space.

residual, *adj.* (16c) Of, relating to, or constituting a residue; remaining; leftover <a residual claim> <a residual functional disability>.

residual, *n.* **1.** A leftover quantity; a remainder. **2.** (*often pl.*) A disability remaining after an illness, injury, or operation. **3.** (*usu. pl.*) A fee paid to a composer or performer for each repeated broadcast (esp. on television) of a film, program, or commercial.

residuary (ri-**zij**-oo-er-ee), *adj.* (18c) Of, relating to, or constituting a residue; residual <a residuary gift>.

residuary, *n.* **1.** Residuary estate. **2.** Residuary legatee.

residuary clause. (18c) *Wills & estates.* A testamentary clause that disposes of any estate property remaining after the satisfaction of all other gifts.

residue. (14c) **1.** Something that is left over after a part is removed or disposed of; a remainder. **2.** Residuary estate.

residuum (ri-**zij**-oo-əm). (17c) **1.** That which remains; a residue. **2.** Residuary estate. Pl. **residua** (ri-**zij**-oo-ə).

resignation, *n.* (14c) **1.** The act or an instance of surrendering or relinquishing an office, right, or claim. **2.** A formal notification of relinquishing an office or position. — **resign,** *vb.*

res integra (rays **in**-tə-grə *also* in-**teg**-rə). [Latin "an entire thing"] Res nova.

res inter alios acta (rays **in**-tər **ay**-lee-ohs **ak**-tə). [Latin "a thing done between others"] **1.** *Contracts.* The common-law doctrine holding that a contract cannot unfavorably affect the rights of a person who is not a party to the contract. **2.** *Evidence.* The rule prohibiting the admission of collateral facts into evidence.

res ipsa loquitur (rays **ip**-sə **loh**-kwə-tər). [Latin "the thing speaks for itself"] (17c) *Torts.* The doctrine providing that, in some circumstances, the mere fact of an accident's occurrence raises an inference of negligence that establishes a prima facie case.

res ipsa loquitur test (rays **ip**-sə **loh**-kwə-tər). (1962) A method for determining whether a defendant has gone beyond preparation and has actually committed an attempt, based on whether the defendant's act itself would have indicated to an observer what the defendant intended to do.

resisting arrest. (1851) The crime of obstructing or opposing a police officer who is making an arrest.

resisting unlawful arrest. (1905) The act of opposing a police officer who is making an unlawful arrest. See Model Penal Code § 3.

res judicata (rays joo-di-**kay**-tə *or* -**kah**-tə). [Latin "a thing adjudicated"] (17c) **1.** An issue that has been definitively settled by judicial decision. **2.** An affirmative defense barring the same parties from litigating a second lawsuit on the same claim, or any other claim arising from the same transaction or series of transactions and that could have been — but was not — raised in the first suit. • The three essential elements are (1) an earlier decision on the issue, (2) a final judgment on the merits, and (3) the involvement of the same parties, or parties in privity with the original parties. Restatement (Second) of Judgments §§ 17, 24 (1982).

res nova (rays **noh**-və). [Latin "new thing"] **1.** An undecided question of law. **2.** A case of first impression.

resolution. (17c) **1.** *Parliamentary law.* A main motion that formally expresses the sense, will, or action of a deliberative assembly (esp. a legislative body).

concurrent resolution. (17c) A resolution passed by one house and agreed to by the other. • It expresses the legislature's opinion on a subject but does not have the force of law.

joint resolution. (17c) A legislative resolution passed by both houses. • It has the force of law and is subject to executive veto.

simple resolution. (18c) A resolution passed by one house only. • It expresses the opinion or affects the internal affairs of the passing house, but it does not have the force of law.

2. Formal action by a corporate board of directors or other corporate body authorizing a particular act, transaction, or appointment.

shareholder resolution. A resolution by shareholders, usu. to ratify the actions of the board of directors.

3. A document containing such an expression or authorization.

resolutory (ri-**zahl**-yə-tor-ee), *adj.* (1818) Operating or serving to annul, dissolve, or terminate <a resolutory clause>.

resort, *n.* Something that one turns to for aid or refuge <the court of last resort>. — **resort,** *vb.*

respite (**res**-pit), *n.* (14c) **1.** A period of temporary delay; an extension of time. **2.** A temporary suspension of a death sentence; a reprieve. **3.** A delay granted to a jury or court for further consideration of a verdict or appeal. — **respite,** *vb.*

respondeat ouster (ri-**spon**-dee-at **ow**-stər). [Law Latin "let him make further answer"] An interlocutory judgment or order that a party who made a dilatory plea that has been denied must now plead on the merits.

respondeat superior (ri-**spon**-dee-at soo-**peer**-ee-ər *or* sə-peer-ee-**or**). [Law Latin "let the superior make answer"] (17c) *Torts.* The doctrine holding an employer or principal liable for the employee's or agent's wrongful acts committed within the scope of the employment or agency.

respondent. (16c) **1.** The party against whom an appeal is taken; APPELLEE. • In some appellate courts, the parties are designated as *petitioner* and *respondent.* In most appellate courts in the United States, the parties are designated as *appellant* and *appellee.* Often the designations depend on whether the appeal is taken by writ of certiorari (or writ of error) or by direct appeal. **2.** The party against whom a motion or petition is filed. **3.** At common law, the defendant in an equity proceeding.

responsibility, *n.* (18c) **1.** LIABILITY (1). **2.** *Criminal law.* A person's mental fitness to answer in court for his or her actions. **3.** *Criminal law.* Guilt. — **responsible,** *adj.*

responsive, *adj.* (15c) Giving or constituting a response; answering <the witness's testimony is not responsive to the question>.

rest, *vb.* (1905) (Of a litigant) to voluntarily conclude presenting evidence in a trial <after the police officer's testimony, the prosecution rested>.

Restatement. One of several influential treatises published by the American Law Institute describing the law in a given area and guiding its development. • The Restatements use a distinctive format of black-letter rules, official comments, illustrations, and reporter's notes. Although the Restatements are frequently cited in cases and commentary, a Restatement provision is not binding on a court unless it has been officially adopted as the law by that jurisdiction's highest court. Restatements have been published in the following areas of law: Agency, Conflict of Laws, Contracts, Employment Law, Foreign Relations Law of the United States, Judgments, Law Governing Lawyers, Property, Restitution, Security, Suretyship and Guaranty, Torts, Trusts, and Unfair Competition.

restater. (1955) An author or reporter of a Restatement.

restitution, *n.* (13c) **1.** A body of substantive law in which liability is based not on tort or contract but on the defendant's unjust enrichment. **2.** The set of remedies associated with that body of law, in which the measure of recovery is usu. based not on the plaintiff's loss, but on the defendant's gain. **3.** Return or restoration of some specific thing to its rightful owner or status. **4.** Compensation for loss; esp., full or partial compensation paid by a criminal to a victim, not awarded in a civil trial for tort, but ordered as part of a criminal sentence or as a condition of probation. — **restitutionary,** *adj.*

restorative justice. An alternative delinquency sanction focused on repairing the harm done, meeting the victim's needs, and holding the offender responsible for his or her actions.

restraining order. (1876) **1.** A court order prohibiting family violence; esp., an order restricting a person from harassing, threatening, and sometimes merely contacting or approaching another specified person. **2.** TEMPORARY RESTRAINING ORDER. **3.** A court order entered to prevent the dissipation or loss of property.

restraint, *n.* (15c) **1.** Confinement, abridgment, or limitation <a restraint on the freedom of speech>. **2.** Prohibition of action; holding back <the victim's family exercised no restraint — they told the suspect exactly what they thought of him>.

restraint of marriage. (16c) A condition (esp. in a gift or bequest) that nullifies the grant to which it applies if the grantee marries or remarries.

restraint of trade. 1. A limitation on business dealings or professional or gainful occupations. **2.** *Antitrust.* An agreement between two or more businesses or a combination of businesses intended to eliminate competition, create a monopoly, artificially raise prices, or otherwise adversely affect the free market.

restraint on alienation. (18c) **1.** A restriction, usu. in a deed of conveyance, on a grantee's ability to sell or transfer real property; a provision that conveys an interest and that, even after the interest has become vested, prevents or discourages the owner from disposing of it at all or from disposing of it in particular ways or to particular persons. **2.** A trust provision that prohibits or penalizes alienation of the trust corpus.

restriction. (15c) **1.** A limitation or qualification. **2.** A limitation (esp. in a deed) placed on the use or enjoyment of property.

resummons. (15c) A second or renewed summons to a party or witness already summoned.

resumption. The taking back of property previously given up or lost.

retail, *n.* The sale of goods or commodities to ultimate consumers, as opposed to the sale for further distribution or processing. — **retail,** *adj.* — **retail,** *vb.*

retailer, *n.* A person or entity engaged in the business of selling personal property to the public or to consumers, as opposed to selling to those who intend to resell the items.

retainage (ri-**tayn**-ij). (1901) A percentage of what a landowner pays a contractor, withheld until the construction has been satisfactorily completed and all mechanic's liens are released or have expired.

retainer, *n.* (18c) **1.** A client's authorization for a lawyer to act in a case <the attorney needed an express retainer before making a settlement offer>. **2.** A fee that a client pays to a lawyer simply to be available when the client needs legal help during a specified period or on a specified matter. **3.** A lump-sum fee paid by the client to engage a lawyer at the outset of a matter. **4.** An advance payment of fees for work that the lawyer will perform in the future. — **retain,** *vb.*

general retainer. (18c) A retainer for a specific length of time rather than for a specific project.

special retainer. (18c) A retainer for a specific case or project.

retaliatory law. (1820) A state law restraining another state's businesses — as by levying taxes — in response to similar restraints imposed by the second state on the first state's businesses.

retirement, *n.* (16c) **1.** Termination of one's own employment or career, esp. upon reaching a certain age or for health reasons; retirement may be voluntary or involuntary. **2.** Withdrawal from action or for privacy <Carol's retirement to her house by the lake>. **3.** Withdrawal from circulation; payment of a debt <retirement of a series of bonds>. — **retire,** *vb.*

retraction, *n.* (14c) **1.** The act of taking or drawing back <retraction of anticipatory repudiation before breach of contract>. **2.** The act of recanting; a statement in recantation <retraction of a defamatory remark>. **3.** *Wills & estates.* A withdrawal of a renunciation <because of her retraction, she took property under her uncle's will>. — **retract,** *vb.*

retreat rule. (1935) *Criminal law.* The doctrine holding that the victim of an assault has a duty to retreat instead of resorting to deadly force in self-defense, unless (1) the victim is at home or in his or her place of business (the so-called *castle doctrine*), or (2) the assailant is a person whom the victim is trying to arrest.

retrial, *n.* (18c) A new trial of an action that has already been tried. — **retry,** *vb.*

retribution, *n.* (14c) **1.** *Criminal law.* Punishment imposed as repayment or revenge for the offense committed; requital. **2.** Something justly deserved; repayment; reward. — **retributive,** *adj.* — **retribute,** *vb.*

retributivism (ri-**trib**-yə-tə-viz-əm). (1966) The legal theory by which criminal punishment is justified, as long as the offender is morally accountable, regardless of whether deterrence or other good consequences would result. • According to retributivism, a criminal is thought to have a debt to pay to society, which is paid by punishment. The punishment is also sometimes said to be society's act of paying back the criminal for the wrong done. Opponents of retributivism sometimes refer to it as "vindictive theory."

retroactive, *adj.* (17c) (Of a statute, ruling, etc.) extending in scope or effect to matters that have occurred in the past. — **retroactivity,** *n.*

retroactive law. (18c) A legislative act that looks backward or contemplates the past, affecting acts or facts that existed before the act came into effect. • A retroactive law is not unconstitutional unless it (1) is in the nature of an ex post facto law or a bill of attainder, (2) impairs the obligation of contracts, (3) divests vested rights, or (4) is constitutionally forbidden.

retrocession. (17c) **1.** The act of ceding something back (such as a territory or jurisdiction). **2.** The return of a title or other interest in property to its former or rightful owner.

return, *n.* (15c) **1.** A court officer's bringing back of an instrument to the court that issued it; return of writ <a sheriff's return of citation>. **2.** A court officer's indorsement on an instrument brought back to the court, reporting what the officer did or found <a return of *nulla bona*>. **3.** Tax return <file your return before April 15>. **4.** (*usu. pl.*) An official report of voting results <election returns>. **5.** Yield or profit <return on an investment>. — **return,** *vb.*

return of writ. (18c) The sheriff's bringing back a writ to the court that issued it, with a short written account (usu. on the back) of the manner in which the writ was executed.

reunification. The return of a child who has been removed from his or her parents because of abuse or neglect by one or both of them.

rev'd. *abbr.* Reversed.

revenue. (15c) Gross income or receipts.

Revenue Procedure. An official statement by the IRS regarding the administration and procedures of the tax laws. — Abbr. Rev. Proc.

Revenue Ruling. An official interpretation by the IRS of the proper application of the tax law to a specific transaction. • Revenue Rulings carry some authoritative weight and may be relied on by the taxpayer who requested the ruling. — Abbr. Rev. Rul.

revenue stamp. (1862) A stamp used as evidence that a tax has been paid.

reversal, *n.* (15c) **1.** An appellate court's overturning of a lower court's decision. **2.** *Securities.* A change in a security's near-term market-price trend.

reverse, *vb.* To overturn (a judgment) on appeal.

reverse-confusion doctrine. *Intellectual property.* The rule that it is unfair competition if the defendant's use of a title that is confusingly similar to the one used by the plaintiff leads the public to believe that the plaintiff's work is the same as the defendant's, or that it is derived from or associated in some manner with the defendant.

reverse-engineering. *Intellectual property.* The process of discovering how an invention works by inspecting and studying it, esp. by taking it apart in order to learn how it works and how to copy it and improve it. — **reverse-engineer,** *vb.*

reverse *Erie* doctrine. The rule that a state court must apply federal law when state law is preempted by federal law or federal law prevails by an *Erie*-like balancing of the facts in situations not already regulated by Congress or the Constitution.

reverse FOIA suit (foy-ə). A lawsuit by the owner of a trade secret or other information exempt from disclosure under a freedom-of-information act to prevent a governmental entity from making that information available to the public.

reversion, *n.* (15c) **1.** The interest that is left after subtracting what the transferor has parted with from what the transferor originally had; specif., a future interest in land arising by operation of law whenever an estate owner grants to another a particular estate, such as a life estate or a term of years, but does not dispose of the entire interest. • A reversion occurs automatically upon termination of the prior estate, as when a life tenant dies. **2.** Loosely, remainder. — **reversionary,** *adj.* — **revert,** *vb.*

reversioner. (17c) **1.** One who possesses the reversion to an estate; the grantor or heir in reversion. **2.** Broadly, one who has a lawful interest in land but not the present possession of it.

reverter. Possibility of reverter.

revest, *vb.* (16c) To vest again or anew <revesting of title in the former owner>.

rev'g. *abbr.* Reversing.

review, *n.* (15c) **1.** Consideration, inspection, or reexamination of a subject or thing. **2.** Plenary power to direct and instruct an agent or subordinate, including the right to remand, modify, or vacate any action by the agent or subordinate, or to act directly in place of the agent or subordinate. — **review,** *vb.*

administrative review. (1928) **1.** Judicial review of an administrative proceeding. **2.** Review of an administrative proceeding within the agency itself.

appellate review. (1837) Examination of a lower court's decision by a higher court, which can affirm, reverse, modify, or vacate the decision.

discretionary review. (1914) The form of appellate review that is not a matter of right but that occurs only with the appellate court's permission.

revision, *n.* (17c) **1.** A reexamination or careful review for correction or improvement. **2.** An altered version of a work.

revival, *n.* (17c) **1.** Restoration to current use or operation; esp., the act of restoring the validity or legal force of an expired contract, an abandoned patent, or a dormant judgment. **2.** *Wills & estates.* The reestablishment of the validity of a revoked will by revoking the will that invalidated the original will or in some other way manifesting the testator's intent to be bound by the earlier will. — **revive,** *vb.*

revivor. (18c) A proceeding to revive an action ended because of either the death of one of the parties or some other circumstance.

revocable (**rev**-ə-kə-bəl), *adj.* (15c) Capable of being canceled or withdrawn <a revocable transfer>.

revocation (rev-ə-**kay**-shən), *n.* (15c) **1.** An annulment, cancellation, or reversal, usu. of an act or power. **2.** *Contracts.* Withdrawal of an offer by the offeror. **3.** *Wills & estates.* Invalidation of a will by the testator, either by destroying the will or by executing a new one. — **revoke,** *vb.*

revolution, *n.* An overthrow of a government, usu. resulting in fundamental political change; a successful rebellion. — **revolutionary,** *adj.* & *n.* — **revolt,** *vb.*

Rev. Proc. *abbr.* Revenue procedure.

Rev. Rul. *abbr.* Revenue ruling.

Rev. Stat. *abbr.* Revised statutes.

reward, *n.* **1.** Something of value, usu. money, given in return for some service or achievement, such as recovering property or providing information that leads to the capture of a criminal. **2.** SALVAGE (3). — **reward,** *vb.*

rezone, *vb.* (1951) To change the zoning boundaries or restrictions of (an area) <rezone the neighborhood>.

RFA. *abbr.* Request for admission.

RFI. *abbr.* Request for instructions.

RFP. *abbr.* **1.** Request for production. **2.** Request for proposal.

RICO (**ree**-koh). *abbr.* (1972) Racketeer Influenced and Corrupt Organizations Act.

rider. An attachment to some document, such as a legislative bill or an insurance policy, that amends or supplements the document. • A rider to a legislative bill often addresses subject matter unrelated to the main purpose of the bill.

RIF. *abbr.* Reduction in force.

right, *n.* (bef. 12c) **1.** That which is proper under law, morality, or ethics <know right from wrong>. **2.** Something that is due to a person by just claim, legal guarantee, or moral principle <the right of liberty>. **3.** A power, privilege, or immunity secured to a person by law <the right to dispose of one's estate>. **4.** A legally enforceable claim that another will do or will not do a given act; a recognized and protected interest the violation of which is a wrong <a breach of duty that infringes one's right>. **5.** (*often pl.*) The interest, claim, or ownership that one has in tangible or intangible property <a debtor's rights in collateral> <publishing rights>. **6.** The privilege of corporate shareholders to purchase newly issued securities in amounts proportionate to their holdings. **7.** The negotiable certificate granting such a privilege to a corporate shareholder.

absolute right. **1.** A right that belongs to every human being, such as the right of personal liberty; a natural right. **2.** An unqualified right; specif., a right that cannot be denied or curtailed except under specific conditions <freedom of thought is an absolute right>.

legal right. **1.** A right created or recognized by law. • The breach of a legal right is usu. remediable by monetary damages. **2.** A right historically recognized by common-law courts. **3.** The capacity of asserting a legally recognized claim against one with a correlative duty to act.

natural right. A right that is conceived as part of natural law and that is therefore thought to exist independently of rights created by government or society, such as the right to life, liberty, and property.

personal right. **1.** A right that forms part of a person's legal status or personal condition, as opposed to the person's estate. **2.** Right *in personam.*

procedural right. (1911) A right that derives from legal or administrative procedure; a right that helps in the protection or enforcement of a substantive right.

property right. (1853) A right to specific property, whether tangible or intangible.

substantial right. (18c) An essential right that potentially affects the outcome of a lawsuit and is capable of legal enforcement and protection, as distinguished from a mere technical or procedural right.

substantive right (**səb**-stən-tiv). (18c) A right that can be protected or enforced by law; a right of substance rather than form.

vested right. A right that so completely and definitely belongs to a person that it cannot be impaired or taken away without the person's consent.

right against self-incrimination. (1911) A criminal defendant's or a witness's constitutional right — under the Fifth Amendment, but waivable under certain conditions — guaranteeing that a person cannot be compelled by the government to testify if the testimony might result in the person's being criminally prosecuted.

rightful, *adj.* **1.** (Of an action) equitable; fair <a rightful dispossession>. **2.** (Of a person) legitimately entitled to a position <a rightful heir>. **3.** (Of an office or piece of property) that one is entitled to <her rightful inheritance>.

right of action. 1. The right to bring a specific case to court. **2.** A right that can be enforced by legal action; a chose in action.

right of assembly. The constitutional right — guaranteed by the First Amendment — of the people to gather peacefully for public expression of religion, politics, or grievances.

right of election. *Wills & estates.* A surviving spouse's statutory right to choose either the gifts given by the deceased spouse in the will or a forced share or a share of the estate as defined in the probate statute.

right of entry. 1. The right of taking or resuming possession of land or other real property in a peaceable manner. **2.** Power of termination. **3.** The right to go into another's real property for a special purpose without committing trespass. • An example is a landlord's right to enter a tenant's property to make repairs. **4.** The right of an alien to go into a jurisdiction for a special purpose. • An example is an exchange student's right to enter another country to attend college.

right of family integrity. A fundamental and substantive due-process right for a family unit to be free of unjustified state interference. • While not specifically mentioned in the U.S. Constitution, this right is said to emanate from it. The contours of the right are nebulous and incompletely defined, but it at least includes the right to bear children, to rear them, and to guide them according to the parents' beliefs, as well as the right of children to be raised by their parents free of unwarranted interference by state officials. The right restricts state action under the Fourteenth Amendment. Interference is not permitted in the absence of a compelling state interest and is reviewed under a strict-scrutiny standard. Most courts require a state to establish by clear and convincing evidence that interference in a familial relationship is justified.

right of first refusal. 1. A potential buyer's contractual right to meet the terms of a third party's higher offer. • For example, if Beth has a right of first refusal on the purchase of Sam's house, and if Terry offers to buy the house for $300,000, then Beth can match this offer and prevent Terry from buying it. **2.** *Family law.* The right of a parent to be offered the opportunity to have custody of a child other than during a usual visitation period before the other parent turns to a third-party caregiver.

right of possession. The right to hold, use, occupy, or otherwise enjoy a given property; esp., the right to enter real property and eject or evict a wrongful possessor.

right of preemption. A potential buyer's contractual right to have the first opportunity to buy, at a specified price, if the seller chooses to sell within the contracted period.

right of privacy. 1. The right to personal autonomy. • The U.S. Constitution does not explicitly provide for a right of privacy or for a general right of personal autonomy, but the Supreme Court has repeatedly ruled that a right of personal autonomy is implied in the "zones of privacy" created by specific constitutional guarantees. **2.** The right of a person and the person's property to be free from unwarranted public scrutiny or exposure.

right of publicity. The right to control the use of one's own name, picture, or likeness and to prevent another from using it for commercial benefit without one's consent.

right of revolution. The inherent right of a people to cast out its rulers, change its polity, or effect radical reforms in its system of government or institutions, by force or general uprising, when the legal and constitutional methods of making such changes have proved inadequate or are so obstructed as to be unavailable.

right of support. *Property.* **1.** A landowner's right to have the land supported by adjacent land and by the underlying earth. **2.** A servitude giving the owner of a house the right to rest timber on the walls of a neighboring house.

right of survivorship. A joint tenant's right to succeed to the whole estate upon the death of the other joint tenant.

right-of-way. 1. The right to pass through property owned by another. • A right-of-way may be established by contract, by longstanding usage, or by public authority (as with a highway). **2.** The right to build and operate a railway line or a highway on land belonging to another, or the land so used. **3.** The right to take precedence in traffic. **4.** The strip of land subject to a nonowner's right to pass through. Pl. **rights-of-way.**

public right-of-way. The right of passage held by the public in general to travel on roads, freeways, and other thoroughfares.

right to bear arms. The constitutional right of persons to own firearms. U.S. Const. amend II.

right to counsel. *Criminal law.* A criminal defendant's constitutional right, guaranteed by the Sixth Amendment, to representation by a court- appointed lawyer if the defendant cannot afford to hire one.

right to die. The right of a terminally ill person to refuse life-sustaining treatment.

right-to-know act. A federal or state statute requiring businesses (such as chemical manufacturers) that produce hazardous substances to disclose information about the substances both to the community where they are produced or stored and to employees who handle them.

right to petition. (17c) The constitutional right — guaranteed by the First Amendment — of the people to make formal requests to the government, as by lobbying or writing letters to public officials.

right to rescind. The remedy accorded to a party to a contract when the other party breaches a duty that arises independently of the contract. • The right to rescind is contrasted with a right of termination, which arises when the other party breaches a duty that arises under the contract.

right to travel. (1838) A person's constitutional right — guaranteed by the Privileges and Immunities Clause — to travel freely between states.

right-to-work law. (1958) A state law that prevents labor–management agreements requiring a person to join a union as a condition of employment.

riot, *n.* (14c) **1.** An assemblage of three or more persons in a public place taking concerted action in a turbulent and disorderly manner for a common purpose (regardless of the lawfulness of that purpose). **2.** An unlawful disturbance of the peace by an assemblage of usu. three or more persons acting with a common purpose in a violent or tumultuous manner that threatens or terrorizes the public or an institution. — **riotous,** *adj.* — **riot,** *vb.*

Riot Act. A 1714 English statute that made it a capital offense for 12 or more rioters to remain together for an hour after a magistrate has officially proclaimed that rioters must disperse. • This statute was not generally accepted in the United States and did not become a part of American common law. It did, however, become a permanent part of the English language in the slang phrase *reading the riot act* (meaning "to reprimand vigorously"), which originally referred to the official command for rioters to disperse.

riparian (ri-**pair**-ee-ən *or* rɪ-), *adj.* (1841) Of, relating to, or located on the bank of a river or stream (or occasionally another body of water, such as a lake) <riparian land> <a riparian owner>.

riparian proprietor. (1808) A person who is in possession of riparian land or who owns an estate in it; a landowner whose property borders on a stream or river.

riparian right. (*often pl.*) (1860) The right of a landowner whose property borders on a body of water or watercourse. • Such a landowner traditionally has the right to make reasonable use of the water.

riparian-rights doctrine. (1921) The rule that owners of land bordering on a waterway have equal rights to use the water passing through or by their property.

ripeness, *n.* **1.** The state of a dispute that has reached, but has not passed, the point when the facts have developed sufficiently to permit an intelligent and useful decision to be made. **2.** The requirement that this state must exist before a court will decide a controversy. — **ripe,** *adj.* — **ripen,** *vb.*

risk, *n.* (17c) **1.** The uncertainty of a result, happening, or loss; the chance of injury, damage, or loss; esp., the existence and extent of the possibility of harm <many feel that skydiving is not worth the risk>. **2.** Liability for injury, damage, or loss if it occurs <the consumer-protection statute placed the risk on the manufacturer instead of the buyer>. **3.** *Insurance.* The chance or degree of probability of loss to the subject matter of an insurance policy <the insurer undertook the risk in exchange for a premium>. **4.** *Insurance.* The amount that an insurer stands to lose <the underwriter took steps to reduce its total risk>. **5.** *Insurance.* A person or thing that an insurer considers a hazard; someone or something that might be covered by an insurance policy <she's a poor risk for health insurance>. **6.** *Insurance.* The type of loss covered by a policy; a hazard from a specified source <this homeowner's policy covers fire risks and flood risks>. — **risk,** *vb.*

risk-averse, *adj.* (Of a person) uncomfortable with volatility or uncertainty; not willing to take risks; very cautious <a risk-averse investor>.

risk of loss. (18c) **1.** The danger or possibility of damage to, destruction of, or misplacement of goods or other property. **2.** Responsibility for bearing the costs and expenses of such damage, destruction, or misplacement.

risk-utility test. (1982) A method of imposing product liability on a manufacturer if the evidence shows that a reasonable person would conclude that the benefits of a product's particular design versus the feasibility of an alternative safer design did not outweigh the dangers inherent in the original design.

robbery, *n.* (12c) The illegal taking of property from the person of another, or in the person's presence, by violence or intimidation; aggravated larceny. • Robbery is usu. a felony, but some jurisdictions classify some robberies as high misdemeanors. — **rob,** *vb.*

aggravated robbery. (1878) Robbery committed by a person who either carries a dangerous weapon — often called *armed robbery* — or inflicts bodily harm on someone during the robbery. • Some statutes also specify that a robbery is aggravated when the victim is a member of a protected class, such as children or the elderly.

armed robbery. (1926) Robbery committed by a person carrying a dangerous weapon, regardless of whether the weapon is revealed or used. • Most states punish armed robbery as an aggravated form of robbery rather than as a separate crime.

highway robbery. **1.** Robbery committed against a traveler on or near a public highway. **2.** Figuratively, a price or fee that is unreasonably high; excessive profit or advantage.

simple robbery. (18c) Robbery that does not involve an aggravating factor or circumstance.

robe. (18c) **1.** The gown worn by a judge while presiding over court. **2.** (*often cap.*) The legal or judicial profession <eminent members of the robe>.

Robert's Rules. **1.** A parliamentary manual titled *Robert's Rules of Order,* originally written in 1875–76 by Henry M. Robert (1837–1923). • The manual went through three editions under its original title and three more (beginning in 1915) under the title *Robert's Rules of Order Revised.* Since 1970 it has been titled *Robert's Rules of Order Newly Revised.* It is the best selling and most commonly adopted parliamentary manual in the United States. **2.** Any parliamentary manual that includes "Robert's Rules" in its title. • The copyright on the first several editions has expired, and many imitators have adapted those editions in varying degrees of faithfulness to the original.

rocket docket. (1987) **1.** An accelerated dispute-resolution process. **2.** A court or judicial district known for its speedy disposition of cases. **3.** A similar administrative process, in which disputes must be decided within a specified time (such as 60 days).

roll, *n.* (14c) **1.** A record of a court's or public office's proceedings. **2.** An official list of the persons and property subject to taxation.

rollover, *n.* **1.** The extension or renewal of a short-term loan; the refinancing of a maturing loan or note. **2.** The transfer of funds (such as IRA funds) to a new investment of the same type, esp.

so as to defer payment of taxes. — **roll over,** *vb.*

rout (rowt), *n.* (15c) The offense that occurs when an unlawful assembly makes some move toward the accomplishment of its participants' common purpose.

routine-activities theory. (1985) The theory that criminal acts occur when (1) a person is motivated to commit the offense, (2) a vulnerable victim is available, and (3) there is insufficient protection to prevent the crime.

royalty. (1839) **1.** *Intellectual property.* A payment — in addition to or in place of an up-front payment — made to an author or inventor for each copy of a work or article sold under a copyright or patent. • Royalties are often paid per item made, used, or sold, or per time elapsed. **2.** *Oil & gas.* A share of the product or profit from real property, reserved by the grantor of a mineral lease, in exchange for the lessee's right to mine or drill on the land.

rptr. *abbr.* Reporter.

R.S. *abbr.* Revised statutes.

rubric (roo-brik). **1.** The title of a statute or code <the rubric of the relevant statute is the Civil Rights Act of 1964>. **2.** A category or designation <assignment of rights falls under the rubric of contract law>. **3.** An authoritative rule, esp. for conducting a public worship service <the rubric dictates whether the congregation should stand or kneel>. **4.** An introductory or explanatory note; a preface <a well-known scholar wrote the rubric to the book's fourth edition>. **5.** An established rule, custom, or law <what is the rubric in the Northern District of Texas regarding appearance at docket call?>.

rule, *n.* (13c) **1.** Generally, an established and authoritative standard or principle; a general norm mandating or guiding conduct or action in a given type of situation. **2.** A regulation governing a court's or an agency's internal procedures. **3.** *Parliamentary law.* A procedural rule (sense 1) for the orderly conduct of business in a deliberative assembly.

rule, *vb.* (13c) **1.** To command or require; to exert control <the dictator ruled the country>. **2.** To decide a legal point <the court ruled on the issue of admissibility>.

rule, the. An evidentiary and procedural rule by which all witnesses are excluded from the courtroom while another witness is testifying <invoking "the rule">. • The phrase "the rule" is used chiefly in the American South and Southwest, but it is a common practice to exclude witnesses before they testify.

Rule 11. *Civil procedure.* In federal practice, the procedural rule requiring the attorney of record or the party (if not represented by an attorney) to sign all pleadings, motions, and other papers filed with the court and — by this signing — to represent that the paper is filed in good faith after an inquiry that is reasonable under the circumstances. • This rule provides for the imposition of sanctions, upon a party's or the court's own motion, if an attorney or party violates the conditions stated in the rule. Fed. R. Civ. P. 11.

rule against perpetuities. (*sometimes cap.*) (18c) *Property.* The common-law rule prohibiting a grant of an estate unless the interest must vest, if at all, no later than 21 years (plus a period of gestation to cover a posthumous birth) after the death of some person alive when the interest was created. • The purpose of the rule was to limit the time that title to property could be suspended out of commerce because there was no owner who had title to the property and who could sell it or exercise other aspects of ownership. If the terms of the contract or gift exceeded the time limits of the rule, the gift or transaction was void.

Rule in Shelley's Case. (18c) *Property.* The rule that if — in a single grant — a freehold estate is given to a person and a remainder is given to the person's heirs, the remainder belongs to the named person and not the heirs, so that the person is held to have a fee simple absolute. • The rule, which dates from the 14th century but draws its name from the famous 16th-century case, has been abolished in most states. *Wolfe v. Shelley,* 76 Eng. Rep. 206 (K.B. 1581).

Rule in Wild's Case. (1842) *Property.* The rule construing a grant to "A and A's children" as a fee tail if A's children do not exist at the effective date of the instrument, and as a joint tenancy if A's children do exist at the effective date. • The rule has been abolished along with the fee tail in most states.

rulemaking, *n.* (1926) The process used by an administrative agency to formulate, amend, or repeal a rule or regulation. — **rulemaking,** *adj.*

formal rulemaking. (1960) Agency rulemaking that, when required by statute or the agency's discretion, must be on the record after an opportunity for an agency hearing, and must comply with certain procedures, such as allowing the submission of evidence and the cross-examination of witnesses.

informal rulemaking. (1968) Agency rulemaking in which the agency publishes a proposed regulation and receives public comments on the regulation, after which the regulation can take effect without the necessity of a formal hearing on the record. • Informal rulemaking is the most common procedure followed by an agency in issuing its substantive rules.

rule of capture. 1. The doctrine that if the donee of a general power of appointment manifests an intent to assume control of the property for all purposes and not just for the purpose of appointing it to someone, the donee captures the property and the property goes to the donee's estate. **2.** *Property.* The principle that wild animals belong to the person who captures them, regardless of whether they were originally on another person's land. **3.** *Oil & gas.* A fundamental principle of oil-and-gas law holding that there is no liability for drainage of oil and gas from under the lands of another so long as there has been no trespass and all relevant statutes and regulations have been observed.

rule of court. (17c) A rule governing the practice or procedure in a given court <federal rules of court>.

rule of decision. (18c) A rule, statute, body of law, or prior decision that provides the basis for deciding or adjudicating a case.

rule of four. (1949) The convention that for certiorari to be granted by the U.S. Supreme Court, four justices must vote in favor of the grant.

rule of inconvenience. (1934) The principle of statutory interpretation holding that a court should not construe a statute in a way that will jeopardize an important public interest or produce a serious hardship for anyone, unless that interpretation is unavoidable.

rule of law. (18c) **1.** A substantive legal principle <under the rule of law known as respondeat superior, the employer is answerable for all wrongs committed by an employee in the course of the employment>. **2.** The supremacy of regular as opposed to arbitrary power <citizens must respect the rule of law>. **3.** The doctrine that every person is subject to the ordinary law within the jurisdiction <all persons within the United States are within the American rule of law>. **4.** The doctrine that general constitutional principles are the result of judicial decisions determining the rights of private individuals in the courts <under the rule of law, Supreme Court caselaw makes up the bulk of what we call

"constitutional law">. **5.** Loosely, a legal ruling; a ruling on a point of law <the *ratio decidendi* of a case is any rule of law reached by the judge as a necessary step in the decision>.

rule of lenity (**len**-ə-tee). The judicial doctrine holding that a court, in construing an ambiguous criminal statute that sets out multiple or inconsistent punishments, should resolve the ambiguity in favor of the more lenient punishment.

rule of necessity. A rule requiring a judge or other official to hear a case, despite bias or conflict of interest, when disqualification would result in the lack of any competent court or tribunal. — Often shortened to *necessity.*

rule of optional completeness. (1983) The evidentiary rule providing that when a party introduces part of a writing or an utterance at trial, the opposing party may require that the remainder of the passage be read to establish the full context. • The rule has limitations: first, no utterance can be received if it is irrelevant, and second, the remainder of the utterance must explain the first part. In many jurisdictions, the rule applies to conversations, to an opponent's admissions, to confessions, and to all other types of writings — even account books. But the Federal Rules of Evidence limit the rule to writings and recorded statements. Fed. R. Evid. 106.

rule of 72. A method for determining how many years it takes to double money invested at a compound interest rate. • For example, at a compound rate of 6%, it takes 12 years (72 divided by 6) for principal to double.

rule of 78. A method for computing the amount of interest that a borrower saves by paying off a loan early, when the interest payments are higher at the beginning of the loan period. • For example, to determine how much interest is saved by prepaying a 12-month loan after 6 months, divide the sum of the digits for the remaining six payments (21) by the sum of the digits for all twelve payments (78) and multiply that percentage by the total interest.

rule of the last antecedent. (1919) An interpretative principle by which a court determines that qualifying words or phrases modify the words or phrases immediately preceding them and not words or phrases more remote, unless the extension is necessary from the context or the spirit of the entire writing. • For example, an application of this rule might mean that, in the phrase *Texas courts, New Mexico courts, and New York courts in the federal system,* the words *in the federal system* might be held to modify only *New York courts* and not *Texas courts* or *New Mexico courts.*

ruling, *n.* (16c) **1.** The outcome of a court's decision either on some point of law or on the case as a whole. **2.** *Parliamentary law.* The chair's decision on a point of order. — **rule,** *vb.*

run, *vb.* (bef. 12c) **1.** To expire after a prescribed period <the statute of limitations had run, so the plaintiff's lawsuit was barred>. **2.** To accompany a conveyance or assignment of (land) <the covenant runs with the land>. **3.** To apply <the injunction runs against only one of the parties in the dispute>.

runaway. (16c) **1.** A person who is fleeing or has escaped from custody, captivity, restraint, or control; esp., a minor who has voluntarily left home without permission and with no intent to return. **2.** An animal or thing that is out of control or has escaped from confinement. — **run away,** *vb.*

runner. (18c) **1.** A law-office employee who delivers papers between offices and files papers in court. **2.** One who solicits personal-injury cases for a lawyer. **3.** A smuggler. **4.** *BrE. Slang.* An escape; flight (from something); a voluntary disappearance.

S

s. *abbr.* **1.** Statute. **2.** SECTION (1). **3.** (*usu. cap.*) Senate.

sabotage (**sab**-ə-tahzh), *n.* (1910) **1.** The destruction, damage, or knowingly defective production of materials, premises, or utilities used for national defense or for war. 18 USCA §§ 2151 et seq. **2.** The willful and malicious destruction of an employer's property or interference with an employer's normal operations, esp. during a labor dispute. — **sabotage,** *vb.*

saboteur (sab-ə-**tər**), *n.* (1921) A person who commits sabotage.

SAET. *abbr.* Substance-abuse evaluation and treatment.

safe, *adj.* **1.** Not exposed to danger; not causing danger <driving at a safe limit of speed>. **2.** Unlikely to be overturned or proved wrong.

safe-deposit box. (1874) A lockbox stored in a bank's vault to secure a customer's valuables. • It usu. takes two keys (one held by the bank and one held by the customer) to open the box.

safe-deposit company. DEPOSITARY (1).

safe harbor. (1960) **1.** An area or means of protection. **2.** A provision (as in a statute or regulation) that affords protection from liability or penalty. • SEC regulations, for example, provide a safe harbor for an issuer's business forecasts that are made in good faith.

safe-haven law. *Family law.* A statute that protects a parent who abandons a baby at a designated place such as a hospital, a physician's office, or a fire station, where it can receive emergency medical assistance as needed.

safe house. A residence where people live under protection, usu. in anonymity.

said, *adj.* (13c) Aforesaid; above-mentioned. • The adjective *said* is obsolescent in legal drafting, its last bastion being patent claims. But even in that context the word is giving way to the ordinary word *the*, which if properly used is equally precise.

salable (**say**-lə-bəl *or* **sayl**-ə-bəl), *adj.* (16c) Fit for sale in the usual course of trade at the usual selling price; merchantable. — **salability** (say-lə-**bil**-ə-tee *or* sayl-ə-**bil**-ə-tee), *n.*

salary. (13c) An agreed compensation for services — esp. professional or semiprofessional services — usu. paid at regular intervals on a yearly basis, as distinguished from an hourly basis. • Salaried positions are usu. exempt from the requirements of the Fair Labor Standards Act (on overtime and the like) but are subject to state regulation.

sale, *n.* (bef. 12c) **1.** The transfer of property or title for a price. See UCC § 2-106(1). **2.** The agreement by which such a transfer takes place. • The four elements are (1) parties competent to contract, (2) mutual assent, (3) a thing capable of being transferred, and (4) a price in money paid or promised.

bona fide sale. A sale made by a seller in good faith, for valuable consideration, and without notice of a defect in title or any other reason not to hold the sale.

compulsory sale. The forced sale of real property in accordance with either an eminent-domain order or an order for a judicial sale arising from nonpayment of taxes.

distress sale. **1.** A form of liquidation in which the seller receives less for the goods than what would be received under normal sales conditions; esp., a going-out-of-business sale. **2.** A foreclosure or tax sale.

forced sale. **1.** Execution sale. **2.** A hurried sale by a debtor because of financial hardship or a creditor's action.

foreclosure sale. The sale of mortgaged property, authorized by a court decree or a power-of-sale clause, to satisfy the debt.

fraudulent sale. A sale made to defraud the seller's creditors by converting into cash property that should be used to satisfy the creditors' claims.

judicial sale. A sale conducted under the authority of a judgment or court order, such as an execution sale.

sale as is. A sale in which the buyer accepts the property in its existing condition unless the seller has misrepresented its quality.

sale on approval. A sale in which completion hinges on the buyer's satisfaction, regardless of whether the goods conform to the contract. • Title and risk of loss remain with the seller until the buyer approves. UCC § 2-326(1)(a).

sheriff's sale. **1.** Execution sale. **2.** Judicial sale.

short sale. *Securities.* A sale of a security that the seller does not own or has not contracted for at the time of sale, and that the seller must borrow to make delivery. • Such a sale is usu. made when the seller expects the security's price to drop. If the price does drop, the seller can make a profit on the difference between the price of the shares sold and the lower price of the shares bought to pay back the borrowed shares.

tax sale. A sale of property because of nonpayment of taxes.

sale or exchange. (1905) **1.** *Tax.* A voluntary transfer of property for value (as distinguished from a gift) resulting in a gain or loss recognized for federal tax purposes. **2.** A transfer of property; esp., a situation in which proceeds of a sale are to be vested in another estate of the same character and use.

sales agreement. (1920) A contract in which ownership of property is presently transferred, or will be transferred in the future, from a seller to a buyer for a fixed sum. UCC § 2-106(1).

salvage (**sal**-vij), *n.* **1.** The rescue of imperiled property. **2.** The property saved or remaining after a fire or other loss, sometimes retained by an insurance company that has compensated the owner for the loss. **3.** Compensation allowed to a person who, having no duty to do so, helps save a ship or its cargo. — **salvage,** *vb.*

same, *pron.* (14c) The very thing just mentioned or described; it or them <two days after receiving the goods, Mr. Siviglio returned same>.

same-actor inference. *Employment law.* The doctrine that when an employee is hired and fired by the same person, and the termination occurs a reasonably short time after the hiring, the termination will be presumed not to be based on a discriminatory reason.

same-conduct test. *Criminal law.* A test for determining whether a later charge arising out of a single incident is barred by the Double Jeopardy Clause; specif., an analysis of whether the later charge requires the state to prove the same conduct that it was required to prove in a previous trial against the same defendant. • The Supreme Court abandoned the *Blockburger* test and adopted the same-conduct test in 1990 (*Grady v. Corbin*, 495 U.S. 508, 110 S.Ct. 2084), but overruled that decision and revived *Blockburger* three years later (*U.S. v. Dixon*, 509 U.S. 688, 113 S.Ct. 2849 (1993)).

same-elements test. **1.** *Blockburger* test. **2.** Legal-elements test.

sampling, *n. Copyright.* The process of taking a small portion of a sound recording and digitally manipulating it as part of a new recording.

sanction (**sangk**-shən), *n.* (15c) **1.** Official approval or authorization <the committee gave sanction to the proposal>. **2.** A penalty or coercive measure that results from failure to comply with a law, rule, or order <a sanction for discovery abuse>.

criminal sanction. (1872) A sanction attached to a criminal conviction, such as a fine or restitution.

death-penalty sanction. (1991) *Civil procedure.* A court's order dismissing the suit or entering a default judgment in favor of the plaintiff because of extreme discovery abuses by a party or because of a party's action or inaction that shows an unwillingness to participate in the case. • Such a sanction is rarely ordered, and is usu. preceded by orders of lesser sanctions that have not been complied with or that have not remedied the problem.

shame sanction. (1991) A criminal sanction designed to stigmatize or disgrace a convicted offender, and often to alert the public about the offender's conviction. • A shame sanction usu. publicly associates the offender with the crime that he or she committed. An example is being required to post a sign in one's yard stating, "Convicted Child Molester Lives Here."

sanction, *vb.* (18c) **1.** To approve, authorize, or support <the court will sanction the trust disposition if it is not against public policy>. **2.** To penalize by imposing a sanction <the court sanctioned the attorney for violating the gag order>.

sanctionable, *adj.* (18c) (Of conduct or action) meriting sanctions; likely to be sanctioned.

sanctions tort. A means of recovery for another party's discovery abuse, whereby the judge orders the abusive party to pay a fine to the injured party for the discovery violation. • This is not a tort in the traditional sense, but rather a form of punishment that results in monetary gain for the injured party.

sanctity of contract. (1831) The principle that the parties to a contract, having duly entered into it, must honor their obligations under it.

sanctuary. (14c) A safe place, esp. where legal process cannot be executed; asylum.

sandbagging, *n.* A trial lawyer's remaining cagily silent when a possible error occurs at trial, with the hope of preserving an issue for appeal if the court does not correct the problem. • Such a tactic does not usu. preserve the issue for appeal because objections must be promptly made to alert the trial judge of the possible error. — **sandbag,** *vb.*

S & L. *abbr.* Savings-and-loan association.

sandpapering, *n.* A lawyer's general preparation of a witness before a deposition or trial.

sane, *adj.* (17c) Having a relatively sound and healthy mind; capable of reason and of distinguishing right from wrong. — **sanity,** *n.* (15c).

sanitary code. A set of ordinances regulating the food and healthcare industries.

sanity hearing. (1925) **1.** An inquiry into the mental competency of a person to stand trial. **2.** A proceeding to determine whether a person should be institutionalized.

satellite litigation. (1983) **1.** One or more lawsuits related to a major piece of litigation that is being conducted in another court <the satellite litigation in state court prevented the federal judge from ruling on the issue>. **2.** Peripheral skirmishes involved in the prosecution of a lawsuit <the plaintiffs called the sanctions "satellite litigation," drummed up by the defendants to deflect attention from the main issues in the case>.

satisfaction, *n.* (14c) **1.** The giving of something with the intention, express or implied, that it is to extinguish some existing legal or moral obligation. • Satisfaction differs from performance because it is always something given as a substitute for or equivalent of something else, while performance is the identical thing promised to be done. **2.** The fulfillment of an obligation; esp., the payment in full of a debt. **3.** Satisfaction piece. **4.** *Wills & estates.* The payment by a testator, during the testator's lifetime, of a legacy provided for in a will; advancement. **5.** *Wills & estates.* A testamentary gift intended to satisfy a debt owed by the testator to a creditor. — **satisfy,** *vb.*

satisfaction of judgment. (17c) **1.** The complete discharge of obligations under a judgment. **2.** The document filed and entered on the record indicating that a judgment has been paid.

satisfaction of lien. (1833) **1.** The fulfillment of all obligations made the subject of a lien. **2.** The document signed by the lienholder releasing the property subject to a lien.

satisfaction of mortgage. (18c) **1.** The complete payment of a mortgage. **2.** A discharge signed by the mortgagee or mortgage holder indicating that the property subject to the mortgage is released or that the mortgage debt has been paid and the mortgage conditions have been fully satisfied.

satisfaction piece. (1831) A written statement that one party (esp. a debtor) has discharged its obligation to another party, who accepts the discharge.

Saturday-night special. (1959) **1.** A handgun that is easily obtained and concealed. **2.** *Corporations.* A surprise tender offer typically held open for a limited offering period (such as one week) to maximize pressure on a shareholder to accept. • These tender offers are now effectively prohibited by section 14(e) of the Williams Act. 15 USCA § 78n(e).

save harmless. To hold harmless.

save-harmless clause. Indemnity clause.

saving, *n.* An exception; a reservation.

saving clause. (17c) **1.** A statutory provision exempting from coverage something that would otherwise be included. • A saving clause is generally used in a repealing act to preserve rights and claims that would otherwise be lost. **2.** Saving-to-suitors clause. **3.** Severability clause.

savings account. A savings-bank depositor's account usu. bearing interest or containing conditions (such as advance notice) to the right of withdrawal.

savings-account trust. Totten trust.

savings-and-loan association. (1884) A financial institution — often organized and chartered like a bank — that primarily makes home-mortgage loans but also usu. maintains checking accounts and provides other banking services. — Often shortened to S & L.

savor, *vb.* (16c) To partake of the character of or bear affinity to (something). • In traditional legal idiom, an interest arising from land is said to "savor of the realty."

S.B. Senate bill.

SBA. *abbr.* Small Business Administration.

sc. *abbr.* Scilicet.

S.C. *abbr.* **1.** Supreme Court. **2.** Same case. • In former practice, when put between two citations, the abbreviation indicated that the same case was reported in both places.

scab. (18c) A person who works under conditions contrary to a union contract; esp., a worker who crosses a union picket line to replace a union worker during a strike.

scale, *n.* **1.** A progression of degrees; esp., a range of wage rates. **2.** A wage according to a range of rates.

scalping, *n.* **1.** The practice of selling something (esp. a ticket) at a price above face value once it becomes scarce (usu. just before a high-demand event begins). **2.** The purchase of a security by an investment adviser before the adviser recommends that a customer buy the same security. • This practice is usu. considered unethical because the customer's purchase will increase the security's price, thus enabling the investment adviser to sell at a profit. **3.** The excessive markup or markdown on a transaction by a market-maker. • This action violates National Association of Securities Dealers guidelines. — **scalp,** *vb.* — **scalper,** *n.*

scandal. 1. Disgraceful, shameful, or degrading acts or conduct. **2.** Defamatory reports or rumors; esp., slander.

scandalous matter. (17c) *Civil procedure.* A matter that is both grossly disgraceful (or defamatory) and irrelevant to the action or defense. • A federal court — upon a party's motion or on its own — can order a scandalous matter struck from a pleading. Fed. R. Civ. P. 12(f).

scandalous subject matter. *Trademarks.* A word, phrase, symbol, or graphic depiction that the U.S. Patent and Trademark Office may refuse to register because it is shockingly offensive to social mores. • Although the Lanham Act uses the phrase "immoral, deceptive, or scandalous subject matter," courts have not distinguished "scandalous" from "immoral."

scatter-point analysis. (1993) A method for studying the effect that minority-population changes have on voting patterns, involving a plotting of the percentage of votes that candidates receive to determine whether voting percentages increase or decrease as the percentages of voters of a particular race increase or decrease.

schedule, *n.* (15c) A written list or inventory; esp., a statement that is attached to a document and that gives a detailed showing of the matters referred to in the document <Schedule B to the title policy lists the encumbrances on the property>. — **schedule,** *vb.* — **scheduled,** *adj.*

scheme. (16c) **1.** A systemic plan; a connected or orderly arrangement, esp. of related concepts <legislative scheme>. **2.** An artful plot or plan, usu. to deceive others <a scheme to defraud creditors>.

schism (**siz**-əm *or* **skiz**-əm). (14c) **1.** A breach or rupture; a division, esp. among members of a group, as of a union. **2.** A separation of beliefs and doctrines by persons of the same organized religion, religious denomination, or sect.

school, *n.* **1.** An institution of learning and education, esp. for children. **2.** The collective body of students under instruction in an institution of learning. **3.** A group of people adhering to the same philosophy or system of beliefs.

school board. An administrative body, made up of a number of directors or trustees, responsible for overseeing public schools within a city, county, or district.

school district. A political subdivision of a state, created by the legislature and invested with local powers of self-government, to build, maintain, fund, and support the public schools within its territory and to otherwise assist the state in administering its educational responsibilities.

Schumer box. In a credit-card agreement, a table that summarizes all the costs for which the cardholder is liable, so that the cardholder can more easily compare credit-card agreements. • The term derives from the name of Senator Charles Schumer, who proposed the disclosure requirements. The box must contain the information listed in 15 USCA § 1637(c)(1)(A)–(B).

Science and Technology Directorate. The division of the Department of Homeland Security responsible for coordinating research and development, including preparing for and responding to terrorist threats involving weapons of mass destruction. — Abbr. S&T.

scienter (sɪ-**en**-tər *or* see-), *n.* [Latin "knowingly"] (1824) **1.** A degree of knowledge that makes a person legally responsible for the consequences of his or her act or omission; the fact of an act's having been done knowingly, esp. as a ground for civil damages or criminal punishment. **2.** A mental state consisting in an intent to deceive, manipulate, or defraud. • In this sense, the term is used most often in the context of securities fraud.

scientific method. An analytical technique by which a hypothesis is formulated and then systematically tested through observation and experimentation.

sci. fa. *abbr.* Scire facias.

scil. *abbr.* Scilicet.

scilicet (**sil**-ə-set *or* -sit). [fr. Latin *scire licet* "that you may know"] (14c) That is to say; namely; VIDELICET. • Like *videlicet*, this word is used in pleadings and other instruments to introduce a more particular statement of matters previously mentioned in general terms. It has never been quite as common, however, as *videlicet*. — Abbr. sc.; scil.; (erroneously) ss.

scintilla (sin-**til**-ə). (13c) A spark or trace <the standard is that there must be more than a scintilla of evidence>. Pl. **scintillas** (sin-**til**-əz).

scintilla-of-evidence rule. (1896) A common-law doctrine holding that if even the slightest amount of relevant evidence exists on an issue, then a motion for summary judgment or for directed verdict cannot be granted and the issue must go to the jury. • Federal courts do not follow this rule, but some states apply it.

scire facias (**sɪ**-ree **fay**-shee-əs). [Law Latin "you are to make known, show cause"] (15c) A writ requiring the person against whom it is issued to appear and show cause why some matter of record should not be annulled or vacated, or why a dormant judgment against that person should not be revived. — Abbr. *sci. fa.*

scofflaw (**skof**-law). (1924) A person who treats the law with contempt; esp., one who avoids various laws that are not easily enforced <some scofflaws carry mannequins in their cars in order to drive in the carpool lane>.

scope note. (1903) In a digest, a précis appearing after a title and showing concisely what subject matter is included and what is excluded.

scope of authority. (1805) *Agency.* The range of reasonable power that an agent has been delegated or might foreseeably be delegated in carrying out the principal's business.

scope of business. The range of activities that are reasonably necessary to operate a commercial venture successfully, as determined by the nature of the venture and the activities of others engaged in the same occupation in the same area.

scope of employment. (1836) The range of reasonable and foreseeable activities that an employee engages in while carrying out the employer's business; the field of action in which a servant is authorized to act in the master–servant relationship.

scope-of-work clause. A contractual provision that highlights in summary fashion what work is to be performed under the contract.

scribe. SECRETARY (3).

scrip. (18c) **1.** A document that entitles the holder to receive something of value. **2.** Money, esp. paper money, that is issued for temporary use.

script. (14c) **1.** An original or principal writing. **2.** Handwriting.

scrivener (**skriv**-[ə]-nər). (14c) A writer; esp., a professional drafter of contracts or other documents.

scrivener's error. Clerical error.

scrivener's exception. (1978) An exemption from the attorney–client privilege whereby the privilege does not attach if the attorney is retained solely to perform a ministerial task for the client, such as preparing a statutory-form deed.

scroll, *n.* (15c) **1.** A roll of paper, esp. one containing a writing; a list. **2.** A draft or outline to be completed at a later time. **3.** A written mark; esp., a character affixed to a signature in place of a seal.

S.Ct. *abbr.* **1.** Supreme Court. **2.** *Supreme Court Reporter.*

S.D. *abbr.* Southern District, in reference to U.S. judicial districts.

S.E. *abbr. South Eastern Reporter.*

seal, *n.* (13c) **1.** A fastening that must be broken before access can be obtained; esp., a device or substance that joins two things, usu. making the seam impervious. **2.** A piece of wax, a wafer, or some other substance affixed to the paper or other material on which a promise, release, or conveyance is written, together with a recital or expression of intention by which the promisor, releasor, or grantor manifests that a piece of wax, wafer, or other substance is a seal. • The purpose of a seal is to secure or prove authenticity. **3.** A design embossed or stamped on paper to authenticate, confirm, or attest; an impression or sign that has legal consequence when applied to an instrument.

corporate seal. (18c) A seal adopted by a corporation for executing and authenticating its corporate and legal instruments.

great seal. **1.** The official seal of the United States, of which the Secretary of State is the custodian. **2.** The official seal of a particular state.

private seal. (16c) A corporate or individual seal, as distinguished from a public seal.

public seal. (16c) A seal used to certify documents belonging to a public authority or government bureau.

seal, *vb.* (14c) **1.** To authenticate or execute (a document) by use of a seal. **2.** To close (an envelope, etc.) tightly; to prevent access to (a document, record, etc.).

sea lane. *Int'l & maritime law.* A designated course or regularly used route for ships, esp. in restricted waters such as harbors and straits.

sealed-container rule. (1961) *Products liability.* The principle that a seller is not liable for a defective product if the seller receives the product from the manufacturer and sells it without knowing of the defect or having a reasonable opportunity to inspect the product.

sealed instrument. (17c) At common law and under some statutes, an instrument to which the bound party has affixed a personal seal, usu. recognized as providing indisputable evidence of the validity of the underlying obligations. • The common-law distinction between sealed and unsealed instruments has been abolished by many states, and the UCC provides that the laws applicable to sealed instruments do not apply to contracts for the sale of goods or negotiable instruments. UCC § 2-203.

sealed will. Mystic will.

sealing of records. (1953) The act or practice of officially preventing access to particular (esp. juvenile-criminal) records, in the absence of a court order.

seaman. *Maritime law.* Under the Jones Act and the Longshore and Harbor Workers' Compensation Act, a person who is attached to a navigating vessel as an employee below the rank of officer and contributes to the function of the vessel or the accomplishment of its mission. • Seamen's injuries are covered under the Jones Act and the general maritime law.

able-bodied seaman. An experienced seaman who is qualified for all seaman's duties and certified by an inspecting authority. — Abbr. AB; ABS.

merchant seaman. A sailor employed by a private vessel, as distinguished from one employed in public or military service.

ordinary seaman. A seaman who has some experience but who is not proficient enough to be classified as an able-bodied seaman.

search, *n.* (14c) **1.** *Criminal procedure.* An examination of a person's body, property, or other area that the person would reasonably be expected to consider as private, conducted by a law-enforcement officer for the purpose of finding evidence of a crime. • Because the Fourth Amendment prohibits unreasonable searches (as well as seizures), a search cannot ordinarily be conducted without probable cause.

administrative search. (1963) A search of public or commercial premises carried out by a regulatory authority to enforce compliance with health, safety, or security regulations. • The probable cause required for an administrative search is less stringent than that required for a search incident to a criminal investigation.

border search. (1922) **1.** A search conducted at the border of a country, esp. at a checkpoint, to exclude illegal aliens and contraband. **2.** Loosely, a search conducted near the border of a country.

checkpoint search. (1973) **1.** A search anywhere on a military installation. **2.** A search in which police officers set up roadblocks and stop motorists to ascertain whether the drivers are intoxicated.

Chimel search. Protective search.

consent search. (1965) A search conducted after a person with the authority to do so voluntarily waives Fourth Amendment rights. • The government has the burden to show that the consent was given freely — not under duress. *Bumper v. North Carolina*, 391 U.S. 543, 548–49, 88 S.Ct. 1788, 1792 (1968).

emergency search. (1971) A warrantless search conducted by a police officer who has probable cause and reasonably believes that, because of a need to protect life or property, there is not enough time to obtain a warrant.

exigent search (**eks**-ə-jənt). (1974) A warrantless search carried out under exigent circumstances, such as an imminent danger to human life or a risk of the destruction of evidence.

inventory search. (1966) A complete search of an arrestee's person before that person is booked into jail. • All possessions found are typically held in police custody.

no-knock search. (1970) A search of property by the police without knocking and announcing their presence and purpose before entry. • A no-knock search warrant may be issued under limited circumstances, as when a prior announcement would probably lead to the destruction of the objects searched for, or would endanger the safety of the police or another person.

private search. A search conducted by a private person rather than by a law-enforcement officer. • Items found during a private search are generally admissible in evidence if the person conducting the search was not acting at the direction of a law-enforcement officer.

protective search. (1967) A search of a detained suspect and the area within the suspect's immediate control, conducted to protect the arresting officer's safety (as from a concealed weapon) and often to preserve evidence. • A protective search can be conducted without a warrant. *Chimel v. California*, 395 U.S. 752, 89 S.Ct. 2034 (1969).

shakedown search. (1952) A usu. unannounced and warrantless search for illicit or contraband material (such as weapons or drugs) in a prisoner's cell.

strip search. (1955) A search of a person conducted after that person's clothes have been removed, the purpose usu. being to find any contraband the person might be hiding.

unreasonable search. (18c) A search conducted without probable cause or other considerations that would make it legally permissible.

voluntary search. (1936) A search in which no duress or coercion was applied to obtain the defendant's consent.

warranted search. (1968) A search conducted under authority of a search warrant.

warrantless search. (1950) A search conducted without obtaining a proper warrant. • Warrantless searches are permissible under exigent circumstances or when conducted incident to an arrest.

zone search. A search of a crime scene (such as the scene of a fire or explosion) by dividing it up into specific sectors.

2. An examination of public documents or records for information; esp., TITLE SEARCH. **3.** *Int'l law.* The wartime process of boarding and examining the contents of a merchant vessel for contraband.

search-and-seizure warrant. Search warrant.

search book. (1912) A lawbook that contains no statements of the law but instead consists of lists or tables of cases, statutes, and the like, used simply to help a researcher find the law. • Most indexes, other than index-digests, are search books.

search incident to arrest. Protective search.

search warrant. (18c) *Criminal law.* A judge's written order authorizing a law-enforcement officer to conduct a search of a specified place and to seize evidence. See Fed. R. Crim. P. 41.

anticipatory search warrant. (1912) A search warrant based on an affidavit showing probable cause that evidence of a certain crime (such as illegal drugs) will be located at a specific place in the future.

blanket search warrant. (1921) **1.** A single search warrant that authorizes the search of more than one area. **2.** An unconstitutional warrant that authorizes the seizure of everything found at a given location, without specifying which items may be seized.

covert-entry search warrant. A warrant authorizing law-enforcement officers to clandestinely enter private premises in the absence of the owner or occupant without prior notice, and to search the premises and collect intangible evidence, esp. photographs and eyewitness information. • Although previously used in federal criminal investigations, these types of warrants were first given express statutory authority by the USA Patriot Act. 18 USCA § 3103a. Information gathered while executing a sneak-and-peek warrant can later be used to support a search warrant under which physical evidence can be seized.

no-knock search warrant. (1972) A search warrant that authorizes the police to enter premises without knocking and announcing their presence and purpose before entry because a prior announcement would lead to the destruction of the objects searched for or would endanger the safety of the police or another person.

sneak-and-peek search warrant. Covert-entry search warrant.

sea rover. **1.** A person who roves the sea for plunder; a pirate. **2.** A pirate vessel.

seasonable, *adj.* (15c) Within the time agreed on; within a reasonable time <seasonable performance of the contract>.

seat, *n.* **1.** Membership and privileges in an organization; esp., membership on a securities or commodities exchange <her seat at the exchange dates back to 1998>. **2.** The center of some activity <the seat of government>.

sec. *abbr.* **1.** (all cap.) Securities and Exchange Commission. **2.** Section.

secession. The process or act of withdrawing, esp. from a religious or political association <the secession from the established church> <the secession of 11 states at the time of the Civil War>.

Second Amendment. The constitutional amendment, ratified with the Bill of Rights in 1791, guaranteeing the right to keep and bear arms as necessary for securing freedom through a well-regulated militia.

secondary, *adj.* (14c) (Of a position, status, use, etc.) subordinate or subsequent.

secondary-effects test. A court's analysis of a regulation affecting free-speech interests to determine whether it is actually intended to diminish or eliminate an indirect harm flowing from the regulated expression. • The test is used to distinguish content-specific regulation from content-neutral regulation. A regulation that is facially content-specific may be treated as content-neutral if its purpose is to diminish or eliminate a secondary effect of the speech, such as a zoning regulation for adult theaters when it is intended to limit crime. The test was first enunciated in *City of Renton v. Playtime Theatres, Inc.*, 475 U.S. 41, 106 S.Ct. 925 (1986).

secondary lender. A wholesale mortgage buyer who purchases first mortgages from banks and savings-and-loan associations, enabling them to restock their money supply and loan more money.

secondary term. *Oil & gas.* The term of an oil-and-gas lease after production has been established, typically lasting "as long thereafter as oil and gas is produced from the premises."

second chair, *n.* (1968) A lawyer who helps the lead attorney in court, usu. by examining some of the witnesses, arguing some of the points of law, and handling parts of the voir dire, opening statement, and closing argument <the young associate was second chair for the fraud case>. — **second-chair,** *vb.*

second-look doctrine. (1962) **1.** Wait-and-see principle. **2.** An approach that courts use to monitor the continuing effectiveness or validity of an earlier order. • For example, a family court may reconsider a waiver of alimony, and a federal court may reconsider a law that Congress has passed a second time after the first law was struck down as unconstitutional.

secret, *n.* (14c) **1.** Something that is kept from the knowledge of others or shared only with those concerned. **2.** Information that cannot be disclosed without a breach of trust; specif., information that is acquired in the attorney–client relationship and that either (1) the client has requested be kept private or (2) the attorney believes would be embarrassing or likely to be detrimental to the client if disclosed. • Under the ABA Code of Professional Responsibility, a lawyer usu. cannot reveal a client's secret unless the client consents after full disclosure. DR 4–101.

secretary. 1. An administrative assistant. **2.** A corporate officer in charge of official correspondence, minutes of board meetings, and records of stock ownership and transfer. **3.** *Parliamentary law.* An officer charged with recording a deliberative assembly's proceedings.

corresponding secretary. An officer in charge of an organization's correspondence, usu. including notices to members.

***financial secretary.* 1.** An officer in charge of billing, collecting, and accounting for dues from the members. **2.** Treasurer.

Secretary General. The chief administrative officer of the United Nations, nominated by the Security Council and elected by the General Assembly.

Secretary of Defense. The member of the President's cabinet who heads the U.S. Department of Defense.

Secretary of Homeland Security. The member of the President's cabinet who heads the U.S. Department of Homeland Security.

Secretary of State. (18c) **1.** The member of the President's cabinet who heads the U.S. Department of State. • The Secretary is the first-ranking member of the cabinet and is also a member of the National Security Council. He or she is fourth in line of succession to the presidency after the Vice President, the Speaker of the House, and the President pro tempore of the Senate. **2.** A state government official who is responsible for the licensing and incorporation of businesses, the administration of elections, and other formal duties. • The secretary of state is elected in some states and appointed in others.

Secretary of the Treasury. The member of the President's cabinet who heads the U.S. Department of the Treasury.

secrete (si-**kreet**), *vb.* (17c) To conceal or secretly transfer (property, etc.), esp. to hinder or prevent officials or creditors from finding it.

secretion of assets. The hiding of property, usu. for the purpose of defrauding an adversary in litigation or a creditor.

secret session. Executive session.

secret will. Mystic will.

section. (16c) **1.** A distinct part or division of a writing, esp. a legal instrument. — Abbr. §; sec.; s. **2.** *Real estate.* A piece of land containing 640 acres, or one square mile. • Traditionally, public lands in the United States were divided into 640-acre squares, each one called a "section."

secular, *adj.* Worldly, as distinguished from spiritual <secular business>.

secured, *adj.* (1875) **1.** (Of a debt or obligation) supported or backed by security or collateral. **2.** (Of a creditor) protected by a pledge, mortgage, or other encumbrance of property that helps ensure financial soundness and confidence.

secured transaction. (1936) A business arrangement by which a buyer or borrower gives collateral to the seller or lender to guarantee payment of an obligation. • Article 9 of the UCC deals with secured transactions.

securities act. (1933) A federal or state law protecting the public by regulating the registration, offering, and trading of securities.

Securities Act of 1933. The federal law regulating the registration and initial public offering of securities, with an emphasis on full public disclosure of financial and other information. 15 USCA §§ 77a–77aa.

securities analyst. A person, usu. an employee of a bank, brokerage, or mutual fund, who studies a company and reports on the company's securities, financial condition, and prospects.

Securities and Exchange Commission. The five-member federal agency that regulates the issuance and trading of securities to protect investors against fraudulent or unfair practices. • The Commission was established by the Securities Exchange Act of 1934.

securities exchange. (1909) **1.** A marketplace or facility for the organized purchase and sale of securities, esp. stocks. **2.** A group of people who organize themselves to create such a marketplace; EXCHANGE (5).

regional securities exchange. A securities exchange that focuses on stocks and bonds of local interest, such as the Boston, Philadelphia, and Midwest stock exchanges.

Securities Exchange Act of 1934. The federal law regulating the public trading of securities. • This law provides for periodic disclosures by issuers of securities and for the registration and supervision of securities exchanges and brokers, and regulates proxy solicitations. The Act also established the SEC. 15 USCA §§ 78a et seq.

Securities Investor Protection Corporation. A federally chartered corporation established under the 1970 Securities Investor Protection Act to protect investors and help brokers in financial trouble. — Abbr. SIPC.

securitize, *vb.* To convert (assets) into negotiable securities for resale in the financial market, allowing the issuing financial institution to remove assets from its books, and thereby improve its capital ratio and liquidity, and to make new loans with the security proceeds if it so chooses. — **securitized, securitizable,** *adj.* — **securitization,** *n.*

security, *n.* (15c) **1.** Collateral given or pledged to guarantee the fulfillment of an obligation; esp., the assurance that a creditor will be repaid (usu. with interest) any money or credit extended to a debtor. **2.** A person who is bound by some type of guaranty; surety. **3.** The state of being secure, esp. from danger or attack. **4.** An instrument that evidences the holder's ownership rights in a firm (e.g., a stock), the holder's creditor relationship with a firm or government (e.g., a bond), or the holder's other rights (e.g., an option). • A security indicates an interest based on an investment in a common enterprise rather than direct participation in the enterprise. Under an important statutory definition, a security is any interest or instrument relating to finances, including a note, stock, treasury stock, bond, debenture, evidence of indebtedness, certificate of interest or participation in a profit-sharing agreement, collateral trust certificate, preorganization certificate or subscription, transferable share, investment contract, voting trust certificate, certificate of deposit for a security, fractional undivided interest in oil, gas, or other mineral rights, or certificate of interest or participation in, temporary or interim certificate for, receipt for, guarantee of, or warrant or right to subscribe to or purchase any of these things. A security also includes any put, call, straddle, option, or privilege on any security, certificate of deposit, group or index of securities, or any such device entered into on a national securities exchange, relating to foreign currency. 15 USCA § 77b(1).

security agreement. An agreement that creates or provides for an interest in specified real or personal property to guarantee the performance of an obligation. • It must provide for a security interest, describe the collateral, and be signed by the debtor. The agreement may include other important covenants and warranties.

Security Council. A principal organ of the United Nations, consisting of five permanent members (China, France, Russia, the United Kingdom, and the United States) and ten additional members elected at stated intervals, charged with the responsibility of maintaining international peace and security, and esp. of preventing or halting wars by diplomatic, economic, or military action.

security for costs. (17c) Money, property, or a bond given to a court by a plaintiff or an appellant to secure the payment of court costs if that party loses.

security interest. (1951) A property interest created by agreement or by operation of law to secure performance of an obligation (esp. repayment of a debt). • Although the UCC limits the creation of a security interest to personal property, the Bankruptcy Code defines the term to mean "a lien created by an agreement." 11 USCA § 101(51).

perfected security interest. (1955) A security interest that complies with the statutory requirements for achieving priority over a trustee in bankruptcy and unperfected interests. • A perfected interest may also have priority over another interest that was perfected later in time.

purchase-money security interest. (1957) A security interest that is created when a buyer uses the lender's money to make the purchase and immediately gives the lender security by using the purchased property as collateral (UCC § 9-107); a security interest that is either (1) taken or retained by the seller of the collateral to secure all or part of its price or (2) taken by a person who by making advances or incurring an obligation gives value to enable the debtor to acquire rights in or the use of collateral if that value is in fact so used. • If a buyer's purchase of a boat, for example, is financed by a bank that loans the amount of the purchase price, the bank's security interest in the boat that secures the loan is a purchase-money security interest. — Abbr. PMSI.

unperfected security interest. (1957) A security interest held by a creditor who has not established priority over any other creditor. • The only priority is over the debtor.

security rating. 1. The system for grading or classifying a security by financial strength, stability, or risk. • Firms such as *Standard and Poor's* and *Moody's* grade securities. **2.** The classification that a given security is assigned to under this system.

sedition, *n.* (14c) **1.** An agreement, communication, or other preliminary activity aimed at inciting treason or some lesser commotion against public authority. **2.** Advocacy aimed at inciting or producing — and likely to incite or produce — imminent lawless action. • At common law, sedition included defaming a member of the royal family or the government. The difference between *sedition* and *treason* is that the former is committed by preliminary steps, while the latter entails some overt act for carrying out the plan. But if the plan is merely for some small commotion, even accomplishing the plan does not amount to treason. — **seditious,** *adj.*

seduction. (16c) The offense that occurs when a man entices a woman of previously chaste character to have unlawful intercourse with him by means of persuasion, solicitation, promises, or bribes, or other means not involving force. • Though seduction was not a crime at common law, many American states made it a statutory crime until the late 20th century. Many states have abolished this offense for persons over the age of legal consent.

seed money. Start-up money for a business venture.

segregation, *n.* (16c) **1.** The act or process of separating.

punitive segregation. (1958) The act of removing a prisoner from the prison population for placement in separate or solitary confinement, usu. for disciplinary reasons.

2. The unconstitutional policy of separating people on the basis of color, nationality, religion, or the like. — **segregate,** *vb.* — **segregative,** *adj.*

de facto segregation. (1958) Segregation that occurs without state authority, usu. on the basis of socioeconomic factors.

de jure segregation. (1963) Segregation that is permitted by law.

seise (seez), *vb.* To invest with seisin or establish as a holder in fee simple; to put in possession <he became seised of half a section of farmland near Amarillo>.

seisin (**see**-zin), *n.* (14c) Possession of a freehold estate in land; ownership.

seisin in deed. (17c) Actual possession of a freehold estate in land, by oneself or by one's tenant or agent, as distinguished from legal possession.

seisin in law. (17c) The right to immediate possession of a freehold estate in land, as when an heir inherits land but has not yet entered it.

seize, *vb.* (13c) **1.** To forcibly take possession (of a person or property). **2.** To place (someone) in possession. **3.** To be in possession (of property). **4.** To be informed of or aware of (something).

seizure, *n.* (15c) The act or an instance of taking possession of a person or property by legal right or process; esp., in constitutional law, a confiscation or arrest that may interfere with a person's reasonable expectation of privacy.

selective disclosure. (1963) The act of divulging part of a privileged communication, or one of several privileged communications, usu. because the divulged portion is helpful to the party giving the information, while harmful portions of the communication are withheld. • Such a disclosure can result in a limited waiver of the privilege for all communications on the same subject matter as the divulged portion.

selective enforcement. (1958) The practice of law-enforcement officers who use wide or even unfettered discretion about when and where to carry out certain laws; esp., the practice of singling a person out for prosecution or punishment under a statute or regulation because the person is a member of a protected group or because the person has exercised or is planning to exercise a constitutionally protected right.

selective prosecution. (1967) **1.** SELECTIVE ENFORCEMENT. **2.** The practice or an instance of a criminal prosecution brought at the discretion of a prosecutor rather than one brought as a matter of course in the normal functioning of the prosecuting authority's office. • Selective prosecution violates the Equal Protection Clause of the Fourteenth Amendment if a defendant is singled out for prosecution when others similarly situated have not been prosecuted and the prosecutor's reasons for doing so are impermissible.

selective prospectivity. (1991) A court's decision to apply a new rule of law in the particular case in which the new rule is announced, but to apply the old rule in all other cases pending at the time the new rule is announced or in which the facts predate the new rule's announcement.

selectman. A municipal officer elected annually in some New England towns to transact business and perform some executive functions.

self-applying, *adj.* (1894) (Of a statute, ordinance, etc.) requiring no more for interpretation than a familiarity with the ordinary meanings of words.

self-dealing, *n.* (1940) Participation in a transaction that benefits oneself instead of another who is owed a fiduciary duty. • For example, a corporate director might engage in self-dealing by participating in a competing business to the corporation's detriment. — **self-deal,** *vb.*

self-defense, *n.* (1651) The use of force to protect oneself, one's family, or one's property from a real or threatened attack. • Generally, a person is justified in using a reasonable amount of force in self-defense if he or she reasonably believes that the danger of bodily harm is imminent and that force is necessary to avoid this danger.

imperfect self-defense. (1882) The use of force by one who makes an honest but unreasonable mistake that force is necessary to repel an attack. • In some jurisdictions, such a self-defender will be charged with a lesser offense than the one committed.

perfect self-defense. (1883) The use of force by one who accurately appraises the necessity and the amount of force to repel an attack.

self-destruct clause. A provision in a trust for a condition that will automatically terminate the trust. • Discretionary trusts, esp. supplemental-needs trusts, often include a self-destruct provision.

self-executing, *adj.* (1857) (Of an instrument) effective immediately without the need of any type of implementing action <the wills had self-executing affidavits attached>. • Legal instruments may be self-executing according to various standards. For example, treaties are self-executing under the Supremacy Clause of the U.S. Constitution (art. VI, § 2) if textually capable of judicial enforcement and intended to be enforced in that manner.

self-help, *n.* (1831) An attempt to redress a perceived wrong by one's own action rather than through the normal legal process. • The UCC and other statutes provide for particular self-help remedies (such as repossession) if the remedy can be executed without breaching the peace. UCC § 9-609.

self-incrimination. (1853) The act of indicating one's own involvement in a crime or exposing oneself to prosecution, esp. by making a statement.

Self-Incrimination Clause. (1925) The clause of the Fifth Amendment to the U.S. Constitution barring the government from compelling criminal defendants to testify against themselves.

self-regulatory organization. A nongovernmental organization that is statutorily empowered to regulate its members by adopting and enforcing rules of conduct, esp. those governing fair, ethical, and efficient practices. — Abbr. SRO.

self-stultification. (1862) The act or an instance of testifying about one's own deficiencies.

sell, *vb.* (bef. 12c) To transfer (property) by sale.

seller. (13c) **1.** A person who sells or contracts to sell goods; a vendor. UCC § 2-103(1)(d). **2.** Generally, a person who sells anything; the transferor of property in a contract of sale.

semble (**sem**-bəl). [Law French] (1817) It seems; it would appear <semble that the parties' intention was to create a binding agreement>. • This term is used chiefly to indicate an obiter dictum in a court opinion or to introduce an uncertain thought or interpretation. — Abbr. sem.; semb.

senate. (13c) **1.** The upper chamber of a bicameral legislature. **2.** (*cap.*) The upper house of the U.S. Congress, composed of 100 members — two from each state — who are elected to six-year terms. — Abbr. S.

senator. (13c) A person who is a member of a senate.

senatorial courtesy. (1884) **1.** The tradition that the President should take care in filling a high-level federal post (such as a judgeship) with a person agreeable to the senators from the nominee's home state, lest the senators defeat confirmation. **2.** Loosely, civility among senators <a decline of senatorial courtesy>.

senility. (18c) Mental feebleness or impairment caused by old age. • A senile person (in the legal, as opposed to the popular, sense) is incompetent to enter into a binding contract or to execute a will. — **senile,** *adj.*

senior, *adj.* (14c) **1.** (Of a debt, etc.) first; preferred, as over junior obligations. **2.** (Of a person) older than someone else. **3.** (Of a person) higher in rank or service. **4.** (Of a man) elder, as distinguished from the man's son who has the same name.

seniority. (15c) **1.** The preferential status, privileges, or rights given to an employee based on the employee's length of service with an employer. • Employees with seniority may receive additional or enhanced benefit packages and obtain competitive advantages over fellow employees in layoff and promotional decisions. **2.** The status of being older or senior.

seniority system. *Employment law.* Any arrangement that recognizes length of service in making decisions about job layoffs and promotions or other advancements.

senior party. *Intellectual property.* In an interference proceeding, the first person to file an application for a property's legal protection, e.g., an invention patent or a trademark registration.

senior status. (1970) The employment condition of a semiretired judge who continues to perform certain judicial duties that the judge is willing and able to undertake.

senior user. *Trademarks.* The first person to use a mark. • That person is usu. found to be the mark's owner.

sensitivity training. (1956) One or more instructional sessions for management and employees, designed to counteract the callous treatment of others, esp. women and minorities, in the workplace.

sentence, *n.* (14c) The judgment that a court formally pronounces after finding a criminal defendant guilty; the punishment imposed on a criminal wrongdoer <a sentence of 20 years in prison>. See Fed. R. Crim. P. 32. — **sentence,** *vb.*

aggregate sentence. (1917) A sentence that arises from a conviction on multiple counts in an indictment.

alternative sentence. (1841) A sentence other than incarceration. • Examples include community service and victim restitution.

blended sentence. In a juvenile-delinquency disposition, a sanction that combines delinquency sanctions and criminal punishment.

concurrent sentences. (1905) Two or more sentences of jail time to be served simultaneously. • For example, if a convicted criminal receives concurrent sentences of 5 years and 15 years, the total amount of jail time is 15 years.

conditional sentence. (1843) A sentence of confinement if the convicted criminal fails to perform the conditions of probation.

consecutive sentences. (1844) Two or more sentences of jail time to be served in sequence. • For example, if a convicted criminal receives consecutive sentences of 20 years and 5 years, the total amount of jail time is 25 years.

death sentence. (1811) A sentence that imposes the death penalty. See Model Penal Code § 210.6.

deferred sentence. (1915) A sentence that will not be carried out if the convicted criminal meets certain requirements, such as complying with conditions of probation.

delayed sentence. (1906) A sentence that is not imposed immediately after conviction, thereby allowing the convicted criminal to satisfy the court (usu. by complying with certain restrictions or conditions during the delay period) that probation is preferable to a prison sentence.

determinate sentence. (1885) A sentence for a fixed length of time rather than for an unspecified duration.

excessive sentence. (1879) A sentence that gives more punishment than is allowed by law.

fixed sentence. **1.** Determinate sentence. **2.** Mandatory sentence.

general sentence. (1891) An undivided, aggregate sentence in a multicount case; a sentence that does not specify the punishment imposed for each count. • General sentences are prohibited.

indeterminate sentence. (1885) **1.** A sentence of an unspecified duration, such as one for a term of 10 to 20 years. **2.** A maximum prison term that the parole board can reduce, through statutory authorization, after the inmate has served the minimum time required by law.

intermittent sentence. (1964) A sentence consisting of periods of confinement interrupted by periods of freedom.

life sentence. (1878) A sentence that imprisons the convicted criminal for life — though in some jurisdictions the prisoner may become eligible for release on good behavior, rehabilitation, or the like.

mandatory sentence. (1926) A sentence set by law with no discretion for the judge to individualize punishment.

maximum sentence. (1898) The highest level of punishment provided by law for a particular crime.

minimum sentence. (1891) The least amount of time that a convicted criminal must serve in prison before becoming eligible for parole.

multiple sentences. (1938) Concurrent or consecutive sentences, if a convicted criminal is found guilty of more than one offense.

nominal sentence. (1852) A criminal sentence in name only; an exceedingly light sentence.

noncustodial sentence. (1971) A criminal sentence (such as probation) not requiring prison time.

presumptive sentence. (1978) An average sentence for a particular crime (esp. provided under sentencing guidelines) that can be raised or lowered based on the presence of mitigating or aggravating circumstances.

prior sentence. (1863) A sentence previously imposed on a criminal defendant for a different offense, whether by a guilty verdict, a guilty plea, or a *nolo contendere.*

split sentence. (1927) A sentence in which part of the time is served in confinement — to expose the offender to the unpleasantness of prison — and the rest on probation.

straight sentence. Determinate sentence.

suspended sentence. (1919) A sentence postponed so that the convicted criminal is not required to serve time unless he or she commits another crime or violates some other court-imposed condition. • A suspended sentence, in effect, is a form of probation.

weekend sentence. Intermittent sentence.

sentence bargain. Plea bargain.

sentenced to time served. (1959) A sentencing disposition whereby a criminal defendant is sentenced to the same jail time that the defendant is credited with serving while in custody awaiting trial. • The sentence results in the defendant's release from custody.

sentence-package rule. (1996) *Criminal procedure.* The principle that a defendant can be resentenced on an aggregate sentence — that is, one arising from a conviction on multiple counts in an indictment — when the defendant successfully challenges part of the conviction, as by successfully challenging some but not all of the counts.

sentencing guidelines. (1970) A set of standards for determining the punishment that a convicted criminal should receive, based on the nature of the crime and the offender's criminal history. • The federal government and several states have adopted sentencing guidelines in an effort to make judicial sentencing more consistent.

sentencing hearing. Presentence hearing.

sentencing phase. Penalty phase.

Sentencing Reform Act of 1984. A federal statute enacted to bring greater uniformity to punishments assessed for federal crimes by creating a committee of federal judges and other officials (the United States Sentencing Commission) responsible for producing sentencing guidelines to be used by the federal courts. 28 USCA § 994(a)(1).

Sentencing Table. A reference guide used by federal courts to calculate the appropriate punishment under the sentencing guidelines by taking into account the gravity of the offense and the convicted person's criminal history.

separable, *adj.* (14c) Capable of being separated or divided <a separable controversy>.

separate, *adj.* (15c) (Of liability, cause of action, etc.) individual; distinct; particular; disconnected.

separate-but-equal doctrine. (1950) The now-defunct doctrine that African-Americans could be segregated if they were provided with equal opportunities and facilities in education, public transportation, and jobs. • This rule was established in *Plessy v. Ferguson*, 163 U.S. 537, 16 S.Ct. 1138 (1896), and overturned in *Brown v. Board of Education*, 347 U.S. 483, 74 S.Ct. 686 (1954).

separate examination. (18c) **1.** The private interrogation of a witness, apart from the other witnesses in the same case. **2.** The interrogation of a wife outside the presence of her husband by a court clerk or notary for the purpose of acknowledging a deed or other instrument. • This was done to ensure that the wife signed without being coerced to do so by her husband.

separate goodwill. Personal goodwill.

separate property. (18c) **1.** Property that a spouse owned before marriage or acquired during marriage by inheritance or by gift from a third party, and in some states property acquired during marriage but after the spouses have entered into a separation agreement and have begun living apart or after one spouse has commenced a divorce action. **2.** In some common-law states, property titled to one spouse or acquired by one spouse individually during marriage. **3.** Property acquired during the marriage in exchange for separate property (in sense 1 or sense 2).

separate-sovereigns rule. (1995) *Criminal procedure.* The principle that a person may be tried twice for the same offense — despite the Double Jeopardy Clause — if the prosecutions are conducted by separate sovereigns, as by the federal government and a state government or by two different states.

separation. (17c) **1.** An arrangement whereby a husband and wife live apart from each other while remaining married, either by mutual consent (often in a written agreement) or by judicial decree; the act of carrying out such an arrangement. **2.** The status of a husband and wife having begun such an arrangement, or the judgment or contract that brought about the arrangement.. **3.** Cessation of a contractual relationship, esp. in an employment situation. — **separate,** *vb.*

separation agreement. (1886) **1.** An agreement between spouses in the process of a divorce or legal separation concerning alimony, maintenance, property division, child custody and support, and the like. **2.** Divorce agreement.

separation of powers. (1896) The division of governmental authority into three branches of government — legislative, executive, and judicial — each with specified duties on which neither of the other branches can encroach; a constitutional doctrine of checks and balances designed to protect the people against tyranny.

separation of witnesses. (1819) The exclusion of witnesses (other than the plaintiff and defendant) from the courtroom to prevent them from hearing the testimony of others.

separation order. **1.** Separation agreement. **2.** ORDER (2).

separation pay. Severance pay.

SEP-IRA. Simplified employee pension plan.

sequester (si-**kwes**-tər), *n.* (14c) **1.** An across-the-board cut in government spending. **2.** A person with whom litigants deposit property being contested until the case has concluded; a sequestrator.

sequester, *vb.* (15c) **1.** To seize (property) by a writ of sequestration. **2.** To segregate or isolate (a jury or witness) during trial.

sequestration (see-kwes-**tray**-shən), *n.* (16c) **1.** The process by which property is removed from the possessor pending the outcome of a dispute in which two or more parties contend for it. **2.** The setting apart of a decedent's personal property when no one has been willing to act as a personal representative for the estate. **3.** The process by which a renounced interest is subjected to judicial management and is distributed as the testator would have wished if he or she had known about the renunciation. **4.** A judicial writ commanding the sheriff or other officer to seize the goods of a person named in the writ. • This writ is sometimes issued against a civil defendant who has defaulted or has acted in contempt of court. **5.** The court-ordered seizure of a bankrupt's estate for the benefit of creditors. **6.** *Int'l law.* The seizure by a belligerent power of enemy assets. **7.** The freezing of a government agency's funds; SEQUESTER (1). **8.** Custodial isolation of a trial jury to prevent tampering and exposure to publicity, or of witnesses to prevent them from hearing the testimony of others.

sequestrator (**see**-kwes-tray-tər). (15c) **1.** An officer appointed to execute a writ of sequestration. **2.** A person who holds property in sequestration.

serendipity doctrine. (1989) *Criminal procedure.* The principle that all evidence discovered during a lawful search is eligible to be admitted into evidence at trial.

serial violation. (1989) *Civil-rights law.* The practice by an employer of committing a series of discriminatory acts against an employee, all of which arise out of the same discriminatory intent or animus. • Such a series of discriminatory acts will usu. be considered a continuing violation. For a claim on the violation to be timely, at least one of the discriminatory acts must have taken place within the time permitted to assert the claim (e.g., 300 days for a Title VII claim).

seriatim (seer-ee-**ay**-tim), *adj.* Occurring in a series.

seriatim, *adv.* [Latin] One after another; in a series; successively <the court disposed of the issues seriatim>.

serious crime. **1.** Serious offense. **2.** FELONY (1).

serological test (seer-ə-**loj**-ə-kəl). (1931) A blood examination to detect the presence of antibodies and antigens, as well as other characteristics, esp. as indicators of disease.

servant. (13c) A person who is employed by another to do work under the control and direction of the employer. • A servant, such as a full-time employee, provides personal services that are integral to an employer's business, so a servant must submit to the employer's control of the servant's time and behavior.

serve, *vb.* (15c) **1.** To make legal delivery of (a notice or process) <a copy of the pleading was served on all interested parties>. **2.** To present (a person) with a notice or process as required by law <the defendant was served with process>.

service, *n.* (15c) **1.** The formal delivery of a writ, summons, or other legal process <after three attempts, service still had not been accomplished>. **2.** The formal delivery of some other legal notice, such as a pleading <be sure that a certificate of service is attached to the motion>.

constructive service. (1808) **1.** Substituted service. **2.** Service accomplished by a method or circumstance that does not give actual notice.

service by publication. (1826) The service of process on an absent or nonresident defendant by publishing a notice in a newspaper or other public medium.

sewer service. *Slang.* The fraudulent service of process on a debtor by a creditor seeking to obtain a default judgment.

substituted service. (1840) Any method of service allowed by law in place of personal service, such as service by mail.

3. The act of doing something useful for a person or company, usu. for a fee <your services were no longer required>. **4.** A person or company whose business is to do useful things for others <a linen service>. **5.** An intangible commodity in the form of human effort, such as labor, skill, or advice <contract for services>.

service, *vb.* (1927) To provide service for; specif., to make interest payments on (a debt) <service the deficit>.

service charge. **1.** A charge assessed for performing a service, such as the charge assessed by a bank against the expenses of maintaining or servicing a customer's checking account. **2.** The sum of (1) all charges payable by the buyer and imposed by the seller as an incident to the extension of credit and (2) charges incurred for investigating the collateral or creditworthiness of the buyer or for commissions for obtaining the credit. UCCC § 2.109.

service life. The period of an asset's expected usefulness. • It may or may not coincide with the asset's depreciable life for income-tax purposes.

servicemark. (1945) *Trademarks.* A name, phrase, or other device used to identify and distinguish the services of a certain provider. • Servicemarks identify and afford protection to intangible things such as services, as distinguished from the protection already provided for marks affixed to tangible things such as goods and products.

servient (**sər**-vee-ənt), *adj.* (17c) (Of an estate) subject to a servitude or easement.

servitude. (16c) **1.** An encumbrance consisting in a right to the limited use of a piece of land or other immovable property without the possession of it; a charge or burden on an estate for another's benefit <the easement by necessity is an equitable servitude>. • Servitudes include easements, irrevocable licenses, profits, and real covenants.

acquired servitude. (1971) A servitude requiring a special mode of acquisition before it comes into existence.

additional servitude. (18c) A servitude imposed on land taken under an eminent-domain proceeding for a different type of servitude, as when a highway is constructed on land condemned for a public sidewalk. • A landowner whose land is burdened by an additional servitude is entitled to further compensation.

apparent servitude. (1834) *Civil law.* A servitude appurtenant that is manifested by exterior signs or constructions, such as a roadway.

conservation servitude. Conservation easement.

equitable servitude. Restrictive covenant.

legal servitude. (18c) *Civil law.* A limitation that the law imposes on the use of an estate for the benefit of the general public or of a particular person or persons.

mineral servitude. (1931) *Louisiana law.* A servitude granting the right to enter another's property to explore for and extract minerals; specif., under the Louisiana Mineral Code, a charge on land in favor of a person or another tract of land, creating a limited right to use the land to explore for and produce minerals.

natural servitude. (18c) **1.** A servitude naturally appurtenant to land, requiring no special mode of acquisition. • An example is the right of land, unencumbered by buildings, to the support of the adjoining land. **2.** *Civil law.* A servitude imposed by law because of the natural situation of the estates. • An example of a natural servitude is a lower estate that is bound to receive waters flowing naturally from a higher estate.

personal servitude. (17c) A servitude granting a specific person certain rights in property.

private servitude. (1922) A servitude vested in a particular person. • Examples include a landowner's personal right-of-way over an adjoining piece of land or a right granted to one person to fish in another's lake.

public servitude. (1805) A servitude vested in the public at large or in some class of indeterminate individuals. • Examples include the right of the public to use a highway over privately owned land and the right to navigate a river the bed of which is privately owned.

servitude appurtenant. (1893) A servitude that is not merely an encumbrance of one piece of land but is accessory to another piece; the right of using one piece of land for the benefit of another, such as the right of support for a building.

servitude in gross. (1884) A servitude that is not accessory to any dominant estate for whose benefit it exists but is merely an encumbrance on a given piece of land.

urban servitude. (1831) A servitude appertaining to the building and construction of houses in a city, such as the right to light and air.

2. The condition of being a servant or slave <under the 15th Amendment, an American citizen's right to vote cannot be denied on account of race, color, or previous condition of servitude>. **3.** The condition of a prisoner who has been sentenced to forced labor <penal servitude>.

involuntary servitude. (18c) The condition of one forced to labor — for pay or not — for another by coercion or imprisonment.

session. (15c) **1.** *Parliamentary law.* A meeting or series of related meetings throughout which a court, legislature, or other deliberative assembly conducts business in a continuing sequence <the court's spring session>.

biennial session. (1854) A legislative session held every two years. • Most state legislatures have biennial sessions, usu. held in odd-numbered years.

closed session. (1956) **1.** Executive session. **2.** A session to which parties not directly involved are not admitted.

executive session. A meeting, usu. held in secret, that only the members and invited nonmembers may attend.

joint session. (1853) The combined meeting of two legislative bodies (such as the House of Representatives and the Senate) to pursue a common agenda.

lame-duck session. (1924) A post-election legislative session in which some of the participants are voting during their last days as elected officials.

open session. (1810) A session to which parties not directly involved are admitted.

plenary session. (1936) A meeting of all the members of a deliberative assembly, not just a committee.

pro forma session. A legislative session held not to conduct business but only to satisfy a constitutional provision that neither house may adjourn for longer than a certain time (usu. three days) without the other house's consent.

regular session. (18c) A session that takes place at fixed intervals or specified times.

special session. (17c) A legislative session, usu. called by the executive, that meets outside its regular term to consider a specific issue or to reduce backlog.

2. The period within any given day during which such a body is assembled and performing its duties <court is in session>. **3.** A trading day in a stock market.

triple witching session. A stock-market session on the third Friday in March, June, September, and December during which stock options, index options and futures contracts all expire. • Stock-market volatility and share volume are often high on these days

session laws. (18c) **1.** A body of statutes enacted by a legislature during a particular annual or biennial session. **2.** The softbound booklets containing these statutes.

set-aside, *n.* (1943) Something (such as a percentage of funds) that is reserved or put aside for a specific purpose.

set aside, *vb.* (18c) (Of a court) to annul or vacate (a judgment, order, etc.) <the judge refused to set aside the default judgment>.

setback, *n.* (1916) *Real estate.* The minimum amount of space required between a lot line and a building line <a 12-foot setback>. • Typically contained in zoning ordinances or deed restrictions, setbacks are designed to ensure that enough light and ventilation reach the property and to keep buildings from being erected too close to property lines.

set down, *vb.* (18c) To schedule (a case) for trial or hearing, usu. by making a docket entry.

setoff, *n.* (18c) **1.** A defendant's counterdemand against the plaintiff, arising out of a transaction independent of the plaintiff's claim. **2.** A debtor's right to reduce the amount of a debt by any sum the creditor owes the debtor; the counterbalancing sum owed by the creditor. — Also written *set-off.* **3.** The balancing of mutual liabilities with respect to a pledge relationship. — **set off,** *vb.*

set out, *vb.* (16c) To recite, explain, narrate, or incorporate (facts or circumstances) <set out the terms of the contract>.

set over, *vb.* (16c) To transfer or convey (property) <to set over the land to the purchaser>.

setting, *n.* The date and time established by a court for a trial or hearing <the plaintiff sought a continuance of the imminent setting>.

special setting. (1916) A preferential setting on a court's calendar, usu. reserved for older cases or cases given priority by law, made either on a party's motion or on the court's own motion. • For example, some jurisdictions authorize a special setting for cases involving a party over the age of 70.

settlement, *n.* (17c) **1.** The conveyance of property — or of interests in property — to provide for one or more beneficiaries, usu. members of the settlor's family, in a way that differs from what the beneficiaries would receive as heirs under the statutes of descent and distribution <in marriage settlements, historically, the wife waived her right to claim dower or to succeed to her husband's property>. **2.** An agreement ending a dispute or lawsuit <the parties reached a settlement the day before trial>. **3.** Payment, satisfaction, or final adjustment <the seller shipped the goods after confirming the buyer's settlement of the account>. **4.** Closing <the settlement on their first home is next Friday>. **5.** *Wills & estates.* The complete execution of an estate by the executor <the settlement of the estate was long and complex>. **6.** The establishment of a legal residence. • This sense was frequently used in poor-relief contexts. — **settle,** *vb.*

settlement credit. (1979) *Civil procedure.* A court's reduction of the amount of a jury verdict — or the effect of the verdict on nonsettling defendants — to account for settlement funds the plaintiff has received from former defendants or from other responsible parties.

settlement-first method. (1996) A means by which to apply a settlement credit to a jury verdict, by first reducing the amount of the verdict by subtracting the amount of all settlements the plaintiff has received on the claim, then reducing the remainder by the percentage of the plaintiff's comparative fault.

settler. (17c) **1.** A person who occupies property with the intent to establish a residence. • The term is usu. applied to an early resident of a country or region. **2.** Settlor.

settle up, *vb.* (1884) To collect, pay, and turn over debts and property (e.g., of a decedent, bankrupt, or insolvent business).

settlor (**set**-lər). (18c) A person who makes a settlement of property; esp., one who sets up a trust.

set up, *vb.* To raise (a defense) <the defendant set up the insanity defense on the murder charge>.

Seventeenth Amendment. The constitutional amendment, ratified in 1913, transferring the power to elect U.S. senators from the state legislatures to the states' voters.

Seventh Amendment. The constitutional amendment, ratified with the Bill of Rights in 1791, guaranteeing the right to a jury trial in federal civil cases that are traditionally considered to be suits at common law and that have an amount in controversy exceeding $20.

seven-years'-absence rule. (1920) The principle that a person who has been missing without explanation for at least seven years is legally presumed dead.

severability clause. (1935) A provision that keeps the remaining provisions of a contract or statute in force if any portion of that contract or statute is judicially declared void, unenforceable, or unconstitutional.

several, *adj.* (15c) **1.** (Of a person, place, or thing) more than one or two but not a lot <several witnesses>. **2.** (Of liability, etc.) separate; particular; distinct, but not necessarily independent <a several obligation>. **3.** (Of things, etc.) different; various <several settlement options>.

severally, *adj.* Distinctly; separately <severally liable>.

several-remedies rule. (1975) A procedural rule that tolls a statute of limitations for a plaintiff who has several available forums (such as a workers'-compensation proceeding and the court system) and who timely files in one forum and later proceeds in another forum, as long as the defendant's right and claims are not affected.

severalty (**sev**-[ə]-rəl-tee). (15c) The state or condition of being separate or distinct <the individual landowners held the land in severalty, not as joint tenants>.

severance, *n.* (15c) **1.** The act of cutting off; the state of being cut off. **2.** *Civil procedure.* The separation, by the court, of the claims of multiple parties either to permit separate actions on each claim or to allow certain interlocutory orders to become final. **3.** The termination of a joint tenancy, usu. by converting it into a tenancy in common. **4.** The removal of anything (such as crops or minerals) attached or affixed to real property, making it personal property rather than a part of the land. • Mineral rights are frequently severed from surface rights on property that may contain oil and gas or other minerals. **5.** Severance pay. — **sever,** *vb.* — **severable,** *adj.*

severance pay. Money (apart from back wages or salary) paid by an employer to a dismissed employee. • The payment may be made in exchange for a release of any claims that the employee might have against the employer.

sex. (14c) **1.** The sum of the peculiarities of structure and function that distinguish a male from a female organism; gender. **2.** Sexual intercourse. **3.** SEXUAL RELATIONS (2).

sex-offender registry. A publicly available list of the names and addresses of sex offenders who have been released from prison. • The registries were started by state statutes known as "Megan's laws." The lists are often posted on the Internet, and some states require publication of the offender's photograph, name, and address in local newspapers.

sex reassignment. Medical treatment intended to effect a sex change; surgery and hormonal treatments designed to alter a person's gender.

sexual activity. Sexual relations.

sexual exploitation. The use of a person, esp. a child, in prostitution, pornography, or other sexually manipulative activity that has caused or could cause serious emotional injury.

sexual harassment. (1973) A type of employment discrimination consisting in verbal or physical abuse of a sexual nature.

hostile-environment sexual harassment. (1986) Sexual harassment in which a work environment is created where an employee is subject to unwelcome verbal or physical sexual behavior that is either severe or pervasive. • This type of harassment might occur, for example, if a group of coworkers repeatedly e-mailed pornographic pictures to a colleague who found the pictures offensive.

quid pro quo sexual harassment. (1982) Sexual harassment in which an employment decision is based on the satisfaction of a sexual demand. • This type of harassment might occur, for example, if a boss fired or demoted an employee who refused to go on a date with the boss.

same-sex sexual harassment. Sexual harassment by a supervisor of an employee of the same sex.

sexually transmitted disease. A disease transmitted only or chiefly by engaging in sexual acts with an infected person. • Common examples are syphilis and gonorrhea. — Abbr. STD.

sexual orientation. (1931) A person's predisposition or inclination toward a particular type of sexual activity or behavior; heterosexuality, homosexuality, or bisexuality. • There has been a trend in recent years to make sexual orientation a protected class, esp. in employment and hate-crime statutes.

sexual predator. A person who has committed many violent sexual acts or who has a propensity for committing violent sexual acts.

sexual relations. (1909) **1.** Sexual intercourse. **2.** Physical sexual activity that does not necessarily culminate in intercourse. • Sexual relations usu. involve the touching of another's breast, vagina, penis, or anus. Both persons (the toucher and the person touched) are said to engage in sexual relations.

S/F. *abbr.* Statute of Frauds.

SG. *abbr.* **1.** Solicitor General. **2.** Surgeon General.

shadow economy. Collectively, the unregistered economic activities that contribute to a country's gross national product. • A shadow economy may involve the legal and illegal production of goods and services, including gambling, prostitution, and drug-dealing, as well as barter transactions and unreported incomes.

shakedown. (1902) **1.** An extortion of money using threats of violence or, in the case of a police officer, threats of arrest. **2.** Shakedown search.

shaken-baby syndrome. The medical condition of a child who has suffered forceful shaking, with resulting brain injury. • Common injuries include retinal hemorrhage and subdural and subarachnoid hemorrhage, with minimal or no signs of external cranial trauma. Many victims suffer blindness or death.

shakeout, *n.* An elimination of weak or nonproductive businesses in an industry, esp. during a period of intense competition or declining prices.

shall, *vb.* (bef. 12c) **1.** Has a duty to; more broadly, is required to <the requester shall send notice> <notice shall be sent>. • This is the mandatory sense that drafters typically intend and that courts typically uphold. **2.** Should (as often interpreted by courts) <all claimants shall request mediation>. **3.** May <no person shall enter the building without first signing the roster>. • When a negative word such as *not* or *no* precedes *shall* (as in the example in angle brackets), the word *shall* often means *may*. What is being negated is permission, not a requirement. **4.** Will (as a future-tense verb) <the corporation shall then have a period of 30 days to object>. **5.** Is entitled to <the secretary shall be reimbursed for all expenses>. • Only sense 1 is acceptable under strict standards of drafting.

sham, *n.* (17c) **1.** Something that is not what it seems; a counterfeit. **2.** A person who pretends to be something that he or she is not; a faker. — **sham,** *vb.* — **sham,** *adj.*

sham exception. (1969) An exception to the *Noerr–Pennington* doctrine whereby a company that petitions the government will not receive First Amendment protection or an exemption from the antitrust laws if its intent in petitioning the government for favorable government action or treatment is really an effort to harm its competitors.

sham transaction. (1937) An agreement or exchange that has no independent economic benefit or business purpose and is entered into solely to create a tax advantage (such as a deduction for a business loss). • The Internal Revenue Service may ignore the purported tax benefits of a sham transaction.

share, *n.* (14c) **1.** An allotted portion owned by, contributed by, or due to someone <each partner's share of the profits>. **2.** One of the definite number of equal parts into which the capital stock of a corporation or joint-stock company is divided <the broker advised his customer to sell the stock shares when the price reaches $29>. • A share represents an equity or ownership interest in the corporation or joint-stock company.

share, *vb.* (16c) **1.** To divide (something) into portions. **2.** To enjoy or partake of (a power, right, etc.).

share acquisition. The acquisition of a corporation by purchasing all or most of its outstanding shares directly from the shareholders; takeover.

sharecropping. An agricultural arrangement in which a landowner leases land to a tenant who, in turn, gives the landlord a portion of the crop as rent. • The landlord usu. provides the seed, fertilizer, and equipment. — **sharecropper,** *n.*

shareholder. (1832) One who owns or holds a share or shares in a company, esp. a corporation.

controlling shareholder. A shareholder who can influence the corporation's activities because the shareholder either owns a majority of outstanding shares or owns a smaller percentage but a significant number of the remaining shares are widely distributed among many others.

dummy shareholder. A shareholder who owns stock in name only for the benefit of the true owner, whose identity is usu. concealed.

interested shareholder. A person who owns enough of a corporation's stock to affect corporate decision-making, usu. at least 15–20% of the corporation's outstanding stock.

majority shareholder. A shareholder who owns or controls more than half the corporation's stock.

minority shareholder. A shareholder who owns less than half the total shares outstanding and thus cannot control the corporation's management or singlehandedly elect directors.

shareholder proposal. A proposal by one or more corporate stockholders to change company policy or procedure. • Ordinarily, the corporation informs all stockholders about the proposal before the next shareholder meeting.

shareware. Software that can be redistributed but not modified and requires all users to pay a license fee.

Sharia (shə-**ree**-ə). The body of Islamic religious law applicable to police, banking, business, contracts, and social issues. • Sharia is a system of laws, rather than a codification of laws, based on the Koran and other Islamic sources.

shark repellent. 1. Takeover defense. **2.** More specifically, a charter or bylaw provision designed to impede hostile bids to acquire a controlling interest in a corporation.

sharp, *adj.* (1886) (Of a clause in a mortgage, deed, etc.) empowering the creditor to take immediate and summary action upon the debtor's default.

sharp practice. (1836) Unethical action and trickery, esp. by a lawyer. — **sharp practitioner,** *n.*

shave, *vb.* (1832) **1.** To purchase (a negotiable instrument) at a greater than usual discount rate. **2.** To reduce or deduct from (a price).

shelter doctrine. (1955) *Commercial law.* The principle that a person to whom a holder in due course has transferred commercial paper, as well as any later transferee, will succeed to the rights of the holder in due course. • As a result, transferees of holders in due course are generally not subject to defenses against the payment of an instrument. This doctrine ensures the free transferability of commercial paper. Its name derives from the idea that the transferees "take shelter" in the rights of the holder in due course.

shelving. *Patents.* The failure to begin or the stopping of commercial use of a patent during a specified period, usu. the term of the license.

shepardize, *vb.* (1928) **1.** (*often cap.*) To determine the subsequent history and treatment of (a case) by using a printed or computerized version of *Shepard's Citators.* **2.** Loosely, to check the precedential value of (a case) by the same or similar means. — **shepardization, shepardizing,** *n.*

sheriff. [Middle English *shire reeve* from Anglo-Saxon *scirgerefa*] A county's chief peace officer, usu. elected, who in most jurisdictions acts as custodian of the county jail, executes civil and criminal process, and carries out judicial mandates within the county.

deputy sheriff. An officer who, acting under the direction of a sheriff, may perform most of the duties of the sheriff's office.

Sherman Antitrust Act. A federal statute, passed in 1890, that prohibits direct or indirect interference with the freely competitive interstate production and distribution of goods. • This Act was amended by the Clayton Act in 1914. 15 USCA §§ 1–7.

***Sherman–Sorrells* doctrine.** (1998) The principle that a defendant may claim as an affirmative defense that he or she was not disposed to commit the offense until a public official (often an undercover police officer) encouraged the defendant to do so. • This entrapment defense, which is recognized in the federal system and a majority of states, was developed in *Sherman v. United States,* 356 U.S. 369, 78 S.Ct. 819 (1958), and *Sorrells v. United States,* 287 U.S. 435, 53 S.Ct. 210 (1932).

shield law. (1971) **1.** A statute that affords journalists the privilege not to reveal confidential sources. **2.** A statute that restricts or prohibits the use, in rape or sexual-assault cases, of evidence about the victim's past sexual conduct.

shifting, *adj.* (1874) (Of a position, place, etc.) changing or passing from one to another <a shifting estate>.

shifting clause. (1813) At common law, a clause under the Statute of Uses prescribing a substituted mode of devolution in the settlement of an estate.

shifting the burden of proof. (1805) In litigation, the transference of the duty to prove a fact from one party to the other; the passing of the duty to produce evidence in a case from one side to another as the case progresses, when one side has made a prima facie showing on a point of evidence, requiring the other side to rebut it by contradictory evidence.

shill. 1. A person who poses as an innocent bystander at a confidence game but actually serves as a decoy for the perpetrators of the scheme. **2.** By-bidder. — **shill,** *vb.*

shingle. A small, usu. dignified sign that marks the office door of a lawyer or other professional.

shin plaster. *Hist. Slang.* **1.** A bank note that has greatly depreciated in value; esp., the paper money of the Republic of Texas in relation to the U.S. dollar. **2.** Paper money in denominations less than one dollar.

ship channel. *Maritime law.* The part of a navigable body of water where the water is deep enough for large vessels to travel safely.

ship's papers. *Maritime law.* The papers that a vessel is required to carry to provide the primary evidence of the ship's national character, ownership, nature and destination of cargo, and compliance with navigation laws. •These papers includes certificates of health, charter-party, muster-rolls, licenses, and bills of lading.

shipwreck. *Maritime law.* **1.** A ship's wreckage. **2.** The injury or destruction of a vessel because of circumstances beyond the owner's control, rendering the vessel incapable of carrying out its mission.

shock the conscience. To cause intense ethical or humanitarian discomfort. • This phrase is used as an equitable standard for gauging whether (1) state action amounts to a violation of a person's substantive-due-process rights, (2) a jury's award is excessive, (3) a fine, jail term, or other penalty is disproportionate to the crime, or (4) a contract is unconscionable.

shop, *n.* (13c) A business establishment or place of employment; a factory, office, or other place of business.

agency shop. A shop in which a union acts as an agent for the employees, regardless of their union membership. • Nonunion members must pay union dues because it is presumed that any collective bargaining will benefit nonunion as well as union members.

closed nonunion shop. A shop in which the employer restricts employment to workers who are unaffiliated with any labor union.

closed shop. A shop in which the employer, by agreement with a union, employs only union members in good standing. • Closed shops were made illegal under the federal Labor-Management Relations Act.

open closed shop. A shop in which the employer hires nonunion workers on the understanding that they will become union members within a specified period.

open shop. **1.** A shop in which the employer hires workers without regard to union affiliation. **2.** Open closed shop.

preferential nonunion shop. A shop in which nonunion members are given preference over main members in employment matters.

preferential union shop. A shop in which union members are given preference over nonunion members in employment matters.

union shop. A shop in which the employer may hire nonunion employees on the condition that they join a union within a specified time (usu. at least 30 days).

shop-book rule. (1898) *Evidence.* An exception to the hearsay rule permitting the admission into evidence of original bookkeeping records if the books' entries were made in the ordinary course of business and the books are authenticated by somebody who maintains them.

shop books. (17c) Records of original entry maintained in the usual course of business by a shopkeeper, trader, or other businessperson.

shoplifting, *n.* (17c) Theft of merchandise from a store or business; specif., larceny of goods from a store or other commercial establishment by willfully taking and concealing the merchandise with the intention of converting the goods to one's personal use without paying the purchase price. — **shoplift,** *vb.*

shop right. (1879) *Patents.* An employer's right to an irrevocable, nonassignable, nonexclusive, royalty-free license in an employee's invention, if the employee conceived and developed the invention during the course of employment and used company funds and materials.

shore. (14c) **1.** Land lying between the lines of high- and low-water mark; lands bordering on the shores of navigable waters below the line of ordinary high water. **2.** Land adjacent to a body of water regardless of whether it is below or above the ordinary high- or low-water mark.

short, *adj.* **1.** Not holding at the time of sale the security or commodity that is being sold in anticipation of a fall in price <the trader was short at the market's close>. **2.** Of or relating to a sale of securities or commodities not in the seller's possession at the time of sale <a short position>.

short-shipped, *adj. Commercial law.* Partially filled; containing fewer units than requested or paid for.

show, *vb.* (12c) To make (facts, etc.) apparent or clear by evidence; to prove.

show cause. To produce a satisfactory explanation or excuse, usu. in connection with a motion or application to a court.

show-cause proceeding. (1922) A usu. expedited proceeding on a show-cause order.

shower (**shoh**-ər), *n.* A person commissioned by a court to take jurors to a place so that they may observe it as they consider a case on which they are sitting.

showing, *n.* (1857) The act or an instance of establishing through evidence and argument; proof <a prima facie showing>.

show trial. (1937) A trial, usu. in a nondemocratic country, that is staged primarily for propagandistic purposes, with the outcome predetermined.

showup, *n.* (1929) A pretrial identification procedure in which a suspect is confronted with a witness to or the victim of a crime. • Unlike a lineup, a showup is a one-on-one confrontation.

shrinkage. (1961) The reduction in inventory caused by theft, breakage, or waste.

shutdown. (1884) A cessation of work production, esp. in a factory.

shut-in royalty clause. *Oil & gas.* A provision in an oil-and-gas lease allowing the lessee to maintain the lease while there is no production from the property because wells capable of production are shut in. • The lessee pays the lessor a shut-in royalty in lieu of production.

shyster (**shɪs**-tər). (1843) A person (esp. a lawyer) whose business affairs are unscrupulous, deceitful, or unethical.

SIB. *abbr.* **1.** Securities and Investment Board. **2.** Survivor-income benefit plan.

sibling. A brother or sister.

sic (sik). [Latin "so, thus"] (1859) Spelled or used as written. • *Sic,* invariably bracketed and usu. set in italics, is used to indicate that a preceding word or phrase in a quoted passage is reproduced as it appeared in the original document <"that case peeked [*sic*] the young lawyer's interest">.

sick leave. 1. An employment benefit allowing a worker time off for sickness, either with or without pay, but without loss of seniority or other benefits. **2.** The time so taken by an employee.

side, *n.* (13c) **1.** The position of a person or group opposing another <the law is on our side>. **2.** Either of two parties in a transaction or dispute <each side put on a strong case>.

sidebar. (1856) **1.** A position at the side of a judge's bench where counsel can confer with the judge beyond the jury's earshot <the judge called the attorneys to sidebar>. **2.** Sidebar conference <during the sidebar, the prosecutor accused the defense attorney of misconduct>. **3.** A short, secondary article within or accompanying a main story in a publication <the sidebar contained information on related topics>. **4.** Sidebar comment.

sidebar comment. (1922) An unnecessary, often argumentative remark made by an attorney or witness, esp. during a trial or deposition <the witness paused

after testifying, then added a sidebar>. — Often shortened to *sidebar.*

sidebar conference. (1925) **1.** A discussion among the judge and counsel, usu. over an evidentiary objection, outside the jury's hearing. **2.** A discussion, esp. during voir dire, between the judge and a juror or prospective juror. — Often shortened to *sidebar.*

side reports. (1943) **1.** Unofficial volumes of case reports. **2.** Collections of cases omitted from the official reports.

sight. (1810) A drawee's acceptance of a draft <payable after sight>. • The term *after sight* means "after acceptance."

sign, *vb.* (15c) **1.** To identify (a record) by means of a signature, mark, or other symbol with the intent to authenticate it as an act or agreement of the person identifying it <both parties signed the contract>. **2.** To agree with or join <the commissioner signed on for a four-year term>.

signal. (1949) **1.** A means of communication, esp. between vessels at sea or between a vessel and the shore. • The international code of signals assigns arbitrary meanings to different arrangements of flags or light displays. **2.** In the citation of legal authority, an abbreviation or notation supplied to indicate some basic fact about the authority. • For example, according to the *Bluebook*, the signal *See* means that the cited authority plainly supports the proposition, while *Cf.* means that the cited authority supports a proposition analogous to (but in some way different from) the main proposition.

signatory (**sig**-nə-tor-ee), *n.* (1866) A person or entity that signs a document, personally or through an agent, and thereby becomes a party to an agreement <eight countries are signatories to the treaty>. — **signatory,** *adj.*

signatory authority. License to make a decision, esp. to withdraw money from an account or to transfer a negotiable instrument.

signature. (16c) **1.** A person's name or mark written by that person or at the person's direction. **2.** *Commercial law.* Any name, mark, or writing used with the intention of authenticating a document. UCC §§ 1-201(37), 3-401(b).

digital signature. (1978) A secure, digital code attached to an electronically transmitted message that uniquely identifies and authenticates the sender. • Digital signatures are esp. important for electronic commerce and are a key component of many electronic message-authentication schemes. Several states have passed legislation recognizing the legality of digital signatures.

electronic signature. An electronic symbol, sound, or process that is either attached to or logically associated with a document (such as a contract or other record) and executed or adopted by a person with the intent to sign the document. • Types of electronic signatures include a typed name at the end of an email, a digital image of a handwritten signature, and the click of an "I accept" button on an e-commerce site.

facsimile signature. (1892) **1.** A signature that has been prepared and reproduced by mechanical or photographic means. **2.** A signature on a document that has been transmitted by a facsimile machine.

unauthorized signature. (1859) A signature made without actual, implied, or apparent authority. • It includes a forgery. UCC § 1-201(43).

signature card. (1902) A financial-institution record consisting of a customer's signature and other information that assists the institution in monitoring financial transactions, as by comparing the signature on the record with signatures on checks, withdrawal slips, and other documents.

signed, sealed, and delivered. (17c) In a certificate of acknowledgment, a statement that the instrument was executed by the person acknowledging it.

silence, *n.* (13c) **1.** A restraint from speaking. • In criminal law, silence includes an arrestee's statements expressing the desire not to speak and requesting an attorney. **2.** A failure to reveal something required by law to be revealed. — **silent,** *adj.*

silent-witness theory. (1973) *Evidence.* A method of authenticating and admitting evidence (such as a photograph), without the need for a witness to verify its authenticity, upon a sufficient showing of the reliability of the process of producing the evidence, including proof that the evidence has not been altered.

silver-platter doctrine. (1958) *Criminal procedure.* The principle that a federal court could admit evidence obtained illegally by a state police officer as long as a federal officer did not participate in or request the search. • The Supreme Court rejected this doctrine in *Elkins v. United States*, 364 U.S. 206, 80 S.Ct. 1437 (1960).

similar happenings. *Evidence.* Events that occur at a time different from the time in dispute and are therefore usu. inadmissible except to the extent that they provide relevant information on issues that would be fairly constant, such as the control of and conditions on land on the day in question.

similarity. *Intellectual property.* The resemblance of one trademark or copyrighted work to another. • How closely a trademark must resemble another to amount to infringement depends on the nature of the product and how much care the typical buyer would be expected to take in making the selection in that particular market.

similiter (si-**mil**-i-tər). [Latin "similarly"] *Common-law pleading.* A party's written acceptance of an opponent's issue or argument; a set form of words by which a party accepts or joins in an issue of fact tendered by the other side.

simple, *adj.* (16c) **1.** (Of a crime) not accompanied by aggravating circumstances. **2.** (Of an estate or fee) heritable by the owner's heirs with no conditions concerning tail. **3.** (Of a contract) not made under seal.

simpliciter (sim-**plis**-i-tər), *adv.* [Latin] (16c) **1.** In a simple or summary manner; simply. **2.** Absolutely; unconditionally; per se.

simultaneous-death act. Uniform Simultaneous Death Act.

simultaneous-death clause. (1953) A testamentary provision mandating that if the testator and beneficiary die in a common disaster, or the order of their deaths is otherwise unascertainable, the testator is presumed to have survived the beneficiary. • If the beneficiary is the testator's spouse, an express exception is often made so that the spouse with the smaller estate is presumed to have survived.

sine (**sɪ**-nee or **sin**-ay), *prep.* [Latin] Without.

sine die (**sɪ**-nee **dɪ**-ee *or* **dɪ**- *or* **sin**-ay **dee**-ay). [Latin "without day"] (17c) With no day being assigned (as for resumption of a meeting or hearing).

sine qua non (**sɪ**-nee kway **non** *or* **sin**-ay kwah **nohn**), *n.* [Latin "without which not"] (17c) An indispensable condition or thing; something on which something else necessarily depends.

single-date-of-removal doctrine. *Civil procedure.* The principle that the deadline for removing a case from state court to federal court is 30 days from the day that any defendant receives a copy of the state-court pleading on which the removal is based. • If a later-served defendant seeks to remove a case to federal court more than 30 days after the day any other defendant received the pleading, the removal is untimely even if effectuated within 30 days after the removing defendant received the pleading. One theory underlying this doctrine is that all defendants must consent to remove a case to federal court, and a defendant who has waited longer than 30 days to remove does not have the capacity to consent to removal. 28 USCA § 1446(b).

single-larceny doctrine. (1969) *Criminal law.* The principle that the taking of different items of property belonging to either the same or different owners at the same time and place constitutes one act of larceny if the theft is part of one larcenous plan, as when it involves essentially one continuous act or if control over the property is exercised simultaneously. • The thief's intent determines the number of occurrences.

single original. (1815) An instrument executed singly, not in duplicate.

single-paragraph form. *Patents.* A style of writing patent claims that uses a colon after the introductory phrase and a semicolon between each element.

SIPA (**see**-pə). *abbr.* Securities Investor Protection Act.

SIPC. *abbr.* Securities Investor Protection Corporation.

sister. (bef. 12c) A female who has one parent or both parents in common with another person.

half sister. A sister who has the same father or the same mother, but not both.

sister-german. A full sister; the daughter of both of one's parents.

stepsister. (15c) The daughter of one's stepparent.

sister-in-law. (15c) The sister of one's spouse or the wife of one's brother. • The wife of one's spouse's brother is also sometimes considered a sister-in-law. Pl. **sisters-in-law.**

sit, *vb.* (14c) **1.** (Of a judge) to occupy a judicial seat <Judge Wilson sits on the trial court for the Eastern District of Arkansas>. **2.** (Of a judge) to hold court or perform official functions <is the judge sitting this week?>. **3.** (Of a court or legislative body) to hold proceedings <the U.S. Supreme Court sits from October to June>.

sit-and-squirm test. A judicial doctrine, used esp. by administrative-law judges in disability-claim cases, whereby a court subjectively determines a set of traits that it expects the claimant to exhibit and denies relief if the claimant fails to exhibit those traits. • The doctrine is adhered to only in some federal circuits and has been expressly rejected in others. Generally, an administrative-law judge may observe a claimant's demeanor in evaluating the credibility of the complaint. Yet it is error for the judge to base a judgment solely on personal observation and not on the record as a whole.

site. A place or location; esp., a piece of property set aside for a specific use.

site assessment. Transactional audit.

site plan. (1937) An illustrated proposal for the development or use of a particular piece of real property. • The illustration is usu. a map or sketch of how the property will appear if the proposal is accepted. Some zoning ordinances require a developer to present a site plan to the city council and to receive council approval before certain projects may be completed.

sit-in, *n.* An organized, passive demonstration in which participants usu. sit (or lie) down and refuse to leave a place as a means of protesting against policies or activities. • Sit-ins originated as a communal act of protesting racial segregation. People who were discriminated against would sit in places that were prohibited to them and refuse to leave. Later the term came to refer to any group protest, as with anti–Vietnam War protests and some labor strikes.

sitting, *n.* (14c) A court session; esp., a session of an appellate court.

en banc sitting. (1944) A court session in which all the judges (or a quorum) participate.

in camera sitting. (1976) A court session conducted by a judge in chambers or elsewhere outside the courtroom.

situation. 1. Condition; position in reference to circumstances <dangerous situation>. **2.** The place where someone or something is occupied; a location <situation near the border>.

situs (sɪ-təs). [Latin] (1834) The location or position (of something) for legal purposes, as in *lex situs*, the law of the place where the thing in issue is situated.

Sixteenth Amendment. The constitutional amendment, ratified in 1913, allowing Congress to tax income.

Sixth Amendment. The constitutional amendment, ratified with the Bill of Rights in 1791, guaranteeing in criminal cases the right to a speedy and public trial by jury, the right to be informed of the nature of the accusation, the right to confront witnesses, the right to counsel, and the right to compulsory process for obtaining favorable witnesses.

S.J.D. Doctor of Juridical Science.

skip person. (1988) *Tax.* A beneficiary who is more than one generation removed from the transferor and to whom assets are conveyed in a generation-skipping transfer. IRC (26 USCA) § 2613(a).

skiptracing agency. (1984) A service that locates persons (such as delinquent debtors, missing heirs, witnesses, stockholders, bondholders, etc.) or missing assets (such as bank accounts).

skyjack, *vb. Slang.* To hijack an aircraft. — **skyjacking,** *n.*

S.L. *abbr.* **1.** Session law. **2.** Statute law.

slamming. The practice by which a long-distance telephone company wrongfully appropriates a customer's service from another company, usu. through an unauthorized transfer or by way of a transfer authorization that is disguised as something else, such as a form to sign up for a free vacation.

slander, *n.* (13c) **1.** A defamatory assertion expressed in a transitory form, esp. speech. • Damages for slander — unlike those for libel — are not presumed and thus must be proved by the plaintiff (unless the defamation is slander per se). **2.** The act of making such a statement. — **slander,** *vb.* — **slanderous,** *adj.*

slander per quod. (18c) Slander that does not qualify as slander per se, thus forcing the plaintiff to prove special damages.

slander per se. (1841) Slander for which special damages need not be proved because it imputes to the plaintiff any one of the following: (1) a crime involving moral turpitude, (2) a loathsome disease (such as a sexually transmitted disease), (3) conduct that would adversely affect one's business or profession, or (4) unchastity (esp. of a woman).

trade slander. Trade defamation that is spoken but not recorded.

slanderer, *n.* (13c) One who commits slander.

slander of title. (18c) A false statement, made orally or in writing, that casts doubt on another person's ownership of property.

SLAPP (slap). *abbr.* A strategic lawsuit against public participation — that is, a suit brought by a developer, corporate executive, or elected official to stifle those who protest against some type of high-dollar initiative or who take an adverse position on a public-interest issue (often involving the environment).

slate. A list of candidates, esp. for political office or a corporation's board of directors, that usu. includes as many candidates for election as there are representatives being elected.

slavery. 1. A situation in which one person has absolute power over the life, fortune, and liberty of another. **2.** The practice of keeping individuals in such a state of bondage or servitude. • Slavery was outlawed by the 13th Amendment to the U.S. Constitution.

slay, *vb.* To kill (a person), esp. in battle.

slayer rule. (1986) The doctrine that neither a person who kills another nor the killer's heirs can share in the decedent's estate.

sleeper. A security that has strong market potential but is underpriced and lacks investor interest.

sleeping on rights. LACHES (1).

slight-evidence rule. (1936) **1.** The doctrine that if evidence establishes the existence of a conspiracy between at least two other people, the prosecution need only offer slight evidence of a defendant's knowing participation or intentional involvement in the conspiracy to secure a conviction. • This rule was first announced in *Tomplain v. United States*, 42 F.2d 202, 203 (5th Cir. 1930). In the decades after *Tomplain*, other circuits adopted the rule, but not until the 1970s did the rule become widespread. Since then, the rule has been widely criticized and, in most circuits, abolished. See, e.g., *United States v. Durrive*, 902 F.2d 1379, 1380 n.* (7th Cir. 1990). But its vitality remains undiminished in some jurisdictions. **2.** The doctrine that only slight evidence of a defendant's participation in a conspiracy need be offered in order to admit a coconspirator's out-of-court statement under the coconspirator exception to the hearsay rule. See Fed. R. Evid. 801(d)(2)(E).

slip-and-fall case. (1952) **1.** A lawsuit brought for injuries sustained in slipping and falling, usu. on the defendant's property. **2.** Loosely, any minor case in tort.

slip decision. Slip opinion.

slip law. (1922) An individual pamphlet in which a single enactment is printed immediately after its passage but before its inclusion in the general laws (such as the session laws or the *U.S. Statutes at Large*).

slipsheet. Slip opinion.

slowdown. An organized effort by workers to decrease production to pressure the employer to take some desired action.

slush fund. Money that is set aside for undesignated purposes, often corrupt ones, and that is not subject to financial procedures designed to ensure accountability.

SM. *abbr.* Servicemark.

Small Business Administration. A federal agency that helps small businesses by assuring them a fair share of government contracts, guaranteeing their loans or lending them money directly, and providing disaster relief. • The agency was established by the Small Business Act of 1953. — Abbr. SBA.

small-business concern. A business qualifying for an exemption from freight undercharges because it is independently owned and operated and is not dominant in its field of operation, with limited numbers of employees and business volume. 15 USCA § 632. — Often shortened to *small business*.

small claim. A claim for damages at or below a specified monetary amount.

small-loan act. A state law fixing the maximum legal interest rate and other terms on small, short-term loans by banks and finance companies.

smart money. 1. Funds held by sophisticated, usu. large investors who are considered capable of minimizing risks and maximizing profits <the smart money has now left this market>. **2.** Punitive damages <although the jury awarded only $7,000 in actual damages, it also awarded $500,000 in smart money>.

smash-and-grab. *Slang.* The act of breaking a window or other glass barrier in order to seize goods beyond it before fleeing. • In a smash-and-grab, the criminal usu. breaks a shop window or a glass display case with a handheld tool and seizes whatever merchandise is nearest.

Smith Act. A 1948 federal antisedition law that criminalizes advocating the forcible or violent overthrow of the government. 18 USCA § 2385.

smoking gun. (1974) A piece of physical or documentary evidence that conclusively impeaches an adversary on an outcome-determinative issue or destroys the adversary's credibility.

Smoot–Hawley Tariff Act. *Hist.* A 1930 protectionist statute that raised tariff rates on most articles imported into the U.S., and provoked U.S. trading partners to institute comparable tariff increases. • This act is often cited as a factor in precipitating and spreading the Great Depression.

smuggling, *n.* (17c) The crime of importing or exporting illegal articles or articles on which duties have not been paid. — **smuggle,** *vb.*

alimentary-canal smuggling. Smuggling carried out by swallowing packets, usu. balloons, filled with contraband, which stays in the smuggler's stomach or intestines during the crossing of a border.

smurf, *n. Slang.* **1.** A person who participates in a money-laundering operation by making transactions of less than $10,000 (the amount that triggers federal reporting requirements) at each of many banks. • The name derives from a cartoon character of the 1980s. **2.** Currency-transaction report.

sneak-and-peek search warrant. Covert-entry search warrant.

SNS. *abbr.* Strategic National Stockpile.

So. *abbr. Southern Reporter.*

sober, *adj.* (14c) **1.** (Of a person) not under the influence of drugs or alcohol. **2.** (Of a person) regularly abstinent or moderate in the use of intoxicating liquors. **3.** (Of a situation, person, etc.) serious; grave. **4.** (Of facts, arguments, etc.) basic; unexaggerated. **5.** (Of a person) rational; having self-control.

sobriety checkpoint. (1984) A part of a roadway at which police officers maintain a roadblock to stop motorists and ascertain whether the drivers are intoxicated.

sobriety test. (1931) A method of determining whether a person is intoxicated. • Common sobriety tests are coordination tests and the use of mechanical devices to measure the blood alcohol content of a person's breath sample.

field sobriety test. (1956) A motor-skills test administered by a peace officer during a stop to determine whether a suspect has been driving while intoxicated. • The test usu. involves checking the suspect's speaking ability or coordination (as by reciting the alphabet or walking in a straight line). — Abbr. FST.

social contract. (1837) The express or implied agreement between citizens and their government by which individuals agree to surrender certain freedoms in exchange for mutual protection; an agreement forming the foundation of a political society. • The term is primarily associated with political philosophers, such as Thomas Hobbes, John Locke, and esp. Jean Jacques Rousseau, though it can be traced back to the Greek Sophists.

social restriction. 1. The curtailment of individuals' liberties ostensibly for the general benefit. **2.** A governmental measure that has this effect.

Social Security Administration. A federal agency in the executive branch responsible for administering the nation's retirement program and its survivors- and disability-insurance program. • The agency was established under the Social Security Act of 1935 and became independent in 1995. — Abbr. SSA.

Social Security Disability Insurance. A benefit for adults with disabilities, paid by the Social Security Administration to wage-earners who have accumulated enough quarters of coverage and then become disabled. • Benefits are also available to disabled adult children and to disabled widows and widowers of qualified wage-earners. — Abbr. SSDI.

social study. Home-study report.

society. (16c) **1.** A community of people, as of a state, nation, or locality, with common cultures, traditions, and interests. **2.** An association or company of persons (usu. unincorporated) united by mutual consent, to deliberate, determine, and act jointly for a common purpose; ORGANIZATION (1). **3.** The general love, affection, and companionship that family members share with one another.

sociopath, *n.* Psychopath. — **sociopathy,** *n.* — **sociopathic,** *adj.*

Socratic method. (18c) A technique of philosophical discussion — and of law-school instruction — by which the questioner (a law professor) questions one or more followers (the law students), building on each answer with another question, esp. an analogy incorporating the answer. • This method takes its name from the Greek philosopher Socrates, who lived in Athens from about 469–399 B.C. His method is a traditional one in law schools, primarily because it forces law students to think through issues rationally and deductively — a skill required in the practice of law. Most law professors who employ this method call on students randomly, an approach designed to teach students to think quickly, without stage fright.

SODDI defense (**sahd**-ee). *Slang.* The some-other-dude-did-it defense; a claim that somebody else committed a crime, usu. made by a criminal defendant who cannot identify the third party.

sodomy (**sod**-ə-mee), *n.* (13c) **1.** Oral or anal copulation between humans, esp. those of the same sex. **2.** Oral or anal copulation between a human and an animal; bestiality. — **sodomize,** *vb.* — **sodomitic,** *adj.* — **sodomist, sodomite,** *n.*

__aggravated sodomy.__ (1965) Criminal sodomy that involves force or results in serious bodily injury to the victim in addition to mental injury and emotional distress. • Some laws provide that sodomy involving a minor is automatically aggravated sodomy.

SOF. *abbr.* Statute of Frauds.

soft dollars. 1. *Securities.* The credits that brokers give their clients in return for the clients' stock-trading business. **2.** The portion of an equity investment that is tax-deductible in the first year.

Software Directive. Directive on the Legal Protection of Computer Programs.

soil bank. A federal agricultural program in which farmers are paid to not grow crops or to grow noncommercial vegetation, to preserve the quality of the soil and stabilize commodity prices by avoiding surpluses.

sole-actor doctrine. (1923) *Agency.* The rule charging a principal with knowledge of the agent's actions, even if the agent acted fraudulently.

solemnity (sə-**lem**-nə-tee). (14c) **1.** A formality (such as a ceremony) required by law to validate an agreement or action <solemnity of marriage>. **2.** The state of seriousness or solemn respectfulness or observance <solemnity of contract>.

solemnity of contract. (1812) The concept that two people may enter into any contract they wish and that the resulting contract is enforceable if formalities are observed and no defenses exist.

solemnize (**sol**-əm-nɪz), *vb.* (14c) To enter into (a marriage, contract, etc.) by a formal act, usu. before witnesses.

solemn occasion. In some states, the serious and unusual circumstance in which the supreme court is constitutionally permitted to render advisory opinions to the remaining branches of government, as when the legislature doubts the legality of proposed legislation and a determination must be made to allow the legislature to exercise its functions. • Some factors that have been considered in determining whether a solemn occasion exists include whether an important question of law is presented, whether the question is urgent, whether the matter is ripe for an opinion, and whether the court has enough time to consider the question.

sole practitioner. (1946) A lawyer who practices law without any partners or associates. — Often shortened to *solo.*

sole proprietorship. (1860) **1.** A business in which one person owns all the assets, owes all the liabilities, and operates in his or her personal capacity. **2.** Ownership of such a business.

solicitation, *n.* (16c) **1.** The act or an instance of requesting or seeking to obtain something; a request or petition <a solicitation for volunteers to handle at least one pro bono case per year>. **2.** The criminal offense of urging, advising, commanding, or otherwise inciting another to commit a crime <convicted of solicitation of murder>. • Solicitation is an inchoate offense distinct from the solicited crime. Under the Model Penal Code, a defendant is guilty of solicitation even if the command or urging was not actually communicated to the solicited person, as long as it was designed to be communicated. Model Penal Code § 5.02(2). **3.** An offer to pay or accept money in exchange for sex <the prostitute was charged with solicitation>. **4.** An attempt or effort to gain business <the attorney's solicitations took the form of radio and television ads>. • The Model Rules of Professional Conduct place certain prohibitions on lawyers' direct solicitation of potential clients. **5.** *Securities.* A request for a proxy; a request to execute, not execute, or revoke a proxy; the furnishing of a form of proxy; or any other communication to security holders under circumstances reasonably calculated to result in the procurement, withholding, or revocation of a proxy. — **solicit,** *vb.*

solicitor. (15c) **1.** A person who seeks business or contributions from others; an advertiser or promoter. **2.** A person who conducts matters on another's behalf; an agent or representative. **3.** The chief law officer of a governmental body or a municipality. **4.** In the United Kingdom, a lawyer who consults with clients and prepares legal documents but is not generally heard in High Court or (in Scotland) Court of Session unless specially licensed. **5.** A prosecutor (in some jurisdictions, such as South Carolina). **6.** A special insurance agent.

solicitor general. (*usu. cap.*) (17c) The second-highest-ranking legal officer in a government (after the attorney general); esp., the chief courtroom lawyer for the executive branch. — Abbr. SG. Pl. **solicitors general.**

solidarity. (1875) The state of being jointly and severally liable (as for a debt). — **solidarily,** *adv.*

solidary (**sol**-ə-der-ee), *adj.* (Of a liability or obligation) joint and several.

solitary confinement. (17c) Separate confinement that gives a prisoner extremely limited access to other people; esp., the complete isolation of a prisoner.

solo, *n.* Sole practitioner.

solvency, *n.* (18c) The ability to pay debts as they come due. — **solvent,** *adj.*

somnambulism (sahm-**nam**-byə-liz-əm). (18c) Sleepwalking. • Generally, a person will not be held criminally responsible for an act performed while in this state.

somnolentia (sahm-nə-**len**-shee-ə). (1879) **1.** The state of drowsiness. **2.** A condition of incomplete sleep resembling drunkenness, during which part of the faculties are abnormally excited while the others are dormant; the combined condition of sleeping and wakefulness producing a temporary state of involuntary intoxication. • To the extent that it destroys moral agency, somnolentia may be a defense to a criminal charge.

son. 1. A person's male child, whether natural or adopted; a male of whom one is the parent. **2.** An immediate male descendant. **3.** *Slang.* Any young male person.

son-in-law. The husband of one's daughter.

Sonny Bono Copyright Term Extension Act. *Copyright.* A federal law extending the copyright term by 20 years for all works published in the U.S. after January 1, 1978, and settling the copyright term for works created before 1978 as 95 years from the original copyright date. • Before the extension, the copyright term was the life of the author plus 50 years. Pub. L. 105-298, 112 Stat. 2827.

Son-of-Sam law. (1981) A state statute that prohibits a convicted criminal from profiting by selling his or her story rights to a publisher or filmmaker. • State law usu. authorizes prosecutors to seize royalties from a convicted criminal and to place the money in an escrow account for the crime victim's benefit. This type of law was first enacted in New York in 1977, in response to the lucrative book deals that publishers offered David Berkowitz, the serial killer who called himself "Son of Sam." In 1992, the U.S. Supreme Court declared New York's Son-of-Sam law unconstitutional as a content-based speech regulation, prompting many states to amend their laws in an attempt to avoid constitutionality problems. *Simon & Schuster, Inc. v. New York State Crime Victims Bd.*, 502 U.S. 105, 112 S.Ct. 501 (1992).

sororicide (sə-**ror**-ə-sɪd). (17c) **1.** The act of killing one's own sister. **2.** A person who kills his or her sister. — **sororicidal,** *adj.*

sound, *adj.* (12c) **1.** (Of health, mind, etc.) good; whole; free from disease or disorder. **2.** (Of property) good; marketable. **3.** (Of discretion) exercised equitably under the circumstances. — **soundness,** *n.*

sound, *vb.* (18c) **1.** To be actionable (in) <her claims for physical injury sound in tort, not in contract>. **2.** To be recoverable (in) <his tort action sounds in damages, not in equitable relief>.

source of law. (1892) Something (such as a constitution, treaty, statute, or custom) that provides authority for legislation and for judicial decisions; a point of origin for law or legal analysis.

South Eastern Reporter. A set of regional lawbooks, part of the West Group's National Reporter System, containing every published appellate decision from Georgia, North Carolina, South Carolina, Virginia, and West Virginia, from 1887 to date. • The first series ran from 1887 to 1939; the second series is the current one. — Abbr. S.E.; S.E.2d.

Southern Reporter. A set of regional lawbooks, part of the West Group's National Reporter System, containing every published appellate decision from Alabama, Florida, Louisiana, and Mississippi, from 1887 to date. • The first series ran from 1887 to 1941; the second series is the current one. — Abbr. So.; So.2d.

South Western Reporter. A set of regional lawbooks, part of the West Group's National Reporter System, containing every published appellate decision from Arkansas, Kentucky, Missouri, Tennessee, and Texas, from 1886 to date. • The first series ran from 1886 to 1928; the second series ran until 1999; the third series is the current one. — Abbr. S.W.; S.W.2d.; S.W.3d.

sovereign, *n.* (13c) **1.** A person, body, or state vested with independent and supreme authority. **2.** The ruler of an independent state. — **sovereign,** *adj.*

sovereign people. (17c) The political body consisting of the collective number of citizens and qualified electors who possess the powers of sovereignty and exercise them through their chosen representatives.

sovereign power. (15c) The power to make and enforce laws.

sovereign right. (16c) A unique right possessed by a state or its agencies that enables it to carry out its official functions for the public benefit, as distinguished from certain proprietary rights that it may possess like any other private person.

sovereign state. (17c) **1.** A state that possesses an independent existence, being complete in itself, without being merely part of a larger whole to whose government it is subject. **2.** A political community whose members are bound together by the tie of common subjection to some central authority, whose commands those members must obey.

sovereignty (**sahv**-[ə-]rin-tee). (18c) **1.** Supreme dominion, authority, or rule. **2.** The supreme political authority of an independent state. **3.** The state itself.

s.p. *abbr.* **1.** *abbr. Sine prole.* **2.** Same principle; same point. • This notation, when inserted between two citations, indicates that the second involves the same principles as the first.

spam. Unsolicited commercial e-mail.

spec. *abbr.* Specification.

special, *adj.* (13c) **1.** Of, relating to, or designating a species, kind, or individual thing. **2.** (Of a statute, rule, etc.) designed for a particular purpose. **3.** (Of powers, etc.) unusual; extraordinary.

special advocate. Guardian ad litem.

special-assessment bond. Special-tax bond.

special-duty doctrine. (1980) *Torts.* The rule that a governmental entity (such as a state or municipality) can be held liable for an individual plaintiff's injury when the entity owed a duty to the plaintiff but not to the general public. • This is an exception to the public-duty doctrine. The special-duty doctrine applies only when the plaintiff has reasonably relied on the governmental entity's assumption of the duty.

special-interest group. An organization that seeks to influence legislation or government policy in favor of a particular interest or issue, esp. by lobbying.

specialist. 1. A lawyer who has been board-certified in a specific field of law. **2.** *Securities.* A securities-exchange member who makes a market in one or more listed securities. • The exchange assigns securities to various specialists and expects them to maintain a fair and orderly market as provided by SEC standards.

special-needs analysis. (1989) *Criminal procedure.* A balancing test used by the Supreme Court to determine whether certain searches (such as administrative, civil-based, or public-safety searches) impose unreasonably on individual rights.

special pleading. (17c) **1.** The common-law system of pleading that required the parties to exchange a series of court papers (such as replications, rebutters, and surrebutters) setting out their contentions in accordance with hypertechnical rules before a case could be tried. • Often, therefore, cases were decided on points of pleading and not on the merits. **2.** The art of drafting pleadings under this system. **3.** An instance of drafting such a pleading. **4.** A responsive pleading that does more than merely deny allegations, as by introducing new matter to justify an otherwise blameworthy act. **5.** An argument that is unfairly slanted toward the speaker's viewpoint because it omits unfavorable facts or authorities and develops only favorable ones.

special plea in error. At common law, a plea alleging some extraneous matter as a ground for defeating a writ of error (such as a release or expiration of the time within which error can be brought), to which the plaintiff in error must reply or demur.

special power of appointment. Limited power of appointment.

special-purpose entity. A business established to perform no function other than to develop, own, and operate a large, complex project (usu. called a *single-purpose project*), esp. so as to limit the number of creditors claiming against the project. — Abbr. SPE.

special-relationship doctrine. (1981) The theory that if a state has assumed control over an individual sufficient to trigger an affirmative duty to protect that individual (as in an involuntary hospitalization or custody), then the state may be liable for the harm inflicted on the individual by a third party. • This is an exception to the general principle prohibiting members of the public from suing state employees for failing to protect them from third parties.

special-use permit. A zoning board's authorization to use property in a way that is identified as a special exception in a zoning ordinance. • Unlike a variance, which is an authorized violation of a zoning ordinance, a special-use permit is a permitted exception. — Abbr. SUP.

species (**spee**-sheez). **1.** A taxonomic class of organisms uniquely distinguished from other classes by shared characteristics and usu. by an inability to interbreed with members of other classes.

candidate species. *Environmental law.* Plants and animals identified by the Fish and Wildlife Service or National Marine Fisheries Service as potentially endangered or threatened but not of high enough priority to develop a proposed listing regulation under the Endangered Species Act. • Candidate species are not protected by federal law.

endangered species. A species in danger of becoming extinct; esp., under federal law, a species that is in danger of extinction throughout all or a significant part of its range. • Federal law excludes from the definition a species of the class Insecta if the Environmental Protection Agency determines that it constitutes a pest whose protection would present a significant risk to the human population. 50 CFR § 81.

threatened species. A species that, within the foreseeable future, is likely to become an endangered species throughout all or a significant part of its range. 16 USCA § 1532(20).

2. A specific class or kind of thing within a larger, general class. • For example, *tort* refers to a general class or genus. *Slander* refers to a specific kind of tort.

specification. (17c) **1.** The act of making a detailed statement, esp. of the measurements, quality, materials, or other items to be provided under a contract. **2.** The statement so made. **3.** *Patents.* The part of a patent application describing how an invention is made and used, the best mode of operation of the claimed invention, and the inventor's claims. • The specification must be clear and complete enough to enable a person of ordinary skill in the art to make and use the invention. It must also disclose the best mode of working the invention. The term may also refer to the description as separate from the claims. — Abbr. spec. **4.** A statement of charges against one who is accused of an offense, esp. a military offense. **5.** The acquisition of title to materials belonging to another person by converting those materials into a new and different form, as by changing grapes into wine, lumber into shelving, or corn into liquor. • The effect is that the original owner of the materials loses the property rights in them and is left with a right of action for their original value. — Abbr. spec.

specific-intent defense. *Criminal law.* A defendant's claim that he or she did not have the capacity (often supposedly because of intoxication or mental illness) to form the intent necessary for committing the crime alleged.

specific performance. (18c) The rendering, as nearly as practicable, of a promised performance through a judgment or decree; specif., a court-ordered remedy that requires precise fulfillment of a legal or contractual obligation when monetary damages are inappropriate or inadequate, as when the sale of real estate or a rare article is involved. • Specific performance is an equitable remedy that lies within the court's discretion to award whenever the common-law remedy is insufficient, either because damages would be inadequate or because the damages could not possibly be established.

specific-purpose rule. *Insurance.* The principle that a nonowner driver of a vehicle is treated as an omnibus insured under the vehicle owner's liability coverage only if the driver's actual use of the vehicle at the time of the accident is the exact use that the owner contemplated when granting permission or consent to the nonowner driver. • The time at which the bailment of the vehicle was to expire must not have passed, the place where the vehicle was being used must be as specified or contemplated by the insured, and the use of the vehicle must comport with the type of use that the insured had in mind when the bailment was created. Otherwise, the permittee's use of the vehicle will be regarded as a conversion.

specious, *adj.* Falsely appearing to be true, accurate, or just <specious argument>.

spectrograph. (1884) An electromagnetic machine that analyzes sound, esp. a human voice, by separating and mapping it into elements of frequency, time lapse, and intensity (represented by a series of horizontal and vertical bar lines) to produce a final voiceprint.

speculation, *n.* (14c) **1.** The buying or selling of something with the expectation of profiting from price fluctuations <he engaged in speculation in the stock market>. **2.** The act or practice of theorizing about matters over which there is no certain knowledge <the public's speculation about the assassination of John F. Kennedy>. — **speculate,** *vb.* — **speculative,** *adj.*

speculator. A knowledgeable, aggressive investor who trades securities to profit from fluctuating market prices.

speech. (bef. 12c) The expression or communication of thoughts or opinions in spoken words; something spoken or uttered.

commercial speech. (1963) Communication (such as advertising and marketing) that involves only the commercial interests of the speaker and the audience, and is therefore afforded lesser First Amendment protection than social, political, or religious speech.

corporate speech. (1959) Speech deriving from a corporation and protected under the First Amendment. • It does not lose protected status simply because of its corporate source.

hate speech. (1988) Speech that carries no meaning other than the expression of hatred for some group, such as a particular race, esp. in circumstances in which the communication is likely to provoke violence.

pure speech. (1943) Words or conduct limited in form to what is necessary to convey the idea. • This type of speech is given the greatest constitutional protection.

seditious speech. (1920) Speech advocating the violent overthrow of government.

symbolic speech. (1966) Conduct that expresses opinions or thoughts, such as a hunger strike or the wearing of a black armband. • Symbolic speech does not enjoy the same constitutional protection that pure speech does.

Speech Clause. The First Amendment provision that "Congress shall make no law . . . abridging the freedom of speech." U.S. Const. amend I.

Speech or Debate Clause. (1965) The clause of the U.S. Constitution giving members of Congress immunity for statements made during debate in either the House or the Senate. • This immunity is extended to other areas where it is necessary to prevent impairment of deliberations and other legitimate legislative activities, such as subpoenaing bank records for an investigation. U.S. Const. art. I, § 6., cl. 1.

speech-plus. Symbolic speech.

speedy trial. (18c) *Criminal procedure.* A trial that the prosecution, with reasonable diligence, begins promptly and conducts expeditiously. • The Sixth Amendment secures the right to a speedy trial. In deciding whether an accused has been deprived of that right, courts generally consider the length of and reason for the delay, and the prejudice to the accused.

Speedy Trial Act of 1974. A federal statute establishing time limits for carrying out the major events (such as information, indictment, arraignment, and trial commencement) in the prosecution of federal criminal cases. 18 USCA §§ 3161–3174.

spending bill. Appropriations bill.

spendthrift, *n.* One who spends lavishly and wastefully; a profligate. — **spendthrift,** *adj.*

spillover theory. (1985) The principle that a severance must be granted only when a defendant can show that a trial with a codefendant would substantially prejudice the defendant's case, as when the jury might wrongly use evidence against the defendant.

spirit of the law. (16c) The general meaning or purpose of the law, as opposed to its literal content.

spiritual, *adj.* Of or relating to ecclesiastical rather than secular matters <spiritual corporation>.

spite fence. (1901) A fence erected solely to annoy a neighbor, as by blocking the neighbor's view or preventing the neighbor from acquiring an easement of light <the court temporarily enjoined the completion of the 25-foot spite fence>.

split, *vb.* **1.** To divide (a cause of action) into segments or parts. **2.** To issue two or more shares for each old share without changing the shareholder's proportional ownership interest.

split fund. Dual fund.

split-funded plan. Employee benefit plan.

split-off, *n.* **1.** The creation of a new corporation by an existing corporation that gives its shareholders stock in the new corporation in return for their stock in the original corporation. **2.** The corporation created by this process.

splitting a cause of action. (1850) Separating parts of a demand and pursuing it piecemeal; presenting only a part of a claim in one lawsuit, leaving the rest for a second suit. • This practice has long been considered procedurally impermissible.

split-up, *n.* The division of a corporation into two or more new corporations. • The shareholders in the original corporation typically receive shares in the new corporations, and the original corporation goes out of business.

spoils system. The practice of awarding government jobs to supporters and friends of the victorious political party.

spoliation (spoh-lee-**ay**-shən), *n.* (18c) **1.** The intentional destruction, mutilation, alteration, or concealment of evidence, usu. a document. • If proved, spoliation may be used to establish that the evidence was unfavorable to the party responsible. **2.** The seizure of personal or real property by violent means; the act of pillaging. **3.** The taking of a benefit properly belonging to another. **4.** *Eccles. law.* The wrongful deprivation of a cleric of his benefice. — **spoliate** (**spoh**-lee-ayt), *vb.* — **spoliator** (**spoh**-lee-ay-tər), *n.*

sponsor. 1. One who acts as a surety for another. **2.** A legislator who proposes a bill. **3.** *Civil law.* One who voluntarily intervenes for another without being requested to do so. **4.** Godparent.

spontaneous abortion. Miscarriage.

spontaneous declaration. (1840) *Evidence.* A statement that is made without time to reflect or fabricate and is related to the circumstances of the perceived occurrence.

spot, *adj.* Made, paid, or delivered immediately <a spot sale> <spot commodities>.

spousal-impoverishment provision. A section of the Medicare Catastrophic Coverage Act allowing the stay-at-home spouse of a person residing in a nursing home to retain certain assets and some joint income, and to earn income without jeopardizing the institutionalized spouse's eligibility for Medicaid. • Before the provision was enacted in 1988, almost all of a couple's joint assets and the noninstitutionalized spouse's income had to go toward the cost of the nursing-home resident's care before Medicaid provided any support. 42 USCA § 1396r-5.

spousal labor. *Family law.* Work by either spouse during the marriage. • This term is typically used in community-property states.

spousal support. Alimony.

spouse. One's husband or wife by lawful marriage; a married person.

innocent spouse. (1924) *Tax.* A spouse who may be relieved of liability for taxes on income that the other spouse did not include on a joint tax return. • The innocent spouse must prove that the other spouse omitted the income, that the innocent spouse did not know and had no reason to know of the omission, and that it would be unfair under the circumstances to hold the innocent spouse liable.

putative spouse. *Family law.* A spouse who believes in good faith that his or her invalid marriage is legally valid.

surviving spouse. A spouse who outlives the other spouse.

spouse-breach. Adultery.

sprinkle power. In a sprinkle trust, the trustee's discretion about when and how much of the trust principal and income are to be distributed to the beneficiaries.

spurious (**spyoor**-ee-əs), *adj.* (16c) **1.** Deceptively suggesting an erroneous origin; fake <spurious trademarks>. **2.**

Of doubtful or low quality <spurious goods that fell apart>. **3.** *Archaic.* Of illegitimate birth <spurious offspring>.

square, *n.* (17c) **1.** A certain portion of land within a city limit. **2.** A space set apart for public use. **3.** In a government survey, an area measuring 24 by 24 miles.

squatter. (18c) **1.** A person who settles on property without any legal claim or title. **2.** A person who settles on public land under a government regulation allowing the person to acquire title upon fulfilling specified conditions.

squatter's rights. (1855) The right to acquire title to real property by adverse possession, or by preemption of public lands.

squeeze-out, *n.* An action taken in an attempt to eliminate or reduce a minority interest in a corporation.

ss. *abbr.* **1.** Sections. **2.** *Subscripsi* (i.e., signed below). **3.** Sans (i.e., without). **4.** (Erroneously) scilicet.

SSA. *abbr.* Social Security Administration.

SSDI. *abbr.* Social Security Disability Insurance.

SSI. *abbr.* Supplemental Security Income.

stabilize, *vb.* **1.** To make firm or steadfast <to stabilize the ship>. **2.** To maintain a particular level or amount <stabilize prices>.

stacking. (1982) **1.** *Insurance.* The process of obtaining benefits from a second policy on the same claim when recovery from the first policy alone would be inadequate.

judicial stacking. The principle that a court can construe insurance policies to permit stacking, under certain circumstances, when the policies do not specifically allow stacking but public policy is best served by permitting it.

policy stacking. Stacking that is permitted by the express terms of an insurance policy.

2. A gerrymandering technique in which a large political or racial group is combined in the same district with a larger opposition group.

staff attorney. **1.** Attorney. **2.** CLERK (5).

stagflation (stag-**flay**-shən), *n.* A period of slow economic growth or recession characterized by high inflation, stagnant consumer demand, and high unemployment. — **stagflationary,** *adj.*

stake, *n.* (bef. 12c) **1.** Something (such as property) deposited by two or more parties with a third party pending the resolution of a dispute; the subject matter of an interpleader. **2.** An interest or share in a business venture. **3.** Something (esp. money) bet in a wager, game, or contest. **4.** A boundary marker used in land surveys.

stakeholder. (18c) **1.** A disinterested third party who holds money or property, the right to which is disputed between two or more other parties. **2.** A person who has an interest or concern in a business or enterprise, though not necessarily as an owner. **3.** One who holds the money or valuables bet by others in a wager.

stalking. (bef. 12c) **1.** The act or an instance of following another by stealth. **2.** The offense of following or loitering near another, often surreptitiously, to annoy or harass that person or to commit a further crime such as assault or battery. • Some statutory definitions include an element that the person being stalked must reasonably feel harassed, alarmed, or distressed about personal safety or the safety of one or more persons for whom that person is responsible. And some definitions include acts such as telephoning another and remaining silent during the call.

stamp, *n.* (15c) An official mark or seal placed on a document, esp. to indicate that a required tax (such as duty or excise tax) has been paid.

stand. Witness stand.

standard, *n.* (15c) **1.** A model accepted as correct by custom, consent, or authority <what is the standard in the ant-farm industry?>. **2.** A criterion for measuring acceptability, quality, or accuracy <the attorney was making a nice living — even by New York standards>. — **standard,** *adj.*

objective standard. (1915) A legal standard that is based on conduct and perceptions external to a particular person. • In tort law, for example, the reasonable-person standard is considered an objective standard because it does not require a determination of what the defendant was thinking.

subjective standard. (1915) A legal standard that is peculiar to a particular person and based on the person's individual views and experiences. • In criminal law, for example, a subjective standard applies to determine premeditation because it depends on the defendant's mental state.

Standard & Poor's. An investment-analysis and -advisory service.

standard of care. (1890) *Torts.* In the law of negligence, the degree of care that a reasonable person should exercise.

standard of need. In public-assistance law, the total subsistence resources required by an individual or family unit as determined by a state and, when unsatisfied by available resources, entitles the individual or family unit to public assistance.

standard of proof. (1922) The degree or level of proof demanded in a specific case, such as "beyond a reasonable doubt" or "by a preponderance of the evidence."

standard of review. The criterion by which an appellate court exercising appellate jurisdiction measures the constitutionality of a statute or the propriety of an order, finding, or judgment entered by a lower court.

Standards for Imposing Lawyer Sanctions. The ABA's 1986 supplement to the Standards for Lawyer Discipline, prescribing a range of sanctions and guidelines for applying them. • Sanctions range from reprimands to disbarment.

Standards for Lawyer Discipline. A set of model rules, created by the ABA in 1979, establishing procedures for disciplining lawyers who violate ethics rules or commit crimes. • The rules stress that the process is an inquiry to determine an attorney's fitness to practice, not to determine a punishment.

standing, *n.* (1924) A party's right to make a legal claim or seek judicial enforcement of a duty or right. • To have standing in federal court, a plaintiff must show (1) that the challenged conduct has caused the plaintiff actual injury, and (2) that the interest sought to be protected is within the zone of interests meant to be regulated by the statutory or constitutional guarantee in question.

third-party standing. (1968) Standing held by someone claiming to protect the rights of others. • For example, in most jurisdictions, only a parent has standing to bring a suit for custody or visitation; in some, however, a third party — for instance, a grandparent or a person with whom the child has substantial contacts — may have standing to bring an action for custody or visitation.

standing by. (14c) **1.** The awaiting of an opportunity to respond, as with assistance. **2.** Silence or inaction when there is a duty to speak or act; esp., the tacit possession of knowledge under circumstances requiring the possessor to reveal the knowledge.

Standing Committee on Rules of Practice and Procedure. A group of judges, lawyers, and legal scholars appointed by the Chief Justice of the United States to advise the Judicial Conference of the United States on possible amendments to the procedural rules in the various federal courts and on other issues relating to the operation of the federal courts. 28 USCA § 331.

standing division. Standing vote.

stand mute. (16c) **1.** (Of a defendant) to refuse to enter a plea to a criminal charge. • Standing mute is treated as a plea of not guilty. **2.** (Of any party) to raise no objections.

standstill agreement. (1934) Any agreement to refrain from taking further action; esp., an agreement by which a party agrees to refrain from further attempts to take over a corporation (as by making no tender offer) for a specified period, or by which financial institutions agree not to call bonds or loans when due.

stand trial. (17c) To submit to a legal proceeding, esp. a criminal prosecution.

staple (**stay**-pəl). **1.** A key commodity such as wool, leather, tin, lead, butter, or cheese (collectively termed *the staple*). **2.** *Patents.* An unpatented thing or material that is a component of a patented product or is used in a patented process, but also has other practical uses. • Patentees may not gain control of the market for staples through tying agreements.

stare decisis (**stahr**-ee di-**sɪ**-sis *or* **stair**-ee), *n.* [Latin "to stand by things decided"] (18c) The doctrine of precedent, under which a court must follow earlier judicial decisions when the same points arise again in litigation.

horizontal stare decisis. The doctrine that a court, esp. an appellate court, must adhere to its own prior decisions, unless it finds compelling reasons to overrule itself.

super stare decisis. The theory that courts must follow earlier court decisions without considering whether those decisions were correct. • Critics argue that strict adherence to old decisions can result in grave injustices and cite as an example the repudiation of *Plessy v. Ferguson*, 163 U.S. 537, 16 S.Ct. 1138 (1896) by *Brown v. Board of Education*, 347 U.S. 483, 74 S.Ct. 686 (1954).

vertical stare decisis. The doctrine that a court must strictly follow the decisions handed down by higher courts within the same jurisdiction.

star paging, *n.* (1873) **1.** A method of referring to a page in an earlier edition of a book, esp. a legal source. • This method correlates the pagination of the later edition with that of the earlier (usu. the first) edition. **2.** By extension, the method of displaying on a computer screen the page breaks that occur in printed documents such as law reports and law reviews. — **star page,** *n.*

stash, *vb.* To hide or conceal (money or property).

stat. *abbr.* Statute.

state, *n.* (16c) **1.** The political system of a body of people who are politically organized; the system of rules by which jurisdiction and authority are exercised over such a body of people <separation of church and state>. **2.** An institution of self-government within a larger political entity; esp., one of the constituent parts of a nation having a federal government <the 50 states>. **3.** (*often cap.*) The people of a state, collectively considered as the party wronged by a criminal deed; esp., the prosecution as the representative of the people <the State rests its case>.

state action. (1893) Anything done by a government; esp., in constitutional law, an intrusion on a person's rights (esp. civil rights) either by a governmental entity or by a private requirement that can be enforced only by governmental action (such as a racially restrictive covenant, which requires judicial action for enforcement).

state-compulsion test. (1978) *Civil-rights law.* The rule that a state is responsible for discrimination that a private party commits while acting under the requirements of state law, as when a restaurant owner is required by state law to refuse service to minorities. *Adickes v. S.H. Kress & Co.*, 398 U.S. 144, 90 S.Ct. 1598 (1970).

stated, *adj.* **1.** Fixed; determined; settled <at the stated time> <settlement for a stated amount>. **2.** Expressed; declared <stated facts>.

State Department. Department of State.

state law. (18c) A body of law in a particular state consisting of the state's constitution, statutes, regulations, and common law.

stateless person. *Int'l law.* A natural person who is not considered a national by any country. • The Convention Relating to Status of Stateless Persons (1954) provides these people with certain protections and obliges them to abide by the laws of the country where they reside.

statement. (18c) **1.** *Evidence.* A verbal assertion or nonverbal conduct intended as an assertion. **2.** A formal and exact presentation of facts. **3.** *Criminal procedure.* An account of a person's knowledge of a crime, taken by the police during their investigation of the offense.

consonant statement. (1889) A witness's previous declaration, testified to by a person to whom the declaration was made and allowed into evidence only after the witness's testimony has been impeached. • This type of evidence would, but for the impeachment of the witness, be inadmissible hearsay.

false statement. (18c) **1.** An untrue statement knowingly made with the intent to mislead. **2.** Any one of three distinct federal offenses: (1) falsifying or concealing a material fact by trick, scheme, or device; (2) making a false, fictitious, or fraudulent representation; and (3) making or using a false document or writing. 18 USCA § 1001.

incriminating statement. (1896) A statement that tends to establish the guilt of someone, esp. the person making it.

prior consistent statement. (1883) A witness's earlier statement that is consistent with the witness's testimony at trial. • A prior consistent statement is not hearsay if it is offered to rebut a charge that the testimony was improperly influenced or fabricated. Fed. R. Evid. 801(d)(1)(B).

prior inconsistent statement. (1885) A witness's earlier statement that conflicts with the witness's testimony at trial. • In federal practice, extrinsic evidence of an unsworn prior inconsistent statement is admissible — if the witness is given an opportunity to explain or deny the statement — for impeachment purposes only. Fed. R. Evid. 613(b). Sworn statements may be admitted for all purposes. Fed. R. Evid. 801(d)(1)(A).

sworn statement. (1831) **1.** A statement given under oath; an affidavit. **2.** A contractor-builder's listing of suppliers and subcontractors, and their respective bids, required by a lending institution for interim financing.

voluntary statement. (1817) A statement made without the influence of duress, coercion, or inducement.

Statement and Account Clause. (1975) The clause of the U.S. Constitution requiring the regular publication of the receipts and expenditures of the federal government. U.S. Const. art. I, § 9, cl. 7.

statement of account. **1.** A report issued periodically (usu. monthly) by a bank to a customer, providing certain information on the customer's account, including the checks drawn and cleared, deposits made, charges debited, and the account balance. **2.** A report issued periodically (usu. monthly) by a creditor to a customer, providing certain information on the customer's account, including the amounts billed, credits given, and the balance due.

statement of defense. The assertions by a defendant; esp., in England, the defendant's answer to the plaintiff's statement of claim.

statement of fact. A form of conduct that asserts or implies the existence or nonexistence of a fact. • The term includes not just a particular statement that a particular fact exists or has existed, but also an assertion that, although perhaps expressed as an opinion, implies the existence of some fact or facts that have led the assertor to hold the opinion in question.

statement of facts. (18c) A party's written presentation of the facts leading up to or surrounding a legal dispute, usu. recited toward the beginning of a brief.

agreed statement of facts. A narrative statement of facts that is stipulated to be correct by the parties and is submitted to a tribunal for a ruling. • When the narrative statement is filed on appeal instead of a report of the trial proceedings, it is called an *agreed statement on appeal.*

statement of intention. *Bankruptcy.* A preliminary statement filed by an individual debtor in a chapter 7 case, in which the debtor details, among other things, whether property of the bankruptcy estate securing any debt will be retained or surrendered and whether the property is claimed as exempt. • The statement must be filed on or before the date of the first creditors' meeting or within 30 days after the bankruptcy petition is filed, whichever is earlier. 11 USCA § 521 (a)(2).

statement of principle. In legislative drafting, a sentence or paragraph that explains the legislature's purpose in passing a statute. • Although a statement of principle often resembles a preamble (usu. both do not appear in a single statute), it differs in that it typically appears in a numbered section of the statute.

statement of the case. In an appellate brief, a short review of what has happened procedurally in the lawsuit and how it reached the present court. • The statement introduces the reviewing court to the case by reciting the facts, procedures, decisions of the court or courts below as they are relevant to the appeal, and the reasons for those decisions.

statement of work. A contractual provision or exhibit that defines what one party (e.g., the seller) is going to do for the other (e.g., the buyer). • The statement of work often covers such terms as (1) inspection and acceptance, (2) quality-assurance requirements, (3) packing and marking, (4) data requirements, and (5) training. There are generally two types of specifications in a statement of work: a performance specification establishing the minimum requirements for items to be supplied, and a design specification establishing the methods to be used in meeting those minimum requirements. — Abbr. SOW.

state of mind. (17c) **1.** The condition or capacity of a person's mind; MENS REA. **2.** Loosely, a person's reasons or motives for committing an act, esp. a criminal act.

state-of-mind exception. (1949) *Evidence.* The principle that an out-of-court declaration of an existing motive is admissible, even when the declarant cannot testify in person. • This principle is an exception to the general rule that hearsay is inadmissible.

state of nature. (16c) The lack of a politically organized society. • The term is a hypothetical construct for the period in human history predating any type of political society.

state of the art. (1910) *Products liability.* The level of pertinent scientific and technical knowledge existing at the time of a product's manufacture, and the best technology reasonably available at the time the product was sold. — **state-of-the-art,** *adj.*

state of the case. The posture of litigation as it develops, as in discovery, at trial, or on appeal.

state of war. A situation in which war has been declared or armed conflict is in progress.

state police. (1843) The department or agency of a state government empowered to maintain order, as by investigating and preventing crimes, and making arrests.

state police power. (1849) The power of a state to enforce laws for the health, welfare, morals, and safety of its citizens, if enacted so that the means are reasonably calculated to protect those legitimate state interests.

state secret. (1822) A governmental matter that would be a threat to the national defense or diplomatic interests of the United States if revealed; information possessed by the government and of a military or diplomatic nature, the disclosure of which would be contrary to the public interest. • State secrets are privileged from disclosure by a witness in an ordinary judicial proceeding.

state sovereignty. (18c) The right of a state to self-government; the supreme authority exercised by each state.

states' rights. (1839) Under the Tenth Amendment, rights neither conferred on the federal government nor forbidden to the states.

state the question. *Parliamentary procedure.* (Of the chair) to formally state a motion as in order and ready for consideration.

stationhouse. 1. A police station or precinct. **2.** The lockup at a police precinct.

station-in-life test. *Family law.* An analysis performed by a court to determine the amount of money reasonably needed to maintain a particular person's accustomed lifestyle. • The elements were first set forth in *Canfield vs. Security-First Nat'l Bank*, 87 P.2d 830, 840 (Cal. 1939). The court takes into account the person's station in society and the costs of the person's support in that station, including housing and related expenses, medical care, further education, and other reasonably necessary expenses, but not including luxuries or extravagant expenditures.

statistical-decision theory. (1966) A method for determining whether a panel of potential jurors was selected from a fair cross section of the community, by calculating the probabilities of selecting a certain number of jurors from a particular group to analyze whether it is statistically probable that the jury pool was selected by mere chance. • This method has been criticized because a pool of potential jurors is not ordinarily selected by mere chance; potential jurors are disqualified for many legitimate reasons.

status. (17c) **1.** A person's legal condition, whether personal or proprietary; the sum total of a person's legal rights, duties, liabilities, and other legal relations, or any particular group of them separately considered <the status of a landowner>. **2.** A person's legal condition regarding personal rights but excluding proprietary relations <the status of a father> <the status of a wife>. **3.** A person's capacities and incapacities, as opposed to other elements of personal status <the status of minors>. **4.** A person's legal condition insofar as it is imposed by the law without the person's consent, as opposed to a condition that the person has acquired by agreement <the status of a slave>.

status quo (**stay**-təs *or* **stat**-əs **kwoh**). [Latin "state in which"] (1807) The situation that currently exists.

status quo ante (**stay**-təs **kwoh an**-tee). [Latin "state in which previously"] (1877) The situation that existed before something else (being discussed) occurred.

statutable (**stach**-ə-tə-bəl), *adj.* (17c) **1.** Prescribed or authorized by statute. **2.** Conforming to the legislative requirements for quality, size, amount, or the like. **3.** (Of an offense) punishable by law.

statute. (14c) A law passed by a legislative body; specif., legislation enacted by any lawmaking body, including legislatures, administrative boards, and municipal courts. • The term *act* is interchangeable as a synonym. For each of the subentries listed below, *act* is sometimes substituted for *statute.* — Abbr. s.; stat.

affirmative statute. (16c) A law requiring that something be done; one that directs the doing of an act.

codifying statute. (1908) A law that purports to be exhaustive in restating the whole of the law on a particular topic, including prior caselaw as well as legislative provisions. • Courts generally presume that a codifying statute supersedes prior caselaw.

compiled statutes. Laws that have been arranged by subject but have not been substantively changed; COMPILATION (2).

consolidating statute. (1886) A law that collects the legislative provisions on a particular subject and embodies them in a single statute, often with minor amendments and drafting improvements. • Courts generally presume that a consolidating statute leaves prior caselaw intact.

construction statute. A legislative directive included in a statute, intended to guide or direct a court's interpretation of the statute. • A construction act can, for example, be a simple statement such as "The word 'week' means seven consecutive days" or a broader directive such as "Words and phrases are to be read in context and construed according to the rules of grammar and common usage. Words and phrases that have acquired a technical or particular meaning, whether by legislative definition or otherwise, are to be construed accordingly."

criminal statute. (18c) A law that defines, classifies, and sets forth punishment for one or more specific crimes.

curative statute. **1.** An act that corrects an error in a statute's original enactment, usu. an error that interferes with interpreting or applying the statute. **2.** Remedial statute.

declaratory statute. (17c) A law enacted to clarify prior law by reconciling conflicting judicial decisions or by explaining the meaning of a prior statute.

directory statute. (1834) A law that indicates only what should be done, with no provision for enforcement.

disabling statute. (18c) A law that limits or curbs certain rights.

enabling statute. (18c) A law that permits what was previously prohibited or that creates new powers; esp., a congressional statute conferring powers on an executive agency to carry out various delegated tasks.

expository statute. Declaratory statute.

general statute. (16c) A law pertaining to an entire community or all persons generally.

mandatory statute. (18c) A law that requires a course of action as opposed to merely permitting it.

model statute. Uniform statute.

negative statute. (16c) A law prohibiting something; a law expressed in negative terms.

nonclaim statute. (18c) **1.** Statute of limitations. **2.** A law that sets a time limit for creditors to bring claims against a decedent's estate. • Unlike a statute of limitations, a nonclaim statute is usu. not subject to tolling and is not waivable.

organic statute. (1856) A law that establishes an administrative agency or local government.

penal statute. (16c) A law that defines an offense and prescribes its corresponding fine, penalty, or punishment.

permissive statute. A statute that allows certain acts but does not command them. • A permissive statute creates a license or privilege, or allows discretion in performing an act.

perpetual statute. (16c) A law containing no provision for repeal, abrogation, or expiration.

prohibitive statute. A statute that forbids all acts that disturb society's peace or forbids certain acts on other grounds. • An example of a noncriminal prohibitive statute is one forbidding the execution of a mentally retarded criminal because a person who lacks mental capacity cannot understand the reason for the punishment.

prospective statute. (1831) A law that applies to future events.

quasi-statute. An executive or administrative order, or a regulation promulgated by a governmental agency, that has the binding effect of legislation.

remedial statute. (18c) A law that affords a remedy.

repealing statute. A statute that revokes, and sometimes replaces, an earlier statute. • A repealing statute may work expressly or by implication.

revised statutes. (18c) Laws that have been collected, arranged, and reenacted as a whole by a legislative body. — Abbr. Rev. Stat.; R.S.

revival statute. (1899) A law that provides for the renewal of actions, of wills, and of the legal effect of documents. • A revival statute cannot resurrect a time-barred criminal prosecution. *Stegner v. California*, 539 U.S. 607, 123 S.Ct. 2446 (2003).

severable statute. (1930) A law that remains operative in its remaining provisions even if a portion of the law is declared unconstitutional.

single-act statute. Long-arm statute.

speaking statute. (2000) A statute to be interpreted in light of the understanding of its terms prevailing at the time of interpretation.

special statute. (17c) A law that applies only to specific individuals, as opposed to everyone.

split-level statute. (1980) A law that includes officially promulgated explanatory materials in addition to its substantive provisions, so that courts are left with two levels of documents to construe.

temporary statute. (17c) **1.** A law that specifically provides that it is to remain in effect for a fixed, limited period. **2.** A law (such as an appropriation statute) that, by its nature, has only a single and temporary operation.

uniform statute. A law drafted with the intention that it will be adopted by all or most of the states; esp., uniform law.

validating statute. (1882) A law that is amended either to remove errors or to add provisions to conform to constitutional requirements.

statute book. (16c) A bound collection of statutes, usu. as part of a larger set of books containing a complete body of statutory law, such as the United States Code Annotated.

statute of distribution. (18c) A state law regulating the distribution of an estate among an intestate's heirs and relatives.

statute of frauds. (18c) **1.** *Hist.* (*cap.*) A 1677 English statute that declared certain contracts judicially unenforceable (but not void) if they were not committed to writing and signed by the party to be charged. • The statute was entitled "An Act for the Prevention of Frauds and Perjuries" (29 Car. 2, ch. 3). **2.** A statute (based on the English Statute of Frauds) designed to prevent fraud and perjury by requiring certain contracts to be in writing and signed by the party to be charged. • Statutes of frauds traditionally apply to the following types of contracts: (1) a contract for the sale or transfer of an interest in land, (2) a contract that cannot be performed within one year of its making, (3) a contract for the sale of goods valued at $500 or more, (4) a contract of an executor or administrator to answer for a decedent's debt, (5) a contract to guarantee the debt or duty of another, and (6) a contract made in consideration of marriage. UCC § 2-201. — Abbr. S/F; SOF.

statute of limitations. (18c) **1.** A law that bars claims after a specified period; specif., a statute establishing a time limit for suing in a civil case, based on the date when the claim accrued (as when the injury occurred or was discovered). • The purpose of such a statute is to require diligent prosecution of known claims, thereby providing finality and predictability in legal affairs and ensuring that claims will be resolved while evidence is reasonably available and fresh. **2.** A statute establishing a time limit for prosecuting a crime, based on the date when the offense occurred.

statute of repose. (18c) A statute barring any suit that is brought after a specified time since the defendant acted (such as by designing or manufacturing a product), even if this period ends before the plaintiff has suffered a resulting injury.

statute of wills. (17c) **1.** (*cap.*) An English statute (enacted in 1540) that established the right of a person to devise real property by will. **2.** A state statute, usu. derived from the English statute, providing for testamentary disposition and if certain requirements for valid execution in that jurisdiction are met.

Statutes at Large. An official compilation of the acts and resolutions that become law from each session of Congress, printed in chronological order.

statutory (**stach**-ə-tor-ee), *adj.* (18c) **1.** Of or relating to legislation <statutory interpretation>. **2.** Legislatively created <the law of patents is purely statutory>. **3.** Conformable to a statute <a statutory act>.

statutory construction. (1813) **1.** The act or process of interpreting a statute. **2.** Collectively, the principles developed by courts for interpreting statutes.

statutory exclusion. *Criminal procedure.* The removal, by law, of certain crimes from juvenile-court jurisdiction.

statutory exposition. (1854) A statute's special interpretation of the ambiguous terms of a previous statute <the statute contained a statutory exposition of the former act>.

statutory law. (17c) The body of law derived from statutes rather than from constitutions or judicial decisions.

statutory right of redemption. (1857) The right of a mortgagor in default to recover property after a foreclosure sale by paying the principal, interest, and other costs that are owed, together with any other measure required to cure the default. • This statutory right exists in many states but is not uniform.

stay, *n.* (16c) **1.** The postponement or halting of a proceeding, judgment, or the like. **2.** An order to suspend all or part of a judicial proceeding or a judgment resulting from that proceeding. — **stay,** *vb.* — **stayable,** *adj.*

automatic stay. Bankruptcy. A bar to all judicial and extrajudicial collection efforts against the debtor or the debtor's property, subject to specific statutory exceptions. 11 USCA §§ 362 (a)–(b). • The policy behind the automatic stay, which is effective upon the filing of the bankruptcy petition, is that all actions against the debtor should be halted pending the determination of creditors' rights and the orderly administration of the debtor's assets free from creditor interference.

STD. *abbr.* Sexually transmitted disease.

steal, *vb.* (bef. 12c) **1.** To take (personal property) illegally with the intent to keep it unlawfully. **2.** To take (something) by larceny, embezzlement, or false pretenses.

step-in-the-dark rule. (1955) *Torts.* The contributory-negligence rule that a person who enters a totally unfamiliar area in the darkness has a duty, in the absence of unusual stress, to refrain from proceeding until first ascertaining whether any dangerous obstacles exist.

sterilization. 1. The act of making (a person or other living thing) permanently unable to reproduce. **2.** The act of depriving (a person or other living thing) of reproductive organs; esp., castration.

stet (stet), *n.* [Latin "let it stand"] (18c) **1.** An order staying legal proceedings, as when a prosecutor determines not to proceed on an indictment and places the case on a stet docket. • The term is used chiefly in Maryland. **2.** An instruction to leave a text as it stands.

stickup. (1904) An armed robbery in which the victim is threatened by the use of weapons.

stillborn, *adj.* (Of an infant) born dead.

sting. (1976) An undercover operation in which law-enforcement agents pose as criminals to catch actual criminals engaging in illegal acts.

stipend (**stɪ**-pend *or* -pənd). **1.** A salary or other regular, periodic payment. **2.** A tribute to support the clergy, usu. consisting of payments in money or grain.

stipulation (stip-yə-**lay**-shən), *n.* (18c) **1.** A material condition or requirement in an agreement; esp., a factual representation that is incorporated into a contract as a term <breach of the stipulation regarding payment of taxes>. • Such a contractual term often appears in a section of the contract called "Representations and Warranties." **2.** A voluntary agreement between opposing parties concerning some relevant point; esp., an agreement relating to a proceeding, made by attorneys representing adverse parties to the proceeding <the plaintiff and defendant entered into a stipulation on the issue of liability>. • A stipulation relating to a pending judicial proceeding, made by a party to the proceeding or the party's attorney, is binding without consideration. **3.** *Roman law.* A formal contract by which a promisor (and only the promisor) became bound by oral question and answer. • By the third century A.D., stipulations were always evidenced in writing. — **stipulate** (**stip**-yə-layt), *vb.* — **stipulative** (**stip**-yə-lə-tiv), *adj.*

stirpital (**stər**-pə-təl), *adj.* (1886) Of or relating to per stirpes distribution.

stirps (stərps), *n.* [Latin "stock"] (17c) A branch of a family; a line of descent. Pl. **stirpes** (**stər**-peez).

stock, *n.* (14c) **1.** The original progenitor of a family; a person from whom a family is descended; BRANCH (1) <George Harper, Sr. was the stock of the Harper

line>. **2.** A merchant's goods that are kept for sale or trade <the car dealer put last year's models on sale to reduce its stock>. **3.** The capital or principal fund raised by a corporation through subscribers' contributions or the sale of shares <Acme's stock is worth far more today than it was 20 years ago>. **4.** A proportional part of a corporation's capital represented by the number of equal units (or shares) owned, and granting the holder the right to participate in the company's general management and to share in its net profits or earnings <Julia sold her stock in Pantheon Corporation>.

stock bonus plan. A special type of profit-sharing plan in which the distribution of benefits consists of the employer-company's own stock.

stockbroker. One who buys or sells stock as agent for another.

stock certificate. An instrument evidencing ownership of shares of stock.

face-amount certificate. **1.** A certificate, investment contract, or other security representing an obligation by its issuer to pay a stated or determinable sum, at a fixed or determinable date or dates more than 24 months after the date of issuance, in consideration of the payment of periodic installments of a stated or determinable amount. **2.** A security representing a similar obligation on the part of the issuer of a face-amount certificate, the consideration for which is the payment of a single lump sum. See 15 USCA § 80a-2(a)(15).

periodic-payment-plan certificate. A certificate, investment contract, or other security providing for a series of periodic payments by the holder and representing an undivided interest in certain specified securities or in a unit or fund of securities purchased wholly or partly with the proceeds of those payments. See 15 USCA § 80a-2(a)(27).

stock in trade. **1.** The inventory carried by a retail business for sale in the ordinary course of business. **2.** The tools and equipment owned and used by a person engaged in a trade. **3.** The equipment and other items needed to run a business.

stock option. **1.** An option to buy or sell a specific quantity of stock at a designated price for a specified period regardless of shifts in market value during the period. **2.** An option that allows a corporate employee to buy shares of corporate stock at a fixed price or within a fixed period. • Such an option is usu. granted as a form of compensation and can qualify for special tax treatment under the Internal Revenue Code.

stock-purchase plan. An arrangement by which an employer corporation allows employees to purchase shares of the corporation's stock.

stock-repurchase plan. A program by which a corporation buys back its own shares in the open market, usu. when the corporation believes the shares are undervalued.

stock sale. *Mergers & acquisitions.* A takeover in which the acquiring corporation buys stock directly from the target corporation's shareholders until it controls all or a majority of the target's stock.

stock split. The issuance of two or more new shares in exchange for each old share without changing the proportional ownership interests of each shareholder. • For example, a 3-for-1 split would give an owner of 100 shares a total of 300 shares, or 3 shares for each share previously owned. A stock split lowers the price per share and thus makes the stock more attractive to potential investors.

reverse stock split. A reduction in the number of a corporation's shares by calling in all outstanding shares and reissuing fewer shares having greater value.

stonewall, *vb.* To persistently refuse to cooperate in an investigation; esp., to refuse to testify or to hand over requested material until every available legal challenge has been exhausted. — **stonewalling,** *n.*

stool pigeon. *Slang.* **1.** An informant, esp. a police informant. **2.** A person who acts as a decoy, esp. on behalf of a gambler or swindler, or for the police to help make an arrest.

stop, *n.* (16c) Under the Fourth Amendment, a temporary restraint that prevents a person from walking away.

stop and frisk, *n.* (1963) A police officer's brief detention, questioning, and search of a person for a concealed weapon when the officer reasonably suspects that the person has committed or is about to commit a crime. • The stop and frisk, which can be conducted without a warrant or probable cause, was held constitutional by the Supreme Court in *Terry v. Ohio,* 392 U.S. 1, 88 S.Ct. 1868 (1968).

stop-notice statute. (1963) A law providing an alternative to a mechanic's lien by allowing a contractor, supplier, or worker to make a claim against the construction lender and, in some instances, the owner for a portion of the undisbursed construction-loan proceeds.

stoppage, *n.* (15c) An obstruction or hindrance to the performance of some act <stoppage of goods or persons in transit for inspection>.

stoppage *in transitu* (in **tran**-si-t[y]oo *or* **tranz**-i-t[y]oo). (18c) The right of a seller of goods to regain possession of those goods from a common carrier under certain circumstances, even though the seller has already parted with them under a contract for sale. • This right traditionally applies when goods are consigned wholly or partly on credit from one person to another, and the consignee becomes bankrupt or insolvent before the goods arrive — in which event the consignor may direct the carrier to deliver the goods to someone other than the consignee (who can no longer pay for them).

store, *n.* (13c) **1.** A place where goods are deposited for purchase or sale. **2.** (*usu. pl.*) A supply of articles provided for the subsistence and accommodation of a ship's crew and passengers. **3.** A place where goods or supplies are stored for future use; a warehouse.

store, *vb.* (13c) To keep (goods, etc.) in safekeeping for future delivery in an unchanged condition.

STR. *abbr.* Suspicious-transaction report.

straight bankruptcy. CHAPTER 7 (2).

strain theory. (18c) The theory that people commit crimes to alleviate stress created by the disjunction between their station in life and the station to which society has conditioned them to aspire.

strand, *n.* (bef. 12c) A shore or bank of an ocean, lake, river, or stream.

stranding, *n. Maritime law.* A ship's drifting, driving, or running aground on a strand. • The type of stranding that occurs determines the method of apportioning the liability for any resulting losses.

accidental stranding. Stranding caused by natural forces, such as wind and waves.

voluntary stranding. Stranding to avoid a more dangerous fate or for fraudulent purposes.

stranger. (14c) **1.** One who is not party to a given transaction; esp., someone other than a party or the party's employee, agent, tenant, or immediate family member. **2.** One not standing toward another in some relation implied in the context; esp., one who is not in privity. **3.** A person who voluntarily pays another person's debt even though the payor cannot be held liable for the debt and the payor's property is not affected by the creditor's rights. • Subrogation does not apply to a stranger if the debtor did not agree to or assign subrogation rights.

stranger in blood. (17c) **1.** One not related by blood, such as a relative by affinity. **2.** Any person not within the consideration of natural love and affection arising from a relationship.

stratagem. (15c) A trick or deception to obtain an advantage, esp. in a military conflict.

strategic alliance. (1983) A coalition formed by two or more persons in the same or complementary businesses to gain long-term financial, operational, or marketing advantages without jeopardizing competitive independence <through their strategic alliance, the manufacturer and distributor of a co-developed product shared development costs>.

straw man. (1896) **1.** A fictitious person, esp. one that is weak or flawed. **2.** A tenuous and exaggerated counterargument that an advocate makes for the sole purpose of disproving it. **3.** A third party used in some transactions as a temporary transferee to allow the principal parties to accomplish something that is otherwise impermissible. **4.** A person hired to post a worthless bail bond for the release of an accused.

straw poll. A nonbinding vote, taken as a way of informally gauging support or opposition but usu. without a formal motion or debate.

stream-of-commerce theory. (1942) **1.** The principle that a state may exercise personal jurisdiction over a defendant if the defendant places a product in the general marketplace and the product causes injury or damage in the forum state, as long as the defendant also takes other acts to establish some connection with the forum state, as by advertising there or by hiring someone to serve as a sales agent there. *Asahi Metal Indus. Co., Ltd. v. Superior Court of Cal.*, 480 U.S. 102, 107 S.Ct. 1026 (1987). **2.** The principle that a person who participates in placing a defective product in the general marketplace is strictly liable for harm caused by the product. Restatement (Second) of Torts § 402A (1979).

strict, *adj.* (15c) **1.** Narrow; restricted <strict construction>. **2.** Rigid; exacting <strict statutory terms>. **3.** Severe <strict punishment>. **4.** Absolute; requiring no showing of fault <strict liability>.

strict scrutiny. (1941) *Constitutional law.* The standard applied to suspect classifications (such as race) in equal-protection analysis and to fundamental rights (such as voting rights) in due-process analysis. • Under strict scrutiny, the state must establish that it has a compelling interest that justifies and necessitates the law in question.

strict test. *Evidence.* The principle that disclosure of a privileged document, even when inadvertent, results in a waiver of the attorney–client privilege regarding the document, unless all possible precautions were taken to protect the document from disclosure.

strike, *n.* (1810) **1.** An organized cessation or slowdown of work by employees to compel the employer to meet the employees' demands; a concerted refusal by employees to work for their employer, or to work at their customary rate of speed, until the employer grants the concessions that they seek.

general strike. A strike organized to affect an entire industry.

illegal strike. **1.** A strike using unlawful procedures. **2.** A strike to obtain unlawful objectives, as in a strike to force an employer to stop doing business with a particular company.

secondary strike. A strike against an employer because that employer has business dealings with another employer directly involved in a dispute with the union.

sit-down strike. A strike in which employees occupy the workplace but do not work.

slowdown strike. A strike in which the workers remain on the job but work at a slower pace to reduce their output.

sympathy strike. A strike by union members who have no grievance against their own employer but who want to show support for another union involved in a labor dispute.

whipsaw strike. A strike against some but not all members of a multiemployer association, called for the purpose of pressuring all the employees to negotiate a labor contract. • Employers whose workers are not on strike have the right to lock out employees to exert counterpressure on the union.

wildcat strike. A strike not authorized by a union or by a collective-bargaining agreement.

2. The removal of a prospective juror from the jury panel <a peremptory strike>. **3.** A failure or disadvantage, as by a criminal conviction <a strike on one's record>. **4.** *Parliamentary law.* A form of the motion to amend by deleting one or more words.

strike, *vb.* (14c) **1.** (Of an employee or union) to engage in a strike <the flight attendants struck to protest the reduction in benefits>. **2.** To remove (a prospective juror) from a jury panel by a peremptory challenge or a challenge for cause <the prosecution struck the panelist who indicated an opposition to the death penalty>. **3.** To expunge, as from a record <motion to strike the prejudicial evidence>.

strike down. (1894) To invalidate (a statute); to declare void.

strike fund. A union fund that provides benefits to its members who are on strike, esp. for subsistence while the members are not receiving wages.

striking a jury. (1859) The selecting of a jury out of all the candidates available to serve on the jury; esp., the selecting of a special jury.

strip, *n.* (16c) **1.** The act of separating and selling a bond's coupons and corpus separately. **2.** The act of a tenant who, holding less than the entire fee in land, spoils or unlawfully takes something from the land.

structure. (15c) **1.** Any construction, production, or piece of work artificially built up or composed of parts purposefully joined together <a building is a structure>. **2.** The organization of elements or parts <the corporate structure>. **3.** A method of constructing parts <the loan's payment structure was a financial burden>.

style, *n.* A case name or designation <the style of the opinion is *Connor v. Gray*>.

s.u. *abbr.* Straight up. • When a prosecutor writes this on a defendant's file, it usu. means that the prosecutor plans to try the case — that is, not enter into a plea bargain.

suable, *adj.* (17c) **1.** Capable of being sued <a suable party>. **2.** Capable of being enforced <a suable contract>. — **suability,** *n.*

sua sponte (s[y]**oo**-ə **spon**-tee). [Latin "of one's own accord; voluntarily"] Without prompting or suggestion; on its own motion <the court took notice sua sponte that it lacked jurisdiction over the case>.

sub (səb). [Latin] Under; upon.

subcontractor. (1834) One who is awarded a portion of an existing contract by a contractor, esp. a general contractor. • For example, a contractor who builds houses typically retains subcontractors to perform specialty work such as installing plumbing, laying carpet, making cabinetry, and landscaping — each subcontractor is paid a somewhat lesser sum than the contractor receives for the work.

subdivision, *n.* (15c) **1.** The division of a thing into smaller parts. **2.** A parcel of land in a larger development. — **subdivide,** *vb.*

subdivision map. (1887) A map that shows how a parcel of land is to be divided into smaller lots, and generally showing the layout and utilities.

subjacent (səb-**jay**-sənt), *adj.* (16c) Located underneath or below <the land's subjacent support>.

subject, *adj.* Referred to above; having relevance to the current discussion <the subject property was then sold to Smith>.

subject, *n.* (14c) **1.** One who owes allegiance to a sovereign and is governed by that sovereign's laws <the monarchy's subjects>. **2.** The matter of concern over which something is created <the subject of the statute>.

subject, *adj.* Referred to above; having relevance to the current discussion <the subject property was then sold to Smith>.

subjection. (14c) **1.** The act of subjecting someone to something <their subjection to torture was unconscionable>. **2.** The condition of a subject in a monarchy; the obligations surrounding such a person <a subject, wherever residing, owes fidelity and obedience to the Crown, while an alien may be released at will from all such ties of subjection>. **3.** The condition of being subject, exposed, or liable; liability <the defendants' subjection to the plaintiffs became clear shortly after the trial began>.

subjective, *adj.* (18c) **1.** Based on an individual's perceptions, feelings, or intentions, as opposed to externally verifiable phenomena <the subjective theory of contract — that the parties must have an actual meeting of the minds — is not favored by most courts>. **2.** Personal; individual <subjective judgments about popular music>.

subjective ethics. Moral relativism.

subjective theory of contract. (1928) The doctrine (now largely outmoded) that a contract is an agreement in which the parties have a subjective meeting of the minds.

subject matter. (16c) **1.** The issue presented for consideration; the thing in which a right or duty has been asserted; the thing in dispute. **2.** Patentable subject matter. — **subject-matter,** *adj.*

subject-matter test. (1974) A method of determining whether an employee's communication with a corporation's lawyer was made at the direction of the employee's supervisors and in the course and scope of the employee's employment, so as to be protected under the attorney–client privilege, despite the fact that the employee is not a member of the corporation's control group. *Harper & Row Pubs., Inc. v. Decker,* 423 F.2d 487 (7th Cir. 1970), *aff'd per curiam by equally divided Court,* 400 U.S. 348, 91 S.Ct. 479 (1971).

subject of a right. (1876) **1.** The owner of a right; the person in whom a legal right is vested. **2.** Object of a right.

subject to liability, *adj.* (Of a person) susceptible to a lawsuit that would result in an adverse judgment; specif., having engaged in conduct that would make the actor liable for another's injury because the actor's conduct is the legal cause of the injury, the injured party having no disability for bringing the lawsuit.

subject to open. (1906) Denoting the future interest of a class of people when this class is subject to a possible increase or decrease in number.

sub judice (səb **joo**-di-see *also* suub **yoo**-di-kay), *adv.* [Latin "under a judge"]

(17c) Before the court or judge for determination; at bar <in the case sub judice, there have been no out-of-court settlements>. • Legal writers sometimes use "case sub judice" where "the present case" would be more comprehensible.

sublease, *n.* A lease by a lessee to a third party, conveying some or all of the leased property for a term shorter than or equal to that of the lessee, who retains a reversion in the lease. — **sublease, sublet,** *vb.*

sublessee. (1882) A third party who receives by lease some or all of the leased property from a lessee.

sublessor. (1884) A lessee who leases some or all of the leased property to a third party.

sublicense. (1880) A license or contract granting to a third party a portion or all of the rights granted to the licensee under an original license.

submission, *n.* (14c) **1.** A yielding, or readiness to yield, to the authority or will of another <his resistance ended in an about-face: complete submission>. **2.** A contract in which the parties agree to refer their dispute to a third party for resolution <in their submission to arbitration, they referred to the rules of the American Arbitration Association>. **3.** An advocate's argument <neither the written nor the oral submissions were particularly helpful>. — **submit,** *vb.*

submission to a finding. The admission to facts sufficient to warrant a finding of guilt.

submission to the jury. (1818) The process by which a judge gives a case to the jury for its consideration and verdict, usu. after all evidence has been presented, arguments have been completed, and jury instructions have been given.

submit, *vb.* To end the presentation of further evidence in (a case) and tender a legal position for decision <case submitted, Your Honor>.

sub nomine (səb **nom**-ə-nee). [Latin] (1861) Under the name of. • This phrase, typically in abbreviated form, is often used in a case citation to indicate that there has been a name change from one stage of the case to another, as in *Guernsey Memorial Hosp. v. Secretary of Health and Human Servs.*, 996 F.2d 830 (6th Cir. 1993), *rev'd sub nom. Shalala v. Guernsey Memorial Hosp.*, 514 U.S. 87, 115 S.Ct. 1232 (1995). — Abbr. *sub nom.*

subordinate (sə-**bor**-də-nit), *adj.* (15c) **1.** Placed in or belonging to a lower rank, class, or position <a subordinate lien>. **2.** Subject to another's authority or control <a subordinate lawyer>.

subordinate (sə-**bor**-də-nayt), *vb.* (17c) To place in a lower rank, class, or position; to assign a lower priority to <subordinate the debt to a different class of claims>.

suborn (sə-**born**), *vb.* [Latin *subonare*, from *sub* "secretly + *ornare* "to furnish; equip"] (16c) **1.** To induce (a person) to commit an unlawful or wrongful act, esp. in a secret or underhanded manner. **2.** To induce (a person) to commit perjury. **3.** To obtain (perjured testimony) from another. — **subornation** (səb-or-**nay**-shən), *n.* — **suborner** (sə-**bor**-nər), *n.*

subornation of perjury. (16c) The crime of persuading another to commit perjury. — Sometimes shortened to *subornation.*

subparagraph form. A style of legal drafting that uses indented subparagraphs for enumerated items; esp., a style of drafting patent claims in this form so as to distinguish clearly between each of the claimed elements.

subpoena (sə-**pee**-nə), *n.* [Latin "under penalty"] (15c) A writ or order commanding a person to appear before a court or other tribunal, subject to a penalty for failing to comply. Pl. **subpoenas.**

alias subpoena (**ay**-lee-əs sə-**pee**-nə). (18c) A second subpoena issued after an initial subpoena has failed.

deposition subpoena. **1.** A subpoena issued to summon a person to make a sworn statement in a time and place other than a trial. **2.** In some jurisdictions, a subpoena duces tecum.

friendly subpoena. A subpoena issued to a person or entity that is willing to testify or produce documents, but only if legally required to do so. • The subpoena may protect the information provider from retaliation from others because the provider is required to comply.

subpoena ad testificandum (sə-**pee**-nə ad tes-tə-fi-**kan**-dəm). [Law Latin] (1807) A subpoena ordering a witness to appear and give testimony.

subpoena duces tecum (sə-**pee**-nə **d**[**y**]**oo**-seez **tee**-kəm *also* **doo**-səz **tay**-kəm). [Law Latin] (18c) A subpoena ordering the witness to appear in court and to bring specified documents, records, or things.

subpoena, *vb.* (17c) **1.** To serve with a subpoena to appear before a court or other tribunal <subpoena the material witnesses>. **2.** To order the production of (documents or other things) by subpoena duces tecum <subpoena the corporate records>.

subpoenal (sə-**pee**-nəl), *adj.* (1969) Required or done under penalty, esp. in compliance with a subpoena.

subrogate (**səb**-rə-gayt), *vb.* (15c) To substitute (a person) for another regarding a legal right or claim.

subrogation (səb-rə-**gay**-shən), *n.* (15c) **1.** The substitution of one party for another whose debt the party pays, entitling the paying party to rights, remedies, or securities that would otherwise belong to the debtor. • For example, a surety who has paid a debt is, by subrogation, entitled to any security for the debt held by the creditor and the benefit of any judgment the creditor has against the debtor, and may proceed against the debtor as the creditor would. Subrogation most commonly arises in relation to insurance policies. **2.** The equitable remedy by which such a substitution takes place. **3.** The principle under which an insurer that has paid a loss under an insurance policy is entitled to all the rights and remedies belonging to the insured against a third party with respect to any loss covered by the policy.

subscription, *n.* (15c) **1.** The act of signing one's name on a document; the signature so affixed. **2.** *Securities.* A written contract to purchase newly issued shares of stock or bonds. **3.** An oral or a written agreement to contribute a sum of money or property, gratuitously or with consideration, to a specific person or for a specific purpose. **4.** RESCRIPT (3). — **subscribe,** *vb.* — **subscriber,** *n.*

subsequent, *adj.* (15c) (Of an action, event, etc.) occurring later; coming after something else.

subsequent remedial measure. (*usu. pl.*) (1956) *Evidence.* An action taken after an event, which, if taken before the event, would have reduced the likelihood of the event's occurrence. • Evidence of subsequent remedial measures, such as repairs made after an accident or the installation of safety equipment, is not admissible to prove negligence, but it may be admitted to prove ownership, control, feasibility, or the like. Fed. R. Evid. 407.

subsidy (**səb**-sə-dee), *n.* (14c) **1.** A grant, usu. made by the government, to any enterprise whose promotion is considered to be in the public interest. • Although governments sometimes make direct payments (such as cash grants), subsidies are usu. indirect. They may take the form of research-and-development support, tax breaks, provision of raw materials at below-market prices, or low-interest loans or low-interest export credits guaranteed by a government agency. **2.** A specific financial contribution by a foreign government or public entity conferring a benefit on exporters to the United States. • Such a subsidy is countervailable under 19 USCA §§ 1671, 1677. — **subsidize,** *vb.*

sub silentio (səb si-**len**-shee-oh). [Latin] (17c) Under silence; without notice being taken; without being expressly mentioned (such as precedent *sub silentio*).

subsistence. (17c) Support; means of support.

substance. (14c) **1.** The essence of something; the essential quality of something, as opposed to its mere form <matter of substance>. **2.** Any matter, esp. an addictive drug <illegal substance> <abuse of a substance>.

substance-abuse evaluation and treatment. (1983) A drug offender's court-ordered participation in a drug rehabilitation program. • This type of treatment is esp. common in DUI cases. — Abbr. SAET.

substantial-capacity test. (1968) *Criminal law.* The Model Penal Code's test for the insanity defense, stating that a person is not criminally responsible for an act if, as a result of a mental disease or defect, the person lacks substantial capacity either to appreciate the criminality of the conduct or to conform the conduct to the law. • This test combines elements of both the *McNaghten* rules and the irresistible-impulse test by allowing consideration of both volitional and cognitive weaknesses. This test was formerly used by the federal courts and many states, but since 1984 many jurisdictions (including the federal courts) — in response to the acquittal by reason of insanity of would-be presidential assassin John Hinckley — have narrowed the insanity defense and adopted a new test resembling the *McNaghten* rules, although portions of the substantial-capacity test continue to be used. Model Penal Code § 4.01.

substantial-cause test. (1929) *Torts.* The principle that causation exists when the defendant's conduct is an important or significant contributor to the plaintiff's injuries.

substantial-certainty test. *Copyright.* The test for deciding whether a second work was copied from the first. • The question is whether a reasonable observer would conclude with substantial certainty that the second work is a copy.

substantial-compliance rule. Substantial-performance doctrine.

substantial-continuity doctrine. A principle for holding a successor corporation liable for the acts of its predecessor corporation, if the successor maintains the same business as the predecessor, with the same employees, doing the same jobs, for the same supervisors, under the same working conditions, and using the same production processes to produce the same products for the same customers.

substantial-evidence rule. (1938) The principle that a reviewing court should uphold an administrative body's ruling if it is supported by evidence on which the administrative body could reasonably base its decision.

substantial-factor test. (1929) Substantial-cause test.

substantially justified. (Of conduct, a position, etc.) having a reasonable basis in law and in fact. • Under the Equal Access to Justice Act, a prevailing party in a lawsuit against the government will be unable to recover its attorney's fees if the government's position is substantially justified.

substantial-performance doctrine. (1936) The rule that if a good-faith attempt to perform does not precisely meet the terms of an agreement or statutory requirements, the performance will still be considered complete if the essential purpose is accomplished, subject to a claim for damages for the shortfall. • Under the Uniform Probate Code, a will that is otherwise void because some formality has not been followed may still be valid under the substantial-performance doctrine. But this rule is not widely followed.

substantial-step test. (1980) *Criminal law.* The Model Penal Code's test for determining whether a person is guilty of attempt, based on the extent of the defendant's preparation for the crime, the criminal intent shown, and any statements personally made that bear on the defendant's actions. Model Penal Code § 5.01(1)(c).

substantiate, *vb.* (17c) To establish the existence or truth of (a fact, etc.), esp. by competent evidence; to verify.

substantive law (**səb**-stən-tiv). (18c) The part of the law that creates, defines, and regulates the rights, duties, and powers of parties.

substitute, *n.* **1.** One who stands in another's place <a substitute for a party>. **2.** *Civil law.* A person named in a will as heir to an estate after the estate has been held and then passed on by another specified person (called the *institute*). **3.** *Parliamentary law.* A form of the motion to amend by replacing one or more words with others. — **substitute,** *vb.*

substituted-judgment doctrine. (1967) A principle that allows a surrogate decision-maker to attempt to establish, with as much accuracy as possible, what healthcare decision an incompetent patient would make if he or she were competent to do so. • The standard of proof is by clear and convincing evidence. Generally, the doctrine is used for a person who was once competent but no longer is.

substitution. (14c) **1.** A designation of a person or thing to take the place of another person or thing. **2.** The process by which one person or thing takes the place of another person or thing. **3.** *Parliamentary law.* An amendment by replacing one or more words with others. **4.** *Civil law.* The designation of a person to succeed another as beneficiary of an estate, usu. involving a fideicommissum.

substitutional, *adj.* (14c) Capable of taking or supplying the position of another <substitutional executor> <substitutional issue>.

substitution-of-judgment doctrine. **1.** *Administrative law.* The standard for reviewing an agency's decision, by which a court uses its own independent judgment in interpreting laws and administrative regulations — rather than deferring to the agency — when the agency's interpretation is not instructive or the regulations do not involve matters requiring the agency's expertise. **2.** *Wills & estates.* The principle that a guardian, conservator, or committee of an incompetent person may make gifts out of that person's estate.

substitution of parties. The replacement of one litigant by another because of the first litigant's death, incompetency, transfer of interest, or, when the litigant is a public official, separation from office.

substraction (səb-**strak**-shən), *n.* (1814) The secret misappropriation of property, esp. from a decedent's estate.

subsume (səb-**s[y]oom**), *vb.* (1825) To judge as a particular instance governed by a general principle; to bring (a case) under a broad rule. — **subsumption** (səb-**səmp**-shən), *n.*

subsurety (səb-**shuur**[-ə]-tee). (1916) A person whose undertaking is given as additional security, usu. conditioned not only on nonperformance by the principal but also on nonperformance by an earlier promisor as well; a surety with the lesser liability in a subsuretyship.

subsuretyship (səb-**shuur**[-ə]-tee-ship). (1967) The relation between two (or more) sureties, in which a principal surety bears the burden of the whole performance that is due from both sureties; a relationship in which one surety acts as a surety for another.

subsurface interest. 1. A landowner's right to the minerals and water below the property. **2.** A similar right held by another through grant by, or purchase from, a landowner.

subterfuge (**səb**-tər-fyooj). (16c) A clever plan or idea used to escape, avoid, or conceal something <a subterfuge to avoid liability under a statute>.

subversion. (14c) The process of overthrowing, destroying, or corrupting <subversion of legal principles> <subversion of the government>.

subversive activity. (1939) A pattern of acts designed to overthrow a government by force or other illegal means.

succession, *n.* (14c) **1.** The act or right of legally or officially taking over a predecessor's office, rank, or duties. **2.** The acquisition of rights or property by inheritance under the laws of descent and distribution; DESCENT (1). — **succeed,** *vb.*

hereditary succession. Intestate succession.

intestate succession. (18c) **1.** The method used to distribute property owned by a person who dies without a valid will. **2.** Succession by the common law of descent.

irregular succession. (17c) Succession by special laws favoring certain persons or the state, rather than heirs (such as testamentary heirs) under the ordinary laws of descent.

legal succession. (18c) The succession established by law, usu. in favor of the nearest relation of a deceased person.

natural succession. (18c) Succession between natural persons, as in descent on the death of an ancestor.

testate succession. (18c) The passing of rights or property by will.

universal succession. Succession to an entire estate of another at death. • This type of succession carries with it the predecessor's liabilities as well as assets. Originally developed by Roman law and later continued by civil law, this concept has now been widely adopted as an option endorsed and authorized by the Uniform Probate Code.

vacant succession. *Civil law.* **1.** A succession that fails either because there are no known heirs or because the heirs have renounced the estate. **2.** An estate that has suffered such a failure.

3. The right by which one group, in replacing another group, acquires all the goods, movables, and other chattels of a corporation. **4.** The continuation of a corporation's legal status despite changes in ownership or management.

successional, *adj.* (14c) Of or relating to acquiring rights or property by inheritance under the laws of descent and distribution.

succession tax. Inheritance tax.

successive-writ doctrine. (1987) *Criminal procedure.* The principle that a second or supplemental petition for a writ of habeas corpus may not raise claims that were heard and decided on the merits in a previous petition.

successor. (14c) **1.** A person who succeeds to the office, rights, responsibilities, or place of another; one who replaces or follows a predecessor. **2.** A corporation that, through amalgamation, consolidation, or other assumption of interests, is vested with the rights and duties of an earlier corporation.

successor in interest. (1832) One who follows another in ownership or control of property. • A successor in interest retains the same rights as the original owner, with no change in substance.

such, *adj.* (bef. 12c) **1.** Of this or that kind <she collects a variety of such things>. **2.** That or those; having just been mentioned <a newly discovered Fabergé egg will be on auction next week; such egg is expected to sell for more than $500,000>.

sudden-onset rule. (1981) The principle that medical testimony is unnecessary to prove causation of the obvious symptoms of an injury that immediately follows a known traumatic incident.

sudden passion. Heat of passion.

sudden-peril doctrine. EMERGENCY DOCTRINE (1).

sue, *vb.* To institute a lawsuit against (another party).

sue facts. (1980) Facts that determine whether a party should bring a lawsuit; esp., facts determining whether a shareholder-derivative action should be instituted under state law.

sue out, *vb.* (15c) **1.** To apply to a court for the issuance of (a court order or writ). **2.** To serve (a complaint) on a defendant.

suffer, *vb.* (14c) **1.** To experience or sustain physical or emotional pain, distress, or injury <suffer grievously><suffer damages>. **2.** To allow or permit (an act, etc.) <to suffer a default>.

sufferance (**səf**-ər-ənts *or* **səf**-rənts). (14c) **1.** Toleration; passive consent. **2.** The state of one who holds land without the owner's permission. **3.** A license implied from the omission to enforce a right.

sufficiency-of-evidence test. (1972) *Criminal procedure.* **1.** The guideline for a grand jury considering whether to indict a suspect: if all the evidence presented were uncontradicted and unexplained, it would warrant a conviction by the fact-trier. **2.** A standard for reviewing a criminal conviction on appeal, based on whether enough evidence exists to justify the fact-trier's finding of guilt beyond a reasonable doubt.

suffrage (**səf**-rij). (14c) **1.** The right or privilege of casting a vote at a public election. **2.** A vote; the act of voting.

suggestibility, *n.* The readiness with which a person accepts another's suggestion. — **suggestible,** *adj.*

suggestio falsi (səg-**jes**-tee-oh **fal**-sɪ *or* **fawl**-sɪ). [Latin] A false representation or misleading suggestion.

suggestion, *n.* (14c) **1.** An indirect presentation of an idea <the client agreed with counsel's suggestion to reword the warranty>. **2.** *Procedure.* A statement of some fact or circumstance that will materially affect the further proceedings in the case <suggestion for rehearing en banc>. **3.** *Archaic. Wills & estates.* Undue influence. — **suggest** (for senses 1 & 2), *vb.*

suggestion of bankruptcy. (1869) A pleading by which a party notifies the court that the party has filed for bankruptcy and that, because of the automatic stay provided by the bankruptcy laws, the court cannot take further action in the case.

suggestion of death. (18c) A pleading filed by a party, or the party's representatives, by which the court is notified that a party to a suit has died.

suggestion of error. (1811) An objection made by a party to a suit, indicating that the court has committed an error or that the party wants a rehearing of a particular issue.

suggestion on the record. A formal written or oral statement informing the court of an important fact that may require a stay of proceedings or affect the court's decision. • Suggestions on the record include suggestion of bankruptcy, suggestion of death, and suggestion of error.

suicide, *n.* (17c) **1.** The act of taking one's own life.

assisted suicide. (1976) The intentional act of providing a person with the medical means or the medical knowledge to commit suicide.

attempted suicide. (1880) An unsuccessful suicidal act.

physician-assisted suicide. A type of assisted suicide.

suicide-by-cop. *Slang.* A form of suicide in which the suicidal person intentionally engages in life-threatening behavior to induce a police officer to shoot the person. • Frequently, the decedent attacks the officer or otherwise threatens the officer's life, but occasionally a third person's life is at risk. A suicide-by-cop is distinguished from other police shootings by three elements. The person must: (1) evince an intent to die; (2) consciously understand the finality of the act; and (3) confront a law enforcement official with behavior so extreme that it compels that officer to act with deadly force.

2. A person who has taken his or her own life. — **suicidal,** *adj.*

suicide clause. *Insurance.* A life-insurance-policy provision either excluding suicide as a covered risk or limiting the insurer's liability in the event of a suicide to the total premiums paid.

sui generis (**s[y]oo**-I *or* **soo**-ee **jen**-ə-ris). [Latin "of its own kind"] (18c) Of its own kind or class; unique or peculiar. • The term is used in intellectual-property law to describe a regime designed to protect rights that fall outside the traditional patent, trademark, copyright, and trade-secret doctrines. For example, a database may not be protected by copyright law if its content is not original, but it could be protected by a sui generis statute designed for that purpose.

sui juris (**s[y]oo**-I *or* **soo**-ee **joor**-is). [Latin "of one's own right; independent"] (17c) **1.** Of full age and capacity. **2.** Possessing full social and civil rights.

suit. (14c) Any proceeding by a party or parties against another in a court of law; CASE (1).

ancillary suit (**an**-sə-ler-ee). (1845) An action, either at law or in equity, that grows out of and is auxiliary to another suit and is filed to aid the primary suit, to enforce a prior judgment, or to impeach a prior decree.

blackmail suit. (1892) A suit filed by a party having no genuine claim but hoping to extract a favorable settlement from a defendant who would rather avoid the expense and inconvenience of litigation.

frivolous suit. (1837) A lawsuit having no legal basis, often filed to harass or extort money from the defendant.

official-capacity suit. A lawsuit that is nominally against one or more individual state employees but that has as the real party in interest the state or a local government.

personal-capacity suit. An action to impose personal, individual liability on a government officer.

plenary suit (**plee**-nə-ree *or* **plen**-ə-ree). (1817) An action that proceeds on formal pleadings under rules of procedure.

strike suit. (1902) A suit (esp. a derivative action), often based on no valid claim, brought either for nuisance value or as leverage to obtain a favorable or inflated settlement.

suit at law. A suit conducted according to the common law or equity, as distinguished from statutory provisions. • Under the current rules of practice in federal and most state courts, the term *civil action* embraces an action both at law and in equity. Fed. R. Civ. P. 2.

suit in equity. A civil suit stating an equitable claim and asking for an exclusively equitable remedy.

suit for exoneration. (1928) A suit in equity brought by a surety to compel the debtor to pay the creditor. • If the debtor has acted fraudulently and is insolvent, a suit for exoneration may include further remedies to ensure that the debtor's assets are applied equitably to the debtor's outstanding obligations.

suit money. (1846) Attorney's fees and court costs allowed or awarded by a court; esp., in some jurisdictions, a husband's payment to his wife to cover her reasonable attorney's fees in a divorce action.

suitor. (16c) **1.** A party that brings a lawsuit; a plaintiff or petitioner. **2.** An individual or company that seeks to take over another company.

sum certain. (16c) **1.** Any amount that is fixed, settled, or exact. **2.** *Commercial law.* In a negotiable instrument, a sum that is agreed on in the instrument or a sum that can be ascertained from the document.

summary, *adj.*(15c) **1.** Short; concise <a summary account of the events on March 6>. **2.** Without the usual formalities; esp., without a jury <a summary trial>. **3.** Immediate; done without delay <the new weapon was put to summary use by the military>. — **summarily** (**səm**-ər-ə-lee *or* sə-**mair**-ə-lee), *adv.*

summary, *n.* (16c) **1.** An abridgment or brief. **2.** A short application to a court without the formality of a full proceeding.

summary judgment. (18c) A judgment granted on a claim or defense about which there is no genuine issue of material fact and upon which the movant is entitled to prevail as a matter of law. • The court considers the contents of the pleadings, the motions, and additional evidence adduced by the parties to determine whether there is a genuine issue of material fact rather than one of law. This procedural device allows the speedy disposition of a controversy without the need for trial. Fed. R. Civ. P. 56.

partial summary judgment. (1924) A summary judgment that is limited to certain issues in a case and that disposes of only a portion of the whole case.

summary of the argument. The part of a brief, esp. an appellate brief, in which the advocate condenses the argument to a précis or synopsis, directing the court to the heart of the argument on each point. • A summary typically runs from one to four pages.

summary procedure. Show-cause proceeding.

summary trial. Summary proceeding.

summation. Closing argument.

summer associate. CLERK (4).

summing up. Closing argument. — **sum up,** *vb.*

summon, *vb.* (13c) To command (a person) by service of a summons to appear in court.

summons, *n.* (13c) **1.** A writ or process commencing the plaintiff's action and requiring the defendant to appear and answer. **2.** A notice requiring a person to appear in court as a juror or witness. Pl. **summonses.**

sum payable. (17c) An amount due; esp., the amount for which the maker of a negotiable instrument becomes liable and must tender in full satisfaction of the debt.

sunset law. (1976) A statute under which a governmental agency or program automatically terminates at the end of a fixed period unless it is formally renewed.

sunshine committee. (2000) An official or quasi-official committee whose proceedings and work are open to public access.

sunshine law. (1972) A statute requiring a governmental department or agency to open its meetings or its records to public access.

SUP. *abbr.* Special-use permit.

sup. ct. *abbr.* Supreme Court.

Superfund. (1977) **1.** The program that funds and administers the cleanup of hazardous-waste sites through a trust fund (financed by taxes on petroleum and chemicals and a tax on certain corporations) created to pay for cleanup pending reimbursement from the liable parties. **2.** The popular name for the act that established this program — the Comprehensive Environmental Response, Compensation, and Liability Act of 1980 (CERCLA).

superior, *adj.* (14c) (Of a rank, office, power, etc.) higher; elevated; possessing greater power or authority; entitled to exert authority or command over another <superior estate> <superior force> <superior agent>. — **superior,** *n.*

superior force. 1. Force majeure. **2.** Act of God. **3.** *Vis major.*

superior-knowledge rule. The doctrine that when a property owner knows or should know that a hazardous condition exists on the property, and the condition is not obvious to a person exercising reasonable care, the owner must make the premises reasonably safe or else warn others of the hazardous condition. Restatement (Second) of Torts § 343A. But the exception is neither automatic nor absolute. See *id.* § 343A(1) & cmt. f.

superlien. (1984) A government's lien that is imposed on a property whose condition violates environmental and public-health and public-safety rules and that has priority over all other liens, so that the government can recover public funds spent on cleanup operations. • A statutory lien is superior to all existing liens and all later-filed liens on the same property. Superliens are sometimes granted to a state's environmental-protection agency. Several states — including Arkansas, Connecticut, Massachusetts, New Hampshire, New Jersey, and Tennessee — have enacted statutes creating superliens on property owned by a party responsible for environmental cleanup.

supersede, *vb.* (17c) **1.** To annul, make void, or repeal by taking the place of <the 1996 statute supersedes the 1989 act>. **2.** To invoke or make applicable the right of supersedeas against (an award of damages) <what is the amount of the bond necessary to supersede the judgment against her?>. — **supersession** (for sense 1), *n.*

supersedeas (soo-pər-**seed**-ee-əs), *n.* [Latin "you shall desist"] (14c) A writ or bond that suspends a judgment creditor's power to levy execution, usu. pending appeal. Pl. **supersedeases** (soo-pər-**see**-dee-əs-iz).

supervisor, *n.* (15c) **1.** One having authority over others; a manager or overseer. • Under the National Labor Relations Act, a supervisor is any individual having authority to hire, transfer, suspend, lay off, recall, promote, discharge, discipline, and handle grievances of other employees, by exercising independent judgment. **2.** The chief administrative officer of a town or county. — **supervisorial** (soo-pər-vɪ-**zor**-ee-əl), *adj.* — **supervision,** *n.*

supervisory control. The control exercised by a higher court over a lower court, as by prohibiting the lower court from acting extrajurisdictionally and by reversing its extrajurisdictional acts.

supplemental, *adj.* (17c) Supplying something additional; adding what is lacking <supplemental rules>.

supplemental register. *Trademarks.* A roll of trademarks that are ineligible for listing on the Principal Register because they are not distinctive. • Marks on the supplemental register are not protected by trademark law, except to the extent that the listing may bar the registration of a similar mark. The listing may be required, however, for the mark to be registered in other countries. 15 USCA § 1091.

Supplemental Security Income. A welfare or needs-based program providing monthly income to the aged, blind, or disabled. • It is authorized by the Social Security Act. — Abbr. SSI.

suppliant (**səp**-lee-ənt). (15c) One who humbly requests something; specif., the actor in a petition of right.

supplier, *n.* **1.** A person engaged, directly or indirectly, in the business of making a product available to consumers. **2.** A person who gives possession of a chattel for another's use or allows someone else to use or occupy it while it is in the person's possession or control.

supply curve. A line on a price-output graph showing the relationship between a good's price and the quantity supplied at a given time.

support, *n.* (14c) **1.** Sustenance or maintenance; esp., articles such as food and clothing that allow one to live in the degree of comfort to which one is accustomed. **2.** One or more monetary payments to a current or former family member for the purpose of helping the recipient maintain an acceptable standard of living. **3.** Basis or foundation. **4.** The bracing of land so that it does not cave in because of another landowner's actions. — **support,** *vb.*

lateral support. Support by the land that lies next to the land under consideration.

subjacent support. Support by the earth that lies underneath the land under consideration.

support obligation. (1938) A secondary obligation or letter-of-credit right that supports the payment or performance of an account, chattel paper, general intangible, document, healthcare-insurance receivable, instrument, or investment property. UCC § 9-102(a)(53).

support order. (1948) A court decree requiring a party (esp. one in a divorce or paternity proceeding) to make payments to maintain a child or spouse, including medical, dental, and educational expenses.

foreign support order. An out-of-state support order.

suppress, *vb.* To put a stop to, put down, or prohibit; to prevent (something) from being seen, heard, known, or discussed <the defendant tried to suppress the incriminating evidence>. — **suppression,** *n.* — **suppressible, suppressive,** *adj.*

suppression of evidence. (18c) **1.** A trial judge's ruling that evidence offered by a party should be excluded because it was illegally acquired. **2.** The destruction of evidence or the refusal to give evidence at a criminal proceeding. • This is usu. considered a crime. **3.** The prosecution's withholding from the defense of evidence that is favorable to the defendant.

suppressio veri (sə-**pres**[**h**]-ee-oh **veer**-ɪ). [Latin] Suppression of the truth; a type of fraud.

supra (**s**[**y**]**oo**-prə). [Latin "above"] (15c) Earlier in this text; used as a citational signal to refer to a previously cited authority.

supralegal, *adj.* Above or beyond the law <a supralegal sovereign>.

supranational, *adj.* Free of the political limitations of nations.

supra protest. (Of a debt) under protest.

supra riparian (**soo**-prə ri-**pair**-ee-ən *or* rɪ-). (1857) Upper riparian; higher up the stream. • This phrase describes the estate, rights, and duties of a riparian owner whose land is situated nearer the source of a stream than the land it is compared to.

supremacy. (16c) The position of having the superior or greatest power or authority.

Supremacy Clause. (1940) The clause in Article VI of the U.S. Constitution declaring that the Constitution, all laws made in furtherance of the Constitution, and all treaties made under the authority of the United States are the "supreme law of the land" and enjoy legal superiority over any conflicting provision of a state constitution or law.

supreme, *adj.* (16c) (Of a court, power, right, etc.) highest; superior to all others.

supreme court. (17c) **1.** (*cap.*) Supreme Court of the United States. **2.** An appellate court existing in most states, usu. as the court of last resort. **3.** In New York, a court of general jurisdiction with trial and appellate divisions. • The Court of Appeals is the court of last resort in New York. **4.** Supreme Court of Judicature. — Abbr. S.C.; S.Ct.; Sup. Ct.

Supreme Court of Appeals. The highest court in West Virginia.

Supreme Court of the United States. The court of last resort in the federal system, whose members are appointed by the President and approved by the Senate. • The Court was established in 1789 by Article III of the U.S. Constitution, which vests the Court with the "judicial power of the United States."

supreme law of the land. (18c) **1.** The U.S. Constitution. **2.** Acts of Congress made in accordance with the U.S. Constitution. **3.** U.S. treaties.

surcharge, *n.* **1.** An additional tax, charge, or cost, usu. one that is excessive. **2.** An additional load or burden. **3.** A second or further mortgage. **4.** The omission of a proper credit on an account. **5.** The amount that a court may charge a fiduciary that has breached its duty. **6.** An overprint on a stamp, esp. one that changes its face value. **7.** The overstocking of an area with animals. — **surcharge,** *vb.*

surety (**shuur**[-ə]-tee). (14c) **1.** A person who is primarily liable for paying another's debt or performing another's obligation. • Although a surety is similar to an insurer, one important difference is that a surety often receives no compensation for assuming liability. A surety differs from a guarantor, who is liable to the creditor only if the debtor does not meet the duties owed to the creditor; the surety is directly liable. **2.** A formal assurance; esp., a pledge, bond, guarantee, or security given for the fulfillment of an undertaking.

surface. 1. The top layer of something, esp. of land. **2.** *Mining law.* An entire portion of land, including mineral deposits, except those specifically reserved. • The meaning of the term varies, esp. when used in legal instruments, depending on the language used, the intention of the parties, the business involved, and the nature and circumstances of the transaction.

surface-damage clause. *Oil & gas.* A lease provision requiring the lessee to pay the lessor or the surface-interest owner for all or for a specified kind or degree of damage to the surface that results from oil-and-gas operations.

Surgeon General. (18c) **1.** The chief medical officer of the U.S. Public Health Service or of a state public-health agency. **2.** The chief officer of the medical departments in the armed forces. — Abbr. SG.

surmise (sər-**mɪz**), *n.* (18c) An idea based on weak evidence; conjecture.

surplus. 1. The remainder of a thing; the residue or excess. **2.** The excess of receipts over disbursements.

surplusage (**sər**-pləs-ij). (15c) **1.** Redundant words in a statute or legal instrument; language that does not add meaning <the court must give effect to every word, reading nothing as mere surplusage>. **2.** Extraneous matter in a pleading <allegations that are irrelevant to the case will be treated as surplusage>.

surprise. (15c) An occurrence for which there is no adequate warning or that affects someone in an unexpected way. • In a trial, the procedural rules are designed to limit surprise — or trial by ambush — as much as possible. For example, the parties in a civil case are permitted to conduct discovery, to determine the essential facts of the case and the identities of possible witnesses, and to inspect relevant documents. At trial, if a party calls a witness who has not been previously identified, the witness's testimony may be excluded if it would unfairly surprise and prejudice the other party. And if a party has diligently prepared the case and is nevertheless taken by surprise on a material point at trial, that fact can sometimes be grounds for a new trial or for relief from the judgment under Rules 59 and 60 of the Federal Rules of Civil Procedure.

surrebuttal (sər-ri-**bət**-əl). (1853) The response to the opposing party's rebuttal in a trial or other proceeding; a rebuttal to a rebuttal <called two extra witnesses in surrebuttal>.

surrebutter (sər-ri-**bət**-ər). *Common-law pleading.* (17c) The plaintiff's answer of fact to the defendant's rebutter.

surrejoinder (sər-ri-**joyn**-dər). *Common-law pleading.* (16c) The plaintiff's answer to the defendant's rejoinder.

surrender, *n.* (15c) **1.** The act of yielding to another's power or control. **2.** The giving up of a right or claim; RELEASE (1). **3.** The return of an estate to the person who has a reversion or remainder, so as to merge the estate into a larger estate. **4.** *Commercial law.* The delivery of an instrument so that the delivery releases the deliverer from all liability. **5.** A tenant's relinquishment of possession before the lease has expired, allowing the landlord to take possession and treat the lease as terminated. — **surrender,** *vb.*

surrender by bail. (18c) A surety's delivery of a prisoner, who had been released on bail, into custody.

surrender by operation of law. (1836) An act that is an equivalent to an agreement by a tenant to abandon property and the landlord to resume possession, as when the parties perform an act so inconsistent with the landlord–tenant relationship that surrender is presumed, or when a tenant performs some act that would not be valid if the estate continued to exist.

surrender of charter. *Corporations.* The dissolution of a corporation by a formal yielding of its charter to the state under which it was created and the subsequent acceptance of that charter by the state.

surreptitious (sər-əp-**tish**-əs), *adj.* (15c) (Of conduct) unauthorized and clandestine; stealthily and usu. fraudulently done <surreptitious interception of electronic communications is prohibited under wiretapping laws>.

surrogacy. 1. The act of performing some function in the place of someone else. **2.** The process of carrying and delivering a child for another person.

- ***gestational surrogacy.*** A pregnancy in which one woman (the genetic mother) provides the egg, which is fertilized, and another woman (the surrogate mother) carries the fetus and gives birth to the child.

- ***traditional surrogacy.*** A pregnancy in which a woman provides her own egg, which is fertilized by artificial insemination, and carries the fetus and gives birth to a child for another person.

surrogate (**sər**-ə-git), *n.* (17c) **1.** A substitute; esp., a person appointed to act in the place of another <in his absence, Sam's wife acted as a surrogate>. **2.** A probate judge <the surrogate held that the will was valid>. **3.** One who acts in place of another. — **surrogate,** *adj.* — **surrogacy** (**sər**-ə-gə-see), **surrogate-ship,** *n.*

surrogate-parenting agreement. (1985) A contract between a woman and typically an infertile couple under which the woman provides her uterus to carry an embryo throughout pregnancy; esp., an agreement between a person (the intentional parent) and a woman (the surrogate mother) providing that the surrogate mother will (1) bear a child for the intentional parent, and (2) relinquish any and all rights to the child.

surrogate's court. Probate court.

surrounding circumstances. (1828) The facts underlying an act, injury, or transaction — usu. one at issue in a legal proceeding.

surtax exemption. (18c) **1.** An exclusion of an item from a surtax. **2.** An item or an amount not subject to a surtax.

surveillance (sər-**vay**-lənts), *n.* (1802) Close observation or listening of a person or place in the hope of gathering evidence. — **surveil** (sər-**vayl**), *vb.*

survey, *n.* (16c) **1.** A general consideration of something; appraisal <a survey of the situation>. **2.** The measuring of a tract of land and its boundaries and contents; a map indicating the results of such measurements <the lender requires a survey of the property before it will issue a loan>. **3.** A governmental department that carries out such measurements <please obtain the boundaries from survey>. **4.** A poll or questionnaire, esp. one examining popular opinion <the radio station took a survey of the concert audience>. **5.** *Maritime law.* A written assessment of the current condition of a vessel or cargo. — **survey,** *vb.*

survival action. (1938) A lawsuit brought on behalf of a decedent's estate for injuries or damages incurred by the decedent immediately before dying. • A survival action derives from the claim that a decedent would have had — such as for pain and suffering — if he or she had survived. In contrast is a claim that the beneficiaries may have in a wrongful-death action, such as for loss of consortium or loss of support from the decedent.

survival clause. *Wills & estates.* A testamentary provision conditioning a bequest on a beneficiary's living for a specified period, often 60 days, after the testator's death. • If the beneficiary dies within the stated period, the testamentary gift usu. accrues to the residuary estate.

surviving, *adj.* (16c) Remaining alive; living beyond the happening of an event so as to entitle one to a distribution of property or income <surviving spouse>.

survivor. (15c) **1.** One who outlives another. **2.** A trustee who administers a trust after the cotrustee has been removed, has refused to act, or has died.

survivorship. (17c) **1.** The state or condition of being the one person out of two or more who remains alive after the others die. **2.** The right of a surviving party having a joint interest with others in an estate to take the whole.

suspect, *n.* (14c) A person believed to have committed a crime or offense.

suspect, *vb.* **1.** To consider (something) to be probable. **2.** To consider (something) possible. **3.** To consider (a person) as having probably committed wrongdoing, but without certain truth.

reasonably suspect. **1.** To consider (something) to be probable under circumstances in which a reasonable person would be led to that conclusion. **2.** To consider (someone) as having probably committed wrongdoing under circumstances in which a reasonable person would be led to that conclusion.

suspect class. (1952) A group identified or defined in a suspect classification.

suspect classification. (1949) *Constitutional law.* A statutory classification based on race, national origin, or alienage, and thereby subject to strict scrutiny under equal-protection analysis. • Examples of laws creating suspect classifications are those permitting only U.S. citizens to receive welfare benefits and setting quotas for the government's hiring of minority contractors.

quasi-suspect classification. A statutory classification based on gender or legitimacy, and therefore subject to intermediate scrutiny under equal-protection analysis. • Examples of laws creating a quasi-suspect classification are those permitting alimony for women only and providing for an all-male draft.

suspend, *vb.* (14c) **1.** To interrupt; postpone; defer <the fire alarm suspended the prosecutor's opening statement>. **2.** To temporarily keep (a person) from performing a function, occupying an office, holding a job, or exercising a right or privilege <the attorney's law license was suspended for violating the Model Rules of Professional Conduct>.

suspend the rules. *Parliamentary law.* To pass a motion that overrides an agenda or other procedural rule, for a limited time and purpose, so that the deliberative assembly may take some otherwise obstructed action.

suspense. (15c) The state or condition of being suspended; temporary cessation <a suspense of judgment>.

suspension. (15c) **1.** The act of temporarily delaying, interrupting, or terminating something <suspension of business operations> <suspension of a statute>. **2.** The state of such delay, interruption, or termination <corporate transfers were not allowed because of the suspension of business>. **3.** The temporary deprivation of a person's powers or privileges, esp. of office or profession; esp., a fairly stringent level of lawyer discipline that prohibits the lawyer from practicing law for a specified period, usu. from several months to several years <suspension of the bar license>. • Suspension may entail requiring the lawyer to pass a legal-ethics bar examination, or to take one or more ethics courses as continuing legal education, before being readmitted to active practice. **4.** The temporary withdrawal from employment, as distinguished from permanent severance <suspension from teaching without pay>.

suspension of trading. The temporary cessation of all trading of a particular stock on a stock exchange because of some abnormal market condition.

suspicion. (14c) The apprehension or imagination of the existence of something wrong based only on inconclusive or slight evidence, or possibly even no evidence.

reasonable suspicion. (18c) A particularized and objective basis, supported by specific and articulable facts, for suspecting a person of criminal activity. • A police officer must have a reasonable suspicion to stop a person in a public place.

suspicious-activity report. (1996) A form that, as of 1996, a financial institution must complete and submit to federal regulatory authorities if it suspects that a federal crime has occurred in the course of a monetary transaction. • This form superseded two earlier forms, the criminal-referral form and the suspicious-transaction report. — Abbr. SAR.

suspicious character. (18c) In some states, a person who is strongly suspected or known to be a habitual criminal and therefore may be arrested or required to give security for good behavior.

suspicious-transaction report. (1993) A checkbox on IRS Form 4789 formerly (1990–1995) requiring banks and other financial institutions to report transactions that might be relevant to a violation of the Bank Secrecy Act or its regulations or that might suggest money-laundering or tax evasion. • This checkbox, like the criminal-referral form, has since been superseded by the suspicious-activity report. — Abbr. STR.

sustain, *vb.* (13c) **1.** To support or maintain, esp. over a long period <enough oxygen to sustain life>. **2.** To nourish and encourage; lend strength to <she helped sustain the criminal enterprise>. **3.** To undergo; suffer <Charles sustained third-degree burns>. **4.** (Of a court) to uphold or rule in favor of <objection sustained>. **5.** To substantiate or corroborate <several witnesses sustained Ms. Sipes's allegation>. **6.** To persist in making (an effort) over a long period <he sustained his vow of silence for the last 16 years of his life>. — **sustainment, sustentation,** *n.* — **sustainable,** *adj.*

S.W. *abbr. South Western Reporter.*

swatting, *n. Slang.* The act of falsely telephoning a report of a serious crime or emergency in progress in order to provoke a response from a law-enforcement agency, esp. the dispatch of a SWAT (Special Weapons and Tactics) team. • Swatting schemes are often elaborate, involving the use of electronic tools to mask the caller's true identity and location, such as voice-changing devices, fake caller-IDs, and the like. — **swatter,** *n.*

swearing-in, *n.* (1900) The administration of an oath to a person who is taking office or testifying in a legal proceeding.

swearing match. (1907) A dispute in which determining a vital fact involves the credibility choice between one witness's word and another's — the two being irreconcilably in conflict and there being no other evidence. • In such a dispute, the fact-finder is generally thought to believe the more reputable witness, such as a police officer over a convicted drug-dealer.

swear out, *vb.* (1850) To obtain the issue of (an arrest warrant) by making a charge under oath <Franklin swore out a complaint against Sutton>.

sweat equity. (1966) Financial equity created in property by the owner's labor in improving the property <the lender required the homeowner to put 300 hours of sweat equity into the property>.

sweating. (1824) *Criminal procedure.* The illegal interrogation of a prisoner by use of threats or similar means to extort information.

sweat-of-the-brow doctrine. *Copyright.* The now-discarded principle that copyrights can protect the labor and expense that went into a work, rather than the work's originality. • The Supreme Court rejected the sweat-of-the-brow doctrine in *Feist Pubs., Inc. v. Rural Tel. Servs. Co.,* 499 U.S. 340, 111 S.Ct. 1282 (1991).

sweatshop. (1890) *Slang.* A business where the employees are overworked and underpaid in extreme conditions; esp., in lawyer parlance, a law firm that requires associates to work so hard that they barely (if at all) maintain a family or social life — though the firm may, in return, pay higher salaries.

swindle, *vb.* (18c) To cheat (a person) out of property <Johnson swindled Norton out of his entire savings> <Johnson swindled Norton's entire savings out of him>. — **swindle,** *n.* — **swindling,** *n.*

swindler. A person who willfully defrauds or cheats another.

swing vote. (1962) The vote that determines an issue when all other voting parties, such as appellate judges, are evenly split.

SYD. *abbr.* Sum of the years' digits.

syllabus (**sil**-ə-bəs). **1.** An abstract or outline of a topic or course of study. **2.** A case summary appearing before the printed judicial opinion in a law report, briefly reciting the facts and the holding of the case. • The syllabus is ordinarily not part of the court's official opinion. Pl. **syllabuses, syllabi** (**sil**-ə-bɪ).

symbiotic-relationship test. (1973) The standard by which a private person may be considered a state actor — and may be liable for violating someone's constitutional rights — if the relationship between the private person and the government is so close that they can fairly be said to be acting jointly. • Private acts by a private person do not generally create liability for violating someone's constitutional rights. But if a private person violates someone's constitutional rights while engaging in state action, the private person, and possibly the government, can be held liable. State action may be shown by proving that the private person and the state have a mutually dependent (symbiotic) relationship. For example, a restaurant in a public parking garage was held to have engaged in discriminatory state action by refusing to serve African-Americans. *Burton v. Wilmington Parking Authority*, 365 U.S. 715, 81 S.Ct. 856 (1961). There, the Court found a symbiotic relationship because the restaurant relied on the garage for its existence and significantly contributed to the municipal parking authority's ability to maintain the garage. But the symbiotic-relationship test is strictly construed. For example, the fact that an entity receives financial support from — or is heavily regulated by — the government is probably insufficient to show a symbiotic relationship.

symbolic, *adj.* (Of a signature) consisting of a symbol or mark.

syndicate (**sin**-di-kit), *n.* (17c) A group organized for a common purpose; esp., an association formed to promote a common interest, carry out a particular business transaction, or (in a negative sense) organize criminal enterprises. — **syndicate** (**sin**-di-kayt), *vb.* — **syndication** (sin-di-**kay**-shən), *n.* — **syndicator** (**sin**-di-kay-tər), *n.*

synopsis (si-**nop**-sis), *n.* (17c) A brief or partial survey; a summary or outline; headnote. — **synopsize** (si-**nop**-sɪz), *vb.*

systematic violation. (1980) *Civil-rights law.* An employer's policy or procedure that discriminates against an employee. • Such a policy or procedure will usu. be considered a continuing violation. So an employee's claim of unlawful discrimination will not be barred as untimely as long as some discriminatory effect of the policy or procedure occurs within the limitations period (e.g., 300 days for a Title VII claim).

T

table, *vb.* (1849) *Parliamentary law.* (Of a deliberative assembly) to set aside the pending business until the assembly votes to resume its consideration. • A matter that has been tabled may be brought up again by a vote of the assembly.

table of cases. (18c) An alphabetical list of the cases cited in a brief or lawbook, usu. prefixed or appended to it, with one or more page or section numbers showing where in the text each case is cited.

tabula rasa (**tab**-yə-lə **rah**-sə *or* -zə). [Latin "scraped tablet"] (16c) A blank tablet ready for writing; a clean slate. Pl. ***tabulae rasae*** (**tab**-yə-lee-**rahs**-ɪ).

tacit (**tas**-it), *adj.* (17c) Implied but not actually expressed; implied by silence or silent acquiescence <a tacit understanding> <a tacit admission>. — **tacitly,** *adv.*

tacking. (18c) **1.** The joining of consecutive periods of possession by different persons to treat the periods as one continuous period; esp., the adding of one's own period of land possession to that of a prior possessor to establish continuous adverse possession for the statutory period. **2.** The joining of a junior lien with the first lien in order to acquire priority over an intermediate lien.

Taft–Hartley Act. Labor–Management Relations Act.

tail, *n.* (14c) The limitation of an estate so that it can be inherited only by the fee owner's issue or class of issue.

tail female. (18c) A limitation to female heirs.

tail general. (15c) **1.** A tail limited to the issue of a particular person, but not to that of a particular couple. **2.** Tail male.

tail male. (17c) A limitation to male heirs.

tail special. (15c) A tail limited to specified heirs of the donee's body.

taint, *n.* (16c) **1.** A conviction of felony. **2.** A person so convicted.

taint, *vb.* (14c) **1.** To imbue with a noxious quality or principle. **2.** To contaminate or corrupt. **3.** To tinge or affect slightly for the worse. — **taint,** *n.*

take, *vb.* (bef. 12c) **1.** To obtain possession or control, whether legally or illegally. **2.** To seize with authority; to confiscate or apprehend. **3.** To acquire (property) for public use by eminent domain; (of a governmental entity) to seize or condemn property. **4.** To acquire possession by virtue of a grant of title, the use of eminent domain, or other legal means; esp., to receive property by will or intestate succession. **5.** To claim one's rights under <she took the Fifth Amendment>.

take back, *vb.* (18c) To revoke; to retract.

take by stealth. (16c) To steal (personal property); to pilfer or filch.

take care of. (16c) **1.** To support or look after (a person). **2.** To pay (a debt). **3.** To attend to (some matter).

take delivery. (1829) To receive something purchased or ordered; esp., to receive a commodity under a futures contract or spot-market contract, or to receive securities recently purchased.

take effect, *vb.* (14c) **1.** To become operative or executed. **2.** To be in force; to go into operation.

takeover. The acquisition of ownership or control of a corporation. • A takeover is typically accomplished by a purchase of shares or assets, a tender offer, or a merger.

friendly takeover. A takeover that is approved by the target corporation.

hostile takeover. A takeover that is resisted by the target corporation.

takeover bid. An attempt by outsiders to wrest control from the incumbent management of a target corporation.

takeover defense. A measure taken by a corporation to discourage hostile takeover attempts.

structural takeover defense. A legal mechanism adopted by a corporation to thwart any future takeover bid without having any financial or operational effect on the target corporation.

transactional takeover defense. A financial or operational transaction designed to make a present or future takeover bid more difficult by raising a company's share price, paying off the bidder, or reducing a bidder's profit.

take the Fifth. (1952) To assert one's right against self-incrimination under the Fifth Amendment.

take the witness. You may now question the witness. • This phrase is a lawyer's courtroom announcement that ends one side's questioning and prompts the other side to begin its questioning. Synonymous phrases are *your witness* and *pass the witness.*

taking, *n.* (14c) **1.** *Criminal & tort law.* The act of seizing an article, with or without removing it, but with an implicit transfer of possession or control.

constructive taking. (1843) An act that does not equal an actual appropriation of an article but that does show an intention to convert it, as when a person entrusted with the possession of goods starts using them contrary to the owner's instructions.

2. *Constitutional law.* The government's actual or effective acquisition of private property either by ousting the owner or by destroying the property or severely impairing its utility. • There is a taking of property when government action directly interferes with or substantially disturbs the owner's use and enjoyment of the property.

actual taking. Physical taking.

de facto taking (di **fak**-toh). (1921) **1.** Interference with the use or value or marketability of land in anticipation of condemnation, depriving the owner of reasonable use and thereby triggering the obligation to pay just compensation. **2.** A taking in which an entity clothed with eminent-domain power substantially interferes with an owner's use, possession, or enjoyment of property.

physical taking. A physical appropriation of an owner's property by an entity clothed with eminent-domain authority.

temporary taking. A government's taking of property for a finite time. • The property owner may be entitled to compensation and damages for any harm done to the property.

Takings Clause. (1955) The Fifth Amendment provision that prohibits the government from taking private property for public use without fairly compensating the owner.

tales (**tay**-leez *or* taylz). [Latin, pl. of *talis* "such," in the phrase *tales de circumstantibus* "such of the bystanders"] (15c) **1.** A supply of additional jurors, usu. drawn from the bystanders at the courthouse, summoned to fill a panel that has become deficient in number because of juror challenges or exemptions. **2.** A writ or order summoning these jurors.

TAM. *abbr.* Technical advice memorandum.

tame, *adj.* (Of an animal) domesticated; accustomed to humans.

tamper, *vb.* (16c) **1.** To meddle so as to alter (a thing); esp., to make changes that are illegal, corrupting, or perverting. **2.** To interfere improperly; to meddle.

tampering, *n.* (17c) **1.** The act of altering a thing; esp., the act of illegally altering a document or product, such as written evidence or a consumer good. See Model Penal Code §§ 224.4, 241.8; 18 USCA § 1365. **2.** The act or an instance of engaging in improper or underhanded dealings, esp. in an attempt to influence. • Tampering with a witness or jury is a criminal offense.

tangible, *adj.* (16c) **1.** Having or possessing physical form; corporeal. **2.** Capable of being touched and seen; perceptible to the touch; capable of being possessed or realized. **3.** Capable of being understood by the mind.

tapper, *n.* (1930) **1.** A person who approaches another for money; a beggar. **2.** By extension, a thief.

tariff, *n.* **1.** A schedule or system of duties imposed by a government on imported or exported goods. • In the United States, tariffs are imposed on imported goods only. **2.** A duty imposed on imported or exported goods under such a system. **3.** A fee that a public utility or telecommunications company may assess for its services. • The tariffs that a provider may charge are limited by statute. **4.** A schedule listing the rates charged for services provided by a public utility, the U.S. Postal Service, or a business (esp. one that must by law file its rates with a public agency). **5.** A scale of sentences and damages for crimes and injuries, arranged by severity. — **tariff,** *vb.*

tarnishment. *Trademarks.* A form of dilution that occurs when a trademark's unauthorized use degrades the mark and diminishes its distinctive quality.

tax, *n.* (14c) A charge, usu. monetary, imposed by the government on persons, entities, transactions, or property to yield public revenue. • Most broadly, the term embraces all governmental impositions on the person, property, privileges, occupations, and enjoyment of the people, and includes duties, imposts, and excises. Although a tax is often thought of as being pecuniary in nature, it is not necessarily payable in money. — **tax,** *vb.*

accrued tax. (1872) A tax that has been incurred but not yet paid or payable.

accumulated-earnings tax. (1957) A penalty tax imposed on a corporation that has retained its earnings in an effort to avoid the income-tax liability arising once the earnings are distributed to shareholders as dividends.

admission tax. A tax imposed as part of the price of being admitted to a particular event.

ad valorem tax. (1810) A tax imposed proportionally on the value of something (esp. real property), rather than on its quantity or some other measure.

alternative minimum tax. (1972) A tax, often a flat rate, potentially imposed on corporations and higher-income individuals to ensure that those taxpayers do not avoid too much (or all) income-tax liability by legitimately using exclusions, deductions, and credits. — Abbr. AMT.

amusement tax. A tax on a ticket to a concert, sporting event, or the like. • The tax is usu. expressed as a percentage of the ticket price.

back tax. (*oft. pl.*) A tax that, though assessed for a previous year or years, remains due and unpaid.

capital-gains tax. (1930) A tax on income derived from the sale of a capital asset. • The federal income tax on capital gains typically has a more favorable tax rate — for example, 20% for an individual and 34% for a corporation — than the otherwise applicable tax rate on ordinary income.

capital-stock tax. **1.** A tax on capital stock in the hands of a stockholder. **2.** A state tax for conducting business in the corporate form, usu. imposed on out-of-state corporations for the privilege of doing business in the state. • The tax is usu. assessed as a percentage of the par or assigned value of a corporation's capital stock.

death tax. **1.** Estate tax. **2.** Inheritance tax.

delinquent tax. A tax not paid when due.

direct tax. (18c) A tax that is imposed on property, as distinguished from a tax on a right or privilege. • A direct tax is presumed to be borne by the person upon whom it is assessed, and not "passed on" to some other person. Ad valorem and property taxes are direct taxes.

estate tax. (1928) A tax imposed on the transfer of property by will or by intestate succession.

estimated tax. (1926) A tax paid quarterly by a taxpayer not subject to withholding (such as a self-employed person) based on either the previous year's tax liability or an estimate of the current year's tax liability.

excess-profits tax. (1918) A tax levied on profits that are beyond a business's normal profits. • This type of tax is usu. imposed only in times of national emergency (such as war) to discourage profiteering.

flat tax. (1952) A tax whose rate remains fixed regardless of the amount of the tax base. • Most sales taxes are flat taxes.

general tax. (16c) **1.** A tax that returns no special benefit to the taxpayer other than the support of governmental programs that benefit all. **2.** A property tax or an ad valorem tax that is imposed for no special purpose except to produce public revenue.

generation-skipping tax. (1977) A tax on a property transfer that skips a generation. • The tax limits the use of generation-skipping techniques as a means of avoiding estate taxes.

generation-skipping transfer tax. (1984) A gift or estate tax imposed on a generation-skipping transfer or a generation-skipping trust. IRC (26 USCA) §§ 2601–2663.

gift tax. (1925) A tax imposed when property is voluntarily and gratuitously transferred. • Under federal law, the gift tax is imposed on the donor, but some states tax the donee.

graduated tax. **1.** A tax employing a rate schedule with higher marginal rates for larger taxable bases (income, property, transfer, etc.) **2.** Progressive tax.

gross-income tax. (1916) A tax on gross income, possibly after the deduction for costs of goods sold, rather than on net profits; an income tax without allowance for expenses or deductions.

gross-receipts tax. A tax on a business's gross receipts, without a deduction for costs of goods sold, or allowance for expenses or deductions.

head tax. **1.** Poll tax. **2.** HEAD MONEY (3).

hidden tax. (1935) A tax that is paid, often unknowingly, by someone other than the person or entity on whom it is levied; esp., a tax imposed on a manufacturer or seller (such as a gasoline producer) who passes it on to consumers in the form of higher sales prices.

income tax. (18c) A tax on an individual's or entity's net income. • The federal income tax — set forth in the Internal Revenue Code — is the federal government's primary source of revenue, and most states also have income taxes.

indirect tax. (18c) A tax on a right or privilege, such as an occupation tax or franchise tax. • An indirect tax is often presumed to be partly or wholly passed on from the nominal taxpayer to another person.

inheritance tax. (18c) **1.** A tax imposed on a person who inherits property from another (unlike an estate tax, which is imposed on the decedent's estate). • There is no federal inheritance tax, but some states have an inheritance tax (though it is creditable or deductible under the federal estate tax). **2.** Loosely, an estate tax.

kiddie tax. (18c) *Slang.* A federal tax imposed on a child's unearned income (above an exempt amount) at the parents' tax rate if the parents' rate is higher and if the child is under 18 years old.

luxury tax. (1925) An excise tax imposed on high-priced items that are not deemed necessities (such as cars costing more than a specified amount).

nanny tax. (1993) *Slang.* A federal social-security tax imposed on the employer of a domestic employee if the employer pays that employee more than a specified amount in total wages in a year. • The term, which is not a technical legal phrase, was popularized in the mid-1990s, when several of President Clinton's nominees were found not to have paid the social-security tax for their nannies.

occupation tax. (1879) An excise tax imposed for the privilege of carrying on a business, trade, or profession. • For example, many states require lawyers to pay an occupation tax.

payroll tax. (1936) **1.** A tax payable by an employer based on its payroll (such as a social-security tax or an unemployment tax). **2.** A tax collected by an employer from its employees' gross pay (such as an income tax or a social-security tax).

personal-property tax. (1863) A tax on personal property (such as jewelry or household furniture) levied by a state or local government.

poll tax. (17c) A fixed tax levied on each person within a jurisdiction. • The 24th Amendment prohibits the federal and state governments from imposing poll taxes as a condition for voting.

progressive tax. (1886) A tax structured so that the effective tax rate increases more than proportionately as the tax base increases, or so that an exemption remains flat or diminishes. • With this type of tax, the percentage of income paid in taxes increases as the taxpayer's income increases. Most income taxes are progressive, so that higher incomes are taxed at a higher rate. But a tax can be progressive without using graduated rates.

property tax. (1808) A tax levied on the owner of property (esp. real property), usu. based on the property's value. • Local governments often impose property taxes to finance school districts, municipal projects, and the like.

regressive tax. (1893) A tax structured so that the effective tax rate decreases as the tax base increases. • With this type of tax, the percentage of income paid in taxes decreases as the taxpayer's income increases. A flat tax (such as the typical sales tax) is usu. considered regressive — despite its constant rate — because it is more burdensome for low-income taxpayers than high-income taxpayers. A growing exemption also produces a regressive tax effect.

sales tax. (1921) A tax imposed on the sale of goods and services, usu. measured as a percentage of their price.

sin tax. (1971) An excise tax imposed on goods or activities that are considered harmful or immoral (such as cigarettes, liquor, or gambling).

special tax. (18c) **1.** A tax levied for a unique purpose. **2.** A tax (such as an inheritance tax) that is levied in addition to a general tax.

specific tax. (18c) A tax imposed as a fixed sum on each article or item of property of a given class or kind without regard to its value.

stamp tax. (18c) A tax imposed by requiring the purchase of a revenue stamp that must be affixed to a legal document (such as a deed or note) before the document can be recorded.

state tax. (18c) **1.** A tax — usu. in the form of a sales or income tax — earmarked for state, rather than federal or municipal, purposes. **2.** A tax levied under a state law.

succession tax. Inheritance tax.

surtax. (1881) An additional tax imposed on something being taxed or on the primary tax itself.

transfer tax. (1890) **1.** A tax imposed on the transfer of property, esp. by will, inheritance, or gift. **2.** Stock-transfer tax. **3.** Generation-skipping transfer tax.

unemployment tax. (1937) A tax imposed on an employer by state or federal law to cover the cost of unemployment insurance. • The Federal Unemployment Tax Act (FUTA) provides for a tax based on a percentage of employee earnings but allows a credit for amounts paid in state unemployment taxes.

unified transfer tax. The federal transfer tax imposed equally on property transferred during life or at death. • Until 1977, gift-tax rates were lower than estate taxes.

use tax. A tax imposed on the use of certain goods that are bought outside the taxing authority's jurisdiction. • Use taxes are designed to discourage the purchase of products that are not subject to the sales tax.

value-added tax. (1935) A tax assessed at each step in the production of a commodity, based on the value added at each step by the difference between the commodity's production cost and its selling price. • A value-added tax — which is levied in several European countries — effectively acts as a sales tax on the ultimate consumer. — Abbr. VAT.

windfall-profits tax. (1973) A tax imposed on a business or industry as a result of a sudden increase in profits. • An example is the tax imposed on oil companies in 1980 for profits resulting from the Arab oil embargo of the 1970s.

withholding tax. (1927) A portion of income tax that is subtracted from salary, wages, dividends, or other income before the earner receives payment. • The most common example is the income tax and social-security tax withheld by an employer from an employee's pay.

taxable, *adj.* (16c) **1.** Subject to taxation <interest earned on a checking account is taxable income>. **2.** (Of legal costs or fees) assessable <expert-witness fees are not taxable court costs>.

taxable distribution. (1927) A generation-skipping transfer from a trust to the beneficiary (i.e., the skip person) that is neither a direct skip nor a taxable termination.

taxable termination. (1988) A taxable event that occurs when (1) an interest in a generation-skipping trust property terminates (as on the death of a skip person's parent who possessed the interest), (2) no interest in the trust is held by a nonskip person, and (3) a distribution may be made to a skip person. • Before the creation of taxable terminations in 1976, a taxpayer could create a trust that paid income to a child for life, then to that child's child for life, and so on without incurring an estate or gift tax liability at the death of each generation's beneficiary.

taxation. (14c) The imposition or assessment of a tax; the means by which the state obtains the revenue required for its activities.

double taxation. (18c) **1.** The imposition of two taxes on the same property during the same period and for the same taxing purpose. **2.** The imposition of two taxes on one corporate profit; esp., the structure of taxation employed by Subchapter C of the Internal Revenue Code, under which corporate profits are taxed twice, once to the corporation when earned and once to the shareholders when the earnings are distributed as dividends.

pass-through taxation. (1998) The taxation of an entity's owners for the entity's income without taxing the entity itself. • Partnerships and S corporations are taxed under this method. So are limited liability companies and limited liability partnerships unless they elect to be taxed as corporations by "checking the box" on their income tax returns. The election is made on Form 8832 (Entity Classification Election). See Treas. Reg. § 301.7701-(3)(b)(1).

tax avoidance. (1927) The act of taking advantage of legally available tax-planning opportunities in order to minimize one's tax liability.

tax base. The total property, income, or wealth subject to taxation in a given jurisdiction; the aggregate value of the property being taxed by a particular tax.

tax-benefit rule. (1942) The principle that if a taxpayer recovers a loss or expense that was deducted in a previous year, the recovery must be included in the current year's gross income to the extent that it was previously deducted.

tax bracket. (1923) A categorized level of income subject to a particular tax rate under federal or state law <28% tax bracket>.

tax court. (1841) **1.** United States Tax Court. **2.** In some states, a court that hears appeals in nonfederal tax cases and can modify or change any valuation, assessment, classification, tax, or final order that is appealed.

Tax Court, U.S. A federal court that hears appeals by taxpayers from adverse IRS decisions about tax deficiencies. • The Tax Court was created in 1942, replacing the Board of Tax Appeals. — Abbr. T.C.

tax credit. (1946) An amount subtracted directly from one's total tax liability, dollar for dollar, as opposed to a deduction from gross income. — Often shortened to *credit.*

child- and dependent-care tax credit. (2001) A tax credit available to a person who is employed full-time and who maintains a household for a dependent child or a disabled spouse or dependent.

earned-income credit. (1927) A refundable federal tax credit on the earned income of a low-income worker with dependent children. • The credit is paid to the taxpayer even if it exceeds the total tax liability. See IRC (26 USCA) § 32. — Abbr. EIC.

foreign tax credit. (1928) A tax credit against U.S. income taxes for a taxpayer who earns income overseas and has paid foreign taxes on that income.

investment tax credit. (1965) A tax credit intended to stimulate business investment in capital goods by allowing a percentage of the purchase price as a credit against the taxpayer's income taxes. • The Tax Reform Act of 1986 generally repealed this credit retroactively for most property placed in service after January 1, 1986. — Abbr. ITC.

unified estate-and-gift tax credit. (1988) A tax credit applied against the federal unified transfer tax. IRC (26 USCA) § 2001(c)(2).

tax-deferred, *adj.* (1948) Not taxable until a future date or event <a tax-deferred retirement plan>.

tax evasion. (1922) The willful attempt to defeat or circumvent the tax law in order to illegally reduce one's tax liability. • Tax evasion is punishable by both civil and criminal penalties.

tax-exempt, *adj.* (1923) **1.** By law not subject to taxation <a tax-exempt charity>. **2.** Bearing interest that is free from income tax <tax-exempt municipal bonds>.

tax-free exchange. (1927) A transfer of property for which the tax law specifically defers (or possibly exempts) income-tax consequences. • For example, a transfer of property to a controlled corporation under IRC (26 USCA) § 351(a) and a like-kind exchange under IRC (26 USCA) § 1031(a).

tax haven. (18c) A jurisdiction, esp. a country, that imposes little or no tax on the profits from transactions carried on there or on persons resident there.

tax home. (18c) A taxpayer's principal business location, post, or station. • Travel expenses are tax-deductible only if the taxpayer is traveling away from home.

tax-identification number. A nine-digit tracking number assigned by the Internal Revenue Service to the tax accounts of businesses and also to entities or individuals who are required to file business tax returns. — Abbr. TIN. — Often shortened to *tax i.d.*

tax incentive. (18c) A governmental enticement, through a tax benefit, to engage in a particular activity, such as the contribution of money or property to a qualified charity.

tax-increment financing. A technique used by a municipality to finance commercial developments usu. involving issuing bonds to finance land acquisition and other up-front costs, and then using the additional property taxes generated from the new development to service the debt. — Abbr. TIF.

tax law. (18c) **1.** Internal Revenue Code. **2.** The statutory, regulatory, constitutional, and common-law rules that constitute the law applicable to taxation. **3.** The area of legal study dealing with taxation.

tax liability. (1932) The amount that a taxpayer legally owes after calculating the applicable tax; the amount of unpaid taxes.

taxpayer. One who pays or is subject to a tax.

taxpayers' bill of rights. (1988) Federal legislation granting taxpayers specific rights when dealing with the Internal Revenue Service, such as the right to have representation and the right to receive written notice of a levy 30 days before enforcement.

taxpayer-standing doctrine. (1977) *Constitutional law.* The principle that a taxpayer has no standing to sue the government for allegedly misspending the public's tax money unless the taxpayer can demonstrate a personal stake and show some direct injury.

tax-preference items. (1971) Certain items that, even though lawfully deducted in arriving at taxable income for regular tax purposes, must be considered in calculating a taxpayer's alternative minimum tax.

tax protest. A taxpayer's formal, usu. written, statement that he or she does not acknowledge a legal or just basis for the tax or a duty to pay it. • The purpose of the protest is to make clear that any payment is made "under protest" and to avoid waiving the right to recover the money paid if the tax is later invalidated.

tax protester. 1. One who files a tax protest. **2.** A person who opposes tax laws and seeks or employs ways, often illegal, to avoid the laws' effects; esp., a person who refuses to pay a tax on grounds that the government has no authority to levy the tax.

tax rate. (1876) A mathematical figure for calculating a tax, usu. expressed as a percentage.

average tax rate. (1895) A taxpayer's tax liability divided by the amount of taxable income.

marginal tax rate. (1939) In a tax scheme, the rate applicable to the last dollar of income earned by the taxpayer. • This concept is useful in calculating the tax effect of receiving additional income or claiming additional deductions.

tax-rate schedule. (1951) A schedule used to determine the tax on a given level of taxable income and based on a taxpayer's status (for example, married filing a joint income-tax return).

tax refund. Money that a taxpayer overpaid and is thus returned by the taxing authority.

tax return. (1870) An income-tax form on which a person or entity reports income, deductions, and exemptions, and on which tax liability is calculated. — Often shortened to *return.*

amended return. (1861) A return filed after the original return, usu. to correct an error in the original.

consolidated return. A return that reflects combined financial information for a group of affiliated corporations.

information return. (1920) A return, such as a W-2, filed by an entity to report some economic information related to, but other than, tax liability.

joint return. (1930) A return filed together by spouses. • A joint return can be filed even if only one spouse had income, but each spouse is usu. individually liable for the tax payment.

separate return. (1913) A return filed by each spouse separately, showing income and liability. • Unlike with a joint return, each spouse is individually liable only for taxes due on the separate return.

tax shelter, *n.* (1952) A financial operation or investment strategy (such as a partnership or real-estate investment trust) that is created primarily for the purpose of reducing or deferring income-tax payments. • The Tax Reform Act of 1986 — by restricting the deductibility of passive losses — sharply limited the effectiveness of tax shelters. — Often shortened to *shelter.* — **tax-sheltered,** *adj.*

tax situs (sɪ-təs). A state or other jurisdiction that has a substantial connection with assets that are subject to taxation.

tax write-off. (1955) A deduction of depreciation, loss, or expense from taxable income.

TBC. *abbr.* Trial before the court.

T-bill. *abbr.* Treasury bill.

T-bond. *abbr.* Treasury bond.

T.C. *abbr.* Tax Court, U.S.

T.C. memo. *abbr.* A memorandum decision of the U.S. Tax Court. — Also abbreviated T.C.M.

teamwork. (1828) Work done by a team; esp., work by a team of animals as a substantial part of one's business, such as farming, express carrying, freight hauling, or transporting material. • In some jurisdictions, animals (such as horses) that work in teams are exempt from execution on a civil judgment.

TECA (**tee**-kə). *abbr.* Temporary Emergency Court of Appeals.

Technical Advice Memorandum. (1967) A publication issued by the national office of the IRS, usu. at a taxpayer's request, to explain some complex or novel tax-law issue. — Abbr. TAM.

telescam. A fraud committed by using telemarketing to induce the victim to disclose sensitive personal information or send money to the perpetrator.

Temporary Assistance to Needy Families. A combined state and federal program that provides limited financial assistance to families in need. 42 USCA §§ 601–603a. • This program replaced Aid to Families with Dependent Children. TANF differs from AFDC because families are limited to no more than five years of assistance, and states have more control over eligibility requirements. — Abbr. TANF.

Temporary Emergency Court of Appeals. *Hist.* A special U.S. court created in 1971 with exclusive jurisdiction over appeals from federal district courts in cases arising under the wage-and-price-control program of the Economic Stabilization Act of 1970. • The court consisted of nine district and circuit judges appointed by the Chief Justice. This court was abolished in 1992. — Abbr. TECA.

temporary restraining order. (1861) **1.** A court order preserving the status quo until a litigant's application for a preliminary or permanent injunction can be heard. • A temporary restraining order may sometimes be granted without notifying the opposing party in advance. **2.** Ex parte injunction. — Often shortened to *restraining order.* — Abbr. TRO.

tenancy. (16c) **1.** The possession or occupancy of land under a lease; a leasehold interest in real estate. **2.** The period of such possession or occupancy. **3.** The possession of real or personal property by right or title, esp. under a conveying instrument such as a deed or will.

cotenancy. (1875) A tenancy with two or more coowners who have unity of possession. • Examples are a joint tenancy and tenancy in common.

entire tenancy. (17c) A tenancy possessed by one person, as opposed to a joint or common tenancy.

general tenancy. (18c) A tenancy that is not of fixed duration under the parties' agreement.

joint tenancy. (17c) A tenancy with two or more coowners who take identical interests simultaneously by the same instrument and with the same right of possession. • A joint tenancy differs from a tenancy in common because each joint tenant has a right of survivorship to the other's share (in some states, this right must be clearly expressed in the conveyance — otherwise, the tenancy will be presumed to be a tenancy in common).

periodic tenancy. (1891) A tenancy that automatically continues for successive periods — usu. month to month or year to year — unless terminated at the end of a period by notice. • A typical example is a month-to-month apartment lease. This type of tenancy originated through court rulings that, when the lessor received a periodic rent, the lease could not be terminated without reasonable notice.

several tenancy. (17c) A tenancy that is separate and not held jointly with another person.

tenancy at sufferance. (18c) A tenancy arising when a person who has been in lawful possession of property wrongfully remains as a holdover after his or her interest has expired. • A tenancy at sufferance takes the form of either a tenancy at will or a periodic tenancy.

tenancy attendant on the inheritance. A tenancy for a term that is vested in a trustee in trust for the owner of the inheritance. • The tenancy is a form of personal property to the trustee.

tenancy at will. (17c) A tenancy in which the tenant holds possession with the landlord's consent but without fixed terms (as for duration or rent); specif., a tenancy that is terminable at the will of either the transferor or the transferee and that has no designated period of duration. • Such a tenancy may be terminated by either party upon fair notice.

tenancy for a term. (17c) A tenancy whose duration is known in years, weeks, or days from the moment of its creation.

tenancy in common. (17c) A tenancy by two or more persons, in equal or unequal undivided shares, each person having an equal right to possess the whole property but no right of survivorship.

tenancy in gross. (1860) A tenancy for a term that is outstanding — that is, one that is unattached to or disconnected from the estate or inheritance, such as one that is in the hands of some third party having no interest in the inheritance.

tenant, *n.* (14c) **1.** One who holds or possesses lands or tenements by any kind of right or title.

dominant tenant. The person who holds a dominant estate and therefore benefits from an easement.

holdover tenant. A person who remains in possession of real property after a previous tenancy (esp. one under a lease) expires, thus giving rise to a tenancy at sufferance. — Sometimes shortened to *holdover.*

prime tenant. A commercial or professional tenant with an established reputation that leases substantial, and usu. the most preferred, space in a commercial development. • A prime tenant is important in securing construction financing and in attracting other desirable tenants.

servient tenant. The person who holds a servient estate and is therefore burdened by an easement.

tenant at sufferance. A tenant who has been in lawful possession of property and wrongfully remains as a holdover after the tenant's interest has expired. • The tenant may become either a tenant at will or a periodic tenant.

tenant for a term. A tenant whose tenancy is for a defined number of years, months, weeks, or days, set when the tenancy is created.

2. One who pays rent for the temporary use and occupation of another's land under a lease or similar arrangement. **3.** *Archaic.* The defendant in a real action (the plaintiff being called a *demandant*).

tenantable repair. (17c) A repair that will render premises fit for present habitation.

tender, *n.* (16c) **1.** A valid and sufficient offer of performance; specif., an unconditional offer of money or performance to satisfy a debt or obligation <a tender of delivery>. • The tender may save the tendering party from a penalty for nonpayment or nonperformance or may, if the other party unjustifiably refuses the tender, place the other party in default.

tender of delivery. (1821) A seller's putting and holding conforming goods at the buyer's disposition and giving the buyer any notification reasonably necessary to take delivery. • The manner, time, and place for tender are determined by the agreement and by Article 2 of the Uniform Commercial Code.

tender of performance. (18c) An obligor's demonstration of readiness, willingness, and ability to perform the obligation; esp., a buyer's demonstration of readiness, willingness, and ability to pay the purchase money, or a seller's offer to deliver merchantable title.• An offer to perform is usu. necessary to hold the defaulting party to a contract liable for breach.

2. Something unconditionally offered to satisfy a debt or obligation. **3.** *Contracts.* Attempted performance that is frustrated by the act of the party for whose benefit it is to take place. • The performance may take the form of either a tender of goods or services, or a tender of payment. Although this sense is quite similar to sense 1, it differs in making the other party's refusal part of the definition itself.

perfect tender. (18c) A seller's tender that meets the contractual terms entered into with the buyer concerning the quality and specifications of the goods sold.

4. An offer or bid put forward for acceptance <a tender for the construction contract>. **5.** Something that serves as a means of payment, such as coin, banknotes, or other circulating medium; money <legal tender>. — **tender,** *vb.*

tender of issue. (1811) *Common-law pleading.* A form attached to a traverse, by which the traversing party refers the issue to the proper mode of trial.

tender-years doctrine. (1954) *Family law.* The doctrine holding that custody of very young children (usu. five years of age and younger) should generally be awarded to the mother in a divorce unless she is found to be unfit. • This doctrine has been rejected in most states and replaced by a presumption of joint custody.

tenement. (14c) **1.** Property (esp. land) held by freehold; an estate or holding of land. **2.** A house or other building used as a residence. **3.** An apartment. **4.** Tenement house.

tenement house. (1858) A low-rent apartment building, usu. in poor condition and at best meeting only minimal safety and sanitary conditions. — Sometimes shortened to *tenement.*

tenendum (tə-**nen**-dəm). [Latin "to be held"] (17c) A clause in a deed designating the kind of tenure by which the things granted are to be held.

Tenth Amendment. The constitutional amendment, ratified as part of the Bill of Rights in 1791, providing that any powers not constitutionally delegated to the federal government, nor prohibited to the states, are reserved for the states or the people.

1031 exchange (**ten**-thər-tee-**wən**). (1972) **1.** An exchange of like-kind property that is exempt from income-tax consequences under IRC (26 USCA) § 1031. **2.** Tax-free exchange.

tenure (**ten**-yər), *n.* (15c) **1.** A right, term, or mode of holding lands or tenements in subordination to a superior. **2.** A status afforded to a teacher or professor as a protection against summary dismissal without sufficient cause. • This status has long been considered a cornerstone of academic freedom. **3.** More generally, the legal protection of a long-term relationship, such as employment. — **tenurial** (ten-**yuur**-ee-əl), *adj.*

term, *n.* (14c) **1.** A word or phrase; esp., an expression that has a fixed meaning in some field <term of art>. **2.** A contractual stipulation <the delivery term provided for shipment within 30 days>.

fundamental term. (1873) **1.** A contractual provision that must be included for a contract to exist; a contractual provision that specifies an essential purpose of the contract, so that a breach of the provision through inadequate performance makes the performance not only defective but essentially different from what had been promised. **2.** A contractual provision that must be included in the contract to satisfy the statute of frauds.

implied term. (18c) A provision not expressly agreed to by the parties but instead read into the contract by a court as being implicit. • An implied term should not, in theory, contradict the contract's express terms.

material term. (1839) A contractual provision dealing with a significant issue such as subject matter, price, payment, quantity, quality, duration, or the work to be done.

nonfundamental term. (1969) Any contractual provision that is not regarded as a fundamental term.

3. (*pl.*) Provisions that define an agreement's scope; conditions or stipulations <terms of sale>. **4.** A fixed period of time; esp., the period for which an estate is granted <term of years>.

attendant term. (1983) A long period (such as 1,000 years) specified as the duration of a mortgage, created to protect the mortgagor's heirs' interest in the land by not taking back title to the land once it is paid for, but rather by assigning title to a trustee who holds the title in trust for the mortgagor and the mortgagor's heirs. • This arrangement gives the heirs another title to the property in case the interest they inherited proves somehow defective. These types of terms have been largely abolished.

satisfied term. (18c) A term of years in land that has satisfied the purpose for which it was created before the term's expiration.

term for deliberating. (1843) The time given a beneficiary to decide whether to accept or reject an inheritance or other succession.

term in gross. (1852) A term that is unattached to an estate or inheritance.

term of years. A fixed period covering a precise number of years.

unexpired term. The remainder of a period prescribed by law or by agreement.

5. The period or session during which a court conducts judicial business <the most recent term was busy indeed>.

additional term. A distinct, added term to a previous term.

adjourned term. (18c) A continuance of a previous or regular term but not a separate term; the same term prolonged.

civil term. The period during which a civil court hears cases.

criminal term. A term of court during which indictments are found and returned, and criminal trials are held.

equity term. (1836) The period during which a court tries only equity cases.

general term. A regular term of court — that is, the period during which a court ordinarily sits.

regular term. (1820) A term of court begun at the time appointed by law and continued, in the court's discretion, until the court lawfully adjourns.

special term. (1803) A term of court scheduled outside the general term, usu. for conducting extraordinary business.

termination, *n.* (15c) **1.** The act of ending something; extinguishment <termination of the partnership by winding up its affairs>. **2.** The end of something in time or existence; conclusion or discontinuance <the insurance policy's termination left the doctor without liability coverage>. — **terminate,** *vb.* — **terminable,** *adj.*

termination fee. A fee paid if a party voluntarily backs out of a deal to sell or purchase a business or a business's assets. • Termination fees are usu. negotiated and agreed on as part of corporate merger or acquisition negotiations. The fee is designed to protect the prospective buyer and to deter the target corporation from entertaining bids from other parties.

termination of parental rights. (1939) *Family law.* The legal severing of a parent's rights, privileges, and responsibilities regarding his or her child. • Termination of a parent's rights frees the child to be adopted by someone else.

termination proceeding. (1939) An administrative action to end a person's or entity's status or relationship.

term of art. (17c) **1.** A word or phrase having a specific, precise meaning in a given specialty, apart from its general meaning in ordinary contexts. • Examples in law include *and his heirs* and *res ipsa loquitur.* **2.** Loosely, a jargonistic word or phrase.

term-of-art canon. (1994) In statutory construction, the principle that if a term has acquired a technical or specialized meaning in a particular context, the term should be presumed to have that meaning if used in that context.

termor (**tər**-mər). (14c) A person who holds lands or tenements for a term of years or for life.

terre-tenant (**tair** ten-ənt). (15c) **1.** One who has actual possession of land; the occupant of land. **2.** One who has an interest in a judgment debtor's land after the judgment creditor's lien has attached to the land (such as a subsequent purchaser). — Also spelled *ter-tenant* (**tər**-ten-ənt).

territorialism. (1977) The traditional approach to choice of law, whereby the place of injury or of contract formation determines which state's law will be applied in a case.

territory, *n.* (14c) **1.** A geographical area included within a particular government's jurisdiction; the portion of the earth's surface that is in a state's exclusive possession and control.

non-self-governing territory. *Int'l law.* A territory that is governed by another country. • These types of territories are rarely allowed representation in the governing country's legislature.

trust territory. *Int'l law.* A territory to which the United Nations' international trusteeship system formerly applied; a territory once administered by the United Nations or a member state for the political, economic, educational, and social advancement of its inhabitants. • All territories that were subject to this system either became independent nations or opted to become part of another nation.

2. A part of the United States not included within any state but organized with a separate legislature (such as Guam and the U.S. Virgin Islands). — **territorial,** *adj.*

territory of a judge. (18c) The territorial jurisdiction of a particular court.

terrorem clause. No-contest clause.

terrorism, *n.* (18c) The use or threat of violence to intimidate or cause panic, esp. as a means of affecting political conduct. See 18 USCA § 2331. — **terrorist,** *adj.* & *n.*

bioterrorism. Terrorism involving the intentional release of harmful biological agents, such as bacteria or viruses, into the air, food, or water supply, esp. of humans.

cyberterrorism. Terrorism committed by using a computer to make unlawful attacks and threats of attack against computers, networks, and electronically stored information, and actually causing the target to fear or experience harm.

domestic terrorism. **1.** Terrorism that occurs primarily within the territorial jurisdiction of the United States. 18 USCA § 2331(5). **2.** Terrorism that is carried out against one's own government or fellow citizens.

ecoterrorism. Terrorism related to environmental issues or animal rights.

international terrorism. Terrorism that occurs primarily outside the territorial jurisdiction of the United

States, or that transcends national boundaries by the means in which it is carried out, the people it is intended to intimidate, or the place where the perpetrators operate or seek asylum. 18 USCA § 2331(1).

state-sponsored terrorism. International terrorism supported by a sovereign government to pursue strategic and political objectives.

state terrorism. Terrorism practiced by a sovereign government, esp. against its own people. • Under international legal principles of sovereignty, a government's conduct that has effects only within its borders is generally not subject to interference from other nations.

terrorizing, *n. Family law.* A parent's or caregiver's act of orally assaulting, bullying, or frightening a child, or causing the child to believe that the world is a hostile place.

***Terry* stop.** STOP AND FRISK.

testable, *adj.* (17c) **1.** Capable of being tested <a testable hypothesis>. **2.** Capable of being transferred by will <today virtually all property is considered testable>. **3.** Capable of making a will <an 18-year-old person is testable in this state>. **4.** Legally qualified to testify as a witness or give evidence <the witness is testable about the statement>.

testacy. The state or condition of a person having died with a valid will.

testament (**tes**-tə-mənt). (14c) **1.** Traditionally, a will disposing of personal property. **2.** WILL (2).

testamentary (tes-tə-**men**-tə-ree *or* -tree), *adj.* (14c) **1.** Of or relating to a will or testament <testamentary intent>. **2.** Provided for or appointed by a will <testamentary guardian>. **3.** Created by a will <testamentary gift>.

testate (**tes**-tayt), *adj.* (15c) Having left a will at death <she died testate>.

testator (**tes**-tay-tər *also* te-**stay**-tər). (14c) A person who has made a will; esp., a person who dies leaving a will. • Because this term is usu. interpreted as applying to both sexes, *testatrix* has become archaic.

teste (**tes**-tee). [Latin *teste meipso* "I myself being a witness"] In drafting, the clause that states the name of a witness and evidences the act of witnessing.

testifier. One who testifies; witness.

testify, *vb.* (14c) **1.** To give evidence as a witness <she testified that the Ford Bronco was at the defendant's home at the critical time>. **2.** (Of a person or thing) to bear witness <the incomplete log entries testified to his sloppiness>.

testimonium clause. (1823) A provision at the end of an instrument (esp. a will) reciting the date when the instrument was signed, by whom it was signed, and in what capacity. • This clause traditionally begins with the phrase "In witness whereof."

testimony, *n.* (14c) Evidence that a competent witness under oath or affirmation gives at trial or in an affidavit or deposition. — **testimonial,** *adj.*

affirmative testimony. (1806) Testimony about whether something occurred or did not occur, based on what the witness saw or heard at the time and place in question.

cumulative testimony. (1818) Identical or similar testimony by more than one witness, and usu. by several, offered by a party usu. to impress the jury with the apparent weight of proof on that party's side. • The trial court typically limits cumulative testimony.

dropsy testimony. (1970) *Slang.* A police officer's false testimony that a fleeing suspect dropped an illegal substance that was then confiscated by the police and used as probable cause for arresting the suspect. • Dropsy testimony is sometimes given when an arrest has been made without probable cause, as when illegal substances have been found through an improper search.

false testimony. (16c) Testimony that is untrue. • This term is broader than *perjury*, which has a state-of-mind element. Unlike perjury, false testimony does not denote a crime.

interpreted testimony. Testimony translated because the witness cannot communicate in the language of the tribunal.

lay opinion testimony. (1942) Evidence given by a witness who is not qualified as an expert but who testifies to opinions or inferences. • In federal court, the admissibility of this testimony is limited to opinions or inferences that are rationally based on the witness's perception and that will be helpful to a clear understanding of the witness's testimony or the determination of a fact in issue. Fed. R. Evid. 701.

nonverbal testimony. (1922) A photograph, drawing, map, chart, or other depiction used to aid a witness in testifying. • The witness need not have made it, but it must accurately represent something that the witness saw.

opinion testimony. (1925) Testimony based on one's belief or idea rather than on direct knowledge of the facts at issue. • Opinion testimony from either a lay witness or an expert witness may be allowed in evidence under certain conditions.

testimony de bene esse (dee **bee**-nee **es**-ee *also* day **ben**-ay **es**-ay). (1805) Testimony taken because it is in danger of being lost before it can be given at a trial or hearing, usu. because of the impending death or departure of the witness. • Such testimony is taken in aid of a pending case, while testimony taken under a bill to perpetuate testimony is taken in anticipation of future litigation.

written testimony. (17c) **1.** Testimony given out of court by deposition or affidavit. • The recorded writing, signed by the witness, is considered testimony. **2.** In some administrative agencies and courts, direct narrative testimony that is reduced to writing, to which the witness swears at a hearing or trial before cross-examination takes place in the traditional way.

test paper. A writing that has been proved genuine and submitted to a jury as a standard by which to determine the authenticity of other writings. • The court decides the test paper's authenticity as a matter of law before it is used by the jury. Direct evidence, such as a witness to the writing's creation or an admission by the party, is preferred, but strong circumstantial evidence is usu. acceptable. In Pennsylvania, a paper or instrument shown to the jury as evidence is still called a *test paper* (sometimes written *test-paper*).

textbook digest. (1922) A legal text whose aim is to set forth the law of a subject in condensed form, with little or no criticism or discussion of the authorities cited, and no serious attempt to explain or reconcile apparently conflicting decisions.

thalweg (**tahl**-vayk *or* -veg). (1831) **1.** A line following the lowest part of a (usu. submerged) valley. **2.** The middle of the primary navigable channel of a waterway, constituting the boundary between states.

Thayer presumption. (1958) A presumption that allows the party against whom the presumption operates to come forward with evidence to rebut the presumption, but that does not shift the burden of proof to that party. See James B. Thayer, *A Preliminary Treatise on Evidence* 31–44 (1898). • Most presumptions that arise in civil trials in federal court are interpreted in this way. Fed. R. Evid. 301.

theft, *n.* (bef. 12c) **1.** The wrongful taking and removing of another's personal property with the intent of depriving the true owner of it; larceny. **2.** Broadly, any act or instance of stealing, including larceny, burglary, embezzlement, and false pretenses. • Many modern penal codes have consolidated such property offenses under the name "theft."

petty theft. A theft of a small quantity of cash or of low-value goods or services. • This offense is usu. a misdemeanor.

theft by deception. (1930) The use of trickery to obtain another's property, esp. by (1) creating or reinforcing a false impression (as about value), (2) preventing one from obtaining information that would affect one's judgment about a transaction, or (3) failing to disclose, in a property transfer, a known lien or other legal impediment. Model Penal Code § 223.

theft by extortion. (1969) Larceny in which the perpetrator obtains property by threatening to (1) inflict bodily harm on anyone or commit any other criminal offense, (2) accuse anyone of a criminal offense, (3) expose any secret tending to subject any person to hatred, contempt, or ridicule, or impair one's credit or business reputation, (4) take or withhold action as an official, or cause an official to take or withhold action, (5) bring about or continue a strike, boycott, or other collective unofficial action, if the property is not demanded or received for the benefit of the group in whose interest the actor purports to act, (6) testify or provide information or withhold testimony or information with respect to another's legal claim or defense, or (7) inflict any other harm that would not benefit the actor. Model Penal Code § 223.4.

theft by false pretext. The use of a false pretext to obtain another's property.

theft of property lost, mislaid, or delivered by mistake. (1973) Larceny in which one obtains control of property the person knows to be lost, mislaid, or delivered by mistake (esp. in the amount of property or identity of recipient) and fails to take reasonable measures to restore the property to the rightful owner. Model Penal Code § 223.5.

theft of services. (1946) The act of obtaining services from another by deception, threat, coercion, stealth, mechanical tampering, or using a false token or device. See Model Penal Code § 223.7.

thence, *adv.* (13c) **1.** From that place; from that time. • In surveying, and in describing land by courses and distances, this word, preceding each course given, implies that the following course is continuous with the one before it <south 240 feet to an iron post, thence west 59 feet>. **2.** On that account; therefore.

thence down the river. (16c) With the meanders of a river. • This phrase appears in the field notes of patent surveyors, indicating that the survey follows a meandering river unless evidence shows that the meander line as written was where the surveyor in fact ran it. Meander lines show the general course of the river and are used in estimating acreage, but are not necessarily boundary lines.

theocracy (thee-**ok**-rə-see). (17c) **1.** Government of a state by those who are believed to be or represent that they are acting under the immediate direction of God or some other divinity. **2.** A state in which power is exercised by ecclesiastics.

theory of law. The legal premise or set of principles on which a case rests.

theory-of-pleading doctrine. (1956) The principle — now outmoded — that one must prove a case exactly as pleaded. • Various modern codes and rules of civil procedure have abolished this strict pleading-and-proof requirement. For example, Fed. R. Civ. P. 15 allows amendment of pleadings to conform to the evidence.

theory of the case. (1800) A comprehensive and orderly mental arrangement of principles and facts, conceived and constructed for the purpose of securing a judgment or decree of a court in favor of a litigant; the particular line of reasoning of either party to a suit, the purpose being to bring together certain facts of the case in a logical sequence and to correlate them in a way that produces in the decision-maker's mind a definite result or conclusion favored by the advocate.

thereabouts, *adv.* (bef. 12c) Near that time or place <Schreuer was seen in Rudolf Place or thereabouts>.

thereafter, *adv.* (bef. 12c) Afterward; later <Skurry was thereafter arrested>.

thereat, *adv.* (bef. 12c) **1.** At that place or time; there. **2.** Because of that; at that occurrence or event.

thereby, *adv.* (bef. 12c) By that means; in that way <Blofeld stepped into the embassy and thereby found protection>.

therefor, *adv.* (bef. 12c) For it or them; for that thing or action; for those things or actions <she lied to Congress but was never punished therefor>.

therefore, *adv.* (14c) **1.** For that reason; on that ground or those grounds <a quorum was not present; therefore, no vote was taken>. **2.** To that end <she wanted to become a tax lawyer, and she therefore applied for the university's renowned LL.M. program in taxation>.

therefrom, *adv.* (13c) From that, it, or them <Hofer had several financial obligations to Ricks, who refused to release Hofer therefrom>.

therein, *adv.* (bef. 12c) **1.** In that place or time <the Dallas/Fort Worth metroplex has a population of about 3 million, and some 20,000 lawyers practice therein>. **2.** Inside or within that thing; inside or within those things <there were 3 school buses with 108 children therein>. **3.** In that regard, circumstance, or particular <therein lies the problem>.

thereinafter, *adv.* (1818) Later in that thing (such as a speech or document) <the book's first reference was innocuous, but the five references thereinafter were libelous per se>.

thereof, *adv.* (bef. 12c) Of that, it, or them <although the disease is spreading rapidly, the cause thereof is unknown>.

thereon, *adv.* (bef. 12c) On that or them <Michaels found the online reports of the cases and relied thereon instead of checking the printed books>.

thereto, *adv.* (bef. 12c) To that place, thing, issue, or the like <the jury awarded $750,000 in actual damages, and it added thereto another $250,000 in punitive damages>.

theretofore, *adv.* (14c) Until that time; before that time <theretofore, the highest award in such a case has been $450,000>.

thereunder, *adv.* (bef. 12c) Under that or them <on the top shelf were three books, and situated thereunder was the missing banknote> <section 1988 was the relevant fee statute, and the plaintiffs were undeniably proceeding thereunder>.

thereupon, *adv.* (13c) **1.** Immediately; without delay; promptly <the writ of execution issued from the court, and the sheriff thereupon sought to find the judgment debtor>. **2.** Thereon. **3.** Therefore.

thief. (bef. 12c) One who steals, esp. without force or violence; one who commits theft or larceny.

common thief. (16c) A thief who has been convicted of theft or larceny more than once.

thieve, *vb.* (bef. 12c) To steal; to commit theft or larceny.

thing. (bef. 12c) **1.** The subject matter of a right, whether it is a material object or not; any subject matter of ownership within the sphere of proprietary or valuable rights. • Things are divided into three categories: (1) things real or immovable, such as land, tenements, and hereditaments, (2) things personal or movable, such as goods and chattels, and (3) things having both real and personal characteristics, such as a title deed and a tenancy for a term. The civil law divided things into corporeal (*tangi possunt*) and incorporeal (*tangi non possunt*). La. Civ. Code art. 461.

accessory thing. A thing that stands in a dependency relationship with another thing (the principal thing). • An accessory thing ordinarily serves the economic or other purpose of the principal thing and shares its legal fate in case of transfer or encumbrance.

corporeal thing. (17c) The subject matter of corporeal ownership; a material object.

incorporeal thing. (17c) The subject matter of incorporeal ownership; any proprietary right apart from the right of full dominion over a material object.

2. Anything that is owned by someone as part of that person's estate or property.

Third Amendment. The constitutional amendment, ratified as part of the Bill of Rights in 1791, prohibiting the quartering of soldiers in private homes except during wartime.

third degree, *n.* (1900) The process of extracting a confession or information from a suspect or prisoner by prolonged questioning, the use of threats, or physical torture <the police gave the suspect the third degree>.

third party, *n.* (1818) A person who is not a party to a lawsuit, agreement, or other transaction but who is usu. somehow implicated in it; someone other than the principal parties. — **third-party,** *adj.*

third-party, *vb.* (1965) To bring (a person or entity) into litigation as a third-party defendant <seeking indemnity, the defendant third-partied the surety>.

third-party check. (1904) A check that the payee indorses to another party — for example, a customer check that the payee indorses to a supplier. • A person who takes a third-party check in good faith and without notice of a security interest can be a holder in due course.

third-party consent. (1942) A person's agreement to official action (such as a search of premises) that affects another person's rights or interests. • To be effective for a search, third-party consent must be based on the consenting person's common authority over the place to be searched or the items to be inspected.

third-party defendant. (1927) A party brought into a lawsuit by the original defendant.

third-party plaintiff. (1857) A defendant who files a pleading in an effort to bring a third party into the lawsuit.

Thirteenth Amendment. The constitutional amendment, ratified in 1865, that abolished slavery and involuntary servitude.

thirty-day letter. (1929) A letter that accompanies a revenue agent's report issued as a result of an Internal Revenue Service audit or the rejection of a taxpayer's claim for refund and that outlines the taxpayer's appeal procedure before the Internal Revenue Service. • If the taxpayer does not request any such procedure within the 30-day period, the IRS will issue a statutory notice of deficiency.

threat, *n.* (bef. 12c) **1.** A communicated intent to inflict harm or loss on another or on another's property, esp. one that might diminish a person's freedom to act voluntarily or with lawful consent <a kidnapper's threats of violence>.

terroristic threat. (1959) A threat to commit any crime of violence with the purpose of (1) terrorizing another, (2) causing the evacuation of a building, place of assembly, or facility of public transportation, (3) causing serious public inconvenience, or (4) recklessly disregarding the risk of causing such terror or inconvenience. Model Penal Code § 211.

2. An indication of an approaching menace <the threat of bankruptcy>. **3.** A person or thing that might well cause harm <Mrs. Harrington testified that she had never viewed her husband as a threat>. — **threaten,** *vb.* — **threatening,** *adj.*

three-strikes law. (1984) *Slang.* A statute prescribing an enhanced sentence, esp. life imprisonment, for a repeat offender's third felony conviction. • About half the states have enacted a statute of this kind.

three wicked sisters. *Slang.* The three doctrines — contributory negligence, the fellow-servant rule, and assumption of the risk — used by 19th-century courts to deny recovery to workers injured on the job.

through lot. A lot that abuts a street at each end.

through rate. The total shipping cost when two or more carriers are involved. • The carriers agree in advance on a through rate, which is typically lower than the sum of the separate rates.

throwaway, *n. Slang.* **1.** An unemancipated minor whose parent or caregiver has forced him or her to leave home. **2.** A runaway whose parent or caregiver refuses to allow him or her to return home.

throwback rule. (1972) *Tax.* **1.** In the taxation of trusts, a rule requiring that an amount distributed in any tax year that exceeds the year's distributable net income must be treated as if it had been distributed in the preceding year. • The beneficiary is taxed in the current year although the computation is made as if the excess had been distributed in the previous year. If the trust did not have undistributed accumulated income in the preceding year, the amount of the throwback is tested against each of the preceding years. IRC (26 USCA) §§ 665–668. **2.** A taxation rule requiring a sale that would otherwise be exempt from state income tax (because the state to which the sale would be assigned for apportionment purposes does not have an income tax, even though the seller's state does) to be attributed to the seller's state and thus subjected to a state-level tax. • This rule applies only if the seller's state has adopted a throwback rule.

throw out, *vb.* (1817) To dismiss (a claim or lawsuit).

ticket, *n.* **1.** A certificate indicating that the person to whom it is issued, or the holder, is entitled to some right or privilege <she bought a bus ticket for Miami>. **2.** CITATION (2) <he got a speeding ticket last week>. **3.** BALLOT (2) <they all voted a straight-party ticket>.

tidal, *adj.* Affected by or having tides. • For a river to be "tidal" at a given spot, the water need not necessarily be salt, but the spot must be one where the tide, in the ordinary and regular course of things, flows and reflows.

tideland. (18c) Land between the lines of the ordinary high and low tides, covered and uncovered successively by the ebb and flow of those tides; land covered and uncovered by the ordinary tides.

tidewater. (18c) Water that falls and rises with the ebb and flow of the tide. • The term is not usu. applied to the open sea, but to coves, bays, and rivers.

tideway. (18c) Land between high- and low-water marks.

TIF. *abbr.* Tax-increment financing.

TILA. *abbr.* Truth in Lending Act.

tillage (**til**-ij), *n.* (15c) A place tilled or cultivated; land under cultivation as opposed to land lying fallow or in pasture.

till-tapping. (1893) *Slang.* Theft of money from a cash register.

time. (bef. 12c) **1.** A measure of duration. **2.** A point in or period of duration at or during which something is alleged to have occurred. **3.** *Slang.* A convicted criminal's period of incarceration.

dead time. (1909) Time that does not count for a particular purpose, such as time not included in calculating an employee's wages or time not credited toward a prisoner's sentence. • The time during which a prisoner has escaped, for example, is not credited toward the prisoner's sentence.

earned time. A credit toward a sentence reduction awarded to a prisoner who takes part in activities designed to lessen the chances that the prisoner will commit a crime after release from prison. • Earned time, which is usu. awarded for taking educational or vocational courses, working, or participating in certain other productive activities, is distinct from good time, which is awarded simply for refraining from misconduct.

flat time. (1943) A prison term that is to be served without the benefit of time-reduction allowances for good behavior and the like.

good time. (1886) The credit awarded to a prisoner for good conduct, which can reduce the duration of the prisoner's sentence.

street time. The time that a convicted person spends on parole or on other conditional release. • If the person's parole is revoked, this time may or may not be credited toward the person's sentence, depending on the jurisdiction and the particular conditions of that person's parole.

time-bar, *n.* (1881) A bar to a legal claim arising from the lapse of a defined length of time, esp. one contained in a statute of limitations. — **time-barred,** *adj.*

time immemorial. (17c) **1.** A point in time so far back that no living person has knowledge or proof contradicting the right or custom alleged to have existed since then. • At common law, that time was fixed as the year 1189, the year that Henry II of England died. **2.** A point in time beyond which legal memory cannot go. **3.** A very long time.

time-place-or-manner restriction. (1974) *Constitutional law.* A government's limitation on when, where, or how a public speech or assembly may occur, but not on the content of that speech or assembly. • As long as such restrictions are narrowly tailored to achieve a legitimate governmental interest, they do not violate the First Amendment.

time-price differential. 1. A figure representing the difference between the current cash price of an item and the total cost of purchasing it on credit. **2.** The difference between a seller's price for immediate cash payment and a different price when payment is made later or in installments.

time-price doctrine. The rule that if a debt arises out of a purchase and sale, the usury laws do not apply. • If a higher price is charged for a deferred payment than for an immediate payment, the difference between the time price and the cash price is deemed compensation to the seller for the risk that the buyer will default and for the interest that the seller could have earned on an immediate payment. Because the buyer can usu. choose to postpone a purchase and save up the cash price, the buyer does not have the same status as a needy borrower who must deal with a potentially predatory lender.

time-sharing, *n.* (1976) Joint ownership or rental of property (such as a vacation condominium) by several persons who take turns occupying the property. — **time-share,** *vb.*

timesheet. (1970) **1.** An employee's record of time spent on the job. **2.** An attorney's daily record of billable and nonbillable hours, used to generate clients' bills.

time value. The price associated with the length of time that an investor must wait until an investment matures or the related income is earned.

timocracy (tı-**mok**-rə-see). (15c) **1.** An aristocracy of property; government by propertied, relatively rich people. **2.** A government in which the rulers' primary motive is the love of honor.

TIN. *abbr.* Tax-identification number.

tin parachute. An employment-contract provision that grants a corporate employee (esp. one below the executive level) severance benefits in the event of a takeover. • These benefits are typically less lucrative than those provided under a golden parachute.

tip, *n.* **1.** A piece of special information; esp., in securities law, advance or inside information passed from one person to another. **2.** A gratuity for service given. • Tip income is taxable. IRC (26 USCA) § 61(a).

title. (15c) **1.** The union of all elements (as ownership, possession, and custody) constituting the legal right to control and dispose of property; the legal link between a person who owns property and the property itself <no one has title to that land>. **2.** Legal evidence of a person's ownership rights in property; an instrument (such as a deed) that constitutes such evidence <record your title with the county clerk>.

aboriginal title. **1.** Land ownership, or a claim of land ownership, by an indigenous people in a place that has been colonized. **2.** Indian title.

absolute title. (17c) An exclusive title to land; a title that excludes all others not compatible with it.

adverse title. (18c) A title acquired by adverse possession.

after-acquired title. (1810) Title held by a person who bought property from a seller who acquired title only after purporting to sell the property to the buyer.

bad title. **1.** Defective title. **2.** Unmarketable title.

clear title. (17c) **1.** A title free from any encumbrances, burdens, or other limitations. **2.** Marketable title.

defeasible title. (17c) A title voidable on the occurrence of a contingency, but not void on its face.

defective title. (17c) A title that cannot legally convey the property to which it applies, usu. because of some conflicting claim to that property.

derivative title. (17c) **1.** A title that results when an already existing right is transferred to a new owner. **2.** The general principle that a transferee of property acquires only the rights held by the transferor and no more.

dormant title. (17c) A title in real property held in abeyance.

doubtful title. (17c) A title that exposes the party holding it to the risk of litigation with an adverse claimant.

equitable title. (17c) A title that indicates a beneficial interest in property and that gives the holder the right to acquire formal legal title. • Before the Statute of Uses (1536), an equitable title was enforceable only in a court of chancery, not of law.

good title. (16c) A title that is legally valid or effective; marketable title.

imperfect title. (18c) A title that requires a further exercise of the granting power to pass land in fee, or that does not convey full and absolute dominion.

just title. In a case of prescription, a title that the possessor received from someone whom the possessor honestly believed to be the real owner, provided that the title was to transfer ownership of the property.

legal title. (17c) A title that evidences apparent ownership but does not necessarily signify full and complete title or a beneficial interest. • Before the Statute of Uses (1536), a legal title was enforceable only in a court of law, not chancery.

marketable title. (18c) A title that a reasonable buyer would accept because it appears to lack any defect and to cover the entire property that the seller has purported to sell; a title that enables a purchaser to hold property in peace during the period of ownership and to have it accepted by a later purchaser who employs the same standards of acceptability.

original title. A title that creates a right for the first time.

paramount title. (18c) **1.** *Archaic.* A title that is the source of the current title; original title. **2.** A title that is superior to another title or claim on the same property.

perfect title. **1.** Fee simple. **2.** A grant of land that requires no further act from the legal authority to constitute an absolute title to the land. **3.** A title that does not disclose a patent defect that may require a lawsuit to defend it. **4.** A title that is good both at law and in equity. **5.** A title that is good and valid beyond all reasonable doubt.

presumptive title. (17c) A title of the lowest order, arising out of the mere occupation or simple possession of property without any apparent right, or any pretense of right, to hold and continue that possession.

record title. (18c) A title as it appears in the public records after the deed is properly recorded.

singular title. (17c) The title by which one acquires property as a singular successor.

tax title. (1831) A title to land purchased at a tax sale.

title by descent. (17c) A title that one acquires by law as an heir of the deceased owner.

title by devise. (1819) A title created by will.

title by estoppel. Title acquired from a person who did not have title at the time of a purported conveyance with a warranty but later acquired the title, which then inures to the benefit of the grantee.

title by prescription. (17c) A title acquired by prescription.

title defective in form. (1836) A title for which some defect appears on the face of the deed, as opposed to a defect that arises from circumstances or extrinsic evidence. • Title defective in form cannot be the basis of prescription.

title of entry. (16c) The right to enter upon lands.

universal title. (17c) A title acquired by a conveyance causa mortis of a stated portion of all the conveyor's property interests so that on the conveyor's death the recipient stands as a universal successor.

unmarketable title. (18c) A title that a reasonable buyer would refuse to accept because of possible conflicting interests in or litigation over the property.

3. The heading of a statute or other legal document <the title of the contract was "Confidentiality Agreement">.

general title. A statute's name that broadly and comprehensively identifies the subject matter addressed by the legislature.

long title. The full, formal title of a statute, usu. containing a brief statement of legislative purpose.

short title. The abbreviated title of a statute by which it is popularly known; a statutory nickname.

4. A subdivision of a statute or code <Title IX>. **5.** The name by which a court case or other legal proceeding is distinguished from others; STYLE (1). **6.** An appellation of office, dignity, or distinction <after the election, he bore the title of mayor for the next four years>.

Title VII of the Civil Rights Act of 1964. A federal law that prohibits employment discrimination and harassment on the basis of race, sex, pregnancy, religion, and national origin, as well as prohibiting retaliation against an employee who opposes illegal harassment or discrimination in the workplace. • This term is often referred to simply as Title VII. 42 USCA §§ 2000e et seq.

Title IX of the Educational Amendments of 1972. A federal statute generally prohibiting sex discrimination and harassment by educational facilities that receive federal funds. • This term is often referred to simply as Title IX. 20 USCA §§ 1681 et seq.

title clearance. The removal of impediments to the marketability of land, esp. through title examinations.

title of right. (1917) A court-issued decree creating, transferring, or extinguishing rights. • Examples include a decree of divorce or judicial separation, an adjudication of bankruptcy, a discharge in bankruptcy, a decree of foreclosure against a mortgagor, an order appointing or removing a trustee, and a grant of letters of administration. In all the examples listed, the judgment operates not as a remedy but as a title of right.

title registration. (1971) A system of registering title to land with a public registry, such as a county clerk's office.

title retention. (1936) A form of lien, in the nature of a chattel mortgage, to secure payment of a loan given to purchase the secured item.

title search. (1965) An examination of the public records to determine whether any defects or encumbrances exist in a given property's chain of title. • A title search is typically conducted by a title company or a real-estate lawyer at a prospective buyer's or mortgagee's request.

title standards. (1938) Criteria by which a real-estate title can be evaluated to determine whether it is defective or marketable. • Many states, through associations of conveyancers and real-estate attorneys, still adhere to title standards.

title theory. (1907) *Property law.* The idea that a mortgage transfers legal title of the property to the mortgagee, who retains it until the mortgage has been satisfied or foreclosed. • Only a few American states — known as *title states, title jurisdictions*, or *title-theory jurisdictions* — have adopted this theory.

title transaction. (1939) A transaction that affects title to an interest in land.

TM. *abbr.* Trademark. • Typically used as a superscript after a mark (^{TM}), it signals only that someone claims ownership of the mark; it does not mean that the mark is registered.

TMEP. *abbr.* Trademark Manual of Examining Procedure.

T-note. *abbr.* Treasury note.

token, *n.* (bef. 12c) **1.** A sign or mark; a tangible evidence of the existence of a fact. **2.** A sign or indication of an intention to do something, as when a buyer places a small order with a vendor to show good faith with a view toward later placing a larger order. **3.** A coin or other legal tender. • Although *token* most commonly refers to a piece of metal, the term may also denote a bill or other medium of exchange.

toll, *n.* **1.** A tax or due paid for the use of something; esp., the consideration paid either to use a public road, highway, or bridge, or to maintain a booth for the sale of goods at a fair or market. **2.** A right to collect such a tax or due. **3.** The privilege of being free from such a tax or due. **4.** A charge for a long-distance telephone call.

toll, *vb.* (15c) **1.** To annul or take away <toll a right of entry>. **2.** (Of a time period, esp. a statutory one) to stop the running of; to abate <toll the limitations period>. **3.** *Hist.* To raise or collect a tax or due for the use of something.

tolling agreement. (1934) An agreement between a potential plaintiff and a potential defendant by which the defendant agrees to extend the statutory limitations period on the plaintiff's claim, usu. so that both parties will have more time to resolve their dispute without litigation.

tolling statute. (1899) A law that interrupts the running of a statute of limitations in certain situations, as when the defendant cannot be served with process in the forum jurisdiction.

tontine (**ton**-teen *or* ton-**teen**), *n.* **1.** A financial arrangement in which a group of participants share in the arrangement's advantages until all but one has died or defaulted, at which time the whole goes to that survivor. **2.** A financial arrangement in which an entire sum goes to the contributing participants still alive and not in default at the end of a specified period.

Torrens system (**tor**-ənz *or* **tahr**-ənz). (1863) A system for establishing title to real estate in which a claimant first acquires an abstract of title and then applies to a court for the issuance of a title certificate, which serves as conclusive evidence of ownership. • This system — named after Sir Robert Torrens, a 19th-century reformer of Australian land laws — has been adopted in the United States by several counties with large metropolitan areas.

tort (tort). (16c) **1.** A civil wrong, other than breach of contract, for which a remedy may be obtained, usu. in the form of damages; a breach of a duty that the law imposes on persons who stand in a particular relation to one another. **2.** (*pl.*) The branch of law dealing with such wrongs.

business tort. A tort that impairs some aspect of an economic interest or business relationship and causes economic loss rather than property damage or bodily harm. • Business torts include tortious interference with contractual relations, intentional interference with prospective economic advantage, unfair business practices, misappropriation of trade secrets, and product disparagement.

constitutional tort. (1966) A violation of one's constitutional rights by a government officer, redressable by a civil action filed directly against the officer. • A constitutional tort committed under color of state law (such as a civil-rights violation) is actionable under 42 USCA § 1983. — Sometimes (informally) shortened to *contort.*

dignitary tort (**dig**-nə-tair-ee). (1996) A tort involving injury to one's reputation or honor. • In the few jurisdictions in which courts use the phrase *dignitary tort* (such as Maine), defamation is commonly cited as an example.

environmental tort. A tort involving exposure to disagreeable or harmful environmental conditions or harm to and degradation of an environment (e.g., the pouring of acid on golf greens). • An environmental tort is usu. harmful to land rather than people, though people may find it unpleasant (e.g., odors from a landfill). By contrast, toxic torts involve exposure to harmful substances that cause personal physical injury or disease.

government tort. (1945) A tort committed by the government through an employee, agent, or instrumentality under its control. • The tort may or may not be actionable, depending on whether the government is entitled to sovereign immunity. A tort action against the U.S. government is regulated by the Federal Tort Claims Act, while a state action is governed by the state's tort claims act.

intentional tort. (1860) A tort committed by someone acting with general or specific intent. • Examples include battery, false imprisonment, and trespass to land.

marital tort. A tort by one spouse against the other. • Since most jurisdictions have abolished interspousal tort immunity, courts have had to decide which tort claims to recognize between married persons. Among those that some, but not all, courts have chosen to recognize are assault and battery, including claims for infliction of sexually transmitted disease, and intentional and negligent infliction of emotional distress.

maritime tort. Any tort within the admiralty jurisdiction.

mass tort. (1940) A civil wrong that injures many people. • Examples include toxic emissions from a factory, the crash of a commercial airliner, and contamination from an industrial-waste-disposal site.

negligent tort. (1865) A tort committed by failure to observe the standard of care required by law under the circumstances.

personal tort. (17c) A tort involving or consisting in an injury to one's person, reputation, or feelings, as distinguished from an injury or damage to real or personal property.

preconception tort. A tort that is committed before the victim has been conceived.

prenatal tort. (1960) **1.** A tort committed against a fetus. • If born alive, a child can sue for injuries resulting from tortious conduct predating the child's birth. **2.** Loosely, any of several torts relating to reproduction, such as those giving rise to wrongful-birth actions, wrongful-life actions, and wrongful-pregnancy actions.

prima facie tort (**prɪ**-mə **fay**-shee-ee *or* -shee *or* -shə). (1938) An unjustified, intentional infliction of harm on another person, resulting in damages, by one or more acts that would otherwise be lawful. • Some jurisdictions have established this tort to provide a remedy for malicious deeds — esp. in business and trade contexts — that are not actionable under traditional tort law.

property tort. (1898) A tort involving damage to property.

public tort. (1949) A minor breach of the law (such as a parking violation) that, although it carries a criminal punishment, is considered a civil offense rather than a criminal one because it is merely a prohibited act (*malum prohibitum*) and not inherently reprehensible conduct (*malum in se*).

quasi-tort. (1809) A wrong for which a nonperpetrator is held responsible; a tort for which one who did not directly commit it can nonetheless be found liable, as when an employer is held liable for a tort committed by an employee.

toxic tort. (1979) A civil wrong arising from exposure to a toxic substance, such as asbestos, radiation, or hazardous waste. • A toxic tort can be remedied by a civil lawsuit (usu. a class action) or by administrative action.

tortfeasor (**tort**-fee-zər). (17c) One who commits a tort; a wrongdoer.

concurrent tortfeasors. (1921) Two or more tortfeasors whose simultaneous actions cause injury to a third party. • Such tortfeasors are jointly and severally liable.

consecutive tortfeasors. (1955) Two or more tortfeasors whose actions, while occurring at different times, combine to cause a single injury to a third party. • Such tortfeasors are jointly and severally liable.

joint tortfeasors. (1822) Two or more tortfeasors who contributed to the claimant's injury and who may be joined as defendants in the same lawsuit.

successive tortfeasors. (1954) Two or more tortfeasors whose negligence occurs at different times and causes different injuries to the same third party.

tortious (**tor**-shəs), *adj.* (16c) **1.** Constituting a tort; wrongful <tortious conduct>. **2.** In the nature of a tort <tortious cause of action>.

tortious interference with contractual relations. (1954) A third party's intentional inducement of a contracting party to break a contract, causing damage to the relationship between the contracting parties.

tortious interference with prospective advantage. (1973) An intentional, damaging intrusion on another's potential business relationship, such as the opportunity of obtaining customers or employment.

tort-of-another doctrine. *Torts.* The principle that a party who must bring or defend an action against a third person based on a tort committed by another person is entitled to seek litigation-related damages from that other person.

tort reform. (1974) A movement to reduce the amount of tort litigation, usu. involving legislation that restricts tort remedies or that caps damages awards (esp. for punitive damages). • Advocates of tort reform argue that it lowers insurance and healthcare costs and prevents windfalls, while opponents contend that it denies plaintiffs the recovery they deserve for their injuries.

torture, *n.* (16c) The infliction of intense pain to the body or mind to punish, to extract a confession or information, or to obtain sadistic pleasure. — **torture,** *vb.*

total, *adj.* (14c) **1.** Whole; not divided; full; complete. **2.** Utter; absolute.

totality-of-the-circumstances test. (1959) *Criminal procedure.* A standard for determining whether hearsay (such as an informant's tip) is sufficiently reliable to establish probable cause for an arrest or search warrant. • Under this test — which replaced *Aguilar–Spinelli*'s two-pronged approach — the reliability of the hearsay is weighed by focusing on the entire situation as described in the probable-cause affidavit, and not on any one specific factor. *Illinois v. Gates*, 462 U.S. 213, 103 S.Ct. 2317 (1983).

total-offset rule. *Torts.* A theory of damages holding that the eroding effect of inflation offsets the accrual of interest on an award and makes it unnecessary to discount future damages to their present value.

to wit (too **wit**), *adv.* (14c) *Archaic.* That is to say; namely <the district attorney amended the complaint to include embezzlement, to wit, "stealing money that the company had entrusted to the accused">. — Sometimes spelled *to-wit*; *towit.*

town meeting. **1.** A legal meeting of a town's qualified voters for the administration of local government or the enactment of legislation. • Town meetings of this type are common in some New

England states. **2.** More generally, any assembly of a town's citizens for the purpose of discussing political, economic, or social issues. **3.** Modernly, a televised event in which one or more politicians meet and talk with representative citizens about current issues.

township. 1. In a government survey, a square tract six miles on each side, containing thirty-six square miles of land. **2.** In some states, a civil and political subdivision of a county. — Abbr. tp.

toxic, *adj.* Having the character or producing the effects of a poison; produced by or resulting from a poison; poisonous.

toxicant (**tok**-si-kənt), *n.* (1879) A poison; a toxic agent; any substance capable of producing toxication or poisoning.

toxicology (tok-si-**kol**-ə-jee). (18c) The branch of medicine that concerns poisons, their effects, their recognition, their antidotes, and generally the diagnosis and therapeutics of poisoning; the science of poisons. — **toxicological** (tok-si-kə-**loj**-i-kəl), *adj.*

toxin, *n.* (1886) **1.** Broadly, any poison or toxicant. **2.** As used in pathology and medical jurisprudence, any diffusible alkaloidal substance — such as the ptomaines, abrin, brucin, or serpent venoms — and esp. the poisonous products of disease-producing bacteria.

tp. *abbr.* Township.

tracing, *n.* (16c) **1.** The process of tracking property's ownership or characteristics from the time of its origin to the present <tracing the vehicle's history>. • Parties in a divorce will be expected to trace the origins of property in existence at the time of marital dissolution in order to characterize each asset as separate or marital property (or as community property in some states). **2.** The act of discovering and following a person's actions or movements <tracing the robber's steps>.

tract. (14c) A specified parcel of land <a 40-acre tract>.

trade, *n.* (14c) **1.** The business of buying and selling or bartering goods or services; commerce. **2.** A transaction or swap. **3.** A business or industry occupation; a craft or profession. — **trade,** *vb.*

trade agreement. 1. An agreement — such as the North American Free Trade Agreement — between two or more nations concerning the buying and selling of each nation's goods. **2.** Collective-bargaining agreement.

trade and commerce. Every business occupation carried on for subsistence or profit and involving the elements of bargain and sale, barter, exchange, or traffic.

trade disparagement. The common-law tort of belittling someone's business, goods, or services with a remark that is false or misleading but not necessarily defamatory. • To succeed at the action, a plaintiff must prove that (1) the defendant made the disparaging remark; (2) the defendant either intended to injure the business, knew the statement was false, or recklessly disregarded whether it was true; and (3) the statement resulted in special damages to the plaintiff, usu. by passing off.

trade dispute. *Int'l law.* A dispute between two or more countries arising from tariff rates or other matters related to international commerce.

trade dress. *Trademarks.* The overall appearance and image in the marketplace of a product or a commercial enterprise. • For a product, trade dress typically comprises packaging and labeling. For an enterprise, it typically comprises design and decor. If a trade dress is distinctive and nonfunctional, it may be protected under trademark law.

trade libel. Trade defamation that is written or recorded.

trademark, *n.* (1838) 1. A word, phrase, logo, or other graphic symbol used by a manufacturer or seller to distinguish its product or products from those of others. • The main purpose of a trademark is to designate the source of goods or services. In effect, the trademark is the commercial substitute for one's signature. To receive federal protection, a trademark must be (1) distinctive rather than merely descriptive or generic; (2) affixed to a product that is actually sold in the marketplace; and (3) registered with the U.S. Patent and Trademark Office. In its broadest sense, the term *trademark* includes a servicemark. Unregistered trademarks are protected under common-law only, and distinguished with the mark "TM." — Often shortened to *mark*. **2.** The body of law dealing with how businesses distinctively identify their products. — Abbr. TM.

abandoned trademark. A mark whose owner has discontinued using it and has no intent to resume using it in the ordinary course of trade, or has allowed it to become a generic term or otherwise to lose its distinctive significance. • Under § 45 of the Lanham Act, nonuse of a mark for three consecutive years is prima facie evidence of abandonment. The owner of an abandoned mark has no trademark rights to exclude others from using it.

arbitrary trademark. A trademark containing common words that do not describe or suggest any characteristic of the product to which the trademark is assigned. • Because arbitrary marks are neither descriptive nor suggestive of the goods or services in connection with which they are used, they are inherently distinctive, require no proof of secondary meaning, and are entitled to strong legal protection. A name that would be generic if used with one product may be arbitrary if used with another. For example, "Bicycle" may be registered to identify playing cards, but it could not be protected as a mark to identify bicycles.

certification trademark. A word, symbol, or device used on goods or services to certify the place of origin, material, mode of manufacture, quality, or other characteristic. See 15 USCA § 1127.

collective trademark. (1941) A trademark or servicemark used by an association, union, or other group either to identify the group's products or services or to signify membership in the group. • Collective marks — such as "Realtor" or "American Peanut Farmers" — can be federally registered under the Lanham Act.

descriptive trademark. A trademark that is a meaningful word in common usage or that merely describes or suggests a product. • This type of trademark is entitled to protection only if it has acquired distinctiveness over time.

disparaging trademark. A trademark that tends to bring a person or class of people into contempt or disrepute. • Section 2(a) of the Lanham Act prohibits the registration of disparaging marks. 15 USCA § 1052(a).

distinctive trademark. A very strong trademark, one that consumers immediately and consistently associate with specific goods and services. • Distinctive trademarks are usu. fanciful, arbitrary, or suggestive, but descriptive trademarks and common names can become distinctive if they become so well known as to acquire a secondary meaning.

famous trademark. A trademark that not only is distinctive but also has been used and heavily advertised or widely accepted in the channels of trade over a long time, and is so well known that consumers immediately associate it with one specific product or service. • Only famous marks are protected from dilution. See 15 USCA § 1125 (c)(1)(A)–(H).

fanciful trademark. A trademark consisting of a made-up or coined word; a distinctive trademark or tradename having no independent meaning. • This type of mark is considered inherently distinctive and thus protected at common law, and is eligible for trademark registration from the time of its first use.

geographically descriptive trademark. A trademark that uses a geographic name to indicate where the goods are grown or manufactured. • This type of mark is protected at common law, and can be registered only on proof that it has acquired distinctiveness over time.

house trademark. A trademark that identifies a company, a division of a company, or a company's product line as the source of a product or service. • A house mark and a product mark often appear together on a label.

product trademark. A trademark that identifies a single good or service, rather than the producing company, a division of a company, or a product line. • A product mark and a house mark often appear together on a label.

prohibited and reserved trademark. A mark that is not protected under the Lanham Act because it either fall into an expressly excluded category or else is similar to a mark granted by statute to another. 15 USCA § 1052.

registered trademark. A trademark that has been filed and recorded with the Patent and Trademark Office. • A federally registered trademark is usu. marked by the symbol "®" or a phrase such as "Registered U.S. Patent & Trademark Office" so that the trademark owner can potentially collect treble damages or the defendant's profits for an infringement. If the symbol is not used, the owner can collect these damages or profits only by proving that the defendant actually knew that the mark was registered.

strong trademark. An inherently distinctive trademark that is used — usu. by the owner only — in a fictitious, arbitrary, and fanciful manner, and is therefore given greater protection than a weak mark under the trademark laws.

suggestive trademark. A trademark that suggests rather than describes the particular characteristics of a product, thus requiring a consumer to use imagination to draw a conclusion about the nature of the product. • A suggestive trademark is entitled to protection without proof of secondary meaning.

technical trademark. A mark that satisfies all the elements of a common-law trademark.

Trademark Office. United States Patent and Trademark Office.

trademark-registration notice. A notice that a mark is protected by registration with the U.S. Patent and Trademark Office, shown by placing a symbol next to the mark. • In the U.S., the R-within-a-circle symbol (®) is common but the legend "Reg. U.S. Pat. Off." is acceptable. Only federally registered marks may use this notice.

Trademark Trial and Appeal Board. An administrative body that hears and decides disputes involving trademark ownership, conflicts between marks, and registrability of marks. — Abbr. TTAB.

tradename. *Intellectual property.* **1.** A name, style, or symbol used to distinguish a company, partnership, or business (as opposed to a product or service); the name under which a business operates. • A tradename is a means of identifying a business — or its products or services — to establish goodwill.

It symbolizes the business's reputation. **2.** A trademark that was not originally susceptible to exclusive appropriation but has acquired a secondary meaning.

trade or business. *Tax.* Any business or professional activity conducted by a taxpayer with the objective of earning a profit. • If the taxpayer can show that the primary purpose and intention is to make a profit, the taxpayer may deduct certain expenses as trade-or-business expenses under the Internal Revenue Code.

trader. 1. A merchant; a retailer; one who buys goods to sell them at a profit. **2.** One who sells goods substantially in the form in which they are bought; one who has not converted them into another form of property by skill and labor. **3.** One who, as a member of a stock exchange, buys and sells securities on the exchange floor either for brokers or on his or her own account. **4.** One who buys and sells commodities and commodity futures for others or for his or her own account in anticipation of a speculative profit.

trade secret. (1862) **1.** A formula, process, device, or other business information that is kept confidential to maintain an advantage over competitors; information — including a formula, pattern, compilation, program, device, method, technique, or process — that (1) derives independent economic value, actual or potential, from not being generally known or readily ascertainable by others who can obtain economic value from its disclosure or use, and (2) is the subject of reasonable efforts, under the circumstances, to maintain its secrecy. • This definition states the majority view, which is found in the Uniform Trade Secrets Act. **2.** Information that (1) is not generally known or ascertainable, (2) provides a competitive advantage, (3) has been developed at the plaintiff's expense and is used continuously in the plaintiff's business, and (4) is the subject of the plaintiff's intent to keep it confidential. • This definition states the minority view, which is found in the Restatement of Torts § 757 cmt. b (1939).

tradesman (**traydz**-mən), *n.* **1.** One who buys and sells things for profit; esp., a shopkeeper. **2.** A shopkeeper's employee. **3.** A mechanic or artisan whose livelihood depends on manual labor; one who is skilled in a trade.

trading. The business of buying and selling, esp. of commodities and securities.

day trading. The act or practice of buying and selling stock shares or other securities on the same day, esp. over the Internet, usu. for the purpose of making a quick profit on the difference between the buying price and the selling price.

secondary trading. The buying and selling of securities in the market between members of the public, involving neither the issuer nor the underwriter of the securities.

short-term trading. Investment in securities only to hold them long enough to profit from market-price fluctuations.

trading curb. A temporary restriction on trading in a particular security to curtail dramatic price movements.

trading halt. A temporary suspension of trading in a particular security for a specific reason, such as an order imbalance or a pending news announcement. • Options can be exercised during a trading halt, and open orders may be canceled.

tradition. (14c) **1.** Past customs and usages that influence or govern present acts or practices. **2.** The delivery of an item or an estate.

traduce (trə-**d**[**y**]**oos**), *vb.* (16c) To slander; calumniate. — **traducement,** *n.*

traffic, *n.* (16c) **1.** Commerce; trade; the sale or exchange of such things as merchandise, bills, and money. **2.** The passing or exchange of goods or commodities from one person to another for an equivalent in goods or money. **3.** People or things being transported along a route. **4.** The passing to and fro of people, animals, vehicles, and vessels along a transportation route.

traffic, *vb.* To trade or deal in (goods, esp. illicit drugs or other contraband) <trafficking in heroin>. — **trafficking,** *n.* — **trafficker,** *n.*

trafficking. The act of transporting, trading, or dealing, esp. in people or illegal goods.

drug trafficking. The act of illegally producing, importing, selling, or supplying significant amounts of a controlled substance.

human trafficking. The illegal recruitment, transportation, transfer, harboring, or receipt of a person, esp. one from another country, with the intent to hold the person captive or exploit the person for labor, services, or body parts. • Human-trafficking offenses include forced prostitution, forced marriages, sweat-shop labor, slavery, and harvesting organs from unwilling donors.

organ trafficking. Illegal trafficking in human body parts, esp. transplantable organs that are offered to the highest bidder or that have been harvested without the consent of the donor or the donor's next of kin. • In international law, organ trafficking is broadly included in the offense of human trafficking.

trafficking in persons. **1.** Human trafficking. **2.** Organ trafficking.

traffic regulation. A prescribed rule of conduct for traffic; a rule intended to promote the orderly and safe flow of traffic.

traitor, *n.* **1.** A person who commits treason against his or her country. **2.** One who betrays a person, a cause, or an obligation. — **traitorous,** *adj.*

tranche (transh), *n.* [French "slice"] *Securities.* **1.** A bond issue derived from a pooling of similar debt obligations. • A tranche usu. differs from other issues by maturity date or rate of return. **2.** A block of bonds designated for sale in a foreign country.

transaction, *n.* (17c) **1.** The act or an instance of conducting business or other dealings; esp., the formation, performance, or discharge of a contract. **2.** Something performed or carried out; a business agreement or exchange. **3.** Any activity involving two or more persons. — **transact,** *vb.* — **transactional,** *adj.*

arm's-length transaction. **1.** A transaction between two unrelated and unaffiliated parties. **2.** A transaction between two parties, however closely related they may be, conducted as if the parties were strangers, so that no conflict of interest arises.

closed transaction. *Tax.* A transaction in which an amount realized on a sale or exchange can be established for the purpose of stating a gain or loss.

colorable transaction. (18c) A sham transaction having the appearance of authenticity; a pretended transaction <the court set aside the colorable transaction>.

transaction-or-occurrence test. (1957) A test used to determine whether, under Fed. R. Civ. P. 13(a), a particular claim is a compulsory counterclaim. • Four different tests have been suggested: (1) Are the legal and factual issues raised by the claim and counterclaim largely the same? (2) Would res judicata bar a later suit on the counterclaim in the absence of the compulsory-counterclaim rule? (3) Will substantially the same evidence support or refute both the plaintiff's claim and the counterclaim? (4) Are the claim and counterclaim logically related?

transcarceration. (1987) The movement of prisoners or institutionalized mentally ill persons from facility to facility, rather than from a prison or an institution back to the community, as when a prisoner is transferred to a halfway house or to a drug-treatment facility.

transcribe, *vb.* (16c) To make a written or typed copy of (spoken material, esp. testimony).

transcript, *n.* (14c) A handwritten, printed, or typed copy of testimony given orally; esp., the official record of proceedings in a trial or hearing, as taken down by a court reporter.

transcription. (16c) **1.** The act or process of transcribing. **2.** Something transcribed; a transcript.

transfer, *n.* (14c) **1.** Any mode of disposing of or parting with an asset or an interest in an asset, including a gift, the payment of money, release, lease, or creation of a lien or other encumbrance. • The term embraces every method — direct or indirect, absolute or conditional, voluntary or involuntary — of disposing of or parting with property or with an interest in property, including retention of title as a security interest and foreclosure of the debtor's equity of redemption. **2.** Negotiation of an instrument according to the forms of law. • The four methods of transfer are by indorsement, by delivery, by assignment, and by operation of law. **3.** A conveyance of property or title from one person to another.

colorable transfer. A sham transfer having the appearance of authenticity; a pretended transfer.

constructive transfer. (1852) A delivery of an item — esp. a controlled substance — by someone other than the owner but at the owner's direction.

incomplete transfer. *Tax.* A decedent's inter vivos transfer that is not completed for federal estate-tax purposes because the decedent retains significant powers over the property's possession or enjoyment. • Because the transfer is incomplete, some or all of the property's value will be included in the transferor's gross estate. IRC (26 USCA) §§ 2036–2038.

inter vivos transfer (**in**-tər **vɪ**-vohs *or* **vee**-vohs). (1930) A transfer of property made during the transferor's lifetime.

testamentary transfer. A transfer made in a will. • The transfer may be of something less than absolute ownership.

transfer in fraud of creditors. (1883) A conveyance of property made in an attempt to prevent the transferor's creditors from making a claim to it.

transfer, *vb.* (14c) **1.** To convey or remove from one place or one person to another; to pass or hand over from one to another, esp. to change over the possession or control of. **2.** To sell or give.

transferable (trans-**fər**-ə-bəl), *adj.* (14c) Capable of being transferred, together with all rights of the original holder.

transferee liability. (1951) *Tax.* The liability of a transferee to pay taxes owed by the transferor. • This liability is limited to the value of the asset transferred. The Internal Revenue Service can, for example, force a donee to pay the gift tax when the donor who made the transfer cannot pay it. IRC (26 USCA) §§ 6901–6905.

transfer of a case. (1843) The removal of a case from the jurisdiction of one court or judge to another by lawful authority.

transferor. (1875) One who conveys an interest in property.

transfer payment. (*usu. pl.*) (1945) A governmental payment to a person who has neither provided goods or services nor invested money in exchange for the payment. • Examples include unemployment compensation and welfare payments.

transferred-intent doctrine. (1957) The rule that if one person intends to harm a second person but instead unintentionally harms a third, the first person's criminal or tortious intent toward the second applies to the third as well. • Thus, the offender may be prosecuted for an intent crime or sued by the third person for an intentional tort.

transfer statute. A provision that allows or mandates the trial of a juvenile as an adult in a criminal court for a criminal act. • Every state has some form of transfer statute. The Supreme Court has held that a juvenile cannot be transferred to criminal court under a discretionary statute "without ceremony — without hearing, without effective assistance of counsel, without a statement of reasons." *Kent v. United States*, 383 U.S. 541, 554, 86 S.Ct. 1045, 1053–54 (1966).

automatic-transfer statute. A law requiring the transfer from delinquency court to criminal court for certain statutorily enumerated offenses if certain statutory requirements are met.

discretionary-transfer statute. A law that allows, but does not mandate, the transfer from delinquency court to criminal court for certain statutorily enumerated offenses if certain statutory requirements are met. • The prosecutor has discretion to request the transfer, and the judge has discretion to order the transfer.

reverse transfer statute. A provision that allows a criminal court to return certain cases to juvenile court.

transient (**tran**-shənt), *adj.* (16c) Temporary; impermanent; passing away after a short time.

transient, *n.* **1.** A person or thing whose presence is temporary or fleeting. **2.** Transient person.

transient person. (18c) One who has no legal residence within a jurisdiction for the purpose of a state venue statute.

transit, *n.* (15c) **1.** The transportation of goods or persons from one place to another. **2.** Passage; the act of passing.

transitory (**tran**-sə-tor-ee *or* **tran**-zə-), *adj.* (14c) Passing from place to place; capable of passing or being changed from one place to another.

translation, *n.* **1.** The transformation of language from one form to another; esp., the systematic rendering of the language of a book, document, or speech into another language. **2.** *Archaic.* The transfer of property. **3.** *Eccles. law.* The removal of a bishop from one diocese to another.

transmit, *vb.* (15c) **1.** To send or transfer (a thing) from one person or place to another. **2.** To communicate.

transmittal letter. (1914) A nonsubstantive letter that establishes a record of delivery, such as a letter to a court clerk advising that a particular pleading is enclosed for filing. • Lawyers have traditionally opened transmittal letters with the phrase "Enclosed please find," even though that phrasing has been widely condemned in business-writing handbooks since the late 19th century. A transmittal letter may properly begin with a range of openers as informal as "Here is" to the more formal "Enclosed is."

transmutation. A change in the nature of something; esp., in family law, the transformation of separate property into marital property, or of marital property into separate property.

transparency. Openness; clarity; lack of guile and attempts to hide damaging information. • The word is used of financial disclosures, organizational policies and practices, lawmaking, and other activities where organizations interaction with the public.

transportation, *n.* (16c) **1.** The movement of goods or persons from one place to another by a carrier. **2.** *Criminal law.* A type of punishment that sends the criminal out of the country to another place (usu. a penal colony) for a specified period. — **transport,** *vb.*

Transportation Security Administration. The federal agency charged with promoting safety and security of air, water, rail, and highway transportation. • The agency was created in the Department of Transportation after the terrorist attacks of September 11, 2001, and was transferred to the Department of Homeland Security in 2002.

transsexual. A person born with the physical characteristics of one sex but who has undergone, or is preparing to undergo, sex-change surgery.

trap, *n.* (bef. 12c) **1.** A device for capturing living creatures, such as a pitfall, snare, or machine that shuts suddenly. **2.** Any device or contrivance by which one may be caught unawares; stratagem; snare. **3.** *Torts.* An ultrahazardous hidden peril of which the property owner or occupier, but not a licensee, has knowledge. • A trap can exist even if it was not designed or intended to catch or entrap anything.

Travel Act. A federal law, enacted in 1961, that prohibits conduct intended to promote, direct, or manage illegal business activities in interstate commerce. • This statute was enacted to create federal jurisdiction over many criminal activities traditionally handled by state and local governments to help those jurisdictions cope with increasingly complex interstate criminal activity. 18 USCA § 1952.

traveled place. (1894) A place where the public has, in some manner, acquired the legal right to travel.

traverse (**trav**-ərs), *n.* (15c) *Common-law pleading.* A formal denial of a factual allegation made in the opposing party's pleading <Smith filed a traverse to Allen's complaint, asserting that he did not knowingly provide false information>. — **traverse** (**trav**-ərs *or* trə-**vərs**), *vb.*

common traverse. (1841) A traverse consisting of a tender of issue — that is, a denial accompanied by a formal offer for decision of the point denied — with a denial that expressly contradicts the terms of the allegation traversed.

cumulative traverse. (1848) A traverse that analyzes a proposition into its constituent parts and traverses them cumulatively. • It amounts to the same thing as traversing the one entire proposition, since the several parts traversed must all make up one entire proposition or point.

general traverse. (17c) A denial of all the facts in an opponent's pleading.

special traverse. (18c) A denial of one material fact in an opponent's pleading; a traverse that explains or qualifies the denial. • The essential parts of a special traverse are an inducement, a denial, and a verification.

traverser, *n.* (14c) One who traverses or denies a pleading.

treason, *n.* (13c) The offense of attempting to overthrow the government of the state to which one owes allegiance, either by making war against the state or by materially supporting its enemies. — **treasonable, treasonous,** *adj.*

Treas. Reg. *abbr.* Treasury regulation.

treasurer. An organization's chief financial officer. • The treasurer's duties typically include prudently depositing (or, if authorized, investing) and safeguarding the organization's funds and otherwise managing its finances; monitoring compliance with any applicable law relating to such finances and filing any required report; disbursing money as authorized; and reporting to the organization on the state of the treasury.

Treasurer of the United States. The officer in the U.S. Department of the Treasury responsible for overseeing the operations of the Bureau of Engraving and Printing and the U.S. Mint.

treasure trove. [Law French "treasure found"] (16c) Valuables (usu. gold or silver) found hidden in the ground or other private place, the owner of which is unknown. • At common law in the United States, the finder of a treasure trove can usu. claim good title against all except the true owner. But until 1996, any treasure trove found in the United Kingdom belonged to the Crown.

Treasuries. (1922) Debt obligations of the federal government backed by the full faith and credit of the government.

treasury. 1. A place or building in which stores of wealth are kept; esp., a place where public revenues are deposited and kept and from which money is disbursed to defray government expenses. **2.** (*cap.*) Department of the Treasury.

Treasury bill. (18c) A short-term debt security issued by the federal government, with a maturity of 13, 26, or 52 weeks. • These bills — auctioned weekly or quarterly — pay interest in the form of the difference between their discounted purchase price and their par value at maturity. — Abbr. T-bill.

Treasury bond. (1858) A long-term debt security issued by the federal government, with a maturity of 10 to 30 years. • These bonds are considered risk-free, but they usu. pay relatively little interest. — Abbr. T-bond.

TIPS bond. A treasury bond whose face value is adjusted to keep pace with the inflation rate. • The acronym TIPS stands for *Treasury inflation-protected securities.* — Abbr. TIPS.

treasury certificate. An obligation of the federal government maturing in one year and on which interest is paid on a coupon basis.

Treasury Department. Department of the Treasury.

Treasury note. (18c) An intermediate-term debt security issued by the federal government, with a maturity of two to ten years. • These notes are considered risk-free, but they usu. pay relatively little interest. — Abbr. T-note.

Treasury Regulation. (1860) A regulation promulgated by the U.S. Treasury Department to explain or interpret a section of the Internal Revenue Code. • Treasury Regulations are binding on all taxpayers. — Abbr. Treas. Reg.

treating-physician rule. The principle that a treating physician's diagnoses and findings about the degree of a social-security claimant's impairment are binding on an administrative-law judge in the absence of substantial contrary evidence.

treaty. An agreement formally signed, ratified, or adhered to between two nations or sovereigns; an international agreement concluded between two or more states in written form and governed by international law.

commercial treaty. A bilateral or multilateral treaty concerning trade or other mercantile activities.

defensive treaty. A treaty in which each party agrees to come to the other's aid if one is attacked by another nation.

nonproliferation treaty. A treaty forbidding the transfer of nuclear weapons from a country with a nuclear arsenal to one that does not have nuclear-weapons capability.

offensive treaty. A treaty in which the parties agree to declare war jointly on another nation and join forces to wage the war.

peace treaty. A treaty signed by heads of state to end a war.

treaty of alliance. A treaty establishing mutual and reciprocal support obligations. • A treaty of alliance may be for support in defense, aggression, or both.

treaty of neutrality. A treaty in which the parties agree not to engage in any aggressive action against one another, whether individually or jointly with others, and not to interfere with the other party's affairs.

Treaty Clause. The constitutional provision giving the President the power to make treaties, with the advice and consent of the Senate. U.S. Const. art. II, § 2.

treaty power. (1835) The President's constitutional authority to make treaties, with the advice and consent of the Senate.

trespass (**tres**-pəs *or* **tres**-pas), *n.* (13c) **1.** An unlawful act committed against the person or property of another; esp., wrongful entry on another's real property. **2.** At common law, a legal action for injuries resulting from an unlawful act of this kind. **3.** *Archaic.* Misdemeanor. — **trespass,** *vb.* — **trespassory** (**tres**-pə-sor-ee), *adj.*

continuing trespass. A trespass in the nature of a permanent invasion on another's rights, such as a sign that overhangs another's property.

criminal trespass. **1.** A trespass on property that is clearly marked against trespass by signs or fences. **2.** A trespass in which the trespasser remains on the property after being ordered off by a person authorized to do so.

innocent trespass. A trespass committed either unintentionally or in good faith.

trespass on the case. (15c) At common law, an action to recover damages that are not the immediate result of a wrongful act but rather a later consequence. • This action was the precursor to a variety of modern-day tort claims, including negligence, nuisance, and business torts. — Often shortened to *case.*

trespass quare clausum fregit (**kwair**-ee-**klaw**-zəm-**free**-jit). [Latin "why he broke the close"] (17c) **1.** A person's unlawful entry on another's land that is visibly enclosed. • This tort consists of doing any of the following without lawful justification: (1) entering upon land in the possession of another, (2) remaining on the land, or (3) placing or projecting any object upon it. **2.** At common law, an action to recover damages resulting from another's unlawful entry on one's land that is visibly enclosed. — Abbr. trespass q.c.f.

trespass to chattels. (1843) The act of committing, without lawful justification, any act of direct physical interference with a chattel possessed by another. • The act must amount to a direct forcible injury.

trespass to try title. (1826) **1.** In some states, an action for the recovery of property unlawfully withheld from an owner who has the immediate right to possession. **2.** A procedure under which a claim to title may be adjudicated.

trespass vi et armis (**vɪ** et **ahr**-mis). [Latin "with force and arms"] (17c) **1.** At common law, an action for damages resulting from an intentional injury to person or property, esp. if by violent means; trespass to the plaintiff's person, as in illegal assault, battery, wounding, or imprisonment, when not under color of legal process, or when the battery, wounding, or imprisonment was in the first instance lawful, but unnecessary violence was used or the imprisonment continued after the process had ceased to be lawful. • This action also lay for injury to relative rights, such as menacing tenants or servants, beating and wounding a spouse, criminal conversation with or seducing a wife, or debauching a daughter or servant. **2.** Trespass *quare clausum fregit.* • In this sense, the "force" is implied by the "breaking" of the close (that is, an enclosed area), even if no real force is used.

trespasser. (14c) One who commits a trespass; one who intentionally and without consent or privilege enters another's property. • In tort law, a landholder owes no duty to unforeseeable trespassers.

innocent trespasser. (1888) One who enters another's land unlawfully, but either inadvertently or believing in a right to do so.

triable, *adj.* (15c) Subject or liable to judicial examination and trial <a triable offense>.

trial. (15c) A formal judicial examination of evidence and determination of legal claims in an adversary proceeding.

bench trial. (1954) A trial before a judge without a jury. • The judge decides questions of fact as well as questions of law.

bifurcated trial. (1945) A trial that is divided into two stages, such as for guilt and punishment or for liability and damages.

joint trial. (18c) A trial involving two or more parties; esp., a criminal trial of two or more persons for the same or similar offenses.

jury trial. (18c) A trial in which the factual issues are determined by a jury, not by the judge.

new trial. (16c) A postjudgment retrial or reexamination of some or all of the issues determined in an earlier judgment. • The trial court may order a new trial by motion of a party or on the court's own initiative. Also, when an appellate court reverses the trial court's judgment, it may remand the case to the trial court for a new trial on some or all of the issues on which the reversal is based. See Fed. R. Civ. P. 59; Fed. R. Crim. P. 33.

political trial. (18c) A trial (esp. a criminal prosecution) in which either the prosecution or the defendant (or both) uses the proceedings as a platform to espouse a particular political belief; a trial of a person for a political crime.

public trial. A trial that anyone may attend or observe.

separate trial. (18c) **1.** *Criminal procedure.* The individual trial of each of several persons jointly accused of a crime. Fed. R. Crim. P. 14. **2.** *Civil procedure.* Within a single action, a distinct trial of a separate claim or issue — or of a group of claims or issues — ordered by the trial judge, usu. to conserve resources or avoid prejudice. Fed. R. Civ. P. 42(b).

summary jury trial. (1984) A settlement technique in which the parties argue before a mock jury, which then reaches a nonbinding verdict that will assist the parties in evaluating their positions.

trial de novo (dee *or* di **noh**-voh). (18c) A new trial on the entire case — that is, on both questions of fact and issues of law — conducted as if there had been no trial in the first instance.

trial in absentia. A trial held without the accused being present. • In the United States, a trial may be held *in absentia* only if the accused has either voluntarily left after the trial has started or else has so disrupted the proceedings that the judge orders the accused's removal as a last resort.

trial on the merits. (18c) A trial on the substantive issues of a case, as opposed to a motion hearing or interlocutory matter.

trial per pais (pər **pay** *or* **pays**). [Law French "trial by the country"] (17c) Trial by jury.

trifurcated trial. (1959) A trial that is divided into three stages, such as for liability, general damages, and special damages.

tribal land. A part of an Indian reservation that is not allotted to or occupied by individual Indians but is held as the tribe's common land.

tribunal (trɪ-**byoo**-nəl). (15c) **1.** A court or other adjudicatory body. **2.** The seat, bench, or place where a judge sits.

tributary (**trib**-yə-ter-ee), *n.* (14c) A stream flowing directly or indirectly into a river.

tribute (**trib**-yoot), *n.* (14c) **1.** An acknowledgment of gratitude or respect. **2.** A contribution that a sovereign raises from its subjects to defray the expenses of state. **3.** Money paid by an inferior sovereign or state to a superior one to secure the latter's friendship and protection.

trigamy (**trig**-ə-mee), *n.* (17c) The act of marrying a person while legally married to someone else and bigamously married to yet another.

tripartite (trɪ-**pahr**-tɪt), *adj.* (15c) Involving, composed of, or divided into three parts or elements <a tripartite agreement>.

TRIPs. *abbr. Intellectual property.* The Agreement on Trade-Related Aspects of Intellectual Property Rights, a treaty that harmonized and strengthened the intellectual-property laws of its signatories by linking the obligation to protect the intellectual-property rights of other members' citizens with a mechanism for settling international trade disputes.

TRO (tee-ahr-**oh**). *abbr.* Temporary restraining order.

trover (**troh**-vər). (16c) A common-law action for the recovery of damages for the conversion of personal property, the damages generally being measured by the property's value.

truancy (**troo**-ən-see), *n.* (18c) The act or state of shirking responsibility; esp., willful and unjustified failure to attend school by one who is required to attend. — **truant,** *adj.* & *n.*

truce. *Int'l law.* A suspension or temporary cessation of hostilities by agreement between belligerent powers.

true and correct. Authentic; accurate; unaltered <we have forwarded a true and correct copy of the expert's report>.

true bill, *n.* (18c) A grand jury's notation that a criminal charge should go before a petty jury for trial <the grand jury returned a true bill, and the state prepared to prosecute>.

true-bill, *vb.* To make or deliver a true bill on <the grand jury true-billed the indictment>.

trust, *n.* (15c) **1.** The right, enforceable solely in equity, to the beneficial enjoyment of property to which another person holds the legal title; a property interest held by one person (the *trustee*) at the request of another (the *settlor*) for the benefit of a third party (the *beneficiary*). • For a trust to be valid, it must involve specific property, reflect the settlor's intent, and be created for a lawful purpose. The two primary types of trusts are *private trusts* and *charitable trusts* (see below). **2.** A fiduciary relationship regarding property and charging the person with title to the property with equitable duties to deal with it for another's benefit; the confidence placed in a trustee, together with the trustee's obligations toward the property and the beneficiary. • A trust arises as a result of a manifestation of an intention to create it. **3.** The property so held; CORPUS (1).

accumulation trust. A trust in which the trustee must accumulate income and gains from sales of trust assets for ultimate disposition with the principal when the trust terminates. • Many states restrict the time over which accumulations may be made or the amount that may be accumulated.

active trust. A trust in which the trustee has some affirmative duty of management or administration besides the obligation to transfer the property to the beneficiary.

annuity trust. A trust from which the trustee must pay a sum certain annually to one or more beneficiaries for their respective lives or for a term of years, and must then either transfer the remainder to or for the use of a qualified charity or retain the remainder for such a use. • The sum certain must not be less than 5% of the initial fair market value of the property transferred to the trust by the donor. A qualified annuity trust must comply with the requirements of IRC (26 USCA) § 664.

asset-protection trust. **1.** A trust designed specifically to insulate assets from the settlor's creditors. • When the trust is created using the law of a state, it is also termed a *domestic asset-protection trust.* It may also be referred to by the name of the specific state, e.g., *Alaska trust, Delaware trust,* or *Nevada trust.* If it is created under foreign law, even though the assets are within the United States, it is also termed an *offshore asset-protection trust.* **2.** Self-settled trust.

blind trust. (1969) A trust in which the settlor places investments under the control of an independent trustee, usu. to avoid a conflict of interest. • The beneficiary has no knowledge of the trust's holdings and no right to participate in the trust's management.

bypass trust. (1981) A trust into which just enough of a decedent's estate passes, so that the estate can take advantage of the unified credit against federal estate taxes. See 26 USCA § 2010.

charitable trust. (18c) A trust created to benefit a specific charity, specific charities, or the general public rather than a private individual or entity. • Charitable trusts are often eligible for favorable tax treatment. If the trust's terms do not specify a charity or a particular charitable purpose, a court may select a charity. See Uniform Trust Act § 405.

Clifford trust. (1941) An irrevocable trust, set up for at least ten years and a day, whereby income from the trust property is paid to the beneficiary but the property itself reverts back to the settlor when the trust expires. • These trusts were often used by parents — with their children as beneficiaries — to shelter investment income, but the Tax Reform Act of 1986 eliminated the tax advantage by imposing the kiddie tax and by taxing the income of settlors with a reversionary interest that exceeds 5% of the trust's value. This term gets its name from *Helvering v. Clifford,* 309 U.S. 331, 60 S.Ct. 554 (1940).

constructive trust. (18c) An equitable remedy that a court imposes against one who has obtained property by wrongdoing. • A constructive trust, imposed to prevent unjust enrichment, creates no fiduciary relationship. Despite its name, it is not a trust at all.

Crummey trust. A trust in which the trustee has the power to distribute or accumulate income and to give the beneficiary the right to withdraw an amount equal to the annual gift exclusion (or a smaller sum) within a reasonable time after the transfer. • This type of trust can have multiple beneficiaries and is often used when the beneficiaries are minors. Gifts to a *Crummey* trust qualify for the annual gift exclusion regardless of the age of the beneficiaries. The trust assets are not required to be distributed to the beneficiaries at age 21. The validity of this type of trust was established in *Crummey v. Commissioner*, 397 F.2d 82 (9th Cir. 1968).

destructible trust. (1953) A trust that can be destroyed by the happening of an event or by operation of law.

discretionary trust. (1837) **1.** A trust in which the settlor has delegated nearly complete or limited discretion to the trustee to decide when and how much income or property is distributed to a beneficiary. • This is perhaps the most common type of trust used in estate planning. **2.** *Crummey* trust.

dynasty trust. A generation-skipping trust funded with the amount that is permanently exempt from generation-skipping tax and designed to last more than two generations. • In 2000, a settlor could contribute $1 million to a dynasty trust. Almost half the states allow dynasty trusts, despite their potential for lasting more than 100 years.

executed trust. A trust in which the estates and interests in the subject matter of the trust are completely limited and defined by the instrument creating the trust and require no further instruments to complete them.

executory trust (eg-**zek**-yə-tor-ee). (18c) A trust in which the instrument creating the trust is intended to be provisional only, and further conveyances are contemplated by the trust instrument before the terms of the trust can be carried out.

express trust. (18c) A trust created with the settlor's express intent, usu. declared in writing; an ordinary trust as opposed to a resulting trust or a constructive trust.

generation-skipping trust. (1976) A trust that is established to transfer (usu. principal) assets to a skip person (a beneficiary more than one generation removed from the settlor). • The transfer is often accomplished by giving some control or benefits (such as trust income) of the assets to a nonskip person, often a member of the generation between the settlor and skip person. This type of trust is subject to a generation-skipping transfer tax. IRC (26 USCA) §§ 2601 et seq.

grantor trust. A trust in which the settlor retains control over the trust property or its income to such an extent that the settlor is taxed on the trust's income. • The types of controls that result in such tax treatment are set out in IRC (26 USCA) §§ 671–677. An example is the revocable trust.

honorary trust. (1844) A noncharitable trust that is of doubtful validity because it lacks a beneficiary capable of enforcing the trust. • Examples include trusts for the care and support of specific animals, or for the care of certain graves. The modern trend is to recognize the validity of such trusts, if the trustee is willing to accept the responsibility. If the trustee fails to carry out the duties, however, a resulting trust arises in favor of the settlor's residuary legatees or next of kin.

illusory trust. (1939) An arrangement that looks like a trust but, because of powers retained in the settlor, has no real substance and is not a completed trust.

indestructible trust. (1909) A trust that, because of the settlor's wishes, cannot be prematurely terminated by the beneficiary.

inter vivos trust (**in**-tər **vɪ**-vohs *or* **vee**-vohs). (1921c) A trust that is created and takes effect during the settlor's lifetime.

irrevocable trust (i-**rev**-ə-kə-bəl). (1837) A trust that cannot be terminated by the settlor once it is created. • In most states, a trust will be deemed irrevocable unless the settlor specifies otherwise.

marital-deduction trust. (1953) A testamentary trust created to take full advantage of the marital deduction; esp., a trust entitling a spouse to lifetime income from the trust and sufficient control over the trust to include the trust property in the spouse's estate at death.

Medicaid-qualifying trust. (1989) A trust deemed to have been created in an effort to reduce someone's assets so that the person may qualify for Medicaid, and that will be included as an asset for purposes of determining the person's eligibility. • A person who wants to apply and qualify for Medicaid, but who has too many assets to qualify, will sometimes set up a trust — or have a spouse or custodian set up a trust — using the applicant's own assets, under which the applicant may be the beneficiary of all or part of the payments from the trust, which are distributed by a trustee with discretion to make trust payments to the applicant. Such a trust may be presumed to have been established for the purpose of attempting to qualify for Medicaid, and may be counted as an asset of the applicant, resulting in a denial of benefits and the imposition of a penalty period during which the applicant cannot reapply. Nonetheless, Medicaid rules allow three types of trusts that do not impair Medicaid eligibility, since the trust assets are not considered the beneficiary's property: *Miller trust*, *pooled trust*, and *under-65 trust*.

pourover trust. (1981) An inter vivos trust that receives property (usu. the residual estate) from a will upon the testator's death.

power-of-appointment trust. (1848) A trust in which property is left in trust for the surviving spouse. • The trustee must distribute income to the spouse for life, and the power of appointment is given to the spouse or to his or her estate. A power-of-appointment trust is commonly used to qualify property for the marital deduction.

precatory trust (**prek**-ə-tor-ee). (1878) A trust that the law will recognize to carry out the wishes of the testator or grantor even though the statement in question is in the nature of an entreaty or recommendation rather than a command.

QTIP trust (**kyoo**-tip). (1985) A trust that is established to qualify for the marital deduction. • Under this trust, the assets are referred to as qualified-terminable-interest property, or QTIP.

resulting trust. (18c) A remedy imposed by equity when property is transferred under circumstances suggesting that the transferor did not intend for the transferee to have the beneficial interest in the property.

self-settled trust. (1969) A trust in which the settlor is also the person who is to receive the benefits from the trust, usu. set up in an attempt to protect the trust assets from creditors. • In most states, such a trust will not protect trust assets from the settlor's creditors. Restatement (Second) of Trusts § 156 (1959).

spendthrift trust. (1878) **1.** A trust that prohibits the beneficiary's interest from being assigned and also prevents a creditor from attaching that interest; a trust by the terms of which a valid restraint is imposed on the voluntary or involuntary transfer of the beneficiary's interest. **2.** A similar trust in which the restraint on alienation results from a statute rather than from the settlor's words in the trust instrument.

split-interest trust. Charitable-remainder trust.

support trust. (1946) A discretionary trust in which the settlor authorizes the trustee to pay to the beneficiary as much income or principal as the trustee believes is needed for support, esp. for "comfortable support" or "support in accordance with the beneficiary's standard of living." • The beneficiary's interest cannot be voluntarily transferred, but creditors who provide necessaries can usu. reach it; general creditors cannot.

testamentary trust (tes-tə-**men**-tə-ree *or* -tree). (1832) A trust that is created by a will and takes effect when the settlor (testator) dies.

Totten trust. (1931) A revocable trust created by one's deposit of money, typically in a savings account, in the depositor's name as trustee for another. • A Totten trust is an early form of "pay on death" account, since it creates no interest in the beneficiary unless the account remained at the depositor's death. Its name derives from the earliest decision in which the court approved the concept, even though the formalities of will execution were not satisfied: *In re Totten*, 71 N.E. 748 (N.Y. 1904). A Totten trust is commonly used to indicate a successor to the account without having to create a will, and thus it is a will substitute.

unitrust. (1971) A trust from which a fixed percentage of the fair market value of the trust's assets, valued annually, is paid each year to the beneficiary.

4. A business combination that aims at monopoly.

business trust. A form of business organization, similar to a corporation, in which investors receive transferable certificates of beneficial interest instead of stock shares.

trustee (trəs-**tee**), *n.* (17c) **1.** One who stands in a fiduciary or confidential relation to another; esp., one who, having legal title to property, holds it in trust for the benefit of another and owes a fiduciary duty to that beneficiary. • Generally, a trustee's duties are to convert to cash all debts and securities that are not qualified legal investments, to reinvest the cash in proper securities, to protect and preserve the trust property, and to ensure that it is employed solely for the beneficiary, in accordance with the directions contained in the trust instrument.

corporate trustee. (1852) A corporation that is empowered by its charter to act as a trustee, such as a bank or trust company.

judicial trustee. (18c) A trustee appointed by a court to execute a trust.

quasi-trustee. (1830) One who benefits from a breach of a trust to a great enough degree to become liable as a trustee.

successor trustee. (1866) A trustee who succeeds an earlier trustee, usu. as provided in the trust agreement.

testamentary trustee (tes-tə-**men**-tə-ree *or* -tree). (1811) A trustee appointed by or acting under a will; one appointed to carry out a trust created by a will.

trustee ad litem (ad **lɪ**-tem *or* -təm). (1921) A trustee appointed by the court.

trustee de son tort (də sawn [*or* son] **tor**[**t**]). (1857) A person who, without legal authority, administers a living person's property to the detriment of the property owner.

trustee ex maleficio (eks mal-ə-**fish**-ee-oh). (1837) A person who is guilty of wrongful or fraudulent conduct and is held by equity to the duty of a trustee, in relation to the subject matter, to prevent him or her from profiting from the wrongdoing.

2. *Bankruptcy.* A person appointed by the U.S. Trustee or elected by creditors or appointed by a judge to administer the bankruptcy estate during a bankruptcy case. • The trustee's duties include (1) collecting and reducing to cash the assets of the estate, (2) operating the debtor's business with court approval if appropriate to preserve the value of business assets, (3) examining the debtor at a meeting of creditors, (4) filing inventories and making periodic reports to the court on the financial condition of the estate, (5) investigating the debtor's financial affairs, (6) examining proofs of claims and objecting to improper claims, (7) furnishing information relating to the bankruptcy to interested parties, and (8) opposing discharge through bankruptcy, if advisable. A trustee is appointed or elected in every Chapter 7 case, and is appointed in every Chapter 12 and Chapter 13 case under the Bankruptcy Code. A trustee is not appointed or elected in a Chapter 11 case unless the court finds that a trustee is needed and appoints one. In most Chapter 11 cases, the bankruptcy estate is administered by the debtor in possession, rather than by a trustee. The role of a bankruptcy trustee varies depending on the type of bankruptcy case. 11 USCA §§ 701–03, 1104, 1202.

trustee, *vb.* (1818) **1.** To serve as trustee. **2.** To place (a person or property) in the hands of one or more trustees. **3.** To appoint (a person) as trustee, often of a bankrupt's estate in order to restrain a creditor from collecting moneys due. **4.** To attach (the effects of a debtor) in the hands of a third person.

trustee, U.S. United States Trustee.

trust fund. (18c) The property held in a trust by a trustee; CORPUS (1).

common trust fund. (1852) A trust fund set up within a trust department to combine the assets of numerous small trusts to achieve greater investment diversification. • Common trust funds are regulated by state law.

trust-fund doctrine. (1892) The principle that the assets of an insolvent company, including paid and unpaid subscriptions to the capital stock, are held as a trust fund to which the company's creditors may look for payment of their claims. • The creditors may follow the property constituting this fund, and may use it to reduce the debts, unless it has passed into the hands of a bona fide purchaser without notice.

trust receipt. 1. A pre-UCC security device — now governed by Article 9 of the Code — consisting of a receipt stating that the wholesale buyer has possession of the goods for the benefit of the financier. • Today there must usu. be a security agreement coupled with a filed financing statement. **2.** A method of financing commercial transactions by which title passes directly from the manufacturer or seller to a banker or lender, who as owner delivers the goods to the dealer on whose behalf the banker or lender is acting, and to whom title ultimately goes when the banker's or lender's primary right has been satisfied.

trusty, *n.* (1855) A convict or prisoner who is considered trustworthy by prison authorities and therefore given special privileges.

truth. (bef. 12c) **1.** A fully accurate account of events; factuality. **2.** *Defamation.* An affirmative defense by which the defendant asserts that the alleged defamatory statement is substantially accurate.

truth, the whole truth, and nothing but the truth. The words used in the common oath administered to a witness who is about to testify <do you swear or affirm that you shall tell the truth, the whole truth and nothing but the truth?>. • The purpose of the second part of the oath is to preclude the possibility of *supressio veri*; the purpose of the third part is to preclude the possibility of *suggestio falsi.*

try, *vb.* (13c) To examine judicially; to examine and resolve (a dispute) by means of a trial.

turnkey, *adj.* (1927) **1.** (Of a product) provided in a state of readiness for immediate use <a turnkey computer network>. **2.** Of, relating to, or involving a product provided in this manner <a turnkey contract>.

turnkey, *n.* A jailer; esp., one charged with keeping the keys to a jail or prison.

turn state's evidence, *vb.* (1846) To cooperate with prosecutors and testify against other criminal defendants <after hours of intense negotiations, the suspect accepted a plea bargain and agreed to turn state's evidence>.

Twelfth Amendment. The constitutional amendment, ratified in 1804, that altered the electoral-college system by separating the balloting for presidential and vice-presidential candidates. • In 1800, members of the Electoral College could cast votes only for the office of President, and Thomas Jefferson and his running mate Aaron Burr each received the same number of votes. The House of Representatives had to break the tie.

twelve-day rule. *Criminal procedure.* A rule in some jurisdictions requiring that a person charged with a felony be given a preliminary examination no later than 12 days after the arraignment on the original warrant.

Twentieth Amendment. The constitutional amendment, ratified in 1933, that changed the date of the presidential and vice-presidential inaugurations from March 4 to January 20, and the date for congressional convention from March 4 to January 3, thereby eliminating the short session of Congress, during which a number of members sat who had not been reelected to office.

Twenty-fifth Amendment. The constitutional amendment, ratified in 1967, that established rules of succession for the presidency and vice presidency in the event of death, resignation, or incapacity. • Article II, § 1 of the Constitution provides for the Vice President to assume the President's powers and duties but does not clearly state that the Vice President also assumes the title of President.

Twenty-first Amendment. The constitutional amendment, ratified in 1933, that repealed the 18th Amendment (which established national Prohibition) and returned the power to regulate alcohol to the states.

Twenty-fourth Amendment. The constitutional amendment, ratified in 1964, that prohibits the federal and state governments from restricting the right to vote in a federal election because of one's failure to pay a poll tax or other tax.

Twenty-second Amendment. The constitutional amendment, ratified in 1951, that prohibits a person from being elected President more than twice (or, if the person succeeded to the office with more than half the predecessor's term remaining, more than once).

Twenty-seventh Amendment. The constitutional amendment, ratified in 1992, that prevents a pay raise for senators and representatives from taking effect until a new Congress convenes. • This amendment was proposed as part of the original Bill of Rights in 1789, but it took 203 years for the required three-fourths of the states to ratify it.

Twenty-sixth Amendment. The constitutional amendment, ratified in 1971, that sets the minimum voting age at 18 for all state and federal elections.

Twenty-third Amendment. The constitutional amendment, ratified in 1961, that allows District of Columbia residents to vote in presidential elections.

twist, *n. Slang.* An informant who provides testimony in exchange for leniency in sentencing, rather than for money.

two-controlled-studies standard. The requirement by the Federal Trade Commission that before the maker of an over-the-counter painkiller can advertise that it is better or has fewer side effects than another brand, the maker must verify the claim in two scientifically controlled studies.

two-dismissal rule. (1944) The rule that a notice of voluntary dismissal operates as an adjudication on the merits — not merely as a dismissal without prejudice — when filed by a plaintiff who has already dismissed the same claim in another court.

two-issue rule. (1929) The rule that if multiple issues were submitted to a trial jury and at least one of them is error-free, the appellate court should presume that the jury based its verdict on the proper issue — not on an erroneous one — and should therefore affirm the judgment.

two-witness rule. (1900) **1.** The rule that, to support a perjury conviction, two independent witnesses (or one witness along with corroborating evidence) must establish that the alleged perjurer gave false testimony. **2.** The rule, as stated in the U.S. Constitution, that no person may be convicted of treason without two witnesses to the same overt act — or unless the accused confesses in open court. U.S. Const. art. IV, § 2, cl. 2.

tying, *adj. Antitrust.* Of or relating to an arrangement whereby a seller sells a product to a buyer only if the buyer purchases another product from the seller <tying agreement>.

tying arrangement. *Antitrust.* (1953) A seller's agreement to sell one product or service only if the buyer also buys a different product or service; a seller's refusal to sell one product or service unless the buyer also buys a different product or service. • The product or service that the buyer wants to buy is known as the *tying product* or *tying service*; the different product or service that the seller insists on selling is known as the *tied product* or *tied service.* Tying arrangements may be illegal under the Sherman or Clayton Act if their effect is too anticompetitive.

U

U3C. *abbr.* Uniform Consumer Credit Code.

uberrimae fidei (yoo-**ber**-ə-mee **fi**-dee-ɪ). [Latin] (1850) Of the utmost good faith.

UCC. *abbr.* **1.** Uniform Commercial Code. **2.** Universal Copyright Convention.

UCCC. *abbr.* Uniform Consumer Credit Code.

UCCJEA. *abbr.* Uniform Child Custody Jurisdiction and Enforcement Act.

UCMJ. *abbr.* Uniform Code of Military Justice.

UCR. *abbr.* Uniform Crime Reports.

UDTPA. *abbr.* Uniform Deceptive Trade Practices Act.

UFCA. *abbr.* Uniform Fraudulent Conveyances Act.

UFTA. *abbr.* Uniform Fraudulent Transfer Act.

UGMA. *abbr.* Uniform Gifts to Minors Act.

ukase (yoo-**kays** *or* **yoo**-kays). (18c) A proclamation or decree, esp. of a final or arbitrary nature. • This term originally referred to a decree issued by a Russian czar.

ULPA. *abbr.* Uniform Limited Partnership Act.

ultimatum (əl-tə-**may**-təm), *n.* (18c) The final and categorical proposal made in negotiating a treaty, contract, or the like. • An ultimatum implies that a rejection might lead to a break-off in negotiations or, in international law, to a cessation of diplomatic relations or even to war. Pl. **ultimatums.**

ultra vires (əl-trə **vɪ**-reez *also* **veer**-eez), *adj.* [Latin "beyond the powers (of)"] (18c) Unauthorized; beyond the scope of power allowed or granted by a corporate charter or by law <the officer was liable for the firm's ultra vires actions>. — **ultra vires,** *adv.*

umpire. (15c) An impartial person appointed to make an award or a final decision, usu. when a matter has been submitted to arbitrators who have failed to agree. • An arbitral submission may provide for the appointment of an umpire. — **umpire,** *vb.*

un-, *prefix.* (bef. 12c) **1.** Not <unassignable>. **2.** Contrary to; against <unconstitutional>.

unanimous (yoo-**nan**-ə-məs), *adj.* (17c) **1.** Agreeing in opinion; being in complete accord <the judges were unanimous in their approval of the recommendation>. **2.** Arrived at by the consent of all <a unanimous verdict>.

unanimous-consent agreement. *Parliamentary law.* An agreement, negotiated between opposing sides debating a motion, regarding the procedure under which the assembly will consider the motion. • The unanimous-consent agreement is a common practice in the U.S. Senate.

unauthorized, *adj.* (16c) Done without authority; specif. (of a signature or indorsement), made without actual, implied, or apparent authority. UCC § 1-201(43).

unauthorized completion. *Commercial law.* The act of filling in missing information in a negotiable instrument either without any authority to do so or without adequate authority. • Unauthorized completion is a personal defense, so it can be raised against any later holder of the instrument who does not have the rights of a holder in due course.

unavailability, *n.* (1855) The status or condition of not being available, as when a witness is exempted by court order from testifying. • Unavailability is recognized under the Federal Rules of Evidence as an exemption to the hearsay rule. Fed. R. Evid. 804.

unavoidable-accident doctrine. (1961) *Torts.* The rule holding no party liable for an accident that was not foreseeable and that could not have been prevented by the exercise of reasonable care. • The modern trend is for courts to ignore this doctrine and to rely instead on the basic concepts of duty, negligence, and proximate cause.

unbanked, *adj.* Lacking a formal relationship with a bank or other financial institution. • Unbanked consumers are the most frequent users of money services businesses.

unborn-widow rule. (1957) The legal fiction, assumed under the rule against perpetuities, that a beneficiary's widow is not alive at the testator's death, and thus a succeeding life estate to her voids any remainders because the interest would not vest within the perpetuities period.

unbroken, *adj.* (14c) Not interrupted; continuous <unbroken possession by the adverse possessor>.

unconditional, *adj.* (17c) Not limited by a condition; not depending on an uncertain event or contingency; absolute.

unconscionability (ən-kon-shə-nə-**bil**-ə-tee). (16c) **1.** Extreme unfairness. • Unconscionability is normally assessed by an objective standard: (1) one party's lack of meaningful choice, and (2) contractual terms that unreasonably favor the other party. **2.** The principle that a court may refuse to enforce a contract that is unfair or oppressive because of procedural abuses during contract formation or because of overreaching contractual terms, esp. terms that are unreasonably favorable to one party while precluding meaningful choice for the other party. • Because unconscionability depends on circumstances at the time the contract is formed, a later rise in market price is irrelevant.

procedural unconscionability. (1973) Unconscionability resulting from improprieties in contract formation (such as oral misrepresentations or disparities in bargaining position) rather than from the terms of the contract itself.

substantive unconscionability. (1973) Unconscionability resulting from actual contract terms that are unduly harsh, commercially unreasonable, and grossly unfair given the existing circumstances.

unconscionable (ən-**kon**-shə-nə-bəl), *adj.* (16c) **1.** (Of a person) having no conscience; unscrupulous <an unconscionable used-car salesman>. **2.** (Of an act or transaction) showing no regard for conscience; affronting the sense of justice, decency, or reasonableness <the contract is void as unconscionable>.

unconstitutional, *adj.* (18c) Contrary to or in conflict with a constitution, esp. the U.S. Constitution <the law is unconstitutional because it violates the First Amendment's free-speech guarantee>.

unconstitutional-conditions doctrine. *Constitutional law.* **1.** The rule that the government cannot condition a person's receipt of a governmental benefit on the waiver of a constitutionally protected right (esp. a right under the First Amendment). • For example, a television station that receives public funds cannot be forced to refrain from endorsing political candidates. **2.** The rule that the government cannot force a defendant to choose between two constitutionally protected rights.

uncopyrightable, *adj.* (Of a work) ineligible for copyright protection either because the work lacks originality or because it is an idea, concept, process, or other abstraction that is not included in one of the eight covered classifications of copyrightable works. 17 USCA §§ 101–106.

uncounseled, *adj.* Without the benefit or participation of legal counsel <an uncounseled conviction> <an uncounseled defendant>.

underinsurance. An agreement to indemnify against property damage up to a certain amount but for less than the property's full value.

underinsured-motorist coverage. Insurance that pays for the insured's losses and injuries negligently caused by a driver does not have enough liability insurance to cover the damages.

under one's hand. (Of a person's signature) affixed manually, as opposed to printed or stamped.

undersigned, *n.* (17c) A person whose name is signed at the end of a document <the undersigned agrees to the terms and conditions set forth above>.

understanding, *n.* (bef. 12c) **1.** The process of comprehending; the act of a person who understands something. **2.** One's personal interpretation of an event or occurrence. **3.** An agreement, esp. of an implied or tacit nature.

under submission. (18c) Being considered by the court; under advisement <the case was under submission in the court of appeals for more than two years>.

undertake, *vb.* (13c) **1.** To take on an obligation or task <he has undertaken to chair the committee on legal aid for the homeless>. **2.** To give a formal promise; guarantee <the merchant undertook that the goods were waterproof>. **3.** To act as surety for (another); to make oneself responsible for (a person, fact, or the like) <her husband undertook her appearance in court>.

undertaking, *n.* (14c) **1.** A promise, pledge, or engagement. **2.** A bail bond.

under the influence. (1879) (Of a driver, pilot, etc.) deprived of clearness of mind and self-control because of drugs or alcohol.

underwriter. 1. Insurer. **2.** One who buys stock from the issuer with an intent to resell it to the public; a person or entity, esp. an investment banker, who guarantees the sale of newly issued securities by purchasing all or part of the shares for resale to the public.

underwriting, *n.* **1.** The act of assuming a risk by insuring it; the insurance of life or property. **2.** The act of agreeing to buy all or part of a new issue of securities to be offered for public sale. — **underwrite,** *vb.*

undisputed, *adj.* Not questioned or challenged; uncontested.

undue, *adj.* (14c) **1.** *Archaic.* Not yet owed; not currently payable <an undue debt>. **2.** Excessive or unwarranted <undue burden> <undue influence>. — **unduly,** *adv.*

undue-burden test. (1992) *Constitutional law.* The Supreme Court test stating that a law regulating abortion will be struck down if it places a substantial obstacle in the path of a woman's right to obtain an abortion. • This test replaced the "trimester analysis" set forth in *Roe v. Wade*, in which the state's ability to restrict abortion increased after each trimester of pregnancy. *Planned Parenthood of Southeastern Pa. v. Casey*, 505 U.S. 833, 112 S.Ct. 2791 (1992).

undue influence. (18c) **1.** The improper use of power or trust in a way that deprives a person of free will and substitutes another's objective. • Consent to a contract, transaction, or relationship or to conduct is voidable if the consent is obtained through undue influence. **2.** *Wills & estates.* Coercion that destroys a testator's free will and substitutes another's objectives in its place. • When a beneficiary actively procures the execution of a will, a presumption of undue influence may be raised, based on the confidential relationship between the influencer and the person influenced.

unemployment. The state or condition of not having a job even though available for work and perhaps seeking it.

structural unemployment. Unemployment resulting from a shift in the demand for a particular product or service.

unencumbered (ən-in-**kəm**-bərd), *adj.* Without any burdens or impediments <unencumbered title to property>.

unenforceable, *adj.* (1804) (Of a contract) valid but incapable of being enforced.

unequal, *adj.* (16c) Not equal in some respect; uneven <unequal treatment under the law>.

unequivocal (ən-i-**kwiv**-ə-kəl), *adj.* (18c) Unambiguous; clear; free from uncertainty.

unethical, *adj.* (1871) Not in conformity with moral norms or standards of professional conduct.

unfair competition. (1876) **1.** Dishonest or fraudulent rivalry in trade and commerce; esp., the practice of endeavoring to pass off one's own goods or products in the market for those of another by means of imitating or counterfeiting the name, brand, size, shape, or other distinctive characteristic of the article or its packaging. **2.** The body of law encompassing various business and privacy torts, all generally based on deceitful trade practices, including passing off, false advertising, commercial disparagement, and misappropriation.

unfair labor practice. Any conduct prohibited by state or federal law governing the relations among employers, employees, and labor organizations. • Examples of unfair labor practices by an employer include (1) interfering with protected employee rights, such as the right to self-organization, (2) discriminating against employees for union-related activities, (3) retaliating against employees who have invoked their rights, and (4) refusing to engage in collective bargaining. Examples of unfair labor practices by a labor organization include causing an employer to discriminate against an employee, engaging in an illegal strike or boycott, causing an employer to pay for work not to be performed (i.e., featherbedding), and refusing to engage in collective bargaining. 29 USCA §§ 151–169.

unfair persuasion. (1931) *Contracts.* A type of undue influence in which a stronger party achieves a result by means that seriously impair the weaker party's free and competent exercise of judgment. • Unfair persuasion is a lesser form of undue influence than duress and misrepresentation. The two primary factors to be considered are the unavailability of independent advice and the susceptibility of the person persuaded.

unfair surprise. (1815) A situation in which a party, having had no notice of some action or proffered evidence, is unprepared to answer or refute it.

unfair trade. An inequitable business practice; esp., the act or an instance of a competitor's repeating of words in a way that conveys a misrepresentation that materially injures the person who first used the words, by appropriating credit of some kind earned by the first user.

Unfair Trade Practices and Consumer Protection Law. A model statute patterned on the Federal Trade Commission Act and proposed by the FTC in 1967 for adoption by the states; a state law providing consumer-protection remedies, including private causes of action, for deceptive trade practices and false advertising. • The Act gives the state attorney general power to regulate unfair and deceptive trade practices. It also gives consumers a right to sue offenders directly. — Abbr. UTP-CPL.

unfit, *adj.* (16c) **1.** Unsuitable; not adapted or qualified for a particular use or service <the buyer returned the unfit goods to the seller and asked for a refund>. **2.** *Family law.* Morally unqualified; incompetent <the judge found the mother unfit and so found that awarding custody of the child to the father was in the child's best interests>.

unfitness of a parent. *Family law.* A parent's failure to exhibit a reasonable concern for, interest in, or responsibility for a child's welfare. • Regardless of the specific ground for an allegation of unfitness, a court considers the parent's actions and the circumstances surrounding the conduct in deciding whether unfitness has been demonstrated.

unforeseen, *adj.* Not foreseen; not expected <unforeseen circumstances>.

unharmed, *adj.* Not injured or damaged.

uniform act. 1. A law drafted with the intention that it will be adopted by all or most of the states; esp., a uniform law. **2.** Uniform statute.

Uniform Adoption Act. A 1994 model statute aimed at achieving uniformity in adoption laws. • The current version of the Act was promulgated in 1994 by the National Conference of Commissioners on Uniform State Laws. State adoption has been largely unsuccessful. Earlier versions, in 1953 and 1971, were amended many times but were enacted in only a few states. — Abbr. UAA.

Uniform Anatomical Gift Act. A 1968 model statute that created protocols that govern the giving and receiving of anatomical gifts. • Under the Act, persons may donate their body or parts of their body for purposes of transplantation, therapy, research, or education. The original Act has been adopted in some form in all 50 states and the District of Columbia. It was revised in 1987, and the revised version has been adopted in some form in at least 22 states. — Abbr. UAGA.

Uniform Child Custody Jurisdiction Act. A 1968 model statute that sets out a standard (based on the child's residence in and connections with the state) by which a state court determines whether it has jurisdiction over a particular child-custody matter or whether it must recognize a custody decree issued by another state's court. • The Uniform Child Custody Jurisdiction Act was replaced in 1997 by the Uniform Child Custody Jurisdiction and Enforcement Act. — Abbr. UCCJA.

Uniform Child Custody Jurisdiction and Enforcement Act. A 1997 model statute that provides uniform methods of expedited interstate custody and visitation orders. • This Act was promulgated as a successor to the Uniform Child Custody Jurisdiction Act. The UCCJEA brings the Uniform Child Custody Jurisdiction Act into conformity with the Parental Kidnapping Prevention Act and the Violence Against Women Act. The Act revises child-custody jurisdiction, giving clearer standards for original jurisdiction and a standard for continuing jurisdiction. The Act also provides a remedial process for enforcing interstate child custody and visitation. — Abbr. UCCJEA.

Uniform Code of Military Justice. 1. Code of Military Justice. **2.** A model code promulgated by the National Conference of Commissioners on Uniform State Laws to govern state military forces when not in federal service. 11 U.L.A. 335 et seq. (1974). — Abbr. UCMJ.

Uniform Commercial Code. A uniform law that governs commercial transactions, including sales of goods, secured transactions, and negotiable instruments. • The Code has been adopted in some form by every state and the District of Columbia. — Abbr. UCC.

Uniform Computer Information Transactions Act. A model law that regulates software licensing and computer-information transactions. • The act draws upon contract law and the Uniform Commercial Code to create a regulatory scheme for licensing, rather than sales or lease, transactions. Among other things, UCITA applies to contracts for the licensing or purchase of software, contracts for software development, and contracts for access to databases through the Internet. It does not cover goods or services contracts within the scope of the UCC. — Abbr. UCITA.

Uniform Consumer Credit Code. A uniform law designed to simplify and modernize the consumer credit and usury laws, to improve consumer understanding of the terms of credit transactions, to protect consumers against unfair practices, and the like. • This Code has been adopted by only a few states. — Abbr. UCCC; U3C.

Uniform Controlled Substances Act. A uniform act, adopted by many states and the federal government, governing the sale, use, and distribution of drugs. 21 USCA §§ 801 et seq.

Uniform Crime Reports. A series of annual criminological studies (each entitled *Crime in the United States*) prepared by the FBI. • The reports include data on eight index offenses, statistics on arrests, and information on offenders, crime rates, and the like. — Abbr. UCR.

Uniform Deceptive Trade Practices Act. A 1964 model state statute that codified many common-law intellectual-property torts, such as trademark infringement, passing off, trade disparagement, and false advertising, and that provided additional consumer protection against other forms of commercial deception. • The Act provides a laundry list of prohibited practices, all involving misrepresentation. — Abbr. UDTPA.

Uniform Determination of Death Act. A 1978 model statute that provides a comprehensive basis for determining death. • This is a technical act that merely defines death clinically and does not deal with suicide, assisted suicide, or the right to die. The Act was revised in 1980. It has been adopted in almost all states.

Uniform Disposition of Community Property at Death Act. A 1971 model statute designed for non-community-property states to preserve the rights of each spouse in property that was community property before the spouses moved to non-community-property states, unless they have severed or altered their community-property rights.

Uniform Division of Income for Tax Purposes Act. A uniform law, adopted by some states, that provides criteria to assist in assigning the total taxable income of a multistate corporation among the various states. — Abbr. UDITPA.

Uniform Divorce Recognition Act. A 1947 model code adopted by some states regarding full-faith-and-credit issues that arise in divorces. — Abbr. UDRA.

Uniform Durable Power of Attorney Act. A 1979 model statute that provides a simple way for a person to deal with his or her property by providing a power of attorney that will survive after the incompetence of the principal. • The Act was revised in 1987 and has been adopted in almost every state.

Uniformed Services Former Spouses' Protection Act. A federal statute that governs the disposition of military pension benefits to former spouses of persons in the armed services. 10 USCA §§ 1401 et seq. • The Act permits state courts to treat military-retirement pay as marital property and to order payment of up to 50% of the retirement pay directly to the former spouse if the spouses were married for at least ten years while the employee served in the military. — Abbr. USFSPA.

Uniform Electronic Transactions Act. A 1999 model law designed to support electronic commerce by providing means for legally recognizing and retaining electronic records, establishing how parties can bind themselves in an electronic transaction, and providing for the use of electronic records by governmental agencies. • UETA covers electronic records and digital signatures but applies only if all parties agree to do business electronically. — Abbr. UETA.

Uniform Enforcement of Foreign Judgments Act. A uniform state law giving the holder of a foreign judgment the right to levy and execute as if it were a domestic judgment.

Uniform Fraudulent Conveyances Act. A model act adopted in 1918 to deal with issues arising from fraudulent conveyances by insolvent persons. • This act differentiated between conduct that was presumed fraudulent and conduct that required an actual intent to commit fraud. — Abbr. UFCA.

Uniform Fraudulent Transfer Act. A model act designed to bring uniformity among the states regarding the definition of, and penalties for, fraudulent transfers. • This act was adopted in 1984 to replace the Uniform Fraudulent Conveyances Act. — Abbr. UFTA.

Uniform Gifts to Minors Act. Uniform Transfers to Minors Act. — Abbr. UGMA.

Uniform Health-Care Decisions Act. A 1993 model statute that facilitates and encourages adults to make advance directives. — Abbr. UHCDA.

Uniform Interstate Family Support Act. A 1992 model statute establishing a one-order system by which an alimony or child-support decree issued by one state can be enforced against a former spouse who resides in another state. • This statute has been adopted in every state and is the basis of jurisdiction in child-support suits. The purpose of the Act is to make the pursuit of interstate child support and paternity more effective, consistent, and efficient by requiring all states to recognize and enforce consistently support orders issued in other states. Before its enactment, there was considerable disparity among the states in the way they handled interstate child-support proceedings, since each state had differing versions of the earlier uniform law, the Uniform Reciprocal Enforcement of Support Act. The Act was revised in 1996 and again in 2001. — Abbr. UIFSA.

Uniform Interstate Juvenile Compact. An agreement that regulates the treatment of juveniles who are not under proper supervision or control, or who have run away or escaped, and who are likely to endanger their own or others' health, morals, or welfare. • The Compact is relied on by the state to transport juvenile runaways back to their home states. It has now been universally adopted in the United States, but not always in its entirety. — Abbr. UIJC.

Uniformity Clause. (1881) The clause of the U.S. Constitution requiring the uniform collection of federal taxes. U.S. Const. art. I, § 8, cl. 1.

Uniform Juvenile Court Act. A 1968 model statute designed to (1) provide for the care, protection, and moral, mental, and physical development of the children who come under its provisions, (2) provide juvenile delinquents with treatment, training, and rehabilitation rather than criminal punishment, (3) attempt to keep families together unless separation of parents and children is necessary for the children's welfare or is in the public interest, (4) provide a judicial procedure for a fair hearing and protection of juvenile delinquents' constitutional and other legal rights, and (5) provide simple interstate procedures to carry out cooperative measures among the juvenile courts of different states. — Abbr. UJCA.

uniform law. An unofficial law proposed as legislation for all the states to adopt exactly as written, the purpose being to promote greater consistency among the states. • All the uniform laws are promulgated by the National Conference of Commissioners on Uniform State Laws. For a complete collection, see *Uniform Laws Annotated*.

Uniform Limited Partnership Act. A model law promulgated in 1916 for adoption by state legislatures to govern the relationship between the partners of a limited partnership. • At one time it was adopted in all states except Louisiana. The National Conference of Commissioners on Uniform State Laws promulgated the Revised Uniform Limited Partnership Act (RULPA) in 1976, and made substantial amendments to it in 1985. The amended RULPA has been adopted by most states. — Abbr. ULPA.

Uniform Mandatory Disposition of Detainers Act. A 1958 model statute requiring a state to timely dispose of any untried charges against a prisoner in that state, on the prisoner's written request. • The Act has been adopted by several states.

Uniform Marriage and Divorce Act. A 1970 model statute that defines marriage and divorce. • Extensively amended in 1973, the Act was an attempt by the National Conference of Commissioners on Uniform State Laws to make marriage and divorce laws more uniform. The Act's greatest significance is that it introduced, as the sole ground for divorce, irreconcilable differences. Although the UMDA has been enacted in part in only a handful of states, it has had an enormous impact on marriage and divorce laws in all states. — Abbr. UMDA.

Uniform Parentage Act. A 1973 model statute that provides a means for determining parenthood for the general welfare of the child and for assigning child support. • The Act abolishes distinctions between legitimate and illegitimate status for children. Instead, it directs courts to determine rights and responsibilities based on the existence of a parent–child relationship. The Act has been adopted in all states. The Act was revised in 2000 and amended in 2002. Among other changes, the revisions provided frameworks for establishing the parentage (esp. paternity) of children born to married or unmarried couples, and set standards and rules for genetic testing. A minority of states have enacted a version of the revised Act.

Uniform Partnership Act. A 1914 model statute intended to bring uniformity to state laws governing general and limited partnerships. • The Act was adopted by almost all the states, but has been superseded in several of them by the Revised Uniform Partnership Act (1994). — Abbr. UPA.

Uniform Premarital Agreement Act. A 1983 model statute that governs the drafting of prenuptial contracts and provides a more certain framework for drafting complete and enforceable agreements. • Under the UPAA, a premarital agreement must be in writing and signed by the parties. It becomes effective only upon marriage. The agreement may govern the parties' assets, support, and obligations during the marriage, at death, and upon divorce. The UPAA has been adopted in some form in about one-third of the states. — Abbr. UPAA.

Uniform Principal and Income Act. A uniform code adopted by some states governing allocation of principal and income in trusts and estates.

Uniform Probate Code. A 1969 model statute that modernizes the rules and doctrines governing intestate succession, probate, and the administration of estates. • It has been extensively amended many times since 1969 and has been enacted in a majority of states. — Abbr. UPC.

Uniform Prudent Investor Act. A 1994 model statute that sets a standard for the acts of a trustee, adopts a prudent-investor standard, and prefers a modern portfolio approach to investing. • Under the Uniform Prudent Investor Act, the trustee is given significant power to delegate the selection of investments. The prudent-investor standard replaces the prudent-person standard of investing. The portfolio approach provides that no investment will be viewed in isolation; rather, it will be viewed as part of the entire portfolio. Under this theory, even though an investor loses trust assets on an investment, if there is an overall positive return, the investor will not be liable to the beneficiaries. — Abbr. UPIA.

Uniform Putative and Unknown Fathers Act. A 1988 model statute aimed at codifying Supreme Court decisions on the rights of an unwed father in relation to his child. • The Act deals primarily with an unwed father's right to notice of a termination and adoption proceeding, to adjudication of paternity, to visitation, and to custody. — Abbr. UPUFA.

Uniform Reciprocal Enforcement of Support Act. A 1950 model statute (now superseded) that sought to unify the way in which interstate support matters were processed and the way in which one jurisdiction's orders were given full faith and credit in another jurisdiction. • This Act, which was amended in 1958 and 1960, was replaced in 1997 with the Uniform Interstate Family Support Act. — Abbr. URESA.

Uniform Simultaneous Death Act. A 1940 model statute creating a rule that a person must survive a decedent by at least 120 hours in order to avoid disputes caused by simultaneous deaths (as in a common disaster) or by quickly successive deaths of persons between whom property or death benefits pass on the death of one survived by the other. • In the absence of the 120-hour period of survival, each person is presumed to have survived the other for purposes of distributing their respective estates. The Act was revised in 1993 and has been adopted in some form by almost every state.

Uniform Status of Children of Assisted Conception Act. A 1988 model statute aimed at ensuring certainty of legal parentage when assisted conception has been used. • The adopting state has the option of regulating or prohibiting contracts with surrogate mothers.

Uniform Trade Secrets Act. A 1979 model statute, enacted by most states, defining *trade secret* differently from the common law by being at once broader (because there is no continuous-use requirement) and narrower (because information "readily ascertainable by proper means" cannot qualify). • The Act has three elements: (1) the information must qualify as a trade secret; (2) it must be misappropriated, either through wrongful means or by breaching a duty of confidentiality; and (3) the owner must have taken reasonable precautions to keep the information secret. — Abbr. UTSA.

Uniform Transfers to Minors Act. A 1983 model statute providing for the transfer of property to a minor and permitting a custodian who acts in a fiduciary capacity to manage investments and apply the income from the property to the minor's support. • The Act has been adopted in most states. It was revised in 1986. — Abbr. UTMA.

unilateral (yoo-nə-**lat**-ər-əl), *adj.* (1802) One-sided; relating to only one of two or more persons or things <unilateral mistake>.

uninsured-motorist coverage. Insurance that pays for the insured's injuries and losses negligently caused by a driver who has no liability insurance.

union, *n.* An organization formed to negotiate with employers, on behalf of workers collectively, about job-related issues such as salary, benefits, hours, and working conditions. • Unions generally represent skilled workers in trades and crafts. — **unionize,** *vb.* — **unionist,** *n.*

closed union. A union with restrictive membership requirements, such as high dues and long apprenticeship periods.

company union. **1.** A union whose membership is limited to the employees of a single company. **2.** A union under company domination.

craft union. A union composed of workers in the same trade or craft, such as carpentry or plumbing, regardless of the industry in which they work.

independent union. A union that is not affiliated with a national or international union.

industrial union. A union composed of workers in the same industry, such as shipbuilding or automobile manufacturing, regardless of their particular trade or craft.

international union. A parent union with affiliates in two or more countries.

local union. A union that serves as the local bargaining unit for a national or international union.

multicraft union. A union composed of workers in different industries.

national union. A parent union with locals in various parts of the United States.

open union. A union with minimal membership requirements.

trade union. A union composed of workers of the same or of several allied trades; a craft union.

union certification. A determination by the National Labor Relations Board or a state agency that a particular union qualifies as the bargaining representative for a segment of a company's workers — a bargaining unit — because it has the support of a majority of the workers in the unit.

unit. The number of shares, often 100, in which a given stock is normally traded.

unital (**yoo**-nə-təl), *adj.* (1860) Of or relating to legal relations that exist between only two persons.

United Nations. An international organization established in 1945 to promote and ensure international peace and security, to promote friendly relations between nations, and to contribute in resolving international problems related to economic, social, cultural, and humanitarian conditions. — Abbr. U.N.

United States Attorney. A lawyer appointed by the President to represent, under the direction of the Attorney General, the federal government in civil and criminal cases in a federal judicial district. • One U.S. Attorney is assigned to each of the federal judicial districts, except for the Northern Mariana Islands and Guam. — Abbr. USA.

Assistant United States Attorney. A lawyer appointed by the Attorney General to act under the direction of the United States Attorney and represent the federal government in civil and criminal cases filed in federal courts. — Abbr. AUSA.

Special Assistant to the United States Attorney. An attorney appointed by the Attorney General for a limited period to assist a United States Attorney in specific cases. 28 USCA § 543. — Abbr. SAUSA.

United States Code. A multivolume published codification of federal statutory law. — Abbr. U.S.C.; USC.

United States Code Annotated. A multivolume publication of the complete text of the United States Code with historical notes, cross-references, and casenotes of federal and state decisions construing specific Code sections. — Abbr. USCA.

United States Court of Appeals. A federal appellate court having jurisdiction to hear cases in one of the 13 judicial circuits of the United States (the First Circuit through the Eleventh Circuit, plus the District of Columbia Circuit and the Federal Circuit).

United States Court of Appeals for the Armed Forces. The primary civilian appellate tribunal responsible for reviewing court-martial convictions from all the military services. 10 USCA §§ 941–950.

United States Court of Appeals for the Federal Circuit. An intermediate-level appellate court with jurisdiction to hear appeals in patent cases, various actions against the United States to recover damages, cases from the U.S. Court of Federal Claims, the U.S. Court of International Trade, the U.S. Court of Appeals for Veterans Claims, the Merit Systems Protection Board, and some administrative agencies. • The Court originated in the 1982 merger of the Court of Customs and Patent Appeals and the U.S. Court of Claims (although the trial jurisdiction of the Court of Claims was given to a new U.S. Claims Court). Among the purposes of its creation were ending forum-shopping in patent suits, settling differences in patent-law doctrines among the circuits, and allowing a single forum to develop the expertise needed to rule on complex technological questions that arise in patent suits. — Abbr. CAFC, Fed. Cir. — Often shortened to *Federal Circuit.*

United States Court of Appeals for Veterans Claims. An Article I federal appellate court that has exclusive jurisdiction to review decisions of the Board of Veterans Appeals. • The Court was created in 1988 as the United States Court of Veterans Appeals; its name was changed in 1998. Its seven judges are appointed by the President and confirmed by the Senate; they serve 15-year terms. Appeals from its decisions are to the U.S. Court of Appeals for the Federal Circuit. 38 USCA §§ 7251 et seq.

United States Court of Federal Claims. A specialized federal court created under Article I of the Constitution in 1982 (with the name *United States Claims Court*) as the successor to the Court of Claims, and renamed in 1992 as the United States Court of Federal Claims. • It has original, nationwide jurisdiction to render a money judgment on any claim against the United States founded on the Constitution, a federal statute, a federal regulation, an express or implied-in-fact contract with the United States, or any other claim for damages not sounding in tort. — Abbr. Cl. Ct.; (formerly) Ct. Cl.

United States Court of International Trade. A court with jurisdiction over any civil action against the United States arising from federal laws governing import transactions or the eligibility of workers, firms, and communities for adjustment assistance under the Trade Act of 1974 (19 USCA §§ 2101–2495). • Its exclusive jurisdiction also includes actions to recover customs duties, to recover on a customs bond, and to impose certain civil penalties for fraud or negligence. See 28 USCA §§ 1581–1584. — Abbr. USCIT; CIT.

United States Customs Court. A court that formerly heard cases involving customs and duties. • Abolished in 1980, its responsibilities have been taken over by the United States Court of International Trade.

United States Customs Service. An agency in the U.S. Department of Homeland Security responsible for collecting import duties on goods, wares, and merchandise, and for enforcing customs and related laws. • The Customs Service was created in 1863. 12 Stat. 665. It was transferred from the Department of the Treasury in 2003.

United States District Court. A federal trial court having jurisdiction to hear civil and criminal cases within its judicial district. • The United States is divided into nearly 100 federal judicial districts. Each state has at least one judicial district. Also, the District of Columbia, Puerto Rico, Guam, the Virgin Islands, and the Northern Mariana Islands each have one district. — Abbr. U.S.D.C.

United States Foreign Intelligence Surveillance Court. An 11-judge court that hears requests from the Attorney General for surveillance warrants under the Foreign Intelligence Surveillance Act. • The court's proceedings and records are normally closed to the public. Its rulings may be reviewed by the Foreign Intelligence Court of Review. — Abbr. FISC.

United States Foreign Intelligence Surveillance Court of Review. A panel comprising three federal judges appointed by the Chief Justice to review decisions of the United States Intelligence Surveillance Court. • The Court was established in 1978 by the Foreign Intelligence Surveillance Act.

United States Magistrate Judge. A federal judicial officer who hears civil and criminal pretrial matters and who may conduct civil trials or criminal misdemeanor trials. 28 USCA §§ 631–639. • Magistrate judges are appointed to renewable eight-year terms under Article I of the U.S. Constitution.

United States Marshals Service. The unit in the U.S. Department of Justice responsible for protecting federal courts and ensuring effective operation of the judicial system. • U.S. marshals make arrests, serve court papers, and enforce court orders. — Abbr. USMS.

United States of America. A federal republic formed after the War of Independence and made up of 48 conterminous states, plus the state of Alaska and the District of Columbia in North America, plus the state of Hawaii in the Pacific. — Abbr. USA; U.S.

United States Reports. The official printed record of U.S. Supreme Court cases. • In a citation, it is abbreviated as U.S., as in 388 U.S. 14 (1967).

United States Secret Service. A law-enforcement agency in the U.S. Department of Homeland Security responsible for providing security for the President, Vice President, certain other government officials, and visiting foreign diplomats, and for protecting U.S. currency by enforcing the laws relating to counterfeiting, forgery, and credit-card fraud. • The Service was transferred from the Department of the Treasury in 2003. — Often shortened to *Secret Service.*

United States Sentencing Commission. An independent commission in the judicial branch of the federal government responsible for setting and regulating guidelines for criminal sentencing in federal courts and for issuing policy statements about their application. • The President appoints its members with the advice and consent of the Senate. It was created under the Sentencing Reform Act 1984. 28 USCA § 991.

United States Sentencing Guidelines. A detailed set of instructions for judges to determine appropriate sentences for federal crimes. — Abbr. USSG.

United States trustee. A federal official who is appointed by the Attorney

General to perform administrative tasks in the bankruptcy process, such as appointing bankruptcy trustees in Chapter 7 and Chapter 11 cases.

Uniting and Strengthening America by Providing Appropriate Tools Required to Intercept and Obstruct Terrorism. USA Patriot Act.

unitization. *Oil & gas.* The collection of producing wells over a reservoir for joint operations such as enhanced-recovery techniques. • Unitization is usu. carried out after primary production has begun to fall off substantially, in order to permit efficient secondary-recovery operations. It is also done to comply with well-spacing requirements established by state law or regulation. Pooling, by contrast, is usu. associated with drilling a single well and operating that well by primary-production techniques. — **unitize** (**yoo**-nə-tɪz), *vb.*

unity, *n.* (13c) **1.** The fact or condition of being one in number; oneness. **2.** Jointness in interest, possession, time, or title. • At common law, all four of these unities were required for the creation of a joint tenancy. — **unitary,** *adj.*

unity of interest. (18c) The requirement that all joint tenants' interests must be identical in nature, extent, and duration.

unity of possession. (18c) The requirement that each joint tenant must be entitled to possession of the whole property.

unity of time. (18c) The requirement that all joint tenants' interests must vest at the same time.

unity of title. (18c) The requirement that all joint tenants must acquire their interests under the same instrument.

unity of seisin (**see**-zin). (1800) The merging of seisin in one person, brought about when the person becomes seised of a tract of land on which he or she already has an easement.

Universal Declaration of Human Rights. An international bill of rights proclaimed by the United Nations in December 1948, being that body's first general enumeration of human rights and fundamental freedoms. • The preamble states that "recognition of the inherent dignity and of the equal and inalienable rights of all members of the human family is the foundation of freedom, justice and peace in the world." The Declaration contains a lengthy list of rights and fundamental freedoms.

universal-inheritance rule. *Wills & estates.* A doctrine holding that an intestate estate escheats to the state only if the decedent leaves no surviving relatives, no matter how distant. • Through the first half of the 20th century, this rule was broadly followed in American jurisdictions. The Uniform Probate Code abandons the universal-inheritance rule and provides that if no member of the third or a nearer parentela survives the decedent, the intestate estate escheats to the state.

unjudicial, *adj.* (16c) Not becoming of or appropriate to a judge.

unjust, *adj.* (14c) Contrary to justice; not just.

unjust enrichment. (1897) **1.** The retention of a benefit conferred by another, without offering compensation, in circumstances where compensation is reasonably expected. **2.** A benefit obtained from another, not intended as a gift and not legally justifiable, for which the beneficiary must make restitution or recompense. **3.** The area of law dealing with unjustifiable benefits of this kind.

unlawful, *adj.* (14c) **1.** Not authorized by law; illegal <in some cities, jaywalking is unlawful>. **2.** Criminally punishable <unlawful entry>. **3.** Involving moral turpitude <the preacher spoke to the congregation about the unlawful activities of gambling and drinking>. — **unlawfully,** *adv.*

unlawful act. (16c) Conduct that is not authorized by law; a violation of a civil or criminal law.

unlawful-detainer proceeding. (1879) An action to return a wrongfully held tenancy (as one held by a tenant after the lease has expired) to its owner.

unliquidated, *adj.* (18c) Not previously specified or determined <unliquidated damages>.

unreasonable, *adj.* (14c) **1.** Not guided by reason; irrational or capricious. **2.** Not supported by a valid exception to the warrant requirement <unreasonable search and seizure>.

unrebuttable, *adj.* Not rebuttable <an unrebuttable presumption>.

unrecorded, *adj.* (16c) Not recorded; esp., not filed in the public record <unrecorded deed>.

unreviewable, *adj.* (1877) Not subject to legal or judicial review <the claim is unreviewable on appeal>.

unsafe, *adj.* (Of a verdict or judgment) likely to be overturned on appeal because of a defect.

unseated, *adj.* (Of land) vacant and neither developed nor cultivated.

unsound, *adj.* (14c) **1.** Not healthy; esp., not mentally well <unsound mind>. **2.** Not firmly made; impaired <unsound foundation>. **3.** Not valid or well founded <unsound argument>.

unsworn, *adj.* (16c) Not sworn <an unsworn statement>.

untenantable (ən-**ten**-ən-tə-bəl), *adj.* (17c) Not capable of being occupied or lived in; not fit for occupancy <the city closed the untenantable housing project>.

untimely, *adj.* (13c) Not timely <an untimely answer>; at an inappropriate time, either too soon or too late.

untrue, *adj.* **1.** (Of something said) not correct; inaccurate. **2.** (Of a person) not faithful or true (to a standard or belief).

UPA. *abbr.* Uniform Partnership Act.

UPAA. *abbr.* Uniform Premarital Agreement Act.

UPC. *abbr.* Uniform Probate Code.

UPIA. *abbr.* Uniform Prudent Investor Act.

UPL. *abbr.* Unauthorized practice of law <the state bar's UPL committee>.

urban, *adj.* Of or relating to a city or town; not rural.

urban renewal. (1954) The process of redeveloping urban areas by demolishing or repairing existing structures or by building new facilities on areas that have been cleared in accordance with an overall plan.

URESA (yə-**ree**-sə). *abbr.* Uniform Reciprocal Enforcement of Support Act.

U.S. *abbr.* **1.** United States. **2.** *United States Reports.*

USA. *abbr.* **1.** United States of America. **2.** United States Army. **3.** United States Attorney.

USAA. *abbr.* United States Arbitration Act.

USAF. *abbr.* United States Air Force.

USAFA. *abbr.* United States Air Force Academy.

usage. (13c) A well-known, customary, and uniform practice, usu. in a specific profession or business.

general usage. (16c) A usage that prevails throughout a country or particular trade or profession; a usage that is not restricted to a local area.

immemorial usage. (17c) A usage that has existed for a very long time; longstanding custom.

local usage. (18c) A practice or method regularly observed in a particular place, sometimes considered by a court in interpreting a document. UCC § 1-205(2)(3).

trade usage. (1864) **1.** A practice or method of dealing having such regular observance in a region, vocation, or trade that it justifies an expectation that it will be observed in a given transaction; a customary practice or set of practices relied on by persons conversant in, or connected with, a trade or business. • While a course of performance or a course of dealing can be established by the parties' testimony, a trade usage is usu. established by expert testimony. **2.** Conventional custom.

USA Patriot Act. A statute enacted in response to the terrorist attacks of September 11, 2001, giving law-enforcement agencies broader authority to collect information on suspected terrorists, to share that information among domestic and foreign intelligence agencies, to make the country's borders more secure, to detain suspects on new types of criminal charges using new criminal procedures, and to give the Treasury Department more authority to investigate and regulate financial institutions that participate in foreign money-laundering. • The title is an acronym of Uniting and Strengthening America by Providing Appropriate Tools Required to Intercept and Obstruct Terrorism. — Often shortened to *Patriot Act.*

USC. *abbr.* United States Code.

USCA. *abbr.* United States Code Annotated.

USCG. *abbr.* United States Coast Guard.

USCGA. *abbr.* United States Coast Guard Academy.

USCIS. *abbr.* United States Citizenship and Immigration Service.

USCIT. *abbr.* United States Court of International Trade.

U.S. Citizenship and Immigration Service. A unit in the U.S. Department of Homeland Security responsible for enforcing the nation's immigration laws. • Its functions were transferred from the former Immigration and Naturalization Service of the U.S. Department of Justice in 2003. — Abbr. USCIS.

USDA. *abbr.* United States Department of Agriculture.

U.S.D.C. *abbr.* United States District Court.

use (yoos), *n.* (bef. 12c) **1.** The application or employment of something; esp., a long-continued possession and employment of a thing for the purpose for which it is adapted, as distinguished from a possession and employment that is merely temporary or occasional <the neighbors complained to the city about the owner's use of the building as a dance club>. **2.** A habitual or common practice <drug use>. **3.** A purpose or end served <the tool had several uses>. **4.** A benefit or profit; esp., the right to take profits from land owned and possessed by another; the equitable ownership of land to which another person holds the legal title <cestui que use>. — **use** (yooz), *vb.*

contingent use. (17c) A use that would be a contingent remainder if it had not been limited by way of use. • An example is a transfer "to A, to the use of B for life, with the remainder to the use of C's heirs."

entire use. A use of property solely for the benefit of a married woman. • When used in the habendum of a trust deed for the benefit of a married woman, this phrase operates to keep her husband from taking anything under the deed.

resulting use. (18c) A use created by implication and remaining with the grantor when the conveyance lacks consideration.

shifting use. (18c) A use arising from the occurrence of a certain event that terminates the preceding use. • In the following example, C has a shifting use that arises when D makes the specified payment: "to A for the use of

B, but then to C when D pays $1,000 to E." This is a type of conditional limitation.

springing use. (17c) A use arising on the occurrence of a future event. • In the following example, B has a springing use that vests when B marries: "to A for the use of B when B marries."

useful, *adj. Patents.* (Of an invention) having a practical application.

useful life. (1923) The estimated length of time that depreciable property will generate income. • Useful life is used to calculate depreciation and amortization deductions.

use in commerce. *Trademarks.* Actual use of a trademark in the advertising, marketing, promotion, sale, or distribution of goods or services.

useless-gesture exception. (1970) *Criminal procedure.* An exception to the knock-and-announce rule whereby police are excused from having to announce their purpose before entering the premises to execute a warrant when it is evident from the circumstances that people inside the premises are of aware of the police officers' authority and purpose.

use plaintiff. *Common-law pleading.* A plaintiff for whom an action is brought in another's name. • For example, when the use plaintiff is an assignee ("A") of a chose in action and sues in the assignor's name ("B"), the assignor's name appears first on the petition's title: "B for the Use of A against C."

user (yooz-ər). (15c) **1.** The exercise or employment of a right or property <the neighbor argued that an easement arose by his continuous user over the last 15 years>. **2.** Someone who uses a thing <the stapler's last user did not put it away>.

end user. (1963) The ultimate consumer for whom a product is designed.

user fee. (1967) A charge assessed for the use of a particular item or facility.

USMA. *abbr.* United States Military Academy.

U.S. Magistrate. United States Magistrate Judge.

USMC. *abbr.* United States Marine Corps.

USMMA. *abbr.* United States Merchant Marine Academy.

USMS. *abbr.* United States Marshals Service.

USN. *abbr.* United States Navy.

USNA. *abbr.* United States Naval Academy.

USPS. *abbr.* United States Postal Service.

USPTO. *abbr.* United States Patent And Trademark Office.

USSG. *abbr.* United States Sentencing Guidelines.

usual, *adj.* (14c) **1.** Ordinary; customary. **2.** Expected based on previous experience, or on a pattern or course of conduct to date.

usurious (yoo-**z[y]oor**-ee-əs *or* yoo-**zhuu**-ree-əs), *adj.* (17c) **1.** Practicing usury <a usurious lender>. **2.** Characterized by usury <a usurious contract>.

usurpation (yoo-sər-**pay**-shən *or* yoo-zər-**pay**-shən), *n.* (14c) The unlawful seizure and assumption of another's position, office, or authority. — **usurp** (yoo-**sərp** *or* yoo-**zərp**), *vb.*

usury (**yoo**-zhə-ree), *n.* (14c) **1.** Historically, the lending of money with interest. **2.** Today, the charging of an illegal rate of interest as a condition to lending money. **3.** An illegally high rate of interest. — **usurer** (**yoo**-zhər-ər), *n.*

usury law. A law prohibiting moneylenders from charging illegally high interest rates.

utilitarian-deterrence theory. (1983) The legal theory that a person should be punished only if the punishment benefits society — that is, only if the punishment would help to deter future harmful conduct.

utilitarianism. (1827) The philosophical and economic doctrine that the best social policy is that which does the most good for the greatest number of people; esp., an ethical theory that judges the rightness or wrongness of actions according to the pleasure they create or the pain they inflict and recommends whatever action creates the greatest good for the greatest number of people. • This is a type of consequentialism. For example, utilitarianism analyzes intellectual-property rights from the point of view of society rather than the individual inventor, author, or artist, and justifies the rights as an incentive for social and technological progress. — **utilitarian,** *adj.* & *n.*

hedonistic utilitarianism. (1943) The theory that the validity of a law should be measured by determining the extent to which it promotes the greatest happiness to the greatest number of citizens. • This theory is found most prominently in the work of Jeremy Bentham, whose "Benthamite utilitarianism" greatly influenced legal reform in nineteenth-century Britain. Hedonistic utilitarianism generally maintains that pleasure is intrinsically good and pain intrinsically bad. Therefore, inflicting pain on an individual, as by punishing a criminal, is justified only if it results in a net increase of pleasure for society by deterring future harmful behavior.

utility. (14c) **1.** The quality of serving some function that benefits society; meritoriousness. **2.** *Patents.* Capacity to perform a function or attain a result for which the patent applicant or holder claims protection as intellectual property. • In patent law, utility is one of the three basic requirements of patentability, the others being nonobviousness and novelty. In the calculation of damages for patent infringement, utility is the benefit or advantage of the patented product or process over the products or processes, if any, that previously had been used to produce similar results. **3.** A business enterprise that performs an essential public service and that is subject to governmental regulation.

public utility. (1895) **1.** A company that provides necessary services to the public, such as telephone lines and service, electricity, and water. • Most utilities operate as monopolies but are subject to governmental regulation. **2.** A person, corporation, or other association that carries on an enterprise for the accommodation of the public, the members of which are entitled as a matter of right to use the enterprises's facilities.

UTMA. *abbr.* Uniform Transfers to Minors Act.

UTSA. *abbr.* Uniform Trade Secrets Act.

utter, *adj.* (15c) Complete; absolute; total <an utter denial>.

utter, *vb.* (15c) **1.** To say, express, or publish <don't utter another word until your attorney is present>. **2.** To put or send (a document) into circulation; esp., to circulate (a forged note) as if genuine <she uttered a counterfeit $50 bill at the grocery store>. — **utterance** (for sense 1), **uttering** (for sense 2), *n.*

uttering. (18c) The crime of presenting a false or worthless instrument with the intent to harm or defraud.

uxor (**ək**-sor), *n.* [Latin] Wife. — Abbr. *ux.*

uxoricide (ək-**sor**-ə-sɪd *or* əg-**zor**-), *n.* (18c) **1.** The murder of one's wife. **2.** A man who murders his wife. — **uxoricidal,** *adj.*

V

v. *abbr.* **1.** Versus. — Also abbreviated *vs.* **2.** Volume. — Also abbreviated *vol.* **3.** Verb. — Also abbreviated *vb.*

VA. *abbr.* Department of Veterans Affairs.

vacancy, *n.* **1.** The state or fact of a lack of occupancy in an office, post, or piece of property. **2.** The time during which an office, post, or piece of property is not occupied. **3.** An unoccupied office, post, or piece of property; an empty place. • Although the term sometimes refers to an office or post that is temporarily filled, the more usual reference is to an office or post that is unfilled even temporarily. An officer's misconduct does not create a vacancy even if a suspension occurs; a vacancy, properly speaking, does not occur until the officer is officially removed.

vacant, *adj.* (13c) **1.** Empty; unoccupied <a vacant office>. • Courts have sometimes distinguished *vacant* from *unoccupied*, holding that *vacant* means completely empty while *unoccupied* means not routinely characterized by the presence of human beings. **2.** Absolutely free, unclaimed, and unoccupied <vacant land>. **3.** (Of an estate) abandoned; having no heir or claimant. — The term implies either abandonment or nonoccupancy for any purpose.

vacate, *vb.* (17c) **1.** To nullify or cancel; make void; invalidate <the court vacated the judgment>. **2.** To surrender occupancy or possession; to move out or leave <the tenant vacated the premises>.

vacation, *n.* (15c) **1.** The act of vacating <vacation of the office> <vacation of the court's order>. **2.** The period between the end of one term of court and the beginning of the next; the space of time during which a court holds no sessions. • The traditional vacations in England were Christmas vacation, beginning December 24 and ending January 6; Easter vacation, beginning Good Friday and ending Easter Tuesday; Whitsun vacation, beginning on the Saturday immediately before and ending the Tuesday immediately after Whitsunday (i.e., Pentecost, the seventh Sunday after Easter); and the long vacation, beginning August 13 and ending October 23. **3.** Loosely, any time when a given court is not in session.

vacatur (və-**kay**-tər), *n.* [Law Latin "it is vacated"] (17c) **1.** The act of annulling or setting aside. **2.** A rule or order by which a proceeding is vacated.

vagrancy (**vay**-grən-see), *n.* (17c) **1.** The state or condition of wandering from place to place without a home, job, or means of support. • Vagrancy is generally considered a course of conduct or a manner of living, rather than a single act. But under some statutes, a single act has been held sufficient to constitute vagrancy. One court held, for example, that the act of prowling about and creeping up on parked cars and their occupants at night, under circumstances suggesting an intent to commit a crime, constitutes vagrancy. See *Smith v. Drew*, 26 P.2d 1040 (Wash. 1933). Many state laws prohibiting vagrancy have been declared unconstitutionally vague. **2.** An instance of such wandering.

vagrant, *adj.* (15c) **1.** Of, relating to, or characteristic of a vagrant; inclined to vagrancy. **2.** Nomadically homeless.

vagrant, *n.* (15c) **1.** At common law, anyone belonging to the several classes of idle or disorderly persons, rogues, and vagabonds. **2.** One who, not having a settled habitation, strolls from place to place; a homeless, idle wanderer. • The term often refers to one who spends time in idleness, lacking any property and without any visible means of support. Under some statutes, a vagrant is an offender against or menace to the public peace, usu. liable to become a public burden.

vague, *adj.* (16c) **1.** Imprecise; not sharply outlined; indistinct; uncertain.

unconstitutionally vague. **1.** (Of a penal legislative provision) so unclear and indefinite as not to give a person of ordinary intelligence the opportunity to know what is prohibited, restricted, or required. **2.** (Of a statute) impermissibly delegating basic policy matters to administrators and judges so such a degree as to lead to arbitrary and discriminatory application.

2. (Of language) describing a distribution around a central norm, as opposed to a neatly bounded class; broadly indefinite; not clearly or concretely expressed. **3.** Characterized by haziness of thought.

vagueness. (18c) **1.** Uncertain breadth of meaning <the phrase "within a reasonable time" is plagued by vagueness — what is reasonable?>. • Though common in writings generally, vagueness raises due-process concerns if legislation does not provide fair notice of what is required, restricted, or prohibited, because enforcement may become arbitrary. **2.** Loosely, ambiguity.

vagueness doctrine. (1957) *Constitutional law.* The doctrine — based on the Due Process Clause — requiring that a criminal statute state explicitly and definitely what acts are prohibited or restricted, so as to provide fair warning and preclude arbitrary enforcement.

valid, *adj.* (16c) **1.** Legally sufficient; binding <a valid contract>. **2.** Meritorious <that is a valid conclusion based on the facts presented in this case>. — **validate,** *vb.* — **validation, validity,** *n.*

valuable, *adj.* Worth a good price; having financial or market value.

valuable papers. Documents that, upon a person's death, are important in carrying out the decedent's wishes and in managing the estate's affairs. • Examples include a will, title documents, stock certificates, powers of attorney, letters to be opened on one's death, and the like. Some statutes require that, to be effective, a holographic will devising realty must be found among the decedent's valuable papers.

valuation, *n.* (16c) **1.** The process of determining the value of a thing or entity. **2.** The estimated worth of a thing or entity. — **value, valuate,** *vb.*

assessed valuation. (1825) The value that a taxing authority gives to property and to which the tax rate is applied.

special-use valuation. (1976) An executor's option of valuating real property in an estate, esp. farmland, based on its current use rather than for its highest potential value.

value, *n.* (14c) **1.** The significance, desirability, or utility of something. **2.** The monetary worth or price of something; the amount of goods, services, or money that something commands in an exchange.

agreed value. A property's value that is fixed by agreement of the parties, esp. the property's owner and the person or entity valuating the property. • An example is a list of property values contained in an insurance policy.

annual value. **1.** The net yearly income derivable from a given piece of property. **2.** One year's rental value of property, less the costs and expenses of maintaining the property.

assessed value. The value of an asset as determined by an appraiser for tax purposes.

cash surrender value. *Insurance.* The amount of money payable when an insurance policy having cash value, such as a whole-life policy, is redeemed before maturity or death. — Abbr. CSV.

fair market value. (18c) The price that a seller is willing to accept and a buyer is willing to pay on the open market and in an arm's-length transaction;

the point at which supply and demand intersect. — Abbr. FMV.

going-concern value. The value of a commercial enterprise's assets or of the enterprise itself as an active business with future earning power, as opposed to the liquidation value of the business or of its assets. • Going-concern value includes, for example, goodwill.

liquidation value. **1.** The value of a business or of an asset when it is sold in liquidation, as opposed to being sold in the ordinary course of business. **2.** Liquidation price.

salvage value. (1917) The value of an asset after it has become useless to the owner; the amount expected to be obtained when a fixed asset is disposed of at the end of its useful life. • Salvage value is used, under some depreciation methods, to determine the allowable tax deduction for depreciation. And under the UCC, when a buyer of goods breaches or repudiates the contract of sale, the seller may, under certain circumstances, either complete the manufacture of any incomplete goods or cease the manufacture and sell the partial product for scrap or salvage value. UCC § 2-704(2).

valued-policy law. A statute requiring insurance companies to pay the full amount of the insurance to the insured in the event of a total loss, regardless of the true value of the property at the time of loss.

value received. (17c) Consideration that has been delivered. • This phrase is commonly used in a bill of exchange or promissory note to show that it was supported by consideration.

vandal. [fr. Latin *Vandalus*, a member of the Germanic tribe known as Vandals] (17c) A malicious destroyer or defacer of works of art, monuments, buildings, or other property.

vandalism, *n.* (18c) **1.** Willful or ignorant destruction of public or private property, esp. of artistic, architectural, or literary treasures. **2.** The actions or attitudes of one who maliciously or ignorantly destroys or disfigures public or private property; active hostility to anything that is venerable or beautiful. — **vandalize,** *vb.* — **vandalistic,** *adj.*

variance. (14c) **1.** A difference or disparity between two statements or documents that ought to agree; esp., in criminal procedure, a difference between the allegations in a charging instrument and the proof actually introduced at trial.

fatal variance. (18c) A variance that either deprives the defendant of fair notice of the charges or exposes the defendant to the risk of double jeopardy. • A fatal variance is grounds for reversing a conviction.

immaterial variance. (18c) A variance too slight to mislead or prejudice the defendant and is thus harmless error.

2. A license or official authorization to depart from a zoning law.

VAT. *abbr.* Value-added tax.

veggie-libel law. *Slang.* Agricultural-disparagement law.

vel non (vel **non**). [Latin "or not"] (1895) Or the absence of it (or them) <this case turns solely on the finding of discrimination vel non>.

venal (**vee**-nəl), *adj.* (17c) **1.** (Of a person) capable of being bribed. **2.** Ready to sell one's services or influence for money or other valuable consideration, usu. for base motives. **3.** Of, relating to, or characterized by corrupt bargaining. **4.** Broadly, purchasable; for sale.

vend, *vb.* (17c) **1.** To transfer to another for money or something else of value. • The term is not commonly applied to real estate, although its derivatives (*vendor* and *vendee*) are. **2.** To make an object of trade, esp. by hawking or peddling. **3.** To utter publicly; to say or state; to publish broadly.

vendee. (16c) A purchaser, usu. of real property; a buyer.

vendetta (ven-**det**-ə), *n.* (1855) A private blood feud in which family members seek revenge on one or more persons outside the family (often members of another family); esp., a private war in which the nearest of kin seek revenge for the slaying of a relative.

vendor. A seller, usu. of real property.

venial (**vee**-nee-əl), *adj.* (14c) (Of a transgression) forgivable; pardonable.

venire (və-**nɪ**-ree *or* -**neer**-ee *or* -**nɪr** *or* -**neer**). (1807) **1.** A panel of persons selected for jury duty and from among whom the jurors are to be chosen.

special venire. A panel of citizens summoned when there is an unexpected need for a larger pool from which to select jurors, or a panel summoned for a particular (usu. capital) case.

2. Venire facias.

venire facias (və-**nɪ**-ree [*or* -**neer**-ee *or* -**nɪr** *or* -**neer**] **fay**-shee-əs). (15c) A writ directing a sheriff to assemble a jury. — Often shortened to *venire.*

venire facias ad respondendum (ad ree-spon-**den**-dəm). A writ requiring a sheriff to summon a person against whom an indictment for a misdemeanor has been issued. • A warrant is now more commonly used.

venire facias de novo (dee *or* di **noh**-voh). (18c) A writ for summoning a jury panel anew because of some impropriety or irregularity in the original jury's return or verdict such that a judgment cannot be entered on it. • The result of a new venire is a new trial. In substance, the writ is a motion for a new trial, but when the party objects to the verdict because of a procedural error (and not an error on the merits), the form of motion was traditionally for a venire facias de novo. — Often shortened to *venire de novo.*

veniremember (və-**nɪ**-ree-mem-bər *or* və-**neer**-ee- *or* və-**neer**-). (1966) A prospective juror; a member of a jury panel.

venture. (16c) An undertaking that involves risk; esp., a speculative commercial enterprise.

venturer, *n.* (16c) **1.** One who risks something, and hopes to gain more, in a business enterprise. **2.** One who participates in an association of two or more parties in a business enterprise.

venue (**ven**-yoo). [Law French "coming"] (16c) *Procedure.* **1.** The proper or a possible place for a lawsuit to proceed, usu. because the place has some connection either with the events that gave rise to the lawsuit or with the plaintiff or defendant. **2.** The territory, such as a country or other political subdivision, over which a trial court has jurisdiction. **3.** Loosely, the place where a conference or meeting is being held. **4.** In a pleading, the statement establishing the place for trial. **5.** In an affidavit, the designation of the place where it was made.

venue facts. (1936) Facts that need to be pleaded or established in a hearing to determine whether venue is proper in a given court.

veracious (və-**ray**-shəs), *adj.* (17c) Truthful; accurate.

veracity (və-**ras**-ət-ee), *n.* (17c) **1.** Truthfulness <the witness's fraud conviction supports the defense's challenge to his veracity>. **2.** Accuracy <you called into question the veracity of Murphy's affidavit>. — **veracious** (və-**ray**-shəs), *adj.*

verbal, *adj.* (15c) **1.** Of, relating to, or expressed in words. **2.** Loosely, of, relating to, or expressed in spoken words.

verbal-act doctrine. (1901) The rule that utterances accompanying conduct that might have legal effect are admissible when the conduct is material to the issue and is equivocal in nature, and when the words help give the conduct its legal significance.

verbatim (vər-**bay**-təm), *adj.* & *adv.* [fr. Latin *verbum* "word"] Word for word. • Courts have repeatedly held that, in the context of the requirement that a trial record must be "verbatim," absolute word-for-word accuracy is not necessary — and insubstantial omissions do not make a transcript "nonverbatim."

verdict. (15c) **1.** A jury's finding or decision on the factual issues of a case. **2.** Loosely, in a nonjury trial, a judge's resolution of the issues of a case.

chance verdict. (1820) A now-illegal verdict, arrived at by hazard or lot.

compromise verdict. (1851) A verdict reached when jurors, to avoid a deadlock, concede some issues so that other issues will be resolved as they want.

defective verdict. (18c) A verdict on which a judgment cannot be based because of irregularities or legal inadequacies.

directed verdict. (1912) A ruling by a trial judge taking a case from the jury because the evidence will permit only one reasonable verdict.

excessive verdict. (1817) A verdict resulting from the jury's passion or prejudice and thereby shocks the court's conscience.

general verdict. (17c) A verdict by which the jury finds in favor of one party or the other, as opposed to resolving specific fact questions.

general verdict with interrogatories. (1878) A general verdict accompanied by answers to written interrogatories on one or more issues of fact that bear on the verdict.

guilty verdict. (18c) A jury's finding that a defendant is guilty of the offense charged.

joint verdict. (1825) A verdict covering two or more parties to a lawsuit.

legally inconsistent verdict. (1975) A verdict in which the same element is found to exist and not to exist, as when a defendant is acquitted of one offense and convicted of another, even though the offenses arise from the same set of facts and an element of the second offense requires proof that the first offense has been committed.

majority verdict. A verdict agreed to by all but one or two jury members. • In some jurisdictions, a civil verdict supported by 10 of 12 jurors is acceptable.

open verdict. A verdict of a coroner's jury finding that the subject "came to his death by means to the jury unknown" or "came to his death at the hands of a person or persons to the jury unknown." • This verdict leaves open either the question whether any crime was committed or the identity of the criminal.

partial verdict. (1829) A verdict by which a jury finds a criminal defendant not guilty of some charges and guilty of other charges.

perverse verdict. (1870) A jury verdict so contrary to the evidence that it justifies the granting of a new trial.

public verdict. (17c) A verdict delivered by the jury in open court.

quotient verdict. (1867) An improper damage verdict that a jury arrives at by totaling what each juror would award and dividing by the number of jurors.

repugnant verdict. (1883) A verdict that contradicts itself in that the defendant is convicted and acquitted of different crimes having identical elements. • Sometimes the inconsistency occurs in a single verdict (*repugnant verdict*), and sometimes it occurs in two separate verdicts (*repugnant verdicts*). Both terms are used mainly in New York.

sealed verdict. (18c) A written verdict put into a sealed envelope when the jurors have agreed on their decision but court is not in session or the jury is continuing to deliberate other counts. • Upon delivering a sealed verdict, the jurors may separate. When court convenes again, this verdict is officially returned with the same effect as if the jury had returned it in open court before separating.

special verdict. (17c) A verdict in which the jury makes findings only on factual issues submitted to them by the judge, who then decides the legal effect of the verdict. See Fed. R. Civ. P. 49.

split verdict. (1886) **1.** A verdict in which one party prevails on some claims, while the other party prevails on others. **2.** *Criminal law.* A verdict finding a defendant guilty on one charge but not guilty on another. **3.** *Criminal law.* A verdict of guilty for one defendant and of not guilty for a codefendant.

true verdict. (16c) A verdict that is reached voluntarily — even if one or more jurors freely compromise their views — and not as a result of an arbitrary rule or order, whether imposed by the jurors themselves, the court, or a court officer.

verdict contrary to law. (18c) A verdict that the law does not authorize a jury to render because the conclusion drawn is not justified by the evidence.

verdict subject to opinion of court. (1820) A verdict that is subject to the court's determination of a legal issue reserved to the court upon the trial, so that judgment is ultimately entered depending on the court's ruling on a point of law.

verification, *n.* (16c) **1.** A formal declaration made in the presence of an authorized officer, such as a notary public, or (in some jurisdictions) under oath but not in the presence of such an officer, whereby one swears to the truth of the statements in the document. • Traditionally, a verification is used as a conclusion for all pleadings that are required to be sworn. **2.** An oath or affirmation that an authorized officer administers to an affiant or deponent. **3.** Loosely, ACKNOWLEDGMENT (5). **4.** Certified copy. **5.** CERTIFICATE OF AUTHORITY (1). **6.** Any act of notarizing. — **verify,** *vb.* — **verifier,** *n.*

verity (**ver**-ə-tee). (14c) Truth; truthfulness; conformity to fact.

versus, *prep.* (15c) Against. — Abbr. v.; vs.

vest, *vb.* (15c) **1.** To confer ownership (of property) upon a person. **2.** To invest (a person) with the full title to property. **3.** To give (a person) an immediate, fixed right of present or future enjoyment. **4.** *Hist.* To put (a person) into possession of land by the ceremony of investiture. — **vesting,** *n.*

vested, *adj.* (18c) Having become a completed, consummated right for present or future enjoyment; not contingent; unconditional; absolute <a vested interest in the estate>.

vested in interest. (18c) Consummated in a way that will result in future possession and use. • Reversions, vested remainders, and any other future use or executory devise that does not depend on an uncertain period or event are all said to be vested in interest.

vested in possession. (18c) Consummated in a way that has resulted in present enjoyment.

vested-rights doctrine. *Constitutional law.* The rule that the legislature cannot take away a right that has been vested by a court's judgment; specif., the principle that it is beyond the province of Congress to reopen a final judgment issued by an Article III court.

vestigial words (ve-**stij**-ee-əl). Statutory words and phrases that, through a succession of amendments, have been made useless or meaningless. • Courts do not allow vestigial words to defeat the fair meaning of a statute.

vesting order. (1873) A court order passing legal title in lieu of a legal conveyance.

veteran. A person who has been honorably discharged from military service.

Veterans Benefits Administration. A unit in the U.S. Department of Veterans Affairs responsible for advising and assisting veterans and their families who apply for veterans' benefits.

Veterans' Employment and Training Service. A unit in the U.S. Department of Labor responsible for administering various programs relating to veterans' employment and training. — Abbr. VETS.

Veterans Health Administration. A unit in the U.S. Department of Veterans Affairs responsible for providing hospital, nursing-home, and medical care to eligible veterans of military service.

veto (**vee**-toh), *n.* [Latin "I forbid"] (17c) **1.** A power of one governmental branch to prohibit an action by another branch; esp., a chief executive's refusal to sign into law a bill passed by the legislature. **2.** VETO MESSAGE. *Pl.* **vetoes.** — **veto,** *vb.*

absolute veto. (1852) An unrestricted veto that is not subject to being overridden.

legislative veto. (1850) *Hist.* A veto allowing Congress to block a federal executive or agency action taken under congressionally delegated authority. • The Supreme Court held the legislative veto unconstitutional in *INS v. Chadha,* 462 U.S. 919, 103 S.Ct. 2764 (1983).

line-item veto. (1858) The executive's power to veto some provisions in a legislative bill without affecting other provisions. • The U.S. Supreme Court declared the presidential line-item veto unconstitutional in 1998. See *Clinton v. City of New York,* 524 U.S. 417, 118 S.Ct. 2091 (1998).

overridden veto. (1971) A veto that the legislature has superseded by again passing the vetoed act, usu. by a supermajority of legislators. • In the federal government, a bill vetoed by the President must receive a two-thirds majority in Congress to override the veto and enact the measure into law.

pocket veto. (1842) A veto resulting from the President's failure to sign a bill passed within the last ten days of the congressional session.

qualified veto. (1853) A veto that is conclusive unless overridden by an extraordinary majority of the legislature. • This is the type of veto power that the President of the United States has.

suspensory veto (sə-**spen**-sə-ree). (1911) A veto that suspends a law until the legislature reconsiders it and then allows the law to take effect if repassed by an ordinary majority.

veto message. (1830) A statement communicating the reasons for the executive's refusing to sign into law a bill passed by the legislature. — Sometimes shortened to *veto.*

veto power. (1883) An executive's conditional power to prevent a bill that has passed the legislature from becoming law.

vex, *vb.* (15c) **1.** To harass, disquiet, or annoy. **2.** To cause physical or emotional distress. — **vexatious,** *adj.* — **vexation,** *n.*

vexation. (15c) The damage that results from trickery or malice.

vexatious (vek-**say**-shəs), *adj.* (16c) (Of conduct) without reasonable or probable cause or excuse; harassing; annoying.

vexatious delay. An insurance company's unjustifiable refusal to satisfy an insurance claim, esp. based on a mere suspicion but no hard facts that the claim is ill-founded.

vexatious suit. (17c) A lawsuit instituted maliciously and without good grounds, meant to create trouble and expense for the party being sued.

vexed question. (17c) **1.** A question often argued about but seemingly never settled. **2.** A question or point that has been decided differently by different tribunals and has therefore been left in doubt.

viable (vɪ-ə-bəl), *adj.* (1832) **1.** Capable of living, esp. outside the womb <a viable fetus>. **2.** Capable of independent existence or standing <a viable lawsuit>. **3.** Capable of succeeding <a viable option>. — **viability** (vɪ-ə-**bil**-ə-tee), *n.*

viatication (vɪ-at-ə-**kay**-shən). [fr. Latin *viaticus* "relating to a road or journey"] The purchase of a terminally or chronically ill policyholder's life insurance in exchange for a lump-sum payment equal to a percentage of the policy's full value.

viator (vɪ-**ay**-tər). **1.** APPARITOR (1). **2.** A terminally or chronically ill life-insurance policyholder who sells the policy to a third party in return for a lump-sum payment equal to a percentage of the policy's face value.

vicarious (vɪ-**kair**-ee-əs), *adj.* (17c) Performed or suffered by one person as substitute for another; indirect; surrogate.

vice (vɪs), *n.* (14c) **1.** A moral failing; an ethical fault. **2.** Wickedness; corruption. **3.** Broadly, any defect or failing.

vice (**vɪ**-see *or* **vɪ**-sə), *prep.* (18c) In the place of; in the stead of. • As a prefix, *vice-* (vɪs) denotes one who takes the place of.

vice president, *n.* (16c) **1.** An officer selected in advance to fill the presidency if the president dies, resigns, is removed from office, or cannot or will not serve. • The Vice President of the United States, who is elected at the same time as the President, serves as presiding officer of the Senate but may cast a vote only to break a tie. On the death, incapacity, resignation, or removal of the President, the Vice President succeeds to the presidency. **2.** A corporate officer of mid-level to high rank, usu. having charge of a department. — Abbr. V.P.; VP. — Also written *vice-president.* — **vice presidency,** *n.* — **vice-presidential,** *adj.*

vicinage (**vis**-ə-nij). [Law French "neighborhood"] (14c) **1.** Vicinity; proximity. **2.** The place where a crime is committed or a trial is held; the place from which jurors are to be drawn for trial; esp., the locale from which the accused is entitled to have jurors selected.

vicious propensity. (1835) An animal's tendency to endanger the safety of persons or property.

vicontiel (vɪ-**kon**-tee-əl), *adj.* (17c) **1.** Of or relating to a viscount. **2.** Of or relating to a sheriff. — Also spelled *vicountiel.*

victim, *n.* (15c) A person harmed by a crime, tort, or other wrong. — **victimize,** *vb.* — **victimization,** *n.*

victim-impact statement. (1981) A statement read into the record during sentencing to inform the judge or jury of the financial, physical, and psychological impact of the crime on the victim and the victim's family.

victim-related adjustment. An increase in punishment available under federal sentencing guidelines when the defendant knew or should have known that the victim bore a particular characteristic — e.g., the victim was unusually vulnerable (because of age or condition) — or was otherwise particularly susceptible to the criminal conduct. See USSG §§ 3A1.1, 1.2.

videlicet (vi-**del**-ə-set *or* -sit). [Latin] (15c) To wit; that is to say; namely; SCILICET. • The term is used primarily to point out, particularize, or make more specific what has been previously stated in general (or occas. obscure) language. One common function is to state the time, place, or manner when that is the essence of the matter at issue. — Abbr. *viz.*

Video Electronics Standards Association. A nonprofit organization that promotes and develops industry-wide standards for computers to ensure interoperability, and encourage innovation and market growth. — Abbr. VESA.

vie (vee). [French] Life. • The term occurs in such Law French phrases as *cestui que vie* and *pur autre vie.*

view, *n.* **1.** The common-law right of prospect — that is, an outlook from the windows of one's house. **2.** An urban servitude that prohibits the obstruction of the outlook from a person's house. **3.** A jury's trip to inspect a place or thing relevant to the case it is considering; the act or proceeding by which a tribunal goes to observe an object that cannot be produced in court because it is immovable or inconvenient to remove. • The appropriate procedures are typically regulated by state statute. At common law, and today in many civil cases, the trial judge's presence is not required. The common practice has been for the jury to be escorted by "showers" who are commissioned for this purpose. Parties and counsel are generally permitted to attend, although this is a matter typically within the trial judge's discretion. **4.** In a real action, a defendant's observation of the thing at issue to ascertain its identity and other circumstances surrounding it.

viewer. (15c) A person, usu. one of several, appointed by a court to investigate certain matters or to examine a particular locality (such as the proposed site of a new road) and to report to the court.

view of an inquest. (1837) A jury's inspection of a place or property to which an inquiry or inquest refers.

vigilance. (16c) Watchfulness; precaution; a proper degree of activity and promptness in pursuing one's rights, in guarding them from infraction, and in discovering opportunities for enforcing one's lawful claims and demands.

vigilant, *adj.* (15c) Watchful and cautious; on the alert; attentive to discover and avoid danger.

vigilante (vij-ə-**lan**-tee). (1856) A person who seeks to avenge a crime by taking the law into his or her own hands.

vigilantism (vij-ə-**lan**-tiz-əm). The act of a citizen who takes the law into his or her own hands by apprehending and punishing suspected criminals.

vindicate, *vb.* (16c) **1.** To clear (a person or thing) from suspicion, criticism, blame, or doubt <DNA tests vindicated the suspect>. **2.** To assert, maintain, or affirm (one's interest) by action <the claimants sought to vindicate their rights through a class-action suit>. **3.** To defend (one's interest) against interference or encroachment <the borrower vindicated its interest in court when the lender tried to foreclose>. — **vindication,** *n.* — **vindicator,** *n.*

vindicatory part (**vin**-də-kə-tor-ee). (1881) The portion of a statute setting forth the penalty for committing a wrong or neglecting a duty.

violation, *n.* (15c) **1.** An infraction or breach of the law; a transgression. **2.** The act of breaking or dishonoring the law; the contravention of a right or duty. **3.** Rape; ravishment. **4.** Under the Model Penal Code, a public-welfare offense. • In this sense, a violation is not a crime. See Model Penal Code § 1.04(5). — **violate,** *vb.* — **violative** (**vɪ**-ə-lay-tiv), *adj.* — **violator,** *n.*

violence. (14c) The use of physical force, usu. accompanied by fury, vehemence, or outrage; esp., physical force unlawfully exercised with the intent to harm. • Some courts have held that violence in labor disputes is not limited to physical contact or injury, but may include picketing conducted with misleading signs, false statements, erroneous publicity, and veiled threats by words and acts.

domestic violence. **1.** Violence between members of a household, usu. spouses; an assault or other violent act committed by one member of a household against another. **2.** The infliction of physical injury, or the creation of a reasonable fear that physical injury or harm will be inflicted, by a parent or a member or former member of a child's household, against a child or against another member of the household.

Violence Against Women Act. A federal statute that established a federal civil-rights action for victims of gender-motivated violence, without the need for a criminal charge. 42 USCA § 13981. • In 2000, the Supreme Court invalidated the statute, holding that neither the Commerce Clause nor the Enforcement Clause of the 14th Amendment authorized Congress to enact the civil-remedy provision of this Act. *United States v. Morrison*, 120 S.Ct. 1740 (2000). — Abbr. VAWA.

violent, *adj.* (14c) **1.** Of, relating to, or characterized by strong physical force <violent blows to the legs>. **2.** Resulting from extreme or intense force <violent death>. **3.** Vehemently or passionately threatening <violent words>.

vir (veer), *n.* [Latin] **1.** An adult male; a man. **2.** A husband. • In the Latin phrases and maxims that once pervaded English law, *vir* generally means "husband," as in the expression *vir et uxor* (husband and wife).

vires (**vɪ**-reez), *n.* (18c) **1.** Natural powers; forces. **2.** Granted powers, esp. when limited.

vir et uxor (**veer** et **ək**-sor). [Latin] Husband and wife.

virtual-representation doctrine. (1945) The principle that a judgment may bind a person who is not a party to the litigation if one of the parties is so closely aligned with the nonparty's interests that the nonparty has been adequately represented by the party in court. • Under this doctrine, for instance, a judgment in a case naming only the husband as a party can be binding on his wife as well.

virtue ethics. *Ethics.* An ethical theory that focuses on the character of the actor rather than on the nature of the act or its consequences. • This approach received its first and perhaps its fullest expression in the works of Aristotle, esp. in his *Ethics.*

vis (vis). [Latin "power"] (17c) **1.** Any force, violence, or disturbance relating to a person or property. **2.** The force of law. • Thus *vim habere* ("to have force") is to be legally valid. Pl. ***vires.***

visa (**vee**-zə). An official indorsement made on a passport, showing that it has been examined and that the bearer is permitted to proceed; a recognition by the country in which a passport-holder wishes to travel that the holder's passport is valid. • A visa is generally required for the admission of aliens into the United States. 8 USCA §§ 1181, 1184.

vis-à-vis (**veez**-ə-**vee**). [French "face to face"] (18c) In relation to; opposite to <the creditor established a preferred position vis-à-vis the other creditors>.

visible means of support. (1846) An apparent method of earning a livelihood. • Vagrancy statutes have long used this phrase to describe those who have no ostensible ability to support themselves.

visitation (viz-ə-**tay**-shən). (14c) **1.** Inspection; superintendence; direction; regulation. **2.** *Family law.* A relative's, esp. a noncustodial parent's, period of access to a child. **3.** The process of inquiring into and correcting corporate irregularities. **4.** VISIT.

grandparent visitation. A grandparent's court-approved access to a grandchild. • The Supreme Court has limited a grandparent's right to have visitation with his or her grandchild if the parent objects, citing a parent's fundamental right to raise his or her child and to make all decisions concerning the child free from state intervention absent a threat to the child's health and safety. *Troxel v. Granville*, 530 U.S. 57, 120 S.Ct. 2054 (2000).

supervised visitation. Visitation, usu. court-ordered, in which a parent may visit with the child or children only in the presence of some other individual. • A court may order supervised visitation when the visiting parent is known or believed to be prone to physical abuse, sexual abuse, or violence.

visitation order. (1944) *Family law.* **1.** An order establishing the visiting times for a noncustodial parent with his or her child. **2.** An order establishing the visiting times for a child and a person with a significant relationship to the child.

visitation right. (1935) **1.** *Family law.* A noncustodial parent's or grandparent's court-ordered privilege of spending time with a child or grandchild who is living with another person, usu. the custodial parent. • The noncustodial parent with visitation rights may sometimes be a parent from whose custody the child has been removed because of abuse or neglect. **2.** *Int'l law.* A belligerent nation's right to search a neutral vessel to find out whether it is carrying contraband or is otherwise engaged in nonneutral service. • If the searched vessel is doing either of these things, the searchers may seize the contraband and carry out an appropriate punishment.

visitor. 1. A person who goes or comes to a particular person or place. **2.** A person appointed to visit, inspect, inquire into, and correct corporate irregularities.

vis major **(vis may-**jər), *n.* [Latin "a superior force"] (17c) **1.** A greater or superior force; an irresistible or overwhelming force of nature; Force majeure. **2.** A loss resulting immediately from a natural cause without human intervention and that could not have been prevented by the exercise of prudence, diligence, and care.

VISTA (vis-tə). *abbr.* (1964) Volunteers in Service to America, a federal program established in 1964 to provide volunteers to help improve the living conditions of people in the poorest areas of the United States, its possessions, and Puerto Rico.

vital statistics. (1837) Public records — usu. relating to matters such as births, marriages, deaths, diseases, and the like — that are statutorily mandated to be kept by a city, state, or other governmental division or subdivision. • On the admissibility of vital statistics, see Fed. R. Evid. 803(9).

vitiate (vish-ee-ayt), *vb.* (16c) **1.** To impair; to cause to have no force or effect <the new statute vitiates any common-law argument that the plaintiffs might have>. **2.** To make void or voidable; to invalidate either completely or in part <fraud vitiates a contract>. **3.** To corrupt morally <Mr. Lawrence complains that his children were vitiated by their governess>. — **vitiation,** *n.* — **vitiator,** *n.*

viva voce (vɪ-və **voh**-see *also* **vee**-və **voh**-chay), *adv.* [Law Latin "with living voice"] (16c) By word of mouth; orally. • In reference to votes, the term means a voice vote was held rather than a vote by ballot. In reference to the examination of witnesses, the term means that oral rather than written testimony was taken.

viz. (viz). *abbr.* [Latin *videlicet*] (16c) Namely; that is to say <the defendant engaged in fraudulent activities, viz., misrepresenting his gross income, misrepresenting the value of his assets, and forging his wife's signature>.

vocation. A person's regular calling or business; one's occupation or profession.

voice exemplar. (1954) A sample of a person's voice used for the purpose of comparing it with a recorded voice to determine whether the speaker is the same person. • Although voiceprint identification was formerly inadmissible, the trend in recent years has been toward admissibility. See Fed. R. Evid. 901.

voiceprint. (1962) A distinctive pattern of curved lines and whorls made by a machine that measures human vocal sounds for the purpose of identifying an individual speaker. • Like fingerprints, voiceprints are thought to be unique to each person.

void, *adj.* (14c) **1.** Of no legal effect; null. • The distinction between *void* and *voidable* is often of great practical importance. Whenever technical accuracy is required, *void* can be properly applied only to those provisions that are of no effect whatsoever — those that are an absolute nullity. — **void, avoid,** *vb.* — **voidness,** *n.*

facially void. (1969) (Of an instrument) patently void upon an inspection of the contents.

void ab initio (ab i-**nish**-ee-oh). (17c) Null from the beginning, as from the first moment when a contract is entered into. • A contract is void ab initio if it seriously offends law or public policy, in contrast to a contract that is merely voidable at the election of one party to the contract.

void for vagueness. (1814) **1.** (Of a deed or other instrument affecting property) having such an insufficient property description as to be unenforceable. **2.** (Of a penal statute) establishing a requirement or punishment without specifying what is required or what conduct is punishable, and therefore void because violative of due process.

2. VOIDABLE. • Although sense 1 above is the strict meaning of *void*, the word is often used and construed as bearing the more liberal meaning of "voidable."

voidable, *adj.* (15c) Valid until annulled; esp., (of a contract) capable of being affirmed or rejected at the option of one of the parties. • This term describes a valid act that may be voided rather than an invalid act that may be ratified. — **voidability,** *n.*

voir dire (vwahr **deer** *also* vor **deer** *or* vor **dɪr**), *n.* [Law French "to speak the truth"] (17c) **1.** A preliminary examination of a prospective juror by a judge or lawyer to decide whether the prospect is qualified and suitable to serve on a jury. • Loosely, the term refers to the jury-selection phase of a trial. **2.** A preliminary examination to test the competence of a witness or evidence. — **voir dire,** *vb.*

volatility. In securities markets, the quality of having sudden and extreme price changes.

volens (**voh**-lenz), *adj.* [Latin] (1872) Willing.

volenti non fit injuria (voh-**len**-tɪ non fit in-**joor**-ee-ə). [Law Latin "to a willing person it is not a wrong," i.e., a person is not wronged by that to which he or she consents] (17c) The principle that a person who knowingly and voluntarily risks danger cannot recover for any resulting injury. • This is the type of affirmative defense that must be pleaded under Fed. R. Civ. P. 8(c).

volition (və-**lish**-ən *or* voh-), *n.* (17c) **1.** The ability to make a choice or determine something. **2.** The act of making a choice or determining something. **3.** The choice or determination that someone makes. — **volitional,** *adj.*

Volstead Act (**vol**-sted). A federal statute enacted in 1919 to prohibit the manufacture, sale, or transportation of liquor. • Sponsored by Andrew Joseph Volstead of Minnesota, a famous Prohibitionist, the statute was passed under the 18th Amendment to the U.S. Constitution. When the 21st Amendment repealed the 18th Amendment in 1933, the Volstead Act was voided.

voluntary, *adj.* (14c) **1.** Done by design or intention <voluntary act>. **2.** Unconstrained by interference; not impelled by outside influence <voluntary statement>. **3.** Without valuable consideration or legal obligation; gratuitous <voluntary gift>. **4.** Having merely nominal consideration <voluntary deed>. — **voluntariness,** *n.* — **voluntarily,** *adv.*

voluntary courtesy. (17c) An act of kindness performed by one person toward another, from the free will of the doer, without any previous request or promise of reward made by the person who is the object of the act. • No promise of remuneration arises from such an act.

voluntary exposure to unnecessary danger. (1883) An intentional act that, from the standpoint of a reasonable person, gives rise to an undue risk of harm. •

The phrase suggests that the actor was consciously willing to take the risk.

voluntary ignorance. (1836) Willful obliviousness; an unknowing or unaware state resulting from the neglect to take reasonable steps to acquire important knowledge.

volunteer. (16c) **1.** A voluntary actor or agent in a transaction; esp., a person who, without an employer's assent and without any justification from legitimate personal interest, helps an employee in the performance of the employer's business. **2.** The grantee in a voluntary conveyance; a person to whom a conveyance is made without any valuable consideration.

vote, *n.* (15c) **1.** The expression of one's preference or opinion in a meeting or election by ballot, show of hands, or other type of communication <the Republican candidate received more votes than the Democratic candidate>. **2.** The total number of votes cast in an election <the incumbent received 60% of the vote>. **3.** The majority or supermajority needed for a certain question <a two-thirds vote>. **4.** The act of voting, usu. by a deliberative assembly <the Senate postponed the vote on the gun-control bill>. — **vote,** *vb.*

voter. (16c) **1.** A person who engages in the act of voting. **2.** A person who has the qualifications necessary for voting.

registered voter. A person who is qualified to vote and whose name is recorded in the voting district where he or she resides.

voting. (16c) The casting of votes for the purpose of deciding an issue.

absentee voting. (1932) **1.** Participation in an election by a qualified voter who is unable to appear at the polls on election day. **2.** The practice of allowing voters to participate in this way.

class voting. (1941) A method of shareholder voting in which different classes of shares vote separately on fundamental corporate changes that affect the rights and privileges of that class.

cumulative voting. (1884) A system in which each voter may cast more than one vote for the same candidate. • Cumulative voting helps a minority elect at least one representative. It is common in shareholder elections.

early voting. (1984) Voting before the day of an election, esp. during a period designated for that purpose. • Unlike with absentee voting, taking advantage of early voting does not require the voter to swear to the inability to come to the polling place on election day.

instant-runoff voting. A system of preferential voting that mimics a runoff election by using each voter's ranked preferences instead of a second round of voting. — Abbr. IRV.

limited voting. A system in which each voter must cast fewer votes than the number of representatives being elected.

low-total voting. A system of weighted preferential voting that adds up the ranked preferences — "1" for a first choice, "2" for a second choice, and so forth — so that the most-preferred candidate wins by having the lowest total.

majority voting. A system in which each voter may cast one vote per representative being elected, and a simple majority is required for election.

noncumulative voting. (1956) A corporate voting system in which a shareholder is limited in board elections to voting no more than the number of shares that he or she owns for a single candidate. • The result is that a majority shareholder will elect the entire board of directors.

plurality voting. Election by plurality.

preferential voting. A system in which each voter ranks the choices in order of preference. • A preferential vote may be transferable or weighted.

proportional voting. A system of transferable preferential voting in a multirepresentative election.

two-round voting. A system in which the voting occurs in two rounds, with the first round determining the candidate's eligibility for the second round. • The second round may be a runoff between the top two candidates from the first round, an election by plurality among candidates who won their political parties' nominations in the first round, or an election by plurality among the candidates from the first round who reached a certain threshold.

voting group. (1972) **1.** A classification of shareholders by the type of stock held for voting on corporate matters. **2.** Collectively, the shareholders falling within such a classification.

Voting Rights Act. The federal law that guarantees a citizen's right to vote, without discrimination based on race, color, or previous condition of servitude. 42 USCA §§ 1971–1974.

voting-stock rights. A stockholder's right to vote stock in the affairs of the company. • Typically, holders of common stock have one vote for each share. Holders of preferred stock usu. have the right to vote when preferred dividends are in default for a specified period.

vouch, *vb.* (14c) **1.** To answer for (another); to personally assure <the suspect's mother vouched for him>. **2.** To call upon, rely on, or cite as authority; to substantiate with evidence <counsel vouched the mathematical formula for determining the statistical probability>.

voucher, *n.* (17c) **1.** Confirmation of the payment or discharge of a debt; a receipt. **2.** A written or printed authorization to disburse money.

vouching-in. (1849) **1.** At common law, a procedural device by which a defendant may give notice of suit to a third party who may be liable to the defendant on the subject-matter of the suit, so that the third party will be bound by the court's decision. • Although this device has been largely replaced by third-party practice, it remains available under the Federal Rules of Civil Procedure. *Humble Oil & Refining Co. v. Philadelphia Ship Maintenance Co.*, 444 F.2d 727, 735 (3d Cir. 1971). **2.** The invitation of a person who is liable to a defendant in a lawsuit to intervene and defend so that, if the invitation is denied and the defendant later sues the person invited, the latter is bound by any determination of fact common to the two lawsuits. See UCC § 2-607. **3.** Impleader.

vouch over, *vb.* (16c) To cite (a person) into court in one's stead.

voyage. *Maritime law.* The passing of a vessel by sea from one place, port, or country to another. • Courts generally hold that the term includes the entire enterprise, not just the route.

foreign voyage. A voyage to a port or place within the territory of a foreign nation. • If the voyage is from one port in a foreign country to another port in the same country, it is considered a foreign voyage.

freighting voyage. A voyage that involves a vessel's transporting cargo between terminal points.

trading voyage. A voyage that contemplates a vessel's touching and stopping at various ports to traffic in, buy and sell, or exchange commodities on the owners' and shippers' account.

voyeur (voy-**yər** *also* vwah-**yər**), *n.* (1900) A person who observes something without participating; esp., one who gains pleasure by secretly observing another's genitals or sexual acts.

voyeurism, *n.* (1900) Gratification derived from observing the genitals or sexual acts of others, usu. secretly. — **voyeuristic,** *adj.*

V.P. *abbr.* Vice president.

vs. *abbr.* Versus.

W

W-2 form. (18c) (1948) *Tax.* A statement of earnings and taxes withheld (including federal, state, and local income taxes and FICA tax) during a given tax year. • The W-2 is prepared by the employer, provided to each employee, and filed with the Internal Revenue Service.

W-4 form. (1955) *Tax.* A form indicating the number of personal exemptions an employee is claiming and that is used by the employer in determining the amount of income to be withheld from the employee's paycheck for federal-income tax purposes.

***Wade* hearing.** (1969) *Criminal law.* A pretrial hearing in which the defendant contests the validity of his or her out-of-court identification. • If the court finds that the identification was tainted by unconstitutional methods, the prosecution cannot use the identification and must link the defendant to the crime by other means. *United States v. Wade*, 388 U.S. 218, 87 S.Ct. 1926 (1967).

wage, *n.* (*usu. pl.*) (14c) Payment for labor or services, usu. based on time worked or quantity produced; specif., compensation of an employee based on time worked or output of production. • Wages include every form of remuneration payable for a given period to an individual for personal services, including salaries, commissions, vacation pay, bonuses, and the reasonable value of board, lodging, payments in kind, tips, and any similar advantage received from the employer. An employer usu. must withhold income taxes from wages.

wage, *vb.* To engage in (a war, etc.).

wage-and-hour law. A law (such as the federal Fair Labor Standards Act) governing minimum wages and maximum working hours for employees.

wage-and-price controls. A system of government-mandated maximum prices that can be charged for different goods and services or paid to various workers in different jobs.

wager, *n.* (14c) **1.** Money or other consideration risked on an uncertain event; a bet or gamble. **2.** A promise to pay money or other consideration on the occurrence of an uncertain event. — **wager,** *vb.* — **wagerer,** *n.*

waif, *n.* (14c) An abandoned article whose owner is unknown, esp. something stolen and thrown away by the thief in flight, usu. through fear of apprehension. • At common law, if a waif, whether stolen or merely abandoned, was seized before the owner reclaimed it, the title vested in the Crown. The owner was thus punished for leaving the property or for failing to pursue the thief and attempting to recover the property. Today, however, the general rule is that a waif passes to the state in trust for the true owner, who may regain it by proving ownership.

wait-and-see principle. (1989) A modification to the rule against perpetuities, under which a court may determine the validity of a contingent future interest based on whether it actually vests within the perpetuities period, rather than on whether it possibly could have vested outside the period.

waiting period. (1897) A period that must expire before some legal right or remedy can be enjoyed or enforced. • For example, many states have waiting periods for the issuance of marriage licenses or the purchase of handguns.

waive, *vb.* (14c) **1.** To abandon, renounce, or surrender (a claim, privilege, right, etc.); to give up (a right or claim) voluntarily. • Ordinarily, to waive a right one must do it knowingly — with knowledge of the relevant facts. **2.** To refrain from insisting on (a strict rule, formality, etc.); to forgo.

waiver (**way**-vər), *n.* (17c) **1.** The voluntary relinquishment or abandonment — express or implied — of a legal right or advantage; FORFEITURE (2) <waiver of notice>. • The party alleged to have waived a right must have had both knowledge of the existing right and the intention of forgoing it.

express waiver. (18c) A voluntary and intentional waiver.

implied waiver. (18c) A waiver evidenced by a party's decisive, unequivocal conduct reasonably inferring the intent to waive.

prospective waiver. (1889) A waiver of something that has not yet occurred, such as a contractual waiver of future claims for discrimination upon settlement of a lawsuit.

subject-matter waiver. A waiver that may result when a party voluntarily discloses a communication or privileged material about a particular topic to a third party. • A party's voluntary disclosure may lead a court to find an implied waiver that extends to all other communications relating to the same subject matter.

2. The instrument by which a person relinquishes or abandons a legal right or advantage <the plaintiff must sign a waiver when the funds are delivered>.

jury waiver. A form signed by a criminal defendant who relinquishes the right to have the trial conducted before a jury.

lien waiver. A written and signed waiver of a subcontractor's mechanic's lien rights, usu. submitted to enable the owner or general contractor to receive a draw on a construction loan.

waiver by election of remedies. (1873) A defense arising when a plaintiff has sought two inconsistent remedies and by a decisive act chooses one of them, thereby waiving the other.

waiver of claims and defenses. (1975) **1.** The intentional relinquishment by a maker, drawer, or other obligor under a contract of the right to assert against the assignee any claims or defenses the obligor has against the assignor. **2.** The contractual clause providing for such a waiver.

waiver of counsel. (1870) A criminal defendant's intentional relinquishment of the right to legal representation. • To be valid, a waiver of counsel must be made voluntarily, knowingly, and intelligently.

waiver of exemption. (1846) **1.** A debtor's voluntary relinquishment of the right to an exemption from a creditor's levy or sale of any part of the debtor's personal property by judicial process. **2.** The contractual clause expressly providing for such a waiver.

waiver of immunity. (1883) The act of giving up the right against self-incrimination and proceeding to testify.

waiver of service. A defendant's voluntary submission to the jurisdiction made by signing an acknowledgment of receipt of the petition and stating that he or she waives all further service.

waiver of tort. (1815) The election to sue in quasi-contract to recover the defendant's unjust benefit, instead of suing in tort to recover damages.

walk, *vb.* (1958) *Slang.* **1.** To be acquitted <though charged with three thefts, Robinson walked each time>. **2.** To escape any type of real punishment <despite the seriousness of the crime, Selvidge paid only $750: he walked>.

walkout. 1. STRIKE (1). **2.** The act of leaving a work assignment, meeting, or other event as a show of protest.

wall. An erection of stone, brick, or other material raised to varying heights, esp.

inside or surrounding a building, for privacy, security, or enclosure.

ancient wall. A party wall that has stood for at least 20 years, thus giving each party an easement right to refuse to allow the other party to remove or substantially change the wall.

party wall. A wall that divides two adjoining, separately owned properties and that is shared by the two property owners as tenants in common.

want of consideration. (18c) The lack of consideration for a contract.

want of jurisdiction. A court's lack of power to act in a particular way or to give certain kinds of relief. • A court may have no power to act at all, may lack authority over a person or the subject matter of a lawsuit, or may have no power to act until the prerequisites for its jurisdiction have been satisfied.

want of prosecution. (17c) Failure of a litigant to pursue the case <dismissal for want of prosecution>. — Abbr. w.o.p.

want of repair. (17c) A defective condition, such as a condition on a highway making it unsafe for ordinary travel.

wanton (**wahn**-tən), *adj.* (14c) Unreasonably or maliciously risking harm while being utterly indifferent to the consequences. • In criminal law, *wanton* usu. connotes malice (in the criminal-law sense), while *reckless* does not.

wantonness, *n.* (14c) Conduct indicating that the actor is aware of the risks but indifferent to the results. • Wantonness usu. suggests a greater degree of culpability than recklessness, and it often connotes malice in criminal-law contexts. — **wanton,** *adj.*

war. 1. Hostile conflict by means of armed forces, carried on between nations, states, or rulers, or sometimes between parties within the same nation or state; a period of such conflict <the Gulf War>. • A state of war may also exist without armed conflict; for example, the treaty formally ending the World War II state of war between the United States and Japan was signed seven years after the fighting ended in 1945.

civil war. An internal armed conflict between people of the same nation.

solemn war. A war formally declared — esp. by public declaration — by one country against another.

war of aggression. A war that the attacking nation initiates for reasons other than self-defense. • This type of war is considered a crime against international peace under customary international law.

2. A dispute or competition between adversaries <fare wars are common in the airline industry>. **3.** A struggle to solve a pervasive problem <America's war against drugs>.

War Clause. (1943) U.S. Const. art. I, § 8, cl. 11–14, giving Congress the power to declare war.

war crime. Conduct that violates international laws governing the conduct of international armed conflicts. • Examples of war crimes are the killing of hostages, abuse of civilians in occupied territories, abuse of prisoners of war, and devastation that is not justified by military necessity.

ward. (15c) **1.** A person, usu. a minor, who is under a guardian's charge or protection.

permanent ward. (1927) A ward who has been assigned a permanent guardian, the rights of the natural parents having been terminated by a juvenile court.

temporary ward. (1901) A minor who is under the supervision of a juvenile court but whose parents' parental rights have not been terminated.

ward of the state. (1832) A person who is housed by, and receives protection and necessities from, the government.

2. A territorial division in a city, usu. defined for purposes of city government. **3.** The act of guarding or protecting something or someone. **4.** *Archaic.* One who guards. **5.** Castle-guard.

warden. (13c) **1.** A person in charge of something <game warden> <port warden>; esp., the official in charge of a prison, jail, or park <prison warden> <game warden>. **2.** SERGEANT-AT-ARMS (4).

wardship. (15c) **1.** Guardianship of a person, usu. a minor. **2.** The condition of being a ward. **3.** *Hist.* The right of the feudal lord to guardianship of a deceased tenant's minor heir until the heir reached the age of majority.

warehouse. A building used to store goods and other items.

warehouse book. A book used by merchants to account for quantities of goods received, shipped, and in stock.

warfare. 1. The act of engaging in war or military conflict. **2.** Loosely, the act of engaging in any type of conflict.

biological warfare. The use of biological or infectious agents in war, usu. by delivering them via airplanes or ballistic missiles.

biochemical warfare. Warfare in which both biological and chemical weapons are used.

chemical warfare. Warfare in which deadly chemical agents, such as nerve gas, are used as weapons, usu. by delivering the chemicals via shells, missiles, or bombs. • Chemical weapons were first used in World War I. The first international treaty forbidding the use of both chemical and biological weapons, the Protocol for the Prohibition of the Use in War of Asphyxiating, Poisonous or Other Gases, and of Biological Methods of Warfare was signed in 1925 and came into force in 1928. The United States is a signatory but with reservations.

economic warfare. **1.** A hostile relationship between two or more countries in which at least one tries to damage the other's economy for economic, political, or military ends. **2.** The collective measures that might be taken to achieve such ends.

guerrilla warfare. Hostilities that are conducted by individuals or small groups who are usu. not part of an organized army and who fight by means of surprise attacks, ambushes, and sabotage. • Formerly, it was thought that the hostilities had to be conducted in enemy-occupied territory. Typically, guerrilla warfare is carried out only when geographical conditions are favorable and when the civilian population is at least partly cooperative.

land warfare. Hostilities conducted on the ground, as opposed to at sea or in the air.

warning. (bef. 12c) The pointing out of a danger, esp. to one who would not otherwise be aware of it. • State and federal laws (such as 21 USCA § 825) require warning labels to be placed on potentially dangerous materials, such as drugs and equipment.

adequate warning. (1885) A warning that reasonably alerts a product's average user to a potential hazard, and the nature and extent of the danger. • Four elements have been articulated as comprising an adequate warning: (1) notice that a severe hazard exists, (2) a description of the hazard's nature, (3) a description of the hazard's possible consequences, and (4) instructions on how to avoid the hazard. In addition, the warning must be prominently displayed, and may have to illustrate the nature and severity of the hazard with pictographs.

war power. (18c) The constitutional authority of Congress to declare war and maintain armed forces (U.S. Const. art. I, § 8, cls. 11–14), and of the President to conduct war as commander-in-chief (U.S. Const. art. II, § 2, cl. 1).

war-powers resolution. (1954) A resolution passed by Congress in 1973 (over the President's veto) restricting the President's authority to involve the United States in foreign hostilities without congressional approval, unless the United States or one of its territories is attacked. 50 USCA §§ 1541–1548.

warrant, *n.* (14c) **1.** A writ directing or authorizing someone to do an act, esp. one directing a law enforcer to make an arrest, a search, or a seizure.

administrative warrant. (1951) A warrant issued by a judge at the request of an administrative agency. • This type of warrant is sought to conduct an administrative search.

arrest warrant. (1894) A warrant, issued only on probable cause, directing a law-enforcement officer to arrest and bring a person to court.

bench warrant. (17c) A writ issued directly by a judge to a law-enforcement officer, esp. for the arrest of a person who has been held in contempt, has been indicted, has disobeyed a subpoena, or has failed to appear for a hearing or trial.

death warrant. (18c) A warrant authorizing a warden or other prison official to carry out a death sentence. • A death warrant typically sets the time and place for a prisoner's execution.

distress warrant. (18c) **1.** A warrant authorizing a court officer to distrain property. **2.** A writ allowing an officer to seize a tenant's goods for failing to pay rent due to the landlord.

escape warrant. (18c) A warrant directing a peace officer to rearrest an escaped prisoner.

extradition warrant. (1876) A warrant for the return of a fugitive from one jurisdiction to another.

fugitive warrant. (1900) A warrant authorizing law-enforcement officers to take into custody a person who has fled from one state to another to avoid prosecution or punishment.

general warrant. (16c) **1.** *Hist.* A warrant issued by the English Secretary of State for the arrest of the author, printer, or publisher of a seditious libel, without naming the persons to be arrested. • General warrants were banned by Parliament in 1766. **2.** A warrant giving a law-enforcement officer broad authority to search and seize unspecified places or persons; a search or arrest warrant that lacks a sufficiently particularized description of the person or thing to be seized or the place to be searched. • General warrants are unconstitutional because they fail to meet the Fourth Amendment's specificity requirements.

John Doe warrant. (1900) A warrant for the arrest of a person whose name is unknown. • A John Doe warrant may be issued, for example, for a person known by sight but not by name. This type of warrant is permitted in a few states, but not in federal practice.

landlord's warrant. (1824) A type of distress warrant from a landlord to seize the tenant's goods, to sell them at public sale, and to compel the tenant to pay rent or observe some other lease stipulation.

outstanding warrant. (1899) An unexecuted arrest warrant.

peace warrant. (18c) A warrant issued by a justice of the peace for the arrest of a specified person.

possessory warrant. (1850) A process, similar to a search warrant, used under certain circumstances by a plaintiff to search for and recover property wrongfully taken or held by another.

preliminary warrant. (1859) A warrant to bring a person to court for a preliminary hearing on probable cause.

rendition warrant. (1881) A warrant requesting the extradition of a fugitive from one jurisdiction to another.

surreptitious-entry warrant. (1985) A warrant authorizing a law officer to enter and observe an ongoing criminal operation (such as an illegal drug lab).

tax warrant. (18c) An official process issued for collecting unpaid taxes and under which property may be seized and sold.

violation warrant. A warrant issued for the arrest of a convict who has violated the terms of probation, parole, or supervised release.

warrant of commitment. A warrant committing a person to custody.

warrant upon indictment or information. (1903) An arrest warrant issued at the request of the prosecutor for a defendant named in an indictment or information. Fed. R. Crim. P. 9.

2. A document conferring authority, esp. to pay or receive money. **3.** An order by which a drawer authorizes someone to pay a particular sum of money to another.

warrant, *vb.* (14) **1.** To guarantee the security of (realty or personalty, or a person) <the store warranted the safety of the customer's jewelry>. **2.** To give warranty of (title); to give warranty of title to (a person) <the seller warrants the property's title to the buyer>. **3.** To promise or guarantee <warrant payment>. **4.** To justify <the conduct warrants a presumption of negligence>. **5.** To authorize <the manager warranted the search of the premises>.

Warrant Clause. (1962) The clause of the Fourth Amendment to the U.S. Constitution requiring that warrants be issued only on probable cause.

warrantee (wor-ən-**tee** *or* wahr-). A person to whom a warranty is given; esp., a person who receives a written warranty. • The term also sometimes applies to the beneficiary of an implied warranty.

warrantor (**wor**-ən-tor *or* -tər *or* **wahr**-). (15c) A person who gives a written warranty or becomes obligated under an implied warranty. See 15 USCA § 2301(5).

warranty (**wor**-ən-tee *or* **wahr**-), *n.* (14c) **1.** *Property.* A covenant by which the grantor in a deed promises to secure to the grantee the estate conveyed in the deed, and pledges to compensate the grantee if the grantee is evicted by someone having better title. • The covenant is binding on the grantor's heirs. Historically, a warrantor was expected to turn over land. But cash compensation could be substituted.

collateral warranty. (16c) A warranty that is made by a stranger to the title, and that consequently runs only to the covenantee and not with the land.

general warranty. (17c) A warranty against the claims of all persons.

special warranty. (17c) A warranty against any person's claim made by, through, or under the grantor or the grantor's heirs.

2. *Contracts.* An express or implied promise that something in furtherance of the contract is guaranteed by one of the contracting parties; esp., a seller's promise that the thing being sold is as represented or promised. • Although a court may treat a misrepresentation as an implied warranty, in general a warranty differs from a representation in four principal ways: (1) a warranty is conclusively presumed to be material, while the burden is on the party claiming breach to show that a representation is material; (2) a warranty must be strictly complied with, while substantial truth is the only requirement for a representation; (3) a warranty is an essential part of a contract, while a representation is usu. only a collateral inducement; and (4) an express warranty is usu. written on the face of the contract, while a representation may be written or oral.

as-is warranty. (1976) A warranty that goods are sold with all existing faults.

construction warranty. (1968) A warranty from the seller or building contractor of a new home that the home is free of structural, electrical, plumbing, and other defects and is fit for its intended purpose.

deceptive warranty. (1975) A warranty containing false or fraudulent representations or promises.

express warranty. (17c) A warranty created by the overt words or actions of the seller. • Under the UCC, an express warranty is created by any of the following: (1) an affirmation of fact or promise made by the seller to the buyer relating to the goods that becomes the basis of the bargain; (2) a description of the goods that becomes part of the basis of the bargain; or (3) a sample or model made part of the basis of the bargain. UCC § 2-313.

extended warranty. (1936) An additional warranty often sold with the purchase of consumer goods (such as appliances and motor vehicles) to cover repair costs not otherwise covered by a manufacturer's standard warranty, by extending either the standard-warranty coverage period or the range of defects covered.

full warranty. A warranty that fully covers labor and materials for repairs. • Under federal law, the warrantor must remedy the consumer product within a reasonable time and without charge after notice of a defect or malfunction. 15 USCA § 2304.

implied warranty. (18c) An obligation imposed by the law when there has been no representation or promise; esp., a warranty arising by operation of law because of the circumstances of a sale, rather than by the seller's express promise.

implied warranty of fitness for a particular purpose. (1923) A warranty — implied by law if the seller has reason to know of the buyer's special purposes for the item — that the item is suitable for those purposes. — Sometimes shortened to *warranty of fitness.*

implied warranty of habitability. (1900) In a residential lease, a warranty from the landlord to the tenant that the leased property is fit to live in and that it will remain so during the term of the lease. • This warranty usu. applies to residential property, but a few courts, esp. in Utah, have applied it to commercial property as well.

implied warranty of merchantability. (1896) A merchant seller's warranty — implied by law — that the thing sold is fit for its ordinary purposes. • Under the UCC, an implied warranty of merchantability arises whenever a merchant sells goods unless the agreement expressly provides otherwise. UCC 2-314. — Sometimes shortened to *warranty of merchantability.*

limited warranty. (1871) A warranty that does not fully cover labor and materials for repairs. • Under federal law, a limited warranty must be clearly labeled as such on the face of the warranty.

personal warranty. (18c) A warranty arising from an obligation to pay all or part of the debt of another.

presentment warranty. (1965) An implied promise concerning the title and credibility of an instrument, made to a payor or acceptor upon presentment of the instrument for payment or acceptance. UCC §§ 3-417, 3-418.

transfer warranty. (1964) **1.** An implied promise concerning the title and credibility of an instrument, made by a transferor to a transferee and, if the transfer is by indorsement, to remote transferees. UCC §§ 3-417, 4-207. **2.** A warranty made by a transferee of a document of title upon a transfer of the document for value to the immediate transferee. UCC § 7-507.

warranty ab initio (ab i-**nish**-ee-oh). (12006) An independent subsidiary promise whose breach does not discharge the contract, but gives to the injured party a right of action for the damage sustained as a result of the breach. • *Ab initio* means that the warranty existed from the contract's inception.

warranty against infringement. A merchant's warranty that the goods being sold or licensed do not violate any patent, copyright, trademark, or other intellectual-property claim. • The warranty does not arise if the buyer provides the seller with the specifications for the goods purchased. Under § 2-312(3) of the Uniform Commercial Code, the warranty against infringement is a part of the warranty of title unless it is explicitly disclaimed.

warranty ex post facto (eks pohst **fak**-toh). (1961) A broken condition for which the injured party could void the contract, but decides instead to continue the contract, with a right of action for the broken condition (which amounts to a breached warranty). • The warranty is *ex post facto* because it was not originally part of the contract. It arises only after the injured party elects to continue the contract, thereby reducing the broken condition to a breached warranty.

warranty of assignment. (18c) An assignor's implied warranty that he or she (1) has the rights assigned, (2) will do nothing to interfere with those rights, and (3) knows of nothing that impairs the value of the assignment.

warranty of title. (18c) A warranty that the seller or assignor of property has title to that property, that the transfer is rightful, and that there are no liens or other encumbrances beyond those that the buyer or assignee is aware of at the time of contracting. • This warranty arises automatically whenever anyone sells goods.

written warranty. (1807) A warranty made in writing; specif., any written affirmation or promise by a supplier of a consumer product to a buyer (for purposes other than resale), forming the basis of the bargain and providing that the material or workmanship is free of defects or will be repaired or replaced free of charge if the product fails to meet the required specifications. 15 USCA § 2301.

3. *Insurance.* A pledge or stipulation by the insured that the facts relating to the person insured, the thing insured, or the risk insured are as stated.

affirmative warranty. A warranty — express or implied — that facts are as stated at the beginning of the policy period. • An affirmative warranty is usu. a condition precedent to the policy taking effect.

executory warranty. A warranty that arises when an insured undertakes to perform some executory stipulation, such as a promise that certain acts will be done or that certain facts will continue to exist.

promissory warranty. A warranty that facts will continue to be as stated throughout the policy period, such that a failure of the warranty provides the insurer with a defense to a claim under the policy.

waste, *n.* (15c) **1.** Permanent harm to real property committed by a tenant (for life or for years) to the prejudice of the heir, the reversioner, or the remainderman.

• In the law of mortgages, any of the following acts by the mortgagor may constitute waste: (1) physical damage, whether intentional or negligent, (2) failure to maintain and repair, except for repair of casualty damage or damage caused by third-party acts, (3) failure to pay property taxes or governmental assessments secured by a lien having priority over the mortgage, so that the payments become delinquent, (4) the material failure to comply with mortgage covenants concerning physical care, maintenance, construction, demolition, or casualty insurance, or (5) keeping the rents to which the mortgagee has the right of possession.

ameliorating waste (ə-**meel**-yə-ray-ting). (1927) A lessee's unauthorized change to the physical character of a lessor's property — technically constituting waste, but in fact resulting in improvement of the property. • Generally, equity will not enjoin such waste.

commissive waste (kə-**mis**-iv). (1868) Waste caused by the affirmative acts of the tenant.

equitable waste. (1842) Waste that abuses a privilege of nonimpeachability at common law, for which equity will restrain the commission of willful, destructive, malicious, or extravagant waste; esp., waste caused by a life tenant who, although ordinarily not responsible for permissive waste, flagrantly damages or destroys the property.

permissive waste. (17c) A tenant's failure to make normal repairs to property so as to protect it from substantial deterioration.

voluntary waste. (16c) Waste resulting from some positive act of destruction.

2. Refuse or superfluous material, esp. that remaining after a manufacturing or chemical process <toxic waste>.

hazardous waste. (1974) Waste that — because of its quantity, concentration, or physical, chemical, or infectious characteristics — may cause or significantly contribute to an increase in mortality or otherwise harm human health or the environment. 42 USCA § 6903(5).

toxic waste. (1964) Hazardous, poisonous substances, such as dichlorodiphenyltrichloroethane (DDT). • Most states regulate the handling and disposing of toxic waste, and several federal statutes (such as the Comprehensive Environmental Response Compensation and Liability Act of 1980 (CERCLA), 42 USCA §§ 9601–9657) regulate the use, transportation, and disposal of toxic waste.

waterboarding. A form of torture in which water is poured over the face of a supine, immobilized victim whose head is pulled back so that the victim cannot avoid inhaling water, and thus experiences the sensation of drowning. • In some variations, fabric or plastic may be draped over the victim's face or the victim may be gagged before the water is poured.

watercourse. (16c) A body of water, usu. of natural origin, flowing in a reasonably definite channel with bed and banks. • The term includes not just rivers and creeks, but also springs, lakes, and marshes in which such flowing streams originate or through which they flow.

ancient watercourse. A watercourse in a channel that has existed from time immemorial.

artificial watercourse. A man-made watercourse, usu. to be used only temporarily. • If the watercourse is of a permanent character and has been maintained for a sufficient length of time, it may be considered a natural watercourse to which riparian rights can attach.

natural watercourse. A watercourse with its origin in the forces of nature. • A natural watercourse does not include surface water, which often flows intermittently and in an indefinite channel. In addition, a natural stream is distinguished from an artificial ditch or canal, which is typically not the subject of riparian rights.

waterfront, *n.* Land or land with buildings fronting a body of water.

watergage, *n.* **1.** A seawall. **2.** An instrument used to measure the height of water.

watermark. 1. A mark indicating the highest or lowest point to which water rises or falls.

***high-water mark.* 1.** The shoreline of a sea reached by the water at high tide. • The high-water mark is usu. computed as a mean or average high tide and not as the extreme height of the water. **2.** In a freshwater lake created by a dam in an unnavigable stream, the highest point on the shore to which the dam can raise the water in ordinary circumstances. **3.** In a river not subject to tides, the line that the river impresses on the soil by covering it long enough to deprive it of agricultural value.

***low-water mark.* 1.** The shoreline of a sea marking the edge of the water at the lowest point of the ordinary ebb tide. **2.** In a river, the point to which the water recedes at its lowest stage.

2. The transparent design or symbol seen when paper is held up to the light, usu. to indicate the genuineness of the document or the document's manufacturer.

waterpower. 1. The force obtained by converting water into energy. **2.** The riparian owner's right consisting of the fall in the stream as it passes over or through the riparian owner's land; the difference of the level between the surface where the stream first touches one's land and the surface where the water leaves the land.

water right. (*often pl.*) (18c) The right to use water from a natural stream or from an artificial canal for irrigation, power, domestic use, and the like; riparian right.

waterscape, *n.* (1842) An aqueduct or passage for water.

way. (bef. 12c) **1.** A passage or path. **2.** A right to travel over another's property.

private way. (17c) **1.** The right to pass over another's land. **2.** A way provided by local authorities primarily to accommodate particular individuals (usu. at the individual's expense) but also for the public's passage.

waybill. *Maritime law.* A document acknowledging the receipt of goods by a carrier or by the shipper's agent and the contract for the transportation of those goods. • Unlike a bill of lading, a waybill is not a document of title and is nonnegotiable. — Abbr. WB.

air waybill. A waybill for goods shipped by air.

ways-and-means committee. (1840) A legislative committee that determines how money will be raised for various governmental purposes.

WC. *abbr.* Workers' compensation.

W.D. *abbr.* Western District, in reference to U.S. judicial districts.

weapon. (bef. 12c) An instrument used or designed to be used to injure or kill someone.

concealed weapon. (1833) A weapon that is carried by a person but that is not visible by ordinary observation.

dangerous weapon. (17c) An object or device that, because of the way it is used, is capable of causing serious bodily injury.

deadly weapon. (16c) Any firearm or other device, instrument, material, or substance that, from the manner in which it is used or is intended to be used, is calculated or likely to produce death. • In some states, the definition encompasses the likelihood of causing either death or serious physical injury.

deadly weapon per se. (1872) A weapon that is deadly in and of itself or would ordinarily result in death by its use <a gun is a deadly weapon per se>.

weapon of mass destruction. (*usu. pl.*) A weapon that is intended to kill human beings, without discriminating between combatants and noncombatants, on a massive scale. • Among the most frequently cited examples are nuclear weapons and chemical weapons. — Abbr. WMD.

wear and tear. (17c) Deterioration caused by ordinary use; the depreciation of property resulting from its reasonable use <the tenant is not liable for normal wear and tear to the leased premises>.

wedge principle. (1951) The argument that relaxation of a constitutionally imposed restraint under specific circumstances may justify further relaxation in broader circumstances. • This principle is most often raised in the context of legalized human euthanasia. But it has frequently been invoked in other contexts, such as the right to protection from unreasonable search and seizure.

weight of the evidence. (17c) The persuasiveness of some evidence in comparison with other evidence <because the verdict is against the great weight of the evidence, a new trial should be granted>.

welfare. (14c) **1.** Well-being in any respect; prosperity.

general welfare. (17c) The public's health, peace, morals, and safety.

public welfare. (16c) A society's well-being in matters of health, safety, order, morality, economics, and politics.

2. A system of social insurance providing assistance to those who are financially in need, as by providing food stamps and family allowances.

corporate welfare. Governmental financial assistance given to a large company, usu. in the form of a subsidy.

welfare state. (1894) A nation in which the government undertakes various social insurance programs, such as unemployment compensation, old-age pensions, family allowances, food stamps, and aid to the blind or deaf.

well, *adv.* (bef. 12c) In a legally sufficient manner; unobjectionable <well-pleaded complaint>.

well, *n.* A hole or shaft sunk into the earth to obtain a fluid, such as water, oil, or natural gas.

well-completion clause. *Oil & gas.* A provision in an oil-and-gas lease specifying that a lessee who starts drilling before the lease terminates has the right to complete the well and to maintain the lease if the drilling achieves production.

well-knowing, *adj.* (17c) Intentional <a well-knowing act or omission>. • This term was formerly used in a pleading to allege scienter.

welshing. (1857) **1.** The act or an instance of evading an obligation, esp. a gambling debt. **2.** The common-law act of larceny in which one receives a deposit to be paid back with additional money depending on the outcome of an event (such as a horse race) but at the time of the deposit the depositee intends to cheat and defraud the depositor by absconding with the money. • Although this term is sometimes thought to be a slur against those hailing from Wales, etymologists have not been able to establish this connection. Authoritative dictionaries record the origin of the term as being unknown. — **welsh,** *vb.* — **welsher,** *n.*

Westlaw. A West Group database for computer-assisted legal research, providing online access to legal resources, including federal and state caselaw, statutes, regulations, legal treatises, legal periodicals, and general and business news. — Abbr. WL.

West Point. United States Military Academy.

Wharton's rule ([h]**wor**-tən). (1940) *Criminal law.* The doctrine that an agreement by two or more persons to commit a particular crime cannot be prosecuted as a conspiracy if the crime could not be committed except by the actual number of participants involved. • But if an additional person participates so as to enlarge the scope of the agreement, all the actors may be charged with conspiracy. The doctrine takes its name from the influential criminal-law author Francis Wharton (1820–1889).

whereabouts, *n.* (17c) The general locale where a person or thing is <her whereabouts are unknown> <the Joneses' present whereabouts is a closely guarded secret>. • As the examples illustrate, this noun, though plural in form, may be construed with either a plural or a singular verb. — **whereabouts,** *adv.* & *conj.*

whereas, *conj.* (14c) **1.** While by contrast; although <McWilliams was stopped at 10:08 p.m. wearing a green hat, whereas the assailant had been identified at 10:04 p.m. wearing a black hat>. **2.** Given the fact that; since <Whereas, the parties have found that their 1994 agreement did not adequately address incidental expenses . . . ; and Whereas, the parties have now decided in an equitable sharing of those expenses . . . ; Now, Therefore, the parties agree to amend the 1994 agreement as follows . . . >. • In sense 2, *whereas* is used to introduce contractual recitals and the like, but modern drafters increasingly prefer a simple heading, such as "Recitals" or "Preamble," and in that way avoid the legalistic *whereases.* — **whereas** (recital or preamble), *n.*

whereas clause. 1. PREAMBLE (1). **2.** RECITAL (2).

whereat, *conj.* (14c) **1.** At or toward which <the point whereat he was aiming>. **2.** As a result of which; whereupon <Pettrucione called Bickley a scurrilous name, whereat a fistfight broke out>.

whereby, *conj.* (13c) By which; through which; in accordance with which <the treaty whereby the warring nations finally achieved peace>.

wherefore, premises considered. (1867) For all these reasons; for the reason or reasons mentioned above. • The phrase is often used to begin the final paragraph of a motion, judgment, contract, or agreement.

wherefrom, *conj.* (14c) From which <the students sent two faxes to the president's office, wherefrom no reply ever came>.

wherein, *conj.* (14c) **1.** In which; where <the jurisdiction wherein Lynn practices>. **2.** During which <they listened intently at the concert, wherein both of them became convinced that the composer's "new" work was a fraud>. **3.** How; in what respect <Fallon demanded to know wherein she had breached any duty>. — **wherein,** *adv.*

whereof, *conj.* (13c) **1.** Of what <Judge Wald knows whereof she speaks>. **2.** Of which <citations whereof even the most responsible are far afield from the true issue>. **3.** Of whom <judges whereof only the most glowing words might be said>.

whereon, *conj.* (13c) On which <the foundation whereon counsel bases this argument>.

whereto, *conj.* (14c) To what place or time <at first, Campbell did not know whereto he was being taken>. — **whereto,** *adv.*

whereupon, *conj.* (14c) **1.** WHEREON <the precedent whereupon the defense bases its argument>. **2.** Soon after and as a result of which; and then <a not-guilty verdict was announced, whereupon a riot erupted>.

wherewith, *conj.* (14c) By means of which <the plaintiff lacked a form of action wherewith to state a compensable claim>.

whim. A passing fancy; an impulse <the jury was instructed to render a verdict based solely on the evidence, not on a whim>.

whistleblower, *n.* (1970) An employee who reports employer wrongdoing to a governmental or law-enforcement agency. • Federal and state laws protect whistleblowers from employer retaliation. — **whistleblowing,** *n.*

whistleblower act. (1984) A federal or state law protecting employees from retaliation for properly disclosing employer wrongdoing such as violating a law or regulation, mismanaging public funds, abusing authority, or endangering public health or safety. • Federal laws containing whistleblower provisions include the Whistleblower Protection Act (5 USCA § 1211), the Occupational Safety and Health Act (29 USCA § 660), CERCLA (42 USCA § 9610), and the Air Pollution and Control Act (42 USCA § 7622).

Whiteacre. (17c) A fictitious tract of land used in legal discourse (esp. law-school hypotheticals) to discuss real-property issues.

whitecapping. (1900) *Criminal law.* The criminal act of threatening a person — usu. a member of a minority group — with violence in an effort to compel the person either to move away or to stop engaging in a certain business or occupation. • Whitecapping statutes were originally enacted to curtail the activities of the Ku Klux Klan.

white-collar crime. (1940) A nonviolent crime usu. involving cheating or dishonesty in commercial matters. • Examples include fraud, embezzlement, bribery, and insider trading.

whitehorse case. (1971) *Slang.* A reported case with facts virtually identical to those of the instant case, so that the disposition of the reported case should determine the outcome of the instant case.

white knight. A person or corporation that rescues the target of an unfriendly corporate takeover, esp. by acquiring a controlling interest in the target corporation or by making a competing tender offer.

white slavery. The practice of forcing a female (or, rarely, a male) to engage in commercial prostitution. • Trafficking in persons for prostitution is prohibited by the Mann Act (18 USCA §§ 2421–2424).

whole law. The law applied by a forum court in a multistate or multinational case after referring to its own choice-of-law rules.

wholesale, *n.* The sale of goods or commodities usu. to a retailer for resale, and not to the ultimate consumer. — **wholesale,** *vb.* — **wholesale,** *adj.*

wholesale dealer. One who sells goods in gross to retail dealers rather than selling in smaller quantities directly to consumers.

wholesaler. One who buys large quantities of goods and resells them in smaller quantities to retailers or other merchants, who in turn sell to the ultimate consumer.

whole-statute rule. The principle of statutory construction that a statute should be considered in its entirety, and that the words used within it should be given their ordinary meanings unless there is a clear indication to the contrary.

wife. A married woman; a woman who has a lawful spouse living.

common-law wife. **1.** The wife in a common-law marriage; a woman who contracts an informal marriage with a spouse and then holds herself out to the community as being married to that spouse. **2.** *Archaic.* Loosely, a concubine.

will, *n.* (bef. 12c) **1.** Wish; desire; choice <employment at will>. **2.** The legal expression of an individual's wishes about the disposition of his or her property after death; esp., a document by which a person directs his or her estate to be distributed upon death <there was no mention of his estranged brother in the will>. — **will,** *vb.*

ambulatory will. (1909) A will that can be altered during the testator's lifetime.

attested will. A will that has been signed by a witness.

bogus will. An unauthentic will, esp. one involving fraud or unauthorized changes.

conditional will. A will that depends on the occurrence of an uncertain event for the will to take effect. • Most jurisdictions hold a conditional will valid even though the testator's death does not result from or on the occasion of the condition mentioned in the will. The courts generally hold that the condition is the inducement for making the will rather than a condition precedent to its operation. See *Eaton v. Brown*, 193 U.S. 411, 24 S.Ct. 487 (1904); *In re Will of Cohen*, 491 A.2d 1292 (N.J. Super. Ct. App. Div. 1985).

contingent will. A will that takes effect only if a specified event occurs.

duplicate will. (1855) A will executed in duplicate originals by a testator who retains one copy and gives the second copy to another person. • The rules applicable to wills apply to both wills, and upon application for probate, both copies must be tendered into the registry of the probate court.

holographic will (hol-ə-**graf**-ik). (1850) A will that is handwritten by the testator. • Such a will is typically unattested. Holographic wills are rooted in the civil-law tradition, having originated in Roman law and having been authorized under the Napoleonic Code. French and Spanish settlers introduced holographic wills in America, primarily in the South and West. Today they are recognized in about half the states.

international will. A will that is executed according to formalities provided in an international treaty or convention, and that will be valid although it may be written in a foreign language by a testator domiciled in another country.

invalid will. (18c) A will that fails to make an effective disposition of property.

joint and mutual will. (1841) A single will executed by two or more people — to dispose of property they own separately, in common, or jointly — requiring the surviving testator to dispose of the property in accordance with the terms of the will. • A joint and mutual will is drafted to be contractually binding on the survivor. The word "joint" indicates the form of the will. The word "mutual" describes the substantive provisions.

joint will. (18c) A single will executed by two or more testators, usu. disposing of their common property by transferring their separate titles to one devisee.

last will. (16c) The most recent will of a deceased; the instrument ultimately fixing the disposition of real and personal property at the testator's death.

lost will. An executed will that cannot be found at the testator's death. • Its contents can be proved by parol evidence in many jurisdictions. But the overwhelming majority of American jurisdictions follow the common-law presumption of revocation if a will is proved to have been in the possession of the testator and has since been lost.

mutual will. (*usu. pl.*) (1837) One of two separate wills in which two persons, usu. a husband and wife, establish identical or similar testamentary provisions disposing of their estates in favor of each other. • It is also possible (though rare) for the testators to execute a single mutual will, as opposed to separate ones. And it is possible (though, again, rare) for more than two parties to execute mutual wills.

mystic will. *Civil law.* A secret will signed by the testator, sealed and delivered to a notary in the presence of three to seven witnesses, accompanied by the testator's declaration that it is a valid will. • The notary is then required to indorse on the envelope containing the will a statement of all the facts surrounding the transaction, and this is signed by the notary and all the witnesses.

nonintervention will. A will that authorizes an independent executor.

notarial will. A will executed by a testator in the presence of two witnesses and a notary public.

nuncupative will (**nəng**-kyə-pay-tiv *or* nəng-**kyoo**-pə-tiv). (18c) An oral will made in contemplation of imminent death, esp. from a recent injury. • Nuncupative wills are invalid in most states. Even in states allowing them, the amount that may be conveyed is usu. limited by statute. Traditionally, only personal property may be conveyed.

oral will. (1853) A will made by the spoken declaration of the testator and usu. dependent on oral testimony for proof.

postnuptial will (pohst-**nəp**-shəl). A will executed after marriage.

pourover will (**por**-oh-vər). (1946) A will giving money or property to an existing trust.

prenuptial will (pree-**nəp**-shəl). (1914) A will executed before marriage. • At common law, marriage automatically revoked a spouse's will, but modern statutes usu. provide that marriage does not revoke a will (although divorce does). But if this marriage was not contemplated by the will and there is nothing otherwise on its face to indicate that the testator intentionally left nothing to any future spouse, the pretermitted spouse may be entitled to a special forced share of the estate. Uniform Probate Code § 2-508.

self-proved will. (1963) A will proved by a self-proving affidavit. • This method of proof, recognized in a growing number of states, eliminates the practical problems of obtaining the live testimony of witnesses.

soldier's will. A soldier's informal oral or written will that is usu. valid despite its noncompliance with normal statutory formalities, as long as the soldier was in actual service at the time the will was made.

unnatural will. (1854) A will that distributes the testator's estate to strangers rather than to the testator's relatives, without apparent reason.

will contest. *Wills & estates.* The litigation of a will's validity, usu. based on allegations that the testator lacked capacity or was under undue influence.

willful, *adj.* (13c) Voluntary and intentional, but not necessarily malicious. — Sometimes spelled *wilful.* — **willfulness,** *n.*

willful blindness. (1927) Deliberate avoidance of knowledge of a crime, esp. by failing to make a reasonable inquiry about suspected wrongdoing despite being aware that it is highly probable.

• A person acts with willful blindness, for example, by deliberately refusing to look inside an unmarked package after being paid by a known drug dealer to deliver it. Willful blindness creates an inference of knowledge of the crime in question. See Model Penal Code § 2.

willfulness. (13c) **1.** The fact or quality of acting purposely or by design; deliberateness; intention. • Willfulness does not necessarily imply malice, but it involves more than just knowledge. **2.** The voluntary, intentional violation or disregard of a known legal duty.

Wills Act. 1. STATUTE OF WILLS (1). **2.** An 1837 English statute that allowed people to dispose of every type of property interest by will and that had an elaborate set of requirements for valid execution. • Some states today continue to adhere to these stringent requirements.

will substitute. A document or instrument that allows a person, upon death, to dispose of an estate in the same or similar manner as a will but without the formalities and expense of a probate proceeding. • The most common will substitutes are trusts, life-insurance plans, and retirement-benefits contracts. The creation of will substitutes has been one of the most important developments in the area of decedents' estates in the past 50 years.

windfall. (15c) An unanticipated benefit, usu. in the form of a profit and not caused by the recipient.

winding up, *n.* (1858) The process of settling accounts and liquidating assets in anticipation of a partnership's or a corporation's dissolution. — **wind up,** *vb.* — **wind up,** *n.*

window-dressing. (1898) The deceptive arrangement of something, usu. facts or appearances, to make it appear more attractive or favorable. • The term is often used to describe the practice of some financial managers, esp. some managers of mutual funds, to sell certain positions at the end of a quarter to make an investment's quarterly performance appear better than it actually was.

WIPO. *abbr.* World Intellectual Property Organization.

wiretapping, *n.* (1904) Electronic or mechanical eavesdropping, usu. done by law-enforcement officers under court order, to listen to private conversations. • Wiretapping is regulated by federal and state law. — **wiretap,** *vb.* — **wiretap,** *n.*

withdrawal, *n.* (18c) **1.** The act of taking back or away; removal <withdrawal of consent>. **2.** The act of retreating from a place, position, or situation <withdrawal from the moot-court competition>. **3.** The removal of money from a depository <withdrawal of funds from the checking account>. **4.** RENUNCIATION (3) <withdrawal from the conspiracy to commit arson>. **5.** RETRACTION (4). **6.** *Parliamentary law.* A motion's removal from consideration by its mover. — **withdraw,** *vb.*

withdrawal of charges. (1842) The removal of charges by the one bringing them, such as a prosecutor.

withdrawal of counsel. (1875) An attorney's termination of his or her role in representing a party in a case. • Normally, the attorney must have the court's permission to withdraw from a case. Permission is usu. sought by a written motion (1) explaining the reason for the requested withdrawal (often, a conflict between attorney and client over a matter such as strategy or fees), and (2) stating whether the client agrees.

withdrawing a juror. (18c) The act or an instance of removing a juror, usu. to obtain a continuance in a case or, sometimes in English practice, to end the case, as when the case has settled, the parties are too anxious to proceed to verdict, or the judge recommends it because the action is not properly before the court.

withholding, *n.* (1940) **1.** The practice of deducting a certain amount from a person's salary, wages, dividends, winnings, or other income, usu. for tax purposes; esp., an employer's practice of taking out a portion of an employee's gross earnings and paying that portion to the government for income-tax and social-security purposes. **2.** The money so deducted. — **withhold,** *vb.*

withholding of evidence. (1848) The act or an instance of obstructing justice by stifling or suppressing evidence knowing that it is being sought in an official investigation or a judicial proceeding.

without delay. (13c) **1.** Instantly; at once. **2.** Within the time reasonably allowed by law.

without impeachment of waste. (16c) (Of a tenant) not subject to an action for waste; not punishable for waste. • This clause is inserted in a lease to give a tenant the right to take certain actions (such as cutting timber) without being held liable for waste. But a tenant cannot abuse the right and will usu. be held liable for maliciously committing waste.

without notice. (16c) Lacking actual or constructive knowledge. • To be a bona fide purchaser, one must buy something "without notice" of another's claim to the item or of defects in the seller's title. To be a holder in due course, one must take a bill or note "without notice" that it is overdue, has been dishonored, or is subject to a claim. UCC § 3-302(a)(2).

without objection. With general consent.

without prejudice, *adv.* (15c) Without loss of any rights; in a way that does not harm or cancel the legal rights or privileges of a party <dismissed without prejudice>.

without recourse. (18c) (In an indorsement) without liability to subsequent holders. • With this stipulation, one who indorses an instrument indicates that he or she has no further liability to any subsequent holder for payment.

without reserve. Of or relating to an auction at which an item will be sold for the highest bid price.

with prejudice, *adv.* With loss of all rights; in a way that finally disposes of a party's claim and bars any future action on that claim <dismissed with prejudice>.

with recourse, *adv.* (In an indorsement) with liability to subsequent holders. • With this stipulation, one who indorses an instrument indicates that he or she remains liable to the holder for payment.

with reserve. Of or relating to an auction at which an item will not be sold unless the highest bid exceeds a minimum price.

with strong hand. With force. • In common-law pleading, this term implies a degree of criminal force, esp. as used in forcible-entry statutes.

witness, *n.* (bef. 12c) **1.** One who sees, knows, or vouches for something <a witness to a testator's signature>. **2.** One who gives testimony under oath or affirmation (1) in person, (2) by oral or written deposition, or (3) by affidavit <the witness to the signature signed the affidavit.>. • A witness must be legally competent to testify. — **witness,** *vb.*

accomplice witness. (1853) A witness who is an accomplice in the crime that the defendant is charged with. • A codefendant cannot be convicted solely on the testimony of an accomplice witness.

alibi witness. (1897) A witness who testifies that the defendant was in a location other than the scene of the crime at the relevant time; a witness who supports the defendant's alibi.

attesting witness. (18c) One who vouches for the authenticity of another's signature by signing an instrument that the other has signed <proof of the will requires two attesting witnesses>.

character witness. (1893) A witness who testifies about another person's character traits or community reputation.

competent witness. (17c) A witness who is legally qualified to testify. • A lay witness who has personal knowledge of the subject matter of the testimony is competent to testify. Fed. R. Evid. 601–602.

corroborating witness. (1853) A witness who confirms or supports someone else's testimony.

court witness. A witness called or recalled to testify by the judge. • The witness called to testify by the court usu. has expertise in the subject matter of the trial and is considered necessary to resolve a conflict in the testimony. The court's discretion to call its own witnesses exists in both civil and criminal cases.

credible witness. (16c) A witness whose testimony is believable.

disinterested witness. (18c) A witness who has no private interest in the matter at issue.

expert witness. (1858) A witness qualified by knowledge, skill, experience, training, or education to provide a scientific, technical, or other specialized opinion about the evidence or a fact issue. Fed. R. Evid. 702–706.

grand-jury witness. (1947) A witness who is called to testify before a grand jury.

hostile witness. (1852) A witness who is biased against the examining party, who is unwilling to testify, or who is identified with an adverse party. • A hostile witness may be asked leading questions on direct examination. Fed. R. Evid. 611(c).

interested witness. (18c) A witness who has a direct and private interest in the matter at issue. • Most jurisdictions provide that a person witnessing a will may not be a devisee under the will. The Uniform Probate Code, however, has abrogated this rule.

lay witness. (1853) A witness who does not testify as an expert and who is therefore restricted to giving an opinion or making an inference that (1) is based on firsthand knowledge, and (2) is helpful in clarifying the testimony or in determining facts. Fed. R. Evid. 701.

material witness. (17c) A witness who can testify about matters having some logical connection with the consequential facts, esp. if few others, if any, know about those matters.

percipient witness. (1913) A witness who has perceived the things about which he or she testifies.

prosecuting witness. (1823) A person who files the complaint that triggers a criminal prosecution and whose testimony the prosecution usu. relies on to secure a conviction.

qualified witness. (1845) A witness who, by explaining the manner in which a business records are made and kept, is able to lay the foundation for the admission of those records under an exception to the hearsay rule. Fed. R. Evid. 803(6).

rebuttal witness. (1891) A witness who contradicts or attempts to contradict evidence previously presented.

res gestae witness. (1894) A witness who, having been at the scene of an incident, can give a firsthand account of what happened.

skilled witness. **1.** Expert witness. **2.** A witness whose degree of knowledge in a particular subject or field is short of the standard for an expert but greater than the knowledge possessed by a typical layperson.

subscribing witness. (17c) One who witnesses the signatures on an instrument and signs at the end of the instrument to that effect.

supernumerary witness. An unrequired witness, such as a third witness to a will where only two are required.

target witness. (1965) **1.** The person who has the knowledge that an investigating body seeks. **2.** A witness who is called before a grand jury and against whom the government is also seeking an indictment.

turncoat witness. (1947) A witness whose testimony was expected to be favorable but who becomes (usu. during the trial) a hostile witness.

zealous witness (**zel**-əs). (1868) A witness who shows partiality toward the litigant that called him or her to testify and who seems eager to help that side in the lawsuit.

witnesseth, *vb.* Shows; records. • This term, usu. set in all capitals, commonly separates the preliminaries in a contract, up through the recitals, from the contractual terms themselves. Modern drafters increasingly avoid it as an antiquated relic. Traditionally, the subject of this verb was *This Agreement*: the sentence, boiled down, was *This Agreement witnesseth* [i.e., shows or records] *that, whereas* [*the parties have agreed to contract with one another*], *the parties therefore agree as follows* .... Many modern contracts erroneously retain the *Witnesseth* even though a new verb appears in the preamble: *This Agreement is between* [one party and the other party]. After the preamble is a period, followed by an all-capped WITNESSETH. It is an example of a form retained long after its utility, and most lawyers do not know what it means or even what purpose it once served.

witness-protection program. (1970) A federal or state program in which a person who testifies against a criminal is assigned a new identity and relocated to another part of the country to avoid retaliation by anyone convicted as a result of that testimony. • The Federal Witness Protection Program was established by the Organized Crime Control Act of 1970 and is administered by the marshals of the U.S. Justice Department.

witness stand. (1853) The space in a courtroom, usu. a boxed area, occupied by a witness while testifying. — Often shortened to *stand.*

witness-tampering. (1924) The act or an instance of obstructing justice by intimidating, influencing, or harassing a witness before or after the witness testifies. • Several state and federal laws, including the Victim and Witness Protection Act of 1982 (18 USCA § 1512), provide criminal penalties for tampering with witnesses or other persons in the context of a pending investigation or official proceeding.

W.L. *abbr.* Westlaw.

wobbler. *Slang.* A crime that can be charged as either a felony or a misdemeanor.

w.o.p. *abbr.* Want of prosecution.

word of art. Term of art.

words actionable in themselves. (18c) Language that is libelous or slanderous per se.

words of limitation. (16c) Language in a conveying instrument — often nonliteral language — describing the extent or quality of an estate. • For example, under long-standing principles of property law, the phrase "to A and her heirs" creates a fee simple in A but gives nothing to A's heirs.

words of procreation (proh-kree-**ay**-shən). (18c) Language in a deed essential to create an estate tail, such as an estate "to A and the heirs of his body.

words of purchase. (17c) Language in a deed or will designating the persons who are to receive the grant. • For example, the phrase "to A for life with a remainder to her heirs" creates a life estate in A and a remainder in A's heirs.

words of severance. In a grant of lands, words showing that the tenants were each to take a distinct share in the property as opposed to undivided portions. • Typical words of severance are *share and share alike, to be divided among, equally,* and *between.*

work, *n.* **1.** Physical and mental exertion to attain an end, esp. as controlled by and for the benefit of an employer; labor.

additional work. **1.** Work that results from a change or alteration in plans concerning the work required, usu. under a construction contract; added work necessary to meet the performance goals under a contract. **2.** Extra work.

extra work. In construction law, work not required under the contract; something done or furnished in addition to the contract's requirements; work entirely outside and independent of the contract and not contemplated by it. • A contractor is usu. entitled to charge for extra work consisting of labor and materials not contemplated by or subsumed within the original contract, at least to the extent that the property owner agrees to a change order. Materials and labor not contemplated by the contract, but that are required by later changes in the plans and specifications, are considered to be extra work.

heavy work. Work involving frequent lifting and carrying of large items. • Under the Social Security Administration regulations for describing a worker's physical limitations, heavy work involves lifting no more than 100 pounds, with frequent lifting or carrying of objects weighing up to 50 pounds. 20 CFR § 404.

inherently dangerous work. Work that can be carried out only by the exercise of special skill and care and that involves a grave risk of serious harm if done unskillfully or carelessly.

light work. Work involving some limited lifting and moving. • Under the Social Security Administration regulations for describing a worker's physical limitations, light work includes walking, standing, sitting while pushing or pulling arm or leg controls, and lifting no more than 20 pounds, with frequent lifting or carrying of objects that weigh up to 10 pounds. 20 CFR § 404.

medium work. Work involving some frequent lifting and moving. • Under the Social Security Administration regulations for describing a worker's physical limitations, medium work includes lifting up to 50 pounds, with frequent lifting or carrying of objects weighing up to 25 pounds. 20 CFR § 404.

sedentary work. Work involving light lifting and only occasional walking or standing. • Under the Social Security Administration regulations for describing a worker's physical limitations, sedentary work involves lifting of no more than ten pounds, occasionally carrying small items such as docket files and small tools, and occasional standing or walking. 20 CFR § 404.

semi-skilled work. Work that may require some alertness and close attention, such as inspecting items or machinery for irregularities, or guarding property or people against loss or injury. 20 CFR § 404.1568(b). — Also written *semiskilled work.*

skilled work. Work requiring the worker to use judgment, deal with the public, analyze facts and figures, or work with abstract ideas at a high level of complexity. 20 CFR § 404.

unskilled work. Work requiring little or no judgment, and involving simple tasks that can be learned quickly on the job. 20 CFR § 404.

very heavy work. Work involving frequent lifting of very large objects and frequent carrying of large objects. • Under the Social Security Administration regulations for describing a worker's physical limitations, very heavy work involves lifting 100 pounds or more, and frequent lifting or carrying of objects weighing 50 pounds or more. 20 CFR § 404.1567(e).

work of necessity. Work reasonably essential to the public's economic, social, or moral welfare as determined by the community standards at a particular time, and (formerly) excepted from the operation of blue laws.

2. *Copyright.* An original expression, in fixed or tangible form (such as paper, audiotape, or computer disk), that may be entitled to common-law or statutory copyright protection. • A work may take many different forms, including art, sculpture, literature, music, crafts, software, and photography.

architectural work. The copyrightable design of a building, as fixed in tangible media such as plans, drawings, and the building itself. 17 USCA § 102(8). • Only the overall design is protected, not each design element.

artistic work. Any visual representation, such as a painting, drawing, map, photograph, sculpture, engraving, or architectural plan.

audiovisual work. A work consisting of related images that are presented in a series, usu. with the aid of a machine, and accompanied by sound. • An example of an audiovisual work is a lecture illustrated with a film strip, or a movie with a soundtrack.

collective work. (1870) **1.** A publication (such as a periodical issue, anthology, or encyclopedia) in which several contributions, constituting separate and independent works in themselves, are assembled into a copyrightable whole. **2.** A selection and arrangement of brief portions of different movies, television shows, or radio shows into a single copyrightable work. • If the selecting and arranging involves any originality, the person who selects and arranges the clips may claim a copyright even if copyright cannot be claimed in the individual component parts.

composite work (kəm-**poz**-it). (1910) An original publication that relates to a variety of subjects and includes discrete selections from many authors. • Although the distinguishable parts are separately protectable, the owner of the composite work — not the individual authors — owns the renewal term, if any. 17 USCA § 304(a).

derivative work. (1965) A copyrightable creation that is based on a preexisting product; a translation, musical arrangement, fictionalization, motion-picture version, abridgment, or any other recast or adapted form of an original work. • Only the holder of the copyright on the original form can produce or permit someone else to produce a derivative work. 17 USCA § 101. — Sometimes shortened to *derivative.*

dramatic work. Any form of nonliterary work created for performance and viewing. • The term includes plays, scripts, films, choreographic works, and similar creations.

joint work. A work created or developed by two or more people whose contributions blend inseparably or interdependently into the whole work. • The cocreators have equal legal rights to register and enjoy the copyright, but this does not affect any other contractually unequal ownership arrangements.

literary work. (18c) A nonaudiovisual work that is expressed in verbal, numerical, or other symbols, such as words or musical notation, and embodied in some type of physical object. • Literary works are one of eight general categories that are eligible for copyright protection. 17 USCA § 102.

pictorial, graphic, and sculptural work. Two- or three-dimensional works of graphic, fine, or applied art that are eligible for copyright protection. • This is one of eight general classifications covered by copyright law. Examples include globes, architectural drawings, photographs, and models. 17 USCA § 102. — Abbr. PGS.

work for hire. A copyrightable work produced either by an employee within the scope of employment or by an independent contractor under a written agreement; esp., a work specially ordered or commissioned for use as (1) a contribution to a collective work, (2) a translation, (3) a supplementary work, (4) a part of a movie or other audiovisual work, (5) a compilation, (6) an instructional text, (7) a test, (8) answer material for a test, or (9) an atlas. • If the work is produced by an independent contractor, the parties must agree expressly in writing that the work will be a work for hire. The employer or commissioning party owns the copyright. 17 USCA § 101.

work of authorship. The product of creative expression, such as literature, music, art, and graphic designs. • Copyright protects a work of authorship if it meets three criteria. First, the work must be original, not a copy. Second, the work must be presented in a fixed medium, such as a computer disk, a canvas, or paper. Finally, some creativity must have been involved in the work's creation, although the amount of creativity required depends on the particular work.

work, *vb.* **1.** To exert effort; to perform, either physically or mentally <lawyers work long hours during trial>. **2.** To function properly; to produce a desired effect <the strategy worked>. **3.** *Patents.* To develop and use (a patented invention, esp. to make it commercially available) <the patentee failed to work the patent>. • Failure to work a patent in a specified amount of time is grounds for a compulsory license in some countries.

worker. 1. One who labors to attain an end; esp., a person employed to do work for another. **2.** A person who offers to perform services for compensation in the employ of another, whether or not the person is so employed at a given time.

workers' compensation. A system of providing benefits to an employee for injuries occurring in the scope of employment. • Most workers'-compensation statutes both hold the employer strictly liable and bar the employee from suing the employer in tort. — Abbr. WC.

workers'-compensation act. A statute by which employers are made responsible for bodily harm to their workers arising out of and in the course of their employment, regardless of the fault of either the employee or the employer.

workers'-compensation board. An agency that reviews cases arising under workers'-compensation statutes and administers the related rules and regulations.

workfare. (1969) A system of requiring a person receiving a public-welfare benefit to earn that benefit by performing a job provided by a government agency or undergoing job training.

work furlough (**fər**-loh). (1960) A prison-treatment program allowing an inmate to be released during the day to work in the community.

workhouse. (17c) A jail for criminals who have committed minor offenses and are serving short sentences.

work-in-process. A product being manufactured or assembled but not yet completed. — Abbr. WIP.

workplace. A person's place of employment or work setting in general..

work product. (1947) Tangible material or its intangible equivalent — in unwritten or oral form — that was either prepared by or for a lawyer or prepared for litigation, either planned or in progress. • Work product is generally exempt from discovery or other compelled disclosure. The term is also used to describe the products of a party's investigation or communications concerning the subject matter of a lawsuit if made (1) to assist in the prosecution or defense of a pending suit, or (2) in reasonable anticipation of litigation. Fed. R. Evid. 26.

fact work product. A lawyer's tangible work product that includes facts but not the lawyer's mental impressions. • Fact work product is subject to a qualified privilege. It is not discoverable unless the party seeking discovery can show (1) a substantial need for the materials and (2) an inability to acquire the information by any other means without undue hardship. See Fed. R. Evid. 26(b)(3).

opinion work product. A lawyer's opinions, mental impressions, conclusions, and legal theories arising from a client's case. • An adversary usu. cannot gain access to this work product despite showing substantial need and undue hardship. Fed. R. Evid. 26(b)(3).

work-product rule. (1954) The rule providing for qualified immunity of an attorney's work product from discovery or other compelled disclosure. Fed. R. Civ. P. 26(b)(3). • The exemption was primarily established to protect an attorney's litigation strategy. *Hickman v. Taylor*, 329 U.S. 495, 67 S.Ct. 385 (1947).

work-release program. (1964) A correctional program allowing a prison inmate — primarily one being readied for discharge — to hold a job outside prison.

World Intellectual Property Organization. An agency of the United Nations Educational, Scientific, and Cultural Organization formed in 1967 to (1) promote intellectual-property protection worldwide through cooperation among nations, and (2) administer multilateral treaties dealing with legal and administrative aspects of intellectual property. • The organization's headquarters are in Geneva, Switzerland. — Abbr. WIPO.

World Trade Organization. The body charged with enforcing intellectual-property provisions of the GATT treaty. • WTO comprises the signatories of the Uruguay Round of GATT negotiations. — Abbr. WTO.

worship. Any form of religious devotion, ritual, or service showing reverence, esp. for a divine being or supernatural power <freedom of worship>.

public worship. **1.** Worship conducted by a religious society according to the society's system of ecclesiastical authority, ritual propriety, and rules and regulations. **2.** Worship under public authority. **3.** Worship in a public place, without privacy or concealment. **4.** Worship allowed by all members of the public equally.

worth, *n.* (bef. 12c) **1.** The monetary value of a thing; the sum of the qualities that render a thing valuable and useful, expressed in the current medium of exchange. **2.** The emotional or sentimental value of something. **3.** The total wealth held by a person or entity.

worthier-title doctrine. (1935) **1.** *Hist.* The common-law doctrine that if a beneficiary of a will would receive an identical interest as an heir under the laws of intestacy, the person takes the interest as an heir rather than as a beneficiary. • The doctrine has been abolished in most states. **2.** *Property.* The doctrine that favors a grantor's intent by construing a grant as a reversion in the grantor instead of as a remainder in the grantor's heirs.

writ (rit). (bef. 12c) A court's written order, in the name of a state or other competent legal authority, commanding the addressee to do or refrain from doing some specified act.

alias writ. (18c) An additional writ issued after another writ of the same kind in the same case. • It derives its name from a Latin phrase that formerly appeared in alias writs: *sicut alias praecipimus*, meaning "as we at another time commanded."

alternative writ. (1827) A common-law writ commanding the person against whom it is issued either to do a specific thing or to show cause why the court should not order it to be done.

counterpart writ. (1841) A copy of an original writ, to be sent to a court in another county where the defendant is located.

extraordinary writ. (17c) A writ issued by a court exercising unusual or discretionary power. • Examples are certiorari, habeas corpus, mandamus, and prohibition.

judicial writ. (16c) **1.** A writ issuing from the court to which the original writ was returnable; a writ issued under the private seal of the court and not under the great seal of England. **2.** Any writ issued by a court.

junior writ. (1839) A writ issued at a later time than a similar writ, such as a later writ issued by a different party or a later writ on a different claim against the same defendant.

optional writ. (18c) At common law, an original writ issued when the plaintiff seeks specific damages, such as payment of a liquidated debt. • The writ commands the defendant either to do a specified thing or to show why the thing has not been done.

original writ. (16c) A writ commencing an action and directing the defendant to appear and answer. • In the United States, this writ has been largely superseded by the summons. At common law, this type of writ was a mandatory letter issuing from the court of chancery under the great seal, and in the king's name, directed to the sheriff of the county where the injury was alleged to have occurred, containing a summary statement of the cause of complaint, and requiring the sheriff in most cases to command the defendant to satisfy the claim or else appear in court to account for not satisfying it.

peremptory writ (pər-**emp**-tə-ree). (18c) At common law, an original writ issued when the plaintiff seeks only general damages, as in an action for trespass. • The writ, which is issued only after the plaintiff gives security for costs, directs the sheriff to have the defendant appear in court.

writ of assistance. A writ to enforce a court's decree transferring real property, the title of which has been previously adjudicated.

writ of course. (17c) A writ issued as a matter of course or granted as a matter of right.

writ of detinue. (17c) A writ in an action for detinue.

writ of ejectment. (17c) The writ in an action of ejectment for the recovery of land.

writ of entry. (16c) A writ that allows a person wrongfully dispossessed of real property to enter and retake the property.

writ of error. (15c) **1.** A writ issued by an appellate court directing a lower court to deliver the record in the case for review.

writ of possession. (17c) A writ issued to recover the possession of land.

writ of prevention. (17c) A writ to prevent the filing of a lawsuit.

writ of protection. (17c) **1.** A writ to protect a witness in a judicial proceeding who is threatened with arrest. **2.** A writ exempting anyone in the Crown's service from arrest in a civil proceeding for a year and a day.

writ of restitution. (17c) **1.** The process of enforcing a civil judgment in a forcible-entry-and-detainer action or enforcing restitution on a verdict in a criminal prosecution for forcible entry and detainer. **2.** A common-law writ issued when a judgment is reversed, whereby all that was lost as a result of the judgment is restored to the prevailing party.

writ of review. (18c) A general form of process issuing from an appellate court to bring up for review the record of the proceedings in the court below; the common-law writ of certiorari.

writ of sequestration. (18c) A writ ordering that a court be given custody of something or that something not be taken from the jurisdiction, such as the collateral for a promissory note. • Such a writ is usu. issued during litigation, often so that the object will be available for attachment or execution after judgment.

writ of supervisory control. (1901) A writ issued to correct an erroneous ruling made by a lower court either when there is no appeal or when an appeal cannot provide adequate relief and the ruling will result in gross injustice.

writ system. (1890) The common-law procedural system under which a plaintiff commences an action by obtaining the appropriate type of original writ.

wrong, *n.* (bef. 12c) Breach of one's legal duty; violation of another's legal right. — **wrong,** *vb.*

civil wrong. (17c) A violation of noncriminal law, such as a tort, a breach of contract or trust, a breach of statutory duty, or a defect in performing a public duty; the breach of a legal duty treated as the subject matter of a civil proceeding.

continuing wrong. (1846) An ongoing wrong that is capable of being corrected by specific enforcement. • An example is the nonpayment of a debt.

intentional wrong. (18c) A wrong in which the *mens rea* amounts to intention, purpose, or design.

legal wrong. (18c) An act that is a violation of the law; an act authoritatively prohibited by a rule of law.

moral wrong. (18c) An act that is contrary to the rule of natural justice.

personal wrong. An invasion of a personal right.

positive wrong. (18c) A wrongful act willfully committed.

private wrong. (16c) An offense committed against a private person and dealt with at the instance of the person injured.

public wrong. (16c) An offense committed against the state or the community at large, and dealt with in a proceeding to which the state is itself a party. • Not all public wrongs are crimes. For example, a person that breaches a contract with the government commits a public wrong, but the offense is a civil one, not a criminal one.

real wrong. An injury to the freehold.

transitory wrong. (2004) A wrong that, once committed, belongs to the irrevocable past. • An example is defamation.

wrong of negligence. (1902) A wrong in which the *mens rea* is a form of mere carelessness, as opposed to wrongful intent.

wrong of strict liability. (1986) A wrong in which a *mens rea* is not required because neither wrongful intent nor culpable negligence is a necessary condition of responsibility.

wrongdoer, *n.* (15c) One who violates the law <both criminals and tortfeasors are wrongdoers>. — **wrongdoing,** *n.*

wrongful, *adj.* (14c) **1.** Characterized by unfairness or injustice <wrongful military invasion>. **2.** Contrary to law; unlawful <wrongful termination>. **3.** (Of a person) not entitled to the position occupied <wrongful possessor>. — **wrongfully,** *adv.*

wrongful-death action. (1926) A lawsuit brought on behalf of a decedent's survivors for their damages resulting from a tortious injury that caused the decedent's death.

wrongful-death statute. (1904) A statute authorizing a decedent's personal representative to bring a wrongful-death action for the benefit of certain beneficiaries.

wrongful-discharge action. (1957) A lawsuit brought by an ex-employee against the former employer, alleging that the termination of employment violated a contract or was illegal.

wrongful dishonor, *n.* (1895) A refusal to accept or pay (a negotiable instrument) when it is properly presented and is payable.

wrongful-eviction action. A lawsuit brought by a former tenant or possessor of real property against one who has put the plaintiff out of possession, alleging that the eviction was illegal.

wrongful-life action. (1963) A lawsuit brought by or on behalf of a child with birth defects, alleging that but for the doctor-defendant's negligent advice, the parents would not have conceived the child or, if they had, would have aborted the fetus to avoid the pain and suffering resulting from the child's congenital defects. • Most jurisdictions reject these claims.

wrongful-pregnancy action. (1979) A lawsuit brought by a parent for damages resulting from a pregnancy following a failed sterilization.

X

X. *abbr.* **1.** Ex dividend. **2.** Ex rights. **3.** Ex distribution. **4.** Ex warrants.

X. 1. A mark serving as the signature of a person who is physically handicapped or illiterate. • The signer's name usu. appears near the mark, and if the mark is to be notarized as a signature, two signing witnesses are ordinarily required in addition to the notary public. **2.** A symbol equivalent to "by" when used in giving dimensions, as in 3 x 5 inches. **3.** A mark placed on a document (such as an application) to indicate a selection, such as "yes" or "no"; esp., a mark on a ballot to indicate a vote.

XD. *abbr.* Ex dividend.

XDIS. *abbr.* Ex distribution.

X-patent. *Patents.* An early U.S. patent, granted before the numbering system set up in the Patent Act of 1836 and so named because an *X* was added to the numbers of existing patents to avoid duplicate numbers.

XR. *abbr.* Ex-rights.

XW. *abbr.* Ex-warrants.

xylon (zɪ-lon), *n.* [fr. Greek *xulon* "wood"] *Archaic.* A Greek punishment apparatus similar to stocks.

XYY-chromosome defense. *Criminal law.* A defense, usu. asserted as the basis for an insanity plea, whereby a male defendant argues that his criminal behavior is due to the genetic abnormality of having an extra Y chromosome, which causes him to have uncontrollable aggressive impulses. • Most courts have rejected this defense because its scientific foundations are uncertain.

XYY syndrome. The abnormal presence of an extra Y chromosome in a male, theoretically resulting in increased aggressiveness and antisocial behavior sometimes resulting in criminal conduct.

Y

yank-cheating, *n.* The illegal practice of inserting paper money into a vending machine, then pulling the money out again after the machine has recognized it, thereby retaining the cash and unlawfully obtaining merchandise.

yardstick theory. *Antitrust.* A method of determining damages for lost profits (and sometimes overcharges) whereby a corporate plaintiff identifies a company similar to the plaintiff but without the impact of the antitrust violation.

yea, *n. Parliamentary law.* An affirmative vote.

yea and nay (**yay / nay**). Yes and no. • In old records, this was a mere assertion and denial without the necessity of an oath.

year. 1. Twelve calendar months beginning January 1 and ending December 31. **2.** A consecutive 365-day period beginning at any point; a span of twelve months.

fiscal year. An accounting period of 12 consecutive months <the company's fiscal year is October 1 to September 30>. • A fiscal year is often different from the calendar year, esp. for tax purposes.

half-year. In legal computation, a period of 182 days.

natural year. Hist. The period of 365 days and about 6 hours, or the time it takes the earth to orbit the sun.

tax year. The period used for computing federal or state income-tax liability, usu. either the calendar year or a fiscal year of 12 months ending on the last day of a month other than December.

year and a day. The common-law time limit fixed for various purposes, such as claiming rights, exemptions, or property (such as rights to wreckage or estrays), or for prosecuting certain acts — so called because a year was formerly counted to include the first and last day, meaning that a year from January 1 was December 31, so a year and a day would then mean a full year from January 1 through January 1.

year-and-a-day rule. (1876) *Criminal law.* The common-law principle that an act causing death is not homicide if the death occurs more than a year and a day after the act was committed. • In Latin, the phrase *year and a day* was commonly rendered *annus et dies.*

Year Books. *Hist.* Books of cases anonymously and fairly regularly reported covering primarily the period from the reign of Edward I to the time of Henry VIII. • The title "Year Books" derives from their being grouped under the regnal years of the sovereigns in whose reigns the reported cases were cited. The reports were probably originally prepared by law teachers and students and later by professional reporters or scribes.

year, day, and waste. *Hist.* A right of the Crown to the profits and waste for a year and a day of the land of persons convicted of petty treason or felony (unless the lord made redemption), after which the Crown had to restore the property to the lord of the fee. The right was abrogated by the Corruption of Blood Act of 1814.

year-end dividend. Dividend.

Year of Our Lord. Anno domini.

year-to-year tenancy. Periodic tenancy.

yeas and nays. The affirmative and negative votes on a bill or resolution before a deliberative assembly.

yellow-dog contract. An employment contract forbidding membership in a labor union. • Such a contract is generally illegal under federal and state law.

yeoman (**yoh**-mən). **1.** *Hist.* An attendant in a royal or noble household. **2.** *Hist.* A commoner; a freeholder (under the rank of gentleman) who holds land yielding 40 shillings per year. **3.** *English law.* One who owns and cultivates property. **4.** A petty officer performing clerical work in the U.S. Navy.

yeoman of the guard. A member of a corps of officers whose primary duties are to ceremonially guard the English royal household. • A yeoman is usu. at least six feet tall, is of the best rank under the gentry, and is generally exempt from arrest on civil process.

yeomanry (**yoh**-mən-ree). **1.** The collective body of yeomen. **2.** Volunteer cavalry units in Great Britain, later transferred to the Territorial Army.

***Yick Wo* doctrine** (yik **woh**). (1958) The principle that a law or ordinance giving a person or entity absolute discretion to give or withhold permission to carry on a lawful business violates the 14th Amendment to the U.S. Constitution. *Yick Wo v. Hopkins*, 118 U.S. 356, 6 S.Ct. 1064 (1886).

yield, *n.* (bef. 12c) Profit expressed as a percentage of the investment.

coupon yield. The annual interest paid on a security (esp. a bond) divided by the security's par value.

current yield. The annual interest paid on a security (esp. a bond) divided by the security's current market price.

discount yield. The yield on a security sold at a discount.

earnings yield. The earnings per share of a security divided by its market price. • The higher the ratio, the better the investment yield.

net yield. The profit or loss on an investment after deducting all appropriate costs and loss reserves.

nominal yield. Coupon yield.

yield, *vb.* **1.** To give up, relinquish, or surrender (a right, etc.) <yield the floor>. **2.** *Parliamentary law.* (Of a motion) to give way to a higher-ranking motion. **3.** *Hist.* To perform a service owed by a tenant to a lord <yield and pay>.

yield spread. The differences in yield between various securities issues.

yield to maturity. The rate of return from an investment if the investment is held until it matures. — Abbr. YTM.

York, Statute of. *Hist.* An English statute passed in York in the twelfth year of Edward II's reign, and including provisions on the subject of attorneys, witnesses, and the taking of inquests by nisi prius.

York–Antwerp rules. *Maritime law.* A set of rules relating to the settlement of maritime losses and disputes arising from bills of lading. • Although these rules have no statutory authority, they are incorporated into almost all bills of lading. The Rules are maintained and updated by the Comité Maritime International (CMI).

your Honor. (16c) A title customarily used when directly addressing a judge or other high official.

Youth Correction Authority Act. A model act, promulgated by the American Law Institute in 1940, that proposed the creation of central state commissions responsible for setting up appropriate agencies that would determine the proper treatment for each youthful offender committed to the agency by the courts. • The Act is noteworthy for its emphasis on rehabilitating juvenile offenders, as opposed to punishing them.

youthful offender. **1.** Offender. **2.** Juvenile delinquent.

yo-yo stock. Volatile stock.

YTM. *abbr.* Yield to maturity.

Z

ZBA. *abbr.* Zero-bracket amount.

zero-bracket amount. A tax deduction formerly available to all individual taxpayers, regardless of whether they itemized their deductions. • In 1944 this was replaced by the standard deduction. — Abbr. ZBA.

zero-tolerance policy. (1990) An established plan or method of action stating that certain acts will not be permitted or condoned. • School districts often have a zero-tolerance policy regarding the use of drugs and alcohol on school premises or at school-sponsored functions. In 1995 Congress enacted a nationwide zero-tolerance statute to combat underage drinking.

ZIFT. *abbr.* Zygote intrafallopian transfer.

zipper clause. *Contracts.* A contractual provision that operates both as an integration clause and as a no-oral-modification clause.

zone. 1. An area that is different or is distinguished from surrounding areas <zone of danger>. **2.** An area in a city or town that, through zoning regulations, is under particular restrictions as to building size, land use, and the like <the capitol is at the center of the height-restriction zone>.

floating zone. An amount of land assigned for a particular use but in no particular location. • An applicant who owns the specified amount of land can apply for a use permit in a specific location.

holding zone. Temporary, low-density zoning used until a community determines how the area should be rezoned.

zone-of-danger rule. (1966) *Torts.* The doctrine allowing the recovery of damages for negligent infliction of emotional distress if the plaintiff was both located in the dangerous area created by the defendant's negligence and frightened by the risk of harm.

zone of employment. *Workers' compensation.* The physical place of employment within which an employee, if injured there, can receive compensation.

zone of interests. (1969) The class or type of interests or concerns that a statute or constitutional guarantee is intended to regulate or protect. • To have standing to challenge a ruling (esp. of an administrative agency), the plaintiff must show that the specific injury suffered comes within the zone of interests protected by the statute on which the ruling was based.

zone of privacy. (1964) *Constitutional law.* A range of fundamental privacy rights that are implied in the express guarantees of the Bill of Rights.

zoning, *n.* (1912) The legislative division of a region, esp. a municipality, into separate districts with different regulations within the districts for land use, building size, and the like. — **zone,** *vb.*

aesthetic zoning. Zoning designed to preserve the aesthetic features or values of an area.

cluster zoning. Zoning that favors planned-unit development by allowing a modification in lot size and frontage requirements under the condition that other land in the development be set aside for parks, schools, or other public needs.

conditional zoning. Zoning in which a governmental body (without definitively committing itself) grants a zoning change subject to conditions that are usu. not imposed on similarly zoned property.

contextual zoning. An approach to zoning that considers appropriate use of a lot based on the scale and types of nearby buildings. • Contextual zoning has been used, for example, to prevent the destruction of older, smaller residences to make room for larger houses disparagingly called "monster homes" or "mc mansions." in established neighborhoods.

contract zoning. **1.** Zoning according to an agreement, by which the landowner agrees to certain restrictions or conditions in exchange for more favorable zoning treatment. • This type of contract zoning is usu. considered an illegal restraint of the government's police power, because by private agreement, the government has committed itself to a particular type of zoning. **2.** Rezoning of property to a less restrictive classification subject to the landowner's agreement to observe specified limitations on the use and physical development of the property that are not imposed on other property in the zone. • This device is esp. used when property is located in a more restrictive zone that borders on a less restrictive zone.

cumulative zoning. A method of zoning in which any use permitted in a higher-use, less intensive zone is permissible in a lower-use, more intensive zone. • For example, under this method, a house could be built in an industrial zone but a factory could not be built in a residential zone.

Euclidean zoning (yoo-**klid**-ee-ən). Zoning by specific and uniform geographical division. • The purpose of Euclidean zoning is to ensure a municipality's orderly development by detailing what uses are permitted and where, and seeing that conflicting land uses are clearly separated. Its name comes from the Supreme Court case that approved it: *Village of Euclid v. Ambler Realty Co.*, 272 U.S. 365, 47 S.Ct. 114 (1926).

exclusionary zoning. Zoning that excludes a specific class or type of business from a district.

floating zoning. Zoning that allots land for particular uses but does not specify the geographic locations for those uses. • This is a type of non-Euclidean zoning. It allows a zoning board to make individual rulings on every application for a particular use and take into account the community's current feelings about where or if the use should be allowed.

incentive zoning. A relaxation in zoning restrictions (such as density limits) that offers an incentive to a developer to provide certain public benefits (such as building low-income housing units).

interim zoning. Temporary emergency zoning pending revisions to existing ordinances or the development of a final zoning plan.

inverse zoning. Zoning that attempts to disperse particular types of property use rather than concentrate them.

non-Euclidean zoning. Zoning that allows a mix of land uses in the same area if the uses are or can be made nonconflicting • For example, a business might be permitted to operate in a residential area if the business adopts a certain architecture to blend in with other structures and has sufficient landscaping and setback to guarantee that nearby residents will not suffer excessive noise, pollution, or other nuisances.

partial zoning. Zoning that affects only a portion of a municipality's territory, and that is usu. invalid because it contradicts the comprehensive zoning plan.

private zoning. The use of restrictive covenants in private agreements to restrict the use and occupancy of real property. • Private zoning often covers such things as lot size, building lines, architectural specifications, and property uses.

reverse spot zoning. Zoning of a large area of land without regard for the zoning of a small piece of land within that area.

spot zoning. Zoning of a particular piece of land without regard for the zoning of the larger area surrounding the land.

zoning map. The map that is created by a zoning ordinance and shows the various zoning districts.

zoning ordinance. (1919) A city ordinance that regulates the use to which land within various parts of the city may be put. • It allocates uses to the various districts of a municipality, as by allocating residences to certain parts and businesses to other parts. A comprehensive zoning ordinance usu. regulates the height of buildings and the proportion of the lot area that must be kept free from buildings.

zygote. A two-celled organism formed by the joining of egg and sperm.

zygote intrafallopian transfer. A procedure in which mature eggs are fertilized in a test tube or petri dish and then injected into a woman's fallopian tubes. — Abbr. ZIFT.

APPENDIX

The Constitution of the United States of America

We the People of the United States, in Order to form a more perfect Union, establish Justice, insure domestic Tranquility, provide for the common defence, promote the general Welfare, and secure the Blessings of Liberty to ourselves and our Posterity, do ordain and establish this Constitution for the United States of America.

Article I

Section 1. All legislative Powers herein granted shall be vested in a Congress of the United States, which shall consist of a Senate and House of Representatives.

Section 2. The House of Representatives shall be composed of Members chosen every second Year by the People of the several States, and the Electors in each State shall have the Qualifications requisite for Electors of the most numerous Branch of the State Legislature.

No Person shall be a Representative who shall not have attained to the Age of twenty five Years, and been seven Years a Citizen of the United States, and who shall not, when elected, be an Inhabitant of that State in which he shall be chosen.

Representatives and direct Taxes shall be apportioned among the several States which may be included within this Union, according to their respective Numbers, which shall be determined by adding to the whole Number of free Persons, including those bound to Service for a Term of Years, and excluding Indians not taxed, three fifths of all other Persons. The actual Enumeration shall be made within three Years after the first Meeting of the Congress of the United States, and within every subsequent Term of ten Years, in such Manner as they shall by Law direct. The Number of Representatives shall not exceed one for every thirty Thousand, but each State shall have at Least one Representative; and until such enumeration shall be made, the State of New Hampshire shall be entitled to chuse three, Massachusetts eight, Rhode Island and Providence Plantations one, Connecticut five, New York six, New Jersey four, Pennsylvania eight, Delaware one, Maryland six, Virginia ten, North Carolina five, South Carolina five, and Georgia three.

When vacancies happen in the Representation from any State, the Executive Authority thereof shall issue Writs of Election to fill such Vacancies.

The House of Representatives shall chuse their Speaker and other Officers; and shall have the sole Power of Impeachment.

Section 3. The Senate of the United States shall be composed of two Senators from each State, chosen by the Legislature thereof, for six Years; and each Senator shall have one Vote.

Immediately after they shall be assembled in Consequence of the first Election, they shall be divided as equally as may be into three Classes. The Seats of the Senators of the first Class shall be vacated at the Expiration of the second Year, of the second Class at the Expiration of the fourth Year, and the third Class at the Expiration of the sixth Year, so that one third may be chosen every second Year; and if Vacancies happen by Resignation, or otherwise, during the Recess of the

Legislature of any State, the Executive thereof may make temporary Appointments until the next Meeting of the Legislature, which shall then fill such Vacancies.

No Person shall be a Senator who shall not have attained to the Age of thirty Years, and been nine Years a Citizen of the United States and who shall not, when elected, be an Inhabitant of that State for which he shall be chosen.

The Vice President of the United States shall be President of the Senate, but shall have no Vote, unless they be equally divided.

The Senate shall chuse their other Officers, and also a President pro tempore, in the Absence of the Vice President, or when he shall exercise the Office of President of the United States.

The Senate shall have the sole Power to try all Impeachments. When sitting for that Purpose, they shall be on Oath or Affirmation. When the President of the United States is tried, the Chief Justice shall preside: And no Person shall be convicted without the Concurrence of two thirds of the Members present.

Judgment in Cases of Impeachment shall not extend further than to removal from Office, and disqualification to hold and enjoy any Office of Honor, Trust or Profit under the United States: but the Party convicted shall nevertheless be liable and subject to Indictment, Trial, Judgment and Punishment, according to Law.

Section 4. The Times, Places and Manner of holding Elections for Senators and Representatives, shall be prescribed in each State by the Legislature thereof; but the Congress may at any time by Law make or alter such Regulations, except as to the Places of chusing Senators.

The Congress shall assemble at least once in every Year, and such Meeting shall be on the first Monday in December, unless they shall by Law appoint a different Day.

Section 5. Each House shall be the Judge of the Elections, Returns and Qualifications of its own Members, and a Majority of each shall constitute a Quorum to do Business; but a smaller Number may adjourn from day to day, and may be authorized to compel the Attendance of absent Members, in such Manner, and under such Penalties as each House may provide.

Each House may determine the Rules of its Proceedings, punish its Members for disorderly Behavior, and, with the Concurrence of two thirds, expel a Member.

Each House shall keep a Journal of its Proceedings, and from time to time publish the same, excepting such Parts as may in their Judgment require Secrecy; and the Yeas and Nays of the Members of either House on any question shall, at the Desire of one fifth of those Present, be entered on the Journal.

Neither House, during the Session of Congress, shall, without the Consent of the other, adjourn for more than three days, nor to any other Place than that in which the two Houses shall be sitting.

Section 6. The Senators and Representatives shall receive a Compensation for their Services, to be ascertained by Law, and paid out of the Treasury of the United States. They shall in all Cases, except Treason, Felony and Breach of the Peace, be privileged from Arrest during their Attendance at the Session of their respective Houses, and in going to and returning from the same; and for any Speech or Debate in either House, they shall not be questioned in any other Place.

No Senator or Representative shall, during the Time for which he was elected, be appointed to any civil Office under the Authority of the United States, which shall have been created, or the Emoluments whereof shall have been encreased during such time; and no Person holding any Office under the United States, shall be a Member of either House during his Continuance in Office.

Section 7. All Bills for raising Revenue shall originate in the House of Representatives; but the Senate may propose or concur with Amendments as on other Bills.

Every Bill which shall have passed the House of Representatives and the Senate, shall, before it become a Law, be presented to the President of the United States; If he approve he shall sign it, but if not he shall return it, with his Objections to the House in which it shall have originated, who shall enter the Objections at large on their Journal, and proceed to reconsider it. If after such Reconsideration two thirds of that House shall agree to pass the Bill, it shall be sent, together with the Objections, to the other House, by which it shall likewise be reconsidered, and if approved by two thirds of that House, it shall become a Law. But in all such Cases the Votes of both Houses shall be determined by yeas and nays, and the Names of the Persons voting for and against the Bill shall be entered on the Journal of each House respectively. If any Bill shall not be returned by the President within ten Days (Sundays excepted) after it shall have been presented to him, the Same shall be a Law, in like Manner as if he had signed it, unless the Congress by their Adjournment prevent its Return, in which Case it shall not be a Law.

Every Order, Resolution, or Vote to which the Concurrence of the Senate and House of Representatives may be necessary (except on a question of Adjournment) shall be presented to the President of the United States; and before the Same shall take Effect, shall be approved by him, or being disapproved by him, shall be repassed by two thirds of the Senate and House of Representatives, according to the Rules and Limitations prescribed in the Case of a Bill.

Section 8. The Congress shall have Power To lay and collect Taxes, Duties, Imposts and Excises, to pay the Debts and provide for the common Defence and general Welfare of the United States; but all Duties, Imposts and Excises shall be uniform throughout the United States;

To borrow Money on the credit of the United States;

To regulate Commerce with foreign Nations, and among the several States, and with the Indian Tribes;

To establish an uniform Rule of Naturalization, and uniform Laws on the subject of Bankruptcies throughout the United States;

To coin Money, regulate the Value thereof, and of foreign Coin, and fix the Standard of Weights and Measures;

To provide for the Punishment of counterfeiting the Securities and current Coin of the United States;

To establish Post Offices and post Roads;

To promote the Progress of Science and useful Arts, by securing for limited Times to Authors and Inventors the exclusive Right to their respective Writings and Discoveries;

To constitute Tribunals inferior to the supreme Court;

To define and punish Piracies and Felonies committed on the high Seas, and Offences against the Law of Nations;

To declare War, grant Letters of Marque and Reprisal, and make Rules concerning Captures on Land and Water;

To raise and support Armies, but no Appropriation of Money to that Use shall be for a longer Term than two Years;

To provide and maintain a Navy;

To make Rules for the Government and Regulation of the land and naval

Forces;

To provide for calling forth the Militia to execute the Laws of the Union, suppress Insurrections and repel Invasions;

To provide for organizing, arming, and disciplining, the Militia, and for governing such Part of them as may be employed in the Service of the United States, reserving to the States respectively, the Appointment of the Officers, and the Authority of training the Militia according to the discipline prescribed by Congress;

To exercise exclusive Legislation in all Cases whatsoever, over such District (not exceeding ten Miles square) as may, by Cession of particular States, and the Acceptance of Congress, become the Seat of the Government of the United States, and to exercise like Authority over all Places purchased by the Consent of the Legislature of the State in which the Same shall be, for the Erection of Forts, Magazines, Arsenals, dock-Yards, and other needful Buildings;—And

To make all Laws which shall be necessary and proper for carrying into Execution the foregoing Powers, and all other Powers vested by this Constitution in the Government of the United States, or in any Department or Officer thereof.

Section 9. The Migration or Importation of such Persons as any of the States now existing shall think proper to admit, shall not be prohibited by the Congress prior to the Year one thousand eight hundred and eight, but a Tax or duty may be imposed on such Importation, not exceeding ten dollars for each Person.

The Privilege of the Writ of Habeas Corpus shall not be suspended, unless when in Cases of Rebellion or Invasion the public Safety may require it.

No Bill of Attainder or ex post facto Law shall be passed.

No Capitation, or other direct, Tax shall be laid, unless in Proportion to the Census or Enumeration herein before directed to be taken.

No Tax or Duty shall be laid on Articles exported from any State.

No Preference shall be given by any Regulation of Commerce or Revenue to the Ports of one State over those of another: nor shall Vessels bound to, or from, one State, be obliged to enter, clear or pay Duties in another.

No Money shall be drawn from the Treasury, but in Consequence of Appropriations made by Law; and a regular Statement and Account of Receipts and Expenditures of all public Money shall be published from time to time.

No Title of Nobility shall be granted by the United States: And no Person holding any Office of Profit or Trust under them, shall, without the Consent of the Congress, accept of any present, Emolument, Office, or Title, of any kind whatever, from any King, Prince, or foreign State.

Section 10. No State shall enter into any Treaty, Alliance, or Confederation; grant Letters of Marque and Reprisal; coin Money; emit Bills of Credit; make any Thing but gold and silver Coin a Tender in Payment of Debts; pass any Bill of Attainder, ex post facto Law, or Law impairing the Obligation of Contracts, or grant any Title of Nobility.

No State shall, without the Consent of the Congress, lay any Imposts or Duties on Imports or Exports, except what may be absolutely necessary for executing its inspection Laws: and the net Produce of all Duties and Imposts, laid by any State on Imports or Exports, shall be for the Use of the Treasury of the United States; and all such Laws shall be subject to the Revision and Controul of the Congress.

No State shall, without the Consent of Congress, lay any Duty of Tonnage, keep Troops, or Ships of War in time of Peace, enter into any Agreement or Compact with another State, or with a foreign Power, or engage in War, unless actually invaded, or in such imminent Danger as will not admit of delay.

Article II

Section 1. The executive Power shall be vested in a President of the United States of America. He shall hold his Office during the Term of four Years, and, together with the Vice President, chosen for the same Term, be elected, as follows:

Each State shall appoint, in such Manner as the Legislature thereof may direct, a Number of Electors, equal to the whole Number of Senators and Representatives to which the State may be entitled in the Congress: but no Senator or Representative, or Person holding an Office of Trust or Profit under the United States, shall be appointed an Elector.

The Electors shall meet in their respective States, and vote by Ballot for two Persons, of whom one at least shall not be an Inhabitant of the same State with themselves. And they shall make a List of all the Persons voted for, and of the Number of Votes for each; which List they shall sign and certify, and transmit sealed to the Seat of the Government of the United States, directed to the President of the Senate. The President of the Senate shall, in the Presence of the Senate and House of Representatives, open all the Certificates, and the Votes shall then be counted. The Person having the greatest Number of Votes shall be the President, if such Number be a Majority of the whole Number of Electors appointed; and if there be more than one who have such Majority, and have an equal Number of Votes, then the House of Representatives shall immediately chuse by Ballot one of them for President; and if no Person have a Majority, then from the five highest on the List the said House shall in like Manner chuse the President. But in chusing the President, the Votes shall be taken by States, the Representation from each State having one Vote; A quorum for this Purpose shall consist of a Member or Members from two thirds of the States, and a Majority of all the States shall be necessary to a Choice. In every Case, after the Choice of the President, the Person having the greatest Number of Votes of the Electors shall be the Vice President. But if there should remain two or more who have equal Votes, the Senate shall chuse from them by Ballot the Vice President.

The Congress may determine the Time of chusing the Electors, and the Day on which they shall give their Votes; which Day shall be the same throughout the United States.

No Person except a natural born Citizen, or a Citizen of the United States, at the time of the Adoption of this Constitution, shall be eligible to the Office of President; neither shall any Person be eligible to that Office who shall not have attained to the Age of thirty five Years, and been fourteen Years a Resident within the United States.

In Case of the Removal of the President from Office, or of his Death, Resignation, or Inability to discharge the Powers and Duties of the said Office, the Same shall devolve on the Vice President, and the Congress may by Law provide for the Case of Removal, Death, Resignation or Inability, both of the President and Vice President, declaring what Officer shall then act as President, and such Officer shall act accordingly, until the Disability be removed, or a President shall be elected.

The President shall, at stated Times, receive for his Services, a Compensation, which shall neither be increased nor diminished during the Period for which he shall have been elected, and he shall not receive within that Period any other Emolument from the United States, or any of them.

Before he enter on the Execution of

his Office, he shall take the following Oath or Affirmation: "I do solemnly swear (or affirm) that I will faithfully execute the Office of President of the United States, and will to the best of my Ability, preserve, protect and defend the Constitution of the United States."

Section 2. The President shall be Commander in Chief of the Army and Navy of the United States, and of the Militia of the several States, when called into the actual Service of the United States; he may require the Opinion, in writing, of the principal Officer in each of the executive Departments, upon any Subject relating to the Duties of their respective Offices, and he shall have Power to grant Reprieves and Pardons for Offences against the United States, except in Cases of Impeachment.

He shall have Power, by and with the Advice and Consent of the Senate, to make Treaties, provided two thirds of the Senators present concur; and he shall nominate, and by and with the Advice and Consent of the Senate, shall appoint Ambassadors, other public Ministers and Consuls, Judges of the supreme Court, and all other Officers of the United States, whose Appointments are not herein otherwise provided for, and which shall be established by Law: but the Congress may by Law vest the Appointment of such inferior Officers, as they think proper, in the President alone, in the Courts of Law, or in the Heads of Departments.

The President shall have Power to fill up all Vacancies that may happen during the Recess of the Senate, by granting Commissions which shall expire at the End of their next Session.

Section 3. He shall from time to time give to the Congress Information of the State of the Union, and recommend to their Consideration such Measures as he shall judge necessary and expedient; he may, on extraordinary Occasions, convene both Houses, or either of them, and in Case of Disagreement between them, with Respect to the Time of Adjournment, he may adjourn them to such Time as he shall think proper; he shall receive Ambassadors and other public Ministers; he shall take Care that the Laws be faithfully executed, and shall Commission all the Officers of the United States.

Section 4. The President, Vice President and all civil Officers of the United States, shall be removed from Office on Impeachment for, and Conviction of, Treason, Bribery, or other high Crimes and Misdemeanors.

Article III

Section 1. The judicial Power of the United States, shall be vested in one supreme Court, and in such inferior Courts as the Congress may from time to time ordain and establish. The Judges, both of the supreme and inferior Courts, shall hold their Offices during good Behaviour, and shall, at stated Times, receive for their Services a Compensation, which shall not be diminished during their Continuance in Office.

Section 2. The judicial Power shall extend to all Cases, in Law and Equity, arising under this Constitution, the Laws of the United States, and Treaties made, or which shall be made, under their Authority;—to all Cases affecting Ambassadors, other public Ministers and Consuls;—to all Cases of admiralty and maritime Jurisdiction;—to Controversies to which the United States shall be a Party;—to Controversies between two or more States;—between a State and Citizens of another State;—between Citizens of different States;—between Citizens of the same State claiming Lands under the Grants of different States, and between a State, or the Citizens thereof, and foreign States, Citizens or Subjects.

In all Cases affecting Ambassadors,

other public Ministers and Consuls, and those in which a State shall be a Party, the supreme Court shall have original Jurisdiction. In all the other Cases before mentioned, the supreme Court shall have appellate Jurisdiction, both as to Law and Fact, with such Exceptions, and under such Regulations as the Congress shall make.

The Trial of all Crimes, except in Cases of Impeachment, shall be by Jury; and such Trial shall be held in the State where the said Crimes shall have been committed; but when not committed within any State, the Trial shall be at such Place or Places as the Congress may by Law have directed.

Section 3. Treason against the United States, shall consist only in levying War against them, or in adhering to their Enemies, giving them Aid and Comfort. No Person shall be convicted of Treason unless on the Testimony of two Witnesses to the same overt Act, or on Confession in open Court.

The Congress shall have Power to declare the Punishment of Treason, but no Attainder of Treason shall work Corruption of Blood, or Forfeiture except during the Life of the Person attainted.

Article IV

Section 1. Full Faith and Credit shall be given in each State to the public Acts, Records, and judicial Proceedings of every other State. And the Congress may by general Laws prescribe the Manner in which such Acts, Records and Proceedings shall be proved, and the Effect thereof.

Section 2. The Citizens of each State shall be entitled to all Privileges and Immunities of Citizens in the several States.

A Person charged in any State with Treason, Felony, or other Crime, who shall flee from Justice, and be found in another State, shall on demand of the executive Authority of the State from which he fled, be delivered up, to be removed to the State having Jurisdiction of the Crime.

No Person held to Service or Labour in one State, under the Laws thereof, escaping into another, shall, in Consequence of any Law or Regulation therein, be discharged from such Service or Labour, but shall be delivered up on Claim of the Party to whom such Service or Labour may be due.

Section 3. New States may be admitted by the Congress into this Union; but no new State shall be formed or erected within the Jurisdiction of any other State; nor any State be formed by the Junction of two or more States, or Parts of States, without the Consent of the Legislatures of the States concerned as well as of the Congress.

The Congress shall have Power to dispose of and make all needful Rules and Regulations respecting the Territory or other Property belonging to the United States; and nothing in this Constitution shall be so construed as to Prejudice any Claims of the United States, or of any particular State.

Section 4. The United States shall guarantee to every State in this Union a Republican Form of Government, and shall protect each of them against Invasion; and on Application of the Legislature, or of the Executive (when the Legislature cannot be convened) against domestic Violence.

Article V

The Congress, whenever two thirds of both Houses shall deem it necessary, shall propose Amendments to this Constitution, or, on the Application of the Legislatures of two thirds of the several States, shall call a Convention for proposing Amendments, which, in either Case, shall be valid to all Intents and Purposes, as Part of this Constitution, when ratified by the Legislatures of three fourths of the several States, or by Conventions in three fourths thereof, as the one or the other Mode of Ratification may be proposed by the Congress; Provided that no Amendment which may be made prior to the Year One thousand eight hundred and eight shall in any Manner affect the first and fourth Clauses in the Ninth Section of the first Article; and that no State, without its Consent, shall be deprived of its equal Suffrage in the Senate.

Article VI

All Debts contracted and Engagements entered into, before the Adoption of this Constitution, shall be as valid against the United States under this Constitution, as under the Confederation.

This Constitution, and the Laws of the United States which shall be made in Pursuance thereof; and all Treaties made, or which shall be made, under the Authority of the United States, shall be the supreme Law of the Land; and the Judges in every State shall be bound thereby, any Thing in the Constitution or Laws of any State to the Contrary notwithstanding.

The Senators and Representatives before mentioned, and the Members of the several State Legislatures, and all executive and judicial Officers, both of the United States and of the several States, shall be bound by Oath or Affirmation, to support this Constitution; but no religious Test shall ever be required as a Qualification to any Office or public Trust under the United States.

Article VII

The Ratification of the Conventions of nine States, shall be sufficient for the Establishment of this Constitution between the States so ratifying the Same.

Articles in addition to, and amendment of, the Constitution of the United States of America, proposed by Congress, and ratified by the Legislatures of the Several States pursuant to the Fifth Article of the original Constitution.

Amendment I [1791]

Congress shall make no law respecting an establishment of religion, or prohibiting the free exercise thereof; or abridging the freedom of speech, or of the press; or the right of the people peaceably to assemble, and to petition the Government for a redress of grievances.

Amendment II [1791]

A well regulated Militia being necessary to the security of a free State, the right of the people to keep and bear Arms, shall not be infringed.

Amendment III [1791]

No Soldier shall, in time of peace be quartered in any house, without the consent of the Owner, nor in time of war, but in a manner to be prescribed by law.

Amendment IV [1791]

The right of the people to be secure in their persons, houses, papers, and effects, against unreasonable searches and seizures, shall not be violated, and no Warrants shall issue, but upon probable cause, supported by Oath or affirmation, and particularly describing the place to be searched, and the persons or things to be seized.

Amendment V [1791]

No person shall be held to answer for a capital, or otherwise infamous crime, unless on a presentment or indictment of a Grand Jury, except in cases arising in the land or naval forces, or in the Militia, when in actual service in time of War or public danger; nor shall any person be subject for the same offence to be twice put in jeopardy of life or limb; nor shall be compelled in any criminal case to be a witness against himself, nor be deprived of life, liberty, or property, without due process of law;

nor shall private property be taken for public use, without just compensation.

Amendment VI [1791]

In all criminal prosecutions, the accused shall enjoy the right to a speedy and public trial, by an impartial jury of the State and district wherein the crime shall have been committed, which district shall have been previously ascertained by law, and to be informed of the nature and cause of the accusation; to be confronted with the witnesses against him; to have compulsory process for obtaining witnesses in his favor, and to have the Assistance of Counsel for his defence.

Amendment VII [1791]

In Suits at common law, where the value in controversy shall exceed twenty dollars, the right of trial by jury shall be preserved, and no fact tried by jury, shall be otherwise re-examined in any Court of the United States, than according to the rules of the common law.

Amendment VIII [1791]

Excessive bail shall not be required, nor excessive fines imposed, nor cruel and unusual punishments inflicted.

Amendment IX [1791]

The enumeration in the Constitution, of certain rights, shall not be construed to deny or disparage others retained by the people.

Amendment X [1791]

The powers not delegated to the United States by the Constitution, nor prohibited by it to the States, are reserved to the States respectively, or to the people.

Amendment XI [1798]

The Judicial power of the United States shall not be construed to extend to any suit in law or equity, commenced or prosecuted against one of the United States by Citizens of another State, or by Citizens or Subjects of any Foreign State.

Amendment XII [1804]

The Electors shall meet in their respective states and vote by ballot for President and Vice-President, one of whom, at least, shall not be an inhabitant of the same state with themselves; they shall name in their ballots the person voted for as President, and in distinct ballots the person voted for as Vice-President, and they shall make distinct lists of all persons voted for as President, and of all persons voted for as Vice-President, and of the number of votes for each, which lists they shall sign and certify, and transmit sealed to the seat of the government of the United States, directed to the President of the Senate;—The President of the Senate shall, in the presence of the Senate and House of Representatives, open all the certificates and the votes shall then be counted;—The person having the greatest Number of votes for President, shall be the President, if such number be a majority of the whole number of Electors appointed; and if no person have such majority, then from the persons having the highest numbers not exceeding three on the list of those voted for as President, the House of Representatives shall choose immediately, by ballot, the President. But in choosing the President, the votes shall be taken by states, the representation from each state having one vote; a quorum for this purpose shall consist of a member or members from two-thirds of the states, and a majority of all the states shall be necessary to a choice. And if the House of Representatives shall not choose a President whenever the right of choice shall devolve upon them before the fourth day of March next following, then the Vice-President shall act as President, as in the case of the death or other constitutional disability of the President.—The person having the greatest number of votes as Vice-

President, shall be the Vice-President, if such number be a majority of the whole number of Electors appointed, and if no person have a majority, then from the two highest numbers on the list, the Senate shall choose the Vice-President; a quorum for the purpose shall consist of two-thirds of the whole number of Senators, and a majority of the whole number shall be necessary to a choice. But no person constitutionally ineligible to the office of President shall be eligible to that of Vice-President of the United States.

Amendment XIII [1865]

Section 1. Neither slavery nor involuntary servitude, except as a punishment for crime whereof the party shall have been duly convicted, shall exist within the United States, or any place subject to their jurisdiction.

Section 2. Congress shall have power to enforce this article by appropriate legislation.

Amendment XIV [1868]

Section 1. All persons born or naturalized in the United States, and subject to the jurisdiction thereof, are citizens of the United States and of the State wherein they reside. No State shall make or enforce any law which shall abridge the privileges or immunities of citizens of the United States; nor shall any State deprive any person of life, liberty, or property, without due process of law; nor deny to any person within its jurisdiction the equal protection of the laws.

Section 2. Representatives shall be apportioned among the several States according to their respective numbers, counting the whole number of persons in each State, excluding Indians not taxed. But when the right to vote at any election for the choice of electors for President and Vice-President of the United States, Representatives in Congress, the Executive and Judicial officers of a State, or the members of the Legislature thereof, is denied to any of the male inhabitants of such State, being twenty-one years of age, and citizens of the United States, or in any way abridged, except for participation in rebellion, or other crime, the basis of representation therein shall be reduced in the proportion which the number of such male citizens shall bear to the whole number of male citizens twenty-one years of age in such State.

Section 3. No person shall be a Senator or Representative in Congress, or elector of President and Vice-President, or hold any office, civil or military, under the United States, or under any State, who, having previously taken an oath, as a member of Congress, or as an officer of the United States, or as a member of any State legislature, or as an executive or judicial officer of any State, to support the Constitution of the United States, shall have engaged in insurrection or rebellion against the same, or given aid or comfort to the enemies thereof. But Congress may by a vote of two-thirds of each House, remove such disability.

Section 4. The validity of the public debt of the United States, authorized by law, including debts incurred for payment of pensions and bounties for services in suppressing insurrection or rebellion, shall not be questioned. But neither the United States nor any State shall assume or pay any debt or obligation incurred in aid of insurrection or rebellion against the United States, or any claim for the loss or emancipation of any slave; but all such debts, obligations and claims shall be held illegal and void.

Section 5. The Congress shall have power to enforce, by appropriate legislation, the provisions of this article.

Amendment XV [1870]

Section 1. The right of citizens of the United States to vote shall not be denied or abridged by the United States or by any State on account of race, color, or previous condition of servitude.

Section 2. The Congress shall have power to enforce this article by appropriate legislation.

Amendment XVI [1913]

The Congress shall have power to lay and collect taxes on incomes, from whatever source derived, without apportionment among the several States, and without regard to any census or enumeration.

Amendment XVII [1913]

[1] The Senate of the United States shall be composed of two Senators from each State, elected by the people thereof, for six years; and each Senator shall have one vote. The electors in each State shall have the qualifications requisite for electors of the most numerous branch of the State legislatures.

[2] When vacancies happen in the representation of any State in the Senate, the executive authority of such State shall issue writs of election to fill such vacancies: *Provided*, That the legislature of any State may empower the executive thereof to make temporary appointments until the people fill the vacancies by election as the legislature may direct.

[3] This amendment shall not be so construed as to affect the election or term of any Senator chosen before it becomes valid as part of the Constitution.

Amendment XVIII [1919]

Section 1. After one year from the ratification of this article the manufacture, sale, or transportation of intoxicating liquors within, the importation thereof into, or the exportation thereof from the United States and all territory subject to the jurisdiction thereof for beverage purposes is hereby prohibited.

Section 2. The Congress and the several States shall have concurrent power to enforce this article by appropriate legislation.

Section 3. This article shall be inoperative unless it shall have been ratified as an amendment to the Constitution by the legislatures of the several States, as provided in the Constitution, within seven years from the date of the submission hereof to the States by the Congress.

Amendment XIX [1920]

[1] The right of citizens of the United States to vote shall not be denied or abridged by the United States or by any State on account of sex.

[2] Congress shall have power to enforce this article by appropriate legislation.

Amendment XX [1933]

Section 1. The terms of the President and Vice President shall end at noon on the 20th day of January, and the terms of Senators and Representatives at noon on the 3d day of January, of the years in which such terms would have ended if this article had not been ratified; and the terms of their successors shall then begin.

Section 2. The Congress shall assemble at least once in every year, and such meeting shall begin at noon on the 3d day of January, unless they shall by law appoint a different day.

Section 3. If, at the time fixed for the beginning of the term of the President, the President elect shall have died, the Vice President elect shall become President. If the President shall not have been chosen before the time fixed for the beginning of his term, or if the President elect shall have failed to qualify, then the Vice President elect shall act as President until a President shall have qualified; and the Congress may by law provide for the case wherein neither a President elect nor a Vice President elect shall have qualified, declaring who shall then act as President, or the manner in which one who is to act shall be selected, and such person shall act accordingly until a President or Vice President shall have qualified.

Section 4. The Congress may by law provide for the case of the death of any of the persons from whom the House of Representatives may choose a President whenever the right of choice shall have devolved upon them, and for the case of the death of any of the persons from whom the Senate may choose a Vice President whenever the right of choice shall have devolved upon them.

Section 5. Sections 1 and 2 shall take effect on the 15th day of October following the ratification of this article.

Section 6. This article shall be inoperative unless it shall have been ratified as an amendment to the Constitution by the legislatures of three-fourths of the several States within seven years from the date of its submission.

Amendment XXI [1933]

Section 1. The eighteenth article of amendment to the Constitution of the United States is hereby repealed.

Section 2. The transportation or importation into any State, Territory, or possession of the United States for delivery or use therein of intoxicating liquors, in violation of the laws thereof, is hereby prohibited.

Section 3. The article shall be inoperative unless it shall have been ratified as an amendment to the Constitution by conventions in the several States, as provided in the Constitution, within seven years from the date of the submission hereof to the States by the Congress.

Amendment XXII [1951]

Section 1. No person shall be elected to the office of the President more than twice, and no person who has held the office of President, or acted as President, for more than two years of a term to which some other person was elected President shall be elected to the office of the President more than once. But this Article shall not apply to any person holding the office of President when this Article was proposed by the Congress, and shall not prevent any person who may be holding the office of President, or acting as President, during the term within which this Article becomes operative from holding the office of President or acting as President during the remainder of such term.

Section 2. This article shall be inoperative unless it shall have been ratified as an amendment to the Constitution by the legislatures of three-fourths of the several States within seven years from the date of its submission to the States by the Congress.

Amendment XXIII [1961]

Section 1. The District constituting the seat of Government of the United States shall appoint in such manner as the Congress may direct:

A number of electors of President and Vice President equal to the whole number of Senators and Representatives in Congress to which the District would be entitled if it were a State, but in no event more than the least populous State; they shall be in addition to those appointed by the States, but they shall be considered, for the purposes of the election of President and Vice President, to be electors appointed by a State; and they shall meet in the District and perform such duties as provided by the twelfth article of amendment.

Section 2. The Congress shall have power to enforce this article by appropriate legislation.

Amendment XXIV [1964]

Section 1. The right of citizens of the United States to vote in any primary or other election for President or Vice President, for electors for President or Vice President, or for Senator or Representative in Congress, shall not be denied or abridged by the United States or any State by reason of failure to pay any poll tax or other tax.

Section 2. The Congress shall have power to enforce this article by appropriate legislation.

Amendment XXV [1967]

Section 1. In case of the removal of the President from office or of his death or resignation, the Vice President shall become President.

Section 2. Whenever there is a vacancy in the office of the Vice President, the President shall nominate a Vice President who shall take office upon confirmation by a majority vote of both Houses of Congress.

Section 3. Whenever the President transmits to the President pro tempore of the Senate and the Speaker of the House of Representatives his written declaration that he is unable to discharge the powers and duties of his office, and until he transmits to them a written declaration to the contrary, such powers and duties shall be discharged by the Vice President as Acting President.

Section 4. Whenever the Vice President and a majority of either the principal officers of the executive departments or of such other body as Congress may by law provide, transmit to the President pro tempore of the Senate and the Speaker of the House of Representatives their written declaration that the President is unable to discharge the powers and duties of his office, the Vice President shall immediately assume the powers and duties of the office as Acting President.

Thereafter, when the President transmits to the President pro tempore of the Senate and the Speaker of the House of Representatives his written declaration that no inability exists, he shall resume the powers and duties of his office unless the Vice President and a majority of either the principal officers of the executive department or of such other body as Congress may by law provide, transmit within four days to the President pro tempore of the Senate and the Speaker of the House of Representatives their written declaration that the President is unable to discharge the powers and duties of his office. Thereupon Congress shall decide the issue, assembling within forty-eight hours for that purpose if not in session. If the Congress, within twenty-one days after receipt of the latter written declaration, or, if Congress is not in session, within twenty-one days after Congress is required to assemble, determines by two-thirds vote of both Houses that the President is unable to discharge the powers and duties of his office, the Vice President shall continue to discharge the same as Acting President; otherwise, the President shall resume the powers and duties of his office.

Amendment XXVI [1971]

Section 1. The right of citizens of the United States, who are eighteen years of age or older, to vote shall not be denied or abridged by the United States or by any State on account of age.

Section 2. The Congress shall have power to enforce this article by appropriate legislation.

Amendment XXVII [1992]

No law, varying the compensation for the services of the Senators and Representatives, shall take effect, until an election of Representatives shall have intervened.